P9-CSU-614

GMAT™

Where do you see yourself in 8 weeks?

How about celebrating your completion of the GMAT™ exam?

Get your FREE 8-week study planner: **mba.com/8-weeks**

Graduate Management Admission Council™

© 2021 Graduate Management Admission Council (GMAC). All rights reserved. GMAT™ and Graduate Management Admission Council™ are trademarks of GMAC in the United States and other countries.

GMAT

GMAT™ Official Guide 2022

Your prep begins here. Designed by the makers of the GMAT™ exam

 **Book + Online + Mobile**

What's included

Book:

- ✓ Over 1,000 practice questions
- ✓ Answer explanations
- ✓ Verbal and Quantitative Review chapters
- ✓ Quick reference quantitative sheets

Online tools:

- ✓ Diagnostic Evaluation
- ✓ Question Bank with over 170 online exclusive questions
- ✓ Flash cards
- ✓ Mobile app

The ONLY source of real GMAT™ questions from past exams

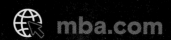 mba.com

GMAT™ Official Prep

GMAT™ OFFICIAL GUIDE 2022

Copyright © 2021 by the Graduate Management Admission Council (GMAC). All rights reserved.

Published by John Wiley & Sons, Inc., Hoboken, New Jersey.

No part of this publication may be reproduced, stored in a retrieval system or transmitted in any form or by any means, electronic, mechanical, photocopying, recording, scanning or otherwise, except as permitted under Sections 107 or 108 of the 1976 United States Copyright Act, without either the prior written permission of the Publisher, or authorization through payment of the appropriate per-copy fee to the Copyright Clearance Center, 222 Rosewood Drive, Danvers, MA 01923, (978) 750-8400, fax (978) 646-8600, or on the web at www.copyright.com. Requests to the Publisher for permission should be addressed to the Permissions Department, John Wiley & Sons, Inc., 111 River Street, Hoboken, NJ 07030, (201) 748-6011, fax (201) 748-6008, or online at http://www.wiley.com/go/permissions.

The publisher and the author make no representations or warranties with respect to the accuracy or completeness of the contents of this work and specifically disclaim all warranties, including without limitation warranties of fitness for a particular purpose. No warranty may be created or extended by sales or promotional materials. The advice and strategies contained herein may not be suitable for every situation. This work is sold with the understanding that the publisher is not engaged in rendering legal, accounting, or other professional services. If professional assistance is required, the services of a competent professional person should be sought. Neither the publisher nor the author shall be liable for damages arising here from. The fact that an organization or Website is referred to in this work as a citation and/or a potential source of further information does not mean that the author or the publisher endorses the information the organization or Website may provide or recommendations it may make. Further, readers should be aware that Internet Websites listed in this work may have changed or disappeared between when this work was written and when it is read.

Trademarks: Wiley, the Wiley logo, and related trademarks are trademarks or registered trademarks of John Wiley & Sons, Inc. and/or its affiliates. The GMAT logo, GMAC™, GMASS™, GMAT™, Graduate Management Admission Council™, and Graduate Management Admission Test™ are trademarks of GMAC in the United States and other countries. All other trademarks are the property of their respective owners. John Wiley & Sons, Inc., is not associated with any product or vendor mentioned in this book.

For general information on our other products and services or to obtain technical support please contact our Customer Care Department within the U.S. at (877) 762-2974, outside the U.S. at (317) 572-3993 or fax (317) 572-4002.

John Wiley & Sons, Inc., also publishes its books in a variety of electronic formats and by print-on-demand. Not all content that is available in standard print versions of this book may appear or be packaged in all book formats. If you have purchased a version of this book that did not include media that is referenced by or accompanies a standard print version, you may request this media by visiting http://booksupport.wiley.com. For more information about Wiley products, visit us at www.wiley.com.

ISBN 978-1-119-79376-2 (pbk); ISBN 978-1-119-79385-4 (ePub)

Printed in the United States of America

SKY10024665_041221

Table of Contents

Dear GMAT™ Test-Taker,

Thank you for your interest in graduate management education. Today more than 7,000 graduate programs around the world use the GMAT exam to establish their MBA, business master's, and other graduate-level management degree programs as hallmarks of excellence. Nine out of ten new MBA enrollments globally are made using a GMAT score.*

By using the *GMAT™ Official Guide* to prepare for the GMAT exam, you're taking a very important step toward achieving your goals and pursuing admission to the MBA or business master's program that is the best fit for you.

This book, *GMAT™ Official Guide 2022*, is designed to help you prepare for and build confidence to do your best on exam day. It's the only guide that features real questions from past exams published by the Graduate Management Admission Council (GMAC), the makers of the GMAT exam.

For more than 60 years, the GMAT exam has helped candidates like you demonstrate their command of the skills needed for success in the classroom and showcase to schools their commitment to pursuing a graduate business degree. Schools use and trust the GMAT exam as part of their admissions process because it's a proven predictor of classroom success and your ability to excel in your chosen program.

The mission of GMAC is to ensure no talent goes undiscovered. We are driven to continue improving the GMAT exam as well as helping you find and connect with the best-fit schools and programs for you. I applaud your commitment to educational success. This guide and the other GMAT™ Official Prep products available at mba.com will give you the confidence to achieve your personal best on the GMAT exam and launch or reinvigorate a rewarding career.

I wish you the best success on all your future educational and professional endeavors.

Sincerely,

Sangeet Chowfla
President & CEO of the Graduate Management Admission Council

---

*Top 100 *Financial Times* full-time MBA programs

GMAT™ Official Guide 2022

1.0   What Is the GMAT™ Exam?

1.0 What Is the GMAT™ Exam?

The Graduate Management Admission Test™ (GMAT™) exam is a standardized exam used in admissions decisions by more than 7,000 graduate management programs, at approximately 2,300 graduate business schools worldwide. It helps you gauge, and demonstrate to schools, your academic potential for success in graduate-level management studies.

The four-part exam measures your Analytical Writing, Integrated Reasoning, Verbal Reasoning, and Quantitative Reasoning skills—higher-order reasoning skills that management faculty, admissions professionals, and employers worldwide have identified as important for incoming students to have. "Higher-order" reasoning skills involve complex judgments, and include critical thinking, analysis, and problem solving. Unlike undergraduate grades and curricula, which vary in their meaning across regions and institutions, your GMAT scores provide a standardized, statistically valid, and reliable measure of how you are likely to perform academically in the core curriculum of a graduate management program. The GMAT exam's validity, fairness, and value in admissions have been well established through numerous academic studies.

The GMAT exam is delivered online or at a test center, entirely in English, and solely on a computer. It is not a test of business knowledge, subject-matter mastery, English vocabulary, or advanced computational skills. The GMAT exam also does not measure other factors related to success in graduate management study, such as job experience, leadership ability, motivation, and interpersonal skills. Your GMAT score is intended to be used as one admissions criterion among other, more subjective, criteria, such as admissions essays and interviews.

1.1 Why Take the GMAT™ Exam?

Taking the GMAT exam helps you stand out in the admissions process and demonstrate your readiness and commitment to pursuing graduate management education. Schools use GMAT scores to help them select the most qualified applicants—because they know that candidates who take the GMAT exam are serious about earning a graduate business degree, and it's a proven predictor of a student's ability to succeed in his or her chosen program. When you consider which programs to apply to, you can look at a school's use of the GMAT exam as one indicator of quality. Schools that use the GMAT exam typically list score ranges or average scores in their class profiles, so you may also find these profiles helpful in gauging the academic competitiveness of a program you are considering and how well your performance on the exam compares with that of the students enrolled in the program.

No matter how you perform on the GMAT exam, you should contact the schools that interest you to learn more and to ask how they use GMAT scores and other criteria (such as your undergraduate grades, essays, and letters of recommendation) in their admissions processes. School admissions offices, websites, and materials published by schools are the key sources of information when you are doing research about where you might want to go to business school.

Myth -vs- **FACT**

M – **If I don't achieve a high score on the GMAT exam, I won't get into my top choice schools.**

F – **There are great schools available for candidates at any GMAT score range.**

Fewer than 50 of the ~200,000 people taking the GMAT exam each year get a perfect score of 800; and many more get into top business school programs around the world each year. Admissions Officers use GMAT scores as one component in their admissions decisions, in conjunction with undergraduate records, application essays, interviews, letters of recommendation, and other information when deciding whom to accept into their programs. Visit School Finder on mba.com to learn about schools that are the best fit for you.

For more information on the GMAT exam, test preparation materials, registration, how to use and send your GMAT scores to schools, and applying to business school, please visit mba.com/gmat.

1.2 GMAT™ Exam Format

The GMAT exam consists of four separately timed sections (see the table on the next page). The Analytical Writing Assessment (AWA) section consists of one essay. The Integrated Reasoning section consists of graphical and data analysis questions in multiple response formats. The Quantitative and Verbal Reasoning sections consist of multiple-choice questions.

The Quantitative and Verbal Reasoning sections of the GMAT exam are computer adaptive, which means that the test draws from a large bank of questions to tailor itself to your ability level, and you won't get many questions that are too hard or too easy for you. The first question will be of medium difficulty. As you answer each question, the computer scores your answer and uses it—as well as your responses to all preceding questions—to select the next question.

Computer-adaptive tests become more difficult the more questions you answer correctly, but if you get a question that seems easier than the last one, it does not necessarily mean you answered the last question incorrectly. The test must cover a range of content, both in the type of question asked and the subject matter presented.

Myth -vs- **FACT**

𝕄 – **Getting an easier question means I answered the last one wrong.**

F – **You should not become distracted by the difficulty level of a question.**

Many different factors contribute to the difficulty of a question, so don't worry when taking the test or waste valuable time trying to determine the difficulty of the question you are answering.

To ensure that everyone receives the same content, the test selects a specific number of questions of each type. The test may call for your next problem to be a relatively hard data sufficiency question involving arithmetic operations. But, if there are no more relatively difficult data sufficiency questions involving arithmetic, you might be given an easier question.

Because the computer uses your answers to select your next questions, you may not skip questions or go back and change your answer to a previous question. If you don't know the answer to a question, try to eliminate as many choices as possible, then select the answer you think is best.

Though the individual questions are different, the mix of question types is the same for every GMAT exam. Your score is determined by the difficulty and statistical characteristics of the questions you answer as well as the number of questions you answer correctly. By adapting to each test-taker, the GMAT exam is able to accurately and efficiently gauge skill levels over a full range of abilities, from very high to very low.

The test includes the types of questions found in this book and in the online question bank found at gmat.wiley.com, but the format and presentation of the GMAT exam questions are different.

Five things to know about GMAT exam questions:

- Only one question or question prompt at a time is presented on the computer screen.
- The answer choices for the multiple-choice questions will be preceded by radio buttons, rather than by letters.
- Different question types appear in random order in the multiple-choice and Integrated Reasoning sections.
- You must choose an answer and confirm your choice before moving on to the next question.
- You may not go back to previous screens to change answers to previous questions.

Format of the GMAT™ Exam

	Questions	Timing
Analytical Writing Assessment	1	30 min.
Integrated Reasoning Multi-Source Reasoning Table Analysis Graphics Interpretation Two-Part Analysis	12	30 min.
Quantitative Reasoning Problem Solving Data Sufficiency	31	62 min.
Verbal Reasoning Reading Comprehension Critical Reasoning Sentence Correction	36	65 min.
	Total Time:	187 min.

On exam day, immediately prior to the start of the first exam section, you will have the flexibility to select your section order for the GMAT exam from three order combinations.

Order #1	Order #2	Order #3
Analytical Writing Assessment	Verbal Reasoning	Quantitative Reasoning
Integrated Reasoning		
Optional 8-minute break		
Quantitative Reasoning	Quantitative Reasoning	Verbal Reasoning
Optional 8-minute break		
Verbal Reasoning	Integrated Reasoning	Integrated Reasoning
	Analytical Writing Assessment	Analytical Writing Assessment

1.3 What Will the Test Experience Be Like?

The GMAT exam offers the flexibility to take the exam either online or at a test center—wherever you feel most comfortable. You may feel more comfortable at home with the online delivery format or prefer the structure and environment of a test center. The choice and flexibility are yours. Both delivery options include the exact same content, structure, two optional 8-minute breaks, scores, and score scales, and scores are uniformly accepted by schools worldwide, so you can choose the option that works best for you.

At the Test Center: The GMAT exam is administered under standardized conditions at over 700 test centers worldwide. Each test center has a proctored testing room with individual computer workstations that allow you to take the exam under quiet conditions and with some privacy. You may not take notes or scratch paper with you into the testing room, but an erasable notepad and marker will be provided for you to use during the test. For more information about exam day, visit mba.com/gmat.

Online: The GMAT Online exam is a remote proctored experience in the comfort of your home or office. You will need a quiet workspace with a desktop or laptop computer that meets minimum system requirements, a webcam, and a reliable internet connection. During your exam you will be able to use a physical whiteboard with up to two dry-erase markers and an eraser and/or an online whiteboard to work through the exam questions (no scratch paper is allowed). For more information about exam day, visit mba.com/gmatonline.

To learn more about accommodations options for the GMAT exam, visit mba.com/accommodations.

1.4 What Is the Content of the GMAT™ Exam Like?

The GMAT exam measures higher-order analytical skills encompassing several types of reasoning. The Analytical Writing Assessment asks you to analyze the reasoning behind an argument and respond in writing; the Integrated Reasoning section asks you to interpret and synthesize information from multiple sources and in different formats to make reasoned conclusions; the Quantitative Reasoning section includes basic arithmetic, algebra, and geometry; and the Verbal Reasoning section asks you to read and comprehend written material and to reason and evaluate arguments.

Test questions may address a variety of subjects, but all the information you need to answer the questions will be included on the exam, with no outside knowledge of the subject matter necessary. The GMAT exam is not a test of business knowledge, English vocabulary, or advanced computational skills. You will need to read and write in English and have basic math and English skills to perform well on the test, but its difficulty comes from analytical and critical thinking abilities.

Myth -vs- **FACT**

M – **My success in business school is not predicted by the GMAT exam.**

F – **False. The GMAT exam measures your critical thinking and reasoning skills, the ones used in business school and beyond in your career.**

The exam measures your ability to make inferences, problem-solve, and analyze data. In fact, some employers even use the GMAT exam to determine your skill sets in these areas. If your program does not require the GMAT exam, you can stand out from the crowd with your performance on the exam and show that you have skills that it takes to succeed in business school.

The questions in this book are organized by question type and from easiest to most difficult, but keep in mind that when you take the test, you may see different types of questions in any order within each section.

1.5 Analytical Writing Assessment Section

The GMAT Analytical Writing Assessment (AWA) section consists of one 30-minute writing task: Analysis of an Argument. The AWA measures your ability to think critically, communicate your ideas, and formulate an appropriate and constructive critique. You will type your essay on a computer keyboard.

For test-taking tips and sample essay responses, see chapter 11.

1.6 Integrated Reasoning Section

The GMAT Integrated Reasoning section highlights the relevant skills that business managers in today's data-driven world need in order to analyze sophisticated streams of data and solve complex problems. It measures your ability to understand and evaluate multiple sources and types of information—graphic, numeric, and verbal—as they relate to one another. This section will require you to use both quantitative and verbal reasoning to solve complex problems and solve multiple problems in relation to one another.

Four types of questions are used in the Integrated Reasoning section:

- Multi-Source Reasoning
- Table Analysis
- Graphics Interpretation
- Two-Part Analysis

Integrated Reasoning questions may require quantitative or verbal reasoning skills, or a combination of both. You will have to interpret graphics and sort tables to extract meaning from data, but advanced statistical knowledge and spreadsheet manipulation skills are not necessary. For both online and test center exams you will have access to an on-screen calculator with basic functions for the Integrated Reasoning section but note that the calculator is ***not*** available on the Quantitative Reasoning section.

To review the Integrated Reasoning question types and test-taking tips, see chapter 10.

For practice questions of each format, with full answer explanations, visit gmat.wiley.com using your unique access code found in the inside front cover of the book.

1.7 Quantitative Reasoning Section

The GMAT Quantitative Reasoning section measures your ability to solve quantitative problems and interpret graphic data.

Two types of multiple-choice questions are used in the Quantitative Reasoning section:

- Problem Solving
- Data Sufficiency

Both are intermingled throughout the Quantitative Reasoning section, and require basic knowledge of arithmetic, elementary algebra, and commonly known concepts of geometry.

To review the basic mathematical concepts that you will need to answer Quantitative Reasoning questions, see the math review in chapter 3. For test-taking tips specific to the question types in the Quantitative Reasoning section, practice questions, and answer explanations, see chapters 4 and 5.

1.8 Verbal Reasoning Section

The GMAT Verbal Reasoning section measures your ability to read and comprehend written material and to reason and evaluate arguments. The Verbal Reasoning section includes reading sections from several different content areas. Although you may be generally familiar with some of the material, neither the reading passages nor the questions assume detailed knowledge of the topics discussed.

Three types of multiple-choice questions are intermingled throughout the Verbal Reasoning section:

- Reading Comprehension
- Critical Reasoning
- Sentence Correction

For test-taking tips specific to each question type in the Verbal Reasoning section, practice questions, and answer explanations, see chapters 7 through 9.

1.9 How Are Scores Calculated?

Verbal Reasoning and Quantitative Reasoning sections are scored on a scale of 6 to 51, in one-point increments. The Total GMAT score ranges from 200 to 800 and is based on your performance in these two sections. Your score is determined by:

- The number of questions you answer
- The number of questions you answer correctly or incorrectly
- The level of difficulty and other statistical characteristics of each question

Your Verbal Reasoning, Quantitative Reasoning, and Total GMAT scores are determined by an algorithm that takes into account the difficulty of the questions that were presented to you and how you answered them. When you answer the easier questions correctly, you get a chance to answer harder questions, making it possible to earn a higher score. After you have completed all the questions on the exam, or when your time is expired, the computer will calculate your scores.

You will receive five scores: Total Score (which is based on your Quantitative Reasoning and Verbal Reasoning scores), Integrated Reasoning Score, and Analytical Writing Assessment Score. The following table summarizes the different types of scores, the scales, and the increments.

Type of Score	Scale	Increments
Total (based on Quantitative Reasoning and Verbal Reasoning)	200–800	10
Quantitative Reasoning	6–51	1
Verbal Reasoning	6–51	1
Integrated Reasoning	1–8	1
Analytical Writing Assessment	0–6	0.5

Your GMAT scores are valid for five years from the date of the exam.

Your GMAT score includes a percentile ranking that compares your skill level with other test-takers from the past three years. The percentile rank of your score shows the percentage of tests taken with scores lower than your score. Every July, percentile ranking tables are updated. Visit mba.com to view the most recent percentile rankings tables.

2.0   How to Prepare

2.0 How to Prepare

2.1 How Should I Prepare to Take the Test?

The GMAT™ exam is designed specifically to measure reasoning skills needed for management education, and the test contains several question formats unique to the GMAT exam. At a minimum, you should be familiar with the test format and the question formats before you sit for the test. Because the GMAT exam is a timed exam, you should practice answering test questions, not only to better understand the question formats and the skills they require, but also to help you learn to pace yourself so you can finish each section when you sit for the exam.

Because the exam measures reasoning rather than subject-matter knowledge, you most likely will not find it helpful to memorize facts. You do not need to study advanced mathematical concepts, but you should be sure your grasp of basic arithmetic, algebra, and geometry is sound enough that you can use these skills in quantitative problem solving. Likewise, you do not need to study advanced vocabulary words, but you should have a firm understanding of basic English vocabulary and grammar for reading, writing, and reasoning.

> ## Myth -vs- FACT
>
> M – **You need very advanced math skills to get a high GMAT score.**
>
> F – **The GMAT exam measures your reasoning and critical thinking abilities, rather than your advanced math skills.**
>
> The GMAT exam only requires basic quantitative skills. You should review the math skills (algebra, geometry, basic arithmetic) presented in this guide (chapter 3) and the *GMAT™ Official Guide Quantitative Review 2022*. The difficulty of GMAT Quantitative Reasoning questions stems from the logic and analysis used to solve the problems and not the underlying math skills.

2.2 Getting Ready for Exam Day

Whether you are testing online or in a test center, it is important to know what to expect to have a successful and worry-free testing experience.

Test Center

While checking into a test center be prepared to:

- Present appropriate identification.
- Provide your palm vein scan (where permitted by law).
- Provide your digital signature stating that you understand and agree to the Test-Taker Rules and Agreement.
- Have a digital photograph taken.

For more information visit mba.com/gmat.

Online

Preparing to take your exam online:

- Check your computer—before your exam day, ensure that your computer meets the minimum system requirements to run the exam.

- Prepare your workspace—identify a quiet place to take your exam and prepare your workspace by ensuring it is clean and all objects are removed except for your computer and whiteboard.

- Whiteboard—if you plan to use a physical whiteboard during your exam, make sure your whiteboard fits the approved dimensions, and you have up to two dry-erase markers, and an eraser.

- Plan ahead—you should plan to begin your check-in process 30 minutes before your scheduled exam time.

For more information visit mba.com/gmatonline.

2.3 How to Use the *GMAT™ Official Guide*

The *GMAT™ Official Guide* series is the largest official source of actual GMAT questions. Use the questions in this study guide to practice different types of GMAT questions. Questions in each chapter are organized by difficulty level from easy to hard, so if you are new to studying, we recommend starting at the beginning of each chapter and working your way through the questions sequentially. You may find certain "easy" questions to be hard and some "hard" questions to be easy; this is not unusual and reflects the fact that different people will often have different perceptions of a question's difficulty level.

You may also find the questions in the *GMAT™ Official Guide* to be easier or harder than questions you see on the Official Practice Exams and/or the actual GMAT exam. This is expected because, unlike the Official Practice Exams, the *GMAT™ Official Guide* is not computer-adaptive and does not adjust to your ability. If you were to complete all of the questions in this book, you would encounter roughly one-third easy questions, one-third medium questions, and one-third hard questions, whereas on the actual exam, you will not likely see such an even mix of questions across difficulty levels.

To find questions of a specific type and difficulty level (e.g., easy arithmetic questions), use the index of questions in chapter 12. Note that the ratio of questions across different content areas in the *GMAT™ Official Guide* in no way reflects the ratio of questions across different content areas on the actual GMAT exam.

Finally, because the GMAT exam is administered on a computer, we encourage you to practice the questions in the *GMAT™ Official Guide* using the Online Question Bank at gmat.wiley.com. All of the questions in this book are available there, and you'll be able to create practice sets and track your progress more easily. The Online Question Bank is also available on your mobile device through the Wiley Efficient Learning mobile app. To access the Online Question Bank on your mobile device, first create an account at gmat.wiley.com and then sign in to your account on the mobile app.

2.4 How to Use Other GMAT™ Official Prep Products

In addition to the *GMAT™ Official Guide*, we recommend using our other GMAT™ Official Prep products.

- **For those who want a realistic simulation of the GMAT exam:** GMAT™ Official Practice Exams 1–6 are the only practice exams that use questions from past GMAT exams and feature the same scoring algorithm and user interface as the real exam, including the online whiteboard tool that is used in the online version of the GMAT exam. The first two practice exams are free to all test-takers and available at mba.com/exam-prep.

- **For those who want more practice questions:** *GMAT™ Official Guide Verbal Review 2022* and *GMAT™ Official Guide Quantitative Review 2022* offer additional questions that are not available in this book.

- **For those who are looking for additional practice with challenging questions:** *GMAT™ Official Advanced Questions* is a compilation of 300 hard Quantitative Reasoning and Verbal Reasoning questions, similar in difficulty level to hard questions found in the *GMAT™ Official Guide* series.

To maximize your studying efforts:

1. Start by learning about the GMAT exam and the question types in the *GMAT™ Official Guide*.

2. Take GMAT™ Official Practice Exam 1 to become familiar with the exam and get a baseline score. Don't worry about your score on the first practice exam! The goal is to become familiar with the exam and set a baseline for measuring your progress.

3. Go to gmat.wiley.com and practice the questions in the *GMAT™ Official Guide*, focusing on areas that require your attention. As you continue to practice, take additional GMAT™ Official Practice Exams to gauge your progress.

4. Before your actual GMAT exam, take a final Official Practice Exam to simulate the real test-taking experience and see how you score.

Remember: the first two GMAT™ Official Practice Exams are part of the free GMAT™ Official Starter Kit, which includes 90 free practice questions and is available to everyone with an mba.com account. GMAT™ Official Practice Exams 3 to 6, additional GMAT™ Official Practice Questions, and other Official Prep products are available for purchase through mba.com/prep.

2.5 General Test-Taking Suggestions

Specific test-taking strategies for individual question types are presented later in this book. The following are general suggestions to help you perform your best on the test.

1. **Use your time wisely.**
   Although the GMAT exam stresses accuracy more than speed, it is important to use your time wisely. On average, you will have about $1\frac{3}{4}$ minutes for each Verbal Reasoning question, about 2 minutes for each Quantitative Reasoning question, and about $2\frac{1}{2}$ minutes for each Integrated Reasoning question. Once you start the test, an onscreen clock will show the time you have left. You can hide this display if you want, but it is a good idea to check the clock periodically to monitor your progress. The clock will automatically alert you when 5 minutes remain for the section you are working on.

2. **Determine your preferred section order before the actual exam.**
   The GMAT exam allows you to select the order in which to take the sections. Use the GMAT™ Official Practice Exams as an opportunity to practice and determine your preferred order. Remember: there is no

Myth -vs- **FACT**

𝑀 – **It is more important to respond correctly to the test questions than it is to finish the test.**

F – **There is a significant penalty for not completing the GMAT exam.**

Pacing is important. If you are stumped by a question, give it your best guess and move on. If you guess incorrectly, the computer program will likely give you an easier question, which you are likely to answer correctly, and the computer will rapidly return to giving you questions matched to your ability. If you don't finish the test, your score will be reduced. Failing to answer five verbal questions, for example, could reduce your score from the 91st percentile to the 77th percentile.

"right" order in which to take the exam; you can practice each order and see which one works best for you.

3. **Answer practice questions ahead of time.**
    After you become generally familiar with all question types, use the practice questions in this book and online at gmat.wiley.com to prepare for the actual test (note that Integrated Reasoning questions are only available online). It may be useful to time yourself as you answer the practice questions to get an idea of how long you will have for each question when you sit for the actual test, as well as to determine whether you are answering quickly enough to finish the test in the allotted time.

4. **Read all test directions carefully.**
    The directions explain exactly what is required to answer each question type. If you read hastily, you may miss important instructions and impact your ability to answer correctly. To review directions during the test, click on the Help icon. But be aware that the time you spend reviewing directions will count against your time allotment for that section of the test.

Myth -vs- **FACT**

M – **The first 10 questions are critical, and you should invest the most time on those.**

F – **All questions count.**

The computer-adaptive testing algorithm uses each answered question to obtain an *initial* estimate. However, as you continue to answer questions, the algorithm self-corrects by computing an updated estimate on the basis of all the questions you have answered, and then administers questions that are closely matched to this new estimate of your ability. Your final score is based on all your responses and considers the difficulty of all the questions you answered. Taking additional time on the first 10 questions will not game the system and can hurt your ability to finish the test.

5. **Read each question carefully and thoroughly.**
    Before you answer a question, determine exactly what is being asked and then select the best choice. Never skim a question or the possible answers; skimming may cause you to miss important information or nuances.

6. **Do not spend too much time on any one question.**
    If you do not know the correct answer, or if the question is too time consuming, try to eliminate answer choices you know are wrong, select the best of the remaining answer choices, and move on to the next question.

    Not completing sections and randomly guessing answers to questions at the end of each test section can significantly lower your score. As long as you have worked on each section, you will receive a score even if you do not finish one or more sections in the allotted time. You will not earn points for questions you never get to see.

7. **Confirm your answers ONLY when you are ready to move on.**
    On the Quantitative Reasoning and Verbal Reasoning sections, once you have selected your answer to a multiple-choice question, you will be asked to confirm it. Once you confirm your response, you cannot go back and change it. You may not skip questions. In the Integrated Reasoning section, there may be several questions based on information provided in the same question prompt. When there is more than one response on a single screen, you can change your response to any of the questions on the screen before moving on to the next screen. However, you may not navigate back to a previous screen to change any responses.

8. **Plan your essay answer before you begin to write.**
    The best way to approach the Analytical Writing Assessment (AWA) section is to read the directions carefully, take a few minutes to think about the question, and plan a response before you begin writing. Take time to organize your ideas and develop them fully but leave time to reread your response and make any revisions that you think would improve it.

This book and other study materials released by the Graduate Management Admission Council (GMAC) are the ONLY source of real questions that have been used on the GMAT exam. All questions that appear or have appeared on the GMAT exam are copyrighted and owned by GMAC, which does not license them to be reprinted elsewhere. Accessing live Integrated Reasoning, Quantitative Reasoning, and/or Verbal Reasoning test questions in advance or sharing test content during or after you take the test is a serious violation, which could cause your scores to be canceled and schools to be notified. In cases of a serious violation, you may be banned from future testing and other legal remedies may be pursued.

To register for the GMAT™ exam go to www.mba.com/gmat

3.0   Math Review

3.0 Math Review

This chapter reviews the basic mathematical concepts, terms, and formulas you should be familiar with in order to answer Quantitative Reasoning questions on the GMAT™ exam. Only a high-level overview is provided, so if you find unfamiliar terms or concepts, consult other resources for a more detailed discussion and explanation.

Knowledge of basic math, while necessary, is seldom sufficient for answering GMAT questions. Unlike traditional math problems you may have encountered in school, GMAT Quantitative Reasoning questions require you to *apply* your knowledge of math. For example, rather than asking you to demonstrate your knowledge of prime factorization by listing a number's prime factors, a GMAT question may require you to *apply* your knowledge of prime factorization and exponents to simplify an algebraic expression with a radical.

To prepare for the GMAT Quantitative Reasoning section, we recommend first reviewing basic mathematical concepts and formulas to ensure you have the foundational knowledge needed to answer the questions before moving on to practicing this knowledge on real GMAT questions from past exams.

Section 3.1, "Value, Order, and Factors," includes the following topics:

1. Numbers and the Number Line
2. Factors, Multiples, Divisibility, and Remainders
3. Exponents
4. Decimals and Place Value
5. Properties of Operations

Section 3.2, "Algebra, Equalities, and Inequalities," includes the following topics:

1. Algebraic Expressions and Equations
2. Linear Equations
3. Factoring and Quadratic Equations
4. Inequalities
5. Functions
6. Formulas and Measurement Conversion

Section 3.3, "Rates, Ratios, and Percents," includes the following topics:

1. Ratio and Proportion
2. Fractions
3. Percents
4. Converting Decimals, Fractions, and Percents
5. Working with Decimals, Fractions, and Percents
6. Rate, Work, and Mixture Problems

Section 3.4, "Statistics, Sets, Counting, Probability, Estimation, and Series," includes the following topics:

1. Statistics
2. Sets
3. Counting Methods
4. Probability
5. Estimation
6. Sequences and Series

Section 3.5, "Geometry," includes the following topics:

1. Lines and Angles
2. Polygons
3. Triangles
4. Quadrilaterals
5. Circles
6. Rectangular Solids and Cylinders
7. Coordinate Geometry

Section 3.6, Reference Sheets

3.1 Value, Order, and Factors

1. Numbers and the Number Line

A. All *real numbers* correspond to points on *the number line*, and all points on the number line correspond to real numbers.

An illustration of the number line below, shows points corresponding to the real numbers $-\frac{3}{2}$, 0.2, and $\sqrt{2}$.

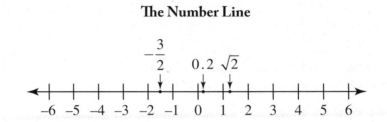

The Number Line

B. On a number line, numbers corresponding to points to the left of zero are *negative* and numbers corresponding to points to the right of zero are *positive*. All real numbers except zero are either positive or negative.

C. For any two numbers on the number line, the number to the left is less than the number to the right. So as shown in the figure above, $-4 < -3 < -\frac{3}{2} < -1$, and $1 < \sqrt{2} < 2$.

D. To say that a number n is between 1 and 4 on the number line means that $n > 1$ and $n < 4$; that is, $1 < n < 4$. If n is "between 1 and 4, inclusive," then $1 \leq n \leq 4$.

E. The *absolute value* of a real number x, denoted $|x|$, is defined to be x if $x \geq 0$ and $-x$ if $x < 0$. A number's absolute value is the distance between that number and zero on the number line. Thus -3 and 3 have the same absolute value, since they are both three units from zero on the number line. The absolute value of any nonzero number is positive.

Examples:

$|-5| = |5| = 5$, $|0| = 0$, and

$\left|\frac{-7}{2}\right| = \frac{7}{2}$.

For any real numbers x and y, $|x + y| \leq |x| + |y|$.

Example:

If $x = 10$ and $y = 2$, then $|x + y| = |12| = 12 = |x| + |y|$.

If $x = 10$ and $y = -2$, then $|x + y| = |8| = 8 < 12 = |x| + |y|$.

2. Factors, Multiples, Divisibility, and Remainders

A. An *integer* is any number in the set $\{\ldots -3, -2, -1, 0, 1, 2, 3, \ldots\}$. For any integer n, the numbers in the set $\{n, n + 1, n + 2, n + 3, \ldots\}$ are *consecutive integers*.

B. If x and y are integers and $x \neq 0$, then x is a *divisor* or *factor* of y if $y = xn$ for some integer n. In this case, y is said to be *divisible* by x or to be a *multiple* of x.

> *Example:*
>
> Since $28 = (7)(4)$, both 4 and 7 are divisors or factors of 28.
>
> But 8 is not a divisor or factor of 28, since there is no integer n such that $28 = 8n$.

C. Dividing a positive integer y by a positive integer x, and then rounding down to the nearest nonnegative integer, yields the *quotient* of the division.

The *remainder* is calculated by multiplying x by the quotient, and then subtracting the result from y. That is, the quotient and the remainder are the unique positive integers q and r, respectively, such that

$y = xq + r$ and $0 \leq r < x$.

> *Example:*
>
> When 28 is divided by 8, the quotient is 3 and the remainder is 4, because $28 = (8)(3) + 4$.

The remainder r is 0 if and only if y is *divisible* by x. In that case, x is a divisor or factor of y, and y is a multiple of x.

> *Example:*
>
> Since 32 divided by 8 yields a remainder of 0, 32 is divisible by 8. So 8 is a divisor or factor of 32, and 32 is a multiple of 8.

When a smaller integer is divided by a larger integer, the quotient is 0 and the remainder is the smaller integer.

> *Example:*
>
> When 5 is divided by 7, the quotient is 0 and the remainder is 5, since $5 = (7)(0) + 5$.

D. Any integer divisible by 2 is an *even integer*; the set of even integers is $\{\ldots -4, -2, 0, 2, 4, 6, 8, \ldots\}$. Integers that are not divisible by 2 are *odd integers*, so $\{\ldots -3, -1, 1, 3, 5, \ldots\}$ is the set of odd integers. For any integer n, the numbers in the set $\{2n, 2n + 2, 2n + 4, \ldots\}$ are *consecutive even integers*, and the numbers in the set $\{2n + 1, 2n + 3, 2n + 5, \ldots\}$ are *consecutive odd integers*.

If at least one factor of a product of integers is even, then the product is even; otherwise, the product is odd. If two integers are both even or both odd, then their sum and their difference are even. Otherwise, their sum and their difference are odd.

E. A *prime* number is a positive integer that has exactly two different positive divisors, 1 and itself. In other words, a prime number is not divisible by any integer other than itself and 1.

> *Example:*
>
> The first six prime numbers are 2, 3, 5, 7, 11, and 13.
>
> But 15 is not a prime number, because it has four different positive divisors: 1, 3, 5, and 15.
>
> And 1 is not a prime number either, because it has only one positive divisor: itself.

Every integer greater than 1 either is prime or can be uniquely expressed as a product of prime factors. An integer greater than 1 that is not prime is called a ***composite number***.

> *Example:*
>
> $14 = (2)(7)$, $81 = (3)(3)(3)(3)$, and
>
> $484 = (2)(2)(11)(11)$ are composite numbers.

3. Exponents

A. An expression of the form k^n means the nth ***power*** of k, or k raised to the nth power, where n is the ***exponent*** and k is the ***base***.

B. A positive integer exponent on a number or a variable indicates how many instances of the number or variable are multiplied together. In other words, when the exponent n is a positive integer, k^n is the product of n instances of k.

> *Examples:*
>
> x^5 means $(x)(x)(x)(x)(x)$; that is, the product in which x is a factor 5 times and there are no other factors. In this example, x^5 is the 5th power of x, or x raised to the 5th power.
>
> The second power of 2, also known as 2 ***squared***, is $2^2 = 2 \times 2 = 4$. The third power of 2, also known as 2 ***cubed***, is $2^3 = 2 \times 2 \times 2 = 8$.

Squaring a number greater than 1, or raising it to any power greater than 1, results in a larger number.

Squaring a number between 0 and 1 results in a smaller number.

> *Examples:*
>
> $3^2 = 9$, and $9 > 3$.
>
> $(0.1)^2 = 0.01$, and $0.01 < 0.1$.

C. A *square root* of a number n is a number x such that $x^2 = n$. Every positive number has two real square roots, one positive and the other negative. The positive square root of n is denoted by $\sqrt{n}$ or by $n^{\frac{1}{2}}$.

> *Example:*
>
> The two square roots of 9 are $\sqrt{9} = 3$ and $-\sqrt{9} = -3$.

Note that for any x, the nonnegative square root of x^2 equals the absolute value of x; that is, $\sqrt{x^2} = |x|$.

The square root of a negative number is not a real number and is called an ***imaginary number***.

D. Every real number r has exactly one real ***cube root***, which is the number s such that $s^3 = r$. The real cube root of r is denoted by $\sqrt[3]{r}$ or by $r^{\frac{1}{3}}$.

> *Examples:*
>
> Since $2^3 = 8$, $\sqrt[3]{8} = 2$.
>
> Similarly, $\sqrt[3]{-8} = -2$ because $(-2)^3 = -8$.

4. Decimals and Place Value

A. In the decimal system, the position of the period or ***decimal point*** determines the ***place values*** of the digits.

> *Example:*
>
> The digits in the number 7,654.321 have the following place values:
>
> | Thousands | | Hundreds | Tens | Ones or units | | Tenths | Hundredths | Thousandths |
> |:---:|:---:|:---:|:---:|:---:|:---:|:---:|:---:|:---:|
> | 7 | , | 6 | 5 | 4 | . | 3 | 2 | 1 |

B. In ***scientific notation***, a decimal is expressed as a number with only one nonzero digit to the left of the decimal point, multiplied by a power of 10. To convert a number expressed in scientific notation to regular decimal notation, move the decimal point by the number of places equal to the absolute value of the exponent on the 10. Move the decimal point to the right if the exponent is positive and to the left if the exponent is negative.

Examples:

In scientific notation, 231 is written as 2.31×10^2, and 0.0231 is written as 2.31×10^{-2}.

You can convert the expression 2.013×10^4 to regular decimal notation by moving the decimal point 4 places to the right, yielding the result 20,130.

Similarly, you can convert the expression 1.91×10^{-4} to regular decimal notation by moving the decimal point 4 places to the left, yielding the result 0.000191.

C. To add or subtract decimals, line up their decimal points. If one of the numbers has fewer digits to the right of its decimal point than another, insert zeros to the right of the last digit.

Examples:

To add 17.6512 and 653.27, insert zeroes to the right of the last digit in 653.27 so that the decimal points line up when the numbers are arranged in a column:

$$
\begin{array}{r}
17.6512 \\
+ \, 653.2700 \\
\hline
670.9212
\end{array}
$$

Likewise, for 653.27 minus 17.6512:

$$
\begin{array}{r}
653.2700 \\
-17.6512 \\
\hline
635.6188
\end{array}
$$

D. To multiply decimals, multiply the numbers as if they were integers and then insert the decimal point in the product so that the number of digits to the right of the decimal point equals the sum of the numbers of digits to the right of the decimal points in the numbers being multiplied, the *multiplicands*.

Example:

To multiply 2.09 by 1.3, first multiply the integers 209 and 13 to obtain 2,717. Since there are $2 + 1 = 3$ digits to the right of the decimal points in the numbers 2.09 and 1.3, put 3 digits in 2,717 to the right of the decimal point to obtain the product:

$$
\begin{array}{r}
2.09 \quad \text{(2 digits to the right)} \\
\times \, 1.3 \quad \text{(1 digit to the right)} \\
\hline
627 \quad\quad\quad\quad\quad\quad\quad \\
2090 \quad\quad\quad\quad\quad\quad \\
\hline
2.717 \quad \text{(2 + 1 = 3 digits to the right)}
\end{array}
$$

E. To divide a number (the ***dividend***) by a decimal (the ***divisor***), move the decimal point of the divisor to the right until the divisor is an integer. Then move the decimal point of the dividend the same number of places to the right and divide as you would integers. The decimal point in the quotient will be directly above the decimal point in the new dividend.

> *Example:*
>
> To divide 698.12 by 12.4, first move the decimal points in both the divisor 12.4 and the dividend 698.12 one place to the right to make the divisor an integer. In other words, replace 698.12/12.4 with 6981.2/124. Then proceed normally with the long division:
>
> $$
> \begin{array}{r}
> 56.3 \\
> 124\overline{)6981.2} \\
> \underline{620} \\
> 781 \\
> \underline{744} \\
> 372 \\
> \underline{372} \\
> 0
> \end{array}
> $$

5. Properties of Operations

Here are some basic properties of arithmetical operations for any real numbers x, y, and z.

A. Addition and Subtraction

$x + 0 = x = x - 0$

$x - x = 0$

$x + y = y + x$

$x - y = -(y - x) = x + (-y)$

$(x + y) + z = x + (y + z)$

If x and y are both positive, then $x + y$ is also positive.

If x and y are both negative, then $x + y$ is negative.

B. Multiplication and Division

$x \times 1 = x = \dfrac{x}{1}$

$x \times 0 = 0$

If $x \neq 0$, then $\dfrac{x}{x} = 1$.

$\dfrac{x}{0}$ is undefined.

$xy = yx$

If $x \neq 0$ and $y \neq 0$, then $\dfrac{x}{y} = \dfrac{1}{\left(\frac{y}{x}\right)}$.

$(xy)z = x(yz)$

$xy + xz = x(y + z)$

If $y \neq 0$, then $\left(\dfrac{x}{y}\right) + \left(\dfrac{z}{y}\right) = \dfrac{(x + z)}{y}$.

If x and y are both positive, then xy is also positive.

If x and y are both negative, then xy is positive.

If x is positive and y is negative, then xy is negative.

If $xy = 0$, then $x = 0$ or $y = 0$, or both.

C. Exponentiation

$x^1 = x$

$x^0 = 1$

If $x \neq 0$, then $x^{-1} = \frac{1}{x}$

$(x^y)^z = x^{yz} = (x^z)^y$

$x^{y+z} = x^y x^z$

If $x \neq 0$, then $x^{y-z} = \frac{x^y}{x^z}$.

$(xz)^y = x^y z^y$

If $z \neq 0$, then $\left(\frac{x}{z}\right)^y = \frac{x^y}{z^y}$.

If $z \neq 0$, then $x^{\frac{y}{z}} = (x^y)^{\frac{1}{z}} = \left(x^{\frac{1}{z}}\right)^y$.

All the practice questions that appear in this chapter are real questions from past GMAT exams and will test the concepts you have just reviewed. The full answer explanations follow the practice question(s) and outline the reasoning for why each answer choice is correct, or incorrect.

PS87710.03*

Practice Question 1

The average distance between the Sun and a certain planet is approximately 2.3×10^{14} inches. Which of the following is closest to the average distance between the Sun and the planet, in kilometers? (1 kilometer is approximately 3.9×10^4 inches.)

- (A) 7.1×10^8
- (B) 5.9×10^9
- (C) 1.6×10^{10}
- (D) 1.6×10^{11}
- (E) 5.9×10^{11}

DS38350.03

Practice Question 2

If x and y are positive, is $x < 10 < y$?

(1) $x < y$ and $xy = 100$

(2) $x^2 < 100 < y^2$

- (A)   Statement (1) ALONE is sufficient, but statement (2) alone is not sufficient.
- (B)   Statement (2) ALONE is sufficient, but statement (1) alone is not sufficient.
- (C)   BOTH statements TOGETHER are sufficient, but NEITHER statement ALONE is sufficient.
- (D)   EACH statement ALONE is sufficient.
- (E)   Statements (1) and (2) TOGETHER are NOT sufficient.

---

*These numbers correlate with the online test bank question number. See the GMAT™ Official Guide Question Index in the back of this book.

DS75160.03
Practice Question 3

Which of the positive numbers x or y is greater?

(1) $y = 2x$

(2) $2x + 5y = 12$

    (A)   Statement (1) ALONE is sufficient, but statement (2) alone is not sufficient.

    (B)   Statement (2) ALONE is sufficient, but statement (1) alone is not sufficient.

    (C)   BOTH statements TOGETHER are sufficient, but NEITHER statement ALONE is sufficient.

    (D)   EACH statement ALONE is sufficient.

    (E)   Statements (1) and (2) TOGETHER are NOT sufficient.

PS10241.03
Practice Question 4

Judy bought a quantity of pens in packages of 5 for \$0.80 per package. She sold all of the pens in packages of 3 for \$0.60 per package. If Judy's profit from the pens was \$8.00, how many pens did she buy and sell?

    (A)   40

    (B)   80

    (C)   100

    (D)   200

    (E)   400

DS10680.03
Practice Question 5

For any positive integer x, the 2-height of x is defined to be the greatest nonnegative integer n such that 2^n is a factor of x. If k and m are positive integers, is the 2-height of k greater than the 2-height of m ?

(1) $k > m$

(2) $\dfrac{k}{m}$ is an even integer.

    (A)   Statement (1) ALONE is sufficient, but statement (2) alone is not sufficient.

    (B)   Statement (2) ALONE is sufficient, but statement (1) alone is not sufficient.

    (C)   BOTH statements TOGETHER are sufficient, but NEITHER statement ALONE is sufficient.

    (D)   EACH statement ALONE is sufficient.

    (E)   Statements (1) and (2) TOGETHER are NOT sufficient.

PS87710.03
Answer Explanation 1

The average distance between the Sun and a certain planet is approximately 2.3×10^{14} inches. Which of the following is closest to the average distance between the Sun and the planet, in kilometers? (1 kilometer is approximately 3.9×10^4 inches.)

    (A) 7.1×10^8

    (B) 5.9×10^9

    (C) 1.6×10^{10}

    (D) 1.6×10^{11}

    (E) 5.9×10^{11}

Arithmetic Measurement Conversion

Convert to kilometers and then estimate.

$$(2.3 \times 10^{14} \text{ in})\left(\frac{1 \text{ km}}{3.9 \times 10^4 \text{ in}}\right) = \frac{2.3 \times 10^{14}}{3.9 \times 10^4} \text{ km}$$

$$= \frac{2.3}{3.9} \times 10^{14-4} \text{ km}$$

$$\approx \frac{2}{4} \times 10^{10}$$

$$= 0.5 \times 10^{10}$$

$$= 5 \times 10^9$$

The correct answer is B.

DS38350.03

Answer Explanation 2

If x and y are positive, is $x < 10 < y$?

(1) $x < y$ and $xy = 100$
(2) $x^2 < 100 < y^2$

Algebra Inequalities

(1) Given that $x < y$, multiply both sides by x, which is positive, to get $x^2 < xy$. Then, since $xy = 100$, it follows that $x^2 < 100$. Similarly, multiply both sides of $x < y$ by y, which is positive, to get $xy < y^2$. Again, since $xy = 100$, it follows that $100 < y^2$.

Combining $x^2 < 100$ and $100 < y^2$ gives $x^2 < 100 < y^2$, from which it follows that $\sqrt{x^2} < \sqrt{100} < \sqrt{y^2}$ and, therefore, $x < 10 < y$, since x and y are both positive; SUFFICIENT.

(2) Given that $x^2 < 100 < y^2$, it follows that $x < 10 < y$ as shown in (1) above; SUFFICIENT.

The correct answer is D; each statement alone is sufficient.

DS75160.03

Answer Explanation 3

Which of the positive numbers x or y is greater?

(1) $y = 2x$
(2) $2x + 5y = 12$

Algebra Order

(1) Given that x is positive and y is twice the value of x, it follows that y is the greater number. This can be seen algebraically by adding x to both sides of $x > 0$ to get $x + x > x$, or $2x > x$, or $y > x$; SUFFICIENT.

(2) Given that $2x + 5y = 12$, then it is possible that $x = 1$ and $y = 2$, and thus it is possible that y is greater than x. However, it is also possible that $x = 2$ and $y = \frac{8}{5}$, and thus it is possible that x is greater than y; NOT sufficient.

The correct answer is A; statement 1 alone is sufficient.

PS10241.03
Answer Explanation 4

Judy bought a quantity of pens in packages of 5 for $0.80 per package. She sold all of the pens in packages of 3 for $0.60 per package. If Judy's profit from the pens was $8.00, how many pens did she buy and sell?

- (A) 40
- (B) 80
- (C) 100
- (D) 200
- (E) 400

Arithmetic Applied Problems; Operations With Decimals

Judy purchased the pens for $\frac{\$0.80}{5}$ = $0.16 each and sold them for $\frac{\$0.60}{3}$ = $0.20 each. Therefore, her profit on each pen was $0.20 − $0.16 = $0.04. If her total profit was $8.00, then she bought and sold $\frac{\$8.00}{\$0.04}$ = 200 pens.

The correct answer is D.

DS10680.03
Answer Explanation 5

For any positive integer x, the 2-height of x is defined to be the greatest nonnegative integer n such that 2^n is a factor of x. If k and m are positive integers, is the 2-height of k greater than the 2-height of m?

(1) $k > m$

(2) $\frac{k}{m}$ is an even integer.

Arithmetic Properties of Numbers

(1) Given that $k > m$, the 2-height of k can be greater than m (choose $k = 4$, which has a 2-height of 2, and choose $m = 2$, which has a 2-height of 1) and the 2-height of k can fail to be greater than m (choose $k = 3$, which has a 2-height of 0, and choose $m = 2$, which has a 2-height of 1); NOT sufficient.

(2) Given that $\frac{k}{m}$ is an even integer, it follows that $\frac{k}{m}$ = 2n for some integer n, or $k = 2mn$. This implies that the 2-height of k is at least one more than the 2-height of m; SUFFICIENT.

The correct answer is B; statement 2 alone is sufficient.

3.2 Algebra, Equalities, and Inequalities

1. Algebraic Expressions and Equations

A. Algebra is based on the operations of arithmetic and on the concept of an ***unknown quantity***, or ***variable***. Letters such as ***x*** or ***n*** are used to represent unknown quantities. Numerical expressions are used to represent known quantities called ***constants***. A combination of variables, constants, and arithmetical operations is called an ***algebraic expression***.

Solving word problems often requires translating verbal expressions into algebraic expressions. The following table lists words and phrases that can be translated as mathematical operations used in algebraic expressions:

3.2 Translating Words into Mathematical Operations

$x + y$	$x - y$	xy	$\dfrac{x}{y}$	x^y
x added to y *x increased by y* *x more than y* *x plus y* *the sum of x and y* *the total of x and y*	*x decreased by y* *difference of x and y* *y fewer than x* *y less than x* *x minus y* *x reduced by y* *y subtracted from x*	*x multiplied by y* *the product of x and y* *x times y*	*x divided by y* *x over y* *the quotient of x and y* *the ratio of x to y*	*x to the power of y* *x to the yth power*
		If $y = 2$: *double x* *twice x*	If $y = 2$: *half of x* *x halved*	If $y = 2$: *x squared*
		If $y = 3$: *triple x*		If $y = 3$: *x cubed*

B. In an algebraic expression, a **term** is either a constant, a variable, or the product of one or more constants and/or variables. The variables in a term may be raised to exponents. A term with no variables is called a **constant term**. The constant in a term that includes one or more variables is called a **coefficient**.

> *Example:*
>
> Suppose Pam has 5 more pencils than Fred has. If F represents the number of pencils Fred has, then the number of pencils Pam has is $F + 5$. This algebraic expression includes two terms: the variable F and the constant term 5.

C. A **polynomial** is an algebraic expression that is a sum of terms and contains exactly one variable. Each term in a polynomial consists of a variable raised to some power and multiplied by some coefficient. If the highest power to which the variable is raised is 1, the expression is called a **first degree** (or **linear**) **polynomial** in that variable. If the highest power to which the variable is raised is 2, the expression is called a **second degree** (or **quadratic**) **polynomial** in that variable.

> *Example:*
>
> The expression $F + 5$ is a linear polynomial in F, since the highest power of F is 1.
>
> The expression $19x^2 - 6x + 3$ is a quadratic polynomial in x, since the highest power of x is 2.
>
> The expression $\dfrac{3x^2}{(2x - 5)}$ is not a polynomial, because it is not a sum of terms that are each a power of x multiplied by a coefficient.

D. Often when working with algebraic expressions, it is necessary to simplify them by factoring or combining **like** terms.

Example:

The expression $6x + 5x$ is equivalent to $(6 + 5)x$, or $11x$.

In the expression $9x - 3y$, 3 is a factor common to both terms: $9x - 3y = 3(3x - y)$.

In the expression $5x^2 + 6y$, there are no like terms and no common factors.

E. In a fraction $\dfrac{n}{d}$, n is the **numerator** and d is the **denominator**. If there are common factors in the numerator and denominator of an algebraic expression, they can be divided out, provided they are not equal to zero.

Example:

If $x \neq 3$, then $\dfrac{(x-3)}{(x-3)} = 1$.

Therefore, $\dfrac{(3xy - 9y)}{(x-3)} = \dfrac{3y(x-3)}{(x-3)} = 3y(1) = 3y$.

F. To multiply two algebraic expressions, multiply each term of one expression by each term of the other expression.

Example:

$$(3x - 4)(9y + x) = 3x(9y + x) - 4(9y + x)$$
$$= 3x(9y) + 3x(x) - 4(9y) - 4(x)$$
$$= 27xy + 3x^2 - 36y - 4x$$

G. An algebraic expression can be evaluated by substituting constants for the variables in the expression.

Example:

If $x = 3$ and $y = -2$, then $3xy - x^2 + y$ can be evaluated as
$3(3)(-2) - (3)^2 + (-2) = -18 - 9 - 2 = -29$.

H. A major focus of algebra is to solve equations involving algebraic expressions. The **solutions** of such an equation are those sets of assignments of constant values to the equation's variables that make the equation true, or "satisfy the equation." An equation may have no solution or one or more solutions. If two or more equations are to be solved together, the solutions must satisfy all the equations simultaneously. The solutions of an equation are also called the **roots** of the equation. These roots can be checked by substituting them into the original equation to determine whether they satisfy the equation.

I. Two equations with the same solution or solutions are **equivalent equations**.

Examples:

The equations $2 + x = 3$ and $4 + 2x = 6$ are equivalent because each has the unique solution $x = 1$. Note that the second equation is the first equation multiplied by 2.

Similarly, the equations $3x - y = 6$ and $6x - 2y = 12$ are equivalent, although in this case each equation has infinitely many solutions. If any value is assigned to x, then $3x - 6$ is a corresponding value for y that will satisfy both equations. For example, $x = 2$ and $y = 0$ is a solution to both equations, and so is $x = 5$ and $y = 9$.

2. Linear Equations

A. A *linear equation* is an equation with a linear polynomial on one side of the equals sign and either a linear polynomial or a constant on the other side, or an equation that can be converted into that form. A linear equation with only one variable is a *linear equation with one unknown*. A linear equation with two variables is *a linear equation with two unknowns*.

Examples:

$5x - 2 = 9 - x$ is a linear equation with one unknown.

$3x + 1 = y - 2$ is a linear equation with two unknowns.

B. To solve a linear equation with one unknown (that is, to find the value of the unknown that satisfies the equation), the unknown should be isolated on one side of the equation. This can be done by performing the same mathematical operations on both sides of the equation. Remember that if the same number is added to or subtracted from both sides of the equation, this does not change the equality; likewise, multiplying or dividing both sides by the same nonzero number does not change the equality.

Example:

To solve the equation $\dfrac{5x - 6}{3} = 4$, isolate the variable x using the following steps:

$$5x - 6 = 12 \quad \text{multiply both sides by 3}$$
$$5x = 18 \quad \text{add 6 to both sides}$$
$$x = \frac{18}{5} \quad \text{divide both sides by 5}$$

The result, $\dfrac{18}{5}$, can be checked by substituting it for x in the original equation to determine whether it satisfies that equation:

$$\frac{\left(5\left(\frac{18}{5}\right) - 6\right)}{3} = \frac{(18 - 6)}{3} = \frac{12}{3} = 4$$

Therefore, $x = \dfrac{18}{5}$ is the solution.

C. If two linear equations with the same two unknowns are equivalent, then they have infinitely many solutions, as illustrated in the second example in 3.2.1.I above. But if two linear equations with the same two unknowns are not equivalent, then they have at most one solution.

There are several methods of solving two linear equations with two unknowns. With any method, if a trivial equation such as $0 = 0$ is reached, then the equations are equivalent and have infinitely many solutions. But if a contradiction is reached, the equations have no solution.

Example:

Consider the two equations: $3x + 4y = 17$ and $6x + 8y = 35$. Note that $3x + 4y = 17$ implies $6x + 8y = 34$, which contradicts the second equation. Thus, no values of x and y can simultaneously satisfy both equations.

If neither a trivial equation nor a contradiction is reached, then a unique solution can be found.

D. One way to solve two linear equations with two unknowns is to express one of the unknowns in terms of the other using one of the equations, then substitute the expression into the remaining equation to obtain an equation with only one unknown. This equation can be solved and the value of the unknown substituted into either of the original equations to find the value of the other unknown.

Example:

The following two equations can be solved for x and y:

$$(1) \quad 3x + 2y = 11$$

$$(2) \quad x - y = 2$$

In equation (2), $x = 2 + y$. So, in equation (1), substitute $2 + y$ for x:

$$3(2 + y) + 2y = 11$$

$$6 + 3y + 2y = 11$$

$$6 + 5y = 11$$

$$5y = 5$$

$$y = 1$$

Since $y = 1$, it follows that $x - 1 = 2$ and $x = 2 + 1 = 3$.

E. Another way to eliminatze one of the unknowns and solve for x and y is by making the coefficients of one of the unknowns the same (disregarding the sign) in both equations and either adding the equations or subtracting one equation from the other.

Example:

Use this method to solve the equations:

$$(1)\ \ 6x + 5y = 29 \text{ and}$$
$$(2)\ \ 4x - 3y = -6$$

Multiply equation (1) by 3 and equation (2) by 5 to get

$$18x + 15\,y = 87 \text{ and}$$
$$20x - 15\,y = -30$$

Adding the two equations eliminates y, yielding $38x = 57$, or $x = \dfrac{3}{2}$.

Finally, substituting $\dfrac{3}{2}$ for x in one of the equations gives $y = 4$. These answers can be checked by substituting both values into both of the original equations.

3. Factoring and Quadratic Equations

A. Some equations can be solved by *factoring*. To do this, first add or subtract expressions to bring all the expressions to one side of the equation, with 0 on the other side. Then try to express the nonzero side as a product of factors that are algebraic expressions. If this is possible, setting any one of the factors equal to 0 will yield a simpler equation, because for any factors x and y, if $xy = 0$, then $x = 0$ or $y = 0$, or both. The solutions of the simpler equations produced in this way will be solutions of the factored equation.

Example:

Factor to find the solutions of the equation $x^3 - 2x^2 + x = -5(x - 1)^2$:

$$x^3 - 2x^2 + x + 5(x - 1)^2 = 0$$
$$x\left(x^2 - 2x + 1\right) + 5(x - 1)^2 = 0$$
$$x(x - 1)^2 + 5(x - 1)^2 = 0$$
$$(x + 5)(x - 1)^2 = 0$$
$$x + 5 = 0 \ \text{ or } \ x - 1 = 0$$
$$x = -5 \ \text{ or } \ x = 1.$$

Therefore, $x = -5$ or $x = 1$.

B. To use factoring to find solutions to equations with algebraic fractions, note that a fraction equals 0 if and only if its numerator equals 0 and its denominator does not.

Example:

Find the solutions of the equation $\dfrac{x(x-3)(x^2+5)}{x-4} = 0$

First note that the numerator must equal 0: $x(x-3)(x^2+5) = 0$.

Therefore, $x = 0$ or $x - 3 = 0$ or $x^2 + 5 = 0$, so $x = 0$ or $x = 3$ or $x^2 + 5 = 0$.

But $x^2 + 5 = 0$ has no real solution because $x + 5 > 0$ for every real number. Thus, the solutions are 0 and 3.

C. The standard form for a ***quadratic equation*** is $ax^2 + bx + c = 0$, where a, b, and c are real numbers and $a \neq 0$.

Examples:

$$x^2 + 6x + 5 = 0$$

$$3x^2 - 2x = 0, \text{ and}$$

$$x^2 + 4 = 0$$

D. Some quadratic equations can easily be solved by factoring.

Example (1):

$$x^2 + 6x + 5 = 0$$
$$(x+5)(x+1) = 0$$
$$x + 5 = 0 \text{ or } x + 1 = 0$$
$$x = -5 \text{ or } x = -1$$

Example (2):

$$3x^2 - 3 = 8x$$
$$3x^2 - 8x - 3 = 0$$
$$(3x+1)(x-3) = 0$$
$$3x + 1 = 0 \text{ or } x - 3 = 0$$
$$x = -\frac{1}{3} \text{ or } x = 3$$

E. A quadratic equation has at most two real roots and may have just one or even no real root.

Examples:

The equation $x^2 - 6x + 9 = 0$ can be expressed as $(x-3)^2 = 0$, or $(x-3)(x-3) = 0$; thus, its only root is 3.

The equation $x^2 + 4 = 0$ has no real root. Since the square of any real number is greater than or equal to zero, $x^2 + 4$ must be greater than zero if x is a real number.

F. An expression of the form $a^2 - b^2$ can be factored as $(a-b)(a+b)$.

Example:

The quadratic equation $9x^2 - 25 = 0$ can be solved as follows:

$$(3x - 5)(3x + 5) = 0$$

$$3x - 5 = 0 \quad \text{or} \quad 3x + 5 = 0$$

$$x = \frac{5}{3} \quad \text{or} \quad x = -\frac{5}{3}$$

G. If a quadratic expression is not easily factored, then its roots can always be found using the ***quadratic formula:*** If $ax^2 + bx + c = 0$ and $a \neq 0$, then the roots are

$$x = \frac{-b + \sqrt{b^2 - 4ac}}{2a} \quad \text{and} \quad x = \frac{-b - \sqrt{b^2 - 4ac}}{2a}$$

These roots are two distinct real numbers unless $b^2 - 4ac \leq 0$.

If $b^2 - 4ac = 0$, then these two expressions both equal $-\dfrac{b}{2a}$, so the equation has only one root.

If $b^2 - 4ac < 0$, then $\sqrt{b^2 - 4ac}$ is not a real number, so the equation has no real roots.

4. Inequalities

A. An ***inequality*** is a statement that uses one of the following symbols:

$\neq$ is not equal to

$>$ is greater than

$\geq$ is greater than or equal to

$<$ is less than

$\leq$ is less than or equal to

Example:

$5x - 3 < 9$ and $6x \geq y$

B. Solving a linear inequality with one unknown is similar to solving a linear equation; the unknown is isolated on one side of the inequality. As in solving an equation, the same number can be added to or subtracted from both sides of the inequality, or both sides of an inequality can be multiplied or divided by a positive number without changing the order of the inequality. However, multiplying or dividing an inequality by a negative number reverses the order of the inequality. Thus, $6 > 2$, but $(-1)(6) < (-1)(2)$.

Example (1):

To solve the inequality $3x - 2 > 5$ for x, isolate x:

$$3x - 2 > 5$$

$$3x > 7 \quad \text{(add 2 to both sides)}$$

$$x > \frac{7}{3} \quad \text{(divide both sides by 3)}$$

Example (2):

To solve the inequality $\dfrac{5x-1}{-2} < 3$ for x, isolate x:

$$\frac{5x-1}{-2} < 3$$

$$5x - 1 > -6 \quad \text{(multiply both sides by } -2)$$

$$5x > -5 \quad \text{(add 1 to both sides)}$$

$$x > -1 \quad \text{(divide both sides by 5)}$$

5. Functions

A. An algebraic expression in one variable can be used to define a ***function*** of that variable. A function is denoted by a letter such as f or g along with the variable in the expression. Function notation provides a short way of writing the result of substituting a value for a variable.

Examples:

(1) The expression $x^3 - 5x^2 + 2$ defines a function f that can be denoted by $f(x) = x^3 - 5x^2 + 2$.

(2) The expression $\dfrac{2z+7}{\sqrt{z+1}}$ defines a function g that can be denoted by $g(z) = \dfrac{2z+7}{\sqrt{z+1}}$.

In these examples, the symbols "$f(x)$" and "$g(z)$" do not represent products. Each is merely the symbol for an algebraic expression, and is read "f of x" or "g of z."

If $x = 1$ is substituted in the first expression, the result can be written $f(1) = -2$, and $f(1)$ is called the "value of f at $x = 1$."

Similarly, if $z = 0$ is substituted in the second expression, then the value of g at $z = 0$ is $g(0) = 7$.

B. Once a function $f(x)$ is defined, it is useful to think of the variable x as an input and $f(x)$ as the corresponding output. In any function there can be at most one output for any given input. However, different inputs can give the same output.

Examples:

If $h(x) = |x + 3|$, then $h(-4) = 1 = h(-2)$.

C. The set of all allowable inputs for a function is called the ***domain*** of the function. For f and g as defined in the examples in 3.2.5.A above, the domain of f is the set of all real numbers and the domain of g is the set of all numbers greater than -1.

The domain of any function can be arbitrarily specified, as in the function defined by "$a(x) = 9x - 5$ for $0 \le x \le 10$." Without such a restriction, the domain is assumed to be all values of x that result in a real number when substituted into the function.

D. The set of all outputs for a function is called the ***range*** of the function.

Examples:

(i) For the function $h(x) = |x + 3|$ considered in the example in 3.2.5.B above, the range is the set of all numbers greater than or equal to 0.

(ii) For the function $a(x) = 9x - 5$ for $0 \le x \le 10$ considered in 3.2.5.C above, the range is the set including every value y such that $-5 \le y \le 85$.

6. Formulas and Measurement Conversion

A. A *formula* is an algebraic equation with specific meanings associated with its variables. To apply a formula in a particular context, find quantities that can be assigned to the formula's variables to match the meanings associated with those variables.

Example:

In the physics formula $F = ma$, the variable F stands for force, the variable m stands for mass, and the variable a stands for acceleration. The standard metric measure of force, the newton, is a force sufficient to accelerate a mass of 1 kilogram by 1 meter/second^2.

So, if we are told that a rock with a mass of 2 kilograms is accelerating at 5 meters/second^2, we can apply the formula $F = ma$ by substituting 2 kilograms for the variable m and 5 meters/second^2 for the variable a, allowing us to calculate the force applied to the rock as 10 newtons.

Note: You do not need to learn physics formulas or terminology used in this example to prepare for the GMAT, but some formulas and terminology may be introduced within specific questions on the exam.

B. Any quantitative relationship between units of measure may be represented as a formula.

Examples:

(i) Since 1 kilometer is 1,000 meters, the relationship between kilometers (k) and meters (m) may be represented by the formula $m = 1000k$.

(ii) The formula $C = \dfrac{5}{9}(F - 32)$ may be used to represent the relationship between measurements of temperature in degrees Celsius (C) and degrees Fahrenheit (F).

C. Except for units of time, if a GMAT question requires converting one unit of measure to another, the relationship between those units will be given.

Example:

A train travels at a constant rate of 25 meters per second. How many kilometers does it travel in 5 minutes? (1 kilometer = 1,000 meters)

Solution: In 1 minute the train travels $(25)(60) = 1,500$ meters, so in 5 minutes it travels 7,500 meters. Since 1 kilometer = 1,000 meters, it follows that 7,500 meters = 7.5 kilometers.

D. In some cases the relationship between units to be converted may be indicated in a table or graph.

Example:

Population by Age Group (in thousands)	
Age	Population
17 years and under	63,376
18–44 years	86,738
45–64 years	43,845
65 years and over	24,051

According to the table above, how many people are 44 years old or younger?

Solution: The table header states that the population figures are given in ***thousands***. The answer in thousands can be obtained by adding 63,376 thousand and 86,738 thousand. The result is 150,114 thousand, which is 150,114,000.

PS21840.03

Practice Question 6

Number of Solid-Colored Marbles in Three Jars			
Jar	Number of red marbles	Number of green marbles	Total number of red and green marbles
P	x	y	80
Q	y	z	120
R	x	z	160

In the table above, what is the number of green marbles in Jar R ?

- (A) 70
- (B) 80
- (C) 90
- (D) 100
- (E) 110

DS71210.03

Practice Question 7

In Mr. Smith's class, what is the ratio of the number of boys to the number of girls?

(1) There are 3 times as many girls as boys in Mr. Smith's class.

(2) The number of boys is $\frac{1}{4}$ of the total number of boys and girls in Mr. Smith's class.

- (A) Statement (1) ALONE is sufficient, but statement (2) alone is not sufficient.
- (B) Statement (2) ALONE is sufficient, but statement (1) alone is not sufficient.
- (C) BOTH statements TOGETHER are sufficient, but NEITHER statement ALONE is sufficient.
- (D) EACH statement ALONE is sufficient.
- (E) Statements (1) and (2) TOGETHER are NOT sufficient.

DS84820.03

Practice Question 8

If x is an integer, is $9^x + 9^{-x} = b$?

(1) $3^x + 3^{-x} = \sqrt{b + 2}$

(2) $x > 0$

    (A)   Statement (1) ALONE is sufficient, but statement (2) alone is not sufficient.

    (B)   Statement (2) ALONE is sufficient, but statement (1) alone is not sufficient.

    (C)   BOTH statements TOGETHER are sufficient, but NEITHER statement ALONE is sufficient.

    (D)   EACH statement ALONE is sufficient.

    (E)   Statements (1) and (2) TOGETHER are NOT sufficient.

DS67730.03

Practice Question 9

What is the total number of executives at Company P?

(1)   The number of male executives is $\dfrac{3}{5}$ the number of female executives.

(2)   There are 4 more female executives than male executives.

    (A)   Statement (1) ALONE is sufficient, but statement (2) alone is not sufficient.

    (B)   Statement (2) ALONE is sufficient, but statement (1) alone is not sufficient.

    (C)   BOTH statements TOGETHER are sufficient, but NEITHER statement ALONE is sufficient.

    (D)   EACH statement ALONE is sufficient.

    (E)   Statements (1) and (2) TOGETHER are NOT sufficient.

DS53060.02

Practice Question 10

Is $x > y$?

(1) $x = y + 2$

(2) $\dfrac{x}{2} = y - 1$

    (A)   Statement (1) ALONE is sufficient, but statement (2) alone is not sufficient.

    (B)   Statement (2) ALONE is sufficient, but statement (1) alone is not sufficient.

    (C)   BOTH statements TOGETHER are sufficient, but NEITHER statement ALONE is sufficient.

    (D)   EACH statement ALONE is sufficient.

    (E)   Statements (1) and (2) TOGETHER are NOT sufficient.

PS21840.03

Answer Explanation 6

Number of Solid-Colored Marbles in Three Jars			
Jar	Number of red marbles	Number of green marbles	Total number of red and green marbles
P	x	y	80
Q	y	z	120
R	x	z	160

In the table above, what is the number of green marbles in Jar R?

(A)   70

(B)   80

(C)   90

(D)   100

(E)   110

Arithmetic; Algebra Interpretation of Tables; Applied Problems

First, set up an equation to find the total number of marbles in the three jars as follows:

$x + y + y + z + x + z = 80 + 120 + 160$

$2x + 2y + 2z = 360$ combine the like terms

$x + y + z = 180$ divide both sides by 2

Then, since it can be seen from the table that the number of green marbles in Jar R is z, solve for z to answer the problem. To do this most efficiently, use the information from the table for Jar P, which is that $x + y = 80$.

$x + y + z = 180$

$80 + z = 180$ substitute 80 for $x + y$

$z = 100$

The correct answer is D.

DS71210.03
Answer Explanation 7

In Mr. Smith's class, what is the ratio of the number of boys to the number of girls?

(1)   There are 3 times as many girls as boys in Mr. Smith's class.

(2)   The number of boys is $\dfrac{1}{4}$ of the total number of boys and girls in Mr. Smith's class.

Algebra Ratio and Proportion

Letting B be the number of boys and G be the number of girls, determine the value of $\dfrac{B}{G}$.

(1)   It is given that $G = 3B$, so $\dfrac{1}{3} = \dfrac{B}{G}$; SUFFICIENT.

(2)   It is given that $B = \dfrac{1}{4}(B + G)$. Therefore, $4B = B + G$, or $3B = G$, or $\dfrac{B}{G} = \dfrac{1}{3}$; SUFFICIENT.

The correct answer is D; each statement alone is sufficient.

DS84820.03
Answer Explanation 8

If x is an integer, is $9^x + 9^{-x} = b$?

(1) $3^x + 3^{-x} = \sqrt{b + 2}$

(2) $x > 0$

Algebra Exponents

When solving this problem, it is helpful to note that $(x^r)(x^{-s}) = x^{r-s}$ and that $(x^r)^2 = x^{2r}$. Note also that $x^0 = 1$.

(1) From this, $3^x + 3^{-x} = \sqrt{b+2}$. Squaring both sides gives:

$$(3^x + 3^{-x})^2 = b + 2$$

$$3^{2x} + 2(3^x)(3^{-x}) + 3^{-2x} = b + 2$$

$$9^x + 2(3^0) + 9^{-x} = b + 2 \quad \text{property of exponents}$$

$$9^x + 2 + 9^{-x} = b + 2 \quad \text{property of exponents}$$

$$9^x + 9^{-x} = b \quad \text{subtract 2 from both sides; SUFFICIENT.}$$

(2) This gives no information about the relationship between x and b; NOT sufficient.

The correct answer is A; statement 1 alone is sufficient.

DS67730.03
Answer Explanation 9

What is the total number of executives at Company P ?

(1) The number of male executives is $\frac{3}{5}$ the number of female executives.

(2) There are 4 more female executives than male executives.

Algebra Simultaneous Equations

Let M be the number of male executives at Company P and let F be the number of female executives at Company P. Determine the value of $M + F$.

(1) Given that $M = \frac{3}{5}F$, it is not possible to determine the value of $M + F$. For example, if $M = 3$ and

$F = 5$, then $M = \frac{3}{5}F$ and $M + F = 8$. However, if $M = 6$ and $F = 10$, then $M = \frac{3}{5}F$ and $M + F = 16$;

NOT sufficient.

(2) Given that $F = M + 4$, it is not possible to determine the value of $M + F$. For example, if $M = 3$ and $F = 7$, then $F = M + 4$ and $M + F = 10$. However, if $M = 4$ and $F = 8$, then $F = M + 4$ and $M + F = 12$; NOT sufficient.

Taking (1) and (2) together, then $F = M + 4$ and $M = \frac{3}{5}F + 4$, so $F = \frac{3}{5}F + 4$. Now solve for F to get $\frac{2}{5}F = 4$

and $F = 10$. Therefore, using $F = 10$ and $F = M + 4$, it follows that $M = 6$, and hence $M + F = 6 + 10 = 16$.

The correct answer is C; both statements together are sufficient.

DS53060.02
Answer Explanation 10

Is $x > y$?

(1) $x = y + 2$

(2) $\frac{x}{2} = y - 1$

Algebra Inequalities

(1) $x = y + 2$ so $x - y = 2$ and since $2 > 0$,
$x - y > 0$ and $x > y$; SUFFICIENT.

(2) The equation given is equivalent to $x = 2y - 2$, which is satisfied both by $x = 0$ and $y = 1$ ($x > y$ is false) and by $x = 4$ and $y = 3$ ($x > y$ is true); NOT sufficient.

The correct answer is A; statement 1 alone is sufficient.

3.3 Rates, Ratios, and Percents

1. Ratio and Proportion

A. The *ratio* of the number x to a nonzero number y may be expressed as $x : y$, or $\frac{x}{y}$, or x to y. The order of the terms is important in a ratio. Unless the absolute values of x and y are equal, $\frac{x}{y} \neq \frac{y}{x}$.

> *Examples:*
>
> The ratio of 2 to 3 may be written as 2:3, or $\frac{2}{3}$, or 2 to 3.
>
> The ratio of the number of months with exactly 30 days to the number with exactly 31 days is 4:7, not 7:4.

B. A *proportion* is a statement that two ratios are equal.

> *Example:*
>
> 2:3 = 8:12 is a proportion.

C. One way to find the value of an unknown variable in a proportion is to cross multiply, then solve the resulting equation.

> *Example:*
>
> To solve for n in the proportion $\frac{2}{3} = \frac{n}{12}$, cross multiply to obtain $3n = 24$, then divide both sides by 3 to find $n = 8$.

D. Some word problems can be solved using ratios.

> *Example:*
>
> If 5 shirts cost a total of \$44, then what is the total cost of 8 shirts at the same cost per shirt?
>
> *Solution:* If c is the cost of the 8 shirts, then $\frac{5}{44} = \frac{8}{c}$. Cross multiplication yields $5c = 8 \times 44 = 352$, so $c = \frac{352}{5} = 70.4$. Thus, the 8 shirts cost a total of \$70.40.

2. Fractions

A. In a fraction $\frac{n}{d}$, n is the **numerator** and d is the **denominator**. The denominator of a fraction can never be 0, because division by 0 is not defined.

B. Two fractions are **equivalent** if they represent the same number. To determine whether two fractions are equivalent, divide each fraction's numerator and denominator by the largest factor the numerator and the denominator have in common, which is called their **greatest common divisor** (gcd). This process is called **reducing each fraction to its lowest terms**. The two fractions are equivalent if and only if reducing each to its lowest terms yields identical results.

> *Example:*
>
> To determine whether $\frac{8}{36}$ and $\frac{14}{63}$ are equivalent, first reduce each to its lowest terms. In the first fraction, the gcd of the numerator 8 and the denominator 36 is 4. Dividing both the numerator and the denominator of $\frac{8}{36}$ by 4 yields $\frac{2}{9}$. In the second fraction, the gcd of the numerator 14 and the denominator 63 is 7. Dividing both the numerator and the denominator of $\frac{14}{63}$ by 7 also yields $\frac{2}{9}$.
>
> Since reducing each fraction to its lowest terms yields the same result, $\frac{8}{36}$ and $\frac{14}{63}$ are equivalent.

C. Two fractions with the same denominator can be added or subtracted by performing the required operation with the numerators, leaving the denominators the same.

> *Example:*
>
> $$\frac{3}{5} + \frac{4}{5} = \frac{3+4}{5} = \frac{7}{5} \text{ and}$$
>
> $$\frac{5}{7} - \frac{2}{7} = \frac{5-2}{7} = \frac{3}{7}$$

D. If two fractions do not have the same denominator, you can add or subtract them by first expressing them as fractions with the same denominator.

> *Examples:*
>
> To add $\frac{3}{5}$ and $\frac{4}{7}$, multiply the numerator and denominator of $\frac{3}{5}$ by 7 to obtain $\frac{21}{35}$.
>
> Then multiply the numerator and denominator of $\frac{4}{7}$ by 5 to obtain $\frac{20}{35}$. Since both fractions are now expressed with the same denominator 35, you can easily add them:
>
> $$\frac{3}{5} + \frac{4}{7} = \frac{21}{35} + \frac{20}{35} = \frac{41}{35}$$

E. To multiply two fractions, simply multiply the two numerators and also multiply the two denominators.

Example:

$$\frac{2}{3} \times \frac{4}{7} = \frac{2 \times 4}{3 \times 7} = \frac{8}{21}$$

F. In general, the *reciprocal* of a fraction $\frac{n}{d}$ is $\frac{d}{n}$, when n and d are not 0.

Example:

The reciprocal of $\frac{4}{7}$ is $\frac{7}{4}$.

G. To divide by a fraction, multiply by the reciprocal of the divisor.

Example:

$$\frac{2}{3} \div \frac{4}{7} = \frac{2}{3} \times \frac{7}{4} = \frac{14}{12} = \frac{7}{6}$$

H. A *mixed number* is written as an integer together with a fraction and equals the sum of the integer and the fraction.

Example:

The mixed number $7\frac{2}{3} = 7 + \frac{2}{3}$

I. To express a mixed number as a fraction, multiply the integer portion of the mixed number by the denominator of the fraction portion of the mixed number. Add this product to the numerator. Then put this sum over the denominator.

Example:

$$7\frac{2}{3} = \frac{(7 \times 3) + 2}{3} = \frac{23}{3}$$

3. Percents

A. The term *percent* means *per hundred* or *number out of 100*.

Example:

The statement that 37 percent, or 37%, of the houses in a city are painted blue means that 37 out of every 100 houses in the city are painted blue.

B. A percent may be greater than 100.

> *Example:*
>
> The statement that the number of blue houses in a city is 150% of the number of red houses means that the city has 150 blue houses for every 100 red houses. Since 150:100 = 3:2, this is equivalent to saying that the city has 3 blue houses for every 2 red houses.

C. A percent need not be an integer.

> *Example:*
>
> The statement that the number of pink houses in a city is 0.5% of the number of blue houses means that the city has 0.5 of a pink house for every 100 blue houses. Since 0.5:100 = 1:200, this is equivalent to saying that the city has 1 pink house for every 200 blue houses.
>
> Similarly, the statement that the number of orange houses is 12.5% of the number of blue houses means that the ratio of orange houses to blue houses is 12.5:100 = 1:8, so there is 1 orange house for every 8 blue houses.

4. Converting Decimals, Fractions, and Percents

A. Decimal numbers may be represented as fractions or sums of fractions.

> *Example:*
>
> $$0.321 = \frac{3}{10} + \frac{2}{100} + \frac{1}{1,000} = \frac{321}{1,000}$$
>
> $$0.0321 = \frac{0}{10} + \frac{3}{100} + \frac{2}{1,000} + \frac{1}{10,000} = \frac{321}{10,000}$$
>
> $$1.56 = 1 + \frac{5}{10} + \frac{6}{100} = \frac{156}{100}$$

B. A percent may be represented as a fraction in which the percent number is the numerator over a denominator of 100. A percent may also be represented as a decimal by moving the decimal point in the percent two places to the left. Conversely, a decimal may be represented as a percent by moving the decimal point two places to the right, then adding a percent sign (%).

> *Examples:*
>
> $$37\% = \frac{37}{100} = 0.37$$
>
> $$300\% = \frac{300}{100} = 3$$
>
> $$0.5\% = \frac{0.5}{100} = 0.005$$

C. To find a certain percent of a number, multiply the number by the percent expressed as a fraction or as a decimal.

> *Examples:*
>
> 20% of $90 = 90\left(\dfrac{20}{100}\right) = 90\left(\dfrac{1}{5}\right) = \dfrac{90}{5} = 18$
>
> 20% of $90 = 90(0.2) = 18$
>
> 250% of $80 = 80\left(\dfrac{250}{100}\right) = 80(2.5) = 200$
>
> 0.5% of $12 = 12\left(\dfrac{0.5}{100}\right) = 12(0.005) = 0.06$

5. Working with Decimals, Fractions, and Percents

A. To find the percent increase or decrease from one quantity to another quantity, first find the amount of the increase or decrease. Then divide this amount by the original quantity, and express this quotient as a percent.

> *Examples:*
>
> Suppose the price of an item increases from \$24 to \$30. To find the percent increase, first note that the amount of the increase is \$30 – \$24 = \$6. Therefore, the percent increase is $\dfrac{6}{24}$ = $0.25 = 25\%$.
>
> Now suppose the price decreases from \$30 to \$24. The amount of the decrease is \$30 – \$24 = \$6. Therefore, the percent decrease is $\dfrac{6}{30}$ = $0.20 = 20\%$.
>
> Note that the percent **increase** from 24 to 30 (25%) does not equal the percent **decrease** from 30 to 24 (20%).

A percent increase and a percent decrease may be greater than 100%.

> *Example:*
>
> Suppose the price of a certain house in 2018 was 300% of its price in 2003. By what percent did the price increase?
>
> *Solution:* If n is the price in 2003, then the percent increase is $\left|\dfrac{(3n-n)}{n}\right| = \left|\dfrac{2n}{n}\right| = 2$, or 200%.

B. If a price is discounted by n percent, then the discounted price is $(100 - n)$ percent of the original price.

Example:

A customer paid $24 for a dress. If that price reflected a 25% discount off the original price of the dress, what was the original price before the discount?

Solution: If p is the original price of the dress, then $0.75p$ is the discounted price, so $0.75p = \$24$. Thus, $p = \$32$, the original price before the discount.

Two discounts may be combined to yield a larger discount.

Example:

A price is discounted by 20%, and then this reduced price is discounted by an additional 30%. These two discounts combined yield an overall discount of what percent?

Solution: If p is the original price of the item, then $0.8p$ is the price after the first discount. The price after the second discount is $(0.7)(0.8)\,p = 0.56p$. This represents an overall discount of 44% (100% − 56%).

C. Gross profit equals revenues minus expenses, or selling price minus cost.

Example:

A certain appliance costs a merchant $30. At what price should the merchant sell the appliance in order to make a gross profit of 50% of the cost of the appliance?

Solution: If s is the selling price of the appliance, then $s - 30 = (0.5)(30)$, or $s = \$45$. Thus, the merchant should sell the appliance for $45.

D. **Simple annual interest** on a loan or investment is computed based only on the original loan or investment amount (the **principal**), and equals (principal) × (interest rate) × (time).

Example:

If $8,000 is invested at 6% simple annual interest, how much interest is earned after 3 months?

Solution: Since the annual interest rate is 6%, the interest for 1 year is $(0.06)(\$8{,}000) = \$480$. There are 12 months in a year, so the interest earned in 3 months is $\left(\frac{3}{12}\right)(\$480) = \$120$

E. **Compound interest** is computed on the principal as well as on any interest already earned.

Compound interest over n periods = (principal) × (1 + interest per period)^n − principal.

Example:

If $10,000 is invested at 10% annual interest, compounded semiannually, what is the balance after 1 year?

Solution: Since the interest is compounded semiannually (every 6 months), the interest rate for each 6-month period is 5%, which is half of the 10% annual rate. Thus, the balance after the first 6 months would be 10,000 + (10,000)(0.05) = $10,500.

For the second 6-month period, the interest is calculated on the $10,500 balance at the end of the first 6-month period. Thus, the balance after 1 year would be 10,500 + (10,500)(0.05) = $11,025.

The balance after one year can also be expressed as $10,000 \times \left(1 + \dfrac{0.10}{2}\right)^2$ dollars.

F. Some GMAT questions require working with decimals, fractions, and percents in graphs.

Example:

DISTRIBUTION OF AL'S WEEKLY NET SALARY

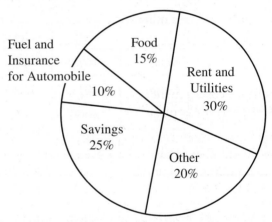

Al's weekly net salary is $350. How many of the categories shown in the chart above were each individually allocated at least $80 of Al's weekly net salary?

Solution: In the circle graph, the relative sizes of the sectors are proportional to their corresponding values, and the sum of the percents given is 100%. Note that $\dfrac{\$80}{\$350}$ is approximately 23%, so

$80 or more of Al's salary was allocated to a category if and only if at least 23% of his salary was allocated to that category. Thus, according to the graph, there were exactly two categories to each of which at least $80 of Al's salary was allocated—the category *Savings* was allocated 25% of his salary, and the category *Rent and Utilities* was allocated 30%.

G. To solve some word problems involving percents and fractions, it can be helpful to organize the given information in a table.

Example:

In a certain production lot, 40% of the toys are red and the remaining toys are green. Half of the toys are small and half are large. If 10% of the toys are red and small, and 40 toys are green and large, how many of the toys are red and large?

Solution: First create a table to organize the information provided:

	Red	Green	Total
Small	10%		50%
Large			50%
Total	40%	60%	100%

Then fill in the missing percents so that the "Red" and "Green" percents in each row add up to the total in that row, and the "Small" and "Large" percents in each column add up to the total in that column:

	Red	Green	Total
Small	10%	40%	50%
Large	30%	20%	50%
Total	40%	60%	100%

Since 20% of the number of toys (n) are green and large, $0.20n = 40$. That is, 40 of the toys are green and large, and the total number of toys $n = 200$. Therefore, 30% of the 200 toys are red and large. Since $(0.3)(200) = 60$, it follows that 60 of the toys are red and large.

6. Rate, Work, and Mixture Problems

A. The distance an object travels equals the average speed at which it travels multiplied by the amount of time it takes to travel that distance. That is, ***distance = rate × time.***

Example:

If a car travels at an average speed of 70 kilometers per hour for 4 hours, how many kilometers does it travel?

Solution: Since distance = rate × time, simply multiply 70 km/hour × 4 hours. Thus, the car travels 280 kilometers in 4 hours.

B. To determine the average rate at which an object travels, divide the total distance traveled by the total amount of traveling time.

Example:

On a 600-kilometer trip, a car traveled half the distance at an average speed of 60 kilometers per hour (kph) and the other half at an average speed of 100 kph. The car did not stop between the two halves of the trip. What was the car's average speed during the trip as a whole?

Solution: First determine the total amount of traveling time. During the first 300 kilometers, the car traveled at 60 kph, so it took $\frac{300}{60} = 5$ hours to travel the first 300 kilometers. During the second 300 kilometers, the car traveled at 100 kph, so it took $\frac{300}{100} = 3$ hours to travel the second 300 kilometers. Thus, the total amount of traveling time was $5 + 3 = 8$ hours, and the car's average speed was $\frac{600 \text{ kilometers}}{8 \text{ hours}} = 75$ kph.

Note that the average speed is not $\frac{(60 + 100)}{2} = 80$ kph.

C. In a ***work problem***, the rates at which certain persons or machines work alone are usually given, and it is necessary to compute the rate at which they work together (or vice versa).

The basic formula for solving work problems is $\frac{1}{r} + \frac{1}{s} = \frac{1}{h}$, where r is the length of time it takes the first person or machine to complete an amount of work when working alone, s is the length of time it takes the second person or machine to complete that same amount of work when working alone, and h is the length of time it takes them to complete that amount of work when they are both working simultaneously.

Example:

Suppose one machine can produce 1,000 bolts in 4 hours, whereas a second machine can produce 1,000 bolts in 5 hours. Then in how many hours can the two machines, working simultaneously at these constant rates, produce 1,000 bolts?

Solution:

$$\frac{1}{4} + \frac{1}{5} = \frac{1}{h}$$

$$\frac{5}{20} + \frac{4}{20} = \frac{1}{h}$$

$$\frac{9}{20} = \frac{1}{h}$$

$$9h = 20$$

$$h = \frac{20}{9} = 2\frac{2}{9}$$

Working together, the two machines can produce 1,000 bolts in $2\frac{2}{9}$ hours.

The same formula can be applied to determine how long it would take one of the people or machines to do a given amount of work alone.

Example:

Suppose that Art and Rita can complete an amount of work in 4 hours when working simultaneously at their respective constant rates, and that Art can complete the same amount of work in 6 hours working alone. Then in how many hours can Rita complete that amount of work working alone?

Solution:

$$\frac{1}{6} + \frac{1}{R} = \frac{1}{4}$$

$$\frac{1}{R} = \frac{1}{4} - \frac{1}{6} = \frac{1}{12}$$

$$R = 12$$

Working alone, Rita can complete the work in 12 hours.

D. In ***mixture problems***, substances with different characteristics are combined, and it is necessary to determine the characteristics of the resulting mixture.

Example:

If 6 kilograms of nuts that cost $1.20 per kilogram are mixed with 2 kilograms of nuts that cost $1.60 per kilogram, then how much does the mixture cost per kilogram?

Solution: The total cost of the 8 kilograms of nuts is 6($1.20) + 2($1.60) = $10.40. Thus, the cost per kilogram is $\frac{\$10.40}{8}$ = $1.30.

More complex mixture problems may involve calculating percents.

Example:

How many liters of a solution that is 15% salt must be added to 5 liters of a solution that is 8% salt so that the resulting solution is 10% salt?

Solution: Let n represent the number of liters of the 15% solution. The amount of salt in the 15% solution [$0.15n$] plus the amount of salt in the 8% solution [$(0.08)(5)$] must equal the amount of salt in the 10% mixture [$0.10(n + 5)$]. Therefore,

$$0.15n + 0.08(5) = 0.10(n + 5)$$

$$15n + 40 = 10n + 50$$

$$5n = 10$$

$$n = 2 \text{ liters}$$

Two liters of the 15% salt solution must be added to the 8% solution to obtain the 10% solution.

PS51061.03
Practice Question 11

As a salesperson, Phyllis can choose one of two methods of annual payment: either an annual salary of $35,000 with no commission or an annual salary of $10,000 plus a 20% commission on her total annual sales. What must her total annual sales be to give her the same annual pay with either method?

- (A) $100,000
- (B) $120,000
- (C) $125,000
- (D) $130,000
- (E) $132,000

DS15161.03
Practice Question 12

For which type of investment, J or K, is the annual rate of return greater?

- (1) Type J returns $115 per $1,000 invested for any one-year period and type K returns $300 per $2,500 invested for any one-year period.
- (2) The annual rate of return for an investment of type K is 12%.
    - (A) Statement (1) ALONE is sufficient, but statement (2) alone is not sufficient.
    - (B) Statement (2) ALONE is sufficient, but statement (1) alone is not sufficient.
    - (C) BOTH statements TOGETHER are sufficient, but NEITHER statement ALONE is sufficient.
    - (D) EACH statement ALONE is sufficient.
    - (E) Statements (1) and (2) TOGETHER are NOT sufficient.

DS07061.03
Practice Question 13

If Car X followed Car Y across a certain bridge that is a $\frac{1}{2}$ mile long, how many seconds did it take Car X to travel across the bridge?

- (1) Car X drove onto the bridge exactly 3 seconds after Car Y drove onto the bridge and drove off the bridge exactly 2 seconds after Car Y drove off the bridge.
- (2) Car Y traveled across the bridge at a constant speed of 30 miles per hour.
    - (A) Statement (1) ALONE is sufficient, but statement (2) alone is not sufficient.
    - (B) Statement (2) ALONE is sufficient, but statement (1) alone is not sufficient.
    - (C) BOTH statements TOGETHER are sufficient, but NEITHER statement ALONE is sufficient.
    - (D) EACH statement ALONE is sufficient.
    - (E) Statements (1) and (2) TOGETHER are NOT sufficient.

PS23461.03
Practice Question 14

If $x > 0$, $\dfrac{x}{50} + \dfrac{x}{25}$ is what percent of x ?

- (A) 6%
- (B) 25%
- (C) 37%
- (D) 60%
- (E) 75%

PS61361.03
Practice Question 15

The cost to rent a small bus for a trip is x dollars, which is to be shared equally among the people taking the trip. If 10 people take the trip rather than 16, how many more dollars, in terms of x, will it cost per person?

(A) $\dfrac{x}{6}$

(B) $\dfrac{x}{10}$

(C) $\dfrac{x}{16}$

(D) $\dfrac{3x}{40}$

(E) $\dfrac{3x}{80}$

PS51061.03
Answer Explanation 11

As a salesperson, Phyllis can choose one of two methods of annual payment: either an annual salary of $35,000 with no commission or an annual salary of $10,000 plus a 20% commission on her total annual sales. What must her total annual sales be to give her the same annual pay with either method?

(A) $100,000
(B) $120,000
(C) $125,000
(D) $130,000
(E) $132,000

Algebra Applied Problems

Letting s be Phyllis's total annual sales needed to generate the same annual pay with either method, the given information can be expressed as $35,000 = $10,000 + 0.2s$. Solve this equation for s.

$$\$35,000 = \$10,000 + 0.2s$$

$$\$25,000 = 0.2s$$

$$\$125,000 = s$$

The correct answer is C.

DS15161.03
Answer Explanation 12

For which type of investment, J or K, is the annual rate of return greater?

(1) Type J returns $115 per $1,000 invested for any one-year period and type K returns $300 per $2,500 invested for any one-year period.

(2) The annual rate of return for an investment of type K is 12%.

Arithmetic Percents

Compare the annual rates of return for Investments J and K.

(1) For Investment J, the annual rate of return is $115 per $1,000 for any one-year period, which can be converted to a percent. For Investment K, the annual rate of return is $300 per $2,500 for any one-year

period, which can also be converted to a percent. These two percents can be compared to determine which is greater; SUFFICIENT.

(2) Investment K has an annual rate of return of 12%, but no information is given about the annual rate of return for Investment J; NOT sufficient.

The correct answer is A; statement 1 alone is sufficient.

DS07061.03
Answer Explanation 13

If Car X followed Car Y across a certain bridge that is a $\frac{1}{2}$ mile long, how many seconds did it take Car X to travel across the bridge?

(1) Car X drove onto the bridge exactly 3 seconds after Car Y drove onto the bridge and drove off the bridge exactly 2 seconds after Car Y drove off the bridge.

(2) Car Y traveled across the bridge at a constant speed of 30 miles per hour.

    (A) Statement (1) ALONE is sufficient, but statement (2) alone is not sufficient.

    (B) Statement (2) ALONE is sufficient, but statement (1) alone is not sufficient.

    (C) BOTH statements TOGETHER are sufficient, but NEITHER statement ALONE is sufficient.

    (D) EACH statement ALONE is sufficient.

    (E) Statements (1) and (2) TOGETHER are NOT sufficient.

Arithmetic Rate Problem

Find the number of seconds that it took Car X to cross the $\frac{1}{2}$-mile bridge.

(1) If Car X drove onto the bridge 3 seconds after Car Y and drove off the bridge 2 seconds after Car Y, then Car X took 1 second less to cross the bridge than Car Y. Since there is no information on how long Car Y took to cross the bridge, there is no way to determine how long Car X took to cross the bridge; NOT sufficient.

(2) If the speed of Car Y was 30 miles per hour, it took Car Y $\frac{1}{60}$ hour = 1 minute = 60 seconds to cross the bridge. However, there is no information on how long Car X took to cross the bridge; NOT sufficient.

Taking (1) and (2) together, Car X took 1 second less than Car Y to cross the bridge and Car Y took 60 seconds to cross the bridge, so Car X took 60 − 1 = 59 seconds to cross the bridge.

The correct answer is C; both statements together are sufficient.

PS23461.03
Answer Explanation 14

If $x > 0$, $\frac{x}{50} + \frac{x}{25}$ is what percent of x ?

    (A) 6%

    (B) 25%

    (C) 37%

    (D) 60%

    (E) 75%

Algebra Arithmetic; Simplifying Algebraic Expressions; Percents

Because we want a percent, use a common denominator of 100 to combine the two terms.

$$\frac{x}{50} + \frac{x}{25} = \frac{2x}{100} + \frac{4x}{100} = \frac{6x}{100} = \left(\frac{6}{100}\right)x, \text{ which is 6\% of } x.$$

The correct answer is A.

PS61361.03
Answer Explanation 15

The cost to rent a small bus for a trip is x dollars, which is to be shared equally among the people taking the trip. If 10 people take the trip rather than 16, how many more dollars, in terms of x, will it cost per person?

(A) $\dfrac{x}{6}$

(B) $\dfrac{x}{10}$

(C) $\dfrac{x}{16}$

(D) $\dfrac{3x}{40}$

(E) $\dfrac{3x}{80}$

Algebra Applied Problems

If 16 people take the trip, the cost per person would be $\dfrac{x}{16}$ dollars. If 10 people take the trip, the cost would be $\dfrac{x}{10}$ dollars. (Note that the lowest common multiple of 10 and 16 is 80.) Thus, if 10 people take the trip, the increase in dollars per person would be $\dfrac{x}{10} - \dfrac{x}{16} = \dfrac{8x}{80} - \dfrac{5x}{80} = \dfrac{3x}{80}$.

The correct answer is E.

3.4 Statistics, Sets, Counting, Probability, Estimation, and Series

1. Statistics

A. One of the most common statistical measures is the *average*, or *(arithmetic) mean*, which locates a type of "center" for the numbers in a set of data. The average or mean of n numbers is defined as the sum of the n numbers divided by n.

> *Example:*
> The average of the 5 numbers 6, 4, 7, 10, and 4 is $\dfrac{(6+4+7+10+4)}{5} = \dfrac{31}{5} = 6.2$.

B. The *median* is another type of center for a set of numbers. To determine the median of a set of n numbers, first order the numbers from least to greatest. If n is odd, the median is defined as the middle number in the list, whereas if n is even, the median is defined as the average of the two middle numbers. The median may be less than, equal to, or greater than the mean of the same set of numbers.

Example:

To find the median of the 5 numbers 6, 4, 7, 10, and 4, first order them from least to greatest: 4, 4, 6, 7, 10. The median is 6, the middle number in this list.

The median of the 6 numbers 4, 6, 6, 8, 9, 12 is $\frac{(6+8)}{2} = 7$. Note that the mean of these 6

numbers is $\frac{(4+6+6+8+9+12)}{6} = \frac{45}{6} = 7.5$.

Often about half of the data in a set is less than the median and about half is greater than the median, but not always.

Example:

For the 15 numbers 3, 5, 7, 7, 7, 7, 7, 7, 8, 9, 9, 9, 9, 10, and 10, the median is 7, but only $\frac{2}{15}$ of the numbers are less than the median.

C. The *mode* of a list of numbers is the number that occurs most frequently in the list.

Example:

The mode of the list of numbers 1, 3, 6, 4, 3, 5 is 3, since 3 is the only number that occurs more than once in the list.

A list of numbers may have more than one mode.

Example:

The list of numbers 1, 2, 3, 3, 3, 5, 7, 10, 10, 10, 20 has two modes, 3 and 10.

D. The degree to which numerical data are spread out or dispersed can be measured in many ways. The simplest measure of dispersion is the *range,* which is defined as the greatest value in the numerical data minus the least value.

Example:

The range of the 5 numbers 11, 10, 5, 13, 21 is 21 − 5 = 16. Note how the range depends on only two values in the data.

E. Another common measure of dispersion is the ***standard deviation.*** Generally speaking, the more the data are spread away from the mean, the greater the standard deviation. The standard deviation of n numbers can be calculated as follows:

(1) Find the arithmetic mean,

(2) Find the differences between the mean and each of the n numbers,

(3) Square each of the differences,

(4) Find the average of the squared differences, and

(5) Take the nonnegative square root of this average.

Example:

The table below is used in calculating the standard deviation of the 5 numbers 0, 7, 8, 10, 10, which have the mean 7.

x	$x - 7$	$(x - 7)^2$
0	−7	49
7	0	0
8	1	1
10	3	9
10	3	9
	Total	68

Standard deviation $\sqrt{\dfrac{68}{5}} \approx 3.7$

Notice that the standard deviation depends on every data value, although it depends most on values farthest from the mean. This is why a data set whose data is grouped closely around the mean will have a smaller standard deviation than will a data set whose data is spread far from the mean.

Consider as a second example the data 6, 6, 6.5, 7.5, 9, which also have mean 7. Note that the numbers in this second example are grouped more closely around the mean of 7 than the numbers in the first example are. As a result, the standard deviation of the numbers in this second example is only about 1.1, significantly lower than the standard deviation of 3.7 in the first example above.

F. There are many ways to display numerical data in order to show how the data are distributed. One simple way is with a ***frequency distribution,*** which is useful for data in which values occur with varying frequencies.

Example:

Consider the following data set of 20 numbers:

−4	0	0	−3	−2	−1	−1	0	−1	−4
−1	−5	0	−2	0	−5	−2	0	0	−1

The data set's frequency distribution can be displayed in a table by listing each different data value x and the frequency f with which x occurs:

Data Value x	Frequency f
−5	2
−4	2
−3	1
−2	3
−1	5
0	7
Total	20

This frequency distribution table can be used to easily compute statistical measures of the data set:

Mean: $= \dfrac{(-5)(2)+(-4)(2)+(-3)(1)+(-2)(3)+(-1)(5)+(0)(7)}{20} = -1.6$

Median: −1 (the average of the 10th and 11th numbers)

Mode: 0 (the number that occurs most frequently)

Range: 0 − (−5) = 5

Standard deviation: $\sqrt{\dfrac{(-5+1.6)^2(2)+(-4+1.6)^2(2)+\ldots+(0+1.6)^2(7)}{20}} \approx 1.7$

G. Some GMAT questions require identifying or computing statistical measures for data displayed in graphs.

Example:

AVERAGE TEMPERATURE AND PRECIPITATION IN CITY X

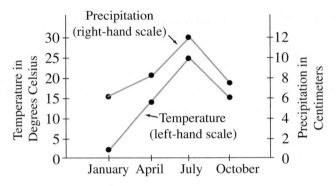

What are the average temperature and precipitation in City X during April?

Solution: Note that the scale on the left applies to the temperature line graph and the one on the right applies to the precipitation line graph. According to the graph, during April the average temperature is approximately 14° Celsius and the average precipitation is approximately 8 centimeters. Since the question is about only the averages during April, the data points shown for January, July, and October are irrelevant.

2. Sets

A. In mathematics a *set* is a collection of numbers or other objects. The objects are called the *elements* of the set. A set with a finite number of elements may be denoted by listing its elements within a pair of braces. The order in which the elements are listed does not matter.

Example:

$\{-5, 0, 1\}$ is the same set as $\{0, 1, -5\}$; that is, $\{-5, 0, 1\} = \{0, 1, -5\}$.

B. If S is a set with a finite number of elements, then the number of elements is denoted by $|S|$.

Example:

$S = \{-5, 0, 1\}$ is a set with $|S| = 3$.

C. If all the elements of a set S are also elements of a set T, then S is a *subset* of T. This relationship is expressed by $S \subseteq T$ or by $T \supseteq S$.

Example:

$\{-5, 0, 1\}$ is a subset of $\{-5, 0, 1, 4, 10\}$; that is, $\{-5, 0, 1\} \subseteq \{-5, 0, 1, 4, 10\}$.

D. The **union** of two sets A and B is the set of all elements that are in A or in B or in both. The union is denoted by $A \cup B$.

Example:

$\{3, 4\} \cup \{4, 5, 6\} = \{3, 4, 5, 6\}$

E. The **intersection** of two sets A and B is the set of all elements that are **both** in A and in B. The intersection is denoted by $A \cap B$.

Example:

$\{3, 4\} \cap \{4, 5, 6\} = \{4\}$

F. Two sets that have no elements in common are said to be **disjoint** or **mutually exclusive**.

Example:

$\{-5, 0, 1\}$ and $\{4, 10\}$ are disjoint.

G. The relationship between sets may be illustrated with a **Venn diagram** in which the sets are represented as regions in a plane. If two sets S and T are not disjoint, and neither is a subset of the other, their intersection $S \cap T$ is represented by the shaded region of the Venn diagram in the figure below.

A Venn Diagram of the Intersection of Two Sets

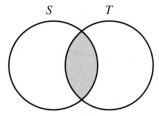

A Venn diagram showing two sets S and T, with their intersection $S \cap T$ shaded.

H. The number of elements in the union of any two finite sets S and T equals the sum of their individual numbers of elements minus the number of elements in their intersection. More concisely, $|S \cup T| = |S| + |T| - |S \cap T|$. This counting method is called the **general addition rule for two sets**.

Example:

$$|\{3, 4\} \cup \{4, 5, 6\}| = |\{3, 4\}| + |\{4, 5, 6\}| - |\{3, 4\} \cap \{4, 5, 6\}| =$$
$$|\{3, 4\}| + |\{4, 5, 6\}| - |\{4\}| = 2 + 3 - 1 = 4.$$

As a special case, if S and T are disjoint, then $|S \cup T| = |S| + |T|$, since $|S \cap T| = 0$.

I. Word problems involving sets can often be solved using Venn diagrams and the general addition rule.

Example:

Each of 25 people is enrolled in history, mathematics, or both. If 20 of them are enrolled in hzistory and 18 are enrolled in mathematics, how many are enrolled in both history and mathematics?

Solution: The 25 people can be divided into three sets: those enrolled in history only, those enrolled in mathematics only, and those enrolled in both history and mathematics. Thus, a Venn diagram may be drawn as follows, where n is the number of people enrolled in both courses, $20 - n$ is the number enrolled in history only, and $18 - n$ is the number enrolled in mathematics only.

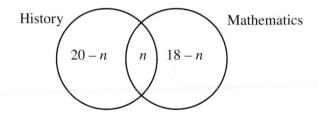

Since there are 25 people total, $(20 - n) + n + (18 - n) = 25$, or $n = 13$. Therefore, 13 people are enrolled in both history and mathematics. Note that $20 + 18 - 13 = 25$, which is an instance of the general addition rule for two sets.

---

3. Counting Methods

A. To count objects and sets of objects without actually listing the elements to be counted, the following *multiplication principle* is essential:

If an object is to be chosen from a set of m objects and a second object is to be chosen from a different set of n objects, then there are mn different possible choices.

Example:

If a meal consists of 1 entree and 1 dessert, and there are 5 entrees and 3 desserts on the menu, then there are $5 \times 3 = 15$ different meals that can be ordered from the menu

---

B. A more general version of the multiplication principle is that the number of possible choices of 1 object apiece out of each of any number of sets is the product of the numbers of objects contained in those sets. So, if 1 object apiece is to be chosen out of each of 3 sets that contain x, y, and z elements, respectively, there are xyz possible choices. And if 1 object apiece is to be chosen out of each of n different sets that each contain exactly m objects apiece, there are m^n possible choices.

Example:

Each time a coin is flipped, there are 2 possible results, heads and tails. If there are 8 consecutive coin flips, then each flip may be mathematically treated as a set containing those 2 possible results. Since there are 8 flips, there are 8 of these sets. Thus, the set of 8 flips has a total of 2^8 possible results.

C. A concept often used with the multiplication principle is the ***factorial***. If n is an integer greater than 1, then n factorial, denoted by $n!$, is defined as the product of all the integers from 1 through n.

Example:

$2! = \times 2 \times 1 = 2$

$3! = 3 \times 2 \times 1 = 6$

$4! = 4 \times 3 \times 2 \times 1 = 24$, etc.

Also, by definition, $0! = 1! = 1$. Two additional equations that may be useful when working with factorials are $n! = (n-1)!(n)$ and $(n+1)! = (n!)(n+1)$.

D. Each possible sequential ordering of the objects in a set is called a ***permutation*** of the set. A permutation can be thought of as a selection process in which objects are selected one by one in a certain order.

The factorial is useful for finding the number of permutations of a given set. If a set of n objects is to be ordered from 1st to n^{th}, then there are n choices for the 1st object, $n-1$ choices remaining for the 2nd object, $n-2$ choices remaining for the 3rd object, and so on, until there is only 1 choice remaining for the nth object. Thus, by the multiplication principle, the number of permutations of a set of n objects is $n(n-1)(n-2) \dots (3)(2)(1) = n!$.

Example:

The number of permutations of the set of letters A, B, and C is $3!$, or 6. The 6 permutations are ABC, ACB, BAC, BCA, CAB, and CBA.

E. Consider a set of n objects from which k objects are to be selected without regard to order, where $0 \le k \le n$. The number of possible complete selections of k objects is denoted by $\binom{n}{k}$ and is called the number of ***combinations*** of n objects taken k at a time. Its numerical value may be calculated as $\binom{n}{k} = \frac{n!}{k!(n-k)!}$. Note that $\binom{n}{k}$ is the number of k-element subsets of a set with n elements. Note also that $\binom{n}{k} = \binom{n}{n-k}$.

Example:

Suppose that $S = \{A, B, C, D, E\}$. The number of 2-element subsets of S, or the number of combinations of the 5 letters in S taken 2 at a time, may be calculated as $\binom{5}{2} = \dfrac{5!}{2!3!} = \dfrac{120}{(2)(6)} = 10$. The 10 subsets are $\{A, B\}, \{A, C\}, \{A, D\}, \{A, E\}, \{B, C\}, \{B, D\}, \{B, E\}, \{C, D\}, \{C, E\}$, and $\{D, E\}$.

Note that $\binom{5}{2} = 10 = \binom{5}{3}$ because every 2-element subset chosen from a set of 5 elements corresponds to a unique 3-element subset consisting of the elements *not* chosen.

4. Probability

A. Many of the ideas discussed above about sets and counting methods are important to the study of **discrete probability**. Discrete probability is concerned with **experiments** that have a finite number of possible **outcomes**. Given such an experiment, an **event** is a particular set of outcomes.

Example:

Rolling a 6-sided die with faces numbered 1 to 6 is an experiment with 6 possible outcomes that may be denoted as 1, 2, 3, 4, 5, and 6, with each number representing the side of the die facing up after the roll. One event in this experiment is that the outcome is 4. This event is denoted $\{4\}$.

Another event in the experiment is that the outcome is an odd number. This event is denoted $\{1, 3, 5\}$.

B. The probability that an event E occurs is a number between 0 and 1, inclusive, and is denoted by $P(E)$. If E is an empty set containing no possible outcomes, then E is **impossible** and $P(E) = 0$. If E is the set of all possible outcomes of the experiment, then E is **certain** to occur and $P(E) = 1$. Otherwise, E is possible but uncertain, and $0 < P(E) < 1$. If F is a subset of E, then $P(F) \leq P(E)$.

C. If the probabilities of any two outcomes of an experiment are identical, those outcomes are said to be **equally likely**. For experiments in which all the individual outcomes are equally likely, the probability of an event E is $P(E) = \dfrac{\text{the number of outcomes in } E}{\text{the total number of possible outcomes}}$.

Example:

Returning to the previous example in which a 6-sided die is rolled once, if the 6 outcomes are equally likely (that is, if the die is fair), then the probability of each outcome is $\dfrac{1}{6}$. The probability that the outcome is an odd number is $P(\{1, 3, 5\}) = \dfrac{|\{1, 3, 5\}|}{6} = \dfrac{3}{6} = \dfrac{1}{2}$.

D. Given two events E and F in an experiment, the following additional events can be defined:

(i) "not E" is the set of outcomes that are not outcomes in E;

(ii) "E or F" is the set of outcomes in E or F or both, that is, $E \cup F$;

(iii) "E and F" is the set of outcomes in both E and F, that is, $E \cap F$.

The probability that E does not occur is $P(\text{not } E) = 1 - P(E)$.

The probability that "E or F" occurs is $P(E \text{ or } F) = P(E) + P(F) - P(E \text{ and } F)$. This is derived using the general addition rule for two sets presented above in 3.4.2.H.

Example:

Consider again the example above in which a 6-sided die is rolled once. Let E be the event $\{1, 3, 5\}$ that the outcome is an odd number. Let F be the event $\{2, 3, 5\}$ that the outcome is a prime number. Then

$P(E \text{ and } F) = P(E \cap F) = P(\{3, 5\}) = \dfrac{|\{3,5\}|}{6} = \dfrac{2}{6} = \dfrac{1}{3}$. Therefore

$P(E \text{ or } F) = P(E) + P(F) - P(E \text{ and } F) = \dfrac{3}{6} + \dfrac{3}{6} - \dfrac{2}{6} = \dfrac{4}{6} = \dfrac{2}{3}$.

Note that the event "E or F" is $E \cup F = \{1, 2, 3, 5\}$, and hence $P(E \text{ or } F) = \dfrac{|\{1,2,3,5\}|}{6} = \dfrac{4}{6} = \dfrac{2}{3}$.

If the event "E and F" is impossible (that is, $E \cap F$ has no outcomes), then E and F are said to be *mutually exclusive* events, and $P(E \text{ and } F) = 0$. In that case $P(E \text{ or } F) = P(E) + P(F)$. This is the special addition rule for the probability of two mutually exclusive events.

E. Two events A and B are said to be *independent* if the occurrence of either event does not alter the probability that the other event occurs. The following multiplication rule holds for any independent events E and F:

$$P(E \text{ and } F) = P(E)P(F).$$

Example:

Returning again to the example of the 6-sided die rolled once, let A be the event $\{2, 4, 6\}$ and B be the event $\{5, 6\}$. Then the probability that A occurs is $P(A) = \dfrac{|A|}{6} = \dfrac{3}{6} = \dfrac{1}{2}$. And **presuming B occurs**, the probability that A occurs is $\dfrac{|A \cap B|}{|B|} = \dfrac{|\{6\}|}{|\{5, 6\}|} = \dfrac{1}{2}$, the same as $P(A)$.

Similarly, the probability that B occurs is $P(B) = \dfrac{|B|}{6} = \dfrac{2}{6} = \dfrac{1}{3}$. And **presuming A occurs**, the probability that B occurs is $\dfrac{|B \cap A|}{|A|} = \dfrac{\{6\}}{|\{2, 4, 6\}|} = \dfrac{1}{3}$, the same as $P(B)$.

Thus, the occurrence of either event does not affect the probability that the other event occurs. Therefore, A and B are independent. So by the multiplication rule for independent events,

$P(A \text{ and } B) = P(A)\, P(B) = \left(\dfrac{1}{2}\right)\left(\dfrac{1}{3}\right) = \dfrac{1}{6}$.

Note that the event "A and B" is $A \cap B = \{6\}$, so $P(A \text{ and } B) = P(\{6\}) = \dfrac{1}{6}$.

It follows from the general addition rule and the multiplication rule above that if E and F are independent, then $P(E \text{ or } F) = P(E) + P(F) - P(E)P(F)$.

F. An event *A* is said to be ***dependent*** on an event *B* if the occurrence of *B* alters the probability that *A* occurs.

The probability of *A* occurring if *B* occurs is represented as $P(A \mid B)$. So the statement that *A* is dependent on *B* may be represented as $P(A \mid B) \neq P(A)$.

The following general multiplication rule holds for any dependent or independent events *A* and *B*:

$P(A \text{ and } B) = P(A \mid B)P(B).$

Example:

Returning to the example of the 6-sided die rolled once, let *A* be the event {4, 6} and *B* be the event {4, 5, 6}. Then the probability that *A* occurs is $P(A) = \dfrac{|A|}{6} = \dfrac{2}{6} = \dfrac{1}{3}$. But **presuming *B* occurs**, the probability that *A* occurs is $P(A \mid B) = \dfrac{|A \cap B|}{|B|} = \dfrac{|\{4,6\}|}{|\{4, 5, 6\}|} = \dfrac{2}{3}$. Thus, $P(A \mid B) \neq P(A)$, so *A* is dependent on *B*.

Similarly, the probability that *B* occurs is $P(B) = \dfrac{|B|}{6} = \dfrac{3}{6} = \dfrac{1}{2}$. But **presuming *A* occurs**, the probability that *B* occurs is $P(B \mid A) = \dfrac{|B \cap A|}{|A|} = \dfrac{|\{4,6\}|}{|\{4,6\}|} = 1$. Thus, $P(B \mid A) \neq P(B)$, so *B* is dependent on *A*.

By the general multiplication rule for events,

$P(A \text{ and } B) = P(A \mid B)P(B) = \left(\dfrac{2}{3}\right)\left(\dfrac{1}{2}\right) = \dfrac{1}{3}$. Similarly, $P(A \text{ and } B) = P(B \mid A)P(A) = (1)\left(\dfrac{1}{3}\right) = \dfrac{1}{3}$.

Note that the event "*A* and *B*" is $A \cap B = \{4, 6\} = A$, so $P(A \text{ and } B) = P(\{4, 6\}) = \dfrac{1}{3} = P(A)$.

G. The rules above may be used together for more complex probability calculations.

Example:

Consider an experiment with events *A*, *B*, and *C* for which $P(A) = 0.23$, $P(B) = 0.40$, and $P(C) = 0.85$. Suppose that events *A* and *B* are mutually exclusive, and that events *B* and *C* are independent. Since *A* and *B* are mutually exclusive, $P(A \text{ or } B) = P(A) + P(B) = 0.23 + 0.40 = 0.63$.

Since *B* and *C* are independent, $P(B \text{ or } C) = P(B) + P(C) - P(B)P(C) = 0.40 + 0.85 - (0.40)(0.85) = 0.91$.

Note that $P(A \text{ or } C)$ and $P(A \text{ and } C)$ cannot be determined using the information given. But since $P(A) + P(C) = 1.08$, which is greater than 1, it cannot equal $P(A \text{ or } C)$, which like any probability must be less than or equal to 1. It follows that *A* and *C* cannot be mutually exclusive and that $P(A \text{ and } C) \geq 0.08$.

Since $A \cap B$ is a subset of *A*, one can also deduce that $P(A \text{ and } C) \leq P(A) = 0.23$.

And since *C* is a subset of $A \cup C$, it follows that $P(A \text{ or } C) \geq P(C) = 0.85$.

Thus, one can conclude that $0.85 \leq P(A \text{ or } C) \leq 1$ and $0.08 \leq P(A \text{ and } C) \leq 0.23$.

---

5. Estimation

A. Often it is too difficult or time-consuming to calculate an exact numerical answer to a complex mathematical question. In these cases, it may be faster and easier to estimate the answer by simplifying the question.

One such estimation technique is to **round** the numbers in the original question: replace each number in the question with a nearby number that has fewer digits. Commonly, a number is rounded to a nearby multiple of some specific power of 10.

For any integer n and real number m, to **round m down** to a multiple of 10^n, simply delete all of m's digits to the right of the one representing multiples of 10^n.

To **round m up** to a multiple of 10^n, first add 10^n to m, then round the result down.

To **round m to the nearest** 10^n, first identify the digit in m that represents a multiple of 10^{n-1}. If this digit is 5 or higher, round m up to a multiple of 10^n. Otherwise, round m down to a multiple of 10^n.

Example:

(i) To round 7651.4 to the nearest hundred (multiple of 10^2), first note that the digit representing tens (multiples of 10^1) is 5.

Since this digit is 5 or higher, round up:

Add 100 to the original number: 7651.4 + 100 = 7751.4.

Then delete all the digits to the right of the one representing multiples of 100 to obtain 7700.

A simple way of thinking of this is that 7700 is closer to 7651.4 than 7600 is, so 7700 is the nearest 100.

(ii) To round 0.43248 to the nearest thousandth (multiple of 10^{-3}), first note that the digit representing ten-thousandths (multiples of 10^{-4}) is 4. Since 4 < 5, round down: simply delete all the digits to the right of the one representing thousandths to obtain 0.432.

B. Rounding can be used to simplify complex arithmetical calculations and produce approximate solutions. The solutions will likely be more accurate, but the calculations more time-consuming, if you retain more digits of the original numbers.

Example:

You can roughly estimate the value of $\dfrac{(298.534 + 58.296)}{1.4822 + 0.937 + 0.014679}$ by rounding the numbers in the dividend to the nearest 10 and the numbers in the divisor to the nearest 0.1:

$$\frac{(298.534 + 58.296)}{1.4822 + 0.937 + 0.014679} \approx \frac{300 + 60}{1.5 + 0.9 + 0} = \frac{360}{2.4} = 150$$

C. In some cases, an estimate can be produced more effectively by rounding to a multiple of a number other than 10, or by rounding to the nearest number that is the square or cube of an integer.

Example:

(i) You can roughly estimate the value of $\dfrac{2447.16}{11.9}$ by noting first that both the dividend and the divisor are close to multiples of 12: 2448 and 12. Thus, $\dfrac{2447.16}{11.9} \approx \dfrac{2448}{12} = 204$.

(ii) You can roughly estimate the value of $\sqrt{\dfrac{8.96}{24.82 \times 4.057}}$ by noting first that each decimal number in the expression is close to the square of an integer: $8.96 \approx 9 = 3^2$, $24.82 \approx 25 = 5^2$, and $4.057 \approx 4 = 2^2$. Thus $\sqrt{\dfrac{8.96}{24.82 \times 4.057}} \approx \sqrt{\dfrac{3^2}{5^2 \times 2^2}} = \sqrt{\dfrac{3^2}{10^2}} = \dfrac{3}{10}$.

D. In some cases, rather than producing a single number as the estimated value of a complex expression, it is more helpful to determine a **range** of possible values for the expression. The **upper bound** of such a range is the smallest number that has been determined to be greater than (or greater than or equal to) the expression's value. The **lower bound** of the range is the largest number that has been determined to be less than (or less than or equal to) the expression's value.

Example:

Consider the equation $x = \dfrac{2.32^2 - 2.536}{2.68^2 + 2.79}$. Note that each decimal in this expression is greater than 2 and less than 3. Therefore, $\dfrac{2^2 - 3}{3^2 + 3} < x < \dfrac{3^2 - 2}{2^2 + 2}$. Simplifying these fractions, we can determine that x is in the range $\dfrac{1}{12} < x < \dfrac{7}{6}$. The lower bound of this range is $\dfrac{1}{12}$, and the upper bound is $\dfrac{7}{6}$.

6. Sequences and Series

A. A **sequence** is any algebraic function whose domain consists of only positive integers. If a function $a(n)$ is a sequence, it may be denoted as a_n. The domain of an **infinite sequence** includes all the positive integers. For any positive integer n, the domain of a **finite sequence of length** n includes only the first n positive integers.

Example:

(i) The function $a(n) = n^2 + \left(\dfrac{n}{5}\right)$ with the domain of all positive integers $n = 1, 2, 3, \ldots$ is an infinite sequence a_n. Its value at $n = 3$ is $a_3 = 3^2 + \dfrac{3}{5} = 9.6$.

(ii) The same function $a(n) = n^2 + \left(\dfrac{n}{5}\right)$ restricted to the domain $\{1, 2, 3\}$ is a finite sequence of length 3 whose range is $\{1.2, 3.4, 9.6\}$.

(iii) Consider the infinite sequence defined by $b_n = (-1)^n (n!)$. A sequence like this may be indicated by listing its values in the order $b_1, b_2, b_3, \ldots, b_n, \ldots$ as follows: $-1, 2, -6, \ldots$, $(-1)^n (n!), \ldots$

The value $(-1)^n (n!)$ is called the nth term of the sequence.

B. A *series* is the sum of the terms in a sequence.

For an infinite sequence $a(n)$, the corresponding *infinite series* is denoted $\sum_{n=1}^{\infty} a(n)$ and is the sum of the infinitely many terms in the sequence, $a_1 + a_2 + a_3 + \dots$

The sum of the first k terms of series a_n is called a *partial sum* of the series and is denoted $\sum_{i=1}^{k} a_i$, or $a_1 + \dots + a_k$.

Example:

The infinite series corresponding to the function $a(n) = n^2 + \left(\frac{n}{5}\right)$ is $\sum_{i=1}^{\infty} n^2 + \left(\frac{n}{5}\right)$ and is the sum of the infinitely many terms $\left(1^2 + \frac{1}{5}\right) + \left(2^2 + \frac{2}{5}\right) + \left(3^2 + \frac{3}{5}\right) + \dots$

For this same function $a(n) = n^2 + \left(\frac{n}{5}\right)$, the partial sum of the first three terms is

$$\sum_{i=1}^{3} a_i = \left(1^2 + \frac{1}{5}\right) + \left(2^2 + \frac{2}{5}\right) + \left(3^2 + \frac{3}{5}\right) = 1.2 + 4.4 + 9.6 = 15.2.$$

PS07310.03

Practice Question 16

The numbers of cars sold at a certain dealership on six of the last seven business days were 4, 7, 2, 8, 3, and 6, respectively. If the number of cars sold on the seventh business day was either 2, 4, or 5, for which of the three values does the average (arithmetic mean) number of cars sold per business day, for the seven business days, equal the median number of cars sold per day for the seven days?

I.   2

II. 4

III. 5

    (A)   II only

    (B)   III only

    (C)   I and II only

    (D)   II and III only

    (E)   I, II, and III

PS02775.03

Practice Question 17

List S consists of 10 consecutive odd integers, and list T consists of 5 consecutive even integers. If the least integer in S is 7 more than the least integer in T, how much greater is the average (arithmetic mean) of the integers in S than the average of the integers in T?

    (A)   2

    (B)   7

    (C)   8

    (D)   12

    (E)   22

PS97920.03
Practice Question 18

If *m* is the average (arithmetic mean) of the first 10 positive multiples of 5 and if *M* is the median of the first 10 positive multiples of 5, what is the value of $M - m$?

(A) −5
(B)   0
(C)   5
(D) 25
(E) 27.5

DS22030.03
Practice Question 19

In a survey of 200 college graduates, 30% said they had received student loans during their college careers, and 40% said they had received scholarships. What percent of those surveyed said that they had received neither student loans nor scholarships during their college careers?

(1)   25% of those surveyed said that they had received scholarships but no loans.
(2)   50% of those surveyed who said that they had received loans also said that they had received scholarships.
   (A)   Statement (1) ALONE is sufficient, but statement (2) alone is not sufficient.
   (B)   Statement (2) ALONE is sufficient, but statement (1) alone is not sufficient.
   (C)   BOTH statements TOGETHER are sufficient, but NEITHER statement ALONE is sufficient.
   (D)   EACH statement ALONE is sufficient.
   (E)   Statements (1) and (2) TOGETHER are NOT sufficient.

DS11040.03
Practice Question 20

A box contains only red chips, white chips, and blue chips. If a chip is randomly selected from the box, what is the probability that the chip will be either white or blue?

(1)   The probability that the chip will be blue is $\frac{1}{5}$.

(2)   The probability that the chip will be red is $\frac{1}{3}$.

   (A)   Statement (1) ALONE is sufficient, but statement (2) alone is not sufficient.
   (B)   Statement (2) ALONE is sufficient, but statement (1) alone is not sufficient.
   (C)   BOTH statements TOGETHER are sufficient, but NEITHER statement ALONE is sufficient.
   (D)   EACH statement ALONE is sufficient.
   (E)   Statements (1) and (2) TOGETHER are NOT sufficient.

PS07310.03
Answer Explanation 16

The numbers of cars sold at a certain dealership on six of the last seven business days were 4, 7, 2, 8, 3, and 6, respectively. If the number of cars sold on the seventh business day was either 2, 4, or 5, for which of the three values does the average (arithmetic mean) number of cars sold per business day, for the seven business days, equal the median number of cars sold per day for the seven days?

I.   2

II.   4

III. 5

    (A)   II only

    (B)   III only

    (C)   I and II only

    (D)   II and III only

    (E)   I, II, and III

Arithmetic Statistics

Listed in numerical order, the given numbers are 2, 3, 4, 6, 7, and 8. If the 7th number were 2 or 4, then the numbers in numerical order would be 2, 2, 3, 4, 6, 7, and 8 or 2, 3, 4, 4, 6, 7, and 8.

In either case the median would be 4 and the average would be $\dfrac{2 + 2 + 3 + 4 + 6 + 7 + 8}{7} = \dfrac{32}{7}$ or $\dfrac{2 + 3 + 4 + 4 + 6 + 7 + 8}{7} = \dfrac{34}{7}$, neither of which equals 4. So, for neither of the values in I or II does the average equal the median. If the 7th number were 5, then the numbers in numerical order would be 2, 3, 4, 5, 6, 7, and 8. The median would be 5 and the average would be $\dfrac{2 + 3 + 4 + 5 + 6 + 7 + 8}{7} = \dfrac{35}{7} = 5$. Thus, for the value in III, the average equals the mean.

The correct answer is B.

PS57720.03
Answer Explanation 17

List S consists of 10 consecutive odd integers, and list T consists of 5 consecutive even integers. If the least integer in S is 7 more than the least integer in T, how much greater is the average (arithmetic mean) of the integers in S than the average of the integers in T?

    (A)   2

    (B)   7

    (C)   8

    (D)   12

    (E)   22

Arithmetic Statistics

Let the integers in S be $s, s + 2, s + 4, \ldots, s + 18$, where s is odd. Let the integers in T be $t, t + 2, t + 4, t + 6, t + 8$, where t is even. Given that $s = t + 7$, it follows that $s - t = 7$. The average of the integers in S is $\dfrac{10s + 90}{10} = s + 9$, and, similarly, the average of the integers in T is $\dfrac{5t + 20}{5} = t + 4$. The difference in these averages is $(s + 9) - (t + 4) = (s - t) + (9 - 4) = 7 + 5 = 12$. Thus, the average of the integers in S is 12 greater than the average of the integers in T.

The correct answer is D.

PS97920.03
Answer Explanation 18

If m is the average (arithmetic mean) of the first 10 positive multiples of 5 and if M is the median of the first 10 positive multiples of 5, what is the value of $M - m$?

(A)   −5
(B)   0
(C)   5
(D)   25
(E)   27.5

Arithmetic Statistics

The first 10 positive multiples of 5 are 5, 10, 15, 20, 25, 30, 35, 40, 45, and 50. From this, the average of the 10 multiples, that is, $\dfrac{\text{sum of values}}{\text{number of values}}$, can be calculated:

$$m = \frac{5 + 10 + 15 + 20 + 25 + 30 + 35 + 40 + 45 + 50}{10} = \frac{275}{10} = 27.5.$$

Since there is an even number of multiples, the median, M, is the average of the middle two numbers, 25 and 30:

$$M = \frac{25 + 30}{2} = 27.5.$$

Therefore, the median minus the average is:

$$M - m = 27.5 - 27.5 = 0.$$

This problem can also be solved as follows. Since the values can be grouped in pairs (i.e., 5 and 50, 10 and 45, 15 and 40, etc.), each of which is symmetric with respect to the median, it follows that the mean and median are equal.

The correct answer is B.

DS22030.03
Answer Explanation 19

In a survey of 200 college graduates, 30% said they had received student loans during their college careers, and 40% said they had received scholarships. What percent of those surveyed said that they had received neither student loans nor scholarships during their college careers?

(1)   25% of those surveyed said that they had received scholarships but no loans.

(2)   50% of those surveyed who said that they had received loans also said that they had received scholarships.

Arithmetic Sets

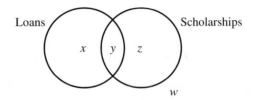

Using the variables shown on the Venn diagram above, determine the value of w. According to the information given, 30% had received student loans, so $x + y = 0.3(200) = 60$ and $x = 60 - y$. Also, 40% had received scholarships, so $y + z = 0.4(200) = 80$ and $z = 80 - y$. Then, since $x + y + z + w = 200$, $w = 200 - x - y - z = 200 - (60 - y) - y - (80 - y) = 60 + y$. Thus, if the value of y can be determined, then the value of w can be determined.

(1)   Since 25% received scholarships but no loans, $z = 80 - y = 0.25(200) = 50$ and $y = 30$; SUFFICIENT.

(2)   Since 50% of those who had received loans had also received scholarships, $0.5(x + y) = y$ and so $0.5(60) = 30 = y$; SUFFICIENT.

The correct answer is D; each statement alone is sufficient.

DS11040.03
Answer Explanation 20

A box contains only red chips, white chips, and blue chips. If a chip is randomly selected from the box, what is the probability that the chip will be either white or blue?

(1)   The probability that the chip will be blue is $\frac{1}{5}$.

(2)   The probability that the chip will be red is $\frac{1}{3}$.

Arithmetic Probability

(1)   Since the probability of drawing a blue chip is known, the probability of drawing a chip that is not blue (in other words, a red or white chip) can also be found. However, the probability of drawing a white or blue chip cannot be determined from this information; NOT sufficient.

(2)   The probability that the chip will be either white or blue is the same as the probability that it will NOT be red. Thus, the probability is $1 - \left(\frac{1}{3}\right) = \left(\frac{2}{3}\right)$; SUFFICIENT.

The correct answer is B; statement 2 alone is sufficient.

3.5 Geometry

1. Lines and Angles

A. In geometry, a *line* is straight and extends without end in both directions. A *line segment* is the part of a line between two points on the line. Those two points are the *endpoints* of the segment.

A Line and a Line Segment

The line above can be referred to as line PQ or line l. The line segment with endpoints P and Q is denoted by $\overline{PQ}$. The length of segment $\overline{PQ}$ is denoted by PQ.

B. If two line segments $\overline{DE}$ and $\overline{FG}$ intersect at a point H, then $\overline{DE}$ is said to *bisect* $\overline{FG}$ if $FH = HG$.

C. The angle at a point B between two line segments $\overline{AB}$ and $\overline{BC}$ is denoted by $\angle ABC$. The angle can be measured as a number n of *degrees* between 0 and 360, and denoted by $n°$. If $\overline{AB}$ and $\overline{BC}$ are segments of the same line AC and have no point other than B in common, then the measure of $\angle ABC$ is 180°.

D. Two angles opposite each other, formed by the intersection of two lines, are called *vertical angles* and are equal in measure.

Vertical Angles

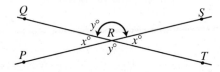

In this figure, $\angle PRQ$ and $\angle SRT$ are one pair of vertical angles, and $\angle QRS$ and $\angle PRT$ are the second pair of vertical angles. Note that $x° + y° = 180°$, since PR and RS are segments of the same line PS.

E. An angle with a measure of 90° is a *right angle.* Two lines intersecting at a right angle are *perpendicular.* The statement that lines l_1 and l_2 are perpendicular is represented as $l_1 \perp l_2$.

Perpendicular Lines Forming a Right Angle

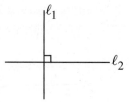

In this figure, perpendicular lines l_1 and l_2 form a right angle, so $l_1 \perp l_2$. The small square at their intersection is a right angle symbol indicating that the lines are perpendicular.

F. Two lines in the same plane that do not intersect are *parallel*. The statement that lines l_1 and l_2 are parallel is represented as $l_1 \parallel l_2$.

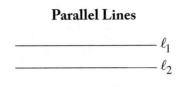

Parallel Lines

In this figure, lines l_1 and l_2 are parallel, so $l_1 \parallel l_2$.

G. If two parallel lines are intersected by a third line, then the angle measures are related as indicated in the figure below, where $x° + y° = 180°$.

Angles Formed by a Line Intersecting Two Parallel Lines

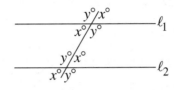

2. Polygons

A. A *polygon* is a closed plane figure formed by three or more line segments, called the *sides* of the polygon. Each side intersects exactly two other sides at their endpoints. The points of intersection of the sides are *vertices.* This chapter will use the term "polygon" to mean a *convex* polygon, that is, a polygon in which each interior angle has a measure of less than 180°. A polygon with three sides is a *triangle*; with four sides, a *quadrilateral*; with five sides, a *pentagon*; and with six sides, a *hexagon*.

Examples:

(i) The following two figures are both polygons. The one on the left is a quadrilateral, and the one on the right is a hexagon.

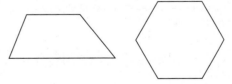

(ii) The three figures below are not polygons.

B. The sum of the interior angle measures of a polygon with *n* sides is $(n-2)180°$.

Examples:

(i) The sum of the interior angle measures of a triangle is 180°.

(ii) The sum of the interior angle measures of a pentagon is $(5-2)180° = (3)180° = 540°$. Note that a pentagon can be partitioned into three triangles, as illustrated below. Therefore, the sum of the angle measures of a pentagon equals the sum of the angle measures of three triangles.

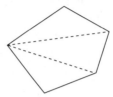

C. The *perimeter* of a polygon is the sum of the lengths of the polygon's sides.

3. Triangles

A. The sum of the lengths of any two sides of any triangle is greater than the length of the third side, as illustrated in the figure below.

Lengths of the Sides of a Triangle

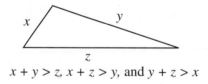

$x + y > z$, $x + z > y$, and $y + z > x$

In this figure, the variables x, y, and z represent the lengths of the triangle's three sides.

B. An *equilateral* triangle is one whose sides are all the same length. All the angles of an equilateral triangle have equal measure. An *isosceles* triangle is one with at least two sides of equal length.

If two sides of a triangle are equal in length, then the two angles opposite those sides are equal in measure. Conversely, if two angles of a triangle are equal in measure, then the sides opposite those angles are equal in length.

Example:

In isosceles triangle ΔPQR below, $x = y$ since $PQ = QR$.

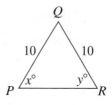

C. A triangle that has a right angle is a ***right*** triangle. In a right triangle, the side opposite the right angle is the ***hypotenuse,*** and the other two sides are the ***legs.*** Any triangle in which the lengths of the sides are in the ratio 3:4:5 is a right triangle.

An important theorem about right triangles is the ***Pythagorean theorem***, which states:

In a right triangle, the square of the length of the hypotenuse equals the sum of the squares of the lengths of the legs.

That is, the Pythagorean theorem states that if a and b are the lengths of the legs of a right triangle, and c is the length of the hypotenuse, then $a^2 + b^2 = c^2$.

Example:

In right triangle $\triangle RST$ below, by the Pythagorean theorem $(RS)^2 + (RT)^2 = (ST)^2$.

Note that $RS = 6$ and $RT = 8$. Therefore, since $6^2 + 8^2 = 36 + 64 = 100 = (ST)^2$ and $ST = \sqrt{100}$, it follows that $ST = 10$.

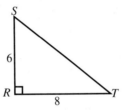

D. In $45°- 45°- 90°$ triangles, the lengths of the sides are in the ratio $1:1:\sqrt{2}$. In $30°- 60°- 90°$ triangles, the lengths of the sides are in the ratio $1:\sqrt{3}:2$.

Examples:

(i) In $45°- 45°- 90°$ triangle $\triangle JKL$ below, $JK = JL = 2$, and $KL = 2\sqrt{2}$.

(ii) In $30°- 60°- 90°$ triangle $\triangle XYZ$ below, $XZ = 3$, $XY = 3\sqrt{3}$, and $YZ = 6$.

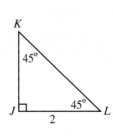 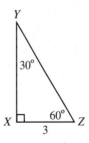

E. The ***altitude*** of a triangle is the segment drawn from a vertex perpendicular to the side opposite that vertex. Relative to that vertex and altitude, the opposite side is called the ***base.***

The area of a triangle equals $\dfrac{(\text{the length of the altitude}) \times (\text{the length of the base})}{2}$.

Example:

In triangle $\triangle ABC$ below, $\overline{BD}$ is the altitude to base $\overline{AC}$, and $\overline{AE}$ is the altitude to base $\overline{BC}$. The area of $\triangle ABC$ is $\dfrac{BD \times AC}{2} = \dfrac{5 \times 8}{2} = 20$. The area also equals $\dfrac{AE \times BC}{2}$. If $\triangle ABC$ is isosceles and $AB = BC$, then altitude $\overline{BD}$ bisects the base; that is, $AD = DC = 4$.

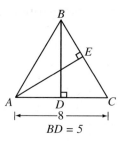

$BD = 5$

F. Any altitude of an equilateral triangle bisects the side to which it is drawn.

Example:

In equilateral triangle $\triangle DEF$ below, $DE = 6$, so $DG = 3$ and $EG = 3\sqrt{3}$.

The area of $\triangle DEF$ is $\dfrac{3\sqrt{3} \times 6}{2} = 9\sqrt{3}$.

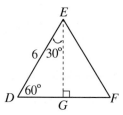

4. Quadrilaterals

A. A *trapezoid* is a quadrilateral with exactly two parallel sides, which are called its **bases.** A trapezoid's **height** is the shortest distance between its bases.

The area of a trapezoid equals $\dfrac{\text{(the sum of the lengths of the bases)} \times \text{(the height)}}{2}$.

Example:

In trapezoid $PQRS$ below, the bases are $\overline{QR}$ and $\overline{PS}$, and the height is 8.

Therefore, the area of $PQRS$ is $(QR + PS) \times \dfrac{8}{2} = (12 + 16) \times \dfrac{8}{2} = 28 \times 4 = 112$.

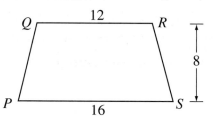

B. A *parallelogram* is a quadrilateral in which both pairs of opposite sides are parallel.

The opposite sides of a parallelogram are equal in length. When one side is taken as the base, the height is the shortest distance between that side and its opposite side.

The *diagonals* of a parallelogram are the two-line segments between its opposite vertices. A parallelogram's diagonals bisect each other.

The area of a parallelogram equals (the length of the base) × (the height).

Example:

In parallelogram $JKLM$ below, $\overline{JK} \parallel \overline{LM}$, and $JK = LM$. Also, $\overline{KL} \parallel \overline{JM}$, and $KL = JM$.

Since the diagonals $\overline{JL}$ and $\overline{KM}$ bisect each other, $KN = NM$ and $JN = NL$.

The area of $JKLM$ is $JM \times 4 = 6 \times 4 = 24$.

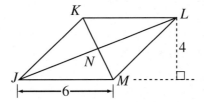

C. A parallelogram with right angles is a *rectangle,* and a rectangle with all sides of equal length is a *square*.

The diagonals of a rectangle are equal in length.

The perimeter of a rectangle equals 2 × (the height + the length of the base).

Example:

In rectangle $WXYZ$ below, the perimeter equals $2(3 + 7) = 20$.

The area of $WXYZ$ is $3 \times 7 = 21$.

Since the diagonals of $WXYZ$ are equal in length, by the Pythagorean theorem

$WY = XZ = \sqrt{9 + 49} = \sqrt{58}$.

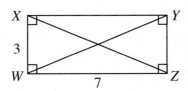

D. On the GMAT exam you may encounter problems involving shapes composed of conjoined polygons.

Example:

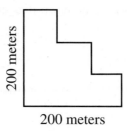

200 meters

200 meters

The figure above shows an aerial view of a piece of land. If all angles shown are right angles, what is the perimeter of the piece of land?

Solution: For reference, label the figure as

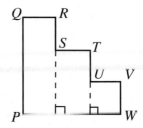

Since all the angles are right angles, $QR + ST + UV = PW$, and $RS + TU + VW = PQ$. Hence, the perimeter of the land is $2PW + 2PQ = 2 \times 200 + 2 \times 200 = 800$ meters.

5. Circles

A. A *circle* is a set of points in a plane that are all located the same distance from a fixed point, the circle's *center*.

A *chord* of a circle is a line segment whose endpoints are on the circle. A chord that passes through the center of the circle is a *diameter* of the circle. A *radius* of a circle is a segment from the center of the circle to a point on the circle. The words "diameter" and "radius" are also used to refer to the lengths of these segments.

The *circumference* of a circle is the distance around the circle. The circumference of a circle of radius r is $2\pi r$, where π is approximately $\frac{22}{7}$ or 3.14.

The area of a circle of radius r is πr^2.

Example:

In the circle below, O is the center, and $\overline{JK}$ and $\overline{PR}$ are chords. $\overline{PR}$ is a diameter and $\overline{OR}$ is a radius. Since $OR = 7$, the circle's circumference is $2\pi(7) = 14\pi$. The circle's area is $\pi(7)^2 = 49\pi$.

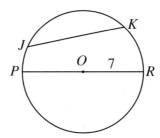

B. An **arc** of a circle is a part of the circle sharing endpoints with a chord of the circle. Any chord defines two arcs with the same endpoints, and the circle is the union of those two arcs. The number of degrees of arc in a circle (that is, the number of degrees in a complete revolution) is 360. If C is the circle's center, m is the circle's circumference, and B and D are points on the circle, an angle $\angle BCD$ of $n°$ defines an arc of length $\dfrac{nm}{360}$ with endpoints B and D.

Example:

In the circle below, O is the center. Suppose the circle's circumference is m.

Since angle $\angle ROT$ has a measure of $60°$, the length of arc RST is $\dfrac{60m}{360} = \dfrac{m}{6}$.

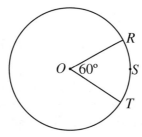

C. A line that has exactly one point in common with a circle is said to be **tangent** to the circle. That common point is called the **point of tangency.**

A radius or diameter with an endpoint at the point of tangency is perpendicular to the tangent line. Conversely, a line that is perpendicular to a radius or diameter at one of its endpoints on the circle is tangent to the circle at that endpoint.

A Tangent to a Circle

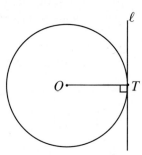

In this figure, line *l* is tangent to the circle, and radius $\overline{OT}$ is perpendicular to *l*.

D. If each vertex of a polygon lies on a circle, then the polygon is ***inscribed*** in the circle and the circle is ***circumscribed*** about the polygon.

If each side of a polygon is tangent to a circle, then the polygon is circumscribed about the circle and the circle is inscribed in the polygon.

Examples:

In the figures below, quadrilateral *PQRS* is inscribed in a circle, and hexagon *ABCDEF* is circumscribed about a circle.

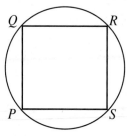
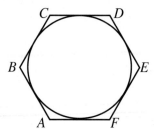

E. A triangle inscribed in a circle so that one of its sides is a diameter of the circle is a right triangle.

Example:

In the circle below with center O, $\overline{XZ}$ is a diameter. Angle $\angle XYZ$ has a measure of 90°.

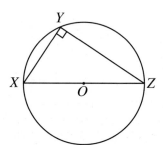

6. Rectangular Solids and Cylinders

A. A ***rectangular solid*** is a three-dimensional figure formed by 6 rectangular surfaces. Each rectangular surface is a ***face***. Each line segment where two faces meet is an ***edge***, and each point at which the edges meet is a ***vertex***.

A rectangular solid has 6 faces, 12 edges, and 8 vertices. Its opposite faces are parallel rectangles with the same dimensions.

A rectangular solid whose edges are all of equal length is a ***cube***.

The ***surface area*** of a rectangular solid is the sum of the areas of all the faces.

The ***volume*** of a rectangular solid equals (length) × (width) × (height).

Example:

In the rectangular solid below, the dimensions are 3, 4, and 8.

The surface area is 2(3 × 4) + 2(3 × 8) + 2(4 × 8) = 136.

The volume is 3 × 8 × 4 = 96.

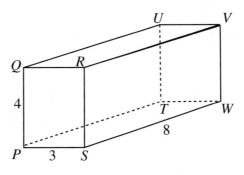

B. A ***right circular cylinder*** is a three-dimensional figure whose ***bases*** are two circles equal in size aligned so that a line segment called the ***axis*** or the ***altitude***, with endpoints at the centers of the circles, is perpendicular to the diameters of both circles. The length of the axis is the cylinder's ***height***.

A Right Circular Cylinder

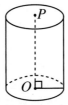

In this figure, points O and P are the centers of the two bases of a right circular cylinder, so $\overline{OP}$ is the cylinder's axis or altitude, and OP is the height.

The surface area of a right circular cylinder with height h and a base of radius r is $2(\pi r^2) + 2\pi rh$ (the sum of the areas of the two bases plus the area of the curved surface).

The volume of a right circular cylinder is $\pi r^2 h$, that is, (area of base) × (height).

Example:

In the right circular cylinder below, the surface area is $2(25\pi) + 2\pi\,(5)(8) = 130\pi$, and the volume is $25\pi\,(8) = 200\pi$.

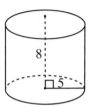

---

7. Coordinate Geometry

A. The figure below shows the (rectangular) ***coordinate plane.*** The horizontal line is called the ***x-axis*** and the perpendicular vertical line is called the ***y-axis.*** The point at which these two axes intersect, designated O, is called the ***origin.*** The axes divide the plane into four quadrants, I, II, III, and IV, as shown.

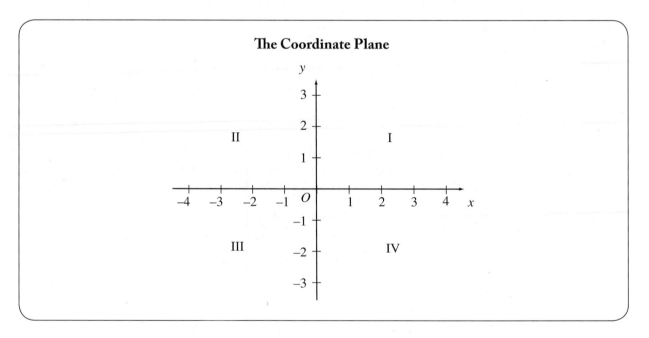

The Coordinate Plane

B. Each point in the coordinate plane has an ***x-coordinate*** and a ***y-coordinate.*** A point is identified by an ordered pair (x, y) of numbers in which the x-coordinate is the first number and the y-coordinate is the second number.

Example:

In the graph below, the (x,y) coordinates of point P are (2,3) since P is 2 units to the right of the y-axis (that is, $x = 2$) and 3 units above the x-axis (that is, $y = 3$).

Similarly, the (x,y) coordinates of point Q are (−4,−3). The origin O has coordinates (0,0).

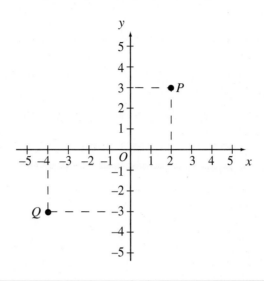

C. One way to find the distance between two points in the coordinate plane is to use the Pythagorean theorem.

Example:

To find the distance between points R and S using the Pythagorean theorem, draw the triangle as shown in the figure below. Note that Z has (x,y) coordinates (−2,−3), $RZ = 7$, and

$ZS = 5$. Therefore, the distance between R and S is $\sqrt{7^2 + 5^2} = \sqrt{74}$.

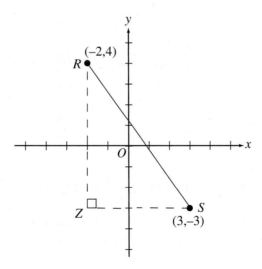

D. For a line in the coordinate plane, the coordinates of each point on the line satisfy a linear equation of the form $y = mx + b$ (or the form $x = a$ if the line is vertical).

In this equation $y = mx + b$, the coefficient m is the line's **slope**, and the constant term b is the line's **y-intercept**.

The y-intercept is the y-coordinate of the point at which the line intersects the y-axis. Similarly, the **x-intercept** is the x-coordinate of the point at which the line intersects the x-axis.

For any two points on the line, the slope is the ratio of the difference in the y-coordinates to the difference in the x-coordinates. Note that after you subtract the y-coordinate of one point from that of the other, it is important to also subtract the x-coordinate of the former point from that of the latter, not the other way around.

If a line's slope is negative, the line slants downward from left to right.

If the slope is positive, the line slants upward.

If the slope is 0, the line is horizontal. The equation of such a line is of the form $y = b$ since $m = 0$.

For a vertical line, slope is not defined.

Example:

In the graph below, each point on the line satisfies the equation $y = -\frac{1}{2}x + 1$. One can verify this for the points $(-2,2)$, $(2,0)$, and $(0,1)$ by substituting the respective coordinates for x and y in the equation.

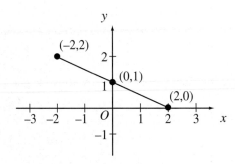

Using the points $(-2, 2)$ and $(2, 0)$, the line's slope may be calculated as:

$$\frac{\text{the difference in the } y\text{-coordinates}}{\text{the difference in the } x\text{-coordinates}} = \frac{0-2}{2-(-2)} = \frac{-2}{4} = -\frac{1}{2}.$$

The y-intercept is 1, which is the value of y when x is set equal to 0 in $y = -\frac{1}{2}x + 1$.

Similarly, the x-intercept may be calculated by setting y equal to 0 in the same equation:

$$-\frac{1}{2}x + 1 = 0$$

$$-\frac{1}{2}x = -1$$

$$x = 2.$$

Thus, the x-intercept is 2.

E. Given any two points (x_1, y_1) and (x_2, y_2) with $x_1 \neq x_2$, the equation of the line passing through these points can be found by applying the definition of slope. The slope is $m = \dfrac{y_2 - y_1}{x_2 - x_1}$. So using the known point (x_1, y_1) and the same slope m, any other point (x, y) on the line must satisfy the equation $m = \dfrac{(y - y_1)}{(x - x_1)}$, or equivalently $(y - y_1) = m(x - x_1)$. Using (x_2, y_2) instead of (x_1, y_1) as the known point would yield an equivalent equation.

Example:

In the graph below, consider the points $(-2, 4)$ and $(3, -3)$.

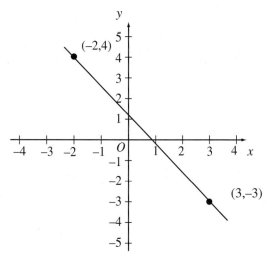

The line's slope is $\dfrac{(-3 - 4)}{(3 - (-2))} = \dfrac{-7}{5}$. So an equation of this line can be found using the point $(3, -3)$ as follows:

$$y - (-3) = \left(-\frac{7}{5}\right)(x - 3)$$

$$y + 3 = \left(-\frac{7}{5}\right)x + \frac{21}{5}$$

$$y = \left(-\frac{7}{5}\right)x + \frac{6}{5}$$

Thus, the y-intercept is $\dfrac{6}{5}$.

The x-intercept can be found as follows:

$$0 = -\frac{7}{5}x + \frac{6}{5}$$

$$\frac{7}{5}x = \frac{6}{5}$$

$$x = \frac{6}{7}$$

Both of these intercepts can be seen on the graph.

F. If two linear equations with unknowns x and y have a unique solution, then the graphs of the equations are two lines that intersect in one point, which is the solution.

If the equations are equivalent, then they represent the same line with infinitely many points or solutions.

If the equations have no solution, then they represent parallel lines, which do not intersect.

G. Any function $f(x)$ can be graphed in the coordinate plane by equating y with the value of the function: $y = f(x)$. So, for any x in the domain of the function f, the point with coordinates $(x, f(x))$ is on the graph of f, and the graph consists entirely of these points.

> *Example:*
>
> Consider the function $f(x) = -\dfrac{7}{5}x + \dfrac{6}{5}$.
>
> If the value of $f(x)$ is equated with the variable y, then the graph of the function in the xy-coordinate plane is simply the graph of the equation $y = -\dfrac{7}{5}x + \dfrac{6}{5}$ considered in the example above.

H. For any function f, the x-intercepts are the solutions of the equation $f(x) = 0$ and the y-intercept is the value $f(0)$.

The graph of a quadratic polynomial function is called a **parabola** and always has a characteristic curved shape, although it may be upside down or have a greater or lesser width.

Example:

Consider a quadratic function defined by $f(x) = x^2 - 1$. One can plot several points $(x, f(x))$ in the coordinate plane to understand the connection between the function and its graph:

x	$f(x)$
-2	3
-1	0
0	-1
1	0
2	3

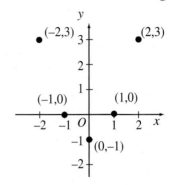

If all the points were graphed for $-2 \leq x \leq 2$, the graph would appear as follows:

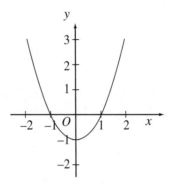

Note that the roots of the equation $f(x) = x^2 - 1 = 0$ are $x = 1$ and $x = -1$; these coincide with the x-intercepts since x-intercepts are found by setting $y = 0$ and solving for x.

Also, the y-intercept is $f(0) = -1$ because this is the value of y corresponding to $x = 0$.

PS22061.03

Practice Question 21

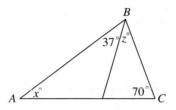

In △ABC above, what is x in terms of z?

(A)   z + 73

(B)   z − 73

(C)   70 − z

(D)   z − 70

(E)   73 − z

DS17061.03

Practice Question 22

What is the maximum number of rectangular blocks, each with dimensions 12 centimeters by 6 centimeters by 4 centimeters, that will fit inside rectangular box X ?

(1)   When box X is filled with the blocks and rests on a certain side, there are 25 blocks in the bottom layer.

(2)   The inside dimensions of box X are 60 centimeters by 30 centimeters by 20 centimeters.

  (A)   Statement (1) ALONE is sufficient, but statement (2) alone is not sufficient.

  (B)   Statement (2) ALONE is sufficient, but statement (1) alone is not sufficient.

  (C)   BOTH statements TOGETHER are sufficient, but NEITHER statement ALONE is sufficient.

  (D)   EACH statement ALONE is sufficient.

  (E)   Statements (1) and (2) TOGETHER are NOT sufficient.

PS29261.03

Practice Question 23

The annual budget of a certain college is to be shown on a circle graph. If the size of each sector of the graph is to be proportional to the amount of the budget it represents, how many degrees of the circle should be used to represent an item that is 15% of the budget?

(A)   15°

(B)   36°

(C)   54°

(D)   90°

(E)   150°

DS48061.03
Practice Question 24

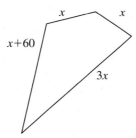

The figure above shows the number of meters in the lengths of the four sides of a jogging path. What is the total distance around the path?

(1)   One of the sides of the path is 120 meters long.

(2)   One of the sides of the path is twice as long as each of the two shortest sides.

    (A)   Statement (1) ALONE is sufficient, but statement (2) alone is not sufficient.

    (B)   Statement (2) ALONE is sufficient, but statement (1) alone is not sufficient.

    (C)   BOTH statements TOGETHER are sufficient, but NEITHER statement ALONE is sufficient.

    (D)   EACH statement ALONE is sufficient.

    (E)   Statements (1) and (2) TOGETHER are NOT sufficient.

DS39161.03
Practice Question 25

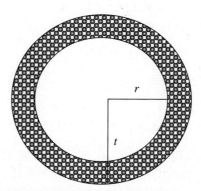

The figure above shows the circular cross section of a concrete water pipe. If the inside radius of the pipe is r feet and the outside radius of the pipe is t feet, what is the value of r ?

(1)   The ratio of $t - r$ to r is 0.15 and $t - r$ is equal to 0.3 feet.

(2)   The area of the concrete in the cross section is 1.29π square feet.

    (A)   Statement (1) ALONE is sufficient, but statement (2) alone is not sufficient.

    (B)   Statement (2) ALONE is sufficient, but statement (1) alone is not sufficient.

    (C)   BOTH statements TOGETHER are sufficient, but NEITHER statement ALONE is sufficient.

    (D)   EACH statement ALONE is sufficient.

    (E)   Statements (1) and (2) TOGETHER are NOT sufficient.

PS22061.03
Answer Explanation 21

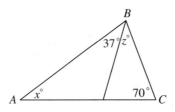

In △ABC above, what is x in terms of z?

    (A) $z + 73$

    (B) $z - 73$

    (C) $70 - z$

    (D) $z - 70$

    (E) $73 - z$

Geometry Angle Measure in Degrees

Since the sum of the degree measures of the angles in a triangle equals 180°,

$x + 37 + z + 70 = 180$. Solve this equation for x.

$$x + 37 + z + 70 = 180$$
$$x + z + 107 = 180$$
$$x + z = 73$$
$$x = 73 - z$$

The correct answer is E.

DS17061.03
Answer Explanation 22

What is the maximum number of rectangular blocks, each with dimensions 12 centimeters by 6 centimeters by 4 centimeters, that will fit inside rectangular box X ?

(1)   When box X is filled with the blocks and rests on a certain side, there are 25 blocks in the bottom layer.

(2)   The inside dimensions of box X are 60 centimeters by 30 centimeters by 20 centimeters.

    (A)   Statement (1) ALONE is sufficient, but statement (2) alone is not sufficient.

    (B)   Statement (2) ALONE is sufficient, but statement (1) alone is not sufficient.

    (C)   BOTH statements TOGETHER are sufficient, but NEITHER statement ALONE is sufficient.

    (D)   EACH statement ALONE is sufficient.

    (E)   Statements (1) and (2) TOGETHER are NOT sufficient.

Geometry Volume

Determine how many rectangular blocks will fit in a rectangular box.

(1)   The side on which the box is resting could be 30 cm by 20 cm. If the blocks are resting on the side that is 6 cm by 4 cm, there would be $\dfrac{30}{6} \times \dfrac{20}{4} = 5 \times 5 = 25$ blocks on the bottom layer. If the box is 12 cm tall, a maximum of 25 blocks would fit inside the box. However, if the box is 48 cm tall, a maximum of 100 blocks would fit inside the box; NOT sufficient.

(2)   If the box is resting on a side that is 30 cm by 20 cm, then $\dfrac{30}{6} \times \dfrac{20}{4} = 5 \times 5 = 25$ blocks will fit on the bottom layer. In this case, the height of the box is 60 cm and $\dfrac{60}{12} = 5$ layers will fit inside the box. If the

box is resting on a side that is 60 cm by 30 cm, then $\dfrac{60}{12} \times \dfrac{30}{6} = 5 \times 5 = 25$ blocks will fit on the bottom layer. In this case, the height of the box is 20 cm and $\dfrac{20}{4} = 5$ layers will fit inside the box. If the box is resting on a side that is 60 cm by 20 cm, then $\dfrac{60}{12} \times \dfrac{20}{4} = 5 \times 5 = 25$ blocks will fit on the bottom layer. In this case, the height of the box is 30 cm and $\dfrac{30}{6} = 5$ layers will fit inside the box. In all cases, the maximum number of blocks that will fit inside the box is $5 \times 25 = 125$; SUFFICIENT.

The correct answer is B; statement 2 alone is sufficient.

PS29261.03
Answer Explanation 23

The annual budget of a certain college is to be shown on a circle graph. If the size of each sector of the graph is to be proportional to the amount of the budget it represents, how many degrees of the circle should be used to represent an item that is 15% of the budget?

(A)   15°
(B)   36°
(C)   54°
(D)   90°
(E)   150°

Geometry; Arithmetic Percents; Interpretation of Graphs

Since there are 360 degrees in a circle, the measure of the central angle in the circle should be $0.15(360°) = 54°$.

The correct answer is C.

DS48061.03
Answer Explanation 24

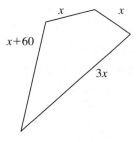

The figure above shows the number of meters in the lengths of the four sides of a jogging path. What is the total distance around the path?

(1)   One of the sides of the path is 120 meters long.
(2)   One of the sides of the path is twice as long as each of the two shortest sides.

    (A)   Statement (1) ALONE is sufficient, but statement (2) alone is not sufficient.
    (B)   Statement (2) ALONE is sufficient, but statement (1) alone is not sufficient.
    (C)   BOTH statements TOGETHER are sufficient, but NEITHER statement ALONE is sufficient.
    (D)   EACH statement ALONE is sufficient.
    (E)   Statements (1) and (2) TOGETHER are NOT sufficient.

Algebra; Geometry Quadrilaterals

Determine the value of $6x + 60$, which can be determined exactly when the value of x can be determined.

(1) Given that one of the sides has length 120, it is possible that $x = 120$, that $3x = 120$, or $x + 60 = 120$. These possibilities generate more than one value for x; NOT sufficient.

(2) Since $x < x + 60$ and $x < 3x$ (the latter because x is positive), the two shortest side lengths are x. One of the two other side lengths is twice this, so it follows that $x + 60 = 2x$, or $x = 60$; SUFFICIENT.

The correct answer is B; statement 2 alone is sufficient.

DS39161.03
Answer Explanation 25

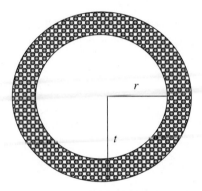

The figure above shows the circular cross section of a concrete water pipe. If the inside radius of the pipe is r feet and the outside radius of the pipe is t feet, what is the value of r?

(1) The ratio of $t - r$ to r is 0.15 and $t - r$ is equal to 0.3 feet.

(2) The area of the concrete in the cross section is 1.29π square feet.

(A) Statement (1) ALONE is sufficient, but statement (2) alone is not sufficient.

(B) Statement (2) ALONE is sufficient, but statement (1) alone is not sufficient.

(C) BOTH statements TOGETHER are sufficient, but NEITHER statement ALONE is sufficient.

(D) EACH statement ALONE is sufficient.

(E) Statements (1) and (2) TOGETHER are NOT sufficient.

Geometry Circles; Area

Determine the value of r.

(1) Since $\dfrac{t - r}{r} = 0.15$ and $t - r = 0.3$, then $\dfrac{0.3}{r} = 0.15$ and $r = \dfrac{0.3}{0.15} = 2$; SUFFICIENT.

(2) The area of the concrete in the cross section is the area of the circular region with radius t minus the area of the circular region with radius r. The area of a circular region with radius R is πR^2, so the area of the concrete in the cross section is $\pi t^2 - \pi r^2$. This area is $1.29\,\pi$, so $\pi t^2 - \pi r^2 = 1.29\,\pi$, and $t^2 - r^2 = 1.29$, from which it is impossible to determine a unique value for r. For example, if $t = \sqrt{2.29}$, then $r = 1$, but if $t = \sqrt{5.29}$, then $r = 2$; NOT sufficient.

The correct answer is A; statement 1 alone is sufficient.

3.6   Reference Sheets

Arithmetic and Decimals

ABSOLUTE VALUE:

$|x|$ is x if $x \geq 0$ and $-x$ if $x < 0$.

For any x and y, $|x + y| \leq |x| + |y|$.

$\sqrt{x^2} = |x|$.

EVEN AND ODD NUMBERS:

Even × Even = Even	Even × Odd = Even
Odd × Odd = Odd	Even + Even = Even
Even + Odd = Odd	Odd + Odd = Even

ADDITION AND SUBTRACTION:

$x + 0 = x = x - 0$

$x - x = 0$

$x + y = y + x$

$x - y = -(y - x) = -y + x$

$(x + y) + z = x + (y + z)$

If x and y are both positive, then $x + y$ is also positive.

If x and y are both negative, then $x + y$ is negative.

DECIMALS:

Add or subtract decimals by lining up their decimal points:

17.6512	653.2700
+ 653.2700	−17.6512
670.9212	635.6188

To multiply decimal A by decimal B:

First, disregard the decimal points, and multiply A and B as if they were integers.

Next, if decimal A has n digits to the right of its decimal point, and decimal B has m digits to the right of its decimal point, place the decimal point so that $A \times B$ has $m + n$ digits to the right of the decimal point.

To divide decimal A by decimal B, first move the decimal points of A and B equally many digits to the right until B is an integer, then divide as you would integers.

QUOTIENTS AND REMAINDERS:

The quotient q and the remainder r of dividing positive integer x by positive integer y are unique positive integers such that

$y = xq + r$ and $0 \leq r < x$.

The remainder r is 0 if and only if y is divisible by x. In that case, x is a factor of y.

MULTIPLICATION AND DIVISION:

$x \times 1 = x = \dfrac{x}{1}$

$x \times 0 = 0$

If $x \neq 0$, then $\dfrac{x}{x} = 1$.

$\dfrac{x}{0}$ is undefined.

$xy = yx$

If $x \neq 0$ and $y \neq 0$, then $\dfrac{x}{y} = \dfrac{1}{\left(\frac{y}{x}\right)}$.

$(xy)z = x(yz)$

$xy + xz = x(y + z)$

If $y \neq 0$, then $\left(\dfrac{x}{y}\right) + \left(\dfrac{z}{y}\right) = \dfrac{(x + z)}{y}$

If x and y are both positive, then xy is also positive.

If x and y are both negative, then xy is positive.

If x is positive and y is negative, then xy is negative.

If $xy = 0$, then $x = 0$ or $y = 0$, or both.

SCIENTIFIC NOTATION:

To convert a number in the scientific notation $A \times 10^n$ into regular decimal notation, move the decimal point in A to the right by n places if n is positive, or to the left by $|n|$ places if n is negative.

To convert a number B from decimal notation to scientific notation, move the decimal point n spaces so that exactly one nonzero digit is to its left. Multiply the result by 10^n if you moved the decimal point to the left or by 10^{-n} if you moved it to the right.

Exponents

SQUARES, CUBES, AND SQUARE ROOTS:

Every positive number has two real square roots, one positive and the other negative. The table below shows the positive square roots rounded to the nearest hundredth.

n	n^2	n^3	$\sqrt{n}$
1	1	1	1
2	4	8	1.41
3	9	27	1.73
4	16	64	2
5	25	125	2.24
6	36	216	2.45
7	49	343	2.65
8	64	512	2.83
9	81	729	3
10	100	1,000	3.16

EXPONENTIATION:

Formula	Example
$x^1 = x$	$2^1 = 2$
$x^0 = 1$	$2^0 = 1$
If $x \neq 0$, then $x^{-1} = \dfrac{1}{x}$.	$2^{-1} = \dfrac{1}{2}$
If $x > 1$ and $y > 1$, then $x^y > x$.	$2^3 = 8 > 2$
If $0 < x < 1$ and $y > 1$, then $x^y < x$.	$0.2^3 = 0.008 < 0.2$
$(x^y)^z = x^{yz} = (x^z)^y$	$(2^3)^4 = 2^{12} = (2^4)^3$
$x^{y+z} = x^y x^z$	$2^7 = 2^3 2^4$
If $x \neq 0$, then $x^{y-z} = \dfrac{x^y}{x^z}$.	$2^{5-3} = \dfrac{2^5}{2^3}$
$(xz)^y = x^y z^y$	$6^4 = 2^4 3^4$
If $z \neq 0$, then $\left(\dfrac{x}{z}\right)^y = \dfrac{x^y}{z^y}$	$\left(\dfrac{3}{4}\right)^2 = \dfrac{3^2}{4^2} = \dfrac{9}{16}$
If $z \neq 0$, then $x^{\frac{y}{z}} = (x^y)^{\frac{1}{z}} = (x^{\frac{1}{z}})^y$.	$4^{\frac{2}{3}} = (4^2)^{\frac{1}{3}} = (4^{\frac{1}{3}})^2$

Algebraic Expressions and Linear Equations

TRANSLATING WORDS INTO MATHEMATICAL OPERATIONS:

$x + y$	$x - y$	xy	$\dfrac{x}{y}$	x^y
x added to y x increased by y x more than y x plus y the sum of x and y the total of x and y	x decreased by y difference of x and y y fewer than x y less than x x minus y x reduced by y y subtracted from x	x multiplied by y the product of x and y x times y If $y = 2$: double x twice x If $y = 3$: triple x	x divided by y x over y the quotient of x and y the ratio of x to y If $y = 2$: half of x x halved	x to the power of y x to the yth power If $y = 2$: x squared If $y = 3$: x cubed

MANIPULATING ALGEBRAIC EXPRESSIONS:

Technique	Example
Factor to combine like terms	$3xy - 9y = 3y(x - 3)$
Divide out common factors	$\dfrac{(3xy - 9y)}{(x - 3)} = \dfrac{3y(x - 3)}{(x - 3)} = 3y(1) = 3y$
Multiply two expressions by multiplying each term of one expression by each term of the other	$(3x - 4)(9y + x) = 3x(9y + x) - 4(9y + x)$ $= 3x(9y) + 3x(x) + -4(9y) + -4(x)$ $= 27xy + 3x^2 - 36y - 4x$
Substitute constants for variables	If $x = 3$ and $y = -2$, then $3xy - x^2 + y$ can be evaluated as $3(3)(-2) - (3)^2 + (-2) = -18 - 9 - 2 = -29$.

SOLVING LINEAR EQUATIONS:

Technique	Example
Isolate a variable on one side of an equation by performing the same operations on both sides of the equation.	Solve the equation $\dfrac{(5x-6)}{3} = 4$ using the following steps: (1) Multiply both sides by 3 to obtain $5x - 6 = 12$. (2) Add 6 to both sides to obtain $5x = 18$. (3) Divide both sides by 5 to obtain $x = \dfrac{18}{5}$.
To solve two equations with two variables x and y: (1) Express x in terms of y using one of the equations. (2) Substitute the expression for x to make the second equation have only the variable y. (3) Solve the second equation for y. (4) Substitute the solution for y into the first equation to find the value of x.	Solve the equations A: $x - y = 2$ and B: $3x + 2y = 11$: (1) From A, $x = 2 + y$. (2) In B, substitute $2 + y$ for x to obtain $3(2 + y) + 2y = 11$. (3) Solve B for y: $6 + 3y + 2y = 11$ $\qquad 6 + 5y = 11$ $\qquad 5y = 5$ $\qquad y = 1.$ (4) Since $y = 1$, it follows from A that $x = 2 + 1 = 3$.
Alternative technique: (1) Multiply both sides of one equation or both equations so that the coefficients on y have the same absolute value in both equations. (2) Add or subtract the two equations to eliminate y and solve for x. (3) Substitute the solution for x into the first equation to find the value of y.	Solve the equations A: $x - y = 2$ and B: $3x + 2y = 11$: (1) Multiply both sides of A by 2 to obtain $2x - 2y = 4$. (2) Add this result to equation B: $2x - 2y + 3x + 2y = 4 + 11$ $\qquad 5x = 15$ $\qquad x = 3.$ (3) Since $x = 3$, it follows from A that $3 - y = 2$, so $y = 1$.

Factoring, Quadratic Equations, and Inequalities

SOLVING EQUATIONS BY FACTORING:

Techniques	Example
(1) Start with a polynomial equation. (2) Add or subtract expressions until 0 is on one side of the equation. (3) Express the nonzero side as a product of factors. (4) Set each factor equal to 0 to find a simple equation yielding a solution to the original equation.	$x^3 - 2x^2 + x = -5(x - 1)^2$ $x^3 - 2x^2 + x + 5(x - 1)^2 = 0$ (i) $x(x^2 - 2x + 1) + 5(x - 1)^2 = 0$ (ii) $x(x - 1)^2 + 5(x - 1)^2 = 0$ (iii) $(x + 5)(x - 1)^2 = 0$ $x + 5 = 0$ or $x - 1 = 0$. Therefore $x = -5$ or $x = 1$.

FORMULAS FOR FACTORING:

$a^2 - b^2 = (a - b)(a + b)$

$a^2 + 2ab + b^2 = (a + b)(a + b)$

$a^2 - 2ab + b^2 = (a - b)(a - b)$

THE QUADRATIC FORMULA:

For any quadratic equation $ax^2 + bx + c = 0$ with $a \neq 0$, the roots are

$$x = \frac{-b + \sqrt{b^2 - 4ac}}{2a} \text{ and } x = \frac{-b - \sqrt{b^2 - 4ac}}{2a}$$

These roots are two distinct real numbers unless $b^2 - 4ac \leq 0$.

If $b^2 - 4ac = 0$, the equation has only one root: $\frac{-b}{2a}$.

If $b^2 - 4ac < 0$, the equation has no real roots.

SOLVING INEQUALITIES:

Explanation	Example
As in solving an equation, the same number can be added to or subtracted from both sides of the inequality, or both sides can be multiplied or divided by a positive number without changing the order of the inequality. But multiplying or dividing an inequality by a negative number reverses the order of the inequality. Thus, $6 > 2$, but $(-1)(6) < (-1)(2)$.	To solve the inequality $\dfrac{(5x - 1)}{-2} < 3$ for x, isolate x as follows: (1) $5x - 1 > -6$ (multiplying both sides by -2, reverse the order of the inequality) (2) $5x > -5$ (add 1 to both sides) (3) $x > -1$ (divide both sides by 5)

Rates, Ratios, and Percentages

FRACTIONS:

Equivalent or Equal Fractions:

Two fractions represent the same number if dividing each fraction's numerator and denominator by their greatest common divisor yields identical results for both fractions.

Adding, Subtracting, Multiplying, and Dividing Fractions:

$$\frac{a}{b} + \frac{c}{d} = \frac{ad}{bd} + \frac{bc}{bd}; \frac{a}{b} - \frac{c}{d} = \frac{ad}{bd} - \frac{bc}{bd}$$

$$\frac{a}{b} \times \frac{c}{d} = \frac{ac}{bd}; \frac{a}{b} \div \frac{c}{d} = \frac{ad}{bc}$$

MIXED NUMBERS:

A mixed number of the form $a\frac{b}{c}$ is equivalent to the fraction $\frac{ac+b}{c}$.

RATE:

distance = rate × time

PROFIT:

Gross profit = Revenues − Expenses, or

Gross profit = Selling price − Cost.

INTEREST:

Simple annual interest =

(principal) × (interest rate) × (time)

Compound interest over n periods =

(principal) × (1 + interest per period)^n − principal

PERCENTS:

$x\% = \frac{x}{100}$.

$x\%$ of y equals $\frac{xy}{100}$.

To convert a percent to a decimal, drop the percent sign, then move the decimal point two digits left.

To convert a decimal to a percent, add a percent sign, then move the decimal point two digits right.

PERCENT INCREASE OR DECREASE:

The percent increase from x to y is

$100\left(\frac{y-x}{x}\right)\%$.

The percent decrease from x to y is

$100\left(\frac{x-y}{x}\right)\%$.

DISCOUNTS:

A price discounted by n percent becomes $(100 − n)$ percent of the original price.

A price discounted by n percent and then by m percent becomes $(100 − n)(100 − m)$ percent of the original price.

WORK:

$\frac{1}{r} + \frac{1}{s} = \frac{1}{h}$, where r is the length of time it takes one person or machine to complete an amount of work when working alone, s is the length of time it takes a second person or machine to complete that same amount of work when working alone, and h is the length of time it takes them to complete that amount of work when they are both working simultaneously.

MIXTURES:

	Number of units of a substance or mixture	Quantity of an ingredient per unit of the substance or mixture	Total quantity of that ingredient in the substance or mixture
Substance A	X	M	X × M
Substance B	Y	N	Y × N
Mixture of A and B	X + Y	$\frac{(X \times M) + (Y \times N)}{X + Y}$	(X × M) + (Y × N)

Statistics, Sets, and Counting Methods

STATISTICS:

Concept	Definition for a set of n numbers ordered from least to greatest	Example with data set $\{4, 4, 5, 7, 10\}$
Mean	The sum of the n numbers, divided by n	$\dfrac{(4+4+5+7+10)}{5} = \dfrac{30}{5} = 6$
Median	The middle number if n is odd; The mean of the two middle numbers if n is even.	5 is the middle number in $\{4, 4, 5, 7, 10\}$.
Mode	The number that appears most frequently in the set	4 is the only number that appears more than once in $\{4, 4, 5, 7, 10\}$.
Range	The largest number in the set minus the smallest	$10 - 4 = 6$
Standard Deviation	Calculated as follows: (1) Find the arithmetic mean, (2) Find the differences between each of the n numbers and the mean, (3) Square each of the differences, (4) Find the average of the squared differences, and (5) Take the nonnegative square root of this average.	(1) The mean is 6. (2) $-2, -2, -1, 1, 4$ (3) $4, 4, 1, 1, 16$ (4) $\dfrac{26}{5} = 5.2$ (5) $\sqrt{5.2}$

SETS:

Concept	Notation for finite sets S and T	Example
Number of elements	$\lvert S \rvert$	$S = \{-5, 0, 1\}$ is a set with $\lvert S \rvert = 3$.
Subset	$S \subseteq T$ (S is a subset of T); $S \supseteq T$ (T is a subset of S)	$\{-5, 0, 1\}$ is a subset of $\{-5, 0, 1, 4, 10\}$.
Union	$S \cup T$	$\{3, 4\} \cup \{4, 5, 6\} = \{3, 4, 5, 6\}$
Intersection	$S \cap T$	$\{3, 4\} \cap \{4, 5, 6\} = \{4\}$
The general addition rule for two sets	$\lvert S \cup T \rvert = \lvert S \rvert + \lvert T \rvert - \lvert S \cap T \rvert$	$\lvert \{3, 4\} \cup \{4, 5, 6\} \rvert =$ $\lvert \{3, 4\} \rvert + \lvert \{4, 5, 6\} \rvert - \lvert \{3, 4\} \cap \{4, 5, 6\} \rvert =$ $\lvert \{3, 4\} \rvert + \lvert \{4, 5, 6\} \rvert - \lvert \{4\} \rvert = 2 + 3 - 1 = 4$.

COUNTING METHODS:

Concept and Equations	Examples
Multiplication Principle: The number of possible choices of 1 element apiece from each of the sets $A_1, A_2, ..., A_n$ is $|A_1| \times |A_2| \times ... \times |A_n|$.	The number of possible choices of 1 element apiece from each of the sets $S = \{-5, 0, 1\}$, $T = \{3, 4\}$, and $U = \{3, 4, 5, 6\}$ is $|S| \times |T| \times |U| = 3 \times 2 \times 4 = 24$.
Factorial: $n! = n \times (n - 1) \times ... \times 1$ $0! = 1! = 1$ $n! = (n - 1)!(n)$	$4! = 4 \times 3 \times 2 \times 1 = 24$ $4! = 3! \times 4$
Permutations: The number of permutations of a set of n objects is $n!$.	The number of permutations of the set of letters A, B, and C is 3!, or 6: ABC, ACB, BAC, BCA, CAB, and CBA.
Combinations: The number of possible complete selections of k objects from a set of n objects is $\binom{n}{k} = \frac{n!}{k!(n-k)!}$.	The number of 2-element subsets of set $\{A, B, C, D, E\}$ is $$\binom{5}{2} = \frac{5!}{2!3!} = \frac{120}{(2)(6)} = 10.$$ The 10 subsets are: $\{A, B\}, \{A, C\}, \{A, D\}, \{A, E\}, \{B, C\}, \{B, D\}, \{B, E\}, \{C, D\}, \{C, E\}$, and $\{D, E\}$.

Probability, Sequences, and Partial Sums

PROBABILITY:

Concept	Definition, Notation, and Equations	Example: Rolling a die with 6 numbered sides once
Event	A set of outcomes of an experiment	The event of the outcome being an odd number is the set $\{1, 3, 5\}$.
Probability	The probability of an event E is a number between 0 and 1, inclusive, and is denoted $P(E)$. If each outcome is equally likely, $P(E) =$ $\dfrac{\text{(the number of possible outcomes in E)}}{\text{(the total number of possible outcomes)}}$.	If the 6 outcomes are equally likely, then the probability of each outcome is $\dfrac{1}{6}$. The probability that the outcome is an odd number is $P(\{1, 3, 5\}) =$ $\dfrac{|\{1,3,5\}|}{6} = \dfrac{3}{6} = \dfrac{1}{2}$.
Conditional Probability	The probability that E occurs if F occurs is $P(E\|F) = \dfrac{\|E \cap F\|}{\|F\|}$.	$P(\{1, 3, 5\}\|\{1, 2\}) = \dfrac{\|\{1\}\|}{\|\{1,2\}\|} = \dfrac{1}{2}$
Not E	The set of outcomes that are not in event E: $P(\text{not } E) = 1 - P(E)$.	$P(\text{not } \{3\}) = \dfrac{6-1}{6} = \dfrac{5}{6}$
E and F	The set of outcomes in both E and F, that is, $E \cap F$; $P(E \text{ and } F) = P(E \cap F) = P(E\|F)P(F)$.	For $E = \{1, 3, 5\}$ and $F = \{2, 3, 5\}$: $P(E \text{ and } F) = P(E \cap F) = P(\{3, 5\}) =$ $\dfrac{\|\{3,5\}\|}{6} = \dfrac{3}{6} = \dfrac{1}{3}$.
E or F	The set of outcomes in E or F or both, that is, $E \cup F$; $P(E \text{ or } F) = P(E) + P(F) - P(E \text{ and } F)$.	For $E = \{1, 3, 5\}$ and $F = \{2, 3, 5\}$: $P(E \text{ or } F) = P(E) + P(F) - P(E \text{ and } F) =$ $\dfrac{3}{6} + \dfrac{3}{6} - \dfrac{2}{6} = \dfrac{4}{6} = \dfrac{2}{3}$.
Dependent and Independent Events	E is dependent on F if $P(E\|F) \neq P(E)$. E and F are independent if neither is dependent on the other. If E and F are independent, $P(E \text{ and } F) = P(E)P(F)$.	For $E = \{2, 4, 6\}$ and $F = \{5, 6\}$: $P(E\|F) = P(E) = \dfrac{1}{2}$, and $P(F\|E) = P(F) = \dfrac{1}{3}$, so E and F are independent. Thus $P(E \text{ and } F) = P(E)P(F) = \left(\dfrac{1}{2}\right)\left(\dfrac{1}{3}\right) = \dfrac{1}{6}$.

SEQUENCE:

An algebraic function whose domain consists of only positive integers.

Example: Function $a(n) = n^2 + \left(\dfrac{n}{5}\right)$ with the domain of all positive integers $n = 1, 2, 3, \ldots$ is an infinite sequence a_n.

PARTIAL SUM:

The sum of the first k terms of series a_n is called a partial sum of the series and is denoted $\sum\limits_{i=1}^{k} a_i$

Example: For this same function $a(n) = n^2 + \left(\dfrac{n}{5}\right)$, the partial sum of the first three terms is

$$\sum_{i=1}^{3} a_i = \left(1^2 + \frac{1}{5}\right) + \left(2^2 + \frac{2}{5}\right) + \left(3^2 + \frac{3}{5}\right).$$

Angles and Polygons

VERTICAL ANGLES:

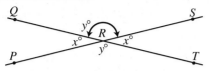

$\angle PRQ$ and $\angle SRT$ are a pair of vertical angles, and so are $\angle QRS$ and $\angle PRT$. Note that $x° + y° = 180°$.

ANGLES FORMED BY A LINE INTERSECTING TWO PARALLEL LINES:

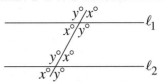

If two parallel lines are intersected by a third line, then the angle measures are related as indicated in the figure above, where $x° + y° = 180°$.

INTERIOR ANGLES OF A POLYGON:

The sum of the interior angle measures of a polygon with n sides is $(n - 2)180°$. For example, the sum of the interior angle measures of a pentagon is $(5 - 2)180° = (3)180° = 540°$.

EQUILATERAL AND ISOSCELES TRIANGLES:

An equilateral triangle's sides are all the same length. An isosceles triangle has at least two sides of equal length.

AREA OF A TRIANGLE:

Area of a triangle $= \dfrac{(\text{length of altitude})(\text{length of base})}{2}$

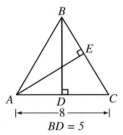

BD = 5

The area of $\triangle ABC$ is $\dfrac{(BD \times AC)}{2} = \dfrac{5 \times 8}{2} = 20$.

If $AB = BC$, then $AD = DC = 4$.

If two sides of a triangle are equal in length, the two angles opposite those sides are equal in measure, and vice versa.

Any altitude of an equilateral triangle bisects the side to which it is drawn.

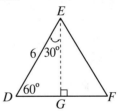

In equilateral triangle $\triangle DEF$, $DE = 6$, so $DG = 3$ and $EG = 3\sqrt{3}$.

AREA OF A TRAPEZOID:

Area of a trapezoid = $\dfrac{\text{(sum of lengths of bases)(height)}}{2}$

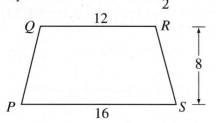

The area of $PQRS$ is $(QR + PS) \times \dfrac{8}{2} = (12 + 16) \times \dfrac{8}{2} = 28 \times 4 = 112$.

AREA OF A PARALLELOGRAM:

The area of a rectangle or other parallelogram = (length of base)(height)

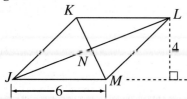

Since the diagonals bisect each other, $KN = NM$ and $JN = NL$. The area of $JKLM$ is $JM \times 4 = 6 \times 4 = 24$.

RIGHT TRIANGLES:

In a right triangle, the side opposite the right angle is the hypotenuse, and the other two sides are the legs.

Any triangle in which the lengths of the sides are in the ratio 3:4:5 is a right triangle.

In 45°– 45°– 90° triangles, the lengths of the sides are in the ratio $1:1:\sqrt{2}$. In 30°– 60°– 90° triangles, the lengths of the sides are in the ratio $1:\sqrt{3}:2$.

The Pythagorean Theorem:

If a and b, are the lengths of the bases of a right triangle, and c is the length of the hypotenuse, then $a^2 + b^2 = c^2$.

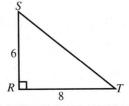

In right triangle $\triangle RST$, RS – 6 and RT – 8. Since $6^2 + 8^2 = 36 + 64 = 100 = (ST)^2$ and $ST = \sqrt{100}$, it follows that $ST = 10$.

Circles, Solids, and Coordinates

CIRCLES:

The circumference of a circle of radius r is $2\pi r$, where π is approximately $\frac{22}{7}$ or 3.14.

The area of a circle of radius r is πr^2.

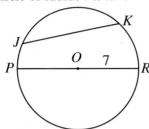

In the circle above, O is the center, and $\overline{JK}$ and $\overline{PR}$ are chords. $\overline{PR}$ is a diameter and $\overline{OR}$ is a radius.

Since $OR = 7$, the circumference is $2\pi(7) = 14\pi$.

The area is $\pi(7)^2 = 49\pi$.

RIGHT CIRCULAR CYLINDERS:

The surface area of a right circular cylinder with height h and a base of radius r is $2(\pi r^2) + 2\pi rh$.

The volume is $\pi r^2 h$, that is, (area of base) × (height).

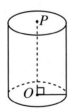

In the right circular cylinder above, where $r = 5$ and $h = 8$, the surface area is $2(25\pi) + 2\pi(5)(8) = 130\pi$.

The volume is $25\pi(8) = 200\pi$.

RECTANGULAR SOLIDS:

Surface area of a rectangular solid = the sum of the areas of all the faces.

Volume of a rectangular solid = (length)(width)(height).

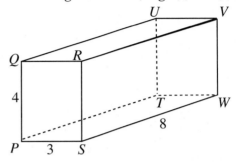

The dimensions of the rectangular solid above are 8, 3, and 4.

The surface area is $2(3 \times 4) + 2(3 \times 8) + 2(4 \times 8) = 136$.

The volume is $8 \times 3 \times 4 = 96$.

LINES IN THE COORDINATE PLANE:

An equation $y = mx + b$ determines a line whose slope is m and whose y-intercept is b.

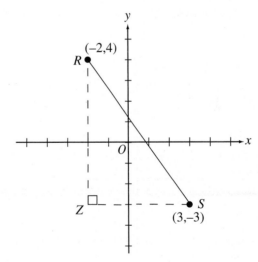

Given any two points (x_1, y_1) and (x_2, y_2) with $x_1 \neq x_2$, the slope is $m = \dfrac{(y_2 - y_1)}{(x_2 - x_1)}$. So using the known point (x_1, y_1) and the same slope m, any other point (x, y) on the line must satisfy the equation $m = \dfrac{(y - y_1)}{(x - x_1)}$.

Above, the line's slope is $\frac{(-3-4)}{(3-(-2))} = \frac{7}{5}$. So an equation of the line can be found using the point $(3,-3)$:

$$y - (-3) = (-\frac{7}{5})(x - 3)$$

$$y + 3 = (-\frac{7}{5})x + \frac{21}{5}$$

$$y = (-\frac{7}{5})x + \frac{6}{5}$$

Thus, the y-intercept is $\frac{6}{5}$.

The x-intercept can be found as follows:

$$0 = (-\frac{7}{5})x + \frac{6}{5}$$

$$(\frac{7}{5})x = \frac{6}{5}$$

$$x = \frac{6}{7}$$

Both of these intercepts can be seen on the graph.

DISTANCES ON THE COORDINATE PLANE:

Use the Pythagorean theorem to find the distance between two points:

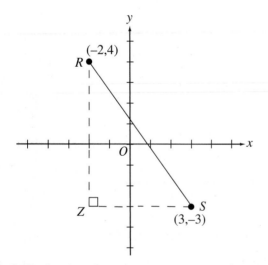

To find the distance between points R and S, draw the triangle as shown. Note that Z has (x,y) coordinates $(-2, -3)$, $RZ = 7$, and $ZS = 5$. Therefore, the distance between R and S is $\sqrt{7^2 + 5^2} = \sqrt{74}$.

PARABOLAS:

The graph of a quadratic polynomial function is a parabola.

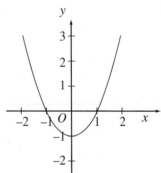

Above is the graph of the quadratic function $f(x) = x^2 - 1$.

4.0 Problem Solving

4.0 Problem Solving

The Quantitative Reasoning section of the GMAT™ exam uses Problem Solving and Data Sufficiency questions to gauge your skill level. This chapter focuses on Problem Solving questions. Remember that quantitative questions require knowledge of the following:

- Arithmetic
- Elementary algebra
- Commonly known concepts of geometry

Problem Solving questions are designed to test your basic mathematical skills and understanding of elementary mathematical concepts, as well as your ability to reason quantitatively, solve quantitative problems, and interpret graphic data. The mathematics knowledge required to answer the questions is no more advanced than what is generally taught in secondary school (or high school) mathematics classes.

In these questions, you are asked to solve each problem and select the best of the five answer choices given. Begin by reading the question thoroughly to determine exactly what information is given and to make sure you understand what is being asked. Scan the answer choices to understand your options. If the problem seems simple, take a few moments to see whether you can determine the answer. Then, check your answer against the choices provided.

If you do not see your answer among the choices, or if the problem is complicated, take a closer look at the answer choices and think again about what the problem is asking. See whether you can eliminate some of the answer choices and narrow down your options. If you are still unable to narrow the answer down to a single choice, reread the question. Keep in mind that the answer will be based solely on the information provided in the question—don't allow your own experience and assumptions to interfere with your ability to find the correct answer to the question.

If you find yourself stuck on a question or unable to select the single correct answer, keep in mind that you have about two minutes to answer each quantitative question. You may run out of time if you take too long to answer any one question; you may simply need to pick the answer that seems to make the most sense. Although guessing is generally not the best way to achieve a high GMAT score, making an educated guess is a good strategy for answering questions you are unsure of. Even if your answer to a particular question is incorrect, your answers to other questions will allow the test to accurately gauge your ability level.

The following pages include test-taking strategies, directions that will apply to questions of this type, sample questions, an answer key, and explanations for all the problems. These explanations present problem solving strategies that could be helpful in answering the questions.

4.1 Test-Taking Strategies

1. **Pace yourself.**

   Consult the on-screen timer periodically. Work as carefully as possible, but do not spend valuable time checking answers or pondering problems that you find difficult.

2. **Use the erasable notepad provided.**

   Working a problem out may help you avoid errors in solving the problem. If diagrams or figures are not presented, it may help to draw your own.

3. **Read each question carefully to determine what is being asked.**

   For word problems, take one step at a time, reading each sentence carefully and translating the information into equations or other useful mathematical representations.

4. **Scan the answer choices before attempting to answer a question.**

   Scanning the answers can prevent you from putting answers in a form that is not given (e.g., finding the answer in decimal form, such as 0.25, when the choices are given in fractional form, such as $\frac{1}{4}$). Also, if the question requires approximations, a shortcut could serve well (e.g., you may be able to approximate 48 percent of a number by using half).

5. **Don't waste time trying to solve a problem that is too difficult for you.**

   Make your best guess and then move on to the next question.

4.2 Section Instructions

Go to www.mba.com/tutorial to view instructions for the section and get a feel for what the test center screens will look like on the actual GMAT exam.

4.3 Practice Questions

Solve the problem and indicate the best of the answer choices given.
<u>Numbers:</u> All numbers used are real numbers.
<u>Figures:</u>   A figure accompanying a Problem Solving question is intended to provide information useful in solving the problem. Figures are drawn. as accurately as possible. Exceptions will be clearly noted. Lines shown as straight are straight, and lines that appear jagged are also straight. The positions of points, angles, regions, etc., exist in the order shown, and angle measures are greater than zero. All figures lie in a plane unless otherwise indicated.

Questions 1 to 99 - Difficulty: Easy

*PC02991

1.   In the figure, the 6 small squares are identical, each with sides of length 1. What is the outer perimeter (shown in bold) of the entire figure?

(A)   8
(B)   12
(C)   16
(D)   20
(E)   24

Performance Time	Ticket Price	Number of Tickets Sold
Thursday night	$40	200
Friday night	$50	240
Saturday afternoon	$40	220
Saturday night	$50	300

PS09868

2.   The table shows a summary of the ticket sales from four performances of a certain play. What is the difference between the maximum and the minimum ticket-sale revenue from a single performance?

(A) $4,000
(B) $5,100
(C) $6,200
(D) $7,000
(E) $9,600

PS10002

3.   During a trip that they took together, Carmen, Juan, Maria, and Rafael drove an average (arithmetic mean) of 80 miles each. Carmen drove 72 miles, Juan drove 78 miles, and Maria drove 83 miles. How many miles did Rafael drive?

(A)   80
(B)   82
(C)   85
(D)   87
(E)   89

PS07308

4.   Each week, a clothing salesperson receives a commission equal to 15 percent of the first $500 in sales and 20 percent of all additional sales that week. What commission would the salesperson receive on total sales for the week of $1,300 ?

(A) $195
(B) $227
(C) $235
(D) $260
(E) $335

PS07799

5.   A certain restaurant that regularly advertises through the mail has 1,040 cover letters and 3,000 coupons in stock. In its next mailing, each envelope will contain 1 cover letter and 2 coupons. If all of the cover letters in stock are used, how many coupons will remain in stock after this mailing?

(A)   920
(B)   1,040
(C)   1,500
(D)   1,960
(E)   2,080

*These numbers correlate with the online test bank question number. See the GMAT™ Official Guide Question Index in the back of this book.

112

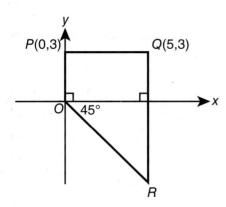

PS02599

6. In the figure above, what are the coordinates of point *R* ?

(A) (3,–5)
(B) (3,–3)
(C) (5,5)
(D) (5,–3)
(E) (5,–5)

PS08877

7. The price of a coat in a certain store is $500. If the price of the coat is to be reduced by $150, by what percent is the price to be reduced?

(A) 10%
(B) 15%
(C) 20%
(D) 25%
(E) 30%

PS05410

8. $\left(\dfrac{1}{2}-\dfrac{1}{3}\right)+\left(\dfrac{1}{3}-\dfrac{1}{4}\right)+\left(\dfrac{1}{4}-\dfrac{1}{5}\right)+\left(\dfrac{1}{5}-\dfrac{1}{6}\right)=$

(A) $-\dfrac{1}{6}$
(B) 0
(C) $\dfrac{1}{3}$
(D) $\dfrac{1}{2}$
(E) $\dfrac{2}{3}$

PS05001

9. While a family was away on vacation, they paid a neighborhood boy $11 per week to mow their lawn and $4 per day to feed and walk their dog. If the family was away for exactly 3 weeks, how much did they pay the boy for his services?

(A) $45
(B) $54
(C) $71
(D) $95
(E) $117

PS17812

10. Last year $48,000 of a certain store's profit was shared by its 2 owners and their 10 employees. Each of the 2 owners received 3 times as much as each of their 10 employees. How much did each owner receive from the $48,000 ?

(A) $12,000
(B) $9,000
(C) $6,000
(D) $4,000
(E) $3,000

PS02295

11. On a vacation, Rose exchanged $500.00 for euros at an exchange rate of 0.80 euro per dollar and spent $\dfrac{3}{4}$ of the euros she received. If she exchanged the remaining euros for dollars at an exchange rate of $1.20 per euro, what was the dollar amount she received?

(A) $60.00
(B) $80.00
(C) $100.00
(D) $120.00
(E) $140.00

x	x	x	y	y	v

v	x	x	y	w	w

PS08461

12. Each of the 12 squares shown is labeled x, y, v, or w. What is the ratio of the number of these squares labeled x or y to the number of these squares labeled v or w?

(A) 1:2
(B) 2:3
(C) 4:3
(D) 3:2
(E) 2:1

PS02382

13. In the xy-coordinate plane, if the point (0,2) lies on the graph of the line $2x + ky = 4$, what is the value of the constant k?

(A) 2
(B) 1
(C) 0
(D) −1
(E) −2

PS01248

14. Bouquets are to be made using white tulips and red tulips, and the ratio of the number of white tulips to the number of red tulips is to be the same in each bouquet. If there are 15 white tulips and 85 red tulips available for the bouquets, what is the greatest number of bouquets that can be made using all the tulips available?

(A) 3
(B) 5
(C) 8
(D) 10
(E) 13

PS07369

15. Over the past 7 weeks, the Smith family had weekly grocery bills of $74, $69, $64, $79, $64, $84, and $77. What was the Smiths' average (arithmetic mean) weekly grocery bill over the 7-week period?

(A) $64
(B) $70
(C) $73
(D) $74
(E) $85

PS14861

16. 125% of 5 =

(A) 5.125
(B) 5.25
(C) 6
(D) 6.125
(E) 6.25

PS02764

17. During a recent storm, 9 neighborhoods experienced power failures of durations 34, 29, 27, 46, 18, 25, 12, 35, and 16 minutes, respectively. For these 9 neighborhoods, what was the median duration, in minutes, of the power failures?

(A) 34
(B) 29
(C) 27
(D) 25
(E) 18

PS02286

18. When traveling at a constant speed of 32 miles per hour, a certain motorboat consumes 24 gallons of fuel per hour. What is the fuel consumption of this boat at this speed measured in miles traveled per gallon of fuel?

(A) $\frac{2}{3}$
(B) $\frac{3}{4}$
(C) $\frac{4}{5}$
(D) $\frac{4}{3}$
(E) $\frac{3}{2}$

PS11906

19. A technician makes a round-trip to and from a certain service center by the same route. If the technician completes the drive to the center and then completes 10 percent of the drive from the center, what percent of the round-trip has the technician completed?

(A) 5%
(B) 10%
(C) 25%
(D) 40%
(E) 55%

PS15957

20. From 2000 to 2003, the number of employees at a certain company increased by a factor of $\frac{1}{4}$. From 2003 to 2006, the number of employees at this company decreased by a factor of $\frac{1}{3}$. If there were 100 employees at the company in 2006, how many employees were there at the company in 2000 ?

(A) 200

(B) 120

(C) 100

(D)   75

(E)   60

PS00984

21. Which of the following statements must be true about the average (arithmetic mean) and the median of 5 consecutive integers?

   I.   The average is one of the integers.

   II. The median is one of the integers.

   III. The median equals the average.

(A) I only

(B) II only

(C) III only

(D) I and II only

(E) I, II, and III

PS15358

22. A collection of 16 coins, each with a face value of either 10 cents or 25 cents, has a total face value of $2.35. How many of the coins have a face value of 25 cents?

(A)   3

(B)   5

(C)   7

(D)   9

(E) 11

PS09707

23. A retailer purchased eggs at $2.80 per dozen and sold the eggs at 3 eggs for $0.90. What was the retailer's gross profit from purchasing and selling 5 dozen eggs? (1 dozen eggs = 12 eggs)

(A) $0.90

(B) $2.40

(C) $4.00

(D) $11.30

(E) $12.00

PS02127

24. In a set of 24 cards, each card is numbered with a different positive integer from 1 to 24. One card will be drawn at random from the set. What is the probability that the card drawn will have either a number that is divisible by both 2 and 3 or a number that is divisible by 7 ?

(A) $\frac{3}{24}$

(B) $\frac{4}{24}$

(C) $\frac{7}{24}$

(D) $\frac{8}{24}$

(E) $\frac{17}{24}$

PS12542

25. If the circumference of a circle inscribed in a square is 25π, what is the perimeter of the square?

(A)   20

(B)   25

(C)   40

(D)   50

(E) 100

PS03972

26. If $1 < x < y < z$, which of the following has the greatest value?

(A) $z(x+1)$

(B) $z(y+1)$

(C) $x(y+z)$

(D) $y(x+z)$

(E) $z(x+y)$

PS00087

27. Set *X* consists of eight consecutive integers. Set *Y* consists of all the integers that result from adding 4 to each of the integers in set *X* and all the integers that result from subtracting 4 from each of the integers in set *X*. How many more integers are there in set *Y* than in set *X* ?

(A)   0
(B)   4
(C)   8
(D)   12
(E)   16

PS05239

28. Of the following, which is the closest to $\dfrac{60.2}{1.03 \times 4.86}$?

(A)   10
(B)   12
(C)   13
(D)   14
(E)   15

PS15402

29. Thabo owns exactly 140 books, and each book is either paperback fiction, paperback nonfiction, or hardcover nonfiction. If he owns 20 more paperback nonfiction books than hardcover nonfiction books, and twice as many paperback fiction books as paperback nonfiction books, how many hardcover nonfiction books does Thabo own?

(A)   10
(B)   20
(C)   30
(D)   40
(E)   50

PS04571

30. If the average (arithmetic mean) of the four numbers 3, 15, 32, and (*N* + 1) is 18, then *N* =

(A)   19
(B)   20
(C)   21
(D)   22
(E)   29

PS13801

31. Abdul, Barb, and Carlos all live on the same straight road, on which their school is also located. The school is halfway between Abdul's house and Barb's house. Barb's house is halfway between the school and Carlos's house. If the school is 4 miles from Carlos's house, how many miles is Abdul's house from Carlos's house?

(A) $1\frac{1}{3}$
(B)   2
(C)   4
(D)   6
(E)   8

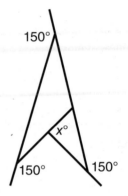

PS00534

32. In the figure shown, what is the value of *x* ?

(A)   60
(B)   80
(C)   85
(D)   90
(E)   95

PS17479

33. During a certain time period, Car X traveled north along a straight road at a constant rate of 1 mile per minute and used fuel at a constant rate of 5 gallons every 2 hours. During this time period, if Car X used exactly 3.75 gallons of fuel, how many miles did Car X travel?

(A)   36
(B)   37.5
(C)   40
(D)   80
(E)   90

PS13707

34. Cheryl purchased 5 identical hollow pine doors and 6 identical solid oak doors for the house she is building. The regular price of each solid oak door was twice the regular price of each hollow pine door. However, Cheryl was given a discount of 25% off the regular price of each solid oak door. If the regular price of each hollow pine door was $40, what was the total price of all 11 doors?

(A) $320
(B) $540
(C) $560
(D) $620
(E) $680

PS01233

35. A certain store will order 25 crates of apples. The apples will be of three different varieties—McIntosh, Rome, and Winesap—and each crate will contain apples of only one variety. If the store is to order more crates of Winesap than crates of McIntosh and more crates of Winesap than crates of Rome, what is the least possible number of crates of Winesap that the store will order?

(A) 7
(B) 8
(C) 9
(D) 10
(E) 11

PS02007

36. A bicycle store purchased two bicycles, one for $250 and the other for $375, and sold both bicycles at a total gross profit of $250. If the store sold one of the bicycles for $450, which of the following could be the store's gross profit from the sale of the other bicycle?

(A) $75
(B) $100
(C) $125
(D) $150
(E) $175

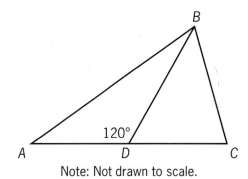

Note: Not drawn to scale.

PS10628

37. In the figure shown, $AC = 2$ and $BD = DC = 1$. What is the measure of angle ABD ?

(A) 15°
(B) 20°
(C) 30°
(D) 40°
(E) 45°

PS12786

38. If $k^2 = m^2$, which of the following must be true?

(A) $k = m$
(B) $k = -m$
(C) $k = |m|$
(D) $k = -|m|$
(E) $|k| = |m|$

PS13831

39. Makoto, Nishi, and Ozuro were paid a total of $780 for waxing the floors at their school. Each was paid in proportion to the number of hours he or she worked. If Makoto worked 15 hours, Nishi worked 20 hours, and Ozuro worked 30 hours, how much was Makoto paid?

(A) $52
(B) $117
(C) $130
(D) $180
(E) $234

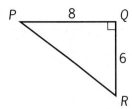

PS05680

40. The figure above shows a path around a triangular piece of land. Mary walked the distance of 8 miles from P to Q and then walked the distance of 6 miles from Q to R. If Ted walked directly from P to R, by what percent did the distance that Mary walked exceed the distance that Ted walked?

(A) 30%

(B) 40%

(C) 50%

(D) 60%

(E) 80%

PS04797

41. If x is a positive integer and $4^x - 3 = y$, which of the following CANNOT be a value of y?

(A) 1

(B) 7

(C) 13

(D) 61

(E) 253

PS05747

42. If $(1 - 1.25)N = 1$, then $N =$

(A) −400

(B) −140

(C) −4

(D) 4

(E) 400

PS14972

43. The quotient when a certain number is divided by $\frac{2}{3}$ is $\frac{9}{2}$. What is the number?

(A) $\frac{4}{27}$

(B) $\frac{1}{3}$

(C) 3

(D) 6

(E) $\frac{27}{4}$

PS06592

44. If a sphere with radius r is inscribed in a cube with edges of length e, which of the following expresses the relationship between r and e?

(A) $r = \frac{1}{2}e$

(B) $r = e$

(C) $r = 2e$

(D) $r = \sqrt{e}$

(E) $r = \frac{1}{4}e^2$

PS13159

45. The price of gasoline at a service station increased from $1.65 per gallon last week to $1.82 per gallon this week. Sally paid $26.40 for gasoline last week at the station. How much more will Sally pay this week at the station for the same amount of gasoline?

(A) $1.70

(B) $2.55

(C) $2.64

(D) $2.72

(E) $2.90

Monthly Charge for Low-Use Telephone
Contract Offered by Company X

Monthly rate (up to 75 message units)	20% less than standard rate of $10.00
Per unit in excess of 75 message units	$0.065

PS02534

46. Based on the rates above, how much would Company X charge a customer with a low-use contract for using 95 message units in a month?

(A) $9.30

(B) $11.30

(C) $12.88

(D) $14.88

(E) $16.18

PS02338

47. If $2x + y = 7$ and $x + 2y = 5$, then $\dfrac{x+y}{3} =$

(A)   1

(B) $\dfrac{4}{3}$

(C) $\dfrac{17}{5}$

(D) $\dfrac{18}{5}$

(E)   4

PS14250

48. City X has a population 4 times as great as the population of City Y, which has a population twice as great as the population of City Z. What is the ratio of the population of City X to the population of City Z ?

(A)   1:8

(B)   1:4

(C)   2:1

(D)   4:1

(E)   8:1

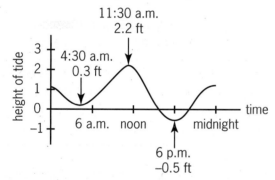

Tides at Bay Cove on July 13

PS05100

49. The graph above shows the height of the tide, in feet, above or below a baseline. Which of the following is closest to the difference, in feet, between the heights of the highest and lowest tides on July 13 at Bay Cove?

(A)   1.7

(B)   1.9

(C)   2.2

(D)   2.5

(E)   2.7

PS06243

50. If $S = 1 + \dfrac{1}{2^2} + \dfrac{1}{3^2} + \dfrac{1}{4^2} + \dfrac{1}{5^2} + \dfrac{1}{6^2} + \dfrac{1}{7^2} + \dfrac{1}{8^2} + \dfrac{1}{9^2} + \dfrac{1}{10^2}$, which of the following is true?

(A) $S > 3$

(B) $S = 3$

(C) $2 < S < 3$

(D) $S = 2$

(E) $S < 2$

PS05308

51. A manufacturer of a certain product can expect that between 0.3 percent and 0.5 percent of the units manufactured will be defective. If the retail price is $2,500 per unit and the manufacturer offers a full refund for defective units, how much money can the manufacturer expect to need to cover the refunds on 20,000 units?

(A)   Between $15,000 and $25,000

(B)   Between $30,000 and $50,000

(C)   Between $60,000 and $100,000

(D)   Between $150,000 and $250,000

(E)   Between $300,000 and $500,000

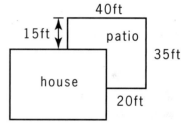

PS05544

52. A flat patio was built alongside a house as shown in the figure above. If all angles are right angles, what is the area of the patio in square feet?

(A)   800

(B)   875

(C)   1,000

(D)   1,100

(E)   1,125

PS10470

53. Which of the following is closest to $\sqrt{\dfrac{4.2(1,590)}{15.7}}$?

(A)   20

(B)   40

(C)   60

(D)   80

(E)   100

PS12114

54. The sum of the weekly salaries of 5 employees is $3,250. If each of the 5 salaries is to increase by 10 percent, then the average (arithmetic mean) weekly salary per employee will increase by

(A) $52.50
(B) $55.00
(C) $57.50
(D) $62.50
(E) $65.00

PS08173

55. Last week Chris earned x dollars per hour for the first 40 hours worked plus 22 dollars per hour for each hour worked beyond 40 hours. If last week Chris earned a total of 816 dollars by working 48 hours, what is the value of x ?

(A)   13
(B)   14
(C)   15
(D)   16
(E)   17

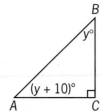

PS07408

56. In the figure above, what is the ratio of the measure of angle B to the measure of angle A ?

(A)   2 to 3
(B)   3 to 4
(C)   3 to 5
(D)   4 to 5
(E)   5 to 6

PS08768

57. The value of $\dfrac{\frac{7}{8}+\frac{1}{9}}{\frac{1}{2}}$ is closest to which of the following?

(A)   2
(B) $\dfrac{3}{2}$
(C)   1
(D) $\dfrac{1}{2}$
(E)   0

PS08025

58. The positive two-digit integers x and y have the same digits, but in reverse order. Which of the following must be a factor of $x + y$?

(A)   6
(B)   9
(C)   10
(D)   11
(E)   14

PS00015

59. In a certain sequence of 8 numbers, each number after the first is 1 more than the previous number. If the first number is −5, how many of the numbers in the sequence are positive?

(A)   None
(B)   One
(C)   Two
(D)   Three
(E)   Four

PS08385

60. A total of s oranges are to be packaged in boxes that will hold r oranges each, with no oranges left over. When n of these boxes have been completely filled, what is the number of boxes that remain to be filled?

(A) $s - nr$
(B) $s - \dfrac{n}{r}$
(C) $rs - n$
(D) $\dfrac{s}{n} - r$
(E) $\dfrac{s}{r} - n$

PS03371

61. If $0 < a < b < c$, which of the following statements must be true?

    I. $2a > b + c$

    II. $c - a > b - a$

    III. $\dfrac{c}{a} < \dfrac{b}{a}$

(A) I only

(B) II only

(C) III only

(D) I and II

(E) II and III

PS00096

62. In the xy-plane, the origin O is the midpoint of line segment PQ. If the coordinates of P are (r,s), what are the coordinates of Q?

(A) (r,s)

(B) $(s,-r)$

(C) $(-s,-r)$

(D) $(-r,s)$

(E) $(-r,-s)$

	Monday	Tuesday	Wednesday	Thursday
Company A	45	55	50	50
Company B	10	30	30	10
Company C	34	28	28	30
Company D	39	42	41	38
Company E	50	60	60	70

PS10568

63. The table shows the numbers of packages shipped daily by each of five companies during a 4-day period. The standard deviation of the numbers of packages shipped daily during the period was greatest for which of the five companies?

(A) A

(B) B

(C) C

(D) D

(E) E

PS15523

64. Company Q plans to make a new product next year and sell each unit of this new product at a selling price of $2. The variable costs per unit in each production run are estimated to be 40% of the selling price, and the fixed costs for each production run are estimated to be $5,040. Based on these estimated costs, how many units of the new product will Company Q need to make and sell in order for their revenue to equal their total costs for each production run?

(A) 4,200

(B) 3,150

(C) 2,520

(D) 2,100

(E) 1,800

PS07197

65. A small business invests $9,900 in equipment to produce a product. Each unit of the product costs $0.65 to produce and is sold for $1.20. How many units of the product must be sold before the revenue received equals the total expense of production, including the initial investment in equipment?

(A) 12,000

(B) 14,500

(C) 15,230

(D) 18,000

(E) 20,000

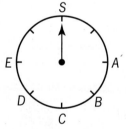

PS05682

66. The dial shown above is divided into equal-sized intervals. At which of the following letters will the pointer stop if it is rotated clockwise from S through 1,174 intervals?

(A) A

(B) B

(C) C

(D) D

(E) E

Estimated Number of Home-Schooled
Students by State, January 2001

State	Number (in thousands)
A	181
B	125
C	103
D	79
E	72

PS12287

67. According to the table shown, the estimated number of home-schooled students in State A is approximately what percent greater than the number in State D ?

(A)   25%

(B)   55%

(C)   100%

(D)   125%

(E)   155%

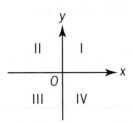

PS02695

68. The graph of the equation $xy = k$, where $k < 0$, lies in which two of the quadrants shown above?

(A)   I and II

(B)   I and III

(C)   II and III

(D)   II and IV

(E)   III and IV

PS00526

69. When n liters of fuel were added to a tank that was already $\frac{1}{3}$ full, the tank was filled to $\frac{7}{9}$ of its capacity. In terms of n, what is the capacity of the tank, in liters?

(A) $\frac{10}{9}n$

(B) $\frac{4}{3}n$

(C) $\frac{3}{2}n$

(D) $\frac{9}{4}n$

(E) $\frac{7}{3}n$

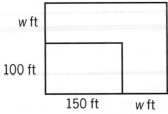

Note: Not drawn to scale.

PS06601

70. The smaller rectangle in the figure above represents the original size of a parking lot before its length and width were each extended by w feet to make the larger rectangular lot shown. If the area of the enlarged lot is twice the area of the original lot, what is the value of w ?

(A)   25

(B)   50

(C)   75

(D)   100

(E)   200

PS02209

71. Kevin invested $8,000 for one year at a simple annual interest rate of 6 percent and invested $10,000 for one year at an annual interest rate of 8 percent compounded semiannually. What is the total amount of interest that Kevin earned on the two investments?

(A) $880

(B) $1,088

(C) $1,253

(D) $1,280

(E) $1,296

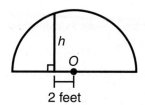

2 feet

PS05957

72. The figure above represents a semicircular archway over a flat street. The semicircle has a center at O and a radius of 6 feet. What is the height h, in feet, of the archway 2 feet from its center?

(A) $\sqrt{2}$

(B) 2

(C) 3

(D) $4\sqrt{2}$

(E) 6

PS01315

73. The harvest yield from a certain apple orchard was 350 bushels of apples. If x of the trees in the orchard each yielded 10 bushels of apples, what fraction of the harvest yield was from these x trees?

(A) $\dfrac{x}{35}$

(B) $1 - \dfrac{x}{35}$

(C) $10x$

(D) $35 - x$

(E) $350 - 10x$

PS00907

74. In a certain fraction, the denominator is 16 greater than the numerator. If the fraction is equivalent to 80 percent, what is the denominator of the fraction?

(A) 32

(B) 64

(C) 72

(D) 80

(E) 120

PS02102

75. Greg assembles units of a certain product at a factory. Each day he is paid $2.00 per unit for the first 40 units that he assembles and $2.50 for each additional unit that he assembles that day. If Greg assembled at least 30 units on each of two days and was paid a total of $180.00 for assembling units on the two days, what is the greatest possible number of units that he could have assembled on one of the two days?

(A) 48

(B) 52

(C) 56

(D) 60

(E) 64

PS00419

76. Which of the following is greatest?

(A) $10\sqrt{3}$

(B) $9\sqrt{4}$

(C) $8\sqrt{5}$

(D) $7\sqrt{6}$

(E) $6\sqrt{7}$

PS14236

77. Al and Ben are drivers for SD Trucking Company. One snowy day, Ben left SD at 8:00 a.m. heading east and Al left SD at 11:00 a.m. heading west. At a particular time later that day, the dispatcher retrieved data from SD's vehicle tracking system. The data showed that, up to that time, Al had averaged 40 miles per hour and Ben had averaged 20 miles per hour. It also showed that Al and Ben had driven a combined total of 240 miles. At what time did the dispatcher retrieve data from the vehicle tracking system?

(A) 1:00 p.m.

(B) 2:00 p.m.

(C) 3:00 p.m.

(D) 5:00 p.m.

(E) 6:00 p.m.

PS02996

78. Of the land owned by a farmer, 90 percent was cleared for planting. Of the cleared land, 40 percent was planted with soybeans and 50 percent of the cleared land was planted with wheat. If the remaining 720 acres of cleared land was planted with corn, how many acres did the farmer own?

(A) 5,832
(B) 6,480
(C) 7,200
(D) 8,000
(E) 8,889

PS00307

79. At the start of an experiment, a certain population consisted of 3 animals. At the end of each month after the start of the experiment, the population size was double its size at the beginning of that month. Which of the following represents the population size at the end of 10 months?

(A) 2^3
(B) 3^2
(C) $2(3^{10})$
(D) $3(2^{10})$
(E) $3(10^2)$

PS03635

80. If $\left(\dfrac{1}{3}+\dfrac{1}{4}+\dfrac{1}{5}+\dfrac{1}{6}\right)=r\left(\dfrac{1}{9}+\dfrac{1}{12}+\dfrac{1}{15}+\dfrac{1}{18}\right)$, then $r=$

(A) $\dfrac{1}{3}$

(B) $\dfrac{4}{3}$

(C) 3
(D) 4
(E) 12

PS03214

81. If x and y are positive integers such that y is a multiple of 5 and $3x + 4y = 200$, then x must be a multiple of which of the following?

(A) 3
(B) 6
(C) 7
(D) 8
(E) 10

PS12764

82. Which of the following expressions can be written as an integer?

I. $\left(\sqrt{82}+\sqrt{82}\right)^2$

II. $(82)\left(\sqrt{82}\right)$

III. $\dfrac{\left(\sqrt{82}\right)\left(\sqrt{82}\right)}{82}$

(A) None
(B) I only
(C) III only
(D) I and II
(E) I and III

PS13101

83. Pumping alone at their respective constant rates, one inlet pipe fills an empty tank to $\dfrac{1}{2}$ of capacity in 3 hours and a second inlet pipe fills the same empty tank to $\dfrac{2}{3}$ of capacity in 6 hours. How many hours will it take both pipes, pumping simultaneously at their respective constant rates, to fill the empty tank to capacity?

(A) 3.25
(B) 3.6
(C) 4.2
(D) 4.4
(E) 5.5

PS02947

84. In the xy-coordinate plane, which of the following points must lie on the line $kx + 3y = 6$ for every possible value of k?

(A) (1,1)
(B) (0,2)
(C) (2,0)
(D) (3,6)
(E) (6,3)

PS11091

85. If $x^2 - 2 < 0$, which of the following specifies all the possible values of x?

    (A) $0 < x < 2$

    (B) $0 < x < \sqrt{2}$

    (C) $-\sqrt{2} < x < \sqrt{2}$

    (D) $-2 < x < 0$

    (E) $-2 < x < 2$

Book Number	Pages in Book	Total Pages Read
1	253	253
2	110	363
3	117	480
4	170	650
5	155	805
6	50	855
7	205	1,060
8	70	1,130
9	165	1,295
10	105	1,400
11	143	1,543
12	207	1,750

PS14467

86. Shawana made a schedule for reading books during 4 weeks (28 days) of her summer vacation. She has checked out 12 books from the library. The number of pages in each book and the order in which she plans to read the books are shown in the table above. She will read exactly 50 pages each day. The only exception will be that she will never begin the next book on the same day that she finishes the previous one, and therefore on some days she may read fewer than 50 pages. At the end of the 28th day, how many books will Shawana have finished?

    (A) 7

    (B) 8

    (C) 9

    (D) 10

    (E) 11

PS07465

87. In Western Europe, x bicycles were sold in each of the years 1990 and 1993. The bicycle producers of Western Europe had a 42 percent share of this market in 1990 and a 33 percent share in 1993. Which of the following represents the decrease in the annual number of bicycles produced and sold in Western Europe from 1990 to 1993?

    (A) 9% of $\dfrac{x}{100}$

    (B) 14% of $\dfrac{x}{100}$

    (C) 75% of $\dfrac{x}{100}$

    (D) 9% of x

    (E) 14% of x

PS06946

88. If k is a positive integer, what is the remainder when $(k + 2)(k^3 - k)$ is divided by 6?

    (A) 0

    (B) 1

    (C) 2

    (D) 3

    (E) 4

PS14989

89. Which of the following fractions is closest to $\dfrac{1}{2}$?

    (A) $\dfrac{4}{7}$

    (B) $\dfrac{5}{9}$

    (C) $\dfrac{6}{11}$

    (D) $\dfrac{7}{13}$

    (E) $\dfrac{9}{16}$

PS12949

90. If $p \neq 0$ and $p - \dfrac{1-p^2}{p} = \dfrac{r}{p}$, then $r =$

(A) $p + 1$

(B) $2p - 1$

(C) $p^2 + 1$

(D) $2p^2 - 1$

(E) $p^2 + p - 1$

PS12760

91. If the range of the six numbers 4, 3, 14, 7, 10, and x is 12, what is the difference between the greatest possible value of x and the least possible value of x?

(A) 0

(B) 2

(C) 12

(D) 13

(E) 15

PS04734

92. What number is 108 more than two-thirds of itself?

(A) 72

(B) 144

(C) 162

(D) 216

(E) 324

PS99551.02

93. A service provider charges c dollars for the first 50 hours of service used per month and 40 cents for each 30 minutes in excess of 50 hours used during the month. If x is an integer greater than 50, which of the following expressions gives this service provider's charge, in dollars, for a month in which x hours of service were used?

(A) $c + 0.40x$

(B) $c + 0.80x$

(C) $c + 0.40(x - 50)$

(D) $c + 0.80(x - 50)$

(E) $c + 0.40(2x - 50)$

PS92820.02

94. A salesperson who had been driving at a speed of 100 kilometers per hour slowed down to a speed of 47 kilometers per hour. Approximately how many miles per hour was the speed reduced? (1 kilometer ≈ 0.625 mile)

(A) 29

(B) 33

(C) 53

(D) 63

(E) 75

PS11396

95. Company P had 15 percent more employees in December than it had in January. If Company P had 460 employees in December, how many employees did it have in January?

(A) 391

(B) 400

(C) 410

(D) 423

(E) 445

PS66740.02

96.

	Recording Time	Viewing Time
Tuesday	4 hours	None
Wednesday	None	1 to 2 hours
Thursday	2 hours	None
Friday	None	2 to 3 hours

The table above shows the numbers of hours of television programs that Jane recorded last week and the numbers of hours she spent viewing these recorded programs. No recorded program was viewed more than once. If h is the number of hours of recorded programs she had not yet viewed by the end of Friday, which of the following intervals represents all of the possible values of h?

(A) $0 \leq h \leq 1$

(B) $1 \leq h \leq 2$

(C) $2 \leq h \leq 3$

(D) $0 \leq h \leq 2$

(E) $1 \leq h \leq 3$

PS93850.02

97. A dance troupe has a total of 50 dancers split into 2 groups. The costumes worn by Group A cost $80 each, and those worn by Group B cost $90 each. If the total cost of all the costumes is $4,270, what is the total cost of the costumes worn by Group B ?

   (A) $1,840
   (B) $2,070
   (C) $2,135
   (D) $2,160
   (E) $2,430

PS07672

98. A doctor prescribed 18 cubic centimeters of a certain drug to a patient whose body weight was 120 pounds. If the typical dosage is 2 cubic centimeters per 15 pounds of body weight, by what percent was the prescribed dosage greater than the typical dosage?

   (A) 8%
   (B) 9%
   (C) 11%
   (D) 12.5%
   (E) 14.8%

PS09899

99. The function f is defined by $f(x) = \sqrt{x} - 10$ for all positive numbers x. If $u = f(t)$ for some positive numbers t and u, what is t in terms of u ?

   (A) $\sqrt{\sqrt{u} + 10}$
   (B) $\left(\sqrt{u} + 10\right)^2$
   (C) $\sqrt{u^2 + 10}$
   (D) $(u + 10)^2$
   (E) $(u^2 + 10)^2$

Questions 100 to 167 - Difficulty: **Medium**

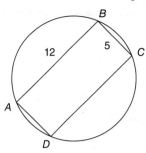

PS77502.01

100. If rectangle $ABCD$ is inscribed in the circle above, what is the area of the circular region?

   (A) 36.00π
   (B) 42.25π
   (C) 64.00π
   (D) 84.50π
   (E) 169.00π

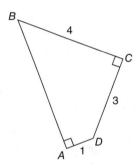

PS58502.01

101. In quadrilateral $ABCD$ above, what is the length of AB ?

   (A) $\sqrt{26}$
   (B) $2\sqrt{5}$
   (C) $2\sqrt{6}$
   (D) $3\sqrt{2}$
   (E) $3\sqrt{3}$

PS98502.01

102. Three-fourths of the area of a rectangular lawn 30 feet wide by 40 feet long is to be enclosed by a rectangular fence. If the enclosure has full width and reduced length rather than full length and reduced width, how much less fence will be needed?

   (A) $2\frac{1}{2}$
   (B) 5
   (C) 10
   (D) 15
   (E) 20

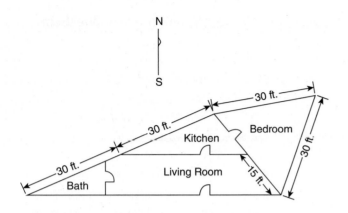

N

S

30 ft.

30 ft.

Bedroom

Kitchen

30 ft.

30 ft.

Living Room

15 ft.

Bath

PS19602.01

103. In the floor plan of an executive's beach house above, the north and south walls of the living room are parallel. What is the floor area, in square feet, of the bedroom?

(A) $450\sqrt{3}$

(B)   450

(C) $225\sqrt{3}$

(D)   225

(E)   It cannot be determined from the information given.

PS40602.01

104. On a scale drawing, a rectangle 1 inch by $1\frac{1}{3}$ inches represents the floor of a room and the indicated scale is 1 inch equals 15 feet. How many square tiles 6 inches on a side will be needed to cover this floor? (1 foot = 12 inches)

(A)   40

(B)   70

(C)   120

(D)   700

(E)   1,200

PS24210.02

105. According to a survey of 200 people, 60 enjoy skiing and 80 enjoy skating. If the number of people who enjoy neither skiing nor skating is 2 times the number of people who enjoy both skiing and skating, how many people surveyed enjoy neither skiing nor skating?

(A)   20

(B)   40

(C)   50

(D)   80

(E)   120

PS45430.02

106.
$$m \oplus p = n$$
$$n \oplus r = m$$
$$n \oplus q = q$$
$$p \oplus q = p$$
$$q \oplus p = r$$

If the relations shown hold for the operation $\oplus$ and the numbers m, n, p, q, and r, then $[(m \oplus p) \oplus q] \oplus p =$

(A) m

(B) n

(C) p

(D) q

(E) r

PS30730.02

107. To rent a tractor, it costs a total of x dollars for the first 24 hours, plus y dollars per hour for each hour in excess of 24 hours. Which of the following represents the cost, in dollars, to rent a tractor for 36 hours?

(A) $x + 12y$

(B) $x + 36y$

(C) $12x + y$

(D) $24x + 12y$

(E) $24x + 36y$

PS49140.02

108. If the mass of 1 cubic centimeter of a certain substance is 7.3 grams, what is the mass, in kilograms, of 1 cubic meter of this substance? (1 cubic meter = 1,000,000 cubic centimeters; 1 kilogram = 1,000 grams)

(A)   0.0073

(B)   0.73

(C)   7.3

(D)   7,300

(E)   7,300,000

PS14031.02

109. If $z \neq 0$ and $z + \dfrac{1 - 2z^2}{z} = \dfrac{w}{z}$, then $w =$

(A) $z + 1$

(B) $z^2 + 1$

(C) $-z^2 + 1$

(D) $-z^2 + z + 1$

(E) $-2z^2 + 1$

PS37631.02

110. For all real numbers a, b, c, d, e, and f, the operation Θ is defined by the equation $(a, b, c) \Theta (d, e, f) = ad + be + cf$. What is the value of $(1, -2, 3) \Theta \left(1, -\dfrac{1}{2}, \dfrac{1}{3}\right)$?

(A) -1

(B) $\dfrac{5}{6}$

(C) 1

(D) $\dfrac{5}{2}$

(E) 3

PS01761

111. If m and p are positive integers and $m^2 + p^2 < 100$, what is the greatest possible value of mp?

(A) 36

(B) 42

(C) 48

(D) 49

(E) 51

PS04482

112. If $\dfrac{x}{y} = \dfrac{c}{d}$ and $\dfrac{d}{c} = \dfrac{b}{a}$, which of the following must be true?

I. $\dfrac{y}{x} = \dfrac{b}{a}$ ✓

II. $\dfrac{x}{a} = \dfrac{y}{b}$ ✓

III. $\dfrac{y}{a} = \dfrac{x}{b}$

(A) I only

(B) II only

(C) I and II only

(D) I and III only

(E) I, II, and III

PS10391

113. If k is an integer and $(0.0025)(0.025)(0.00025) \times 10^k$ is an integer, what is the least possible value of k?

(A) -12

(B) -6

(C) 0

(D) 6

(E) 12

PS07325

114. If $a(a + 2) = 24$ and $b(b + 2) = 24$, where $a \ne b$, then $a + b =$

(A) -48

(B) -2

(C) 2

(D) 46

(E) 48

PS68850.02

115. In the xy plane, the distance between the origin and the point $(4,5)$ is the same as the distance between which of the following two points?

(A) $(-3,2)$ and $(-7,8)$

(B) $(-2,1)$ and $(3,5)$

(C) $(-2,-4)$ and $(1,0)$

(D) $(3,2)$ and $(8,7)$

(E) $(4,1)$ and $(-1,-4)$

PS05560

116. In a recent election, Ms. Robbins received 8,000 votes cast by independent voters, that is, voters not registered with a specific political party. She also received 10 percent of the votes cast by those voters registered with a political party. If N is the total number of votes cast in the election and 40 percent of the votes cast were cast by independent voters, which of the following represents the number of votes that Ms. Robbins received?

(A) $0.06N + 3,200$

(B) $0.1N + 7,200$

(C) $0.4N + 7,200$

(D) $0.1N + 8,000$

(E) $0.06N + 8,000$

PS01080.02

117. The profit P, in dollars, for any given month at a certain company is defined by $P = I - C$, where I represents total income, in dollars, and C represents total costs, in dollars, for the month. For each of the first 4 months of the year, $C = I + 32,000$; and for each of the next 3 months, $I = C + 36,000$. If $I = C + 10,000$ for each of the 5 remaining months of the year, what was the company's total profit for the 12-month year?

(A) $10,000

(B) $30,000

(C) $40,000

(D) $50,000

(E) $70,000

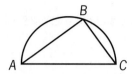

PS11308

118. In the figure shown, the triangle is inscribed in the semicircle. If the length of line segment AB is 8 and the length of line segment BC is 6, what is the length of arc ABC ?

(A) 15π
(B) 12π
(C) 10π
(D) 7π
(E) 5π

PS15517

119. A manufacturer makes and sells 2 products, P and Q. The revenue from the sale of each unit of P is $20.00 and the revenue from the sale of each unit of Q is $17.00. Last year the manufacturer sold twice as many units of Q as P. What was the manufacturer's average (arithmetic mean) revenue per unit sold of these 2 products last year?

(A) $28.50
(B) $27.00
(C) $19.00
(D) $18.50
(E) $18.00

PS11756

120. A worker carries jugs of liquid soap from a production line to a packing area, carrying 4 jugs per trip. If the jugs are packed into cartons that hold 7 jugs each, how many jugs are needed to fill the last partially filled carton after the worker has made 17 trips?

(A) 1
(B) 2
(C) 4
(D) 5
(E) 6

PS69400.02

121. Last year a state senate consisting of only Republican and Democrat members had 20 more Republican members than Democrat members. This year the senate has the same number of members as last year, but it has 2 fewer Republican members than last year. If this year the number of Republican members is $\frac{2}{3}$ the number of senate members, how many members does the senate have this year?

(A) 33
(B) 36
(C) 42
(D) 45
(E) 48

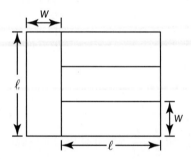

PS02820

122. The figure shown above represents a modern painting that consists of four differently colored rectangles, each of which has length ℓ and width w. If the area of the painting is 4,800 square inches, what is the width, in inches, of each of the four rectangles?

(A) 15
(B) 20
(C) 25
(D) 30
(E) 40

PS44321.02

123. Sam has $800 in his account. He will deposit $1 in his account one week from now, $2 two weeks from now, and each week thereafter he will deposit an amount that is $1 greater than the amount that he deposited one week before. If there are no other transactions, how much money will Sam have in his account 50 weeks from now?

(A) $850
(B) $1,200
(C) $1,675
(D) $2,075
(E) $3,350

PS30720.02

124. A certain state's milk production was 980 million pounds in 2007 and 2.7 billion pounds in 2014. Approximately how many more million gallons of milk did the state produce in 2014 than in 2007 ? (1 billion = 10^9 and 1 gallon = 8.6 pounds.)

(A)   100
(B)   200
(C)   1,700
(D)   8,200
(E)   14,800

PS09737

125. Working simultaneously and independently at an identical constant rate, four machines of a certain type can produce a total of x units of product P in 6 days. How many of these machines, working simultaneously and independently at this constant rate, can produce a total of $3x$ units of product P in 4 days?

(A)   24
(B)   18
(C)   16
(D)   12
(E)   8

PS01622

126. The symbol Δ denotes one of the four arithmetic operations: addition, subtraction, multiplication, or division. If $6 \Delta 3 \leq 3$, which of the following must be true?

I. $2 \Delta 2 = 0$
II. $2 \Delta 2 = 1$
III. $4 \Delta 2 = 2$

(A)   I only
(B)   II only
(C)   III only
(D)   I and II only
(E)   I, II, and III

PS04448

127. If $mn \neq 0$ and 25 percent of n equals $37\frac{1}{2}$ percent of m, what is the value of $\frac{12n}{m}$?

(A)   18
(B) $\frac{32}{3}$
(C)   8
(D)   3
(E) $\frac{9}{8}$

PS02555

128. Last year Joe grew 1 inch and Sally grew 200 percent more than Joe grew. How many inches did Sally grow last year?

(A)   0
(B)   1
(C)   2
(D)   3
(E)   4

Technique	Percent of Consumers
Television ads	35%
Coupons	22%
Store displays	18%
Samples	15%

PS10307

129. The table shows partial results of a survey in which consumers were asked to indicate which one of six promotional techniques most influenced their decision to buy a new food product. Of those consumers who indicated one of the four techniques listed, what fraction indicated either coupons or store displays?

(A) $\frac{2}{7}$
(B) $\frac{1}{3}$
(C) $\frac{2}{5}$
(D) $\frac{4}{9}$
(E) $\frac{1}{2}$

PS36090.02

130. If 65 percent of a certain firm's employees are full-time and if there are 5,100 more full-time employees than part-time employees, how many employees does the firm have?

(A) 8,250
(B) 10,200
(C) 11,050
(D) 16,500
(E) 17,000

PS09708

131. The cost C, in dollars, to remove p percent of a certain pollutant from a pond is estimated by using the formula $C = \dfrac{100{,}000p}{100 - p}$. According to this estimate, how much more would it cost to remove 90 percent of the pollutant from the pond than it would cost to remove 80 percent of the pollutant?

(A) $500,000
(B) $100,000
(C) $50,000
(D) $10,000
(E) $5,000

PS11121

132. If $xy \neq 0$ and $x^2y^2 - xy = 6$, which of the following could be y in terms of x?

I. $\dfrac{1}{2x}$

II. $-\dfrac{2}{x}$

III. $\dfrac{3}{x}$

(A) I only
(B) II only
(C) I and II
(D) I and III
(E) II and III

PS00633

133. $\sqrt{4.8 \times 10^9}$ is closest in value to

(A)   2,200
(B)   70,000
(C)   220,000
(D)   7,000,000
(E) 22,000,000

PS21260.02

134. In a certain high school, 80 percent of the seniors are taking calculus, and 60 percent of the seniors who are taking calculus are also taking physics. If 10 percent of the seniors are taking neither calculus nor physics, what percent of the seniors are taking physics?

(A) 40%
(B) 42%
(C) 48%
(D) 58%
(E) 80%

PS81711.02

135. If the units digit of $\dfrac{5{,}610.37}{10^k}$ is 6, what is the value of k?

(A)   3
(B)   2
(C)   1
(D) −1
(E) −2

PS08865

136. Three printing presses, R, S, and T, working together at their respective constant rates, can do a certain printing job in 4 hours. S and T, working together at their respective constant rates, can do the same job in 5 hours. How many hours would it take R, working alone at its constant rate, to do the same job?

(A)   8
(B) 10
(C) 12
(D) 15
(E) 20

PS51950.02
137.

Results of a Poll

Company	Number Who Own Stock in the Company
AT&T	30
IBM	48
GM	54
FORD	75
US Air	83

In a poll, 200 subscribers to *Financial Magazine X* indicated which of five specific companies they own stock in. The results are shown in the table above. If 15 of the 200 own stock in both IBM and AT&T, how many of those polled own stock in neither company?

(A)   63
(B)   93
(C)   107
(D)   122
(E)   137

PS07112
138. For a party, three solid cheese balls with diameters of 2 inches, 4 inches, and 6 inches, respectively, were combined to form a single cheese ball. What was the approximate diameter, in inches, of the new cheese ball? (The volume of a sphere is $\frac{4}{3}\pi r^3$, where r is the radius.)

(A)   12
(B)   16
(C) $\sqrt[3]{16}$
(D) $3\sqrt[3]{8}$
(E) $2\sqrt[3]{36}$

PS02325
139. The sum of all the integers k such that $-26 < k < 24$ is

(A)   0
(B)   −2
(C)   −25
(D)   −49
(E)   −51

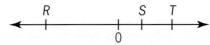

PS08399
140. The number line shown contains three points R, S, and T, whose coordinates have absolute values r, s, and t, respectively. Which of the following equals the average (arithmetic mean) of the coordinates of the points R, S, and T?

(A) s
(B) $s + t - r$
(C) $\dfrac{r - s - t}{3}$
(D) $\dfrac{r + s + t}{3}$
(E) $\dfrac{s + t - r}{3}$

PS94530.02
141. Tanks A and B are each in the shape of a right circular cylinder. The interior of Tank A has a height of 10 meters and a circumference of 8 meters, and the interior of Tank B has a height of 8 meters and a circumference of 10 meters. The capacity of Tank A is what percent of the capacity of Tank B?

(A)   75%
(B)   80%
(C)   100%
(D)   120%
(E)   125%

PS05962
142. Mark and Ann together were allocated n boxes of cookies to sell for a club project. Mark sold 10 boxes less than n and Ann sold 2 boxes less than n. If Mark and Ann have each sold at least one box of cookies, but together they have sold less than n boxes, what is the value of n?

(A)   11
(B)   12
(C)   13
(D)   14
(E)   15

PS07601.02

143.
$$\begin{array}{r} 3P5 \\ + 4QR \\ \hline 8S4 \end{array}$$

In the correctly worked addition problem shown, P, Q, R, and S are digits. If $Q = 2P$, which of the following could be the value of S?

(A)   3
(B)   4
(C)   5
(D)   7
(E)   9

PS04089

144. A certain high school has 5,000 students. Of these students, x are taking music, y are taking art, and z are taking both music and art. How many students are taking neither music nor art?

(A) $5,000 - z$
(B) $5,000 - x - y$
(C) $5,000 - x + z$
(D) $5,000 - x - y - z$
(E) $5,000 - x - y + z$

PS06133

145. Each person who attended a company meeting was either a stockholder in the company, an employee of the company, or both. If 62 percent of those who attended the meeting were stockholders and 47 percent were employees, what percent were stockholders who were <u>not</u> employees?

(A)   34%
(B)   38%
(C)   45%
(D)   53%
(E)   62%

Accounts	Amount Budgeted	Amount Spent
Payroll	$110,000	$117,000
Taxes	40,000	42,000
Insurance	2,500	2,340

PS08441

146. The table shows the amount budgeted and the amount spent for each of three accounts in a certain company. For which of these accounts did the amount spent differ from the amount budgeted by more than 6 percent of the amount budgeted?

(A)   Payroll only
(B)   Taxes only
(C)   Insurance only
(D)   Payroll and Insurance
(E)   Taxes and Insurance

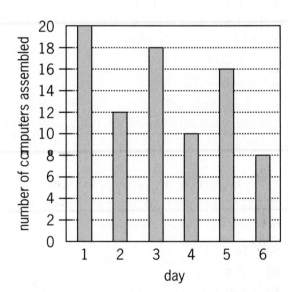

PS15111

147. The graph shows the number of computers assembled during each of 6 consecutive days. From what day to the next day was the percent change in the number of computers assembled the greatest in magnitude?

(A)   From Day 1 to Day 2
(B)   From Day 2 to Day 3
(C)   From Day 3 to Day 4
(D)   From Day 4 to Day 5
(E)   From Day 5 to Day 6

PS02704
148. If $n = 20! + 17$, then n is divisible by which of the following?

    I. 15
    II. 17
    III. 19

    (A) None
    (B) I only
    (C) II only
    (D) I and II
    (E) II and III

PS39811.02
149. Exchange Rates in a Particular Year

$$\$1 = 5.3 \text{ francs}$$
$$\$1 = 1.6 \text{ marks}$$

An American dealer bought a table in Germany for 480 marks and sold the same table in France for 2,385 francs. What was the dealer's gross profit on the two transactions in dollars?

    (A) $0
    (B) $50
    (C) $100
    (D) $150
    (E) $200

PS41450.02
150. One inch represents 20 miles on Map K and one inch represents 30 miles on Map L. An area of 3 square inches represents how many more square miles on Map L than on Map K ?

    (A) 30
    (B) 400
    (C) 500
    (D) 900
    (E) 1,500

PS02600
151. The product of two negative numbers is 160. If the lesser of the two numbers is 4 less than twice the greater, what is the greater number?

    (A) −20
    (B) −16
    (C) −10
    (D) −8
    (E) −4

PS10546
152. According to a certain estimate, the depth $N(t)$, in centimeters, of the water in a certain tank at t hours past 2:00 in the morning is given by $N(t) = -20(t - 5)^2 + 500$ for $0 \le t \le 10$. According to this estimate, at what time in the morning does the depth of the water in the tank reach its maximum?

    (A) 5:30   420
    (B) 7:00   500
    (C) 7:30   490
    (D) 8:00   480
    (E) 9:00   420

PS50750.02
153. The sides of a square region, measured to the nearest centimeter, are 6 centimeters long. The least possible value of the actual area of the square region is

    (A) 36.00 sq cm
    (B) 35.00 sq cm
    (C) 33.75 sq cm
    (D) 30.25 sq cm
    (E) 25.00 sq cm

PS04617
154. After driving to a riverfront parking lot, Bob plans to run south along the river, turn around, and return to the parking lot, running north along the same path. After running 3.25 miles south, he decides to run for only 50 minutes more. If Bob runs at a constant rate of 8 minutes per mile, how many miles farther south can he run and still be able to return to the parking lot in 50 minutes?

    (A) 1.5
    (B) 2.25
    (C) 3.0
    (D) 3.25
    (E) 4.75

PS12577

155. Alex deposited x dollars into a new account that earned 8 percent annual interest, compounded annually. One year later Alex deposited an additional x dollars into the account. If there were no other transactions and if the account contained w dollars at the end of two years, which of the following expresses x in terms of w?

 (A) $\dfrac{w}{1+1.08}$

 (B) $\dfrac{w}{1.08+1.16}$

 (C) $\dfrac{w}{1.16+1.24}$

 (D) $\dfrac{w}{1.08+(1.08)^2}$

 (E) $\dfrac{w}{(1.08)^2+(1.08)^3}$

PS05973

156. M is the sum of the reciprocals of the consecutive integers from 201 to 300, inclusive. Which of the following is true?

 (A) $\dfrac{1}{3}<M<\dfrac{1}{2}$

 (B) $\dfrac{1}{5}<M<\dfrac{1}{3}$

 (C) $\dfrac{1}{7}<M<\dfrac{1}{5}$

 (D) $\dfrac{1}{9}<M<\dfrac{1}{7}$

 (E) $\dfrac{1}{12}<M<\dfrac{1}{9}$

PS00428

157. Working simultaneously at their respective constant rates, Machines A and B produce 800 nails in x hours. Working alone at its constant rate, Machine A produces 800 nails in y hours. In terms of x and y, how many hours does it take Machine B, working alone at its constant rate, to produce 800 nails?

 (A) $\dfrac{x}{x+y}$

 (B) $\dfrac{y}{x+y}$

 (C) $\dfrac{xy}{x+y}$

 (D) $\dfrac{xy}{x-y}$

 (E) $\dfrac{xy}{y-x}$

PS63210.02

158. Carol purchased one basket of fruit consisting of 4 apples and 2 oranges and another basket of fruit consisting of 3 apples and 5 oranges. Carol is to select one piece of fruit at random from each of the two baskets. What is the probability that one of the two pieces of fruit selected will be an apple and the other will be an orange?

 (A) $\dfrac{1}{4}$

 (B) $\dfrac{1}{2}$

 (C) $\dfrac{1}{24}$

 (D) $\dfrac{5}{24}$

 (E) $\dfrac{13}{24}$

PS94421.02

159. Last year Brand X shoes were sold by dealers in 403 different regions worldwide, with an average (arithmetic mean) of 98 dealers per region. If last year these dealers sold an average of 2,488 pairs of Brand X shoes per dealer, which of the following is closest to the total number of pairs of Brand X shoes sold last year by the dealers worldwide?

(A) 10^4
(B) 10^5
(C) 10^6
(D) 10^7
(E) 10^8

10, 4, 26, 16

PS08966

160. What is the median of the numbers shown?

(A) 10
(B) 13
(C) 14
(D) 15
(E) 16

	Number of Marbles in Each of Three Bags	Percent of Marbles in Each Bag That Are Blue (to the nearest tenth)
Bag P	37	10.8%
Bag Q	x	66.7%
Bag R	32	50.0%

PS03823

161. If $\frac{1}{3}$ of the total number of marbles in the three bags listed in the table above are blue, how many marbles are there in bag Q?

(A) 5
(B) 9
(C) 12
(D) 23
(E) 46

Age Category (in years)	Number of Employees
Less than 20	29
20–29	58
30–39	36
40–49	21
50–59	10
60–69	5
70 and over	2

PS11600

162. The table above gives the age categories of the 161 employees at Company X and the number of employees in each category. According to the table, if m is the median age, in years, of the employees at Company X, then m must satisfy which of the following?

(A) $20 \leq m \leq 29$
(B) $25 \leq m \leq 34$
(C) $30 \leq m \leq 39$
(D) $35 \leq m \leq 44$
(E) $40 \leq m \leq 49$

PS70371.02

163. If k and n are positive integers such that $n > k$, then $k! + (n - k) \cdot (k - 1)!$ is equivalent to which of the following?

(A) $k \cdot n!$
(B) $k! \cdot n$
(C) $(n - k)!$
(D) $n \cdot (k + 1)!$
(E) $n \cdot (k - 1)!$

PS02749

164. Ron is 4 inches taller than Amy, and Barbara is 1 inch taller than Ron. If Barbara's height is 65 inches, what is the median height, in inches, of these three people?

(A) 60
(B) 61
(C) 62
(D) 63
(E) 64

PS02777

165. If x and y are positive numbers such that $x + y = 1$, which of the following could be the value of $100x + 200y$?

   I.   80
   II.   140
   III.   199

(A) II only
(B) III only
(C) I and II
(D) I and III
(E) II and III

PS02017

166. If X is the hundredths digit in the decimal $0.1X$ and if Y is the thousandths digit in the decimal $0.02Y$, where X and Y are nonzero digits, which of the following is closest to the greatest possible value of $\dfrac{0.1X}{0.02Y}$?

(A) 4
(B) 5
(C) 6
(D) 9
(E) 10

PS28101.02

167. If each of the 12 teams participating in a certain tournament plays exactly one game with each of the other teams, how many games will be played?

(A) 144
(B) 132
(C) 66
(D) 33
(E) 23

Questions 168 to 262 - Difficulty: Hard

PS60231.02

168. If the length of a diagonal of a square is $2\sqrt{x}$, what is the area of the square in terms of x?

(A) $\sqrt{x}$
(B) $\sqrt{2x}$
(C) $2\sqrt{x}$
(D) x
(E) $2x$

PS13724

169. Clarissa will create her summer reading list by randomly choosing 4 books from the 10 books approved for summer reading. She will list the books in the order in which they are chosen. How many different lists are possible?

(A)   6
(B)   40
(C)   210
(D) 5,040
(E) 151,200

PS10982

170. If n is a positive integer and the product of all the integers from 1 to n, inclusive, is divisible by 990, what is the least possible value of n?

(A) 8
(B) 9
(C) 10
(D) 11
(E) 12

PS02111

171. The probability that event M will not occur is 0.8 and the probability that event R will not occur is 0.6. If events M and R cannot both occur, which of the following is the probability that either event M or event R will occur?

(A) $\dfrac{1}{5}$
(B) $\dfrac{2}{5}$
(C) $\dfrac{3}{5}$
(D) $\dfrac{4}{5}$
(E) $\dfrac{12}{25}$

PS16410

172. The total cost for Company X to produce a batch of tools is $10,000 plus $3 per tool. Each tool sells for $8. The gross profit earned from producing and selling these tools is the total income from sales minus the total production cost. If a batch of 20,000 tools is produced and sold, then Company X's gross profit per tool is

(A) $3.00

(B) $3.75

(C) $4.50

(D) $5.00

(E) $5.50

PS07357

173. If Q is an odd number and the median of Q consecutive integers is 120, what is the largest of these integers?

(A) $\dfrac{Q-1}{2}+120$

(B) $\dfrac{Q}{2}+119$

(C) $\dfrac{Q}{2}+120$

(D) $\dfrac{Q+119}{2}$

(E) $\dfrac{Q+120}{2}$

PS02649

174. A ladder of a fire truck is elevated to an angle of 60° and extended to a length of 70 feet. If the base of the ladder is 7 feet above the ground, how many feet above the ground does the ladder reach?

(A) 35

(B) 42

(C) $35\sqrt{3}$

(D) $7+35\sqrt{3}$

(E) $7+42\sqrt{3}$

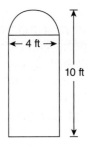

PS13827

175. The window in the figure above consists of a rectangle and a semicircle with dimensions as shown. What is the area, in square feet, of the window?

(A) $40+8\pi$

(B) $40+2\pi$

(C) $32+8\pi$

(D) $32+4\pi$

(E) $32+2\pi$

PS00562

176. If there are fewer than 8 zeros between the decimal point and the first nonzero digit in the decimal expansion of $\left(\dfrac{t}{1,000}\right)^4$, which of the following numbers could be the value of t?

I. 3

II. 5

III. 9

(A) None

(B) I only

(C) II only

(D) III only

(E) II and III

PS08280

177. A three-digit code for certain locks uses the digits 0, 1, 2, 3, 4, 5, 6, 7, 8, 9 according to the following constraints. The first digit cannot be 0 or 1, the second digit must be 0 or 1, and the second and third digits cannot both be 0 in the same code. How many different codes are possible?

(A) 144

(B) 152

(C) 160

(D) 168

(E) 176

PS02903

178. Jackie has two solutions that are 2 percent sulfuric acid and 12 percent sulfuric acid by volume, respectively. If these solutions are mixed in appropriate quantities to produce 60 liters of a solution that is 5 percent sulfuric acid, approximately how many liters of the 2 percent solution will be required?

(A) 18
(B) 20
(C) 24
(D) 36
(E) 42

PS16259

179. If Jake loses 8 pounds, he will weigh twice as much as his sister. Together they now weigh 278 pounds. What is Jake's present weight, in pounds?

(A) 131
(D) 135
(C) 139
(D) 147
(E) 188

PS03768

180. For each student in a certain class, a teacher adjusted the student's test score using the formula $y = 0.8x + 20$, where x is the student's original test score and y is the student's adjusted test score. If the standard deviation of the original test scores of the students in the class was 20, what was the standard deviation of the adjusted test scores of the students in the class?

(A) 12
(B) 16
(C) 28
(D) 36
(E) 40

PS01987

181. Last year 26 members of a certain club traveled to England, 26 members traveled to France, and 32 members traveled to Italy. Last year no members of the club traveled to both England and France, 6 members traveled to both England and Italy, and 11 members traveled to both France and Italy. How many members of the club traveled to at least one of these three countries last year?

(A) 52
(B) 67
(C) 71
(D) 73
(E) 79

PS16088

182. A store reported total sales of $385 million for February of this year. If the total sales for the same month last year was $320 million, approximately what was the percent increase in sales?

(A) 2%
(B) 17%
(C) 20%
(D) 65%
(E) 83%

PS11065

183. When positive integer x is divided by positive integer y, the remainder is 9. If $\frac{x}{y} = 96.12$, what is the value of y?

(A) 96
(B) 75
(C) 48
(D) 25
(E) 12

PS16802

184. If $x(2x + 1) = 0$ and $\left(x + \frac{1}{2}\right)(2x - 3) = 0$, then $x =$

(A) -3
(B) $-\frac{1}{2}$
(C) 0
(D) $\frac{1}{2}$
(E) $\frac{3}{2}$

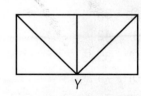

PS08219

185. Figures X and Y above show how eight identical triangular pieces of cardboard were used to form a square and a rectangle, respectively. What is the ratio of the perimeter of X to the perimeter of Y?

(A) $2:3$
(B) $\sqrt{2}:2$
(C) $2\sqrt{2}:3$
(D) $1:1$
(E) $\sqrt{2}:1$

PS04711

186. A certain experimental mathematics program was tried out in 2 classes in each of 32 elementary schools and involved 37 teachers. Each of the classes had 1 teacher and each of the teachers taught at least 1, but not more than 3, of the classes. If the number of teachers who taught 3 classes is n, then the least and greatest possible values of n, respectively, are

(A) 0 and 13
(B) 0 and 14
(C) 1 and 10
(D) 1 and 9
(E) 2 and 8

PS16214

187. For the positive numbers, n, $n+1$, $n+2$, $n+4$, and $n+8$, the mean is how much greater than the median?

(A) 0
(B) 1
(C) $n+1$
(D) $n+2$
(E) $n+3$

PS08313

188. The interior of a rectangular carton is designed by a certain manufacturer to have a volume of x cubic feet and a ratio of length to width to height of 3:2:2. In terms of x, which of the following equals the height of the carton, in feet?

(A) $\sqrt[3]{x}$

(B) $\sqrt[3]{\dfrac{2x}{3}}$

(C) $\sqrt[3]{\dfrac{3x}{2}}$

(D) $\dfrac{2}{3}\sqrt[3]{x}$

(E) $\dfrac{3}{2}\sqrt[3]{x}$

PS16810

189. The present ratio of students to teachers at a certain school is 30 to 1. If the student enrollment were to increase by 50 students and the number of teachers were to increase by 5, the ratio of students to teachers would then be 25 to 1. What is the present number of teachers?

(A) 5
(B) 8
(C) 10
(D) 12
(E) 15

PS16811

190. What is the smallest integer n for which $25^n > 5^{12}$?

(A) 6
(B) 7
(C) 8
(D) 9
(E) 10

PS16122

191. Sixty percent of the members of a study group are women, and 45 percent of those women are lawyers. If one member of the study group is to be selected at random, what is the probability that the member selected is a woman lawyer?

(A) 0.10
(B) 0.15
(C) 0.27
(D) 0.33
(E) 0.45

PS06570

192. Each year for 4 years, a farmer increased the number of trees in a certain orchard by $\dfrac{1}{4}$ of the number of trees in the orchard the preceding year. If all of the trees thrived and there were 6,250 trees in the orchard at the end of the 4-year period, how many trees were in the orchard at the beginning of the 4-year period?

(A) 1,250
(B) 1,563
(C) 2,250
(D) 2,560
(E) 2,752

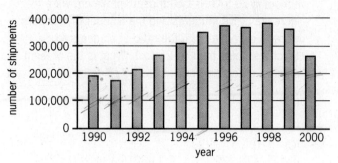

Number of Shipments of Manufactured Homes
in the United States, 1990–2000

PS00422

193. According to the chart shown, which of the following is closest to the median annual number of shipments of manufactured homes in the United States for the years from 1990 to 2000, inclusive?

(A)   250,000
(B)   280,000
(C)   310,000
(D)   325,000
(E)   340,000

PS08209

194. For the positive integers a, b, and k, $a^k \| b$ means that a^k is a divisor of b, but a^{k+1} is not a divisor of b. If k is a positive integer and $2^k \| 72$, then k is equal to

(A)   2
(B)   3
(C)   4
(D)   8
(E)   18

PS06674

195. A certain characteristic in a large population has a distribution that is symmetric about the mean m. If 68 percent of the distribution lies within one standard deviation d of the mean, what percent of the distribution is less than $m + d$?

(A)   16%
(B)   32%
(C)   48%
(D)   84%
(E)   92%

PS07459

196. Four extra-large sandwiches of exactly the same size were ordered for m students, where $m > 4$. Three of the sandwiches were evenly divided among the students. Since 4 students did not want any of the fourth sandwich, it was evenly divided among the remaining students. If Carol ate one piece from each of the four sandwiches, the amount of sandwich that she ate would be what fraction of a whole extra-large sandwich?

(A) $\dfrac{m+4}{m(m-4)}$

(B) $\dfrac{2m-4}{m(m-4)}$

(C) $\dfrac{4m-4}{m(m-4)}$

(D) $\dfrac{4m-8}{m(m-4)}$

(E) $\dfrac{4m-12}{m(m-4)}$

PS05888

197. Which of the following equations has $1 + \sqrt{2}$ as one of its roots?

(A) $x^2 + 2x - 1 = 0$
(B) $x^2 - 2x + 1 = 0$
(C) $x^2 + 2x + 1 = 0$
(D) $x^2 - 2x - 1 = 0$
(E) $x^2 - x - 1 = 0$

PS07730

198. In Country C, the unemployment rate among construction workers dropped from 16 percent on September 1, 1992, to 9 percent on September 1, 1996. If the number of construction workers was 20 percent greater on September 1, 1996, than on September 1, 1992, what was the approximate percent change in the number of unemployed construction workers over this period?

(A)   50% decrease
(B)   30% decrease
(C)   15% decrease
(D)   30% increase
(E)   55% increase

PS06215

199. In a box of 12 pens, a total of 3 are defective. If a customer buys 2 pens selected at random from the box, what is the probability that neither pen will be defective?

(A) $\dfrac{1}{6}$

(B) $\dfrac{2}{9}$

(C) $\dfrac{6}{11}$

(D) $\dfrac{9}{16}$

(E) $\dfrac{3}{4}$

PS13244

200. At a certain fruit stand, the price of each apple is 40 cents and the price of each orange is 60 cents. Mary selects a total of 10 apples and oranges from the fruit stand, and the average (arithmetic mean) price of the 10 pieces of fruit is 56 cents. How many oranges must Mary put back so that the average price of the pieces of fruit that she keeps is 52 cents?

(A) 1

(B) 2

(C) 3

(D) 4

(E) 5

PS04688

201. A pharmaceutical company received $3 million in royalties on the first $20 million in sales of the generic equivalent of one of its products and then $9 million in royalties on the next $108 million in sales. By approximately what percent did the ratio of royalties to sales decrease from the first $20 million in sales to the next $108 million in sales?

(A) 8%

(B) 15%

(C) 45%

(D) 52%

(E) 56%

Times at Which the Door
Opened from 8:00 to 10:00

8:00	8:06	8:30	9:05
8:03	8:10	8:31	9:11
8:04	8:18	8:54	9:29
8:04	8:19	8:57	9:31

PS06497

202. The light in a restroom operates with a 15-minute timer that is reset every time the door opens as a person goes in or out of the room. Thus, after someone enters or exits the room, the light remains on for only 15 minutes unless the door opens again and resets the timer for another 15 minutes. If the times listed above are the times at which the door opened from 8:00 to 10:00, approximately how many minutes during this two-hour period was the light off?

(A) 10

(B) 25

(C) 35

(D) 40

(E) 70

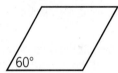

PS07536

203. The parallelogram shown has four sides of equal length. What is the ratio of the length of the shorter diagonal to the length of the longer diagonal?

(A) $\dfrac{1}{2}$

(B) $\dfrac{1}{\sqrt{2}}$

(C) $\dfrac{1}{2\sqrt{2}}$

(D) $\dfrac{1}{\sqrt{3}}$

(E) $\dfrac{1}{2\sqrt{3}}$

PS00041

204. If p is the product of the integers from 1 to 30, inclusive, what is the greatest integer k for which 3^k is a factor of p?

(A) 10
(B) 12
(C) 14
(D) 16
(E) 18

PS04651

205. If $n = 3^8 - 2^8$, which of the following is NOT a factor of n?

(A) 97
(B) 65
(C) 35
(D) 13
(E)   5

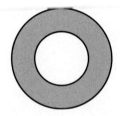

PS12078

206. In the figure shown, if the area of the shaded region is 3 times the area of the smaller circular region, then the circumference of the larger circle is how many times the circumference of the smaller circle?

(A) 4
(B) 3
(C) 2
(D) $\sqrt{3}$
(E) $\sqrt{2}$

PS12177

207. Club X has more than 10 but fewer than 40 members. Sometimes the members sit at tables with 3 members at one table and 4 members at each of the other tables, and sometimes they sit at tables with 3 members at one table and 5 members at each of the other tables. If they sit at tables with 6 members at each table except one and fewer than 6 members at that one table, how many members will be at the table that has fewer than 6 members?

(A) 1
(B) 2
(C) 3
(D) 4
(E) 5

PS07081

208. In order to complete a reading assignment on time, Terry planned to read 90 pages per day. However, she read only 75 pages per day at first, leaving 690 pages to be read during the last 6 days before the assignment was to be completed. How many days in all did Terry have to complete the assignment on time?

(A) 15
(B) 16
(C) 25
(D) 40
(E) 46

PS13996

209. If $s > 0$ and $\sqrt{\dfrac{r}{s}} = s$, what is r in terms of s?

(A) $\dfrac{1}{s}$
(B) $\sqrt{s}$
(C) $s\sqrt{s}$
(D) s^3
(E) $s^2 - s$

PS12536

210. If $3 < x < 100$, for how many values of x is $\dfrac{x}{3}$ the square of a prime number?

(A) Two
(B) Three
(C) Four
(D) Five
(E) Nine

PS07547
211. A researcher plans to identify each participant in a certain medical experiment with a code consisting of either a single letter or a pair of distinct letters written in alphabetical order. What is the least number of letters that can be used if there are 12 participants, and each participant is to receive a different code?

(A) 4
(B) 5
(C) 6
(D) 7
(E) 8

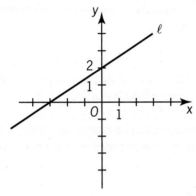

PS06948
212. The graph of which of the following equations is a straight line that is parallel to line ℓ in the figure above?

(A) $3y - 2x = 0$
(B) $3y + 2x = 0$
(C) $3y + 2x = 6$
(D) $2y - 3x = 6$
(E) $2y + 3x = -6$

PS06562
213. An object thrown directly upward is at a height of h feet after t seconds, where $h = -16(t - 3)^2 + 150$. At what height, in feet, is the object 2 seconds after it reaches its maximum height?

(A)   6
(B)   86
(C) 134
(D) 150
(E) 166

PS16107
214. Which of the following is equivalent to the pair of inequalities $x + 6 > 10$ and $x - 3 \leq 5$?

(A) $2 \leq x < 16$
(B) $2 \leq x < 4$
(C) $2 < x \leq 8$
(D) $4 < x \leq 8$
(E) $4 \leq x < 16$

PS16823
215. David has d books, which is 3 times as many as Jeff and $\frac{1}{2}$ as many as Paula. How many books do the three of them have altogether, in terms of d ?

(A) $\frac{5}{6}d$

(B) $\frac{7}{3}d$

(C) $\frac{10}{3}d$

(D) $\frac{7}{2}d$

(E) $\frac{9}{2}d$

PS16824
216. There are 8 teams in a certain league and each team plays each of the other teams exactly once. If each game is played by 2 teams, what is the total number of games played?

(A) 15
(B) 16
(C) 28
(D) 56
(E) 64

PS07491
217. At his regular hourly rate, Don had estimated the labor cost of a repair job as $336 and he was paid that amount. However, the job took 4 hours longer than he had estimated and, consequently, he earned $2 per hour less than his regular hourly rate. What was the time Don had estimated for the job, in hours?

(A) 28
(B) 24
(C) 16
(D) 14
(E) 12

PS16828

218. If $\dfrac{p}{q} < 1$, and p and q are positive integers, which of the following must be greater than 1 ?

(A) $\sqrt{\dfrac{p}{q}}$

(B) $\dfrac{p}{q^2}$

(C) $\dfrac{p}{2q}$

(D) $\dfrac{q}{p^2}$

(E) $\dfrac{q}{p}$

PS16830

219. To mail a package, the rate is x cents for the first pound and y cents for each additional pound, where $x > y$. Two packages weighing 3 pounds and 5 pounds, respectively, can be mailed separately or combined as one package. Which method is cheaper, and how much money is saved?

(A) Combined, with a savings of $x - y$ cents
(B) Combined, with a savings of $y - x$ cents
(C) Combined, with a savings of x cents
(D) Separately, with a savings of $x - y$ cents
(E) Separately, with a savings of y cents

PS16831

220. If money is invested at r percent interest, compounded annually, the amount of the investment will double in approximately $\dfrac{70}{r}$ years. If Pat's parents invested $5,000 in a long-term bond that pays 8 percent interest, compounded annually, what will be the approximate total amount of the investment 18 years later, when Pat is ready for college?

(A) $20,000
(B) $15,000
(C) $12,000
(D) $10,000
(E) $9,000

PS16832

221. On a recent trip, Cindy drove her car 290 miles, rounded to the nearest 10 miles, and used 12 gallons of gasoline, rounded to the nearest gallon. The actual number of miles per gallon that Cindy's car got on this trip must have been between

(A) $\dfrac{290}{12.5}$ and $\dfrac{290}{11.5}$

(B) $\dfrac{295}{12}$ and $\dfrac{285}{11.5}$

(C) $\dfrac{285}{12}$ and $\dfrac{295}{12}$

(D) $\dfrac{285}{12.5}$ and $\dfrac{295}{11.5}$

(E) $\dfrac{295}{12.5}$ and $\dfrac{285}{11.5}$

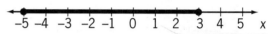

PS16833

222. Which of the following inequalities is an algebraic expression for the shaded part of the number line above?

(A) $|x| \le 3$
(B) $|x| \le 5$
(C) $|x - 2| \le 3$
(D) $|x - 1| \le 4$
(E) $|x + 1| \le 4$

PS16835

223. In a small snack shop, the average (arithmetic mean) revenue was $400 per day over a 10-day period. During this period, if the average daily revenue was $360 for the first 6 days, what was the average daily revenue for the last 4 days?

(A) $420
(B) $440
(C) $450
(D) $460
(E) $480

PS05882

224. If y is the smallest positive integer such that 3,150 multiplied by y is the square of an integer, then y must be

(A) 2

(B) 5

(C) 6

(D) 7

(E) 14

PS16116

225. If $[x]$ is the greatest integer less than or equal to x, what is the value of $[-1.6] + [3.4] + [2.7]$?

(A) 3

(B) 4

(C) 5

(D) 6

(E) 7

PS06558

226. In the first week of the year, Nancy saved \$1. In each of the next 51 weeks, she saved \$1 more than she had saved in the previous week. What was the total amount that Nancy saved during the 52 weeks?

(A) \$1,326

(B) \$1,352

(C) \$1,378

(D) \$2,652

(E) \$2,756

PS16100

227. In a certain sequence, the term x_n is given by the formula $x_n = 2x_{n-1} - \frac{1}{2}(x_{n-2})$ for all $n \geq 2$. If $x_0 = 3$ and $x_1 = 2$, what is the value of x_3 ?

(A) 2.5

(B) 3.125

(C) 4

(D) 5

(E) 6.75

PS08570

228. During a trip, Francine traveled x percent of the total distance at an average speed of 40 miles per hour and the rest of the distance at an average speed of 60 miles per hour. In terms of x, what was Francine's average speed for the entire trip?

(A) $\dfrac{180 - x}{2}$

(B) $\dfrac{x + 60}{4}$

(C) $\dfrac{300 - x}{5}$

(D) $\dfrac{600}{115 - x}$

(E) $\dfrac{12,000}{x + 200}$

PS00564

229. If $n = (33)^{43} + (43)^{33}$, what is the units digit of n ?

(A) 0

(B) 2

(C) 4

(D) 6

(E) 8

PS13691

230. Team A and Team B are competing against each other in a game of tug-of-war. Team A, consisting of 3 males and 3 females, decides to line up male, female, male, female, male, female. The lineup that Team A chooses will be one of how many different possible lineups?

(A) 9

(B) 12

(C) 15

(D) 36

(E) 720

PS08480

231. A border of uniform width is placed around a rectangular photograph that measures 8 inches by 10 inches. If the area of the border is 144 square inches, what is the width of the border, in inches?

(A) 3

(B) 4

(C) 6

(D) 8

(E) 9

PS09403

232. If $d = \dfrac{1}{2^3 \times 5^7}$ is expressed as a terminating decimal, how many nonzero digits will d have?

(A) One

(B) Two

(C) Three

(D) Seven

(E) Ten

PS03513

233. For any positive integer n, the sum of the first n positive integers equals $\dfrac{n(n+1)}{2}$. What is the sum of all the even integers between 99 and 301 ?

(A) 10,100

(B) 20,200

(C) 22,650

(D) 40,200

(E) 45,150

PS91151.02

234. November 16, 2001, was a Friday. If each of the years 2004, 2008, and 2012 had 366 days, and the remaining years from 2001 through 2014 had 365 days, what day of the week was November 16, 2014 ?

(A) Sunday

(B) Monday

(C) Tuesday

(D) Wednesday

(E) Thursday

PS06498

235. How many prime numbers between 1 and 100 are factors of 7,150 ?

(A) One

(B) Two

(C) Three

(D) Four

(E) Five

PS08732

236. A sequence of numbers a_1, a_2, a_3, ... is defined as follows: $a_1 = 3$, $a_2 = 5$, and every term in the sequence after a_2 is the product of all terms in the sequence preceding it, e.g., $a_3 = (a_1)(a_2)$ and $a_4 = (a_1)(a_2)(a_3)$. If $a_n = t$ and $n > 2$, what is the value of a_{n+2} in terms of t ?

(A) $4t$

(B) t^2

(C) t^3

(D) t^4

(E) t^8

PS08552

237. Last year the price per share of Stock X increased by k percent and the earnings per share of Stock X increased by m percent, where k is greater than m. By what percent did the ratio of price per share to earnings per share increase, in terms of k and m ?

(A) $\dfrac{k}{m}\%$

(B) $(k - m)\%$

(C) $\dfrac{100(k-m)}{100+k}\%$

(D) $\dfrac{100(k-m)}{100+m}\%$

(E) $\dfrac{100(k-m)}{100+k+m}\%$

PS04677

238. Of the 300 subjects who participated in an experiment using virtual-reality therapy to reduce their fear of heights, 40 percent experienced sweaty palms, 30 percent experienced vomiting, and 75 percent experienced dizziness. If all of the subjects experienced at least one of these effects and 35 percent of the subjects experienced exactly two of these effects, how many of the subjects experienced only one of these effects?

(A) 105

(B) 125

(C) 130

(D) 180

(E) 195

PS56710.02

239. The outer dimensions of a closed rectangular cardboard box are 8 centimeters by 10 centimeters by 12 centimeters, and the six sides of the box are uniformly $\frac{1}{2}$ centimeter thick. A closed canister in the shape of a right circular cylinder is to be placed inside the box so that it stands upright when the box rests on one of its sides. Of all such canisters that would fit, what is the outer radius, in centimeters, of the canister that occupies the maximum volume?

(A)   3.5
(B)   4
(C)   4.5
(D)   5
(E)   5.5

PS03686

240. If $m^{-1} = -\frac{1}{3}$, then m^{-2} is equal to

(A)   −9
(B)   −3
(C) $-\frac{1}{9}$
(D) $\frac{1}{9}$
(E)   9

PS07555

241. A photography dealer ordered 60 Model X cameras to be sold for $250 each, which represents a 20 percent markup over the dealer's initial cost for each camera. Of the cameras ordered, 6 were never sold and were returned to the manufacturer for a refund of 50 percent of the dealer's initial cost. What was the dealer's approximate profit or loss as a percent of the dealer's initial cost for the 60 cameras?

(A)   7% loss
(B)   13% loss
(C)   7% profit
(D)   13% profit
(E)   15% profit

PS04305

242. Seven pieces of rope have an average (arithmetic mean) length of 68 centimeters and a median length of 84 centimeters. If the length of the longest piece of rope is 14 centimeters more than 4 times the length of the shortest piece of rope, what is the maximum possible length, in centimeters, of the longest piece of rope?

(A)   82
(B)   118
(C)   120
(D)   134
(E)   152

PS16146

243. What is the difference between the sixth and the fifth terms of the sequence 2, 4, 7, … whose nth term is $n + 2^{n-1}$?

(A)   2
(B)   3
(C)   6
(D)   16
(E)   17

PS02405

244. From the consecutive integers −10 to 10, inclusive, 20 integers are randomly chosen with repetitions allowed. What is the least possible value of the product of the 20 integers?

(A) $(-10)^{20}$
(B) $(-10)^{10}$
(C)   0
(D) $-(10)^{19}$
(E) $-(10)^{20}$

PS05140

245. The letters D, G, I, I, and T can be used to form 5-letter strings such as DIGIT or DGIIT. Using these letters, how many 5-letter strings can be formed in which the two occurrences of the letter I are separated by at least one other letter?

(A)   12
(B)   18
(C)   24
(D)   36
(E)   48

PS00574

246. $\dfrac{0.99999999}{1.0001} - \dfrac{0.99999991}{1.0003} =$

(A) 10^{-8}

(B) $3(10^{-8})$

(C) $3(10^{-4})$

(D) $2(10^{4})$

(E) 10^{-4}

PS03144

247. Last Sunday a certain store sold copies of Newspaper A for $1.00 each and copies of Newspaper B for $1.25 each, and the store sold no other newspapers that day. If r percent of the store's revenue from newspaper sales was from Newspaper A and if p percent of the newspapers that the store sold were copies of Newspaper A, which of the following expresses r in terms of p?

(A) $\dfrac{100p}{125 - p}$

(B) $\dfrac{150p}{250 - p}$

(C) $\dfrac{300p}{375 - p}$

(D) $\dfrac{400p}{500 - p}$

(E) $\dfrac{500p}{625 - p}$

PS16890

248. For the past n days, the average (arithmetic mean) daily production at a company was 50 units. If today's production of 90 units raises the average to 55 units per day, what is the value of n?

(A) 30

(B) 18

(C) 10

(D) 9

(E) 7

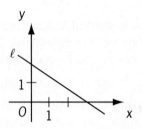

PS16893

249. In the coordinate system above, which of the following is the equation of line ℓ?

(A) $2x - 3y = 6$

(B) $2x + 3y = 6$

(C) $3x + 2y = 6$

(D) $2x - 3y = -6$

(E) $3x - 2y = -6$

PS16894

250. If a two-digit positive integer has its digits reversed, the resulting integer differs from the original by 27. By how much do the two digits differ?

(A) 3

(B) 4

(C) 5

(D) 6

(E) 7

PS16896

251. In an electric circuit, two resistors with resistances x and y are connected in parallel. In this case, if r is the combined resistance of these two resistors, then the reciprocal of r is equal to the sum of the reciprocals of x and y. What is r in terms of x and y?

(A) xy

(B) $x + y$

(C) $\dfrac{1}{x + y}$

(D) $\dfrac{xy}{x + y}$

(E) $\dfrac{x + y}{xy}$

PS16897

252. Xavier, Yvonne, and Zelda each try independently to solve a problem. If their individual probabilities for success are $\frac{1}{4}$, $\frac{1}{2}$, and $\frac{5}{8}$, respectively, what is the probability that Xavier and Yvonne, but not Zelda, will solve the problem?

   (A) $\frac{11}{8}$

   (B) $\frac{7}{8}$

   (C) $\frac{9}{64}$

   (D) $\frac{5}{64}$

   (E) $\frac{3}{64}$

PS16898

253. If $\frac{1}{x} - \frac{1}{x+1} = \frac{1}{x+4}$, then x could be

   (A) 0
   (B) –1
   (C) –2
   (D) –3
   (E) –4

PS16899

254. $\left(\frac{1}{2}\right)^{-3} \left(\frac{1}{4}\right)^{-2} \left(\frac{1}{16}\right)^{-1} =$

   (A) $\left(\frac{1}{2}\right)^{-48}$

   (B) $\left(\frac{1}{2}\right)^{-11}$

   (C) $\left(\frac{1}{2}\right)^{-6}$

   (D) $\left(\frac{1}{8}\right)^{-11}$

   (E) $\left(\frac{1}{8}\right)^{-6}$

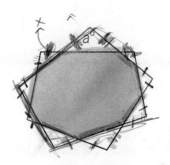

PS00947

255. The figure shown above consists of a shaded 9-sided polygon and 9 unshaded isosceles triangles. For each isosceles triangle, the longest side is a side of the shaded polygon and the two sides of equal length are extensions of the two adjacent sides of the shaded polygon. What is the value of a ?

   (A) 100
   (B) 105
   (C) 110
   (D) 115
   (E) 120

PS01648

256. List T consists of 30 positive decimals, none of which is an integer, and the sum of the 30 decimals is S. The estimated sum of the 30 decimals, E, is defined as follows. Each decimal in T whose tenths digit is even is rounded up to the nearest integer, and each decimal in T whose tenths digit is odd is rounded down to the nearest integer; E is the sum of the resulting integers. If $\frac{1}{3}$ of the decimals in T have a tenths digit that is even, which of the following is a possible value of $E - S$?

   I.   –16
   II.   6
   III.   10

   (A) I only
   (B) I and II only
   (C) I and III only
   (D) II and III only
   (E) I, II, and III

PS16115
257. If $5 - \dfrac{6}{x} = x$, then x has how many possible values?

(A) None

(B) One

(C) Two

(D) A finite number greater than two

(E) An infinite number

PS16904
258. Seed mixture X is 40 percent ryegrass and 60 percent bluegrass by weight; seed mixture Y is 25 percent ryegrass and 75 percent fescue. If a mixture of X and Y contains 30 percent ryegrass, what percent of the weight of the mixture is X ?

(A) 10%

(B) $33\dfrac{1}{3}\%$

(C) 40%

(D) 50%

(E) $66\dfrac{2}{3}\%$

PS49220.02
259.

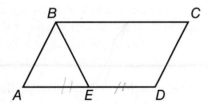

In the figure above, ABCD is a parallelogram and E is the midpoint of side AD. The area of triangular region ABE is what fraction of the area of quadrilateral region BCDE ?

(A) $\dfrac{1}{2}$

(B) $\dfrac{1}{3}$

(C) $\dfrac{1}{4}$

(D) $\dfrac{1}{5}$

(E) $\dfrac{1}{6}$

PS14203
260. How many of the integers that satisfy the inequality $\dfrac{(x+2)(x+3)}{x-2} \geq 0$ are less than 5 ?

(A) 1

(B) 2

(C) 3

(D) 4

(E) 5

PS07712
261. Of the 150 houses in a certain development, 60 percent have air-conditioning, 50 percent have a sunporch, and 30 percent have a swimming pool. If 5 of the houses have all three of these amenities and 5 have none of them, how many of the houses have exactly two of these amenities?

(A) 10

(B) 45

(C) 50

(D) 55

(E) 65

PS08886
262. The value of $\dfrac{2^{-14} + 2^{-15} + 2^{-16} + 2^{-17}}{5}$ is how many times the value of $2^{(-17)}$?

(A) $\dfrac{3}{2}$

(B) $\dfrac{5}{2}$

(C) 3

(D) 4

(E) 5

4.4 Answer Key

1.	B	33.	E	65.	D	97.	E	129.	D
2.	D	34.	C	66.	E	98.	D	130.	E
3.	D	35.	C	67.	D	99.	D	131.	A
4.	C	36.	E	68.	D	100.	B	132.	E
5.	A	37.	C	69.	D	101.	C	133.	B
6.	E	38.	E	70.	B	102.	B	134.	D
7.	E	39.	D	71.	E	103.	C	135.	B
8.	C	40.	B	72.	D	104.	E	136.	E
9.	E	41.	B	73.	A	105.	E	137.	E
10.	B	42.	C	74.	D	106.	E	138.	E
11.	D	43.	C	75.	C	107.	A	139.	D
12.	E	44.	A	76.	B	108.	D	140.	E
13.	A	45.	D	77.	B	109.	C	141.	B
14.	B	46.	A	78.	D	110.	E	142.	A
15.	C	47.	B	79.	D	111.	D	143.	A
16.	E	48.	E	80.	C	112.	C	144.	E
17.	C	49.	E	81.	E	113.	E	145.	D
18.	D	50.	E	82.	E	114.	B	146.	D
19.	E	51.	D	83.	B	115.	B	147.	D
20.	B	52.	C	84.	B	116.	E	148.	C
21.	E	53.	A	85.	C	117.	B	149.	D
22.	B	54.	E	86.	B	118.	E	150.	E
23.	C	55.	D	87.	D	119.	E	151.	D
24.	C	56.	D	88.	A	120.	B	152.	B
25.	E	57.	A	89.	D	121.	E	153.	D
26.	E	58.	D	90.	D	122.	B	154.	A
27.	C	59.	C	91.	D	123.	D	155.	D
28.	B	60.	E	92.	E	124.	B	156.	A
29.	B	61.	B	93.	D	125.	B	157.	E
30.	C	62.	E	94.	B	126.	C	158.	E
31.	D	63.	B	95.	B	127.	A	159.	E
32.	D	64.	A	96.	E	128.	D	160.	B

161.	B	182.	C	203.	D	224.	E	245.	D
162.	A	183.	B	204.	C	225.	A	246.	D
163.	E	184.	B	205.	C	226.	C	247.	D
164.	E	185.	C	206.	C	227.	C	248.	E
165.	E	186.	A	207.	E	228.	E	249.	B
166.	D	187.	B	208.	B	229.	A	250.	A
167.	C	188.	B	209.	D	230.	D	251.	D
168.	E	189.	E	210.	B	231.	A	252.	E
169.	D	190.	B	211.	B	232.	B	253.	C
170.	D	191.	C	212.	A	233.	B	254.	B
171.	C	192.	D	213.	B	234.	A	255.	A
172.	C	193.	C	214.	D	235.	D	256.	B
173.	A	194.	B	215.	C	236.	D	257.	C
174.	D	195.	D	216.	C	237.	D	258.	B
175.	E	196.	E	217.	B	238.	D	259.	B
176.	A	197.	D	218.	E	239.	C	260.	D
177.	B	198.	B	219.	A	240.	D	261.	D
178.	E	199.	C	220.	A	241.	D	262.	C
179.	E	200.	E	221.	D	242.	D		
180.	B	201.	C	222.	E	243.	E		
181.	B	202.	B	223.	D	244.	E		

4.5 Answer Explanations

The following discussion is intended to familiarize you with the most efficient and effective approaches to the kinds of problems common to Problem Solving questions. The particular questions in this chapter are generally representative of the kinds of Problem Solving questions you will encounter on the GMAT exam. Remember that it is the problem solving strategy that is important, not the specific details of a particular question.

Questions 1 to 99 - Difficulty: Easy

*PS02991

1. In the figure, the 6 small squares are identical, each with sides of length 1. What is the outer perimeter (shown in bold) of the entire figure?

(A)   8
(B)   12
(C)   16
(D)   20
(E)   24

Geometry Perimeter

The labeled figure shows the 6 horizontal sides of the boundary, 4 sides of length 1 and 2 sides of length 2, and the 6 vertical sides of the boundary, 2 sides of length 1 and 1 side each of lengths a, b, c, and d. The perimeter is the sum of the lengths of these 12 sides, or $4(1) + 2(2) + 2(1) + a + b + c + d$, or $10 + a + b + c + d$. To determine the value of $a + b + c + d$, note that the vertical width of the squares is 2. On the left side, this vertical width is the sum of the lengths of 3 vertical sides of the boundary, 1 side of length 1 and 1 side each of lengths a and b, and thus $2 = 1 + a + b$, or $a + b = 1$. On the right side, this vertical width is the sum of the lengths of 3 vertical sides of the boundary, 1 side of length 1 and 1 side each of lengths c and d, and thus $2 = 1 + c + d$, or $c + d = 1$. Therefore, the perimeter is $10 + (a + b) + (c + d) = 10 + 1 + 1 = 12$.

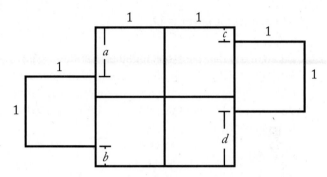

The correct answer is B.

Performance Time	Ticket Price	Number of Tickets Sold
Thursday night	$40	200
Friday night	$50	240
Saturday afternoon	$40	220
Saturday night	$50	300

PS09868

2. The table shows a summary of the ticket sales from four performances of a certain play. What is the difference between the maximum and the minimum ticket-sale revenue from a single performance?

(A) $4,000
(B) $5,100
(C) $6,200
(D) $7,000
(E) $9,600

Arithmetic Interpretation of Tables

For each performance, the product of the ticket price and the number of tickets sold is the ticket-sale revenue. The following table shows these values.

---

*These numbers correlate with the online test bank question number. See the GMAT™ Official Guide Question Index in the back of this book.

155

Performance Time	Ticket-sale Revenue
Thursday night	200($40) = $8,000
Friday night	240($50) = $12,000
Saturday afternoon	220($40) = $8,800
Saturday night	300($50) = $15,000

From these values it follows that for a single performance, the maximum ticket-sale revenue is $15,000 and the minimum ticket-sale revenue is $8,000, and therefore the difference between these two revenues is $15,000 − $8,000 = $7,000.

The correct answer is D.

PS10002

3. During a trip that they took together, Carmen, Juan, Maria, and Rafael drove an average (arithmetic mean) of 80 miles each. Carmen drove 72 miles, Juan drove 78 miles, and Maria drove 83 miles. How many miles did Rafael drive?

   (A) 80
   (B) 82
   (C) 85
   (D) 87
   (E) 89

Arithmetic Statistics

Let C, J, M, and R be the numbers of miles, respectively, that Carmen, Juan, Maria, and Rafael drove. Since the average of the numbers of miles they drove is 80, it follows that

$$\frac{C + J + M + R}{4} = 80 \text{, or } C + J + M + R = 4(80)$$

= 320. It is given that $C = 72, J = 78$, and $M = 83$. Therefore, $72 + 78 + 83 + R = 320$, or $R = 87$.

The correct answer is D.

PS07308

4. Each week, a clothing salesperson receives a commission equal to 15 percent of the first $500 in sales and 20 percent of all additional sales that week. What commission would the salesperson receive on total sales for the week of $1,300 ?

   (A) $195
   (B) $227
   (C) $235
   (D) $260
   (E) $335

Arithmetic Applied Problems

The commission on the total sales can be calculated as follows:

$$\begin{array}{l} \text{commission on} \\ \text{first \$500} \end{array} + \begin{array}{l} \text{commission on} \\ \text{amount over \$500} \end{array}$$

$$= \quad (0.15)(\$500) + (0.20)(\$1,300 - \$500)$$

$$= \qquad \qquad \$75 + \$160$$

Therefore, the commission on the total sales is $75 + $160 = $235.

The correct answer is C.

PS07799

5. A certain restaurant that regularly advertises through the mail has 1,040 cover letters and 3,000 coupons in stock. In its next mailing, each envelope will contain 1 cover letter and 2 coupons. If all of the cover letters in stock are used, how many coupons will remain in stock after this mailing?

   (A)   920
   (B)   1,040
   (C)   1,500
   (D)   1,960
   (E)   2,080

Arithmetic Applied Problems

In the next mailing there will be 1,040 cover letters and 2(1,040) = 2,080 coupons. Therefore, after the next mailing the number of coupons remaining in stock will be 3,000 − 2,080 = 920.

The correct answer is A.

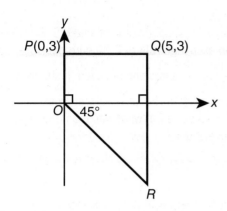

PS02599

6. In the figure above, what are the coordinates of point R?

    (A) (3,–5)
    (B) (3,–3)
    (C) (5,5)
    (D) (5,–3)
    (E) (5,–5)

Geometry Simple Coordinate Geometry; Triangles

In the figure, each of the points M and R has x-coordinate 5 because these two points lie on a vertical line that contains Q and it is given that the x-coordinate of Q is 5. Also, the measure of $\angle MRO$ is 45°, and hence $OM = MR$, because $\triangle OMR$ is a right triangle and it is given that the measure of $\angle ROM$ is 45°. Since it is given that $OM = 5$, it follows that $MR = 5$ and the coordinates of R are $(5,y) = (5,-5)$.

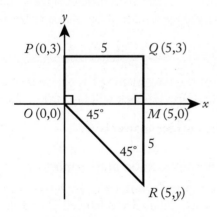

The correct answer is E.

PS08877

7. The price of a coat in a certain store is $500. If the price of the coat is to be reduced by $150, by what percent is the price to be reduced?

    (A) 10%
    (B) 15%
    (C) 20%
    (D) 25%
    (E) 30%

Arithmetic Percents

A reduction of $150 from $500 represents a percent decrease of $\left(\dfrac{150}{500} \times 100\right)\% = 30\%$.

Therefore, the price of the coat was reduced by 30%.

The correct answer is E.

PS05410

8. $\left(\dfrac{1}{2} - \dfrac{1}{3}\right) + \left(\dfrac{1}{3} - \dfrac{1}{4}\right) + \left(\dfrac{1}{4} - \dfrac{1}{5}\right) + \left(\dfrac{1}{5} - \dfrac{1}{6}\right) =$

    (A) $-\dfrac{1}{6}$
    (B) 0
    (C) $\dfrac{1}{3}$
    (D) $\dfrac{1}{2}$
    (E) $\dfrac{2}{3}$

Arithmetic Operations on Rational Numbers

The parentheses can be removed without any change of signs, and after doing this most of the terms can be additively cancelled as shown below.

$$\frac{1}{2} - \frac{\cancel{1}}{\cancel{3}} + \frac{\cancel{1}}{\cancel{3}} - \frac{\cancel{1}}{\cancel{4}} + \frac{\cancel{1}}{\cancel{4}} - \frac{\cancel{1}}{\cancel{5}} + \frac{\cancel{1}}{\cancel{5}} - \frac{1}{6} = \frac{1}{2} - \frac{1}{6}$$
$$= \frac{1}{3}$$

The correct answer is C.

PS05001
9. While a family was away on vacation, they paid a neighborhood boy $11 per week to mow their lawn and $4 per day to feed and walk their dog. If the family was away for exactly 3 weeks, how much did they pay the boy for his services?

(A) $45
(B) $54
(C) $71
(D) $95
(E) $117

Arithmetic Applied Problems

A period of exactly 3 weeks consists of exactly $3(7) = 21$ days. Therefore, the boy was paid for 3 weeks of mowing the lawn and for 21 days of feeding and walking the dog, for a total pay of $3(\$11) + 21(\$4) = \$33 + \$84 = \$117$.

The correct answer is E.

PS17812
10. Last year $48,000 of a certain store's profit was shared by its 2 owners and their 10 employees. Each of the 2 owners received 3 times as much as each of their 10 employees. How much did each owner receive from the $48,000 ?

(A) $12,000
(B) $9,000
(C) $6,000
(D) $4,000
(E) $3,000

Algebra First-Degree Equations

Let A be the amount received by each owner and let B be the amount received by each employee. From the given information it follows that $A = 3B$ and $2A + 10B = 48,000$. Thus, $2(3B) + 10B = 48,000$, or $16B = 48,000$, or $B = 3,000$. Therefore, the amount received by each owner was $A = 3B = 3(\$3,000) = \$9,000$.

The correct answer is B.

PS02295
11. On a vacation, Rose exchanged $500.00 for euros at an exchange rate of 0.80 euro per dollar and spent $\frac{3}{4}$ of the euros she received. If she exchanged the remaining euros for dollars at an exchange rate of $1.20 per euro, what was the dollar amount she received?

(A) $60.00
(B) $80.00
(C) $100.00
(D) $120.00
(E) $140.00

Arithmetic Operations with Rational Numbers

At the exchange rate of 0.80 euro per dollar, Rose exchanged $500.00 for $(0.80)(500) = 400$ euros. She spent $\frac{3}{4}(400) = 300$ euros, had $400 - 300 = 100$ euros left, and exchanged them for dollars at the exchange rate of $1.20 per euro. Therefore, the dollar amount she received was $(1.20)(100) = \$120.00$.

The correct answer is D.

x	x	x	y	y	v
v	x	x	y	w	w

PS08461
12. Each of the 12 squares shown is labeled x, y, v, or w. What is the ratio of the number of these squares labeled x or y to the number of these squares labeled v or w ?

(A) 1:2
(B) 2:3
(C) 4:3
(D) 3:2
(E) 2:1

Arithmetic Ratio and Proportion

By a direct count, there are 8 squares labeled x or y (5 labeled x, 3 labeled y) and there are 4 squares labeled v or w (2 labeled v, 2 labeled w). Therefore, the ratio of the number of squares labeled x or y to the number of squares labeled v or w is 8:4, which reduces to 2:1.

The correct answer is E.

PS02382
13. In the *xy*-coordinate plane, if the point (0,2) lies on the graph of the line $2x + ky = 4$, what is the value of the constant *k*?

(A) 2
(B) 1
(C) 0
(D) −1
(E) −2

Algebra First-Degree Equations

It is given that the point (0,2) lies on the graph of $2x + ky = 4$. Therefore, $2(0) + k(2) = 4$, or $0 + 2k = 4$, or $k = 2$.

The correct answer is A.

PS01248
14. Bouquets are to be made using white tulips and red tulips, and the ratio of the number of white tulips to the number of red tulips is to be the same in each bouquet. If there are 15 white tulips and 85 red tulips available for the bouquets, what is the greatest number of bouquets that can be made using all the tulips available?

(A) 3
(B) 5
(C) 8
(D) 10
(E) 13

Arithmetic Applied Problems; Properties of Numbers

Because all the tulips are to be used and the same number of white tulips will be in each bouquet, the number of white tulips in each bouquet times the number of bouquets must equal the total number of white tulips, or 15. Thus, the number of bouquets must be a factor of 15, and so the number must be 1, 3, 5, or 15. Also, the number of red tulips in each bouquet times the number of bouquets must equal the total number of red tulips, or 85. Thus, the number of bouquets must be a factor of 85, and so the number must be 1, 5, 17, or 85. Since the number of bouquets must be 1, 3, 5, or 15, and the number of bouquets must be 1, 5, 17, or 85, it follows that the number of bouquets must be 1 or 5, and thus the greatest number of bouquets that can be made is 5. Note that each of the 5 bouquets will have 3 white tulips, because

(5)(3) = 15, and each of the 5 bouquets will have 17 red tulips, because (5)(17) = 85.

The correct answer is B.

PS07369
15. Over the past 7 weeks, the Smith family had weekly grocery bills of $74, $69, $64, $79, $64, $84, and $77. What was the Smiths' average (arithmetic mean) weekly grocery bill over the 7-week period?

(A) $64
(B) $70
(C) $73
(D) $74
(E) $85

Arithmetic Statistics

The average weekly grocery bill over the 7-week period can be calculated by dividing the total of the 7 weekly grocery bills by 7.

$$= \frac{\$74+\$69+\$64+\$79+\$64+\$84+\$77}{7}$$

$$= \frac{\$511}{7} = \$73$$

An alternate method is suggested by the fact that the bills, in dollars, are close to 70. Note that if all the bills were 70, then the average would be 70. This method makes use of the amount by which the bills are over 70 or under 70.

bill	amount over 70	amount under 70
74	4	*
69	*	1
64	*	6
79	9	*
64	*	6
84	14	*
77	7	*
total	34	13

Therefore, since 34 > 13, the average is over 70 by $\frac{34-13}{7} = \frac{21}{7} = 3$, so 73.

Tip: When calculating an average value where the values are roughly clustered together, it is often quicker to pick a fixed value and add to this fixed value the average of the signed differences from the fixed value. In the solution above, the fixed value was 70 and the signed differences are 4, –1, –6, 9, –6, 14, and 7.

Additional Example: Calculate the average of 99, 102, 101, 98, and 96. Letting 100 be the fixed value, the average can be calculated as follows:

$$100 + \frac{-1 + 2 + 1 - 2 - 4}{5} = 100 - \frac{4}{5}$$
$$= 100 - 0.8 = 99.2$$

Note that these values cluster more closely to 99 than to 100, but 100 is probably simpler to work with.

The correct answer is C.

PS14861

16. 125% of 5 =

(A) 5.125
(B) 5.25
(C) 6
(D) 6.125
(E) 6.25

Arithmetic Percents

125% of 5 represents $\frac{125}{100} \times 5$, or $1.25 \times 5 = 6.25$.

The correct answer is E.

PS02764

17. During a recent storm, 9 neighborhoods experienced power failures of durations 34, 29, 27, 46, 18, 25, 12, 35, and 16 minutes, respectively. For these 9 neighborhoods, what was the median duration, in minutes, of the power failures?

(A) 34
(B) 29
(C) 27
(D) 25
(E) 18

Arithmetic Statistics

To determine the median of these 9 numbers, put the numbers in numerical order in a list and determine the middle value in the list:

12, 16, 18, 25, **27**, 29, 34, 35, 46

From this list it follows that the median is 27.

The correct answer is C.

PS02286

18. When traveling at a constant speed of 32 miles per hour, a certain motorboat consumes 24 gallons of fuel per hour. What is the fuel consumption of this boat at this speed measured in miles traveled per gallon of fuel?

(A) $\frac{2}{3}$

(B) $\frac{3}{4}$

(C) $\frac{4}{5}$

(D) $\frac{4}{3}$

(E) $\frac{3}{2}$

Arithmetic Operations With Rational Numbers

If the motorboat consumes 24 gallons of fuel in 1 hour, then it consumes 1 gallon of fuel in $\frac{1}{24}$ hour. If the motorboat travels 32 miles in 1 hour, then it travels $\frac{32}{24} = \frac{4}{3}$ miles in $\frac{1}{24}$ hour, which is the length of time it takes to consume 1 gallon of fuel. Thus, the motorboat travels $\frac{4}{3}$ miles per gallon of fuel.

The correct answer is D.

PS11906

19. A technician makes a round-trip to and from a certain service center by the same route. If the technician completes the drive to the center and then completes 10 percent of the drive from the center, what percent of the round-trip has the technician completed?

(A) 5%
(B) 10%
(C) 25%
(D) 40%
(E) 55%

Arithmetic Percents

In completing the drive to the service center, the technician has completed 50% of the round-trip. The drive from the center is the other 50% of the round-trip. In completing 10% of the drive from the center, the technician has completed an additional 10% of 50%, or 5% of the round-trip. Thus, the technician has completed $50\% + 5\% = 55\%$ of the round-trip.

The correct answer is E.

PS15957

20. From 2000 to 2003, the number of employees at a certain company increased by a factor of $\frac{1}{4}$. From 2003 to 2006, the number of employees at this company decreased by a factor of $\frac{1}{3}$. If there were 100 employees at the company in 2006, how many employees were there at the company in 2000 ?

(A) 200

(B) 120

(C) 100

(D) 75

(E) 60

Algebra First-Degree Equations

Let N be the number of employees in 2000. In 2003 there were $\frac{1}{4}(\text{number in 2000}) = \frac{1}{4}N$ more employees than in 2000, for a total of $N + \frac{1}{4}N = \frac{5}{4}N$ employees. In 2006 there were $\frac{1}{3}(\text{number in 2003}) = \frac{1}{3}\left(\frac{5}{4}\right)N$ fewer employees than in 2003, for a total of $\frac{5}{4}N - \frac{1}{3}\left(\frac{5}{4}N\right) = \frac{5}{6}N$ employees. It is given that there were 100 employees in 2006, so $\frac{5}{6}N = 100$, or $N = \frac{6}{5}(100) = 120$.

The correct answer is B.

PS00984

21. Which of the following statements must be true about the average (arithmetic mean) and the median of 5 consecutive integers?

I.   The average is one of the integers.

II.   The median is one of the integers.

III. The median equals the average.

(A) I only

(B) II only

(C) III only

(D) I and II only

(E) I, II, and III

Algebra Statistics

If n is the least of the 5 consecutive integers then, in increasing order, the integers are

$n,\ n+1,\ n+2,\ n+3,\ n+4.$

Statement I must be true because the average of the integers is $\dfrac{n+(n+1)+(n+2)+(n+3)+(n+4)}{5}$, or $\dfrac{5n+10}{5} = n+2$, and $n+2$ is one of the integers.

Statement II must be true because the median is the middle number in the list, which is $n + 2$, and $n + 2$ is one of the integers.

Statement III must be true because $n + 2$ is both the average and the median.

The correct answer is E.

PS15358

22. A collection of 16 coins, each with a face value of either 10 cents or 25 cents, has a total face value of $2.35. How many of the coins have a face value of 25 cents?

(A) 3

(B) 5

(C) 7

(D) 9

(E) 11

Algebra First-Degree Equations

Let x represent the number of coins each with a face value of 25 cents. Then, since there are 16 coins in all, $16 - x$ represents the number of coins each with a face value of 10 cents. The total face value of the coins is $2.35 or 235 cents so,

$25x + 10(16 - x) = 235$ given

$25x + 160 - 10x = 235$ distributive property

$15x + 160 = 235$ combine like terms

$15x = 75$ subtract 160 from both sides

$x = 5$ divide both sides by 15

Therefore, 5 of the coins have a face value of 25 cents.

The correct answer is B.

PS09707

23. A retailer purchased eggs at $2.80 per dozen and sold the eggs at 3 eggs for $0.90. What was the retailer's gross profit from purchasing and selling 5 dozen eggs? (1 dozen eggs = 12 eggs)

(A) $0.90
(B) $2.40
(C) $4.00
(D) $11.30
(E) $12.00

Arithmetic Applied Problems

The retailer's cost was $2.80 per dozen eggs and the retailer's revenue was $0.90 per 3 eggs, or 4($0.90) = $3.60 per dozen eggs. Therefore, the retailer's profit for 5 dozen eggs—revenue minus cost for 5 dozen eggs—was 5($3.60 – $2.80) = 5($0.80) = $4.00.

The correct answer is C.

PS02127

24. In a set of 24 cards, each card is numbered with a different positive integer from 1 to 24. One card will be drawn at random from the set. What is the probability that the card drawn will have either a number that is divisible by both 2 and 3 or a number that is divisible by 7 ?

(A) $\dfrac{3}{24}$

(B) $\dfrac{4}{24}$

(C) $\dfrac{7}{24}$

(D) $\dfrac{8}{24}$

(E) $\dfrac{17}{24}$

Arithmetic Probability

The desired probability is N divided by 24, where N is the number of positive integers from 1 through 24 that are either divisible by both 2 and 3, or divisible by 7. Since an integer is divisible by both 2 and 3 if and only if the integer is divisible by 6, it follows that N is the number of positive integers from 1 through 24 that are either divisible by 6 or divisible by 7. There are 4 numbers from 1 through 24 that are divisible by 6, namely 6, 12,

18, and 24. There are 3 numbers from 1 through 24 that are divisible by 7, namely 7, 14, and 21. Since these numbers are all different from each other, it follows that $N = 4 + 3 = 7$ and the desired probability is $\dfrac{N}{24} = \dfrac{7}{24}$.

The correct answer is C.

PS12542

25. If the circumference of a circle inscribed in a square is 25π, what is the perimeter of the square?

(A) 20
(B) 25
(C) 40
(D) 50
(E) 100

Geometry Circles; Circumference; Perimeter

The solution of this problem relies on the following:

(i) If d represents the diameter of a circle, then the circumference of the circle is given by πd.

(ii) If the side length of a square is represented by s, then the perimeter of the square is given by $4s$.

(iii) As shown in the figure below, for any circle inscribed in a square, the length of the diameter of the circle is equal to the length of a side of the square.

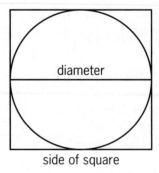

side of square

It is given that the circumference of the circle is 25π. Therefore, from (i), $d = 25$. From (iii), $s = d$, so $s = 25$. Lastly, from (ii), the perimeter of the square is $4(25) = 100$.

The correct answer is E.

PS03972
26. If $1 < x < y < z$, which of the following has the greatest value?

(A) $z(x + 1)$

(B) $z(y + 1)$

(C) $x(y + z)$

(D) $y(x + z)$

(E) $z(x + y)$

Algebra Inequalities

This problem can be solved by calculating each of the options for a fixed and appropriate choice of values of the variables. For example, if $x = 2$, $y = 3$, and $z = 4$, then $1 < x < y < z$ and the values of the options are as follows:

(A) $z(x + 1) = 4(2 + 1) = 12$

(B) $z(y + 1) = 4(3 + 1) = 16$

(C) $x(y + z) = 2(3 + 4) = 14$

(D) $y(x + z) = 3(2 + 4) = 18$

(E) $z(x + y) = 4(2 + 3) = 20$

Alternatively, this problem can also be solved algebraically.

E is greater than each of A and B:

$$\underset{A}{z(x + 1) = zx + z} \quad \underset{\text{use } 1 < y}{<} \quad \underset{E}{zx + zy = z(x + y)}$$

$$\underset{B}{z(y + 1) = zy + z} \quad \underset{\text{use } 1 < x}{<} \quad \underset{E}{zy + zx = z(y + x)}$$

E is greater than each of C and D:

$$\underset{C}{x(y + z) = xy + xz} \quad \underset{\text{use } x < z}{<} \quad \underset{E}{zy + xz = z(y + x)}$$

$$\underset{D}{y(x + z) = yx + yz} \quad \underset{\text{use } y < z}{<} \quad \underset{E}{zx + yz = z(x + y)}$$

The correct answer is E.

PS00087
27. Set X consists of eight consecutive integers. Set Y consists of all the integers that result from adding 4 to each of the integers in set X and all the integers that result from subtracting 4 from each of the integers in set X. How many more integers are there in set Y than in set X?

(A) 0

(B) 4

(C) 8

(D) 12

(E) 16

Arithmetic Operations with Integers

Since the 8 consecutive integers in Set X are not specified, let Set $X = \{3, 4, 5, 6, 7, 8, 9, 10\}$. The following table shows Set X and Set Y whose elements were obtained by adding 4 to each element of Set X and subtracting 4 from each element of Set X. The elements of Set Y that are also in Set X are marked with an asterisk, *. There are 8 unmarked elements in Set Y, so Set Y has 8 more elements than Set X.

Set X	Set Y	
	Add 4	Subtract 4
3	7*	−1
4	8*	0
5	9*	1
6	10*	2
7	11	3*
8	12	4*
9	13	5*
10	14	6*

The correct answer is C.

PS05239
28. Of the following, which is the closest to $\dfrac{60.2}{1.03 \times 4.86}$?

(A) 10

(B) 12

(C) 13

(D) 14

(E) 15

Arithmetic Estimation

Replace the three numbers appearing in the expression with three nearby integers that allow the arithmetic operations to be carried out easily to get an approximation.

$$\frac{60.2}{1.03 \times 4.86} \approx \frac{\overset{12}{\cancel{60}}}{1 \times \cancel{5}^{\,1}} = \frac{12}{1 \times 1} = 12$$

The correct answer is B.

PS15402

29. Thabo owns exactly 140 books, and each book is either paperback fiction, paperback nonfiction, or hardcover nonfiction. If he owns 20 more paperback nonfiction books than hardcover nonfiction books, and twice as many paperback fiction books as paperback nonfiction books, how many hardcover nonfiction books does Thabo own?

(A) 10

(B) 20

(C) 30

(D) 40

(E) 50

Algebra Simultaneous First-Degree Equations

Let F represent the number of paperback fiction books that Thabo owns; N_p, the number of paperback nonfiction books; and N_h, the number of hardcover nonfiction books. It is given that $F + N_p + N_h = 140$, $N_p = N_h + 20$, and $F = 2N_p = 2(N_h + 20)$. It follows that

$$
\begin{aligned}
F + N_p + N_h &= 140 \text{ given} \\
2(N_h + 20) + (N_h + 20) + N_h &= 140 \text{ by substitution} \\
4N_h + 60 &= 140 \text{ combine like terms} \\
4N_h &= 80 \text{ subtract 60 from both sides} \\
N_h &= 20 \text{ divide both sides by 4}
\end{aligned}
$$

The correct answer is B.

PS04571

30. If the average (arithmetic mean) of the four numbers 3, 15, 32, and $(N + 1)$ is 18, then $N =$

(A) 19

(B) 20

(C) 21

(D) 22

(E) 29

Arithmetic Statistics

From the given information and the definition of average, it follows that

$$\frac{3 + 15 + 32 + (N + 1)}{4} = 18, \text{ or } \frac{51 + N}{4} = 18.$$

Multiplying both sides of the last equation by 4 gives $51 + N = 72$. Therefore, $N = 72 - 51 = 21$.

The correct answer is C.

PS13801

31. Abdul, Barb, and Carlos all live on the same straight road, on which their school is also located. The school is halfway between Abdul's house and Barb's house. Barb's house is halfway between the school and Carlos's house. If the school is 4 miles from Carlos's house, how many miles is Abdul's house from Carlos's house?

(A) $1\frac{1}{3}$

(B) 2

(C) 4

(D) 6

(E) 8

Geometry Applied Problems

In the diagram, A represents the location of Abdul's house, S represents the location of the school, B represents the location of Barb's house, and C represents the location of Carlos's house. Because the school is halfway between Abdul's house and Barb's house, S is the midpoint of $\overline{AB}$, and because Barb's house is halfway between the school and Carlos's house, B is the midpoint of $\overline{SC}$. Therefore, $AS = SB = BC$. Finally, since $SC = 4$, it follows that $AS = SB = BC = 2$ and hence $AC = 2 + 2 + 2 = 6$.

The correct answer is D.

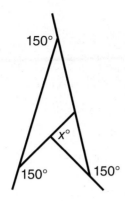

150°

x°

150°   150°

PS00534

32. In the figure shown, what is the value of x ?

    (A)   60

    (B)   80

    (C)   85·

    (D)   90

    (E)   95

Geometry Angles and Their Measure

The revised figure shows three angles, each with measure 150°, and their three corresponding supplementary angles, each with measure 30°. Since the sum of the measures of the angles in $\triangle PQR$ is 180°, it follows that the measure of $\angle PRQ$ is 180° − (30°+ 30°) = 120°, and hence the measure of $\angle SRT$ is 180° − 120° = 60°. Finally, since the sum of the measures of the angles in $\triangle RST$ is 180°, it follows that $x° = 180° − (30° + 60°) = 90°$.

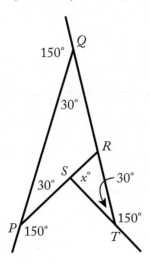

150°   Q

30°

R

S   x°

30°   30°

P 150°

150°

T

The correct answer is D.

PS17479

33. During a certain time period, Car X traveled north along a straight road at a constant rate of 1 mile per minute and used fuel at a constant rate of 5 gallons every 2 hours. During this time period, if Car X used exactly 3.75 gallons of fuel, how many miles did Car X travel?

    (A)   36

    (B)   37.5

    (C)   40

    (D)   80

    (E)   90

Arithmetic Applied Problems

The car used fuel at the rate of 5 gallons every 2 hours, and thus after using 3.75 gallons of fuel, the car had traveled for $(3.75)\left(\dfrac{2}{5}\right)$ hours.

One way to obtain this value is indicated by the calculations in following table.

5 gal	corresponds to	2 hr	Given
1 gal	corresponds to	$\dfrac{2}{5}$ hr	Divide by 5
3.75 gal	corresponds to	$(3.75)\left(\dfrac{2}{5}\right)$ hr	Multiply by 3.75

Since $(3.75)\left(\dfrac{2}{5}\right)=\left(\dfrac{15}{4}\right)\left(\dfrac{2}{5}\right)=\dfrac{3}{2}$ hours = 90 minutes, the car drove for 90 minutes at a rate of 1 mile per minute. Therefore, the total distance the car drove was

distance = rate × time = $\left(1\,\dfrac{\text{mi}}{\text{min}}\right)(90\text{ min}) = $ 90 miles.

The correct answer is E.

PS13707

34. Cheryl purchased 5 identical hollow pine doors and 6 identical solid oak doors for the house she is building. The regular price of each solid oak door was twice the regular price of each hollow pine door. However, Cheryl was given a discount of 25% off the regular price of each solid oak door. If the regular price of each hollow pine door was $40, what was the total price of all 11 doors?

    (A) $320

    (B) $540

    (C) $560

    (D) $620

    (E) $680

Algebra Applied Problems; Percents

The price of each pine door is $40, so the price of 5 pine doors is 5($40) = $200. The price of each oak door is twice that of a pine door, and thus $80, which becomes (0.75)($80) = $60 when the 25% discount is applied. Therefore, the price of 6 oak doors at the 25% discount is 6($60) = $360, and hence the total price of all 11 doors is $200 + $360 = $560.

The correct answer is C.

PS01233

35. A certain store will order 25 crates of apples. The apples will be of three different varieties—McIntosh, Rome, and Winesap—and each crate will contain apples of only one variety. If the store is to order more crates of Winesap than crates of McIntosh and more crates of Winesap than crates of Rome, what is the least possible number of crates of Winesap that the store will order?

(A) 7
(B) 8
(C) 9
(D) 10
(E) 11

Arithmetic Applied Problems

Let M, R, and W be the numbers of crates, respectively, of McIntosh, Rome, and Winesap apples. From the given information it follows that $M + R + W = 25$ and $M \leq R < W$. Find the least possible value of W such that positive integer values of M, R, and W satisfy these two conditions.

Since the values 8, 8, and 9 for M, R, and W satisfy these two conditions, $W = 9$ is possible. Thus, the least possible value of W is less than or equal to 9. It is not possible for the value of W to be less than 9, since if the value of W were less than 9, then $M + R + W < 25$. This is because in this case, the greatest possible values of M, R, and W would be 7, 7, and 8, which have a sum less than 25. Therefore, the least possible value of W is 9.

The correct answer is C.

PS02007

36. A bicycle store purchased two bicycles, one for $250 and the other for $375, and sold both bicycles at a total gross profit of $250. If the store sold one of the bicycles for $450, which of the following could be the store's gross profit from the sale of the other bicycle?

(A) $75
(B) $100
(C) $125
(D) $150
(E) $175

Arithmetic Profit and Loss

Let $450 and R be the individual revenues from selling the two bicycles. Then the unknown profit from selling one of the bicycles is either $R - $250 or $R - $375.

$$\text{total profit} = (\text{total revenue}) - (\text{total cost})$$
$$\$250 = (\$450 + \$R) - (\$250 + \$375)$$
$$\$250 = \$R - \$175$$
$$\$425 = \$R$$

From this it follows that the unknown profit is either $425 - $250 = $175 or $425 - $375 = $50.

The correct answer is E.

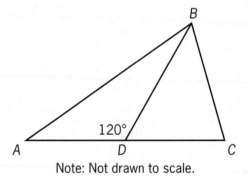

Note: Not drawn to scale.

PS10628

37. In the figure shown, $AC = 2$ and $BD = DC = 1$. What is the measure of angle ABD?

(A) 15°
(B) 20°
(C) 30°
(D) 40°
(E) 45°

Geometry Triangles

Since $AC = AD + DC$, and it is given that $AC = 2$ and $DC = 1$, it follows that $AD = 1$. Therefore, $AD = BD = 1$ and $\triangle ABD$ is an isosceles triangle where the measure of $\angle ABD$ is equal to the measure of $\angle BAD$. Letting $x°$ be the common degree measure of these two angles, it follows that $x° + x° + 120° = 180°$, or $2x° = 60°$, or $x° = 30°$.

The correct answer is C.

PS12786

38. If $k^2 = m^2$, which of the following must be true?

(A) $k = m$
(B) $k = -m$
(C) $k = |m|$
(D) $k = -|m|$
(E) $|k| = |m|$

Algebra Simplifying Algebraic Expressions

One method of solving this problem is to take the nonnegative square root of both sides of the equation $k^2 = m^2$ and then since $\sqrt{u^2} = |u|$ for all real numbers u, it follows that $|k| = \sqrt{k^2} = \sqrt{m^2} = |m|$.

The table below shows that each of the other answer choices can be true but can also be false. For each pair of values for k and m, it is true that $k^2 = m^2$.

	True for		False for	
	k	m	k	m
A $k = m$	3	3	3	-3
B $k = -m$	-3	3	3	3
C $k = |m|$	3	-3	-3	-3
D $k = -|m|$	-3	-3	3	-3

The correct answer is E.

PS13831

39. Makoto, Nishi, and Ozuro were paid a total of $780 for waxing the floors at their school. Each was paid in proportion to the number of hours he or she worked. If Makoto worked 15 hours, Nishi worked 20 hours, and Ozuro worked 30 hours, how much was Makoto paid?

(A) $52
(B) $117
(C) $130
(D) $180
(E) $234

Arithmetic Ratio and Proportion

Makoto, Nishi, and Ozuro worked a total of $15 + 20 + 30 = 65$ hours and were paid a total of $780. Since Makoto worked 15 of the 65 hours and he was paid in proportion to the number of hours he worked, his pay was $\frac{15}{65}(\$780)$. To determine which of the answer choices equals this amount of money, note that $\frac{15}{65}$ can be reduced to $\frac{3}{13}$ by dividing the numerator and denominator by 5. Also note that 780 can be factored as $(10)(78) = (10)(2)(39) = (10)(2)(3)(13)$. Then calculate $\frac{3}{\cancel{13}}(10)(2)(3)(\cancel{13}) = (3)(10)(2)(3) = 180$.

Tip: In problems requiring calculations with fractions, it can be helpful to reduce fractions and utilize cancellation, as much as possible.

The correct answer is D.

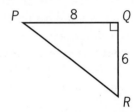

PS05680

40. The figure above shows a path around a triangular piece of land. Mary walked the distance of 8 miles from P to Q and then walked the distance of 6 miles from Q to R. If Ted walked directly from P to R, by what percent did the distance that Mary walked exceed the distance that Ted walked?

(A) 30%
(B) 40%
(C) 50%
(D) 60%
(E) 80%

Geometry Pythagorean Theorem

Mary walked a distance of $6 + 8 = 14$ miles. The distance that Ted walked, PR, can be found by using the Pythagorean theorem $6^2 + 8^2 = (PR)^2$, or $(PR)^2 = 100$. Taking square roots, it follows that Ted walked 10 miles. Therefore, the distance Mary walked exceeded the distance Ted walked by $14 - 10 = 4$ miles and 4 is 40% of 10.

The correct answer is B.

PS04797
41. If x is a positive integer and $4^x - 3 = y$, which of the following CANNOT be a value of y?

(A)   1

(B)   7

(C)   13

(D)   61

(E)   253

Arithmetic Exponents

This can be solved by calculating the value of $4^x - 3$ for the first few positive integer values of x.

x	4^x	$4^x - 3$	answer choice
1	4	1	A
2	16	13	C
3	64	61	D
4	256	253	E

Alternatively, this can be solved by observing that 4^x always has units digit 4 or 6—the product of two integers with units digit 4 has units digit 6, the product of two integers with units digit 6 has units digit 4, etc.—and therefore any integer that does not have units digit $4 - 3 = 1$ or $6 - 3 = 3$ cannot be the value of $4^x - 3$ for some positive integer value of x.

The correct answer is B.

PS05747
42. If $(1 - 1.25)N = 1$, then $N =$

(A)   −400

(B)   −140

(C)   −4

(D)   4

(E)   400

Algebra Operations with Rational Numbers

Since $(1 - 1.25)N = -0.25N = -\frac{1}{4}N$, the equation becomes $-\frac{1}{4}N = 1$, which has solution $N = -4$.

The correct answer is C.

PS14972
43. The quotient when a certain number is divided by $\frac{2}{3}$ is $\frac{9}{2}$. What is the number?

(A) $\frac{4}{27}$

(B) $\frac{1}{3}$

(C)   3

(D)   6

(E) $\frac{27}{4}$

Arithmetic Operations with Rational Numbers

Let N be the unknown number. The quotient when N is divided by $\frac{2}{3}$ is $N \div \frac{2}{3}$, which equals $N \times \frac{3}{2} = \frac{3}{2}N$ (invert and multiply). Since this quotient equals $\frac{9}{2}$, it follows that $\frac{3}{2}N = \frac{9}{2}$.

Therefore, $N = \left(\frac{9}{2}\right)\left(\frac{2}{3}\right) = 3$.

Tip: Sometimes a correct method of calculation will be intuitively evident if difficult-to-conceptualize numbers are replaced with easy-to-conceptualize numbers. For example, if the first sentence had instead been "The quotient when a certain number is divided by 2 is 3" (i.e., after dividing a certain number by 2, the result is 3), then it may be intuitively evident that the number can be obtained by multiplying 2 and 3. Thus, for this problem, the number can be obtained by multiplying $\frac{2}{3}$ and $\frac{9}{2}$.

The correct answer is C.

PS06592
44. If a sphere with radius r is inscribed in a cube with edges of length e, which of the following expresses the relationship between r and e?

(A) $r = \frac{1}{2}e$

(B) $r = e$

(C) $r = 2e$

(D) $r = \sqrt{e}$

(E) $r = \frac{1}{4}e^2$

Geometry Volume

The solution to this problem relies on the following:

(i) The distance between two opposite faces of a cube is the same as the edge length of the cube.

(ii) The radius of a sphere is $\frac{1}{2}$ the diameter of the sphere.

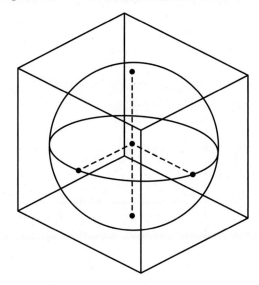

A sphere inscribed in a cube touches, but does not extend beyond, each of the 6 sides of the cube. In the figure above of a sphere inscribed in a cube, the vertical dashed segment is a diameter of the sphere. It extends from the bottom face of the cube to the top face of the cube. From (i) the length of this segment is the same as the edge length of the cube. Thus, the diameter of the sphere is equal to the edge length of the cube. Therefore, from (ii), the radius of the sphere is equal to half the edge length of the cube, or $r = \frac{1}{2}e$.

The correct answer is A.

PS13159

45. The price of gasoline at a service station increased from $1.65 per gallon last week to $1.82 per gallon this week. Sally paid $26.40 for gasoline last week at the station. How much more will Sally pay this week at the station for the same amount of gasoline?

(A) $1.70
(B) $2.55
(C) $2.64
(D) $2.72
(E) $2.90

Arithmetic Applied Problems

Since $1.82 − $1.65 = $0.17, Sally paid $0.17 per gallon more this week than last week. Therefore, the total additional amount that Sally paid this week over last week is the number of gallons Sally purchased times $0.17.

Number of gallons purchased last week:

$$\frac{\text{total paid last week}}{\text{price per gallon last week}} = \frac{26.40}{1.65}$$

Number of gallons purchased this week: $\frac{26.40}{1.65}$

Total additional amount paid this week:

$$(\$0.17)\frac{26.40}{1.65} = (\$0.17)(16) = \$2.72.$$

One way to lessen the arithmetic computations is to work with integers and factor.

$$0.17\left(\frac{26.4}{1.65}\right) = \frac{(17)(264)}{1,650} \quad \begin{array}{l}\text{multiply numerator and}\\ \text{denominator by 1,000}\\ \text{for ease of calculation}\end{array}$$

$$= \frac{(17)(3 \times 8 \times 11)}{3 \times 5 \times 11 \times 10} \quad \text{factor}$$

$$= \frac{(17)(\cancel{3} \times 8 \times \cancel{11})}{\cancel{3} \times 5 \times \cancel{11} \times 10} \quad \text{identify common factors}$$

$$= \frac{17 \times 8}{50} \quad \text{cancel common factors}$$

$$= \frac{136}{50} \quad \text{multiply}$$

$$= \frac{13.6}{5} \quad \begin{array}{l}\text{divide numerator and}\\ \text{denominator by 10}\end{array}$$

$$= 2.72 \quad \text{divide}$$

The correct answer is D.

Monthly Charge for Low-Use Telephone
Contract Offered by Company *X*

Monthly rate (up to 75 message units)	20% less than standard rate of $10.00
Per unit in excess of 75 message units	$0.065

PS02534

46. Based on the rates above, how much would Company *X* charge a customer with a low-use contract for using 95 message units in a month?

(A) $9.30
(B) $11.30
(C) $12.88
(D) $14.88
(E) $16.18

Arithmetic Interpretation of Tables

The low-use contract charge for using 95 message units in a month is the monthly rate plus the charge for messages in excess of 75.

Monthly rate	+ Charge for excess	= Total charge
$(100\% - 20\%)(\$10)$	$+ (95 - 75)(\$0.065)$	$=$
$(0.8)(\$10)$	$+ (20)(\$0.065)$	$=$
$\$8.00$	$+ \$1.30$	$= \$9.30$

Note that the product $(20)(0.065)$ can be obtained by multiplying 0.065 by 10 and then doubling the result.

The correct answer is A.

PS02338
47. If $2x + y = 7$ and $x + 2y = 5$, then $\dfrac{x+y}{3} =$

(A) 1

(B) $\dfrac{4}{3}$

(C) $\dfrac{17}{5}$

(D) $\dfrac{18}{5}$

(E) 4

Algebra Simultaneous Equations

Adding the equations $2x + y = 7$ and $x + 2y = 5$ gives $3x + 3y = 12$, or $x + y = 4$. Dividing both sides of the last equation by 3 gives $\dfrac{x+y}{3} = \dfrac{4}{3}$.

The correct answer is B.

PS14250
48. City X has a population 4 times as great as the population of City Y, which has a population twice as great as the population of City Z. What is the ratio of the population of City X to the population of City Z ?

(A) 1:8

(B) 1:4

(C) 2:1

(D) 4:1

(E) 8:1

Arithmetic Ratio and Proportion

Let X, Y, and Z be the populations of Cities X, Y, and Z, respectively. It is given that $X = 4Y$,

and $Y = 2Z$ or $Z = \dfrac{Y}{2}$. Then, $\dfrac{X}{Z} = \dfrac{4Y}{\dfrac{Y}{2}} =$
$(4Y)\left(\dfrac{2}{Y}\right) = \dfrac{8}{1}$.

The correct answer is E.

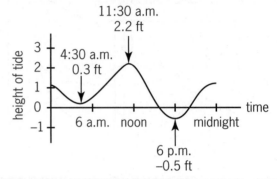

Tides at Bay Cove on July 13

PS05100
49. The graph above shows the height of the tide, in feet, above or below a baseline. Which of the following is closest to the difference, in feet, between the heights of the highest and lowest tides on July 13 at Bay Cove?

(A) 1.7

(B) 1.9

(C) 2.2

(D) 2.5

(E) 2.7

Arithmetic Interpretation of Graphs and Tables

From the graph, the highest tide is 2.2 ft above the baseline and the lowest tide is 0.5 ft below the baseline. Therefore, the difference between the heights of the highest tide and the lowest tide is $[2.2 - (-0.5)]$ ft $= (2.2 + 0.5)$ ft $= 2.7$ ft.

The correct answer is E.

PS06243
50. If $S = 1 + \dfrac{1}{2^2} + \dfrac{1}{3^2} + \dfrac{1}{4^2} + \dfrac{1}{5^2} + \dfrac{1}{6^2} + \dfrac{1}{7^2} + \dfrac{1}{8^2} + \dfrac{1}{9^2} + \dfrac{1}{10^2}$, which of the following is true?

(A) $S > 3$

(B) $S = 3$

(C) $2 < S < 3$

(D) $S = 2$

(E) $S < 2$

Arithmetic Estimation

Because $\frac{1}{3^2}$ is less than $\frac{1}{2^2}$ and each of $\frac{1}{5^2}$,

$\frac{1}{6^2},\frac{1}{7^2},\frac{1}{8^2},\frac{1}{9^2}$, and $\frac{1}{10^2}$ is less than $\frac{1}{4^2}$,

$1+\frac{1}{2^2}+\frac{1}{3^2}+\frac{1}{4^2}+\frac{1}{5^2}+\frac{1}{6^2}+\frac{1}{7^2}+\frac{1}{8^2}+\frac{1}{9^2}+\frac{1}{10^2}$

$<1+2\left(\frac{1}{2^2}\right)=1\frac{1}{2}$ $+7\left(\frac{1}{4^2}\right)=\frac{7}{16}$

Therefore, $S<1\frac{1}{2}+\frac{7}{16}<2$.

The correct answer is E.

PS05308
51. A manufacturer of a certain product can expect that between 0.3 percent and 0.5 percent of the units manufactured will be defective. If the retail price is $2,500 per unit and the manufacturer offers a full refund for defective units, how much money can the manufacturer expect to need to cover the refunds on 20,000 units?

(A)   Between $15,000 and $25,000
(B)   Between $30,000 and $50,000
(C)   Between $60,000 and $100,000
(D)   Between $150,000 and $250,000
(E)   Between $300,000 and $500,000

Arithmetic Applied Problems

The expected number of defective units is between 0.3% and 0.5% of 20,000, or between $(0.003)(20,000)=60$ and $(0.005)(20,000)=100$. Since each unit has a retail price of $2,500, the amount of money needed to cover the refunds for the expected number of defective units is between 60($2,500) and 100($2,500), or between $150,000 and $250,000.

The correct answer is D.

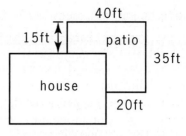

PS05544
52. A flat patio was built alongside a house as shown in the figure above. If all angles shown are right angles, what is the area of the patio in square feet?

(A)   800
(B)   875
(C)   1,000
(D)   1,100
(E)   1,125

Geometry Area

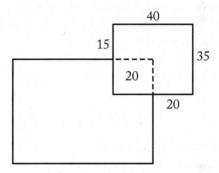

The area of the patio can be calculated by imagining the patio to be a rectangle of dimensions 40 ft by 35 ft that has a lower-left square corner of dimensions 20 ft by 20 ft covered up, as shown in the figure above. The area of the patio will be the area of the uncovered part of the rectangle, and therefore the area of the patio, in square feet, is $(40)(35)-(20)(20)=1,400-400=1,000$.

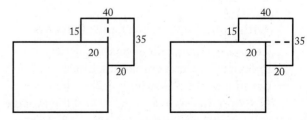

Alternatively, the area of the patio can be calculated by dividing the patio into two rectangles and adding the areas of the two rectangles. This can be done in two ways:

by using rectangles of dimensions 20 ft by 35 ft and 20 ft by 15 ft, as shown in the figure above on the left (for a total area of 700 ft² + 300 ft² = 1,000 ft²), or by using rectangles of dimensions 40 ft by 15 ft and 20 ft by 20 ft, as shown in the figure above on the right (for a total area of 600 ft² + 400 ft² = 1,000 ft²).

The correct answer is C.

PS10470

53. Which of the following is closest to $\sqrt{\dfrac{4.2(1,590)}{15.7}}$?

(A) 20
(B) 40
(C) 60
(D) 80
(E) 100

Arithmetic Estimation

Replace the numbers that appear with nearly equal values that are perfect squares and then evaluate the resulting expression:

$$\sqrt{\frac{4(1,600)}{16}} = \sqrt{\frac{4 \times 16 \times 100}{16}} = \sqrt{4 \times 100}$$

$$= \sqrt{4} \times \sqrt{100} = 2 \times 10 = 20.$$

The correct answer is A.

PS12114

54. The sum of the weekly salaries of 5 employees is $3,250. If each of the 5 salaries is to increase by 10 percent, then the average (arithmetic mean) weekly salary per employee will increase by

(A) $52.50
(B) $55.00
(C) $57.50
(D) $62.50
(E) $65.00

Arithmetic Applied Problems; Percents

Let S_1, S_2, S_3, S_4, and S_5 be the salaries, in dollars, of the 5 employees. Since the sum of the 5 salaries is 3,250, then $S_1 + S_2 + S_3 + S_4 + S_5 = 3,250$ and the average salary is $\dfrac{S_1 + S_2 + S_3 + S_4 + S_5}{5} = \dfrac{3,250}{5} = 650.$

After each salary is increased by 10%, the salaries

will be $(1.1)S_1, (1.1)S_2, (1.1)S_3, (1.1)S_4$, and $(1.1)S_5$ and the average salary, in dollars, will be

$$\frac{(1.1)S_1 + (1.1)S_2 + (1.1)S_3 + (1.1)S_4 + (1.1)S_5}{5} =$$

$$1.1 \times \left(\frac{S_1 + S_2 + S_3 + S_4 + S_5}{5} \right) = 1.1 \times 650 = 715.$$

Therefore, the increase in the average salary is $715 - 650 = 65.$

The correct answer is E.

PS08173

55. Last week Chris earned x dollars per hour for the first 40 hours worked plus 22 dollars per hour for each hour worked beyond 40 hours. If last week Chris earned a total of 816 dollars by working 48 hours, what is the value of x ?

(A) 13
(B) 14
(C) 15
(D) 16
(E) 17

Algebra Applied Problems

Chris worked 40 hours at a rate of x per hour, $48 - 40 = 8$ hours at a rate of $22 per hour, and earned a total of $816.

$40x + 8(22) = 816$	given information
$40x + 176 = 816$	multiply 8 and 22
$40x = 640$	subtract 176 from both sides
$x = 16$	divide both sides by 40

The correct answer is D.

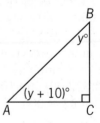

PS07408

56. In the figure above, what is the ratio of the measure of angle B to the measure of angle A ?

(A) 2 to 3
(B) 3 to 4
(C) 3 to 5
(D) 4 to 5
(E) 5 to 6

Geometry Angles

Because the sum of the degree measures of the three interior angles of a triangle is 180, it follows that $y + (y + 10) + 90 = 180$. Therefore, $2y = 80$, and hence $y = 40$. The ratio of the measure of angle B to the measure of angle A can now be determined: $\dfrac{y}{y+10} = \dfrac{40}{50} = \dfrac{4}{5}$.

The correct answer is D.

PS08768
57. The value of $\dfrac{\dfrac{7}{8} + \dfrac{1}{9}}{\dfrac{1}{2}}$ is closest to which of the following?

(A)   2

(B) $\dfrac{3}{2}$

(C)   1

(D) $\dfrac{1}{2}$

(E)   0

Arithmetic Estimation

First, note that division by $\dfrac{1}{2}$ is the same as multiplication by $\dfrac{2}{1}$ (invert and multiply), so,

$\left(\dfrac{7}{8} + \dfrac{1}{9}\right) \div \dfrac{1}{2} = \left(\dfrac{7}{8} + \dfrac{1}{9}\right) \times \dfrac{2}{1} = \left(\dfrac{7}{8} + \dfrac{1}{9}\right) \times 2$. Then, because the question asks for the value "closest to" and not the exact value, estimate $\left(\dfrac{7}{8} + \dfrac{1}{9}\right) \times 2 \approx$

$\left(\dfrac{7}{8} + \dfrac{1}{8}\right) \times 2$ and calculate $\left(\dfrac{7+1}{8}\right) \times 2 = \dfrac{8}{8} \times 2 = 2$.

Alternatively, calculate $\dfrac{7}{8} + \dfrac{1}{9}$ using the common denominator of 72, $\dfrac{7}{8} + \dfrac{1}{9} = \dfrac{63}{72} + \dfrac{8}{72} = \dfrac{71}{72}$, then estimate $\dfrac{71}{72} \approx \dfrac{72}{72} = 1$, then calculate $1(2) = 2$.

The correct answer is A.

PS08025
58. The positive two-digit integers x and y have the same digits, but in reverse order. Which of the following must be a factor of $x + y$?

(A)   6

(B)   9

(C)   10

(D)   11

(E)   14

Arithmetic Properties of Numbers

Let m and n be digits. If $x = 10m + n$, then $y = 10n + m$. Adding x and y gives $x + y = (10m + n) + (10n + m) = 11m + 11n = 11(m + n)$, and therefore 11 is a factor of $x + y$.

The correct answer is D.

PS00015
59. In a certain sequence of 8 numbers, each number after the first is 1 more than the previous number. If the first number is –5, how many of the numbers in the sequence are positive?

(A)   None

(B)   One

(C)   Two

(D)   Three

(E)   Four

Arithmetic Sequences

The sequence consists of eight consecutive integers beginning with –5:

$$-5, \ -4, \ -3, \ -2, \ -1, \ 0, \ 1, \ 2$$

In this sequence exactly two of the numbers are positive.

The correct answer is C.

PS08385
60. A total of s oranges are to be packaged in boxes that will hold r oranges each, with no oranges left over. When n of these boxes have been completely filled, what is the number of boxes that remain to be filled?

(A) $s - nr$

(B) $s - \dfrac{n}{r}$

(C) $rs - n$

(D) $\dfrac{s}{n} - r$

(E) $\dfrac{s}{r} - n$

Algebra Algebraic Expressions

If s oranges are packed r oranges to a box with no oranges left over, then the number of boxes that will be filled is $\frac{s}{r}$. If n of these boxes are already filled, then $\frac{s}{r} - n$ boxes remain to be filled.

The correct answer is E.

PS03371

61. If $0 < a < b < c$, which of the following statements must be true?

   I. $2a > b + c$

   II. $c - a > b - a$

   III. $\dfrac{c}{a} < \dfrac{b}{a}$

   (A)   I only

   (B)   II only

   (C)   III only

   (D)   I and II

   (E)   II and III

Algebra Inequalities

Given $0 < a < b < c$, Statement I is not necessarily true. If, for example, $a = 1$, $b = 2$, and $c = 3$, then $0 < a < b < c$, but $2a = 2(1) < 2 + 3 = b + c$.

Given $0 < a < b < c$, then $c > b$, and subtracting a from both sides gives $c - a > b - a$. Therefore, Statement II is true.

Given $0 < a < b < c$, Statement III is not necessarily true. If, for example, $a = 1$, $b = 2$, and $c = 3$, then $0 < a < b < c$, but $\dfrac{c}{a} = \dfrac{3}{1} > \dfrac{2}{1} = \dfrac{b}{a}$.

The correct answer is B.

PS00096

62. In the xy-plane, the origin O is the midpoint of line segment PQ. If the coordinates of P are (r,s), what are the coordinates of Q?

   (A) (r,s)

   (B) $(s,-r)$

   (C) $(-s,-r)$

   (D) $(-r,s)$

   (E) $(-r,-s)$

Algebra Coordinate Geometry

Since the answer choices are different when $(r,s) = (1,2)$, determine which answer choice has the property that O is the midpoint of $\overline{PQ}$.

(A) NO

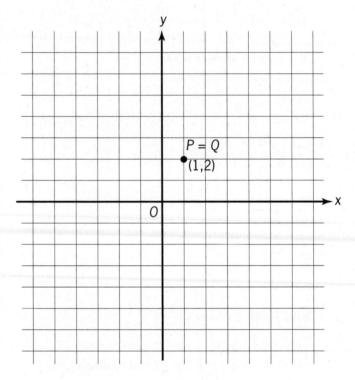

(B) NO

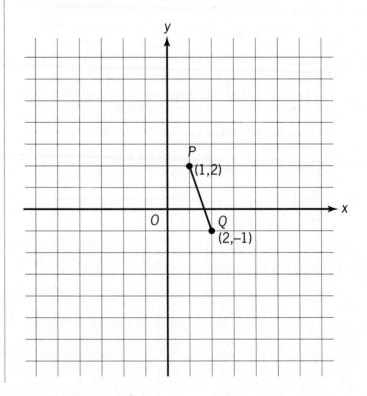

(C) NO

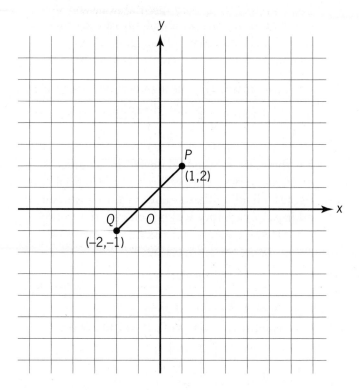

(E) YES

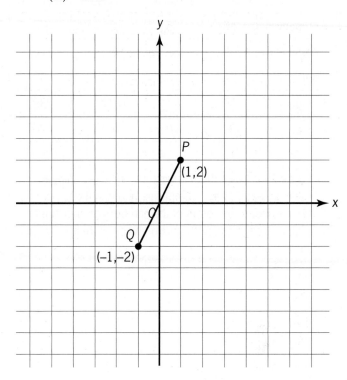

(D) NO

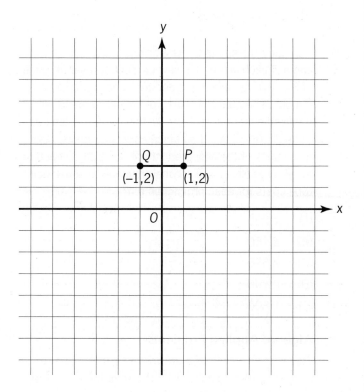

Alternatively, this problem can be solved algebraically. Let (x,y) be the coordinates of Q. The midpoint of (r,s) and (x,y) is $\left(\dfrac{r+x}{2}, \dfrac{s+y}{2} \right)$. Since the midpoint is $(0,0)$, it follows that $\dfrac{r+x}{2} = 0$ and $\dfrac{s+y}{2} = 0$. Therefore, $r+x = 0$ and $s+y = 0$, or $x = -r$ and $y = -s$, and so, $(x,y) = (-r,-s)$.

The correct answer is E.

	Monday	Tuesday	Wednesday	Thursday
Company A	45	55	50	50
Company B	10	30	30	10
Company C	34	28	28	30
Company D	39	42	41	38
Company E	50	60	60	70

PS10568

63. The table shows the numbers of packages shipped daily by each of five companies during a 4-day period. The standard deviation of the numbers of packages shipped daily during the period was greatest for which of the five companies?

(A) A
(B) B
(C) C
(D) D
(E) E

Arithmetic Statistics

Since the standard deviation of a data set is a measure of how widely the data are scattered about their mean, find the mean number of packages shipped by each company and then calculate the deviations of the company's data from its mean.

For Company A, the mean number of packages shipped is $\dfrac{45 + 55 + 2(50)}{4} = 50$ and the deviations from this mean are -5, 5, 0, and 0. Note that the numbers of packages allow for quick calculations of the means. For example, for Company A the total number of packages is the sum of $45 + 55 = 100$ and $50 + 50 = 100$, and for Company D the total number of packages is the sum of $39 + 41 = 80$ and $42 + 38 = 80$.

The following table shows the means and deviations for the 5 companies.

	mean	deviations from mean
Company A	50	-5, 5, 0, 0
Company B	**20**	**-10, 10, 10, -10**
Company C	30	4, -2, -2, 0
Company D	40	-1, 2, 1, -2
Company E	60	-10, 0, 0, 10

This table shows that the magnitude of each of the 4 deviations for Company B is greater than or equal to the magnitude of any of the other deviations, which strongly suggests that the standard deviation is greatest for Company B.

For those interested, the standard deviations can be calculated as $\sqrt{\dfrac{\text{sum of (deviations)}^2}{4}}$. However, since we only wish to determine which company has the greatest standard deviation, it suffices to calculate the values of "sum of (deviations)^2", because dividing these values by 4 followed by taking a square root will not change their order (that is, the greatest will still be the greatest).

	(deviations)^2	sum of (deviations)^2
Company A	25, 25, 0, 0	40
Company B	**100, 100, 100, 100**	**400**
Company C	16, 4, 4, 0	24
Company D	1, 4, 1, 4	10
Company E	100, 0, 0, 100	200

The correct answer is B.

PS15523

64. Company Q plans to make a new product next year and sell each unit of this new product at a selling price of $2. The variable costs per unit in each production run are estimated to be 40% of the selling price, and the fixed costs for each production run are estimated to be $5,040. Based on these estimated costs, how many units of the new product will Company Q need to make and sell in order for their revenue to equal their total costs for each production run?

(A) 4,200
(B) 3,150
(C) 2,520
(D) 2,100
(E) 1,800

Algebra Applied Problems

Let x be the desired number of units to be sold at a price of $2 each. Then the revenue for selling these units is $2x$, and the total cost for selling these units is $(40\%)(\$2.00)x = \$0.80x$ plus a fixed cost of $5,040.

revenue = total cost — given requirement

$$2x = 0.8x + 5{,}040 \quad \text{given information}$$

$$1.2x = 5{,}040 \quad \text{subtract } 0.8x \text{ from both sides}$$

$$x = 4{,}200 \quad \text{divide both sides by 1.2}$$

The correct answer is A.

PS07197

65. A small business invests $9,900 in equipment to produce a product. Each unit of the product costs $0.65 to produce and is sold for $1.20. How many units of the product must be sold before the revenue received equals the total expense of production, including the initial investment in equipment?

(A) 12,000

(B) 14,500

(C) 15,230

(D) 18,000

(E) 20,000

Arithmetic Rate

Let n be the number of units desired. Then, in dollars, the revenue received is $1.2n$ and the total expense is $9{,}900 + 0.65n$. These two amounts are equal when $1.2n = 9{,}900 + 0.65n$, or $0.55n = 9{,}900$. Therefore,

$$n = \frac{9{,}900}{0.55} = \frac{990{,}000}{55} = \frac{90{,}000}{5} = 18{,}000.$$

The correct answer is D.

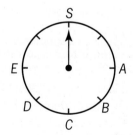

PS05682

66. The dial shown above is divided into equal-sized intervals. At which of the following letters will the pointer stop if it is rotated clockwise from S through 1,174 intervals?

(A) A

(B) B

(C) C

(D) D

(E) E

Arithmetic Properties of Numbers

There are 8 intervals in each complete revolution. Dividing 8 into 1,174 gives 146 with remainder 6. Therefore, 1,174 intervals is equivalent to 146 complete revolutions followed by an additional 6 intervals measured clockwise from S, which places the pointer at E.

The correct answer is E.

Estimated Number of Home-Schooled Students by State, January 2001

State	Number (in thousands)
A	181
B	125
C	103
D	79
E	72

PS12287

67. According to the table shown, the estimated number of home-schooled students in State A is approximately what percent greater than the number in State D ?

(A) 25%

(B) 55%

(C) 100%

(D) 125%

(E) 155%

Arithmetic Percents

The percent increase from the number in State D to the number in State A is

$$= \left(\frac{181{,}000 - 79{,}000}{79{,}000} \times 100 \right)\% \quad \text{expression for percent increase}$$

$$= \left(\frac{181 - 79}{79} \times 100 \right)\% \quad \text{reduce fraction}$$

$$= \left(\frac{102}{79} \times 100 \right)\% \quad \text{subtract}$$

$$\approx \left(\frac{100}{80} \times 100 \right)\% \quad \text{approximate}$$

$$= (1.25 \times 100)\% \quad \text{divide}$$

$$= 125\% \quad \text{multiply}$$

The correct answer is D.

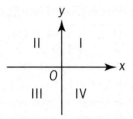

PS02695

68. The graph of the equation $xy = k$, where $k < 0$, lies in which two of the quadrants shown above?

(A) I and II

(B) I and III

(C) II and III

(D) II and IV

(E) III and IV

Algebra Coordinate Geometry

If a point lies on the graph of $xy = k$, then the product of the point's x- and y-coordinates is k. Since k is negative, it follows that for any such point, the product of the point's x- and y-coordinates is negative. Therefore, for any such point, the point's x- and y-coordinates have opposite signs, and hence the point must be in quadrant II or in quadrant IV.

The correct answer is D.

PS00526

69. When n liters of fuel were added to a tank that was already $\frac{1}{3}$ full, the tank was filled to $\frac{7}{9}$ of its capacity. In terms of n, what is the capacity of the tank, in liters?

(A) $\frac{10}{9}n$

(B) $\frac{4}{3}n$

(C) $\frac{3}{2}n$

(D) $\frac{9}{4}n$

(E) $\frac{7}{3}n$

Algebra Applied Problems

Let C represent the capacity of the tank, in liters. It follows that

$$\frac{1}{3}C + n = \frac{7}{9}C \qquad \text{given}$$

$$n = \frac{7}{9}C - \frac{1}{3}C \qquad \text{subtract } \frac{1}{3}C \text{ from both sides}$$

$$n = \frac{4}{9}C \qquad \text{combine like terms}$$

$$\frac{9}{4}n = C \qquad \text{divide both sides by } \frac{4}{9}$$

The correct answer is D.

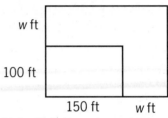

Note: Not drawn to scale.

PS06601

70. The smaller rectangle in the figure above represents the original size of a parking lot before its length and width were each extended by w feet to make the larger rectangular lot shown. If the area of the enlarged lot is twice the area of the original lot, what is the value of w?

(A) 25

(B) 50

(C) 75

(D) 100

(E) 200

Geometry Area

From the given information it follows that $(100 + w)(150 + w) = 2(100)(150)$, or $(100 + w)(150 + w) = (200)(150)$. This is a quadratic equation that can be solved by several methods. One method is by inspection. The left side is clearly equal to the right side when $w = 50$. Another method is by factoring. Expanding the left side gives $(100)(150) + 250w + w^2 = (200)(150)$, or $w^2 + 250w - (100)(150) = 0$. Factoring the left side gives $(w - 50)(w + 300) = 0$, which has $w = 50$ as its only positive solution.

The correct answer is B.

PS02209

71. Kevin invested $8,000 for one year at a simple annual interest rate of 6 percent and invested $10,000 for one year at an annual interest rate of 8 percent compounded semiannually. What is the total amount of interest that Kevin earned on the two investments?

(A) $880

(B) $1,088

(C) $1,253

(D) $1,280

(E) $1,296

Arithmetic Applied Problems

<u>Interest on $8,000 investment:</u> For simple interest, recall that the amount of interest is

(Principal) × (Interest rate) × (Time)	=	($8,000)(0.06)(1)
	=	$480

<u>Interest on $10,000 investment:</u> For compound interest, recall that the amount of interest is the final investment value minus the principal, which is equal to $P\left(1+\dfrac{r}{n}\right)^{nt} - P$, where

P	=	principal	=	$10,000
r	=	annual interest rate	=	0.08
n	=	periods per year	=	2
t	=	number of years	=	1

Substitute these values and calculate the result:

$$10,000\left(1+\dfrac{0.08}{2}\right)^{(2)(1)} - 10,000$$

$10,000(1.04)^2 - 10,000$	arithmetic
$10,000(1.04^2 - 1)$	factor out 10,000
$10,000(1.0816 - 1)$	square 1.04
$10,000(0.0816)$	subtract
816	multiply

Therefore, the total amount of interest on the two investments is $480 + $816 = $1,296.

Tip: The algebraic identity $(a+b)^2 = a^2 + 2ab + b^2$ is sometimes useful in squaring numbers quickly. For example, $1.04^2 = (1+0.04)^2$ can be obtained by adding the following three numbers: square of 1, double the product of 1 and 0.04, and square of 0.04. Another example is $305^2 = (300+5)^2$.

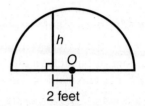

a	b	a^2	$2ab$	b^2
1	0.04	1	0.08	0.0016
300	5	90,000	3,000	25

Thus, 1.04^2 can be calculated by $1 + 0.08 + 0.0016$ and 305^2 can be calculated by $90,000 + 3,000 + 25$. The additions are especially easy when, as is the case with these examples, the nonzero digits of the numbers being added all have different place values. This is often the case when b is relatively small compared to a.

The correct answer is E.

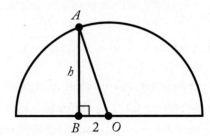

2 feet

PS05957

72. The figure above represents a semicircular archway over a flat street. The semicircle has a center at O and a radius of 6 feet. What is the height h, in feet, of the archway 2 feet from its center?

(A) $\sqrt{2}$

(B)   2

(C)   3

(D) $4\sqrt{2}$

(E)   6

Geometry Circles; Pythagorean Theorem

In the figure, $\triangle ABO$ is a right triangle with legs of lengths 2 and h. From the Pythagorean theorem, it follows that $(AO)^2 = 2^2 + h^2 = 4 + h^2$. Also, $AO = 6$ since the radius of the semicircle is 6. Thus, $6^2 = 4 + h^2$, or $36 = 4 + h^2$, or $h^2 = 32$. Therefore, $h = \sqrt{32} = \sqrt{16 \cdot 2} = 4\sqrt{2}$.

A

h

B 2 *O*

The correct answer is D.

PS01315

73. The harvest yield from a certain apple orchard was 350 bushels of apples. If x of the trees in the orchard each yielded 10 bushels of apples, what fraction of the harvest yield was from these x trees?

(A) $\dfrac{x}{35}$

(B) $1 - \dfrac{x}{35}$

(C) $10x$

(D) $35 - x$

(E) $350 - 10x$

Algebra Algebraic Expressions

Since each of the x trees yielded 10 bushels, the total number of bushels yielded by these trees was $10x$. Since the yield of the entire orchard was 350 bushels, $\dfrac{10x}{350} = \dfrac{x}{35}$ was the fraction of the total yield from these x trees.

The correct answer is A.

PS00907

74. In a certain fraction, the denominator is 16 greater than the numerator. If the fraction is equivalent to 80 percent, what is the denominator of the fraction?

(A) 32

(B) 64

(C) 72

(D) 80

(E) 120

Algebra First-Degree Equations

Let n be the numerator of the fraction. Then $n + 16$ is the denominator of the fraction. From the given information it follows that

$\dfrac{n}{n+16} = 80\%$, which is solved below.

$$\dfrac{n}{n+16} = \dfrac{4}{5} \qquad \text{convert 80\% to a fraction}$$

$$5n = 4(n+16) \qquad \text{clear fractions}$$

$$5n = 4n + 64 \qquad \text{simplify}$$

$$n = 64 \qquad \text{subtract } 4n \text{ from both sides}$$

Therefore, the denominator of the fraction is $n + 16 = 64 + 16 = 80$.

The correct answer is D.

PS02102

75. Greg assembles units of a certain product at a factory. Each day he is paid $2.00 per unit for the first 40 units that he assembles and $2.50 for each additional unit that he assembles that day. If Greg assembled at least 30 units on each of two days and was paid a total of $180.00 for assembling units on the two days, what is the greatest possible number of units that he could have assembled on one of the two days?

(A) 48

(B) 52

(C) 56

(D) 60

(E) 64

Arithmetic Applied Problems

Since the task is to find the greatest number of units Greg could have assembled on one of the days, start by checking the answer choice with the greatest value (in this case, E).

E Number of units assembled on day with greatest number: 64

Pay: $40(\$2.00) + 24(\$2.50) = \$80.00 + \$60.00 = \$140.00$

Pay for other day: $180.00 − $140.00 = $40

Number of units assembled on other day: $\dfrac{\$40}{\$2} = 20$

Conclusion: Because $20 < 30$, the greatest number is NOT 64.

D Number of units assembled on day with greatest number: 60

Pay: $40(\$2.00) + 20(\$2.50) = \$80.00 + \$50.00 = \$130.00$

Pay for other day: $180.00 − $130.00 = $50

Number of units assembled on other day: $\dfrac{\$50}{\$2} = 25$

Conclusion: Because $25 < 30$, the greatest number is NOT 60.

C Number of units assembled on day with greatest number: 56

Pay: $40(\$2.00) + 16(\$2.50) = \$80.00 + \$40.00 = \$120.00$

Pay for other day: $180.00 − $120.00 = $60

Number of units assembled on other day:
$$\frac{\$60}{\$2} = 30$$

Conclusion: Because $30 \geq 30$, the greatest number IS 56.

Note that neither 48 nor 52 can be the greatest because $56 > 48$ and $56 > 52$.

The correct answer is C.

PS00419

76. Which of the following is greatest?

(A) $10\sqrt{3}$

(B) $9\sqrt{4}$

(C) $8\sqrt{5}$

(D) $7\sqrt{6}$

(E) $6\sqrt{7}$

Arithmetic Operations on Radical Expressions

Since all the expressions represent positive numbers, the expression that has the greatest squared value will be the expression that has the greatest value.

$\left(10\sqrt{3}\right)^2 = 100 \times 3 = 300$ (not greatest)

$\left(9\sqrt{4}\right)^2 = 81 \times 4 = 324$ (greatest)

$\left(8\sqrt{5}\right)^2 = 64 \times 5 = 320$ (not greatest)

$\left(7\sqrt{6}\right)^2 = 49 \times 6 = 294$ (not greatest)

$\left(6\sqrt{7}\right)^2 = 36 \times 7 = 252$ (not greatest)

The correct answer is B.

PS14236

77. Al and Ben are drivers for SD Trucking Company. One snowy day, Ben left SD at 8:00 a.m. heading east and Al left SD at 11:00 a.m. heading west. At a particular time later that day, the dispatcher retrieved data from SD's vehicle tracking system. The data showed that, up to that time, Al had averaged 40 miles per hour and Ben had averaged 20 miles per hour. It also showed that Al and Ben had driven a combined total of 240 miles. At what time did the dispatcher retrieve data from the vehicle tracking system?

(A) 1:00 p.m.

(B) 2:00 p.m.

(C) 3:00 p.m.

(D) 5:00 p.m.

(E) 6:00 p.m.

Algebra Applied Problems

Let t be the number of hours after 8:00 a.m. that Ben drove. Then Al, who began 3 hours after Ben began and thus drove 3 hours less than Ben, drove $(t - 3)$ hours. First, find the total distance each drove in terms of t.

	rate	time	distance = rate × time
Al	40	$t - 3$	$40(t - 3)$
Ben	20	t	$20t$

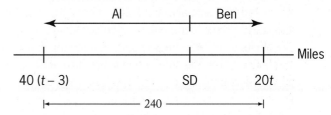

Since the combined total distance that Al and Ben drove was 240 miles, it follows that $40(t - 3) + 20t = 240$. Solve for t.

$$
\begin{aligned}
40(t - 3) + 20t &= 240 \quad \text{given} \\
60t - 120 &= 240 \quad \text{expand and combine like terms} \\
60t &= 360 \quad \text{add 120 to both sides} \\
t &= 6 \quad \text{divide both sides by 60}
\end{aligned}
$$

Therefore, the data was retrieved 6 hours after 8:00 a.m., which was 2:00 p.m.

The correct answer is B.

PS02996

78. Of the land owned by a farmer, 90 percent was cleared for planting. Of the cleared land, 40 percent was planted with soybeans and 50 percent of the cleared land was planted with wheat. If the remaining 720 acres of cleared land was planted with corn, how many acres did the farmer own?

(A) 5,832

(B) 6,480

(C) 7,200

(D) 8,000

(E) 8,889

Arithmetic Applied Problems; Percents

Corn was planted on $100\% - (40\% + 50\%) = 10\%$ of the cleared land, and the cleared land represents 90% of the farmer's land. Therefore, corn was planted on 10% of 90%, or $(0.10)(0.90) = 0.09 = 9\%$, of the farmer's land. It is given that corn was planted on 720 acres, so if x is the number of acres the farmer owns, then

$0.09x = 720$ and $x = \dfrac{720}{0.09} = 8,000$.

The correct answer is D.

PS00307

79. At the start of an experiment, a certain population consisted of 3 animals. At the end of each month after the start of the experiment, the population size was double its size at the beginning of that month. Which of the following represents the population size at the end of 10 months?

(A) 2^3

(B) 3^2

(C) $2(3^{10})$

(D) $3(2^{10})$

(E) $3(10^2)$

Arithmetic Applied Problems; Sequences

The population doubles each month, so multiply the previous month's population by 2 to get the next month's population. Thus, at the end of the 1st month the population will be $(3)(2)$, at the end of the 2nd month the population will be $(3)(2)(2)$, at the end of the 3rd month the population will be $(3)(2)(2)(2)$, and so on. Therefore, at the end of the 10th month the population will be the product of 3 and ten factors of 2, which equals $3(2^{10})$.

The correct answer is D.

PS03635

80. If $\left(\dfrac{1}{3} + \dfrac{1}{4} + \dfrac{1}{5} + \dfrac{1}{6}\right) = r\left(\dfrac{1}{9} + \dfrac{1}{12} + \dfrac{1}{15} + \dfrac{1}{18}\right)$, then $r =$

(A) $\dfrac{1}{3}$

(B) $\dfrac{4}{3}$

(C) 3

(D) 4

(E) 12

Arithmetic Operations with Rational Numbers

$$\left(\dfrac{1}{3} + \dfrac{1}{4} + \dfrac{1}{5} + \dfrac{1}{6}\right) = r\left(\dfrac{1}{9} + \dfrac{1}{12} + \dfrac{1}{15} + \dfrac{1}{18}\right)$$

$$\left(\dfrac{1}{3} + \dfrac{1}{4} + \dfrac{1}{5} + \dfrac{1}{6}\right) = r\left(\dfrac{1}{3}\right)\left(\dfrac{1}{3} + \dfrac{1}{4} + \dfrac{1}{5} + \dfrac{1}{6}\right)$$

$$1 = r\left(\dfrac{1}{3}\right)$$

$$3 = r$$

Alternatively,

$$\left(\dfrac{1}{3} + \dfrac{1}{4} + \dfrac{1}{5} + \dfrac{1}{6}\right) = r\left(\dfrac{1}{9} + \dfrac{1}{12} + \dfrac{1}{15} + \dfrac{1}{18}\right)$$

$$\left(\dfrac{20}{60} + \dfrac{15}{60} + \dfrac{12}{60} + \dfrac{10}{60}\right) = r\left(\dfrac{20}{180} + \dfrac{15}{180} + \dfrac{12}{180} + \dfrac{10}{180}\right)$$

$$\left(\dfrac{20 + 15 + 12 + 10}{60}\right) = r\left(\dfrac{20 + 15 + 12 + 10}{180}\right)$$

$$\left(\dfrac{20 + 15 + 12 + 10}{60}\right)\left(\dfrac{20 + 15 + 12 + 10}{60}\right) \times \left(\dfrac{180}{20 + 15 + 12 + 10}\right) \times \left(\dfrac{180}{20 + 15 + 12 + 10}\right) = r$$

$$\dfrac{180}{60} = r$$

$$3 = r$$

The correct answer is C.

PS03214

81. If x and y are positive integers such that y is a multiple of 5 and $3x + 4y = 200$, then x must be a multiple of which of the following?

(A) 3

(B) 6

(C) 7

(D) 8

(E) 10

Arithmetic Properties of Numbers

Since y is a multiple of 5, consider the following table:

y	$4y$	$3x = 200 - 4y$	$x = \dfrac{200 - 4y}{3}$	Is x a positive integer?
5	20	180	60	**yes**
10	40	160	$\dfrac{160}{3}$	no
15	60	140	$\dfrac{140}{3}$	no
20	80	120	40	**yes**
25	100	100	$\dfrac{100}{3}$	no
30	120	80	$\dfrac{80}{3}$	no
35	140	60	20	**yes**
40	160	40	$\dfrac{40}{3}$	no
45	180	20	$\dfrac{20}{3}$	no
50	200	0	0	no

The only positive integers x that satisfy the $3x + 4y = 200$, where y is a multiple of 5, are 60, 40, and 20; each is a multiple of 10.

Note: It is not necessary to perform all of the calculations shown here, nor is it necessary to fill out the table completely. Using "number sense" to see the patterns (e.g., numbers in the second column increase by 20 while numbers in the third column decrease by 20) will shorten the work considerably.

The correct answer is E.

PS12764
82. Which of the following expressions can be written as an integer?

I. $\left(\sqrt{82} + \sqrt{82}\right)^2$

II. $(82)\left(\sqrt{82}\right)$

III. $\dfrac{\left(\sqrt{82}\right)\left(\sqrt{82}\right)}{82}$

(A) None
(B) I only
(C) III only
(D) I and II
(E) I and III

Arithmetic Operations with Radical Expressions

Expression I represents an integer because $\left(\sqrt{82} + \sqrt{82}\right)^2 = \left(2\sqrt{82}\right)^2 = (4)(82)$.

Expression II does not represent an integer because $(82)\sqrt{82} = \sqrt{82^3}$ and $82^3 = 2^3 \times 41^3$ is not a perfect square. Regarding this last assertion, note that the square of any integer has the property that each of its distinct prime factors is repeated an even number of times. For example, $24^2 = (2^3 \times 3)^2 = 2^6 \times 3^2$ has the prime factor 2 repeated 6 times and the prime factor 3 repeated twice. Expression III represents an integer, because $\dfrac{\left(\sqrt{82}\right)\left(\sqrt{82}\right)}{82} = \dfrac{82}{82} = 1$.

The correct answer is E.

PS13101
83. Pumping alone at their respective constant rates, one inlet pipe fills an empty tank to $\dfrac{1}{2}$ of capacity in 3 hours and a second inlet pipe fills the same empty tank to $\dfrac{2}{3}$ of capacity in 6 hours. How many hours will it take both pipes, pumping simultaneously at their respective constant rates, to fill the empty tank to capacity?

(A) 3.25
(B) 3.6
(C) 4.2
(D) 4.4
(E) 5.5

Arithmetic Applied Problems

The first pipe can fill $\dfrac{1}{2}$ of the tank in 3 hours, which is equivalent to the rate of filling $\dfrac{1}{2} \div 3 = \dfrac{1}{6}$ of the tank per hour. The second pipe can fill $\dfrac{2}{3}$ of the tank in 6 hours, which is equivalent to the rate of filling $\frac{2}{3} \div 6 = \frac{1}{9}$ of the tank per hour. Together, they can fill the tank at a rate of $\frac{1}{6} + \frac{1}{9} = \frac{5}{18}$ of the tank per hour. Thus, when both pipes are used at the same time, they will fill the tank in $\frac{18}{5} = 3.6$ hours.

The correct answer is B.

PS02947

84. In the *xy*-coordinate plane, which of the following points must lie on the line $kx + 3y = 6$ for every possible value of k ?

(A) (1,1)

(B) (0,2)

(C) (2,0)

(D) (3,6)

(E) (6,3)

Algebra Coordinate Geometry

Substitute the various answer choices for (x,y) into $kx + 3y = 6$ and determine whether the resulting equation has all real numbers for its solution. Note that it is not necessary to solve the resulting equations, but for completeness the solutions are given.

		equation for k	solution for k
A	(1,1)	$k + 3 = 6$	3
B	(0,2)	$0 + 3(2) = 6$	**all real numbers**
C	(2,0)	$2k + 3(0) = 6$	3
D	(3,6)	$3k + 3(6) = 6$	-4
E	(6,3)	$6k + 3(3) = 6$	-0.5

Alternatively, the linear equation $kx + 3y = 6$ can be solved for a unique value of k if $x \neq 0$, so if the equation is true for every possible value of k, then $x = 0$ and $(x,y) = (0, 2)$ is the only answer choice that could be the correct answer.

The correct answer is B.

PS11091

85. If $x^2 - 2 < 0$, which of the following specifies all the possible values of x ?

(A) $0 < x < 2$

(B) $0 < x < \sqrt{2}$

(C) $-\sqrt{2} < x < \sqrt{2}$

(D) $-2 < x < 0$

(E) $-2 < x < 2$

Algebra Inequalities

The corresponding equality $x^2 - 2 = 0$ has two solutions, $x = \sqrt{2}$ and $x = -\sqrt{2}$, and thus there are three intervals to test for inclusion in the solution of the inequality: $x < -\sqrt{2}, -\sqrt{2} < x < \sqrt{2}$, and $x > \sqrt{2}$, labeled I_1, I_2, and I_3, respectively, in the figure below.

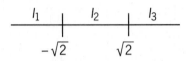

Next, choose a value from each of these intervals to test whether the inequality holds:

From I_1, for example, choose $x = -2$; the inequality becomes $(-2)^2 - 2 < 0$ (False).

From I_2, for example, choose $x = 0$; the inequality becomes $(0)^2 - 2 < 0$ (True).

From I_3, for example, choose $x = 2$; the inequality becomes $(2)^2 - 2 < 0$ (False).

Therefore, the solution consists of only values in I_2.

Alternatively, the expression $x^2 - 2$ can be factored as $(x - \sqrt{2})(x + \sqrt{2})$. The value of the factor $(x - \sqrt{2})$ is 0 at $x = \sqrt{2}$, negative for values of x less than $\sqrt{2}$, and positive for values of x greater than $\sqrt{2}$. Similarly, the value of the factor $(x + \sqrt{2})$ is 0 at $x = -\sqrt{2}$, negative for values of x less than $-\sqrt{2}$, and positive for values of x greater than $-\sqrt{2}$. Using the number line, this information can be summarized as shown below:

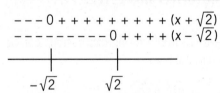

Then, as shown below, vertical lines through the zeros partition the number line into three intervals I_1, I_2, and I_3.

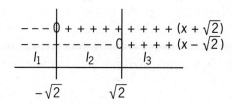

I_1: $x < -\sqrt{2}$, where both factors are negative, so the product

$(x - \sqrt{2})(x + \sqrt{2})$ is positive.

I_2: $-\sqrt{2} < x < \sqrt{2}$, where one factor is positive and the other is negative, so the

product $(x - \sqrt{2})(x + \sqrt{2})$ is negative.

I_3: $x > \sqrt{2}$, where both factors are positive, so the product

$(x - \sqrt{2})(x + \sqrt{2})$ is positive.

Therefore, the solution consists of only values in I_2.

The correct answer is C.

Book Number	Pages in Book	Total Pages Read
1	253	253
2	110	363
3	117	480
4	170	650
5	155	805
6	50	855
7	205	1,060
8	70	1,130
9	165	1,295
10	105	1,400
11	143	1,543
12	207	1,750

PS14467

86. Shawana made a schedule for reading books during 4 weeks (28 days) of her summer vacation. She has checked out 12 books from the library. The number of pages in each book and the order in which she plans to read the books are shown in the table above. She will read exactly 50 pages each day. The only exception will be that she will never begin the next book on the same day that she finishes the previous one, and therefore on some days she may read fewer than 50 pages. At the end of the 28th day, how many books will Shawana have finished?

(A)   7
(B)   8
(C)   9
(D)   10
(E)   11

Arithmetic Operations with Integers

Book 1: 6 days—50 pages on each of Days 1–5, 3 pages on Day 6 [5(50) + 3 = 253]

Book 2: 3 days—50 pages on each of Days 7 and 8, 10 pages on Day 9 [2(50) + 10 = 110]

Book 3: 3 days—50 pages on each of Days 10 and 11, 17 pages on Day 12 [2(50) + 17 = 117]

Book 4: 4 days—50 pages on each of Days 13–15, 20 pages on Day 16 [3(50) + 20 = 170]

Book 5: 4 days—50 pages on each of Days 17–19, 5 pages on Day 20 [3(50) + 5 = 155]

Book 6: 1 day—50 pages on Day 21 [1(50) = 50]

Book 7: 5 days—50 pages on each of Days 22–25, 5 pages on Day 26 [4(50) + 5 = 205]

Book 8: 2 days—50 pages on Day 27, 20 pages on Day 28 [50 + 20 = 70]

At this point, Shawana has read on a total of 28 days and has finished 8 books.

The correct answer is B.

PS07465

87. In Western Europe, x bicycles were sold in each of the years 1990 and 1993. The bicycle producers of Western Europe had a 42 percent share of this market in 1990 and a 33 percent share in 1993. Which of the following represents the decrease in the annual number of bicycles produced and sold in Western Europe from 1990 to 1993?

(A)   9% of $\dfrac{x}{100}$

(B)   14% of $\dfrac{x}{100}$

(C)   75% of $\dfrac{x}{100}$

(D)   9% of x

(E)   14% of x

Arithmetic Percents

Of the x bicycles sold in Western Europe in 1990, 42% of them were produced in Western Europe. It follows that the number of bicycles produced and sold in Western Europe in 1990 was $0.42x$. Similarly, of the x bicycles sold in Western Europe in 1993, 33% were produced in Western Europe. It follows that the number of bicycles produced and sold in Western Europe in 1993 was $0.33x$. Therefore, the decrease in the annual number of bicycles produced and sold in Western Europe from 1990 to 1993 was $0.42x - 0.33x = 0.09x$, which is 9% of x.

The correct answer is D.

PS06946

88.   If k is a positive integer, what is the remainder when $(k + 2)(k^3 - k)$ is divided by 6 ?

(A)   0

(B)   1

(C)   2

(D)   3

(E)   4

Algebra Properties of Numbers

Since k can be any positive integer, the remainder must be the same regardless of the value of k. If $k = 2$, for example, then $(k + 2)(k^3 - k) =$ $(2 + 2)(2^3 - 2) = (4)(6)$, which is a multiple of 6, and therefore, the remainder when divided by 6 is 0.

Alternatively, factor the given expression:

$$(k + 2)(k^3 - k) = (k + 2)(k)(k^2 - 1)$$
$$= (k + 2)(k)(k + 1)(k - 1)$$

Now, rearrange the factors in ascending order $(k - 1)(k)(k + 1)(k + 2)$, and observe that for any positive integer k, the factors are 4 consecutive integers, two of which are even and one of which is divisible by 3. Therefore, $(k + 2)(k^3 - k)$ is divisible by both 2 and 3. Thus, $(k + 2)(k^3 - k)$ is divisible by 6 with 0 remainder.

The correct answer is A.

PS14989

89.   Which of the following fractions is closest to $\dfrac{1}{2}$?

(A) $\dfrac{4}{7}$

(B) $\dfrac{5}{9}$

(C) $\dfrac{6}{11}$

(D) $\dfrac{7}{13}$

(E) $\dfrac{9}{16}$

Arithmetic Fractions

A fraction equals $\dfrac{1}{2}$ if its numerator is half its denominator. Thus, to compare the answer choices with $\dfrac{1}{2}$, rewrite $\dfrac{1}{2}$ to have the same denominators as the answer choices. This will allow for an easy determination of the distance to $\dfrac{1}{2}$.

answer choice	value	rewrite of $\dfrac{1}{2}$	distance to $\dfrac{1}{2}$
A	$\dfrac{4}{7}$	$\dfrac{3.5}{7}$	$\dfrac{0.5}{7}$
B	$\dfrac{5}{9}$	$\dfrac{4.5}{9}$	$\dfrac{0.5}{9}$
C	$\dfrac{6}{11}$	$\dfrac{5.5}{11}$	$\dfrac{0.5}{11}$
D	$\dfrac{7}{13}$	$\dfrac{6.5}{13}$	$\dfrac{0.5}{13}$
E	$\dfrac{9}{16}$	$\dfrac{8}{16}$	$\dfrac{1}{16}$

Clearly, $\dfrac{0.5}{13}$ is smaller than each of $\dfrac{0.5}{7}$, $\dfrac{0.5}{9}$, and $\dfrac{0.5}{11}$ because the numerators are equal, and thus larger denominators correspond to smaller values. Also, $\dfrac{0.5}{13} = \dfrac{1}{26}$ is smaller than $\dfrac{1}{16}$. Therefore, $\dfrac{7}{13}$ is closest to $\dfrac{1}{2}$.

The correct answer is D.

PS12949

90. If $p \neq 0$ and $p - \dfrac{1-p^2}{p} = \dfrac{r}{p}$, then $r =$

(A) $p + 1$
(B) $2p - 1$
(C) $p^2 + 1$
(D) $2p^2 - 1$
(E) $p^2 + p - 1$

Algebra Simplifying Algebraic Expressions

$p - \dfrac{1-p^2}{p} = \dfrac{r}{p}$	given
$p^2 - (1 - p^2) = r$	multiply both sides by p
$2p^2 - 1 = r$	combine like terms

The correct answer is D.

PS12760

91. If the range of the six numbers 4, 3, 14, 7, 10, and x is 12, what is the difference between the greatest possible value of x and the least possible value of x?

(A)   0
(B)   2
(C)   12
(D)   13
(E)   15

Arithmetic Statistics

The range of the six numbers 3, 4, 7, 10, 14, and x is 12. If x were neither the greatest nor the least of the six numbers, then the greatest and least of the six numbers would be 14 and 3. But, this cannot be possible because the range of the six numbers would be $14 - 3 = 11$ and not 12 as stated. Therefore, x must be either the greatest or the least of the six numbers. If x is the greatest of

the six numbers, then 3 is the least, and $x - 3 = 12$. It follows that $x = 15$. On the other hand, if x is the least of the six numbers, then 14 is the greatest, and $14 - x = 12$. It follows that $x = 2$. Thus, there are only two possible values of x, namely 15 and 2, and so the difference between the greatest and least possible values of x is $15 - 2 = 13$.

The correct answer is D.

PS04734

92. What number is 108 more than two-thirds of itself?

(A)   72
(B)   144
(C)   162
(D)   216
(E)   324

Algebra First-Degree Equations

Let x be the number that is 108 more than two-thirds of itself. Then, $108 + \dfrac{2}{3}x = x$. Solve for x as follows:

$$108 + \dfrac{2}{3}x = x$$

$$108 = \dfrac{1}{3}x$$

$$324 = x$$

The correct answer is E.

PS99551.02

93. A service provider charges c dollars for the first 50 hours of service used per month and 40 cents for each 30 minutes in excess of 50 hours used during the month. If x is an integer greater than 50, which of the following expressions gives this service provider's charge, in dollars, for a month in which x hours of service were used?

(A) $c + 0.40x$
(B) $c + 0.80x$
(C) $c + 0.40(x - 50)$
(D) $c + 0.80(x - 50)$
(E) $c + 0.40(2x - 50)$

Algebra Algebraic Expressions

For x hours of service used in the month, the charge is c dollars for the first 50 hours used, leaving $(x - 50)$ hours to be charged at 40 cents per half hour, which is equivalent to 80 cents per hour. Therefore, the total charge, in dollars, for a month in which x hours of service were used is $c + 0.80(x - 50)$.

The correct answer is D.

PS92820.02

94. A salesperson who had been driving at a speed of 100 kilometers per hour slowed down to a speed of 47 kilometers per hour. Approximately how many miles per hour was the speed reduced? (1 kilometer ≈ 0.625 mile)

(A)   29
(B)   33
(C)   53
(D)   63
(E)   75

Arithmetic Measurement Conversion

$(100 - 47) \dfrac{km}{hr}$ amount of reduction

$53 \dfrac{km}{hr}$ subtract

$\left(53 \dfrac{\cancel{km}}{hr}\right)\left(0.625 \dfrac{mi}{\cancel{km}}\right)$ 1 km = 0.625 mi

$(50)(0.6) \dfrac{mi}{hr}$ estimate

$30 \dfrac{mi}{hr}$ multiply

From the calculations above it follows that speed was reduced, in miles per hour, by a little more than 30; among the answer choices, only 33 is a reasonable choice. The exact value is 33.125, and this can be found by multiplying 53 and 0.625 or, since $(53)\left(\dfrac{625}{1,000}\right) = (53)\left(\dfrac{5}{8}\right) = \dfrac{265}{8}$, dividing 265 by 8.

The correct answer is B.

PS11396

95. Company P had 15 percent more employees in December than it had in January. If Company P had 460 employees in December, how many employees did it have in January?

(A)   391
(B)   400
(C)   410
(D)   423
(E)   445

Arithmetic Percents

It is given that 460 is 115% of the number of employees in January. Therefore, the number of employees in January was

$$\dfrac{460}{1.15} = \dfrac{460}{1.15}\left(\dfrac{100}{100}\right) = \left(\dfrac{460}{115}\right)(100) = (4)(100) = 400.$$

The correct answer is B.

PS66740.02

96.

	Recording Time	Viewing Time
Tuesday	4 hours	None
Wednesday	None	1 to 2 hours
Thursday	2 hours	None
Friday	None	2 to 3 hours

The table above shows the numbers of hours of television programs that Jane recorded last week and the numbers of hours she spent viewing these recorded programs. No recorded program was viewed more than once. If h is the number of hours of recorded programs she had not yet viewed by the end of Friday, which of the following intervals represents all of the possible values of h?

(A) $0 \leq h \leq 1$
(B) $1 \leq h \leq 2$
(C) $2 \leq h \leq 3$
(D) $0 \leq h \leq 2$
(E) $1 \leq h \leq 3$

Arithmetic Inequalities

By the end of Friday Jane had recorded a total of $4 + 2 = 6$ hours of programs, and she had viewed between $1 + 2 = 3$ hours and $2 + 3 = 5$ hours of these programs. Therefore, the number of hours of recorded programs that Jane had not yet viewed by the end of Friday was between $6 - 5 = 1$ and $6 - 3 = 3$.

The correct answer is E.

PS93850.02

97. A dance troupe has a total of 50 dancers split into 2 groups. The costumes worn by Group A cost $80 each, and those worn by Group B cost $90 each. If the total cost of all the costumes is $4,270, what is the total cost of the costumes worn by Group B ?

(A) $1,840
(B) $2,070
(C) $2,135
(D) $2,160
(E) $2,430

Algebra Applied Problems; First-Degree Equations

Let n be the number of dancers in Group B. Then the number of dancers in Group A is $50 - n$, and we are given that $(50 - n)(\$80) + (n)(\$90) = \$4,270$.

$(50 - n)(80) + 90n = 4{,}270$	given
$(50 - n)(8) + 9n = 427$	divide both sides by 10
$400 - 8n + 9n = 427$	distributive law
$n = 27$	combine like terms and subtract 400 from each side

Therefore, the total cost of the costumes worn by Group B is $27(\$90) = \$2,430$.

The correct answer is E.

PS07672

98. A doctor prescribed 18 cubic centimeters of a certain drug to a patient whose body weight was 120 pounds. If the typical dosage is 2 cubic centimeters per 15 pounds of body weight, by what percent was the prescribed dosage greater than the typical dosage?

(A) 8%
(B) 9%
(C) 11%
(D) 12.5%
(E) 14.8%

Arithmetic Percents

If the typical dosage is 2 cubic centimeters per 15 pounds of body weight, then the typical dosage for a person who weighs 120 pounds is $2\left(\dfrac{120}{15}\right) = 2(8) = 16$ cubic centimeters. The prescribed dosage of 18 cubic centimeters is, therefore, $\left(\left(\dfrac{18 - 16}{16}\right) \times 100\right)\%$ or 12.5% greater than the typical dosage.

The correct answer is D.

PS09899

99. The function f is defined by $f(x) = \sqrt{x} - 10$ for all positive numbers x. If $u = f(t)$ for some positive numbers t and u, what is t in terms of u ?

(A) $\sqrt{\sqrt{u} + 10}$
(B) $\left(\sqrt{u} + 10\right)^2$
(C) $\sqrt{u^2 + 10}$
(D) $(u + 10)^2$
(E) $(u^2 + 10)^2$

Algebra Functions

Because $f(x) = \sqrt{x} - 10$ it follows that $f(t) = \sqrt{t} - 10$. The problem states that $u = f(t)$, so by substitution $u = \sqrt{t} - 10$. To express t in terms of u, isolate t on one side of the equation:

$$u = \sqrt{t} - 10 \quad \text{given}$$
$$u + 10 = \sqrt{t} \quad \text{add 10 to both sides}$$
$$(u + 10)^2 = t \quad \text{square both sides}$$

Therefore, t in terms of u is $(u + 10)^2$.

The correct answer is D.

Questions 100 to 167 - Difficulty: **Medium**

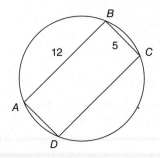

PS77502.01

100. If rectangle *ABCD* is inscribed in the circle above, what is the area of the circular region?

(A) 36.00π

(B) 42.25π

(C) 64.00π

(D) 84.50π

(E) 169.00π

Geometry Circles; Rectangles

The diagonal $\overline{AC}$ is the hypotenuse of right triangle $\triangle ABC$ that is inscribed in the circle, and thus $\overline{AC}$ is a diameter of the circle. Applying the Pythagorean theorem gives $(AC)^2 = 12^2 + 5^2 = 144 + 25 = 169$, or $AC = 13$.

Therefore, the radius of the circle is $\frac{13}{2} = 6.5$ and the area of the circle is $\pi(6.5)^2 = 42.25\pi$.

Note that the computation of $(6.5)^2$ can be avoided by observing that $\pi(6)^2 = 36\pi$ which shows that answer choice A is too small and $\pi(8)^2 = 64\pi$ which shows that answer choices C, D, and E are too large.

Tip: If a, b, and c are positive integers such that $a^2 + b^2 = c^2$, then they are called a Pythagorean triple because a, b, and c can be the side lengths of

a right triangle. The two best known Pythagorean triples are 3, 4, 5 and 5, 12, 13. Thus, for the problem above, once 5 and 12 are identified as the legs of a right triangle, the hypotenuse can be immediately identified without calculation as 13. Note that any positive integer multiple of a Pythagorean triple is a Pythagorean triple: If $a^2 + b^2 = c^2$ is true, then $(5a)^2 + (5b)^2 = (5c)^2$ is true, and thus if a, b, c is a Pythagorean triple, then $5a$, $5b$, $5c$ is a Pythagorean triple. Using this principle, it follows that 6, 8, 10 (2 times the triple 3, 4, 5) and 15, 36, 39 (3 times the triple 5, 12, 13) are also Pythagorean triples.

The correct answer is B.

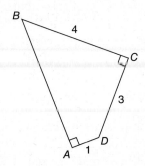

PS58502.01

101. In quadrilateral *ABCD* above, what is the length of *AB* ?

(A) $\sqrt{26}$

(B) $2\sqrt{5}$

(C) $2\sqrt{6}$

(D) $3\sqrt{2}$

(E) $3\sqrt{3}$

Geometry Quadrilaterals; Pythagorean Theorem

First, apply the Pythagorean theorem to $\triangle BCD$ to get $(BD)^2 = 3^2 + 4^2 = 25$, or $BD = 5$. Next, apply the Pythagorean theorem to $\triangle DAB$ to get $1^2 + (AB)^2 = 5^2$, or $(AB)^2 = 24$. Therefore, $AB = \sqrt{24} = 2\sqrt{6}$.

The correct answer is C.

PS98502.01

102. Three-fourths of the area of a rectangular lawn 30 feet wide by 40 feet long is to be enclosed by a rectangular fence. If the enclosure has full width and reduced length rather than full length and reduced width, how much less fence will be needed?

(A) $2\frac{1}{2}$

(B) 5

(C) 10

(D) 15

(E) 20

Geometry Rectangles

Let L ft be the reduced length. Then from $(30 \text{ ft})(L \text{ ft}) = \frac{3}{4}(30 \text{ ft})(40 \text{ ft})$ it follows that $L = 30$, and hence in this case the amount of fence needed is $2(30 \text{ ft} + 30 \text{ ft}) = 120$ ft. Let W ft be the reduced width. Then from $(W \text{ ft})(40 \text{ ft}) = \frac{3}{4}(30 \text{ ft})(40 \text{ ft})$ it follows that $W = 22.5$, and hence in this case the amount of fence needed is $2(22.5 \text{ ft} + 40 \text{ ft}) = 125$ ft. Therefore, the former case requires 5 ft less fence than the latter case.

The correct answer is B.

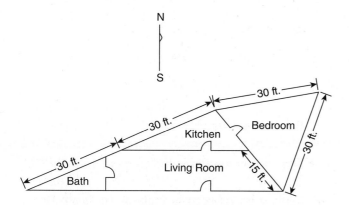

PS19502.01

103. In the floor plan of an executive's beach house above, the north and south walls of the living room are parallel. What is the floor area, in square feet, of the bedroom?

(A) $450\sqrt{3}$

(B) 450

(C) $225\sqrt{3}$

(D) 225

(E) It cannot be determined from the information given.

Geometry Triangles; Area

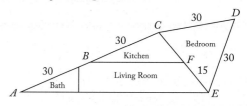

Using the labels in the figure above, it is given that $\overline{BF}$ is parallel to $\overline{AE}$ and so $\frac{BC}{AC} = \frac{CF}{CE}$ because, if a line parallel to one side of a triangle intersects the other two sides, it cuts off segments that are proportional to these sides. Therefore, $\frac{30}{30 + 30} = \frac{CF}{CF + 15}$ or $\frac{1}{2} = \frac{CF}{CF + 15}$. Solving for CF gives $CF + 15 = 2CF$ and so $CF = 15$. It follows that $CE = 15 + 15 = 30$, ΔCDE is equilateral, and each of its angles measures $60°$. Then, ΔCDF is a $30° - 60° - 90°$ triangle with its sides in the ratio $1 : \sqrt{3} : 2$, from which it follows that $DF = 15\sqrt{3}$. Thus, the area, in square feet, of ΔCDE, which is the bedroom, is $\frac{1}{2}(30)(15\sqrt{3}) = 225\sqrt{3}$.

The correct answer is C.

PS40602.01

104. On a scale drawing, a rectangle 1 inch by $1\frac{1}{3}$ inches represents the floor of a room and the indicated scale is 1 inch equals 15 feet. How many square tiles 6 inches on a side will be needed to cover this floor? (1 foot = 12 inches)

(A) 40

(B) 70

(C) 120

(D) 700

(E) 1,200

Geometry Quadrilaterals; Area

In feet, the floor is $(1)(15)$ feet = 15 feet by $\left(1\frac{1}{3}\right)(15) = 20$ feet with an area of $(15)(20) = 300$ square feet and each tile is $\frac{1}{2}$ foot by $\frac{1}{2}$ foot with an area of $\left(\frac{1}{2}\right)\left(\frac{1}{2}\right) = \frac{1}{4}$ square feet. The number of tiles needed to cover the floor is then $\dfrac{300}{\frac{1}{4}} = 1{,}200.$

Alternatively, in inches, the floor is $(1)(15)(12)$ inches = 180 inches by $\left(1\dfrac{1}{3}\right)(15)(12) = 240$ inches with an area of $(180)(240)$ square inches and each tile is 6 inches by 6 inches with an area of $(6)(6)$ square inches. The number of tiles needed to cover the floor is then $\dfrac{(180)(240)}{(6)(6)} = \left(\dfrac{180}{6}\right)\left(\dfrac{240}{6}\right) = (30)(40) = 1{,}200.$

The correct answer is E.

PS24210.02

105. According to a survey of 200 people, 60 enjoy skiing and 80 enjoy skating. If the number of people who enjoy neither skiing nor skating is 2 times the number of people who enjoy both skiing and skating, how many people surveyed enjoy neither skiing nor skating?

(A) 20
(B) 40
(C) 50
(D) 80
(E) 120

Algebra Sets

Determine the number of people who enjoy neither skiing nor skating.

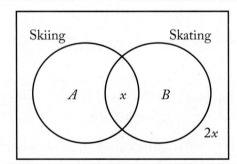

Consider the Venn diagram above, where A represents the number of people who enjoy skiing

only, B represents the number of people who enjoy skating only, and x is the number of people who enjoy both skiing and skating. As stated, the number of people who enjoy neither is twice the number who enjoy both, so $2x$ represents the number of people who enjoy neither skiing nor skating. From the given information, it follows that $60 = A + x$, $80 = B + x$, and $200 = A + x + B + 2x = (A + x) + (B + x) + x$. By substitution, $200 = 60 + 80 + x$, so $x = 60$ and $2x = 120$.

The correct answer is E.

PS45430.02

106.
$$m \oplus p = n$$
$$n \oplus r = m$$
$$n \oplus q = q$$
$$p \oplus q = p$$
$$q \oplus p = r$$

If the relations shown hold for the operation $\oplus$ and the numbers m, n, p, q, and r, then $[(m \oplus p) \oplus q] \oplus p =$

(A) m
(B) n
(C) p
(D) q
(E) r

Algebra Formulas

$$[(m \oplus p) \oplus q] \oplus p \quad \text{given}$$
$$[n \oplus q] \oplus p \quad m \oplus p = n$$
$$q \oplus p \quad n \oplus q = q$$
$$r \quad q \oplus p = r$$

The correct answer is E.

PS30730.02

107. To rent a tractor, it costs a total of x dollars for the first 24 hours, plus y dollars per hour for each hour in excess of 24 hours. Which of the following represents the cost, in dollars, to rent a tractor for 36 hours?

(A) $x + 12y$
(B) $x + 36y$
(C) $12x + y$
(D) $24x + 12y$
(E) $24x + 36y$

Algebra Algebraic Expressions

Determine the cost to rent a tractor for 36 hours if the cost is x dollars for the first 24 hours and y dollars for each hour in excess of 24 hours.

The cost will be x dollars for the first 24 hours plus y dollars for each of $36 - 24 = 12$ hours. Thus the total cost of renting the tractor for 36 hours is $(x + 12y)$ dollars.

The correct answer is A.

PS49140.02

108. If the mass of 1 cubic centimeter of a certain substance is 7.3 grams, what is the mass, in kilograms, of 1 cubic meter of this substance? (1 cubic meter = 1,000,000 cubic centimeters; 1 kilogram = 1,000 grams)

(A)   0.0073
(B)   0.73
(C)   7.3
(D)   7,300
(E)   7,300,000

Arithmetic Measurement Conversion

Determine the mass, in kilograms, of 1 cubic meter of a substance if the mass of 1 cubic centimeter of this substance is 7.3 grams.

1 cubic meter is 1,000,000 cubic centimeters and each cubic centimeter has a mass of 7.3 grams, so 1 cubic meter has a mass of $7.3(1,000,000) = 7,300,000$ grams. Then, since 1 kilogram = 1,000 grams,

$$7,300,000 \text{ grams} = \frac{7,300,000}{1,000}$$

$= 7,300$ kilograms.

The correct answer is D.

PS14031.02

109. If $z \neq 0$ and $z + \dfrac{1 - 2z^2}{z} = \dfrac{w}{z}$, then $w =$

(A) $z + 1$
(B) $z^2 + 1$
(C) $-z^2 + 1$
(D) $-z^2 + z + 1$
(E) $-2z^2 + 1$

Algebra Simplifying Algebraic Expressions

Multiplying both sides of $\dfrac{w}{z} = z + \dfrac{1 - 2z^2}{z}$ by z

gives $w = z\left(z + \dfrac{1 - 2z^2}{z} \right) = z^2 + (1 - 2z^2) = 1 - z^2$.

The correct answer is C.

PS37631.02

110. For all real numbers a, b, c, d, e, and f, the operation Θ is defined by the equation $(a, b, c) \Theta (d, e, f) = ad + be + cf$. What is the value of $(1, -2, 3) \Theta \left(1, -\dfrac{1}{2}, \dfrac{1}{3}\right)$?

(A) -1
(B) $\dfrac{5}{6}$
(C) 1
(D) $\dfrac{5}{2}$
(E) 3

Algebra Formulas

By definition, $(1, -2, 3) \Theta \left(1, -\dfrac{1}{2}, \dfrac{1}{3}\right) =$
$(1)(1) + (-2)\left(-\dfrac{1}{2}\right) + (3)\left(\dfrac{1}{3}\right) = 1 + 1 + 1 = 3$.

The correct answer is E.

PS01761

111. If m and p are positive integers and $m^2 + p^2 < 100$, what is the greatest possible value of mp?

(A)   36
(B)   42
(C)   48
(D)   49
(E)   51

Arithmetic Operations with Integers

Trying various integer values for m and corresponding values of p that satisfy $m^2 + p^2 < 100$ might be the quickest way to solve this problem. First, $m < 10$ and $p < 10$; otherwise, $m^2 + p^2 < 100$ is not true.

If $m = 9$, then for $m^2 + p^2 < 100$ to be true, $p < \sqrt{100 - 81} = \sqrt{19}$, so $p \leq 4$, and the greatest possible value for mp is $(9)(4) = 36$.

Similarly, if $m = 8$, then $p < \sqrt{100-64} = \sqrt{36}$, so $p \le 5$, and the greatest possible value for mp is $(8)(5) = 40$.

If $m = 7$, then $p < \sqrt{100-49} = \sqrt{51}$, so $p \le 7$, and the greatest possible value for mp is $(7)(7) = 49$.

If $m = 6$, then $p < \sqrt{100-36} = \sqrt{64}$, so $p \le 7$, and the greatest possible value for mp is $(6)(7) = 42$.

If $m \le 5$ and $p \le 9$, it follows that $mp \le 45$.

Thus, the greatest possible value for mp is 49.

The correct answer is D.

PS04482
112. If $\dfrac{x}{y} = \dfrac{c}{d}$ and $\dfrac{d}{c} = \dfrac{b}{a}$, which of the following must be true?

   I. $\dfrac{y}{x} = \dfrac{b}{a}$

   II. $\dfrac{x}{a} = \dfrac{y}{b}$

   III. $\dfrac{y}{a} = \dfrac{x}{b}$

(A)   I only
(B)   II only
(C)   I and II only
(D)   I and III only
(E)   I, II, and III

Algebra Ratio and Proportion

Equation I is true:

$\dfrac{x}{y} = \dfrac{c}{d}$ given

$\dfrac{y}{x} = \dfrac{d}{c}$ take reciprocals

$\dfrac{d}{c} = \dfrac{b}{a}$ given

$\dfrac{y}{x} = \dfrac{b}{a}$ use last two equations

Equation II is true:

$\dfrac{y}{x} = \dfrac{b}{a}$ Equation I (shown true)

$y = \dfrac{bx}{a}$ multiply both sides by x

$\dfrac{y}{b} = \dfrac{x}{a}$ divide both sides by b

Equation III is false, since otherwise it would follow that:

$y = \dfrac{bx}{a}$ from above

$\dfrac{y}{a} = \dfrac{bx}{a^2}$ divide both sides by a

$\dfrac{x}{b} = \dfrac{bx}{a^2}$ use Equation III (assumed true)

$x = \dfrac{b^2 x}{a^2}$ multiply both sides by b

From this it follows that Equation III will hold only if $\dfrac{b^2}{a^2} = 1$, which can be false. For example, if $x = a = c = 1$ and $y = b = d = 2$ (a choice of values for which $\dfrac{x}{y} = \dfrac{c}{d}$ and $\dfrac{d}{c} = \dfrac{b}{a}$ are true), then $\dfrac{b^2}{a^2} \ne 1$ and Equation III is $\dfrac{2}{1} = \dfrac{1}{2}$, which is false.

The correct answer is C.

PS10391
113. If k is an integer and $(0.0025)(0.025)(0.00025) \times 10^k$ is an integer, what is the least possible value of k?

(A)   −12
(B)   −6
(C)   0
(D)   6
(E)   12

Arithmetic Properties of Numbers

Let $N = (0.0025)(0.025)(0.00025) \times 10^k$. Rewriting each of the decimals as an integer times a power of 10 gives $N = (25 \times 10^{-4})(25 \times 10^{-3})(25 \times 10^{-5}) \times 10^k = (25)^3 \times 10^{k-12}$. Since the units digit of $(25)^3$ is 5, it follows that if $k = 11$, then the tenths digit of N would be 5, and thus N would not be an integer; and if $k = 12$, then N would be $(25)^3 \times 10^0 = (25)^3$, which is an integer. Therefore, the least value of k such that N is an integer is 12.

The correct answer is E.

PS07325
114. If $a(a + 2) = 24$ and $b(b + 2) = 24$, where $a \neq b$, then $a + b =$

(A) −48

(B) −2

(C) 2

(D) 46

(E) 48

Algebra Second-Degree Equations

$a(a + 2) = 24$	given
$a^2 + 2a = 24$	use distributive property
$a^2 + 2a - 24 = 0$	subtract 24 from both sides
$(a + 6)(a - 4) = 0$	factor

So, $a + 6 = 0$, which means that $a = -6$, or $a - 4 = 0$, which means $a = 4$. The equation with the variable b has the same solutions, and so $b = -6$ or $b = 4$.

Since $a \neq b$, then $a = -6$ and $b = 4$, which means $a + b = -6 + 4 = -2$, or $a = 4$ and $b = -6$, which means that $a + b = 4 + (-6) = -2$

The correct answer is B.

PS68850.02
115. In the xy plane, the distance between the origin and the point $(4,5)$ is the same as the distance between which of the following two points?

(A) $(-3,2)$ and $(-7,8)$

(B) $(-2,1)$ and $(3,5)$

(C) $(-2,-4)$ and $(1,0)$

(D) $(3,2)$ and $(8,7)$

(E) $(4,1)$ and $(-1,-4)$

Geometry Simple Coordinate Geometry

Determine the pair of points for which the distance between them is the same as the distance between the origin and the point $(4,5)$.

First, the distance between the origin and the point $(4,5)$ is $\sqrt{(4-0)^2 + (5-0)^2} = \sqrt{16 + 25} = \sqrt{41}$. The distance between

A $(-3,2)$ and $(-7,8)$ is

$\sqrt{(-3-(-7))^2 + (2-8)^2} = \sqrt{16 + 36} \neq \sqrt{41}$

B $(-2,1)$ and $(3,5)$ is $\sqrt{(-2-3)^2 + (1-5)^2} = \sqrt{25 + 16} = \sqrt{41}$.

Since there is only one correct answer, no more calculations are necessary, but for completeness, the distance between

C $(-2,-4)$ and $(1,0)$ is $\sqrt{(-2-1)^2 + (-4-0)^2} = \sqrt{9 + 16} \neq \sqrt{41}$

D $(3,2)$ and $(8,7)$ is $\sqrt{(3-8)^2 + (2-7)^2} = \sqrt{25 + 25} \neq \sqrt{41}$

E $(4,1)$ and $(-1,-4)$ is $\sqrt{(4-(-1))^2 + (1-(-4))^2} = \sqrt{25 + 25} \neq \sqrt{41}$.

The correct answer is B.

PS05560
116. In a recent election, Ms. Robbins received 8,000 votes cast by independent voters, that is, voters not registered with a specific political party. She also received 10 percent of the votes cast by those voters registered with a political party. If N is the total number of votes cast in the election and 40 percent of the votes cast were cast by independent voters, which of the following represents the number of votes that Ms. Robbins received?

(A) $0.06N + 3,200$

(B) $0.1N + 7,200$

(C) $0.4N + 7,200$

(D) $0.1N + 8,000$

(E) $0.06N + 8,000$

Algebra Percents

If N represents the total number of votes cast and 40% of the votes cast were cast by independent voters, then 60% of the votes cast, or $0.6N$ votes, were cast by voters registered with a political party. Ms. Robbins received 10% of these, and so Ms. Robbins received $(0.10)(0.6N) = 0.06N$ votes cast by voters registered with a political party. Thus, Ms. Robbins received $0.06N$ votes cast by voters registered with a political party and 8,000 votes cast by independent voters, so she received $0.06N + 8,000$ votes in all.

The correct answer is E.

PS01080.02

117. The profit P, in dollars, for any given month at a certain company is defined by $P = I - C$, where I represents total income, in dollars, and C represents total costs, in dollars, for the month. For each of the first 4 months of the year, $C = I + 32{,}000$; and for each of the next 3 months, $I = C + 36{,}000$. If $I = C + 10{,}000$ for each of the 5 remaining months of the year, what was the company's total profit for the 12-month year?

(A) $10,000
(B) $30,000
(C) $40,000
(D) $50,000
(E) $70,000

Arithmetic Applied Problems

For each of the first 4 months, total costs exceeded total income by $32,000, and hence for each of 4 months total profit was –$32,000. Also, for each of the next 3 months, total income exceeded total costs by $36,000, and hence for each of 3 months total profit was $36,000. Finally, for each of the remaining 5 months, total income exceeded total costs by $10,000, and hence for each of 5 months total profit was $10,000. Therefore, the total profit for the 12-month year was 4(–$32,000) + 3($36,000) + 5($10,000) = $30,000.

Alternatively, the given equations can be easily manipulated to obtain the values of $I - C$ for each month, as shown below.

Given Equation	Value of $I - C$	Number of Months	Net Profit
$C = I + 32{,}000$	$I - C = -32{,}000$	4	–$128,000
$I = C + 36{,}000$	$I - C = 36{,}000$	3	$108,000
$I = C + 10{,}000$	$I - C = 10{,}000$	5	$50,000

Adding the values in the right-most column gives the total profit for the 12-month year: –$128,000 + $108,000 + $50,000 = $30,000.

The correct answer is B.

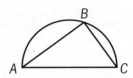

PS11308

118. In the figure shown, the triangle is inscribed in the semicircle. If the length of line segment AB is 8 and the length of line segment BC is 6, what is the length of arc ABC?

(A) 15π
(B) 12π
(C) 10π
(D) 7π
(E) 5π

Geometry Circles; Triangles

Because $\triangle ABC$ is inscribed in a semicircle, $\angle ABC$ is a right angle. Applying the Pythagorean theorem gives $(AB)^2 + (BC)^2 = (AC)^2$. Then substituting the given lengths, $8^2 + 6^2 = (AC)^2$, and so $(AC)^2 = 100$ and $AC = 10$. Thus, the diameter of the circle is 10, the circumference of the entire circle is 10π, and the length of arc ABC is half the circumference of the circle, or 5π.

The correct answer is E.

PS15517

119. A manufacturer makes and sells 2 products, P and Q. The revenue from the sale of each unit of P is $20.00 and the revenue from the sale of each unit of Q is $17.00. Last year the manufacturer sold twice as many units of Q as P. What was the manufacturer's average (arithmetic mean) revenue per unit sold of these 2 products last year?

(A) $28.50
(B) $27.00
(C) $19.00
(D) $18.50
(E) $18.00

Arithmetic Statistics

Let x represent the number of units of Product P the manufacturer sold last year. Then $2x$ represents the number of units of Product Q the manufacturer sold last year, and $x + 2x = 3x$ represents the total number of units of Products P and Q the manufacturer sold last year. The total revenue from the sale of Products P and Q was

$(20x) + \$(17(2x)) = \$(54x)$, so the average revenue per unit sold was $\dfrac{\$(54x)}{3x} = \$18$.

The correct answer is E.

PS11756

120. A worker carries jugs of liquid soap from a production line to a packing area, carrying 4 jugs per trip. If the jugs are packed into cartons that hold 7 jugs each, how many jugs are needed to fill the last partially filled carton after the worker has made 17 trips?

(A)   1
(B)   2
(C)   4
(D)   5
(E)   6

Arithmetic Remainders

Carrying 4 jugs per trip, the worker carries a total of $4(17) = 68$ jugs in 17 trips. At 7 jugs per carton, these jugs will completely fill 9 cartons with 5 jugs left over since $(9)(7) + 5 = 68$. To fill the 10th carton, $7 - 5 = 2$ jugs are needed.

The correct answer is B.

PS69400.02

121. Last year a state senate consisting of only Republican and Democrat members had 20 more Republican members than Democrat members. This year the senate has the same number of members as last year, but it has 2 fewer Republican members than last year. If this year the number of Republican members is $\dfrac{2}{3}$ the number of senate members, how many members does the senate have this year?

(A)   33
(B)   36
(C)   42
(D)   45
(E)   48

Algebra First-Degree Equations

Let D be the number of Democrat members last year. Then $D + 20$ is the number of Republican members last year and $(D + 20) - 2 = D + 18$ is the number of Republican members this year. Since the total number of members this year is the same as last year, it follows that there are 2

more Democrat members this year than last year, and so the number of Democrat members this year is $D + 2$ and the total number of members this year is $2D + 20$. Using the fact that this year the number of Republican members is $\dfrac{2}{3}$ the total number of members, the value of D can be found.

$D + 18 = \dfrac{2}{3}(2D + 20)$	given
$3(D + 18) = 2(2D + 20)$	multiply both sides by 3
$3D + 54 = 4D + 40$	distributive law
$D = 14$	subtract both $3D$ and 40 from both sides

Therefore, the total number of members this year is $2D + 20 = 2(14) + 20 = 48$.

The correct answer is E.

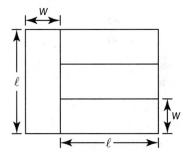

PS02820

122. The figure shown above represents a modern painting that consists of four differently colored rectangles, each of which has length ℓ and width w. If the area of the painting is 4,800 square inches, what is the width, in inches, of each of the four rectangles?

(A)   15
(B)   20
(C)   25
(D)   30
(E)   40

Geometry Area

From the figure, $\ell = 3w$, and the area of the painting is $\ell(w + \ell)$. Substituting $3w$ for ℓ gives $3w(w + 3w) = 3w(4w) = 12w^2$. It is given that the area is 4,800 square inches, so $12w^2 = 4{,}800$, $w^2 = 400$, and $w = 20$.

The correct answer is B.

PS44321.02
123. Sam has $800 in his account. He will deposit $1 in his account one week from now, $2 two weeks from now, and each week thereafter he will deposit an amount that is $1 greater than the amount that he deposited one week before. If there are no other transactions, how much money will Sam have in his account 50 weeks from now?

(A) $850
(B) $1,200
(C) $1,675
(D) $2,075
(E) $3,350

Arithmetic Series and Sequences

Determine the amount Sam will have in his account after 50 weeks if the account starts with $800 and Sam deposits $1 more each week than he deposited the week before.

Sam's deposits over the 50-week period will be $1 + 2 + 3 + \ldots + 48 + 49 + 50 = (1 + 50) + (2 + 49) + (3 + 48) + \ldots + (25 + 26) = (25)(51) = \$1,275$. Thus, after 50 weeks Sam will have $\$800 + \$1,275 = \$2,075$.

The correct answer is D.

PS30720.02
124. A certain state's milk production was 980 million pounds in 2007 and 2.7 billion pounds in 2014. Approximately how many more million gallons of milk did the state produce in 2014 than in 2007 ? (1 billion $= 10^9$ and 1 gallon = 8.6 pounds.)

(A)   100
(B)   200
(C)   1,700
(D)   8,200
(E)   14,800

Arithmetic Measurement Conversion

Using 2.7 billion = 2,700 million, the amount of increase in millions of gallons can be calculated as follows.

The amount of increase is:
$(2,700 - 980)$ million pounds = 1,720 million pounds

To convert pounds into gallons:

$$(1,720 \text{ million } \cancel{\text{pounds}})\left(\frac{1 \text{ gallon}}{8.6 \ \cancel{\text{pounds}}}\right)$$
$$= 200 \text{ million gallons}$$

The correct answer is B.

PS09737
125. Working simultaneously and independently at an identical constant rate, 4 machines of a certain type can produce a total of x units of product P in 6 days. How many of these machines, working simultaneously and independently at this constant rate, can produce a total of 3x units of product P in 4 days?

(A)   24
(B)   18
(C)   16
(D)   12
(E)   8

Algebra Applied Problems

Define a *machine day* as 1 machine working for 1 day. Then, 4 machines each working 6 days is equivalent to $(4)(6) = 24$ machine days. Thus, x units of product P were produced in 24 machine days, and $3x$ units of product P will require $(3)(24) = 72$ machine days, which is equivalent to $\frac{72}{4} = 18$ machines working independently and simultaneously for 4 days.

The correct answer is B.

PS01622
126. The symbol Δ denotes one of the four arithmetic operations: addition, subtraction, multiplication, or division. If $6 \Delta 3 \leq 3$, which of the following must be true?

I. $2 \Delta 2 = 0$
II. $2 \Delta 2 = 1$
III. $4 \Delta 2 = 2$

(A)   I only
(B)   II only
(C)   III only
(D)   I and II only
(E)   I, II, and III

Arithmetic Operations with Integers

If Δ represents addition, subtraction, multiplication, or division, then $6 \Delta 3$ is equal to either $6 + 3 = 9$, or $6 - 3 = 3$, or $6 \times 3 = 18$, or $6 \div 3 = 2$. Since it is given that $6 \, \Delta \, 3 \leq 3$, Δ represents either subtraction or division.

Statement I is true for subtraction since $2 - 2 = 0$ but not true for division since $2 \div 2 = 1$.

Statement II is not true for subtraction since $2 - 2 = 0$ but is true for division since $2 \div 2 = 1$.

Statement III is true for subtraction since $4 - 2 = 2$ and is true for division since $4 \div 2 = 2$. Therefore, only Statement III must be true.

The correct answer is C.

PS04448

127. If $mn \neq 0$ and 25 percent of n equals $37\frac{1}{2}$ percent of m, what is the value of $\dfrac{12n}{m}$?

   (A)   18

   (B) $\dfrac{32}{3}$

   (C)   8

   (D)   3

   (E) $\dfrac{9}{8}$

Algebra Percents; First-Degree Equations

It is given that $(25\%)n = (37.5\%)m$, or $0.25n = 0.375m$. The value of $\dfrac{12n}{m}$ can be found by first finding the value of $\dfrac{n}{m}$ and then multiplying the result by 12. Doing this gives $\dfrac{12n}{m} = \left(\dfrac{0.375}{0.25}\right)(12) = 18$. Alternatively, the numbers involved allow for a series of simple equation transformations to be carried out, such as the following:

$0.25n = 0.375m$	given
$25n = 37.5m$	multiply both sides by 100
$50n = 75m$	multiply both sides by 2
$2n = 3m$	divide both sides by 25
$12n = 18m$	multiply both sides by 6
$\dfrac{12n}{m} = 18$	divide both sides by m

The correct answer is A.

PS02555

128. Last year Joe grew 1 inch and Sally grew 200 percent more than Joe grew. How many inches did Sally grow last year?

   (A)   0

   (B)   1

   (C)   2

   (D)   3

   (E)   4

Arithmetic Percents

Joe grew 1 inch last year and Sally grew 200 percent more than Joe grew, so Sally grew 1 inch plus 200 percent of 1 inch or $1 + 2(1) = 3$ inches.

The correct answer is D.

Technique	Percent of Consumers
Television ads	35%
Coupons	22%
Store displays	18%
Samples	15%

PS10307

129. The table shows partial results of a survey in which consumers were asked to indicate which one of six promotional techniques most influenced their decision to buy a new food product. Of those consumers who indicated one of the four techniques listed, what fraction indicated either coupons or store displays?

   (A) $\dfrac{2}{7}$

   (B) $\dfrac{1}{3}$

   (C) $\dfrac{2}{5}$

   (D) $\dfrac{4}{9}$

   (E) $\dfrac{1}{2}$

Arithmetic Percents; Ratio and Proportion

Let T be the total number of consumers who were asked. Then the table shows $35\% + 22\% + 18\% + 15\% = 90\%$ of this total, or

$0.9T$ consumers. Also, the number of consumers who indicated either coupons or store displays was $0.22T + 0.18T = 0.4T$. Therefore, the number of consumers who indicated either coupons or store displays divided by the number of consumers shown in the table is $\dfrac{0.4T}{0.9T} = \dfrac{4}{9}$.

The correct answer is D.

PS36090.02

130. If 65 percent of a certain firm's employees are full-time and if there are 5,100 more full-time employees than part-time employees, how many employees does the firm have?

(A)   8,250
(B)   10,200
(C)   11,050
(D)   16,500
(E)   17,000

Algebra Simultaneous Equations

Let T represent the total number of employees the firm has; F, the number of full-time employees; and P, the number of part-time employees. Since 65 percent of the firm's employees are full-time, it follows that 35 percent are part-time. Thus, $F = 0.65T$ and $P = 0.35T$. However, $F = P + 5,100$, so $0.65T = 0.35T + 5,100$, so $0.30T = 5,100$, and $T = \dfrac{5,100}{0.30} = 17,000$.

The correct answer is E.

PS09708

131. The cost C, in dollars, to remove p percent of a certain pollutant from a pond is estimated by using the formula $C = \dfrac{100,000p}{100 - p}$. According to this estimate, how much more would it cost to remove 90 percent of the pollutant from the pond than it would cost to remove 80 percent of the pollutant?

(A) $500,000
(B) $100,000
(C) $50,000
(D) $10,000
(E) $5,000

Algebra; Arithmetic Simplifying Algebraic Expressions; Operations on Rational Numbers

Removing 90% of the pollutant from the pond would cost $\dfrac{(100,000)(90)}{100 - 90} = \dfrac{9,000,000}{10} = 900,000$ dollars, and removing 80% of the pollutant would cost $\dfrac{(100,000)(80)}{100 - 80} = \dfrac{8,000,000}{20} = 400,000$ dollars. The difference is, then, $\$900,000 - \$400,000 = \$500,000$.

The correct answer is A.

PS11121

132. If $xy \neq 0$ and $x^2y^2 - xy = 6$, which of the following could be y in terms of x?

I. $\dfrac{1}{2x}$

II. $\dfrac{2}{x}$

III. $\dfrac{3}{x}$

(A)   I only
(B)   II only
(C)   I and II
(D)   I and III
(E)   II and III

Algebra Second-Degree Equations

$$x^2y^2 - xy = 6 \quad \text{given}$$
$$x^2y^2 - xy - 6 = 0 \quad \text{subtract 6 from both sides}$$
$$(xy + 2)(xy - 3) = 0 \quad \text{factor}$$

So, $xy + 2 = 0$, which means $xy = -2$ and $y = -\dfrac{2}{x}$, or $xy - 3 = 0$, which means that $xy = 3$ and $y = \dfrac{3}{x}$. Thus, y in terms of x could be given by the expressions in II or III.

The correct answer is E.

PS00633

133. $\sqrt{4.8 \times 10^9}$ is closest in value to

(A)   2,200
(B)   70,000
(C)   220,000
(D)   7,000,000
(E)   22,000,000

Arithmetic Operations on Radical Expressions

$$\sqrt{4.8} \times \sqrt{10^9} = \sqrt{48 \times 10^8} \quad \text{substitute } 48 \times 10^8$$
$$\text{for } 4.8 \times 10^9$$

$$= \sqrt{48} \times \sqrt{10^8} \quad \sqrt{ab} = \sqrt{a} \times \sqrt{b}$$

$$\approx \sqrt{49} \times \sqrt{10^8} \quad 49 \approx 48$$

and then

$$\sqrt{49} \times \sqrt{10^8} = 7 \times 10^4 \quad \sqrt{49} = 7, \ \sqrt{10^8} = \sqrt{(10^4)^2} = 10^4$$

$$= 70,000$$

The correct answer is B.

PS21260.02

134. In a certain high school, 80 percent of the seniors are taking calculus, and 60 percent of the seniors who are taking calculus are also taking physics. If 10 percent of the seniors are taking neither calculus nor physics, what percent of the seniors are taking physics?

(A)   40%
(B)   42%
(C)   48%
(D)   58%
(E)   80%

Arithmetic Sets

Determine what percent of the seniors at a certain high school are taking physics.

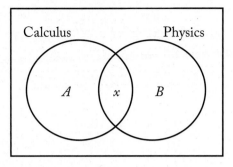

Consider the Venn diagram above, where A represents the percent of the seniors who are taking calculus only, B represents the percent of the seniors who are taking physics only, and x is the percent of the seniors who are taking both calculus and physics. As stated, 80 percent of the seniors are taking calculus, so $A + x = 0.8$, and 60 percent of the seniors taking calculus are taking physics, so $x = (0.8)(0.6) = 0.48$. Also, $A + x + B = 0.9$ since 10 percent of the seniors are taking neither calculus nor physics. It follows that $B = 0.9 - (A + x) = 0.9 - 0.8 = 0.1$. Therefore, the percent of the seniors who are taking physics is given by $B + x = 0.1 + 0.48 = 0.58$ or 58 percent.

The correct answer is D.

PS81711.02

135. If the units digit of $\dfrac{5,610.37}{10^k}$ is 6, what is the value of k?

(A)   3
(B)   2
(C)   1
(D)   −1
(E)   −2

Arithmetic Exponents

As shown in the table below, the units digit of $\dfrac{5,610.37}{10^k}$ is 6 when $k = 2$.

$$\frac{5,610.37}{10^{-2}} = \frac{5,610.37}{0.01} = 561,037$$

$$\frac{5,610.37}{10^{-1}} = \frac{5,610.37}{0.1} = 56,103.7$$

$$\frac{5,610.37}{10^0} = \frac{5,610.37}{1} = 5,610.37$$

$$\frac{5,610.37}{10^1} = \frac{5,610.37}{10} = 56\mathbf{1}.037$$

$$\frac{5,610.37}{10^2} = \frac{5,610.37}{100} = 5\mathbf{6}.1037$$

$$\frac{5,610.37}{10^3} = \frac{5,610.37}{1,000} = \mathbf{5}.61037$$

The correct answer is B.

PS08865

136. Three printing presses, R, S, and T, working together at their respective constant rates, can do a certain printing job in 4 hours. S and T, working together at their respective constant rates, can do the same job in 5 hours. How many hours would it take R, working alone at its constant rate, to do the same job?

(A)   8
(B)   10
(C)   12
(D)   15
(E)   20

Algebra Applied Problems

Let r be the portion of the job that printing press R, working alone, completes in 1 hour; and let s and t be the corresponding portions, respectively, for printing press S and printing press T. From the given information, it follows that $r + s + t = \frac{1}{4}$ and $s + t = \frac{1}{5}$. Subtracting these two equations gives $r = \frac{1}{4} - \frac{1}{5} = \frac{1}{20}$. It follows that printing press R, working alone, will complete $\frac{1}{20}$ of the job in 1 hour, and therefore printing press R, working alone, will complete the job in 20 hours.

The correct answer is E.

PS51950.02

137.

Results of a Poll

Company	Number Who Own Stock in the Company
AT&T	30
IBM	48
GM	54
FORD	75
US Air	83

In a poll, 200 subscribers to *Financial Magazine X* indicated which of five specific companies they own stock in. The results are shown in the table above. If 15 of the 200 own stock in both IBM and AT&T, how many of those polled own stock in neither company?

(A)   63
(B)   93
(C)   107
(D)   122
(E)   137

Arithmetic Sets; Interpretation of Tables

Since 48 of the 200 subscribers polled own stock in IBM and 15 of these 48 subscribers also own stock in AT&T, it follows that $48 - 15 = 33$ subscribers own stock in IBM but not in AT&T, as shown in the Venn diagram below. Similarly, $30 - 15 = 15$ of the 200 subscribers own stock in AT&T but not in IBM. Therefore, if n is the number of those polled who do not own stock in either IBM or AT&T, then $33 + 15 + 15 + n = 200$, or $n = 137$.

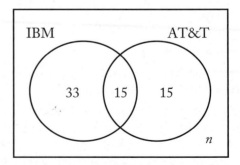

The correct answer is E.

PS07112

138. For a party, three solid cheese balls with diameters of 2 inches, 4 inches, and 6 inches, respectively, were combined to form a single cheese ball. What was the approximate diameter, in inches, of the new cheese ball? (The volume of a sphere is $\frac{4}{3}\pi r^3$, where r is the radius.)

(A) 12

(B) 16

(C) $\sqrt[3]{16}$

(D) $3\sqrt[3]{8}$

(E) $2\sqrt[3]{36}$

Geometry Volume

Since the diameters of the cheese balls are given as 2 inches, 4 inches, and 6 inches, the radii of the cheese balls are 1 inch, 2 inches, and 3 inches, respectively. Using $V = \frac{4}{3}\pi r^3$, the combined volume of the 3 cheese balls is $\frac{4}{3}\pi\left(1^3 + 2^3 + 3^3\right)$ or $\frac{4}{3}\pi(36)$ cubic inches.

Thus, if R represents the radius of the new cheese ball, then the volume of the new cheese ball is $\frac{4}{3}\pi R^3 = \frac{4}{3}\pi(36)$ and $R^3 = 36$, from which it follows that $R = \sqrt[3]{36}$ inches. Therefore, the diameter of the new cheese ball is $2R = 2\sqrt[3]{36}$ inches.

The correct answer is E.

PS02325

139. The sum of all the integers k such that $-26 < k < 24$ is

(A)   0

(B)   −2

(C) −25

(D) −49

(E) −51

Arithmetic Operations on Integers

In the sum of all integers k such that $-26 < k < 24$, the positive integers from 1 through 23 can be paired with the negative integers from −1 through −23. The sum of these pairs is 0 because $a + (-a) = 0$ for all integers a. Therefore, the sum of all integers k such that $-26 < k < 24$ is $-25 + (-24) + (23)(0) = -49$.

The correct answer is D.

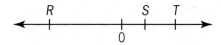

PS08399

140. The number line shown contains three points R, S, and T, whose coordinates have absolute values r, s, and t, respectively. Which of the following equals the average (arithmetic mean) of the coordinates of the points R, S, and T?

(A) s

(B) $s + t - r$

(C) $\dfrac{r - s - t}{3}$

(D) $\dfrac{r + s + t}{3}$

(E) $\dfrac{s + t - r}{3}$

Arithmetic Absolute Value; Number Line

Because point R is to the left of 0 on the number line, the coordinate of R is negative. It is given that r is the absolute value of the coordinate of R and so the coordinate of R is $-r$. Because points S and T are to the right of 0 on the number line, their coordinates are positive. It is given that s and t are the absolute values of the coordinates of S and T, and so the coordinates of S and T are s and t. The arithmetic mean of the coordinates of R, S, and T is $\dfrac{s + t - r}{3}$.

The correct answer is E.

PS94530.02

141. Tanks A and B are each in the shape of a right circular cylinder. The interior of Tank A has a height of 10 meters and a circumference of 8 meters, and the interior of Tank B has a height of 8 meters and a circumference of 10 meters. The capacity of Tank A is what percent of the capacity of Tank B?

(A) 75%

(B) 80%

(C) 100%

(D) 120%

(E) 125%

Geometry Volume

The interior circumference of Tank A is 8 meters, so $8 = 2\pi r$, where r is the interior radius of Tank A. It follows that $r = \dfrac{4}{\pi}$ and the capacity of Tank A is $\pi\left(\dfrac{4}{\pi}\right)^2(10) = \dfrac{160}{\pi}$.

The interior circumference of Tank B is 10 meters, so $10 = 2\pi R$, where R is the interior radius of Tank B. It follows that $R = \dfrac{5}{\pi}$ and the capacity of Tank B is $\pi\left(\dfrac{5}{\pi}\right)^2 (8) = \dfrac{200}{\pi}$. Thus,

$$\frac{\text{capacity of Tank A}}{\text{capacity of Tank B}} = \frac{\dfrac{160}{\pi}}{\dfrac{200}{\pi}} = \frac{4}{5} \text{ or } 80 \text{ percent.}$$

The correct answer is B.

PS05962

142. Mark and Ann together were allocated n boxes of cookies to sell for a club project. Mark sold 10 boxes less than n and Ann sold 2 boxes less than n. If Mark and Ann have each sold at least one box of cookies, but together they have sold less than n boxes, what is the value of n?

(A) 11
(B) 12
(C) 13
(D) 14
(E) 15

Algebra Inequalities

Mark sold $n - 10$ boxes and Ann sold $n - 2$ boxes. Because each person sold at least one box, it follows that $n - 10 \geq 1$ and $n - 2 \geq 1$, which implies that $n \geq 11$. On the other hand, together they sold less than n boxes, so $(n - 10) + (n - 2) < n$, which implies that $n < 12$. Therefore, n is an integer such that $n \geq 11$ and $n < 12$, which implies that $n = 11$.

The correct answer is A.

PS07601.02

143.

$$\begin{array}{r} 3P5 \\ + 4QR \\ \hline 8S4 \end{array}$$

In the correctly worked addition problem shown, P, Q, R, and S are digits. If $Q = 2P$, which of the following could be the value of S?

(A) 3
(B) 4
(C) 5
(D) 7
(E) 9

Arithmetic Place Value

Step 1: Analysis of the units column.

By considering the sum of the unit digits, $5 + R = 4$ or $5 + R = 14$. Since $R \geq 0$, we have $5 + R \geq 5$, and thus $5 + R = 4$ is not possible. Therefore, $5 + R = 14$. It follows that $R = 9$ and 1 is carried to the tens column.

Step 2: Analysis of the tens and hundreds columns.

Since $3 + 4 = 7$ and the hundreds digit of $8S4$ is 8, it follows that 1 must have been carried from the tens column to the hundreds column. Therefore, the sum of the tens digits must be $S + 10$, and hence $1 + P + Q = S + 10$, where the 1 was carried from the units column.

Step 3: Apply the assumption $Q = 2P$ to rule out answer choices B, C, and D.

Substituting $2P$ for Q in the equation $1 + P + Q = S + 10$ gives $1 + P + 2P = S + 10$, which can be rewritten as $S = 3P - 9 = 3(P - 3)$. This shows that S is divisible by 3, and therefore, answer choices B, C, and D can NOT be correct.

Step 4: Show that $S = 9$ is not possible.

If $S = 9$, then we have $9 = 3(P - 3)$. Solving this equation gives $P = 6$. However, from $Q = 2P$, it follows that $Q = 12$, which is not a digit. Therefore, $S = 9$ is not possible and answer choice E is NOT correct.

The only possibility remaining is $S = 3$. Although it is not necessary to verify that $S = 3$ is consistent, one can show that $S = 3$ leads to the following for the sum:

$$\begin{array}{r} 345 \\ + \ 489 \\ \hline 834 \end{array}$$

The correct answer is A.

PS04089

144. A certain high school has 5,000 students. Of these students, x are taking music, y are taking art, and z are taking both music and art. How many students are taking neither music nor art?

(A)   5,000 – z
(B)   5,000 – x – y
(C)   5,000 – x + z
(D)   5,000 – x – y – z
(E)   5,000 – x – y + z

Algebra Sets

Since x students are taking music, y students are taking art, and z students are taking both music and art, the number of students taking only music is $x - z$, and the number of students taking only art is $y - z$, as illustrated by the following Venn diagram.

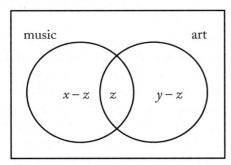

Therefore, the number of students taking neither music nor art is
$5,000 - [(x - z) + z + (y - z)] = 5,000 - x - y + z.$

The correct answer is E.

PS06133

145. Each person who attended a company meeting was either a stockholder in the company, an employee of the company, or both. If 62 percent of those who attended the meeting were stockholders and 47 percent were employees, what percent were stockholders who were <u>not</u> employees?

(A)   34%
(B)   38%
(C)   45%
(D)   53%
(E)   62%

Arithmetic Sets

Let M represent the number of meeting attendees. Then, since 62% of M or $0.62M$ were

stockholders and 47% of M or $0.47M$ were employees, it follows that $0.62M + 0.47M = 1.09M$ were either stockholders, employees, or both. Since $1.09M$ exceeds M, the excess $1.09M - M = 0.09M$ must be the number of attendees who were both stockholders and employees, leaving the rest $0.62M - 0.09M = 0.53M$, or 53%, of the meeting attendees to be stockholders but not employees.

The correct answer is D.

Accounts	Amount Budgeted	Amount Spent
Payroll	$110,000	$117,000
Taxes	40,000	42,000
Insurance	2,500	2,340

PS08441

146. The table shows the amount budgeted and the amount spent for each of three accounts in a certain company. For which of these accounts did the amount spent differ from the amount budgeted by more than 6 percent of the amount budgeted?

(A)   Payroll only
(B)   Taxes only
(C)   Insurance only
(D)   Payroll and Insurance
(E)   Taxes and Insurance

Arithmetic Percents

For Payroll, 6% of the budgeted amount is $(0.06)(\$110,000) = \$6,600$. Since $\$117,000 - \$110,000 = \$7,000 > \$6,600$, the amount spent differed from the amount budgeted by more than 6%.

For Taxes, 6% of the budgeted amount is $(0.06)(\$40,000) = \$2,400$. Since $\$42,000 - \$40,000 = \$2,000 < \$2,400$, the amount spent did not differ from the amount budgeted by more than 6%.

For Insurance, 6% of the budgeted amount is $(0.06)(\$2,500) = \$150$. Since $\$2,500 - \$2,340 = \$160 > \$150$, the amount spent differed from the amount budgeted by more than 6%.

Thus, the amount spent differed from the amount budgeted by more than 6% for Payroll and Insurance.

The correct answer is D.

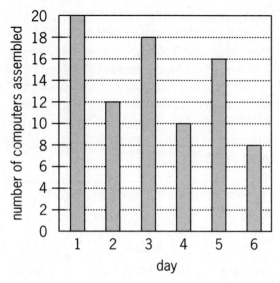

PS15111

147. The graph shows the number of computers assembled during each of 6 consecutive days. From what day to the next day was the percent change in the number of computers assembled the greatest in magnitude?

(A) From Day 1 to Day 2
(B) From Day 2 to Day 3
(C) From Day 3 to Day 4
(D) From Day 4 to Day 5
(E) From Day 5 to Day 6

Arithmetic Percents

The following table shows the percent change from each day to the next and the magnitude of the percent change.

PS02704

148. If $n = 20! + 17$, then n is divisible by which of the following?

I.   15
II. 17
III. 19

(A) None
(B) I only
(C) II only
(D) I and II
(E) II and III

Arithmetic Properties of Numbers

Because 20! is the product of all integers from 1 through 20, it follows that 20! is divisible by each integer from 1 through 20. In particular, 20! is divisible by each of the integers 15, 17, and 19. Since 20! and 17 are both divisible by 17, their sum is divisible by 17, and hence the correct answer will include II. If n were divisible by 15, then $n - 20!$ would be divisible by 15. But, $n - 20! = 17$ and 17 is not divisible by 15. Therefore, the correct answer does not include I. If n were divisible by 19, then $n - 20!$ would be divisible by 19. But, $n - 20! = 17$ and 17 is not divisible by 19. Therefore, the correct answer does not include III.

The correct answer is C.

Time Period	Percent Change	Magnitude of Percent Change
From Day 1 to Day 2	$\left(\dfrac{12-20}{20} \times 100\right)\% = \left(-\dfrac{8}{20} \times 100\right)\% = -40\%$	40
From Day 2 to Day 3	$\left(\dfrac{18-12}{12} \times 100\right)\% = \left(\dfrac{6}{12} \times 100\right)\% = 50\%$	50
From Day 3 to Day 4	$\left(\dfrac{10-18}{18} \times 100\right)\% = \left(-\dfrac{8}{18} \times 100\right)\% \approx -44\%$	44
From Day 4 to Day 5	$\left(\dfrac{16-10}{10} \times 100\right)\% = \left(\dfrac{6}{10} \times 100\right)\% = 60\%$	60
From Day 5 to Day 6	$\left(\dfrac{8-16}{16} \times 100\right)\% = \left(-\dfrac{8}{16} \times 100\right)\% = -50\%$	50

The correct answer is D.

PS39811.02
149. Exchange Rates in a Particular Year

$$\$1 = 5.3 \text{ francs}$$
$$\$1 = 1.6 \text{ marks}$$

An American dealer bought a table in Germany for 480 marks and sold the same table in France for 2,385 francs. What was the dealer's gross profit on the two transactions in dollars?

(A) $0
(B) $50
(C) $100
(D) $150
(E) $200

Arithmetic Measurement Conversion

Given that $1 = 1.6 marks, it follows that $\frac{\$1}{1.6} = 1$ mark and 480 marks $= 480 \left(\frac{\$1}{1.6} \right) =$ $300. Similarly, given that $1 = 5.3 francs, it follows that $\frac{\$1}{5.3} = 1$ franc and 2,385 francs $= 2,385 \left(\frac{\$1}{5.3} \right) = \$450$. The gross profit on the two transactions is $450 − $300 = $150.

The correct answer is D.

PS41450.02
150. One inch represents 20 miles on Map K and one inch represents 30 miles on Map L. An area of 3 square inches represents how many more square miles on Map L than on Map K ?

(A) 30
(B) 400
(C) 500
(D) 900
(E) 1,500

Arithmetic Measurement Conversion

On Map K, 1 square inch represents $20^2 = 400$ square miles, and hence 3 square inches represents $3(400) = 1,200$ square miles. On Map L, 1 square inch represents $30^2 = 900$ square miles, and hence 3 square inches represents $3(900) = 2,700$ square miles. Therefore, an area of 3 square inches on Map L represents $2,700 − 1,200 = 1,500$ square miles more than 3 square inches on Map K.

The correct answer is E.

PS02600
151. The product of two negative numbers is 160. If the lesser of the two numbers is 4 less than twice the greater, what is the greater number?

(A) −20
(B) −16
(C) −10
(D) −8
(E) −4

Algebra Second-Degree Equations

Let x and y be the two numbers, where x is the lesser of the two numbers and y is the number desired. From the given information it follows that $xy = 160$ and $x = 2y − 4$, from which it follows that $(2y − 4)y = 160$. Dividing both sides of the last equation by 2 gives $(y − 2)y = 80$. Thus, 80 is to be written as a product of two negative numbers, one that is 2 less than the other. Trying simple factorizations of 80 quickly leads to the value of y: $(−40)(−2) = 80$, $(−20)(−4) = 80$, $(−10)(−8) = 80$. Therefore, $y = −8$. Note that because −8 is one of the answer choices, it is not necessary to ensure there are no other negative solutions to the equation $(y − 2)y = 80$.

Alternatively, $(y − 2)y = 80$ can be written as $y^2 − 2y − 80 = 0$. Factoring the left side gives $(y + 8)(y − 10) = 0$, and $y = −8$ is the only negative solution.

The correct answer is D.

PS10546
152. According to a certain estimate, the depth $N(t)$, in centimeters, of the water in a certain tank at t hours past 2:00 in the morning is given by $N(t) = −20(t − 5)^2 + 500$ for $0 \le t \le 10$. According to this estimate, at what time in the morning does the depth of the water in the tank reach its maximum?

(A) 5:30
(B) 7:00
(C) 7:30
(D) 8:00
(E) 9:00

Algebra Functions

When $t = 5$, the value of $−20(t − 5)^2 + 500$ is 500. For all values of t between 0 and 10, inclusive, except $t = 5$, the value of $-20(t - 5)^2$ is negative and $-20(t - 5)^2 + 500 < 500$. Therefore, the tank reaches its maximum depth 5 hours after 2:00 in the morning, which is 7:00 in the morning.

The correct answer is B.

PS50750.02

153. The sides of a square region, measured to the nearest centimeter, are 6 centimeters long. The least possible value of the actual area of the square region is

(A)   36.00 sq cm

(B)   35.00 sq cm

(C)   33.75 sq cm

(D)   30.25 sq cm

(E)   25.00 sq cm

Geometry Area

Determine the least possible area of a square region if, when measured to the nearest centimeter, the sides are 6 centimeters long.

Let s represent the length of the side of the square region. Then, $5.5 \le s < 6.5$. It follows that $(5.5)^2 \le s^2 < (6.5)^2$ or $30.25 \le s^2 < 42.25$, and the least possible value for the area of the region is 30.25 sq cm.

The correct answer is D.

PS04617

154. After driving to a riverfront parking lot, Bob plans to run south along the river, turn around, and return to the parking lot, running north along the same path. After running 3.25 miles south, he decides to run for only 50 minutes more. If Bob runs at a constant rate of 8 minutes per mile, how many miles farther south can he run and still be able to return to the parking lot in 50 minutes?

(A)   1.5

(B)   2.25

(C)   3.0

(D)   3.25

(E)   4.75

Algebra Applied Problems

After running 3.25 miles south, Bob has been running for $(3.25 \text{ miles})\left(8\dfrac{\text{minutes}}{\text{mile}}\right) = 26$ minutes. Thus, if t is the number of additional minutes that Bob can run south before turning around, then the number of minutes that Bob will run north, after turning around, will be $t + 26$. Since Bob will be running a total of 50 minutes after the initial 26 minutes of running, it follows that $t + (t + 26) = 50$, or $t = 12$. Therefore, Bob can run south an additional

$\dfrac{12 \text{ minutes}}{8\dfrac{\text{minutes}}{\text{mile}}} = 1.5$ miles before turning around.

The correct answer is A.

PS12577

155. Alex deposited x dollars into a new account that earned 8 percent annual interest, compounded annually. One year later Alex deposited an additional x dollars into the account. If there were no other transactions and if the account contained w dollars at the end of two years, which of the following expresses x in terms of w?

(A) $\dfrac{w}{1 + 1.08}$

(B) $\dfrac{w}{1.08 + 1.16}$

(C) $\dfrac{w}{1.16 + 1.24}$

(D) $\dfrac{w}{1.08 + (1.08)^2}$

(E) $\dfrac{w}{(1.08)^2 + (1.08)^3}$

Algebra Applied Problems

At the end of the first year, the value of Alex's initial investment was $x(1.08)$ dollars, and after he deposited an additional x dollars into the account, its value was $[x(1.08) + x]$ dollars. At the end of the second year, the value was w dollars, where $w = [x(1.08) + x](1.08) = x(1.08)^2 + x(1.08) = x[(1.08)^2 + 1.08]$. Thus, $x = \dfrac{w}{1.08 + (1.08)^2}$.

The correct answer is D.

PS05973
156. *M* is the sum of the reciprocals of the consecutive integers from 201 to 300, inclusive. Which of the following is true?

(A) $\dfrac{1}{3} < M < \dfrac{1}{2}$

(B) $\dfrac{1}{5} < M < \dfrac{1}{3}$

(C) $\dfrac{1}{7} < M < \dfrac{1}{5}$

(D) $\dfrac{1}{9} < M < \dfrac{1}{7}$

(E) $\dfrac{1}{12} < M < \dfrac{1}{9}$

Arithmetic Estimation

$M = \dfrac{1}{201} + \dfrac{1}{202} + \dfrac{1}{203} + \ldots + \dfrac{1}{298} + \dfrac{1}{299} + \dfrac{1}{300}$	Given
$> \dfrac{1}{300} + \dfrac{1}{300} + \dfrac{1}{300} + \ldots + \dfrac{1}{300} + \dfrac{1}{300} + \dfrac{1}{300}$	See Note 1 below

Note 1: 300 is greater than each of 201, 202, 203, ..., 298, and 299, so the reciprocal of 300 is less than the reciprocal of each of 201, 202, 203, ..., 298, and 299 and the sum in line 2 of the table above, $(100)\left(\dfrac{1}{300}\right) = \dfrac{1}{3}$, is less than the sum of line 1. Thus, $\dfrac{1}{3} < M$.

$M = \dfrac{1}{201} + \dfrac{1}{202} + \dfrac{1}{203} + \ldots + \dfrac{1}{298} + \dfrac{1}{299} + \dfrac{1}{300}$	Given
$< \dfrac{1}{200} + \dfrac{1}{200} + \dfrac{1}{200} + \ldots + \dfrac{1}{200} + \dfrac{1}{200} + \dfrac{1}{200}$	See Note 2 below

Note 2: 200 is less than each of 201, 202, 203, ..., 298, and 299, so the reciprocal of 200 is greater than the reciprocal of each of 201, 202, 203, ..., 298, and 299 and the sum in line 2 of the table above, $(100)\left(\dfrac{1}{200}\right) = \dfrac{1}{2}$, is greater than the sum of line 1. Thus, $\dfrac{1}{2} > M$ or $M < \dfrac{1}{2}$. Combining the results $\dfrac{1}{3} < M$ and $M < \dfrac{1}{2}$ gives $\dfrac{1}{3} < M < \dfrac{1}{2}$.

The correct answer is A.

PS00428
157. Working simultaneously at their respective constant rates, Machines *A* and *B* produce 800 nails in *x* hours. Working alone at its constant rate, Machine *A* produces 800 nails in *y* hours. In terms of *x* and *y*, how many hours does it take Machine *B*, working alone at its constant rate, to produce 800 nails?

(A) $\dfrac{x}{x+y}$

(B) $\dfrac{y}{x+y}$

(C) $\dfrac{xy}{x+y}$

(D) $\dfrac{xy}{x-y}$

(E) $\dfrac{xy}{y-x}$

Algebra Applied Problems

Let R_A and R_B be the constant rates, in nails per hour, at which Machines A and B work, respectively. Then it follows from the given information that $R_A + R_B = \dfrac{800}{x}$ and $R_A = \dfrac{800}{y}$.

Hence, $\dfrac{800}{y} + R_B = \dfrac{800}{x}$, or

$$R_B = \dfrac{800}{x} - \dfrac{800}{y} = 800\left(\dfrac{1}{x} - \dfrac{1}{y}\right) = 800\left(\dfrac{y-x}{xy}\right).$$

Therefore, the time, in hours, it would take Machine *B* to produce 800 nails is given by

$$\dfrac{800}{800\left(\dfrac{y-x}{xy}\right)} = \dfrac{xy}{y-x}.$$

The correct answer is E.

PS63210.02

158. Carol purchased one basket of fruit consisting of 4 apples and 2 oranges and another basket of fruit consisting of 3 apples and 5 oranges. Carol is to select one piece of fruit at random from each of the two baskets. What is the probability that one of the two pieces of fruit selected will be an apple and the other will be an orange?

(A) $\dfrac{1}{4}$

(B) $\dfrac{1}{2}$

(C) $\dfrac{1}{24}$

(D) $\dfrac{5}{24}$

(E) $\dfrac{13}{24}$

Arithmetic Probability

There are 6 pieces of fruit in the first basket and 8 pieces of fruit in the second basket. By the multiplication principle, the number of selections of a piece of fruit from the first basket and a piece of fruit from the second basket is $(6)(8) = 48$. Of these selections, $(4)(5) = 20$ are such that an apple is selected from the first basket and an orange is selected from the second basket, and $(2)(3) = 6$ are such that an orange is selected from the first basket and an apple is selected from the second basket. Therefore, there is a total of $20 + 6 = 26$ selections in which one apple is chosen and one orange is chosen, and hence the probability of such a selection is $\dfrac{26}{48} = \dfrac{13}{24}$.

Alternatively, the desired probability is the sum of the probabilities of two disjoint events. In the first event, an apple is selected from the first basket and an orange is selected from the second basket; the probability of this event is $\left(\dfrac{4}{6}\right)\left(\dfrac{5}{8}\right) = \dfrac{20}{48}$.

In the second event, an orange is selected from the first basket and an apple is selected from the second basket; the probability of this event is $\left(\dfrac{2}{6}\right)\left(\dfrac{3}{8}\right) = \dfrac{6}{48}$. Therefore, the desired probability is $\dfrac{20}{48} + \dfrac{6}{48} = \dfrac{26}{48} = \dfrac{13}{24}$.

The correct answer is E.

PS94421.02

159. Last year Brand X shoes were sold by dealers in 403 different regions worldwide, with an average (arithmetic mean) of 98 dealers per region. If last year these dealers sold an average of 2,488 pairs of Brand X shoes per dealer, which of the following is closest to the total number of pairs of Brand X shoes sold last year by the dealers worldwide?

(A) 10^4

(B) 10^5

(C) 10^6

(D) 10^7

(E) 10^8

Arithmetic Estimation; Exponents

Since the average number of dealers per region is 98, it follows that $\dfrac{\text{number of dealers}}{403} = 98$, and thus the number of dealers is $(98)(403)$. Also, since the average number of pairs sold per dealer is 2,488, it follows that $\dfrac{\text{number of pairs sold}}{(98)(403)} = 2{,}488$, and thus the number of pairs sold is $(98)(403)(2{,}488)$, which is approximately $(100)(400)(2500) = (10^2)(4 \times 10^2)(25 \times 10^2)$. Therefore, the total number of pairs sold is approximately $(4)(25) \times 10^{2+2+2} = 100 \times 10^6 = 10^8$.

The correct answer is E.

10, 4, 26, 16

PS08966

160. What is the median of the numbers shown?

(A) 10

(B) 13

(C) 14

(D) 15

(E) 16

Arithmetic Statistics

To determine the median of these 4 numbers, put the numbers in numerical order in a list and determine the average of the two middle values in the list:

4, **10**, **16**, 26

From this list it follows that the median is the average of 10 and 16, which is $\dfrac{10+16}{2} = 13$.

The correct answer is B.

	Number of Marbles in Each of Three Bags	Percent of Marbles in Each Bag That Are Blue (to the nearest tenth)
Bag P	37	10.8%
Bag Q	$\times$	66.7%
Bag R	32	50.0%

PS03823

161. If $\dfrac{1}{3}$ of the total number of marbles in the three bags listed in the table above are blue, how many marbles are there in bag Q?

(A) 5
(B) 9
(C) 12
(D) 23
(E) 46

Algebra Percents

What is the value of x, the number of marbles in bag Q? From the given information and rounded to the nearest integer, bag P has $(37)(0.108) = 4$ blue marbles, bag Q has $(x)(0.667) = \dfrac{2}{3}x$ blue marbles, and bag R has $(32)(0.5) = 16$ blue marbles. Therefore, the total number of blue marbles is equal to $4 + \dfrac{2}{3}x + 16 = 20 + \dfrac{2}{3}x$. It is given that $\dfrac{1}{3}$ of the total number of marbles are blue, so the total number of blue marbles is also equal to $\dfrac{1}{3}(37 + x + 32) = \dfrac{1}{3}x + 23$. It follows that $20 + \dfrac{2}{3}x = \dfrac{1}{3}x + 23$, or $\dfrac{1}{3}x = 3$, or $x = 9$.

The correct answer is B.

Age Category (in years)	Number of Employees
Less than 20	29
20–29	58
30–39	36
40–49	21
50–59	10
60–69	5
70 and over	2

PS11600

162. The table above gives the age categories of the 161 employees at Company X and the number of employees in each category. According to the table, if m is the median age, in years, of the employees at Company X, then m must satisfy which of the following?

(A) $20 \le m \le 29$
(B) $25 \le m \le 34$
(C) $30 \le m \le 39$
(D) $35 \le m \le 44$
(E) $40 \le m \le 49$

Arithmetic Statistics

The median of 161 ages is the 81st age when the ages are listed in order. Since 29 of the ages are less than 20, the median age must be greater than or equal to 20. Since 58 of the ages are between 20 and 29, a total of $29 + 58 = 87$ of the ages are less than or equal to 29, and thus the median age is less than or equal to 29. Therefore, the median age is greater than or equal to 20 and less than or equal to 29.

The correct answer is A.

PS70371.02

163. If k and n are positive integers such that $n > k$, then $k! + (n - k) \cdot (k - 1)!$ is equivalent to which of the following?

(A) $k \cdot n!$
(B) $k! \cdot n$
(C) $(n - k)!$
(D) $n \cdot (k + 1)!$
(E) $n \cdot (k - 1)!$

Algebra Simplifying Algebraic Expressions

$k! + (n-k) \cdot (k-1)!$ given

$k \cdot (k-1)! + (n-k) \cdot (k-1)!$ $k! = k \cdot (k-1)!$

$[k + (n-k)] \cdot (k-1)!$ factor out $(k-1)!$

$n \cdot (k-1)!$ combine like terms

The correct answer is E.

PS02749

164. Ron is 4 inches taller than Amy, and Barbara is 1 inch taller than Ron. If Barbara's height is 65 inches, what is the median height, in inches, of these three people?

(A)   60

(B)   61

(C)   62

(D)   63

(F)   64

Arithmetic Operations with Integers

Let R, A, and B be the heights, respectively and in inches, of Ron, Amy, and Barbara. It is given that $R = 4 + A$, $B = 1 + R$, and $B = 65$. Therefore, $R = B - 1 = 65 - 1 = 64$ and $A = R - 4 = 64 - 4 = 60$. From this it follows that the three heights, in inches, are 60, 64, and 65. The median of these three heights is 64.

The correct answer is E.

PS02777

165. If x and y are positive numbers such that $x + y = 1$, which of the following could be the value of $100x + 200y$?

I.   80

II.   140

III.   199

(A)   II only

(B)   III only

(C)   I and II

(D)   I and III

(E)   II and III

Algebra Simultaneous Equations; Inequalities

Since $x + y = 1$, then $y = 1 - x$ and $100x + 200y$ can be expressed as $100x + 200(1 - x) = 200 - 100x$. Test each value.

   I.   If $200 - 100x = 80$, then $x = \dfrac{200-80}{100} = 1.2$ and $y = 1 - 1.2 = -0.2$.

Since y must be positive, 80 cannot be a value of $100x + 200y$.

   II.   If $200 - 100x = 140$, then $x = \dfrac{200-140}{100} = 0.6$ and $y = 1 - 0.6 = 0.4$, so 140 can be a value of $100x + 200y$.

   III.   If $200 - 100x = 199$, then $x = \dfrac{200-199}{100} = 0.01$ and $y = 1 - 0.01 = 0.99$, so 199 can be a value of $100x + 200y$

The correct answer is E.

PS02017

166. If X is the hundredths digit in the decimal $0.1X$ and if Y is the thousandths digit in the decimal $0.02Y$, where X and Y are nonzero digits, which of the following is closest to the greatest possible value of $\dfrac{0.1x}{0.02y}$?

(A)   4

(B)   5

(C)   6

(D)   9

(E)   10

Arithmetic Operations with Decimals; Place Value

The greatest possible value of $\dfrac{0.1X}{0.02Y}$ will occur when $0.1X$ has the greatest possible value and $0.02Y$ has the least possible value. Since X and Y are nonzero digits, this means than X must be 9 and Y must be 1. The greatest possible value of $\dfrac{0.1X}{0.02Y}$ is then $\dfrac{0.19}{0.021} \approx 9.05$, which is closest to 9.

The correct answer is D.

PS28101.02

167. If each of the 12 teams participating in a certain tournament plays exactly one game with each of the other teams, how many games will be played?

(A)   144

(B)   132

(C)   66

(D)   33

(E)   23

Arithmetic Elementary Combinatorics

Since each of the 12 teams will play exactly one game with each of the other teams, the number of games that will be played is equal to the number of selections of 2 teams, without regard to order, from 12 teams. This is the number of combinations of 12 teams taken 2 at a time, which is equal to

$$\binom{12}{2} = \frac{12!}{2!(12-2)!} = \frac{(\cancel{10!})(11)(12)}{(2)(\cancel{10!})} = 66.$$

Alternatively, each of the 12 teams will play each of the 11 other teams. The product $(12)(11)$ counts each of the games twice since, for example, this product separately counts "Team A plays Team B" and "Team B plays Team A". Therefore, the number of games that will be played is $\dfrac{(12)(11)}{2} = 66$.

The correct answer is C.

Questions 168 to 262 - Difficulty: **Hard**

PS60231.02

168. If the length of a diagonal of a square is $2\sqrt{x}$, what is the area of the square in terms of x?

(A) $\sqrt{x}$

(B) $\sqrt{2x}$

(C) $2\sqrt{x}$

(D) x

(E) $2x$

Geometry Pythagorean Theorem; Rectangles

Let s be the length of a side of the square. Then the area of the square is s^2. By the Pythagorean theorem we have $s^2 + s^2 = (2\sqrt{x})^2$, or $2s^2 = 4x$. Therefore, the area of the square is $s^2 = 2x$.

The correct answer is E.

PS13724

169. Clarissa will create her summer reading list by randomly choosing 4 books from the 10 books approved for summer reading. She will list the books in the order in which they are chosen. How many different lists are possible?

(A)   6

(B)   40

(C)   210

(D)   5,040

(E)   151,200

Arithmetic Elementary Combinatorics

Any of the 10 books can be listed first. Any of the 9 books remaining after the first book is listed can be listed second. Any of the 8 books remaining after the first and second books are listed can be listed third. Any of the 7 books remaining after the first, second, and third books are listed can be listed fourth. By the multiplication principle, there are $(10)(9)(8)(7) = 5,040$ different lists possible.

The correct answer is D.

PS10982

170. If n is a positive integer and the product of all the integers from 1 to n, inclusive, is divisible by 990, what is the least possible value of n?

(A)   8

(B)   9

(C)   10

(D)   11

(E)   12

Arithmetic Properties of Numbers

For convenience, let N represent the product of all integers from 1 through n. Then, since N is divisible by 990, every prime factor of 990 must also be a factor of N. The prime factorization of 990 is $2 \times 3^2 \times 5 \times 11$, and therefore, 11 must be a factor of N. Then, the least possible value of N with factors of $2, 5, 3^2$, and 11 is $1 \times 2 \times 3 \times \cdots \times 11$, and the least possible value of n is 11.

The correct answer is D.

PS02111

171. The probability that event M will <u>not</u> occur is 0.8 and the probability that event R will <u>not</u> occur is 0.6. If events M and R cannot both occur, which of the following is the probability that either event M or event R will occur?

(A) $\dfrac{1}{5}$

(B) $\dfrac{2}{5}$

(C) $\dfrac{3}{5}$

(D) $\dfrac{4}{5}$

(E) $\dfrac{12}{25}$

Arithmetic Probability

Let $P(M)$ be the probability that event M will occur, let $P(R)$ be the probability that event R will occur, and let $P(M$ and $R)$ be the probability that events M and R both occur. Then the probability that either event M or event R will occur is $P(M) + P(R) - P(M$ and $R)$. From the given information, it follows that $P(M) = 1.0 - 0.8 = 0.2$, $P(R) = 1.0 - 0.6 = 0.4$, and $P(M$ and $R) = 0$. Therefore, the probability that either event M or event R will occur is

$0.2 + 0.4 - 0 = 0.6 = \dfrac{3}{5}$.

The correct answer is C.

PS16410

172. The total cost for Company X to produce a batch of tools is $10,000 plus $3 per tool. Each tool sells for $8. The gross profit earned from producing and selling these tools is the total income from sales minus the total production cost. If a batch of 20,000 tools is produced and sold, then Company X's gross profit per tool is

(A) $3.00
(B) $3.75
(C) $4.50
(D) $5.00
(E) $5.50

Arithmetic Applied Problems

The total cost to produce 20,000 tools is $10,000 + \$3(20,000) = \$70,000$. The revenue resulting from the sale of 20,000 tools is $\$8(20,000) = \$160,000$. The gross profit is $\$160,000 - \$70,000 = \$90,000$, and the gross profit per tool is $\dfrac{\$90,000}{20,000} = \$4.50$.

The correct answer is C.

PS07357

173. If Q is an odd number and the median of Q consecutive integers is 120, what is the largest of these integers?

(A) $\dfrac{Q-1}{2} + 120$

(B) $\dfrac{Q}{2} + 119$

(C) $\dfrac{Q}{2} + 120$

(D) $\dfrac{Q+119}{2}$

(E) $\dfrac{Q+120}{2}$

Arithmetic Statistics

For an odd number of data values, the median is the middle number. Thus, 120 is the middle number, and so half of the $Q - 1$ remaining values are at most 120 and the other half of the $Q - 1$ remaining values are at least 120. In particular, $\dfrac{Q-1}{2}$ data values lie to the right of 120 when the data values are listed in increasing order from left to right, and so the largest data value is $120 + \dfrac{Q-1}{2}$. Alternatively, it is evident that (B), (C), or (E) cannot be correct since these expressions do not have an integer value when Q is odd. For the list consisting of the single number 120 (i.e., if $Q = 1$), (D) fails because $\dfrac{Q+119}{2} = \dfrac{1+119}{2} = 60 \neq 120$ and (A) does not fail because $\dfrac{Q-1}{2} + 120 = \dfrac{1-1}{2} + 120 = 120$.

The correct answer is A.

PS02649

174. A ladder of a fire truck is elevated to an angle of 60° and extended to a length of 70 feet. If the base of the ladder is 7 feet above the ground, how many feet above the ground does the ladder reach?

(A) 35
(B) 42
(C) $35\sqrt{3}$
(D) $7 + 35\sqrt{3}$
(E) $7 + 42\sqrt{3}$

Geometry Triangles

The solution to this problem relies on the relationships of the side lengths of a 30°-60°-90° triangle, as shown in the figure below.

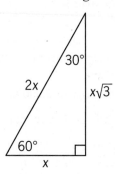

The figure below shows these relationships applied to the ladder on the fire truck. The ladder has length of 70 feet, so $70 = 2x$ and $x = 35$, as shown in the figure.

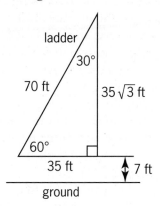

Therefore, the ladder reaches $7 + 35\sqrt{3}$ feet above the ground.

Tip: For more information on 30°– 60°– 90° triangles, please refer to 3.5.3.D section of the Math Review chapter.

The correct answer is D.

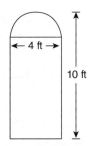

PS13827

175. The window in the figure above consists of a rectangle and a semicircle with dimensions as shown. What is the area, in square feet, of the window?

(A) $40 + 8\pi$

(B) $40 + 2\pi$

(C) $32 + 8\pi$

(D) $32 + 4\pi$

(E) $32 + 2\pi$

Geometry Area

The semicircle has a radius of 2 ft, and thus its area is $\frac{1}{2}\pi(2^2) = 2\pi$ ft^2. The rectangle has dimensions 4 ft by 8 ft, where $8 = 10 - 2$ is the full height of the window minus the radius of the semicircle, and thus has area $(4)(8) = 32$ ft^2. Therefore, in square feet, the area of the window is $32 + 2\pi$.

The correct answer is E.

PS00562

176. If there are fewer than 8 zeros between the decimal point and the first nonzero digit in the decimal expansion of $\left(\dfrac{t}{1,000}\right)^4$, which of the following numbers could be the value of t?

I.   3
II.   5
III. 9

(A)   None

(B)   I only

(C)   II only

(D)   III only

(E)   II and III

Arithmetic Properties of Numbers; Decimals

Since $\left(\dfrac{t}{1,000}\right)^4 = \left(t \times \dfrac{1}{1,000}\right)^4 = t^4 \times \left(\dfrac{1}{1,000}\right)^4 = t^4 \times \dfrac{1}{1,000^4}$ and $(1,000)^4 = (10^3)^4 = 10^{12}$, it follows that $\left(\dfrac{t}{1,000}\right)^4 = t^4 \times \dfrac{1}{10^{12}} = t^4 \times 10^{-12}$.

The following table illustrates the effect that multiplication by 10^{-1}, 10^{-2}, 10^{-3}, and 10^{-4} has on the placement of the decimal point of 52.7, a number chosen only for illustrative purposes.

multiplication by	resulting number	placement of decimal point
10^{-1}	5.27	1 place left of original
10^{-2}	0.527	2 places left of original
10^{-3}	0.0527	3 places left of original
10^{-4}	0.00527	4 places left of original

Therefore, the decimal point of $t^4 \times 10^{-12}$ is 12 positions to the left of the decimal point of t^4. Now consider the value of $t^4 \times 10^{-12}$ for the three given values of t.

t	t^4	$t^4 \times 10^{-12}$	# zeros after decimal point
3	81	0.000000000081	10
5	625	0.000000000625	9
9	6,561	0.000000006561	8

From the table above it follows that NONE of these values of t is such that $t^4 \times 10^{-12}$ has fewer than 8 zeros between the decimal point and the first nonzero digit.

The correct answer is A.

PS08280

177. A three-digit code for certain locks uses the digits 0, 1, 2, 3, 4, 5, 6, 7, 8, 9 according to the following constraints. The first digit cannot be 0 or 1, the second digit must be 0 or 1, and the second and third digits cannot both be 0 in the same code. How many different codes are possible?

(A) 144
(B) 152
(C) 160
(D) 168
(E) 176

Arithmetic Elementary Combinatorics

Since the first digit cannot be 0 or 1, there are 8 digits possible for the first digit. Since the second digit must be 0 or 1, there are 2 digits possible for the second digit. If there were no other restrictions, all 10 digits would be possible for the third digit, making the total number of possible codes $8 \times 2 \times 10 = 160$. But, the additional restriction that the second and third digits cannot both be 0 in the same code eliminates the 8 codes 2-0-0, 3-0-0, 4-0-0, 5-0-0, 6-0-0, 7-0-0, 8-0-0, and 9-0-0. Therefore, there are 160 − 8 = 152 possible codes.

The correct answer is B.

PS02903

178. Jackie has two solutions that are 2 percent sulfuric acid and 12 percent sulfuric acid by volume, respectively. If these solutions are mixed in appropriate quantities to produce 60 liters of a solution that is 5 percent sulfuric acid, approximately how many liters of the 2 percent solution will be required?

(A) 18
(B) 20
(C) 24
(D) 36
(E) 42

Algebra Simultaneous Equations

Let x represent the quantity of the 2% sulfuric acid solution in the mixture, from which it follows that the 2% sulfuric acid solution contributes $0.02x$ liters of sulfuric acid to the mixture. Let y represent the quantity of the 12% sulfuric acid solution in the mixture, from which it follows that the 12% sulfuric acid solution contributes $0.12y$ liters of sulfuric acid to the mixture. Since there are 60 liters of the mixture, $x + y = 60$. The quantity of sulfuric acid in the mixture, which is 5% sulfuric acid, is then $(0.05)(60) = 3$ liters. Therefore, $0.02x + 0.12y = 3$. Substituting $60 - x$ for y gives $0.02x + 0.12(60 - x) = 3$. Then,

$$0.02x + 0.12(60 - x) = 3 \quad \text{given}$$
$$0.02x + 7.2 - 0.12x = 3 \quad \text{use distributive property}$$
$$7.2 - 0.1x = 3 \quad \text{combine like terms}$$
$$-0.1x = -4.2 \quad \text{subtract 7.2 from both sides}$$
$$x = 42 \quad \text{divide both sides by } -0.1$$

The correct answer is E.

PS16259

179. If Jake loses 8 pounds, he will weigh twice as much as his sister. Together they now weigh 278 pounds. What is Jake's present weight, in pounds?

(A) 131
(B) 135
(C) 139
(D) 147
(E) 188

Algebra Systems of Equations

Let J represent Jake's weight and S represent his sister's weight. Then $J - 8 = 2S$ and $J + S = 278$. Solve the second equation for S and get $S = 278 - J$. Substituting the expression for S into the first equation gives

$$J - 8 = 2(278 - J)$$
$$J - 8 = 556 - 2J$$
$$J + 2J = 556 + 8$$
$$3J = 564$$
$$J = 188$$

The correct answer is E.

PS03768

180. For each student in a certain class, a teacher adjusted the student's test score using the formula $y = 0.8x + 20$, where x is the student's original test score and y is the student's adjusted test score. If the standard deviation of the original test scores of the students in the class was 20, what was the standard deviation of the adjusted test scores of the students in the class?

  (A)   12
  (B)   16
  (C)   28
  (D)   36
  (E)   40

Arithmetic Statistics

The solution to this problem relies on the statistical properties summarized in the following table:

Data Set Values	Mean	Standard Deviation
x	μ	σ
$ax + b$	$a\mu + b$	$a\sigma$

The standard deviation of the original test scores was 20. Therefore, when the teacher multiplied each student's score by 0.8 and then added 20, the standard deviation of the set of adjusted scores is $0.8(20) = 16$.

The correct answer is B.

PS01987

181. Last year 26 members of a certain club traveled to England, 26 members traveled to France, and 32 members traveled to Italy. Last year no members of the club traveled to both England and France, 6 members traveled to both England and Italy, and 11 members traveled to both France and Italy. How many members of the club traveled to at least one of these three countries last year?

  (A)   52
  (B)   67
  (C)   71
  (D)   73
  (E)   79

Arithmetic Applied Problems

The numbers in the following diagram represent the numbers of members of the club who traveled to the indicated countries, and these numbers can be determined as follows. Since no members traveled to both England and France, both regions that form the overlap of England and France are labeled with 0. It follows that none of the 6 members who traveled to both England and Italy traveled to France, and so the region corresponding to England and Italy only is labeled with 6. It also follows that none of the 11 members who traveled to both France and Italy traveled to England, and so the region corresponding to France and Italy only is labeled with 11. At this point it can be determined that $26 - 6 = 20$ members traveled to England only, $26 - 11 = 15$ members traveled to France only, and $32 - (6 + 11) = 15$ members traveled to Italy only.

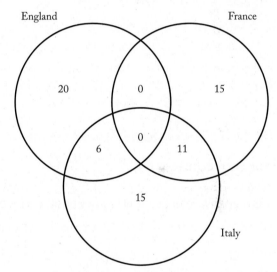

From the diagram it follows that $20 + 15 + 6 + 11 + 15 = 67$ members traveled to at least one of these three countries.

The correct answer is B.

PS16088

182. A store reported total sales of $385 million for February of this year. If the total sales for the same month last year was $320 million, approximately what was the percent increase in sales?

(A) 2%
(B) 17%
(C) 20%
(D) 65%
(E) 83%

Arithmetic Percents

The percent increase in sales from last year to this year is 100 times the quotient of the difference in sales for the two years divided by the sales last year. Thus, the percent increase is

$$\frac{385-320}{320} \times 100 = \frac{65}{320} \times 100$$

$$= \frac{13}{64} \times 100$$

$$\approx \frac{13}{65} \times 100$$

$$= \frac{1}{5} \times 100$$

$$= 20\%$$

The correct answer is C.

PS11065

183. When positive integer x is divided by positive integer y, the remainder is 9. If $\frac{x}{y} = 96.12$, what is the value of y?

(A) 96
(B) 75
(C) 48
(D) 25
(E) 12

Arithmetic Properties of Numbers

The remainder is 9 when x is divided by y, so $x = yq + 9$ for some positive integer q. Dividing both sides by y gives $\frac{x}{y} = q + \frac{9}{y}$.
But, $\frac{x}{y} = 96.12 = 96 + 0.12$. Equating the two expressions for $\frac{x}{y}$ gives $q + \frac{9}{y} = 96 + 0.12$.
Thus, $q = 96$ and $\frac{9}{y} = 0.12$.

$$9 = 0.12\,y$$

$$y = \frac{9}{0.12}$$

$$y = 75$$

The correct answer is B.

PS16802

184. If $x(2x+1) = 0$ and $\left(x+\frac{1}{2}\right)(2x-3) = 0$, then $x =$

(A) -3
(B) $-\frac{1}{2}$
(C) 0
(D) $\frac{1}{2}$
(E) $\frac{3}{2}$

Algebra Second-Degree Equations; Simultaneous Equations

Setting each factor equal to 0, it can be seen that the solution set to the first equation is $\left\{0, -\frac{1}{2}\right\}$ and the solution set to the second equation is $\left\{-\frac{1}{2}, \frac{3}{2}\right\}$. Therefore, $-\frac{1}{2}$ is the solution to both equations.

The correct answer is B.

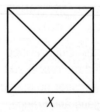
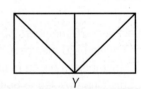

X   Y

PS08219

185. Figures X and Y above show how eight identical triangular pieces of cardboard were used to form a square and a rectangle, respectively. What is the ratio of the perimeter of X to the perimeter of Y?

(A) 2:3
(B) $\sqrt{2}$:2
(C) $2\sqrt{2}$:3
(D) 1:1
(E) $\sqrt{2}$:1

Geometry Perimeter

Because Figure X is a square and the diagonals of a square are the same length, are perpendicular, and bisect each other, it follows that each triangular piece is a $45°$–$45°$–$90°$ triangle. Thus, the length of each side of the square is $a\sqrt{2}$, and the perimeter is $4a\sqrt{2}$. The perimeter of the rectangle is $2(a + 2a) = 6a$. It follows that the ratio of the perimeter of the square to the perimeter of the rectangle is

$$\frac{4a\sqrt{2}}{6a} = \frac{2\sqrt{2}}{3}, \text{ or } 2\sqrt{2} : 3.$$

The correct answer is C.

PS04711

186. A certain experimental mathematics program was tried out in 2 classes in each of 32 elementary schools and involved 37 teachers. Each of the classes had 1 teacher and each of the teachers taught at least 1, but not more than 3, of the classes. If the number of teachers who taught 3 classes is n, then the least and greatest possible values of n, respectively, are

(A)   0 and 13

(B)   0 and 14

(C)   1 and 10

(D)   1 and 9

(E)   2 and 8

Algebra Simultaneous Equations; Inequalities

It is given that $2(32) = 64$ classes are taught by 37 teachers. Let k, m, and n be the number of teachers who taught, respectively, 1, 2, and 3 of the classes. Then $k + m + n = 37$ and $k + 2m + 3n = 64$. Subtracting these two equations gives $m + 2n = 64 - 37 = 27$, or $2n = 27 - m$, and therefore $2n \leq 27$. Because n is an integer, it follows that $n \leq 13$ and B cannot be the answer. Since $n = 0$ is possible, which can be seen by using $m = 27$ and $k = 10$ (obtained by solving $2n = 27 - m$ with $n = 0$, then by solving $k + m + n = 37$ with $n = 0$ and $m = 27$), the answer must be A.

It is not necessary to ensure that $n = 13$ is possible to answer the question. However, it is not difficult to see that $k = 23$, $m = 1$, and $n = 13$ satisfy the given conditions.

The correct answer is A.

PS16214

187. For the positive numbers, n, $n + 1$, $n + 2$, $n + 4$, and $n + 8$, the mean is how much greater than the median?

(A)   0

(B)   1

(C) $n + 1$

(D) $n + 2$

(E) $n + 3$

Algebra Statistics

Since the five positive numbers n, $n + 1$, $n + 2$, $n + 4$, and $n + 8$ are in ascending order, the median is the third number, which is $n + 2$. The mean of the five numbers is

$$\frac{n + (n + 1) + (n + 2) + (n + 4) + (n + 8)}{5}$$

$$= \frac{5n + 15}{5}$$

$$= n + 3$$

Since $(n + 3) - (n + 2) = 1$, the mean is 1 greater than the median.

The correct answer is B.

PS08313

188. The interior of a rectangular carton is designed by a certain manufacturer to have a volume of x cubic feet and a ratio of length to width to height of 3:2:2. In terms of x, which of the following equals the height of the carton, in feet?

(A) $\sqrt[3]{x}$

(B) $\sqrt[3]{\dfrac{2x}{3}}$

(C) $\sqrt[3]{\dfrac{3x}{2}}$

(D) $\dfrac{2}{3}\sqrt[3]{x}$

(E) $\dfrac{3}{2}\sqrt[3]{x}$

Geometry; Arithmetic Volume; Ratio and Proportion

For convenience, assume the carton's interior has length, width, and height of 3, 2, and 2, respectively, and a volume of $x = 12$. Now determine which of the answer choices is equal to the height, which is equal to 2.

answer choice	value when $x = 12$	equal to 2?
A $\sqrt[3]{x}$	$\sqrt[3]{12}$	no
B $\sqrt[3]{\dfrac{2x}{3}}$	$\sqrt[3]{8}$	**yes**
C $\sqrt[3]{\dfrac{3x}{2}}$	$\sqrt[3]{18}$	no
D $\dfrac{2}{3}\sqrt[3]{x}$	$\dfrac{2}{3}\sqrt[3]{12}$	no
E $\dfrac{3}{2}\sqrt[3]{x}$	$\dfrac{3}{2}\sqrt[3]{12}$	no

answer choice	(answer choice)^3	equal to $\dfrac{2x}{3}$?
A $\sqrt[3]{x}$	x	no
B $\sqrt[3]{\dfrac{2x}{3}}$	$\dfrac{2x}{3}$	**yes**
C $\sqrt[3]{\dfrac{3x}{2}}$	$\dfrac{3x}{2}$	no
D $\dfrac{2}{3}\sqrt[3]{x}$	$\dfrac{8}{27}x$	no
E $\dfrac{3}{2}\sqrt[3]{x}$	$\dfrac{27}{8}x$	no

Alternatively, this problem can be solved using algebra. Letting c represent the constant of proportionality, the length, width, and height of the carton can be expressed as $3c, 2c,$ and $2c$, respectively. The volume of the carton is then $(3c)(2c)(2c) = 12c^3$. Since it is given that the volume is x, it follows that $12c^3 = x$. Now solve for c in terms of x and then express the height, $2c$, in terms of x.

$$12c^3 = x \qquad \text{given}$$

$$c^3 = \frac{x}{12} \qquad \text{divide both sides by 12}$$

$$c = \sqrt[3]{\frac{x}{12}} \qquad \text{take the cube root of both sides}$$

$$2c = 2\sqrt[3]{\frac{x}{12}} \qquad \begin{array}{l}\text{multiply both sides by 2,}\\\text{because the height is } 2c\end{array}$$

$$2c = \sqrt[3]{8}\sqrt[3]{\frac{x}{12}} \qquad \sqrt[3]{8} = 2$$

$$2c = \sqrt[3]{8\left(\frac{x}{12}\right)} \qquad \text{use the rule } \left(\sqrt[3]{a}\right)\left(\sqrt[3]{b}\right) = \sqrt[3]{ab}$$

$$2c = \sqrt[3]{\frac{2x}{3}} \qquad \text{cancel common factors}$$

If the last few steps seem too complicated, note that the initial expression for $2c$, namely $2\sqrt[3]{\dfrac{x}{12}}$, can be cubed and compared with the cubes of the answer choices. The table below shows these comparisons with $\left(2\sqrt[3]{\dfrac{x}{12}}\right)^3 = 8\left(\dfrac{x}{12}\right) = \dfrac{2x}{3}$.

The correct answer is B.

PS16810

189. The present ratio of students to teachers at a certain school is 30 to 1. If the student enrollment were to increase by 50 students and the number of teachers were to increase by 5, the ratio of students to teachers would then be 25 to 1. What is the present number of teachers?

(A) 5
(B) 8
(C) 10
(D) 12
(E) 15

Algebra Applied Problems

After noting that $\dfrac{\text{number of students}}{\text{number of teachers}} = \dfrac{30}{1}$ implies that the number of students is 30 times the number of teachers, this problem can be solved with arithmetic, as shown in the table below, by guessing the present number of teachers, increasing the numbers of students and teachers as specified, then checking to see if the resulting ratio is equal to $\dfrac{25}{1}$.

Present Number of Teachers	Present Number of Students	Teachers Increased by 5	Students Increased by 50	Resulting Ratio	Equal to $\frac{25}{1}$?
5	150	10	200	$\frac{200}{10} = \frac{20}{1}$	no
8	240	13	290	$\frac{290}{13} = \frac{22\frac{4}{13}}{1}$	no
10	300	15	350	$\frac{350}{15} = \frac{23\frac{1}{3}}{1}$	no
12	360	17	410	$\frac{410}{17} = \frac{24\frac{2}{17}}{1}$	no
15	450	20	500	$\frac{500}{20} = \frac{25}{1}$	yes

Therefore, the present number of teachers is 15.

Alternatively, the problem can be solved using algebra.

The following table summarizes the given information, where s represents the present number of students and t represents the present number of teachers:

	Number of Students	Number of Teachers	$\frac{Students}{Teachers}$	Equation After Cross Multiplying
Present	s	t	$\frac{s}{t} = \frac{30}{1}$	$s = 30t$
After Increases	$s + 50$	$t + 5$	$\frac{s+50}{t+5} = \frac{25}{1}$	$s + 50 = 25(t+5)$

Determine the value of t using $s = 30t$ (Equation 1) and $s + 50 = 25(t + 5) = 25t + 125$ (Equation 2).

$$
\begin{aligned}
s + 50 &= 25t + 125 &&\text{equation 2} \\
30t + 50 &= 25t + 125 &&\text{substitution from Equation 1} \\
5t + 50 &= 125 &&\text{subtract } 25t \text{ from both sides} \\
5t &= 75 &&\text{subtract 50 from both sides} \\
t &= 15 &&\text{divide both sides by 5}
\end{aligned}
$$

Therefore, the present number of teachers is 15.

The correct answer is E.

PS16811
190. What is the smallest integer n for which $25^n > 5^{12}$?

(A) 6
(B) 7
(C) 8
(D) 9
(E) 10

Arithmetic Operations with Rational Numbers

Because $5^2 = 25$, a common base is 5. Rewrite the left side with 5 as a base: $25^n = (5^2)^n = 5^{2n}$. It follows that the desired integer is the least integer n for which $5^{2n} > 5^{12}$. This will be the least integer n for which $2n > 12$, or the least integer n for which $n > 6$, which is 7.

The correct answer is B.

PS16122
191. Sixty percent of the members of a study group are women, and 45 percent of those women are lawyers. If one member of the study group is to be selected at random, what is the probability that the member selected is a woman lawyer?

(A) 0.10
(B) 0.15
(C) 0.27
(D) 0.33
(E) 0.45

Arithmetic Probability

For simplicity, suppose there are 100 members in the study group. Since 60 percent of the members are women, there are 60 women in the group. Also, 45 percent of the women are lawyers so there are $0.45(60) = 27$ women lawyers in the study group. Therefore the probability of selecting a woman lawyer is $\frac{27}{100} = 0.27$.

The correct answer is C.

PS06570
192. Each year for 4 years, a farmer increased the number of trees in a certain orchard by $\frac{1}{4}$ of the number of trees in the orchard the preceding year. If all of the trees thrived and there were 6,250 trees in the orchard at the end of the 4-year period, how many trees were in the orchard at the beginning of the 4-year period?

(A) 1,250
(B) 1,563
(C) 2,250
(D) 2,560
(E) 2,752

Arithmetic Operations on Rational Numbers

Let N be the number of trees in the orchard at the beginning of the 4-year period. Since the number of trees increases by a factor of $\frac{1}{4}$ each year, the number of trees after the first year is $N + \frac{1}{4}N = \frac{5}{4}N$. Note that this shows algebraically that an increase by a factor of $\frac{1}{4}$ corresponds to multiplication by $\frac{5}{4}$. Therefore, the number of trees after the second year is $\frac{5}{4}$ times $\frac{5}{4}N$, which equals $\left(\frac{5}{4}\right)^2 N$. Similarly, the number of trees after the third year is $\left(\frac{5}{4}\right)^3 N$ and the number of trees after the fourth year is $\left(\frac{5}{4}\right)^4 N$. Since the number of trees after the fourth year is 6,250, it follows that $\left(\frac{5}{4}\right)^4 N = 6,250$. Next, solve for N:

$\left(\frac{5}{4}\right)^4 N$	$= 6,250$	given
$\left(\frac{5^4}{4^4}\right)N$	$= 6,250$	property of exponents
N	$= 6,250 \div \frac{5^4}{4^4}$	divide both sides by $\frac{5^4}{4^4}$
N	$= 6,250 \times \frac{4^4}{5^4}$	invert and multiply
N	$= 2 \times 5^5 \times \frac{4^4}{5^4}$	factor 6,250
N	$= 2 \times 5 \times 4^4$	cancel common factors
N	$= 2,560$	multiply

The correct answer is D.

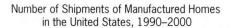

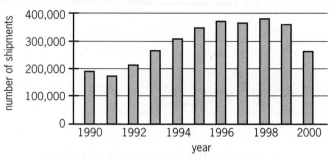

Number of Shipments of Manufactured Homes
in the United States, 1990–2000

PS00422

193. According to the chart shown, which of the following is closest to the median annual number of shipments of manufactured homes in the United States for the years from 1990 to 2000, inclusive?

(A) 250,000
(B) 280,000
(C) 310,000
(D) 325,000
(E) 340,000

Arithmetic Interpretation of Graphs and Tables; Statistics

From the chart, the approximate numbers of shipments are as follows:

Year	Number of Shipments
1990	190,000
1991	180,000
1992	210,000
1993	270,000
1994	310,000
1995	350,000
1996	380,000
1997	370,000
1998	390,000
1999	360,000
2000	270,000

Since there are 11 entries in the table and 11 is an odd number, the median of the numbers of shipments is the 6th entry when the numbers of shipments are arranged in order from least to greatest. In order, from least to greatest, the first 6 entries are:

Number of Shipments
180,000
190,000
210,000
270,000
270,000
310,000

The 6th entry is 310,000.

The correct answer is C.

PS08209

194. For the positive integers a, b, and k, $a^k \| b$ means that a^k is a divisor of b, but a^{k+1} is not a divisor of b. If k is a positive integer and $2^k \| 72$, then k is equal to

(A) 2
(B) 3
(C) 4
(D) 8
(E) 18

Arithmetic Property of Numbers

Since $72 = (2^3)(3^2)$, it follows that 2^3 is a divisor of 72 and 2^4 is not a divisor of 72. Therefore, $2^3 \| 72$, and hence $k = 3$.

The correct answer is B.

PS06674

195. A certain characteristic in a large population has a distribution that is symmetric about the mean m. If 68 percent of the distribution lies within one standard deviation d of the mean, what percent of the distribution is less than $m + d$?

(A) 16%
(B) 32%
(C) 48%
(D) 84%
(E) 92%

Arithmetic Statistics

Since 68% lies between $m - d$ and $m + d$, a total of $(100 - 68)\% = 32\%$ lies to the left of $m - d$ and to the right of $m + d$. Because the distribution is symmetric about m, half of the 32% lies to the right of $m + d$. Therefore, 16% lies to the right of $m + d$, and hence $(100 - 16)\% = 84\%$ lies to the left of $m + d$.

The correct answer is D.

PS07459

196. Four extra-large sandwiches of exactly the same size were ordered for m students, where $m > 4$. Three of the sandwiches were evenly divided among the students. Since 4 students did not want any of the fourth sandwich, it was evenly divided among the remaining students. If Carol ate one piece from each of the four sandwiches, the amount of sandwich that she ate would be what fraction of a whole extra-large sandwich?

(A) $\dfrac{m+4}{m(m-4)}$

(B) $\dfrac{2m-4}{m(m-4)}$

(C) $\dfrac{4m-4}{m(m-4)}$

(D) $\dfrac{4m-8}{m(m-4)}$

(E) $\dfrac{4m-12}{m(m-4)}$

Algebra Applied Problems

Since each of 3 of the sandwiches was evenly divided among m students, each piece was $\dfrac{1}{m}$ of a sandwich. Since the fourth sandwich was evenly divided among $m - 4$ students, each piece was $\dfrac{1}{m-4}$ of the fourth sandwich. Carol ate 1 piece from each of the four sandwiches, so she ate a total of

$$(3)\frac{1}{m} + \frac{1}{m-4} = \frac{3(m-4)+m}{m(m-4)} = \frac{4m-12}{m(m-4)}$$

The correct answer is E.

PS05888

197. Which of the following equations has $1 + \sqrt{2}$ as one of its roots?

(A) $x^2 + 2x - 1 = 0$

(B) $x^2 - 2x + 1 = 0$

(C) $x^2 + 2x + 1 = 0$

(D) $x^2 - 2x - 1 = 0$

(E) $x^2 - x - 1 = 0$

Algebra Second-Degree Equations

This problem can be solved by working backwards to construct a quadratic equation with $1 + \sqrt{2}$ as a root that does not involve radicals.

$x = 1 + \sqrt{2}$	set x to the desired value
$x - 1 = \sqrt{2}$	subtract 1 from both sides
$(x-1)^2 = 2$	square both sides
$x^2 - 2x + 1 = 2$	expand the left side
$x^2 - 2x - 1 = 0$	subtract 2 from both sides

The correct answer is D.

PS07730

198. In Country C, the unemployment rate among construction workers dropped from 16 percent on September 1, 1992, to 9 percent on September 1, 1996. If the number of construction workers was 20 percent greater on September 1, 1996, than on September 1, 1992, what was the approximate percent change in the number of unemployed construction workers over this period?

(A) 50% decrease

(B) 30% decrease

(C) 15% decrease

(D) 30% increase

(E) 55% increase

Arithmetic Percents

Letting N represent the number of construction workers on September 1, 1992, the information given in the problem is as follows:

(1) On September 1, 1992, the unemployment rate among construction workers was 16 percent, so the **number** of unemployed construction workers on September 1, 1992, was **0.16N**.

(2) On September 1, 1996, the **number** of construction workers was 20 percent greater than on September 1, 1992, so the **number** of construction workers on September 1, 1996, was **1.2N**.

(3) On September 1, 1996, the unemployment rate among construction workers was 9 percent, so the **number** of unemployed construction workers on September 1, 1996, was **0.09(1.2N)**.

As a fraction, the percent change in the **number** of unemployed construction workers from September 1, 1992, to September 1, 1996, is given by:

$$\frac{\text{number in 1996} - \text{number in 1992}}{\text{number in 1992}} = \frac{0.09(1.2N) - 0.16N}{0.16N}$$ substitution of expressions from (1) and (3)

$$= \frac{(0.09)(1.2) - 0.16}{0.16}$$ divide numerator and denominator by N

$$= \frac{9(12) - 160}{160}$$ multiply numerator and denominator by 1,000 for ease of calculation

$$= \frac{108 - 160}{160}$$ multiply

$$= -\frac{52}{160}$$ subtract

$$= -\frac{13}{40}$$ divide numerator and denominator by 4

$$\approx -\frac{13}{39}$$ $39 \approx 40$

$$\approx -\frac{1}{3}$$ divide numerator and denominator by 13

Then, as a percent, $-\frac{1}{3}$ represents a decrease of about 30%.

The correct answer is B.

PS06215

199. In a box of 12 pens, a total of 3 are defective. If a customer buys 2 pens selected at random from the box, what is the probability that neither pen will be defective?

(A) $\frac{1}{6}$

(B) $\frac{2}{9}$

(C) $\frac{6}{11}$

(D) $\frac{9}{16}$

(E) $\frac{3}{4}$

Arithmetic Probability

The probability that the first pen selected is not defective is $\frac{9}{12} = \frac{3}{4}$ (9 pens are not defective out of a total of 12 pens). Assuming the first pen selected is not defective, the probability that

the second pen is not defective is $\frac{8}{11}$ (this time 8 pens are not defective out of a total of 11 pens). Therefore, using the multiplication rule for dependent events, the probability that both pens are not defective is $\left(\frac{3}{4}\right)\left(\frac{8}{11}\right) = \frac{6}{11}$.

Alternatively, by a direct count using the number of combinations of n objects taken k at a time (see section 3.4.3 *Counting Methods* in the Math Review chapter), there are

$\binom{9}{2} = \frac{(9)(8)}{2} = 36$ ways to select 2 non-defective pens from the 9 non-defective pens, and there are $\binom{12}{2} = \frac{(12)(11)}{2} = 66$ ways to select 2 pens from the 12 pens. Therefore, the probability that the 2 pens selected are not defective is

$$\frac{\text{number of ways to select 2 non-defective pens}}{\text{number of ways to select 2 pens}} =$$

$\frac{36}{66} = \frac{6}{11}$.

The correct answer is C.

PS13244

200. At a certain fruit stand, the price of each apple is 40 cents and the price of each orange is 60 cents. Mary selects a total of 10 apples and oranges from the fruit stand, and the average (arithmetic mean) price of the 10 pieces of fruit is 56 cents. How many oranges must Mary put back so that the average price of the pieces of fruit that she keeps is 52 cents?

(A) 1
(B) 2
(C) 3
(D) 4
(E) 5

Algebra Statistics

This problem can be solved using arithmetic or algebra.

<u>With algebra</u>

Let x be the number of oranges Mary selected originally. It follows that the number of apples Mary selected is $10 - x$ since the number of pieces of fruit she selected originally was 10. The average price of the 10 pieces of fruit is 56 cents so,

$$\frac{40(10 - x) + 60x}{10} = 56 \quad \text{given}$$

$$40(10 - x) + 60x = 560 \quad \text{multiply both sides by 10}$$

$$400 - 40x + 60x = 560 \quad \text{distributive property}$$

$$400 + 20x = 560 \quad \text{combine like terms}$$

$$20x = 160 \quad \text{subtract 400 from each term}$$

$$x = 8 \quad \text{divide both sides by 20}$$

Thus, Mary originally selected 8 oranges and 2 apples.

If y represents the number of oranges that Mary must put back, then $8 - y$ is the number of oranges she keeps. So, with the 2 apples, the total number of pieces of fruit she keeps is $2 + (8 - y)$. The average price of these $2 + (8 - y)$ pieces of fruit is 52 cents so,

$$\frac{40(2) + 60(8 - y)}{2 + (8 - y)} = 52 \quad \text{given}$$

$$40(2) + 60(8 - y) = 52[2 + (8 - y)] \quad \text{multiply both sides by } 2 + (8 - y)$$

$$40(2) + 60(8 - y) = 52(10 - y) \quad \text{combine like terms}$$

$$80 + 480 - 60y = 520 - 52y \quad \text{distributive property}$$

$$560 - 60y = 520 - 52y \quad \text{combine like terms}$$

$$560 = 520 + 8y \quad \text{add } 60y \text{ to both sides}$$

$$40 = 8y \quad \text{subtract 520 from both sides}$$

$$5 = y \quad \text{divide both sides by 8}$$

Therefore, Mary must put back 5 oranges so that the average price of the 2 apples and 3 oranges she keeps is $\frac{40(2) + 60(3)}{5} = \frac{260}{5} = 52$ cents.

<u>With arithmetic</u>

In order to know how many oranges Mary should put back to decrease the average price of the pieces of fruit she is buying to 52 cents, the number of oranges she originally selected needs to be determined. Consider the following table:

Number of apples	Number of oranges	Average price (cents)	Average = 56 cents?
1	9	$\frac{1(40) + 9(60)}{10} = \frac{580}{10} = 58$	no
2	8	$\frac{2(40) + 8(60)}{10} = \frac{560}{10} = 56$	**yes**

Thus, Mary originally selected 2 apples and 8 oranges.

Next, determine how many oranges Mary must put back so that the average price of the pieces of fruit she keeps is 52 cents, consider the following table:

Number of apples	Number of oranges put back	Number of oranges kept	Average price (cents)	Average = 52 cents?
2	1	7	$\dfrac{2(40)+7(60)}{9}=\dfrac{500}{9}=55\dfrac{5}{9}$	no
2	2	6	$\dfrac{2(40)+6(60)}{8}=\dfrac{440}{8}=55$	no
2	3	5	$\dfrac{2(40)+5(60)}{7}=\dfrac{380}{7}=54\dfrac{2}{7}$	no
2	4	4	$\dfrac{2(40)+4(60)}{6}=\dfrac{320}{6}=53\dfrac{1}{3}$	no
2	5	3	$\dfrac{2(40)+3(60)}{5}=\dfrac{260}{5}=52$	**yes**

Therefore, Mary must put back 5 oranges.

Note: It is not necessary to perform all of the calculations shown here. It should be obvious, for example, that $\dfrac{500}{9}, \dfrac{380}{7}$, and $\dfrac{320}{6}$ are not whole numbers and therefore cannot equal 52. Nor is it necessary to increment the number of oranges she must put back by 1. For this problem, a good guess might be 4, thinking she might need to put back half the oranges she selected originally. Since putting back 4 oranges doesn't bring the average price down enough, the only other choice is 5, which is the correct answer.

Note that the steps are explained in great detail here. Having good algebraic manipulation skills would make most of the steps fairly automatic.

The correct answer is E.

PS04688

201. A pharmaceutical company received $3 million in royalties on the first $20 million in sales of the generic equivalent of one of its products and then $9 million in royalties on the next $108 million in sales. By approximately what percent did the ratio of royalties to sales decrease from the first $20 million in sales to the next $108 million in sales?

(A)   8%
(B)   15%
(C)   45%
(D)   52%
(E)   56%

Arithmetic Percents

The ratio of royalties to sales for the first $20 million in sales is $\dfrac{3}{20}$, and the ratio of royalties to sales for the next $108 million in sales is $\dfrac{9}{108}=\dfrac{1}{12}$. Now calculate the percent decrease from $\dfrac{3}{20}$ to $\dfrac{1}{12}$.

$$\dfrac{\dfrac{1}{12}-\dfrac{3}{20}}{\dfrac{3}{20}}\times100=\left(\dfrac{1}{12}-\dfrac{3}{20}\right)\times\dfrac{20}{3}\times100$$

$$=\left(\dfrac{1\times20}{12\times3}-\dfrac{3\times20}{20\times3}\right)\times100$$

$$=\left(\dfrac{5}{9}-1\right)\times100$$

$$=-\dfrac{4}{9}\times100$$

$$\approx-0.44\times100$$

$$\approx45\% \text{ decrease}$$

An alternate way to calculate the percent decrease from $\dfrac{3}{20}$ to $\dfrac{1}{12}$ is to scale the values up until they are integers, which allows for a simpler calculation. Multiplying each of these values by 60 gives $60 \times \frac{3}{20} = 9$ and $60 \times \frac{1}{12} = 5$, respectively, so the problem reduces to calculating the percent decrease from 9 to 5. Therefore,

$$\frac{5-9}{9} \times 100 = -\frac{4}{9} \times 100 \approx -0.44 \times 100 \approx 45\%$$

decrease.

The correct answer is C.

Times at Which the Door
Opened from 8:00 to 10:00

8:00	8:06	8:30	9:05
8:03	8:10	8:31	9:11
8:04	8:18	8:54	9:29
8:04	8:19	8:57	9:31

PS06497

202. The light in a restroom operates with a 15-minute timer that is reset every time the door opens as a person goes in or out of the room. Thus, after someone enters or exits the room, the light remains on for only 15 minutes unless the door opens again and resets the timer for another 15 minutes. If the times listed above are the times at which the door opened from 8:00 to 10:00, approximately how many minutes during this two-hour period was the light off?

(A) 10
(B) 25
(C) 35
(D) 40
(E) 70

Arithmetic Operations with Integers

In the table given above, read down the columns looking for pairs of consecutive times that are more than 15 minutes apart. The following table shows all such pairs:

Consecutive times more than 15 minutes apart	Minutes between times door opens	Minutes that light is on	Minutes that light is off
8:31 and 8:54	54 − 31 = 23	15	23 − 15 = 8
9:11 and 9:29	29 − 11 = 18	15	18 − 15 = 3
9:31 and 10:00	60 − 31 = 29	15	29 − 15 = 14
Total time light is off			25

The correct answer is B.

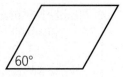

PS07536

203. The parallelogram shown has four sides of equal length. What is the ratio of the length of the shorter diagonal to the length of the longer diagonal?

(A) $\frac{1}{2}$

(B) $\frac{1}{\sqrt{2}}$

(C) $\frac{1}{2\sqrt{2}}$

(D) $\frac{1}{\sqrt{3}}$

(E) $\frac{1}{2\sqrt{3}}$

Geometry Quadrilaterals; Triangles

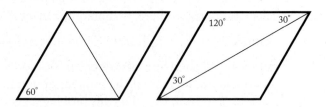

First, opposite angles of a parallelogram have equal measure, and the sum of the measures of adjacent angles is 180°. This means that each of the angles adjacent to the angle labeled 60° has measure 120°.

Since all four sides of the parallelogram have equal length, say x units, the shorter diagonal divides the parallelogram into two isosceles triangles. An isosceles triangle with one angle measuring 60° is equilateral, and so the shorter diagonal has length x units.

The longer diagonal divides the parallelogram into two isosceles triangles with one angle measuring 120° and each of the other angles measuring $\frac{180-120}{2} = 30°$, as shown in the figure above on the right.

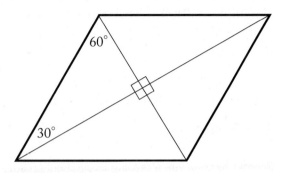

Then, because the diagonals of a parallelogram are perpendicular and bisect each other, the two diagonals divide the parallelogram into four 30°–60°–90° triangles, each with hypotenuse x units long. The sides of a 30°–60°–90° triangle are in the ratio of $1 : \sqrt{3} : 2$ and so, if y represents the length of the side opposite the 60° angle, then $\frac{x}{2} = \frac{y}{\sqrt{3}}$ and $y = \frac{x\sqrt{3}}{2}$. But, y is half the length of the longer diagonal, so the longer diagonal has length $x\sqrt{3}$ units. Therefore, the ratio of the length of the shorter diagonal to the length of the longer diagonal is $\frac{x}{x\sqrt{3}} = \frac{1}{\sqrt{3}}$.

The correct answer is D.

PS00041

204. If p is the product of the integers from 1 to 30, inclusive, what is the greatest integer k for which 3^k is a factor of p?

(A)   10
(B)   12
(C)   14
(D)   16
(E)   18

Arithmetic Properties of Numbers

The table below shows the numbers from 1 to 30, inclusive, that have at least one factor of 3 and how many factors of 3 each has.

Multiples of 3 Between 1 and 30	Number of Factors of 3
3	1
$6 = 2 \times 3$	1
$9 = 3 \times 3$	2
$12 = 2 \times 2 \times 3$	1
$15 = 3 \times 5$	1
$18 = 2 \times 3 \times 3$	2
$21 = 3 \times 7$	1
$24 = 2 \times 2 \times 2 \times 3$	1
$27 = 3 \times 3 \times 3$	3
$30 = 2 \times 3 \times 5$	1

The sum of the numbers in the right column is 14. Therefore, 3^{14} is the greatest power of 3 that is a factor of the product of the first 30 positive integers.

The correct answer is C.

PS04651

205. If $n = 3^8 - 2^8$, which of the following is NOT a factor of n?

(A)   97
(B)   65
(C)   35
(D)   13
(E)   5

Arithmetic Properties of Numbers

Since $3^8 - 2^8$ is the difference of the perfect squares $(3^4)^2$ and $(2^4)^2$, then $3^8 - 2^8 = (3^4 + 2^4)(3^4 - 2^4)$. But $3^4 - 2^4$ is also the difference of the perfect squares $(3^2)^2$ and $(2^2)^2$ so $3^4 - 2^4 = (3^2 + 2^2)(3^2 - 2^2)$ and therefore $3^8 - 2^8 = (3^4 + 2^4)(3^2 + 2^2)(3^2 - 2^2)$. It follows that $3^8 - 2^8$ can be factored as $(81 + 16)(9 + 4)(9 - 4) = (97)(13)(5)$. Therefore, 7 is not a factor of $3^8 - 2^8$, and hence $35 = 5 \times 7$ is not a factor of $3^8 - 2^8$. It is easy to see that each of 97, 13, and 5 is a factor of $3^8 - 2^8$, and so is 65, since $65 = 5 \times 13$, although this additional analysis is not needed to arrive at the correct answer.

The correct answer is C.

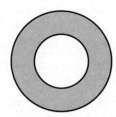

PS12078

206. In the figure shown, if the area of the shaded region is 3 times the area of the smaller circular region, then the circumference of the larger circle is how many times the circumference of the smaller circle?

(A) 4

(B) 3

(C) 2

(D) $\sqrt{3}$

(E) $\sqrt{2}$

Geometry Circles

Let R represent the radius of the larger circle and r represent the radius of the smaller circle. Then the area of the shaded region is the area of the larger circular region minus the area of the smaller circular region, or $\pi R^2 - \pi r^2$. It is given that the area of the shaded region is three times the area of the smaller circular region, and so $\pi R^2 - \pi r^2 = 3\pi r^2$. Then $R^2 - r^2 = 3r^2$, and so $R^2 = 4r^2$ and $R = 2r$. The circumference of the larger circle is $2\pi R = 2\pi(2r) = 2(2\pi r)$, which is 2 times the circumference of the smaller circle.

The correct answer is C.

PS12177

207. Club X has more than 10 but fewer than 40 members. Sometimes the members sit at tables with 3 members at one table and 4 members at each of the other tables, and sometimes they sit at tables with 3 members at one table and 5 members at each of the other tables. If they sit at tables with 6 members at each table except one and fewer than 6 members at that one table, how many members will be at the table that has fewer than 6 members?

(A) 1

(B) 2

(C) 3

(D) 4

(E) 5

Arithmetic Properties of Numbers

Let n be the number of members that Club X has. Since the members can be equally divided into groups of 4 each with 3 left over, and the members can be equally divided into groups of 5 each with 3 left over, it follows that $n - 3$ is divisible by both 4 and 5. Therefore, $n - 3$ must be a multiple of $(4)(5) = 20$. Also, because the only multiple of 20 that is greater than 10 and less than 40 is 20, it follows that $n - 3 = 20$, or $n = 23$. Finally, when these 23 members are divided into the greatest number of groups of 6 each, there will be 5 members left over, since $23 = (3)(6) + 5$.

The correct answer is E.

PS07081

208. In order to complete a reading assignment on time, Terry planned to read 90 pages per day. However, she read only 75 pages per day at first, leaving 690 pages to be read during the last 6 days before the assignment was to be completed. How many days in all did Terry have to complete the assignment on time?

(A) 15

(B) 16

(C) 25

(D) 40

(E) 46

Algebra Applied Problems

Let n be the number of days that Terry read at the slower rate of 75 pages per day. Then $75n$ is the number of pages Terry read at this slower rate, and $75n + 690$ is the total number of pages Terry needs to read. Also, $n + 6$ is the total number of days that Terry will spend on the reading assignment. The requirement that Terry average 90 pages per day is equivalent to $\dfrac{75n + 690}{n + 6} = 90$.

Then

$$\frac{75n + 690}{n + 6} = 90$$

$$75n + 690 = 90n + 540$$

$$150 = 15n$$

$$10 = n$$

Therefore, the total number of days that Terry has to complete the assignment on time is $n + 6 = 10 + 6 = 16$.

The correct answer is B.

PS13996

209. If $s > 0$ and $\sqrt{\dfrac{r}{s}} = s$, what is r in terms of s?

(A) $\dfrac{1}{s}$

(B) $\sqrt{s}$

(C) $s\sqrt{s}$

(D) s^3

(E) $s^3 - s$

Algebra Equations

Solve the equation for r as follows:

$$\sqrt{\dfrac{r}{s}} = s$$

$\dfrac{r}{s} = s^2$ square both sides of the equation

$r = s^3$ multiply both sides by s

The correct answer is D.

PS12536

210. If $3 < x < 100$, for how many values of x is $\dfrac{x}{3}$ the square of a prime number?

(A) Two

(B) Three

(C) Four

(D) Five

(E) Nine

Arithmetic Properties of Numbers

If $\dfrac{x}{3}$ is the square of a prime number, then possible values of $\dfrac{x}{3}$ are $2^2, 3^2, 5^2, 7^2, \ldots$. Therefore, possible values of x are $3 \times 2^2 = 12$, $3 \times 3^2 = 27$, $3 \times 5^2 = 75$, $3 \times 7^2 = 147$, …. Since only three of these values, namely 12, 27, and 75, are between 3 and 100, there are three values of x such that $\dfrac{x}{3}$ is the square of a prime number.

The correct answer is B.

PS07547

211. A researcher plans to identify each participant in a certain medical experiment with a code consisting of either a single letter or a pair of distinct letters written in alphabetical order. What is the least number of letters that can be used if there are 12 participants, and each participant is to receive a different code?

(A) 4

(B) 5

(C) 6

(D) 7

(E) 8

Arithmetic Elementary Combinatorics

None of the essential aspects of the problem is affected if the letters are restricted to be the first n letters of the alphabet, for various positive integers n. With the 3 letters a, b, and c, there are 6 codes: a, b, c, ab, ac, and bc. With the 4 letters a, b, c, and d, there are 10 codes: a, b, c, d, ab, ac, ad, bc, bd, and cd. Clearly, more than 12 codes are possible with 5 or more letters, so the least number of letters that can be used is 5.

The correct answer is B.

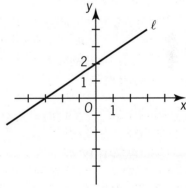

PS06948

212. The graph of which of the following equations is a straight line that is parallel to line ℓ in the figure above?

(A) $3y - 2x = 0$

(B) $3y + 2x = 0$

(C) $3y + 2x = 6$

(D) $2y - 3x = 6$

(E) $2y + 3x = -6$

Algebra Coordinate Geometry

From the graph, line ℓ contains points $(-3,0)$ and $(0,2)$, so the slope of line ℓ is $\dfrac{0-2}{-3-0} = \dfrac{2}{3}$.

Any line parallel to line ℓ has slope $\dfrac{2}{3}$. Rewrite each of the equations given in the answer choices in slope-intercept form $y = mx + b$, where m is the slope and b is the y-intercept, to find the equation whose graph is a line with slope $\dfrac{2}{3}$. For answer choice A, $3y - 2x = 0$ so $3y = 2x$ and $y = \dfrac{2}{3}x$. The graph of this equation is a line with slope $\dfrac{2}{3}$.

The correct answer is A.

PS06562

213. An object thrown directly upward is at a height of h feet after t seconds, where $h = -16(t - 3)^2 + 150$. At what height, in feet, is the object 2 seconds after it reaches its maximum height?

(A)   6
(B)   86
(C)   134
(D)   150
(E)   166

Algebra Applied Problems

Since $(t - 3)^2$ is positive when $t \neq 3$ and zero when $t = 3$, it follows that the *minimum* value of $(t - 3)^2$ occurs when $t = 3$. Therefore, the *maximum* value of $-16(t - 3)^2$, and also the maximum value of $-16(t - 3)^2 + 150$, occurs when $t = 3$. Hence, the height 2 seconds after the maximum height is the value of h when $t = 5$, or $-16(5 - 3)^2 + 150 = 86$.

The correct answer is B.

PS16107

214. Which of the following is equivalent to the pair of inequalities $x + 6 > 10$ and $x - 3 \leq 5$?

(A) $2 \leq x < 16$
(B) $2 \leq x < 4$
(C) $2 < x \leq 8$
(D) $4 < x \leq 8$
(E) $4 \leq x < 16$

Algebra Inequalities

Solve the inequalities separately and combine the results.

$$x + 6 > 10$$
$$x > 4$$
$$x - 3 \leq 5$$
$$x \leq 8$$

Since $x > 4$, then $4 < x$. Combining $4 < x$ and $x \leq 8$ gives $4 < x \leq 8$.

The correct answer is D.

PS16823

215. David has d books, which is 3 times as many as Jeff and $\dfrac{1}{2}$ as many as Paula. How many books do the three of them have altogether, in terms of d ?

(A) $\dfrac{5}{6}d$

(B) $\dfrac{7}{3}d$

(C) $\dfrac{10}{3}d$

(D) $\dfrac{7}{2}d$

(E) $\dfrac{9}{2}d$

Algebra Applied Problems; Simultaneous Equations

Let J be the number of books that Jeff has, and let P be the number of books Paula has. Then, the given information about David's books can be expressed as $d = 3J$ and $d = \dfrac{1}{2}P$. Solving these two equations for J and P gives $\dfrac{d}{3} = J$ and $2d = P$.

Thus, $d + J + P = d + \dfrac{d}{3} + 2d = 3\dfrac{1}{3}d = \dfrac{10}{3}d$.

The correct answer is C.

PS16824

216. There are 8 teams in a certain league and each team plays each of the other teams exactly once. If each game is played by 2 teams, what is the total number of games played?

(A)   15
(B)   16
(C)   28
(D)   56
(E)   64

Arithmetic Operations on Rational Numbers

Since no team needs to play itself, each team needs to play 7 other teams. In addition, each game needs to be counted only once, rather than once for each team that plays that game. Since two teams play each game, $\frac{8 \times 7}{2} = 28$ games are needed.

The correct answer is C.

PS07491

217. At his regular hourly rate, Don had estimated the labor cost of a repair job as $336 and he was paid that amount. However, the job took 4 hours longer than he had estimated and, consequently, he earned $2 per hour less than his regular hourly rate. What was the time Don had estimated for the job, in hours?

(A) 28
(B) 24
(C) 16
(D) 14
(E) 12

Algebra Second-Degree Equations

For ease of calculation later, note that $336 = 6 \times 7 \times 8$.

To avoid fairly extensive algebraic manipulation, consider starting with the answer choices by checking to see which one satisfies the conditions of the problem.

Estimated		Actual	
Number of hours	Per hour pay†	Number of hours	Per hour pay
A 28	$\frac{\$336}{28} = \$12^*$	32	$\frac{\$336}{32} \neq \$10^{**}$
B 24	$\frac{\$336}{24} = \$14$	28	$\frac{\$336}{28} = \$12$
C 16	$\frac{\$336}{16} = \$21$	20	$\frac{\$336}{20} \neq \$19$
D 14	$\frac{\$336}{14} = \$24$	18	$\frac{\$336}{18} \neq \$22$
E 12	$\frac{\$336}{12} = \$28$	16	$\frac{\$336}{16} \neq \$26$

† Note that Don used his regular hourly rate to estimate the labor cost of the repair job, so if he estimated $336 for his labor for a t-hour job, then his regular hourly rate was $\frac{\$336}{t}$.

*Cancel wherever possible

$$\frac{336}{28} = \frac{6 \times \cancel{7} \times \cancel{8}^2}{\cancel{7} \times \cancel{4}} = 12$$

**This would need to be $12 - 2 = 10$ in order for (A) 28 to be correct.

The correct answer is B.

PS16828

218. If $\frac{p}{q} < 1$, and p and q are positive integers, which of the following must be greater than 1 ?

(A) $\sqrt{\dfrac{p}{q}}$

(B) $\dfrac{p}{q^2}$

(C) $\dfrac{p}{2q}$

(D) $\dfrac{q}{p^2}$

(E) $\dfrac{q}{p}$

Arithmetic Properties of Numbers

Since p and q are positive integers, $0 < \dfrac{p}{q} < 1$.

A   Since $\dfrac{p}{q} < 1$, then $q > p$. Taking the square root of both sides of the inequality gives $\sqrt{q} > \sqrt{p}$. Then, $\sqrt{\dfrac{p}{q}} = \dfrac{\sqrt{p}}{\sqrt{q}}$, so here the denominator will still be larger than the numerator. CANNOT be greater than 1.

B   Squaring the denominator increases the denominator, which decreases the value of the fraction. CANNOT be greater than 1.

C   Multiplying the denominator by 2 increases the denominator, which decreases the value of the fraction. CANNOT be greater than 1.

D   Since $\dfrac{p}{q} < 1$, then $q > p$. When $p^2 < q$, this expression will be greater than 1, but p^2 need not be less than q. For example, if $p = 2$ and $q = 100$, $\dfrac{p}{q} = \dfrac{2}{100}$ and $\dfrac{q}{p^2} = \dfrac{100}{2^2} = \dfrac{100}{4} = 25 > 1$.

However, if $p = 3$ and $q = 4$, then $\dfrac{p}{q} = \dfrac{3}{4}$

and $\dfrac{q}{p^2} = \dfrac{4}{3^2} = \dfrac{4}{9} < 1$. NEED NOT be

greater than 1.

E   Again, since $\dfrac{p}{q} < 1$, then $q > p$. Thus,

the reciprocal, $\dfrac{q}{p}$, always has a value

greater than 1 because the numerator will

always be a larger positive integer than the
denominator. MUST be greater than 1.

The correct answer is E.

PS16830

219. To mail a package, the rate is *x* cents for the first
pound and *y* cents for each additional pound, where
$x > y$. Two packages weighing 3 pounds and 5
pounds, respectively, can be mailed separately or
combined as one package. Which method is cheaper,
and how much money is saved?

(A)   Combined, with a savings of $x - y$ cents

(B)   Combined, with a savings of $y - x$ cents

(C)   Combined, with a savings of *x* cents

(D)   Separately, with a savings of $x - y$ cents

(E)   Separately, with a savings of *y* cents

Algebra Applied Problems

Shipping the two packages separately would cost
$1x + 2y$ for the 3-pound package and $1x + 4y$
for the 5-pound package. Shipping them together
(as a single 8-pound package) would cost
$1x + 7y$. By calculating the sum of the costs for
shipping the two packages separately minus the
cost for shipping the one combined package, it
is possible to determine the difference in cost, as
shown.

$((1x + 2y) + (1x + 4y)) - (1x + 7y)$ (cost for 3 lb.
                                        + cost for 5 lb.)
                                        − cost for 8 lb.

$= (2x + 6y) - (1x + 7y)$ combine like
                             terms

$= 2x + 6y - 1x - 7y$ distribute the
                         negative

$= x - y$ combine like
             terms

Since $x > y$, this value is positive, which means it
costs more to ship two packages separately. Thus
it is cheaper to mail one combined package at a
cost savings of $x - y$ cents.

The correct answer is A.

PS16831

220. If money is invested at *r* percent interest, compounded
annually, the amount of the investment will double in
approximately $\dfrac{70}{r}$ years. If Pat's parents invested
$5,000 in a long-term bond that pays 8 percent
interest, compounded annually, what will be the
approximate total amount of the investment 18 years
later, when Pat is ready for college?

(A) $20,000

(B) $15,000

(C) $12,000

(D) $10,000

(E) $9,000

Algebra Applied Problems

Since the investment will double in
$\dfrac{70}{r} = \dfrac{70}{8} = 8.75 \approx 9$ years, the value of the
investment over 18 years can be approximated by
doubling its initial value twice. Therefore, the
approximate value will be $(\$5,000)(2)(2) =$
$20,000.

The correct answer is A.

PS16832

221. On a recent trip, Cindy drove her car 290 miles,
rounded to the nearest 10 miles, and used 12 gallons

of gasoline, rounded to the nearest gallon. The actual number of miles per gallon that Cindy's car got on this trip must have been between

(A) $\dfrac{290}{12.5}$ and $\dfrac{290}{11.5}$

(B) $\dfrac{295}{12}$ and $\dfrac{285}{11.5}$

(C) $\dfrac{285}{12}$ and $\dfrac{295}{12}$

(D) $\dfrac{285}{12.5}$ and $\dfrac{295}{11.5}$

(E) $\dfrac{295}{12.5}$ and $\dfrac{285}{11.5}$

Arithmetic Estimation

The lowest number of miles per gallon can be calculated using the lowest possible miles and the highest amount of gasoline. Also, the highest number of miles per gallon can be calculated using the highest possible miles and the lowest amount of gasoline.

Since the miles are rounded to the nearest 10 miles, the number of miles is between 285 and 295. Since the gallons are rounded to the nearest gallon, the number of gallons is between 11.5 and 12.5. Therefore, the lowest number of miles per gallon is $\dfrac{\text{lowest miles}}{\text{highest gallons}} = \dfrac{285}{12.5}$ and the highest number of miles per gallon is $\dfrac{\text{highest miles}}{\text{lowest gallons}} = \dfrac{295}{11.5}$.

The correct answer is D.

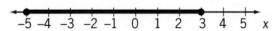

PS16833

222. Which of the following inequalities is an algebraic expression for the shaded part of the number line above?

(A) $|x| \le 3$

(B) $|x| \le 5$

(C) $|x - 2| \le 3$

(D) $|x - 1| \le 4$

(E) $|x + 1| \le 4$

Algebra Inequalities

The number line above shows $-5 \le x \le 3$. To turn this into absolute value notation, as all the choices are written, the numbers need to be opposite signs of the same value.

Since the distance between –5 and 3 is 8 $(3 - (-5) = 8)$, that distance needs to be split in half with –4 to one side and 4 to the other. Each of these two values is 1 more than the values in the inequality above, so adding 1 to all terms in the inequality gives $-4 \le x + 1 \le 4$, which is the same as $|x + 1| \le 4$.

The correct answer is E.

PS16835

223. In a small snack shop, the average (arithmetic mean) revenue was $400 per day over a 10-day period. During this period, if the average daily revenue was $360 for the first 6 days, what was the average daily revenue for the last 4 days?

(A) $420

(B) $440

(C) $450

(D) $460

(E) $480

Arithmetic; Algebra Statistics; Applied Problems

Let x be the average daily revenue for the last 4 days. Using the formula $\text{average} = \dfrac{\text{sum of values}}{\text{number of values}}$, the information regarding the average revenues for the 10-day and 6-day periods can be expressed as follows and solved for x:

$$\$400 = \frac{6(\$360) + 4x}{10}$$

$\$4,000 = \$2,160 + 4x$ \quad multiply both sides by 10

$\$1,840 = 4x$ \quad subtract $2,160 from both sides

$\$460 = x$ \quad divide both sides by 4

The correct answer is D.

PS05882

224. If y is the smallest positive integer such that 3,150 multiplied by y is the square of an integer, then y must be

(A) 2
(B) 5
(C) 6
(D) 7
(E) 14

Arithmetic Properties of Numbers

To find the smallest positive integer y such that $3,150y$ is the square of an integer, first find the prime factorization of 3,150 by a method similar to the following:

$$3,150 = 10 \times 315$$

$$= (2 \times 5) \times (3 \times 105)$$

$$= 2 \times 5 \times 3 \times (5 \times 21)$$

$$= 2 \times 5 \times 3 \times 5 \times (3 \times 7)$$

$$= 2 \times 3^2 \times 5^2 \times 7$$

To be a perfect square, $3,150y$ must have an even number of each of its prime factors. At a minimum, y must have one factor of 2 and one factor of 7 so that $3,150y$ has two factors of each of the primes 2, 3, 5, and 7. The smallest positive integer value of y is then $(2)(7) = 14$.

The correct answer is E.

PS16116

225. If $[x]$ is the greatest integer less than or equal to x, what is the value of $[-1.6] + [3.4] + [2.7]$?

(A) 3
(B) 4
(C) 5
(D) 6
(E) 7

Arithmetic Profit and Loss

The greatest integer that is less than or equal to −1.6 is −2. It cannot be −1 because −1 is greater than −1.6. The greatest integer that is less than or equal to 3.4 is 3. It cannot be 4 because 4 is greater than 3.4. The greatest integer that is less than or equal to 2.7 is 2. It cannot be 3 because 3 is greater than 2.7. Therefore, $[-1.6] + [3.4] + [2.7] = -2 + 3 + 2 = 3$.

The correct answer is A.

PS06558

226. In the first week of the year, Nancy saved $1. In each of the next 51 weeks, she saved $1 more than she had saved in the previous week. What was the total amount that Nancy saved during the 52 weeks?

(A) $1,326
(B) $1,352
(C) $1,378
(D) $2,652
(E) $2,756

Arithmetic Operations on Rational Numbers

In dollars, the total amount saved is the sum of $1, (1 + 1), (1 + 1 + 1)$, and so on, up to and including the amount saved in the 52nd week, which was $52. Therefore, the total amount saved in dollars was $1 + 2 + 3 + \ldots + 50 + 51 + 52$. This sum can be easily evaluated by grouping the terms as $(1 + 52) + (2 + 51) + (3 + 50) + \ldots + (26 + 27)$, which results in the number 53 added to itself 26 times. Therefore, the sum is $(26)(53) = 1,378$.

Alternatively, the formula for the sum of the first n positive integers is $\dfrac{n(n+1)}{2}$. Therefore, the sum of the first 52 positive integers is $\dfrac{52(53)}{2} = 26(53) = 1,378$.

The correct answer is C.

PS16100

227. In a certain sequence, the term x_n is given by the formula $x_n = 2x_{n-1} - \dfrac{1}{2}(x_{n-2})$ for all $n \geq 2$. If $x_0 = 3$ and $x_1 = 2$, what is the value of x_3 ?

(A) 2.5
(B) 3.125
(C) 4
(D) 5
(E) 6.75

Algebra Simplifying Algebraic Expressions

Given the formula $x_n = 2x_{n-1} - \frac{1}{2}(x_{n-2})$ with $x_0 = 3$ and $x_1 = 2$, then

$$x_2 = 2x_1 - \frac{1}{2}x_0$$
$$= 2(2) - \frac{1}{2}(3)$$
$$= \frac{5}{2}$$
$$x_3 = 2x_2 - \frac{1}{2}x_1$$
$$= 2\left(\frac{5}{2}\right) - \frac{1}{2}(2)$$
$$= 5 - 1$$
$$= 4$$

The correct answer is C.

PS08570

228. During a trip, Francine traveled x percent of the total distance at an average speed of 40 miles per hour and the rest of the distance at an average speed of 60 miles per hour. In terms of x, what was Francine's average speed for the entire trip?

(A) $\frac{180 - x}{2}$

(B) $\frac{x + 60}{4}$

(C) $\frac{300 - x}{5}$

(D) $\frac{600}{115 - x}$

(E) $\frac{12,000}{x + 200}$

Algebra Applied Problems

Assume for simplicity that the total distance of Francine's trip is 100 miles. Then the table below gives all of the pertinent information.

Distance	Rate	Time = $\frac{\text{Distance}}{\text{Rate}}$
x	40	$\frac{x}{40}$
$100 - x$	60	$\frac{100 - x}{60}$

The total time for Francine's trip is

$$\frac{x}{40} + \frac{100 - x}{60} = \frac{3x}{120} + \frac{2(100 - x)}{120}$$
$$= \frac{3x + 2(100 - x)}{120}$$
$$= \frac{3x + 200 - 2x}{120}$$
$$= \frac{x + 200}{120}$$

Francine's average speed over the entire trip is

$$\frac{\text{total distance}}{\text{total time}} = \frac{100}{\frac{x + 200}{120}} = \frac{12,000}{x + 200}.$$

The correct answer is E.

PS00564

229. If $n = (33)^{43} + (43)^{33}$, what is the units digit of n?

(A) 0
(B) 2
(C) 4
(D) 6
(E) 8

Arithmetic Properties of Numbers

When a polynomial is raised to a power, the last term in the expression is the last term of the polynomial raised to that power. For example, $(a + b)^2 = a^2 + 2ab + b^2$. We can think of 33 as the binomial $10 \cdot 3 + 3$ whose last term is the units digit 3. Thus, the units digit of 33^2 is $3^2 = 9$. Similarly, for 33^3 we have $3^3 = 27$, so the units digit of 33^3 is 7. The patterns for powers of 33 and 43 are shown in the table below.

power of 33	units digit	power of 43	units digit
33^1	3	43^1	3
33^2	9	43^2	9
33^3	7	43^3	7
33^4	1	43^4	1
33^5	3	43^5	3
33^6	9	43^6	9
33^7	7	43^7	7
33^8	1	43^8	1
$\vdots$	$\vdots$	$\vdots$	$\vdots$
33^{32}	1	43^{32}	1
33^{33}	3	43^{33}	3
$\vdots$	$\vdots$		
33^{40}	1		
33^{41}	3		
33^{42}	9		
33^{43}	7		

From the table above, the units digit of 33^{43} is 7 and the units digit of 43^{33} is 3. Since $7 + 3 = 10$, the units digit of $33^{43} + 43^{33}$ is 0.

The correct answer is A.

PS13691

230. Team A and Team B are competing against each other in a game of tug-of-war. Team A, consisting of 3 males and 3 females, decides to line up male, female, male, female, male, female. The lineup that Team A chooses will be one of how many different possible lineups?

(A) 9
(B) 12
(C) 15
(D) 36
(E) 720

Arithmetic Elementary Combinatorics

Any of the 3 males can be first in the line, and any of the 3 females can be second. Either of the 2 remaining males can be next, followed by either of the 2 remaining females. The last 2 places in the line are filled with the only male left followed by the only female left. By the multiplication principle, there are $3 \times 3 \times 2 \times 2 \times 1 \times 1 = 36$ different lineups possible.

The correct answer is D.

PS08480

231. A border of uniform width is placed around a rectangular photograph that measures 8 inches by 10 inches. If the area of the border is 144 square inches, what is the width of the border, in inches?

(A) 3
(B) 4
(C) 6
(D) 8
(E) 9

Algebra Second-Degree Equations

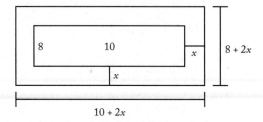

Note: Figure not drawn to scale.

Let x be the width, in inches, of the border. The photograph with the border has dimensions $(10 + 2x)$ inches and $(8 + 2x)$ inches with an area of $(10 + 2x)(8 + 2x) = (80 + 36x + 4x^2)$ square inches. The photograph without the border has dimensions 10 inches and 8 inches with an area of $(10)(8) = 80$ square inches. The area of the border is then the difference between the areas of the photograph with and without the border or $(80 + 36x + 4x^2) - 80 = 36x + 4x^2$ square inches. It is given that the area of the border is 144 square inches so,

$$36x + 4x^2 = 144$$
$$4x^2 + 36x - 144 = 0$$
$$x^2 + 9x - 36 = 0$$
$$(x - 3)(x + 12) = 0$$

So, $x - 3 = 0$, which means $x = 3$, or $x + 12 = 0$, which means $x = -12$.

Thus, after discarding $x = -12$ since the width of the border must be positive, $x = 3$.

The correct answer is A.

PS09403

232. If $d = \dfrac{1}{2^3 \times 5^7}$ is expressed as a terminating decimal, how many nonzero digits will d have?

(A)   One

(B)   Two

(C)   Three

(D)   Seven

(E)   Ten

Arithmetic Operations on Rational Numbers

It will be helpful to use the fact that a factor that is an integer power of 10 has no effect on the number of nonzero digits a terminating decimal has.

$$\frac{1}{2^3 \times 5^7} = \frac{1}{2^3 \times 5^3} \times \frac{1}{5^4}$$

$$= \left(\frac{1}{2 \times 5}\right)^3 \times \left(\frac{1}{5}\right)^4$$

$$= \left(\frac{1}{10}\right)^3 \times \left(\frac{1}{5}\right)^4$$

$$= 10^{-3} \times (0.2)^4$$

$$= 10^{-3} \times (0.0016)$$

$$= 0.0000016$$

The correct answer is B.

PS03513

233. For any positive integer n, the sum of the first n positive integers equals $\frac{n(n+1)}{2}$. What is the sum of all the even integers between 99 and 301 ?

(A)   10,100

(B)   20,200

(C)   22,650

(D)   40,200

(E)   45,150

Algebra Simplifying Expressions; Arithmetic Computation with Integers

Note: The approach given below does not rely on the given formula.

To determine how many integers are to be summed, consider the following:

5 even integers have 10 as their first two digits, namely 100, 102, 104, 106, 108; 5 even integers have 11 as their first two digits, namely 110, 112, 114, 116, 118;

⋮

5 even integers have 28 as their first two digits, namely 280, 282, 284, 286, 288;

5 even integers have 29 as their first two digits, namely 290, 292, 294, 296, 298.

The first two digits range from 10 through 29, so there are $29 - 10 + 1 = 20$ such pairs of two digits. Thus there are $20(5) = 100$ even integers between 100 and 298. Including 300, there are 101 even integers between 99 and 301.

These even integers are listed below.

1st	2nd	3rd	4th	...	50th	51st	52nd	...	98th	99th	100th	101st
100	102	104	106	...	198	200	202	...	294	296	298	300

To sum, pair the integers

1st and 101st	$100 + 300 = 400$	
2nd and 100th	$102 + 298 = 400$	
3rd and 99th	$104 + 296 = 400$	$50(400) = 20{,}000$
4th and 98th	$106 + 294 = 400$	
⋮		
50th and 52nd	$198 + 202 = 400$	
51st	$= 200$	$+ \quad 200$

$$20{,}200$$

Alternatively, let S represent the sum. Then,

$$S = 100 + 102 + 104 + \ldots + 296 + 298 + 300$$
next, rewrite the sum

$$S = 300 + 298 + 296 + \ldots + 104 + 102 + 100$$
then add the two equations

$$2S = 400 + 400 + 400 + \ldots + 400 + 400 + 400$$
now divide by 2

$$S = 200 + 200 + 200 + \ldots + 200 + 200 + 200$$
there are 101 terms in S, so

$$S = 101(200) = 20{,}200.$$

The correct answer is B.

PS91151.02
234. November 16, 2001, was a Friday. If each of the years 2004, 2008, and 2012 had 366 days, and the remaining years from 2001 through 2014 had 365 days, what day of the week was November 16, 2014 ?

(A) Sunday

(B) Monday

(C) Tuesday

(D) Wednesday

(E) Thursday

Arithmetic Operations with Integers

The number of days between November 16, 2001, and November 16, 2014, is $10(365) + 3(366) = 4,748$ and, because $4,748 = 7(678) + 2$, it follows that $4,748$ days is 678 weeks plus 2 days. Then, 678 weeks from Friday, November 16, 2001, is Friday, November 14, 2014, and 2 days from Friday, November 14, 2014, is Sunday, November 16, 2014.

The correct answer is A.

PS06498
235. How many prime numbers between 1 and 100 are factors of 7,150 ?

(A) One

(B) Two

(C) Three

(D) Four

(E) Five

Arithmetic Rate

To find the number of prime numbers between 1 and 100 that are factors of 7,150, find the prime factorization of 7,150 using a method similar to the following:

$$7,150 = 10 \times 715$$
$$= (2 \times 5) \times (5 \times 143)$$
$$= 2 \times 5 \times 5 \times (11 \times 13)$$

Thus, 7,150 has four prime factors: 2, 5, 11, and 13.

The correct answer is D.

PS08732
236. A sequence of numbers a_1, a_2, a_3, ... is defined as follows: $a_1 = 3$, $a_2 = 5$, and every term in the sequence after a_2 is the product of all terms in the sequence preceding it, e.g., $a_3 = (a_1)(a_2)$ and $a_4 = (a_1)(a_2)(a_3)$. If $a_n = t$ and $n > 2$, what is the value of a_{n+2} in terms of t?

(A) $4t$

(B) t^2

(C) t^3

(D) t^4

(E) t^8

Algebra Sequences

It is given that $a_n = (a_1)(a_2) \dots (a_{n-1})$ and $a_n = t$. Therefore, $a_{n+1} = (a_1)(a_2) \dots (a_{n-1})(a_n) = (a_n)(a_n) = t^2$ and $a_{n+2} = (a_1)(a_2) \dots (a_n)(a_{n+1}) = (a_{n+1})(a_{n+1}) = (t^2)(t^2) = t^4$.

The correct answer is D.

PS08552
237. Last year the price per share of Stock X increased by k percent and the earnings per share of Stock X increased by m percent, where k is greater than m. By what percent did the ratio of price per share to earnings per share increase, in terms of k and m?

(A) $\dfrac{k}{m}\%$

(B) $(k - m)\%$

(C) $\dfrac{100(k-m)}{100+k}\%$

(D) $\dfrac{100(k-m)}{100+m}\%$

(E) $\dfrac{100(k-m)}{100+k+m}\%$

Algebra Percents

Although this problem can be solved algebraically, the answer can also be identified by choosing numerical values for the variables, calculating the percent increase in the ratio, and comparing the result with the corresponding numerical values of the answer choices. To this end, let the original price per share be $1,000 and earnings per share be $200, where $k = 10$ and $m = 5$. Note that $k > m$ for these values.

	Before increase	After increase
price	$1,000	1.1($1,000) = $1,100
earnings	$200	1.05($200) = $210
$\dfrac{\text{price}}{\text{earnings}}$	$\dfrac{1,000}{200} = 5$	$\dfrac{1,100}{210} = \dfrac{110}{21}$

Therefore, the percent increase in the ratio of price per share to earnings per share is

$$\left(\dfrac{\dfrac{110}{21} - 5}{5} \times 100 \right)\% = \left(\dfrac{110 - 105}{(5)(21)} \times 100 \right)\% = \dfrac{500}{105}\%$$

Now substitute $k = 10$ and $m = 5$ into the answer choices to determine which answer choice gives $\dfrac{500}{105}\%$.

A $\dfrac{10}{5}\%$ NO

B $(10 - 5)\%$ NO

C $\dfrac{100(5)}{100 + 10}\% = \dfrac{500}{110}\%$ NO

D $\dfrac{100(5)}{100 + 5}\% = \dfrac{500}{105}\%$ **YES**

E $\dfrac{100(5)}{100 + 10 + 5}\% = \dfrac{500}{115}\%$ NO

The correct answer is D.

PS04677

238. Of the 300 subjects who participated in an experiment using virtual-reality therapy to reduce their fear of heights, 40 percent experienced sweaty palms, 30 percent experienced vomiting, and 75 percent experienced dizziness. If all of the subjects experienced at least one of these effects and 35 percent of the subjects experienced exactly two of these effects, how many of the subjects experienced only one of these effects?

(A) 105
(B) 125
(C) 130
(D) 180
(E) 195

Arithmetic Applied Problems

Let a be the number who experienced only one of the effects, b be the number who experienced exactly two of the effects, and c be the number who experienced all three of the effects. Then

$a + b + c = 300$, since each of the 300 participants experienced at least one of the effects. From the given information, $b = 105$ (35% of 300), which gives $a + 105 + c = 300$, or $a + c = 195$ (Eq. 1). Also, if the number who experienced sweaty palms (40% of 300, or 120) is added to the number who experienced vomiting (30% of 300, or 90), and this sum is added to the number who experienced dizziness (75% of 300, or 225), then each participant who experienced only one of the effects is counted exactly once, each participant who experienced exactly two of the effects is counted exactly twice, and each participant who experienced all three of the effects is counted exactly 3 times. Therefore, $a + 2b + 3c = 120 + 90 + 225 = 435$. Using $b = 105$, it follows that $a + 2(105) + 3c = 435$, or $a + 3c = 225$ (Eq. 2). Then solving the system defined by Eq. 1 and Eq. 2,

$$\begin{cases} a + c = 195 \\ a + 3c = 225 \end{cases} \quad \text{multiply 1st equation by } -3$$

$$\begin{cases} -3a - 3c = -585 \\ a + 3c = 225 \end{cases} \quad \text{add equations}$$

$-2a = -360$, or $a = 180$

The correct answer is D.

PS56710.02

239. The outer dimensions of a closed rectangular cardboard box are 8 centimeters by 10 centimeters by 12 centimeters, and the six sides of the box are uniformly $\dfrac{1}{2}$ centimeter thick. A closed canister in the shape of a right circular cylinder is to be placed inside the box so that it stands upright when the box rests on one of its sides. Of all such canisters that would fit, what is the outer radius, in centimeters, of the canister that occupies the maximum volume?

(A) 3.5
(B) 4
(C) 4.5
(D) 5
(E) 5.5

Geometry Rectangular Solids and Cylinders

Since the inner distances between pairs of opposite sides of the box are $\dfrac{1}{2} + \dfrac{1}{2} = 1$ centimeters less than their corresponding outer distances, the inner dimensions of the box are 7 cm by 9 cm by 11 cm. Thus, there are three possibilities for the inner dimensions of the side on which the box rests: (a) 7 cm by 9 cm; (b) 7 cm by 11 cm; (c) 9 cm by 11 cm. For each of these possibilities, the outer diameter of the cylinder is at most the inner length of the shortest edge of the side on which the box rests and the outer height of the cylinder is at most the inner length of the remaining edge (i.e., the inner height of the box for that possibility).

Using the fact that the volume of a right circular cylinder of diameter d and height h is $\pi\left(\dfrac{d}{2}\right)^2 h$, it follows that, for the three possibilities given above, the maximum volume, in cubic centimeters, of the cylinder would be, respectively

$$\pi\left(\frac{7}{2}\right)^2(11) = \frac{7\pi}{4}(7)(11),\ \pi\left(\frac{7}{2}\right)^2(9) = \frac{7\pi}{4}(7)(9),$$

and $\pi\left(\dfrac{9}{2}\right)^2(7) = \dfrac{7\pi}{4}(9)(9)$. Of these three

possibilities, the last represents the greatest volume, and corresponds to a cylinder having an outer radius of $\dfrac{9}{2} = 4.5$ cm.

The correct answer is C.

PS03686
240. If $m^{-1} = -\dfrac{1}{3}$, then m^{-2} is equal to

(A) −9

(B) −3

(C) $-\dfrac{1}{9}$

(D) $\dfrac{1}{9}$

(E) 9

Arithmetic Negative Exponents

Using rules of exponents, $m^{-2} = m^{-1 \times 2} = \left(m^{-1}\right)^2$,

and since $m^{-1} = -\dfrac{1}{3}$, $m^{-2} = \left(-\dfrac{1}{3}\right)^2 = \dfrac{1}{9}$.

The correct answer is D.

PS07555
241. A photography dealer ordered 60 Model X cameras to be sold for $250 each, which represents a 20 percent markup over the dealer's initial cost for each camera. Of the cameras ordered, 6 were never sold and were returned to the manufacturer for a refund of 50 percent of the dealer's initial cost. What was the dealer's approximate profit or loss as a percent of the dealer's initial cost for the 60 cameras?

(A) 7% loss

(B) 13% loss

(C) 7% profit

(D) 13% profit

(E) 15% profit

Arithmetic Percents

Given that $250 is 20% greater than a camera's initial cost, it follows that the initial cost for each camera was $\left(\$\dfrac{250}{1.2}\right)$. Therefore, the initial cost for the 60 cameras was $60\left(\$\dfrac{250}{1.2}\right)$. The total revenue is the sum of the amount obtained from selling $60 - 6 = 54$ cameras for $250 each and the $\left(\dfrac{1}{2}\right)\left(\$\dfrac{250}{1.2}\right)$ refund for each of 6 cameras, or $(54)(\$250) + (6)\left(\dfrac{1}{2}\right)\left(\$\dfrac{250}{1.2}\right)$. The total profit, as a percent of the total initial cost, is

$$\left(\frac{(\text{total revenue}) - (\text{total initial cost})}{(\text{total initial cost})} \times 100\right)\% =$$

$$\left(\left(\frac{(\text{total revenue})}{(\text{total initial cost})} - 1\right) \times 100\right)\%.\ \text{Using}$$

the numerical expressions obtained above,

$$\frac{(\text{total revenue})}{(\text{total initial cost})} - 1$$

$$= \frac{(54)(250)+6\left(\frac{1}{2}\right)\left(\frac{250}{1.2}\right)}{(60)\left(\frac{250}{1.2}\right)}-1 \quad \text{by substitution}$$

$$= \frac{54+3\left(\frac{1}{1.2}\right)}{(60)\left(\frac{1}{1.2}\right)}-1 \quad \text{by canceling 250s}$$

$$= \frac{54(1.2)+3}{60}-1 \quad \begin{array}{l}\text{by multiplying}\\ \text{top and bottom by 1.2}\\ \text{and then canceling 1.2}\end{array}$$

$$= \frac{67.8}{60}-1$$

$$= 1.13-1$$

$$= 0.13$$

Finally, $(0.13 \times 100)\% = 13\%$, which represents a profit since it is positive.

The correct answer is D.

PS04305

242. Seven pieces of rope have an average (arithmetic mean) length of 68 centimeters and a median length of 84 centimeters. If the length of the longest piece of rope is 14 centimeters more than 4 times the length of the shortest piece of rope, what is the maximum possible length, in centimeters, of the longest piece of rope?

(A) 82
(B) 118
(C) 120
(D) 134
(E) 152

Algebra Statistics

Let $a, b, c, d, e, f,$ and g be the lengths, in centimeters, of the pieces of rope, listed from least to greatest. From the given information it follows that $d = 84$ and $g = 4a + 14$. Therefore, listed from least to greatest, the lengths are $a, b, c, 84, e, f,$ and $4a + 14$. The maximum value of $4a + 14$ will occur when the maximum value of a is used, and this

will be the case only if the shortest 3 pieces all have the same length. Therefore, listed from least to greatest, the lengths are $a, a, a, 84, e, f,$ and $4a + 14$. The maximum value for $4a + 14$ will occur when e and f are as small as possible. Since e and f are to the right of the median, they must be at least 84 and so 84 is the least possible value for each of e and f. Therefore, listed from least to greatest, the lengths are $a, a, a, 84, 84, 84,$ and $4a + 14$. Since the average length is 68, it follows that

$$\frac{a+a+a+84+84+84+(4a+14)}{7} = 68, \text{ or } a = 30.$$

Hence, the maximum length of the longest piece is $(4a + 14) = [4(30) + 14] = 134$ centimeters.

The correct answer is D.

PS16146

243. What is the difference between the sixth and the fifth terms of the sequence 2, 4, 7, ... whose nth term is $n + 2^{n-1}$?

(A) 2
(B) 3
(C) 6
(D) 16
(E) 17

Algebra Simplifying Algebraic Expressions

According to the given formula, the sixth term of the sequence is $6 + 2^{6-1} = 6 + 2^5$ and the fifth term is $5 + 2^{5-1} = 5 + 2^4$. Then,

$$\left(6 + 2^5\right) - \left(5 + 2^4\right) = (6-5) + \left(2^5 - 2^4\right)$$
$$= 1 + 2^4(2-1)$$
$$= 1 + 2^4$$
$$= 1 + 16$$
$$= 17$$

The correct answer is E.

PS02405
244. From the consecutive integers –10 to 10, inclusive, 20 integers are randomly chosen with repetitions allowed. What is the least possible value of the product of the 20 integers?

(A) $(-10)^{20}$

(B) $(-10)^{10}$

(C) 0

(D) $-(10)^{19}$

(E) $-(10)^{20}$

Arithmetic Properties of Numbers

If –10 is chosen an odd number of times and 10 is chosen the remaining number of times (for example, choose –10 once and choose 10 nineteen times, or choose –10 three times and choose 10 seventeen times), then the product of the 20 chosen numbers will be $-(10)^{20}$. Note that $-(10)^{20}$ is less than $-(10)^{19}$, the only other negative value among the answer choices.

The correct answer is E.

PS05140
245. The letters D, G, I, I, and T can be used to form 5-letter strings such as DIGIT or DGIIT. Using these letters, how many 5-letter strings can be formed in which the two occurrences of the letter I are separated by at least one other letter?

(A) 12

(B) 18

(C) 24

(D) 36

(E) 48

Arithmetic Elementary Combinatorics

There are 6 ways to select the locations of the 2 occurrences of the letter I, and this number can be determined by listing all such ways as shown below, where the symbol * is used in place of the letters D, G, and T:

I*I**, I**I*, I***I, *I*I*, *I**I, **I*I

Alternatively, the number of ways to select the locations of the 2 occurrences of the letter I can be determined by using $\binom{5}{2} - 4 =$

$\dfrac{5!}{(2!)(3!)} - 4 = 10 - 4 = 6$, which is the number of

ways to select 2 of the 5 locations minus the 4 ways in which the 2 selected locations are adjacent.

For each of these 6 ways to select the locations of the 2 occurrences of the letter I, there are 6 ways to select the locations of the letters D, G, and T, which can be determined by using $3! = 6$ or by listing all such ways:

DGT, DTG, GDT, GTD, TDG, TGD

It follows that the number of ways to select the locations of the 5 letters to form 5-letter strings is $(6)(6) = 36$.

The correct answer is D.

PS00574
246. $\dfrac{0.99999999}{1.0001} - \dfrac{0.99999991}{1.0003} =$

(A) 10^{-8}

(B) $3(10^{-8})$

(C) $3(10^{-4})$

(D) $2(10^{-4})$

(E) 10^{-4}

Arithmetic Operations on Rational Numbers

Calculations with lengthy decimals can be avoided by writing 0.99999999 as $1 - 10^{-8}$, 0.99999991 as $1 - 9(10^{-8})$, 1.0001 as $1 + 10^{-4}$, and 1.0003 as $1 + 3(10^{-4})$. Doing this gives

$$\frac{1-10^{-8}}{1+10^{-4}} - \frac{1-9\left(10^{-8}\right)}{1+3\left(10^{-4}\right)}$$

$$= \frac{\left[1+10^{-4}\right]\left[1-10^{-4}\right]}{1+10^{-4}} - \frac{1-9\left(10^{-8}\right)}{1+3\left(10^{-4}\right)}$$

$$= \frac{1-10^{-4}}{1} - \frac{1-9(10^{-8})}{1+3\left(10^{-4}\right)}$$

$$= \frac{\left[1-10^{-4}\right]\left[1+3\left(10^{-4}\right)\right]-\left[1-9\left(10^{-8}\right)\right]}{1+3\left(10^{-4}\right)}$$

$$= \frac{1+3\left(10^{-4}\right)-10^{-4}-3\left(10^{-8}\right)-1+9\left(10^{-8}\right)}{1+3\left(10^{-4}\right)}$$

$$= \frac{2\left(10^{-4}\right)+6\left(10^{-8}\right)}{1+3\left(10^{-4}\right)}$$

$$= \frac{\left[2\left(10^{-4}\right)\right]\left[1 + 3\left(10^{-4}\right)\right]}{1 + 3\left(10^{-4}\right)}$$

$$= 2\left(10^{-4}\right)$$

The correct answer is D.

PS03144

247. Last Sunday a certain store sold copies of Newspaper A for $1.00 each and copies of Newspaper B for $1.25 each, and the store sold no other newspapers that day. If r percent of the store's revenue from newspaper sales was from Newspaper A and if p percent of the newspapers that the store sold were copies of Newspaper A, which of the following expresses r in terms of p ?

(A) $\dfrac{100p}{125 - p}$

(B) $\dfrac{150p}{250 - p}$

(C) $\dfrac{300p}{375 - p}$

(D) $\dfrac{400p}{500 - p}$

(E) $\dfrac{500p}{625 - p}$

Algebra Percents

Because the number of newspapers sold at the store last Sunday is not given, assume for simplicity that number is 1,000. Also, the value of p is not given, so choose a convenient value to work with, say $p = 60$. In the table that follows, the chosen numbers are in **boldface**.

	Newspaper A	Newspaper B	Total
Percent of papers sold	**$p = 60$**	40	100
Number sold	600	400	**1,000**
Revenue	600($1) = $600	400($1.25) = $500	$1,100
Percent of revenue (r)	$\dfrac{600}{1,100} \times 100 = \dfrac{600}{11}$		

Now, check the answer choices using $p = 60$ to see which one yields $\dfrac{600}{11}$.

(A) $\dfrac{100p}{125 - p} = \dfrac{100(60)}{125 - 60} = \dfrac{6,000}{65}$

No (65 doesn't have 11 as a factor)

(B) $\dfrac{150p}{250 - p} = \dfrac{150(60)}{250 - 60} = \dfrac{9,000}{190}$

No (190 doesn't have 11 as a factor)

(C) $\dfrac{300p}{375 - p} = \dfrac{300(60)}{375 - 60} = \dfrac{18,000}{315}$

No (315 doesn't have 11 as a factor)

(D) $\dfrac{400p}{500 - p} = \dfrac{400(60)}{500 - 60} = \dfrac{24,000}{440}$

Yes (440 has 11 as a factor) $\dfrac{24,000}{440} = \dfrac{600}{11}$

(E) $\dfrac{500p}{625 - p} = \dfrac{500(60)}{625 - 60} = \dfrac{30,000}{565}$

No (565 doesn't have 11 as a factor)

The correct answer is D.

PS16890

248. For the past n days, the average (arithmetic mean) daily production at a company was 50 units. If today's production of 90 units raises the average to 55 units per day, what is the value of n ?

(A) 30

(B) 18

(C) 10

(D) 9

(E) 7

Arithmetic; Algebra Statistics; Applied Problems; Simultaneous Equations

Let x be the total production of the past n days.

Using the formula $\text{average} = \dfrac{\text{sum of values}}{\text{number of values}}$, the information in the problem can be expressed in the following two equations

$$50 = \frac{x}{n}$$ daily average of 50 units over the past n days

$$55 = \frac{x + 90}{n + 1}$$ increased daily average when including today's 90 units

Solving the first equation for x gives $x = 50n$. Then substituting $50n$ for x in the second equation gives the following that can be solved for n:

$$55 = \frac{50n + 90}{n + 1}$$

$55(n + 1) = 50n + 90$ multiply both sides by $(n + 1)$

$55n + 55 = 50n + 90$ distribute the 55

$5n = 35$ subtract $50n$ and 55 from both sides

$n = 7$ divide both sides by 5

The correct answer is E.

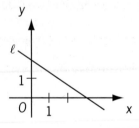

PS16893
249. In the coordinate system above, which of the following is the equation of line ℓ ?

(A) $2x - 3y = 6$

(B) $2x + 3y = 6$

(C) $3x + 2y = 6$

(D) $2x - 3y = -6$

(E) $3x - 2y = -6$

Geometry Simple Coordinate Geometry

From the figure above, it is given that line ℓ passes through $(0,2)$ and $(3,0)$. The slope-intercept form for the equation of a line is $y = mx + b$, where m is the slope and b is the y-intercept. The slope is $\frac{2 - 0}{0 - 3} = -\frac{2}{3}$ and

the y-intercept is 2. Therefore, the equation is $y = -\frac{2}{3}x + 2$, which can be rewritten as

$2x + 3y = 6$.

Alternatively, determine which of the answer choice equations is true for both $(x,y) = (0,2)$ and $(x,y) = (3,0)$.

		true for $(x,y) = (0,2)$?	true for $(x,y) = (3,0)$?
A	$2x - 3y = 6$	$0 - 6 = 6$ false	$6 - 0 = 6$ true
B	$2x + 3y = 6$	$0 + 6 = 6$ **true**	$6 + 0 = 6$ **true**
C	$3x + 2y = 6$	$0 + 4 = 6$ false	$9 + 0 = 6$ false
D	$2x - 3y = -6$	$0 - 6 = -6$ true	$6 - 0 = -6$ false
E	$3x - 2y = -6$	$0 - 4 = -6$ false	$9 - 0 = -6$ false

The correct answer is B.

PS16894
250. If a two-digit positive integer has its digits reversed, the resulting integer differs from the original by 27. By how much do the two digits differ?

(A)   3

(B)   4

(C)   5

(D)   6

(E)   7

Algebra Applied Problems

Let the one two-digit integer be represented by $10t + s$, where s and t are digits, and let the other integer with the reversed digits be represented by $10s + t$. The information that the difference between the integers is 27 can be expressed in the following equation, which can be solved for the answer.

$(10s + t) - (10t + s) = 27$

$10s + t - 10t - s = 27$ distribute the negative

$9s - 9t = 27$ combine like terms

$s - t = 3$ divide both sides by 9

Thus, it is seen that the two digits s and t differ by 3.

The correct answer is A.

PS16896

251. In an electric circuit, two resistors with resistances x and y are connected in parallel. In this case, if r is the combined resistance of these two resistors, then the reciprocal of r is equal to the sum of the reciprocals of x and y. What is r in terms of x and y?

(A) xy

(B) $x + y$

(C) $\dfrac{1}{x + y}$

(D) $\dfrac{xy}{x + y}$

(E) $\dfrac{x + y}{xy}$

Algebra Applied Problems

Note that two numbers are reciprocals of each other if and only if their product is 1. Thus the reciprocals of r, x, and y are $\dfrac{1}{r}$, $\dfrac{1}{x}$, and $\dfrac{1}{y}$, respectively. So, according to the problem, $\dfrac{1}{r} = \dfrac{1}{x} + \dfrac{1}{y}$. To solve this equation for r, begin by creating a common denominator on the right side by multiplying the first fraction by $\dfrac{y}{y}$ and the second fraction by $\dfrac{x}{x}$:

$$\frac{1}{r} = \frac{1}{x} + \frac{1}{y}$$

$$\frac{1}{r} = \frac{y}{xy} + \frac{x}{xy}$$

$$\frac{1}{r} = \frac{x + y}{xy} \qquad \text{combine the fractions on the right side}$$

$$r = \frac{xy}{x + y} \qquad \text{invert the fractions on both sides}$$

The correct answer is D.

PS16897

252. Xavier, Yvonne, and Zelda each try independently to solve a problem. If their individual probabilities for success are $\dfrac{1}{4}$, $\dfrac{1}{2}$, and $\dfrac{5}{8}$, respectively, what is the probability that Xavier and Yvonne, but not Zelda, will solve the problem?

(A) $\dfrac{11}{8}$

(B) $\dfrac{7}{8}$

(C) $\dfrac{9}{64}$

(D) $\dfrac{5}{64}$

(E) $\dfrac{3}{64}$

Arithmetic Probability

Since the individuals' probabilities are independent, they can be multiplied to figure out the combined probability. The probability of Xavier's success is given as $\dfrac{1}{4}$, and the probability of Yvonne's success is given as $\dfrac{1}{2}$. Since the probability of Zelda's success is given as $\dfrac{5}{8}$, then the probability of her NOT solving the problem is $1 - \dfrac{5}{8} = \dfrac{3}{8}$.

Thus, the combined probability is

$$\left(\frac{1}{4}\right)\left(\frac{1}{2}\right)\left(\frac{3}{8}\right) = \frac{3}{64}.$$

The correct answer is E.

PS16898

253. If $\dfrac{1}{x} - \dfrac{1}{x+1} = \dfrac{1}{x+4}$, then x could be

(A) 0

(B) −1

(C) −2

(D) −3

(E) −4

Algebra Second-Degree Equations

Solve the equation for x. Begin by multiplying all the terms by $x(x+1)(x+4)$ to eliminate the denominators.

$$\frac{1}{x} - \frac{1}{x+1} = \frac{1}{x+4}$$

$$(x+1)(x+4) - x(x+4) = x(x+1)$$

$(x+4)(x+1-x) = x(x+1)$ factor the $(x+4)$ out front on the left side

$(x+4)(1) = x(x+1)$ simplify

$(x+4) = x^2 + x$ distribute the x on the right side

$4 = x^2$ subtract x from both sides

$\pm 2 = x$ take the square root of both sides

Both -2 and 2 are square roots of 4 since $\left(-2^2\right) = 4$ and $\left(2^2\right) = 4$. Thus, x could be -2.

This problem can also be solved as follows. Rewrite the left side as, $\dfrac{(x+1)-x}{x(x+1)} = \dfrac{1}{x(x+1)}$, then set equal to the right side to get

$\dfrac{1}{x(x+1)} = \dfrac{1}{x+4}$. Next, cross multiply:

$(1)(x+4) = x(x+1)(1)$. Therefore, $x+4 = x^2 + x$, or $x^2 = 4$, so $x = \pm 2$.

The correct answer is C.

PS16899

254. $\left(\dfrac{1}{2}\right)^{-3} \left(\dfrac{1}{4}\right)^{-2} \left(\dfrac{1}{16}\right)^{-1} =$

(A) $\left(\dfrac{1}{2}\right)^{-48}$

(B) $\left(\dfrac{1}{2}\right)^{-11}$

(C) $\left(\dfrac{1}{2}\right)^{-6}$

(D) $\left(\dfrac{1}{8}\right)^{-11}$

(E) $\left(\dfrac{1}{8}\right)^{-6}$

Arithmetic Operations on Rational Numbers

It is clear from the answer choices that all three factors need to be written with a common denominator, and they thus become

$$\left(\frac{1}{2}\right)^{-3} = \left(\frac{1}{2}\right)^{-3}$$

$$\left(\frac{1}{4}\right)^{-2} = \left(\left(\frac{1}{2}\right)^2\right)^{-2} = \left(\frac{1}{2}\right)^{-4}$$

$$\left(\frac{1}{16}\right)^{-1} = \left(\left(\frac{1}{2}\right)^4\right)^{-1} = \left(\frac{1}{2}\right)^{-4}$$

So, $\left(\dfrac{1}{2}\right)^{-3} \left(\dfrac{1}{4}\right)^{-2} \left(\dfrac{1}{16}\right)^{-1} =$

$$\left(\frac{1}{2}\right)^{-3}\left(\frac{1}{2}\right)^{-4}\left(\frac{1}{2}\right)^{-4} = \left(\frac{1}{2}\right)^{-3-4-4} = \left(\frac{1}{2}\right)^{-11}.$$

The correct answer is B.

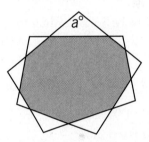

PS00947

255. The figure shown above consists of a shaded 9-sided polygon and 9 unshaded isosceles triangles. For each isosceles triangle, the longest side is a side of the shaded polygon and the two sides of equal length are extensions of the two adjacent sides of the shaded polygon. What is the value of a?

(A)   100

(B)   105

(C)   110

(D)   115

(E)   120

Geometry Polygons

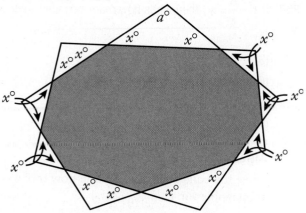

Let $x°$ represent the measure of each base angle of the triangle with vertex angle labeled $a°$. Each base angle of this triangle and one base angle of a triangle with which it shares a vertex are vertical angles and have the same measure. Thus, the base angles of these triangles also have measure $x°$. This pattern continues for the base angles of each pair of triangles that share a vertex, so each base angle of each of the 9 triangles has measure $x°$, as shown above. Also, the vertex angle of each of the 9 triangles has measure $a° = 180° − 2x°$.

Each interior angle of the shaded polygon has measure $(180 − x)°$ since each forms a straight angle with an angle that has measure $x°$, and the sum of the measures is $(9)(180 − x)°$. But the sum of the interior angles of a polygon with n sides is $(n − 2)(180°)$, so the sum of the interior angles of a 9-sided polygon is $(7)(180°) = 1,260°$. Therefore, $(9)(180 − x)° = 1,260°$ and $x = 40$. Finally, $a = 180 − 2x = 180 − 2(40) = 100$.

The correct answer is A.

PS01648

256. List T consists of 30 positive decimals, none of which is an integer, and the sum of the 30 decimals is S. The estimated sum of the 30 decimals, E, is defined as follows. Each decimal in T whose tenths digit is even is rounded up to the nearest integer, and each decimal in T whose tenths digit is odd is rounded down to the nearest integer; E is the sum of the resulting integers.

If $\frac{1}{3}$ of the decimals in T have a tenths digit that is even, which of the following is a possible value of $E − S$?

I. $−16$

II. 6

III. 10

(A)   I only

(B)   I and II only

(C)   I and III only

(D)   II and III only

(E)   I, II, and III

Arithmetic Operations on Rational Numbers

First, consider $E − S$ as the total of the "contributions" made by the decimals in T with even tenths digits and the "contributions" made by the decimals in T with odd tenths digits, as shown in the following tables.

	Decimals with even tenth digit	Example
Number that occurs in T	$\frac{1}{3}(30) = 10$	
Max possible tenth digit	8	14.89999
Contribution each makes to $E − S$	Greater than 0.1	$15 − 14.89999$ $= 0.10001$
Total contribution to $E − S$	Greater than $10(0.1)$ $= 1$	
Min possible tenth digit	0	14.00001
Contribution each makes to $E − S$	Less than 1	$15 − 14.00001$ $= 0.99999$
Total contribution to $E − S$	Less than $10(1) = 10$	
Summary	$1 <$ (evens' contribution to $E − S$) < 10	

	Decimals with odd tenth digit	Example
Number that occurs in T	$\frac{2}{3}(30) = 20$	
Max possible tenth digit	9	14.9999
Contribution each makes to $E - S$	Greater than -1	$14 - 14.9999$ $= -0.9999$
Total contribution to $E - S$	Greater than $20(-1)$ $= -20$	
Min possible tenth digit	1	14.1
Contribution each makes to $E - S$	Less than or equal to -0.1	$14 - 14.1$ $= -0.1$
Total contribution to $E - S$	Less than or equal to $20(-0.1) = -2$	
Summary	$-20 <$ (odds' contribution to $E - S$) ≤ -2	

Adding the summary inequalities from the tables gives

$1 + (-20) <$ (evens' contribution to $E - S$) + (odds' contribution to $E - S$) $< 10 + (-2)$ or $-19 < E - S < 8$. Thus, the possible values of $E - S$ include -16 and 6, but not 10.

Note that if T contains 10 repetitions of 1.8 and 20 repetitions of 1.9, then
$S = 10(1.8) + 20(1.9) = 18 + 38 = 56$,
$E = 10(2) + 20(1) = 20 + 20 = 40$, and
$E - S = 40 - 56 = -16$.

However, if T contains 10 repetitions of 1.2 and 20 repetitions of 1.1, then
$S = 10(1.2) + 20(1.1) = 12 + 22 = 34$,
$E = 10(2) + 20(1) = 20 + 20 = 40$, and
$E - S = 40 - 34 = 6$.

The correct answer is B.

PS16115
257. If $5 - \dfrac{6}{x} = x$, then x has how many possible values?

(A) None

(B) One

(C) Two

(D) A finite number greater than two

(E) An infinite number

Algebra Second-Degree Equations

Solve the equation to determine how many values are possible for x.

$$5 - \frac{6}{x} = x$$
$$5x - 6 = x^2$$
$$0 = x^2 - 5x + 6$$
$$0 = (x - 3)(x - 2)$$
$$x = 3 \text{ or } 2$$

The correct answer is C.

PS16904
258. Seed mixture X is 40 percent ryegrass and 60 percent bluegrass by weight; seed mixture Y is 25 percent ryegrass and 75 percent fescue. If a mixture of X and Y contains 30 percent ryegrass, what percent of the weight of the mixture is X ?

(A) 10%

(B) $33\frac{1}{3}\%$

(C) 40%

(D) 50%

(E) $66\frac{2}{3}\%$

Algebra Applied Problems

Let X be the amount of seed mixture X in the final mixture, and let Y be the amount of seed mixture Y in the final mixture. The final mixture of X and Y needs to contain 30 percent ryegrass seed, so any other kinds of grass seed are irrelevant to the solution to this problem. The information about the ryegrass percentages for X,

Y, and the final mixture can be expressed in the following equation and solved for X.

$$0.40X + 0.25Y = 0.30(X + Y)$$

$0.40X + 0.25Y = 0.30X + 0.30Y$	distribute the 0.30 on the right side
$0.10X = 0.05Y$	subtract $0.30X$ and $0.25Y$ from both sides
$X = 0.5Y$	divide both sides by 0.10

Using this, the percent of the weight of the combined mixture $(X + Y)$ that is X is

$$\frac{X}{X+Y} = \frac{0.5Y}{0.5Y+Y} = \frac{0.5Y}{1.5Y} = \frac{0.5}{1.5} = 0.33\overline{3} = 33\frac{1}{3}\%$$

The correct answer is B.

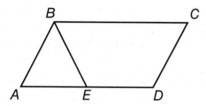

PS49220.02

259. In the figure above, *ABCD* is a parallelogram and *E* is the midpoint of side *AD*. The area of triangular region *ABE* is what fraction of the area of quadrilateral region *BCDE* ?

(A) $\frac{1}{2}$

(B) $\frac{1}{3}$

(C) $\frac{1}{4}$

(D) $\frac{1}{5}$

(E) $\frac{1}{6}$

Geometry Area

The area of $\triangle ABE$ is $\frac{1}{2}(AE)h$, where h is the height of parallelogram *ABCD*. Since *E* is the midpoint of *AD*, $AE = \frac{1}{2}AD$. So the area of $\triangle ABE$ is $\left(\frac{1}{2}\right)\left(\frac{1}{2}AD\right)h = \frac{1}{4}(AD)h$. Since the area of *ABCD* is $(AD)h$, the area of *BCDE* is

$(AD)h - \frac{1}{4}(AD)h = \frac{3}{4}(AD)h$. It follows that

$$\frac{\text{area of } ABE}{\text{area of } BCDE} = \frac{\frac{1}{4}(AD)h}{\frac{3}{4}(AD)h} = \frac{1}{3}.$$

The correct answer is B.

PS14203

260. How many of the integers that satisfy the inequality $\frac{(x+2)(x+3)}{x-2} \geq 0$ are less than 5 ?

(A) 1

(B) 2

(C) 3

(D) 4

(E) 5

Algebra Inequalities

Note: This explanation is very detailed. However, many of the steps should become more automatic with additional practice in solving nonlinear inequalities.

The expression $\frac{(x+2)(x+3)}{x-2}$ contains three binomials, namely $x + 2$, $x + 3$, and $x - 2$, that determine for what values of x each binomial is zero, negative, and positive. The table below summarizes these values.

Binomial	Zero for	Negative for	Positive for
$x + 3$	$x = -3$	$x < -3$	$x > -3$
$x + 2$	$x = -2$	$x < -2$	$x > -2$
$x - 2$	$x = 2$	$x < 2$	$x > 2$

Note that, although $x - 2 = 0$ when $x = 2$, $\frac{(x+2)(x+3)}{x-2}$ is undefined for $x = 2$. However, $\frac{(x+2)(x+3)}{x-2} = 0$ when $x = -3$ and when $x = -2$. Both of these values are integers less than 5. (i)

The number line below shows the information in the table above. The vertical segments at $x = -3$, $x = -2$, and $x = 2$ partition the number line into 4 intervals:

I_1, where $x < -3$

I_2, where $-3 < x < -2$

I_3, where $-2 < x < 2$

I_4, where $x > 2$.

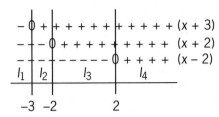

I_1: All three binomials are negative, so the inequality $\dfrac{(x+2)(x+3)}{x-2} \geq 0$ is NOT satisfied.

I_2: Contains no integers, so need not be considered further.

I_3: Two binomials are positive, one is negative so the inequality $\dfrac{(x+2)(x+3)}{x-2} \geq 0$ is NOT satisfied.

I_4: All three binomials are positive, so the inequality $\dfrac{(x+2)(x+3)}{x-2} \geq 0$ is satisfied. The integers in this interval that are less than 5 are 3 and 4. (ii)

From (i) and (ii), there are 4 integers, namely -3, -2, 3, and 4, for which $\dfrac{(x+2)(x+3)}{x-2} \geq 0$.

The correct answer is D.

PS07712

261. Of the 150 houses in a certain development, 60 percent have air-conditioning, 50 percent have a sunporch, and 30 percent have a swimming pool. If 5 of the houses have all three of these amenities and 5 have none of them, how many of the houses have exactly two of these amenities?

(A) 10

(B) 45

(C) 50

(D) 55

(E) 65

Arithmetic Sets

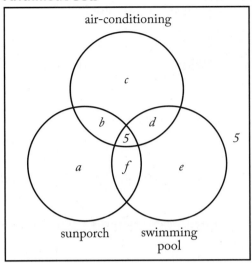

Since 60% of the 150 houses have air-conditioning, $b + c + d + 5 = 0.6(150) = 90$, so $b + c + d = 85$ (i). Similarly, since 50% have a sunporch, $a + b + f + 5 = 0.5(150) = 75$, so $a + b + f = 70$ (ii). Likewise, since 30% have a swimming pool, $d + e + f + 5 = 0.3(150) = 45$, so $d + e + f = 40$ (iii). Adding equations (i), (ii), and (iii) gives $(b + c + d) + (a + b + f) + (d + e + f) = 195$, or $a + 2b + c + 2d + e + 2f = 195$ (iv). But $a + b + c + d + e + f + 5 + 5 = 150$, or $a + b + c + d + e + f = 140$ (v). Subtracting equation (v) from equation (iv) gives $b + d + f = 55$, so 55 houses have exactly two of the amenities.

The correct answer is D.

PS08886

262. The value of $\dfrac{2^{-14} + 2^{-15} + 2^{-16} + 2^{-17}}{5}$ is how many times the value of $2^{(-17)}$?

(A) $\dfrac{3}{2}$

(B) $\dfrac{5}{2}$

(C) 3

(D) 4

(E) 5

Arithmetic Negative Exponents

If the value of $\dfrac{2^{-14}+2^{-15}+2^{-16}+2^{-17}}{5}$ is x times

the value of 2^{-17}, then

$$x(2^{-17}) = \dfrac{2^{-14}+2^{-15}+2^{-16}+2^{-17}}{5}$$

$$x = \dfrac{\dfrac{2^{-14}+2^{-15}+2^{-16}+2^{-17}}{5}}{2^{-17}}$$

$$= \dfrac{2^{-14}+2^{-15}+2^{-16}+2^{-17}}{5} \times 2^{17}$$

$$= \dfrac{(2^{-14}+2^{-15}+2^{-16}+2^{-17}) \times 2^{17}}{5}$$

$$= \dfrac{2^{-14+17}+2^{-15+17}+2^{-16+17}+2^{-17+17}}{5}$$

$$= \dfrac{2^{3}+2^{2}+2^{1}+2^{0}}{5}$$

$$= \dfrac{8+4+2+1}{5}$$

$$= 3$$

The correct answer is C.

To register for the GMAT™ exam go to www.mba.com/gmat

5.0   Data Sufficiency

5.0 Data Sufficiency

Data Sufficiency questions appear in the Quantitative Reasoning section of the GMAT™ exam. Multiple-choice Data Sufficiency questions are intermingled with Problem Solving questions throughout the section. You will have 62 minutes to complete the Quantitative Reasoning section of the GMAT exam, or about 2 minutes to answer each question. These questions require knowledge of the following topics:

- Arithmetic
- Elementary algebra
- Commonly known concepts of geometry

Data Sufficiency questions are designed to measure your ability to analyze a quantitative problem, recognize which given information is relevant, and determine at what point there is sufficient information to solve a problem. In these questions, you are to classify each problem according to the five fixed answer choices, rather than find a solution to the problem.

Each Data Sufficiency question consists of a question, often accompanied by some initial information, and two statements, labeled (1) and (2), which contain additional information. You must decide whether the information in each statement is sufficient to answer the question or—if neither statement provides enough information—whether the information in the two statements together is sufficient. It is also possible that the statements, in combination, do not give enough information to answer the question.

Begin by reading the initial information and the question carefully. Next, consider the first statement. Does the information provided by the first statement enable you to answer the question? Go on to the second statement. Try to ignore the information given in the first statement when you consider whether the second statement provides information that, by itself, allows you to answer the question. Now you should be able to say, for each statement, whether it is sufficient to determine the answer.

Next, consider the two statements in tandem. Do they, together, enable you to answer the question?

Look again at your answer choices. Select the one that most accurately reflects whether the statements provide the information required to answer the question.

5.1 Test-Taking Strategies

1. Do not waste valuable time solving a problem.

You only need to determine whether sufficient information is given to solve it.

2. Consider each statement separately.

First, decide whether each statement alone gives sufficient information to solve the problem. Be sure to disregard the information given in statement (1) when you evaluate the information given in statement (2). If either, or both, of the statements give(s) sufficient information to solve the problem, select the answer corresponding to the description of which statement(s) give(s) sufficient information to solve the problem.

3. Judge the statements in tandem if neither statement is sufficient by itself.

It is possible that the two statements together do not provide sufficient information. Once you decide, select the answer corresponding to the description of whether the statements together give sufficient information to solve the problem.

4. Answer the question asked.

For example, if the question asks, "What is the value of y ?" for an answer statement to be sufficient, you must be able to find one and only one value for y. Being able to determine minimum or maximum values for an answer (e.g., $y = x + 2$) is not sufficient, because such answers constitute a range of values rather than the specific value of y.

5. Be very careful not to make unwarranted assumptions based on the images represented.

Figures are not necessarily drawn to scale; they are generalized figures showing little more than intersecting line segments and the relationships of points, angles, and regions. For example, if a figure described as a rectangle looks like a square, do *not* conclude that it is actually a square just by looking at the figure.

If statement 1 is sufficient, then the answer must be **A or D.**

If statement 2 is not sufficient, then the answer must be **A.**

If statement 2 is sufficient, then the answer must be **D.**

If statement 1 is not sufficient, then the answer must be **B, C, or E.**

If statement 2 is sufficient, then the answer must be **B.**

If statement 2 is not sufficient, then the answer must be **C or E.**

If both statements together are sufficient, then the answer must be **C.**

If both statements together are still not sufficient, then the answer must be **E.**

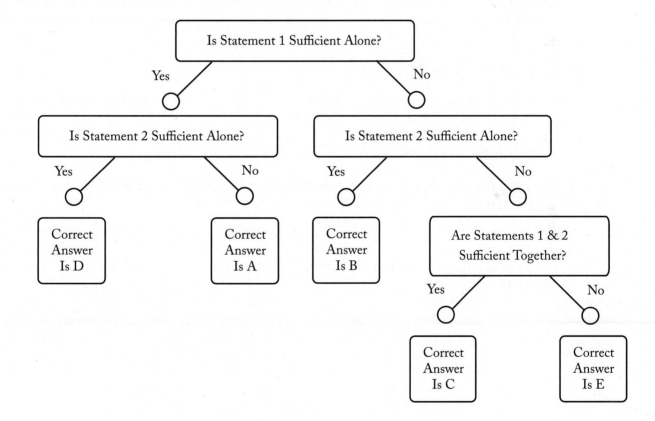

5.2 Section Instructions

Go to www.mba.com/tutorial to view instructions for the section and get a feel for what the test center screens will look like on the actual GMAT exam.

5.3 Practice Questions

Each Data Sufficiency problem consists of a question and two statements, labeled (1) and (2), which contain certain data. Using these data and your knowledge of mathematics and everyday facts (such as the number of days in July or the meaning of the word *counterclockwise*), decide whether the data given are sufficient for answering the question and then indicate one of the following answer choices:

A   Statement (1) ALONE is sufficient, but statement (2) alone is not sufficient.
B   Statement (2) ALONE is sufficient, but statement (1) alone is not sufficient.
C   BOTH statements TOGETHER are sufficient, but NEITHER statement ALONE is sufficient.
D   EACH statement ALONE is sufficient.
E   Statements (1) and (2) TOGETHER are NOT sufficient.

<u>Note:</u> In Data Sufficiency problems that ask for the value of a quantity, the data given in the statements are sufficient only when it is possible to determine exactly one numerical value for the quantity.

<u>Example:</u>

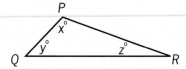

In, $\triangle PQR$ what is the value of x ?

(1) $PQ = PR$

(2) $y = 40$

<u>Explanation:</u> According to statement (1) $PQ = PR$; therefore, $\triangle PQR$ is isosceles and $y = z$. Since $x + y + z = 180$, it follows that $x + 2y = 180$. Since statement (1) does not give a value for y, you cannot answer the question using statement (1) alone. According to statement (2), $y = 40$; therefore, $x + z = 140$. Since statement (2) does not give a value for z, you cannot answer the question using statement (2) alone. Using both statements together, since $x + 2y = 180$ and the value of y is given, you can find the value of x. Therefore, BOTH statements (1) and (2) TOGETHER are sufficient to answer the questions, but NEITHER statement ALONE is sufficient.

<u>Numbers:</u> All numbers used are real numbers.

<u>Figures:</u>
• Figures conform to the information given in the question, but will not necessarily conform to the additional information given in statements (1) and (2).
• Lines shown as straight are straight, and lines that appear jagged are also straight.
• The positions of points, angles, regions, etc., exist in the order shown, and angle measures are greater than zero.
• All figures lie in a plane unless otherwise indicated.

Questions 263 to 348 - Difficulty: Easy

*DS02562
263. What is the number of pages of a certain journal article?

(1) The size of each page is $5\frac{1}{2}$ inches by 8 inches.
(2) The average (arithmetic mean) number of words per page is 250.

DS10471
264. If a certain vase contains only roses and tulips, how many tulips are there in the vase?

(1) The number of roses in the vase is 4 times the number of tulips in the vase.
(2) There is a total of 20 flowers in the vase.

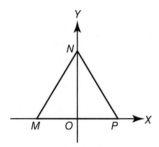

DS18950.02
265. In the xy-coordinate plane above, what are the coordinates of point N ?

(1) Triangle MNP is equilateral.
(2) Point M has coordinates (−4,0).

DS03802
266. The cost of 10 pounds of apples and 2 pounds of grapes was $12. What was the cost per pound of apples?

(1) The cost per pound of grapes was $2.
(2) The cost of 2 pounds of apples was less than the cost of 1 pound of grapes.

DS05863
267. What was the median annual salary for the employees at Company X last year?

St 1 (1) Last year there were 29 employees at Company X.
St 2 (2) Last year 12 employees at Company X had an annual salary of $24,000.

DS03422
268. How many basic units of currency X are equivalent to 250 basic units of currency Y ?

(1) 100 basic units of currency X are equivalent to 625 basic units of currency Y.
(2) 2,000 basic units of currency X are equivalent to 12,500 basic units of currency Y.

DS16840.02
269. In the xy-coordinate plane, what are the x-coordinates of the four vertices of square JKMN ?

(1) J and M are on the x-axis, and K and N are on the y-axis.
(2) The center of the square is at the origin.

DS12265
270. A company bought 3 printers and 1 scanner. What was the price of the scanner?

(1) The total price of the printers and the scanner was $1,300.
(2) The price of each printer was 4 times the price of the scanner.

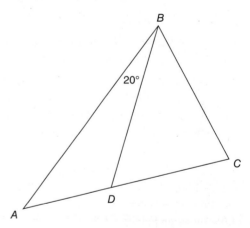

DS17639
271. In the figure above, point D is on $\overline{AC}$. What is the degree measure of ∠BAC ?

(1) The measure of ∠BDC is 60°.
(2) The degree measure of ∠BAC is less than the degree measure of ∠BCD.

*These numbers correlate with the online test bank question number. See the GMAT™ Official Guide Question Index in the back of this book.

261

DS07822

272. Each of the 256 solid-colored marbles in a box is either blue, green, or purple. What is the ratio of the number of blue marbles to the number of purple marbles in the box?

(1) The number of green marbles in the box is 4 times the number of blue marbles in the box.

(2) There are 192 green marbles in the box.

DS15940

273. A certain mixture of paint requires blue, yellow, and red paints in ratios of 2:3:1, respectively, and no other ingredients. If there are ample quantities of the blue and red paints available, is there enough of the yellow paint available to make the desired amount of the mixture?

(1) Exactly 20 quarts of the mixture are needed.

(2) Exactly 10 quarts of the yellow paint are available.

DS50241.02

274. There are 2 groups of students who took a history test. Was the average (arithmetic mean) score of the students in Group A higher than the average score of the students in Group B who took the test?

(1) Of the students who took the test, 10 were in Group A and 12 were in Group B.

(2) On the test, the highest score achieved was achieved by a Group B student and the lowest score achieved was achieved by a Group A student.

DS05338

275. The research funds of a certain company were divided among three departments, X, Y, and Z. Which one of the three departments received the greatest proportion of the research funds?

(1) The research funds received by departments X and Y were in the ratio 3 to 5, respectively.

(2) The research funds received by departments X and Z were in the ratio 2 to 1, respectively.

DS03138

276. In a certain class, some students donated cans of food to a local food bank. What was the average (arithmetic mean) number of cans donated per student in the class?

(1) The students donated a total of 56 cans of food.

(2) The total number of cans donated was 40 greater than the total number of students in the class.

DS00254

277. Each of the n employees at a certain company has a different annual salary. What is the median of the annual salaries of the n employees?

(1) When the annual salaries of the n employees are listed in increasing order, the median is the 15th salary.

(2) The sum of the annual salaries of the n employees is $913,500.

DS10687

278. In a recent town election, what was the ratio of the number of votes in favor of a certain proposal to the number of votes against the proposal?

(1) There were 60 more votes in favor of the proposal than against the proposal.

(2) There were 240 votes in favor of the proposal.

DS02541

279. How many men are in a certain company's vanpool program?

(1) The ratio of men to women in the program is 3 to 2.

(2) The men and women in the program fill 6 vans.

DS08054

280. Each of the marbles in a jar is either red or white or blue. If one marble is to be selected at random from the jar, what is the probability that the marble will be blue?

(1) There are a total of 24 marbles in the jar, 8 of which are red.

(2) The probability that the marble selected will be white is $\frac{1}{2}$.

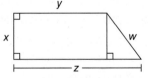

DS04594

281. In the figure above, what is the value of z ?

(1) $x = y = 1$

(2) $w = 2$

DS04630

282. What is the value of 10 percent of y ?

(1) 5 percent of y is 60.

(2) y is 80 percent of 1,500.

DS12062

283. Last semester, Professor K taught two classes, A and B. Each student in class A handed in 7 assignments, and each student in class B handed in 5 assignments. How many students were in class A ?

  (1)   The students in both classes combined handed in a total of 85 assignments.

  (2)   There were 10 students in class B.

DS06802

284. Was the amount of John's heating bill for February greater than it was for January?

  (1)   The ratio of the amount of John's heating bill for February to that for January was $\frac{26}{25}$.

  (2)   The sum of the amounts of John's heating bills for January and February was $183.60.

DS06662

285. If sequence S has 120 terms, what is the 105th term of S ?

  (1)   The first term of S is –8.

  (2)   Each term of S after the first term is 10 more than the preceding term.

DS15650.02

286. If all of the six faces of a concrete block are rectangular, what is the volume of the block?

  (1)   Each of the four lateral faces of the block has an area of 200 square inches.

  (2)   The top of the block is square and has an area of 400 square inches.

DS00858

287. Machine R and machine S work at their respective constant rates. How much time does it take machine R, working alone, to complete a certain job?

  (1)   The amount of time that it takes machine S, working alone, to complete the job is $\frac{3}{4}$ the amount of time that it takes machine R, working alone, to complete the job.

  (2)   Machine R and machine S, working together, take 12 minutes to complete the job.

DS06065

288. If $u > 0$ and $v > 0$, which is greater, u^v or v^u ?

  (1) $u = 1$

  (2) $v > 2$

DS00660

289. What was the range of the selling prices of the 30 wallets sold by a certain store yesterday?

  (1) $\frac{1}{3}$ of the wallets had a selling price of $24 each.

  (2)   The lowest selling price of the wallets was $\frac{1}{3}$ the highest selling price of the wallets.

DS08723

290. Three houses are being sold through a real estate agent. What is the asking price for the house with the second-largest asking price?

  (1)   The difference between the greatest and the least asking price is $130,000.

  (2)   The difference between the two greater asking prices is $85,000.

DS04605

291. If $a + b + c = 12$, what is the value of b ?

  (1) $a + b = 8$

  (2) $b + c = 6$

DS11254

292. Is $rw = 0$?

  (1) $-6 < r < 5$

  (2) $6 < w < 10$

DS06633

293. Is $x = \frac{1}{y}$?

  (1) $xy = 1$

  (2) $\frac{1}{xy} = 1$

DS07949

294. How many people in a group of 50 own neither a fax machine nor a laser printer?

  (1)   The total number of people in the group who own a fax machine or a laser printer or both is less than 50.

  (2)   The total number of people in the group who own both a fax machine and a laser printer is 15.

DS06475

295. What is the value of w^{-2} ?

  (1) $w^{-1} = \frac{1}{2}$

  (2) $w^3 = 8$

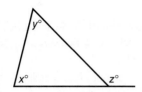

Note: Figure not drawn to scale

DS27860.02

296. What is the value of z in the figure above?

   (1)   x = 50

   (2)   y = 35

DS07839

297. A certain investment earned a fixed rate of 4 percent interest per year, compounded annually, for five years. The interest earned for the third year of the investment was how many dollars greater than that for the first year?

   (1)   The amount of the investment at the beginning of the second year was $4,160.00.

   (2)   The amount of the investment at the beginning of the third year was $4,326.40.

DS06397

298. What is the circumference of circle C ?

   (1)   The radius of circle C is 2π.

   (2)   The center of circle C is located at point (7,8) in the xy-plane.

DS07813

299. What is the value of t ?

   (1) $s + t = 6 + s$

   (2) $t^3 = 216$

DS11109

300. For a certain car repair, the total charge consisted of a charge for parts, a charge for labor, and a 6 percent sales tax on both the charge for parts and the charge for labor. If the charge for parts, excluding sales tax, was $50.00, what was the total charge for the repair?

   (1)   The sales tax on the charge for labor was $9.60.

   (2)   The total sales tax was $12.60.

DS06905

301. George has a total of B books in his library, 25 of which are hardcover fiction books. What is the value of B ?

   (1)   40 of the B books are fiction and the rest are nonfiction.

   (2)   60 of the B books are hardcovers and the rest are paperbacks.

DS12031

302. Is $w + h^4$ positive?

   (1)   h is positive.

   (2)   w is positive.

DS15377

303. If a is a 3-digit integer and b is a 3-digit integer, is the units digit of the product of a and b greater than 5 ?

   (1)   The units digit of a is 4.

   (2)   The units digit of b is 7.

DS02450

304. In each of the last five years, Company K donated p percent of its annual profits to a certain scholarship fund. Did Company K donate more than $10,000 to the scholarship fund last year?

   (1)   Two years ago, Company K had annual profits of $3 million and donated $15,000 to the scholarship fund.

   (2)   Last year, Company K had annual profits of $2.5 million.

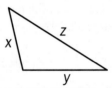

DS06901

305. Is the area of the triangular region above less than 20 ?

   (1) $x^2 + y^2 \neq z^2$

   (2) $x + y < 13$

DS04366

306. A, B, C, and D are points on a line. If C is the midpoint of line segment AB and if D is the midpoint of line segment CB, is the length of line segment DB greater than 5 ?

   (1)   The length of line segment AC is greater than 8.

   (2)   The length of line segment CD is greater than 6.

DS11805

307. The people in a line waiting to buy tickets to a show are standing one behind the other. Adam and Beth are among the people in the line, and Beth is standing behind Adam with a number of people between them. If the number of people in front of Adam plus the number of people behind Beth is 18, how many people in the line are behind Beth?

   (1)   There are a total of 32 people in the line.

   (2)   23 people in the line are behind Adam.

DS08730
308. Square *ABCD* is inscribed in circle *O*. What is the area of square region *ABCD* ?

    (1) The area of circular region *O* is 64π.
    (2) The circumference of circle *O* is 16π.

DS12533
309. Lines *k* and *m* are parallel to each other. Is the slope of line *k* positive?

    (1) Line *k* passes through the point (3,2).
    (2) Line *m* passes through the point (–3,2).

DS19520
310. In cross section, a tunnel that carries one lane of one-way traffic is a semicircle with radius 4.2 m. Is the tunnel large enough to accommodate the truck that is approaching the entrance to the tunnel?

    (1) The maximum width of the truck is 2.4 m.
    (2) The maximum height of the truck is 4 m.

DS13122
311. In a certain group of 50 people, how many are doctors who have a law degree?

    (1) In the group, 36 people are doctors.
    (2) In the group, 18 people have a law degree.

DS01544
312. Of a group of 50 households, how many have at least one cat or at least one dog, but not both?

    (1) The number of households that have at least one cat and at least one dog is 4.
    (2) The number of households that have no cats and no dogs is 14.

DS02441
313. Robin invested a total of $12,000 in two investments, X and Y, so that the investments earned the same amount of simple annual interest. How many dollars did Robin invest in investment Y ?

    (1) Investment X paid 3 percent simple annual interest, and investment Y paid 6 percent simple annual interest.
    (2) Robin invested more than $1,000 in investment X.

DS03999
314. In a real estate office that employs *n* salespeople, *f* of them are females and *x* of the females are new employees. What is the value of *n* ?

    (1) If an employee were randomly selected from the *n* employees, the probability of selecting a female would be $\frac{2}{3}$.
    (2) If an employee were randomly selected from the *f* female employees, the probability of selecting a new employee would be $\frac{1}{2}$.

DS09315
315. Is $\frac{x+1}{y+1} > \frac{x}{y}$?

    (1) $0 < x < y$
    (2) $xy > 0$

DS01216
316. Do at least 60 percent of the students in Pat's class walk to school?

    (1) At least 60 percent of the female students in Pat's class walk to school.
    (2) The number of students in Pat's class who walk to school is twice the number of students who do not walk to school.

DS03628
317. A certain plumber charges $92 for each job completed in 4 hours or less and $23 per hour for each job completed in more than 4 hours. If it took the plumber a total of 7 hours to complete two separate jobs, what was the total amount charged by the plumber for the two jobs?

    (1) The plumber charged $92 for one of the two jobs.
    (2) The plumber charged $138 for one of the two jobs.

DS02585
318. If *x* and *y* are positive numbers, is $\frac{x+1}{y+1} > \frac{x}{y}$?

    (1) $x > 1$
    (2) $x < y$

DS01619
319. If *a* and *b* are positive integers, is $\frac{a}{b} < \frac{9}{11}$? ?

    (1) $\frac{a}{b} < 0.818$
    (2) $\frac{b}{a} > 1.223$

DS04536

320. Every object in a box is either a sphere or a cube, and every object in the box is either red or green. How many objects are in the box?

    (1)   There are six cubes and five green objects in the box.

    (2)   There are two red spheres in the box.

DS01425

321. If x and y are positive integers, is xy even?

    (1) $x^2 + y^2 - 1$ is divisible by 4.

    (2) $x + y$ is odd.

DS14502

322. If a and b are integers, is $a + b + 3$ an odd integer?

    (1) ab is an odd integer.

    (2) $a - b$ is an even integer.

DS08308

323. If x and y are positive integers, what is the value of $\sqrt{x} + \sqrt{y}$?

    (1) $x + y = 15$

    (2) $\sqrt{xy} = 6$

DS05312

324. A certain truck uses $\frac{1}{12} + kv^2$ gallons of fuel per mile when its speed is v miles per hour, where k is a constant. At what speed should the truck travel so that it uses $\frac{5}{12}$ gallon of fuel per mile?

    (1)   The value of k is $\frac{1}{10,800}$.

    (2)   When the truck travels at 30 miles per hour, it uses $\frac{1}{6}$ gallon of fuel per mile.

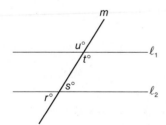

DS48710.02

325. In the figure shown, is $\ell_1 \parallel \ell_2$?

    (1) $r = s$

    (2) $t = u$

DS51531.02

326. What is the volume of the right circular cylinder X ?

    (1)   The height of X is 20.

    (2)   The base of X has area 25π.

DS76502.01

327. If r and s are positive integers, is $r + s$ even?

    (1) r is even.

    (2) s is even.

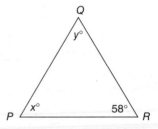

DS27502.01

328. In the figure above, $\triangle PQR$ has angle measures as shown. Is $x < y$?

    (1) $PQ = QR$

    (2) $PR > QR$

DS10602.01

329. If S is a set of odd integers and 3 and -1 are in S, is -15 in S ?

    (1)   5 is in S.

    (2)   Whenever two numbers are in S, their product is in S.

DS01602.01

330. Is the integer x a 3-digit integer?

    (1) x is the square of an integer.

    (2) $90 < x < 150$

DS11602.01

331. If the 1st term of a sequence is 0 and the 2nd term is 1, is the 5th term 2 ?

    (1)   Each odd-numbered term is either 0 or 2.

    (2)   The 3rd term is 2.

DS21602.01

332. Is the sum of four particular integers even?

    (1)   Two of the integers are odd and two are even.

    (2)   The average (arithmetic mean) of the four integers is an integer.

DS70602.01

333. If a school district paid a total of $35 per desk for *x* desks and a total of $30 per table for *y* tables, what was the total amount that the district paid for these desks and tables?

    (1)   The total amount the district paid for the *y* tables was $900.

    (2)   *x* = 90, and the total amount the district paid for the *x* desks was 3.5 times the total amount the district paid for the *y* tables.

DS90602.01

334. Three children inherited a total of *X* dollars. If the oldest child inherited $7,000 more than the youngest child, and the youngest child inherited $9,000 less than the middle child, what is the value of *X* ?

    (1)   The middle child inherited $27,000.

    (2)   The youngest child and the middle child together inherited a total of $45,000.

DS41602.01

335. If $xyz \neq 0$, what is the value of $\dfrac{x^4 z^2}{z^2 y^2}$?

    (1) $y^2 = x^4$

    (2) $x = 2$ and $y = 4$

DS81602.01

336. If *a* and *b* are integers, and $b > 0$, does $\dfrac{a-1}{b+1} = \dfrac{a}{b}$?

    (1) $a = b - 4$

    (2) $a = -b$

DS12602.01

337. In a sequence of numbers in which each term is 2 more than the preceding term, what is the fourth term?

    (1)   The last term is 90.

    (2)   The first term is 2.

DS32602.01

338. Is the integer *p* divisible by 5 ?

    (1)   *p* is divisible by 10.

    (2)   *p* is not divisible by 15.

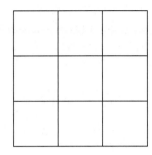

DS52602.01

339. The 9 squares above are to be filled with *x*'s and *o*'s, with only one symbol in each square. How many of the squares will contain an *x* ?

    (1)   More than $\dfrac{1}{2}$ of the number of squares will contain an *o*.

    (2)   Each of the 4 corner squares will contain an *x*.

DS72602.01

340. Is the sum of two integers divisible by 10 ?

    (1)   One of the integers is even.

    (2)   One of the integers is a multiple of 5.

DS22602.01

341. Is *x* an integer?

    (1) $x^3 = 8$

    (2) $x = \sqrt{4}$

DS42602.01

342. If a building has 6,000 square meters of floor space, how many offices are in the building?

    (1)   Exactly $\dfrac{1}{4}$ of the floor space is not used for offices.

    (2)   There are exactly 20 executive offices and each of these occupies 3 times as much floor space as the average for all of the remaining offices.

DS43602.01

343. If *p*, *r*, and *s* are consecutive integers in ascending order and *x* is the average (arithmetic mean) of the three integers, what is the value of *x* ?

    (1)   Twice *x* is equal to the sum of *p*, *r*, and *s*.

    (2)   The sum of *p*, *r*, and *s* is zero.

DS53602.01

344. If *m* and *n* are integers, what is the value of $m + n$?

    (1) $(x + m)(x + n) = x^2 + 5x + mn$ and $x \neq 0$.

    (2) $mn = 4$

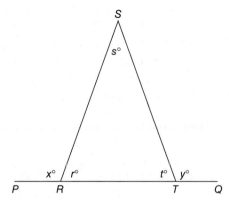

DS63602.01

345. In the figure above, *RST* is a triangle with angle measures as shown and *PRTQ* is a line segment. What is the value of $x + y$?

    (1) $s = 40$

    (2) $r = 70$

DS04602.0

346. If *R*, *S*, and *T* are points on a line, and if *R* is 5 meters from *T* and 2 meters from *S*, how far is *S* from *T* ?

    (1)   *R* is between *S* and *T*.

    (2)   *S* is to the left of *R*, and *T* is to the right of *R*.

DS65602.01

347. Is *n* equal to zero?

    (1)   The product of *n* and some nonzero number is 0.

    (2)   The sum of *n* and 0 is 0.

DS45602.01

348. On a map, $\frac{1}{2}$ inch represents 100 miles. According to this map, how many miles is City X from City Y ?

    (1)   City X is 3 inches from City Y on the map.

    (2)   Cities X and Y are each 300 miles from City Z.

Questions 349 to 426 - Difficulty: Medium

DS07502.01

349. What is the remainder when the positive integer *n* is divided by 5 ?

    (1)   When *n* is divided by 3, the quotient is 4 and the remainder is 1.

    (2)   When *n* is divided by 4, the remainder is 1.

DS37502.01

350. If *r* and *s* are positive numbers and θ is one of the operations, $+$, $-$, $\times$, or $\div$, which operation is θ ?

    (1)   If $r = s$, then $r\ \theta\ s = 0$.

    (2)   If $r \neq s$, then $r\ \theta\ s \neq s\ \theta\ r$.

DS57502.01

351. In any sequence of *n* nonzero numbers, a pair of consecutive terms with opposite signs represents a sign change. For example, the sequence -2, 3, -4, 5 has three sign changes. Does the sequence of nonzero numbers s_1, s_2, s_3, ..., s_n have an even number of sign changes?

    (1) $s_k = (-1)^k$ for all positive integers *k* from 1 to *n*.

    (2)   *n* is odd.

DS86502.01

352. Jack picked 76 apples. Of these, he sold 4*y* apples to Juanita and 3*t* apples to Sylvia. If he kept the remaining apples, how many apples did he keep? (*t* and *y* are positive integers.)

    (1) $y \geq 15$ and $t = 2$

    (2) $y = 17$

DS47502.01

353. What number is 6 more than $x + y$?

    (1)   *y* is 3 less than *x*.

    (2)   *y* is twice *x*.

DS08502.01

354. The total price of 5 pounds of regular coffee and 3 pounds of decaffeinated coffee was $21.50. What was the price of the 5 pounds of regular coffee?

    (1)   If the price of the 5 pounds of regular coffee had been reduced 10 percent and the price of the 3 pounds of decaffeinated coffee had been reduced 20 percent, the total price would have been $18.45.

    (2)   The price of the 5 pounds of regular coffee was $3.50 more than the price of the 3 pounds of decaffeinated coffee.

DS38502.01

355. If *a* and *b* are integers, is $a^5 < 4^b$?

    (1) $a^3 = -27$

    (2) $b^2 = 16$

DS28502.01

356. If each side of parallelogram *P* has length 1, what is the area of *P* ?

    (1)   One angle of *P* measures 45 degrees.

    (2)   The altitude of *P* is $\frac{\sqrt{2}}{2}$.

DS49502.01

357. If x is an integer greater than 0, what is the remainder when x is divided by 4 ?

    (1) The remainder is 3 when $x + 1$ is divided by 4.
    (2) The remainder is 0 when $2x$ is divided by 4.

DS00602.01

358. A certain painting job requires a mixture of yellow, green, and white paint. If 12 quarts of paint are needed for the job, how many quarts of green paint are needed?

    (1) The ratio of the amount of green paint to the amount of yellow and white paint combined needs to be 1 to 3.
    (2) The ratio of the amount of yellow paint to the amount of green paint needs to be 3 to 2.

DS69502.01

359. Is the average (arithmetic mean) of the numbers x, y, and z greater than z ?

    (1) $z - x < y - z$
    (2) $x < z < y$

DS30602.01

360. Is the point Q on the circle with center C ?

    (1) R is a point on the circle and the distance from Q to R is equal to the distance from Q to C.
    (2) S is a point on the circle and the distance from Q to S is equal to the distance from S to C.

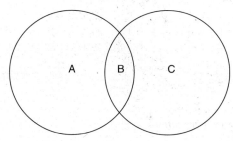

DS59502.01

361. In the figure above, if A, B, and C are the areas, respectively, of the three nonoverlapping regions formed by the intersection of two circles of equal area, what is the value of $B + C$?

    (1) $A + 2B + C = 24$
    (2) $A + C = 18$ and $B = 3$

DS61602.01

362. A company produces a certain toy in only 2 sizes, small or large, and in only 2 colors, red or green. If, for each size, there are equal numbers of red and green toys in a certain production lot, what fraction of the total number of green toys is large?

    (1) In the production lot, 400 of the small toys are green.
    (2) In the production lot, $\frac{2}{3}$ of the toys produced are small.

DS51602.01

363. Is quadrilateral $PQRS$ a parallelogram?

    (1) Adjacent sides PQ and QR have the same length.
    (2) Adjacent sides RS and SP have the same length.

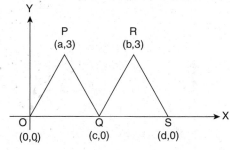

DS71602.01

364. In the figure above, the vertices of $\triangle OPQ$ and $\triangle QRS$ have coordinates as indicated. Do $\triangle OPQ$ and $\triangle QRS$ have equal areas?

    (1) $b = 2a$
    (2) $d = 2c$

DS92602.01

365. After the first two terms in a sequence of numbers, each term in the sequence is formed by adding all of the preceding terms. Is 12 the fifth term in the sequence?

    (1) The sum of the first 3 terms in the sequence is 6.
    (2) The fourth term in the sequence is 6.

DS13602.01

366. Jones has worked at Firm X twice as many years as Green, and Green has worked at Firm X four years longer than Smith. How many years has Green worked at Firm X ?

    (1) Jones has worked at Firm X 9 years longer than Smith.
    (2) Green has worked at Firm X 5 years less than Jones.

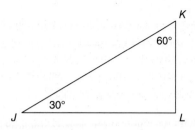

DS83602.01

367. In △*JKL* shown above, what is the length of segment *JL* ?

   (1)   *JK* = 10

   (2)   *KL* = 5

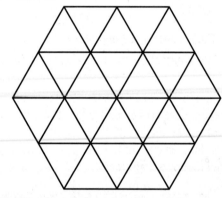

DS24602.01

368. A six-sided mosaic contains 24 triangular pieces of tile of the same size and shape, as shown in the figure above. If the sections of tile fit together perfectly, how many square centimeters of tile are in the mosaic?

   (1)   Each side of each triangular piece of tile is 9 centimeters long.

   (2)   The mosaic can be put inside a rectangular frame that is 40 centimeters wide.

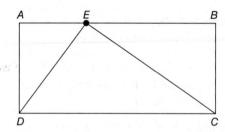

DS34602.01

369. If, in the figure above, *ABCD* is a rectangular region, what is the value of the ratio $\dfrac{\text{area of } \triangle EDA}{\text{area of } \triangle EBC}$?

   (1)   *AD* = 4

   (2)   *AE* = 2 and *EB* = 4

DS64602.01

370. A noncompressible ball in the shape of a sphere is to be passed through a square opening in a board. What is the perimeter of the opening?

   (1)   The radius of the ball is equal to 2 inches.

   (2)   The square opening is the smallest square opening through which the ball will fit.

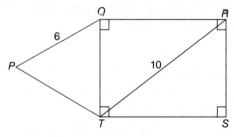

DS74602.01

371. In the figure above, what is the area of region *PQRST* ?

   (1)   *PQ* = *RS*

   (2)   *PT* = *QT*

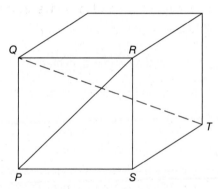

DS84602.01

372. The figure above represents a box that has the shape of a cube. What is the volume of the box?

   (1)   *PR* = 10 cm

   (2)   *QT* = $5\sqrt{6}$ cm

DS94602.01

373. If *x* and *y* are the lengths of the legs of a right triangle, what is the value of *xy* ?

   (1)   The hypotenuse of the triangle is $10\sqrt{2}$.

   (2)   The area of the triangular region is 50.

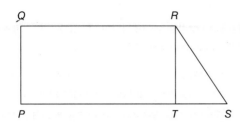

DS75602.01

374. In the figure above, *PQRT* is a rectangle. What is the length of segment *PQ* ?

   (1)   The area of region *PQRS* is 39 and *TS* = 6.
   (2)   The area of region *PQRT* is 30 and *QR* = 10.

DS08420

375. On June 1, Mary paid Omar $360 for rent and utilities for the month of June. Mary moved out early, and Omar refunded the money she paid for utilities, but not for rent, for the days in June after she moved out. How many dollars did Omar refund to Mary?

   (1)   Mary moved out on June 24.
   (2)   The amount Mary paid for utilities was less than $\frac{1}{5}$ the amount Mary paid for rent.

DS04057

376. If $x = 2t$ and $y = \frac{t}{3}$, what is the value of $x^2 - y^2$?

   (1) $t^2 - 3 = 6$
   (2) $t^3 = -27$

DS02939

377. The 10 students in a history class recently took an examination. What was the maximum score on the examination?

   (1)   The mean of the scores was 75.
   (2)   The standard deviation of the scores was 5.

DS01341

378. Last school year, each of the 200 students at a certain high school attended the school for the entire year. If there were 8 cultural performances at the school during the last school year, what was the average (arithmetic mean) number of students attending each cultural performance?

   (1)   Last school year, each student attended at least one cultural performance.
   (2)   Last school year, the average number of cultural performances attended per student was 4.

DS14569

379. A clothing manufacturer makes jackets that are wool or cotton or a combination of wool and cotton. The manufacturer has 3,000 pounds of wool and 2,000 pounds of cotton on hand. Is this enough wool and cotton to make at least 1,000 jackets?

   (1)   Each wool jacket requires 4 pounds of wool, and no cotton.
   (2)   Each cotton jacket requires 6 pounds of cotton, and no wool.

DS05377

380. If *n* is an integer, what is the greatest common divisor of 12 and *n* ?

   (1)   The product of 12 and *n* is 432.
   (2)   The greatest common divisor of 24 and *n* is 12.

DS11287

381. Each month, Jim receives a base salary plus a 10 percent commission on the price of each car he sells that month. If Jim sold 15 cars last month, what was the total amount of base salary and commissions that Jim received that month?

   (1)   Last month, Jim's base salary was $3,000.
   (2)   Last month, Jim sold 3 cars whose prices totaled $60,000 and 5 cars whose prices totaled $120,000.

DS17615

382. If *x* is a positive integer greater than 1, what is the value of *x* ?

   (1)   2*x* is a common factor of 18 and 24.
   (2)   *x* is a factor of 6.

DS13408

383. By what percentage was the price of a certain television set discounted for a sale?

   (1)   The price of the television set before it was discounted for the sale was 25 percent greater than the discounted price.
   (2)   The price of the television set was discounted by $60 for the sale.

DS05049

384. Jack wants to use a circular rug on his rectangular office floor to cover two small circular stains, each less than $\frac{\pi}{100}$ square feet in area and each more than 3 feet from the nearest wall. Can the rug be placed to cover both stains?

   (1)   Jack's rug covers an area of 9π square feet.

   (2)   The centers of the stains are less than 4 feet apart.

DS24751.01

385. A paint mixture was formed by mixing exactly 3 colors of paint. By volume, the mixture was $x\%$ blue paint, $y\%$ green paint, and $z\%$ red paint. If exactly 1 gallon of blue paint and 3 gallons of red paint were used, how many gallons of green paint were used?

   (1) $x = y$

   (2) $z = 60$

×	a	b	c
a	d	e	f
b	e	g	h
c	f	h	j

DS05772

386. In the multiplication table above, each letter represents an integer. What is the value of c?

   (1) $c = f$

   (2) $h \neq 0$

DS09379

387. If n is an integer, is $(0.1)^n$ greater than $(10)^n$?

   (1) $n > -10$

   (2) $n < 10$

DS19199

388. For a basic monthly fee of F yen (¥F), Naoko's first cell phone plan allowed him to use a maximum of 420 minutes on calls during the month. Then, for each of x additional minutes he used on calls, he was charged ¥M, making his total charge for the month ¥T, where $T = F + xM$. What is the value of F?

   (1)   Naoko used 450 minutes on calls the first month and the total charge for the month was ¥13,755.

   (2)   Naoko used 400 minutes on calls the second month and the total charge for the month was ¥13,125.

DS13949

389. Is the sum of the prices of the 3 books that Shana bought less than $48?

   (1)   The price of the most expensive of the 3 books that Shana bought is less than $17.

   (2)   The price of the least expensive of the 3 books that Shana bought is exactly $3 less than the price of the second most expensive book.

DS12943

390. If r and t are three-digit positive integers, is r greater than t?

   (1)   The tens digit of r is greater than each of the three digits of t.

   (2)   The tens digit of r is less than either of the other two digits of r.

DS14788

391. Is the product of two positive integers x and y divisible by the sum of x and y?

   (1) $x = y$

   (2) $x = 2$

DS24571.01

392. If a and b are constants, is the expression $\dfrac{x+b}{\sqrt{x+a}}$ defined for $x = -2$?

   (1) $a = 5$

   (2) $b = 6$

DS05330

393. A company makes and sells two products, P and Q. The costs per unit of making and selling P and Q are $8.00 and $9.50, respectively, and the selling prices per unit of P and Q are $10.00 and $13.00, respectively. In one month the company sold a total of 834 units of these products. Was the total profit on these items more than $2,000.00?

   (1)   During the month, more units of P than units of Q were sold.

   (2)   During the month, at least 100 units of Q were sold.

DS03045

394. Jill has applied for a job with each of two different companies. What is the probability that she will get job offers from both companies?

   (1)   The probability that she will get a job offer from neither company is 0.3.

   (2)   The probability that she will get a job offer from exactly one of the two companies is 0.5.

DS46420.02

395. A certain computer company produces two different monitors, P and Q. In 2010, what was the net profit from the sale of the two monitors?

    (1)   Of the company's expenses in 2010, rent and utilities totaled $500,000.

    (2)   In 2010, the company sold 50,000 units of monitor P at $300 per unit and 30,000 units of monitor Q at $650 per unit.

DS01257

396. A conveyor belt moves bottles at a constant speed of 120 centimeters per second. If the conveyor belt moves a bottle from a loading dock to an unloading dock, is the distance that the conveyor belt moves the bottle less than 90 meters? (1 meter = 100 centimeters)

    (1)   It takes the conveyor belt less than 1.2 minutes to move the bottle from the loading dock to the unloading dock.

    (2)   It takes the conveyor belt more than 1.1 minutes to move the bottle from the loading dock to the unloading dock.

DS02706

397. If x, y, and z are positive numbers, what is the value of the average (arithmetic mean) of x and z ?

    (1) $x - y = y - z$

    (2) $x^2 - y^2 = z$

DS04428

398. The rectangular rug shown in the figure above has an accent border. What is the area of the portion of the rug that excludes the border?

    (1)   The perimeter of the rug is 44 feet.

    (2)   The width of the border on all sides is 1 foot.

DS06537

399. If $y \neq 2xz$, what is the value of $\dfrac{2xz + yz}{2xz - y}$?

    (1) $2x + y = 3$

    (2) $z = 2$

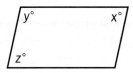

DS04852

400. In the parallelogram shown, what is the value of x ?

    (1) $y = 2x$

    (2) $x + z = 120$

DS06096

401. In a product test of a common cold remedy, x percent of the patients tested experienced side effects from the use of the drug and y percent experienced relief of cold symptoms. What percent of the patients tested experienced both side effects and relief of cold symptoms?

    (1)   Of the 1,000 patients tested, 15 percent experienced neither side effects nor relief of cold symptoms.

    (2)   Of the patients tested, 30 percent experienced relief of cold symptoms without side effects.

DS13588

402. Is $x < 5$?

    (1) $x^2 > 5$

    (2) $x^2 + x < 5$

DS72951.01

403. Three roommates—Bela, Gyorgy, and Janos—together saved money for a trip. The amount that Bela saved was equal to 8% of his monthly income. The amount that Gyorgy saved was exactly $\dfrac{1}{3}$ of the total amount saved by all 3 roommates. What was the total amount saved for the trip by all 3 roommates?

    (1)   Bela had a monthly income of $2,000.

    (2)   Janos saved 1.5 times as much for the trip as Bela.

DS11257

404. Is zp negative?

    (1) $pz^4 < 0$

    (2) $p + z^4 = 14$

DS04157
405. In each game of a certain tournament, a contestant either loses 3 points or gains 2 points. If Pat had 100 points at the beginning of the tournament, how many games did Pat play in the tournament?

   (1) At the end of the tournament, Pat had 104 points.
   (2) Pat played fewer than 10 games.

DS05631
406. At the beginning of the year, the Finance Committee and the Planning Committee of a certain company each had n members, and no one was a member of both committees. At the end of the year, 5 members left the Finance Committee and 3 members left the Planning Committee. How many members did the Finance Committee have at the beginning of the year?

   (1) The ratio of the total number of members who left at the end of the year to the total number of members at the beginning of the year was 1:6.
   (2) At the end of the year, 21 members remained on the Planning Committee.

DS15561
407. If $xy \neq 0$, is $x^3 + y^3 > 0$?

   (1) $x + y > 0$
   (2) $xy > 0$

DS13541
408. Max purchased a guitar for a total of $624, which consisted of the price of the guitar and the sales tax. Was the sales tax rate greater than 3 percent?

   (1) The price of the guitar that Max purchased was less than $602.
   (2) The sales tax for the guitar that Max purchased was less than $30.

DS75271.01
409. A pentagon with 5 sides of equal length and 5 interior angles of equal measure is inscribed in a circle. Is the perimeter of the pentagon greater than 26 centimeters?

   (1) The area of the circle is 16π square centimeters.
   (2) The length of each diagonal of the pentagon is less than 8 centimeters.

DS13841.01
410. If $2.00X$ and $3.00Y$ are 2 numbers in decimal form with thousandths digits X and Y, is $3(2.00X) > 2(3.00Y)$?

   (1) $3X < 2Y$
   (2) $X < Y - 3$

DS50351.01
411. The length, width, and height of a rectangular box, in centimeters, are L, W, and H. If the volume of this box is V cubic centimeters and the total area of the 6 sides of this box is A square centimeters, what is the value of $\frac{V}{A}$?

   (1) At least 2 of L, W, and H are equal to 5.
   (2) L, W, and H all have the same value.

DS06027
412. What is the sum of a certain pair of consecutive odd integers?

   (1) At least one of the integers is negative.
   (2) At least one of the integers is positive.

DS45530.01
413. Is $x = y$?

   (1) $\frac{2x}{3} - \frac{y}{3} = \frac{1}{3}$
   (2) $\frac{x}{4} - \frac{y}{4} = 0$

DS08197
414. The sum of 4 different odd integers is 64. What is the value of the greatest of these integers?

   (1) The integers are consecutive odd numbers.
   (2) Of these integers, the greatest is 6 more than the least.

DS13130
415. Was the number of books sold at Bookstore X last week greater than the number of books sold at Bookstore Y last week?

   (1) Last week, more than 1,000 books were sold at Bookstore X on Saturday and fewer than 1,000 books were sold at Bookstore Y on Saturday.
   (2) Last week, less than 20 percent of the books sold at Bookstore X were sold on Saturday and more than 20 percent of the books sold at Bookstore Y were sold on Saturday.

DS47651.01

416. A rectangular solid has length, width, and height of L cm, W cm, and H cm, respectively. If these dimensions are increased by $x\%$, $y\%$, and $z\%$, respectively, what is the percentage increase in the total surface area of the solid?

    (1) L, W, and H are in the ratios of 5:3:4.
    (2) $x = 5$, $y = 10$, $z = 20$

DS08091.01

417. A certain list, L, contains a total of n numbers, not necessarily distinct, that are arranged in increasing order. If L_1 is the list consisting of the first n_1 numbers in L and L_2 is the list consisting of the last n_2 numbers in L, is 17 a mode for L ?

    (1) 17 is a mode for L_1 and 17 is a mode for L_2.
    (2) $n_1 + n_2 = n$

DS04540

418. From May 1 to May 30 in the same year, the balance in a checking account increased. What was the balance in the checking account on May 30 ?

    (1) If, during this period of time, the increase in the balance in the checking account had been 12 percent, then the balance in the account on May 30 would have been $504.
    (2) During this period of time, the increase in the balance in the checking account was 8 percent.

DS08365

419. A merchant discounted the sale price of a coat and the sale price of a sweater. Which of the two articles of clothing was discounted by the greater dollar amount?

    (1) The percent discount on the coat was 2 percentage points greater than the percent discount on the sweater.
    (2) Before the discounts, the sale price of the coat was $10 less than the sale price of the sweater.

DS01168

420. If the positive integer n is added to each of the integers 69, 94, and 121, what is the value of n ?

    (1) $69 + n$ and $94 + n$ are the squares of two consecutive integers.
    (2) $94 + n$ and $121 + n$ are the squares of two consecutive integers.

DS71521.01

421. If a merchant purchased a sofa from a manufacturer for $400 and then sold it, what was the selling price of the sofa?

    (1) The selling price of the sofa was greater than 140 percent of the purchase price.
    (2) The merchant's gross profit from the purchase and sale of the sofa was $\frac{1}{3}$ of the selling price.

DS05269

422. Last year, in a certain housing development, the average (arithmetic mean) price of 20 new houses was $160,000. Did more than 9 of the 20 houses have prices that were less than the average price last year?

    (1) Last year the greatest price of one of the 20 houses was $219,000.
    (2) Last year the median of the prices of the 20 houses was $150,000.

DS14527

423. For a certain city's library, the average cost of purchasing each new book is $28. The library receives $15,000 from the city each year; the library also receives a bonus of $2,000 if the total number of items checked out over the course of the year exceeds 5,000. Did the library receive the bonus last year?

    (1) The library purchased an average of 50 new books each month last year and received enough money from the city to cover this cost.
    (2) The lowest number of items checked out in one month was 459.

$$7, 9, 6, 4, 5, x$$

DS89950.01

424. If x is a number in the list above, what is the median of the list?

    (1) $x > 7$
    (2) The median of the list equals the arithmetic mean of the list.

DS15045

425. Three dice, each of which has its 6 sides numbered 1 through 6, are tossed. The sum of the 3 numbers that are facing up is 12. Is at least 1 of these numbers 5 ?

    (1) None of the 3 numbers that are facing up is divisible by 3.
    (2) Of the numbers that are facing up, 2, but not all 3, are equal.

DS01324
426. On the number line, point *R* has coordinate *r* and point *T* has coordinate *t*. Is $t < 0$?

    (1) $-1 < r < 0$
    (2) The distance between *R* and *T* is equal to r^2.

Questions 427 to 502 - Difficulty: **Hard**

DS11210.02
427. Did the population of Town C increase by at least 100 percent from the year 2000 to the year 2010?

    (1) The population of Town C in 2000 was $\frac{2}{3}$ of the population in 2005.
    (2) The population of Town C increased by a greater number of people from 2005 to 2010 than it did from 2000 to 2005.

DS06659
428. *S* is a set of points in the plane. How many distinct triangles can be drawn that have three of the points in *S* as vertices?

    (1) The number of distinct points in *S* is 5.
    (2) No three of the points in *S* are collinear.

DS16078
429. Stores L and M each sell a certain product at a different regular price. If both stores discount their regular price of the product, is the discount price at Store M less than the discount price at Store L?

    (1) At Store L the discount price is 10 percent less than the regular price; at Store M the discount price is 15 percent less than the regular price.
    (2) At Store L the discount price is $5 less than the regular store price; at Store M the discount price is $6 less than the regular price.

DS16529
430. If *d* denotes a decimal, is $d \geq 0.5$?

    (1) When *d* is rounded to the nearest tenth, the result is 0.5.
    (2) When *d* is rounded to the nearest integer, the result is 1.

DS08231
431. In the two-digit integers 3■ and 2▲, the symbols ■ and ▲ represent different digits, and the product (3■)(2▲) is equal to 864. What digit does ■ represent?

    (1) The sum of ■ and ▲ is 10.
    (2) The product of ■ and ▲ is 24.

$$\underset{M}{\bullet} \rule{4cm}{0.4pt} \ell$$

DS07262
432. Two points, *N* and *Q* (not shown), lie to the right of point *M* on line ℓ. What is the ratio of the length of *QN* to the length of *MQ*?

    (1) Twice the length of *MN* is 3 times the length of *MQ*.
    (2) Point *Q* is between points *M* and *N*.

DS05639
433. Did the sum of the prices of three shirts exceed $60?

    (1) The price of the most expensive of the shirts exceeded $30.
    (2) The price of the least expensive of the shirts exceeded $20.

DS03057
434. What is the total number of coins that Bert and Claire have?

    (1) Bert has 50 percent more coins than Claire.
    (2) The total number of coins that Bert and Claire have is between 21 and 28.

DS05668
435. A telephone station has *x* processors, each of which can process a maximum of *y* calls at any particular time, where *x* and *y* are positive integers. If 500 calls are sent to the station at a particular time, can the station process all of the calls?

    (1) $x = 600$
    (2) $100 < y < 200$

	Price per Flower
Roses	$1.00
Daisies	$0.50

DS07953
436. Kim and Sue each bought some roses and some daisies at the prices shown above. If Kim bought the same total number of roses and daisies as Sue, was the price of Kim's purchase of roses and daisies higher than the price of Sue's purchase of roses and daisies?

    (1) Kim bought twice as many daisies as roses.
    (2) Kim bought 4 more roses than Sue bought.

DS14406

437. Jazz and blues recordings accounted for 6 percent of the $840 million revenue from the sales of recordings in Country Y in 2000. What was the revenue from the sales of jazz and blues recordings in Country Y in 1998 ?

    (1)   Jazz and blues recordings accounted for 5 percent of the revenue from the sales of recordings in Country Y in 1998.

    (2)   The revenue from the sales of jazz and blues recordings in Country Y increased by 40 percent from 1998 to 2000.

DS06315

438. On a certain nonstop trip, Marta averaged x miles per hour for 2 hours and y miles per hour for the remaining 3 hours. What was her average speed, in miles per hour, for the entire trip?

    (1) $2x + 3y = 280$

    (2) $y = x + 10$

DS12730

439. If x is a positive integer, what is the value of $\sqrt{x + 24} - \sqrt{x}$?

    (1) $\sqrt{x}$ is an integer.

    (2) $\sqrt{x + 24}$ is an integer.

DS13982

440. A tank is filled with gasoline to a depth of exactly 2 feet. The tank is a cylinder resting horizontally on its side, with its circular ends oriented vertically. The inside of the tank is exactly 6 feet long. What is the volume of the gasoline in the tank?

    (1)   The inside of the tank is exactly 4 feet in diameter.

    (2)   The top surface of the gasoline forms a rectangle that has an area of 24 square feet.

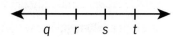

DS16197

441. Of the four numbers represented on the number line above, is r closest to zero?

    (1) $q = -s$

    (2) $-t < q$

DS18414

442. A group consisting of several families visited an amusement park where the regular admission fees were ¥5,500 for each adult and ¥4,800 for each child. Because there were at least 10 people in the group, each paid an admission fee that was 10% less than the regular admission fee. How many children were in the group?

    (1)   The total of the admission fees paid for the adults in the group was ¥29,700.

    (2)   The total of the admission fees paid for the children in the group was ¥4,860 more than the total of the admission fees paid for the adults in the group.

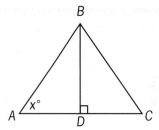

DS16536

443. What is the area of triangular region ABC above?

    (1)   The product of BD and AC is 20.

    (2) $x = 45$

DS05265

444. In the xy-coordinate plane, is point R equidistant from points $(-3, -3)$ and $(1, -3)$?

    (1)   The x-coordinate of point R is -1.

    (2)   Point R lies on the line $y = -3$.

DS09603

445. What is the ratio of the average (arithmetic mean) height of students in class X to the average height of students in class Y ?

    (1)   The average height of the students in class X is 120 centimeters.

    (2)   The average height of the students in class X and class Y combined is 126 centimeters.

DS04631

446. Is the positive two-digit integer N less than 40 ?

    (1)   The units digit of N is 6 more than the tens digit.

    (2) N is 4 less than 4 times the units digit.

DS06318
447. If $2^{x+y} = 4^8$, what is the value of y ?

  (1) $x^2 = 81$

  (2) $x - y = 2$

DS03680
448. Each week a certain salesman is paid a fixed amount equal to $300, plus a commission equal to 5 percent of the amount of his sales that week over $1,000. What is the total amount the salesman was paid last week?

  (1)   The total amount the salesman was paid last week is equal to 10 percent of the amount of his sales last week.

  (2)   The salesman's sales last week totaled $5,000.

DS01383
449. At a bakery, all donuts are priced equally and all bagels are priced equally. What is the total price of 5 donuts and 3 bagels at the bakery?

  (1)   At the bakery, the total price of 10 donuts and 6 bagels is $12.90.

  (2)   At the bakery, the price of a donut is $0.15 less than the price of a bagel.

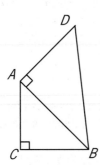

DS06869
450. In the figure above, is the area of triangular region ABC equal to the area of triangular region DBA ?

  (1) $(AC)^2 = 2(AD)^2$

  (2) $\triangle ABC$ is isosceles.

DS08105
451. If r and s are positive integers, can the fraction $\dfrac{r}{s}$ be expressed as a decimal with only a finite number of nonzero digits?

  (1) s is a factor of 100.

  (2) r is a factor of 100.

DS16384
452. If $r > 0$ and $s > 0$, is $\dfrac{r}{s} < \dfrac{s}{r}$?

  (1) $\dfrac{r}{3s} = \dfrac{1}{4}$

  (2) $s = r + 4$

DS06789
453. If k is an integer such that $56 < k < 66$, what is the value of k ?

  (1)   If k were divided by 2, the remainder would be 1.

  (2)   If $k + 1$ were divided by 3, the remainder would be 0.

DS13965
454. If x is a positive integer, then is x prime?

  (1) $3x + 1$ is prime.

  (2) $5x + 1$ is prime.

$$k,\ n,\ 12,\ 6,\ 17$$

DS00172
455. What is the value of n in the list above?

  (1) $k < n$

  (2)   The median of the numbers in the list is 10.

DS07508
456. If x and y are integers, what is the value of $x + y$?

  (1) $3 < \dfrac{x + y}{2} < 4$

  (2) $2 < x < y < 5$

DS00764
457. Last year, if Arturo spent a total of $12,000 on his mortgage payments, real estate taxes, and home insurance, how much did he spend on his real estate taxes?

  (1)   Last year, the total amount that Arturo spent on his real estate taxes and home insurance was $33\dfrac{1}{3}$ percent of the amount that he spent on his mortgage payments.

  (2)   Last year, the amount that Arturo spent on his real estate taxes was 20 percent of the total amount he spent on his mortgage payments and home insurance.

DS06038
458. If a, b, c, and d are positive numbers, is $\dfrac{a}{b} < \dfrac{c}{d}$?

  (1) $0 < \dfrac{c - a}{d - b}$

  (2) $\left(\dfrac{ad}{bc}\right)^2 < \dfrac{ad}{bc}$

DS12008
459. Is the number of members of Club X greater than the number of members of Club Y ?

(1) Of the members of Club X, 20 percent are also members of Club Y.

(2) Of the members of Club Y, 30 percent are also members of Club X.

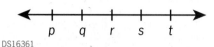

DS16361
460. On the number line above, *p*, *q*, *r*, *s*, and *t* are five consecutive even integers in increasing order. What is the average (arithmetic mean) of these five integers?

(1) $q + s = 24$

(2) The average (arithmetic mean) of *q* and *r* is 11.

DS06657
461. If $\lceil x \rceil$ denotes the least integer greater than or equal to *x*, is $\lceil x \rceil = 0$?

(1) $-1 < x < 1$

(2) $x < 0$

DS12718
462. If *x* and *y* are integers, is $x > y$?

(1) $x + y > 0$

(2) $y^x < 0$

DS03046
463. If *r* and *s* are the roots of the equation $x^2 + bx + c = 0$, where *b* and *c* are constants, is $rs < 0$?

(1) $b < 0$

(2) $c < 0$

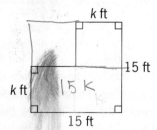

DS02888
464. The figure above represents an L-shaped garden. What is the value of *k* ?

(1) The area of the garden is 189 square feet.

(2) The perimeter of the garden is 60 feet.

DS01049
465. The only articles of clothing in a certain closet are shirts, dresses, and jackets. The ratio of the number of shirts to the number of dresses to the number of jackets in the closet is 9:4:5, respectively. If there are more than 7 dresses in the closet, what is the total number of articles of clothing in the closet?

(1) The total number of shirts and jackets in the closet is less than 30.

(2) The total number of shirts and dresses in the closet is 26.

TOTAL EXPENSES FOR THE FIVE DIVISIONS OF COMPANY H

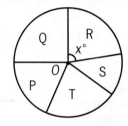

DS16542
466. The figure above represents a circle graph of Company H's total expenses broken down by the expenses for each of its five divisions. If *O* is the center of the circle and if Company H's total expenses are $5,400,000, what are the expenses for Division R ?

(1) $x = 94$

(2) The total expenses for Divisions S and T are twice as much as the expenses for Division R.

DS13641
467. If *x* is negative, is $x < -3$?

(1) $x^2 > 9$

(2) $x^3 < -9$

DS04897
468. What is the number of cans that can be packed in a certain carton?

(1) The interior volume of this carton is 2,304 cubic inches.

(2) The exterior of each can is 6 inches high and has a diameter of 4 inches.

279

r	s	t
u	v	w
x	y	z

DS08301

469. Each of the letters in the table above represents one of the numbers 1, 2, or 3, and each of these numbers occurs exactly once in each row and exactly once in each column. What is the value of *r*?

   (1) $v + z = 6$

   (2) $s + t + u + x = 6$

DS00328

470. Material A costs $3 per kilogram, and Material B costs $5 per kilogram. If 10 kilograms of Material K consists of *x* kilograms of Material A and *y* kilograms of Material B, is $x > y$?

   (1) $y > 4$

   (2)   The cost of the 10 kilograms of Material K is less than $40.

DS16164

471. At what speed was a train traveling on a trip when it had completed half of the total distance of the trip?

   (1)   The trip was 460 miles long and took 4 hours to complete.

   (2)   The train traveled at an average rate of 115 miles per hour on the trip.

DS12047

472. Tom, Jane, and Sue each purchased a new house. The average (arithmetic mean) price of the three houses was $120,000. What was the median price of the three houses?

   (1)   The price of Tom's house was $110,000.

   (2)   The price of Jane's house was $120,000.

DS13958

473. What is the value of *x* if $x^3 < x^2$?

   (1) $-2 < x < 2$

   (2)   *x* is an integer greater than −2.

DS08451

474. For any integers *x* and *y*, min(*x*, *y*) and max(*x*, *y*) denote the minimum and the maximum of *x* and *y*, respectively. For example, min(5, 2) = 2 and max(5, 2) = 5. For the integer *w*, what is the value of min(10, *w*)? *think harder*

   (1) $w = \max(20, z)$ for some integer *z*

   (2) $w = \max(10, w)$

DS01473

475. A certain bookcase has 2 shelves of books. On the upper shelf, the book with the greatest number of pages has 400 pages. On the lower shelf, the book with the least number of pages has 475 pages. What is the median number of pages for all of the books on the 2 shelves?

   (1)   There are 25 books on the upper shelf.

   (2)   There are 24 books on the lower shelf.

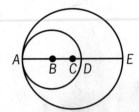

DS12070

476. In the figure above, points *A*, *B*, *C*, *D*, and *E* lie on a line. *A* is on both circles, *B* is the center of the smaller circle, *C* is the center of the larger circle, *D* is on the smaller circle, and *E* is on the larger circle. What is the area of the region inside the larger circle and outside the smaller circle?

   (1) $AB = 3$ and $BC = 2$

   (2) $CD = 1$ and $DE = 4$

DS08995

477. In planning for a car trip, Joan estimated both the distance of the trip, in miles, and her average speed, in miles per hour. She accurately divided her estimated distance by her estimated average speed to obtain an estimate for the time, in hours, that the trip would take. Was her estimate within 0.5 hour of the actual time that the trip took?

   (1)   Joan's estimate for the distance was within 5 miles of the actual distance.

   (2)   Joan's estimate for her average speed was within 10 miles per hour of her actual average speed.

DS12239
478. A certain list consists of 3 different numbers. Does the median of the 3 numbers equal the average (arithmetic mean) of the 3 numbers?

  (1) The range of the 3 numbers is equal to twice the difference between the greatest number and the median.

  (2) The sum of the 3 numbers is equal to 3 times one of the numbers.

DS12806
479. Line ℓ lies in the xy-plane and does not pass through the origin. What is the slope of line ℓ? *draw out, all lines / possib*

  (1) The x-intercept of line ℓ is twice the y-intercept of line ℓ.

  (2) The x- and y-intercepts of line ℓ are both positive.

$$y = ax - 5$$
$$y = x + 6$$
$$y = 3x + b$$

DS07713
480. In the xy-plane, the straight-line graphs of the three equations above each contain the point (p,r). If a and b are constants, what is the value of b?

  (1) $a = 2$

  (2) $r = 17$

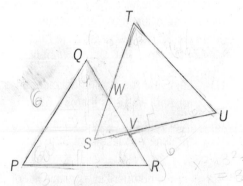

DS06861
481. In the figure above, PQR and STU are identical equilateral triangles, and PQ = 6. What is the perimeter of polygon PQWTUVR?

  (1) Triangle SWV has perimeter 9. ✗

  (2) VW has length 3.5. ✗

DS09973
482. The range of the numbers in set S is x, and the range of the numbers in set T is y. If all of the numbers in set T are also in set S, is x greater than y?

  (1) Set S consists of 7 numbers.

  (2) Set T consists of 6 numbers.

DS13857
483. The hypotenuse of a right triangle is 10 cm. What is the perimeter, in centimeters, of the triangle?

  (1) The area of the triangle is 25 square centimeters.

  (2) The 2 legs of the triangle are of equal length.

Shipment	S1	S2	S3	S4	S5	S6
Fraction of the Total Value of the Six Shipments	$\frac{1}{4}$	$\frac{1}{5}$	$\frac{1}{6}$	$\frac{3}{20}$	$\frac{2}{15}$	$\frac{1}{10}$

DS01427
484. Six shipments of machine parts were shipped from a factory on two trucks, with each shipment entirely on one of the trucks. Each shipment was labeled either S1, S2, S3, S4, S5, or S6. The table shows the value of each shipment as a fraction of the total value of the six shipments. If the shipments on the first truck had a value greater than $\frac{1}{2}$ of the total value of the six shipments, was S3 shipped on the first truck?

  (1) S2 and S4 were shipped on the first truck.

  (2) S1 and S6 were shipped on the second truck.

DS11723
485. If x, y, and z are three-digit positive integers and if $x = y + z$, is the hundreds digit of x equal to the sum of the hundreds digits of y and z?

  (1) The tens digit of x is equal to the sum of the tens digits of y and z.

  (2) The units digit of x is equal to the sum of the units digits of y and z.

	Favorable	Unfavorable	Not Sure
Candidate M	40	20	40
Candidate N	30	35	35

DS05162

486. The table above shows the results of a survey of 100 voters who each responded "Favorable" or "Unfavorable" or "Not Sure" when asked about their impressions of Candidate M and of Candidate N. What was the number of voters who responded "Favorable" for both candidates?

   (1) The number of voters who did not respond "Favorable" for either candidate was 40.

   (2) The number of voters who responded "Unfavorable" for both candidates was 10.

DS00340

487. A school administrator will assign each student in a group of n students to one of m classrooms. If $3 < m < 13 < n$, is it possible to assign each of the n students to one of the m classrooms so that each classroom has the same number of students assigned to it?

   (1) It is possible to assign each of $3n$ students to one of m classrooms so that each classroom has the same number of students assigned to it.

   (2) It is possible to assign each of $13n$ students to one of m classrooms so that each classroom has the same number of students assigned to it.

DS19120.02

488. At a certain clothing store, customers who buy 2 shirts pay the regular price for the first shirt and a discounted price for the second shirt. The store makes the same profit from the sale of 2 shirts that it makes from the sale of 1 shirt at the regular price. For a customer who buys 2 shirts, what is the discounted price of the second shirt?

   (1) The regular price of each of the 2 shirts the customer buys at the clothing store is $16.

   (2) The cost to the clothing store of each of the 2 shirts the customer buys is $12.

DS07441

489. If q, s, and t are all different numbers, is $q < s < t$?

   (1) $t - q = |t - s| + |s - q|$

   (2) $t > q$

DS11538

490. What is the median number of employees assigned per project for the projects at Company Z?

   (1) 25 percent of the projects at Company Z have 4 or more employees assigned to each project.

   (2) 35 percent of the projects at Company Z have 2 or fewer employees assigned to each project.

DS04409

491. Last year, a certain company began manufacturing product X and sold every unit of product X that it produced. Last year the company's total expenses for manufacturing product X were equal to $100,000 plus 5 percent of the company's total revenue from all units of product X sold. If the company made a profit on product X last year, did the company sell more than 21,000 units of product X last year?

   (1) The company's total revenue from the sale of product X last year was greater than $110,000.

   (2) For each unit of product X sold last year, the company's revenue was $5.

DS01641

492. Beginning in January of last year, Carl made deposits of $120 into his account on the 15th of each month for several consecutive months and then made withdrawals of $50 from the account on the 15th of each of the remaining months of last year. There were no other transactions in the account last year. If the closing balance of Carl's account for May of last year was $2,600, what was the range of the monthly closing balances of Carl's account last year?

   (1) Last year the closing balance of Carl's account for April was less than $2,625.

   (2) Last year the closing balance of Carl's account for June was less than $2,675.

DS16368

493. Are all of the numbers in a certain list of 15 numbers equal?

   (1) The sum of all the numbers in the list is 60.

   (2) The sum of any 3 numbers in the list is 12.

DS16565

494. If the average (arithmetic mean) of six numbers is 75, how many of the numbers are equal to 75?

   (1) None of the six numbers is less than 75.

   (2) None of the six numbers is greater than 75.

DS16188
495. What amount did Jean earn from the commission on her sales in the first half of 1988 ?

 (1) In 1988 Jean's commission was 5 percent of the total amount of her sales.

 (2) The amount of Jean's sales in the second half of 1988 averaged $10,000 per month more than in the first half.

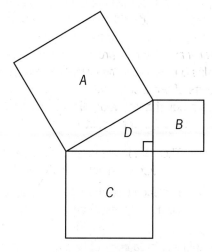

DS16572
496. In the figure above, if the area of triangular region D is 4, what is the length of a side of square region A ?

 (1) The area of square region B is 9.

 (2) The area of square region C is $\frac{64}{9}$.

DS16168
497. If n is a positive integer and $k = 5.1 \times 10^n$, what is the value of k ?

 (1) $6{,}000 < k < 500{,}000$

 (2) $k^2 = 2.601 \times 10^9$

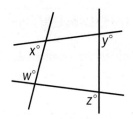

DS06875
498. What is the value of $x + y$ in the figure above?

 (1) $w = 95$

 (2) $z = 125$

DS16370
499. If n and k are positive integers, is $\sqrt{n+k} > 2\sqrt{n}$?

 (1) $k > 3n$

 (2) $n + k > 3n$

has to be
+ (can't √(-))

DS16589
500. In a certain business, production index p is directly proportional to efficiency index e, which is in turn directly proportional to investment index i. What is p if $i = 70$?

 (1) $e = 0.5$ whenever $i = 60$.

 (2) $p = 2.0$ whenever $i = 50$.

DS16085
501. If n is a positive integer, what is the tens digit of n ?

 (1) The hundreds digit of 10n is 6.

 (2) The tens digit of $n + 1$ is 7.

DS16204
502. What is the value of $\frac{2t + t - x}{t - x}$?

 (1) $\frac{2t}{t - x} = 3$

 (2) $t - x = 5$

5.4 Answer Key

263.	E	299.	D	335.	D	371.	C	407.	A
264.	C	300.	D	336.	B	372.	D	408.	A
265.	C	301.	E	337.	B	373.	B	409.	D
266.	A	302.	B	338.	A	374.	B	410.	D
267.	E	303.	C	339.	C	375.	E	411.	C
268.	D	304.	C	340.	E	376.	D	412.	C
269.	E	305.	E	341.	D	377.	E	413.	B
270.	C	306.	B	342.	E	378.	B	414.	D
271.	A	307.	C	343.	D	379.	C	415.	C
272.	C	308.	D	344.	A	380.	D	416.	C
273.	C	309.	E	345.	A	381.	E	417.	A
274.	E	310.	C	346.	D	382.	A	418.	C
275.	C	311.	E	347.	D	383.	A	419.	E
276.	C	312.	C	348.	A	384.	C	420.	D
277.	E	313.	A	349.	A	385.	D	421.	B
278.	C	314.	E	350.	A	386.	E	422.	B
279.	E	315.	A	351.	C	387.	E	423.	D
280.	C	316.	B	352.	C	388.	B	424.	A
281.	C	317.	B	353.	C	389.	C	425.	C
282.	D	318.	B	354.	D	390.	C	426.	C
283.	C	319.	D	355.	A	391.	C	427.	C
284.	A	320.	E	356.	D	392.	A	428.	C
285.	C	321.	D	357.	A	393.	E	429.	C
286.	C	322.	D	358.	A	394.	C	430.	B
287.	C	323.	C	359.	A	395.	E	431.	D
288.	C	324.	D	360.	E	396.	A	432.	A
289.	E	325.	E	361.	D	397.	E	433.	B
290.	E	326.	C	362.	B	398.	E	434.	C
291.	C	327.	C	363.	E	399.	E	435.	A
292.	E	328.	D	364.	B	400.	D	436.	B
293.	D	329.	C	365.	D	401.	E	437.	B
294.	E	330.	C	366.	D	402.	B	438.	A
295.	D	331.	E	367.	D	403.	C	439.	E
296.	C	332.	D	368.	A	404.	E	440.	D
297.	D	333.	B	369.	B	405.	E	441.	A
298.	A	334.	D	370.	C	406.	D	442.	C

443.	A	455.	C	467.	A	479.	A	491.	B
444.	A	456.	D	468.	E	480.	D	492.	C
445.	E	457.	B	469.	D	481.	A	493.	B
446.	D	458.	B	470.	B	482.	E	494.	D
447.	B	459.	C	471.	E	483.	D	495.	E
448.	D	460.	D	472.	B	484.	B	496.	D
449.	A	461.	C	473.	B	485.	A	497.	D
450.	C	462.	C	474.	D	486.	A	498.	C
451.	A	463.	B	475.	C	487.	B	499.	A
452.	D	464.	A	476.	D	488.	B	500.	B
453.	E	465.	D	477.	E	489.	A	501.	A
454.	E	466.	A	478.	D	490.	C	502.	A

5.5 Answer Explanations

The following discussion of Data Sufficiency is intended to familiarize you with the most efficient and effective approaches to the kinds of problems common to Data Sufficiency. The particular questions in this chapter are generally representative of the kinds of Data Sufficiency questions you will encounter on the GMAT exam. Remember that it is the problem solving strategy that is important, not the specific details of a particular question.

Questions 263 to 348 - Difficulty: Easy

*DS02562

263. What is the number of pages of a certain journal article?

    (1) The size of each page is $5\frac{1}{2}$ inches by 8 inches.

    (2) The average (arithmetic mean) number of words per page is 250.

Arithmetic Applied Problems

(1) Given that each page is $5\frac{1}{2}$ inches by 8 inches, any positive integer can be the number of pages of the journal article. For example, it is possible that the journal article consists of 10 pages, each $5\frac{1}{2}$ inches by 8 inches. However, it is also possible that the journal article consists of 20 pages, each $5\frac{1}{2}$ inches by 8 inches. Therefore, the number of pages cannot be determined; NOT sufficient.

(2) Given that the average number of words per page is 250, any positive integer can be the number of pages of the journal article. For example, it is possible that the journal article consists of 10 pages and contains a total of 10(250) = 2,500 words, and in this case the average number of words per page is $\frac{2,500}{10}$ = 250. However, it is also possible that the journal article consists of 20 pages and contains a total of 20(250) = 5,000 words, and in this case the average number of words per page is also $\frac{5,000}{20}$ = 250. Therefore, the number of pages cannot be determined; NOT sufficient.

Taking (1) and (2) together, it is still not possible to determine the number of pages because each of the examples used above satisfies both (1) and (2).

The correct answer is E;
both statements together are still not sufficient.

DS10471

264. If a certain vase contains only roses and tulips, how many tulips are there in the vase?

    (1) The number of roses in the vase is 4 times the number of tulips in the vase.

    (2) There is a total of 20 flowers in the vase.

Arithmetic Ratio and Proportion

The task is to determine the number of tulips in the vase.

(1) This says that for every tulip in the vase, there are 4 roses so the ratio of roses to tulips is 4:1. Because there could be 4 roses and 1 tulip or there could be 20 roses and 5 tulips, the number of tulips cannot be uniquely determined; NOT sufficient.

(2) This says the total number of roses and tulips in the vase is 20. Because there could be 10 roses and 10 tulips or there could be 15 roses and 5 tulips, the number of tulips cannot be uniquely determined; NOT sufficient.

From (1), the ratio of roses to tulips is 4:1 so $\frac{1}{5}$ of the flowers in the vase are tulips. From (2), there are 20 flowers in the vase. So, taking (1) and (2) together, the number of tulips in the vase is $\frac{1}{5}(20)$ = 4.

The correct answer is C;
both statements together are sufficient.

---

*These numbers correlate with the online test bank question number. See the GMAT™ Official Guide Question Index in the back of this book.

286

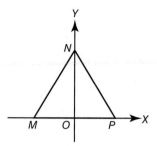

DS18950.02

265. In the *xy*-coordinate plane above, what are the coordinates of point *N* ?

(1)   Triangle *MNP* is equilateral.

(2)   Point *M* has coordinates (−4,0).

Geometry Simple Coordinate Geometry

(1)   Given that Δ*MNP* is equilateral, the figure below shows that when *M* and *P* are close together, then *N* will be closer to the *x*-axis than when *M* and *P* are further apart. Therefore, it is not possible to determine the coordinates of *N*; NOT sufficient.

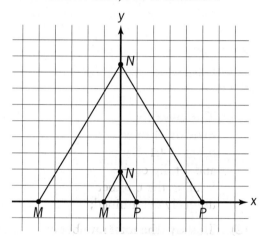

Tip: When solving Data Sufficiency problems it is often helpful to consider contrasting extreme scenarios when they exist, such as *M* and *P* close together and far apart above. Another example is when a quadrilateral can be any rectangle—consider the scenario when the rectangle is a square and the scenario when the rectangle is long with a small width.

(2)   Given only that point *M* has coordinates (−4,0), the *y*-coordinate of *N* can be any positive real number and the *x*-coordinate of *P* can be any positive real number; NOT sufficient.

Taking (1) and (2) together gives an equilateral triangle with vertex *M* having coordinates

(−4,0). Using properties of equilateral triangles, Δ*MNO* is a 30°-60°-90° triangle with shorter leg $\overline{MO}$ of length 4. Therefore, the longer leg $\overline{ON}$ has length $4\sqrt{3}$ and the coordinates of *N* are $(0, 4\sqrt{3})$.

The correct answer is C; both statements together are sufficient.

DS03802

266. The cost of 10 pounds of apples and 2 pounds of grapes was $12. What was the cost per pound of apples?

(1)   The cost per pound of grapes was $2.

(2)   The cost of 2 pounds of apples was less than the cost of 1 pound of grapes.

Arithmetic Applied Problems

Determine the cost per pound of apples.

(1)   The cost per pound of grapes was $2. The cost of 2 pounds of grapes was 2($2) = $4. The cost of the 10 pounds of apples was $12 − $4 = $8. The cost per pound of the apples was $\frac{\$8}{10}$ = $0.80; SUFFICIENT.

(2)   Intuitively, since (2) involves an inequality, it seems as if it wouldn't give enough information to determine the unique cost per pound of apples. A good strategy might be to guess multiple values for the costs per pound of apples and grapes that satisfy the condition given in the problem (the cost of 10 pounds of apples and 2 pounds of grapes is $12) and look for values that also meet the condition in (2), namely that the cost of 2 pounds of apples is less than the cost of 1 pound of grapes. For example:

Cost per pound of apples	Cost per pound of grapes	Total cost of 10 pounds of apples and 2 pounds of grapes, in dollars	Is total cost $12?	Is the cost of 2 pounds of apples less than the cost of 1 pound of grapes?
$1	$1	10(1) + 2(1)	yes	No, 2(1) ≮ 1
$0.50	$3.50	10(0.5) + 2(3.5)	yes	Yes, 2(0.50) < 3.50
$0.60	$3.00	10(0.6) + 2(3)	yes	Yes, 2(0.60) < 3.00

As shown in the table, the cost per pound of apples could be $0.50 or $0.60, so the cost per pound of apples cannot be uniquely determined; NOT sufficient.

The correct answer is A; statement 1 alone is sufficient.

DS05863

267. What was the median annual salary for the employees at Company X last year?

(1) Last year there were 29 employees at Company X.

(2) Last year 12 employees at Company X had an annual salary of $24,000.

Arithmetic Statistics

(1) Given that there were 29 employees, the median salary is the 15th salary in a list of 29 positive numbers, but we cannot determine the value of any of the numbers; NOT sufficient.

(2) Given that 12 employees had an annual salary of $24,000, the median salary is the median of a list of 12 or more positive numbers, of which 12 are equal to $24,000. If there were only 12 employees, then the median salary would be $24,000. However, if there were more than 2(12) = 24 employees and all but 12 of the employees had an annual salary of $30,000, then the median salary would be $30,000; NOT sufficient.

Taking (1) and (2) together, if 12 employees had an annual salary of $24,000 and the remaining 17 employees had an annual salary of $20,000, then the median salary would be $20,000. However, if 12 employees had an annual salary of $24,000 and the remaining 17 employees had an annual salary of $30,000, then the median salary would be $30,000.

Tip: If more than half the numbers in a list of numbers have the same value, then the median of the list will be that value, regardless of the values of the remaining numbers.

The correct answer is E; both statements together are still not sufficient.

DS03422

268. How many basic units of currency X are equivalent to 250 basic units of currency Y ?

(1) 100 basic units of currency X are equivalent to 625 basic units of currency Y.

(2) 2,000 basic units of currency X are equivalent to 12,500 basic units of currency Y.

Arithmetic Ratio and Proportion

(1) The equivalency of 100 basic units of currency X and 625 basic units of currency Y means that 1 basic unit of currency Y is equivalent to $\frac{100}{625}$ basic units of currency X. Therefore, 250 basic units of currency Y are equivalent to $(250)\left(\frac{100}{625}\right)$ basic units of currency X; SUFFICIENT.

(2) The equivalency of 2,000 basic units of currency X and 12,500 basic units of currency Y means that 1 basic unit of currency Y is equivalent to $\frac{2,000}{12,500}$ basic units of currency X. Therefore, 250 basic units of currency Y are equivalent to $(250)\left(\frac{2,000}{12,500}\right)$ basic units of currency X; SUFFICIENT.

Tip: For Data Sufficiency questions in which the task is to determine a specific value, there is no need to perform calculations to get the value in its simplest form. The goal is to determine whether the value can be uniquely determined, not to find the actual value in its simplest form.

The correct answer is D; each statement alone is sufficient.

DS16840.02

269. In the xy-coordinate plane, what are the x-coordinates of the four vertices of square JKMN ?

(1) J and M are on the x-axis, and K and N are on the y-axis.

(2) The center of the square is at the origin.

Geometry Simple Coordinate Geometry

(1) Given that J and M are on the x-axis, and K and N are on the y-axis, it is possible that

the four vertices are $J = (-1,0)$, $M = (1,0)$, $K = (0,-1)$, and $N = (0,1)$, and thus the x-coordinates of the four vertices could be -1, 1, and 0. However, it is also possible that the four vertices are $J = (-2,0)$, $M = (2,0)$, $K = (0,-2)$, and $N = (0,2)$, and thus the x-coordinates of the four vertices could be -2, 2, and 0; NOT sufficient.

(2) Given that the center of the square is $(0,0)$, it is not possible to determine the x-coordinates of the four vertices because, for each of the examples given in (1) above, the center of the square is $(0,0)$; NOT sufficient.

Taking (1) and (2) together, it is not possible to determine the x-coordinates of the four vertices because each of the examples given above satisfies both (1) and (2).

The correct answer is E; both statements together are still not sufficient.

DS12265

270. A company bought 3 printers and 1 scanner. What was the price of the scanner?

(1) The total price of the printers and the scanner was $1,300.

(2) The price of each printer was 4 times the price of the scanner.

Algebra Simultaneous Equations

Let P_1, P_2, and P_3 be the prices, in dollars, of the 3 printers and let S be the price, in dollars, of the scanner. What is the value of S?

(1) Given that $P_1 + P_2 + P_3 + S = 1,300$, it is clear that the value of S cannot be determined; NOT sufficient.

(2) Given that $P_1 = P_2 = P_3 = 4S$, it is possible that $P_1 = P_2 = P_3 = 400$ and $S = 100$. On the other hand, it is also possible that $P_1 = P_2 = P_3 = 800$ and $S = 200$; NOT sufficient.

Taking (1) and (2) together, substituting $P_1 = 4S$, $P_2 = 4S$, and $P_3 = 4S$ into $P_1 + P_2 + P_3 + S = 1,300$ gives $4S + 4S + 4S + S = 1,300$, or $13S = 1,300$, and therefore $S = 100$.

The correct answer is C; both statements together are sufficient.

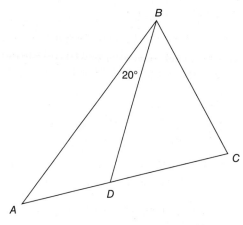

DS17639

271. In the figure above, point D is on $\overline{AC}$. What is the degree measure of $\angle BAC$?

(1) The measure of $\angle BDC$ is 60°.

(2) The degree measure of $\angle BAC$ is less than the degree measure of $\angle BCD$.

Geometry Angles

(1) Given that the measure of $\angle BDC$ is 60°, it follows that the measure of $\angle BDA$ is $180° - 60° = 120°$. Therefore, since the measures of the angles in a triangle add to 180°, the measure of $\angle BAC$ is $180 - (20° + 120°) = 40°$; SUFFICIENT.

(2) Given that the degree measure of $\angle BAC$ is less than the degree measure of $\angle BCD$, when the line segment $\overline{AC}$ rotates a few degrees counterclockwise about point A and point D stays on $\overline{AC}$, then the degree measure of $\angle BAC$ decreases (and the degree measure of $\angle BCD$ increases, and the degree measure of $\angle ABD$ remains 20°). Therefore, the degree measure of $\angle BAC$ can vary; NOT sufficient.

The correct answer is A; statement 1 alone is sufficient.

DS07822

272. Each of the 256 solid-colored marbles in a box is either blue, green, or purple. What is the ratio of the number of blue marbles to the number of purple marbles in the box?

(1) The number of green marbles in the box is 4 times the number of blue marbles in the box.

(2) There are 192 green marbles in the box.

Arithmetic Ratio and Proportion

Let B, G, and P be the numbers of marbles, respectively, that are blue, green, and purple. From the given information it follows that $B + G + P = 256$. What is the value of $\frac{B}{P}$?

(1) Given that $G = 4B$, it is possible that $\frac{B}{P} = \frac{1}{251}$ (choose $B = 1$, $G = 4$, and $P = 251$) and it is possible that $\frac{B}{P} = \frac{1}{123}$ (choose $B = 2$, $G = 8$, and $P = 246$); NOT sufficient.

(2) Given that $G = 192$, it is possible that $\frac{B}{P} = \frac{1}{63}$ (choose $B = 1$, $G = 192$, and $P = 63$) and it is possible that $\frac{B}{P} = \frac{1}{31}$ (choose $B = 2$, $G = 192$, and $P = 62$); NOT sufficient.

Taking (1) and (2) together, it follows from $G = 4B$ and $G = 192$ that $192 = 4B$, or $B = 48$. Thus, $B + G + P = 256$ becomes $48 + 192 + P = 256$, and so $P = 256 - 48 - 192 = 16$. Therefore, $\frac{B}{P} = \frac{48}{16}$.

The correct answer is C; both statements together are sufficient.

DS15940

273. A certain mixture of paint requires blue, yellow, and red paints in ratios of 2:3:1, respectively, and no other ingredients. If there are ample quantities of the blue and red paints available, is there enough of the yellow paint available to make the desired amount of the mixture?

(1) Exactly 20 quarts of the mixture are needed.
(2) Exactly 10 quarts of the yellow paint are available.

Arithmetic Ratios

Given that the mixture requires blue paint, yellow paint, and red paint in the ratios 2:3:1, it follows that $\frac{3}{2 + 3 + 1} = \frac{1}{2}$ of the mixture will be yellow paint. Determining whether there is enough yellow paint available depends on how much of the mixture is needed and how much yellow paint is available.

(1) This indicates that exactly 20 quarts of the paint mixture are needed, so $\frac{1}{2}(20) = 10$ quarts of yellow paint are needed. However, there is no information about how much yellow paint is available; NOT sufficient.

(2) This indicates that exactly 10 quarts of yellow paint are available, but there is no information about how much of the mixture or how much yellow paint is needed; NOT sufficient.

Taking (1) and (2) together, 10 quarts of yellow paint are needed and 10 quarts are available.

The correct answer is C; both statements together are sufficient.

DS50241.02

274. There are 2 groups of students who took a history test. Was the average (arithmetic mean) score of the students in Group A higher than the average score of the students in Group B who took the test?

(1) Of the students who took the test, 10 were in Group A and 12 were in Group B.

(2) On the test, the highest score achieved was achieved by a Group B student and the lowest score achieved was achieved by a Group A student.

Arithmetic Statistics

(1) Given that 10 of the scores were by students in Group A and 12 of the scores were by students in Group B, the following table shows two possibilities.

A scores	B scores	A average	B average	A average > B average?
10 scores of 8	12 scores of 1	8	1	yes
10 scores of 1	12 scores of 8	1	8	no

Therefore, it is not possible to determine whether the average score of the students in Group A is higher than the average score of the students in Group B; NOT sufficient.

(2) Given that the highest score achieved was achieved by a Group B student and the lowest score achieved was achieved by a

Group A student, the following table shows two possibilities.

A scores	B scores	A average	B average	A average > B average?
1, 7, 7	2, 2, 8	5	4	yes
1, 1, 1	8, 8, 8	1	8	no

Therefore, it is not possible to determine whether the average score of the students in Group A is higher than the average score of the students in Group B; NOT sufficient.

Taking (1) and (2) together, the table below shows that it is not possible to determine whether the average score of the students in Group A is higher than the average score of the students in Group B.

A scores		B scores		A average	B average	A average > B average?
score	frequency	score	frequency			
2	1	3	11	4.7	4	yes
5	9	15	1			
score	frequency	score	frequency			
2	1	6	12	4.7	6	no
5	9					

The correct answer is E; both statements together are still not sufficient.

DS05338
275. The research funds of a certain company were divided among three departments, X, Y, and Z. Which one of the three departments received the greatest proportion of the research funds?

(1) The research funds received by departments X and Y were in the ratio 3 to 5, respectively.

(2) The research funds received by departments X and Z were in the ratio 2 to 1, respectively.

Algebra Order; Ratio

Let x, y, and z be the research funds, respectively, of departments X, Y, and Z. Which of

$\dfrac{x}{x+y+z}$, $\dfrac{y}{x+y+z}$, or $\dfrac{z}{x+y+z}$ is the greatest, or respectively, which of x, y, or z is the greatest?

(1) Given that $\dfrac{x}{y} = \dfrac{3}{5}$ where x and y are positive, it follows that $x < y$. However, nothing is known about z other than z is positive, so it cannot be determined which of x, y, or z is the greatest; NOT sufficient.

(2) Given that $\dfrac{x}{z} = \dfrac{2}{1}$ where x and z are positive, it follows that $z < x$. However, nothing is known about y other than y is positive, so it cannot be determined which of x, y, or z is the greatest; NOT sufficient.

Taking (1) and (2) together, it follows from (1) that $x < y$ and it follows from (2) that $z < x$. Therefore, $z < x < y$ and y is the greatest.

The correct answer is C; both statements together are sufficient.

DS03138
276. In a certain class, some students donated cans of food to a local food bank. What was the average (arithmetic mean) number of cans donated per student in the class?

(1) The students donated a total of 56 cans of food.

(2) The total number of cans donated was 40 greater than the total number of students in the class.

Arithmetic Statistics

Let s be the number of students and let c be the number of cans. What is the value of $\dfrac{c}{s}$?

(1) Given that $c = 56$, it is not possible to determine the value of $\dfrac{c}{s}$ because nothing is known about the value of s other than s is a positive integer; NOT sufficient.

(2) Given that $c = 40 + s$, it is not possible to determine the value of $\dfrac{c}{s}$. For example, if $c = 40$ and $s = 40$, then $\dfrac{c}{s} = 1$. However,

if $c = 80$ and $s = 40$, then $\frac{c}{s} = 2$; NOT sufficient.

Taking (1) and (2) together, it follows that $40 + s = c = 56$, or $s = 56 - 40 = 16$. Therefore, $c = 56$, $s = 16$, and $\frac{c}{s} = \frac{56}{16}$.

**The correct answer is C;
both statements together are sufficient.**

DS00254

277. Each of the n employees at a certain company has a different annual salary. What is the median of the annual salaries of the n employees?

(1) When the annual salaries of the n employees are listed in increasing order, the median is the 15th salary.

(2) The sum of the annual salaries of the n employees is $913,500.

Arithmetic Statistics

(1) Given that the median is the 15th salary and all n salaries are different, it follows that there are 14 salaries less than the 15th salary and 14 salaries greater than the 15th salary, for a total of 29 employee salaries. However, there is no information about what any of the salaries actually are, so the median of the salaries cannot be determined; NOT sufficient.

(2) Given that the sum of the annual salaries is $913,500, the median salary cannot be uniquely determined. To determine more than one possible value for the median salary, use common divisibility rules to find factors of $913,500.

For example, 913,500 is divisible by 5 because it ends in 0. Then, because $913,500 = 5(182,700)$, there could be 5 salaries, each $182,700. But the salaries must be all different, so we need 5 different salaries that total $913,500. They could be the salaries shown in the table below. Note that the pattern starts with the 3rd (middle) salary of $182,700, then the 2nd and 4th

salaries are "paired" in that one is decreased and the other is increased by the same amount from $182,700. Likewise, for the 1st and 5th salaries. The median is $182,700.

Salary #	Salary
1	$182,698
2	$182,699
3	**$182,700**
4	$182,701
5	$182,702
Total	$913,500

Also, 913,500 is divisible by 9 because the sum of its digits is divisible by 9 and $913,500 = 9(101,500)$. Using ideas similar to those used in the first example, there could be 9 different salaries that total $913,500. Using the same technique as in the first example, these salaries could be those shown below. All 9 salaries are listed to reinforce the technique. They need not be written out as part of the solution.

Salary #	Salary
1	$101,496
2	$101,497
3	$101,498
4	$101,499
5	**$101,500**
6	$101,501
7	$101,502
8	$101,503
9	$101,504
Total	$913,500

Therefore, the median salary could be $182,700 or $101,500; NOT sufficient.

Taking (1) and (2) together, there are 29 different salaries and their sum is $913,500, but this information is not sufficient to uniquely determine the median.

Salary number	Salary (Example I)	Salary (Example II)
1	$30,100	$30,100
2	$30,200	$30,200
3	$30,300	$30,300
⋮	⋮	⋮
14	$31,400	$31,380
15	**$31,500**	**$31,540**
16	$31,600	$31,580
⋮	⋮	⋮
27	$32,700	$32,700
28	$32,800	$32,800
29	$32,900	$32,900
Total	$913,500	$913,500

Note that 913,500 = 29(31,500). The table above shows two examples, each consisting of 29 different salaries (not all are shown, however) that were obtained using techniques similar to those used in the previous examples. Note that, in both examples, the 1st salary is $1,400 less than $31,500 and the 29th is $1,400 more than $31,500, the 2nd salary is $1,300 less than $31,500 and the 28th is $1,300 more than $31,500, and so on. The salary columns in both examples are identical except for the 14th, 15th, and 16th salaries, which were used to obtain different medians.

In each example, the median is the 15th salary, so (1) is satisfied, and the sum of the salaries is $913,500, so (2) is satisfied. But the median in one case is $31,500 and the median in the other case is $31,540.

The correct answer is E; both statements together are still not sufficient.

DS10687
278. In a recent town election, what was the ratio of the number of votes in favor of a certain proposal to the number of votes against the proposal?

(1) There were 60 more votes in favor of the proposal than against the proposal.

(2) There were 240 votes in favor of the proposal.

Arithmetic Ratio and Proportion

Let F be the number of votes in favor and let A be the number of votes against. What is the value of $\frac{F}{A}$?

(1) Given that $F = 60 + A$, it is possible that $\frac{F}{A} = 2$ (choose $F = 120$ and $A = 60$) and it is possible that $\frac{F}{A} = 3$ (choose $F = 90$ and $A = 30$); NOT sufficient.

(2) Given that $F = 240$, it is possible that $\frac{F}{A} = 1$ (choose $F = 240$ and $A = 240$) and it is possible that $\frac{F}{A} = 2$ (choose $F = 240$ and $A = 120$); NOT sufficient.

Taking (1) and (2) together, substitute $F = 240$ into $F = 60 + A$ to get $240 = 60 + A$, or $A = 180$. Therefore, $\frac{F}{A} = \frac{240}{180}$.

The correct answer is C; both statements together are sufficient.

DS02541
279. How many men are in a certain company's vanpool program?

(1) The ratio of men to women in the program is 3 to 2.

(2) The men and women in the program fill 6 vans.

Arithmetic Applied Problems

Let m be the number of men in the program and let w be the number of women in the program. What is the value of m ?

(1) Given that $\frac{m}{w} = \frac{3}{2}$, it is not possible to determine the value of m. For example, if $m = 3$ and $w = 2$, then $\frac{m}{w} = \frac{3}{2}$ is true; and if $m = 6$ and $w = 4$, then $\frac{m}{w} = \frac{3}{2}$ is true; NOT sufficient.

(2) Given that the men and women fill 6 vans, it is clearly not possible to determine the value of m; NOT sufficient.

Taking (1) and (2) together, it is still not possible to determine the value of m. Even if it is assumed that each van has the same maximum capacity, it is possible that $m = 18$ and $w = 12$ (a total of 30 people, which would fill 6 vans each having a capacity of 5 people) and it is possible that $m = 36$ and $w = 24$ (a total of 60 people, which would fill 6 vans each having a capacity of 10 people).

**The correct answer is E;
both statements together are still not sufficient.**

DS08054

280. Each of the marbles in a jar is either red or white or blue. If one marble is to be selected at random from the jar, what is the probability that the marble will be blue?

(1) There are a total of 24 marbles in the jar, 8 of which are red.

(2) The probability that the marble selected will be white is $\frac{1}{2}$.

Arithmetic Probability

This problem can be solved by determining the number of marbles in the jar and the number that are blue.

(1) This indicates that there are 24 marbles in the jar and 8 of them are red. The number of marbles that are blue is not known; NOT sufficient.

(2) This indicates neither the number of marbles in the jar nor the number that are blue; NOT sufficient.

Taking (1) and (2) together, there are 24 marbles in the jar, 8 of which are red and $\frac{1}{2}(24) = 12$ of which are white. Then, the number of blue marbles is $24 - 8 - 12 = 4$, and the probability that one marble selected at random will be blue is $\frac{4}{24} = \frac{1}{6}$.

**The correct answer is C;
both statements together are sufficient.**

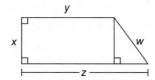

DS04594

281. In the figure above, what is the value of z ?

(1) $x = y = 1$

(2) $w = 2$

Geometry Triangles; Pythagorean Theorem

(1) Given that $x = y = 1$, the length of the base of the triangle to the right, which equals $z - y = z - 1$, can vary, and thus the value of z can vary; NOT sufficient.

(2) Given that $w = 2$, all dimensions of the rectangle to the left can vary, and thus the value of z can vary; NOT sufficient.

Taking (1) and (2) together, then $z = y + (z - y) = 1 + (z - 1)$, and the value of $z - 1$ can be determined by applying the Pythagorean theorem to the triangle that has hypotenuse of length $w = 2$ and sides of lengths $x = 1$ and $z - 1$. Specifically, the Pythagorean theorem gives $1^2 + (z - 1)^2 = 2^2$, or $1 + (z - 1)^2 = 4$, and solving this equation gives $(z - 1)^2 = 3$, or $z - 1 = \sqrt{3}$, or $z = 1 + \sqrt{3}$.

**The correct answer is C;
both statements together are sufficient.**

DS04630

282. What is the value of 10 percent of y ?

(1) 5 percent of y is 60.

(2) y is 80 percent of 1,500.

Arithmetic Percents

This problem can be solved by determining the value of y.

(1) If 5 percent of y is 60, then $0.05y = 60$ and $y = \frac{60}{0.05} = 1,200$; SUFFICIENT.

(2) If y is 80 percent of 1,500, then $y = (0.80)(1,500) = 1,200$; SUFFICIENT.

**The correct answer is D;
each statement alone is sufficient.**

DS12062

283. Last semester, Professor K taught two classes, A and B. Each student in class A handed in 7 assignments, and each student in class B handed in 5 assignments. How many students were in class A ?

(1)   The students in both classes combined handed in a total of 85 assignments.

(2)   There were 10 students in class B.

Algebra Simultaneous Equations

Let a be the number of students in class A and let b be the number of students in class B. Then the students in class A handed in a total of $7a$ assignments and the students in class B handed in a total of $5b$ assignments. What is the value of a ?

(1)   Given that $7a + 5b = 85$, it is not possible to determine the value of a. For example, it is possible that $a = 5$ and $b = 10$, since $7(5) + 5(10) = 85$. On the other hand, it is also possible that $a = 10$ and $b = 3$, since $7(10) + 5(3) = 85$; NOT sufficient.

(2)   Given that $b = 10$, it is not possible to determine the value of a. For example, it is possible that $a = b = 10$; and it is also possible that $a = 5$ and $b = 10$; NOT sufficient.

Taking (1) and (2) together, substituting $b = 10$ into $7a + 5b = 85$ gives $7a + 5(10) = 85$, or $7a = 35$, or $a = 5$.

**The correct answer is C;
both statements together are sufficient.**

DS06802

284. Was the amount of John's heating bill for February greater than it was for January?

(1)   The ratio of the amount of John's heating bill for February to that for January was $\frac{26}{25}$.

(2)   The sum of the amounts of John's heating bills for January and February was $183.60.

Arithmetic Applied Problems

Let J and F be the amounts, respectively and in dollars, of the heating bills for January and February. Is $F > J$?

(1)   Given that $\frac{F}{J} = \frac{26}{25}$, it follows that $\frac{F}{J} > 1$. Multiplying both sides of the inequality $\frac{F}{J} > 1$ by the positive quantity J gives $F > J$; SUFFICIENT.

(2)   Given that $J + F = 183.60$, it is not possible to determine whether $F > J$. For example, if $J = 83.60$ and $F = 100.00$, then $J + F = 183.60$ and $F > J$. On the other

hand, if $J = 100.00$ and $F = 83.60$, then $J + F = 183.60$ and $F < J$; NOT sufficient.

**The correct answer is A;
statement 1 alone is sufficient.**

DS06662

285. If sequence S has 120 terms, what is the 105th term of S ?

(1)   The first term of S is –8.

(2)   Each term of S after the first term is 10 more than the preceding term.

Arithmetic Sequences

This problem can be solved by determining at least one term of the sequence and how each term is derived from the preceding term(s).

(1)   This indicates that the first term of the sequence is –8, but does not indicate how subsequent terms are derived; NOT sufficient.

(2)   This indicates how each term is derived from the preceding term, but does not indicate at least one term of the sequence; NOT sufficient.

Taking (1) and (2) together, the first term is –8 and each subsequent term is 10 more than the preceding term from which the 105th term can be determined.

**The correct answer is C;
both statements together are sufficient.**

DS15650.02

286. If all of the six faces of a concrete block are rectangular, what is the volume of the block?

(1)   Each of the four lateral faces of the block has an area of 200 square inches.

(2)   The top of the block is square and has an area of 400 square inches.

Geometry Rectangular Solids

The figure below shows the block, where the dimensions of the top and bottom of the block are a inches by b inches and the height of the block is c inches. Determine the volume of the block, or equivalently, determine the value of abc.

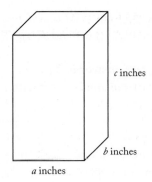

c inches

b inches

a inches

(1) Given that each of the four lateral faces of the block has an area of 200 square inches, it is possible that $a = 20$, $b = 20$, and $c = 10$ (because for these values we have $ac = bc = 200$), and thus it is possible that $abc = 4{,}000$. However, it is also possible that $a = 10$, $b = 10$, and $c = 20$ (because for these values we have $ac = bc = 200$), and thus it is possible that $abc = 2{,}000$; NOT sufficient.

(2) Given that the top of the block is square and has an area of 400 square inches, it follows that $a = b$ and $ab = 400$. However, it is not possible to determine the value of abc, since more than one value of c is possible, and hence more than one value of $abc = (ab)c = 400c$ is possible; NOT sufficient.

Taking (1) and (2) together, it follows from (2) that $ab = a^2 = 400$, and thus $a = b = 20$. Therefore, from (1) we have $ac = 200$, or $20c = 200$, or $c = 10$, and hence $abc = (20)(20)(10) = 4{,}000$.

The correct answer is C; both statements together are sufficient.

DS00858

287. Machine R and machine S work at their respective constant rates. How much time does it take machine R, working alone, to complete a certain job?

(1) The amount of time that it takes machine S, working alone, to complete the job is $\frac{3}{4}$ the amount of time that it takes machine R, working alone, to complete the job.

(2) Machine R and machine S, working together, take 12 minutes to complete the job.

Algebra Applied Problems

(1) Given that machine S takes $\frac{3}{4}$ as long as machine R to complete the job, if the rate of

each machine were doubled, then machine S would still take $\frac{3}{4}$ as long as machine R to complete the job and machine R, working alone, would then take half as long to complete the job as compared to before the rates were doubled; NOT sufficient.

(2) Given that machine R and machine S, working together, take 12 minutes to complete the job, if machine S is extremely slow and thus contributes very little when the machines are working together, then it would take machine R, working alone, only a little more than 12 minutes to complete the job. However, if machine S, working alone, takes only a few seconds less than 12 minutes to complete the job, and thus machine R contributes very little when the machines are working together, then it would take machine R, working alone, a long time to complete the job; NOT sufficient.

Taking (1) and (2) together, let t be the time it takes for machine R, working alone, to complete the job. Then the time it takes machine S, working alone, to complete the job is $\frac{3}{4}t$. Thus, the individual constant rates of machines R and S are, respectively, $\frac{1}{t}$ and $\frac{1}{\frac{3}{4}t} = \left(\frac{4}{3}\right)\frac{1}{t}$, and their combined rate is $\left(1 + \frac{4}{3}\right)\frac{1}{t} = \frac{7}{3t}$. Since it takes 12 minutes to complete the job when the machines are working together, it follows that $\left(\frac{7}{3t}\right)(12) = 1$, which can be solved for t.

The correct answer is C; both statements together are sufficient.

DS06065

288. If $u > 0$ and $v > 0$, which is greater, u^v or v^u?

(1) $u = 1$

(2) $v > 2$

Arithmetic Exponents

(1) Given that $u = 1$, then $u^v = 1^v = 1$ and $v^u = v^1 = v$. If $v = 2$, then $u^v = 1$ is less than

$v^u = 2$. However, if $v = 0.5$, then $u^v = 1$ is greater than $v^u = 0.5$; NOT sufficient.

(2) Given that $v > 2$, it is possible that u^v is less than v^u (for example, if $u = 1$ and $v = 4$, then $u^v = 1^4 = 1$ and $v^u = 4^1 = 4$), and it is possible that u^v is greater than v^u (for example, if $u = 3$ and $v = 4$, then $u^v = 3^4 = 81$ and $v^u = 4^3 = 64$); NOT sufficient.

Taking (1) and (2) together, it follows from (1) that $u^v = 1$ and $v^u = v$, and it follows from (2) that $v > 2$. Therefore, $u^v = 1 < 2 < v = v^u$, and so v^u is greater than u^v.

**The correct answer is C;
both statements together are sufficient.**

DS00660

289. What was the range of the selling prices of the 30 wallets sold by a certain store yesterday?

(1) $\frac{1}{3}$ of the wallets had a selling price of $24 each.

(2) The lowest selling price of the wallets was $\frac{1}{3}$ the highest selling price of the wallets.

Arithmetic Statistics

Since the range of a data set is the greatest value in the data set minus the least value in the data set, this problem can be solved if the least selling price and the greatest selling price of the wallets sold by the store yesterday can be determined.

(1) This indicates that 10 of the wallets had a selling price of $24 each, but does not indicate the least selling price or the greatest selling price of the wallets sold by the store yesterday; NOT sufficient.

(2) This indicates that $L = \frac{1}{3} G$, where L represents the least selling price and G represents the greatest selling price, but does not give enough information to determine $G - L$; NOT sufficient.

Taking (1) and (2) together, the least and greatest selling prices of the wallets sold by the store yesterday could be $10 and $30 for a range of $30 − $10 = $20, or the least and greatest selling prices of the wallets sold by the store yesterday could be $20 and $60 for a range of $60 − $20 = $40.

**The correct answer is E;
both statements together are still not sufficient.**

DS08723

290. Three houses are being sold through a real estate agent. What is the asking price for the house with the second-largest asking price?

(1) The difference between the greatest and the least asking price is $130,000.

(2) The difference between the two greater asking prices is $85,000.

Algebra Simultaneous Equations

Let x, y, and z, where $x \le y \le z$, be the asking prices of the three houses. This problem can be solved by determining the value of y.

(1) This indicates that $z - x = \$130{,}000$, but does not give the value of y; NOT sufficient.

(2) This indicates that $z - y = \$85{,}000$, but does not give the value of y; NOT sufficient.

Taking (1) and (2) together, x, y, and z could be $100,000, $145,000, and $230,000, respectively, in which case the second highest selling price is $145,000, or they could be $200,000, $245,000, and $330,000, respectively, in which case the second highest selling price is $245,000.

**The correct answer is E;
both statements together are still not sufficient.**

DS04605

291. If $a + b + c = 12$, what is the value of b ?

(1) $a + b = 8$

(2) $b + c = 6$

Algebra Simultaneous Equations

(1) Given that $a + b = 8$, it follows from $(a + b) + c = 12$ that $8 + c = 12$, or $c = 4$. However, the value of b still cannot be determined. For example, if $a = 6$, $b = 2$, and $c = 4$, then $a + b + c = 12$ and $a + b = 8$. On the other hand, if $a = 4$, $b = 4$, and $c = 4$, then $a + b + c = 12$ and $a + b = 8$; NOT sufficient.

(2) Given that $b + c = 6$, it follows from $a + (b + c) = 12$ that $a + 6 = 12$, or $a = 6$. However, the value of b still cannot be

determined. For example, if $a = 6$, $b = 3$, and $c = 3$, then $a + b + c = 12$ and $b + c = 6$. On the other hand, if $a = 6$, $b = 2$, and $c = 4$, then $a + b + c = 12$ and $b + c = 6$; NOT sufficient.

Taking (1) and (2) together, it follows from (1) that $c = 4$ and it follows from (2) that $a = 6$. Substituting these values in $a + b + c = 12$ gives $6 + b + 4 = 12$, or $b = 2$.

The correct answer is C; both statements together are sufficient.

DS11254
292. Is $rw = 0$?

   (1) $-6 < r < 5$

   (2) $6 < w < 10$

Algebra Inequalities

This problem can be solved if it can be determined that either or both of r and w is zero or that neither r nor w is zero.

   (1)   This indicates that r can be, but does not have to be, zero and gives no indication of the value of w; NOT sufficient.

   (2)   This indicates that w cannot be zero, but gives no indication of the value of r; NOT sufficient.

Taking (1) and (2) together, r could be zero, in which case $rw = 0$ **or** r could be nonzero, in which case $rw \neq 0$.

The correct answer is E; both statements together are still not sufficient.

DS06633
293. Is $x = \dfrac{1}{y}$?

   (1) $xy = 1$

   (2) $\dfrac{1}{xy} = 1$

Algebra Equations

   (1)   This indicates that neither x nor y can be zero because if $x = 0$ or $y = 0$, then $xy = 0$. Since $xy = 1$ and $y \neq 0$, then dividing both sides by y gives $x = \dfrac{1}{y}$; SUFFICIENT.

   (2)   This indicates that neither x nor y can be zero because if $x = 0$ or $y = 0$, then $xy = 0$, and division by zero is undefined. Multiplying both sides of the equation $\dfrac{1}{xy} = 1$ by x gives $\dfrac{1}{y} = x$; SUFFICIENT.

The correct answer is D; each statement alone is sufficient.

DS07949
294. How many people in a group of 50 own neither a fax machine nor a laser printer?

   (1)   The total number of people in the group who own a fax machine or a laser printer or both is less than 50.

   (2)   The total number of people in the group who own both a fax machine and a laser printer is 15.

Algebra Sets

   (1)   This indicates that the total number who own either a fax machine or a laser printer or both is less than 50, but does not indicate how much less than 50 the total number is. Thus, the number of people in the group who own neither a fax machine nor a laser printer cannot be determined; NOT sufficient.

   (2)   This indicates that, of the 50 people, 15 own both a fax machine and a laser printer, but does not indicate how many own one or the other. Thus, the number of people in the group who own neither a fax machine nor a laser printer cannot be determined; NOT sufficient.

Taking (1) and (2) together, it is known that 15 people own both a fax machine and a laser printer and that the total number who own either a fax machine or a laser printer or both is less than 50, but the exact number who own neither still cannot be determined. For example, if 20 people own only a fax machine and 10 people own only a laser printer, then both (1) and (2) are true and the number of people who own neither a fax machine nor a laser printer is $50 - 20 - 10 - 15 = 5$. However, if 10 people own only a fax machine and 10 people own only a laser printer, then both (1) and (2) are true and the number of people who own neither a fax machine nor a laser printer is $50 - 10 - 10 - 15 = 15$.

The correct answer is E;
both statements together are still not sufficient.

DS06475

295. What is the value of w^{-2} ?

(1) $w^{-1} = \dfrac{1}{2}$

(2) $w^3 = 8$

Algebra Exponents

(1) Since $w^{-1} = \dfrac{1}{2}$, then $(w^{-1})^2 = \left(\dfrac{1}{2}\right)^2 = \dfrac{1}{4}$ or $w^{-2} = \dfrac{1}{4}$; SUFFICIENT.

(2) Since $w^3 = 8$, then $w = \sqrt[3]{8} = 2$ and $w^{-2} = 2^{-2} = \dfrac{1}{4}$; SUFFICIENT.

The correct answer is D;
each statement alone is sufficient.

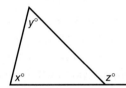

Note: Figure not drawn to scale

DS27860.02

296. What is the value of z in the figure above?

(1) $x = 50$

(2) $y = 35$

Geometry Angles

Determine the value of z, where $z = x + y$.

(1) Given that the value of x is 50, if the value of y were 50, for example, the value of z would be 100. On the other hand, if the value of y were 35, the value of z would be 85; NOT sufficient.

(2) Given that the value of y is 35, if the value of x were 50, for example, the value of z would be 85. On the other hand, if the value of x were 65, the value of z would be 100; NOT sufficient.

Taking (1) and (2) together, the value of z is $50 + 35 = 85$.

The correct answer is C;
both statements together are sufficient.

DS07839

297. A certain investment earned a fixed rate of 4 percent interest per year, compounded annually, for five years. The interest earned for the third year of the investment was how many dollars greater than that for the first year?

(1) The amount of the investment at the beginning of the second year was $4,160.00.

(2) The amount of the investment at the beginning of the third year was $4,326.40.

Arithmetic Applied Problems; Percents

This problem can be solved by determining the dollar amount of the interest earned for the third year minus the dollar amount of interest earned in the first year, or, in symbols, $[A(1.04)^3 - A(1.04)^2] - [A(1.04)^1 - A]$, where A represents the dollar amount of the investment. This can be determined if the value of A can be determined.

(1) This indicates that $A(1.04)^1 = \$4,160.00$, since the amount of the investment at the beginning of the second year is the same as the amount of the investment at the end of the first year. Thus, the value of A can be determined by dividing 4,160.00 by 1.04; SUFFICIENT.

(2) This indicates that $A(1.04)^2 = \$4,326.40$, since the amount of the investment at the beginning of the third year is the same as the amount of the investment at the end of the second year. Thus, the value of A can be determined by dividing 4,326.40 by $(1.04)^2$; SUFFICIENT.

The correct answer is D;
each statement alone is sufficient.

DS06397

298. What is the circumference of circle C ?

(1) The radius of circle C is 2π.

(2) The center of circle C is located at point (7,8) in the xy-plane.

Geometry Circles

What is the value of $2\pi r$, where r is the radius of circle C?

(1) Given that $r = 2\pi$, the value of $2\pi r$ is $2\pi \cdot 2\pi$; SUFFICIENT.

(2) Given that the center of circle C is located at $(7,8)$, the radius of circle C can be any positive real number, and therefore the value of $2\pi r$ cannot be determined; NOT sufficient.

The correct answer is A; statement 1 alone is sufficient.

DS07813
299. What is the value of t?

(1) $s + t = 6 + s$

(2) $t^3 = 216$

Algebra Equations

(1) Given that $s + t = 6 + s$, subtracting s from both sides gives $t = 6$; SUFFICIENT.

(2) Given that $t^3 = 216$, taking the cube root of both sides gives $t = 6$; SUFFICIENT.

The correct answer is D; each statement alone is sufficient.

DS11109
300. For a certain car repair, the total charge consisted of a charge for parts, a charge for labor, and a 6 percent sales tax on both the charge for parts and the charge for labor. If the charge for parts, excluding sales tax, was $50.00, what was the total charge for the repair?

(1) The sales tax on the charge for labor was $9.60.

(2) The total sales tax was $12.60.

Arithmetic Applied Problems; Percents

To find the total charge, T, for the repair, requires determining the value, in dollars, of $T = (1.06)(50 + L) = 53 + 1.06L$, where L represents the charge, in dollars, for labor. This value can be determined if the value of L can be determined.

(1) This indicates that $0.06L = 9.60$, from which L can be determined by dividing 9.60 by 0.06; SUFFICIENT.

(2) This indicates that $(0.06)(50 + L) = 12.60$. So, $3.00 + 0.06L = 12.60$ or $0.06L = 9.60$, which is the same as the equation in (1); SUFFICIENT.

The correct answer is D; each statement alone is sufficient.

DS06905
301. George has a total of B books in his library, 25 of which are hardcover fiction books. What is the value of B?

(1) 40 of the B books are fiction and the rest are nonfiction.

(2) 60 of the B books are hardcovers and the rest are paperbacks.

Arithmetic Applied Problems

Since 25 of George's B books are hardcover fiction, it is reasonable to assume that some of George's books might be paperback and some might be nonfiction. Therefore, the following table might be useful in determining, if possible, the value of B.

Fiction		Nonfiction		B
Hardcover	Paperback	Hardcover	Paperback	
25				

(1) If 40 of the B books are fiction, then $40 - 25 = 15$ are paperback fiction. This information is shown in the following table.

Fiction		Nonfiction		B
Hardcover	Paperback	Hardcover	Paperback	
25	15			

The rest are nonfiction, but there is no indication how many are nonfiction. Note that the table has two blank cells under Nonfiction and these can be filled with any numbers, which implies that the value of B cannot be uniquely determined; NOT sufficient.

(2) If 60 of the B books are hardcovers, then $60 - 25 = 35$ are hardcover nonfiction. This information is shown in the following table.

Fiction		Nonfiction		B
Hardcover	Paperback	Hardcover	Paperback	
25		35		

The rest are paperbacks, but there is no indication of how many are paperbacks. The table has two blank cells under paperback, and these can be filled with any numbers, which implies that the value of B cannot be uniquely determined; NOT sufficient.

Taking the information from both (1) and (2), shown in the following table, is still not sufficient to uniquely determine the value of B.

Fiction		Nonfiction		B
Hardcover	Paperback	Hardcover	Paperback	
25	15	35		

The table has one blank cell under Paperback that can be filled with any number, which implies that the value of B cannot be uniquely determined.

The correct answer is E;
both statements together are still not sufficient.

DS12031
302. Is $w + h^4$ positive?

(1) h is positive.

(2) w is positive.

Arithmetic Properties of Numbers

(1) Given that h is positive, then $w + h^4$ can be positive (for example, when $w = 1$ and $h = 1$) and $w + h^4$ can be negative (for example, when $w = -2$ and $h = 1$); NOT sufficient.

(2) Given that w is positive, then because $h^4 \geq 0$, it follows that $w + h^4 \geq w + 0 = w$ and thus $w + h^4 > 0$ since $w > 0$; SUFFICIENT.

The correct answer is B;
statement 2 alone is sufficient.

DS15377
303. If a is a 3-digit integer and b is a 3-digit integer, is the units digit of the product of a and b greater than 5 ?

(1) The units digit of a is 4.

(2) The units digit of b is 7.

Arithmetic Operations with Integers

Determine whether the units digit of the product of the two 3-digit integers a and b is greater than 5.

(1) It is given that the units digit of a is 4. If the units digit of b is 0 or 1, then the units digit of ab is not greater than 5. However, if the units digit of b is 2, then the units digit of ab is greater than 5; NOT sufficient.

(2) It is given that the units digit of b is 7. If the units digit of a is 0, then the units digit of ab is not greater than 5. However, if the units digit of a is 1, then the units digit of ab is greater than 5; NOT sufficient.

Taking (1) and (2) together, the units digit of a is 4 and the units digit of b is 7. Therefore, the units digit of ab is 8, which is greater than 5.

The correct answer is C;
both statements together are sufficient.

DS02450
304. In each of the last five years, Company K donated p percent of its annual profits to a certain scholarship fund. Did Company K donate more than $10,000 to the scholarship fund last year?

(1) Two years ago, Company K had annual profits of $3 million and donated $15,000 to the scholarship fund.

(2) Last year, Company K had annual profits of $2.5 million.

Arithmetic Applied Problems; Percents

(1) Although the given information allows the value of p to be determined (see further below), no information is available about Company K's profit last year; NOT sufficient.

(2) It is given that Company K's profit last year was $2.5 million. However, no information is available about the value of p or how much Company K donated to the scholarship fund last year; NOT sufficient.

Taking (1) and (2) together, from (1) it follows that 15,000 is p% of 3 million, so $15{,}000 = \left(\dfrac{p}{100}\right)(3{,}000{,}000)$, or $p = \dfrac{(100)(15{,}000)}{3{,}000{,}000} = \dfrac{15}{30} = 0.5$.

Using the value of p and (2), it follows that the amount Company K donated to the scholarship fund last year was $(0.5\%)(\$2.5\text{ million}) = (0.005)(\$2{,}500{,}000) = \$12{,}500$. Therefore, Company K donated more than $10,000 to the scholarship fund last year.

Tip: If a Data Sufficiency problem asks a question about the value of something, it is not necessary to determine a specific decimal, a reduced fraction, or any other representation for this value if it is known that only one such value exists. Thus, in the previous paragraph, it is not necessary to solve for p (it is enough to know that a unique value of p can be found) and it is not necessary to evaluate the product $(p\%)(\$2.5 \text{ million})$, since whatever the product is, it will either be greater than \$10,000, and the answer to the question will be "yes," or not be greater than \$10,000, and the answer to the question will be "no."

The correct answer is C; both statements together are sufficient.

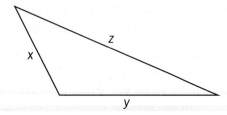

DS06901

305. Is the area of the triangular region above less than 20 ?

(1) $x^2 + y^2 \neq z^2$

(2) $x + y < 13$

Geometry Triangles; Area

Determine whether the area of the given triangle is less than 20.

(1)   This indicates that the triangle is not a right triangle but gives no information about the size of the triangle so its area could be less than 20, but it could also be 20 or greater; NOT sufficient.

(2)   Stating that the sum of the lengths of two sides of the triangle is less than 13 gives very little information about the size of the triangle and no information about the shape of the triangle. Therefore, it is not possible to determine whether the area is less than 20.

For example, the triangle could be a right triangle with a base of 4 (that is, $y = 4$) and a height of 3 (that is, $x = 3$). Then $x + y < 13$ and the area is $\frac{1}{2}(4)(3) = 6$, which is less than 20.

The triangle could also be a right triangle with a base of 6.99 (that is, $y = 6.99$) and a

height of 6 (that is, $x = 6$). Then $x + y < 13$ and the area is $\frac{1}{2}(6.99)(6) = (6.99)(3) = 20.97$, which is greater than 20; NOT sufficient.

Taking (1) and (2) together is still not sufficient to determine whether the area of the triangle is less than 20. Statement (1) indicates that the triangle is not a right triangle and statement (2) gives some information about the size of the triangle, but neither gives information specific enough to determine whether the area of the triangle is less than 20.

For example, the triangle could be obtuse, as shown in the figure below, where $h < x$ because h and x are the lengths of a leg and hypotenuse, respectively, of a right triangle.

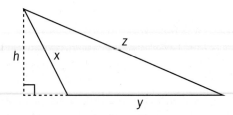

If A represents the area of the triangle, which satisfies (1) because it is not a right triangle, then $A = \frac{1}{2}hy$, and because $h < x$, $\frac{1}{2}hy < \frac{1}{2}xy$, so $A < \frac{1}{2}xy$. If $x = y = 6$, then $x + y < 13$, which satisfies (2), and $A < \frac{1}{2}(6)(6)$ or $A < 18$. Therefore, a triangle that satisfies both (1) and (2) and has area less than 20 is possible.

However, the triangle could also be acute as shown in the figure below, where $h < x$ because h and x are the lengths of a leg and hypotenuse, respectively, of a right triangle.

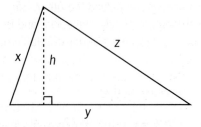

Since the task is to determine whether the area of the triangle is less than 20, choose values for y and h so that the area of the triangle is exactly 20. The values 6 and $6\frac{2}{3}$ give the area

$A = \frac{1}{2} by = \frac{1}{2}(6\frac{2}{3})(6) = 20$. Note that any value of x such that $6\frac{2}{3} < x < 7$ will satisfy (1). Therefore, a triangle that satisfies both (1) and (2) and has area 20 is possible.

**The correct answer is E;
both statements together are still not sufficient.**

DS04366
306. *A*, *B*, *C*, and *D* are points on a line. If *C* is the midpoint of line segment *AB* and if *D* is the midpoint of line segment *CB*, is the length of line segment *DB* greater than 5 ?

(1) The length of line segment *AC* is greater than 8.

(2) The length of line segment *CD* is greater than 6.

Geometry Lines and Segments

It is given that *C* is the midpoint of $\overline{AB}$, so $AC = CB = \frac{1}{2}(AB)$. It is given that *D* is the midpoint of $\overline{CB}$, so $CD = DB = \frac{1}{2}(CB)$. Determine if $DB > 5$.

(1) Given that $AC > 8$, it follows that $CB > 8$ since $AC = CB$, and so $DB = \frac{1}{2}(CB) > \frac{1}{2}(8)$ or $DB > 4$. However, this means that *DB* could be 6 and $6 > 5$ or *DB* could be 4.1 and $4.1 < 5$; NOT sufficient.

(2) Given that $CD > 6$, it follows that $DB > 6$ since $CD = DB$; SUFFICIENT.

**The correct answer is B;
statement 2 alone is sufficient.**

DS11805
307. The people in a line waiting to buy tickets to a show are standing one behind the other. Adam and Beth are among the people in the line, and Beth is standing behind Adam with a number of people between them. If the number of people in front of Adam plus the number of people behind Beth is 18, how many people in the line are behind Beth?

(1) There are a total of 32 people in the line.

(2) 23 people in the line are behind Adam.

Arithmetic Order

Beth is standing in line behind Adam with a number of people between them. Let *x* be the number of people ahead of Adam, let *y* be the number of people between Adam and Beth, and let *z* be the number of people behind Beth. It is given that $x + z = 18$. Determine *z*.

(1) This indicates that there are 32 people in the line. Two of these people are Adam and Beth, so there are 30 other people in line besides Adam and Beth. Therefore, $x + y + z = 30$ and $x + z = 18$. From this, $y = 12$, but *z* cannot be determined uniquely. For example, if $x = 5$, then $z = 13$, but if $x = 10$, then $z = 8$; NOT sufficient.

(2) This indicates that $y + 1 + z = 23$ because the people behind Adam consist of the people between Adam and Beth, Beth herself, and the people behind Beth. If, for example, $y = 4$, then $z = 18$, but if $y = 9$, then $z = 13$; NOT sufficient.

Taking (1) and (2) together, $y = 12$ from (1) and $y + z = 22$ from (2). Therefore, $z = 10$, and there are 10 people in line behind Beth.

**The correct answer is C;
both statements together are sufficient.**

DS08730
308. Square *ABCD* is inscribed in circle *O*. What is the area of square region *ABCD* ?

(1) The area of circular region *O* is 64π.

(2) The circumference of circle *O* is 16π.

Geometry Circles; Area

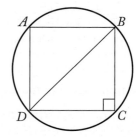

Since the area of square *ABCD* is the square of its side length, to solve this problem it is necessary to determine the side length of *ABCD*. From the figure, a diameter of the circle coincides with a diagonal of the square. If the length of a diameter of the circle can be determined, then the length of a diagonal of the square can be determined, from which the side length of the square can be determined using the Pythagorean theorem.

(1) This indicates that the area of the circle is 64π, so letting r represent the radius of the circle, $\pi r^2 = 64\pi$. Thus, $r^2 = 64$, $r = 8$, and $d = 2(8) = 16$, where d represents the length of the diameter of the circle and also the diagonal of the square; SUFFICIENT.

(2) This indicates that the circumference of the circle is 16π, so letting d represent the length of the diameter of the circle as well as the diagonal of the square, $\pi d = 16\pi$. Thus, $d = 16$; SUFFICIENT.

**The correct answer is D;
each statement alone is sufficient.**

DS12533
309. Lines k and m are parallel to each other. Is the slope of line k positive?

(1) Line k passes through the point (3,2).
(2) Line m passes through the point (–3,2).

Geometry Coordinate Geometry

(1) This indicates that line k passes through the point (3,2). One point is not enough to determine whether the slope of line k is positive. If, for example, line k also passes through the point (0,0), then the slope of line k is $\dfrac{2-0}{3-0} = \dfrac{2}{3}$, which is positive. But if line k also passes through the point (5,0), then the slope of line k is $\dfrac{2-0}{3-5} = \dfrac{2}{-2}$, which is negative; NOT sufficient.

(2) This indicates that line m passes through the point (–3,2). One point is not enough to determine whether the slope of line m is positive. If, for example, line m also passes through the point (0,0), then the slope of line m is $\dfrac{2-0}{-3-0} = \dfrac{2}{-3}$, which is negative. In this case, the slope of line k is also negative since parallel lines k and m have the same

slope. But if line m also passes through the point (0,5), then the slope of line m is $\dfrac{2-5}{-3-0} = \dfrac{-3}{-3}$, which is positive. In this case, the slope of line k is also positive since parallel lines k and m have the same slope; NOT sufficient.

Taking (1) and (2) together gives no more information than (1) or (2) alone and so whether the slope of line k is positive cannot be determined.

**The correct answer is E;
both statements together are still not sufficient.**

DS19520
310. In cross section, a tunnel that carries one lane of one-way traffic is a semicircle with radius 4.2 m. Is the tunnel large enough to accommodate the truck that is approaching the entrance to the tunnel?

(1) The maximum width of the truck is 2.4 m.
(2) The maximum height of the truck is 4 m.

Geometry Circles; Pythagorean Theorem

(1) Given that the maximum width of the truck is 2.4 m, it is possible that the tunnel is large enough (for example, if the maximum height of the truck is sufficiently small) and it is possible that the tunnel is not large enough (for example, if the maximum height of the truck is sufficiently large); NOT sufficient.

(2) Given that the maximum height of the truck is 4 m, it is possible that the tunnel is large enough (for example, if the maximum width is sufficiently small) and it is possible that the tunnel is not large enough (for example, if the maximum width of the truck is sufficiently large); NOT sufficient.

Taking (1) and (2) together, it is possible for the truck to pass through the tunnel, because even if the truck were rectangular with width 2.4 m and height 4 m, the truck could pass through the tunnel if it were centered in the tunnel as shown in the diagram. In this position, it follows from the Pythagorean theorem that every point on the truck is located at most a distance of

$\sqrt{(1.2)^2 + 4^2}$ meters from the center axis of the tunnel, and this distance is less than 4.2 meters, the radius of the tunnel, since $(1.2)^2 + 4^2 = 17.44$ is less than $(4.2)^2 = 17.64$.

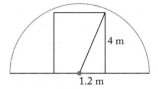

**The correct answer is C;
both statements together are sufficient.**

DS13122

311. In a certain group of 50 people, how many are doctors who have a law degree?

    (1) In the group, 36 people are doctors.

    (2) In the group, 18 people have a law degree.

Arithmetic Sets

(1) Given that there are 36 people who are doctors, there is no information about how many of the 36 people have a law degree, and therefore it cannot be determined how many of the 36 people are doctors with a law degree; NOT sufficient.

(2) Given that there are 18 people who have a law degree, there is no information about how many of the 18 people are doctors, and therefore it cannot be determined how many of the 18 people are doctors with a law degree; NOT sufficient.

Taking (1) and (2) together, if n is the number of doctors with a law degree, the contingency table below shows that more than one value of n is possible by assigning appropriate values in the column labeled "not a doctor."

	doctor	not a doctor	total
law degree	n		18
no law degree	$36 - n$		32
total	36	14	50

For example, the first table below gives $n = 10$ and the second table below gives $n = 12$.

	doctor	not a doctor	total
law degree	n	8	18
no law degree	$36 - n$	6	32
total	36	14	50

	doctor	not a doctor	total
law degree	n	6	18
no law degree	$36 - n$	8	32
total	36	14	50

**The correct answer is E;
both statements together are still not sufficient.**

DS01544

312. Of a group of 50 households, how many have at least one cat or at least one dog, but not both?

    (1) The number of households that have at least one cat and at least one dog is 4.

    (2) The number of households that have no cats and no dogs is 14.

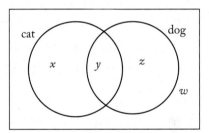

Arithmetic Sets

Using the labels on the Venn diagram, $w + x + y + z = 50$. Determine the value of $x + z$.

(1) This indicates that $y = 4$, so $w + x + z = 46$, but the value of $x + z$ cannot be uniquely determined; NOT sufficient.

(2) This indicates that $w = 14$, so $x + y + z = 36$, but the value of $x + z$ cannot be uniquely determined; NOT sufficient.

Taking (1) and (2) together, $14 + x + 4 + z = 50$, so $x + z = 50 - 14 - 4 = 32$.

**The correct answer is C;
both statements together are sufficient.**

DS02441

313. Robin invested a total of $12,000 in two investments, X and Y, so that the investments earned the same amount of simple annual interest. How many dollars did Robin invest in investment Y ?

(1) Investment X paid 3 percent simple annual interest, and investment Y paid 6 percent simple annual interest.

(2) Robin invested more than $1,000 in investment X.

Algebra Applied Problems

For investments X and Y, let r_X and r_Y be the annual percentage interest rates, respectively, and let x and y be the investment amounts, respectively and in dollars. Then $x + y = 12{,}000$ and $r_X \cdot x = r_Y \cdot y$. What is the value of y ?

(1) Given that $r_X = 3$ and $r_Y = 6$, then from $r_X \cdot x = r_Y \cdot y$ it follows that $3x = 6y$, or $x = 2y$. Therefore, $x + y = 12{,}000$ becomes $2y + y = 12{,}000$, or $3y = 12{,}000$, or $y = 4{,}000$; SUFFICIENT.

(2) Given that $x > 1{,}000$, it is not possible to determine the value of y. For example, $y = 4{,}000$ is possible (choose $r_X = 3$, $r_Y = 6$, and $x = 8{,}000$) and $y = 6{,}000$ is possible (choose $r_X = 3$, $r_Y = 3$, and $x = 6{,}000$); NOT sufficient.

The correct answer is A; statement 1 alone is sufficient.

DS03999

314. In a real estate office that employs n salespeople, f of them are females and x of the females are new employees. What is the value of n ?

(1) If an employee were randomly selected from the n employees, the probability of selecting a female would be $\dfrac{2}{3}$.

(2) If an employee were randomly selected from the f female employees, the probability of selecting a new employee would be $\dfrac{1}{2}$.

Arithmetic Probability

(1) Given that $\dfrac{f}{n} = \dfrac{2}{3}$, it is possible that $n = 3$ (choose $f = 2$ and $x = 1$) and it is possible

that $n = 6$ (choose $f = 4$ and $x = 2$); NOT sufficient.

(2) Given that $\dfrac{x}{f} = \dfrac{1}{2}$, the value of n cannot be determined because $\dfrac{x}{f} = \dfrac{1}{2}$ is true for each of the two choices of values of n, f, and x that were used in (1); NOT sufficient.

Taking (1) and (2) together is still not sufficient because both (1) and (2) hold for each of the two choices of values of n, f, and x that were used in (1).

The correct answer is E; both statements together are still not sufficient.

DS09315

315. Is $\dfrac{x+1}{y+1} > \dfrac{x}{y}$?

(1) $0 < x < y$

(2) $xy > 0$

Algebra Inequalities

(1) Given that $0 < x < y$, the following steps show how to obtain $\dfrac{x+1}{y+1} > \dfrac{x}{y}$.

y	$>$	x	given
$xy + y$	$>$	$xy + x$	add xy to both sides
$y(x+1)$	$>$	$x(y+1)$	factor
$\dfrac{x+1}{y+1}$	$>$	$\dfrac{x}{y}$	divide both sides by $y(y+1)$

In the last step, the direction of the inequality is not changed because both y and $y + 1$ are positive, and hence the product $y(y + 1)$ is positive. These steps can be discovered by performing standard algebraic manipulations that transform $\dfrac{x+1}{y+1} > \dfrac{x}{y}$ into $y > x$, and then verifying that it is mathematically valid to reverse the steps; SUFFICIENT.

(2) Given that $xy > 0$, it is possible that $\dfrac{x+1}{y+1} > \dfrac{x}{y}$ can be true (choosing $x = 1$ and $y = 2$, the inequality becomes $\dfrac{2}{3} > \dfrac{1}{2}$) and it is possible that $\dfrac{x+1}{y+1} > \dfrac{x}{y}$ can be false

(choosing $x = -1$ and $y = -2$, the inequality becomes $\frac{0}{-1} > \frac{-1}{-2}$ or $0 > \frac{1}{2}$); NOT sufficient.

The correct answer is A; statement 1 alone is sufficient.

DS01216

316. Do at least 60 percent of the students in Pat's class walk to school?

(1) At least 60 percent of the female students in Pat's class walk to school.

(2) The number of students in Pat's class who walk to school is twice the number of students who do not walk to school.

Arithmetic Percents

This problem can be solved by determining the total number of students in Pat's class and the number who walk to school.

(1) This indicates that at least 60% of the female students in Pat's class walk to school. However, it does not give any information about the other students in Pat's class; NOT sufficient.

(2) Letting x represent the number of students in Pat's class who do not walk to school, this indicates that $2x$ students in Pat's class walk to school and that the total number of students in Pat's class is $x + 2x = 3x$. From this, the percent of students in Pat's class who walk to school is $\left[\frac{2x}{3x}100\right]\% = \left[\frac{2}{3}(100)\right]\%$; SUFFICIENT.

The correct answer is B; statement 2 alone is sufficient.

DS03628

317. A certain plumber charges $92 for each job completed in 4 hours or less and $23 per hour for each job completed in more than 4 hours. If it took the plumber a total of 7 hours to complete two separate jobs, what was the total amount charged by the plumber for the two jobs?

(1) The plumber charged $92 for one of the two jobs.

(2) The plumber charged $138 for one of the two jobs.

Arithmetic Applied Problems

Find the total amount charged for two jobs lasting a total of 7 hours if the plumber charges $92 for a job lasting 4 hours or less and $23 per hour for a job lasting more than 4 hours.

(1) This indicates that one of the two jobs lasted 4 hours or less. If that job lasted 2 hours, then the other job lasted 5 hours, and the charge for that job would be ($23)(5) = $115, making the total for the two jobs $92 + $115 = $207. However, if the jobs lasted 1 hour and 6 hours, respectively, then the total charge for the two jobs would be $92 + (6)($23) = $92 + $138 = $230; NOT sufficient.

(2) This indicates that one job lasted $\frac{\$138}{\$23} = 6$ hours. Therefore, the other job lasted for 1 hour and the charge for that job was $92, making the total charge for the two jobs $92 + $138 = $230; SUFFICIENT.

The correct answer is B; statement 2 alone is sufficient.

DS02585

318. If x and y are positive numbers, is $\frac{x+1}{y+1} > \frac{x}{y}$?

(1) $x > 1$

(2) $x < y$

Algebra Inequalities

Since y is positive, multiplying both sides of the inequality $\frac{x+1}{y+1} > \frac{x}{y}$ by $y(y+1)$ gives $y(x+1) > x(y+1)$ or $xy + y > xy + x$, which is equivalent to $y > x$. So, determining whether the inequality $\frac{x+1}{y+1} > \frac{x}{y}$ is true is equivalent to determining whether the inequality $y > x$ is true.

(1) This indicates that $x > 1$. If, for example, $x = 3$ and $y = 4$, then $y > x$ is true. However, if $x = 4$ and $y = 3$, then $y > x$ is not true; NOT sufficient.

(2) This indicates that $x < y$, so $y > x$ is true; SUFFICIENT.

The correct answer is B; statement 2 alone is sufficient.

DS01619
319. If a and b are positive integers, is $\dfrac{a}{b} < \dfrac{9}{11}$?

   (1) $\dfrac{a}{b} < 0.818$

   (2) $\dfrac{b}{a} > 1.223.$

Arithmetic Inequalities

If $11a < 9b$ and b is positive, then $\dfrac{11a}{b} < 9$ and $\dfrac{a}{b} < \dfrac{9}{11}$. Therefore, this problem can be solved by determining if $11a < 9b$.

   (1)   From this,

$\dfrac{a}{b} <$	0.818	given
$a <$	$0.818b$	multiply both sides by b, which is positive
$11a <$	$8.998b$	multiply both sides by 11

Then, since $8.998b < 9b$, it follows that $11a < 9b$; SUFFICIENT.

   (2)   From this,

$\dfrac{b}{a} >$	1.223	given
$b >$	$1.223a$	multiply both sides by a, which is positive
$9b >$	$11.007a$	multiply both sides by 9

Then, since $11.007a > 11a$, it follows that $9b > 11a$; SUFFICIENT.

**The correct answer is D;
each statement alone is sufficient.**

DS04536
320. Every object in a box is either a sphere or a cube, and every object in the box is either red or green. How many objects are in the box?

   (1)   There are six cubes and five green objects in the box.

   (2)   There are two red spheres in the box.

Arithmetic Sets

This problem can be solved using a contingency table set up as shown below, where T represents the number to be determined.

	cube	sphere	total
red			
green			
total			T

   (1)   The following table displays the information that there are 6 cubes and 5 green objects:

	cube	sphere	total
red			
green			5
total	6		T

It is obvious that there is not enough information to determine a unique value for T; NOT sufficient.

   (2)   The following table displays the information that there are 2 red spheres:

	cube	sphere	total
red		2	
green			
total			T

It is obvious that there is not enough information to determine a unique value for T; NOT sufficient.

The following table displays the information from (1) and (2) taken together:

	cube	sphere	total
red		2	
green			5
total	6		T

It is obvious that there is still not enough information to determine a unique value for T.

**The correct answer is E;
both statements together are still not sufficient.**

DS01425
321. If x and y are positive integers, is xy even?

   (1) $x^2 + y^2 - 1$ is divisible by 4.

   (2) $x + y$ is odd.

Arithmetic Properties of Numbers

Determine whether the product of two positive integers, x and y, is even.

(1)   This indicates that $x^2 + y^2 - 1$ is divisible by 4, so $x^2 + y^2 - 1 = 4q$ for some integer q. Then $x^2 + y^2 = 4q + 1$, which means $x^2 + y^2$ is odd. Both x^2 and y^2 cannot be even because, in that case, their sum would be even, and both cannot be odd because, in that case, their sum would also be even. Therefore, one of x^2 and y^2 is even, and the other is odd. It follows that one of x or y is even and the other is odd, so xy is even; SUFFICIENT.

(2)   If $x + y$ is odd, then one of x and y is even and the other is odd because if both were even or both were odd, the sum would be even. It follows that xy is even; SUFFICIENT.

The correct answer is D; each statement alone is sufficient.

DS14502

322. If a and b are integers, is $a + b + 3$ an odd integer?

(1) ab is an odd integer.

(2) $a - b$ is an even integer.

Arithmetic Properties of Numbers

Determine whether $a + b + 3$ is odd for integers a and b.

(1)   This indicates that, since ab is odd, both a and b are odd because if one of a or b is even or both a and b are even, then ab is even. Therefore, $a + b$ is even and $a + b + 3$ is odd; SUFFICIENT.

(2)   This indicates that, since $a - b$ is even, both a and b are even or both are odd because if one of them is even and the other is odd, then $a - b$ is odd. Therefore, $a + b$ is even, and $a + b + 3$ is odd; SUFFICIENT.

The correct answer is D; each statement alone is sufficient.

DS08308

323. If x and y are positive integers, what is the value of $\sqrt{x} + \sqrt{y}$?

(1) $x + y = 15$

(2) $\sqrt{xy} = 6$

Algebra Operations with Radicals

(1)   Given that $x + y = 15$, the table below shows two possible values of $\sqrt{x} + \sqrt{y}$ for positive integer values of x and y.

x	y	$x + y$	$\sqrt{x} + \sqrt{y}$
1	14	15	$1 + \sqrt{14}$
4	11	15	$2 + \sqrt{11}$

Although it is reasonable to believe that $1 + \sqrt{14}$ is not equal to $2 + \sqrt{11}$, this can be verified as follows.

$1 + \sqrt{14}$ is less than 5:

$$1 + \sqrt{14} < 1 + \sqrt{16} = 1 + 4 = 5$$

$2 + \sqrt{11}$ is greater than 5:

$$2 + \sqrt{11} > 2 + \sqrt{9} = 2 + 3 = 5$$

Therefore, there is more than one possible value of $\sqrt{x} + \sqrt{y}$; NOT sufficient.

(2)   Given that $\sqrt{xy} = 6$, the table below shows two possible values of $\sqrt{x} + \sqrt{y}$ for positive integer values of x and y.

x	y	$\sqrt{xy}$	$\sqrt{x} + \sqrt{y}$
1	36	6	$1 + 6 = 7$
4	9	6	$2 + 3 = 5$

Therefore, $\sqrt{x} + \sqrt{y}$ can have more than one possible value; NOT sufficient.

Taking (1) and (2) together, $x + y = 15$ and $\sqrt{xy} = 6$, or by squaring both sides of the second equation, $x + y = 15$ and $xy = 36$. Thus, x and y are positive integers with a product of 36, and so there are only five possibilities, all of which are shown in the table below.

Note that it is not necessary to consider the additional possibilities obtained by interchanging the values of x and y, since the value of $\sqrt{x} + \sqrt{y}$ would not be changed.

x	y	xy	$x + y$
1	36	36	37
2	18	36	20
3	**12**	**36**	**15**
4	9	36	13
6	6	36	12

From the table above, it follows that only the choice of 3 and 12 gives a sum of 15, satisfying (1) as well as (2), so $\sqrt{x}+\sqrt{y}=\sqrt{3}+\sqrt{12}$.

Tip: The solution above made use of the assumption that both x and y are positive integers. However, if you desire practice in solving simultaneous equations, use algebra to solve the equations $x + y = 15$ and $\sqrt{xy} = 6$ to show that only two solutions exist: $(x, y) = (3,12)$ and $(x, y) = (12,3)$.

**The correct answer is C;
both statements together are sufficient.**

DS05312

324. A certain truck uses $\frac{1}{12} + kv^2$ gallons of fuel per mile when its speed is v miles per hour, where k is a constant. At what speed should the truck travel so that it uses $\frac{5}{12}$ gallon of fuel per mile?

(1) The value of k is $\frac{1}{10,800}$.

(2) When the truck travels at 30 miles per hour, it uses $\frac{1}{6}$ gallon of fuel per mile.

Algebra Applied Problems

This problem can be solved by determining the positive value of v so that $\frac{1}{12} + kv^2 = \frac{5}{12}$.

(1) This indicates the value of k and so the value of v can be determined by solving

$$\frac{1}{12} + \frac{1}{10,800}v^2 = \frac{5}{12} \text{ for } v;$$

SUFFICIENT.

(2) This indicates that $\frac{1}{12} + k(30)^2 = \frac{1}{6}$. The value of k can be determined by solving this equation for k. Then that value of k can be substituted into $\frac{1}{12} + kv^2 = \frac{5}{12}$, which can then be solved for the value of v; SUFFICIENT.

**The correct answer is D;
each statement alone is sufficient.**

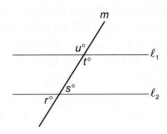

DS48710.02

325. In the figure shown, is $\ell_1 \parallel \ell_2$?

(1) $r = s$

(2) $t = u$

Geometry Lines

(1) Given that $r = s$, it is not possible to determine whether ℓ_1 is parallel to ℓ_2 because the two angles with measures indicated by $r°$ and $s°$ are vertical angles, and thus $r = s$ is true regardless of whether ℓ_1 is parallel to ℓ_2; NOT sufficient.

(2) Given that $t = u$, it is not possible to determine whether ℓ_1 is parallel to ℓ_2 because the two angles with measures indicated by $t°$ and $u°$ are vertical angles, and thus $t = u$ is true regardless of whether ℓ_1 is parallel to ℓ_2; NOT sufficient.

Taking (1) and (2) together, it is still not possible to determine whether ℓ_1 is parallel to ℓ_2 because both pairs of angles that are involved are vertical angles, and thus both (1) and (2) hold regardless of whether ℓ_1 is parallel to ℓ_2.

**The correct answer is E;
both statements together are still not sufficient.**

DS51531.02

326. What is the volume of the right circular cylinder X?

(1) The height of X is 20.

(2) The base of X has area 25π.

Geometry Volume

Determine the volume of right circular cylinder X.

(1) Given that the height of X is 20, if the radius of X were 20, then the volume of X would be $8,000\pi$. On the other hand, if the radius of X were 1, then the volume of X would be 20π; NOT sufficient.

(2)   Given that the area of the base is 25π, if the height of X were 1, then the volume of X would be 25π. On the other hand, if the height were 20, then the volume of X would be 500π; NOT sufficient.

Taking (1) and (2) together, the volume of X is $(25\pi)(20) = 500\pi$.

**The correct answer is C;
both statements together are sufficient.**

DS76502.01

327.   If r and s are positive integers, is $r + s$ even?

(1) r is even.

(2) s is even.

Arithmetic Properties of Integers

An integer m is even if and only if m is divisible by 2, or equivalently, if and only if $m = 2M$ for some integer M. Is $r + s$ even?

(1)   Given that r is even, $r + s$ could be even (choose $r = 2$ and $s = 2$) and $r + s$ could be odd (choose $r = 2$ and $s = 1$); NOT sufficient.

(2)   Given that s is even, $r + s$ could be even (choose $r = 2$ and $s = 2$) and $r + s$ could be odd (choose $r = 1$ and $s = 2$); NOT sufficient.

Taking (1) and (2) together, let R and S be integers such that $r = 2R$ and $s = 2S$. Then $r + s = 2R + 2S = 2(R + S)$, where $R + S$ is an integer. Therefore, $r + s$ is even.

**The correct answer is C;
both statements together are sufficient.**

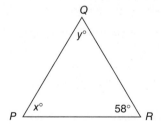

DS27502.01

328.   In the figure above, $\triangle PQR$ has angle measures as shown. Is $x < y$?

(1) $PQ = QR$

(2) $PR > QR$

Geometry Triangles

(1)   Given that $PQ = QR$, it follows that the angle at vertex R has the same measure as the angle at vertex P, or $58 = x$. Therefore, using $x + y + 58 = 180$ gives $58 + y + 58 = 180$, or $y = 64$. Since the values of both x and y are now known, it can be determined whether $x < y$; SUFFICIENT.

(2)   Given that $PR > QR$, it follows that the measure of the angle at vertex Q is greater than the measure of the angle at vertex P, or $y > x$; SUFFICIENT.

**The correct answer is D;
each statement alone is sufficient.**

DS10602.01

329.   If S is a set of odd integers and 3 and -1 are in S, is -15 in S ?

(1)   5 is in S.

(2)   Whenever two numbers are in S, their product is in S.

Arithmetic Operations with Integers

(1)   Given that S is a set of odd integers that contains $3, -1$, and 5, it is not possible to determine whether -15 is also in S.

If S is the set of all odd integers, then -15 is in S.

If $S = \{-1, 3, 5\}$, then -15 is not in S; NOT sufficient.

(2)   Given that S is a set of odd integers that contains 3 and -1 and for any pair of integers in S, their product is also in S, it is not possible to determine whether -15 is in S.

If S is the set of all odd integers, then -15 is in S. Note that the set of all odd integers contains 3 and -1 and the product of any two odd integers is an odd integer.

If $S = \{\ldots, -27, -9, -3, -1, 1, 3, 9, 27, \ldots\}$, then -15 is not in S because S does not contain an integer divisible by 5. Note that $(3)(-1) = -3, (3)(-3) = -9, (3)(-9) = -27$, etc.; $(-1)(-1) = 1, (3)(1) = 3, (3)(3) = 9, (3)(9) = 27$, etc., so the product of any two numbers in S is also in S; NOT sufficient.

Taking (1) and (2) together along with the information given in the question itself, it follows that −15 is in S. From the information given in the question, S contains 3 and −1. From (1), S also contains 5. From (2), S contains (3)(5) = 15 and (−1)(15) = −15.

The correct answer is C; both statements together are sufficient.

DS01602.01

330. Is the integer x a 3-digit integer?

    (1)   x is the square of an integer.

    (2) $90 < x < 150$

Arithmetic Properties of Integers

    (1)   Given that x is the square of an integer, both $x = 16$ (not a 3-digit integer) and $x = 100$ (a 3-digit integer) are possible; NOT sufficient.

    (2)   Given that $90 < x < 150$, both $x = 95$ (not a 3-digit integer) and $x = 100$ (a 3-digit integer) are possible; NOT sufficient.

From (1) and (2) taken together, it follows that x is among the numbers …, 81, 100, 121, 144, 169, … and $90 < x < 150$. Therefore, x must be one of the three numbers 100, 121, 144, and hence x must be a 3-digit integer.

The correct answer is C; both statements together are sufficient.

DS11602.01

331. If the 1st term of a sequence is 0 and the 2nd term is 1, is the 5th term 2 ?

    (1)   Each odd-numbered term is either 0 or 2.

    (2)   The 3rd term is 2.

Arithmetic Series and Sequences

Let the sequence be 0, 1, a, b, c. Is $c = 2$?

    (1)   Given that $a = 0$ or $a = 2$, and $c = 0$ or $c = 2$, it is possible that $c = 2$ (consider the sequence 0, 1, 2, 2, 2) and it is possible that $c \neq 2$ (consider the sequence 0, 1, 2, 0, 0); NOT sufficient.

    (2)   Given that $a = 2$, the same examples given in (1) show that it is not possible to determine whether $c = 2$; NOT sufficient.

Taking (1) and (2) together, it is still not possible to determine whether $c = 2$ because the same examples were used for both (1) and (2).

The correct answer is E; both statements together are still not sufficient.

DS21602.01

332. Is the sum of four particular integers even?

    (1)   Two of the integers are odd and two are even.

    (2)   The average (arithmetic mean) of the four integers is an integer.

Arithmetic Properties of Integers

    (1)   Given that two of the integers are odd and two of the integers are even, the sum of the four integers must be the sum of an even integer (this being the sum of the two odd integers) and an even integer (this being the sum of the two even integers). Since the sum of two even integers is even, it follows that the sum of the four integers is even; SUFFICIENT.

    (2)   Given that the average of the four integers is an integer, it follows that the sum of the four integers divided by four is an integer, and hence the sum of the integers is four times an integer. Since four times an integer is even, it follows that the sum of the four integers is even; SUFFICIENT.

The correct answer is D; each statement alone is sufficient.

DS70602.01

333. If a school district paid a total of $35 per desk for x desks and a total of $30 per table for y tables, what was the total amount that the district paid for these desks and tables?

    (1)   The total amount the district paid for the y tables was $900.

    (2)   x = 90, and the total amount the district paid for the x desks was 3.5 times the total amount the district paid for the y tables.

Algebra Simultaneous Equations

Determine the value of $35x + 30y$.

    (1)   Given that $30y = 900$, it follows that $y = 30$. However, it is not possible to determine

the value of $35x + 30y = 35x + 900$ because more than one possible value of x is possible; NOT sufficient.

(2) Given that $x = 90$ and $35x = 3.5(30y)$, it follows that $(35)(90) = (3.5)(30)y$, or $y = \dfrac{35}{3.5} \times \dfrac{90}{30} = 10 \times 3 = 30$, and therefore $35x + 30y = 35(90) + 30(30)$; SUFFICIENT.

**The correct answer is B;
statement 2 alone is sufficient.**

DS90602.01

334. Three children inherited a total of *X* dollars. If the oldest child inherited $7,000 more than the youngest child, and the youngest child inherited $9,000 less than the middle child, what is the value of *X* ?

(1) The middle child inherited $27,000.

(2) The youngest child and the middle child together inherited a total of $45,000.

Algebra Simultaneous Equations

Let A, B, and C be the amounts inherited, respectively and in dollars, of the oldest, middle, and youngest child. It is given that $A = 7{,}000 + C$ and $C = B - 9{,}000$. Then $A = 7{,}000 + (B - 9{,}000) = B - 2{,}000$. Determine the value of $A + B + C$, or equivalently, determine the value of $(B - 2{,}000) + B + (B - 9{,}000) = 3B - 11{,}000$.

(1) Given that $B = 27{,}000$, it follows that $3B - 11{,}000 = 70{,}000$; SUFFICIENT.

(2) Given that $B + C = 45{,}000$, then using $C = B - 9{,}000$ it follows that $B + (B - 9{,}000) = 45{,}000$, which can be solved to obtain $B = 27{,}000$. Therefore, $3B - 11{,}000 = 70{,}000$; SUFFICIENT.

**The correct answer is D;
each statement alone is sufficient.**

DS41602.01

335. If $xyz \neq 0$, what is the value of $\dfrac{x^4 z^2}{z^2 y^2}$?

(1) $y^2 = x^4$

(2) $x = 2$ and $y = 4$

Algebra Simplifying Algebraic Expressions

What is the value of $\dfrac{x^4 z^2}{z^2 y^2}$? Equivalently (since $z \neq 0$), what is the value of $\dfrac{x^4}{y^2}$?

(1) Given that $y^2 = x^4$, then dividing both sides of this equation by y^2 gives $1 = \dfrac{x^4}{y^2}$; SUFFICIENT.

(2) Given that $x = 2$ and $y = 4$, then $\dfrac{x^4}{y^2} = \dfrac{2^4}{4^2} = \dfrac{16}{16} = 1$; SUFFICIENT.

**The correct answer is D;
each statement alone is sufficient.**

DS81602.01

336. If *a* and *b* are integers, and $b > 0$, does $\dfrac{a-1}{b+1} = \dfrac{a}{b}$?

(1) $a = b - 4$

(2) $a = -b$

Algebra Ratios

(1) Given that $a = b - 4$, then $\dfrac{a-1}{b+1} = \dfrac{a}{b}$ can be true (use $a = -2$ and $b = 2$) and $\dfrac{a-1}{b+1} = \dfrac{a}{b}$ can be false (use $a = -3$ and $b = 1$); NOT sufficient.

(2) Given that $a = -b$, then

$\dfrac{a-1}{b+1} = \dfrac{-b-1}{b+1} = \dfrac{-(b+1)}{b+1} = -1$ and

$\dfrac{a}{b} = \dfrac{-b}{b} = -1$; SUFFICIENT.

**The correct answer is B;
statement 2 alone is sufficient.**

DS12602.01

337. In a sequence of numbers in which each term is 2 more than the preceding term, what is the fourth term?

(1) The last term is 90.

(2) The first term is 2.

Arithmetic Series and Sequences

(1) Given that the last term is 90, then the sequence could be 2, 4, 6, 8, …, 90 with the fourth term equal to 8, and the sequence could be 84, 86, 88, 90 with the fourth term equal to 90; NOT sufficient.

(2) Given that the first term is 2, then the second term must be 2 + 2 = 4, the third term must be 4 + 2 = 6, and the fourth term must be 6 + 2 = 8; SUFFICIENT.

**The correct answer is B;
statement 2 alone is sufficient.**

DS32602.01

338. Is the integer *p* divisible by 5 ?

(1) *p* is divisible by 10.

(2) *p* is not divisible by 15.

Arithmetic Properties of Integers

(1) If *p* is divisible by 10, then *p* = 10*q* for some integer *q*. So, *p* = (5)(2*q*) and *p* is divisible by 5; SUFFICIENT.

(2) If *p* is not divisible by 15, then *p* could be 20, for example, and 20 is divisible by 5. But, *p* could also be 21, for example, and 21 is not divisible by 5; NOT sufficient.

**The correct answer is A;
statement 1 alone is sufficient.**

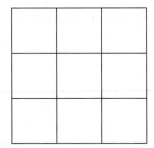

DS52602.01

339. The 9 squares above are to be filled with *x*'s and *o*'s, with only one symbol in each square. How many of the squares will contain an *x* ?

(1) More than $\frac{1}{2}$ of the number of squares will contain an *o*.

(2) Each of the 4 corner squares will contain an *x*.

Arithmetic Properties of Numbers

(1) If more than $\frac{1}{2}$ of the squares will contain an *o*, then 5, 6, 7, 8, or 9 of the squares will contain an *o*. The rest will contain *x*'s, and so 4, 3, 2, 1, or 0 of the squares will contain an *x*; NOT sufficient.

(2) Since each of the 4 corner squares will contain an *x*, the number of squares that will contain an *x* could be 4, 5, 6, 7, 8, or 9; NOT sufficient.

Taking (1) and (2) together, from (1), the number of squares containing *x*'s will be 4, 3, 2, 1, or 0, while from (2), the number of squares containing *x*'s will be 4, 5, 6, 7, 8, or 9. Therefore, the number of squares containing *x*'s will be 4.

**The correct answer is C;
both statements together are sufficient.**

DS72602.01

340. Is the sum of two integers divisible by 10 ?

(1) One of the integers is even.

(2) One of the integers is a multiple of 5.

Arithmetic Properties of Integers

(1) If one of the integers is 10, which is even, and the other is 2, then 10 + 2 = 12, which is not divisible by 10. However, if the other integer is 20, then 10 + 20 = 30, which is divisible by 10; NOT sufficient.

(2) Note that the examples in (1) also satisfy (2); NOT sufficient.

Since the examples used to show that (1) is not sufficient also show that (2) is not sufficient, it follows that (1) and (2) taken together are not sufficient.

**The correct answer is E;
both statements together are still not sufficient.**

DS22602.01

341. Is *x* an integer?

(1) $x^3 = 8$

(2) $x = \sqrt{4}$

Algebra Exponents and Radicals

(1) If $x^3 = 8$, then $x = \sqrt[3]{8} = 2$, which is an integer; SUFFICIENT.

(2) If $x = \sqrt{4}$, then $x = 2$, which is an integer; SUFFICIENT.

**The correct answer is D;
each statement alone is sufficient.**

DS42602.01
342. If a building has 6,000 square meters of floor space, how many offices are in the building?

    (1) Exactly $\frac{1}{4}$ of the floor space is not used for offices.

    (2) There are exactly 20 executive offices and each of these occupies 3 times as much floor space as the average for all of the remaining offices.

Algebra Simultaneous Equations

(1) This says that exactly $\frac{3}{4}(6,000) =$ 4,500 square meters of floor space are used for offices since exactly $\frac{1}{4}$ (6,000) = 1,500 square meters of the floor space are not used for offices. No information is given about the configuration of the 4,500 square meters used for offices. Therefore, the number of offices in the building cannot be determined; NOT sufficient.

(2) While this says there are exactly 20 executive offices and each occupies 3 times the average space of the other offices, no information is given about how much of the 6,000 square meters of floor space in the building is used for offices nor how the offices are configured. Therefore, the number of offices in the building cannot be determined; NOT sufficient.

Taking (1) and (2) together, 4,500 square meters of space are used for offices which include 20 executive offices, and each executive office occupies 3 times as much floor space as the average of all of the remaining offices. However, no information is given about the actual size of an executive office or about the actual average size of the remaining offices. Therefore, the number of offices in the building cannot be determined. The examples in the table verify this:

Non-executive		Executive			
Number	Size (m²)	Number	Size (m²)	Total number of offices	Total space used for offices
30	50	20	150	30 + 20 = 50	30(50) + 20(150) = 4,500
15	60	20	180	15 + 20 = 35	15(60) + 20(180) = 4,500

The correct answer is E; both statements together are still not sufficient.

DS43602.01
343. If p, r, and s are consecutive integers in ascending order and x is the average (arithmetic mean) of the three integers, what is the value of x?

    (1) Twice x is equal to the sum of p, r, and s.
    (2) The sum of p, r, and s is zero.

Algebra Statistics

(1) It is given that twice x is equal to the sum of p, r, and s, or $2x = p + r + s$. Because x is the average of p, r, and s, it follows that $3x = p + r + s$ and so $2x = 3x$. Therefore, $x = 0$; SUFFICIENT

(2) It is given that $p + r + s = 0$. Since $x = \frac{p+r+s}{3}$, it follows that $x = \frac{0}{3} = 0$; SUFFICIENT.

The correct answer is D; each statement alone is sufficient.

DS53602.01
344. If m and n are integers, what is the value of $m + n$?

    (1) $(x + m)(x + n) = x^2 + 5x + mn$ and $x \neq 0$.
    (2) $mn = 4$

Algebra Simplifying Algebraic Expressions

(1) Since it is given that $(x + m)(x + n) = x^2 + 5x + mn$ and it is also true that $(x + m)(x + n) = x^2 + (m + n)x + mn$, it follows that $m + n = 5$; SUFFICIENT.

(2) Given that $mn = 4$, it is possible that $m = 1$ and $n = 4$, which means that $m + n = 5$. But it is also possible that $m = 2$ and $n = 2$, which means that $m + n = 4$; NOT sufficient.

The correct answer is A; statement 1 alone is sufficient.

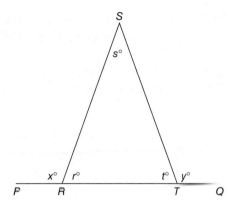

DS63602.01

345. In the figure above, *RST* is a triangle with angle measures as shown and *PRTQ* is a line segment. What is the value of $x + y$?

(1) $s = 40$

(2) $r = 70$

Geometry Triangles

(1) Given that $s = 40$, then $180 = 40 + r + t$ and $140 = r + t$. Also, $x + r = 180$ and $t + y = 180$, so $(x + y) + (r + t) = 360$, which means that $(x + y) + 140 = 360$. Therefore, $(x + y) = 360 - 140 = 220$; SUFFICIENT.

(2) If $r = 70$, then $x = 180 - 70 = 110$. Since $r + s + t = 180$, then $s + t = 180 - r = 180 - 70 = 110$, from which it follows that $x = s + t$. By similar reasoning, $y = r + s = 70 + s$. Therefore, the value of $x + y$ depends on the values of s and t, which can be any two positive integers whose sum is 110. For example, if $s = 70$ and $t = 40$, then $x + y = 110 + 140 = 250$, but if $s = 50$ and $t = 60$, then $x + y = 110 + 120 = 230$; NOT sufficient.

The correct answer is A; statement 1 alone is sufficient.

DS04602.01

346. If *R*, *S*, and *T* are points on a line, and if *R* is 5 meters from *T* and 2 meters from *S*, how far is *S* from *T*?

(1) *R* is between *S* and *T*.

(2) *S* is to the left of *R*, and *T* is to the right of *R*.

Geometry Lines and Segments

(1) It is given that *R* is between *S* and *T*, so the placement of *R*, *S*, and *T* is shown by either

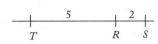

or

In either case, the distance from *S* to *T* is 7 meters; SUFFICIENT.

(2) It is given that *S* is to the left of *R*, and *T* is to the right of *R*, so the placement of *R*, *S*, and *T* is shown by

The distance from *S* to *T* is 7 meters; SUFFICIENT.

The correct answer is D; each statement alone is sufficient.

DS65602.01

347. Is *n* equal to zero?

(1) The product of *n* and some nonzero number is 0.

(2) The sum of *n* and 0 is 0.

Arithmetic Properties of Numbers

(1) If *x* represents a nonzero number, then from (1), $nx = 0$. If the product of two numbers is 0, one or both of the numbers must be 0. Since *x* is nonzero, it follows that $n = 0$; SUFFICIENT.

(2) Given $n + 0 = 0$, then by a property of the integer 0, namely that $n + 0 = n$ for any number *n*, it follows that $n = 0$; SUFFICIENT.

The correct answer is D; each statement alone is sufficient.

DS45602.01

348. On a map, $\frac{1}{2}$ inch represents 100 miles. According to this map, how many miles is City X from City Y?

(1) City X is 3 inches from City Y on the map.

(2) Cities X and Y are each 300 miles from City Z.

Algebra Measurement Conversion

(1) Letting d represent the distance, in miles, from City X to City Y, given that City X is 3 inches from City Y on a map where $\frac{1}{2}$ inch represents 100 miles, the following proportion can be solved for d.

$$\frac{\frac{1}{2}}{3} = \frac{100}{d} ; \text{SUFFICIENT.}$$

(2) Given that each of Cities X and Y is 300 miles from City Z, if points X, Y, and Z representing these cities on the map are on a straight line, then the distance between Cities X and Y is $300 + 300 = 600$ miles. However, if points X, Y, and Z are the vertices of a triangle on the map, the distance is less than 600 miles because the length of the third side of a triangle is less than the sum of the lengths of the other two sides; NOT sufficient.

The correct answer is A; statement 1 alone is sufficient.

Questions 349 to 426 - Difficulty: **Medium**

DS07502.01

349. What is the remainder when the positive integer n is divided by 5 ?

(1) When n is divided by 3, the quotient is 4 and the remainder is 1.

(2) When n is divided by 4, the remainder is 1.

Arithmetic Properties of Integers

(1) Given that the quotient is 4 and the remainder is 1 when n is divided by 3, it follows that $n = (3)(4) + 1 = 13$. Since 13 is 3 more than a multiple of 5, the remainder when n is divided by 5 is 3; SUFFICIENT.

(2) Given that the remainder is 1 when n is divided by 4, $n = 5$ is possible (has remainder 0 when divided by 5) and $n = 9$ is possible (has remainder 4 when divided by 5); NOT sufficient.

The correct answer is A; statement 1 alone is sufficient.

DS37502.01

350. If r and s are positive numbers and θ is one of the operations, $+$, $-$, $\times$, or $\div$, which operation is θ ?

(1) If $r = s$, then $r \; \theta \; s = 0$.

(2) If $r \neq s$, then $r \; \theta \; s \neq s \; \theta \; r$.

Arithmetic Arithmetic Operations

(1) Given that 0 is always the result when the operation is applied to the same two positive numbers, then the operation can be subtraction (because $r - r = 0$ is true for all positive numbers r), but the operation cannot be addition (because $1 + 1 \neq 0$), multiplication (because $1 \times 1 \neq 0$), or division (because $1 \div 1 \neq 0$). Therefore, the operation must be subtraction; SUFFICIENT.

(2) Given that if $r \neq s$, then $r \; \theta \; s \neq s \; \theta \; r$, or equivalently (by forming the logical contrapositive), if $r \; \theta \; s = s \; \theta \; r$, then $r = s$, it is not possible to determine the operation θ. Subtraction satisfies this condition, because from $r - s = s - r$ it follows that $2r = 2s$ and $r = s$. Division satisfies this condition, because from $r \div s = s \div r$, or $\frac{r}{s} = \frac{s}{r}$, it follows that $r^2 = s^2$ and $r = s$ (the possibility $r = -s$ is excluded because r and s are nonzero positive numbers). Therefore, both subtraction and division satisfy this condition; NOT sufficient.

The correct answer is A; statement 1 alone is sufficient.

DS57502.01

351. In any sequence of n nonzero numbers, a pair of consecutive terms with opposite signs represents a sign change. For example, the sequence -2, 3, -4, 5 has three sign changes. Does the sequence of nonzero numbers s_1, s_2, s_3, ..., s_n have an even number of sign changes?

(1) $s_k = (-1)^k$ for all positive integers k from 1 to n.

(2) n is odd.

Arithmetic Series and Sequences

(1) Given that $s_k = (-1)^k$ for all positive integers k from 1 to n, the table below shows for the first 5 values of n the corresponding sequence and number of sign changes.

_n = 3:_

k	$(-1)^k$	Sequence	Number of sign changes
1	−1		
2	1	−1, 1, −1	2
3	−1		

_n = 4:_

k	$(-1)^k$	Sequence	Number of sign changes
1	−1		
2	1		
3	−1	−1, 1, −1, 1	3
4	1		

The examples above show that if $n = 3$, then the sequence has an even number of sign changes and if $n = 4$ the sequence has an odd number of sign changes; NOT sufficient.

(2) Taking $n = 3$, which is odd, the sequence could be either of the sequences below:

Example I: −1, 1, −1

Example II: 3, −5, −2

The sequence in Example I has 2 sign changes (an even number of sign changes) and the sequence in Example II has 1 sign change (an odd number of sign changes); NOT sufficient.

Taking (1) and (2) together, the table below shows for the first 3 odd values of n the corresponding sequence and number of sign changes.

n	sequence	number of sign changes	even or odd?
1	−1	0	even
3	−1, 1, −1	2	even
5	−1, 1, −1, 1, −1	4	even

Since each successive odd value of n puts the values 1 and −1 after the last term of the preceding sequence, which is −1, each successive odd value of n increases the number of sign changes by 2.

Therefore, when n is odd, the sequence s_1, s_2, s_3, ... , s_n has an even number of sign changes.

The correct answer is C; both statements together are sufficient.

DS86502.01

352. Jack picked 76 apples. Of these, he sold 4y apples to Juanita and 3t apples to Sylvia. If he kept the remaining apples, how many apples did he keep? (_t_ and _y_ are positive integers.)

(1) $y \geq 15$ and $t = 2$

(2) $y = 17$

Algebra Simultaneous Equations

Determine the value of the nonnegative integer $76 - 4y - 3t$.

(1) Given that $y \geq 15$ and $t = 2$, it follows that $76 - 4y - 3t = 76 - 4y - 6 = 70 - 4y$ could have the value $70 - 4(15) = 10$, $70 - 4(16) = 6$, or $70 - 4(17) = 2$; NOT sufficient.

(2) Given that $y = 17$, it follows that $76 - 4y - 3t = 76 - 68 - 3t = 8 - 3t$ could have the value $8 - 3(1) = 5$ or $8 - 3(2) = 2$; NOT sufficient.

Taking (1) and (2) together, it follows that $76 - 4y - 3t = 76 - 4(17) - 3(2) = 2$.

The correct answer is C; both statements together are sufficient.

DS47502.01

353. What number is 6 more than $x + y$?

(1) _y_ is 3 less than _x_.

(2) _y_ is twice _x_.

Algebra Simultaneous Equations

Determine the value of $x + y + 6$.

(1) Given that $y = x - 3$, $x + y + 6$ could be 15 (use $x = 6$ and $y = 3$) and $x + y + 6$ could be 21 (use $x = 9$ and $y = 6$); NOT sufficient.

(2) Given that $y = 2x$, $x + y + 6$ could be 9 (use $x = 1$ and $y = 2$) and $x + y + 6$ could be 12 (use $x = 2$ and $y = 4$); NOT sufficient.

Taking (1) and (2) together, then $y = x - 3$ and $y = 2x$ both hold. Therefore, $x - 3 = 2x$, or $x = -3$, and hence $y = 2(-3) = -6$. It follows that $x + y + 6 = (-3) + (-6) + 6 = -3$.

**The correct answer is C;
both statements together are sufficient.**

DS08502.01

354. The total price of 5 pounds of regular coffee and 3 pounds of decaffeinated coffee was $21.50. What was the price of the 5 pounds of regular coffee?

(1) If the price of the 5 pounds of regular coffee had been reduced 10 percent and the price of the 3 pounds of decaffeinated coffee had been reduced 20 percent, the total price would have been $18.45.

(2) The price of the 5 pounds of regular coffee was $3.50 more than the price of the 3 pounds of decaffeinated coffee.

Algebra Simultaneous Equations

Let x be the price of 5 pounds of regular coffee and let y be the price of 3 pounds of decaffeinated coffee. Then $x + y = 21.5$, or $y = 21.5 - x$. Determine the value of x.

(1) Given that $0.9x + 0.8y = 18.45$, the value of x can be determined because substituting $y = 21.5 - x$ into $0.9x + 0.8y = 18.45$ gives a single equation with unknown x, and that equation can be solved for a unique value of x; SUFFICIENT.

Alternatively (see the Tip below), $y = 21.5 - x$ and $0.9x + 0.8y = 18.45$ are equations of nonparallel lines in the coordinate plane and thus have a single point of intersection. One way to ensure that the lines are not parallel is to solve each equation for y in terms of x and note that the coefficients of x are different. In this case, $y = 21.5 - x$ gives a coefficient of x equal to -1 and $0.9x + 0.8y = 18.45$ gives a coefficient of x equal to $-\dfrac{0.9}{0.8}$.

(2) Given that $x = 3.5 + y$, the value of x can be determined because substituting $y = 21.5 - x$ into $x = 3.5 + y$ gives a single equation with unknown x, and that equation can be solved for a unique value of x; SUFFICIENT.

Alternatively (see the Tip below), $y = 21.5 - x$ and $x = 3.5 + y$ are equations of nonparallel lines in the coordinate plane and thus have a single point of intersection. One way to ensure that the lines are not

parallel is to solve each equation for y in terms of x and note that the coefficients of x are different. In this case, $y = 21.5 - x$ gives a coefficient of x equal to -1 and $x = 3.5 + y$ gives a coefficient of x equal to 1.

Tip: Data Sufficiency problems involving simultaneous equations usually do not have to be solved. Instead, it is typically enough to determine whether no solution exists, exactly one solution exists, or more than one solution exists, and this can often be accomplished by graphical methods.

**The correct answer is D;
each statement alone is sufficient.**

DS38502.01

355. If a and b are integers, is $a^5 < 4^b$?

(1) $a^3 = -27$

(2) $b^2 = 16$

Arithmetic Exponents

(1) Given that $a^3 = -27$, it follows that $a = -3$, and hence $a < 0$. Therefore, $a^5 < 0$ (the 5th power of a negative number is negative), from which it follows that $a^5 < 4^b$ because a^5 is less than zero and 4 raised to an integer power is greater than zero; SUFFICIENT.

(2) Given that $b^2 = 16$, it follows that $b = 4$ or $b = -4$, but there is no restriction on the value of a. If $a = 1$ and $b = 4$, then $a^5 = 1$ is less than $4^b = 4^4$. However, if $a = 5$ and $b = 4$, then $a^5 = 5^5$ is greater than $4^b = 4^4$; NOT sufficient.

**The correct answer is A;
statement 1 alone is sufficient.**

DS28502.01

356. If each side of parallelogram P has length 1, what is the area of P ?

(1) One angle of P measures 45 degrees.

(2) The altitude of P is $\dfrac{\sqrt{2}}{2}$.

Geometry Quadrilaterals; Area

The figure below shows parallelogram P, its altitude h, and an interior angle with degree measure θ. The area of a parallelogram is its base times its altitude. Therefore, the area of parallelogram P is $(h)(1) = h$. Determine the value of h.

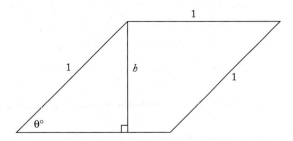

(1) Given that $\theta = 45$, it follows that the right triangle in the figure with hypotenuse 1 and side length h is a 45°–45°–90° triangle. Therefore, the length of each of its legs is $\dfrac{\sqrt{2}}{2}$ times the length of its hypotenuse, and hence $h = \dfrac{\sqrt{2}}{2}$; SUFFICIENT.

(2) Given that $h = \dfrac{\sqrt{2}}{2}$, it follows from the comments above that the area of P is $h = \dfrac{\sqrt{2}}{2}$; SUFFICIENT.

The correct answer is D; each statement alone is sufficient.

DS49502.01

357. If x is an integer greater than 0, what is the remainder when x is divided by 4 ?

(1) The remainder is 3 when $x + 1$ is divided by 4.

(2) The remainder is 0 when $2x$ is divided by 4.

Arithmetic Properties of Integers

(1) Given that the remainder is 3 when $x + 1$ is divided by 4, or equivalently, that $x + 1$ is 3 more than a multiple of 4, then it follows that x is 2 more than a multiple of 4, or equivalently, that the remainder is 2 when $x + 1$ is divided by 4; SUFFICIENT.

(2) Given that the remainder is 0 when $2x$ is divided by 4, it is possible that the remainder when x is divided by 4 is 0 (choose $x = 4$; then $2x = 8$ has remainder 0 and $x = 4$ has remainder 0) and it is possible that the remainder when x is divided by 4 is 2 (choose $x = 6$; then $2x = 12$ has remainder 0 and $x = 6$ has remainder 2); NOT sufficient.

The correct answer is A; statement 1 alone is sufficient.

DS00602.01

358. A certain painting job requires a mixture of yellow, green, and white paint. If 12 quarts of paint are needed for the job, how many quarts of green paint are needed?

(1) The ratio of the amount of green paint to the amount of yellow and white paint combined needs to be 1 to 3.

(2) The ratio of the amount of yellow paint to the amount of green paint needs to be 3 to 2.

Algebra Ratios; Simultaneous Equations

This problem involves 3 quantities:

The number of quarts of yellow paint, represented by Y; the number of quarts of green paint, represented by G; and the number of quarts of white paint, represented by W.

It is given that $Y + G + W = 12$.

The task is to uniquely determine the value of G, which is possible only if there is enough information to eliminate Y and W from $Y + G + W = 12$, so that only G is left.

(1) Using the variables introduced above, this gives $\dfrac{G}{Y + W} = \dfrac{1}{3}$ or $3G = Y + W$. Substituting $3G$ for $Y + W$ in $Y + G + W = 12$ gives $4G = 12$, which yields a unique value of G; SUFFICIENT.

(2) Using the variables introduced above, this gives $\dfrac{Y}{G} = \dfrac{3}{2}$ or $Y = \dfrac{3}{2}G$. Then, by substitution, $\dfrac{3}{2}G + G + W = 12$. Because the value of W can vary, the value of G cannot be uniquely determined; NOT sufficient.

The correct answer is A; statement 1 alone is sufficient.

DS69502.01

359. Is the average (arithmetic mean) of the numbers x, y, and z greater than z ?

(1) $z - x < y - z$

(2) $x < z < y$

Algebra Inequalities

Determine whether $\dfrac{x+y+z}{3} > z$, or
$x + y + z > 3z$. Equivalently, determine whether
$x + y > 2z$.

(1) Given that $z - x < y - z$, it follows by
     adding $x + z$ to each side that $2z < x + y$;
     SUFFICIENT.

(2) Given that $x < z < y$, consider the following
     table:

x	z	y	$x + y$	$2z$
1	2	4	5	4
1	3	4	5	6

The table shows that if $x < z < y$, then it is
possible that the inequality $x + y > 2z$ is true and
it is possible that the inequality $x + y > 2z$ is false;
NOT sufficient.

The correct answer is A;
statement 1 alone is sufficient.

DS30602.01

360. Is the point Q on the circle with center C ?

(1) R is a point on the circle and the distance from Q
     to R is equal to the distance from Q to C.

(2) S is a point on the circle and the distance from Q
     to S is equal to the distance from S to C.

Geometry Circles

Given a circle with center C, determine whether
the point Q is on this circle. In what follows, the
distance from one point X to another point Y will
be denoted XY. For example, the distance from Q
to R will be denoted QR.

(1) If R is on circle C (that is, the circle with
     center C), then $\overline{CR}$ is the radius of the
     circle. The perpendicular bisector of $\overline{CR}$
     consists of all points that are equidistant
     from C and R. Since $QR = QC$, it follows
     that Q is a point on the perpendicular
     bisector of $\overline{CR}$. The figure below shows
     several possible locations for Q, some of
     which are on circle C and some of which are
     not on circle C; NOT sufficient.

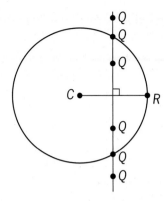

(2) Given that S is on circle C, it follows that SC is
     the radius of circle C. Since it is also given that
     $QS = SC$, this means that Q is on a circle with
     center S (hereafter called circle S) and circle
     S has the same radius as circle C. The figure
     below shows both circle C and circle S as well
     as several possible locations for Q, at least
     one of which is on circle C and at least one of
     which is not on circle C; NOT sufficient.

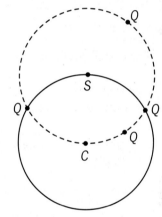

Taking (1) and (2) together, consider two cases:
$R = S$ and $R \neq S$.

Case 1: $R = S$

$QR = QC$	given in (1)
$QS = QC$	substitution of S for R since $S = R$
$SC = QC$	substitution of SC for QS since $QS = SC$ is given in (2)
$RC = QC$	substitution of R for S since $R = S$

Since R and Q are equidistant from C and R is on
circle C, it follows that Q is on circle C.

Case 2: $R \neq S$

To satisfy (1), Q must be on the perpendicular
bisector of $\overline{CR}$, and to satisfy (2), Q must be on
circle S which has the same radius as circle C.

The figure below shows that Q need not be on circle C.

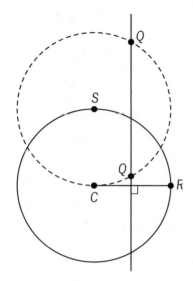

Therefore, it is possible that Q is on circle C (as in Case 1) and it is possible that Q is not on circle C (as in Case 2); NOT sufficient.

**The correct answer is E;
both statements together are still not sufficient.**

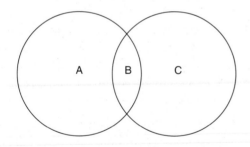

DS59502.01

361. In the figure above, if A, B, and C are the areas, respectively, of the three nonoverlapping regions formed by the intersection of two circles of equal area, what is the value of $B + C$?

(1)　　$A + 2B + C = 24$

(2)　　$A + C = 18$ and $B = 3$

Geometry Circles; Area

It is given that the area of the left circle is equal to the area of the right circle, or $A + B = B + C$. Subtracting B from each side of this equation gives $A = C$. Determine the value of $B + C$.

(1)　　Given that $A + 2B + C = 24$, it follows from $A = C$ that $C + 2B + C = 24$,

or $2B + 2C = 24$, or $B + C = 12$; SUFFICIENT.

(2)　　Given that $A + C = 18$ and $B = 3$, it follows from $A = C$ that the first equation is equivalent to $C + C = 18$, or $C = 9$. Therefore, $B = 3$ and $C = 9$, and hence $B + C = 12$; SUFFICIENT.

**The correct answer is D;
each statement alone is sufficient.**

DS61602.01

362. A company produces a certain toy in only 2 sizes, small or large, and in only 2 colors, red or green. If, for each size, there are equal numbers of red and green toys in a certain production lot, what fraction of the total number of green toys is large?

(1)　In the production lot, 400 of the small toys are green.

(2)　In the production lot, $\frac{2}{3}$ of the toys produced are small.

Algebra Ratios

Let x be the number of small toys of each color, and let y be the number of large toys of each color. The contingency table below gives a summary of the information given. Determine the value of $\dfrac{y}{x + y}$.

	small	large	total
red	x	y	$x + y$
green	x	y	$x + y$
total	$2x$	$2y$	$2x + 2y$

(1)　Given that $x = 400$, it is clearly not possible to determine the value of $\dfrac{y}{x + y} = \dfrac{y}{400 + y}$; NOT sufficient.

(2)　Given that $\dfrac{2}{3}$ of the toys are small, then because there are $(2x + 2y)$ toys altogether and $2x$ small toys, it follows that $\dfrac{2x}{2x + 2y} = \dfrac{2}{3}$. Therefore, $3(2x) = 2(2x + 2y)$, or $x = 2y$, and hence $\dfrac{y}{x + y} = \dfrac{y}{2y + y} = \dfrac{y}{3y} = \dfrac{1}{3}$; SUFFICIENT.

**The correct answer is B;
statement 2 alone is sufficient.**

DS51602.01

363. Is quadrilateral *PQRS* a parallelogram?

   (1)   Adjacent sides *PQ* and *QR* have the same length.

   (2)   Adjacent sides *RS* and *SP* have the same length.

Geometry Quadrilaterals

   (1)   Given that $PQ = QR$, it is not possible to determine whether quadrilateral *PQRS* is a parallelogram. For example, if quadrilateral *PQRS* is a square, then $PQ = QR$ and quadrilateral *PQRS* is a parallelogram. However, if quadrilateral *PQRS* is as shown in the figure below, then $PQ = QR$ and quadrilateral *PQRS* is not a parallelogram; NOT sufficient.

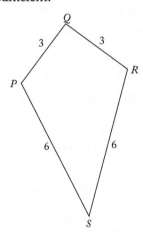

   (2)   Given that $RS = SP$, it is not possible to determine whether quadrilateral *PQRS* is a parallelogram. For example, if quadrilateral *PQRS* is a square, then $RS = SP$ and quadrilateral *PQRS* is a parallelogram. However, if quadrilateral *PQRS* is as shown in the figure above, then $RS = SP$ and quadrilateral *PQRS* is not a parallelogram; NOT sufficient.

Taking (1) and (2) together, it is not possible to determine whether quadrilateral *PQRS* is a parallelogram because the same examples used in (1) also satisfy (2).

**The correct answer is E;
both statements together are still not sufficient.**

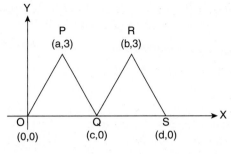

DS71602.01

364. In the figure above, the vertices of $\triangle OPQ$ and $\triangle QRS$ have coordinates as indicated. Do $\triangle OPQ$ and $\triangle QRS$ have equal areas?

   (1) $b = 2a$

   (2) $d = 2c$

Geometry Triangles; Area

The area of $\triangle OPQ$ is $\dfrac{1}{2}(c-0)(3-0) = \dfrac{3}{2}c$ and

the area of $\triangle QRS$ is $\dfrac{1}{2}(d-c)(3-0) = \dfrac{3}{2}(d-c)$.

Determine whether $\dfrac{3}{2}c = \dfrac{3}{2}(d-c)$, or

equivalently, whether $d = 2c$.

   (1)   Given that $b = 2a$, it is not possible to determine whether $d = 2c$. For example, if $a = 2$, $b = 4$, $c = 3$, and $d = 6$, then $d = 2c$. However, if $a = 2$, $b = 4$, $c = 3$, and $d = 10$, then $d \neq 2c$; NOT sufficient.

   (2)   Given that $d = 2c$, then as explained in the preliminary comments above, it follows that $\triangle OPQ$ and $\triangle QRS$ have equal areas; SUFFICIENT.

**The correct answer is B;
statement 2 alone is sufficient.**

DS92602.01

365. After the first two terms in a sequence of numbers, each term in the sequence is formed by adding all of the preceding terms. Is 12 the fifth term in the sequence?

   (1)   The sum of the first 3 terms in the sequence is 6.

   (2)   The fourth term in the sequence is 6.

Algebra Series and Sequences

If the first term is *a* and the second term is *b*, then the third term is $a + b$, the fourth term is $a + b + (a + b) = 2a + 2b$, and the fifth term is $a + b + (a + b) + (2a + 2b) = 4a + 4b$. Is $4a + 4b = 12$?

(1) It is given that the sum of the first 3 terms is 6, and since the sum of the first 3 terms is the fourth term, it follows that $2a + 2b = 6$. Therefore $a + b = 3$ and $4(a + b) = 4a + 4b = 12$; SUFFICIENT.

(2) It is given that the fourth term is 6. Since the fourth term is $2a + 2b$, the same reasoning used in (1) applies, and $4a + 4b = 12$; SUFFICIENT.

The correct answer is D; each statement alone is sufficient.

DS13602.01

366. Jones has worked at Firm *X* twice as many years as Green, and Green has worked at Firm *X* four years longer than Smith. How many years has Green worked at Firm *X* ?

(1) Jones has worked at Firm *X* 9 years longer than Smith.

(2) Green has worked at Firm *X* 5 years less than Jones.

Algebra Simultaneous Equations

Let J, G, and S be the number of years Jones, Green, and Smith, respectively, have worked at Firm X. Then $J = 2G$ and $G = 4 + S$. What is the value of G ?

(1) Given that $J = 9 + S$, then from $J = 2G$ it follows that $2G = 9 + S$. From $G = 4 + S$ it follows that $S = G - 4$, and therefore $G - 4$ can be substituted for S in the equation $2G = 9 + S$ to obtain $2G = 9 + (G - 4)$, or $G = 5$; SUFFICIENT.

(2) Given that $G = J - 5$, it follows from $J = 2G$ that $G = 2G - 5$, or $G = 5$; SUFFICIENT.

The correct answer is D; each statement alone is sufficient.

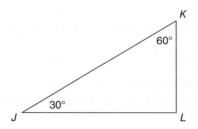

DS83602.01

367. In $\triangle JKL$ shown above, what is the length of segment *JL* ?

(1) $JK = 10$

(2) $KL = 5$

Geometry Triangles

Since $\triangle JKL$ is a 30°–60°–90° triangle, its side lengths are in the ratio $1 : \sqrt{3} : 2$. Therefore, if the length of $\overline{KL}$ is represented by x, then the length of $\overline{JL}$ is represented by $x\sqrt{3}$, and the length of $\overline{JK}$ is represented by $2x$.

(1) $JK = 10$, so $2x = 10$ and $x = 5$. Therefore, from above, $JL = 5\sqrt{3}$; SUFFICIENT.

(2) $KL = 5$, so $x = 5$ and $JL = 5\sqrt{3}$; SUFFICIENT.

The correct answer is D; each statement alone is sufficient.

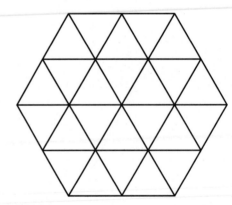

DS24602.01

368. A six-sided mosaic contains 24 triangular pieces of tile of the same size and shape, as shown in the figure above. If the sections of tile fit together perfectly, how many square centimeters of tile are in the mosaic?

(1) Each side of each triangular piece of tile is 9 centimeters long.

(2) The mosaic can be put inside a rectangular frame that is 40 centimeters wide.

Geometry Triangles; Area

(1) It is given that each side of each triangle is 9 centimeters long. The height of each triangle can be determined using the ratios for 30°–60°–90° triangles, and thus the area of each of the 24 triangular tiles can be determined. Then, multiplying by 24

will give the area of the tile in the mosaic; SUFFICIENT.

(2) It is given that the mosaic can be put inside a rectangular frame that is 40 centimeters wide. This means that the distance from A to E on the figure below is a maximum of 40 centimeters, but no information is given on the exact width of the mosaic. There is also no information on the distance from C to G; NOT sufficient.

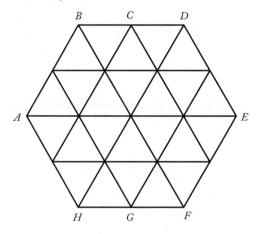

The correct answer is A; statement 1 alone is sufficient.

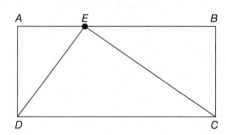

DS34602.01

369. If, in the figure above, $ABCD$ is a rectangular region, what is the value of the ratio $\dfrac{\text{area of } \triangle EDA}{\text{area of } \triangle EBC}$?

(1) $AD = 4$

(2) $AE = 2$ and $EB = 4$

Geometry Triangles

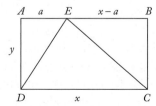

Using the figure above,

$$\frac{\text{area of } \triangle EDA}{\text{area of } \triangle EBC} = \frac{\frac{1}{2}ay}{\frac{1}{2}(x-a)y} = \frac{a}{x-a}.$$

(1) In the notation introduced in the figure above, this gives $y = 4$. However, the desired ratio depends only on the value of a and x and no information is given for these values; NOT sufficient.

(2) In the notation introduced in the figure above, this gives $a = 2$ and $x - a = 4$. With these values for a and $x - a$, the value of the desired ratio can be determined; SUFFICIENT.

The correct answer is B; statement 2 alone is sufficient.

DS64602.01

370. A noncompressible ball in the shape of a sphere is to be passed through a square opening in a board. What is the perimeter of the opening?

(1) The radius of the ball is equal to 2 inches.

(2) The square opening is the smallest square opening through which the ball will fit.

Geometry Quadrilaterals; Perimeter

(1) The radius of the ball is 2 inches, so the diameter of the ball is 4 inches. The square opening must be at least 4 inches on a side, so the perimeter of the opening must be at least 16 inches. However, there is not enough information to determine the exact perimeter of the opening; NOT sufficient.

(2) Knowing that the square opening is the smallest through which the ball will fit is not enough information to determine the perimeter of the opening because there is no information on the diameter of the ball; NOT sufficient.

Given (1) and (2), the perimeter of the square opening must be at least 16 inches and as small as possible. Therefore, the perimeter of the square opening is 16 inches.

The correct answer is C; both statements together are sufficient.

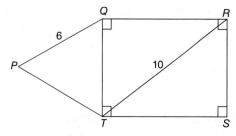

DS74602.01

371. In the figure above, what is the area of region *PQRST*?

(1) $PQ = RS$

(2) $PT = QT$

Geometry Triangles; Area

From the figure, region *PQRST* is composed of $\triangle PQT$ and quadrilateral *QRST*, which is a rectangle because each of its angles is a right angle. The area of region *PQRST* is the sum of the areas of $\triangle PQT$ and rectangle *QRST*.

(1)   Given $PQ = RS$, it follows from $PQ = 6$ and $RS = QT$ that $QT = 6$. The area of rectangle *QRST* can be determined because both its length and width can be determined. Note that the length of rectangle *QRST* is $\sqrt{10^2 - 6^2} = 8$ by the Pythagorean theorem, or by observing that 10 and 6 are double the hypotenuse length and shortest leg length of a 3-4-5 right triangle. Therefore, determining whether more than one value is possible for the area of region *PQRST* is equivalent to determining whether more than one value is possible for the area of $\triangle PQT$. The figure below shows the side lengths that are known and arc *AB*, which is a portion of the circle with center *Q* and radius 6.

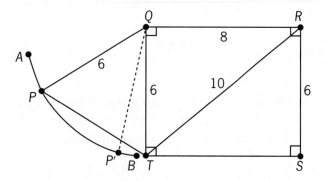

Note that any of the points on *AB*, for example point *P′*, is a possible location for point *P*. Since the area of $\triangle PQT$ is small when *P* is very close to *T*, it follows that the area of $\triangle PQT$ cannot be determined, and hence the area of region *PQRST* cannot be determined; NOT sufficient.

Alternatively, there are two cases in which the area of $\triangle PQT$ can be explicitly calculated. If $PT = 6$, then $\triangle PQT$ is equilateral and its area is $9\sqrt{3}$. If $PT = 8$, then $\triangle PQT$ is isosceles and its area is $8\sqrt{5}$.

(2)   Given $PT = QT$, it follows that $\triangle PQT$ is isosceles with side $PQ = 6$.

Example I: If $PT = QT = 6$, then $\triangle PQT$ is equilateral with sides of length 6 and the length of rectangle *QRST* is $\sqrt{10^2 - 6^2} = 8$ by the Pythagorean theorem. Thus, the area of region *PQRST* has a certain value that could be calculated, but for the purposes here the value will not be needed.

Example II: If $PT = QT = 8$, then $QR = \sqrt{10^2 - 6^2} = 6$ by the Pythagorean theorem. The figure below shows the side lengths that are known. The area of region *PQRST* is greater than in Example I, because in both examples the area of the rectangle is the same and the area of the 6-8-8 isosceles triangle is greater than the area of the 6-6-6 equilateral triangle; NOT sufficient.

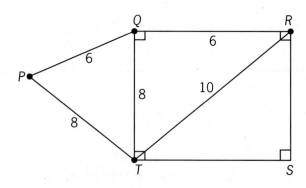

Taking (1) and (2) together, from (1) rectangle *QRST* which has length 8 and width 6, and thus its area is 48, and from (1) and (2)

ΔPQT is equilateral with sides of length 6, and thus its area can be determined. Therefore, the area of region $PQRST$ can be determined. If you wish to further review geometry, note that the areas of the triangle in Examples I and II are, respectively, $9\sqrt{3}$ and $3\sqrt{55}$.

**The correct answer is C;
both statements together are sufficient.**

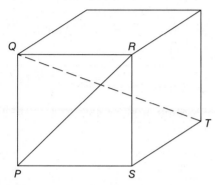

DS84602.01

372. The figure above represents a box that has the shape of a cube. What is the volume of the box?

(1) $PR = 10$ cm

(2) $QT = 5\sqrt{6}$ cm

Geometry Volume

Letting s represent the side length of the cube, if the value of s can be determined, then the volume of the cube, s^3, can be determined.

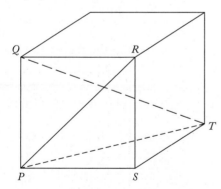

(1) It is given that $PR = 10$. Applying the Pythagorean theorem to ΔPSR, it follows that $10^2 = 2s^2$, from which the value of s can be determined; SUFFICIENT.

(2) It is given that $QT = 5\sqrt{6}$. Applying the Pythagorean theorem to ΔPST, it follows that $PT^2 = 2s^2$. Then applying the Pythagorean theorem to ΔQPT,

it follows that $QT^2 = QP^2 + PT^2$ or $(5\sqrt{6})^2 = s^2 + 2s^2 = 3s^2$, from which the value of s can be determined; SUFFICIENT.

**The correct answer is D;
each statement alone is sufficient.**

DS94602.01

373. If x and y are the lengths of the legs of a right triangle, what is the value of xy?

(1) The hypotenuse of the triangle is $10\sqrt{2}$.

(2) The area of the triangular region is 50.

Geometry Triangles; Area; Pythagorean Theorem

(1) Given that the hypotenuse of the triangle is $10\sqrt{2}$, it follows that $x^2 + y^2 = (10\sqrt{2})^2 = 200$.
It is possible that $x = y = 10$ ($x^2 + y^2 = 200$), in which case $xy = 100$. However, it is also possible that $x = 5\sqrt{6}$ and $y = 5\sqrt{2}$ ($(5\sqrt{6})^2 + (5\sqrt{2})^2 = 150 + 50 = 200$), in which case $xy = 50\sqrt{3}$; NOT sufficient.

(2) Given that the area of the triangle is 50, it follows that $\frac{xy}{2} = 50$, so $xy = 100$; SUFFICIENT.

**The correct answer is B;
statement 2 alone is sufficient.**

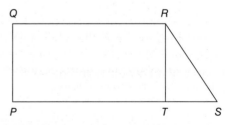

DS75602.01

374. In the figure above, $PQRT$ is a rectangle. What is the length of segment PQ?

(1) The area of region $PQRS$ is 39 and $TS = 6$.

(2) The area of region $PQRT$ is 30 and $QR = 10$.

Geometry Quadrilaterals

Since $PQRT$ is a rectangle, $\overline{QR}$ is parallel to $\overline{PT}$, and since $\overline{PT}$ is part of the same line as $\overline{PS}$, it follows that $\overline{QR}$ is parallel to $\overline{PS}$. Therefore, quadrilateral $PQRS$ is a trapezoid with area given by $\frac{1}{2}(QR+PS)(PQ)$.

(1) Given that the area of $PQRS$ is 39, it follows that $\frac{1}{2}(QR+PS)(PQ) = 39$. But, $PS = PT + TS$, where $TS = 6$, and $QR = PT$ since $PQRT$ is a rectangle. Therefore,

$$39 = \frac{1}{2}(2PT+6)(PQ) \text{ or}$$

$78 = (2PT+6)(PQ)$. This equation has two unknowns, namely PT and PQ, and many values for PT and PQ satisfy the equation; NOT sufficient.

(2) Since $PQRT$ is a rectangle with area given by $(QR)(QP)$, from (2), $30 = (10)(QP)$, so $QP = 3$; SUFFICIENT.

The correct answer is B; statement 2 alone is sufficient.

DS08420

375. On June 1, Mary paid Omar $360 for rent and utilities for the month of June. Mary moved out early, and Omar refunded the money she paid for utilities, but not for rent, for the days in June after she moved out. How many dollars did Omar refund to Mary?

(1) Mary moved out on June 24.

(2) The amount Mary paid for utilities was less than $\frac{1}{5}$ the amount Mary paid for rent.

Algebra Applied Problems; Proportions

This problem could be solved by making a table of possible amounts Mary could have paid for rent and utilities for the month of June, such that they total $360, as shown below.

Rent	Utilities
$300	$60
$310	$50
$320	$40
$330	$30
$340	$20
$350	$10

(1) Given that Mary moved out on June 24, Omar refunded the amount she paid for 6 days of utilities or $\frac{6}{30} = \frac{1}{5}$ of the amount

she paid for the whole month. As seen from the table, this amount varies, so $\frac{1}{5}$ of the total amount varies. Therefore, the amount Omar refunded to Mary cannot be uniquely determined; NOT sufficient.

Note that a third column, as shown below, could be added to the table to confirm that $\frac{1}{5}$ of the amount she paid for utilities for the whole month varies. Adding this column will aid in determining whether (1) and (2) together are sufficient. Amounts shown in **boldface** satisfy (1).

Rent	Utilities	$\frac{1}{5}$ Utilities
$300	$60	**$12**
$310	$50	**$10**
$320	$40	**$8**
$330	$30	**$6**
$340	$20	**$4**
$350	$10	**$2**

(2) Given that the amount Mary paid for utilities was less than $\frac{1}{5}$ the amount she paid for rent, the amount Omar refunded to Mary cannot be uniquely determined. To verify this, another column can be added to the table to show $\frac{1}{5}$ the amount Mary paid for rent and to show the amounts she paid for utilities that are less than $\frac{1}{5}$ the amount she paid for rent. Amounts shown *underlined* in the table below satisfy (2); NOT sufficient.

Rent	Utilities	$\frac{1}{5}$ Utilities	$\frac{1}{5}$ Rent
$300	$60	**$12**	$60
$310	$50	**$10**	$62
$320	$40	**$8**	$64
$330	$30	**$6**	$66
$340	$20	**$4**	$68
$350	$10	**$2**	$70

Taking (1) and (2) together, observe that there are several amounts in boldface in the third column that satisfy (1) and corresponding amounts underlined in the second column that satisfy (2). Therefore, the amount Omar refunded to Mary cannot be uniquely determined.

The correct answer is E; both statements together are still not sufficient.

DS04057

376. If $x = 2t$ and $y = \dfrac{t}{3}$, what is the value of $x^2 - y^2$?

    (1) $t^2 - 3 = 6$

    (2) $t^3 = -27$

Algebra Simplifying Algebraic Expressions

This problem can be solved by determining the value of $x^2 - y^2 = (2t)^2 - \left(\dfrac{t}{3}\right)^2 = 4t^2 - \dfrac{t^2}{9}$, and this can be determined if the value of t^2 or the value of t can be determined.

    (1)   This indicates that $t^2 - 3 = 6$ and so $t^2 = 6 + 3 = 9$; SUFFICIENT.

    (2)   This indicates that $t^3 = -27$ and so $t = -3$; SUFFICIENT.

The correct answer is D; each statement alone is sufficient.

DS02939

377. The 10 students in a history class recently took an examination. What was the maximum score on the examination?

    (1)   The mean of the scores was 75.

    (2)   The standard deviation of the scores was 5.

Arithmetic Statistics

    (1)   Given that the mean of the scores was 75, then all 10 scores could have been 75 and the maximum score would be 75. However, it is also possible that the scores were 74, 76, and 8 scores of 75, and the maximum score would be 76; NOT sufficient.

    (2)   Given that the standard deviation of the scores was 5, it is not possible to determine the maximum score because adding a fixed nonzero number to each of the scores will not change the standard deviation but doing this will change the maximum score; NOT sufficient.

Taking (1) and (2) together, it seems reasonable that the maximum still cannot be determined, but since the method used in (2) above changes the mean, something more explicit is needed. The standard deviation of the 10 scores is

$$\sqrt{\dfrac{\text{sum of (deviations)}^2}{10}}\,,$$ where each "deviation" is

the (unsigned) difference between the score and 75 (the mean of the scores). Thus, the standard deviation of the 10 scores will be 5 if the sum of squares of the deviations is 250. The following table shows two possibilities for the 10 scores, each with a mean of 75 and a standard deviation of 5.

Scores	Deviations from 75	Sum of (deviations)^2
70, 70, 70, 70, 70 80, 80, 80, 80, 80	5, 5, 5, 5, 5 5, 5, 5, 5, 5	$10(5^2) = 250$
70, 70, 70, 70, 75 75, 75, 80, 80, 85	5, 5, 5, 5, 0 0, 0, 5, 5, 10	$6(5^2) + 10^2 = 250$

Since the maximum of the upper list of scores is 80 and the maximum of the lower list of scores is 85, it follows that the maximum score cannot be determined.

Tip: For any list of numbers, the sum of the *signed* deviations from the mean is 0. This allows for an easy verification that the mean of each list above is 75. For example, the signed deviations for the second list are –5, –5, –5, –5, 0, 0, 0, 5, 5, and 10, which add to 0. This idea is also useful in constructing various lists of numbers that have the same mean, such as the two lists above.

The correct answer is E; both statements together are still not sufficient.

DS01341

378. Last school year, each of the 200 students at a certain high school attended the school for the entire year. If there were 8 cultural performances at the school during the last school year, what was the average (arithmetic mean) number of students attending each cultural performance?

    (1)   Last school year, each student attended at least one cultural performance.

    (2)   Last school year, the average number of cultural performances attended per student was 4.

Arithmetic Statistics

Determine the average number of students attending each of 8 cultural performances at a school that has 200 students.

(1) This indicates that each student attended at least one cultural performance, but the average number of students attending each performance cannot be uniquely determined. It could be as low as $\frac{200}{8} = 25$ students if each student attended exactly one performance, or it could be as high as $\frac{200}{1} = 200$ if each student attended every performance; NOT sufficient.

(2) This indicates that, since the average number of performances attended per student was 4, $\frac{\text{total attendance at performances}}{\text{total number of students}} = 4$, so the total attendance at the performances is $(4)(200) = 800$ students. It follows that the average number of students attending each performance is $\frac{800}{8} = 100$; SUFFICIENT.

The correct answer is B; statement 2 alone is sufficient.

DS14569

379. A clothing manufacturer makes jackets that are wool or cotton or a combination of wool and cotton. The manufacturer has 3,000 pounds of wool and 2,000 pounds of cotton on hand. Is this enough wool and cotton to make at least 1,000 jackets?

(1) Each wool jacket requires 4 pounds of wool, and no cotton.

(2) Each cotton jacket requires 6 pounds of cotton, and no wool.

Arithmetic Applied Problems

(1) Given that each wool jacket requires 4 pounds of wool and no cotton, then at most a total of 750 wool jackets can be made (because $\frac{3,000}{4} = 750$), and possibly no other jackets. Therefore, it is possible that there is enough wool and cotton to make at least 1,000 jackets (for example, if there is enough cotton to make 250 cotton jackets) and it is possible that there is not enough wool and cotton to make at least 1,000 jackets (for example, if there is less than the amount of cotton needed to make 250 cotton jackets); NOT sufficient.

(2) Given that each cotton jacket requires 6 pounds of cotton and no wool, then at most a total of 333 cotton jackets can be made (because rounding $\frac{2,000}{6}$ down to the nearest integer gives 333), and possibly no other jackets. Therefore, it is possible that there is enough wool and cotton to make at least 1,000 jackets (for example, if there is enough wool to make 667 wool jackets), and it is possible that there is not enough wool and cotton to make at least 1,000 jackets (for example, if there is less than the amount of wool needed to make 667 wool jackets); NOT sufficient.

Taking (1) and (2) together, there is enough wool and cotton to make 750 wool jackets and 333 cotton jackets for a total of 1,083 jackets.

The correct answer is C; both statements together are sufficient.

DS05377

380. If n is an integer, what is the greatest common divisor of 12 and n?

(1) The product of 12 and n is 432.

(2) The greatest common divisor of 24 and n is 12.

Arithmetic Properties of Integers

(1) This says $12n = 432$. The value of n can be determined by solving this equation. Then, using that value for n, the greatest common divisor of n and 12 can be determined; SUFFICIENT.

(2) This says 12 is the greatest common divisor of 24 and n. It follows that 12 is a divisor of n. Since 12 is a divisor of itself, 12 is also a common divisor of 12 and n. Because 12 is the greatest of the divisors of 12, it follows that 12 is the greatest common divisor of 12 and n; SUFFICIENT.

The correct answer is D; each statement alone is sufficient.

DS11287
381. Each month, Jim receives a base salary plus a 10 percent commission on the price of each car he sells that month. If Jim sold 15 cars last month, what was the total amount of base salary and commissions that Jim received that month?

   (1) Last month, Jim's base salary was $3,000.
   (2) Last month, Jim sold 3 cars whose prices totaled $60,000 and 5 cars whose prices totaled $120,000.

Arithmetic Applied Problems

Determine the total of Jim's base salary plus a 10% commission on the price of each of the 15 cars he sold last month.

   (1) This indicates that Jim's base salary was $3,000 but gives no information about the prices of the 15 cars he sold last month; NOT sufficient.

   (2) This indicates that Jim's commission on 8 cars that he sold last month can be determined but gives no information about his base salary or about the prices of the other 7 cars he sold last month; NOT sufficient.

Taking (1) and (2) together gives Jim's base salary and information about the prices of 8 of the 15 cars he sold last month, but does not provide information about the selling prices of the other 7 cars he sold.

The correct answer is E; both statements together are still not sufficient.

DS17615
382. If x is a positive integer greater than 1, what is the value of x?

   (1) $2x$ is a common factor of 18 and 24.
   (2) x is a factor of 6.

Arithmetic Properties of Numbers

   (1) Given that $2x$, where x is an integer greater than 1, is a common factor of 18 and 24, then $2x$ is an even integer greater than or equal to 4 that is a factor of 18 and 24. The factors of 18 are 1, 2, 3, 6, 9, and 18. The factors of 24 are 1, 2, 3, 4, 6, 8, 12, and 24. Since the only even integer greater than or equal to 4 that belongs to both lists is 6, it follows that $2x = 6$, or $x = 3$; SUFFICIENT.

   (2) Given that x, an integer greater than 1, is a factor of 6, then x could be 2, 3, or 6; NOT sufficient.

The correct answer is A; statement 1 alone is sufficient.

DS13408
383. By what percent was the price of a certain television set discounted for a sale?

   (1) The price of the television set before it was discounted for the sale was 25 percent greater than the discounted price.
   (2) The price of the television set was discounted by $60 for the sale.

Arithmetic Percents

Let B represent the price, in dollars, for the television before the sale and let D represent the discounted price, in dollars. The percent by which B was discounted to obtain D can be determined if the value of $\dfrac{B-D}{B}$ can be determined.

   (1) This indicates that B is 25% greater than D or that $B = 1.25D$. Then,
   $$\frac{B-D}{B} = \frac{1.25D - D}{1.25D} = \frac{0.25}{1.25} = 0.2 \text{ or } 20\%;$$
   SUFFICIENT.

   (2) This indicates that $D = B - 60$, but B is unknown. For example, B could be 100 and the value of $\dfrac{B-D}{B}$ would be $\dfrac{60}{100}$, or B could be 500 and the value of $\dfrac{B-D}{B}$ would be $\dfrac{60}{500}$; NOT sufficient.

The correct answer is A; statement 1 alone is sufficient.

DS05049
384. Jack wants to use a circular rug on his rectangular office floor to cover two small circular stains, each less than $\dfrac{\pi}{100}$ square feet in area and each more than 3 feet from the nearest wall. Can the rug be placed to cover both stains?

   (1) Jack's rug covers an area of 9π square feet.
   (2) The centers of the stains are less than 4 feet apart.

Geometry Applied Problems; Circles

(1) Given that the rug covers an area of 9π ft^2 and because the stains have a combined area of only $2\left(\dfrac{\pi}{100}\right) = \dfrac{\pi}{50}$ ft^2, it is possible that the rug could cover both stains. However, since there is no information about the size of the rectangular floor or the location of the stains, it is also possible that the rug could not cover both stains; NOT sufficient.

(2) Given that the centers of the stains are less than 4 ft apart, it is not possible to determine whether the rug could cover the stains because there is no information about the size of the rug; NOT sufficient.

Taking (1) and (2) together, because the area of each circular stain is less than $\dfrac{\pi}{100}$ ft^2, it follows that the radius of each circular stain is less than 0.1 ft ($\pi r^2 < \dfrac{1}{100}\pi$ implies $r^2 < \dfrac{1}{100}$, or $r < \dfrac{1}{10} = 0.1$). Hence, every point in either of the circular stains is less than $(2 + 0.1) = 2.1$ ft from the midpoint of the centers of the stains— midpoint to center of stain is 2 ft, center of stain to any point in stain is less than 0.1 ft. Also, because the area of the circular rug is 9π ft^2, it follows that the radius of the rug is 3 ft ($\pi r^2 = 9$ π implies $r^2 = 9$, or $r = 3$). By placing the rug so that its center is at the midpoint of the centers of the stains, the rug will cover all points within a distance of 3 ft from the midpoint, which includes every point in each of the stains, because every point in each of the stains is less than 2.1 ft from the midpoint.

The correct answer is C; both statements together are sufficient.

DS24751.01

385. A paint mixture was formed by mixing exactly 3 colors of paint. By volume, the mixture was x% blue paint, y% green paint, and z% red paint. If exactly 1 gallon of blue paint and 3 gallons of red paint were used, how many gallons of green paint were used?

(1) $x = y$

(2) $z = 60$

Algebra First-Degree Equations

Letting T represent the total number of gallons of the paint in the mixture, and B, G, and R the amounts of blue paint, green paint, and red paint, respectively, in the mixture, then $B = \dfrac{x}{100}T$, $G = \dfrac{y}{100}T$, and $R = \dfrac{z}{100}T$. It is given that $\dfrac{x}{100}T = 1$ and $\dfrac{z}{100}T = 3$, from which it follows that $z = 3x$. Also, since there are exactly three colors of paint, $x + y + z = 100$ and $B + G + R = T$. Determine the value of G, or equivalently, the value $\dfrac{y}{100}T$.

(1) Given that $x = y$ and $\dfrac{x}{100}T = 1$, it follows that $\dfrac{y}{100}T = 1$; SUFFICIENT.

(2) Given that $z = 60$ and $\dfrac{z}{100}T = 3$, it follows that $T = 5$. Knowing that the total amount of paint in the mixture is 5 gallons of which 1 gallon is blue paint and 3 gallons are red paint, the amount of green paint can be determined; SUFFICIENT.

The correct answer is D; each statement alone is sufficient.

×	a	b	c
a	d	e	f
b	e	g	h
c	f	h	j

DS05772

386. In the multiplication table above, each letter represents an integer. What is the value of c ?

(1) $c = f$

(2) $h \neq 0$

Arithmetic Properties of Numbers

The table above is a multiplication table, so $a \times a = d$, $a \times b = e$, $a \times c = f$, etc.

(1) Given that $c = f$, it is not possible to uniquely determine the value of c, as shown in the tables below in which $c = f$, but $c = 1$ in the first table and $c = 2$ in the second table; NOT sufficient.

×	1	1	1
1	1	1	1
1	1	1	1
1	1	1	1

×	1	1	2
1	1	1	2
1	1	1	2
2	2	2	4

(2) In the two tables above, $h \neq 0$, but $c = 1$ in the first table and $c = 2$ in the second table; NOT sufficient.

Taking (1) and (2) together, the tables above satisfy both statements since $c = f$ in both tables and $h \neq 0$ in both tables, but $c = 1$ in the first table and $c = 2$ in the second table. Therefore, it is not possible to uniquely determine the value of c; NOT sufficient

The answer is E;
both statements together are still not sufficient.

DS09379
387. If n is an integer, is $(0.1)^n$ greater than $(10)^n$?

(1) $n > -10$
(2) $n < 10$

Arithmetic Exponents

$(0.1)^n = \dfrac{1}{10^n}$ will be greater than 10^n if 1 is greater than 10^{2n}, and this will be the case if and only if $n < 0$. Determine if $n < 0$.

(1) This indicates that n is greater than -10. This includes nonnegative values of n as well as negative values of n; NOT sufficient.

(2) This indicates that n is less than 10, but this includes negative values of n as well as nonnegative values of n; NOT sufficient.

Taking (1) and (2) together, n can have any value between -10 and 10 and can therefore be negative or nonnegative.

The correct answer is E;
both statements together are still not sufficient.

DS19199
388. For a basic monthly fee of F yen (¥F), Naoko's first cell phone plan allowed him to use a maximum of 420 minutes on calls during the month. Then, for each of x additional minutes he used on calls, he was charged ¥M, making his total charge for the month ¥T, where $T = F + xM$. What is the value of F ?

(1) Naoko used 450 minutes on calls the first month and the total charge for the month was ¥13,755.
(2) Naoko used 400 minutes on calls the second month and the total charge for the month was ¥13,125.

Algebra Simultaneous Equations

(1) Given that Naoko used 450 minutes and was charged ¥13,125, it follows that $F + (450 - 420)M = 13,755$, or $F + 30M = 13,755$. However, the value of F cannot be determined. For example, $F = 13,005$ and $M = 25$ is possible, and $F = 13,035$ and $M = 24$ is possible; NOT sufficient.

(2) Given that Naoko used 400 minutes and was charged ¥13,125, it follows that $F = 13,125$, since Naoko did not use more than 420 minutes; SUFFICIENT.

The correct answer is B;
statement 2 alone is sufficient.

DS13949
389. Is the sum of the prices of the 3 books that Shana bought less than $48 ?

(1) The price of the most expensive of the 3 books that Shana bought is less than $17.
(2) The price of the least expensive of the 3 books that Shana bought is exactly $3 less than the price of the second most expensive book.

Arithmetic Operations with Integers; Order

Let B_1, B_2, and B_3 be the prices, in dollars and in numerical order, of the 3 books. Thus, $B_1 \leq B_2 \leq B_3$. Determine whether $B_1 + B_2 + B_3 < 48$.

(1) Given that $B_3 < 17$, it is possible that $B_1 + B_2 + B_3 < 48$ (choose $B_1 = B_2 = 15$ and $B_3 = 16$) and it is possible that $B_1 + B_2 + B_3 > 48$ (choose $B_1 = B_2 = 16$ and $B_3 = 16.5$); NOT sufficient.

(2) Given that $B_1 = B_2 - 3$, it is possible that $B_1 + B_2 + B_3 < 48$ (choose $B_1 = 3$, $B_2 = 6$, and $B_3 = 10$) and it is possible that $B_1 + B_2 + B_3 > 48$ (choose $B_1 = 3$, $B_2 = 6$, and $B_3 = 48$); NOT sufficient.

Taking (1) and (2) together, from (1) and the information given it follows that $B_3 < 17$ and $B_2 \leq B_3 < 17$, or $B_2 < 17$. Also, from $B_2 < 17$ and (2), it follows that $B_1 < 17 - 3$, or $B_1 < 14$. Therefore, $B_1 + B_2 + B_3$ is the sum of 3 numbers—a number less than 14, a number less than 17, and a number less than 17—and thus $B_1 + B_2 + B_3 < 14 + 17 + 17 = 48$.

The correct answer is C; both statements together are sufficient.

DS12943

390. If r and t are three-digit positive integers, is r greater than t?

(1) The tens digit of r is greater than each of the three digits of t.

(2) The tens digit of r is less than either of the other two digits of r.

Arithmetic Properties of Numbers

(1) Each of the examples below are such that the tens digit of r (equal to 4 in both examples) is greater than each of the three digits of t.

Example I: $r = 242$ and $t = 222$.

Example II: $r = 242$ and $t = 333$.

Note that r is greater than t in Example I and r is not greater than t in Example II; NOT sufficient.

(2) Given that the tens digit of r is less than either of the other two digits of r, there is no information about the three-digit integer t; NOT sufficient.

Taking (1) and (2) together, the hundreds digit of r is greater than the tens digit of r by (2) and the tens digit of r is greater than the hundreds digit of t by (1). Therefore, the hundreds digit of r is greater than the hundreds digit of t and it follows that r is greater than t.

The correct answer is C; both statements together are sufficient.

DS14788

391. Is the product of two positive integers x and y divisible by the sum of x and y?

(1) $x = y$

(2) $x = 2$

Arithmetic Properties of Numbers

(1) Given that $x = y$, then xy could be divisible by $x + y$ (for example, if $x = y = 2$, then $xy = 4$ is divisible by $x + y = 4$) and xy could fail to be divisible by $x + y$ (for example, if $x = y = 3$, then $xy = 9$ is not divisible by $x + y = 6$); NOT sufficient.

(2) Given that $x = 2$, then xy could be divisible by $x + y$ (for example, if $x = y = 2$, then $xy = 4$ is divisible by $x + y = 4$) and xy could fail to be divisible by $x + y$ (for example, if $x = 2$ and $y = 3$, then $xy = 6$ is not divisible by $x + y = 5$); NOT sufficient.

Taking (1) and (2) together, it follows that $x = y = 2$, and so $xy = 4$ is divisible by $x + y = 4$.

The correct answer is C; both statements together are sufficient.

DS24571.01

392. If a and b are constants, is the expression $\dfrac{x+b}{\sqrt{x+a}}$ defined for $x = -2$?

(1) $a = 5$

(2) $b = 6$

Algebra Functions

In the set of real numbers, the radical expression $\dfrac{x+b}{\sqrt{x+a}}$ is defined for all values of x for which $\sqrt{x+a}$ is a nonzero real number, from which it follows that $\dfrac{x+b}{\sqrt{x+a}}$ is defined for all values of x such that $x > -a$. If $-2 > -a$ or equivalently if $a > 2$, then $\dfrac{x+b}{\sqrt{x+a}}$ is defined for $x = -2$. Determine if $a > 2$.

(1) If $a = 5$, then $a > 2$; SUFFICIENT.

(2) Given information only about the value of b, if $a = 5$, for example, then a is greater than 2. On the other hand, if $a = -5$, then a is not greater than 2; NOT sufficient.

The correct answer is A; statement 1 alone is sufficient.

DS05330

393. A company makes and sells two products, P and Q. The costs per unit of making and selling P and Q are $8.00 and $9.50, respectively, and the selling prices per unit of P and Q are $10.00 and $13.00, respectively. In one month the company sold a total of 834 units of these products. Was the total profit on these items more than $2,000.00 ?

    (1) During the month, more units of P than units of Q were sold.
    (2) During the month, at least 100 units of Q were sold.

Arithmetic Applied Problems

It is given that the profit on each unit of P is $10.00 − $8.00 = $2.00, and the profit on each unit of Q is $13.00 − $9.50 = $3.50. Also if p and q represent the number of units of Products P and Q made and sold, then it is given that $p + q = 834$. Determining if the total profit on these items was more than $2,000 requires determining how many units of at least one of the products were sold.

    (1) This indicates that $p > q$, but does not give a specific value for p or q; NOT sufficient.
    (2) This indicates that $q \geq 100$, but does not give a specific value for q; NOT sufficient.

Taking (1) and (2) together, $p > q$ and $q \geq 100$, so $p > 100$, but a specific value for p or q cannot be determined.

**The correct answer is E;
both statements together are still not sufficient.**

DS03045

394. Jill has applied for a job with each of two different companies. What is the probability that she will get job offers from both companies?

    (1) The probability that she will get a job offer from neither company is 0.3.
    (2) The probability that she will get a job offer from exactly one of the two companies is 0.5.

Arithmetic Probability

Let $P(2)$ be the probability that she will get a job offer from both companies, $P(1)$ be the probability that she will get a job offer from exactly one of the companies, and $P(0)$ be the probability that she will get a job offer from neither company. Then $P(2) + P(1) + P(0) = 1$. What is the value of $P(2)$?

    (1) Given that $P(0) = 0.3$, it follows that $P(2) + P(1) + 0.3 = 1$, or $P(2) + P(1) = 0.7$.

However, the value of $P(2)$ cannot be determined, since nothing is known about the value of $P(1)$ other than $0 \leq P(1) \leq 0.7$; NOT sufficient.

    (2) (2) Given that $P(1) = 0.5$, it follows that $P(2) + 0.5 + P(0) = 1$, or $P(2) + P(0) = 0.5$. However, the value of $P(2)$ cannot be determined, since nothing is known about the value of $P(0)$ other than $0 \leq P(1) \leq 0.5$; NOT sufficient.

Taking (1) and (2) together, it follows that $P(2) + 0.5 + 0.3 = 1$, or $P(2) = 0.2$.

**The correct answer is C;
both statements together are sufficient.**

DS46420.02

395. A certain computer company produces two different monitors, P and Q. In 2010, what was the net profit from the sale of the two monitors?

    (1) Of the company's expenses in 2010, rent and utilities totaled $500,000.
    (2) In 2010, the company sold 50,000 units of monitor P at $300 per unit and 30,000 units of monitor Q at $650 per unit.

Arithmetic Applied Problems

The net profit from the sale of the two monitors is the total revenue, R, from the sale of the two monitors minus the total cost, C, of the two monitors, or $R − C$. Determine the value of $R − C$.

    (1) Given that the rent and utilities totaled $500,000, it is not possible to determine the value of $R − C$ because we only know that $C \geq 500,000$ and we do not know anything about the value of R; NOT sufficient.
    (2) Given that $R = 50,000(\$300) + 30,000(\$650)$, it is not possible to determine the value of $R − C$ because we do not know anything about the value of C; NOT sufficient.

Taking (1) and (2) together, it is not possible to determine the value of $R − C$ because from (2) the value of R is fixed and from both (1) and (2) we can only conclude that $C \geq 500,000$, and therefore more than one value of $R − C$ is possible.

**The correct answer is E;
both statements together are still not sufficient.**

DS01257

396. A conveyor belt moves bottles at a constant speed of 120 centimeters per second. If the conveyor belt moves a bottle from a loading dock to an unloading dock, is the distance that the conveyor belt moves the bottle less than 90 meters? (1 meter = 100 centimeters)

 (1) It takes the conveyor belt less than 1.2 minutes to move the bottle from the loading dock to the unloading dock.

 (2) It takes the conveyor belt more than 1.1 minutes to move the bottle from the loading dock to the unloading dock.

Arithmetic Applied Problems

Since the rate at which the conveyor belt moves is given as 120 centimeters per second, which is equivalent to $\frac{120}{100} = 1.2$ meters per second, the conveyor will move less than 90 meters if it moves for less than $\frac{90}{1.2} = 75$ seconds.

 (1) This indicates that the length of time the conveyor belt moves is less than 1.2 minutes, which is equivalent to $(1.2)(60) = 72$ seconds and $72 < 75$; SUFFICIENT.

 (2) This indicates that the length of time the conveyor belt moves is more than 1.1 minutes, which is equivalent to $(1.1)(60) = 66$ seconds, but does not indicate how much more than 66 seconds the conveyor moves. If the conveyor moves for 70 seconds $(70 > 66)$, for example, it moves less than 90 meters since $70 < 75$. However, if the conveyor belt moves for 80 seconds $(80 > 66)$, then it moves more than 90 meters since $80 > 75$; NOT sufficient.

The correct answer is A; statement 1 alone is sufficient.

DS02706

397. If x, y, and z are positive numbers, what is the value of the average (arithmetic mean) of x and z?

 (1) $x - y = y - z$

 (2) $x^2 - y^2 = z$

Algebra Statistics; Simplifying Algebraic Expressions

Determine the unique value of $\frac{x+z}{2}$.

 (1) Given $x - y = y - z$, it follows that $2y = x + z$, so $y = \frac{x+z}{2}$. Without values for x and z or at least a way to determine their sum, the value of $\frac{x+z}{2}$ cannot be uniquely determined; NOT sufficient.

 (2) Given $x^2 - y^2 = z$, it is not possible to uniquely determine the value of $\frac{x+z}{2}$ as shown by the examples in the table below.

x	y	$x^2 - y^2$	z	$\frac{x+z}{2}$
3	2	$9 - 4$	5	$\frac{3+5}{2} = 4$
5	4	$25 - 16$	9	$\frac{5+9}{2} = 7$

Taking (1) and (2) together, $z = 2y - x$ from (1) and $z = x^2 - y^2$ from (2), so $2y - x = x^2 - y^2$. Then,

$$2y - x = x^2 - y^2 \qquad \text{given}$$
$$2y = x^2 - y^2 + x \quad \text{add } x \text{ to both sides}$$
$$y^2 + 2y = x^2 + x \qquad \text{add } y^2 \text{ to both sides}$$

To see that there is more than one pair of values for x and y that satisfy this equation, choose $x = 1$, for example, and determine whether the equation $y^2 + 2y = 1^2 + 1 = 2$ or $y^2 + 2y - 2 = 0$ has at least one real number solution. Note that the equation has the form $ay^2 + by + c = 0$ and it will have two real number solutions if the discriminant $b^2 - 4ac$ is positive. Here, the discriminant is $2^2 - 4(1)(-2) = 12$, which is positive, so the equation $y^2 + 2y - 2 = 0$ has two real number solutions.

Since the values of x and y cannot be uniquely determined, the value of z cannot be uniquely determined. Therefore, the value of $\frac{x+z}{2}$ cannot be uniquely determined.

The correct answer is E; both statements together are still not sufficient.

DS04428

398. The rectangular rug shown in the figure above has an accent border. What is the area of the portion of the rug that excludes the border?

(1)   The perimeter of the rug is 44 feet.

(2)   The width of the border on all sides is 1 foot.

Geometry Rectangles; Perimeter

(1)   Given that the perimeter of the rug is 44 ft, then the rectangular rug could have area 121 ft^2 (length = 11 ft and width = 11 ft) and the rectangular rug could have area 96 ft^2 (length = 16 ft and width = 6 ft). Moreover, no information is given about the width of the accent border, so even if the area of the rectangular rug could be determined, it would still not be possible to determine the area of the portion of the rug that excludes the border; NOT sufficient.

(2)   Given that the width of the border is 1 ft, the area of the portion of the rug that excludes the border is $(L-2)(W-2)$ ft^2, where L ft and W ft are the length and width, respectively, of the rug. If $L = W = 11$, then $(L-2)(W-2) = 81$. However, if $L = 16$ and $W = 6$, then $(L-2)(W-2) = 56$; NOT sufficient.

Taking (1) and (2) together, the area could be 81 ft^2 or 56 ft^2 as shown by the examples in (1) and (2).

The correct answer is E;
both statements together are still not sufficient.

DS06537
399. If $y \neq 2xz$, what is the value of $\dfrac{2xz + yz}{2xz - y}$?

(1) $2x + y = 3$

(2) $z = 2$

Algebra Simplifying Algebraic Expressions

The task is to determine the value of $\dfrac{2xz + yz}{2xz - y} = \dfrac{z(2x + y)}{2xz - y}$.

(1)   This indicates $2x + y = 3$, and so $\dfrac{2xz + yz}{2xz - y} = \dfrac{3z}{2xz - y}$. However, this is not enough to determine the value of $\dfrac{2xz + yz}{2xz - y}$. For example, if $x = 1$, $y = 1$, and $z = 2$, then $2x + y = 3$ and $\dfrac{2xz + yz}{2xz - y} = 2$, but if $x = 0$,

$y = 3$, and $z = 2$, then $2x + y = 3$ and $\dfrac{2xz + yz}{2xz - y} = -2$; NOT sufficient.

(2)   This indicates that $z = 2$, and so $\dfrac{2xz + yz}{2xz - y} = \dfrac{4x + 2y}{4x - y}$. However, this is not enough to determine the value of $\dfrac{2xz + yz}{2xz - y}$. For example, if $x = 1$, $y = 1$, and $z = 2$, then $\dfrac{2xz + yz}{2xz - y} = 2$, but if $x = 0$, $y = 3$, and $z = 2$, then $\dfrac{2xz + yz}{2xz - y} = -2$; NOT sufficient.

Taking (1) and (2) together is not enough to determine the value of $\dfrac{2xz + yz}{2xz - y}$ because the same examples used to show that (1) is not sufficient were also used to show that (2) is not sufficient.

The correct answer is E;
both statements together are still not sufficient.

DS04852
400. In the parallelogram shown, what is the value of x ?

(1) $y = 2x$

(2) $x + z = 120$

Geometry Angles

(1)   Given that $y = 2x$ and the fact that adjacent angles of a parallelogram are supplementary, it follows that $180 = x + y = x + 2x = 3x$, or $180 = 3x$. Solving this equation gives $x = 60$; SUFFICIENT.

(2)   Given that $x + z = 120$ and the fact that opposite angles of a parallelogram have the same measure, it follows that $120 = x + z = x + x$, or $120 = 2x$. Solving this equation gives $x = 60$; SUFFICIENT.

The correct answer is D;
each statement alone is sufficient.

DS06096

401. In a product test of a common cold remedy, x percent of the patients tested experienced side effects from the use of the drug and y percent experienced relief of cold symptoms. What percent of the patients tested experienced both side effects and relief of cold symptoms?

(1) Of the 1,000 patients tested, 15 percent experienced neither side effects nor relief of cold symptoms.

(2) Of the patients tested, 30 percent experienced relief of cold symptoms without side effects.

Algebra Sets

The Venn diagram below represents the numbers of patients who experienced neither, one, or both side effects and relief. In the diagram,

a = number who experienced side effects only,
b = number who experienced both,
c = number who experienced relief only,
d = number who experienced neither,

where $T = a + b + c + d$ is the total number of patients. Note that $a + b = \dfrac{x}{100}T$ and $b + c = \dfrac{y}{100}T$.
Determine the value of $\dfrac{b}{T}$.

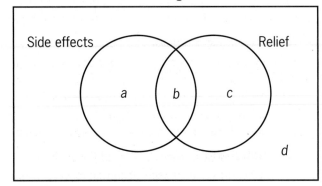

(1) Given that 1,000 patients were tested and $(0.15)(1,000) = 150$ patients experienced neither side effects nor relief, it follows that $a + b + c + d = 1,000$ and $d = 150$. Therefore, $a + b + c + 150 = 1,000$, or $a + b + c = 850$. However, there is no information about how the remaining 850 patients are assigned to the other categories. Thus, the percent of patients who experienced both side effects and relief could be any value between 0% and 85%; NOT sufficient.

(2) Given that 30% of the patients experienced relief without side effects, there is no information about how the remaining 70% of the patients are assigned to the other categories. Thus, the percent of patients who experienced both side effects and relief could be any value between 0% and 70%; NOT sufficient.

Taking (1) and (2) together, it follows that 150 patients experienced neither side effects nor relief and $(0.3)(1,000) = 300$ patients experienced relief only. Therefore, from $a + b + c + d = T$ it follows that $a + b + 300 + 150 = 1,000$, or $a + b = 550$. However, it is still not possible to determine a unique value of $\dfrac{b}{T} = \dfrac{b}{1,000}$, the percent of patients who experienced both side effects and relief. For example, it is possible that $a = 300$ and $b = 250$ (that is, the percent who experienced both could be 25%), and it is possible that $a = 250$ and $b = 300$ (that is, the percent who experienced both could be 30%).

**The correct answer is E;
both statements together are still not sufficient.**

DS13588

402. Is $x < 5$?

(1) $x^2 > 5$
(2) $x^2 + x < 5$

Algebra Inequalities

(1) Given that $x^2 > 5$, then $x < 5$ can be true (for example, if $x = -3$) and $x < 5$ can be false (for example, if $x = 6$); NOT sufficient.

(2) Given that $x^2 + x < 5$, then $x < 5 - x^2$. Also, since $x^2 \geq 0$ is true for any real number x, it follows that $-x^2 \leq 0$, or after adding 5 to both sides, $5 - x^2 \leq 5$. From $x < 5 - x^2$ and $5 - x^2 \leq 5$, it follows that $x < 5$; SUFFICIENT.

**The correct answer is B;
statement 2 alone is sufficient.**

DS72951.01

403. Three roommates—Bela, Gyorgy, and Janos—together saved money for a trip. The amount that Bela saved was equal to 8% of his monthly income. The amount that Gyorgy saved was exactly $\frac{1}{3}$ of the total amount saved by all 3 roommates. What was the total amount saved for the trip by all 3 roommates?

    (1) Bela had a monthly income of $2,000.

    (2) Janos saved 1.5 times as much for the trip as Bela.

Algebra First-Degree Equations

Letting B, G, and J represent the amounts saved by Bela, Gyorgy, and Janos, respectively, then $B = 0.08I$, where I represents Bela's monthly income, $G = \frac{1}{3}(B + G + J)$, and $G = \frac{1}{2}(B + J)$. Determine the value of $B + G + J$.

    (1) This allows the value of B to be determined, but gives no information about the values of G or J; NOT sufficient.

    (2) This gives the relationship between the values of J and B, but no information to determine the value of either B or J; NOT sufficient.

Taking (1) and (2) together, the values of both B and J can be determined as can the value of G since $G = \frac{1}{2}(B + J)$. Thus, the value of $B + G + J$ can be determined.

**The correct answer is C;
both statements together are sufficient.**

DS11257

404. Is zp negative?

    (1) $pz^4 < 0$

    (2) $p + z^4 = 14$

Arithmetic Properties of Numbers

    (1) Given that $pz^4 < 0$, zp can be negative (choose $p = -2$ and $z = 2$) and zp can be nonnegative (choose $p = -2$ and $z = -2$); NOT sufficient.

    (2) Given that $p + z^4 = 14$, the same examples used to show that (1) is not sufficient can be used for (2); NOT sufficient.

Taking (1) and (2) together is of no more help than either (1) or (2) taken separately because the same examples used to show that (1) is not sufficient also show that (2) is not sufficient.

**The correct answer is E;
both statements together are still not sufficient.**

DS04157

405. In each game of a certain tournament, a contestant either loses 3 points or gains 2 points. If Pat had 100 points at the beginning of the tournament, how many games did Pat play in the tournament?

    (1) At the end of the tournament, Pat had 104 points.

    (2) Pat played fewer than 10 games.

Arithmetic Computation with Integers

Pat either lost 3 points or gained 2 points in each game she played. Therefore, since she had 100 points at the beginning of the tournament, her score at the end of the tournament was $100 - 3x + 2y$, where x and y represent, respectively, the number of games in which she lost 3 points and the number of games in which she gained 2 points. Determine the value of $x + y$.

    (1) This indicates that $100 - 3x + 2y = 104$, but no information is given about the values of x or y. For example, the values of x and y could be 0 and 2, respectively, so that $x + y = 2$ or the values of x and y could be 2 and 5, respectively, so that $x + y = 7$; NOT sufficient.

    (2) This indicates that Pat played fewer than 10 games, but in each of the examples above, Pat played fewer than 10 games; NOT sufficient.

Since the examples given satisfy both (1) and (2), taking (1) and (2) together does not give enough information to determine the value of $x + y$.

**The correct answer is E;
both statements together are still not sufficient.**

DS05631

406. At the beginning of the year, the Finance Committee and the Planning Committee of a certain company each had n members, and no one was a member of both committees. At the end of the year, 5 members

left the Finance Committee and 3 members left the Planning Committee. How many members did the Finance Committee have at the beginning of the year?

(1) The ratio of the total number of members who left at the end of the year to the total number of members at the beginning of the year was 1:6.

(2) At the end of the year, 21 members remained on the Planning Committee.

Algebra Applied Problems

(1) It is given that $\dfrac{8}{2n} = \dfrac{1}{6}$, since a total of $3 + 5 = 8$ members left at the end of the year and there were a total of $n + n = 2n$ members at the beginning of the year. It follows that $(8)(6) = (2n)(1)$, or $n = 24$; SUFFICIENT.

(2) It is given that $n - 3 = 21$, since 3 members from the original n members left the Planning Committee at the end of the year. It follows that $n = 21 + 3 = 24$; SUFFICIENT.

The correct answer is D; each statement alone is sufficient.

DS15561
407. If $xy \neq 0$, is $x^3 + y^3 > 0$?

(1) $x + y > 0$

(2) $xy > 0$

Algebra Inequalities

i. Because it is given that $xy \neq 0$, it follows that $x \neq 0$ and $y \neq 0$. Therefore, the cases where $x = 0$ and/or $y = 0$ need not be considered.

ii. If $a > b$, then $a^3 > b^3$ is true for all nonzero a and b. This can be proved algebraically and can be verified by looking at a chart of values such as the one below which shows that as a increases, so does a^3.

a	a^3
−3	−27
−2	−8
−1	−1
1	1
2	8
3	27

(1) Given that $x + y > 0$, so $x > -y$. From ii. above, it follows that $x^3 > (-y)^3$. Then, $x^3 > -y^3$ and $x^3 + y^3 > 0$; SUFFICIENT.

(2) Given that $xy > 0$, it is possible that $x^3 + y^3 > 0$. For example, if $x = y = 1$, then $xy > 0$ and $x^3 + y^3 > 0$. However, it is also possible that $x^3 + y^3 < 0$. For example, if $x = y = -1$, then $xy > 0$ and $x^3 + y^3 < 0$; NOT sufficient.

The correct answer is A; statement 1 alone is sufficient.

DS13541
408. Max purchased a guitar for a total of $624, which consisted of the price of the guitar and the sales tax. Was the sales tax rate greater than 3 percent?

(1) The price of the guitar that Max purchased was less than $602.

(2) The sales tax for the guitar that Max purchased was less than $30.

Arithmetic Applied Problems; Percents

Letting P be the price, in dollars, of the guitar and $r\%$ be the sales tax rate, it is given that $P\left(1 + \dfrac{r}{100}\right) = 624$. Determine if $r > 3$.

(1) Given that $P < 602$, then $624 = P\left(1 + \dfrac{r}{100}\right) < 602\left(1 + \dfrac{r}{100}\right)$, and so $1 + \dfrac{r}{100} > \dfrac{624}{602}$. Therefore, $\dfrac{r}{100} > \dfrac{624}{602} - 1 = \dfrac{22}{602} = \dfrac{11}{301} > \dfrac{3}{100}$, because $(11)(100) > (3)(301)$, and so $r > 100\left(\dfrac{3}{100}\right) = 3$; SUFFICIENT.

(2) Given that the sales tax was less than $30, it is not possible to determine whether the sales tax rate was greater than 3%. Since $(0.03)(\$624) = \$18.72$, a 3% sales tax rate on the price corresponds to a sales tax that is less than $18.72, since the price is less than $624. Therefore, it is possible that the sales tax is less than $30 and the sales tax rate is less than 3%, since any sales tax rate less than 3% would give a sales tax that is less than $18.72 (and hence less than $30).

However, it is also possible that the sales tax is less than $30 and the sales tax rate is 4% (which is greater than 3%), since a 4% sales tax rate implies $P\left(1+\dfrac{4}{100}\right)=624$, or $P=\dfrac{62,400}{104}=600$, and thus the sales tax would be $0.04(\$600)=\$24<\$30$; NOT sufficient.

The correct answer is A; statement 1 alone is sufficient.

DS75271.01

409. A pentagon with 5 sides of equal length and 5 interior angles of equal measure is inscribed in a circle. Is the perimeter of the pentagon greater than 26 centimeters?

   (1) The area of the circle is 16π square centimeters.

   (2) The length of each diagonal of the pentagon is less than 8 centimeters.

Geometry Polygons

A regular pentagon can be partitioned into 5 isosceles triangles, one of which is shown in the figure below. The vertex angle of each of these triangles has measure $72°$. If $s=r$, then each of the 5 triangles would be equilateral with vertex angle measuring $60°$, not $72°$. If $s<r$, then the vertex of each of the 5 triangles would measure less than $60°$. Therefore, $s>r$. If P represents the perimeter, determine if $P>26$.

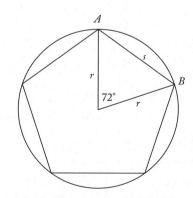

   (1) This gives $r=4$, so the circumference of the circle is 8π. The length of arc $\widehat{AB}$ is $\left(\dfrac{72}{360}\right)(8\pi)=\dfrac{8\pi}{5}$. Also, $s<\dfrac{8\pi}{5}$ because a straight line is the shortest distance between two points, so $P<8\pi$, or equivalently,

$\dfrac{P}{8}<\pi$. If $P>26$ were true, then $\dfrac{P}{8}>3.25$ would be true. But $3.25>\pi$ so $\dfrac{P}{8}>\pi$, which contradicts $\dfrac{P}{8}<\pi$ and so contradicts $P>26$. It follows that the answer to "Is P greater than 26?" is definitively "no"; SUFFICIENT.

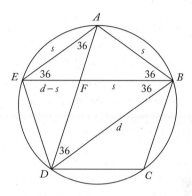

   (2) Diagonals $\overline{AD}$, $\overline{BD}$, and $\overline{BE}$ are shown in the figure above. Using these diagonals, each with length d, plus the facts that all the sides of the pentagon are the same length, the degree measure of each of the pentagon's interior angles is 108, and the base angles of an isosceles triangle have equal degree measures, the angle measures, in degrees, shown in the figure can be verified. Also it can be shown that $\triangle ABF$ is isosceles (the degree measure of $\angle FAB$ is $108-36=72$ and the degree measure of $\angle AFB$ is $180-(36+72)=72$), so $FB=s$. It follows that $\triangle AFE$ and $\triangle BFD$ are similar and their sides are in proportion. Thus, if d represents the length of each diagonal of the pentagon, then $\dfrac{s}{d}=\dfrac{d-s}{s}$ or $s^2=d(d-s)=d^2-ds$.

It follows that $d=\dfrac{s\pm\sqrt{s^2+4(1)s^2}}{2(1)}$, which simplifies to $d=\dfrac{1+\sqrt{5}}{2}s$. (Note that $d=\dfrac{s-\sqrt{s^2+4(1)s^2}}{2(1)}=\dfrac{1-\sqrt{5}}{2}s$ has been discarded because $\dfrac{1-\sqrt{5}}{2}$ is negative and $\dfrac{1-\sqrt{5}}{2}s$ cannot be a length.) It is given that $d < 8$ from which it follows that

$\dfrac{1+\sqrt{5}}{2}s < 8$ and thus $s < \dfrac{16}{1+\sqrt{5}}$. Since

$P = 5s$, it follows that $P < \dfrac{80}{1+\sqrt{5}} =$

$\left(\dfrac{80}{1+\sqrt{5}}\right)\left(\dfrac{1-\sqrt{5}}{1-\sqrt{5}}\right) = \dfrac{80(1-\sqrt{5})}{-4} =$

$20(\sqrt{5} - 1)$. It is true that $20(\sqrt{5} - 1)$

< 26 because if $20(\sqrt{5} - 1) \geq 26$, then

$(\sqrt{5} - 1) \geq \dfrac{13}{10}$, and $\sqrt{5} \geq \dfrac{23}{10}$,

from which it follows that $5 \geq \dfrac{529}{100}$ or

$5 \geq 5.29$. But, this is not true and so $20(\sqrt{5} - 1) < 26$ and $P < 26$. Therefore, the answer to the question "Is P greater than 26?" is definitively "no"; SUFFICIENT.

The correct answer is D;
each statement alone is sufficient.

DS13841.01

410. If $2.00X$ and $3.00Y$ are 2 numbers in decimal form with thousandths digits X and Y, is $3(2.00X) > 2(3.00Y)$?

  (1) $3X < 2Y$

  (2) $X < Y - 3$

Arithmetic Operations with Integers

The decimals $3(2.00X)$ and $2(3.00Y)$ can also

be expressed as $3\left(2 + \dfrac{X}{1{,}000}\right) = 6 + \dfrac{3X}{1{,}000}$

and $2\left(3 + \dfrac{Y}{1{,}000}\right) = 6 + \dfrac{2Y}{1{,}000}$. Then,

$3(2.00X) > 2(3.00Y)$ only if $3X > 2Y$. Determine if $3X > 2Y$ is true.

  (1) Given that $3X < 2Y$, it follows that $3X > 2Y$ is not true and so $3(2.00X) > 2(3.00Y)$ is not true for all integer values of X and Y from 0 through 9; SUFFICIENT.

  (2) Given that $X < Y - 3$, if $X = 0$, then the possible values for Y are 4, 5, 6, 7, 8, and 9. For each of these values, $3X > 2Y$ is not true. If $X = 1$, then the possible values for Y are 5, 6, 7, 8, and 9 and for each of these values, $3X > 2Y$ is not true. If $X = 2$, then the possible values for Y are 6, 7, 8, and 9

and for each of these values, $3X > 2Y$ is not true. If $X = 3$, then the possible values for Y are 7, 8, and 9 and for each of these values, $3X > 2Y$ is not true. If $X = 4$, then the possible values for Y are 8 and 9 and for each of these values, $3X > 2Y$ is not true. If $X = 5$, then the only possible value for Y is 9 and for this value, $3X > 2Y$ is not true. If $X \geq 6$, there are no integer values from 0 through 9 for which $X < Y - 3$. In all possible cases, $3X > 2Y$ is not true, so $3(2.00X) > 2(3.00Y)$ is not true; SUFFICIENT.

Alternatively, if $X < Y - 3$, then $X + 3 < Y$. If $3X > 2Y$ were true, or equivalently, if $Y < \dfrac{3}{2}X$ were true, then $X + 3 < Y < \dfrac{3}{2}X$ would be true, from which it follows that $X + 3 < \dfrac{3}{2}X$ would be true. But, this would imply $X > 6$ is true, which cannot be true because if $X + 3 < Y$, then $Y > 9$, and Y cannot be greater than 9 because Y is a digit.

The correct answer is D;
each statement alone is sufficient.

DS50351.01

411. The length, width, and height of a rectangular box, in centimeters, are L, W, and H. If the volume of this box is V cubic centimeters and the total area of the 6 sides of this box is A square centimeters, what is the value of $\dfrac{V}{A}$?

  (1) At least 2 of L, W, and H are equal to 5.

  (2) L, W, and H all have the same value.

Geometry Volume; Surface Area

For a rectangular box with dimensions L, W, and H, $V = LWH$ and $A = 2(LW + LH + WH)$.

Determine the value of $\dfrac{V}{A}$.

  (1) Given that at least 2 of the dimensions are 5, if $L = W = 5$ and $H = 1$, then
$\dfrac{V}{A} = \dfrac{(5)(5)(1)}{2[(5)(5)+(2)(5)(1)]} = \dfrac{25}{70} = \dfrac{5}{14}$.
However, if $L = W = 5$ and $H = 2$, then
$\dfrac{V}{A} = \dfrac{(5)(5)(2)}{2[(5)(5)+(2)(5)(2)]} = \dfrac{50}{90} = \dfrac{5}{9}$;
NOT sufficient.

(2) Given that L, W, and H all have the same value, then letting s represent that value, $\dfrac{V}{A} = \dfrac{s^3}{2(3s^2)}$ and this value differs as s differs; NOT sufficient.

Taking (1) and (2) together, $L = W = H = 5$ and a unique value for $\dfrac{V}{A}$ can be determined.

**The correct answer is C;
both statements together are sufficient.**

DS06027
412. What is the sum of a certain pair of consecutive odd integers?

(1) At least one of the integers is negative.

(2) At least one of the integers is positive.

Arithmetic Properties of Numbers

(1) Given that at least one of the integers is negative, the sum could be −4 (if the integers were −3 and −1) and the sum could be 0 (if the integers were −1 and 1); NOT sufficient.

(2) Given that at least one of the integers is positive, the sum could be 0 (if the integers were −1 and 1) and the sum could be 4 (if the integers were 1 and 3); NOT sufficient.

Taking (1) and (2) together, the smaller of the two numbers cannot be less than −1 (otherwise (2) would not be true) and the larger of the two numbers cannot be greater than 1 (otherwise (1) would not be true). Therefore, the integers must be −1 and 1, and the sum must be 0.

**The correct answer is C;
both statements together are sufficient.**

DS45530.01
413. Is $x = y$?

(1) $\dfrac{2x}{3} - \dfrac{y}{3} = \dfrac{1}{3}$

(2) $\dfrac{x}{4} - \dfrac{y}{4} = 0$

Algebra First-Degree Equations

(1) Given that $\dfrac{2x}{3} - \dfrac{y}{3} = \dfrac{1}{3}$, or equivalently $2x - y = 1$, it is not possible to determine

whether $x = y$ is true. For example, if $x = 1$ and $y = 1$, then $2(1) - 1 = 1$ and $x = y$. However, if $x = 2$ and $y = 3$, then $2(2) - 3 = 1$ and $x \neq y$; NOT sufficient.

(2) Given that $\dfrac{x}{4} - \dfrac{y}{4} = 0$, then multiplying both sides by 4 gives $x - y = 0$, which means $x = y$; SUFFICIENT.

**The correct answer is B;
statement 2 alone is sufficient.**

DS08197
414. The sum of 4 different odd integers is 64. What is the value of the greatest of these integers?

(1) The integers are consecutive odd numbers.

(2) Of these integers, the greatest is 6 more than the least.

Arithmetic Properties of Numbers

Determine the greatest of four odd integers whose sum is 64.

(1) This indicates that the integers are consecutive odd integers. Letting z represent the greatest of the four integers, it follows that $(z - 6) + (z - 4) + (z - 2) + z = 64$, from which a unique value of z can be determined; SUFFICIENT.

(2) Letting w, x, y, and z represent four different odd integers, where $w < x < y < z$, this indicates that $z - w = 6$ or $w = z - 6$. This means that $x = z - 4$ and $y = z - 2$ since w, x, y, and z must be different odd integers and it must be true that $w < x < y < z$. From $w + x + y + z = 64$, it follows that $(z - 6) + (z - 4) + (z - 2) + z = 64$ from which a unique value of z can be determined; SUFFICIENT.

**The correct answer is D;
each statement alone is sufficient.**

DS13130
415. Was the number of books sold at Bookstore X last week greater than the number of books sold at Bookstore Y last week?

(1) Last week, more than 1,000 books were sold at Bookstore X on Saturday and fewer than 1,000 books were sold at Bookstore Y on Saturday.

(2)   Last week, less than 20 percent of the books sold at Bookstore X were sold on Saturday and more than 20 percent of the books sold at Bookstore Y were sold on Saturday.

Arithmetic Inequalities

Determine if Bookstore X sold more books last week than Bookstore Y.

(1)   This indicates that Bookstore X sold more books on Saturday than Bookstore Y, but it gives no information about the numbers of books sold by the two bookstores on the other days of last week; NOT sufficient.

(2)   This gives information about the percents of the books sold last week that were sold on Saturday, but it gives no information about the actual numbers of books sold at the two bookstores last week. Therefore, a comparison of the numbers of books sold last week by Bookstore X and Bookstore Y is not possible; NOT sufficient.

Taking (1) and (2) together, if x represents the number of books that Bookstore X sold on Saturday and T_X represents the total number of books that Bookstore X sold last week, then $x > 1,000$ and $x < 0.2T_X$. It follows that $1,000 < 0.2T_X$ and so $T_X > 5,000$. Similarly, if y represents the number of books that Bookstore Y sold on Saturday and T_Y represents the total number of books that Bookstore Y sold last week, then $y < 1,000$ and $y > 0.2T_Y$. It follows that $0.2T_Y < 1,000$, and so $T_Y < 5,000$. Combining the inequalities gives $T_Y < 5,000 < T_X$, and so $T_Y < T_X$, which means that Bookstore X sold more books last week than Bookstore Y.

**The correct answer is C;
both statements together are sufficient.**

DS47651.01

416. A rectangular solid has length, width, and height of L cm, W cm, and H cm, respectively. If these dimensions are increased by x%, y%, and z%, respectively, what is the percentage increase in the total surface area of the solid?

(1) L, W, and H are in the ratios of 5:3:4.

(2) $x = 5$, $y = 10$, $z = 20$

Geometry Surface Area

The total surface area of a rectangular solid with dimensions l, w, and h is given by $2(lw + lh + wh)$.

(1)   This gives the relationships among the dimensions of the solid, but gives no information about the percentages by which the dimensions are increased; NOT sufficient.

(2)   This gives the percentages by which the dimensions are increased, but gives no information about the dimensions themselves; NOT sufficient.

Taking (1) and (2) together gives both the relationships among the dimensions and the percentages by which the dimensions are increased. From the ratios given in (1) and letting the constant of proportionality be 1, which causes no loss of generality, $L = 5$, $W = 3$, and $H = 4$. The dimensions of the enlarged solid can be determined by multiplying L by 1.05, W by 1.1, and H by 1.2. The percent increase in the surface area of the solid is given by

$$\frac{\text{SA of enlarged solid} - \text{SA of original solid}}{\text{SA of original solid}} \times 100,$$

where SA is short for surface area. The total surface area of the original solid and the enlarged solid can be determined by substituting their dimensions into the formula for total surface area. Thus, the percent increase can be determined. Note that it is not necessary to do the actual calculations.

**The correct answer is C;
both statements together are sufficient.**

DS08091.01

417. A certain list, L, contains a total of n numbers, not necessarily distinct, that are arranged in increasing order. If L_1 is the list consisting of the first n_1 numbers in L and L_2 is the list consisting of the last n_2 numbers in L, is 17 a mode for L?

(1)   17 is a mode for L_1 and 17 is a mode for L_2.

(2) $n_1 + n_2 = n$

Arithmetic Statistics

A mode for a list is the most frequently occurring member (or members) of the list. The table below shows all mode(s) for several lists and also shows that a list may have more than one mode.

List	Mode(s)
3, 5, 5, 8, 9	5
3, 5, 5, 8, 8	5, 8
5, 5, 8, 8, 8	8
3, 3, 3, 3, 3	3

(1) Given that 17 is a mode for L_1 and 17 is a mode for L_2, the examples below show three possibilities for L_1, L_2, and L when $n = 13$, where * denotes unspecified numbers not equal to 17 such that the numbers are arranged in increasing numerical order.

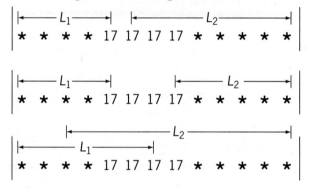

In each of these examples, one or more of the 17s belongs to each of L_1 and L_2. This must be the case because 17 is a mode for L_1 and thus 17 must belong to L_1, and similarly for L_2.

Also, none of the numbers less than 17 can appear more times in L_1 (and hence in L) than 17 appears in L_1, since 17 is a mode for L_1. Similarly, none of the numbers greater than 17 can appear more times in L_2 (and hence in L) than 17 appears in L_2. That is, 17 appears in L at least as many times as any number less than 17 appears in L, and 17 appears in L at least as many times as any number greater than 17 appears in L. Therefore, 17 appears in L at least as many times as any other number in L, and hence 17 is a mode for L; SUFFICIENT.

(2) Given that $n_1 + n_2 = n$, the first example below shows that 17 could be a mode for L and the second example below shows that 5 could be the (only) mode for L.

$$
\begin{array}{cccccccc}
\vert\!\leftarrow\!L_1\!\rightarrow\!\vert & & \vert\!\leftarrow\!\!\!\!&\!\!\!\!L_2\!\!\!\!&\!\!\!\!\rightarrow\!\vert \\
1 & 2 & 3 & 17 & 17 & 18 & 19
\end{array}
$$

$$
\begin{array}{cccccccc}
\vert\!\leftarrow\!L_1\!\rightarrow\!\vert & & \vert\!\leftarrow\!\!\!\!&\!\!\!\!L_2\!\!\!\!&\!\!\!\!\rightarrow\!\vert \\
5 & 5 & 5 & 16 & 17 & 18 & 19
\end{array}
$$

Therefore, it is possible that 17 is a mode for L and it is possible that 17 is not a mode for L; NOT sufficient.

The correct answer is A; statement 1 alone is sufficient.

DS04540

418. From May 1 to May 30 in the same year, the balance in a checking account increased. What was the balance in the checking account on May 30 ?

(1) If, during this period of time, the increase in the balance in the checking account had been 12 percent, then the balance in the account on May 30 would have been $504.

(2) During this period of time, the increase in the balance in the checking account was 8 percent.

Arithmetic Applied Problems; Percents

(1) Given that the amount on May 30 would have been $504 if the increase had been 12%, it follows that the amount on May 1 was $ $\dfrac{504}{1.12}$ = $450. However, the balance on May 30 cannot be determined because the (actual) percent increase is not given. For example, if the increase had been 10%, then the balance on May 30 would have been (1.1)($450) = $495, which is different from $504; NOT sufficient.

(2) Given that the increase was 8%, the amount on May 30 could be $108 (if the amount on May 1 was $100) and the amount on May 30 could be $216 (if the amount on May 1 was $200); NOT sufficient.

Taking (1) and (2) together, it follows that the amount on May 30 was ($450)(1.08) = $486.

**The correct answer is C;
both statements together are sufficient.**

DS08365

419. A merchant discounted the sale price of a coat and the sale price of a sweater. Which of the two articles of clothing was discounted by the greater dollar amount?

   (1) The percent discount on the coat was 2 percentage points greater than the percent discount on the sweater.

   (2) Before the discounts, the sale price of the coat was $10 less than the sale price of the sweater.

Arithmetic Applied Problems; Percents

   (1) Given that the discount on the coat was 2 percentage points greater than the discount on the sweater, the sweater could have been discounted by the greater dollar amount ($30 sweater with 10% discount is a discount of $3; $20 coat with 12% discount is a discount of $2.40) and the coat could have been discounted by the greater dollar amount ($110 sweater with 10% discount is a discount of $11; $100 coat with 12% discount is a discount of $12); NOT sufficient.

   (2) Given that the coat's sale price was $10 less than the sweater's sale price, the same examples used to show that (1) is not sufficient can be used for (2); NOT sufficient.

Taking (1) and (2) together is of no more help than either (1) or (2) taken separately because the same examples used to show that (1) is not sufficient also show that (2) is not sufficient.

**The correct answer is E;
both statements together are still not sufficient.**

DS01168

420. If the positive integer n is added to each of the integers 69, 94, and 121, what is the value of n?

   (1) 69 + n and 94 + n are the squares of two consecutive integers.

   (2) 94 + n and 121 + n are the squares of two consecutive integers.

Algebra Computation with Integers

   (1) Given that 69 + n and 94 + n are squares of consecutive integers and differ by 25 (that is, (94 + n) − (69 + n) = 25), look for consecutive integers whose squares differ by 25. It would be wise to start with 10^2 = 100 since 94 + n will be greater than 94.

10^2 = 100
           } difference is 21
11^2 = 121
           } difference is 23
12^2 = 144
           } difference is 25
13^2 = 169

Then, the consecutive integers whose squares differ by 25 are 69 + n = 144 and 94 + n = 169. The value of n can be determined from either equation.

To be sure that the value for n is unique, consider algebraically that the difference of the squares of consecutive integers is 25. So, $(x + 1)^2 − x^2 = 25$, from which it follows that $x^2 + 2x + 1 − x^2 = 25$ and $2x + 1 = 25$. This equation has a unique solution; SUFFICIENT.

   (2) Given that 94 + n and 121 + n are squares of consecutive integers and differ by 27 (that is, (121 + n) − (94+ n) = 27), look for consecutive integers whose squares differ by 27. It would be wise to start with 12^2 = 144 since 121 + n will be greater than 121.

12^2 = 144
           } difference is 25
13^2 = 169
           } difference is 27
14^2 = 196

Then, the consecutive integers whose squares differ by 27 are 94 + n = 169 and 121 + n = 196. The value of n can be determined from either equation; SUFFICIENT.

Tip: Since this and other such problems can be solved quickly using numbers, it might be helpful to have rapid recall of the perfect squares, possibly through 20^2.

**The correct answer is D;
each statement alone is sufficient.**

DS71521.01

421. If a merchant purchased a sofa from a manufacturer for $400 and then sold it, what was the selling price of the sofa?

(1) The selling price of the sofa was greater than 140 percent of the purchase price.

(2) The merchant's gross profit from the purchase and sale of the sofa was $\frac{1}{3}$ of the selling price.

Algebra Applied Problems

Letting s represent the selling price of the sofa, in dollars, determine the value of s.

(1) The condition that the selling price of the sofa was greater than 140 percent of the purchase price is equivalent to $s > 1.4(400)$, from which it is not possible to determine the selling price; NOT sufficient.

(2) Given that the gross profit from the purchase and sale of the sofa was $\frac{1}{3}$ of the selling price, it follows that $s - 400 = \frac{1}{3}s$ since gross profit is defined to be the selling price minus the purchase price. From this, a unique value of s can be determined; SUFFICIENT.

The correct answer is B; statement 2 alone is sufficient.

DS05269

422. Last year, in a certain housing development, the average (arithmetic mean) price of 20 new houses was $160,000. Did more than 9 of the 20 houses have prices that were less than the average price last year?

(1) Last year the greatest price of one of the 20 houses was $219,000.

(2) Last year the median of the prices of the 20 houses was $150,000.

Arithmetic Statistics

(1) Given that the greatest of the prices was $219,000, the table below shows two possibilities in which the average price was $160,000.

Example I		Example II	
price	frequency	price	frequency
$101,000	1	$119,000	1
$160,000	18	$159,000	18
$219,000	1	$219,000	1

In Example I, note that 101,000 + 219,000 = 320,000 = 160,000 + 160,000, so the sum of the prices is 20($160,000) and the average price is $160,000. Example II is then obtained from Example I by transferring $1,000 from each of the $160,000 prices to the $101,000 price, and thus the sum of the prices in Example II is also 20($160,000).

Example I shows that only 1 of the prices could have been less than the average price, and Example II shows that 19 of the prices could have been less than the average price; NOT sufficient.

(2) Given that the median of the 20 prices was $150,000, then when the prices are listed in numerical order from least to greatest, the average of the 10th and 11th prices is $150,000. Therefore, the 10th price must be less than or equal to $150,000, since if the 10th price was greater than $150,000, then both prices would be greater than $150,000 and their average would be greater than $150,000 (the median), contrary to what is given. Moreover, since the first 9 prices are less than or equal to the 10th price, it follows that the first 10 prices are each less than or equal to $150,000. Therefore, at least 10 of the prices are less than the average price; SUFFICIENT.

The correct answer is B; statement 2 alone is sufficient.

DS14527

423. For a certain city's library, the average cost of purchasing each new book is $28. The library receives $15,000 from the city each year; the library also receives a bonus of $2,000 if the total number of items checked out over the course of the year exceeds 5,000. Did the library receive the bonus last year?

(1)   The library purchased an average of 50 new books each month last year and received enough money from the city to cover this cost.

(2)   The lowest number of items checked out in one month was 459.

Arithmetic Applied Problems

(1)   Given that the library purchased an average of 50 new books each month, for the entire year the library purchased a total of $(50)(12) = 600$ books for a total cost of $(600)(\$28) = \$16,800$. Excluding any possible bonus, the library received \$15,000 from the city. Since this amount received from the city is not enough to cover the cost of the books, and the information provided in (1) says that the total amount received from the city was enough to cover the cost of the books, it follows that the library received a bonus; SUFFICIENT.

(2)   Given that the least number of books checked out in one month was 459, it follows that the total number of books checked out for the year was at least $(12)(459) = 5,508$. Since this is greater than 5,000, it follows that the total number of books checked out for the year was greater than 5,000 and the library received a bonus; SUFFICIENT.

The correct answer is D; each statement alone is sufficient.

DS89950.01

$$7, 9, 6, 4, 5, x$$

424.   If x is a number in the list above, what is the median of the list?

(1) $x > 7$

(2)   The median of the list equals the arithmetic mean of the list.

Arithmetic Statistics

(1)   The given numbers in the list, in order, are $4, 5, 6, 7, 9$. From (1), $x > 7$, so the list could be $4, 5, 6, 7, x, 9$ or the list could be $4, 5, 6, 7, 9, x$. In either case, the two middle numbers are 6 and 7 and the median is $\frac{6+7}{2} = \frac{13}{2}$; SUFFICIENT.

(2)   The mean of the list is $\frac{7+9+6+4+5+x}{6} = \frac{31+x}{6}$, which depends on the value of x. Likewise, the median depends on the value of x. If $x = 2$, then the list is $2, 4, 5, 6, 7, 9$, which has median $\frac{5+6}{2} = \frac{11}{2}$ and arithmetic mean $\frac{31+2}{6} = \frac{33}{6} = \frac{11}{2}$, thereby satisfying (2).

However, if $x = 8$, then the list is $4, 5, 6, 7, 8, 9$, which has median $\frac{6+7}{2} = \frac{13}{2}$ and arithmetic mean $\frac{31+8}{6} = \frac{39}{6} = \frac{13}{2}$, thereby satisfying (2); NOT sufficient.

The correct answer is A; statement 1 alone is sufficient.

DS15045

425.   Three dice, each of which has its 6 sides numbered 1 through 6, are tossed. The sum of the 3 numbers that are facing up is 12. Is at least 1 of these numbers 5 ?

(1)   None of the 3 numbers that are facing up is divisible by 3.

(2)   Of the numbers that are facing up, 2, but not all 3, are equal.

Arithmetic Properties of Integers

When three dice, each with its 6 faces numbered 1 through 6, are tossed and the sum of the three integers facing up is 12, the possible outcomes are $\{1, 5, 6\}, \{2, 4, 6\}, \{2, 5, 5\}, \{3, 3, 6\}, \{3, 4, 5\}$, and $\{4, 4, 4\}$. Determine if, in the outcome described, at least one of the numbers is 5.

(1)   This indicates that none of the numbers is divisible by three. The outcome could be $\{4, 4, 4\}$. In this case, none of the three numbers is 5. On the other hand, the outcome could be $\{2, 5, 5\}$. In this case, at least one of the numbers is 5; NOT sufficient.

(2)   This indicates that two of the numbers, but not all three, are equal. The outcome could be $\{3, 3, 6\}$. In this case, none of the three numbers is 5. On the other hand, the outcome could be $\{2, 5, 5\}$. In this case,

at least one of the numbers is 5; NOT sufficient.

Taking (1) and (2) together, of the possible outcomes {1, 5, 6}, {2, 4, 6}, {3, 3, 6}, and {3, 4, 5} are eliminated because they do not satisfy (1), and {4, 4, 4} is eliminated because it does not satisfy (2). This leaves only {2, 5, 5}, and at least one number is 5.

**The correct answer is C;
both statements together are sufficient.**

DS01324
426. On the number line, point R has coordinate r and point T has coordinate t. Is $t < 0$?

(1) $-1 < r < 0$

(2) The distance between R and T is equal to r^2.

Arithmetic Number Line

(1) This indicates that point R is between -1 and 0 on the number line, but gives no information about the location of the point T; NOT sufficient.

(2) This gives information about R and T in relation to one another, namely that the distance between them is r^2, but it gives no information about the actual location of T. Note that the distance between two points on the number line is the positive difference between their coordinates. Thus statement (2) gives $|r - t| = r^2$. Whether $t < 0$ is true cannot be determined; NOT sufficient.

Taking (1) and (2) together,

$$-1 < r < 0 \quad \text{given in (1)}$$
$$0 < r^2 < -r \quad \text{multiply by } r, \text{which is negative}$$
$$0 < |r - t| < -r \quad |r - t| = r^2 \text{ by (2)}$$
$$-(-r) < r - t < -r \quad \text{if } |a| < b, \text{then } -b < a < b$$
$$r < r - t < -r \quad -(-r) = r$$
$$0 < -t < -2r \quad \text{subtract } r$$
$$0 > t > 2r \quad \text{multiply by } -1$$

Therefore, $t < 0$. SUFFICIENT.

**The correct answer is C;
both statements together are sufficient.**

DS11210.02
427. Did the population of Town C increase by at least 100 percent from the year 2000 to the year 2010 ?

(1) The population of Town C in 2000 was $\frac{2}{3}$ of the population in 2005.

(2) The population of Town C increased by a greater number of people from 2005 to 2010 than it did from 2000 to 2005.

Algebra Percents

Determine whether the population of Town C increased by at least 100 percent from the year 2000 to the year 2010.

(1) Given that the population of Town C in 2000 was $\frac{2}{3}$ of the population in 2005, it is impossible to determine whether the population of Town C increased by at least 100 percent from the year 2000 to the year 2010 because no information is given that helps to determine the population in 2010; NOT sufficient.

(2) Given that the population of Town C increased by a greater number of people from 2005 to 2010 than it did from 2000 to 2005, it is not possible to determine whether the population of Town C increased by at least 100 percent from the year 2000 to the year 2010 because no information is given that helps determine the increase from 2000 to 2005; NOT sufficient.

Taking (1) and (2) together, from (1) the population in 2000 was $\frac{2}{3}$ of the population in 2005, so if P represents the population in 2005, then the population increase from 2000 to 2005 is $P - \frac{2}{3}P = \frac{1}{3}P$. From (2), the population increase from 2005 to 2010 was greater than $\frac{1}{3}P$, so the population increase from 2000 to 2010 was greater than $\frac{1}{3}P + \frac{1}{3}P = \frac{2}{3}P$. Thus, the percent increase from 2000 to 2010 is given by increase in population from 2000 to 2010 ÷ population in 2000, which

$$\frac{\text{increase in population from 2000 to 2010}}{\text{population in 2000}}, \text{which}$$

is greater than $\dfrac{\frac{2}{3}P}{\frac{2}{3}P} = 1$ or 100%.

**The correct answer is C;
both statements together are sufficient.**

DS06659

428. S is a set of points in the plane. How many distinct triangles can be drawn that have three of the points in S as vertices?

   (1)   The number of distinct points in S is 5.

   (2)   No three of the points in S are collinear.

Arithmetic Elementary Combinatorics

   (1)   Given that the number of points in S is 5, the number of triangles can be 0 (if the points are collinear) and the number of triangles can be greater than 0 (if the points are not all collinear); NOT sufficient.

   (2)   Given that no three points of S are collinear, the number of triangles can be 1 (if S consists of 3 points) and the number of triangles can be 4 (if S consists of 4 points); NOT sufficient.

Taking (1) and (2) together, the number of distinct triangles must be $\binom{5}{3} = \dfrac{5!}{3!(5-3)!} = 10$, which is the number of combinations of 5 points taken 3 at a time.

**The correct answer is C;
both statements together are sufficient.**

DS16078

429. Stores L and M each sell a certain product at a different regular price. If both stores discount their regular price of the product, is the discount price at Store M less than the discount price at Store L?

   (1)   At Store L the discount price is 10 percent less than the regular price; at Store M the discount price is 15 percent less than the regular price.

   (2)   At Store L the discount price is $5 less than the regular store price; at Store M the discount price is $6 less than the regular price.

Arithmetic Percents

Let L_r and L_d be the regular and discounted prices, respectively, at Store L, and let M_r and M_d be the regular and discounted prices, respectively, at Store M. Determine if $M_d < L_d$.

   (1)   Knowing that $L_d = (1 - 0.10)L_r = 0.90L_r$ and that $M_d = (1 - 0.15)M_r = 0.85M_r$ gives no information for comparing M_d and L_d; NOT sufficient.

   (2)   Knowing that $L_d = L_r - 5$ and that $M_d = M_r - 6$ gives no information for comparing M_d and L_d; NOT sufficient.

Taking (1) and (2) together gives $0.90L_r = L_r - 5$ and $0.85 M_r = M_r - 6$, from which it follows that $0.10L_r = 5$ or $L_r = 50$ and $0.15M_r = 6$ or $M_r = 40$. Then $L_d = 50 - 5 = 45$ and $M_d = 40 - 6 = 34$. Therefore, $M_d < L_d$.

**The correct answer is C;
both statements together are sufficient.**

DS16529

430. If d denotes a decimal, is $d \geq 0.5$?

   (1)   When d is rounded to the nearest tenth, the result is 0.5.

   (2)   When d is rounded to the nearest integer, the result is 1.

Arithmetic Rounding; Estimating

   (1)   In this case, for example, the value of d could range from the decimal 0.45 to 0.54. Some of these, such as 0.51 or 0.52, are greater than or equal to 0.5, and others, such as 0.47 or 0.48, are less than 0.5; NOT sufficient.

   (2)   When the result of rounding d to the nearest integer is 1, d could range in value from the decimal 0.50 to 1.49, which are greater than or equal to 0.5; SUFFICIENT.

**The correct answer is B;
statement 2 alone is sufficient.**

DS08231

431. In the two-digit integers 3■ and 2▲, the symbols ■ and ▲ represent different digits, and the product (3■)(2▲) is equal to 864. What digit does ■ represent?

   (1)   The sum of ■ and ▲ is 10.

   (2)   The product of ■ and ▲ is 24.

Arithmetic Properties of Numbers

(1) Given that the sum of the digits ■ and ▲ is 10, the table below shows the 9 possibilities for the digits ■ and ▲ with the corresponding values for the product ■▲.

(■,▲)	■ + ▲	■▲
(1,9) or (9,1)	10	9
(2,8) or (8,2)	10	16
(3,7) or (7,3)	10	21
(4,6) or (6,4)	**10**	**24**

Because the units digit of (3■)(2▲) is equal to the units digit of ■▲, it follows that (3■)(2▲) is equal to (34)(26) = 884 or (36)(24) = 864. Given that (3■)(2▲) = 864, ■ = 6; SUFFICIENT.

(2) Given that the product of the digits ■ and ▲ is 24, the table below shows the 4 possibilities for the digits ■ and ▲ with the corresponding values for the product ■▲.

(■,▲)	■▲	(3■)(2▲)
(3,8)	24	(33)(28) = 924
(4,6)	24	(34)(26) = 884
(6,4)	**24**	**(36)(24) = 864**
(8,3)	24	(38)(23) = 874

Given that (3■)(2▲) = 864, ■ = 6; SUFFICIENT.

The correct answer is D; each statement alone is sufficient.

DS07262

•——————————————— ℓ
    M

432. Two points, *N* and *Q* (not shown), lie to the right of point *M* on line ℓ. What is the ratio of the length of *QN* to the length of *MQ* ?

(1) Twice the length of *MN* is 3 times the length of *MQ*.
(2) Point *Q* is between points *M* and *N*.

Algebra Order

(1) Given that twice the length of *MN* is 3 times the length of *MQ*, it follows that the points are ordered from left to right as *M*, *Q*, and *N*. Thus, letting *MQ* = *x* and *QN* = *y*, it is given that $2(x + y) = 3x$ and

the value of $\frac{y}{x}$ is to be determined. The given equation can be rewritten as $2x + 2y = 3x$, or $2y = x$, or $\frac{y}{x} = \frac{1}{2}$; SUFFICIENT.

(2) Given that *Q* is between *M* and *N*, the ratio of *QN* to *MQ* can be close to zero (if *Q* and *N* are close together and both far from *M*) and the ratio of *QN* to *MQ* can be large (if *M* and *Q* are close together and both far from *N*); NOT sufficient.

The correct answer is A; statement 1 alone is sufficient.

DS05639

433. Did the sum of the prices of three shirts exceed $60 ?

(1) The price of the most expensive of the shirts exceeded $30.
(2) The price of the least expensive of the shirts exceeded $20.

Arithmetic Applied Problems

(1) Given that the price of the most expensive shirt exceeded $30, the sum of the prices of the shirts can be under $60 (if the prices were $10, $10, and $35) and the sum of the prices of the shirts can be over $60 (if the prices were $10, $10, and $50); NOT sufficient.

(2) Given that the price of the least expensive shirt exceeded $20, it follows that the sum of the prices of the shirts exceeds 3($20) = $60; SUFFICIENT.

The correct answer is B; statement 2 alone is sufficient.

DS03057

434. What is the total number of coins that Bert and Claire have?

(1) Bert has 50 percent more coins than Claire.
(2) The total number of coins that Bert and Claire have is between 21 and 28.

Arithmetic Computation with Integers

Determine the total number of coins Bert and Claire have. If *B* represents the number of coins that Bert has and *C* represents the number of coins that Claire has, determine *B* + *C*.

(1) Bert has 50% more coins than Claire, so $B = 1.5C$, and $B + C = 1.5C + C = 2.5C$, but the value of C can vary; NOT sufficient.

(2) The total number of coins Bert and Claire have is between 21 and 28, so $21 < B + C < 28$ and, therefore, $B + C$ could be 22, 23, 24, 25, 26, or 27; NOT sufficient.

Taking (1) and (2) together, $21 < 2.5C < 28$ and then $\dfrac{21}{2.5} < C < \dfrac{28}{2.5}$ or $8.4 < C < 11.2$.

If $C = 9$, then $B = (1.5)(9) = 13.5$; if $C = 10$, then $B = (1.5)(10) = 15$; and if $C = 11$, then $B = (1.5)(11) = 16.5$. Since B represents a number of coins, B is an integer. Therefore, $B = 15$, $C = 10$, and $B + C = 25$.

The correct answer is C;
both statements together are sufficient.

DS05668

435. A telephone station has x processors, each of which can process a maximum of y calls at any particular time, where x and y are positive integers. If 500 calls are sent to the station at a particular time, can the station process all of the calls?

(1) $x = 600$
(2) $100 < y < 200$

Algebra Applied Problems

At a particular time, the telephone station can process a maximum of xy calls, where x and y are positive integers. Determine whether $xy \geq 500$.

(1) Given that $x = 600$, it follows that $xy \geq 600$ since $y \geq 1$ (y is a positive integer); SUFFICIENT.

(2) Given that $100 < y < 200$, $xy < 500$ is possible (if $x = 3$ and $y = 150$) and $xy \geq 500$ is possible (if $x = 10$ and $y = 150$); NOT sufficient.

The correct answer is A;
statement 1 alone is sufficient.

	Price per Flower
Roses	$1.00
Daisies	$0.50

DS07953

436. Kim and Sue each bought some roses and some daisies at the prices shown above. If Kim bought the same total number of roses and daisies as Sue, was the price of Kim's purchase of roses and daisies higher than the price of Sue's purchase of roses and daisies?

(1) Kim bought twice as many daisies as roses.
(2) Kim bought 4 more roses than Sue bought.

Algebra Applied Problems

Let R_K be the number of roses that Kim bought, let R_S be the number of roses that Sue bought, and let T be the total number of roses and daisies each bought. Then Kim bought $(T - R_K)$ daisies and Sue bought $(T - R_S)$ daisies.

For the roses and daisies, Kim paid a total of $\$[R_K + \frac{1}{2}(T - R_K)] = \$\frac{1}{2}(R_K + T)$ and Sue paid a total of $\$[R_S + \frac{1}{2}(T - R_S)] = \$\frac{1}{2}(R_S + T)$.

Determine whether $\frac{1}{2}(R_K + T) > \frac{1}{2}(R_S + T)$, or equivalently, determine whether $R_K > R_S$.

(1) Given that $T - R_K = 2R_K$, or $T = 3R_K$, it is not possible to determine whether $R_K > R_S$ because no information is provided about the value of R_S; NOT sufficient.

(2) Given that $R_K = R_S + 4$, it follows that $R_K > R_S$; SUFFICIENT.

The correct answer is B;
statement 2 alone is sufficient.

DS14406

437. Jazz and blues recordings accounted for 6 percent of the $840 million revenue from the sales of recordings in Country Y in 2000. What was the revenue from the sales of jazz and blues recordings in Country Y in 1998?

(1) Jazz and blues recordings accounted for 5 percent of the revenue from the sales of recordings in Country Y in 1998.

(2) The revenue from the sales of jazz and blues recordings in Country Y increased by 40 percent from 1998 to 2000.

Arithmetic Percents

It is given that jazz and blues recordings accounted for 6% of the $840 million revenue of recordings in Country Y in 2000. Determine the revenue from the sales of jazz and blues recordings in 1998.

(1) This indicates that jazz and blues recordings accounted for 5% of the revenue from the sales of recordings in Country Y in 1998. However, no information is given to indicate what the revenue from the sales of recordings was in 1998. Therefore, the revenue from sales of jazz and blues recordings in 1998 cannot be determined; NOT sufficient.

(2) This indicates that the revenue from the sales of jazz and blues recordings in Country Y increased by 40% from 1998 to 2000. Letting R_{1998} and R_{2000} represent the revenue from the sales of jazz and blues recordings in 1998 and 2000, respectively, then $R_{2000} = 1.4R_{1998}$, and so $(0.06)(\$840 \text{ million}) = 1.4R_{1998}$, from which R_{1998} can be determined; SUFFICIENT.

The correct answer is B; statement 2 alone is sufficient.

DS06315

438. On a certain nonstop trip, Marta averaged x miles per hour for 2 hours and y miles per hour for the remaining 3 hours. What was her average speed, in miles per hour, for the entire trip?

(1) $2x + 3y = 280$

(2) $y = x + 10$

Algebra Rate Problems

Marta traveled a total of $(2x + 3y)$ miles in

$2 + 3 = 5$ hours for an average speed

of $\left(\dfrac{2x+3y}{5}\right)$ miles per hour. Determine the value

of $\dfrac{2x+3y}{5}$.

(1) Given that $2x + 3y = 280$, it follows that $\dfrac{2x+3y}{5} = \dfrac{280}{5}$; SUFFICIENT.

(2) Given that $y = x + 10$, it follows that $\dfrac{2x+3y}{5} = \dfrac{2x+3(x+10)}{5} = x + 6.$

Therefore, the value of $\dfrac{2x+3y}{5}$ can be 56 (if $x = 50$ and $y = 60$) and the value of $\dfrac{2x+3y}{5}$ can be 61 (if $x = 55$ and $y = 65$); NOT sufficient.

The correct answer is A; statement 1 alone is sufficient.

DS12730

439. If x is a positive integer, what is the value of $\sqrt{x+24} - \sqrt{x}$?

(1) $\sqrt{x}$ is an integer.

(2) $\sqrt{x+24}$ is an integer.

Arithmetic Operations with Radicals

Determine the value of $\sqrt{x+24} - \sqrt{x}$.

(1) This says $\sqrt{x}$ is an integer, so x is a perfect square. Because there are infinitely many perfect squares, it would seem reasonable that $\sqrt{x+24} - \sqrt{x}$, cannot be uniquely determined. The table below verifies this; NOT sufficient.

x	$\sqrt{x}$	$\sqrt{x+24}$	$\sqrt{x+24} - \sqrt{x}$
1	1	$\sqrt{25} = 5$	4
25	5	$\sqrt{49} = 7$	2

(2) This says $\sqrt{x+24}$ is an integer, so $x + 24$ is a perfect square. Because there are infinitely many perfect squares, it would seem reasonable that $\sqrt{x+24} - \sqrt{x}$, cannot be uniquely determined. The table below verifies this; NOT sufficient.

$\sqrt{x+24}$	x	$\sqrt{x}$	$\sqrt{x+24} - \sqrt{x}$
$5 = \sqrt{1+24}$	1	1	4
$7 = \sqrt{25+24}$	25	5	2

Taking (1) and (2) together, $x = 1$ and $x = 25$ satisfy both (1) and (2) but give different values for $\sqrt{x+24} - \sqrt{x}$, the value of $\sqrt{x+24} - \sqrt{x}$ cannot be uniquely determined.

The correct answer is E; both statements together are still not sufficient.

DS13982

440. A tank is filled with gasoline to a depth of exactly 2 feet. The tank is a cylinder resting horizontally on its side, with its circular ends oriented vertically. The inside of the tank is exactly 6 feet long. What is the volume of the gasoline in the tank?

(1) The inside of the tank is exactly 4 feet in diameter.

(2) The top surface of the gasoline forms a rectangle that has an area of 24 square feet.

Geometry Cylinders; Volume

(1) Given that the diameter of the cylindrical tank is 4 ft, it follows that its radius is 2 ft. Therefore, the radius and height of the cylindrical tank are known, and hence its volume can be determined: $\pi r^2 h = \pi(2)^2(4)$ ft³. Since the tank is filled with gasoline to a depth of 2 ft, exactly half of the tank is filled with gasoline, and thus the volume of the gasoline can be determined; SUFFICIENT.

(2) Given that the top surface of the gasoline forms a rectangle with area 24 ft², the figure below shows that the diameter of the cylindrical tank is 4 ft, and therefore the volume of the gasoline can be determined. Note that the figure below shows that it is not possible for LESS than half of the tank to be filled with gasoline (that is, it is not possible for the diameter to be less than 4 ft) and it is not possible for MORE than half of the tank to be filled with gasoline (that is, it is not possible for the diameter to be greater than 4 ft).

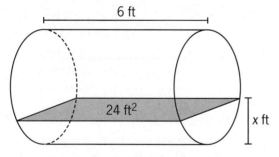

Less than half filled is not possible: The first figure in the right column shows a circular vertical cross-section of the cylindrical tank, where O is the center, r ft is the radius, and $\overline{AC}$ marks the location of the top surface of the gasoline.

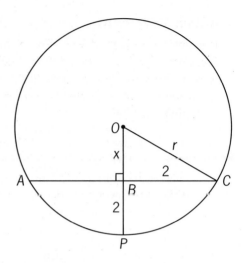

Because the depth of the gasoline is 2 ft, we have $BP = 2$. Because the surface of the gasoline forms a rectangle with area 24 ft² and length 6 ft, it follows that the width of the rectangle is 4 ft (that is, $AC = 4$), and hence $BC = 2$. From $OP = OB + BP$ it follows that $r = x + 2$ and from $\triangle OBC$ it follows that $r < x + 2$. Since r cannot be simultaneously equal to $x + 2$ and less than $x + 2$, the case in which the tank is less than half filled with gasoline is not possible.

More than half filled is not possible: The figure below shows a circular vertical cross-section of the cylindrical tank, where O is the center, r ft is the radius, and $\overline{A'C'}$ marks the location of the top surface of the gasoline.

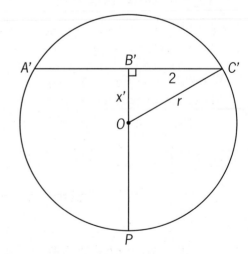

Because the depth of the gasoline is 2 ft, we have $B'P = 2$. Because the surface of the gasoline forms a rectangle with area 24 ft² and length 6 ft, it follows that the width of the rectangle is 4 ft (that is, $A'C' = 4$), and hence $B'C' = 2$. From $B'P = B'O + OP$ it follows that $2 = x' + r$ and from $\triangle OB'C'$ it follows that $2 < r$. Since 2 cannot be simultaneously equal to $x' + r$ and less than r, the case in which the tank is more than half filled with gasoline is not possible.

The above analysis shows that the diameter of the cylindrical tank is 4 ft, and therefore the volume of the gasoline can be determined as in (1) above; SUFFICIENT.

The correct answer is D; each statement alone is sufficient.

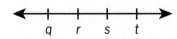

DS16197

441. Of the four numbers represented on the number line above, is r closest to zero?

(1) $q = -s$

(2) $-t < q$

Algebra Order

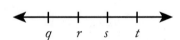

Referring to the figure above, in which it may be assumed that $q, r, s,$ and t are different numbers, determine if r is closest to 0.

(1) Since $q = -s$, one of q and s is positive and the other is negative. Since s is to the right of q, then s is positive and q is negative. Also, 0 is halfway between q and s, so q and s are the same distance from 0. If $r = 0$, then, of $q, r, s,$ and t, r is closest to 0 because it IS 0. If $r \neq 0$ then either (i) $q < 0 < r < s < t$ or (ii) $q < r < 0 < s < t$.

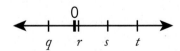

(i) If $q < 0 < r < s < t$, as shown above, r is closer to 0 than s is because r is between 0 and s, and r is clearly closer to 0 than t is because t is farther away from 0 than s is. Also, since q and s are the same distance from 0 and r is closer to

0 than s is, then r is closer to 0 than q is. Therefore, r is closest to 0.

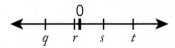

(ii) If $q < r < 0 < s < t$, as shown above, r is closer to 0 than q is because r is between 0 and q. Also, r is closer to 0 than s is because r is closer to 0 than q is and q and s are the same distance from 0. Moreover, r is closer to 0 than t is because t is farther away from 0 than s is. Therefore, r is closest to 0.

In each case, r is closest to 0; SUFFICIENT.

(2) If $-t < q$, then $-t$ is to the left of q. If $t = 5, s = 4, r = 3,$ and $q = -2$, then $-5 < -2$, so (2) is satisfied. In this case, q is closest to 0. On the other hand, if $t = 5, s = 4, r = -1,$ and $q = -2$, then $-5 < -2$, so (2) is satisfied, but r is closest to 0; NOT sufficient.

The correct answer is A; statement 1 alone is sufficient.

DS18414

442. A group consisting of several families visited an amusement park where the regular admission fees were ¥5,500 for each adult and ¥4,800 for each child. Because there were at least 10 people in the group, each paid an admission fee that was 10% less than the regular admission fee. How many children were in the group?

(1) The total of the admission fees paid for the adults in the group was ¥29,700.

(2) The total of the admission fees paid for the children in the group was ¥4,860 more than the total of the admission fees paid for the adults in the group.

Arithmetic Simultaneous Equations

Determine the number of children in a group of at least 10 people who visited an amusement park.

(1) This indicates that $(0.9)(5,500)A = 29,700$, where A represents the number of adults in the group. From this, the number of adults can be determined. However, the number of children in the group cannot be determined without additional information about the

exact number of people in the group; NOT sufficient.

(2) If C and A represent the numbers of children and adults, respectively, in the group, this indicates that $(0.9)(4,800)C = (0.9)(5,500)A + 4,860$, or $48C = 55A + 54$, or $48C - 55A = 54$, which is a single equation with two variables from which unique values of C and A cannot be determined, even under the assumptions that C and A are integers such that $C + A \geq 10$. For example, the values of C and A could be 8 and 6, respectively, since $(48)(8) - (55)(6) = 54$, or the values of C and A could be 63 and 54, respectively, since $(48)(63) - (55)(54) = 54$; NOT sufficient.

Taking (1) and (2) together, it follows that

$$A = \frac{29,700}{(0.9)(5,500)} = 6 \text{ and}$$

$$C = \frac{(0.9)(5,500)(6) + 4,860}{(0.9)(4,800)} = 8.$$

The correct answer is C; both statements together are sufficient.

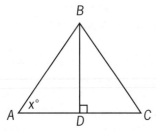

DS16536

443. What is the area of triangular region ABC above?

(1) The product of BD and AC is 20.

(2) $x = 45$

Geometry Triangles; Area

The area of $\triangle ABC = \dfrac{BD \times AC}{2}$.

(1) The product of BD and AC is given as 20, so the area of $\triangle ABC$ is $\dfrac{20}{2}$ or 10; SUFFICIENT.

(2) With the measurement of x being 45, it is concluded that $\triangle ABD$ is a 45°–45°–90° right triangle, where the length of side BD is equal to the length of side AD. However, with no lengths of any side known, there

is not enough information to calculate the area; NOT sufficient.

The correct answer is A; statement 1 alone is sufficient.

DS05265

444. In the xy-coordinate plane, is point R equidistant from points $(-3,-3)$ and $(1,-3)$?

(1) The x-coordinate of point R is -1.

(2) Point R lies on the line $y = -3$.

Algebra Coordinate Geometry

(1) Since the x-coordinate of R is -1, R lies on the line with equation $x = -1$. The figure below shows points $A(-3,-3)$ and $B(1,-3)$, the line $x = -1$, and R with x-coordinate -1 and arbitrary y-coordinate y.

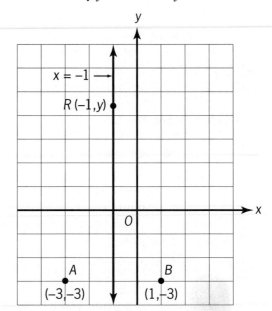

Since the point $(-1,-3)$ is the midpoint of the horizontal segment $\overline{AB}$ and the vertical line $x = -1$ contains $(-1,-3)$, the line $x = -1$ is the perpendicular bisector of $\overline{AB}$. Every point on the perpendicular of $\overline{AB}$ is equidistant from A and B. Since R is on the line $x = -1$, R is equidistant from A and B.

Alternatively, by the distance formula, the distance between $(-3,-3)$ and R is

$$\sqrt{\left(-3-(-1)\right)^2 + (-3-y)^2} = \sqrt{(-2)^2 + (-3-y)^2}$$
$$= \sqrt{4 + (-3-y)^2}$$

Also by the distance formula, the distance between $(1,-3)$ and R is

$$\sqrt{(1-(-1))^2+(-3-y)^2} = \sqrt{2^2+(-3-y)^2}$$
$$= \sqrt{4+(-3-y)^2}$$

Since the distance between $(-3,-3)$ and R is the same as the distance between $(1,-3)$ and R, it follows that R is equidistant from $(-3,-3)$ and $(1,-3)$; SUFFICIENT.

(2)   Given that R is on the line $y = -3$, the y-coordinate of R is -3. Since the x-coordinate of R is not specified, R could be at multiple locations on the line $y = -3$, as shown in the chart and figure below; NOT sufficient.

x-coordinate	distance from $(-3,-3)$	distance from $(1,-3)$	equidistant?
−1	2	2	yes
3	6	2	no

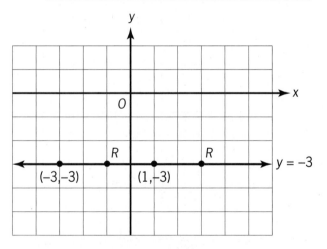

**The correct answer is A;
statement 1 alone is sufficient.**

DS09603
445. What is the ratio of the average (arithmetic mean) height of students in class X to the average height of students in class Y ?

(1)   The average height of the students in class X is 120 centimeters.

(2)   The average height of the students in class X and class Y combined is 126 centimeters.

Arithmetic Statistics

(1)   Given that the average height of the students in class X is 120 cm, but given no information about the average height of the students in class Y, the desired ratio cannot be determined; NOT sufficient.

(2)   Given that the average height of the students in class X and class Y combined is 126 cm, the ratio of the averages of the individual classes cannot be determined. For example, if class X consists of 10 students, each of whom has height 120 cm, and class Y consists of 10 students, each of whom has height 132 cm, then the average height of the students in class X and class Y combined is $\dfrac{10(120)+10(132)}{20} = 126$ cm and the ratio of the averages of the individual classes is $\dfrac{120}{132}$. However, if class X consists of 10 students, each of whom has height 120 cm and class Y consists of 20 students, each of whom has height 129 cm, then the average height of the students in class X and class Y combined is $\dfrac{10(120)+20(129)}{30} = 126$ cm and the ratio of the averages of the individual classes is $\dfrac{120}{129}$; NOT sufficient.

Taking (1) and (2) together is of no more help than either (1) or (2) taken separately because the same examples used to show that (2) is not sufficient include the information from (1).

**The correct answer is E;
both statements together are still not sufficient.**

DS04631
446. Is the positive two-digit integer N less than 40 ?

(1)   The units digit of N is 6 more than the tens digit.

(2) N is 4 less than 4 times the units digit.

Arithmetic Place Value

Determine if the two-digit integer N is less than 40. Letting the tens digit be t and the units digit be u, then $N = 10t + u$. Determine if $10t + u < 40$.

(1) Given that $u = t + 6$, then
$N = 10t + (t + 6) = 11t + 6$. Since u is a digit,
$u = t + 6 \leq 9$, so $t \leq 3$. Therefore,
$N = 11t + 6 \leq 11(3) + 6 = 39$;
SUFFICIENT.

(2) Given that $N = 4u - 4$, then since u is a
digit and $u \leq 9$, it follows that
$N = 4u - 4 \leq 4(9) - 4 = 32$; SUFFICIENT.

**The correct answer is D;
each statement alone is sufficient.**

DS06318
447. If $2^{x + y} = 4^8$, what is the value of y?

(1) $x^2 = 81$

(2) $x - y = 2$

Algebra Exponents

Since $4^8 = (2^2)^8 = 2^{16}$, the equation $2^{x + y} = 4^8$
becomes $2^{x + y} = 2^{16}$, which is equivalent to
$x + y = 16$

(1) Given that $x^2 = 81$, then both $x = 9$ and
$x = -9$ are possible. Therefore, $y = 7$ is possible
(choose $x = 9$) and $y = 25$ is possible (choose
$x = -9$); NOT sufficient.

(2) Given that $x - y = 2$, it follows that
$-x + y = -2$. Adding the last equation
to $x + y = 16$ gives $2y = 14$, or $y = 7$;
SUFFICIENT.

**The correct answer is B;
statement 2 alone is sufficient.**

DS03680
448. Each week a certain salesman is paid a fixed amount
equal to $300, plus a commission equal to 5 percent of
the amount of his sales that week over $1,000. What is
the total amount the salesman was paid last week?

(1) The total amount the salesman was paid last
week is equal to 10 percent of the amount of his
sales last week.

(2) The salesman's sales last week totaled $5,000.

Algebra Applied Problems

Let P be the salesman's pay for last week and let S be
the amount of his sales last week. Then $P = 300 +
0.05(S - 1,000)$. Determine the value of P.

(1) Given $P = 0.10S$, then $0.10S =
300 + 0.05(S - 1,000)$. This equation can

be solved for a unique value of S, from
which the value of P can be determined;
SUFFICIENT.

(2) Given $S = 5,000$, then $P =
300 + 0.05(5,000 - 1,000)$; SUFFICIENT.

**The correct answer is D;
each statement alone is sufficient.**

DS01383
449. At a bakery, all donuts are priced equally and all bagels
are priced equally. What is the total price of 5 donuts
and 3 bagels at the bakery?

(1) At the bakery, the total price of 10 donuts and
6 bagels is $12.90.

(2) At the bakery, the price of a donut is $0.15 less
than the price of a bagel.

Algebra Simultaneous Equations

Let x be the price, in dollars, of each donut and
let y be the price, in dollars, of each bagel. Find
the value of $5x + 3y$.

(1) Given that $10x + 6y = 12.90$, since
$5x + 3y = \frac{1}{2}(10x + 6y)$, it follows that
$5x + 3y = \frac{1}{2}(12.90)$; SUFFICIENT.

(2) Given that $x = y - 0.15$, then $5x + 3y =
5(y - 0.15) + 3y = 8y - 0.75$, which varies as
y varies; NOT sufficient.

**The correct answer is A;
statement 1 alone is sufficient.**

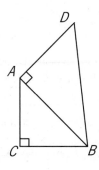

DS06869
450. In the figure above, is the area of triangular region
ABC equal to the area of triangular region DBA?

(1) $(AC)^2 = 2(AD)^2$

(2) $\triangle ABC$ is isosceles.

Geometry Triangles; Area

(1) Given that $(AC)^2 = 2(AD)^2$, the table below shows two possible assignments for the 5 side lengths in the figure above. The Pythagorean theorem can be used to verify the values given for AB and BD.

AC	AD	BC	AB	BD
$\sqrt{2}$	1	$\sqrt{2}$	2	$\sqrt{5}$
$\sqrt{2}$	1	1	$\sqrt{3}$	2

For the first row, the area of $\triangle ABC$ is $\frac{1}{2}(\sqrt{2})(\sqrt{2}) = 1$, the area of $\triangle DBA$ is $\frac{1}{2}(1)(2) = 1$, and the areas are equal.

For the second row the area of $\triangle ABC$ is $\frac{1}{2}(\sqrt{2})(1) = \frac{1}{2}\sqrt{2}$, the area of $\triangle DBA$ is $\frac{1}{2}(1)(\sqrt{3}) = \frac{1}{2}\sqrt{3}$, and the areas are not equal; NOT sufficient.

(2) Given that $\triangle ABC$ is an isosceles triangle, the first row in the table above shows that $\triangle ABC$ and $\triangle DBA$ can have the same area. To show that $\triangle ABC$ and $\triangle DBA$ can have different areas, consider the figure below, where A, B, C, and D are positioned so that $\triangle ABC$ is isosceles and $\triangle ABC$ and $\triangle DBA$ have different areas; NOT sufficient.

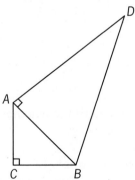

Taking (1) and (2) together, as shown in the figure below, let $AC = BC = x$ be the length of the legs of $\triangle ABC$. Using the Pythagorean theorem for $\triangle ABC$, it follows that $AB = \sqrt{2}x$. Using $(AC)^2 = 2(AD)^2$, it follows that $x^2 = 2(AD)^2$, or $AD = \frac{x}{\sqrt{2}}$. Therefore, the area of $\triangle ABC$ is $\frac{1}{2}x^2$ and the area of $\triangle DBA$ is $\frac{1}{2}\left(\frac{1}{\sqrt{2}}x\right)(\sqrt{2}x) = \frac{1}{2}x^2$, and the areas are equal.

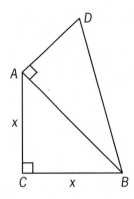

The correct answer is C; both statements together are sufficient.

DS08105

451. If r and s are positive integers, can the fraction $\frac{r}{s}$ be expressed as a decimal with only a finite number of nonzero digits?

(1) s is a factor of 100.

(2) r is a factor of 100.

Arithmetic Properties of Numbers

(1) It is given that s is a factor of 100, then $s = 1$, 2, 4, 5, 10, 20, 25, 50, or 100. Multiply the numerator and denominator of $\frac{r}{s}$, where s is one of the factors of 100, by 1 according to the following chart.

If s is equal to	then multiply $\frac{r}{s}$ by	to get
1	$1 = \frac{100}{100}$	$\frac{100r}{100}$
2	$1 = \frac{50}{50}$	$\frac{50r}{100}$
4	$1 = \frac{25}{25}$	$\frac{25r}{100}$
5	$1 = \frac{20}{20}$	$\frac{20r}{100}$
10	$1 = \frac{10}{10}$	$\frac{10r}{100}$
20	$1 = \frac{5}{5}$	$\frac{5r}{100}$
25	$1 = \frac{4}{4}$	$\frac{4r}{100}$
50	$1 = \frac{2}{2}$	$\frac{2r}{100}$
100	$1 = \frac{1}{1}$	$\frac{r}{100}$

In each case, the resulting fraction is a multiple of r divided by 100, and the decimal representation will have a finite number of nonzero digits. For example, if $\frac{r}{s} = \frac{3}{25}$, use $1 = \frac{4}{4}$. Then $\frac{3}{25} \times \frac{4}{4} = \frac{12}{100} = 0.12$, which has only a finite number of nonzero digits; SUFFICIENT.

(2) It is given that r is a factor of 100, then $r = 1, 2, 4, 5, 10, 20, 25, 50,$ or 100. If $r = 4$ and $s = 5$, then $\frac{r}{s} = \frac{4}{5} = 0.8$, which has only a finite number of nonzero digits. However, if $r = 5$, and $s = 6$, then $\frac{r}{s} = \frac{5}{6} = 0.83333333...$, which does not have a finite number of nonzero digits; NOT sufficient.

The correct answer is A;
statement 1 alone is sufficient.

DS16384
452. If $r > 0$ and $s > 0$, is $\frac{r}{s} < \frac{s}{r}$?

(1) $\frac{r}{3s} = \frac{1}{4}$

(2) $s = r + 4$

Algebra Ratios

Given positive numbers r and s, determine if $\frac{r}{s} < \frac{s}{r}$.

(1) If $\frac{r}{3s} = \frac{1}{4}$, then $\frac{r}{s} = \frac{3}{4}$, $\frac{s}{r} = \frac{4}{3}$, and so $\frac{r}{s} < \frac{s}{r}$, since $\frac{3}{4} < \frac{4}{3}$; SUFFICIENT.

(2) If $s = r + 4$, then $\frac{r}{s} = \frac{r}{r+4}$ and $\frac{s}{r} = \frac{r+4}{r}$. Since $r + 4 > r$, $\frac{r}{r+4} < 1$ and $\frac{r+4}{r} > 1$, so $\frac{r}{s} < \frac{s}{r}$; SUFFICIENT.

The correct answer is D;
each statement alone is sufficient.

DS06789
453. If k is an integer such that $56 < k < 66$, what is the value of k ?

(1) If k were divided by 2, the remainder would be 1.

(2) If $k + 1$ were divided by 3, the remainder would be 0.

Arithmetic Properties of Integers

Determine the value of the integer k, where $56 < k < 66$.

(1) It is given that the remainder is 1 when k is divided by 2, which implies that k is odd. Therefore, the value of k can be $57, 59, 61, 63,$ or 65; NOT sufficient.

(2) It is given that the remainder is 0 when $k + 1$ is divided by 3, which implies that $k + 1$ is divisible by 3. Since $56 < k < 66$ (equivalently, $57 < k + 1 < 67$), the value of $k + 1$ can be $60, 63,$ or 66 so the value of k can be $59, 62,$ or 65; NOT sufficient.

Taking (1) and (2) together, 59 and 65 appear in both lists of possible values for k; NOT sufficient.

The correct answer is E;
both statements together are still not sufficient.

DS13965
454. If x is a positive integer, then is x prime?

(1) $3x + 1$ is prime.

(2) $5x + 1$ is prime.

Arithmetic Properties of Numbers

Determine if the positive integer x is prime.

(1) This indicates that $3x + 1$ is prime. If $x = 2$, then $3x + 1 = 7$ is prime and so is x. However, if $x = 6$, then $3x + 1 = 19$ is prime, but 6 is not prime; NOT sufficient.

(2) This indicates that $5x + 1$ is prime. If $x = 2$, then $5x + 1 = 11$ is prime and so is x. However, if $x = 6$, then $5x + 1 = 31$ is prime, but 6 is not prime; NOT sufficient.

Because the same examples were used to establish that neither (1) nor (2) is sufficient, it is not possible to determine whether x is prime from the given information.

The correct answer is E;
both statements together are still not sufficient.

$$k, n, 12, 6, 17$$

DS00172
455. What is the value of n in the list above?

(1) $k < n$

(2) The median of the numbers in the list is 10.

Arithmetic Statistics

Given the list $k, n, 12, 6, 17$, determine the value of n.

(1) Although $k < n$, no information is given about the value of k or n; NOT sufficient.

(2) Since the median of the numbers in the list is 10 and there are 5 numbers in the list, 10 is one of those 5 numbers. Therefore, $n = 10$ or $k = 10$. If $n = 10$, then the value of n has been determined. However, if $k = 10$, then n can be any number that is 10 or less, so the value of n cannot be determined; NOT sufficient.

Taking (1) and (2) together, if $k < n$ and the median of the list is 10, then 12 and 17 are to the right of the median and the list in ascending order is either $6, k, n, 12, 17$ or $k, 6, n, 12, 17$. In either case, n is the middle number, and since the median is 10, $n = 10$.

**The correct answer is C;
both statements together are sufficient.**

DS07508
456. If x and y are integers, what is the value of $x + y$?

(1) $3 < \dfrac{x+y}{2} < 4$

(2) $2 < x < y < 5$

Arithmetic Computation with Integers

Determine the value of $x + y$ for integers x and y.

(1) Given that $3 < \dfrac{x+y}{2} < 4$, then $6 < x + y < 8$. Since $x + y$ is an integer and 7 is the only integer greater than 6 and less than 8, it follows that the value of $x + y$ is 7; SUFFICIENT.

(2) Given that $2 < x < y < 5$, then $2 < x < 5$, and hence $x = 3$ or $x = 4$. Likewise, $2 < y < 5$, and hence $y = 3$ or $y = 4$. With the additional restriction that $x < y$, it follows that $x = 3$ and $y = 4$, and thus $x + y = 7$; SUFFICIENT.

**The correct answer is D;
each statement alone is sufficient.**

DS00764
457. Last year, if Arturo spent a total of $12,000 on his mortgage payments, real estate taxes, and home

insurance, how much did he spend on his real estate taxes?

(1) Last year, the total amount that Arturo spent on his real estate taxes and home insurance was $33\dfrac{1}{3}$ percent of the amount that he spent on his mortgage payments.

(2) Last year, the amount that Arturo spent on his real estate taxes was 20 percent of the total amount he spent on his mortgage payments and home insurance.

Arithmetic Applied Problems

Let M, R, and H be the amounts that Arturo spent last year on mortgage payments, real estate taxes, and home insurance, respectively. Given that $M + R + H = 12,000$, determine the value of R.

(1) Given that $R + H = \dfrac{1}{3}M$ and $M + R + H = 12,000$, then $M + \dfrac{1}{3}M = 12,000$, or $M = 9,000$. However, the value of R cannot be determined, since it is possible that $R = 2,000$ (use $M = 9,000$ and $H = 1,000$) and it is possible that $R = 1,000$ (use $M = 9,000$ and $H = 2,000$); NOT sufficient.

(2) Given that $R = \dfrac{1}{5}(M + H)$, or $5R = M + H$ and $M + R + H = 12,000$, which can be rewritten as $(M + H) + R = 12,000$, then $5R + R = 12,000$, or $R = 2,000$; SUFFICIENT.

**The correct answer is B;
statement 2 alone is sufficient.**

DS06038
458. If a, b, c, and d are positive numbers, is $\dfrac{a}{b} < \dfrac{c}{d}$?

(1) $0 < \dfrac{c-a}{d-b}$

(2) $\left(\dfrac{ad}{bc}\right)^2 < \dfrac{ad}{bc}$

Algebra Inequalities

Determine whether $\dfrac{a}{b} < \dfrac{c}{d}$, where a, b, c, and d are positive numbers.

(1) Given that $0 < \dfrac{c-a}{d-b}$, then $a = 2$, $b = 3$, $c = 6$, and $d = 8$ are possible values for a, b, c,

and d because $\dfrac{c-a}{d-b} = \dfrac{6-2}{8-3} = \dfrac{4}{5}$ and $\dfrac{4}{5} > 0$.

For these values, $\dfrac{a}{b} < \dfrac{c}{d}$ is true because

$\dfrac{2}{3} < \dfrac{6}{8}$.

On the other hand, $a = 4$, $b = 6$, $c = 2$, and d

$= 3$ are also possible values of a, b, c, and d

because $\dfrac{c-a}{d-b} = \dfrac{2-4}{3-6} = \dfrac{2}{3}$ and $\dfrac{2}{3} > 0$. For

these values, $\dfrac{a}{b} < \dfrac{c}{d}$ is false because $\dfrac{4}{6} = \dfrac{2}{3}$;

NOT sufficient.

(2) Given that $\left(\dfrac{ad}{bc}\right)^2 < \dfrac{ad}{bc}$, then

$\dfrac{ad}{bc} < 1$ dividing both sides by the

positive number $\dfrac{ad}{bc}$

$\dfrac{ad}{b} < c$ multiplying both sides by the

positive number c

$\dfrac{a}{b} < \dfrac{c}{d}$ dividing both sides by the positive

number d; SUFFICIENT

**The correct answer is B;
statement 2 alone is sufficient.**

DS12008

459. Is the number of members of Club X greater than the number of members of Club Y ?

(1) Of the members of Club X, 20 percent are also members of Club Y.

(2) Of the members of Club Y, 30 percent are also members of Club X.

Arithmetic Sets

(1) Given that 20 percent of the members of Club X are also members of Club Y, these 20 percent could be the only members of Club Y, in which case all the members of Club Y belong to Club X and Club X would have a greater number of members than Club Y. However, these 20 percent could form only a tiny portion of the members of Club Y and Club Y would have a greater number of members than Club X; NOT sufficient.

(2) Given that 30 percent of the members of Club Y are also members of Club X, these 30 percent could be the only members of Club X, in which case all the members of Club X belong to Club Y and Club Y would have a greater number of members than Club X. However, these 30 percent could form only a tiny portion of the members of Club X and Club X would have a greater number of members than Club Y; NOT sufficient.

Taking (1) and (2) together, the Venn diagram below shows the numbers of members in one or both of Club X and Club Y. For example, b is the number of members of Club X that are also members of Club Y, and b is the number of members of Club Y that are also members of Club X. We are to determine whether $a + b$, the number of members of Club X, is greater than $b + c$, the number of members of Club Y.

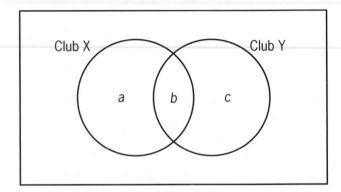

$b \quad = \dfrac{1}{5}(a + b) \quad$ from (1) and $20\% = \dfrac{1}{5}$

$5b \quad = a + b \quad$ multiply both sides by 5

$b \quad = \dfrac{3}{10}(b + c) \quad$ from (2) and $30\% = \dfrac{3}{10}$

$\dfrac{10}{3}b \quad = b + c \quad$ multiply both sides by $\dfrac{10}{3}$

The 2nd equation above says that the number of members of Club X is $5b$ and the 4th equation above says that the number of members of Club Y is $\dfrac{10}{3}b$. Since 5 is greater than $\dfrac{10}{3}$, it follows that the number of members of Club X is greater than the number of members of Club Y.

**The correct answer is C;
both statements together are sufficient.**

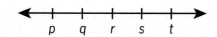

DS16361

460. On the number line above, p, q, r, s, and t are five consecutive even integers in increasing order. What is the average (arithmetic mean) of these five integers?

(1) $q + s = 24$

(2) The average (arithmetic mean) of q and r is 11.

Arithmetic Properties of Numbers

Since p, q, r, s, and t are consecutive even integers listed in numerical order, the 5 integers can also be given as $p, p + 2, p + 4, p + 6$, and $p + 8$. Determine the average of these 5 integers, which is the value

of $\dfrac{p + (p + 2) + (p + 4) + (p + 6) + (p + 8)}{5} =$

$\dfrac{5p + 20}{5} = p + 4$

(1) Given that $q + s = 24$, then $(p + 2) + (p + 6) = 24$. Therefore, $2p + 8 = 24$, or $p = 8$, and hence $p + 4 = 12$; SUFFICIENT.

(2) Given that $\dfrac{q + r}{2} = 11$, then $q + r = (2)(11) = 22$, or $(p + 2) + (p + 4) = 22$. Therefore, $2p + 6 = 22$, or $p = 8$, and hence $p + 4 = 12$; SUFFICIENT.

The correct answer is D; each statement alone is sufficient.

DS06657

461. If $\lceil x \rceil$ denotes the least integer greater than or equal to x, is $\lceil x \rceil = 0$?

(1) $-1 < x < 1$

(2) $x < 0$

Algebra Functions

Determine if $\lceil x \rceil$, the least integer greater than or equal to x, is equal to 0, which is the same as determining if x satisfies $-1 < x \leq 0$.

(1) Given that $-1 < x < 1$, then it is possible that $\lceil x \rceil = 0$ (for example, if $x = 0$, then $\lceil x \rceil = 0$) and it is possible that $\lceil x \rceil \neq 0$ (for example, if $x = \dfrac{1}{2}$, then $\lceil x \rceil = 1 \neq 0$); NOT sufficient.

(2) Given that $x < 0$, then it is possible that $\lceil x \rceil = 0$ (for example, if $x = -\dfrac{1}{2}$, then $\lceil x \rceil = 0$) and it is possible that $\lceil x \rceil \neq 0$ (for example, if $x = -5$, then $\lceil x \rceil = -5 \neq 0$); NOT sufficient.

Taking (1) and (2) together gives $-1 < x < 0$, which implies that $\lceil x \rceil = 0$.

The correct answer is C; both statements together are sufficient.

DS12718

462. If x and y are integers, is $x > y$?

(1) $x + y > 0$

(2) $y^x < 0$

Arithmetic Properties of Integers

Determine if the integer x is greater than the integer y.

(1) It is given that $x + y > 0$, and so $-x < y$. If, for example, $x = -3$ and $y = 4$, then $x + y = -3 + 4 = 1 > 0$ and $x < y$. On the other hand, if $x = 4$ and $y = -3$, then $x + y = 4 - 3 = 1 > 0$ and $x > y$; NOT sufficient.

(2) It is given that $y^x < 0$, so $y < 0$. If, for example, $x = 3$ and $y = -2$, then $(-2)^3 = -8 < 0$ and $x > y$. On the other hand, if $x = -3$ and $y = -2$, then $(-2)^{-3} = -\dfrac{1}{8} < 0$ and $x < y$; NOT sufficient.

Taking (1) and (2) together, from (2) y is negative and from (1) $-x$ is less than y. Therefore, $-x$ is negative, and hence x is positive. Since x is positive and y is negative, it follows that $x > y$.

The correct answer is C; both statements together are sufficient.

DS03046

463. If r and s are the roots of the equation $x^2 + bx + c = 0$, where b and c are constants, is $rs < 0$?

(1) $b < 0$

(2) $c < 0$

Algebra Second-Degree Equations

Determine whether the product of the roots to $x^2 + bx + c = 0$, where b and c are constants, is negative.

If r and s are the roots of the given equation, then $(x - r)(x - s) = x^2 + bx + c$. This implies that $x^2 - (r + s)x + rs = x^2 + bx + c$, and so $rs = c$. Therefore, rs is negative if and only if c is negative.

(1) Given that $b < 0$, then c could be negative or positive. For example, if $b = -1$ and $c = -6$, then the given equation would be $x^2 - x - 6 = (x - 3)(x + 2) = 0$, and the product of its roots would be $(3)(-2)$, which is negative. On the other hand, if $b = -6$ and $c = 5$, then the given equation would be $x^2 - 6x + 5 = (x - 5)(x - 1) = 0$, and the product of its roots would be $(5)(1)$, which is positive; NOT sufficient.

(2) Given that $c < 0$, it follows from the explanation above that $rs < 0$; SUFFICIENT.

The correct answer is B;
statement 2 alone is sufficient.

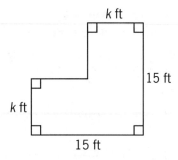

DS02888

464. The figure above represents an L-shaped garden. What is the value of k ?

(1) The area of the garden is 189 square feet.

(2) The perimeter of the garden is 60 feet.

Geometry Polygons

Imagine the garden to be a 15-foot square, from which a $(15 - k)$-foot square has been removed from the top left corner, as shown by the dashed line in the figure below.

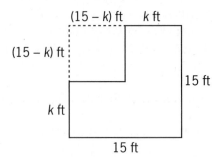

(1) Given that the area of the garden is 189 square feet, the area of the garden is the area of the 15-foot square, which is $15^2 = 225$ square feet, minus the area of the $(15 - k)$-foot square, which is $(15 - k)^2$, so $189 = 225 - (15 - k)^2$. Thus, $(15 - k)^2 = 36$, from which it follows that $15 - k = -6$ or $15 - k = 6$. Because $15 - k$ represents the side of a square, $15 - k = 6$, so $k = 9$; SUFFICIENT.

(2) Given that the perimeter of the garden is 60 feet, then, starting at the top and going clockwise around the garden, $60 = k + 15 + 15 + k + (15 - k) + (15 - k)$. Because $k + k - k - k = 0$ and $15 + 15 + 15 + 15 = 60$, the perimeter will be 60 for any value of k between 0 and 15; NOT sufficient.

The correct answer is A;
statement 1 alone is sufficient.

DS01049

465. The only articles of clothing in a certain closet are shirts, dresses, and jackets. The ratio of the number of shirts to the number of dresses to the number of jackets in the closet is 9:4:5, respectively. If there are more than 7 dresses in the closet, what is the total number of articles of clothing in the closet?

(1) The total number of shirts and jackets in the closet is less than 30.

(2) The total number of shirts and dresses in the closet is 26.

Arithmetic Ratio and Proportion

Letting s, d, and j represent, respectively, the numbers of shirts, dresses, and jackets in the closet, then $s = 9x$, $d = 4x$, and $j = 5x$, where x is a positive integer. It is given that $4x > 7$, and so $4x \geq 8$ or $x \geq 2$ since x is an integer. Determine the value of $9x + 4x + 5x = 18x$.

(1) This indicates that $9x + 5x < 30$, and so $14x \leq 28$ or $x \leq 2$ since x is an integer. It follows from $x \geq 2$ and $x \leq 2$ that $x = 2$ and $18x = 36$; SUFFICIENT.

(2) This indicates that $9x + 4x = 26$ or $13x = 26$, or $x = 2$. It follows that $18x = 36$; SUFFICIENT.

The correct answer is D; each statement alone is sufficient.

TOTAL EXPENSES FOR THE
FIVE DIVISIONS OF COMPANY H

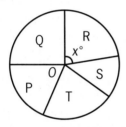

DS16542
466. The figure above represents a circle graph of Company H's total expenses broken down by the expenses for each of its five divisions. If O is the center of the circle and if Company H's total expenses are $5,400,000, what are the expenses for Division R?

(1) $x = 94$
(2) The total expenses for Divisions S and T are twice as much as the expenses for Division R.

Geometry Circles

In this circle graph, the expenses of Division R are equal to the value of $\frac{x}{360}$ multiplied by $5,400,000, or $15,000x$. Therefore, it is necessary to know the value of x in order to determine the expenses for Division R.

(1) The value of x is given as 94, so the expenses of Division R can be determined; SUFFICIENT.

(2) This gives a comparison among the expenses of some of the divisions of Company H, but no information is given about the value of x; NOT sufficient.

The correct answer is A; statement 1 alone is sufficient.

DS13641
467. If x is negative, is $x < -3$?

(1) $x^2 > 9$
(2) $x^3 < -9$

Algebra Properties of Numbers

(1) Given that $x^2 > 9$, it follows that $x < -3$ or $x > 3$, a result that can be obtained in a variety of ways. For example, consider the equivalent inequality $\left(|x|\right)^2 > 9$ that reduces to $|x| > 3$, or consider when the two factors of $x^2 - 9$ are both positive and when the two factors of $x^2 - 9$ are both negative, or consider where the graph of the parabola $y = x^2 - 9$ is above the x-axis, etc. Since it is also given that x is negative, it follows that $x < -3$; SUFFICIENT.

(2) Given that $x^3 < -9$, if $x = -4$, then $x^3 = -64$, and so $x^3 < -9$ and it is true that $x < -3$. However, if $x = -3$, then $x^3 = -27$, and so $x^3 < -9$, but it is not true that $x < -3$; NOT sufficient.

The correct answer is A; statement 1 alone is sufficient.

DS04897
468. What is the number of cans that can be packed in a certain carton?

(1) The interior volume of this carton is 2,304 cubic inches.
(2) The exterior of each can is 6 inches high and has a diameter of 4 inches.

Geometry Rectangular Solids and Cylinders

(1) No information about the size of the cans is given; NOT sufficient.

(2) No information about the size of the carton is given; NOT sufficient.

Taking (1) and (2) together, there is still not enough information to answer the question. If the carton is a rectangular solid that is 1 inch by 1 inch by 2,304 inches and the cans are cylindrical with the given dimensions, then 0 cans can be packed into the carton. However, if the carton is a rectangular solid that is 16 inches by 12 inches by 12 inches and the cans are cylindrical with the given dimensions, then 1 or more cans can be packed into the carton.

**The correct answer is E;
both statements together are still not sufficient.**

r	s	t
u	v	w
x	y	z

DS08301

469. Each of the letters in the table above represents one of the numbers 1, 2, or 3, and each of these numbers occurs exactly once in each row and exactly once in each column. What is the value of *r* ?

(1) *v* + *z* = 6
(2) *s* + *t* + *u* + *x* = 6

Arithmetic Properties of Numbers

In the following discussion, "row/column convention" means that each of the numbers 1, 2, and 3 appears exactly once in any given row and exactly once in any given column.

(1) Given that *v* + *z* = 6, then both *v* and *z* are equal to 3, since no other sum of the possible values is equal to 6. Applying the row/column convention to row 2, and then to row 3, it follows that neither *u* nor *x* can be 3. Since neither *u* nor *x* can be 3, the row/column convention applied to column 1 forces *r* to be 3; SUFFICIENT.

(2) If *u* = 3, then *s* + *t* + *x* = 3. Hence, *s* = *t* = *x* = 1, since the values these variables can have does not permit another possibility. However, this assignment of values would violate the row/column convention for row 1, and thus *u* cannot be 3. If *x* = 3, then *s* + *t* + *u* = 3. Hence, *s* = *t* = *u* = 1, since the values these variables can have does not permit another possibility. However, this assignment of values would violate the

row/column convention for row 1, and thus *x* cannot be 3. Since neither *u* nor *x* can be 3, the row/column convention applied to column 1 forces *r* to be 3; SUFFICIENT.

**The correct answer is D;
each statement alone is sufficient.**

DS00328

470. Material A costs $3 per kilogram, and Material B costs $5 per kilogram. If 10 kilograms of Material K consists of *x* kilograms of Material A and *y* kilograms of Material B, is *x* > *y* ?

(1) *y* > 4
(2) The cost of the 10 kilograms of Material K is less than $40.

Algebra Inequalities

Since *x* + *y* = 10, the relation *x* > *y* is equivalent to *x* > 10 − *x*, or *x* > 5.

(1) The given information is consistent with *x* = 5.5 and *y* = 4.5, and the given information is also consistent with *x* = *y* = 5. Therefore, it is possible for *x* > *y* to be true and it is possible for *x* > *y* to be false; NOT sufficient.

(2) Given that 3*x* + 5*y* < 40, or 3*x* + 5(10 − *x*) < 40, then 3*x* − 5*x* < 40 − 50. It follows that −2*x* < −10, or *x* > 5; SUFFICIENT.

**The correct answer is B;
statement 2 alone is sufficient.**

DS16164

471. At what speed was a train traveling on a trip when it had completed half of the total distance of the trip?

(1) The trip was 460 miles long and took 4 hours to complete.
(2) The train traveled at an average rate of 115 miles per hour on the trip.

Arithmetic Applied Problems

Determine the speed of the train when it had completed half the total distance of the trip.

(1) Given that the train traveled 460 miles in 4 hours, the train could have traveled at the constant rate of 115 miles per hour for 4 hours, and thus it could have been traveling 115 miles per hour when it had completed half the total distance of the trip. However,

the train could have traveled 150 miles per hour for the first 2 hours (a distance of 300 miles) and 80 miles per hour for the last 2 hours (a distance of 160 miles), and thus it could have been traveling 150 miles per hour when it had completed half the total distance of the trip; NOT sufficient.

(2) Given that the train traveled at an average rate of 115 miles per hour, each of the possibilities given in the explanation for (1) could occur, since 460 miles in 4 hours gives an average speed of $\frac{460}{4} = 115$ miles per hour; NOT sufficient.

Assuming (1) and (2), each of the possibilities given in the explanation for (1) could occur. Therefore, (1) and (2) together are not sufficient.

The correct answer is E;
both statements together are still not sufficient.

DS12047
472. Tom, Jane, and Sue each purchased a new house. The average (arithmetic mean) price of the three houses was $120,000. What was the median price of the three houses?

(1) The price of Tom's house was $110,000.

(2) The price of Jane's house was $120,000.

Arithmetic Statistics

Let T, J, and S be the purchase prices for Tom's, Jane's, and Sue's new houses. Given that the average purchase price is 120,000, or $T + J + S = 3(120,000)$, determine the median purchase price.

(1) Given $T = 110,000$, the median could be 120,000 (if $J = 120,000$ and $S = 130,000$) or 125,000 (if $J = 125,000$ and $S = 125,000$); NOT sufficient.

(2) Given $J = 120,000$, the following two cases include every possibility consistent with $T + J + S = (3)(120,000)$, or $T + S = (2)(120,000)$.

(i) $T = S = 120,000$

(ii) One of T or S is less than 120,000 and the other is greater than 120,000.

In each case, the median is clearly 120,000; SUFFICIENT.

The correct answer is B;
statement 2 alone is sufficient.

DS13958
473. What is the value of x if $x^3 < x^2$?

(1) $-2 < x < 2$

(2) x is an integer greater than −2.

Algebra Inequalities

The inequality $x^3 < x^2$ is equivalent to $x^3 - x^2 < 0$, or $x^2(x - 1) < 0$. Since this inequality is false for $x = 0$, it follows that $x \neq 0$, and hence $x^2 > 0$. Therefore, $x^2(x - 1) < 0$ can only hold if $x - 1 < 0$, or if $x < 1$. Thus, the problem is equivalent to determining the value of x given that $x \neq 0$ and $x < 1$.

(1) Given that $-2 < x < 2$, it is not possible to determine the value of x. For example, the value of x could be −1 (note that −1 < 1) and the value of x could be 0.5 (note that 0.125 < 0.25); NOT sufficient.

(2) Given that the value of x is an integer greater than −2, then the value of x must be among the integers $-1, 0, 1, 2, 3, \ldots$. However, from the discussion above, $x \neq 0$ and $x < 1$, so the value of x can only be −1; SUFFICIENT.

The correct answer is B;
statement 2 alone is sufficient.

DS08451
474. For any integers x and y, min(x, y) and max(x, y) denote the minimum and the maximum of x and y, respectively. For example, min(5, 2) = 2 and max(5, 2) = 5. For the integer w, what is the value of min(10, w) ?

(1) $w = \max(20, z)$ for some integer z.

(2) $w = \max(10, w)$

Arithmetic Properties of Numbers

If $w \geq 10$, then $(10, w) = 10$, and if $w < 10$, then $(10, w) = w$. Therefore, the value of min(10, w) can be determined if the value of w can be determined.

(1) Given that $w = \max(20, z)$ then $w \geq 20$. Hence, $w \geq 10$, and so min(10, w) = 10; SUFFICIENT.

(2) Given that $w = \max(10, w)$, then $w \geq 10$, and so min(10, w) = 10; SUFFICIENT.

The correct answer is D;
each statement alone is sufficient.

DS01473

475. A certain bookcase has 2 shelves of books. On the upper shelf, the book with the greatest number of pages has 400 pages. On the lower shelf, the book with the least number of pages has 475 pages. What is the median number of pages for all of the books on the 2 shelves?

(1) There are 25 books on the upper shelf.
(2) There are 24 books on the lower shelf.

Arithmetic Statistics

(1) The information given says nothing about the number of books on the lower shelf. If there are fewer than 25 books on the lower shelf, then the median number of pages will be the number of pages in one of the books on the upper shelf or the average number of pages in two books on the upper shelf. Hence, the median will be at most 400. If there are more than 25 books on the lower shelf, then the median number of pages will be the number of pages in one of the books on the lower shelf or the average number of pages in two books on the lower shelf. Hence, the median will be at least 475; NOT sufficient.

(2) An analysis very similar to that used in (1) shows the information given is not sufficient to determine the median; NOT sufficient.

Given both (1) and (2), it follows that there is a total of 49 books. Therefore, the median will be the 25th book when the books are ordered by number of pages. Since the 25th book in this ordering is the book on the upper shelf with the greatest number of pages, the median is 400. Therefore, (1) and (2) together are sufficient.

**The correct answer is C;
both statements together are sufficient.**

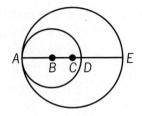

DS12070

476. In the figure above, points A, B, C, D, and E lie on a line. A is on both circles, B is the center of the smaller circle, C is the center of the larger circle, D is on the smaller circle, and E is on the larger circle. What is the area of the region inside the larger circle and outside the smaller circle?

(1) $AB = 3$ and $BC = 2$
(2) $CD = 1$ and $DE = 4$

Geometry Circles

If R is the radius of the larger circle and r is the radius of the smaller circle, then the desired area is $\pi R^2 - \pi r^2$. Thus, if both the values of R and r can be determined, then the desired area can be determined.

(1) Given that $AB = r = 3$ and $BC = 2$, then $AB + BC = R = 3 + 2 = 5$; SUFFICIENT.

(2) Given that $CD = 1$ and $DE = 4$, then $CD + DE = R = 1 + 4 = 5$. Since $\overline{AE}$ is a diameter of the larger circle, then $AD + DE = 2R$. Also, since $\overline{AD}$ is a diameter of the smaller circle, then $AD = 2r$. Thus, $2r + DE = 2R$ or $2r + 4 = 10$, and so $r = 3$; SUFFICIENT.

**The correct answer is D;
each statement alone is sufficient.**

DS08995

477. In planning for a trip, Joan estimated both the distance of the trip, in miles, and her average speed, in miles per hour. She accurately divided her estimated distance by her estimated average speed to obtain an estimate for the time, in hours, that the trip would take. Was her estimate within 0.5 hour of the actual time that the trip took?

(1) Joan's estimate for the distance was within 5 miles of the actual distance.

(2) Joan's estimate for her average speed was within 10 miles per hour of her actual average speed.

Arithmetic Applied Problems; Estimating

(1) Given that the estimate for the distance was within 5 miles of the actual distance, it is not possible to determine whether the estimate of the time (that is, the estimated distance divided by the estimated average speed) was within 0.5 hour of the actual time because nothing is known about the estimated average speed; NOT sufficient.

(2) Given that the estimate for the average speed was within 10 miles per hour of the actual average speed, it is not possible to determine whether the estimate of the time (that is, the estimated distance divided by the estimated average speed) was within 0.5 hour of the actual time because nothing is known about the estimated distance; NOT sufficient.

Taking (1) and (2) together, the table below shows two possibilities for the estimated distance, estimated average speed, actual distance, and actual average speed that are consistent with the information given in (1) and (2).

estimated distance	estimated speed	actual distance	actual speed
20 miles	$20 \frac{\text{miles}}{\text{hour}}$	20 miles	$20 \frac{\text{miles}}{\text{hour}}$
20 miles	$20 \frac{\text{miles}}{\text{hour}}$	20 miles	$10 \frac{\text{miles}}{\text{hour}}$

In the first row of the table, the estimate of the time and the actual time are each equal to 1 hour, and so the estimate of the time is within 0.5 hour of the actual time. In the second row of the table, the estimate of the time is 1 hour and the actual time is $\frac{20}{10} = 2$ hours, and so the estimate of the time is not within 0.5 hour of the actual time.

The correct answer is E; both statements together are still not sufficient.

DS12239

478. A certain list consists of 3 different numbers. Does the median of the 3 numbers equal the average (arithmetic mean) of the 3 numbers?

(1) The range of the 3 numbers is equal to twice the difference between the greatest number and the median.

(2) The sum of the 3 numbers is equal to 3 times one of the numbers.

Arithmetic Statistics

Let the numbers be x, y, and z so that $x < y < z$. Determine whether $y = \frac{x + y + z}{3}$, or equivalently, whether $3y = x + y + z$, or equivalently, whether $2y = x + z$.

(1) Given that the range is equal to twice the difference between the greatest number and the median, it follows that $z - x = 2(z - y)$, or $z - x = 2z - 2y$, or $2y = x + z$; SUFFICIENT.

(2) Given that the sum of the 3 numbers equals 3 times one of the numbers, it follows that $x + y + z = 3x$ or $x + y + z = 3y$ or $x + y + z = 3z$. If $x + y + z = 3x$, then $y + z = 2x$, or $(y - x) + (z - x) = 0$. Also, if $x + y + z = 3z$, then $x + y = 2z$, or $0 = (z - x) + (z - y)$. In each of these cases, the sum of two positive numbers is zero, which is impossible. Therefore, it must be true that $x + y + z = 3y$, from which it follows that $x + z = 2y$, and hence by the initial comments, the median of the 3 numbers equals the average of the 3 numbers; SUFFICIENT.

The correct answer is D; each statement alone is sufficient.

DS12806
479. Line ℓ lies in the xy-plane and does not pass through the origin. What is the slope of line ℓ ?

    (1)   The x-intercept of line ℓ is twice the y-intercept of line ℓ.

    (2)   The x- and y-intercepts of line ℓ are both positive.

Geometry Coordinate Geometry

Since the line does not pass through the origin, the line is either vertical and given by the equation $x = c$ for some constant c such that $c \neq 0$, or the line is not vertical and given by the equation $y = mx + b$ for some constants m and b such that $b \neq 0$. Determine whether the line is not vertical, and if so, determine the slope of the line, which is the value of m.

    (1)   Given that the x-intercept of the line is twice the y-intercept of the line, it follows that the line is not vertical, since a vertical line that does not pass through the origin will not have a y-intercept. Thus, the line is given by the equation $y = mx + b$. The x-intercept of the line is the solution to $0 = mx + b$, or $mx = -b$, which has solution $x = -\dfrac{b}{m}$, and the y-intercept of the line is b. Therefore, $-\dfrac{b}{m} = 2b$. Since $b \neq 0$, both sides of the last equation can be divided by b to get $-\dfrac{1}{m} = 2$, or $m = -\dfrac{1}{2}$; SUFFICIENT.

    (2)   Given that the x- and y-intercepts of the line are both positive, it is not possible to determine the slope of the line. For example, if the line is given by $y = -x + 1$, then the x-intercept is 1 (solve $-x + 1 = 0$), the y-intercept is 1 ($b = 1$), and the slope is -1. However, if the line is given by $y = -2x + 2$, then the x-intercept is 1 (solve $-2x + 2 = 0$), the y-intercept is 2 ($b = 2$), and the slope is -2; NOT sufficient.

The correct answer is A; statement 1 alone is sufficient.

$$y = ax - 5$$
$$y = x + 6$$
$$y = 3x + b$$

DS07713
480. In the xy-plane, the straight-line graphs of the three equations above each contain the point (p, r). If a and b are constants, what is the value of b ?

    (1) $a = 2$

    (2) $r = 17$

Algebra Coordinate Geometry

Since (p, r) is on each of the lines, each of the following three equations is true:

    (i) $r = ap - 5$

    (ii) $r = p + 6$

    (iii) $r = 3p + b$

Determine the value of b.

    (1)   Given that $a = 2$, Equations (i) and (ii) become $r = 2p - 5$ and $r = p + 6$. Subtracting equations gives $0 = p - 11$, or $p = 11$. Now using $r = p + 6$, it follows that $r = 11 + 6 = 17$. Finally, using $p = 11$ and $r = 17$ in Equation (iii) gives $17 = 3(11) + b$, or $b = 17 - 33 = -16$; SUFFICIENT.

    (2)   Given that $r = 17$, Equation (ii) becomes $17 = p + 6$, and so $p = 17 - 6 = 11$. Using $r = 17$ and $p = 11$, Equation (iii) becomes $17 = 3(11) + b$, or $b = 17 - 33 = -16$; SUFFICIENT.

The correct answer is D; each statement alone is sufficient.

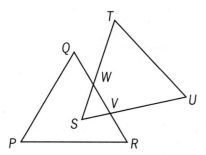

DS06861

481. In the figure above, *PQR* and *STU* are identical equilateral triangles, and *PQ* = 6. What is the perimeter of polygon *PQWTUVR* ?

(1) Triangle *SWV* has perimeter 9.

(2) *VW* has length 3.5.

Geometry Triangles; Perimeter

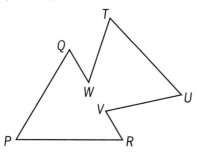

The figure above shows polygon *PQWTUVR*. Note that it is identical to the figure of the equilateral triangles *PQR* and *STU*, except that segments $\overline{SW}$, $\overline{WV}$, and $\overline{VS}$ are missing.

(1) It is given that $\triangle SWV$ has perimeter 9; it follows that $SW + WV + VS = 9$. Since $\triangle PQR$ and $\triangle STU$ are identical equilateral triangles with side length 6, the perimeter of *PQWTUVR* = (perimeter of $\triangle PQR$ + perimeter of $\triangle STU$) − (perimeter of $\triangle SWV$), and this number can be uniquely determined; SUFFICIENT.

(2) It is given that $\overline{VW}$ has length 3.5; it is not possible to determine the perimeter of *PQWTUVR*. It could be that $\triangle SWV$ is equilateral, in which case the perimeter of $\triangle SWV$ is known and the perimeter of *PQWTUVR* can be determined. However, without knowing *SW* and *VS* or a means to determine them, the perimeter of *PQWTUVR* cannot be determined; NOT sufficient.

The correct answer is A; statement 1 alone is sufficient.

DS09973

482. The range of the numbers in set *S* is *x*, and the range of the numbers in set *T* is *y*. If all of the numbers in set *T* are also in set *S*, is *x* greater than *y* ?

(1) Set *S* consists of 7 numbers.

(2) Set *T* consists of 6 numbers.

Arithmetic Statistics

Set *S* has a range of *x*, set *T* has a range of *y*, and *T* is a subset of *S*. Determine if *x* is greater than *y*.

(1) It is given that *S* contains exactly 7 numbers, but nothing additional is known about *T*. Thus, if $S = \{1, 2, 3, 4, 5, 6, 7\}$ and $T = \{1, 2, 3, 4, 5, 6\}$, then $x = 7 - 1 = 6$, $y = 6 - 1 = 5$, and *x* is greater than *y*. On the other hand, if $S = \{1, 2, 3, 4, 5, 6, 7\}$ and $T = \{1, 3, 4, 5, 6, 7\}$, then $x = 7 - 1 = 6$, $y = 7 - 1 = 6$, and *x* is not greater than *y*; NOT sufficient.

(2) It is given that *T* contains exactly 6 numbers, but nothing additional is known about *T*. Since the same examples given in (1) can also be used in (2), it cannot be determined if *x* is greater than *y*; NOT sufficient.

Taking (1) and (2) together, the examples used in (1) can be used to show that it cannot be determined if *x* is greater than *y*.

The correct answer is E; both statements together are still not sufficient.

DS13857

483. The hypotenuse of a right triangle is 10 cm. What is the perimeter, in centimeters, of the triangle?

(1) The area of the triangle is 25 square centimeters.

(2) The 2 legs of the triangle are of equal length.

Geometry Triangles

If *x* and *y* are the lengths of the legs of the triangle, then it is given that $x^2 + y^2 = 100$. Determining the value of $x + y + 10$, the perimeter of the triangle, is equivalent to determining the value of $x + y$.

(1) Given that the area is 25, then $\frac{1}{2}xy = 25$, or $xy = 50$. Since $(x + y)^2 = x^2 + y^2 + 2xy$, it follows that $(x + y)^2 = 100 + 2(50)$, or $x + y = \sqrt{200}$; SUFFICIENT.

(2) Given that $x = y$, since $x^2 + y^2 = 100$, it follows that $2x^2 = 100$, or $x = \sqrt{50}$. Hence, $x + y = x + x = 2x = 2\sqrt{50}$; SUFFICIENT.

The correct answer is D;
each statement alone is sufficient.

Shipment	S1	S2	S3	S4	S5	S6
Fraction of the Total Value of the Six Shipments	$\frac{1}{4}$	$\frac{1}{5}$	$\frac{1}{6}$	$\frac{3}{20}$	$\frac{2}{15}$	$\frac{1}{10}$

DS01427

484. Six shipments of machine parts were shipped from a factory on two trucks, with each shipment entirely on one of the trucks. Each shipment was labeled either S1, S2, S3, S4, S5, or S6. The table shows the value of each shipment as a fraction of the total value of the six shipments. If the shipments on the first truck had a value greater than $\frac{1}{2}$ of the total value of the six shipments, was S3 shipped on the first truck?

(1) S2 and S4 were shipped on the first truck.

(2) S1 and S6 were shipped on the second truck.

Arithmetic Operations on Rational Numbers

Given that the shipments on the first truck had a value greater than $\frac{1}{2}$ of the total value of the 6 shipments, determine if S3 was shipped on the first truck.

To avoid dealing with fractions, it will be convenient to create scaled values of the shipments by multiplying each fractional value by 60, which is the least common denominator of the fractions. Thus, the scaled values associated with S1, S2, S3, S4, S5, and S6 are 15, 12, 10, 9, 8, and 6, respectively. The given information is that the scaled value of the shipments on the first truck is greater than $\left(\frac{1}{2}\right)(60) = 30$.

(1) Given that the first truck includes shipments with scaled values 12 and 9, it may or may not be the case that S3 (the shipment with scaled value 10) is on the first truck. For example, the first truck could contain only S2, S3, and S4, for a total scaled value $12 + 10 + 9 = 31 > 30$. Or, the first truck could contain only S1, S2, and S4,

for a total scaled value $15 + 12 + 9 = 36 > 30$; NOT sufficient.

(2) Given that the second truck includes shipments with scaled values 15 and 6, the second truck cannot contain S3. Otherwise, the second truck would contain shipments with scaled values 15, 6, and 10, for a total scaled value $15 + 6 + 10 = 31$, leaving at most a total scaled value 29 (which is not greater than 30) for the first truck; SUFFICIENT.

The correct answer is B;
statement 2 alone is sufficient.

DS11723

485. If x, y, and z are three-digit positive integers and if $x = y + z$, is the hundreds digit of x equal to the sum of the hundreds digits of y and z?

(1) The tens digit of x is equal to the sum of the tens digits of y and z.

(2) The units digit of x is equal to the sum of the units digits of y and z.

Arithmetic Place Value

Letting $x = 100a + 10b + c$, $y = 100p + 10q + r$, and $z = 100t + 10u + v$, where a, b, c, p, q, r, t, u, and v are digits, determine if $a = p + t$.

(1) It is given that $b = q + u$ (which implies that $c + v \leq 9$ because if $c + v > 9$, then in the addition process a ten would need to be carried over to the tens column and b would be $q + u + 1$). Since b is a digit, $0 \leq b \leq 9$. Hence, $0 \leq q + u \leq 9$, and so $0 \leq 10(q + u) \leq 90$. Therefore, in the addition process, there are no hundreds to carry over from the tens column to the hundreds column, so $a = p + t$; SUFFICIENT.

(2) It is given that $c = r + v$. If $x = 687$, $y = 231$, and $z = 456$, then, $y + z = 231 + 456 = 687 = x$, $r + v = 1 + 6 = 7 = c$, and $p + t = 2 + 4 = 6 = a$. On the other hand, if $x = 637$, $y = 392$, and $z = 245$, then $y + z = 392 + 245 = 637 = x$, $r + v = 2 + 5 = 7 = c$, and $p + t = 3 + 2 = 5 \neq 6 = a$; NOT sufficient.

The correct answer is A;
statement 1 alone is sufficient.

	Favorable	Unfavorable	Not Sure
Candidate M	40	20	40
Candidate N	30	35	35

DS05162

486. The table above shows the results of a survey of 100 voters who each responded "Favorable" or "Unfavorable" or "Not Sure" when asked about their impressions of Candidate M and of Candidate N. What was the number of voters who responded "Favorable" for both candidates?

(1) The number of voters who did not respond "Favorable" for either candidate was 40.

(2) The number of voters who responded "Unfavorable" for both candidates was 10.

Arithmetic Sets

Let x, y, and z, respectively, be the numbers of voters who responded "Favorable," "Unfavorable," and "Not Sure" to both candidates. The table below gives a more complete tabulation of the survey results. For example, since 20 voters responded "Unfavorable" for Candidate M and y of those 20 voters also responded "Unfavorable" for Candidate N, it follows that $20 - y$ of those 20 voters responded "Unfavorable" for Candidate M only. Determine the value of x, the number of voters who responded "Favorable" for both candidates.

	Favorable	Unfavorable	Not Sure
M and N	x	y	z
M only	$40 - x$	$20 - y$	$40 - z$
N only	$30 - x$	$35 - y$	$35 - z$

(1) It is given that the number of voters who did not respond "Favorable" for either candidate was 40. Also, from the table above the number of voters who responded "Favorable" for at least one candidate was $(40 - x) + (30 - x) + x = 70 - x$. Since there were 100 voters, it follows that $(70 - x) + 40 = 100$, which can be solved for a unique value of x; SUFFICIENT.

(2) It is given that the number of voters who responded "Unfavorable" for both candidates was 10, or $y = 10$. However, there is not enough information to determine

the value of x. This can be seen by choosing different integer values for x between 0 and 30, inclusive, and using each value to complete the table above (choose $z = 5$ for completeness, for example); NOT sufficient.

The correct answer is A; statement 1 alone is sufficient.

DS00340

487. A school administrator will assign each student in a group of n students to one of m classrooms. If $3 < m < 13 < n$, is it possible to assign each of the n students to one of the m classrooms so that each classroom has the same number of students assigned to it?

(1) It is possible to assign each of $3n$ students to one of m classrooms so that each classroom has the same number of students assigned to it.

(2) It is possible to assign each of $13n$ students to one of m classrooms so that each classroom has the same number of students assigned to it.

Arithmetic Properties of Numbers

Determine if n is divisible by m.

(1) Given that $3n$ is divisible by m, then n is divisible by m if $m = 9$ and $n = 27$ (note that $3 < m < 13 < n$, $3n = 81$, and $m = 9$, so $3n$ is divisible by m) and n is not divisible by m if $m = 9$ and $n = 30$ (note that $3 < m < 13 < n$, $3n = 90$, and $m = 9$, so $3n$ is divisible by m); NOT sufficient.

(2) Given that $13n$ is divisible by m, then $13n = qm$, or $\dfrac{n}{m} = \dfrac{q}{13}$, for some integer q.

Since 13 is a prime number that divides qm (because $13n = qm$) and 13 does not divide m (because $m < 13$), it follows that 13 divides q.

Therefore, $\dfrac{q}{13}$ is an integer, and since $\dfrac{n}{m} = \dfrac{q}{13}$, then $\dfrac{n}{m}$ is an integer. Thus, n is divisible by m; SUFFICIENT.

The correct answer is B; statement 2 alone is sufficient.

DS19120.02

488. At a certain clothing store, customers who buy 2 shirts pay the regular price for the first shirt and a discounted price for the second shirt. The store makes the same profit from the sale of 2 shirts that it makes from the sale of 1 shirt at the regular price. For a customer who buys 2 shirts, what is the discounted price of the second shirt?

(1) The regular price of each of the 2 shirts the customer buys at the clothing store is $16.

(2) The cost to the clothing store of each of the 2 shirts the customer buys is $12.

Arithmetic Applied Problems

Solving this problem relies on the definition of profit: profit = selling price − cost.

(1) Given that the regular price of each of the 2 shirts is $16, the discounted price cannot be uniquely determined because no information is given about the rate of discount, the amount of discount, or the cost; NOT sufficient.

(2) Recall that profit = selling price − cost. Since the store makes the same profit from the sale of 2 shirts as it makes from the sale of 1 shirt at the regular price, the profit from the second shirt is $0. It follows that the selling price (that is, the discounted price) of the second shirt equals its cost.

Given that the cost of each of the shirts is $12, it follows that the discounted price of the second shirt is $12; SUFFICIENT.

**The correct answer is B;
statement 2 alone is sufficient.**

DS07441

489. If q, s, and t are all different numbers, is $q < s < t$?

(1) $t - q = |t - s| + |s - q|$

(2) $t > q$

Algebra Absolute Value

(1) Given $t - q = |t - s| + |s - q|$, it follows that $t - q > 0$, since $|t - s| + |s - q|$ is a sum of two positive numbers. Therefore, $t > q$. If s is NOT between q and t, then either s is to the

left of q or s is to the right of t. The number lines below show these two possibilities.

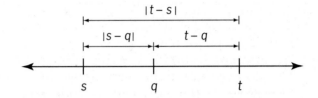

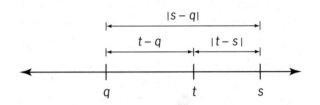

However, $t - q = |t - s| + |s - q|$ is not true for either of these possibilities, since for each possibility the distance between t and q (which equals $t - q$) is less than the sum of the distance between t and s (which equals $|t - s|$) and the distance between s and q (which equals $|s - q|$). Therefore, if $t - q = |t - s| + |s - q|$ is true, then s must be between q and t, and it follows that $q < s < t$; SUFFICIENT.

(2) Given $t > q$, it is possible that $q < s < t$ is true (for example, when s is between t and q) and it is also possible that $q < s < t$ is false (for example, when s is greater than t); NOT sufficient.

**The correct answer is A;
statement 1 alone is sufficient.**

DS11538

490. What is the median number of employees assigned per project for the projects at Company Z?

(1) 25 percent of the projects at Company Z have 4 or more employees assigned to each project.

(2) 35 percent of the projects at Company Z have 2 or fewer employees assigned to each project.

Arithmetic Statistics

(1) Although 25 percent of the projects have 4 or more employees, there is essentially no

information about the middle values of the numbers of employees per project. For example, if there were a total of 100 projects, then the median could be 2 (75 projects that have exactly 2 employees each and 25 projects that have exactly 4 employees each) or the median could be 3 (75 projects that have exactly 3 employees each and 25 projects that have exactly 4 employees each); NOT sufficient.

(2)   Although 35 percent of the projects have 2 or fewer employees, there is essentially no information about the middle values of the numbers of employees per project. For example, if there were a total of 100 projects, then the median could be 3 (35 projects that have exactly 2 employees each and 65 projects that have exactly 3 employees each) or the median could be 4 (35 projects that have exactly 2 employees each and 65 projects that have exactly 4 employees each); NOT sufficient.

Given both (1) and (2), $100 - (25 + 35)$ percent = 40 percent of the projects have exactly 3 employees. Therefore, when the numbers of employees per project are listed from least to greatest, 35 percent of the numbers are 2 or less and $(35 + 40)$ percent = 75 percent are 3 or less, and hence the median is 3.

**The correct answer is C;
both statements together are sufficient.**

DS04409

491. Last year, a certain company began manufacturing product X and sold every unit of product X that it produced. Last year the company's total expenses for manufacturing product X were equal to $100,000 plus 5 percent of the company's total revenue from all units of product X sold. If the company made a profit on product X last year, did the company sell more than 21,000 units of product X last year?

(1)   The company's total revenue from the sale of product X last year was greater than $110,000.

(2)   For each unit of product X sold last year, the company's revenue was $5.

Algebra Applied Problems

Recall that Profit = Revenue − Expenses and for this company the profit on product X last year was positive. Then, letting R represent total revenue, in dollars, from all units of product X sold, profit = $R - (100,000 + 0.05R)$ = $0.95R - 100,000$. So,

$$0.95R - 100,000 > 0.$$

(1)   This says $R > 110,000$, but gives no information on how many units were sold or the price at which they were sold. Therefore, whether the company sold more than 21,000 units cannot be determined; NOT sufficient.

number sold	unit price	R, in dollars	number sold > 21,000 ?
1,200	$100	120,000	no
22,000	$10	220,000	yes

Note that a calculator is not needed to verify that the profit (which is given in dollars by 95% of $R - 100,000$) is positive for each of these two values of R. For example,

10% of 120,000	=	12,000	move decimal point 1 place to the left
5% of 120,000	=	6,000	5% is $\frac{1}{2}$ of 10%
120,000 − 6,000	=	114,000	$R - 5\%$ of $R =$ 95% of R
114,000 − 100,000	=	14,000	95% of $R - 100,000$

(2)   This says the unit price was $5. If x represents the number of units sold, then $R = 5x$ and, by substitution, the requirement that the profit is positive becomes $0.95(5x) - 100,000 > 0$.

$$0.95(5x) - 100,000 > 0 \quad \text{given}$$

$$0.95(5x) > 100,000 \quad \text{add 100,000 to both sides}$$

$$0.95x > 20,000 \quad \text{divide both sides by 5}$$

$$x > \frac{20,000}{0.95} \quad \text{divide both sides by 0.95}$$

$$x > \frac{20,000}{\frac{19}{20}} \qquad 0.95 = \frac{95}{100} = \frac{19}{20}$$

$$x > (20,000)\left(\frac{20}{19}\right) \quad \text{invert divisor and multiply}$$

$$x > 20,000 + (20,000)\left(\frac{1}{19}\right) \qquad \frac{20}{19} = 1 + \frac{1}{19}$$

$$x > 20,000 + 1,000 \qquad \frac{1}{19} > \frac{1}{20}, (20,000)\frac{1}{20} = 1,000$$

$$x > 21,000 \quad \text{add}$$

Therefore, the company sold more than 21,000 units; SUFFICIENT.

The correct answer is B; statement 2 alone is sufficient.

DS01641

492. Beginning in January of last year, Carl made deposits of $120 into his account on the 15th of each month for several consecutive months and then made withdrawals of $50 from the account on the 15th of each of the remaining months of last year. There were no other transactions in the account last year. If the closing balance of Carl's account for May of last year was $2,600, what was the range of the monthly closing balances of Carl's account last year?

(1) Last year the closing balance of Carl's account for April was less than $2,625.

(2) Last year the closing balance of Carl's account for June was less than $2,675.

Arithmetic Statistics

It is given that the closing balance for May was $2,600 and the closing balance for each month either increases by $120 or decreases by $50 relative to the closing balance for the previous month, depending on when the withdrawals began. Therefore, the closing balance for June was either $2,720 or $2,550, and the closing balance for April was either $2,480 or $2,650. The table below shows these possibilities for 5 of the months that the withdrawals could have

begun. The values in the last two rows of the table remain the same for later months that the withdrawals could have begun.

Withdrawals began	Close April	Close May	Close June
Apr 15	$2,650	$2,600	$2,550
May 15	$2,650	$2,600	$2,550
Jun 15	$2,480	$2,600	$2,550
Jul 15	$2,480	$2,600	$2,720
Aug 15	$2,480	$2,600	$2,720

(1) Given that the closing balance for April was less than $2,625, it follows from the table above that the withdrawals could have begun in June or in any later month. For each of these possibilities, the balance at the beginning of January was $2,600 − 5($120) = $2,000, since each of the 5 transactions made before the end of May were $120 deposits. Therefore, the range of the monthly closing balances of the account can vary because the range will depend on how many of the transactions made after May were $120 deposits and how many were $50 withdrawals; NOT sufficient.

(2) Given that the closing balance for June was less than $2,675, it follows from the table above that the withdrawals could have begun in June or in any earlier month. For each of these possibilities,

the balance at the end of December was $2,600 − 7($50) = $2,250, since each of the 7 transactions made after the end of May were $50 withdrawals. Therefore, the range of the monthly closing balances of the account can vary because the range will depend on how many of the transactions made before May were $120 deposits and how many were $50 withdrawals; NOT sufficient.

Taking (1) and (2) together, withdrawals started in June or later by (1) and withdrawals started in June or earlier by (2), so withdrawals started in June. Therefore, each of the monthly closing balances of the account is known, and thus the range of these monthly closing balances can be determined.

The correct answer is C; both statements together are sufficient.

DS16368
493. Are all of the numbers in a certain list of 15 numbers equal?

(1)   The sum of all the numbers in the list is 60.
(2)   The sum of any 3 numbers in the list is 12.

Arithmetic Properties of Numbers

(1)   It is given that the sum of the 15 numbers in the list is 60, it is possible that they are all equal to 4 since 15(4) = 60. It is also possible that 10 of the numbers are each 6 and the other 5 are each 0 since 10(6) + 5(0) = 60; NOT sufficient.

(2)   It is given that the sum of any 3 numbers in the list is 12. Let $a_1, a_2, a_3, \ldots, a_{15}$ represent the 15 numbers, then, $a_1 + a_2 + a_3 = 12$ and $a_2 + a_3 + a_4 = 12$. It follows that $a_1 + a_2 + a_3 = a_2 + a_3 + a_4$, so $a_1 = a_4$. Likewise, $a_1 + a_2 + a_3 = a_2 + a_3 + a_5$, so $a_1 = a_5$. Continuing this pattern will result in a_1 equal to each of $a_4, a_5, \ldots, a_{15}$. Also, $a_1 + a_3 + a_4 = a_2 + a_3 + a_4$, so $a_1 = a_2$. Furthermore, $a_1 + a_4 + a_5 = a_3 + a_4 + a_5$, so $a_1 = a_3$. Therefore, a_1 is equal to each of $a_2, a_3, a_4, a_5, \ldots, a_{15}$; SUFFICIENT.

The correct answer is B; statement 2 alone is sufficient.

DS16565
494. If the average (arithmetic mean) of six numbers is 75, how many of the numbers are equal to 75 ?

(1)   None of the six numbers is less than 75.
(2)   None of the six numbers is greater than 75.

Arithmetic Statistics

If the average of six numbers is 75, then $\frac{1}{6}$ of the sum of the numbers is 75. Therefore, the sum of the numbers is (6)(75).

(1)   If one of the numbers is greater than 75, then we can write that number as $75 + x$ for some positive number x. Consequently, the sum of the 6 numbers must be at least $(5)(75) + (75 + x) = (6)(75) + x$, which is greater than (6)(75), contrary to the fact that the sum is equal to (6)(75). Hence, none of the numbers can be greater than 75. Since none of the numbers can be less than 75 (given information) and none of the numbers can be greater than 75, it follows that each of the numbers is equal to 75; SUFFICIENT.

(2)   If one of the numbers is less than 75, then we can write that number as $75 − x$ for some positive number x. Consequently, the sum of the 6 numbers must be at most $(5)(75) + (75 − x) = (6)(75) − x$, which is less than (6)(75), contrary to the fact that the sum is equal to (6)(75). Hence, none of the numbers can be less than 75. Since none of the numbers can be less than 75 and none of the numbers can be greater than 75 (given information), it follows that each of the numbers is equal to 75; SUFFICIENT.

The correct answer is D; each statement alone is sufficient.

DS16188
495. What amount did Jean earn from the commission on her sales in the first half of 1988 ?

(1)   In 1988 Jean's commission was 5 percent of the total amount of her sales.
(2)   The amount of Jean's sales in the second half of 1988 averaged $10,000 per month more than in the first half.

Arithmetic Applied Problems

Let A be the amount of Jean's sales in the first half of 1988. Determine the value of A.

(1) If the amount of Jean's sales in the first half of 1988 was \$10,000, then her commission in the first half of 1988 would have been (5%)(\$10,000) = \$500. On the other hand, if the amount of Jean's sales in the first half of 1988 was \$100,000, then her commission in the first half of 1988 would have been (5%)(\$100,000) = \$5,000; NOT sufficient.

(2) No information is given that relates the amount of Jean's sales to the amount of Jean's commission; NOT sufficient.

Given (1) and (2), from (1) the amount of Jean's commission in the first half of 1988 is (5%)A. From (2) the amount of Jean's sales in the second half of 1988 is A + \$60,000. Both statements together do not give information to determine the value of A.

**The correct answer is E;
both statements together are still not sufficient.**

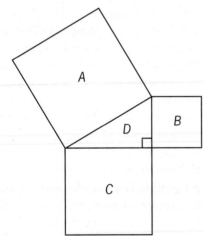

DS16572

496. In the figure above, if the area of triangular region D is 4, what is the length of a side of square region A?

(1) The area of square region B is 9.

(2) The area of square region C is $\dfrac{64}{9}$.

Geometry Area

Let x be the length of a side of square region C and y be the length of a side of square region B.

Then the area of triangular region D is $\dfrac{1}{2}xy$ and it is given that $\dfrac{1}{2}xy = 4$, or $xy = 8$. The

Pythagorean theorem can be used to find the length of a side of square region A if the values of both x and y can be determined.

(1) Given that the area of square region B is 9, it follows that $y^2 = 9$, or $y = 3$. Since $xy = 8$, the value of x can be determined, and therefore the values of both x and y can be determined; SUFFICIENT.

(2) Given that the area of square region C is $\dfrac{64}{9}$, it follows that $x^2 = \dfrac{64}{9}$, or $x = \dfrac{8}{3}$. Since $xy = 8$, the value of y can be determined, and therefore the values of both x and y can be determined; SUFFICIENT.

**The correct answer is D;
each statement alone is sufficient.**

DS16168

497. If n is a positive integer and $k = 5.1 \times 10^n$, what is the value of k?

(1) $6,000 < k < 500,000$

(2) $k^2 = 2.601 \times 10^9$

Arithmetic Properties of Numbers

(1) It is given that $6,000 < k < 500,000$ consider the following table:

n	k
1	51
2	510
3	5,100
4	51,000
5	510,000
6	5,100,000

From the table, there is only one value of k between 6,000 and 500,000, so k can be uniquely determined; SUFFICIENT.

(2) It is given that $k = 5.1 \times 10^n$, which is positive, and $k^2 = 2.601 \times 10^9$, it follows that $k = \sqrt{2.601 - 10^9}$, so k can be uniquely determined; SUFFICIENT.

**The correct answer is D;
each statement alone is sufficient.**

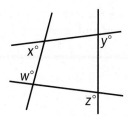

DS06875

498. What is the value of $x + y$ in the figure above?

(1) $w = 95$

(2) $z = 125$

Geometry Angles

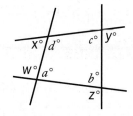

In the figure above, a, b, c, and d are the degree measures of the interior angles of the quadrilateral formed by the four lines and $a + b + c + d = 360$. Then

$w + x + y + z$

$= (180 - a) + (180 - d) + (180 - c) + (180 - b)$

$= 720 - (a + b + c + d)$

$= 720 - 360$

$= 360.$

Determine the value of $x + y$.

(1)   Given that $w = 95$, then $95 + x + y + z = 360$ and $x + y + z = 265$. If $z = 65$, for example, then $x + y = 200$. On the other hand, if $z = 100$, then $x + y = 165$; NOT sufficient.

(2)   Given that $z = 125$, then $w + x + y + 125 = 360$ and $w + x + y = 235$. If $w = 35$, for example, then $x + y = 200$. On the other hand, if $w = 100$, then $x + y = 135$; NOT sufficient.

Taking (1) and (2) together, $95 + x + y + 125 = 360$, and so $x + y = 140$.

The correct answer is C; both statements together are sufficient.

DS16370

499. If n and k are positive integers, is $\sqrt{n+k} > 2\sqrt{n}$?

(1) $k > 3n$

(2) $n + k > 3n$

Algebra Inequalities

Determine if $\sqrt{n+k} > 2\sqrt{n}$. Since each side is positive, squaring each side preserves the inequality, so $\sqrt{n+k} > 2\sqrt{n}$ is equivalent to $(\sqrt{n+k})(\sqrt{n+k}) > (2\sqrt{n})(2\sqrt{n})$, which in turn is equivalent to $n + k > 4n$, or to $k > 3n$.

(1)   Given that $k > 3n$, then $\sqrt{n+k} > 2\sqrt{n}$; SUFFICIENT.

(2)   Given that $n + k > 3n$, then $k > 2n$. However, it is possible for $k > 2n$ to be true and $k > 3n$ to be false (for example, $k = 3$ and $n = 1$) and it is possible for $k > 2n$ to be true and $k > 3n$ to be true (for example, $k = 4$ and $n = 1$); NOT sufficient.

The correct answer is A; statement 1 alone is sufficient.

DS16589

500. In a certain business, production index p is directly proportional to efficiency index e, which is in turn directly proportional to investment index i. What is p if $i = 70$?

(1) $e = 0.5$ whenever $i = 60$.

(2) $p = 2.0$ whenever $i = 50$.

Arithmetic Proportions

(1)   This gives only values for e and i, and, while p is directly proportional to e, the nature of this proportion is unknown. Therefore, p cannot be determined; NOT sufficient.

(2)   Since p is directly proportional to e, which is directly proportional to i, then p is directly proportional to i. Therefore, the following proportion can be set up: $\dfrac{p}{i} = \dfrac{2.0}{50}$. If $i = 70$, then $\dfrac{p}{70} = \dfrac{2.0}{50}$. Through cross multiplying, this equation yields $50p = 140$, or $p = 2.8$; SUFFICIENT.

The preceding approach is one method that can be used. Another approach is as follows: It is given that $p = Ke = K(Li) = (KL)i$, where K and L are the proportionality constants, and the value of $70KL$ is to be determined. Statement (1) allows us to determine the value of L, but gives nothing about K, and thus (1) is not sufficient. Statement (2) allows us to determine the value of KL, and thus (2) is sufficient.

The correct answer is B; statement 2 alone is sufficient.

DS16085

501. If n is a positive integer, what is the tens digit of n?

(1) The hundreds digit of $10n$ is 6.

(2) The tens digit of $n + 1$ is 7.

Arithmetic Properties of Numbers

(1) It is given that the hundreds digit of $10n$ is 6, recall that multiplying a positive integer by 10 puts a 0 in units place, moves the integer's units digit to tens place, its tens digit to hundreds place, and so on. For example, if $n = 3{,}542$, then $10n = 35{,}420$. Thus, if the hundreds digit of $10n$ is 6, then the tens digit of n is 6; SUFFICIENT.

(2) It is given that the tens digit of $n + 1$ is 7, it is not possible to determine the tens digit of n. If $n + 1 = 70$, then $n = 69$ and the tens digit of n is 6. However, if $n + 1 = 71$, then $n = 70$ and the tens digit of n is 7; NOT sufficient.

The correct answer is A; statement 1 alone is sufficient.

DS16204

502. What is the value of $\dfrac{2t + t - x}{t - x}$?

(1) $\dfrac{2t}{t - x} = 3$

(2) $t - x = 5$

Algebra Simplifying Algebraic Expressions

Determine the value of $\dfrac{2t + t - x}{t - x}$.

(1) Since $\dfrac{2t}{t - x} = 3$ and

$$\frac{2t + t - x}{t - x} = \frac{2t}{t - x} + \frac{t - x}{t - x} = \frac{2t}{t - x} + 1,$$

it follows that $\dfrac{2t + t - x}{t - x} = 3 + 1$;

SUFFICIENT.

(2) Given that $t - x = 5$, it follows that $\dfrac{2t + t - x}{t - x} = \dfrac{2t + 5}{5} = \dfrac{2}{5}t + 1$, which can vary when the value of t varies. For example, $\dfrac{2}{5}t + 1 = 3$ if $t = 5$ (choose $x = 0$ to have $t - x = 5$) and $\dfrac{2}{5}t + 1 = 5$ if $t = 10$ (choose $x = 5$ to have $t - x = 5$); NOT sufficient.

The correct answer is A; statement 1 alone is sufficient.

6.0 Verbal Review

6.0 Verbal Reasoning

The Verbal Reasoning section of the GMAT™ exam uses multiple-choice questions to measure your skills in reading and comprehending written material, reasoning, evaluating arguments, and correcting written material to conform to standard written English. This section includes content on a variety of topics, but neither the passages nor the questions assume knowledge of the topics discussed. Intermingled throughout the section are three main types of questions: Reading Comprehension, Critical Reasoning, and Sentence Correction.

Reading Comprehension questions are based on passages consisting of generally between 200 to 350 words. Each passage is followed by several questions that require you to understand, analyze, apply, and evaluate information and concepts presented in the passage.

Critical Reasoning questions are based on passages typically less than 100 words in length. Unlike Reading Comprehension passages, each Critical Reasoning passage is associated with just one question. This question requires you to logically analyze, evaluate, or reason about an argument, situation, or plan presented in the passage.

Sentence Correction questions are not based on passages. Instead, each Sentence Correction question presents a single sentence in which words are underlined. This question asks you to replace the underlined section with an answer choice—either the original underlined wording or a substitute for that wording—that makes the sentence as a whole express its intended meaning most correctly and effectively. This task requires you to know and apply the stylistic conventions and grammatical rules of standard written English.

You will have 65 minutes to complete the Verbal Reasoning section, or an average of about $1\frac{3}{4}$ minutes to answer each question. Including the time needed to read the Reading Comprehension passages, the average time you require to answer each Reading Comprehension question will probably be slightly longer than the overall Verbal Reasoning section average. On the other hand, the average time you require to answer a Sentence Correction question will probably be shorter than the Verbal Reasoning section average if you work efficiently and manage your time wisely.

To prepare for the Verbal Reasoning section, you may wish to first review basic concepts of textual analysis and logical reasoning to ensure that you have the foundational skills needed to answer the questions, before moving on to practice applying this knowledge on retired questions from past GMAT exams.

6.1 Verbal Review

To prepare for the Verbal Reasoning section and to succeed in graduate business programs, you will need some basic skills in analyzing and evaluating written texts and the ideas they express. This chapter explains some basic concepts that are useful in developing these skills. Only a high-level summary is provided, so if you find unfamiliar terms or concepts, you should consult other resources for a more detailed discussion and explanation.

The following concepts will help you develop different skills you may require in answering questions in the Verbal Reasoning section of the GMAT exam.

Section 6.2, "Analyzing Passages," includes the following topics:

1. Arguments
2. Explanations
3. Narratives and Descriptions

Section 6.3, "Inductive Reasoning," includes the following topics:

1. Inductive Arguments
2. Generalizations and Predictions
3. Causal Reasoning
4. Analogies

Section 6.4, "Deductive Reasoning," includes the following topics:

1. Deductive Arguments
2. Logical Operators
3. Reasoning with Logical Operators
4. Necessity, Probability, and Possibility
5. Quantifiers
6. Reasoning with Quantifiers

Section 6.5, "Grammar and Style," includes the following topics:

1. Subjects and Objects
2. Number and Person
3. Tense and Mood
4. Modifiers
5. Clauses and Conjunctions
6. Style

6.2 Analyzing Passages

1. Arguments

A. An *argument* presents one or more ideas as reasons to accept one or more other ideas. Often some of these ideas are not explicitly expressed, but are to be implicitly understood.

> *Example:*
> The sidewalk is dry, so it must not have rained last night.
> In this example, the observation that the sidewalk is dry is presented as a reason to agree with the statement that it didn't rain last night. The argument also takes it to be implicitly understood that rain typically leaves sidewalks wet.

B. A *premise* is an idea that an argument explicitly or implicitly presents as a reason to accept another idea. An argument may include any number of premises.

The words and phrases below often immediately precede a stated premise:

after all	*for one thing*	*moreover*
because	*furthermore*	*seeing that*
for	*given that*	*since*
for the reason that	*in light of the fact that*	*whereas*

> *Example:*
> Our mayor should not support the proposal to expand the freeway, because the benefits of the expansion would not justify the cost. Furthermore, most voters oppose the expansion.
>
> This is an example of an argument with two explicit premises. The word *because* introduces the first premise, that the benefits of the expansion would not justify the cost. The word *furthermore* introduces the second premise, that most voters oppose the expansion. Together, these premises argue that the mayor should not support the proposal.

C. A *conclusion* is an idea in support of which an argument presents one or more premises. When there is more than one conclusion in an argument, a *main conclusion* is a conclusion that is not presented to support any further conclusion, whereas an *intermediate conclusion* is a conclusion presented to support a further conclusion.

The words and phrases below often immediately precede a stated conclusion:

clearly	*it follows that*	*suggests that*
entails that	*proves*	*surely*
hence	*shows that*	*therefore*
implies that	*so*	*thus*

> *Example:*
> Julia just hiked fifteen kilometers, so she must have burned a lot of calories. Surely she's hungry now.
>
> This is an example of an argument with a premise, an intermediate conclusion, and a main conclusion. The word *so* introduces the intermediate conclusion, that Julia must have burned a lot of calories. The word *surely* introduces the main conclusion, that Julia is hungry now. The premise that Julia just hiked fifteen kilometers is presented to support the intermediate conclusion, which in turn is presented to support the main conclusion.

In an argument, conclusions may be stated before, between, or after premises. There may be no indicator words to signal which statements are premises and which are conclusions. To identify the premises and conclusions in these cases, consider which statements the author is presenting as reasons to accept which other statements. The reasons presented are the premises, and the statements the author is trying to persuade readers to accept are the conclusions.

Example:
For healthy eating, Healthful Brand Donuts are the best donuts you can buy. Unlike any other donuts on the market, Healthful Brand Donuts contain plenty of fiber and natural nutrients.

In this argument, the author is obviously trying to persuade the reader that Healthful Brand Donuts are the best donuts to buy for healthy eating. Thus, the first sentence is the conclusion. The statement about Healthful Brand Donuts' ingredients is presented as a reason to accept that conclusion, so it is a premise. Since the author's intentions are clear, no indicator words are used.

All the practice questions that appear in this chapter are real questions from past GMAT exams and will test the concepts you have just reviewed. The full answer explanations follow the practice question(s) and outline the reasoning for why each answer choice is correct, or incorrect.

CR63800.03*

Practice Question 1

Thyrian lawmaker: Thyria's Cheese Importation Board inspects all cheese shipments to Thyria and rejects shipments not meeting specified standards. Yet only one percent is ever rejected. Therefore, since the health consequences and associated economic costs of not rejecting that one percent are negligible, whereas the board's operating costs are considerable, for economic reasons alone the board should be disbanded.

Consultant: I disagree. The threat of having their shipments rejected deters many cheese exporters from shipping substandard product.

The consultant responds to the lawmaker's argument by

    (A)   rejecting the lawmaker's argument while proposing that the standards according to which the board inspects imported cheese should be raised

    (B)   providing evidence that the lawmaker's argument has significantly overestimated the cost of maintaining the board

    (C)   objecting to the lawmaker's introducing into the discussion factors that are not strictly economic

    (D)   pointing out a benefit of maintaining the board which the lawmaker's argument has failed to consider

    (E)   shifting the discussion from the argument at hand to an attack on the integrity of the cheese inspectors

CR32900.03

Practice Question 2

One summer, floods covered low-lying garlic fields situated in a region with a large mosquito population. Since mosquitoes lay their eggs in standing water, flooded fields would normally attract mosquitoes, yet no mosquitoes were found in the fields. Diallyl sulfide, a major component of garlic, is known to repel several species of insects, including mosquitoes, so it is likely that diallyl sulfide from the garlic repelled the mosquitoes.

Which of the following, if true, most strengthens the argument?

    (A)   Diallyl sulfide is also found in onions but at concentrations lower than in garlic.

    (B)   The mosquito population of the region as a whole was significantly smaller during the year in which the flooding took place than it had been in previous years.

    (C)   By the end of the summer, most of the garlic plants in the flooded fields had been killed by waterborne fungi.

    (D)   Many insect species not repelled by diallyl sulfide were found in the flooded garlic fields throughout the summer.

    (E)   Mosquitoes are known to be susceptible to toxins in plants other than garlic, such as marigolds.

*These numbers correlate with the online test bank question number. See the GMAT™ Official Guide Question Index in the back of this book.

386

CR63800.03
Answer Explanation 1

Argument Construction

Situation   The Thyrian lawmaker argues that the Cheese Importation Board should be disbanded, because its operating costs are high and it rejects only a small percentage of the cheese it inspects. The consultant disagrees, pointing out that the board's inspections deter those who export cheese to Thyria from shipping substandard cheese.

Reasoning   *What strategy does the consultant use in the counterargument?* The consultant indicates to the lawmaker that there is a reason to retain the board that the lawmaker has not considered. The benefit the board provides is not that it identifies a great deal of substandard cheese and rejects it (thus keeping the public healthy), but that the possibility that their cheese could be found substandard is what keeps exporters from attempting to export low-quality cheese to Thyria.

A   The consultant does reject the lawmaker's argument, but the consultant does not propose higher standards. Indeed, in suggesting that the board should be retained, the consultant implies that the board's standards are appropriate.

B   The consultant does not provide any evidence related to the board's cost.

C   The only point the lawmaker raises that is not strictly economic is about the health consequences of disbanding the board, but the consultant does not address this point at all.

D   **Correct.** This statement properly identifies the strategy the consultant employs in his or her counterargument. The consultant points out that the board provides a significant benefit that the lawmaker did not consider.

E   The consultant does not attack the integrity of the cheese inspectors; to the contrary, the consultant says that their inspections deter the cheese exporters from shipping substandard cheese.

The correct answer is D.

CR32900.03
Answer Explanation 2

Argument Evaluation

Situation   When summer floods covered garlic fields in an area with many mosquitoes, no mosquitoes were found in the fields, even though flooded fields would normally attract mosquitoes to lay their eggs in the water. Diallyl sulfide, which is found in garlic, repels mosquitoes and some other insect species, and likely accounts for the lack of mosquitoes in the area.

Reasoning   *Given the facts cited, what would provide additional evidence that diallyl sulfide from the garlic made mosquitoes avoid the flooded fields?* The argument would be strengthened by any independent evidence suggesting that diallyl sulfide pervaded the flooded fields or excluding other factors that might explain the absence of mosquitoes in the fields.

A   This could strengthen the argument if mosquitoes also avoid flooded onion fields, but we do not know whether they do.

B   This would weaken the argument by suggesting that the general mosquito population decline, rather than the diallyl sulfide, could explain the absence of mosquitoes in the fields.

C   It is not clear how this would affect the amount of diallyl sulfide in the flooded fields, so this does not provide evidence that the diallyl sulfide repelled the mosquitoes.

D   **Correct.** This provides evidence that there was no factor other than diallyl sulfide that reduced insect populations in the flooded garlic fields.

E   If anything, this would weaken the argument, since it is at least possible that some of these toxins were present in the flooded fields.

The correct answer is D.

D. A *valid* argument is one whose conclusions follow from its premises. The premises and conclusions need not be true in order for an argument to be valid. An argument with false premises is valid as long as the conclusion *would* follow if the premises *were* true. A *sound* argument is a valid argument with true premises.

Examples:
i) Everyone who tries fried eggplant is guaranteed to love the taste. So if you try it, you'll love the taste too.
In example i), the premise is false if taken literally: in reality, not everyone who tries fried eggplant is guaranteed to love the taste. Thus, example i) is not a sound argument. Nonetheless, it is a valid argument, because if everyone who tried fried eggplant were guaranteed to love the taste, it would follow logically that you too would love the taste if *you* tried it.

ii) Some people who try fried eggplant dislike the taste. So if you try it, you'll probably dislike the taste too.
In example ii), the only premise is true: in reality, some people who try fried eggplant dislike the taste. Nonetheless, example ii) is an invalid argument, and thus is not sound. The mere fact that *some* people dislike the taste of fried eggplant doesn't entail that *you personally* will *probably* dislike the taste.

E. An *assumption* is an idea whose truth is taken for granted. An assumption may be a premise in an argument, an idea about a cause or an effect in a causal explanation, or any other type of unsupported idea in a descriptive passage. A conclusion is never an assumption—an argument presents reasons to agree with a conclusion rather than taking its truth for granted.

A passage may also rely on *implicit assumptions* that the author considers too obvious to state explicitly. Although unstated, such assumptions are needed to fill in gaps in the explicit material. An argument or explanation is weak and vulnerable to criticism if it relies on implausible or clearly false assumptions.

F. A *necessary assumption* of an argument is an idea that must be true in order for the argument's stated premises to adequately support one of the argument's conclusions. In other words, a necessary assumption is one that the argument requires in order to work.

Example:
Mario has booked a flight scheduled to arrive at 5:00 p.m.—which should allow him to get here around 6:30 p.m. So, by 7:00 p.m. we will be going out to dinner with Mario.

In this argument, one necessary assumption is that the plane Mario is booked on will arrive not significantly later than the scheduled time. A second necessary assumption is that Mario managed to catch his flight. Unless these and all of the argument's other necessary assumptions are true, the argument's stated premises would not adequately support the conclusion.

CR49110.03

Practice Question 3

The spacing of the four holes on a fragment of a bone flute excavated at a Neanderthal campsite is just what is required to play the third through sixth notes of the diatonic scale—the seven-note musical scale used in much of Western music since the Renaissance. Musicologists therefore hypothesize that the diatonic musical scale was developed and used thousands of years before it was adopted by Western musicians.

Which of the following, if true, most strongly supports the hypothesis?

(A) Bone flutes were probably the only musical instrument made by Neanderthals.

(B) No musical instrument that is known to have used a diatonic scale is of an earlier date than the flute found at the Neanderthal campsite.

(C) The flute was made from a cave-bear bone and the campsite at which the flute fragment was excavated was in a cave that also contained skeletal remains of cave bears.

(D) Flutes are the simplest wind instrument that can be constructed to allow playing a diatonic scale.

(E) The cave-bear leg bone used to make the Neanderthal flute would have been long enough to make a flute capable of playing a complete diatonic scale.

CR49110.03

Answer Explanation 3

Argument Evaluation

Situation   The arrangement of the holes in a bone fragment from a Neanderthal campsite matches part of the scale used in Western music since the Renaissance. Musicologists hypothesize from this that the scale was developed thousands of years before Western musicians adopted it.

Reasoning   *Which of the options, if true, would provide the most support for the musicologists' hypothesis?* One way to approach this question is to ask yourself, "If this option were false, would the hypothesis be *less* likely to be true?" If the Neanderthal bone fragment could *not* have been part of a flute that encompassed *the entire* seven-note diatonic scale, then the bone fragment's existence would not provide strong support for the hypothesis.

A   To the extent that this is even relevant, it tends to weaken the hypothesis; it makes less likely the possibility that Neanderthals used other types of musical instruments employing the diatonic scale.

B   This also weakens the hypothesis because it states that there is no known evidence of a certain type that would support the hypothesis.

C   The fact that the cave-bear bone fragment that was apparently a flute came from a site where many other cave-bear skeletal remains were found has little bearing on the hypothesis, and in no way supports it.

D   This does not strengthen the hypothesis, for even if the option were false—even if a simpler instrument could be constructed that employed the diatonic scale—the existence of a flute employing the diatonic scale would provide no less support for the hypothesis.

E   **Correct.** This option most strongly supports the hypothesis.

The correct answer is E.

G. A *sufficient assumption* of an argument is an idea whose truth would ensure that the argument's main conclusion follows from the argument's stated premises.

> *Example:*
> The study of poetry is entirely without value, since poetry has no practical use.
>
> For this argument, one sufficient assumption would be that the study of what has no practical use is entirely without value. This assumption, together with the argument's stated premise, would sufficiently support the conclusion: if both the premise and the assumption are true, then the conclusion must also be true. Another sufficient assumption would be that the study of literature with no practical use is entirely without value, and poetry is a type of literature. Although these two distinct assumptions are each sufficient, neither one is necessary.

H. Arguments fall into several broad categories determined by the types of conclusions they support.

    i. A *prescriptive* argument supports a conclusion about what should or should not be done. Prescriptive arguments advocate adopting or rejecting policies, procedures, strategies, goals, laws, or ethical norms.

> *Example:*
> Our company's current staff is too small to handle our upcoming project. So, to ensure the project's success, the company should hire more employees.
>
> Another prescriptive argument can be found in the example in 6.2.1.B above, which concludes that the mayor should not support the proposed freeway expansion.

    ii. An *evaluative* argument supports a conclusion that something is good or bad, desirable or undesirable, without advocating any particular policy or course of action.

> *Example:*
> This early novel is clearly one of the greatest of all time. Not only did it pioneer brilliantly innovative narrative techniques, but it did so with exceptional grace, subtlety, and sophistication.

    iii. An *interpretive* argument supports a conclusion about the underlying significance of something. An interpretive argument may support or oppose an account of the meaning, importance, or implications of a set of observations, a theory, an artistic or literary work, or a historical event.

> *Example:*
> Many famous authors have commented emphatically on this early novel, either praising or condemning it. This suggests that the novel has had an enormous influence on later fiction.

iv. A *causal* argument supports a conclusion that one or more phenomena did or did not causally contribute to one or more effects. A causal argument may support or oppose an account of the causes, reasons, or motivations underlying an event, condition, decision, or outcome. For example, a causal argument may support or oppose an account of the influences underlying a literary or artistic style or movement.

> *Example:*
> Our houseplant started to thrive only when we moved it to a sunny window. So probably the reason it was sickly before then was that it wasn't getting enough sunlight.
>
> Another causal argument can be found in the example in 6.2.1.C above, which concludes that Julia must be hungry now.

v. A basic *factual* argument supports a factual conclusion that does not fit into any of the other categories explained above.

> *Example:*
> All dogs are mammals. Rover is a dog. Therefore, Rover is a mammal.

CR96370.03

Practice Question 4

The tulu, a popular ornamental plant, does not reproduce naturally, and is only bred and sold by specialized horticultural companies. Unfortunately, the tulu is easily devastated by a contagious fungal rot. The government ministry plans to reassure worried gardeners by requiring all tulu plants to be tested for fungal rot before being sold. However, infected plants less than 30 weeks old have generally not built up enough fungal rot in their systems to be detected reliably. And many tulu plants are sold before they are 24 weeks old.

Which of the following, if performed by the government ministry, could logically be expected to overcome the problem with their plan to test for the fungal rot?

(A) Releasing a general announcement that tulu plants less than 30 weeks old cannot be effectively tested for fungal rot

(B) Requiring all tulu plants less than 30 weeks old to be labeled as such

(C) Researching possible ways to test tulu plants less than 24 weeks old for fungal rot

(D) Ensuring that tulu plants are not sold before they are 30 weeks old

(E) Quarantining all tulu plants from horticultural companies at which any case of fungal rot has been detected until those tulu plants can be tested for fungal rot

CR96370.03

Answer Explanation 4

Evaluation of a Plan

Situation   There is a contagious fungal rot that devastates the tulu, a popular ornamental plant. To reassure worried gardeners, the government ministry plans to require that tulu plants be tested for the rot before being sold. However, many tulu plants are sold before they are 24 weeks old, yet fungal rot in plants less than 30 weeks old generally cannot be detected reliably.

Reasoning   *What could the government ministry do to overcome the problem?* The problem arises from the fact that tulu plants are frequently sold before they are 24 weeks old, which is too soon for any fungal rot that is present to have built up enough in their root systems to be detected. Since the goal of the testing is to ensure that infected tulu plants are not sold, an obvious solution would be to make sure that no plants are sold before they are old enough for fungal rot to have built up to a detectable level. Thus, tulu plants should not be sold before they are 30 weeks old.

A   Releasing such an announcement would help overcome the problem if it guaranteed that no one would buy or sell tulu plants before the plants were 30 weeks old, but it is far from certain that it would guarantee this.

B   Similar to A, introducing such labeling would help overcome the problem if it guaranteed that no one would buy or sell tulu plants before the plants were 30 weeks old, but it is far from certain that it would guarantee this.

C   There is no guarantee that such research will be successful at reducing the age at which tulu plants can be reliably tested.

D   **Correct.** If the government *ensures* that no tulu plants less than 30 weeks of age are sold, then the specific problem mentioned in the passage would be overcome.

E   This will not help overcome the problem. Such a quarantine program might lead horticultural companies to start selling tulu plants *only* if they are less than 24 weeks old, thereby minimizing the chance of quarantine by minimizing the chance of detection.

The correct answer is D.

2. Explanations

A. A *causal explanation* asserts that one or more factors do or may causally contribute to one or more effects. A causal explanation is not necessarily an argument, and doesn't have to include any premises or conclusions. However, a causal explanation may be a premise or conclusion in an argument.

The words and phrases below often indicate a causal explanation:

as a result	due to	results in
because	leads to	that's why
causes	produces	thereby
contributes to	responsible for	thus

Note that some of these words can also be used to indicate premises or conclusions in arguments. In such cases you may need to determine whether the author is presenting reasons to accept a conclusion or is simply stating that one or more factors causally contribute to one or more effects. If the author is simply explaining what caused an effect, and is not trying to persuade the reader that the effect is real, then the passage is a causal explanation but not an argument.

Just as an argument may include premises, intermediate conclusions, and main conclusions, a causal explanation may assert that one or more causes produced one or more intermediate effects that in turn produced further effects.

Example:
Julia just hiked fifteen kilometers, thereby burning a lot of calories. That's why she's hungry now.

This is an example of a causal explanation asserting that a causal factor (Julia's fifteen-kilometer hike) produced an intermediate effect (Julia burning a lot of calories) that in turn produced a further effect (Julia being hungry now). The word *thereby* introduces the intermediate effect, and the phrase *that's why* introduces the final effect. This explanation assumes that you already know that Julia is hungry now; it does not present reasons to believe she is hungry, but rather explains why she is hungry, and therefore is not an argument.

CR03570.03

Practice Question 5

While many people think of genetic manipulation of food crops as being aimed at developing larger and larger plant varieties, some plant breeders have in fact concentrated on discovering or producing dwarf varieties, which are roughly half as tall as normal varieties.

Which of the following would, if true, most help to explain the strategy of the plant breeders referred to above?

(A) Plant varieties used as food by some are used as ornamentals by others.

(B) The wholesale prices of a given crop decrease as the supply of it increases.

(C) Crops once produced exclusively for human consumption are often now used for animal feed.

(D) Short plants are less vulnerable to strong wind and heavy rains.

(E) Nations with large industrial sectors tend to consume more processed grains.

CR03570.03

Answer Explanation 5

Evaluation of a Plan

Situation   Some plant breeders have concentrated on discovering or producing certain species of food crop plants to be roughly half as tall as normal varieties.

Reasoning   *Why would some plant breeders concentrate on discovering or producing smaller varieties of certain food crops?* Presumably these breeders would not seek smaller varieties of plant crops unless the smaller size conveyed some benefit. If short plants were less vulnerable to strong wind and heavy rains, they would be apt to be more productive, other things being equal. Plant breeders would have reason to try to discover or produce such more productive varieties.

A   This statement doesn't indicate whether those who use the plants as ornamentals desire shorter varieties.

B   At most this suggests that higher productivity is not as much of an advantage as it otherwise would be. But there is nothing in the passage that indicates that smaller varieties would be more productive than normal-sized plants.

C   No reason is given for thinking that smaller varieties of plants are more conducive to use for animal feed than are larger varieties.

D   Correct. This answer choice is correct because—unlike the other choices—it helps explain why smaller plant varieties could sometimes be preferable to larger varieties. A plant that is less vulnerable to wind and rain is apt to suffer less damage. This is a clear advantage that would motivate plant breeders to try to discover or produce smaller varieties.

E   This has no direct bearing on the question posed. Processed grains are not even mentioned in the passage, let alone linked to smaller plant varieties.

The correct answer is D.

B. An *observation* is a claim that some state of affairs has been observed or is otherwise directly known. In the example of a causal explanation above, the statements that Julia just hiked fifteen kilometers and that she is hungry now are observations. Assuming that her burning of calories is not directly known or observed, the statement that she burned a lot of calories is not an observation.

C. A *hypothesis* is a tentative factual idea whose truth is not known and not taken for granted. A hypothesis may serve as an argument's conclusion. Causal explanations are often hypotheses. A passage may discuss *alternative hypotheses*, such as competing causal explanations for the same observation. In some cases, a passage may present pros and cons of two or more alternative hypotheses without arguing for any one of them as a conclusion.

Example:
A bush in our yard just died. The invasive insects we've seen around the yard lately might be responsible. Or the bush might not have gotten enough water. It's been a dry summer.

In this example, two alternative hypotheses are considered. The first hypothesis presents the observation that invasive insects have been in the yard as a possible causal explanation for the observed death of the bush. This hypothesis would require an implicit assumption that these insects are capable of injuring bushes of the species in question. The second hypothesis presents the observation that it's been a dry summer as an alternative causal explanation for the observed death of the bush. This hypothesis would require the assumption that the dry weather resulted in the bush not getting enough water. The passage presents observations in tentative support of each hypothesis but does not decisively argue for either of them as a conclusion.

This passage refers to Questions 6–9.

Line   Biologists have advanced two theories to explain why schooling of fish occurs in so many fish species. Because schooling is particularly widespread among species of small fish, both theories assume that schooling offers the advantage of some protection from predators.

(5)   Proponents of theory A dispute the assumption that a school of thousands of fish is highly visible. Experiments have shown that any fish can be seen, even in very clear water, only within a sphere of 200 meters in diameter. When fish are in a compact group, the spheres of visibility overlap. Thus the chance of a predator finding the school is only slightly greater than the chance of the predator finding a single fish swimming alone. Schooling is advantageous to the individual fish because a predator's chance of finding any particular fish swimming in the school is much smaller than its chance of finding at least one of the same group of fish if the fish were dispersed
(10)   throughout an area.

        However, critics of theory A point out that some fish form schools even in areas where predators are abundant and thus little possibility of escaping detection exists. They argue that the school continues to be of value to its members even after detection. They advocate theory B, the "confusion effect," which can be explained in two different ways.

(15)   Sometimes, proponents argue, predators simply cannot decide which fish to attack. This indecision supposedly results from a predator's preference for striking prey that is distinct from the rest of the school in appearance. In many schools the fish are almost identical in appearance, making it difficult for a predator to select one. The second explanation for the "confusion effect" has to do with the sensory confusion caused by a large number of prey moving around the predator. Even if the predator makes the decision to attack a particular fish, the
(20)   movement of other prey in the school can be distracting. The predator's difficulty can be compared to that of a tennis player trying to hit a tennis ball when two are approaching simultaneously.

Questions 6–9 refer to the passage.

RC73100-01.03

Practice Question 6

According to the passage, theory B states that which of the following is a factor that enables a schooling fish to escape predators?

(A)   The tendency of fish to form compact groups

(B)   The movement of other fish within the school

(C)   The inability of predators to detect schools

(D)   The ability of fish to hide behind one another in a school

(E)   The great speed with which a school can disperse

RC73100-03.03

Practice Question 7

According to the passage, both theory A and theory B have been developed to explain how

(A)   fish hide from predators by forming schools

(B)   forming schools functions to protect fish from predators

(C)   schooling among fish differs from other protective behaviors

(D)   small fish are able to make rapid decisions

(E)   small fish are able to survive in an environment densely populated by large predators

RC73100-05.03

Practice Question 8

According to one explanation of the "confusion effect," a fish that swims in a school will have greater advantages for survival if it

(A)   tends to be visible for no more than 200 meters

(B)   stays near either the front or the rear of a school

(C)   is part of a small school rather than a large school

(D)   is very similar in appearance to the other fish in the school

(E)   is medium-sized

RC73100-06.03

Practice Question 9

The author is primarily concerned with

(A)   discussing different theories

(B)   analyzing different techniques

(C)   defending two hypotheses

(D)   refuting established beliefs

(E)   revealing new evidence

RC73100-01.03

Answer Explanation 6

According to the passage, theory B states that which of the following is a factor that enables a schooling fish to escape predators?

(A)   The tendency of fish to form compact groups

(B)   The movement of other fish within the school

(C)   The inability of predators to detect schools

(D)   The ability of fish to hide behind one another in a school

(E)   The great speed with which a school can disperse

Supporting Idea

This question depends on understanding what the passage states about theory B, the "confusion effect." One element of theory B is that predators may experience sensory confusion created by large numbers of moving fish in a school.

A   The compactness of groups of schooling fish is an element of theory A, not theory B.

B   **Correct.** It is the movement of schooling fish around a predator that creates sensory confusion in the predator; this movement may distract the predator and help to protect individual fish in the school.

C   According to the passage's description of theory A, predators are actually slightly more likely to detect schools than they are to detect individual fish.

D   Theory B does not involve fish hiding behind one another, but rather moving around the predator.

E   The passage does not discuss the speed of dispersal of schools of fish.

The correct answer is B.

RC73100-03.03

Answer Explanation 7

According to the passage, both theory A and theory B have been developed to explain how

(A)   fish hide from predators by forming schools

(B)   forming schools functions to protect fish from predators

(C)   schooling among fish differs from other protective behaviors

(D)   small fish are able to make rapid decisions

(E)   small fish are able to survive in an environment densely populated by large predators

Supporting Idea

The passage states in its first paragraph that two theories were developed to explain why schooling occurs in so many fish species and that they both assume that schooling helps protect fish from predators.

A   While theory A involves an explanation of how schooling makes an individual fish less likely to be found by predators, theory B explains how schooling protects fish even when they are detected by predators.

B   **Correct.** Both theory A and theory B begin with the assumption that schooling provides protection from predators, and each theory offers a different explanation for how that protection occurs.

C   The passage does not discuss protective behaviors other than schooling.

D   The decision-making ability of predators, not schooling fish, is discussed in the passage; schooling is presented as an instinctive behavior.

E   The passage suggests that only theory B helps explain schooling behavior in environments where many predators, large or otherwise, are found, and that theory A explains schooling in areas where predators are not as abundant.

The correct answer is B.

RC73100-05.03
Answer Explanation 8

According to one explanation of the "confusion effect," a fish that swims in a school will have greater advantages for survival if it

- (A) tends to be visible for no more than 200 meters
- (B) stays near either the front or the rear of a school
- (C) is part of a small school rather than a large school
- (D) is very similar in appearance to the other fish in the school
- (E) is medium-sized

Inference

The "confusion effect" is discussed in the third and fourth paragraphs. The first explanation of the "confusion effect" proposes that because predators prefer to select distinctive prey, they find it difficult to select one fish from among many that look the same.

A   The 200-meter visibility of fish is part of the explanation for theory A, not theory B (the "confusion effect").

B   The location of an individual fish within a school is not discussed in the passage as being important to the "confusion effect."

C   The size of a school of fish is not discussed as an element of the "confusion effect."

D   Correct. Because predators, according to the "confusion effect," prefer to select prey that is distinct from the rest of the school, a fish that is similar in appearance to the other fish in its school would most likely enjoy a survival advantage.

E   The size of a fish relative to the other fish in its school would most likely contribute to its ability to survive: that is, if it resembled other fish in size, it would be safer, based on what the passage says about the "confusion effect." Furthermore, the passage gives no reason to think that merely being medium-sized would confer any advantage (unless the other fish were medium-sized as well).

The correct answer is D.

RC73100-06.03
Answer Explanation 9

The author is primarily concerned with

- (A) discussing different theories
- (B) analyzing different techniques
- (C) defending two hypotheses
- (D) refuting established beliefs
- (E) revealing new evidence

Main Idea

Determining the author's primary concern depends on understanding the focus of the passage as a whole. The author presents two theories that purport to account for why fish, particularly small fish, tend to school, and explains the arguments of proponents of each theory.

A   **Correct.** The author discusses two theories—identified as theory A and theory B—that account for the tendency of fish to school.

B   The author is not concerned with different techniques in the passage.

C   The two theories of why fish school could be referred to as hypotheses, but the author is not primarily concerned with defending them; rather, the passage explains how each attempts to account for the phenomenon in question.

D   The author presents, rather than refutes, beliefs about why fish tend to school.

E   The author reveals no evidence, new or otherwise, in the passage. The passage is a general discussion of scientific opinions based on existing evidence.

The correct answer is A.

3. Narratives and Descriptions

A. A *narrative* describes a chronological sequence of related events. A narrative is not in itself an argument or a causal explanation, but may contain one or more arguments or causal explanations, or be contained within them.

The words and phrases below often indicate narrative sequence:

after	earlier	then
afterwards	later	thereafter
before	previously	until
beforehand	since	while
during	subsequently	when

Example:

While Julia was hiking fifteen kilometers, she burned a lot of calories. **Afterwards**, she felt hungry.

This is an example of a narrative describing a chronological sequence of three events. The word *while* indicates that Julia's hike and her burning of calories happened at the same time. The word *afterwards* indicates that her hunger arose soon after the first two events. Although it is reasonable to assume that these events were causally related, the narrative doesn't actually say that they were. Thus, it is not an explicit causal explanation. And since the narrative simply reports the events without presenting any premises as reasons to accept any particular conclusion, it is not an argument either.

B. Not all passages are arguments, causal explanations, or narratives. Passages may also report on views, findings, innovations, places, societies, artistic works, devices, organisms, etc. without arguing for any conclusion, explaining any causal relationships, or narrating how any sequence of events unfolded over time.

C. Similarly, not all statements in a passage serve as premises, conclusions, observations to be explained, hypotheses, or reports of events. Some other roles that statements may play in passages include:

- Providing background information to help the reader understand the substance of the passage
- Describing details of something the passage is discussing
- Expressing the author's attitude toward material presented in the passage
- Providing examples to illustrate and clarify general statements
- Summarizing ideas that the passage is arguing against

6.3 Inductive Reasoning

1. Inductive Arguments

A. In an *inductive argument,* the premises are intended to support a conclusion but not to absolutely prove it. For example, the premises may provide evidence suggesting that the conclusion is likely to be true, without ruling out the possibility that the conclusion might nonetheless be false despite the evidence provided.

B. An inductive argument may be *strengthened* by providing further evidence or other reasons that directly support the argument's conclusion, or that make the argument's premises more compelling as reasons to accept its conclusion. Conversely, an inductive argument may be *weakened* or undermined by providing evidence or reasons that directly cast doubt on the argument's conclusion, or that make the argument's premises less compelling as reasons to accept the conclusion. Below we will consider examples of how various types of inductive arguments may be evaluated, strengthened, and weakened.

2. Generalizations and Predictions

A. An argument by *generalization* typically involves using one or more premises about a sample or subset of a population to support a conclusion about that population as a whole.

Example:
Of the eight apartments currently available for lease in this building, six are studio apartments. So probably about $\frac{3}{4}$ of all the apartments in the building are studio apartments.

In this example, the apartments currently available for lease in the building are a *sample* of the *population* of all the apartments in the building. Since six of the eight apartments currently available for lease are studio apartments, $\frac{3}{4}$ of the apartments in the sample are studio apartments.

This observation is used to argue by generalization that the population as a whole is probably similar to the sample; in other words, that probably about $\frac{3}{4}$ of all the apartments in the building are studio apartments.

B. A related type of argument by generalization uses premises about an entire population to support a conclusion about a subset of that population.

Example:

About $\frac{3}{4}$ of all the apartments in the building are studio apartments. So probably about $\frac{3}{4}$ of the apartments on the building's second floor are studio apartments.

In this example, a premise about the proportion of studio apartments among the entire population (all the apartments in the building) is used to support the conclusion that a similar proportion holds among a subset of the population (the apartments only on the second floor).

C. A *predictive* argument by generalization uses a premise about the sample of a population observed so far to support a conclusion about another sample of the population that has not yet been observed.

Example:

Of the eight apartments I have visited in this building so far, six have been studio apartments. So probably about six out of the next eight apartments I visit in the building will also be studio apartments.

In this example, the apartments the author has visited in the building are a sample consisting of only the apartments observed so far. The observation about the proportion of studio apartments in this sample is used to support a prediction that roughly the same proportion of studio apartments will be found among another sample, which consists of the next eight apartments in the building to be visited.

CR51800.03

Practice Question 10

In the United States, of the people who moved from one state to another when they retired, the percentage who retired to Florida has decreased by three percentage points over the past 10 years. Since many local businesses in Florida cater to retirees, these declines are likely to have a noticeably negative economic effect on these businesses and therefore on the economy of Florida.

Which of the following, if true, most seriously weakens the argument given?

(A) People who moved from one state to another when they retired moved a greater distance, on average, last year than such people did ten years ago.

(B) People were more likely to retire to North Carolina from another state last year than people were ten years ago.

(C) The number of people who moved from one state to another when they retired has increased significantly over the past ten years.

(D) The number of people who left Florida when they retired to live in another state was greater last year than it was ten years ago.

(E) Florida attracts more people who move from one state to another when they retire than does any other state.

CR51800.03

Answer Explanation 10

Argument Evaluation

Situation   Of those people who move to another state when they retire, the percentage moving to Florida has declined. This trend is apt to harm Florida's economy because many businesses there cater to retirees.

Reasoning   *Which of the options most weakens the argument?* The argument draws its conclusion from data about the *proportion* of emigrating retirees moving to Florida. Yet what matters more directly to the conclusion (and to Florida's economy) is the *absolute number* of retirees immigrating to Florida. That number could have remained constant, or even risen, if the absolute number of emigrating retirees itself increased while the proportion going to Florida decreased.

A   This has no obvious bearing on the argument one way or another. It makes it more likely, perhaps, that a person in a distant state will retire to Florida, but less likely that one in a neighboring state will do so.

B   This has no bearing on whether fewer people have been retiring to Florida over the last ten years.

C   **Correct.** This is the option that most seriously weakens the argument.

D   This makes it *more* likely that Florida's economy will be harmed because of decreasing numbers of retirees, but has no real bearing on the argument which concludes specifically that *declines in the proportion of emigrating retirees moving to Florida* will have a negative effect on the state's economy.

E   This is irrelevant. At issue is how the numbers of retirees in Florida from one year compare to the next, not how those numbers compare with numbers of retirees in other states.

The correct answer is C.

D. The strength of an argument by generalization depends largely on how similar the observed sample is to the overall population, or to the unobserved sample about which a prediction is made. If the sample is selected in a way that is likely to make it differ from the overall population in relevant respects, the argument is flawed in that it relies on a ***biased sample***.

> *Example:*
> In a telephone survey of our city's residents, about four out of every five respondents stated that they usually answer the phone when it rings. So probably about four out of every five residents of our city usually answer the phone when it rings.
>
> In this example, the sample consists of respondents to the telephone survey. People who usually answer the phone when it rings are more likely to respond to telephone surveys than are people who usually don't answer the phone. The way the sample was selected (via a telephone survey) makes it likely that a much greater proportion of respondents in the sample than of all the city's residents usually answer the phone when it rings. Therefore, the argument is flawed in that the sample is biased.

E. The strength of an argument generalizing from a sample also depends in part on how large the sample is. The larger the sample, the stronger the argument. This is partly because a smaller sample is statistically more likely to differ greatly from the broader population in its members' characteristics. An argument by generalization that relies on too small a sample to adequately justify the conclusion involves a ***hasty generalization***.

Example:

A coin came up heads five of the eight times Beth flipped it. This suggests that the coin she flipped is weighted so that it tends to come up heads more frequently than tails.

In this example, the sample consists of eight flips of the coin, and the population consists of all potential flips of the same coin. The sample is not clearly biased, because Beth's flips of the coin would not clearly be more likely to come up heads or tails than anyone else's flips of the same coin would. However, the sample is far too small to adequately justify the conclusion that the coin is weighted to favor heads. A coin flipped eight times is quite likely to come up heads more or fewer than exactly four times simply by chance, even if it is not weighted to favor one side. Therefore, this argument is flawed in that it involves a hasty generalization. If Beth and other people flipped the coin thousands or millions of times, and still observed that it comes up heads five out of every eight times, the argument would be stronger. No matter how many times the coin had been flipped to confirm this observed pattern, there would still remain at least some possibility that the coin was not weighted to favor heads and that the results had occurred purely by chance.

F. An argument by generalization is weaker when its conclusion is more precise, and stronger when its conclusion is vaguer, given the same premises. This is because a sample is unlikely to precisely match the population it's drawn from. A conclusion that allows for a broader range of potential mismatches between sample and population is more likely to be true, given the same evidence. An argument whose conclusion is too precise to be justified by the evidence presented is flawed in that it involves the *fallacy of specificity*.

Example:

Biologists carefully caught, weighed, and released fifty frogs out of the hundreds in a local lake. These fifty frogs weighed an average of 32.86 grams apiece. Therefore, the frogs in the lake must also weigh an average of 32.86 grams apiece.

In this example, it is quite possible that the sample is biased, because frogs of certain types might have been easier for the biologists to catch. But even if we assume that the biologists avoided any sampling bias, it would be statistically unlikely that the average weight of the sampled frogs so precisely matched the average weight of all the frogs in the lake. Thus, the conclusion is unjustifiably precise, and the argument suffers from the fallacy of specificity. A much stronger argument might use the same evidence to support the conclusion that the frogs in the lake have an average weight of between 25 and 40 grams apiece. Since that conclusion would still be true even given a range of potential mismatches between the sample and the population, it is better justified by the same evidence.

3. Causal Reasoning

A. In causal arguments, premises about presumed causal relationships or correlations between phenomena are presented to support conclusions about causes and effects. Causal reasoning is intrinsically challenging, because causal relationships can't be directly observed, and there is no scientific or philosophical consensus about the nature of causality. To say that one phenomenon causally contributes to another generally implies that if the former phenomenon appears, the latter is more likely to subsequently appear. It also implies that the presence of the former phenomenon is part of a reasonable explanation for the appearance of the latter.

> *Example:*
> Bushes of the species in our yard tend to die after several weeks without water. Therefore, they must require water at least every few weeks to survive.
>
> In this example, the premise is the observation that when one phenomenon appears (the bushes receive no water for several weeks), another phenomenon is more likely to subsequently occur (the bushes die). The conclusion is effectively that a period of several weeks without water causes bushes of that species to die.

B. A causal argument may also rely on a generally observed correlation as support for the conclusion that a particular instance of one phenomenon caused a particular instance of another.

> *Example:*
> A bush in our yard just died. There's been no rain this summer, and no one has been watering the yard. Bushes of the species in our yard tend to die after several weeks without water. Therefore, the bush probably died because it didn't get enough water.
>
> In this example, a particular instance of one phenomenon (one bush of a specific species dying) is observed to follow a particular instance of another phenomenon (the bush went without any water for weeks). A generalization is then presented that instances of the former phenomenon (bushes of that species dying) generally tend to follow instances of the latter (bushes of that species not getting any water for weeks). These premises together support the conclusion that the lack of water caused the observed death of the particular bush in question.

C. Causal arguments may be weakened by observing other correlations that suggest alternative causal explanations that could be used in competing arguments. In order to evaluate the relative strengths of two alternative explanations, it is often helpful to find or experimentally create conditions in which one possible cause is present and the other is absent.

Example:
Causal Argument 1: Bushes of the species in our yard tend to die after several weeks without water. Therefore, they must require water at least every few weeks to survive.

Causal Argument 2: Bushes of this species grow only in a region in which dry weather always coincides with extreme heat. So the heat may be the main reason why these bushes tend to die after periods without water.

Experiment 1: Ensure some of the bushes receive water regularly during a period of extreme heat, and see how well they survive.

Experiment 2: Keep some of the bushes dry during cooler weather, and see how well they survive.

A finding that the bushes survive well in Experiment 1 but not in Experiment 2 would strengthen Argument 1 and weaken Argument 2.

Conversely, a finding that the bushes survive well in Experiment 2 but not in Experiment 1 would strengthen Argument 2 and weaken Argument 1.

A finding that the bushes consistently die in both experiments would strengthen both arguments, suggesting that either heat or drought alone will kill the bushes.

A finding that the bushes survive well in both experiments would weaken both arguments, suggesting that some factor other than drought or heat may be partially or entirely responsible for killing the bushes, or alternatively that both drought and heat must occur together in order to kill the bushes.

D. In setting up experiments to test causal hypotheses, it is important to avoid experimental conditions that might introduce or eliminate other potential causes that have not been considered.

Examples:
i) To run Experiment 1 mentioned above, a scientist planted some of the bushes in a tropical rainforest in which daily rainfall and extreme heat typically occur together.

ii) To run Experiment 2 mentioned above, a scientist planted some of the bushes under an awning where rain could not reach them in cooler weather.

Both versions of the two experiments are problematic because they introduce other causal variables. In example i), different soil conditions, insect populations, and humidity levels in the rainforest might make it harder or easier for the bushes to survive, independently of the heat and rainfall. In example ii), putting the bushes under an awning would likely reduce their exposure to sunlight, which might make it harder or easier for the bushes to survive regardless of the heat and rainfall. These flaws in experimental design would cast doubt on any argument that cited these versions of the experiments as evidence to strengthen or weaken Causal Argument 1 or Causal Argument 2.

Also note that testing a causal hypothesis through experimentation typically involves reasoning by generalization: a conclusion about a broad population is based on observations of the population sample in the experiment. Thus, causal reasoning based on experimentation is vulnerable to the same flaws previously discussed in 6.3.2 Generalizations and Predictions. A causal argument will be weak if it generalizes from a sample that is too small or selected in a biased way. Under these conditions, an apparent correlation is likely to arise merely by coincidence or due to extraneous factors, without indicating a real causal relationship.

E. Even when some kind of causal association between two phenomena clearly exists, it may be difficult to determine which phenomenon is the cause and which is the effect, or whether both phenomena are caused by a third, underlying phenomenon.

Example:
A certain type of earthworm is far more frequently found in the soil under healthy bushes of the species in our yard than in the soil under sickly bushes of that species.

Even if the earthworms' presence is clearly causally associated with the bushes' health, the causal relationship could be that:

i) the earthworms improve the bushes' health, or

ii) healthier bushes attract the earthworms, or

iii) particular soil conditions both improve the bushes' health and attract the earthworms.

More than one of these causal relationships, and others, may be true at the same time. To untangle the causal relationships, it would be helpful to conduct experiments or field observations to evaluate how healthy the bushes are in the same soil conditions without earthworms; how attracted the earthworms are to those soil conditions without the bushes; and whether the earthworms tend to appear around healthier bushes even in much different soil conditions.

F. Even reliable, consistent correlations between two phenomena may arise by sheer coincidence. To determine whether this is the case, it is helpful to test whether stopping one of the phenomena from occurring also results in the other ceasing to occur. Even when no such test is possible, it is also helpful to consider whether or not there is any plausible, specific way that one of the phenomena could cause the other.

Example:

For years, Juan has arrived at work at a hair salon every weekday at exactly 8 a.m. Five hundred miles to the north, over the same period, Ashley has arrived at work at a car dealership every weekday at exactly 8:01 a.m. Therefore, Juan's daily arrival time must causally determine when Ashley arrives at work.

In this example, even though for years Juan's arrival at work has been very consistently and reliably followed by Ashley's a moment later, the argument is absurdly weak because there does not seem to be any obvious way that Juan's arrival time could causally determine Ashley's arrival time. Nonetheless, it would be possible to test the hypothesis in the argument's conclusion by persuading Juan to change his arrival times in various ways, then seeing whether Ashley's arrival times also consistently changed in the same ways. Without a plausible reason for the two arrival times to be connected, quite a lot of evidence of this type would be required to reasonably overcome the suspicion that the observed correlation is purely coincidental. Alternatively, a discovery that Juan and Ashley knew each other and had reason to coordinate their work schedules might provide a plausible causal connection between their arrival times and greatly strengthen the argument.

This passage refers to Questions 11–14.

Line   Findings from several studies on corporate mergers and acquisitions during the 1970s and 1980s raise questions about why firms initiate and consummate such transactions. One study showed, for example, that acquiring firms were on average unable to maintain acquired firms' pre-merger levels of profitability. A second study concluded that post-acquisition gains to most acquiring firms were not adequate to cover the premiums paid to obtain

(5)   acquired firms. A third demonstrated that, following the announcement of a prospective merger, the stock of the prospective acquiring firm tends to increase in value much less than does that of the firm for which it bids. Yet mergers and acquisitions remain common, and bidders continue to assert that their objectives are economic ones. Acquisitions may well have the desirable effect of channeling a nation's resources efficiently from less to more efficient sectors of its economy, but the individual executives arranging these deals must see them as

(10)   advancing either their own or their companies' private economic interests. It seems that factors having little to do with corporate economic interests explain acquisitions. These factors may include the incentive compensation of executives, lack of monitoring by boards of directors, and managerial error in estimating the value of firms targeted for acquisition. Alternatively, the acquisition acts of bidders may derive from modeling: a manager does what other managers do.

Questions 11–14 refer to the passage.

RC00034-01

Practice Question 11

The primary purpose of the passage is to

(A)   review research demonstrating the benefits of corporate mergers and acquisitions and examine some of the drawbacks that acquisition behavior entails

(B)   contrast the effects of corporate mergers and acquisitions on acquiring firms and on firms that are acquired

(C)   report findings that raise questions about a reason for corporate mergers and acquisitions and suggest possible alternative reasons

(D)   explain changes in attitude on the part of acquiring firms toward corporate mergers and acquisitions

(E)   account for a recent decline in the rate of corporate mergers and acquisitions

RC00034-03
Practice Question 12

It can be inferred from the passage that the author would be most likely to agree with which of the following statements about corporate acquisitions?

    (A)   Their known benefits to national economies explain their appeal to individual firms during the 1970s and 1980s.

    (B)   Despite their adverse impact on some firms, they are the best way to channel resources from less to more productive sectors of a nation's economy.

    (C)   They are as likely to occur because of poor monitoring by boards of directors as to be caused by incentive compensation for managers.

    (D)   They will be less prevalent in the future, since their actual effects will gain wider recognition.

    (E)   Factors other than economic benefit to the acquiring firm help to explain the frequency with which they occur.

RC00034-04
Practice Question 13

The author of the passage mentions the effect of acquisitions on national economies most probably in order to

    (A)   provide an explanation for the mergers and acquisitions of the 1970s and 1980s overlooked by the findings discussed in the passage

    (B)   suggest that national economic interests played an important role in the mergers and acquisitions of the 1970s and 1980s

    (C)   support a noneconomic explanation for the mergers and acquisitions of the 1970s and 1980s that was cited earlier in the passage

    (D)   cite and point out the inadequacy of one possible explanation for the prevalence of mergers and acquisitions during the 1970s and 1980s

    (E)   explain how modeling affected the decisions made by managers involved in mergers and acquisitions during the 1970s and 1980s

RC00034-07
Practice Question 14

The author of the passage implies that which of the following is a possible partial explanation for acquisition behavior during the 1970s and 1980s?

    (A)   Managers wished to imitate other managers primarily because they saw how financially beneficial other firms' acquisitions were.

    (B)   Managers miscalculated the value of firms that were to be acquired.

    (C)   Lack of consensus within boards of directors resulted in their imposing conflicting goals on managers.

    (D)   Total compensation packages for managers increased during that period.

    (E)   The value of bidding firms' stock increased significantly when prospective mergers were announced.

RC00034-01
Answer Explanation 11

The primary purpose of the passage is to

    (A)   review research demonstrating the benefits of corporate mergers and acquisitions and examine some of the drawbacks that acquisition behavior entails

    (B)   contrast the effects of corporate mergers and acquisitions on acquiring firms and on firms that are acquired

    (C)   report findings that raise questions about a reason for corporate mergers and acquisitions and suggest possible alternative reasons

    (D)   explain changes in attitude on the part of acquiring firms toward corporate mergers and acquisitions

    (E)   account for a recent decline in the rate of corporate mergers and acquisitions

Main Idea

This question requires understanding what the passage as a whole is trying to do. The passage begins by citing three studies that demonstrate that when firms acquire other firms, there is not necessarily a worthwhile economic gain. The passage then cites economic interests as the reason given by firms when they acquire other firms but calls into question the veracity of this reasoning. The passage then goes on to speculate as to why mergers and acquisitions occur.

A   The research cited in the passage calls into question whether mergers and acquisitions are beneficial to firms.

B   The passage is not concerned with comparing the relative effects of mergers and acquisitions on the acquired and acquiring firms.

C   **Correct.** The passage surveys reports that question the reason given by firms when they acquire other firms and suggests other reasons for these acquisitions.

D   The passage does not indicate that there has been a change in the attitude of acquiring firms toward mergers and acquisitions.

E   The passage does not indicate that there has been a decline in the rate of mergers and acquisitions.

The correct answer is C.

RC00034-03

Answer Explanation 12

It can be inferred from the passage that the author would be most likely to agree with which of the following statements about corporate acquisitions?

(A)   Their known benefits to national economies explain their appeal to individual firms during the 1970s and 1980s.

(B)   Despite their adverse impact on some firms, they are the best way to channel resources from less to more productive sectors of a nation's economy.

(C)   They are as likely to occur because of poor monitoring by boards of directors as to be caused by incentive compensation for managers.

(D)   They will be less prevalent in the future, since their actual effects will gain wider recognition.

(E)   Factors other than economic benefit to the acquiring firm help to explain the frequency with which they occur.

Inference

This question requires understanding what view the author has about a particular issue. The three studies cited by the passage all suggest that mergers and acquisitions do not necessarily bring economic benefit to the acquiring firms. The author concludes therefore that *factors having little to do with corporate economic interests explain acquisitions* and then goes on to speculate as to what the reasons may actually be.

A   The passage indicates that while mergers and acquisitions may benefit the national economy, the appeal of mergers and acquisitions must be tied to companies' *private economic interests*.

B   The passage makes no judgment as to the best way for firms to channel resources from less to more efficient economic sectors.

C   The passage makes no comparison between the influence of poor monitoring by boards and that of executive incentives.

D   The passage makes no prediction as to future trends in the market for mergers and acquisitions.

E   **Correct.** The passage states that factors other than economic interests drive mergers and acquisitions.

The correct answer is E.

RC00034-04

Answer Explanation 13

The author of the passage mentions the effect of acquisitions on national economies most probably in order to

   (A)   provide an explanation for the mergers and acquisitions of the 1970s and 1980s overlooked by the findings discussed in the passage

   (B)   suggest that national economic interests played an important role in the mergers and acquisitions of the 1970s and 1980s

   (C)   support a noneconomic explanation for the mergers and acquisitions of the 1970s and 1980s that was cited earlier in the passage

   (D)   cite and point out the inadequacy of one possible explanation for the prevalence of mergers and acquisitions during the 1970s and 1980s

   (E)   explain how modeling affected the decisions made by managers involved in mergers and acquisitions during the 1970s and 1980s

Evaluation

This question requires understanding why a piece of information is included in the passage. After the passage cites the results of the three studies on mergers and acquisitions, which call into question the economic benefits of acquisitions, it indicates that firms nonetheless claim that their objectives are economic. The passage then states that while acquisitions *may well have* a desirable effect on national economies, the results of the studies suggest that factors other than economic interest must drive executives to arrange mergers and acquisitions.

   A   The passage does not mention national economies as part of an explanation for the occurrence of mergers and acquisitions.

   B   The passage suggests that the effect of acquisitions on national economies is not tied to any explanations for why acquisitions occur.

   C   The effect of acquisitions on national economies is not mentioned in the passage as an explanation for why acquisitions occur.

   D   **Correct.** The passage uses the mention of national economies as part of a larger point questioning the stated motivations behind firms' efforts to acquire other firms.

   E   In the passage, modeling is unrelated to the idea that acquisitions may have a desirable effect on national economies.

The correct answer is D.

RC00034-07

Answer Explanation 14

The author of the passage implies that which of the following is a possible partial explanation for acquisition behavior during the 1970s and 1980s?

   (A)   Managers wished to imitate other managers primarily because they saw how financially beneficial other firms' acquisitions were.

   (B)   Managers miscalculated the value of firms that were to be acquired.

   (C)   Lack of consensus within boards of directors resulted in their imposing conflicting goals on managers.

   (D)   Total compensation packages for managers increased during that period.

   (E)   The value of bidding firms' stock increased significantly when prospective mergers were announced.

Inference

This question requires recognizing what can be inferred from the information in the passage. After providing the results of the studies of mergers and acquisitions, the author concludes that even though acquiring firms state that their objectives are economic, *factors having little to do with corporate economic interests explain acquisitions* (lines 10–11). Among alternative explanations, the author points to *managerial error in estimating the value of firms targeted for acquisition* (lines 12–13) as possibly contributing to acquisition behavior in the 1970s and 1980s.

A   While the passage indicates that managers may have modeled their behavior on other managers, it does not provide a reason for why this would be so.

B   **Correct.** The author states that one explanation for acquisition behavior may be that managers erred when they estimated the value of firms being acquired.

C   The author discusses a lack of monitoring by boards of directors but makes no mention of consensus within these boards.

D   The author does not discuss compensation packages for managers.

E   The passage does not state how significantly the value of the bidding firm's stock increased upon announcing a merger but only that it increased less in value than did the stock of the prospective firm being acquired.

The correct answer is B.

4. Analogies

A. In an argument by *analogy*, at least two things are observed to be similar in certain respects. The argument then presents a claim about one of those two things as a reason to accept a similar claim about the other.

> *Example:*
> Laotian cuisine and Thai cuisine use many of the same ingredients and cooking techniques. Ahmed enjoys Thai cuisine. So if he tried Laotian cuisine, he would probably enjoy it too.
>
> In this example, Laotian cuisine and Thai cuisine are observed to be similar in the ingredients and cooking techniques they use. The argument then presents a claim about Thai cuisine: that Ahmed enjoys it. By analogy, the argument concludes that a similar claim is probably true of Laotian cuisine: Ahmed would enjoy it if he tried it.

B. For an argument by analogy to work properly, the observed similarities between the two things must be *relevant* to the question of whether those two things also share the further similarity indicated by the conclusion. The argument in the example above meets this standard. Since the ingredients and cooking techniques used in a particular cuisine generally influence whether a particular person would enjoy that cuisine, the observed similarities in ingredients and cooking techniques between Laotian and Thai cuisine are highly relevant to the question of how similar the two cuisines are likely to be with regard to how much Ahmed enjoys them. Alternatively, if the observed similarities are not very relevant to the conclusion, the argument is weak.

Example:
Laotian cuisine and Latvian cuisine both originated in nations whose English names start with the letter *L*. Ahmed enjoys Latvian cuisine. So if he tried Laotian cuisine, he would probably enjoy it too.

In this example, Laotian cuisine and Latvian cuisine are observed to be similar with respect to the English names of the nations in which they originated. Since the English spelling of a nation's name would be unlikely to influence how much a particular person enjoys that nation's cuisine, this observed similarity is irrelevant to the question of how similar Laotian and Latvian cuisine are likely to be with regard to how much Ahmed enjoys them. Thus, the analogy is absurd, and the argument is deeply flawed. To salvage the argument, it would be necessary to present a convincing reason why the observed similarities are relevant after all—for example, by presenting evidence that Ahmed is a very unusual person whose enjoyment of food is intensely affected by English spellings.

C. A reasonable argument by analogy may be strengthened by pointing out additional relevant similarities between the two things being compared, or weakened by pointing out relevant dissimilarities between them.

Example:
Beth and Alan are both children living on the same block in the Hazelfern School District. Beth attends Tubman Primary School. So probably Alan does too.

Pointing out that Beth and Alan are both in the same grade—a similarity that would make it even more likely that they attend the same school, might strengthen this moderately reasonable argument. On the other hand, the argument might be weakened by pointing out that Beth is eight years older than Alan—a dissimilarity suggesting that Alan may be too young to attend the same school Beth attends.

CR28310.03

Practice Question 15

Which of the following most logically completes the passage?

The figures in portraits by the Spanish painter El Greco (1541–1614) are systematically elongated. In El Greco's time, the intentional distortion of human figures was unprecedented in European painting. Consequently, some critics have suggested that El Greco had an astigmatism, a type of visual impairment, that resulted in people appearing to him in the distorted way that is characteristic of his paintings. However, this suggestion cannot be the explanation, because _____.

(A) several twentieth-century artists have consciously adopted from El Greco's paintings the systematic elongation of the human form

(B) some people do have elongated bodies somewhat like those depicted in El Greco's portraits

(C) if El Greco had an astigmatism, then, relative to how people looked to him, the elongated figures in his paintings would have appeared to him to be distorted

(D) even if El Greco had an astigmatism, there would have been no correction for it available in the period in which he lived

(E) there were non-European artists, even in El Greco's time, who included in their works human figures that were intentionally distorted

CR28310.03
Answer Explanation 15

Argument Evaluation

Situation Figures in portraits by the Spanish painter El Greco are elongated. Some critics infer that this was because El Greco suffered from an astigmatism that made people appear elongated to him. But this explanation cannot be correct.

Reasoning *Which option would most logically complete the argument?* We need something that provides the best reason for thinking that the explanation suggested by critics—astigmatism—cannot be right. The critics' explanation might seem to work because ordinarily an artist would try to paint an image of a person so that the image would have the same proportions as the perceived person. So if people seemed to El Greco to have longer arms and legs than they actually had, the arms and legs of the painted figures should appear to others to be longer than people's arms and legs normally are. This is how the explanation seems to make sense. But if astigmatism were the explanation, then the elongated images in his pictures should have appeared to El Greco to be too long: he would have perceived the images as longer than they actually are—and therefore as inaccurate representations of what he perceived. So astigmatism cannot be a sufficient explanation for the elongated figures in his paintings.

A Even if subsequent artists intentionally depicted human forms as more elongated than human figures actually are, and they did so to mimic El Greco's painted figures, that does not mean that El Greco's figures were intentionally elongated.

B Although this option provides another possible explanation for El Greco's elongated figures, it provides no evidence that the people El Greco painted had such elongated figures.

C **Correct**. El Greco would have perceived the images of people in his paintings as too long, relative to his perception of the people themselves. This means that even if El Greco did have astigmatism, that factor would not provide an answer to the question, Why did El Greco paint images that he knew were distorted?

D The absence of an ability to correct astigmatism in El Greco's day does not undermine the hypothesis that it was astigmatism that caused El Greco to paint elongated figures.

E Again, this suggests another possible explanation for the distortion—namely, that El Greco did it deliberately—but it does not provide any reason to think that this is the correct explanation (and that the critics' explanation is actually incorrect).

The correct answer is C.

6.4 Deductive Reasoning

1. Deductive Arguments

A. In a ***deductive argument***, the premises are intended to absolutely prove the conclusion. In a valid deductive argument, if the premises are true, then the conclusion **must** also be true. In an argument presented as deductive, if there is any possibility of the premises being true while the conclusion is false, then the reasoning is flawed. However, a flawed deductive argument might work perfectly well as an inductive argument, provided that the author doesn't improperly present the premises as **proving** the conclusion.

2. Logical Operators

A. A ***logical operator*** expresses how the truth of one statement or idea is related to the truth of another. The basic types of logical operators are ***negations***, ***logical conjunctions***, ***disjunctions***, and ***implications***.

B. The *negation* of a statement is false because the statement itself is true, and vice versa. A negation is generally indicated by words and phrases such as *not, it is false that, it is not the case that, etc.*

Note that statements in ordinary speech and writing are often vague, ambiguous, context-sensitive, or subjective—they may be true in one sense and false in another, they may be only partly true, or their truth may be indeterminate. If a statement is true in a particular way or to a particular degree, the statement's negation is false in the same way and to the same degree.

Example:
The negation of the statement "The cat is on the mat" may be expressed as "The cat is not on the mat." "The cat is on the mat" is true because "The cat is not on the mat" is false, and vice versa—but only if both statements refer to the same cat and the same mat, in the same sense, and the same context. If the first statement is uttered while the cat is sleeping on the mat, but then the cat wakes up and leaves before the second sentence is uttered, then the context has changed, so the second utterance does not express the negation of the first. And if the cat is only partly on the mat when both statements are uttered, then the second statement as uttered is *partly* false to the degree that, and in the same sense that, the first is partly true.

C. The *logical conjunction* of two statements expresses the idea that both are true. The following words and terms often indicate a logical conjunction of two statements *A* and *B*:

A and B	*A even though B*	*not only A but also B*
Although A, B	*A. Furthermore, B.*	*A, whereas B*
A but B	*A, however B*	

In standard written English, the use of the conjunction indicators *and, furthermore*, and *not only . . . but also* usually implies that the *A* and *B* are relevant to each other or being mentioned for similar reasons—for example, that both are being presented as premises supporting the same conclusion. On the other hand, the conjunction indicators *although, but, even though, however*, and *whereas* convey the idea that there is some tension or conflict between *A* and *B*; for example, that it is surprising for both *A* and *B* to be true, or that *A* supports a conclusion that conflicts with a conclusion that *B* supports, or that *A* and *B* differ in some other unexpected way.

Examples:
i) Raul has worked for this company a long time, **and** he is searching for another job.

ii) **Although** Raul has worked for this company a long time, he is searching for another job.

Both the examples above state that Raul has worked for the company for a long time, and that he is searching for another job. But in example ii), the use of *although* may suggest that it is *surprising* that Raul is searching for another job, given that he has worked for the company a long time. In contrast, the use of *and* in example i) may suggest that it is *unsurprising* that Raul is searching for another job now that he has worked for the company a long time.

D. A *disjunction* indicates that either one of two statements is true. A disjunction of two statements *A* and *B* is usually expressed as *A or B, either A or B*, or *A unless B*.

An *inclusive disjunction* indicates that *A* and *B* might both be true, whereas an *exclusive disjunction* indicates that *A* and *B* are not both true. It is often unclear whether a disjunction expressed in English is meant to be inclusive or exclusive. For clarity, it may be helpful to write *A or B or both* to indicate an inclusive disjunction, or to write *A or B but not both* to indicate an exclusive disjunction.

Examples:

i) It will **either** rain **or** snow tomorrow.

ii) It will rain tomorrow **unless** it snows.

These examples both express the idea that at least one of the two statements "It will rain tomorrow" and "It will snow tomorrow" is true. In each case, it isn't entirely clear whether the author also means to imply that it won't **both** rain **and** snow tomorrow. The author could clarify by stating

iii) Tomorrow it will rain or snow, or both. (*inclusive disjunction*)

or iv) Tomorrow it will either rain or snow, but not both. (*exclusive disjunction*)

E. A *conditional* indicates that the truth of one statement would require or entail the truth of another—in other words, that the second statement could be properly inferred from the first. The following expressions all indicate the same conditional relationship between two statements *A* and *B*:

A would mean that B	*B if A*	*A only if B*
If A, then B	*Not A unless B*	*B provided that A*

Conditional statements of these forms don't imply that *A* is actually true, nor that *B* is. Thus, they don't present *A* as a reason to believe that *B*. So in a conditional statement, *A* is not a premise and *B* is not a conclusion. In other words, a conditional statement is not an argument. But a conditional statement *if A then B* does imply that assuming *A* as a premise, if appropriate, would allow one to correctly infer *B* as a conclusion.

Examples:

i) It will snow tonight **only if** the temperature falls below 5 degrees Celsius.

ii) It **won't** snow tonight **unless** the temperature falls below 5 degrees Celsius.

iii) **If** it snows tonight, it'll mean the temperature has fallen below 5 degrees Celsius.

These examples all express the idea that snow tonight would require temperatures below 5 degrees Celsius. They do not say that it actually will snow tonight, nor that temperatures actually will be below 5 degrees Celsius. But they do suggest, for example, that observing snow tonight would allow one to correctly infer that the temperature must be below 5 degrees Celsius.

Although conditionals are often used to express or suggest causal claims, their meaning is not necessarily causal. In the examples above, there is no implication that snow tonight would cause the temperature to fall below 5 degrees Celsius.

Also note that none of these examples say or imply that if the temperature falls below 5 degrees Celsius tonight, then it will necessarily snow. That is, a conditional of the form *if A, then B* doesn't necessarily imply that *if B, then A*.

F. If two statements *A and B* are *logically equivalent*, then they are both true or false under the same conditions, and each can be correctly inferred from the other. In other words, if *A then B*, and if *B then A*. When precision is needed, this can be expressed by writing *A if and only if B*.

3. Reasoning with Logical Operators

A. Here is a list of some basic types of logically equivalent statements formed with various combinations of the logical operators. In this list, the word *not* is used to express negation, the word *and* is used to express logical conjunction, the word *or* is used to express inclusive disjunction, and the expression *if . . . then* is used to express implication.

Logical Equivalences with Logical Operators		
A and B	is logically equivalent to	*B and A*
not (A and B)	is logically equivalent to	*not-A or not-B*
A or B	is logically equivalent to	*B or A*
not (A or B)	is logically equivalent to	*not-A and not-B* (in other words, *neither A nor B)*
if A then B	is logically equivalent to	*if not-B then not-A*
if A then (B and C)	is logically equivalent to	*(if A then B) and (if A then C)*
if A then (B or C)	is logically equivalent to	*(if A then B) or (if A then C)*
if (A or B) then C	is logically equivalent to	*(if A then C) and (if B then C)*

B. When two statements are logically equivalent, either one can be used as a premise to support the other as a conclusion in a valid argument. So for any line in the list above, an argument in which a statement of the form on the left is used as a premise to support a statement of the form on the right is valid. So is an argument in which a statement of the form on the right is used as a premise to support a statement of the form on the left.

Examples:
The second line in the list above says that for any two statements *A* and *B*, the statement *not (A and B)* is logically equivalent to the statement *not-A or not-B*. This gives us two valid arguments:

i) *not (A and B), therefore not-A or not-B*

and ii) *not-A or not-B, therefore not (A and B)*

Let's consider a specific example in standard written English. The statement *Ashley and Tim don't both live in this neighborhood* is logically equivalent to *Either Ashley doesn't live in this neighborhood or Tim doesn't*. This yields two **valid** arguments:

iii) Ashley and Tim don't both live in this neighborhood. Therefore, either Ashley doesn't live in this neighborhood or Tim doesn't.

and iv) Either Ashley doesn't live in this neighborhood or Tim doesn't. Therefore, Ashley and Tim don't both live in this neighborhood.

C. Here is a list of several more forms of valid argument that use the logical operators, and several forms of invalid argument with which they are often confused.

Valid and Invalid Inferences with Logical Operators	
Valid: *A and B, therefore A*	**Invalid:** *A, therefore A and B*
Valid: *A, therefore A or B*	**Invalid:** *A or B, therefore A*
Valid: *not–A and not–B, therefore not (A and B)*	**Invalid:** *not (A and B), therefore not–A and not–B*
Valid: *not (A or B), therefore not–A or not–B*	**Invalid:** *not–A or not–B, therefore not (A or B)*
Valid: *if A, then B; and A; therefore B*	**Invalid:** *if A, then B; and B; therefore A*
Valid: *if A, then B; and not–B; therefore not–A*	**Invalid:** *if A, then B; and not–A; therefore not–B*

On the actual GMAT exam, you will sometimes need to judge whether or not an argument is valid.

Examples:
The third line in the previous table says that ***not–A and not–B, therefore not (A and B)*** is valid, whereas ***not (A and B), therefore not–A and not–B*** is invalid. So a simple example of a **valid** argument would be:

i) Ashley doesn't live in this neighborhood, and Tim doesn't either. Therefore, it's not true that Ashley and Tim both live in this neighborhood

Whereas a superficially similar but **invalid** argument would be:

ii) It's not true that Ashley and Tim both live in this neighborhood. Therefore, Ashley doesn't live in this neighborhood, and Tim doesn't either.

Similarly, the fifth line in the previous table says that ***if A, then B; and A; therefore B*** is valid, whereas ***if A, then B; and B; therefore A*** is invalid. So another **valid** argument would be:

iii) If Ashley lives in this neighborhood, so does Tim. And Ashley does live in this neighborhood. So Tim must too.

However, example iii) should not be confused with the similar **invalid** argument:

iv) If Ashley lives in this neighborhood, so does Tim. And Tim does live in this neighborhood. So Ashley must too.

CR88310.03

Practice Question 16

Museums that house Renaissance oil paintings typically store them in environments that are carefully kept within narrow margins of temperature and humidity to inhibit any deterioration. Laboratory tests have shown that the kind of oil paint used in these paintings actually adjusts to climatic changes quite well. If, as some museum directors believe, **paint is the most sensitive substance in these works**, then by relaxing the standards for temperature and humidity control, **museums can reduce energy costs without risking damage to these paintings**. Museums would be rash to relax those standards, however, since results of preliminary tests indicate that gesso, a compound routinely used by Renaissance artists to help paint adhere to the canvas, is unable to withstand significant variations in humidity.

In the argument above, the two portions in **boldface** play which of the following roles?

(A) The first is an objection that has been raised against the position taken by the argument; the second is the position taken by the argument.

(B) The first is the position taken by the argument; the second is the position that the argument calls into question.

(C) The first is a judgment that has been offered in support of the position that the argument calls into question; the second is a circumstance on which that judgment is, in part, based.

(D) The first is a judgment that has been offered in support of the position that the argument calls into question; the second is that position.

(E) The first is a claim that the argument calls into question; the second is the position taken by the argument.

CR88310.03

Answer Explanation 16

Argument Evaluation

Situation   Museums house Renaissance paintings under strictly controlled climatic conditions to prevent deterioration. This is costly. But the paint in these works actually adjusts well to climate changes. On the other hand, another compound routinely used in these paintings, gesso, does not react well to changes in humidity.

Reasoning   *What roles do the two boldfaced statements play in the argument?* The first statement is not asserted by the author of the argument, but rather attributed as a belief to some museum directors. What the argument itself asserts is that IF this belief is true THEN the second boldfaced statement is true. But the argument then goes on to offer evidence that the first statement is false and so concludes that museum directors would be ill-advised to assume that the second statement was true.

A   This option mistakenly claims that the argument adopts the second statement as its position, when in fact the argument calls this position into question.

B   Rather than adopting the first statement, the argument offers evidence that calls it into question.

C   This option contends that the first statement is a judgment that is based on the second; in fact the opposite is true.

D   **Correct**. This option properly identifies the roles the two portions in boldface play in the argument.

E   While the argument does call the first statement into question, it also calls the second statement into question as well.

The correct answer is D.

4. Necessity, Probability, and Possibility

A. A statement may be qualified with words or phrases expressing the likelihood that the statement is true. In the most basic cases, these words or phrases indicate that:

- The statement is *necessarily* true; that is, there is a 100 percent chance the statement is true; or

- The statement is *probably* true; that is, there is a substantial chance that the statement is true;

- The statement is *possibly* true; that is, the odds are greater than 0 percent but less than 100 percent that the statement is true.

Note that in ordinary English, saying that a claim is possibly true or probably true usually implies that the claim is not necessarily true.

B. The table below categorizes words and phrases often used to indicate various degrees of probability:

Words Indicating Necessity, Probability, and Possibility		
Necessity	Probability	Possibility
certainly	*probably*	*can*
clearly	*likely*	*could*
definitely	*more likely than not*	*may*
must		*maybe*
necessarily		*might*
surely		*perhaps*
		possibly

Note that in standard written English, the meanings of **probably** and **likely** are vague. In some contexts these terms might imply a high degree of probability, such as a 95 percent chance, whereas in other contexts they might be used to indicate a substantial chance below 50 percent. It is best not to assign any very precise meaning to these terms when you encounter them on the GMAT exam.

C. The table below lists several forms of valid argument involving necessity, probability, and possibility, and several forms of invalid argument with which they are often confused.

Valid and Invalid Inferences with Necessity, Probability, and Possibility	
Valid: *Probably A, therefore possibly A*	**Invalid:** *Possibly A, therefore probably A*
Valid: *Possibly (A and B), therefore possibly A and possibly B*	**Invalid:** *Possibly A and possibly B, therefore possibly (A and B)*
Valid: *Probably (A and B), therefore probably A and probably B*	**Invalid:** *Probably A and probably B, therefore probably (A and B)*
Valid: *Probably A or probably B, therefore probably (A or B)*	**Invalid:** *Probably (A or B), therefore probably A or probably B*
Valid: *Necessarily A or necessarily B, therefore necessarily (A or B)*	**Invalid:** *Necessarily (A or B), therefore necessarily A or necessarily B*

Examples:

The second line in the previous table says that **possibly (A and B), therefore possibly A and possibly B** is valid, whereas **possibly A and possibly B, therefore possibly (A and B) is** invalid. So a simple **valid** argument would be:

i) It's possible that Tim and Ashley both live in this house. So it's possible that Tim lives in this house, and it's also possible that Ashley does.

Whereas a superficially similar but **invalid** argument would be:

ii) It's possible that Tim lives in this house. It is also possible that Ashley lives in this house. So possibly both Tim and Ashley live in this house.

To see that argument ii) is invalid, suppose that you know for certain that the house has only one resident, but you don't know whether that resident is Tim, Ashley, or someone else. In that case the premises of argument ii) would be true, but its conclusion would be false. Thus, the conclusion can't be correctly inferred from the premises.

5. Quantifiers

A. A *quantifier* is a word or phrase that indicates proportion, number, or amount. In this section we will consider ordinary nonmathematical quantifiers used in the Verbal Reasoning section. Some basic examples of quantifiers are *all*, *most*, *some*, and *none*.

   i. A *universal quantifier* such as *all* indicates a reference to 100 percent of the individuals in a category or to the entirety of some collective.

   ii. A quantifier such as *most* indicates a reference to more than 50 percent of the individuals in a category. In standard written English, *most* sometimes implies *not all*, but not always—its meaning is somewhat vague. It is often helpful to write either *most but not all*, or else *most or all*, to indicate which meaning is intended.

   iii. An *existential quantifier* such as *some* indicates a reference to one or more individuals in a category or to at least a portion of some collective. In English it is often quite unclear whether *some* is being used to imply *not all*. For clarity it is often helpful to write *only some*, to indicate that *not all* is implied, or else *at least some*, to indicate the meaning *some or all*. When used with a plural noun, *some* may also imply *more than one*.

   iv. A quantifier such as *no* or *none of* indicates something is being denied about all the individuals in a category or about the entirety of some collective.

   v. Other common nonmathematical quantifiers have more nuanced meanings. For example, *a few* has the vague meaning of a relatively small number more than two. The upper limit of what counts as *a few* depends on the context: the expression *a few Europeans* might indicate a reference to many thousands of people (still a tiny part of Europe's overall population), whereas *a few residents in our building* would probably indicate a reference to only three or four people if the building had only fifteen residents.

CR13750.03

Practice Question 17

Codex Berinensis, a Florentine copy of an ancient Roman medical treatise, is undated but contains clues to when it was produced. Its first 80 pages are by a single copyist, but the remaining 20 pages are by three different copyists, which indicates some significant disruption. Since a letter in handwriting, identified as that of the fourth copyist, mentions a plague that killed many people in Florence in 1148, Codex Berinensis was probably produced in that year.

Which of the following, if true, most strongly supports the hypothesis that Codex Berinensis was produced in 1148 ?

   (A) Other than Codex Berinensis, there are no known samples of the handwriting of the first three copyists.

   (B) According to the account by the fourth copyist, the plague went on for 10 months.

   (C) A scribe would be able to copy a page of text the size and style of Codex Berinensis in a day.

   (D) There was only one outbreak of plague in Florence in the 1100s.

   (E) The number of pages of Codex Berinensis produced by a single scribe becomes smaller with each successive change of copyist.

CR13750.03
Answer Explanation 17

Argument Evaluation

Situation   The Florentine copy of an ancient Roman work is undated but provides clues as to the time it was produced. The first 80 pages of Codex Berinensis are the work of one copyist. The fact that the last 20 pages are the work of a succession of three different copyists is an indication of serious turmoil at the time the copying was done. Since a letter in the fourth copyist's handwriting reveals that a plague killed many people there in 1148, Codex Berinensis was probably produced in that year.

Reasoning   *Which information supports the hypothesis dating the Codex to 1148?* Consider the basis of the hypothesis: the succession of copyists indicating the work was significantly disrupted, and the fourth copyist's letter indicating the plague of 1148 caused serious loss of life. From this, it is argued that the plague of 1148 was the reason for the multiple copyists and that the work can thus be dated to that year. What if there were multiple plagues?

In that case, Codex Berinensis could have been produced at another time. If, instead, only one plague occurred in the 1100s, the elimination of that possibility supports the hypothesis that the work was done in 1148.

A   Examples of the copyists' handwriting might help date Codex Berinensis; the absence of handwriting samples does not help support 1148 as the date.

B   The length of the plague, while it may account for the succession of copyists, does not help support the particular year the work was done.

C   The amount of work a copyist could achieve each day does not provide any information about the year the work appeared.

D   **Correct.** This statement properly identifies a circumstance that supports the hypothesis.

E   The productivity or tenure of the various copyists is irrelevant to establishing the date.

The correct answer is D.

B. The table below categorizes some of the basic English quantifier words by their meanings.

Basic English Quantifier Words			
"All" and similar quantifier words	**"Most" and similar quantifier words**	**"Some" and similar quantifier words**	**"No" and similar quantifier words**
all	generally	a number	never
always	a majority	a portion	no
any	most	any	none
both	more than half	at least one	not any
each	usually	occasionally	not one
every		one or more	nowhere
everywhere		some	
whenever		sometimes	
wherever		somewhere	

Note that the meaning of *any* varies greatly in different contexts. The sentence *Any of the students would prefer chocolate ice cream* means *Each of the students would prefer chocolate ice cream.* But confusingly, the sentence *I don't know whether any of the students would prefer chocolate ice cream* means *I don't know whether one or more of the students would prefer chocolate ice cream.*

C. In standard written English, using quantifiers in a declarative statement usually implies that there is at least one individual in each of the categories mentioned, and that any collective mentioned exists. However, this rule does not always apply in hypothetical statements, in conditionals, or with the quantifier *any*.

Examples:
i) **All** life forms native to planets other than Earth **are** carbon-based.

ii) **Any** life forms native to planets other than Earth **would be** carbon-based.

In statement i), the word *all* and the indicative verb form *are* suggests the opinion that there actually exist some life forms native to planets other than Earth. But in statement ii), the word *any* and the conditional verb form *would be* shows the author is carefully avoiding any implication about whether or not there are life forms native to planets other than Earth.

D. Superficially similar statements with two or more quantifiers can have very different meanings depending on word order and nuances of phrasing.

Examples:
i) There must be some beverage that is the favorite of every student in the class.

ii) Each student in the class must have some favorite beverage.

Statement i) suggests that there must be a *particular* beverage that is all the students' favorite. In other words, every student in the class must have *the same* favorite beverage. Statement ii) only suggests that each individual student must have one or another favorite beverage. In other words, the students in the class may have *different* favorite beverages from each other.

E. A *count noun* refers to a countable number of individuals, whereas a *mass noun* refers to a collective quantity rather than to individuals. Only count nouns can be plural; words used as mass nouns always have a singular form. English diction sometimes requires that you use a different quantifier with a count noun than with a similar mass noun. Sentence Correction questions may also test this skill.

Examples:
Correct: i) She drank many of the sodas in the refrigerator.
Correct: ii) She drank much of the soda in the refrigerator.
Incorrect: iii) She drank many of the soda in the refrigerator.

In example i), *many* is used correctly with the count noun *sodas*, meaning *cans or bottles of soda.* Example ii) *much* is used correctly with the mass noun *soda*, which refers to the soda in the refrigerator collectively rather than to individual containers of soda. Example iii) is grammatically incorrect because it uses *many* with *soda* as a mass noun.

Except in certain technical mathematical contexts, the comparative quantifiers *less* and *least* are typically used with mass nouns for comparisons of amount or degree, whereas *fewer* and *fewest* are used with count nouns for comparisons of number.

> *Examples:*
> **Correct:** Fewer deliveries arrived today than yesterday.
> **Incorrect:** Less deliveries arrived today than yesterday.
>
> Since the plural form of *deliveries* clearly indicates it is a count noun, the appropriate comparison word is *fewer*, not *less*.

6. Reasoning with Quantifiers

A. Here is a list of a few types of logically equivalent statements formed with some of the basic quantifiers above. In this list, the letters *A* and *B* stand in for noun phrases, and the word *some* is used to mean *one or more*. For simplicity we use the plural in each statement, but this does not necessarily mean that a singular meaning is excluded. Similar equivalences hold when quantifiers are used with mass nouns.

Logical Equivalences with Quantifiers		
All As are Bs	is logically equivalent to	*No As are not Bs.*
Some As are Bs	is logically equivalent to	*Some Bs are As.*
No As are Bs	is logically equivalent to	*No Bs are As.*
Some As are not Bs	is logically equivalent to	*Not all As are Bs.*

Notice that *All As are Bs* is **not** equivalent to *All Bs are As*, and that *Some As are not Bs* is **not** equivalent to *Some Bs are not As*.

> *Examples:*
> i) The true statement *All ostriches are birds* is obviously not equivalent to the false statement *All birds are ostriches*.
>
> ii) The true statement *Some birds are not ostriches* is obviously not equivalent to the false statement *Some ostriches are not birds*.

B. As explained previously, when two statements are logically equivalent, either one can be used as a premise to support the other as a conclusion in a valid argument. This principle applies to equivalences involving quantifiers just as it does to equivalences using logical operators.

C. A *syllogism* is a simple form of argument in which two premises containing quantifiers are used to support a conclusion that also contains quantifiers.

Here is a list of several forms of valid syllogism, and several forms of invalid syllogism with which they are sometimes confused. As explained previously, the letters *A, B,* and *C* stand in for noun phrases, and the word *some* is used to mean *one or more*.

Valid and Invalid Syllogisms
Valid: *All As are Bs. All Bs are Cs. So all As are Cs.*
—**Invalid:** *All As are Bs. All Bs are Cs. So all Cs are As.*
—**Invalid:** *All As are Bs. All Cs are Bs. So all As are Cs.*
—**Invalid:** *All Bs are As. All Bs are Cs. So all As are Cs.*
Valid: *Some As are Bs. All Bs are Cs. So some As are Cs.*
—**Invalid:** *All As are Bs. Some Bs are Cs. So some As are Cs.*
—**Invalid:** *Some As are Bs. Some Bs are Cs. So some As are Cs.*
Valid: *All As are Bs. No Bs are Cs. So no As are Cs.*
—**Invalid:** *No As are Bs. All Bs are Cs. So no As are Cs.*
—**Invalid:** *No As are Bs. No Bs are Cs. So all As are Cs.*
—**Invalid:** *No As are Bs. All Bs are Cs. So some As are not Cs.*

Examples:

The first line of the previous table states that the syllogism *All As are Bs. All Bs are Cs. So all As are Cs* is valid. A simple example of a **valid** syllogism following this pattern would be:

i) All the trees in the local park were planted by the town arborist. All the trees planted by that arborist have also been labeled by her. So all the trees in the local park must have been labeled by the arborist.

But a superficially similar but obviously **invalid** syllogism would follow the pattern in the second line of the table (*All As are Bs. All Bs are Cs. So all Cs are As*):

ii) All the trees in the local park were planted by the town arborist. All the trees the arborist has planted have also been labeled by her. So all the trees that have been labeled by the arborist must be in the local park.

To see that argument ii) is invalid, consider that even if both premises are true, the arborist might also have labeled trees outside the park (possibly including some trees she didn't plant).

Another **invalid** syllogism would follow the pattern in the third line of the table (*All As are Bs. All Cs are Bs. So all As are Cs*):

iii) All the trees in the local park were planted by the town arborist. All the trees the arborist has labeled are trees she planted. So all the trees in the local park must have been labeled by the arborist.

To see that argument iii) is invalid, consider that even if both premises are true, the arborist might not have labeled many of the trees she planted, including many or all of those in the park.

The pattern in the fourth line of the table (*All Bs are As. All Bs are Cs. So all As are Cs*) yields yet another **invalid** syllogism:

iv) All the trees the town arborist has planted are in the local park. All the trees planted by that arborist have also been labeled by her. So all the trees in the local park must have been labeled by the arborist.

To see that argument iv) is invalid, consider that even if both premises are true, the park might contain many trees that the arborist neither planted nor labeled.

D. Note that some of the quantifier words in the table "Basic English Quantifier Words" in section 6.4.5.B refer specifically to time or place. For example, **whenever** means **every time**, **usually** means **most times**, and **never** means **at no time**. Understanding these meanings may allow you to paraphrase these arguments into more standardized forms to check their validity.

Example:

Max **never** goes running when the sidewalks are icy. The sidewalks are **usually** icy on January mornings, so Max must not go running on most January mornings.

This example can be paraphrased as follows:

No times when Max goes running are times the sidewalks are icy. Most January mornings are times the sidewalks are icy. So most January mornings are not times when Max goes running.

Thus, this argument is a valid syllogism of the form ***No As are Bs. Most Cs are Bs. So most Cs are not As.***

6.5 Grammar and Style

1. Subjects and Objects

A. A complete declarative sentence generally includes at least a **subject** (a noun, pronoun, or noun phrase) and a verb. Many verbs also require a second noun, pronoun, or noun phrase as the **direct object**. Some even require an additional component, which may be a noun, pronoun, or noun phrase, sometimes preceded by a preposition. If any one of these components is missing, the sentence is incomplete and is called a **sentence fragment**.

Examples:

i) **Complete Sentence:** The brown package arrived quickly.

Sentence fragment with subject missing: Arrived quickly.

Sentence fragment with verb missing: The brown package quickly.

In example i), the complete sentence includes a subject, *the brown package*, the verb *arrived*, and the adverb *quickly*. The first sentence fragment is missing a subject. The second sentence fragment is missing a verb.

ii) **Complete Sentence:** I mailed the package yesterday.

Sentence Fragment with direct object missing: I mailed yesterday.

In example ii), the complete sentence includes the subject *I*, the verb *mailed*, the direct object *the package*, and the adverb *yesterday*. In standard written English, the verb *to mail* typically requires a direct object naming something that is mailed. Although the word *yesterday* can be a noun, yesterday is not something that can be mailed, so in this context *yesterday* is clearly being used as an adverb. Thus, the sentence fragment is missing the direct object the verb requires.

iii) **Complete Sentence:** He put the package on your desk.

Sentence Fragment with direct object missing: He put on your desk.

Sentence Fragment with indirect object missing: He put the package.

In example iii), the complete sentence includes the subject *he*, the verb *put*, the direct object *the package*, and the prepositional phrase *on your desk*, which contains the indirect object *your desk*. The verb *to put* requires both a direct object naming something that is put somewhere and a phrase indicating where that thing is put. The first sentence fragment is missing the required direct object. The second sentence fragment is missing the required indirect object in a prepositional phrase. Note that this final sentence fragment could also be completed with an adverb of location such as *right there* or *downstairs* rather than with a prepositional phrase.

SC93410.03

Practice Question 18

In a review of 2,000 studies of human behavior that date back to the 1940s, two Swiss <u>psychologists, declaring that since most of the studies had failed to control for such variables as social class and family size,</u> none could be taken seriously.

- (A) psychologists, declaring that since most of the studies had failed to control for such variables as social class and family size,
- (B) psychologists, declaring that most of the studies failed in not controlling for such variables like social class and family size, and
- (C) psychologists declared that since most of the studies, having failed to control for such variables as social class and family size,
- (D) psychologists declared that since most of the studies fail in controlling for such variables like social class and family size,
- (E) psychologists declared that since most of the studies had failed to control for variables such as social class and family size,

SC93410.03
Answer Explanation 18

Verb Form; Diction

The subject of the sentence, *two Swiss psychologists*, needs a main verb. The *ing* verb form *declaring* cannot, on its own, be the main verb of a correct English sentence. Furthermore, the clause that addresses the reason for not taking the studies seriously also needs a subject (*most of the studies*) and a verb (*had failed*).

A   The sentence needs a verb form that agrees in person and number with the subject, *two Swiss psychologists*, and that is in the appropriate tense.

B   In addition to the problem with *declaring*, explained above, in this version of the sentence the phrase *failed in not controlling for* is awkward and does not mean the same thing as *failed to control for*. Also, the expression *such X like Y* is incorrect in English; the correct usage is *such X as Y*.

C   The correct form for the sentence's main verb *declared* is used here, but *having failed* is a participial form and as such cannot be the main verb in the clause.

D   English has a rule of sequence of tenses: once a verb form is marked for past tense, the following verb forms that describe the same object or event have to be in the past tense as well. Thus, *fail* is the wrong verb form. The expression *such X like Y* is incorrect in English; the correct usage is *such X as Y*.

E   **Correct.** The subject *two Swiss psychologists* is followed by a verb in the past tense (*declared*); the dependent clause *since . . . family size* also has the correct verb form (*had failed*).

The correct answer is E.

> **B.** In some cases sentence fragments are grammatically acceptable.

> *Examples:*
> i) The greater the thread count, the higher the price.
>
> ii) Better a small nutritious meal than a large unwholesome one.
>
> iii) Here today, gone tomorrow.
>
> iv) No idea.
>
> Examples i) and ii) show grammatically standard ways of expressing comparisons without an explicit verb. Equivalent complete sentences would be:
>
> ***Whenever the thread count is greater, the price is higher*** and
>
> ***A small nutritious meal is better than a large unwholesome one.***
>
> Example iii) is a grammatically correct conventional saying with no subject and no verb. An equivalent complete sentence might be ***What is here today is gone tomorrow.***
>
> Example iv) would be a grammatically correct but informal reply to a question. In some contexts, an equivalent complete sentence might be ***I have no idea.***

C. The grammatical subject of a complete English sentence may be a placeholder pronoun that doesn't actually refer to anything. The two standard placeholder pronouns are *it* and *there*.

> *Examples:*
> i) **It** was raining yesterday.
>
> ii) **There** are several reasons to prefer this theory to the proposed alternative.
>
> In example i), the subject pronoun *it* does not refer to any actual entity that was raining. In example ii), the subject pronoun *there* does not refer to any place where the reasons are.

D. In a declarative sentence, the subject precedes the verb, and the direct and indirect objects follow the verb. But in some cases alternative word orders are also grammatically correct.

> *Examples:*
> i) "Tell me about it," said his uncle.
>
> ii) In neither case could I find the needed information.
>
> In example i), the direct object is the quotation *"Tell me about it."* The direct object precedes the verb *said*, which in turn precedes the subject *his uncle*. This word order is grammatically acceptable for direct quotations, especially in standard English writing.
>
> Example ii) starts with a prepositional phrase *in neither case* that modifies the auxiliary verb *could*. The subject *I* is embedded between *could* and the main verb *find*. This word order is grammatically acceptable, especially in formal contexts.

E. Most pronouns take different forms as grammatical subjects than they take as direct and indirect objects. A common grammatical error is to use subject pronouns as objects, or vice versa. Although this is often acceptable in casual speech, it is considered ungrammatical in formal writing.

> *Examples:*
> **Correct:** **He** and Nina visited Paul and **me**.
> **Incorrect use of object pronoun as subject:** Nina and **him** visited Paul and me.
> **Incorrect use of subject pronoun as object:** He and Nina visited Paul and **I**.
>
> In these sentences, the subject pronoun *he* is the correct one to use in the sentence's grammatical subject phrase *He and Nina*; the object form *him* is incorrect. And the object pronoun *me* is the correct one to use in the sentence's direct object phrase *Paul and me*; the subject form *I* is incorrect.

2. Number and Person

A. Standard written English makes few distinctions of number and person in verb forms, but most verbs change form with a third-person singular subject in the present tense. The verb *to be* also has distinct forms in the past tense and with the subject *I* in the present tense. The form a verb takes must be consistent with the number and person of the grammatical subject.

Examples:
Correct: Every one of the circuits **has** a separate switch.
Incorrect: Every one of the circuits **have** a separate switch.

In these sentences, the subject is the noun phrase *every one of the circuits*. It is singular, because every one of the circuits is being considered individually. Although *circuits* is plural and immediately precedes the verb, it is not the grammatical subject. Thus, the correct verb form is the singular form *has*, not the plural form *have*.

B. As a pronoun, *each* is singular. When *each* is used directly before a noun, the noun is singular. But *each* may also be used after a plural subject, with a plural verb form.

Examples:
i) **Each** has a separate switch.

ii) **Each circuit** has a separate switch.

iii) **The circuits each** have separate switches.

These three examples are all grammatically correct. In example i), the subject is the singular pronoun *each*. In example ii), the subject is the singular *each circuit*. In example iii), the subject is the plural *the circuits*, and *each* serves as an adverb.

Note that in examples i) and ii), the direct object a *separate switch* is also singular, whereas in example iii), the direct object *separate switches* is plural. This is appropriate because in examples i) and ii), each circuit and its switch are being considered separately, whereas in example iii), they are all being considered collectively. In example iii), the meaning is unclear whether each individual circuit has several separate switches, or whether the circuits have only one switch apiece. When precision is important, wordings like that in example iii) should be avoided.

C. In some cases, a term may take a plural verb form when used to refer to multiple individuals but a singular verb form when used to refer to a collective or quantity.

Examples:
i) Six dollars **were** withdrawn from the box, one at a time.

ii) Six dollars **is** a high price for that.

iii) The staff **are** working well together.

iv) The staff **is** larger than it used to be.

v) A number of the trees **are** now flowering.

vi) The number of trees now flowering **is** large.

These examples are all grammatically correct.

In example i), the subject *six dollars* is plural because it refers to six separate dollar bills.

In example ii), the subject *six dollars* is singular because it refers to a single amount of money.

In example iii), the subject *the staff* is plural because it refers to separate staff members working together.

In example iv), the subject *the staff* is singular because it refers to the staff as a single group that has become larger, rather than to individual staff members, who are not being described as having become larger.

In example v), the subject *a number of the trees* is plural because it refers to multiple trees, which are flowering, rather than to the number, which is not flowering.

In example vi), the subject *the number of trees* is singular because it refers to a number, which is large, rather than to the trees, which are not being described as large.

D. A pronoun often has an *antecedent*—a noun, a noun phrase, or another pronoun appearing elsewhere in the discourse. A pronoun and its antecedent share the same referent. When a pronoun has an antecedent, it should be clear what the antecedent is, and the pronoun should agree with the antecedent in person, number, and gender. Similarly, where a noun or noun phrase has the same referent as another noun or noun phrase, the two terms should agree in number.

Examples:

Correct: The agency regularly releases **reports**, but **they** have become less frequent this year.

Incorrect: The agency regularly releases reports, but **it** has become less frequent this year.

Incorrect: The agency is reporting regularly, but **they** have become less frequent this year.

In the correct example above, the plural pronoun *they* clearly refers to the plural antecedent *reports*.

In the first incorrect example, the grammatical antecedent for the singular pronoun *it* appears to be the singular *the agency*, but the resulting sentence makes no sense. Evidently the intended antecedent is supposed to be something like *the release of reports*. But because that phrase doesn't actually appear, the sentence is confusing.

In the second incorrect example, the plural *they* has no plural antecedent in the sentence. The noun *the agency* is clearly singular in this sentence, since it is used with the singular verb form *is*. Without a plural antecedent for *they*, the sentence is confusing and unclear.

SC06684

Practice Question 19

Faced with an estimated $2 billion budget gap, the city's mayor proposed a nearly 17 percent reduction in the amount allocated the previous year to maintain the city's major cultural institutions and to subsidize hundreds of local arts groups.

(A) proposed a nearly 17 percent reduction in the amount allocated the previous year to maintain the city's major cultural institutions and to subsidize

(B) proposed a reduction from the previous year of nearly 17 percent in the amount it was allocating to maintain the city's major cultural institutions and for subsidizing

(C) proposed to reduce, by nearly 17 percent, the amount from the previous year that was allocated for the maintenance of the city's major cultural institutions and to subsidize

(D) has proposed a reduction from the previous year of nearly 17 percent of the amount it was allocating for maintaining the city's major cultural institutions, and to subsidize

(E) was proposing that the amount they were allocating be reduced by nearly 17 percent from the previous year for maintaining the city's major cultural institutions and for the subsidization

SC06684

Answer Explanation 19

Rhetorical Construction; Parallelism

The original sentence contains no errors. It uses the parallel construction *to maintain* and *to subsidize* to show clearly the two areas where the *17 percent reduction* in funds will be applied. In addition, the *17 percent reduction* is closely followed by *the amount allocated the previous year*, making it clear what is being reduced by 17 percent.

A   **Correct.** The sentence uses parallel construction and a well-placed modifier.

B   *To maintain* and *for subsidizing* are not parallel. The sentence is imprecise, and *it* does not have a clear antecedent.

C   *For the maintenance* and *to subsidize* are not parallel, and the sentence is wordy.

D   *For maintaining* and *to subsidize* are not parallel, *it* does not have a clear antecedent, and the sentence structure makes it unclear just what the writer is claiming.

E   *Maintaining* and *the subsidization* are not parallel, *they* does not have a clear antecedent, and the sentence structure makes it unclear just what the writer is claiming.

The correct answer is A.

3. Tense and Mood

A. The table below summarizes some of the main English tenses, with examples:

English Tenses		
Simple Present	**Simple Past**	**Simple Future**
We <u>eat</u> dinner at 6 every evening.	We <u>ate</u> dinner yesterday evening.	We <u>will eat</u> dinner tomorrow evening.
Present Progressive	**Past Progressive**	**Future Progressive**
We <u>are eating</u> dinner now.	We <u>were eating</u> dinner when you called.	We <u>will be eating</u> dinner when you arrive.
Present Perfect	**Past Perfect**	**Future Perfect**
We <u>have eaten</u> dinner already this evening.	We <u>had eaten</u> dinner before you called.	We <u>will have eaten</u> dinner before you arrive.
Present Perfect Progressive	**Past Perfect Progressive**	**Future Perfect Progressive**
We <u>have been eating</u> dinner for about ten minutes now.	We <u>had been eating</u> dinner for only ten minutes when dessert was served.	We <u>will have been eating</u> dinner for at least ten minutes by the time you arrive.

B. Standard written English generally uses the present progressive tense to describe events as currently occurring. The simple present tense is often reserved instead for describing events and conditions as occurring at indefinite or unspecified times, or as recurring. However, in compound sentences either the present progressive or the simple present may be used to describe events as hypothetical or occurring in the future.

Examples:
i) The dog **is barking** loudly.

ii) The dog **barks** loudly.

iii) If the dog **is barking** loudly, it will wake you up.

iv) If the dog **barks** loudly, it will wake you up.

These examples are all grammatically correct. In example i), the present progressive *is barking* indicates that the sentence is describing an event happening now, rather than the dog's general tendency to bark loudly. But in example ii), the simple present *barks* indicates that the sentence is describing the dog's general habit; the dog is inclined to bark loudly, but might not be doing so right at this moment. Examples iii) and iv) both describe hypothetical future events, but the use of the present progressive *is barking* in example iii) more clearly refers to prolonged barking, whereas the simple present *barks* in example iv) could refer to either prolonged barking or a single bark.

C. For a sentence with two or more verbs to make sense, the verbs' tenses must be aligned so that the timing of the events described is coherent. Progressive tenses are generally used to describe situations ongoing at a particular time, while perfect tenses are used to describe either situations that occurred up to a particular time or situations that occurred earlier but are still considered relevant to the time being discussed.

Examples:
i) **Correct:** I enjoyed my visit to Tianjin, a city whose history I had researched beforehand.
Incorrect: I enjoyed my visit to Tianjin, a city whose history I have researched beforehand.

In example i), the past perfect *had researched* is used correctly in describing a situation that occurred earlier than the main event described with the simple past *enjoyed*. In this context it is incorrect to use the present perfect *have researched*, because that would imply that the main event (the speaker's enjoying a stay in Tianjin) is occurring now—an implication contradicted by the use of the simple past *enjoyed*.

ii) **Correct:** When the researcher begins the next experiment, she will be working in a new laboratory.
Incorrect: When the researcher begins the next experiment, she was working in a new laboratory.

In example ii), the simple present *begins* is correctly used in a *when* clause to describe a future event. Therefore, the future progressive *will be working* is correctly used to describe a situation as ongoing at the time of that future event. However, it would make no sense to use the past progressive *was working* to describe a situation as ongoing at the time of that future event. The use of *was working* would signify a situation that was ongoing at the time of a past event.

SC02457

Practice Question 20

Being a United States citizen since 1988 and born in Calcutta in 1940, author Bharati Mukherjee has lived in England and Canada, and first came to the United States in 1961 to study at the Iowa Writers' Workshop.

- (A) Being a United States citizen since 1988 and born in Calcutta in 1940, author Bharati Mukherjee has
- (B) Having been a United States citizen since 1988, she was born in Calcutta in 1940; author Bharati Mukherjee
- (C) Born in Calcutta in 1940, author Bharati Mukherjee became a United States citizen in 1988; she has
- (D) Being born in Calcutta in 1940 and having been a United States citizen since 1988, author Bharati Mukherjee
- (E) Having been born in Calcutta in 1940 and being a United States citizen since 1988, author Bharati Mukherjee

SC02457

Answer Explanation 20

Verb Form; Rhetorical Construction

Being . . . since 1988 and born in Calcutta in 1940 is an awkward, wordy construction, which presents an unclear and potentially confusing chronological order. Since in the correct version of the sentence the original phrase (*being . . .*) has been made into a main clause, a semi-colon should separate it from the second main clause beginning *she has lived*.

A   The phrases are expressed in an illogical and potentially confusing sequence.

B   *Having been* suggests that the citizenship came chronologically before the birth. The pronoun *she* is the subject of the first clause; since the author's name is mentioned only after the semicolon, *she* has no clear referent.

C   **Correct.** In this sentence, the sequence of events is expressed logically, grammatically, and concisely in each independent clause.

D   The progressive verb forms *being born* and *having been* illogically suggest continuous action and fail to establish a logical time sequence. The sentence is wordy and awkward.

E   The progressive verb forms *having been born* and *being* illogically suggest continuous action and fail to establish a logical time sequence. The sentence is wordy and awkward.

The correct answer is C.

   D. All the verb forms considered above are in the ***indicative mood***, which is generally used in statements describing actual or expected situations. In contrast, the ***subjunctive mood*** and the ***conditional mood*** are used in certain statements concerning orders, requests, wishes, and hypothetical or imaginary situations.

   i. The ***present subjunctive*** of a verb is simply the verb's bare infinitive without ***to***. It is used in certain constructions to indicate an action being prescribed, required, requested, etc.

> *Examples:*
> **Correct:** He asked that they try the cake.
> **Incorrect:** He asked that they tried the cake.
>
> In these sentences, the present subjunctive ***try*** is the correct verb form to use when describing a requested action. The simple past ***tried*** is incorrect, even though ***asked*** is in the past tense.

   ii. The ***past subjunctive*** is generally identical in form to the simple past tense, except that in formal writing the past subjunctive of ***to be*** is always ***were***, even with singular subjects. The past subjunctive is used in simple statements and in the antecedents of conditionals to indicate that the situation described is not real.

> *Examples:*
> **Correct:** I wish I were on vacation now.
> **Incorrect:** I wish I am on vacation now.
>
> In these sentences, ***were*** is the correct verb form to use in describing a wish for a vacation that is not actually happening. Although the wish is for a vacation in the present moment, the simple present ***am*** is incorrect because the sentence indicates the vacation is not presently occurring.

   iii. The ***past perfect subjunctive*** is identical in form to the past perfect and is used in simple statements and in the antecedents of conditionals to indicate that a situation was not real at some earlier time.

Examples:
Correct: I wish I **had gone** on vacation yesterday.
Incorrect: I wish I **went** on vacation yesterday.

In these sentences, the past perfect subjunctive **had gone** is the correct verb form to use in describing a wish for an imaginary past event to have occurred. The simple past tense **went** is incorrect because the sentence indicates the event did not actually occur.

iv. In conditional statements about unreal, imaginary situations, the past subjunctive or past perfect subjunctive should be used in the antecedent clause, while the verb in the consequent clause should be in the **conditional mood**. Like the past, present, and future tenses, the conditional mood comes in a simple form (**would eat**), a progressive form (**would be eating**), a perfect form (**would have eaten**), and a perfect progressive form (**would have been eating**). Conditional verb forms can also be formed with **could** and **should**.

Examples:
Correct: If I **were** on vacation now, I **would go** to the beach.
Incorrect: If I were on vacation now, I **am going** to the beach.
Incorrect: If I **would be** on vacation now, I would go to the beach.

In these conditional sentences describing an imaginary, unreal situation, the past subjunctive **were** is the correct verb form in the antecedent clause, and the conditional **would go** is the correct verb form in the consequent clause. When a conditional sentence describes an imaginary situation, it is incorrect to use a non-conditional verb form in the consequent clause or to use a conditional verb form in the antecedent clause.

E. Verb forms with **would, could,** and **should** can also be used in various contexts to describe actual, potential, or prescribed actions or situations.

Examples:
i) I **would like** to go on vacation next week.

ii) I really **could go** on vacation next week.

iii) I **should go** on vacation next week.

In these sentences the verb forms with **would, could,** and **should** are used to describe an actual desire in example i), an actual capacity in example ii), and a prescriptive judgment in example iii). In example i), the form **would like** is essentially a formal or polite substitute for the simple present **want**.

4. Modifiers

A. Adjectives modify nouns and noun phrases, whereas adverbs modify verbs, adjectives, other adverbs, and entire clauses. In standard written English, it is incorrect to use an adjective in place of an adverb or vice versa.

> *Examples:*
> **Correct:** She played the piano really well.
> **Incorrect in formal writing:** She played the piano really good.
> **Incorrect in formal writing:** She played the piano real well.
>
> In the correct form of the sentence above, the adverb *well* modifies the verb *played*, and the adverb *really* modifies the adverb *well*. In formal writing, it is incorrect to use an adjective such as *good* to modify a verb or to use an adjective such as *real* to modify an adverb. However, both of the sentences labeled above as "incorrect in formal writing" would often be acceptable in casual speech.

B. Entire phrases may also modify nouns, verbs, and other parts of speech. Careful word ordering and phrasing is often needed to unambiguously indicate which sentence element a phrase is modifying. In most cases it is helpful to put the modifier close to the element it is intended to modify.

> *Examples:*
> **Ambiguous Grammar:** She saw a boy petting a dog with her binoculars.
>
> **Unambiguous Grammar:** Through her binoculars, she saw a boy petting a dog.
>
> **Unambiguous Grammar:** She saw a boy who had her binoculars and was petting a dog.
>
> **Unambiguous Grammar:** She saw a boy using her binoculars to pet a dog.
>
> **Unambiguous Grammar:** She saw a boy who was petting a dog that had her binoculars.
>
> The sentence with ambiguous grammar is confusing because it is unclear whether the prepositional phrase *with her binoculars* is meant to modify *saw*, or *boy*, or *petting*, or *dog*. Rewording and reorganizing the sentence in any of the four grammatically unambiguous ways above clarifies which meaning is intended.

Practice Question 21

Unlike the original National Museum of Science and Technology in Italy, where the models are encased in glass or operated only by staff members, the Virtual Leonardo Project, an online version of the museum, encourages visitors to "touch" each exhibit, which thereby activates the animated functions of the piece.

- (A) exhibit, which thereby activates
- (B) exhibit, in turn an activation of
- (C) exhibit, and it will activate
- (D) exhibit and thereby activate
- (E) exhibit which, as a result, activates

SC95430.03

Answer Explanation 21

Grammatical Construction; Logical Predication

The relative pronoun *which* requires an antecedent, and there is none provided in this sentence. It makes more sense to make the visitors the agents responsible for the action of both the verbs—*touch* and *activate*. Because to "*touch*" is an infinitive, the second verb form must be, as well, though the *to* may be implied.

A   *Which* has no antecedent in the sentence, so it is unclear what activated the display.

B   *In turn an activation . . .* seems to be the subject of a new clause, but it has no verb, so the sentence is incomplete.

C   There is no antecedent for *it* because *touch* is a verb.

D   **Correct.** The agent of the action is clearly indicated by the grammatical structure of the sentence; visitors are encouraged *to "touch" . . . and thereby (to) activate.*

E   *Which* has no antecedent in this sentence.

The correct answer is D.

> C. A dangling modifier is one that has been misplaced so that it grammatically modifies the wrong sentence element or no sentence element at all.

> *Examples:*
> **Correct:** i) Concerned that the snake might be poisonous, the workers decided to leave it untouched.
>
> **Incorrect:** ii) Concerned that it might be poisonous, the snake was left untouched by the workers.
>
> **Incorrect:** iii) Concerned that the snake might be poisonous, the decision of the workers was to leave it untouched.
>
> **Incorrect:** iv) Concerned that the snake might be poisonous, it was decided the workers would leave it untouched.
>
> In general, an adjective phrase at the beginning of a sentence modifies the following noun phrase, which is typically the sentence's grammatical subject. Thus, example i) above correctly expresses the intended meaning that the workers were concerned the snake might be poisonous. Example ii) incorrectly indicates that the snake was concerned, and example iii) incorrectly indicates that the decision was concerned. In example iv), there is no sentence element that could plausibly be modified by the phrase ***concerned that the snake might be poisonous***; the sentence's grammatical subject ***it*** is a dummy pronoun that doesn't refer to anything.

5. Clauses and Conjunctions

A. A *clause* is a part of a sentence containing at least a subject and a verb. Sentences may contain several types of clauses:

- An *independent clause* is one that could stand alone as a separate sentence with its meaning intact.

- A *subordinate clause* modifies an independent clause, usually by providing a time, place, or reason, but cannot stand on its own as a separate sentence with its meaning fully intact.

- A *relative clause* modifies a noun or verb in another clause. Often a relative clause starts with a relative pronoun such as *what, who, which,* or *that,* or a relative adverb such as *when, where,* or *why,* but in some cases these elements may be preceded by a preposition or omitted altogether.

- A *noun clause* looks like a relative clause, but serves as a noun in the sentence rather than as a modifier.

Examples:
i) They shipped the package last week, and it will arrive on time.

In example i), the two clauses *they shipped the package last week* and *it will arrive on time* are independent, because each can stand alone as a separate sentence with its meaning intact.

ii) **If they shipped the package last week**, it will arrive on time.

In example ii), the clause *if they shipped the package last week* is a subordinate clause. It cannot stand on its own, but rather states a condition under which the main clause *it will arrive on time* is true.

iii) The package that they shipped last week will arrive on time.

In example iii), the clause *that they shipped last week* is a relative clause modifying the subject of the main clause *The package will arrive on time.* The relative clause specifies which package will arrive on time. Omitting the relative pronoun *that* from this sentence would also be grammatically acceptable.

iv) I'm not sure which package they shipped last week.

In example iv), the noun clause *which package they shipped last week* does not modify any noun, but itself serves as the direct object of the sentence.

B. Appropriate punctuation or connectives must be used to separate clauses from other clauses or sentence components. Failure to do so may result in an ungrammatical *run-on sentence*.

Examples:
Correct: i) The players decided to cancel the game; playing during the storm would have been unpleasant.

Correct: ii) The players decided to cancel the game **because** playing during the storm would have been unpleasant.

Correct: iii) The players decided to cancel the game, **which** would have been unpleasant to play during the storm.

Incorrect: iv) The players decided to cancel the game, playing during the storm would have been unpleasant.

Incorrect: v) The players decided to cancel the game would have been unpleasant to play during the storm.

Example i) correctly uses a semicolon to separate two independent clauses; example ii) correctly uses *because* to separate an independent clause from a subordinate clause; and example iii) correctly uses a comma and *which* to separate an independent clause from a relative clause. Example iv) is incorrect because it uses only a comma between two independent clauses, failing to separate them adequately. Example v) ungrammatically runs two clauses together into a monstrous hybrid clause in which the subject of *would have been* is unclear.

SC02605

Practice Question 22

As a result of record low temperatures, the water pipes on the third floor froze, <u>which caused the heads of the sprinkler system to burst, which released torrents of water</u> into offices on the second floor.

- (A) which caused the heads of the sprinkler system to burst, which released torrents of water
- (B) which caused the heads of the sprinkler system to burst and which released torrents of water
- (C) which caused the heads of the sprinkler system to burst, torrents of water were then released
- (D) causing the heads of the sprinkler system to burst, then releasing torrents of water
- (E) causing the heads of the sprinkler system to burst and release torrents of water

SC02605
Answer Explanation 22

Logical Predication; Grammatical Construction

This sentence describes a causal sequence of events leading to flooded second-floor offices. One of the steps, sprinkler heads bursting, was presumably simultaneous with the release of torrents of water, so it is best to present these events as actions attached to the same subject (*heads of the sprinkler system*). The sentence as given attempts to explain the sequence in a chain of relative clauses, using the pronoun *which* to introduce successive steps. The precise reference of this relative pronoun is somewhat obscure—it appears to refer to the entire preceding clause—and the sequence separates the simultaneous bursting of heads and releasing of water into two temporally separate events.

A   The reference of the second *which* is obscure, and the sentence implausibly separates bursting heads and releasing of torrents into two temporally separate events.

B   Joining the relative pronouns with the conjunction *and* makes the freezing of the water pipes the subject of both *caused . . .* and *released . . .* Thus, it seems to indicate, somewhat implausibly, that the freezing of the pipes directly released torrents of water independently of its causing the sprinkler heads to burst.

C   The passive verb *were . . . released* obscures the causal sequence behind the releasing of torrents of water. The introduction of a new independent clause without a conjunction is ungrammatical and makes this version a run-on sentence.

D   As in (B), the structure of this version makes the freezing of the pipes the subject of both *causing . . .* and *releasing . . . .* The introduction of the sequential marker *then* divides the bursting of heads and releasing of torrents of water into two separate events in the sequence. It indicates, implausibly, that the pipes' freezing directly released torrents of water after it had also caused the sprinkler heads to burst.

E   **Correct.** The elimination of the relative pronouns clarifies the causal sequence of events, and the double infinitives *to burst* and (*to*) *release* underscores the simultaneity of these events.

The correct answer is E.

C.   *Grammatical conjunctions* connect sentence components and show the relationship between them. Grammatical conjunctions include not only words such as ***and*** that indicate logical conjunctions, but also words that indicate disjunctions, implications, premise-conclusion relationships, cause-effect relationships, relationships in time and space, and other types of relationship between sentence components. There are three types of conjunctions:

   i.   *Coordinating conjunctions* connect at least two components of the same type, such as two clauses, two noun phrases, two verbs, two adjectives, or two adverbs. English coordinating conjunctions include ***and, but, for, nor, or, so***, and ***yet***. Of these, ***for*** and ***so*** are used as conjunctions only between clauses.

   ii.   *Correlative conjunctions* consist of two words or phrases, each preceding one sentence component. Some common correlative conjunctions include ***both/and, either/or, neither/nor***, and ***not only/but also***. Most correlative conjunctions require that the two sentence components they connect be of the same grammatical type.

   iii.   *Subordinating conjunctions* connect an independent clause to a subordinate clause. They generally indicate that the subordinate clause expresses the time, place, manner, or condition in which the statement in the independent clause holds. There are many subordinating conjunctions, including ***as, because, if, once, though, unless, until, where, when, whether or not***, and ***while***.

Examples:

i) I sat **and** relaxed in the easy chair.

ii) I **not only** sat **but also** relaxed in the easy chair.

iii) I relaxed **as** I sat in the easy chair.

All these examples are grammatically correct. In example i), the verbs *sat* and *relaxed* are joined by the coordinating conjunction *and*, while in example ii), the same two verbs are joined by the correlative conjunction *not only/but also*. In example iii), the subordinating conjunction *as* joins the independent clause *I relaxed* to the subordinate clause *I sat in the easy chair*. The subordinate clause indicates the situation in which the statement in the independent clause *I relaxed* holds.

Note that in each example, deleting the conjunction and either one of the components it connects leaves a grammatically correct sentence. For instance, in example i), deleting *sat and* would leave the grammatically correct sentence *I relaxed in the easy chair*. In contrast, *I sat and relaxing in the easy chair* would be grammatically incorrect, because deleting *sat and* from *I sat and relaxing in the easy chair* would leave the verbless sentence fragment *I relaxing in the easy chair*.

D. In many cases, using a conjunction to connect two components of different grammatical types is grammatically incorrect. This error frequently occurs with correlative conjunctions and in lists using coordinating conjunctions.

Examples:
Correct: i) I went to both **a park** and **the downtown library**.
Incorrect: ii) I went both **to a park** and **the downtown library**.

Correct: iii) I went to **a park**, **a movie theater**, and then **the downtown library**.
Incorrect: iv) I <u>went to</u> **a park**, **a movie theater**, and then went to **the downtown library**.

In example i), the correlative conjunction *both/and* is correctly used to connect two noun phrases: *a park* and *the downtown library*. In example ii), *both/and* incorrectly connects the prepositional phrase *to the park* to the noun phrase *the downtown library*. In example iii), the coordinating conjunction *and then* is used correctly to connect three noun phrases in a list: *a park*, *a movie theater*, and *the downtown library*. In example iv), *and then* is used incorrectly because at least two components in the list differ in grammatical type: *a movie theater* is a noun phrase, whereas *went to the downtown library* is a verb phrase. Given this grammatical error, it is unclear whether the first component in the list is supposed to be the noun phrase *a park* or the verb phrase *went to a park*.

SC74010.03
Practice Question 23

Tropical bats play important roles in the rain forest ecosystem, aiding in the dispersal of cashew, date, and fig seeds; <u>pollinating banana, breadfruit, and mango trees; and indirectly help produce</u> tequila by pollinating agave plants.

    (A)   pollinating banana, breadfruit, and mango trees; and indirectly help produce

    (B)   pollinating banana, breadfruit, and mango trees; and indirectly helping to produce

    (C)   pollinating banana, breadfruit, and mango trees; and they indirectly help to produce

    (D)   they pollinate banana, breadfruit, and mango trees; and indirectly help producing

    (E)   they pollinate banana, breadfruit, and mango trees; indirectly helping the producing of

SC74010.03
Answer Explanation 23

Logical Predication; Parallelism

This sentence expresses a list of the roles tropical bats play in the rain forest ecosystem. Since these roles are enumerated in a list, and since the first member of the list is already provided, it is necessary to maintain the same structure for the rest of the members of the list in order to maintain parallelism and clarity. Note that semicolons separate the members of the list, leaving the commas to mark series of items within each member of the list.

A   In this version, the third member of the list does not maintain the *ing* verb form that the two previous members use.

B   **Correct.** This version correctly maintains the parallel structure (*aiding in . . .; pollinating . . .; and helping . . .*).

C   In this version, the third member of the list does not maintain the *ing* verb form of the two previous members of the list. In addition, this member of the list includes a subject (*they*) while the other members do not, again violating parallelism.

D   In order to maintain parallelism the verb that is the member of the list has to be in the *ing* form, not its complement. Thus, the *ing* has to be on the verb *help*, not on *produce*.

E   Although this version maintains parallelism throughout, the phrase *helping the producing* is an incorrect construction in English.

The correct answer is B.

6. Style

    A. Sentences that are grammatically correct and unambiguous may nonetheless be poorly written in various ways. For example, they may contain more words than needed to convey the intended meaning, or be confusing and annoying to the reader. A few common errors of this type include redundancy, unnecessary use of noun phrases in place of verbs, and inappropriate use of passive voice or other convoluted verbal constructions.

Examples:

Correct: i) Bananas are almost always harvested green and allowed to ripen in transit or on supermarket shelves.

Incorrect: ii) With regard to how bananas are harvested and allowed to ripen, they are almost always harvested green and allowed to ripen in transit or on supermarket shelves.

Incorrect: iii) Bananas are almost always harvested green, and the ripening of the bananas is allowed in transit or on supermarket shelves.

Incorrect: iv) Bananas are almost always harvested green, and it is allowed that they ripen in transit or on supermarket shelves.

In example i), the wording is straightforward and concise. Example ii) incorrectly starts with a redundant announcement of the sentence's topic. The reader can easily see that the sentence is about how bananas are harvested and allowed to ripen without the phrase *with regard to how bananas are harvested and allowed to ripen*, so that phrase is a pointless distraction. In example iii), the noun phrase *the ripening of the bananas* is an unnecessarily wordy substitute for example i)'s simple infinitive *to ripen*. In example iv), the construction *it is allowed that they ripen* is an unnecessarily wordy substitute for example i)'s simple *allowed to ripen*.

The variety of common stylistic errors in standard English writing is too vast for this review chapter to survey adequately. To learn about more types of stylistic error, consult guides to writing styles. Keep in mind that opinions differ about what constitutes good writing style, and that different guidebooks may contradict each other in the stylistic practices they recommend. The GMAT exam does not test familiarity with specific and potentially controversial stylistic rules advocated by any single style guide.

SC92120.03

Practice Question 24

With corn, soybean, and wheat reserves <u>being low enough so</u> a poor harvest would send prices skyrocketing, grain futures brokers and their clients are especially interested in weather that could affect crops.

- (A) being low enough so
- (B) so low such that
- (C) so low that
- (D) that are low enough so
- (E) that are so low such that

CR09351.03

Practice Question 25

<u>To Josephine Baker, Paris was her home long before it was fashionable to be an expatriate</u>, and she remained in France during the Second World War as a performer and an intelligence agent for the Resistance.

- (A) To Josephine Baker, Paris was her home long before it was fashionable to be an expatriate,
- (B) For Josephine Baker, long before it was fashionable to be an expatriate, Paris was her home,
- (C) Josephine Baker made Paris her home long before to be an expatriate was fashionable,
- (D) Long before it was fashionable to be an expatriate, Josephine Baker made Paris her home,
- (E) Long before it was fashionable being an expatriate, Paris was home to Josephine Baker,

SC92120.03
Answer Explanation 24

Idiom; Rhetorical Construction

This sentence opens with a long participial phrase (*With . . . skyrocketing*) that describes conditions within which the action of the main clause (*grain futures brokers . . . crops*) occurs. The opening phrase compares one economic condition (grain reserve levels) with another (prices), using the idiomatic expression *so low that*. Some of the phrases used in expressing this kind of comparison are wordy and indirect (*being low enough so*). Thus, they are not standard in written English, even though they may be accepted in some informal speaking contexts.

A   This phrase is wordy and unidiomatic.

B   This phrase combines two idioms (*so . . . that* and *such that*) in a way that does not clearly make sense. It is wordy and redundant; both *so . . . that* and *such* signal comparison.

C   **Correct.** This wording is standard, clear, and direct.

D   The relative clause introduced by *that are* makes this phrase unnecessarily wordy and cumbersome; *enough* and *so* are redundant.

E   This version of the phrase is the most redundant of all—piling comparative terms one upon the other (*that are so* and *such*). The repetition obscures instead of develops meaning.

The correct answer is C.

CR09351.03
Answer Explanation 25

Rhetorical Construction; Parallelism

This compound sentence (consisting of two independent clauses joined by the coordinating conjunction *and*) would be most clearly expressed if Josephine Baker were the subject of the first clause since *she* is the subject of the second clause: *Josephine Baker made Paris her home* would clearly parallel *she remained in France*. The adverb clause *long . . . expatriate* is best placed before the main first clause.

A   *To Josephine Baker . . . her* is redundant and awkward; the subject of the first main clause is *Paris* rather than *Baker*.

B   *For Josephine Baker . . . her* is redundant and awkward; putting two introductory elements together before the main clause is awkward.

C   Inversion of the expected word order in *to be an expatriate was unfashionable* is awkward.

D   **Correct.** The clearest, most economical order for this sentence is to put the adverb clause first, and make *Baker* the subject of the first main clause, parallel to *she* in the second.

E   *Being* is awkward; *Baker* should be the subject of the first main clause, parallel to *she* in the second main clause.

The correct answer is D.

To register for the GMAT™ exam go to www.mba.com/gmat

7.0   Reading Comprehension

7.0 Reading Comprehension

Reading Comprehension questions appear in the Verbal Reasoning section of the GMAT™. They refer to written passages consisting of generally between 200 to 350 words. The passages discuss topics in the social sciences, humanities, physical and biological sciences, and such business-related fields as marketing, economics, and human resource management. Each passage is accompanied by a short series of questions asking you to interpret the text, apply the information you gather from the reading, and make inferences (or informed assumptions) based on the reading. For these questions, you will see a split computer screen. The written passage will remain visible on the left side as each question associated with that passage appears, in turn, on the right side. You will see only one question at a time. However, the number of questions associated with each passage may vary.

As you move through the Reading Comprehension sample questions, try to determine a process that works best for you. You might begin by reading a passage carefully and thoroughly. Some test takers prefer to skim the passages the first time through, or even to read the first question before reading the passage. You may want to reread any sentences that present complicated ideas or that introduce terms new to you. Read each question and series of answers carefully. Make sure you understand exactly what the question is asking and what the answer choices are.

If you need to, you may reread any parts of the passage relevant to answering the question that you are currently viewing, but you will not be able to return to other questions after you have answered them and moved on. Some questions ask explicitly about particular portions of the passages. In some cases, the portion referred to is highlighted while the relevant question is displayed. In such cases, the question will explicitly refer to the highlighted part.

The following pages describe what Reading Comprehension questions are designed to measure, the directions that will precede the questions, and the various question types. This chapter also provides test-taking strategies, sample questions, and detailed explanations of all the questions. The explanations further illustrate how Reading Comprehension questions evaluate basic reading skills.

7.1 What Is Measured

GMAT Reading Comprehension questions measure your ability to understand, analyze, apply, and evaluate information and concepts presented in written form. All questions are to be answered on the basis of what is stated or implied in the reading material, and no specific prior knowledge of the material is required. Success in all types of GMAT questions—except those that are purely mathematical—requires strong reading skills. Thus, for some examinees, Critical Reasoning, Sentence Correction, and word-based Quantitative questions inevitably test reading comprehension in addition to the skills that they primarily target. But they do so only indirectly and only at the level of proficiency needed to demonstrate the skills that are directly targeted. By contrast, the Reading Comprehension questions are designed to focus directly on various components of Reading Comprehension and to measure different levels of skill in those components.

Generally speaking, reading comprehension skills are divided into two fundamental categories: *Identify Stated Idea* and *Identify Inferred Idea*.

- *Identify Stated Idea* refers to your ability to understand the passage as a whole and its constituent parts. To answer questions related to this skill category, you need not do anything further with the information. The skills required for *Identify Stated Idea* are typically prerequisites for those in the second category, *Identify Inferred Idea*, but questions targeting either of these fundamental skill types may be just as difficult as those targeting the other.

- *Identify Inferred Idea* refers to your ability to use information in a passage for purposes such as inferring additional information on the basis of what is given, applying the information to further contexts, critiquing the views expressed in the passage, and evaluating the ways in which the writing is structured.

More specifically, GMAT Reading Comprehension questions evaluate your ability to do the following:

- **Understand complex, sophisticated nontechnical writing.**
  Effective reading involves understanding not only words and phrases in context but also the overall messages conveyed by the writer. Although the questions do not directly measure your vocabulary knowledge (they will not ask you to show that you know the standard meanings of terms), some of them may test your ability to interpret special meanings of terms as they are used in the reading passages.

- **Understand the purposes and functions of passage components, and the logical and rhetorical relationships among concepts and pieces of information.**
  Questions that focus on this type of skill may ask you, for example, to determine how part of a passage relates to other parts, to identify the strong and weak points of an argument, or to evaluate the relative importance of arguments and ideas in a passage.

- **Draw inferences from facts and statements.**
  With a little reflection, anyone who thoroughly comprehends a text should be able to determine what further information can be inferred from it. The inference questions will ask you to reach conclusions on the basis of factual statements, authors' claims and opinions, or other components of a reading passage.

- **Understand and follow the development of quantitative concepts in written material.**
  Reading Comprehension questions do not measure mathematical knowledge. However, the passages sometimes contain quantitative information or opinions about such matters as percentages, proportions, trends, probabilities, or statistics, expressed in ways that should be understandable without technical mathematical training. You may be asked to interpret, evaluate, or apply such quantitative information, or to draw inferences from it. In some cases, you might need to use some very simple arithmetic.

There are six kinds of Reading Comprehension questions, each kind focusing on a different skill. But there is inevitably some peripheral overlap between the skills tested by one kind of question and those tested by others. For example, identifying a passage's main point often requires recognizing the logical or rhetorical structure of the text, while drawing inferences or applying information often requires accurately understanding of the passage's main and supporting ideas.

During the test, no labels will indicate which kind of Reading Comprehension question you are looking at, but each question's wording will clearly indicate what you need to do. Most of the Reading Comprehension question types will be represented among the several Reading Comprehension sets in your test, but you may not see all the types.

The Reading Comprehension questions fall into the following categories:

1. Main Idea

Each passage is a unified whole—that is, the individual sentences and paragraphs support and develop one central point and have a single unified purpose. Sometimes you will be told the central point in the passage itself, and sometimes you will need to determine the central point from the overall organization or development of the passage. A Main Idea question may ask you to

- recognize an accurate summary, restatement, or paraphrase of the main idea of a passage
- identify the author's primary purpose or objective in writing the passage
- assign a title that summarizes, briefly and pointedly, the main idea developed in the passage.

Main Idea questions are usually easy to identify as such. They generally ask explicitly about the main idea or main purpose, using phrases such as:

Which of the following most accurately expresses the main idea of the passage?,

The primary purpose of the passage as a whole is to . . . , or

In the passage, the author seeks primarily to. . . .

Incorrect answer choices for these questions often take the form of ideas in the passage that are subsidiary or tangential to the main point, statements that are superficially similar to but demonstrably distinct from the main point, or statements that are simply outside the scope of the passage even though they may be conceptually related to it.

As you read a passage, you may find it helpful to consider the rhetorical strategy the author is using. For example, is the author primarily reporting facts, events, or other writers' views; arguing for a point of view; or commenting on others' views or on events or states of affairs? Identifying the rhetorical strategy is essential in answering Main Idea questions that ask about the passage's purpose, but can also help focus your thoughts for those that ask about a main idea as such. The two major rhetorical strategies in reading passages are argumentation and exposition, each involving different kinds of Main Idea questions.

In passages primarily involving argumentation, the correct answer to a Main Idea question will typically be a paraphrase or description of the main conclusion of the passage's main argument. This conclusion is the main position the passage is intended to persuade readers to accept. The main conclusion is sometimes, but not always, stated explicitly in the passage. When it is not, the passage will make it clear to careful, perceptive readers what the author is arguing for. The correct answer choice may also briefly mention the reasons given in support of the position. For example, the answer choice might begin with the words *An analysis of recent findings supports the hypothesis that. . .*

The answer to a Main Idea question about an expository passage can take various forms, depending on the author's purpose and focus. In general, the answer will summarize the most important overall idea or theme discussed throughout the passage, or the overall purpose of the passage. For example, the answer to a Main Idea question about a narrative passage may be either a concise one-sentence summary of the events described or a statement of the overall outcome of the events, depending on the author's focus. And the answer to a Main Idea question about the purpose of a descriptive passage might be a sentence fragment that begins with the words *To describe the roles of. . .*

2. Supporting Idea

These questions measure your ability to comprehend ideas directly expressed in a passage and differentiate them from ideas that are neither expressed nor implied in the passage. They also measure your ability to differentiate supporting ideas from the main idea and from ideas implied by the author but not explicitly stated.

Like Main Idea questions, Supporting Idea questions simply assess whether you understand the messages conveyed in the writing, without asking you to do anything further with the information. **Supporting** refers not only to ideas expressed as premises supporting a main conclusion, but also to other ideas other than the main idea. Since each GMAT Reading Comprehension passage has an overall main point or purpose, every part of the passage can be thought of as supporting that main point or purpose in some way, either directly or tangentially. Therefore, Supporting Idea questions may ask you to understand and identify anything (other than the main point) that is stated in the passage.

Correct answers to Supporting Idea questions almost never consist of verbatim quotations from the passage, so you will need to be able to recognize paraphrases or more abstract expressions of the passage material. Among the passage components you may be asked to understand and recognize are:

- a premise of an argument
- a tangential point such as an acknowledgment of a potential objection to the author's position
- an example given to illustrate a principle or generalization
- a counterexample intended to provide evidence against a principle or generalization
- a fact cited as background information relevant to the main idea or to a subsidiary idea
- a component of a complex explanation, description, or narration
- a brief statement of a position against which the author's reasoning is directed
- a descriptive detail used to support or elaborate on the main idea.

Whereas questions about the main idea ask you to determine the meaning of the passage as a whole, questions about supporting ideas ask you to determine the meanings of individual phrases, sentences, and paragraphs that contribute to the meaning of the passage as a whole. In many cases, these questions can be thought of as asking for the main point of one small part of the passage. Supporting Idea questions often contain key phrases such as:

According to the passage . . . ,

Which of the following does the author cite as . . . ,

The passage mentions which of the following . . . , or

Which of the following does the author propose. . . .

Answering Supporting Idea questions requires remembering or quickly locating the relevant information in the passage. Occasionally, it may be possible to answer a question by quickly glancing to find the needed information without first fully reading through the passage, but as a general strategy, that could be risky and even time-consuming. Supporting Idea questions typically require a good understanding of the relationships among parts of the passage. In many cases, they will ask you to identify a piece of information that plays a specified role or is presented in a specified context. Thus, they may contain phrases such as:

Which of the following does the author offer as an objection to . . . ,

According to the passage, new businesses are more likely to fail if they . . . , or

The passage compares the sea turtle's thermoregulation to. . . .

3. Inference

Inference questions ask about ideas that are not explicitly stated in a passage but are implied by the author or otherwise follow logically from the information in the passage. Unlike questions about supporting ideas, which ask about information directly expressed in a passage, inference questions ask about ideas or meanings that must be inferred from the information directly stated.

Authors often make their points in indirect ways, suggesting ideas without actually stating them. Inference questions measure your ability to understand an author's intended meaning in parts of a passage where the meaning is only suggested. They sometimes also measure your ability to understand further implications that clearly follow from the information in the passage, even if the author does not clearly intend them to be inferred. Therefore, when you read a passage, you should concentrate not only on the explicit meaning of the author's words, but also on the subtler meanings and unstated implications of those words. Inference questions do not ask about obscure or tenuous implications that are very remote from the passage; rather, they ask about things that any astute, observant reader should be able to infer from the passage after a little reflection.

You may be asked to draw inferences in order to identify:

- a likely cause of a phenomenon or situation described in the passage
- a likely effect of a phenomenon or situation described in the passage
- a specific instance or subset based on a generalization given in the passage.

For example, if the passage indicates that all reptiles have a certain property and also mentions that crocodiles are reptiles, you could infer that crocodiles have the property in question.

- a statement that the author (or someone referred to in the passage) likely considers true or false
- an evaluative position that the author (or someone referred to in the passage) likely holds.

For example, it may be possible to infer from the author's word choices that she or he disapproves of something discussed in the passage.

- the intended meaning of a word or phrase based on how that word or phrase is used in the passage. However, GMAT questions will not ask you to define a word used in the passage with a standard meaning that could be accurately guessed from background vocabulary knowledge.

In some cases, the inference you are asked to draw will follow from a single statement or series of statements in the passage. In other cases, it will require you to consider together two or more separate parts of the passage. The relevant parts may be close together or far apart, but they will always be significant aspects of the passage, not irrelevant or highly obscure details. The question may refer explicitly to one or more portions of the passage, or it may require you to locate or remember the relevant information.

Inference questions often contain phrases such as:

Which of the following statements about . . . is most strongly supported by the passage?,

It can be inferred from the passage that . . . ,

If the claims made by the author about . . . are true, which of the following is most likely also true?,

The passage implies that . . . , or

The information in the passage suggests that. . . .

Some of the inferences might depend on commonly known and obviously true facts in addition to the information supplied by the passage. For example, if the passage says that an event happened during a snowstorm, you could reasonably infer that the weather was not hot at that time and place.

Incorrect answer choices for inference questions are often statements that appear superficially related to the passage but are not supported by the information in question. When the question asks what can be inferred from a specific part of the passage, you should be careful not to select an answer that follows from some other part of the passage but not from the part in question.

Incorrect answer choices are often true statements even though they are not supported by the information in the passage. Conversely, the correct answer could be a false statement implied by false information in the passage. For example, when the author explains why a theory is mistaken, you might be asked to infer that if the theory were true, such incorrect information would also have to be true.

Occasionally, it may not be possible to tell merely from a question's wording whether you are being asked to infer something or rather to recognize something directly expressed. For example, a question beginning "*In the passage, the author suggests . . .*" might be asking you to note that the author explicitly makes a certain suggestion in the passage. More typically, a question beginning "*The passage suggests . . .*" will be asking you to identify an idea the text implies but does not explicitly state. However, if you understand the passage and the relationships and implications of its parts, you will be able to find the correct answer without having to worry about how the test writers classified the question.

4. Application

Application questions measure your ability to discern relationships between situations or ideas presented in the passage and other situations or ideas beyond the direct scope of the passage. The most crucial skill involved in answering application questions is that of abstracting key features or principles from one context and applying them effectively to other contexts. This skill is often needed when working with scholarly, legal, professional, or business writings.

Application questions are often hypothetical or speculative, and therefore may contain words such as *would, could, might,* or *should,* or phrases such as *most clearly exemplifies, is most similar to,* or *is most likely ruled out by.* Some application questions pose analogies between passage topics and other topics.

Because application questions can be about the relationships of the passage to topics outside its scope, you should not expect to be able to eliminate any answer choice based on whether or not its topic appears in the passage. For instance, all the answer choices for an analogy question relating to a passage's explanation of a water-treatment process might refer to book-publishing processes.

Here are some major application types you may encounter on the exam:

A. *Analogies.* These could involve:

- a function or purpose similar to the function or purpose of something described in the passage.

A question might ask, for instance, *In which of the following is the role played by a computer program most analogous to the role of the protein molecule in the pesticide discussed in the passage?*

- a method or procedure similar to one described in the passage but used in a different context
- a goal or purpose similar to the goal or purpose of something discussed in the passage.

For example, a protest demonstration's goal of changing one country's environmental policies would be more analogous to a politician's goal of changing another country's food safety regulations than to an employee's goal of finding a new job.

- a part–whole relationship similar to a part–whole relationship described in the passage.

This could be, for example, a relationship between an organism and its ecosystem, or between a book chapter and the book as a whole.

- a logical relationship similar to the relationship between parts of the passage or between elements of someone's reasoning described in the passage.

B. *Principles, policies, and procedures.* You may be asked to identify, for example:

- a rule or policy that if enforced could help bring about a goal presented in the passage
- a principle that is not explicitly formulated in the passage but underlies the author's reasoning
- a generalization supported by a range of specific instances referred to in the passage
- an action or situation violating or conforming to a rule or policy mentioned in the passage
- a potential solution to a problem discussed in the passage
- an alternative approach that could have the same effect as one discussed in the passage.

C. *Extensions of the author's rhetorical strategies.* These include such things as:

- an example effectively illustrating a point made by the author
- a prediction about how the author would likely respond to an objection to her or his position
- an additional topic that could be relevantly added to the discussion in the passage
- an idea the passage does not express but implies that the author would probably accept or reject.

D. *What-if scenarios.* You might need to identify, for example:

- a hypothetical extension of a trend or series of developments described in the passage
- how a researcher's conclusions would have been logically affected if some observed data had been different from the data reported in the passage
- how circumstances would likely have been different if developments described in the passage had not occurred
- how someone whose views are described in the passage would likely respond if that person read the passage.

5. Evaluation

Evaluation questions require you to analyze and evaluate a passage's organization and logic. They fall into two broad subcategories: analysis and critique.

Analysis-type evaluation questions require you to determine how parts of the passage work in relation to each other. These questions often ask about the author's purpose. Unlike Main Idea questions about authors' purposes, they do not ask you to identify the entire passage's overall purpose, but rather the purposes of specific elements within the passage, and the relationships among those purposes. However, some evaluation questions may ask you to identify the logical structure of the passage or of a portion of the passage.

Critique-type evaluation questions require you to judge the strengths, weaknesses, relevance, or effectiveness of parts of the passage, as well as the relationships of those parts to potential objections or justifications. These questions often involve some of the same types of reasoning encountered in Critical Reasoning questions. Reading Comprehension evaluation questions require neither technical knowledge of formal logic nor familiarity with specialized terms of logic or argumentation. You can answer these questions using the information in the passage and careful reasoning.

Evaluation questions often contain phrases such as:

> *The purpose of . . . ,*
>
> *. . . most accurately describes the structure of . . . ,*
>
> *. . . most strengthens . . . ,*
>
> *. . . would most justify . . . ,*
>
> *. . . is most vulnerable to the objection that . . . ,* or
>
> *Which . . . additional information would most help. . . .*

Answer choices are often abstract and might not contain any words or concepts that appear in the passage. For example, a question that asks about a paragraph's function might have an answer choice such as: ***It rejects a theory presented in the preceding paragraph and offers some criteria that an alternative theory would need to meet.***

Here are some major application types that you may encounter in the test:

A. *Analysis*. Answers to these questions might be, for example, statements about:

- how the passage as a whole is constructed.

In such cases, the answer will sometimes be expressed as an abstract summary of the elements that make up the passage.

- how a portion of the passage is constructed
- the purpose or function of one part of the passage.

For instance, does that part of the passage define a term, compare or contrast two ideas, present a new idea, or refute an idea?

- how one portion of the passage relates logically or rhetorically to surrounding parts
- how the author tries to persuade readers to accept his or her assertions
- a likely reason or motivation for a view the author expresses or attributes to someone else.

B. *Critique*. In these questions, you may be asked to identify, for example:

- an assumption involved in the author's reasoning or in someone else's reasoning discussed in the passage
- crucial gaps in the information provided in the passage

- a potential discovery that would help resolve an issue discussed in the passage

- a statement that, if true, would strengthen or weaken the author's reasoning or someone else's reasoning presented in the passage

- a potential counterexample to a general claim made in the passage.

6. Style and Tone

Effective reading often depends on recognizing and evaluating both the author's attitude toward a topic and the effect the author intends the writing to have on readers. These are often implicit in the passage's style and tone rather than stated explicitly.

Some questions focus directly and exclusively on the style or tone of the passage as a whole. They often involve phrases such as:

The overall tone of the passage can be most accurately described as . . . ,

The passage, as a whole, functions primarily as a . . . , or

The author's approach to . . . can be most accurately described as. . . .

In the answer choices, you may be asked to select an adjective or adjective phrase that accurately describes the overall tone of the passage—for instance, ***critical, questioning, objective, dismissive,*** or ***enthusiastic***. Answer choices may also be noun phrases such as ***advocacy for a political position, a sarcastic portrayal of a historical trend,*** or ***a journalistic exploration of some attempts to solve a problem***. Or the answer choices may be more complex clauses or full sentences.

To answer questions about style and tone, you will typically have to consider the language of the passage or a large section of the passage as a whole. It takes more than one pointed, critical word to give an entire passage or section a critical tone. Sometimes, style and tone questions ask what audience the passage was probably intended for or what type of publication it would most appropriately appear in. To answer any question involving style and tone, you must ask yourself what attitudes or objectives a passage's words convey beyond their literal meanings.

You may sometimes need to consider style and tone in answering any type of Reading Comprehension question, even a question that does not explicitly ask about that aspect of the passage. Some question types are more likely than others to involve this type of consideration. An inference question, for example, may ask you to infer the author's attitude toward a topic. You may also need to consider the passage's tone in order to confidently identify the passage's main purpose. And some evaluation questions require you to recognize the rhetorical approach the author takes in a portion of the passage.

7.2 Test-Taking Strategies

1. **Do not expect to be completely familiar with material presented in the passages.**
   You may find some passages easier to understand than others, but all passages are designed to present a challenge. If you have some familiarity with the material presented in a passage, do not let this knowledge influence your choice of answers to the questions. Answer all questions on the basis of what is **stated or implied** in the passage itself.

2. **Analyze each passage carefully, because the questions require you to have a specific and detailed understanding of the passages.**

   You may find it easier to analyze a passage first before moving to the questions. Alternatively, you may prefer to skim the passage the first time and read more carefully once you understand the questions. You may even want to read the question before reading the passage. You should choose the method most suitable for you.

3. **Focus on key words and phrases, trying to maintain an overall sense of what is discussed in the passage.**

   Keep the following in mind:

   - Note how each fact relates to an idea or an argument

   - Note where the passage moves from one idea to the next

   - Distinguish the passage's main idea from its supporting ideas

   - Determine what conclusions are reached and why.

4. **Read the questions carefully, making sure you understand what is asked.**

   An answer choice that accurately restates information in the passage may be incorrect if it does not answer the question. Refer back to the passage for clarification if you need to.

5. **Read all the answer choices carefully.**

   Never assume that you have selected the best answer without first reading all the choices.

6. **Select the choice that answers the question best in terms of the information given in the passage.**

   Do not rely on outside knowledge of the material to help you answer the questions.

7. **Remember that comprehension—not speed—is the critical success factor on the Reading Comprehension section.**

7.3 Section Instructions

Go to www.mba.com/tutorial to view instructions for the section and get a feel for what the test center screens will look like on the actual GMAT exam.

7.4 Practice Questions

Each of the Reading Comprehension questions is based on the content of a passage. After reading the passage answer all questions pertaining to it on the basis of what is stated or implied in the passage. For each question, select the best answer of the choices given. On the actual GMAT exam, you will see no more than four questions per passage.

Questions 503 to 543 - Difficulty: Easy

Line   Scientists long believed that two nerve clusters in the human hypothalamus, called suprachiasmatic nuclei (SCNs), were what controlled our circadian rhythms. Those rhythms are the biological cycles
(5)   that recur approximately every 24 hours in synchronization with the cycle of sunlight and darkness caused by Earth's rotation. Studies have demonstrated that in some animals, the SCNs control daily fluctuations in blood pressure, body
(10)   temperature, activity level, and alertness, as well as the nighttime release of the sleep-promoting agent melatonin. Furthermore, cells in the human retina dedicated to transmitting information about light levels to the SCNs have recently been discovered.
(15)   Four critical genes governing circadian cycles have been found to be active in every tissue, however, not just the SCNs, of flies, mice, and humans. In addition, when laboratory rats that usually ate at will were fed only once a day, peak
(20)   activity of a clock gene in their livers shifted by 12 hours, whereas the same clock gene in the SCNs remained synchronized with light cycles. While scientists do not dispute the role of the SCNs in controlling core functions such as the regulation of
(25)   body temperature and blood pressure, scientists now believe that circadian clocks in other organs and tissues may respond to external cues other than light—including temperature changes—that recur regularly every 24 hours.

Questions 503–505 refer to the passage.

*RC00504-01
503. The primary purpose of the passage is to

(A)   challenge recent findings that appear to contradict earlier findings

(B)   present two sides of an ongoing scientific debate

(C)   report answers to several questions that have long puzzled researchers

(D)   discuss evidence that has caused a long-standing belief to be revised

(E)   attempt to explain a commonly misunderstood biological phenomenon

RC00504-05
504. The passage mentions each of the following as a function regulated by the SCNs in some animals EXCEPT

(A)   activity level
(B)   blood pressure
(C)   alertness
(D)   vision
(E)   temperature

*These numbers correlate with the online test bank question number. See the GMAT™ Official Guide Question Index in the back of this book.

455

RC00504-04

505. The author of the passage would probably agree with which of the following statements about the SCNs?

    (A)   The SCNs are found in other organs and tissues of the body besides the hypothalamus.

    (B)   The SCNs play a critical but not exclusive role in regulating circadian rhythms.

    (C)   The SCNs control clock genes in a number of tissues and organs throughout the body.

    (D)   The SCNs are a less significant factor in regulating blood pressure than scientists once believed.

    (E)   The SCNs are less strongly affected by changes in light levels than they are by other external cues.

Line   In their study of whether offering a guarantee of service quality will encourage customers to visit a particular restaurant, Tucci and Talaga have found that the effect of such guarantees is mixed. For
(5)   higher-priced restaurants, there is some evidence that offering a guarantee increases the likelihood of customer selection, probably reflecting the greater financial commitment involved in choosing an expensive restaurant. For lower-priced restaurants,
(10)   where one expects less assiduous service, Tucci and Talaga found that a guarantee could actually have a negative effect: a potential customer might think that a restaurant offering a guarantee is worried about its service. Moreover, since customers understand a
(15)   restaurant's product and know what to anticipate in terms of service, they are empowered to question its quality. This is not generally true in the case of skilled activities such as electrical work, where, consequently, a guarantee might have greater customer appeal.
(20)   For restaurants generally, the main benefit of a service guarantee probably lies not so much in customer appeal as in managing and motivating staff. Staff members would know what service standards are expected of them and also know that the success
(25)   of the business relies on their adhering to those standards. Additionally, guarantees provide some basis for defining the skills needed for successful service in areas traditionally regarded as unskilled, such as waiting tables.

Questions 506–508 refer to the passage.

RC00525-01

506. The primary purpose of the passage is to

(A)   question the results of a study that examined the effect of service-quality guarantees in the restaurant industry

(B)   discuss potential advantages and disadvantages of service-quality guarantees in the restaurant industry

(C)   examine the conventional wisdom regarding the effect of service-quality guarantees in the restaurant industry

(D)   argue that only certain restaurants would benefit from the implementation of service-quality guarantees

(E)   consider the impact that service-quality guarantees can have on the service provided by a restaurant

RC00525-02

507. It can be inferred that the author of the passage would agree with which of the following statements about the appeal of service guarantees to customers?

(A)   Such guarantees are likely to be somewhat more appealing to customers of restaurants than to customers of other businesses.

(B)   Such guarantees are likely to be more appealing to customers who know what to anticipate in terms of service.

(C)   Such guarantees are likely to have less appeal in situations where customers are knowledgeable about a business's product or service.

(D)   In situations where a high level of financial commitment is involved, a service guarantee is not likely to be very appealing.

(E)   In situations where customers expect a high level of customer service, a service guarantee is likely to make customers think that a business is worried about its service.

RC00525-07

508. According to the passage, Tucci and Talaga found that service guarantees, when offered by lower-priced restaurants, can have which of the following effects?

(A)   Customers' developing unreasonably high expectations regarding service

(B)   Customers' avoiding such restaurants because they fear that the service guarantee may not be fully honored

(C)   Customers' interpreting the service guarantee as a sign that management is not confident about the quality of its service

(D)   A restaurant's becoming concerned that its service will not be assiduous enough to satisfy customers

(E)   A restaurant's becoming concerned that customers will be more emboldened to question the quality of the service they receive

Line   One proposal for preserving rain forests is
to promote the adoption of new agricultural
technologies, such as improved plant varieties and
use of chemical herbicides, which would increase
(5)   productivity and slow deforestation by reducing
demand for new cropland. Studies have shown
that farmers in developing countries who have
achieved certain levels of education, wealth, and
security of land tenure are more likely to adopt such
(10)   technologies. But these studies have focused on
villages with limited land that are tied to a market
economy rather than on the relatively isolated, self-
sufficient communities with ample land characteristic
of rain-forest regions. A recent study of the Tawahka
(15)   people of the Honduran rain forest found that farmers
with some formal education were more likely to
adopt improved plant varieties but less likely to
use chemical herbicides and that those who spoke
Spanish (the language of the market economy) were
(20)   more likely to adopt both technologies. Nonland
wealth was also associated with more adoption of
both technologies, but availability of uncultivated land
reduced the incentive to employ the productivity-
enhancing technologies. Researchers also measured
(25)   land-tenure security: in Tawahka society, kinship ties
are a more important indicator of this than are legal
property rights, so researchers measured it by a
household's duration of residence in its village. They
found that longer residence correlated with more
(30)   adoption of improved plant varieties but less adoption
of chemical herbicides.

Questions 509–510 refer to the passage.

RC00455-03

509.   The passage suggests that in the study mentioned in
line 14 the method for gathering information about
security of land tenure reflects which of the following
pairs of assumptions about Tawahka society?

(A)   The security of a household's land tenure
depends on the strength of that household's
kinship ties, and the duration of a household's
residence in its village is an indication of the
strength of that household's kinship ties.

(B)   The ample availability of land makes security of
land tenure unimportant, and the lack of a need
for secure land tenure has made the concept of
legal property rights unnecessary.

(C)   The strength of a household's kinship ties is
a more reliable indicator of that household's
receptivity to new agricultural technologies than
is its quantity of nonland wealth, and the duration
of a household's residence in its village is a more
reliable indicator of that household's security of
land tenure than is the strength of its kinship ties.

(D)   Security of land tenure based on kinship ties
tends to make farmers more receptive to the use
of improved plant varieties, and security of land
tenure based on long duration of residence in a
village tends to make farmers more receptive to
the use of chemical herbicides.

(E)   A household is more likely to be receptive to the
concept of land tenure based on legal property
rights if it has easy access to uncultivated land,
and a household is more likely to uphold the
tradition of land tenure based on kinship ties
if it possesses a significant degree of nonland
wealth.

RC00455-05

510. According to the passage, the proposal mentioned in line 1 is aimed at preserving rain forests by encouraging farmers in rain-forest regions to do each of the following EXCEPT

(A)   adopt new agricultural technologies

(B)   grow improved plant varieties

(C)   decrease their use of chemical herbicides

(D)   increase their productivity

(E)   reduce their need to clear new land for cultivation

Line   The argument for "monetizing"—or putting a monetary value on—ecosystem functions may be stated thus: Concern about the depletion of natural resources is widespread, but this concern, in the

(5) absence of an economic argument for conservation, has not translated into significant conservational progress. Some critics blame this impasse on environmentalists, whom they believe fail to address the economic issues of environmental degradation.

(10) Conservation can appear unprofitable when compared with the economic returns derived from converting natural assets (pristine coastlines, for example) into explicitly commercial ones (such as resort hotels). But according to David Pearce, that illusion stems

(15) from the fact that "services" provided by ecological systems are not traded on the commodities market, and thus have no readily *quantifiable* value. To remedy this, says Pearce, one has to show that all ecosystems have economic value—indeed, that all

(20) ecological services are economic services. Tourists visiting wildlife preserves, for example, create jobs and generate income for national economies; undisturbed forests and wetlands regulate water runoff and act as water-purifying systems, saving

(25) millions of dollars worth of damage to property and to marine ecosystems. In Gretchen Daily's view, monetization, while unpopular with many environmentalists, reflects the dominant role that economic considerations play in human behavior,

(30) and the expression of economic value in a common currency helps inform environmental decision-making processes.

Questions 511–514 refer to the passage.

RC00344-02

511. Information in the passage suggests that David Pearce would most readily endorse which of the following statements concerning monetization?

(A) Monetization represents a strategy that is attractive to both environmentalists and their critics.

(B) Monetization is an untested strategy, but it is increasingly being embraced by environmentalists.

(C) Monetization should at present be restricted to ecological services and should only gradually be extended to such commercial endeavors as tourism and recreation.

(D) Monetization can serve as a means of representing persuasively the value of environmental conservation.

(E) Monetization should inform environmental decision-making processes only if it is accepted by environmentalist groups.

RC00344-04

512. Which of the following most clearly represents an example of an "ecological service" as that term is used in line 20 ?

(A) A resort hotel located in an area noted for its natural beauty

(B) A water-purifying plant that supplements natural processes with nontoxic chemicals

(C) A wildlife preserve that draws many international travelers

(D) A nonprofit firm that specializes in restoring previously damaged ecosystems

(E) A newsletter that keeps readers informed of ecological victories and setbacks

RC00344-05

513. According to the passage, Daily sees monetization as an indication of which of the following?

(A) The centrality of economic interests to people's actions

(B) The reluctance of the critics of environmentalism to acknowledge the importance of conservation

(C) The inability of financial interests and ecological interests to reach a common ideological ground

(D) The inevitability of environmental degradation

(E) The inevitability of the growth of ecological services in the future

RC00344-06

514. Which of the following can be inferred from the passage concerning the environmentalists mentioned in line 8 ?

(A) They are organized in opposition to the generation of income produced by the sale of ecological services.

(B) They are fewer in number but better organized and better connected to the media than their opponents.

(C) They have sometimes been charged with failing to use a particular strategy in their pursuit of conservational goals.

(D) They have been in the forefront of publicizing the extent of worldwide environmental degradation.

(E) They define environmental progress differently and more conservatively than do other organized groups of environmentalists.

Line   Much research has been devoted to investigating what motivates consumers to try new products. Previous consumer research suggests that both the price of a new product and the way it is advertised
(5)   affect consumers' perceptions of the product's performance risk (the possibility that the product will not function as consumers expect and/or will not provide the desired benefits). Some of this research has concluded that a relatively high price will reduce
(10)   a consumer's perception of the performance risk associated with purchasing a particular product, while other studies have reported that price has little or no effect on perceived performance risk. These conflicting findings may simply be due to the nature
(15)   of product advertisements: a recent study indicates that the presentation of an advertised message has a marked effect on the relationship between price and perceived performance risk.
       Researchers have identified consumers' perception
(20)   of the credibility of the source of an advertised message—i.e., the manufacturer—as another factor affecting perceived performance risk: one study found that the greater the source credibility, the lower the consumer's perception of the risk of purchasing
(25)   an advertised new product. However, past research suggests that the relationship between source credibility and perceived performance risk may be more complex: source credibility may interact with price in a subtle way to affect consumers' judgments
(30)   of the performance risk associated with an advertised product.

Questions 515–518 refer to the passage.

RC00359-01

515. According to the passage, the studies referred to in line 12 reported which of the following about the effect of price on consumers' perception of the performance risk associated with a new product?

(A)   Although most consumers regard price as an important factor, their perception of the performance risk associated with a new product is ultimately determined by the manufacturer's reputation.

(B)   Price interacts with the presentation of an advertised message to affect perceived performance risk.

(C)   Price does not significantly affect consumers' perception of the performance risk associated with a new product.

(D)   Consumers tend to regard price as more important than the manufacturer's credibility when they are buying from that manufacturer for the first time.

(E)   Consumers are generally less concerned about a new product's performance risk when that product is relatively expensive.

RC00359-03

516. The "past research" mentioned in line 25 suggests which of the following about perceived performance risk?

(A)   The more expensive a new product is, the more likely consumers may be to credit advertised claims about that product.

(B)   The more familiar consumers are with a particular manufacturer, the more willing they may be to assume some risk in the purchase of a new product being advertised by that manufacturer.

(C)   Consumers' perception of the performance risk associated with a new product being advertised may be influenced by an interplay between the product's price and the manufacturer's credibility.

(D)   Consumers may be more likely to believe that a product will function as it is advertised to do when they have bought products from a particular manufacturer before.

(E)   The price of a particular advertised product may have less impact than the manufacturer's credibility on consumers' assessment of the performance risk associated with that product.

RC00359-05

517. The passage is primarily concerned with

   (A) challenging the implications of previous research into why consumers try new products

   (B) suggesting new marketing strategies for attracting consumers to new products

   (C) reconciling two different views about the effect of price on consumers' willingness to try new products

   (D) describing a new approach to researching why consumers try new products

   (E) discussing certain findings regarding why consumers try new products

RC00359-06

518. Which of the following, if true, would most tend to weaken the conclusion drawn from "some of this research" (line 8)?

   (A) In a subsequent study, consumers who were asked to evaluate new products with relatively low prices had the same perception of the products' performance risk as did consumers who were shown the same products priced more expensively.

   (B) In a subsequent study, the quality of the advertising for the products that consumers perceived as having a lower performance risk was relatively high, while the quality of the advertising for the products that consumers perceived as having a higher performance risk was relatively poor.

   (C) In a subsequent study, the products that consumers perceived as having a lower performance risk were priced higher than the highest priced products in the previous research.

   (D) None of the consumers involved in this research had ever before bought products from the manufacturers involved in the research.

   (E) Researchers found that the higher the source credibility for a product, the more consumers were willing to pay for it.

Line   Historians remain divided over the role of banks in facilitating economic growth in the United States in the late eighteenth and early nineteenth centuries. Some scholars contend

(5)   that banks played a minor role in the nation's growing economy. Financial institutions, they argue, appeared only after the economy had begun to develop, and once organized, followed conservative lending practices, providing aid to

(10)   established commercial enterprises but shunning those, such as manufacturing and transportation projects, that were more uncertain and capital-intensive (i.e., requiring greater expenditures in the form of capital than in

(15)   labor).
    A growing number of historians argue, in contrast, that banks were crucial in transforming the early national economy. When state legislatures began granting more bank charters

(20)   in the 1790s and early 1800s, the supply of credit rose accordingly. Unlike the earliest banks, which had primarily provided short-term loans to well-connected merchants, the banks of the early nineteenth century issued credit widely. As Paul

(25)   Gilje asserts, the expansion and democratization of credit in the early nineteenth century became the driving force of the American economy, as banks began furnishing large amounts of capital to transportation and industrial enterprises. The

(30)   exception, such historians argue, was in the South; here, the overwhelmingly agrarian nature of the economy generated outright opposition to banks, which were seen as monopolistic institutions controlled by an elite group of

(35)   planters.

Questions 519–523 refer to the passage.

RC00419-01

519. The primary purpose of the passage is to

(A) compare the economic role played by southern banks with the economic role played by banks in the rest of the United States during the late eighteenth and early nineteenth centuries

(B) reevaluate a conventional interpretation of the role played by banks in the American economy during the late eighteenth and early nineteenth centuries

(C) present different interpretations of the role played by banks in the American economy during the late eighteenth and early nineteenth centuries

(D) analyze how the increasing number of banks in the late eighteenth and early nineteenth centuries affected the American economy

(E) examine how scholarly opinion regarding the role played by banks in the American economy during the late eighteenth and early nineteenth centuries has changed over time

RC00419-02

520. The passage suggests that the scholars mentioned in line 4 would argue that the reason banks tended not to fund manufacturing and transportation projects in the late eighteenth and early nineteenth centuries was that

(A) these projects, being well established and well capitalized, did not need substantial long-term financing from banks

(B) these projects entailed a level of risk that was too great for banks' conservative lending practices

(C) banks preferred to invest in other, more speculative projects that offered the potential for higher returns

(D) bank managers believed that these projects would be unlikely to contribute significantly to economic growth in the new country

(E) bank managers believed funding these projects would result in credit being extended to too many borrowers

RC00419-04

521. The passage suggests that Paul Gilje would be most likely to agree with which of the following claims about the lending practices of the "earliest banks" (see line 21)?

    (A) These lending practices were unlikely to generate substantial profits for banks.

    (B) These lending practices only benefited a narrow sector of the economy.

    (C) The restrictive nature of these lending practices generated significant opposition outside of the South.

    (D) The restrictive nature of these lending practices forced state legislatures to begin granting more bank charters by the early nineteenth century.

    (E) These lending practices were likely to be criticized by economic elites as being overly restrictive.

RC00419 05

522. The passage suggests that the opposition to banks in the South in the early nineteenth century stemmed in part from the perception that banks

    (A) did not benefit more than a small minority of the people

    (B) did not support the interests of elite planters

    (C) were too closely tied to transportation and industrial interests

    (D) were unwilling to issue the long-term loans required by agrarian interests

    (E) were too willing to lend credit widely

RC00419-06

523. Which of the following statements best describes the function of the last sentence of the passage?

    (A) It provides evidence tending to undermine the viewpoint of the scholars mentioned in line 5.

    (B) It resolves a conflict over the role of banks summarized in the first paragraph.

    (C) It clarifies some of the reasons state legislatures began granting more bank charters.

    (D) It qualifies a claim made earlier in the passage about the impact of banks on the American economy in the early nineteenth century.

    (E) It supports a claim made earlier in the passage about how the expansion of credit affected the economy.

Line   In recent years, Western business managers have been heeding the exhortations of business journalists and academics to move their companies toward long-term, collaborative "strategic partnerships" with
(5)   their external business partners (e.g., suppliers). The experts' advice comes as a natural reaction to numerous studies conducted during the past decade that compared Japanese production and supply practices with those of the rest of the world. The
(10)   link between the success of a certain well-known Japanese automaker and its effective management of its suppliers, for example, has led to an unquestioning belief within Western management circles in the value of strategic partnerships. Indeed, in the automobile
(15)   sector all three United States manufacturers and most of their European competitors have launched programs to reduce their total number of suppliers and move toward having strategic partnerships with a few.
(20)   However, new research concerning supplier relationships in various industries demonstrates that the widespread assumption of Western managers and business consultants that Japanese firms manage their suppliers primarily through strategic
(25)   partnerships is unjustified. Not only do Japanese firms appear to conduct a far smaller proportion of their business through strategic partnerships than is commonly believed, but they also make extensive use of "market-exchange" relationships, in which
(30)   either party can turn to the marketplace and shift to different business partners at will, a practice usually associated with Western manufacturers.

Questions 524–527 refer to the passage.

RC00458-01

524. The passage is primarily concerned with

(A)   examining economic factors that may have contributed to the success of certain Japanese companies

(B)   discussing the relative merits of strategic partnerships as compared with those of market-exchange relationships

(C)   challenging the validity of a widely held assumption about how Japanese firms operate

(D)   explaining why Western companies have been slow to adopt a particular practice favored by Japanese companies

(E)   pointing out certain differences between Japanese and Western supplier relationships

RC00458-02

525. According to the passage, the advice referred to in line 6 was a response to which of the following?

(A)   A recent decrease in the number of available suppliers within the United States automobile industry

(B)   A debate within Western management circles during the past decade regarding the value of strategic partnerships

(C)   The success of certain European automobile manufacturers that have adopted strategic partnerships

(D)   An increase in demand over the past decade for automobiles made by Western manufacturers

(E)   Research comparing Japanese business practices with those of other nations

RC00458-03

526. The author mentions "the success of a certain well-known Japanese automaker" in lines 10–11, most probably in order to

(A)   demonstrate some of the possible reasons for the success of a certain business practice

(B)   cite a specific case that has convinced Western business experts of the value of a certain business practice

(C)   describe specific steps taken by Western automakers that have enabled them to compete more successfully in a global market

(D)   introduce a paradox about the effect of a certain business practice in Japan

(E)   indicate the need for Western managers to change their relationships with their external business partners

RC00458-05

527. Which of the following is cited in the passage as evidence supporting the author's claim about what the new research referred to in line 20 demonstrates?

(A)   The belief within Western management circles regarding the extent to which Japanese firms rely on strategic partnerships

(B)   The surprising number of European and United States businesses that have strategic partnerships with their suppliers

(C)   The response of Western automobile manufacturers to the advice that they adopt strategic partnerships with their suppliers

(D)   The prevalence of "market-exchange" relationships between Japanese firms and their suppliers

(E)   The success of a particular Japanese automobile manufacturer that favors strategic partnerships with its suppliers

Line   In an effort to explain why business acquisitions often fail, scholars have begun to focus on the role of top executives of acquired companies. Acquired companies that retain their top executives tend to

(5)   have more successful outcomes than those that do not. Furthermore, existing research suggests that retaining the highest-level top executives, such as the CEO (chief executive officer) and COO (chief operating officer), is related more positively to postacquisition

(10)   success than retaining lower-ranked top executives. However, this explanation, while insightful, suffers from two limitations. First, the focus on positional rank does not recognize the variation in length of service that may exist in top executive posts across companies,

(15)   nor does it address which particular top executives (with respect to length of service) should be retained to achieve a successful acquisition outcome. Second, the relationship between retained top executives and acquisition outcomes offered by existing research

(20)   is subject to opposing theoretical explanations related to length of service. The resource-based view (RBV) suggests that keeping acquired company top executives with longer organizational tenure would lead to more successful outcomes, as those executives

(25)   have idiosyncratic and nontransferable knowledge of the acquired company that would be valuable for the effective implementation of the acquisition. The opposing position, offered by the upper echelons perspective (UEP), suggests that retaining top

(30)   executives having short organizational tenure would lead to more successful outcomes, as they would have the adaptability to manage most effectively during the uncertainty of the acquisition process.
        Responding to these limitations, Bergh conducted

(35)   a study of executive retention and acquisition outcome that focused on the organizational tenure of retained company top executives in 104 acquisitions, followed over 5 years. Bergh considered the acquisition successful if the acquired company was

(40)   retained and unsuccessful if it was divested. Bergh's findings support the RBV position. Apparently, the benefits of long organizational tenure lead to more successful outcomes than the benefits of short organizational tenure. While longer tenured top

(45)   executives may have trouble adapting to change, it appears that their perspectives and knowledge bases offer unique value after the acquisition. Although from the UEP position it seems sensible to retain less tenured executives and allow more tenured

(50)   ones to leave, such a strategy appears to lower the probability of acquisition success.

Questions 528–531 refer to the passage.

RC00497-02

528. According to the passage, the research mentioned in line 6 suggests which of the following about lower-ranked top executives and postacquisition success?

(A) Given that these executives are unlikely to contribute to postacquisition success, little effort should be spent trying to retain them.

(B) The shorter their length of service, the less likely it is that these executives will play a significant role in postacquisition success.

(C) These executives are less important to postacquisition success than are more highly ranked top executives.

(D) If they have long tenures, these executives may prove to be as important to postacquisition success as are more highly ranked top executives.

(E) Postacquisition success is unlikely if these executives are retained.

RC00497-03

529. The resource-based view, as described in the passage, is based on which of the following ideas?

(A) The managerial skills of top executives become strongest after the first five years of their tenure.

(B) Company-specific knowledge is an important factor in the success of an acquisition process.

(C) The amount of nontransferable knowledge possessed by long-tenured top executives tends to be underestimated.

(D) Effective implementation of an acquisition depends primarily on the ability of executives to adapt to change.

(E) Short-tenured executives are likely to impede the implementation of a successful acquisition strategy.

RC00497-04

530. The passage suggests that Bergh and a proponent of the upper echelons perspective would be most likely to disagree over which of the following?

(A) Whether there is a positive correlation between short organizational tenure and managerial adaptability

(B) Whether there is a positive correlation between long organizational tenure and the acquisition of idiosyncratic and nontransferable knowledge

(C) Whether adaptability is a useful trait for an executive who is managing an acquisition process

(D) Whether retaining less-tenured top executives of an acquired company is an optimal strategy for achieving postacquisition success

(E) Whether retaining highest-level top executives of acquired companies is more important than retaining lower-ranked top executives

RC00497-05

531. According to the passage, prior to Bergh's study, research on the role of top executives of acquired companies in business acquisition success was limited in which of the following ways?

(A) It did not address how the organizational tenure of top executives affects postacquisition success.

(B) It did not address why some companies have longer-tenured CEOs than others.

(C) It did not consider strategies for retaining long-tenured top executives of acquired companies.

(D) It failed to differentiate between the contribution of highest-level top executives to postacquisition success and that of lower-ranked top executives.

(E) It underestimated the potential contribution that lower-level top executives can make to postacquisition success.

Line   When Jamaican-born social activist Marcus
            Garvey came to the United States in 1916, he
            arrived at precisely the right historical moment.
            What made the moment right was the return of
(5)   African American soldiers from the First World War
            in 1918, which created an ideal constituency for
            someone with Garvey's message of unity, pride,
            and improved conditions for African American
            communities.
(10)   Hoping to participate in the traditional American
            ethos of individual success, many African American
            people entered the armed forces with enthusiasm,
            only to find themselves segregated from white
            troops and subjected to numerous indignities. They
(15)   returned to a United States that was as segregated
            as it had been before the war. Considering similar
            experiences, anthropologist Anthony F. C. Wallace
            has argued that when a perceptible gap arises
            between a culture's expectations and the reality of
(20)   that culture, the resulting tension can inspire a
            revitalization movement: an organized, conscious
            effort to construct a culture that fulfills long-
            standing expectations.
            Some scholars have argued that Garvey created
(25)   the consciousness from which he built, in the 1920s,
            the largest revitalization movement in
            African American history. But such an argument only
            tends to obscure the consciousness of
            identity, strength, and sense of history that already
(30)   existed in the African American community. Garvey
            did not create this consciousness; rather, he gave
            this consciousness its political expression.

Questions 532–535 refer to the passage.

RC00017-02

532. According to the passage, which of the following
     contributed to Marcus Garvey's success?

   (A)   He introduced cultural and historical
         consciousness to the African American
         community.

   (B)   He believed enthusiastically in the traditional
         American success ethos.

   (C)   His audience had already formed a
         consciousness that made it receptive to his
         message.

   (D)   His message appealed to critics of African
         American support for United States military
         involvement in the First World War.

   (E)   He supported the movement to protest
         segregation that had emerged prior to his arrival
         in the United States.

RC00017-03

533. The passage suggests that many African American
     people responded to their experiences in the armed
     forces in which of the following ways?

   (A)   They maintained as civilians their enthusiastic
         allegiance to the armed forces.

   (B)   They questioned United States involvement in the
         First World War.

   (C)   They joined political organizations to protest the
         segregation of African American troops and the
         indignities they suffered in the military.

   (D)   They became aware of the gap between their
         expectations and the realities of American
         culture.

   (E)   They repudiated Garvey's message of pride and
         unity.

RC00017-04

534. It can be inferred from the passage that the "scholars" mentioned in line 24 believe which of the following to be true?

(A) Revitalization resulted from the political activism of returning African American soldiers following the First World War.

(B) Marcus Garvey had to change a number of prevailing attitudes in order for his mass movement to find a foothold in the United States.

(C) The prevailing sensibility of the African American community provided the foundation of Marcus Garvey's political appeal.

(D) Marcus Garvey hoped to revitalize consciousness of cultural and historical identity in the African American community.

(E) The goal of the mass movement that Marcus Garvey helped bring into being was to build on the pride and unity among African Americans.

RC00017-05

535. According to the passage, many African American people joined the armed forces during the First World War for which of the following reasons?

(A) They wished to escape worsening economic conditions in African American communities.

(B) They expected to fulfill ideals of personal attainment.

(C) They sought to express their loyalty to the United States.

(D) They hoped that joining the military would help advance the cause of desegregation.

(E) They saw military service as an opportunity to fulfill Marcus Garvey's political vision.

Line   Arboria is floundering in the global marketplace, incurring devastating losses in market position and profits. The problem is not Arboria's products, but Arboria's trade policy. Arboria faces the prospect

(5)   of continuing economic loss until Arborian business and political leaders recognize the fundamental differences between Arborian and foreign economic systems. Today the key trade issue is not free trade versus protectionism but diminishing trade versus

(10)   expanding trade.

    Arboria is operating with an obsolete trade policy, an artifact of the mid-1940s when Arboria and Whorfland dominated the global economy, tariffs were the principal obstacle to trade, and Arborian

(15)   supremacy was uncontested in virtually all industries. In the intervening decades, economic circumstances have shifted radically. Arborian trade policy has not.

    Today, Arboria's trade policy seems paralyzed by the relentless conflict between proponents of

(20)   "free" and "fair" trade. The free traders argue that Arborian markets should be open, and the movement of goods and services across national borders unrestrained. The fair traders assert that access to Arborian markets should be restricted until Arborian

(25)   businesses are granted equal access to foreign markets. They contend that free trade is impossible while other nations erect barriers to Arborian exports.

    Both are correct: fair trade requires equal access and equal access leads to free trade. But both sides

(30)   base their positions on the same two outdated premises:

1. Global commerce is conducted under the terms of the General Agreement on Tariffs and Trade (GATT) and dominated by Arboria and similar economic

(35)   systems abroad.
2. Multilateral negotiations are the most effective way to resolve pressing trade issues.

    Both assumptions are wrong. The 40-year-old GATT

(40)   now covers less than 7 percent of global commerce. World trade is no longer dominated by the free-trade economies; nearly 75 percent is conducted by economic systems operating with principles at odds with those of Arboria. Forging a multilateral

(45)   trade policy consensus among so many diverse economic systems has become virtually impossible. And while multilateral talks drag on, Arboria misses opportunities for trade expansion.

Questions 536–543 refer to the passage.

RC38200-01.01

536. Which of the following best states the difference between free trade and fair trade, as explained in the passage?

(A) Free trade requires no trade tariffs whatsoever, whereas fair trade assumes multilateral agreement on tariffs for goods of equal worth.

(B) Free trade is based on the unrestricted movement of goods across all national boundaries, whereas fair trade is based on a nation's restriction of commerce with each nation that erects trade barriers to the first nation's exports.

(C) The trade policies of countries like Arboria are based on the principles of free trade, whereas the trade policies of other types of world economies are based on fair trade.

(D) Free-trade nations negotiate individual trade agreements with each of their trading partners, whereas fair-trade nations conduct multilateral trade negotiations.

(E) Free trade assumes a constant level of global commerce, whereas fair trade promotes a steady expansion of international trade.

RC38200-02.01

537. It can be inferred that the author of the passage would most likely agree with which of the following statements about multilateral trade negotiations?

(A) They are the most effective way to resolve trade problems.

(B) They are most effective in dealing with fair-trade issues between nations.

(C) They have only recently begun to make an impact on world trade.

(D) Arborian reliance on multilateral trade negotiations, while appropriate in the past, is inadequate for today's global marketplace.

(E) The principles of multilateral trade negotiations are incompatible with current Arborian foreign trade policy.

RC38200-03.01

538. Which of the following statements best summarizes the author's opinion of "free traders" and "fair traders"?

(A) The free and the fair traders' continuing debate provides a healthy and effective forum for examining Arborian trade policy.

(B) The proponents of fair trade are essentially correct, while those who advocate free trade are not.

(C) The proponents of free trade are better able to deal with current economic problems than are the fair traders.

(D) Neither the free nor the fair traders can come up with a workable trade policy because neither takes multilateral negotiations into account.

(E) The proponents of both free and fair trade have based their positions on out-of-date premises that do not reflect current economic conditions.

RC38200-04.01

539. The author mentions all of the following as characteristic of world trade in the mid-1940s EXCEPT:

(A) Arboria played a major role in the global marketplace.

(B) Whorfland played a major role in the global marketplace.

(C) Tariffs were the main obstacle to trade.

(D) Fair-trade economies dominated international trade.

(E) Arborian manufacturers were unsurpassed in most industries.

RC38200-05.01

540. In presenting the argument in the passage, the author uses all of the following EXCEPT:

(A) statistical information about global commerce

(B) definitions of terms concerning world trade

(C) generalizations about Arboria's economic system

(D) historical background of Arborian trade policy

(E) an example of an economic system whose principles differ from those of Arboria

RC38200-06.01

541. The author asserts which of the following about Arboria's trade policy?

(A) A dramatic revision of Arboria's trade policy will be necessary unless Arborian manufacturers improve the quality of their goods.

(B) The most crucial issue facing Arborian trade policymakers is that of free trade versus protectionism.

(C) Arboria's current trade policy was essentially developed during the 1940s and has changed little since that time.

(D) Arboria's trade policy is widely emulated throughout the world, to the extent that most international commerce is modeled on Arboria's principles.

(E) Arboria's trade policy has evolved gradually over the last eighty years, constantly readjusting itself in response to shifts in global commerce.

RC38200-07.01

542. The passage is primarily concerned with

(A) illustrating the erosion of Arboria's position in the world marketplace

(B) examining the differences between "free" and "fair" traders

(C) advocating a reassessment of Arboria's trade policy

(D) criticizing the terms of the General Agreement on Tariffs and Trade (GATT)

(E) comparing the different economic circumstances of Arboria's trade partners

RC38200-08.01

543. The author implies that the main obstacle to a truly effective Arborian trade policy is the

(A) weak position that Arboria currently holds in the global marketplace

(B) inability of Arborian leaders to recognize that foreign economic systems are based on principles fundamentally different from their own

(C) dominance of the supporters of free trade in the conflict between free-trade and fair-trade advocates

(D) apparent inability of Arborian industries to produce goods that are competitive in the world market

(E) protectionism that characterizes the foreign trade policies of so many of Arboria's trade partners

Questions 544 to 591 - Difficulty: **Medium**

Line   In *Winters v. United States* (1908), the Supreme
Court held that the right to use waters flowing through
or adjacent to the Fort Berthold Indian Reservation
was reserved to American Indians by the treaty
(5)   establishing the reservation. Although this treaty did
not mention water rights, the Court ruled that the
federal government, when it created the reservation,
intended to deal fairly with American Indians by
reserving for them the waters without which their
(10)   lands would have been useless. Later decisions,
citing Winters, established that courts can find federal
rights to reserve water for particular purposes if
(1) the land in question lies within an enclave under
exclusive federal jurisdiction; (2) the land has been
(15)   formally withdrawn from federal public lands—i.e.,
withdrawn from the stock of federal lands available
for private use under federal land use laws—and set
aside or reserved; and (3) the circumstances reveal
the government intended to reserve water as well as
(20)   land when establishing the reservation.
        Some American Indian tribes have also established
water rights through the courts based on their
traditional diversion and use of certain waters prior
to the United States' acquisition of sovereignty. For
(25)   example, the Rio Grande pueblos already existed
when the United States acquired sovereignty over
New Mexico in 1848. Although they at that time
became part of the United States, the pueblo lands
never formally constituted a part of federal public
(30)   lands; in any event, no treaty, statute, or executive
order has ever designated or withdrawn the pueblos
from public lands as American Indian reservations.
This fact, however, has not barred application of the
Winters doctrine. What constitutes an American Indian
(35)   reservation is a question of practice, not of legal
definition, and the pueblos have always been treated
as reservations by the United States. This pragmatic
approach is buttressed by *Arizona v. California*
(1963), wherein the Supreme Court indicated that
(40)   the manner in which any type of federal reservation
is created does not affect the application to it of the
Winters doctrine. Therefore, the reserved water rights
of Pueblo Indians have priority over other citizens'
water rights as of 1848, the year in which pueblos
(45)   must be considered to have become reservations.

Questions 544–551 refer to the passage.

RC74000-01.01

544. According to the passage, which of the following was true of the treaty establishing the Fort Berthold Indian Reservation?

(A)   It was challenged in the Supreme Court a number of times.

(B)   It was rescinded by the federal government, an action that gave rise to the Winters case.

(C)   It cited American Indians' traditional use of the land's resources.

(D)   It failed to mention water rights to be enjoyed by the reservation's inhabitants.

(E)   It was modified by the Supreme Court in *Arizona v. California*.

RC74000-02.01

545. The passage suggests that, if the criteria discussed in lines 10–20 of the text were the only criteria for establishing a reservation's water rights, which of the following would be true?

(A)   The water rights of the inhabitants of the Fort Berthold Indian Reservation would not take precedence over those of other citizens.

(B)   Reservations established before 1848 would be judged to have no water rights.

(C)   There would be no legal basis for the water rights of the Rio Grande pueblos.

(D)   Reservations other than American Indian reservations could not be created with reserved water rights.

(E)   Treaties establishing reservations would have to mention water rights explicitly in order to reserve water for a particular purpose.

RC74000-03.01

546. Which of the following most accurately summarizes the relationship between *Arizona v. California*, as that decision is described in the passage, and the criteria discussed in lines 10–20?

(A)   *Arizona v. California* abolishes these criteria and establishes a competing set of criteria for applying the Winters doctrine.

(B)   *Arizona v. California* establishes that the Winters doctrine applies to a broader range of situations than those defined by these criteria.

(C)   *Arizona v. California* represents the sole example of an exception to the criteria as they were set forth in the Winters doctrine.

(D)   *Arizona v. California* does not refer to the Winters doctrine to justify water rights, whereas these criteria do rely on the Winters doctrine.

(E)   *Arizona v. California* applies the criteria derived from the Winters doctrine only to federal lands other than American Indian reservations.

RC74000-04.01

547. The "pragmatic approach" mentioned in lines 37–38 of the passage is best defined as one that

(A)   grants recognition to reservations that were never formally established but that have traditionally been treated as such

(B)   determines the water rights of all citizens in a particular region by examining the actual history of water usage in that region

(C)   gives federal courts the right to reserve water along with land even when it is clear that the government originally intended to reserve only the land

(D)   bases the decision to recognize the legal rights of a group on the practical effect such a recognition is likely to have on other citizens

(E)   dictates that courts ignore precedents set by such cases as *Winters v. United States* in deciding what water rights belong to reserved land

RC74000-05.01

548. It can be inferred from the passage that the Winters doctrine has been used to establish which of the following?

(A)   A rule that the government may reserve water only by explicit treaty or agreement

(B)   A legal distinction between federal lands reserved for American Indians and federal lands reserved for other purposes

(C)   Criteria governing when the federal government may set land aside for a particular purpose

(D)   The special status of American Indian tribes' rights to reserved land

(E)   The federal right to reserve water implicitly as well as explicitly under certain conditions

RC74000-06.01

549. The author cites the fact that the Rio Grande pueblos were never formally withdrawn from public lands primarily in order to do which of the following?

(A)   Suggest why it might have been argued that the Winters doctrine ought not to apply to pueblo lands

(B)   Imply that the United States never really acquired sovereignty over pueblo lands

(C)   Argue that the pueblo lands ought still to be considered part of federal public lands

(D)   Support the argument that the water rights of citizens other than American Indians are limited by the Winters doctrine

(E)   Suggest that federal courts cannot claim jurisdiction over cases disputing the traditional diversion and use of water by Pueblo Indians

RC74000-07.01

550. The primary purpose of the passage is to

(A)   trace the development of laws establishing American Indian reservations

(B)   explain the legal bases for the water rights of American Indian tribes

(C)   question the legal criteria often used to determine the water rights of American Indian tribes

(D)   discuss evidence establishing the earliest date at which the federal government recognized the water rights of American Indians

(E)   point out a legal distinction between different types of American Indian reservations

RC74000-08.01

551. The passage suggests that the legal rights of citizens other than American Indians to the use of water flowing into the Rio Grande pueblos are

(A)   guaranteed by the precedent set in *Arizona v. California*

(B)   abolished by the Winters doctrine

(C)   deferred to the Pueblo Indians whenever treaties explicitly require this

(D)   guaranteed by federal land-use laws

(E)   limited by the prior claims of the Pueblo Indians

Line   In corporate purchasing, competitive scrutiny is typically limited to suppliers of items that are directly related to end products. With "indirect" purchases (such as computers, advertising, and legal services),

(5) which are not directly related to production, corporations often favor "supplier partnerships" (arrangements in which the purchaser forgoes the right to pursue alternative suppliers), which can inappropriately shelter suppliers from rigorous

(10) competitive scrutiny that might afford the purchaser economic leverage. There are two independent variables—availability of alternatives and ease of changing suppliers—that companies should use to evaluate the feasibility of subjecting suppliers of

(15) indirect purchases to competitive scrutiny. This can create four possible situations.

   In Type 1 situations, there are many alternatives and change is relatively easy. Open pursuit of alternatives—by frequent competitive bidding, if

(20) possible—will likely yield the best results. In Type 2 situations, where there are many alternatives but change is difficult—as for providers of employee health-care benefits—it is important to continuously test the market and use the results to secure

(25) concessions from existing suppliers. Alternatives provide a credible threat to suppliers, even if the ability to switch is constrained. In Type 3 situations, there are few alternatives, but the ability to switch without difficulty creates a threat that companies

(30) can use to negotiate concessions from existing suppliers. In Type 4 situations, where there are few alternatives and change is difficult, partnerships may be unavoidable.

Questions 552–556 refer to the passage.

RC00394-02

552. Which of the following can be inferred about supplier partnerships, as they are described in the passage?

(A) They cannot be sustained unless the goods or services provided are available from a large number of suppliers.

(B) They can result in purchasers paying more for goods and services than they would in a competitive-bidding situation.

(C) They typically are instituted at the urging of the supplier rather than the purchaser.

(D) They are not feasible when the goods or services provided are directly related to the purchasers' end products.

(E) They are least appropriate when the purchasers' ability to change suppliers is limited.

RC00394-03

553. Which of the following best describes the relation of the second paragraph to the first?

(A) The second paragraph offers proof of an assertion made in the first paragraph.

(B) The second paragraph provides an explanation for the occurrence of a situation described in the first paragraph.

(C) The second paragraph discusses the application of a strategy proposed in the first paragraph.

(D) The second paragraph examines the scope of a problem presented in the first paragraph.

(E) The second paragraph discusses the contradictions inherent in a relationship described in the first paragraph.

RC00394-04

554. It can be inferred that the author of the passage would be most likely to make which of the following recommendations to a company purchasing health care benefits for its employees?

(A) Devise strategies for circumventing the obstacles to replacing the current provider of health care benefits.

(B) Obtain health care benefits from a provider that also provides other indirect products and services.

(C) Obtain bids from other providers of health care benefits in order to be in a position to negotiate a better deal with the current provider.

(D) Switch providers of health care benefits whenever a different provider offers a more competitive price.

(E) Acknowledge the difficulties involved in replacing the current provider of health care benefits and offer to form a partnership with the provider.

RC00394-05

555. Which of the following is one difference between Type 2 situations and Type 4 situations, as they are described in the passage?

(A) The number of alternative suppliers available to the purchaser

(B) The most effective approach for the purchaser to use in obtaining competitive bids from potential suppliers

(C) The degree of difficulty the purchaser encounters when changing suppliers

(D) The frequency with which each type of situation occurs in a typical business environment

(E) The likelihood that any given purchase will be an indirect purchase

RC00394-06

556. According to the passage, which of the following factors distinguishes an indirect purchase from other purchases?

(A) The ability of the purchasing company to subject potential suppliers of the purchased item to competitive scrutiny

(B) The number of suppliers of the purchased item available to the purchasing company

(C) The methods of negotiation that are available to the purchasing company

(D) The relationship of the purchased item to the purchasing company's end product

(E) The degree of importance of the purchased item in the purchasing company's business operations

Line   Carotenoids, a family of natural pigments, form
an important part of the colorful signals used by
many animals. Animals acquire carotenoids either
directly (from the plants and algae that produce
(5)   them) or indirectly (by eating insects) and store them
in a variety of tissues. Studies of several animal
species have shown that when choosing mates,
females prefer males with brighter carotenoid-based
coloration. Owens and Olson hypothesize that the
(10)   presence of carotenoids, as signaled by coloration,
would be meaningful in the context of mate selection
if carotenoids were either rare or required for
health. The conventional view is that carotenoids
are meaningful because they are rare: healthier
(15)   males can forage for more of the pigments than
can their inferior counterparts. Although this may be
true, there is growing evidence that carotenoids are
meaningful also because they are required: they are
used by the immune system and for detoxification
(20)   processes that are important for maintaining health.
It may be that males can use scarce carotenoids
either for immune defense and detoxification or for
attracting females. Males that are more susceptible
to disease and parasites will have to use their
(25)   carotenoids to boost their immune systems, whereas
males that are genetically resistant will use fewer
carotenoids for fighting disease and will advertise
this by using the pigments for flashy display instead.

Questions 557–561 refer to the passage.

RC00423-01

557. According to the "conventional view" referred to in
line 13 of the passage, brighter carotenoid-based
coloration in certain species suggests that an
individual

(A)   lives in a habitat rich in carotenoid-bearing plants
and insects

(B)   has efficient detoxification processes

(C)   has a superior immune system

(D)   possesses superior foraging capacity

(E)   is currently capable of reproducing

RC00423-02

558. The idea that carotenoid-based coloration is significant
partly because carotenoids are required for health
suggests that a lack of bright coloration in a male is
most likely to indicate which of the following?

(A)   Inefficient detoxification processes

(B)   Immunity to parasite infestation

(C)   Low genetic resistance to disease

(D)   Lack of interest in mating

(E)   Lack of carotenoid-storing tissues

RC00423-03

559. The passage suggests that relatively bright carotenoid-
based coloration is a signal of which of the following
characteristics in males of certain animal species?

(A)   Readiness for mating behavior

(B)   Ability to fight

(C)   Particular feeding preferences

(D)   Recovery from parasite infestation

(E)   Fitness as a mate

RC00423-04

560. The passage implies which of the following about the
insects from which animals acquire carotenoids?

(A)   They do not produce carotenoids themselves.

(B)   They use carotenoids primarily for coloration.

(C)   They maintain constant levels of carotenoids in
their tissues.

(D)   They are unable to use carotenoids to boost
their immune system.

(E)   They are available in greater abundance than are
carotenoid-bearing plants.

RC00423-05

561. Information in the passage suggests that which of the following is true of carotenoids that a male animal uses for detoxification processes?

(A) They were not acquired directly from plants and algae.

(B) They cannot be replenished through foraging.

(C) They cannot be used simultaneously to brighten coloration.

(D) They do not affect the animal's susceptibility to parasites.

(E) They increase the chances that the animal will be selected as a mate.

Line   Linda Kerber argued in the mid-1980s that after the American Revolution (1775–1783), an ideology of "republican motherhood" resulted in a surge of educational opportunities for women in the United
(5)   States. Kerber maintained that the leaders of the new nation wanted women to be educated in order to raise politically virtuous sons. A virtuous citizenry was considered essential to the success of the country's republican form of government;
(10)   virtue was to be instilled not only by churches and schools, but by families, where the mother's role was crucial. Thus, according to Kerber, motherhood became pivotal to the fate of the republic, providing justification for an unprecedented attention to female
(15)   education.
      Introduction of the "republican motherhood" thesis dramatically changed historiography. Prior to Kerber's work, educational historians barely mentioned women and girls; Thomas Woody's
(20)   1929 work is the notable exception. Examining newspaper advertisements for academies, Woody found that educational opportunities increased for both girls and boys around 1750. Pointing to "An Essay on Woman" (1753) as reflecting a shift in
(25)   view, Woody also claimed that practical education for females had many advocates before the Revolution. Woody's evidence challenges the notion that the Revolution changed attitudes regarding female education, although it may have accelerated
(30)   earlier trends. Historians' reliance on Kerber's "republican motherhood" thesis may have obscured the presence of these trends, making it difficult to determine to what extent the Revolution really changed women's lives.

Questions 562–566 refer to the passage.

RC00349-02

562. According to the passage, Kerber maintained that which of the following led to an increase in educational opportunities for women in the United States after the American Revolution?

(A)   An unprecedented demand by women for greater educational opportunities in the decades following the Revolution

(B)   A new political ideology calling for equality of opportunity between women and men in all aspects of life

(C)   A belief that the American educational system could be reformed only if women participated more fully in that system

(D)   A belief that women needed to be educated if they were to contribute to the success of the nation's new form of government

(E)   A recognition that women needed to be educated if they were to take an active role in the nation's schools and churches

RC00349-03

563. According to the passage, within the field of educational history, Thomas Woody's 1929 work was

(A)   innovative because it relied on newspaper advertisements as evidence

(B)   exceptional in that it concentrated on the period before the American Revolution

(C)   unusual in that it focused on educational attitudes rather than on educational practices

(D)   controversial in its claims regarding educational opportunities for boys

(E)   atypical in that it examined the education of girls

RC00349-04

564. The passage suggests that Woody would have agreed with which of the following claims regarding "An Essay on Woman"?

(A) It expressed attitudes concerning women's education that were reflected in new educational opportunities for women after 1750.

(B) It persuaded educators to offer greater educational opportunities to women in the 1750s.

(C) It articulated ideas about women's education that would not be realized until after the American Revolution.

(D) It offered one of the most original arguments in favor of women's education in the United States in the eighteenth century.

(E) It presented views about women's education that were still controversial in Woody's own time.

RC00349-05

565. The passage suggests that, with regard to the history of women's education in the United States, Kerber's work differs from Woody's primarily concerning which of the following?

(A) The extent to which women were interested in pursuing educational opportunities in the eighteenth century

(B) The extent of the support for educational opportunities for girls prior to the American Revolution

(C) The extent of public resistance to educational opportunities for women after the American Revolution

(D) Whether attitudes toward women's educational opportunities changed during the eighteenth century

(E) Whether women needed to be educated in order to contribute to the success of a republican form of government

RC00349-06

566. According to the passage, Kerber argued that political leaders thought that the form of government adopted by the United States after the American Revolution depended on which of the following for its success?

(A) Women assuming the sole responsibility for instilling political virtue in children

(B) Girls becoming the primary focus of a reformed educational system that emphasized political virtue

(C) The family serving as one of the primary means by which children were imbued with political virtue

(D) The family assuming many of the functions previously performed by schools and churches

(E) Men and women assuming equal responsibility for the management of schools, churches, and the family

Line   In the Sonoran Desert of northwestern Mexico and
southern Arizona, the flowers of several species of
columnar cacti—cardon, saguaro, and organ
pipe—were once exclusively pollinated at night by
(5)   nectar-feeding bats, as their close relatives in arid
tropical regions of southern Mexico still are. In these
tropical regions, diurnal (daytime) visitors to columnar
cactus flowers are ineffective pollinators because,
by sunrise, the flowers' stigmas become unreceptive
(10)   or the flowers close. Yet the flowers of the Sonoran
Desert cacti have evolved to remain open after sunrise,
allowing pollination by such diurnal visitors as bees and
birds. Why have these cacti expanded their range of
pollinators by remaining open and receptive in daylight?
(15)   This development at the northernmost range of
columnar cacti may be due to a yearly variation in the
abundance—and hence the reliability—of migratory
nectar-feeding bats. Pollinators can be unreliable
for several reasons. They can be dietary generalists
(20)   whose fidelity to a particular species depends on
the availability of alternative food sources. Or, they
can be dietary specialists, but their abundance may
vary widely from year to year, resulting in variable
pollination of their preferred food species. Finally, they
(25)   may be dietary specialists, but their abundance may
be chronically low relative to the availability of flowers.
    Recent data reveals that during spring in the
Sonoran Desert, the nectar-feeding bats are
specialists feeding on cardon, saguaro, and
(30)   organpipe flowers. However, whereas cactus-flower
abundance tends to be high during spring, bat
population densities tend to be low except near
maternity roosts. Moreover, in spring, diurnal cactus-
pollinating birds are significantly more abundant in
(35)   this region than are the nocturnal bats. Thus, with bats
being unreliable cactus-flower pollinators, and daytime
pollinators more abundant and therefore more reliable,
selection favors the cactus flowers with traits that
increase their range of pollinators. While data suggest
(40)   that population densities of nectar-feeding bats are
also low in tropical areas of southern Mexico, where
bats are the exclusive pollinators of many species
of columnar cacti, cactus-flower density and bat
population density appear to be much more evenly
(45)   balanced there: compared with the Sonoran Desert's
cardon and saguaro, columnar cacti in southern Mexico
produce far fewer flowers per night. Accordingly,
despite their low population density, bats are able to
pollinate nearly 100 percent of the available flowers.

Questions 567–569 refer to the passage.

RC00633-01

567. The primary purpose of the passage is to

(A)   compare the adaptive responses of several
species of columnar cacti in the Sonoran Desert
with those in the arid tropical regions of southern
Mexico

(B)   discuss some of the possible causes of the
relatively low abundance of migratory nectar-
feeding bats in the Sonoran Desert

(C)   provide a possible explanation for a particular
evolutionary change in certain species of
columnar cacti in the Sonoran Desert

(D)   present recent findings that challenge a
particular theory as to why several species
of columnar cacti in the Sonoran Desert have
expanded their range of pollinators

(E)   compare the effectiveness of nocturnal and
diurnal pollination for several different species of
columnar cacti in the Sonoran Desert

RC00633-02

568. According to the passage, which of the following types
of nectar-feeding pollinators is likely to be an unreliable
pollinator of a particular cactus flower?

(A)   A dietary specialist whose abundance is typically
high in relation to that of the flower

(B)   A dietary specialist whose abundance is at times
significantly lower than that of the flower

(C)   A dietary generalist for whom that flower's
nectar is not a preferred food but is the most
consistently available food

(D)   A dietary generalist for whom that flower's nectar
is slightly preferred to other available foods

(E)   A dietary generalist that evolved from a species
of dietary specialists

RC00633-06

569. According to the passage, present-day columnar cacti in the Sonoran Desert differ from their close relatives in southern Mexico in that the Sonoran cacti

(A) have flowers that remain open after sunset

(B) are pollinated primarily by dietary specialists

(C) can be pollinated by nectar-feeding bats

(D) have stigmas that are unreceptive to pollination at night

(E) are sometimes pollinated by diurnal pollinators

Line   Manufacturers have to do more than build large manufacturing plants to realize economies of scale. It is true that as the capacity of a manufacturing operation rises, costs per unit of output fall as plant

(5)   size approaches "minimum efficient scale," where the cost per unit of output reaches a minimum, determined roughly by the state of existing technology and size of the potential market. However, minimum efficient scale cannot be fully realized unless a steady

(10)   "throughput" (the flow of materials through a plant) is attained. The throughput needed to maintain the optimal scale of production requires careful coordination not only of the flow of goods through the production process, but also of the flow of input from

(15)   suppliers and the flow of output to wholesalers and final consumers. If throughput falls below a critical point, unit costs rise sharply and profits disappear. A manufacturer's fixed costs and "sunk costs" (original capital investment in the physical plant) do not

(20)   decrease when production declines due to inadequate supplies of raw materials, problems on the factory floor, or inefficient sales networks. Consequently, potential economies of scale are based on the physical and engineering characteristics of the

(25)   production facilities—that is, on tangible capital—but realized economies of scale are operational and organizational, and depend on knowledge, skills, experience, and teamwork—that is, on organized human capabilities, or intangible capital.

(30)   The importance of investing in intangible capital becomes obvious when one looks at what happens in new capital-intensive manufacturing industries. Such industries are quickly dominated, not by the first firms to acquire technologically sophisticated plants of

(35)   theoretically optimal size, but rather by the first to exploit the full potential of such plants. Once some firms achieve this, a market becomes extremely hard to enter. Challengers must construct comparable plants and do so after the first movers have already

(40)   worked out problems with suppliers or with new production processes. Challengers must create distribution networks and marketing systems in markets where first movers have all the contacts and know-how. And challengers must recruit management

(45)   teams to compete with those that have already mastered these functional and strategic activities.

Questions 570–574 refer to the passage.

RC00121-01

570. The passage suggests that in order for a manufacturer in a capital-intensive industry to have a decisive advantage over competitors making similar products, the manufacturer must

(A) be the first in the industry to build production facilities of theoretically optimal size

(B) make every effort to keep fixed and sunk costs as low as possible

(C) be one of the first to operate its manufacturing plants at minimum efficient scale

(D) produce goods of higher quality than those produced by direct competitors

(E) stockpile raw materials at production sites in order to ensure a steady flow of such materials

RC00121-02

571. The passage suggests that which of the following is true of a manufacturer's fixed and sunk costs?

(A) The extent to which they are determined by market conditions for the goods being manufactured is frequently underestimated.

(B) If they are kept as low as possible, the manufacturer is very likely to realize significant profits.

(C) They are the primary factor that determines whether a manufacturer will realize economies of scale.

(D) They should be on a par with the fixed and sunk costs of the manufacturer's competitors.

(E) They are not affected by fluctuations in a manufacturing plant's throughput.

RC00121-03

572. In the context of the passage as a whole, the second paragraph serves primarily to

(A) provide an example to support the argument presented in the first paragraph

(B) evaluate various strategies discussed in the first paragraph

(C) introduce evidence that undermines the argument presented in the first paragraph

(D) anticipate possible objections to the argument presented in the first paragraph

(E) demonstrate the potential dangers of a commonly used strategy

RC00121-05

573. The passage LEAST supports the inference that a manufacturer's throughput could be adversely affected by

   (A)   a mistake in judgment regarding the selection of a wholesaler

   (B)   a breakdown in the factory's machinery

   (C)   a labor dispute on the factory floor

   (D)   an increase in the cost per unit of output

   (E)   a drop in the efficiency of the sales network

RC00121-07

574. The primary purpose of the passage is to

   (A)   point out the importance of intangible capital for realizing economies of scale in manufacturing

   (B)   show that manufacturers frequently gain a competitive advantage from investment in large manufacturing facilities

   (C)   argue that large manufacturing facilities often fail because of inadequate investment in both tangible and intangible capital

   (D)   suggest that most new industries are likely to be dominated by firms that build large manufacturing plants early

   (E)   explain why large manufacturing plants usually do not help manufacturers achieve economies of scale

Line   A small number of the forest species of
         lepidoptera (moths and butterflies, which exist as
         caterpillars during most of their life cycle) exhibit
         regularly recurring patterns of population growth
(5)   and decline—such fluctuations in population are
         known as population cycles. Although many different
         variables influence population levels, a regular pattern
         such as a population cycle seems to imply a
         dominant, driving force. Identification of that driving
(10)   force, however, has proved surprisingly elusive
         despite considerable research. The common
         approach of studying causes of population cycles by
         measuring the mortality caused by different agents,
         such as predatory birds or parasites, has been
(15)   unproductive in the case of lepidoptera. Moreover,
         population ecologists' attempts to alter cycles by
         changing the caterpillars' habitat and by reducing
         caterpillar populations have not succeeded. In short,
         the evidence implies that these insect populations, if
(20)   not self-regulating, may at least be regulated by an
         agent more intimately connected with the insect than
         are predatory birds or parasites.
             Recent work suggests that this agent may be a
         virus. For many years, viral disease had been reported
(25)   in declining populations of caterpillars, but population
         ecologists had usually considered viral disease to
         have contributed to the decline once it was underway
         rather than to have initiated it. The recent work has
         been made possible by new techniques of molecular
(30)   biology that allow viral DNA to be detected at low
         concentrations in the environment. Nuclear
         polyhedrosis viruses are hypothesized to be the
         driving force behind population cycles in lepidoptera
         in part because the viruses themselves follow an
(35)   infectious cycle in which, if protected from direct
         sunlight, they may remain virulent for many years
         in the environment, embedded in durable crystals of
         polyhedrin protein. Once ingested by a caterpillar,
         the crystals dissolve, releasing the virus to infect
(40)   the insect's cells. Late in the course of the infection,
         millions of new virus particles are formed and
         enclosed in polyhedrin crystals. These crystals
         reenter the environment after the insect dies and
         decomposes, thus becoming available to infect
(45)   other caterpillars.
             One of the attractions of this hypothesis is its broad
         applicability. Remarkably, despite significant differences
         in habitat and behavior, many species of lepidoptera
         have population cycles of similar length, between eight
(50)   and eleven years. Nuclear polyhedrosis viral infection is
         one factor these disparate species share.

RC00120-05

575. The primary purpose of the passage is to

(A)   describe the development of new techniques that
      may help to determine the driving force behind
      population cycles in lepidoptera

(B)   present evidence that refutes a particular theory
      about the driving force behind population cycles
      in lepidoptera

(C)   present a hypothesis about the driving force
      behind population cycles in lepidoptera

(D)   describe the fluctuating patterns of population
      cycles in lepidoptera

(E)   question the idea that a single driving force is
      behind population cycles in lepidoptera

RC00120-06

576. It can be inferred from the passage that the mortality
      caused by agents such as predatory birds or parasites
      was measured in an attempt to

(A)   develop an explanation for the existence of
      lepidoptera population cycles

(B)   identify behavioral factors in lepidoptera that
      affect survival rates

(C)   identify possible methods for controlling
      lepidoptera population growth

(D)   provide evidence that lepidoptera populations
      are self-regulating

(E)   determine the life stages of lepidoptera at which
      mortality rates are highest

RC00120-01

577. Which of the following, if true, would most weaken the author's conclusion in lines 18–22 ?

   (A) New research reveals that the number of species of birds and parasites that prey on lepidoptera has dropped significantly in recent years.

   (B) New experiments in which the habitats of lepidoptera are altered in previously untried ways result in the shortening of lepidoptera population cycles.

   (C) Recent experiments have revealed that the nuclear polyhedrosis virus is present in a number of predators and parasites of lepidoptera.

   (D) Differences among the habitats of lepidoptera species make it difficult to assess the effects of weather on lepidoptera population cycles.

   (E) Viral disease is typically observed in a large proportion of the lepidoptera population.

RC00120-02

578. According to the passage, before the discovery of new techniques for detecting viral DNA, population ecologists believed that viral diseases

   (A) were not widely prevalent among insect populations generally

   (B) affected only the caterpillar life stage of lepidoptera

   (C) were the driving force behind lepidoptera population cycles

   (D) attacked already declining caterpillar populations

   (E) infected birds and parasites that prey on various species of lepidoptera

RC00120-03

579. According to the passage, nuclear polyhedrosis viruses can remain virulent in the environment only when

   (A) the polyhedrin protein crystals dissolve

   (B) caterpillar populations are in decline

   (C) they are present in large numbers

   (D) their concentration in a particular area remains low

   (E) they are sheltered from direct sunlight

RC00120-04

580. It can be inferred from the passage that while inside its polyhedrin protein crystals, the nuclear polyhedrosis virus

   (A) is exposed to direct sunlight

   (B) is attractive to predators

   (C) cannot infect caterpillars' cells

   (D) cannot be ingested by caterpillars

   (E) cannot be detected by new techniques of molecular biology

Line   Resin is a plant secretion that hardens when exposed to air; fossilized resin is called amber. Although Pliny in the first century recognized that amber was produced from "marrow discharged by

(5)   trees," amber has been widely misunderstood to be a semiprecious gem and has even been described in mineralogy textbooks. Confusion also persists surrounding the term "resin," which was defined before rigorous chemical analyses were available.

(10)   Resin is often confused with gum, a substance produced in plants in response to bacterial infections, and with sap, an aqueous solution transported through certain plant tissues. Resin differs from both gum and sap in that scientists have not determined a

(15)   physiological function for resin.

     In the 1950s, entomologists posited that resin may function to repel or attract insects. Fraenkel conjectured that plants initially produced resin in nonspecific chemical responses to insect attack

(20)   and that, over time, plants evolved that produced resin with specific repellent effects. But some insect species, he noted, might overcome the repellent effects, actually becoming attracted to the resin. This might induce the insects to feed on those

(25)   plants or aid them in securing a breeding site. Later researchers suggested that resin mediates the complex interdependence, or "coevolution," of plants and insects over time. Such ideas led to the development of the specialized discipline of chemical

(30)   ecology, which is concerned with the role of plant chemicals in interactions with other organisms and with the evolution and ecology of plant antiherbivore chemistry (plants' chemical defenses against attack by herbivores such as insects).

Questions 581–584 refer to the passage.

RC00223-03

581. According to the passage, which of the following is true of plant antiherbivore chemistry?

(A) Changes in a plant's antiherbivore chemistry may affect insect feeding behavior.

(B) A plant's repellent effects often involve interactions between gum and resin.

(C) A plant's antiherbivore responses assist in combating bacterial infections.

(D) Plant antiherbivore chemistry plays only a minor role in the coevolution of plants and insects.

(E) Researchers first studied repellent effects in plants beginning in the 1950s.

RC00223-04

582. Of the following topics, which would be most likely to be studied within the discipline of chemical ecology as it is described in the passage?

(A) Seeds that become attached to certain insects, which in turn carry away the seeds and aid in the reproductive cycle of the plant species in question

(B) An insect species that feeds on weeds detrimental to crop health and yield, and how these insects might aid in agricultural production

(C) The effects of deforestation on the life cycles of subtropical carnivorous plants and the insect species on which the plants feed

(D) The growth patterns of a particular species of plant that has proved remarkably resistant to herbicides

(E) Insects that develop a tolerance for feeding on a plant that had previously been toxic to them, and the resultant changes within that plant species

RC00223-05

583. The author refers to "bacterial infections" (see line 11) most likely in order to

(A)   describe the physiological function that gum performs in plants

(B)   demonstrate that sap is not the only substance that is transported through a plant's tissues

(C)   explain how modern chemical analysis has been used to clarify the function of resin

(D)   show that gum cannot serve as an effective defense against herbivores

(E)   give an example of how confusion has arisen with regard to the nature of resin

RC00223-07

584. The author of the passage refers to Pliny most probably in order to

(A)   give an example of how the nature of amber has been misunderstood in the past

(B)   show that confusion about amber has long been more pervasive than confusion about resin

(C)   make note of the first known reference to amber as a semiprecious gem

(D)   point out an exception to a generalization about the history of people's understanding of amber

(E)   demonstrate that Pliny believed amber to be a mineral

Line   During the 1980s, many economic historians studying Latin America focused on the impact of the Great Depression of the 1930s. Most of these historians argued that although the Depression
(5)   began earlier in Latin America than in the United States, it was less severe in Latin America and did not significantly impede industrial growth there. The historians' argument was grounded in national government records concerning tax revenues and
(10)   exports and in government-sponsored industrial censuses, from which historians have drawn conclusions about total manufacturing output and profit levels across Latin America. However, economic statistics published by Latin American
(15)   governments in the early twentieth century are neither reliable nor consistent; this is especially true of manufacturing data, which were gathered from factory owners for taxation purposes and which therefore may well be distorted. Moreover,
(20)   one cannot assume a direct correlation between the output level and the profit level of a given industry as these variables often move in opposite directions. Finally, national and regional economies are composed of individual firms and industries,
(25)   and relying on general, sweeping economic indicators may mask substantial variations among these different enterprises. For example, recent analyses of previously unexamined data on textile manufacturing in Brazil and Mexico suggest that the
(30)   Great Depression had a more severe impact on this Latin American industry than scholars had recognized.

RC00333-01

585. The primary purpose of the passage is to

(A) compare the impact of the Great Depression on Latin America with its impact on the United States

(B) criticize a school of economic historians for failing to analyze the Great Depression in Latin America within a global context

(C) illustrate the risks inherent in comparing different types of economic enterprises to explain economic phenomena

(D) call into question certain scholars' views concerning the severity of the Great Depression in Latin America

(E) demonstrate that the Great Depression had a more severe impact on industry in Latin America than in certain other regions

RC00333-02

586. Which of the following conclusions about the Great Depression is best supported by the passage?

(A) It did not impede Latin American industrial growth as much as historians had previously thought.

(B) It had a more severe impact on the Brazilian and the Mexican textile industries than it had on Latin America as a region.

(C) It affected the Latin American textile industry more severely than it did any other industry in Latin America.

(D) The overall impact on Latin American industrial growth should be reevaluated by economic historians.

(E) Its impact on Latin America should not be compared with its impact on the United States.

RC00333-04

587. Which of the following, if true, would most strengthen the author's assertion regarding economic indicators in lines 25–27 ?

   (A)   During an economic depression, European textile manufacturers' profits rise while their industrial output remains steady.

   (B)   During a national economic recession, United States microchips manufacturers' profits rise sharply while United States steel manufacturers' profits plunge.

   (C)   During the years following a severe economic depression, textile manufacturers' output levels and profit levels increase in Brazil and Mexico but not in the rest of Latin America.

   (D)   Although Japanese industry as a whole recovers after an economic recession, it does not regain its previously high levels of production.

   (E)   While European industrial output increases in the years following an economic depression, total output remains below that of Japan or the United States.

Line   Among the myths taken as fact by the
environmental managers of most corporations is
the belief that environmental regulations affect all
competitors in a given industry uniformly. In reality,
(5)   regulatory costs—and therefore compliance—
fall unevenly, economically disadvantaging some
companies and benefiting others. For example, a
plant situated near a number of larger
noncompliant competitors is less likely to attract
(10)   the attention of local regulators than is an isolated
plant, and less attention means lower costs.

     Additionally, large plants can spread compliance
costs such as waste treatment across a larger
revenue base; on the other hand, some smaller
(15)   plants may not even be subject to certain
provisions such as permit or reporting
requirements by virtue of their size. Finally, older
production technologies often continue to generate
toxic wastes that were not regulated when the
(20)   technology was first adopted. New regulations
have imposed extensive compliance costs on
companies still using older industrial coal-fired
burners that generate high sulfur dioxide and
nitrogen oxide outputs, for example, whereas new
(25)   facilities generally avoid processes that would
create such waste products. By realizing that they
have discretion and that not all industries are
affected equally by environmental regulation,
environmental managers can help their companies
(30)   to achieve a competitive edge by anticipating
regulatory pressure and exploring all possibilities for
addressing how changing regulations will affect their
companies specifically.

Questions 588–591 refer to the passage.

RC00272-02

588. It can be inferred from the passage that a large plant
might have to spend more than a similar but smaller
plant on environmental compliance because the larger
plant is

(A) more likely to attract attention from local
regulators

(B) less likely to be exempt from permit and
reporting requirements

(C) less likely to have regulatory costs passed on to
it by companies that supply its raw materials

(D) more likely to employ older production
technologies

(E) more likely to generate wastes that are more
environmentally damaging than those generated
by smaller plants

RC00272-04

589. According to the passage, which of the following
statements about sulfur dioxide and nitrogen oxide
outputs is true?

(A) Older production technologies cannot be
adapted so as to reduce production of these
outputs as waste products.

(B) Under the most recent environmental regulations,
industrial plants are no longer permitted to
produce these outputs.

(C) Although these outputs are environmentally
hazardous, some plants still generate them as
waste products despite the high compliance
costs they impose.

(D) Many older plants have developed innovative
technological processes that reduce the
amounts of these outputs generated as waste
products.

(E) Since the production processes that generate
these outputs are less costly than alternative
processes, these less expensive processes are
sometimes adopted despite their acknowledged
environmental hazards.

RC00272-06

590. Which of the following best describes the relationship of the statement about large plants (lines 12–17) to the passage as a whole?

(A) It presents a hypothesis that is disproved later in the passage.

(B) It highlights an opposition between two ideas mentioned in the passage.

(C) It provides examples to support a claim made earlier in the passage.

(D) It exemplifies a misconception mentioned earlier in the passage.

(E) It draws an analogy between two situations described in the passage.

RC00272-07

591. The primary purpose of the passage is to

(A) address a widespread environmental management problem and suggest possible solutions

(B) illustrate varying levels of compliance with environmental regulation among different corporations

(C) describe the various alternatives to traditional methods of environmental management

(D) advocate increased corporate compliance with environmental regulation

(E) correct a common misconception about the impact of environmental regulations

Questions 592 to 651 - Difficulty: **Hard**

Line   Two works published in 1984 demonstrate contrasting approaches to writing the history of United States women. Buel and Buel's biography of Mary Fish (1736–1818) makes little effort to
(5)   place her story in the context of recent historiography on women. Lebsock, meanwhile, attempts not only to write the history of women in one southern community, but also to redirect two decades of historiographical debate as to
(10) whether women gained or lost status in the nineteenth century as compared with the eighteenth century. Although both books offer the reader the opportunity to assess this controversy regarding women's status, only Lebsock's deals with
(15) it directly. She examines several different aspects of women's status, helping to refine and resolve the issues. She concludes that while women gained autonomy in some areas, especially in the private sphere, they lost it in
(20) many aspects of the economic sphere. More importantly, she shows that the debate itself depends on frame of reference: in many respects, women lost power in relation to men, for example, as certain jobs (delivering babies, supervising
(25) schools) were taken over by men. Yet women also gained power in comparison with their previous status, owning a higher proportion of real estate, for example. In contrast, Buel and Buel's biography provides ample raw material for
(30) questioning the myth, fostered by some historians, of a colonial golden age in the eighteenth century but does not give the reader much guidance in analyzing the controversy over women's status.

Questions 592–597 refer to the passage.

RC00109-01

592. The primary purpose of the passage is to

    (A) examine two sides of a historiographical debate

    (B) call into question an author's approach to a historiographical debate

    (C) examine one author's approach to a historiographical debate

    (D) discuss two authors' works in relationship to a historiographical debate

    (E) explain the prevalent perspective on a historiographical debate

RC00109-02

593. The author of the passage mentions the supervision of schools primarily in order to

    (A) remind readers of the role education played in the cultural changes of the nineteenth century in the United States

    (B) suggest an area in which nineteenth-century American women were relatively free to exercise power

    (C) provide an example of an occupation for which accurate data about women's participation are difficult to obtain

    (D) speculate about which occupations were considered suitable for United States women of the nineteenth century

    (E) illustrate how the answers to questions about women's status depend on particular contexts

RC00109-03

594. With which of the following characterizations of Lebsock's contribution to the controversy concerning women's status in the nineteenth-century United States would the author of the passage be most likely to agree?

(A) Lebsock has studied women from a formerly neglected region and time period.

(B) Lebsock has demonstrated the importance of frame of reference in answering questions about women's status.

(C) Lebsock has addressed the controversy by using women's current status as a frame of reference.

(D) Lebsock has analyzed statistics about occupations and property that were previously ignored.

(E) Lebsock has applied recent historiographical methods to the biography of a nineteenth-century woman.

RC00109-04

595. According to the passage, Lebsock's work differs from Buel and Buel's work in that Lebsock's work

(A) uses a large number of primary sources

(B) ignores issues of women's legal status

(C) refuses to take a position on women's status in the eighteenth century

(D) addresses larger historiographical issues

(E) fails to provide sufficient material to support its claims

RC00109-05

596. The passage suggests that Lebsock believes that compared to nineteenth-century American women, eighteenth-century American women were

(A) in many respects less powerful in relation to men

(B) more likely to own real estate

(C) generally more economically independent

(D) more independent in conducting their private lives

(E) less likely to work as school superintendents

RC00109-06

597. The passage suggests that Buel and Buel's biography of Mary Fish provides evidence for which of the following views of women's history?

(A) Women have lost power in relation to men since the colonial era.

(B) Women of the colonial era were not as likely to be concerned with their status as were women in the nineteenth century.

(C) The colonial era was not as favorable for women as some historians have believed.

(D) Women had more economic autonomy in the colonial era than in the nineteenth century.

(E) Women's occupations were generally more respected in the colonial era than in the nineteenth century.

Line   Acting on the recommendation of a British
government committee investigating the high
incidence in white lead factories of illness among
employees, most of whom were women, the Home
(5)   Secretary proposed in 1895 that Parliament enact
legislation that would prohibit women from holding
most jobs in white lead factories. Although the
Women's Industrial Defence Committee (WIDC),
formed in 1892 in response to earlier legislative
(10)   attempts to restrict women's labor, did not discount
the white lead trade's potential health dangers, it
opposed the proposal, viewing it as yet another
instance of limiting women's work opportunities.
    Also opposing the proposal was the Society for
(15)   Promoting the Employment of Women (SPEW),
which attempted to challenge it by investigating the
causes of illness in white lead factories. SPEW
contended, and WIDC concurred, that controllable
conditions in such factories were responsible for
(20)   the development of lead poisoning. SPEW provided
convincing evidence that lead poisoning could be
avoided if workers were careful and clean and if
already extant workplace safety regulations were
stringently enforced. However, the Women's Trade
(25)   Union League (WTUL), which had ceased in the late
1880s to oppose restrictions on women's labor,
supported the eventually enacted proposal, in part
because safety regulations were generally not being
enforced in white lead factories, where there were
(30)   no unions (and little prospect of any) to pressure
employers to comply with safety regulations.

Questions 598–600 refer to the passage.

RC00558-01

598. The passage suggests that WIDC differed from WTUL
in which of the following ways?

(A)   WIDC believed that the existing safety regulations
were adequate to protect women's health,
whereas WTUL believed that such regulations
needed to be strengthened.

(B)   WIDC believed that unions could not succeed
in pressuring employers to comply with such
regulations, whereas WTUL believed that unions
could succeed in doing so.

(C)   WIDC believed that lead poisoning in white
lead factories could be avoided by controlling
conditions there, whereas WTUL believed that
lead poisoning in such factories could not
be avoided no matter how stringently safety
regulations were enforced.

(D)   At the time that the legislation concerning white
lead factories was proposed, WIDC was primarily
concerned with addressing health conditions
in white lead factories, whereas WTUL was
concerned with improving working conditions in
all types of factories.

(E)   At the time that WIDC was opposing legislative
attempts to restrict women's labor, WTUL had
already ceased to do so.

RC00558-02

599. Which of the following, if true, would most clearly support the contention attributed to SPEW in lines 17–20 ?

(A) Those white lead factories that most strongly enforced regulations concerning worker safety and hygiene had the lowest incidences of lead poisoning among employees.

(B) The incidence of lead poisoning was much higher among women who worked in white lead factories than among women who worked in other types of factories.

(C) There were many household sources of lead that could have contributed to the incidence of lead poisoning among women who also worked outside the home in the late nineteenth century.

(D) White lead factories were more stringent than were certain other types of factories in their enforcement of workplace safety regulations.

(E) Even brief exposure to the conditions typically found in white lead factories could cause lead poisoning among factory workers.

RC00558-06

600. The passage is primarily concerned with

(A) presenting various groups' views of the motives of those proposing certain legislation

(B) contrasting the reasoning of various groups concerning their positions on certain proposed legislation

(C) tracing the process whereby certain proposed legislation was eventually enacted

(D) assessing the success of tactics adopted by various groups with respect to certain proposed legislation

(E) evaluating the arguments of various groups concerning certain proposed legislation

Line   It is an odd but indisputable fact that the
seventeenth-century English women who are
generally regarded as among the forerunners of
modern feminism are almost all identified with the
(5)   Royalist side in the conflict between Royalists and
Parliamentarians known as the English Civil Wars.
Since Royalist ideology is often associated with the
radical patriarchalism of seventeenth-century
political theorist Robert Filmer—a patriarchalism
(10)   that equates family and kingdom and asserts the
divinely ordained absolute power of the king and,
by analogy, of the male head of the household—
historians have been understandably puzzled by the
fact that Royalist women wrote the earliest
(15)   extended criticisms of the absolute subordination
of women in marriage and the earliest systematic
assertions of women's rational and moral equality
with men. Some historians have questioned the
facile equation of Royalist ideology with Filmerian
(20)   patriarchalism; and indeed, there may have been
no consistent differences between Royalists and
Parliamentarians on issues of family organization
and women's political rights, but in that case one
would expect early feminists to be equally divided
(25)   between the two sides.
     Catherine Gallagher argues that Royalism
engendered feminism because the ideology of
absolute monarchy provided a transition to an
ideology of the absolute self. She cites the example
(30)   of the notoriously eccentric author Margaret
Cavendish (1626–1673), duchess of Newcastle.
Cavendish claimed to be as ambitious as any
woman could be, but knowing that as a woman she
was excluded from the pursuit of power in the real
(35)   world, she resolved to be mistress of her own
world, the "immaterial world" that any person can
create within her own mind—and, as a writer, on
paper. In proclaiming what she called her
"singularity," Cavendish insisted that she was a
(40)   self-sufficient being within her mental empire, the
center of her own subjective universe rather than a
satellite orbiting a dominant male planet. In
justifying this absolute singularity, Cavendish
repeatedly invoked the model of the absolute
(45)   monarch, a figure that became a metaphor for the
self-enclosed, autonomous nature of the individual
person. Cavendish's successors among early
feminists retained her notion of woman's sovereign
self, but they also sought to break free from the
(50)   complete political and social isolation that her
absolute singularity entailed.

Questions 601–606 refer to the passage.

RC00433-02

601. The author of the passage refers to Robert Filmer (see
line 9) primarily in order to

(A)   show that Royalist ideology was somewhat more
radical than most historians appear to realize

(B)   qualify the claim that patriarchalism formed the
basis of Royalist ideology

(C)   question the view that most early feminists were
associated with the Royalist faction

(D)   highlight an apparent tension between Royalist
ideology and the ideas of early feminists

(E)   argue that Royalists held conflicting opinions
on issues of family organization and women's
political rights

RC00433-11

602. The passage suggests which of the following about the seventeenth-century English women mentioned in line 2 ?

(A) Their status as forerunners of modern feminism is not entirely justified.

(B) They did not openly challenge the radical patriarchalism of Royalist Filmerian ideology.

(C) Cavendish was the first among these women to criticize women's subordination in marriage and assert women's equality with men.

(D) Their views on family organization and women's political rights were diametrically opposed to those of both Royalist and Parliamentarian ideology.

(E) Historians would be less puzzled if more of them were identified with the Parliamentarian side in the English Civil Wars.

RC00433-04

603. The passage suggests that Margaret Cavendish's decision to become an author was motivated, at least in part, by a desire to

(A) justify her support for the Royalist cause

(B) encourage her readers to work toward eradicating Filmerian patriarchalism

(C) persuade other women to break free from their political and social isolation

(D) analyze the causes for women's exclusion from the pursuit of power

(E) create a world over which she could exercise total control

RC00433-08

604. The phrase "a satellite orbiting a dominant male planet" (lines 41–42) refers most directly to

(A) Cavendish's concept that each woman is a sovereign self

(B) the complete political and social isolation of absolute singularity

(C) the immaterial world that a writer can create on paper

(D) the absolute subordination of women in a patriarchal society

(E) the metaphorical figure of the absolute monarch

RC00433-06

605. The primary purpose of the passage is to

(A) trace the historical roots of a modern sociopolitical movement

(B) present one scholar's explanation for a puzzling historical phenomenon

(C) contrast two interpretations of the ideological origins of a political conflict

(D) establish a link between the ideology of an influential political theorist and that of a notoriously eccentric writer

(E) call attention to some points of agreement between opposing sides in an ideological debate

RC00433-09

606. Which of the following, if true, would most clearly undermine Gallagher's explanation of the link between Royalism and feminism?

(A) Because of their privileged backgrounds, Royalist women were generally better educated than were their Parliamentarian counterparts.

(B) Filmer himself had read some of Cavendish's early writings and was highly critical of her ideas.

(C) Cavendish's views were highly individual and were not shared by the other Royalist women who wrote early feminist works.

(D) The Royalist and Parliamentarian ideologies were largely in agreement on issues of family organization and women's political rights.

(E) The Royalist side included a sizable minority faction that was opposed to the more radical tendencies of Filmerian patriarchalism.

Line   Frazier and Mosteller assert that medical research could be improved by a move toward larger, simpler clinical trials of medical treatments. Currently, researchers collect far more background information
(5)   on patients than is strictly required for their trials—substantially more than hospitals collect—thereby escalating costs of data collection, storage, and analysis. Although limiting information collection could increase the risk that researchers will overlook
(10)   facts relevant to a study, Frazier and Mosteller contend that such risk, never entirely eliminable from research, would still be small in most studies. Only in research on entirely new treatments are new and unexpected variables likely to arise.
(15)   Frazier and Mosteller propose not only that researchers limit data collection on individual patients but also that researchers enroll more patients in clinical trials, thereby obtaining a more representative sample of the total population with
(20)   the disease under study. Often researchers restrict study participation to patients who have no ailments besides those being studied. A treatment judged successful under these ideal conditions can then be evaluated under normal conditions. Broadening the
(25)   range of trial participants, Frazier and Mosteller suggest, would enable researchers to evaluate a treatment's efficacy for diverse patients under various conditions and to evaluate its effectiveness for different patient subgroups. For example, the value
(30)   of a treatment for a progressive disease may vary according to a patient's stage of disease. Patients' ages may also affect a treatment's efficacy.

Questions 607–611 refer to the passage.

RC00312-01

607. The passage is primarily concerned with

(A)   identifying two practices in medical research that may affect the accuracy of clinical trials

(B)   describing aspects of medical research that tend to drive up costs

(C)   evaluating an analysis of certain shortcomings of current medical research practices

(D)   describing proposed changes to the ways in which clinical trials are conducted

(E)   explaining how medical researchers have traditionally conducted clinical trials and how such trials are likely to change

RC00312-03

608. Which of the following can be inferred from the passage about a study of the category of patients referred to in lines 20–22 ?

(A)   Its findings might have limited applicability.

(B)   It would be prohibitively expensive in its attempt to create ideal conditions.

(C)   It would be the best way to sample the total population of potential patients.

(D)   It would allow researchers to limit information collection without increasing the risk that important variables could be overlooked.

(E)   Its findings would be more accurate if it concerned treatments for a progressive disease than if it concerned treatments for a nonprogressive disease.

RC00312-04

609. It can be inferred from the passage that a study limited to patients like those mentioned in lines 20–22 would have which of the following advantages over the kind of study proposed by Frazier and Mosteller?

   (A)   It would yield more data and its findings would be more accurate.

   (B)   It would cost less in the long term, though it would be more expensive in its initial stages.

   (C)   It would limit the number of variables researchers would need to consider when evaluating the treatment under study.

   (D)   It would help researchers to identify subgroups of patients with secondary conditions that might also be treatable.

   (E)   It would enable researchers to assess the value of an experimental treatment for the average patient.

RC00312-05

610. The author mentions patients' ages (line 32) primarily in order to

   (A)   identify the most critical variable differentiating subgroups of patients

   (B)   cast doubt on the advisability of implementing Frazier and Mosteller's proposals about medical research

   (C)   indicate why progressive diseases may require different treatments at different stages

   (D)   illustrate a point about the value of enrolling a wide range of patients in clinical trials

   (E)   substantiate an argument about the problems inherent in enrolling large numbers of patients in clinical trials

RC00312-06

611. According to the passage, which of the following describes a result of the way in which researchers generally conduct clinical trials?

   (A)   They expend resources on the storage of information likely to be irrelevant to the study they are conducting.

   (B)   They sometimes compromise the accuracy of their findings by collecting and analyzing more information than is strictly required for their trials.

   (C)   They avoid the risk of overlooking variables that might affect their findings, even though doing so raises their research costs.

   (D)   Because they attempt to analyze too much information, they overlook facts that could emerge as relevant to their studies.

   (E)   In order to approximate the conditions typical of medical treatment, they base their methods of information collection on those used by hospitals.

Line   There are recent reports of apparently drastic
declines in amphibian populations and of extinctions
of a number of the world's endangered amphibian
species. These declines, if real, may be signs of a
(5)   general trend toward extinction, and many
environmentalists have claimed that immediate
environmental action is necessary to remedy
this "amphibian crisis," which, in their view, is an
indicator of general and catastrophic environmental
(10)   degradation due to human activity.
    To evaluate these claims, it is useful to make a
preliminary distinction that is far too often ignored.
A declining population should not be confused with
an endangered one. An endangered population is
(15)   always rare, almost always small, and, by definition,
under constant threat of extinction even without a
proximate cause in human activities. Its disappearance,
however unfortunate, should come as no great
surprise. Moreover, chance events—which may
(20)   indicate nothing about the direction of trends in
population size—may lead to its extinction. The
probability of extinction due to such random factors
depends on the population size and is independent of
the prevailing direction of change in that size.
(25)   For biologists, population declines are potentially
more worrisome than extinctions. Persistent
declines, especially in large populations, indicate a
changed ecological context. Even here, distinctions
must again be made among declines that are only
(30)   apparent (in the sense that they are part of habitual
cycles or of normal fluctuations), declines that take
a population to some lower but still acceptable
level, and those that threaten extinction (e.g., by
taking the number of individuals below the minimum
(35)   viable population). Anecdotal reports of population
decreases cannot distinguish among these
possibilities, and some amphibian populations have
shown strong fluctuations in the past.
    It is indisputably true that there is simply not
(40)   enough long-term scientific data on amphibian
populations to enable researchers to identify real
declines in amphibian populations. Many fairly
common amphibian species declared all but extinct
after severe declines in the 1950s and 1960s
(45)   have subsequently recovered, and so might
the apparently declining populations that have
generated the current appearance of an amphibian
crisis. Unfortunately, long-term data will not soon
be forthcoming, and postponing environmental
(50)   action while we wait for it may doom species and
whole ecosystems to extinction.

Questions 612–617 refer to the passage.

RC00229-01

612. The primary purpose of the passage is to

(A)   assess the validity of a certain view

(B)   distinguish between two phenomena

(C)   identify the causes of a problem

(D)   describe a disturbing trend

(E)   allay concern about a particular phenomenon

RC00229-02

613. It can be inferred from the passage that the author
believes which of the following to be true of the
environmentalists mentioned in lines 5–6 ?

(A)   They have wrongly chosen to focus on anecdotal
reports rather than on the long-term data that
are currently available concerning amphibians.

(B)   Their recommendations are flawed because
their research focuses too narrowly on a single
category of animal species.

(C)   Their certainty that population declines in general
are caused by environmental degradation is not
warranted.

(D)   They have drawn premature conclusions
concerning a crisis in amphibian populations
from recent reports of declines.

(E)   They have overestimated the effects of chance
events on trends in amphibian populations.

RC00229-03

614. It can be inferred from the passage that the author
believes which of the following to be true of the
amphibian extinctions that have recently been
reported?

(A)   They have resulted primarily from human
activities causing environmental degradation.

(B)   They could probably have been prevented if
timely action had been taken to protect the
habitats of amphibian species.

(C)   They should not come as a surprise, because
amphibian populations generally have been
declining for a number of years.

(D)   They have probably been caused by a
combination of chance events.

(E)   They do not clearly constitute evidence of
general environmental degradation.

RC00229-04

615. According to the passage, each of the following is true of endangered amphibian species EXCEPT:

   (A)   They are among the rarest kinds of amphibians.

   (B)   They generally have populations that are small in size.

   (C)   They are in constant danger of extinction.

   (D)   Those with decreasing populations are the most likely candidates for immediate extinction.

   (E)   They are in danger of extinction due to events that sometimes have nothing to do with human activities.

RC00229-05

616. Which of the following most accurately describes the organization of the passage?

   (A)   A question is raised, a distinction regarding it is made, and the question is answered.

   (B)   An interpretation is presented, its soundness is examined, and a warning is given.

   (C)   A situation is described, its consequences are analyzed, and a prediction is made.

   (D)   Two interpretations of a phenomenon are described, and one of them is rejected as invalid.

   (E)   Two methods for analyzing a phenomenon are compared, and further study of the phenomenon is recommended.

RC00229-06

617. Which of the following best describes the function of the sentence in lines 35–38 ?

   (A)   To give an example of a particular kind of study

   (B)   To cast doubt on an assertion made in the previous sentence

   (C)   To raise an objection to a view presented in the first paragraph

   (D)   To provide support for a view presented in the first paragraph

   (E)   To introduce an idea that will be countered in the following paragraph

Line   While the most abundant and dominant species
within a particular ecosystem is often crucial in
perpetuating the ecosystem, a "keystone" species,
here defined as one whose effects are much larger
(5)   than would be predicted from its abundance, can
also play a vital role. But because complex species
interactions may be involved, identifying a keystone
species by removing the species and observing
changes in the ecosystem is problematic. It might
(10)   seem that certain traits would clearly define a species
as a keystone species; for example,
Pisaster ochraceus is often a keystone predator
because it consumes and suppresses mussel
populations, which in the absence of this starfish
(15)   can be a dominant species. But such predation on a
dominant or potentially dominant species occurs in
systems that do as well as in systems that do not
have species that play keystone roles. Moreover,
whereas *P. ochraceus* occupies an unambiguous
(20)   keystone role on wave-exposed rocky headlands,
in more wave-sheltered habitats the impact of
P. ochraceus predation is weak or nonexistent,
and at certain sites sand burial is responsible for
eliminating mussels. Keystone status appears to
(25)   depend on context, whether of particular
geography or of such factors as community
diversity (for example, a reduction in species
diversity may thrust more of the remaining species
into keystone roles) and length of species
(30)   interaction (since newly arrived species in particular
may dramatically affect ecosystems).

Questions 618–621 refer to the passage.

RC00556-03

618. The passage mentions which of the following as
a factor that affects the role of *P. ochraceus* as a
keystone species within different habitats?

(A)   The degree to which the habitat is sheltered from
waves

(B)   The degree to which other animals within a
habitat prey on mussels

(C)   The fact that mussel populations are often not
dominant within some habitats occupied by
P. ochraceus

(D)   The size of the *P. ochraceus* population within
the habitat

(E)   The fact that there is great species diversity
within some habitats occupied by *P. ochraceus*

RC00556-04

619. Which of the following hypothetical experiments most
clearly exemplifies the method of identifying species'
roles that the author considers problematic?

(A)   A population of seals in an Arctic habitat is
counted in order to determine whether it is the
dominant species in that ecosystem.

(B)   A species of fish that is a keystone species in
one marine ecosystem is introduced into another
marine ecosystem to see whether the species
will come to occupy a keystone role.

(C)   In order to determine whether a species of
monkey is a keystone species within a particular
ecosystem, the monkeys are removed from that
ecosystem and the ecosystem is then studied.

(D)   Different mountain ecosystems are compared to
determine how geography affects a particular
species' ability to dominate its ecosystem.

(E)   In a grassland experiencing a changing climate,
patterns of species extinction are traced in order
to evaluate the effect of climate changes on
keystone species in that grassland.

RC00556-05

620. Which of the following, if true, would most clearly support the argument about keystone status advanced in the last sentence of the passage (lines 24–31)?

(A) A species of bat is primarily responsible for keeping insect populations within an ecosystem low, and the size of the insect population in turn affects bird species within that ecosystem.

(B) A species of iguana occupies a keystone role on certain tropical islands, but does not play that role on adjacent tropical islands that are inhabited by a greater number of animal species.

(C) Close observation of a savannah ecosystem reveals that more species occupy keystone roles within that ecosystem than biologists had previously believed.

(D) As a keystone species of bee becomes more abundant, it has a larger effect on the ecosystem it inhabits.

(E) A species of moth that occupies a keystone role in a prairie habitat develops coloration patterns that camouflage it from potential predators.

RC00556-06

621. The passage suggests which of the following about the identification of a species as a keystone species?

(A) Such an identification depends primarily on the species' relationship to the dominant species.

(B) Such an identification can best be made by removing the species from a particular ecosystem and observing changes that occur in the ecosystem.

(C) Such an identification is likely to be less reliable as an ecosystem becomes less diverse.

(D) Such an identification seems to depend on various factors within the ecosystem.

(E) Such an identification can best be made by observing predation behavior.

Line   Conodonts, the spiky phosphatic remains (bones
and teeth composed of calcium phosphate) of
tiny marine animals that probably appeared about
520 million years ago, were once among the most
(5)   controversial of fossils. Both the nature of the
organism to which the remains belonged and the
function of the remains were unknown. However,
since the 1981 discovery of fossils preserving not
just the phosphatic elements but also other remains
(10)   of the tiny soft-bodied animals (also called conodonts)
that bore them, scientists' reconstructions of the
animals' anatomy have had important implications
for hypotheses concerning the development of the
vertebrate skeleton.
(15)   The vertebrate skeleton had traditionally been
regarded as a defensive development, champions of
this view postulating that it was only with the much
later evolution of jaws that vertebrates became
predators. The first vertebrates, which were soft-
(20)   bodied, would have been easy prey for numerous
invertebrate carnivores, especially if these early
vertebrates were sedentary suspension feeders.
Thus, traditionalists argued, these animals developed
coverings of bony scales or plates, and teeth were
(25)   secondary features, adapted from the protective
bony scales. Indeed, external skeletons of this
type are common among the well-known fossils of
ostracoderms, jawless vertebrates that existed from
approximately 500 to 400 million years ago.
(30)   However, other paleontologists argued that many of
the definitive characteristics of vertebrates, such as
paired eyes and muscular and skeletal adaptations
for active life, would not have evolved unless the
first vertebrates were predatory. Teeth were more
(35)   primitive than external armor according to this view,
and the earliest vertebrates were predators.
     The stiffening notochord along the back of the
body, V-shaped muscle blocks along the sides,
and posterior tail fins help to identify conodonts as
(40)   among the most primitive of vertebrates. The lack of
any mineralized structures apart from the elements
in the mouth indicates that conodonts were more
primitive than the armored jawless fishes such as the
ostracoderms. It now appears that the hard parts that
(45)   first evolved in the mouth of an animal improved its
efficiency as a predator, and that aggression rather
than protection was the driving force behind the origin
of the vertebrate skeleton.

Questions 622–624 refer to the passage.

RC00073-01
622. According to the passage, the anatomical evidence
provided by the preserved soft bodies of conodonts
led scientists to conclude that

(A)   conodonts had actually been invertebrate
carnivores

(B)   conodonts' teeth were adapted from protective
bony scales

(C)   conodonts were primitive vertebrate suspension
feeders

(D)   primitive vertebrates with teeth appeared earlier
than armored vertebrates

(E)   scientists' original observations concerning
the phosphatic remains of conodonts were
essentially correct

RC00073-03
623. The second paragraph in the passage serves primarily to

(A)   outline the significance of the 1981 discovery of
conodont remains to the debate concerning the
development of the vertebrate skeleton

(B)   contrast the traditional view of the development
of the vertebrate skeleton with a view derived
from the 1981 discovery of conodont remains

(C)   contrast the characteristics of the ostracoderms
with the characteristics of earlier soft-bodied
vertebrates

(D)   explain the importance of the development of
teeth among the earliest vertebrate predators

(E)   present the two sides of the debate concerning
the development of the vertebrate skeleton

RC00073-08

624. It can be inferred that on the basis of the 1981 discovery of conodont remains, paleontologists could draw which of the following conclusions?

    (A)   The earliest vertebrates were sedentary suspension feeders.

    (B)   Ostracoderms were not the earliest vertebrates.

    (C)   Defensive armor preceded jaws among vertebrates.

    (D)   Paired eyes and adaptations for activity are definitive characteristics of vertebrates.

    (E)   Conodonts were unlikely to have been predators.

Line Jon Clark's study of the effect of the modernization of a telephone exchange on exchange maintenance work and workers is a solid contribution to a debate that encompasses two lively issues in the history and
(5) sociology of technology: technological determinism and social constructivism.

Clark makes the point that the characteristics of a technology have a decisive influence on job skills and work organization. Put more strongly, technology can
(10) be a primary determinant of social and managerial organization. Clark believes this possibility has been obscured by the recent sociological fashion, exemplified by Braverman's analysis, that emphasizes the way machinery reflects social choices. For
(15) Braverman, the shape of a technological system is subordinate to the manager's desire to wrest control of the labor process from the workers. Technological change is construed as the outcome of negotiations among interested parties who seek to incorporate
(20) their own interests into the design and configuration of the machinery. This position represents the new mainstream called social constructivism.

The constructivists gain acceptance by misrepresenting technological determinism:
(25) technological determinists are supposed to believe, for example, that machinery imposes appropriate forms of order on society. The alternative to constructivism, in other words, is to view technology as existing outside society, capable of directly
(30) influencing skills and work organization.

Clark refutes the extremes of the constructivists by both theoretical and empirical arguments. Theoretically he defines "technology" in terms of relationships between social and technical variables.
(35) Attempts to reduce the meaning of technology to cold, hard metal are bound to fail, for machinery is just scrap unless it is organized functionally and supported by appropriate systems of operation and maintenance. At the empirical level Clark shows how
(40) a change at the telephone exchange from maintenance-intensive electromechanical switches to semielectronic switching systems altered work tasks, skills, training opportunities, administration, and organization of workers. Some changes Clark
(45) attributes to the particular way management and labor unions negotiated the introduction of the technology, whereas others are seen as arising from the capabilities and nature of the technology itself. Thus Clark helps answer the question: "When is
(50) social choice decisive and when are the concrete characteristics of technology more important?"

Questions 625–632 refer to the passage.

RC00013-01

625. The primary purpose of the passage is to

(A) advocate a more positive attitude toward technological change

(B) discuss the implications for employees of the modernization of a telephone exchange

(C) consider a successful challenge to the constructivist view of technological change

(D) challenge the position of advocates of technological determinism

(E) suggest that the social causes of technological change should be studied in real situations

RC00013-02

626. Which of the following statements about the modernization of the telephone exchange is supported by information in the passage?

(A) The new technology reduced the role of managers in labor negotiations.

(B) The modernization was implemented without the consent of the employees directly affected by it.

(C) The modernization had an impact that went significantly beyond maintenance routines.

(D) Some of the maintenance workers felt victimized by the new technology.

(E) The modernization gave credence to the view of advocates of social constructivism.

RC00013-03

627. Which of the following most accurately describes Clark's opinion of Braverman's position?

(A) He respects its wide-ranging popularity.

(B) He disapproves of its misplaced emphasis on the influence of managers.

(C) He admires the consideration it gives to the attitudes of the workers affected.

(D) He is concerned about its potential to impede the implementation of new technologies.

(E) He is sympathetic to its concern about the impact of modern technology on workers.

628. The information in the passage suggests that which of the following statements from hypothetical sociological studies of change in industry most clearly exemplifies the social constructivists' version of technological determinism?

(A) It is the available technology that determines workers' skills, rather than workers' skills influencing the application of technology.

(B) All progress in industrial technology grows out of a continuing negotiation between technological possibility and human need.

(C) Some organizational change is caused by people; some is caused by computer chips.

(D) Most major technological advances in industry have been generated through research and development.

(E) Some industrial technology eliminates jobs, but educated workers can create whole new skills areas by the adaptation of the technology.

629. The information in the passage suggests that Clark believes that which of the following would be true if social constructivism had not gained widespread acceptance?

(A) Businesses would be more likely to modernize without considering the social consequences of their actions.

(B) There would be greater understanding of the role played by technology in producing social change.

(C) Businesses would be less likely to understand the attitudes of employees affected by modernization.

(D) Modernization would have occurred at a slower rate.

(E) Technology would have played a greater part in determining the role of business in society.

630. According to the passage, constructivists employed which of the following to promote their argument?

(A) Empirical studies of business situations involving technological change

(B) Citation of managers supportive of their position

(C) Construction of hypothetical situations that support their view

(D) Contrasts of their view with a misstatement of an opposing view

(E) Descriptions of the breadth of impact of technological change

631. The author of the passage uses the expression "are supposed to" in line 25 primarily in order to

(A) suggest that a contention made by constructivists regarding determinists is inaccurate

(B) define the generally accepted position of determinists regarding the implementation of technology

(C) engage in speculation about the motivation of determinists

(D) lend support to a comment critical of the position of determinists

(E) contrast the historical position of determinists with their position regarding the exchange modernization

632. Which of the following statements about Clark's study of the telephone exchange can be inferred from information in the passage?

(A) Clark's reason for undertaking the study was to undermine Braverman's analysis of the function of technology.

(B) Clark's study suggests that the implementation of technology should be discussed in the context of conflict between labor and management.

(C) Clark examined the impact of changes in the technology of switching at the exchange in terms of overall operations and organization.

(D) Clark concluded that the implementation of new switching technology was equally beneficial to management and labor.

(E) Clark's analysis of the change in switching systems applies only narrowly to the situation at the particular exchange that he studied.

Line   Because the framers of the United States
Constitution (written in 1787) believed that protecting
property rights relating to inventions would encourage
the new nation's economic growth, they gave
(5)   Congress—the national legislature—a constitutional
mandate to grant patents for inventions. The resulting
patent system has served as a model for those in
other nations. Recently, however, scholars have
questioned whether the American system helped
(10)   achieve the framers' goals. These scholars have
contended that from 1794 to roughly 1830, American
inventors were unable to enforce property rights
because judges were "antipatent" and routinely
invalidated patents for arbitrary reasons. This
(15)   argument is based partly on examination of court
decisions in cases where patent holders ("patentees")
brought suit alleging infringement of their patent
rights. In the 1820s, for instance, 75 percent
of verdicts were decided against the patentee.
(20)   The proportion of verdicts for the patentee began to
increase in the 1830s, suggesting to these scholars
that judicial attitudes toward patent rights began
shifting then.
        Not all patent disputes in the early nineteenth
(25)   century were litigated, however, and litigated
cases were not drawn randomly from the
population of disputes. Therefore the rate of
verdicts in favor of patentees cannot be used
by itself to gauge changes in judicial attitudes
(30)   or enforceability of patent rights. If early judicial
decisions were prejudiced against patentees, one
might expect that subsequent courts—allegedly
more supportive of patent rights—would reject
the former legal precedents. But pre-1830
(35)   cases have been cited as frequently as later
decisions, and they continue to be cited today,
suggesting that the early decisions, many of
which clearly declared that patent rights were
a just recompense for inventive ingenuity,
(40)   provided a lasting foundation for patent law.
The proportion of judicial decisions in favor of
patentees began to increase during the 1830s
because of a change in the underlying population
of cases brought to trial. This change was partly
(45)   due to an 1836 revision to the patent system:
an examination procedure, still in use today, was
instituted in which each application is scrutinized
for its adherence to patent law. Previously,
patents were automatically granted upon payment
(50)   of a $30 fee.

RC00650-02

633.   The passage implies that which of the following was
a reason that the proportion of verdicts in favor of
patentees began to increase in the 1830s?

(A)   Patent applications approved after 1836 were
more likely to adhere closely to patent law.

(B)   Patent laws enacted during the 1830s better
defined patent rights.

(C)   Judges became less prejudiced against
patentees during the 1830s.

(D)   After 1836, litigated cases became less
representative of the population of patent
disputes.

(E)   The proportion of patent disputes brought to trial
began to increase after 1836.

RC00650-03

634.   The passage implies that the scholars mentioned in
line 8 would agree with which of the following criticisms
of the American patent system before 1830?

(A)   Its definition of property rights relating to
inventions was too vague to be useful.

(B)   Its criteria for the granting of patents were not
clear.

(C)   It made it excessively difficult for inventors to
receive patents.

(D)   It led to excessive numbers of patent-
infringement suits.

(E)   It failed to encourage national economic growth.

RC00650-06

635.   It can be inferred from the passage that the frequency
with which pre-1830 cases have been cited in court
decisions is an indication that

(A)   judicial support for patent rights was strongest in
the period before 1830

(B)   judicial support for patent rights did not increase
after 1830

(C)   courts have returned to judicial standards that
prevailed before 1830

(D)   verdicts favoring patentees in patent-infringement
suits did not increase after 1830

(E)   judicial bias against patentees persisted after
1830

RC00650-07

636. It can be inferred from the passage that the author and the scholars referred to in line 21 disagree about which of the following aspects of the patents defended in patent-infringement suits before 1830 ?

(A) Whether the patents were granted for inventions that were genuinely useful

(B) Whether the patents were actually relevant to the growth of the United States economy

(C) Whether the patents were particularly likely to be annulled by judges

(D) Whether the patents were routinely invalidated for reasons that were arbitrary

(E) Whether the patents were vindicated at a significantly lower rate than patents in later suits

RC00650-08

637. The author of the passage cites which of the following as evidence challenging the argument referred to in lines 14 15 ?

(A) The proportion of cases that were decided against patentees in the 1820s

(B) The total number of patent disputes that were litigated from 1794 to 1830

(C) The fact that later courts drew upon the legal precedents set in pre-1830 patent cases

(D) The fact that the proportion of judicial decisions in favor of patentees began to increase during the 1830s

(E) The constitutional rationale for the 1836 revision of the patent system

Line　　Jacob Burckhardt's view that Renaissance European women "stood on a footing of perfect equality" with Renaissance men has been repeatedly cited by feminist scholars as a prelude to their
(5)　　presentation of rich historical evidence of women's inequality. In striking contrast to Burckhardt, Joan Kelly in her famous 1977 essay, "Did Women Have a Renaissance?" argued that the Renaissance was a period of economic and social decline for women
(10)　　relative both to Renaissance men and to medieval women. Recently, however, a significant trend among feminist scholars has entailed a rejection of both Kelly's dark vision of the Renaissance and Burckhardt's rosy one. Many recent works by these
(15)　　scholars stress the ways in which differences among Renaissance women—especially in terms of social status and religion—work to complicate the kinds of generalizations both Burckhardt and Kelly made on the basis of their observations about
(20)　　upper-class Italian women.

　　The trend is also evident, however, in works focusing on those middle- and upper-class European women whose ability to write gives them disproportionate representation in the historical
(25)　　record. Such women were, simply by virtue of their literacy, members of a tiny minority of the population, so it is risky to take their descriptions of their experiences as typical of "female experience" in any general sense. Tina Krontiris, for example, in
(30)　　her fascinating study of six Renaissance women writers, does tend at times to conflate "women" and "women writers," assuming that women's gender, irrespective of other social differences, including literacy, allows us to view women as a homogeneous
(35)　　social group and make that group an object of analysis. Nonetheless, Krontiris makes a significant contribution to the field and is representative of those authors who offer what might be called a cautiously optimistic assessment of Renaissance
(40)　　women's achievements, although she also stresses the social obstacles Renaissance women faced when they sought to raise their "oppositional voices." Krontiris is concerned to show women intentionally negotiating some power for themselves

(45)　　(at least in the realm of public discourse) against potentially constraining ideologies, but in her sober and thoughtful concluding remarks, she suggests that such verbal opposition to cultural stereotypes was highly circumscribed; women seldom attacked
(50)　　the basic assumptions in the ideologies that oppressed them.

Questions 638–644 refer to the passage.

RC00313-01

638. The author of the passage discusses Krontiris primarily to provide an example of a writer who

(A)　is highly critical of the writings of certain Renaissance women

(B)　supports Kelly's view of women's status during the Renaissance

(C)　has misinterpreted the works of certain Renaissance women

(D)　has rejected the views of both Burckhardt and Kelly

(E)　has studied Renaissance women in a wide variety of social and religious contexts

RC00313-02

639. According to the passage, Krontiris's work differs from that of the scholars mentioned in line 12 in which of the following ways?

(A)　Krontiris's work stresses the achievements of Renaissance women rather than the obstacles to their success.

(B)　Krontiris's work is based on a reinterpretation of the work of earlier scholars.

(C)　Krontiris's views are at odds with those of both Kelly and Burkhardt.

(D)　Krontiris's work focuses on the place of women in Renaissance society.

(E)　Krontiris's views are based exclusively on the study of a privileged group of women.

RC00313-03

640. According to the passage, feminist scholars cite Burckhardt's view of Renaissance women primarily for which of the following reasons?

(A) Burckhardt's view forms the basis for most arguments refuting Kelly's point of view.

(B) Burckhardt's view has been discredited by Kelly.

(C) Burckhardt's view is one that many feminist scholars wish to refute.

(D) Burckhardt's work provides rich historical evidence of inequality between Renaissance women and men.

(E) Burckhardt's work includes historical research supporting the arguments of the feminist scholars.

RC00313-04

641. It can be inferred that both Burckhardt and Kelly have been criticized by the scholars mentioned in line 12 for which of the following?

(A) Assuming that women writers of the Renaissance are representative of Renaissance women in general

(B) Drawing conclusions that are based on the study of an atypical group of women

(C) Failing to describe clearly the relationship between social status and literacy among Renaissance women

(D) Failing to acknowledge the role played by Renaissance women in opposing cultural stereotypes

(E) Failing to acknowledge the ways in which social status affected the creative activities of Renaissance women

RC00313-05

642. The author of the passage suggests that Krontiris incorrectly assumes that

(A) social differences among Renaissance women are less important than the fact that they were women

(B) literacy among Renaissance women was more prevalent than most scholars today acknowledge

(C) during the Renaissance, women were able to successfully oppose cultural stereotypes relating to gender

(D) Renaissance women did not face many difficult social obstacles relating to their gender

(E) in order to attain power, Renaissance women attacked basic assumptions in the ideologies that oppressed them

RC00313-06

643. The last sentence in the passage serves primarily to

(A) suggest that Krontiris's work is not representative of recent trends among feminist scholars

(B) undermine the argument that literate women of the Renaissance sought to oppose social constraints imposed on them

(C) show a way in which Krontiris's work illustrates a "cautiously optimistic" assessment of Renaissance women's achievements

(D) summarize Krontiris's view of the effect of literacy on the lives of upper- and middle-class Renaissance women

(E) illustrate the way in which Krontiris's study differs from the studies done by Burckhardt and Kelly

RC00313-08

644. The author of the passage implies that the women studied by Krontiris are unusual in which of the following ways?

(A) They faced obstacles less formidable than those faced by other Renaissance women.

(B) They have been seen by historians as more interesting than other Renaissance women.

(C) They were more concerned about recording history accurately than were other Renaissance women.

(D) Their perceptions are more likely to be accessible to historians than are those of most other Renaissance women.

(E) Their concerns are likely to be of greater interest to feminist scholars than are the ideas of most other Renaissance women.

Line When asteroids collide, some collisions cause an asteroid to spin faster; others slow it down. If asteroids are all monoliths—single rocks—undergoing random collisions, a graph of their rotation rates

(5) should show a bell-shaped distribution with statistical "tails" of very fast and very slow rotators. If asteroids are rubble piles, however, the tail representing the very fast rotators would be missing, because any loose aggregate spinning faster than once every few

(10) hours (depending on the asteroid's bulk density) would fly apart. Researchers have discovered that all but five observed asteroids obey a strict limit on rate of rotation. The exceptions are all smaller than 200 meters in diameter, with an abrupt cutoff for

(15) asteroids larger than that.

The evident conclusion—that asteroids larger than 200 meters across are multicomponent structures or rubble piles—agrees with recent computer modeling of collisions, which also finds a transition at that

(20) diameter. A collision can blast a large asteroid to bits, but after the collision those bits will usually move slower than their mutual escape velocity. Over several hours, gravity will reassemble all but the fastest pieces into a rubble pile. Because collisions among

(25) asteroids are relatively frequent, most large bodies have already suffered this fate. Conversely, most small asteroids should be monolithic, because impact fragments easily escape their feeble gravity.

Questions 645–648 refer to the passage.

RC00524-02

645. The passage implies which of the following about the five asteroids mentioned in line 12 ?

(A) Their rotation rates are approximately the same.

(B) They have undergone approximately the same number of collisions.

(C) They are monoliths.

(D) They are composed of fragments that have escaped the gravity of larger asteroids.

(E) They were detected only recently.

RC00524-04

646. The discovery of which of the following would call into question the conclusion mentioned in line 16 ?

(A) An asteroid 100 meters in diameter rotating at a rate of once per week

(B) An asteroid 150 meters in diameter rotating at a rate of 20 times per hour

(C) An asteroid 250 meters in diameter rotating at a rate of once per week

(D) An asteroid 500 meters in diameter rotating at a rate of once per hour

(E) An asteroid 1,000 meters in diameter rotating at a rate of once every 24 hours

RC00524-06

647. According to the passage, which of the following is a prediction that is based on the strength of the gravitational attraction of small asteroids?

(A) Small asteroids will be few in number.

(B) Small asteroids will be monoliths.

(C) Small asteroids will collide with other asteroids very rarely.

(D) Most small asteroids will have very fast rotation rates.

(E) Almost no small asteroids will have very slow rotation rates.

RC00524-07

648. The author of the passage mentions "escape velocity" (see line 22) in order to help explain which of the following?

(A) The tendency for asteroids to become smaller rather than larger over time

(B) The speed with which impact fragments reassemble when they do not escape an asteroid's gravitational attraction after a collision

(C) The frequency with which collisions among asteroids occur

(D) The rotation rates of asteroids smaller than 200 meters in diameter

(E) The tendency for large asteroids to persist after collisions

Line Most attempts by physicists to send particles faster than the speed of light involve a remarkable phenomenon called quantum tunneling, in which particles travel through solid barriers that appear
(5) to be impenetrable. If you throw a ball at a wall, you expect it to bounce back, not to pass straight through it. Yet subatomic particles perform the equivalent feat. Quantum theory says that there is a distinct, albeit small, probability that such a particle
(10) will tunnel its way through a barrier; the probability declines exponentially as the thickness of the barrier increases. Though the extreme rapidity of quantum tunneling was noted as early as 1932, not until 1955 was it hypothesized—by Wigner and
(15) Eisenbud—that tunneling particles sometimes travel faster than light. Their grounds were calculations that suggested that the time it takes a particle to tunnel through a barrier increases with the thickness of the barrier until tunneling time
(20) reaches a maximum; beyond that maximum, tunneling time stays the same regardless of barrier thickness. This would imply that once maximum tunneling time is reached, tunneling speed will increase without limit as barrier thickness increases. Several recent
(25) experiments have supported this hypothesis that tunneling particles sometimes reach superluminal speed. According to measurements performed by Raymond Chiao and colleagues, for example, photons can pass through an optical filter at 1.7 times the
(30) speed of light.

RC00301-04

649. The author of the passage mentions calculations about tunneling time and barrier thickness in order to

(A)   suggest that tunneling time is unrelated to barrier thickness

(B)   explain the evidence by which Wigner and Eisenbud discovered the phenomenon of tunneling

(C)   describe data recently challenged by Raymond Chiao and colleagues

(D)   question why particles engaged in quantum tunneling rarely achieve extremely high speeds

(E)   explain the basis for Wigner and Eisenbud's hypothesis

RC00301-03

650. The passage implies that if tunneling time reached no maximum in increasing with barrier thickness, then

(A)   tunneling speed would increase with barrier thickness

(B)   tunneling speed would decline with barrier thickness

(C)   tunneling speed would vary with barrier thickness

(D)   tunneling speed would not be expected to increase without limit

(E)   successful tunneling would occur even less frequently than it does

RC00301-02

651. Which of the following statements about the earliest scientific investigators of quantum tunneling can be inferred from the passage?

(A)   They found it difficult to increase barrier thickness continually.

(B)   They anticipated the later results of Chiao and his colleagues.

(C)   They did not suppose that tunneling particles could travel faster than light.

(D)   They were unable to observe instances of successful tunneling.

(E)   They made use of photons to study the phenomenon of tunneling.

7.5 Answer Key

503.	D	533.	D	563.	E	593.	E	623.	E
504.	D	534.	B	564.	A	594.	B	624.	B
505.	B	535.	B	565.	B	595.	D	625.	C
506.	B	536.	B	566.	C	596.	C	626.	C
507.	C	537.	D	567.	C	597.	C	627.	B
508.	C	538.	E	568.	B	598.	E	628.	A
509.	A	539.	D	569.	E	599.	A	629.	B
510.	C	540.	E	570.	C	600.	B	630.	D
511.	D	541.	C	571.	E	601.	D	631.	A
512.	C	542.	C	572.	A	602.	E	632.	C
513.	A	543.	B	573.	D	603.	E	633.	A
514.	C	544.	D	574.	A	604.	D	634.	E
515.	C	545.	C	575.	C	605.	B	635.	B
516.	C	546.	B	576.	A	606.	C	636.	D
517.	E	547.	A	577.	B	607.	D	637.	C
518.	A	548.	E	578.	D	608.	A	638.	D
519.	C	549.	A	579.	E	609.	C	639.	E
520.	B	550.	B	580.	C	610.	D	640.	C
521.	B	551.	E	581.	A	611.	A	641.	B
522.	A	552.	B	582.	E	612.	A	642.	A
523.	D	553.	C	583.	A	613.	D	643.	C
524.	C	554.	C	584.	D	614.	E	644.	D
525.	E	555.	A	585.	D	615.	D	645.	C
526.	B	556.	D	586.	D	616.	B	646.	D
527.	D	557.	D	587.	B	617.	C	647.	B
528.	C	558.	C	588.	B	618.	A	648.	E
529.	B	559.	E	589.	C	619.	C	649.	E
530.	D	560.	A	590.	C	620.	B	650.	D
531.	A	561.	C	591.	E	621.	D	651.	C
532.	C	562.	D	592.	D	622.	D		

7.6 Answer Explanations

The following discussion of Reading Comprehension is intended to familiarize you with the most efficient and effective approaches to the kinds of problems common to Reading Comprehension. The particular questions in this chapter are generally representative of the kinds of Reading Comprehension questions you will encounter on the GMAT exam. Remember that it is the problem solving strategy that is important, not the specific details of a particular question.

Questions 503 to 543 - Difficulty: **Easy**

Questions 503–505 refer to the passage on page 455.

*RC00504-01
503. The primary purpose of the passage is to

(A)   challenge recent findings that appear to contradict earlier findings

(B)   present two sides of an ongoing scientific debate

(C)   report answers to several questions that have long puzzled researchers

(D)   discuss evidence that has caused a long-standing belief to be revised

(E)   attempt to explain a commonly misunderstood biological phenomenon

Main Idea

This question depends on understanding the passage as a whole. The passage begins by describing a long-held belief regarding humans' circadian rhythms: that the SCNs control them. It then goes on to explain that new findings have led scientists to believe that other organs and tissues may be involved in regulating the body's circadian rhythms as well.

A   The passage does not challenge the more-recent findings. Furthermore, the recent findings that the passage recounts do not contradict earlier findings; rather, when placed alongside those earlier findings, they have led scientists to reach additional conclusions.

B   The passage does not discuss a two-sided debate; no findings or conclusions are disputed by any figures in the passages.

C   There is only one question at issue in the passage: whether the SCN alone control human circadian rhythms. Furthermore, nothing in the passage suggests that researchers have been puzzled for a long time about this.

D   Correct. The new evidence regarding circadian rhythm–related gene activity in all the body's tissue has led scientists to revise their long–standing belief that the SCN alone control circadian rhythms.

E   The biological phenomenon of circadian rhythms is not, at least as far as the passage is concerned, misunderstood. Its causes are being investigated and refined.

The correct answer is D.

RC00504-05
504. The passage mentions each of the following as a function regulated by the SCNs in some animals EXCEPT

(A)   activity level

(B)   blood pressure

(C)   alertness

(D)   vision

(E)   temperature

---

*These numbers correlate with the online test bank question number. See the GMAT™ Official Guide Question Index in the back of this book.

519

Supporting Idea

This question asks about what is NOT specifically mentioned in the passage with regard to functions regulated by the SCN. Those functions, as identified in the passage, are blood pressure, body temperature, activity level, alertness, and the release of melatonin.

A   The passage includes activity level in its list of functions regulated by the SCN.

B   The passage includes blood pressure in its list of functions regulated by the SCN.

C   The passage includes alertness in its list of functions regulated by the SCN.

D   **Correct.** While the passage does say that cells in the human retina transmit information to the SCN, there is no suggestion that the SCN reciprocally control vision.

E   The passage includes temperature in its list of functions regulated by the SCN.

The correct answer is D.

RC00504-04

505. The author of the passage would probably agree with which of the following statements about the SCNs?

(A)   The SCNs are found in other organs and tissues of the body besides the hypothalamus.

(B)   The SCNs play a critical but not exclusive role in regulating circadian rhythms.

(C)   The SCNs control clock genes in a number of tissues and organs throughout the body.

(D)   The SCNs are a less significant factor in regulating blood pressure than scientists once believed.

(E)   The SCNs are less strongly affected by changes in light levels than they are by other external cues.

Application

The author of the passage states in the second paragraph, *Four critical genes governing circadian cycles have been found to be active in every tissue, however, not just in the SCNs, of flies, mice, and humans.* The author goes on in that paragraph to point out that though scientists still accept the role of SCNs in *controlling core functions*, they *now believe that circadian clocks in other organs and tissues may respond to external cues other than light . . . that recur regularly every 24 hours.* The author nowhere disputes these beliefs, and so it is reasonable to conclude that the author of the passage agrees that these beliefs are true.

A   The author states that the SCNs are nerve clusters in the hypothalamus, and nothing in the passage contradicts or undermines the supposition that they are only in the hypothalamus.

B   **Correct.** The author indicates in the second paragraph that while scientists still believe that the SCNs control core circadian function, they also believe that circadian clocks found elsewhere in the body have an effect as well. Because the author nowhere disputes these beliefs, it is reasonable to conclude that the author would agree that SCNs play a critical but not exclusive role in regulating circadian rhythms.

C   The evidence offered in the second paragraph about the activity of the clock gene in rat livers suggests that these clock genes are not under the SCNs' control. The passage does not suggest that the SCNs control any of the non-SCN controllers of circadian rhythms.

D   The author states in the second paragraph that scientists do not dispute the idea that the SCNs regulate blood pressure.

E   The first paragraph indicates that the SCNs respond to light levels; clock genes in other tissues are the ones that may respond to other external cues.

The correct answer is B.

Questions 506–508 refer to the passage on page 457.

RC00525-01
506. The primary purpose of the passage is to

(A) question the results of a study that examined the effect of service-quality guarantees in the restaurant industry

(B) discuss potential advantages and disadvantages of service-quality guarantees in the restaurant industry

(C) examine the conventional wisdom regarding the effect of service-quality guarantees in the restaurant industry

(D) argue that only certain restaurants would benefit from the implementation of service-quality guarantees

(E) consider the impact that service-quality guarantees can have on the service provided by a restaurant

Main Idea

This question depends on understanding the passage as a whole. The first paragraph describes Tucci and Talaga's findings regarding the effect of service-quality guarantees: that they have different, more positive results for higher-priced restaurants than for lower-priced ones, which could be affected negatively. The second paragraph explains that a particular benefit from service guarantees could accrue to restaurants generally.

A The passage does not question the results of Tucci and Talaga's study; rather, the passage appears to accept the results of the study as accurate.

B **Correct.** The potential advantages involve the management and motivation of service staff, as well as, for higher-priced restaurants, a greater likelihood of being selected by customers over other restaurants. Potential disadvantages for lower-priced restaurants include the possibility that potential customers may believe that such restaurants are concerned about the quality of their service.

C The passage does not indicate whether there is any conventional wisdom regarding service-quality guarantees in the restaurant industry.

D The second paragraph of the passage suggests that restaurants in general could potentially enjoy some benefits from the implementation of service-quality guarantees. For lower-priced restaurants, these benefits could offset the possible negative effects of service-quality guarantees described in the first paragraph.

E The second paragraph of the passage indicates an effect that service-quality guarantees could have on a restaurant's staff and the service that the staff provides, but this is only one of the subsidiary points contributing to the focus of the passage as a whole. The first is more concerned with the question of what effect these guarantees would have on whether customers choose to patronize that restaurant.

The correct answer is B.

RC00525-02
507. It can be inferred that the author of the passage would agree with which of the following statements about the appeal of service guarantees to customers?

(A) Such guarantees are likely to be somewhat more appealing to customers of restaurants than to customers of other businesses.

(B) Such guarantees are likely to be more appealing to customers who know what to anticipate in terms of service.

(C) Such guarantees are likely to have less appeal in situations where customers are knowledgeable about a business's product or service.

(D) In situations where a high level of financial commitment is involved, a service guarantee is not likely to be very appealing.

(E) In situations where customers expect a high level of customer service, a service guarantee is likely to make customers think that a business is worried about its service.

Inference

This question asks for an inference from the passage about the author's view of why and how service guarantees would appeal to customers. The question does not ask specifically about service guarantees in the context of restaurants, but rather service guarantees in general. The end of the first paragraph addresses this general question: a service guarantee may appeal most to customers in the case of activities whose quality they are less likely to know how to question.

A   The author states that a service guarantee might have greater appeal in the case of skilled activities than it would for restaurant customers.

B   According to the author, customers who know what to expect in terms of service—a group that includes restaurant customers—would likely find service guarantees less appealing.

C   **Correct.** The author makes clear that service guarantees would be less appealing to restaurant customers when they know what to expect in terms of the quality of service.

D   The passage provides some evidence that where a high level of financial commitment is involved, a service guarantee may be more rather than less appealing than in other situations. In discussing higher-priced restaurants, which require a relatively high level of financial commitment, the author states that Tucci and Talaga found evidence that a service guarantee would likely appeal to customers.

E   The author implies that customers of higher-priced restaurants expect a high level of service, certainly a level higher than that expected by customers of lower-priced restaurants. But it is at lower-priced restaurants that Tucci and Talaga found that a service guarantee makes customers think a given restaurant is concerned about its service.

The correct answer is C.

508. According to the passage, Tucci and Talaga found that service guarantees, when offered by lower-priced restaurants, can have which of the following effects?

(A)   Customers' developing unreasonably high expectations regarding service

(B)   Customers' avoiding such restaurants because they fear that the service guarantee may not be fully honored

(C)   Customers' interpreting the service guarantee as a sign that management is not confident about the quality of its service

(D)   A restaurant's becoming concerned that its service will not be assiduous enough to satisfy customers

(E)   A restaurant's becoming concerned that customers will be more emboldened to question the quality of the service they receive

Supporting Idea

This question requires identifying Tucci and Talaga's findings regarding service guarantees offered by lower-priced restaurants. The passage states directly that these researchers found in these situations that a guarantee could lead potential customers to think that the restaurant has concerns about its service.

A   The passage does not report that Tucci and Talaga found that service guarantees create unreasonably high expectations regarding service.

B   The passage does not report that Tucci and Talaga found that customers doubted that service guarantees would be honored.

C   **Correct.** The passage explicitly indicates that Tucci and Talaga found that potential customers of lower-priced restaurants could interpret service guarantees as indicating worries about the quality of service.

D   The passage indicates that Tucci and Talaga found that customers might think that lower-priced restaurants are offering service guarantees because they are concerned that the quality of their service is too low, but the passage does not indicate that service guarantees lead such restaurants to have concerns about the quality of their service, and in fact it may be that such guarantees could lead to improvements in service.

E   The passage indicates that service guarantees offered at lower-priced restaurants may empower customers to question the quality of service, but it does not indicate that service guarantees lead restaurants to have concerns about this.

The correct answer is C.

Questions 509–510 refer to the passage on page 459.

Main Idea Summary

The passage primarily reports some research findings regarding the extent to which farmers in certain types of rain forest regions are likely to adopt technologies that would increase productivity and slow deforestation by reducing demand for new cropland. It begins by noting that some studies have not included the types of farming communities that are characteristic of rainforest regions. The latter part of the passage describes some research regarding these previously omitted communities. The findings of that research provide evidence of how various factors may influence whether farmers in those communities adopt improved plant varieties and/or chemical herbicides.

RC00455-03

509. The passage suggests that in the study mentioned in line 14 the method for gathering information about security of land tenure reflects which of the following pairs of assumptions about Tawahka society?

(A)   The security of a household's land tenure depends on the strength of that household's kinship ties, and the duration of a household's residence in its village is an indication of the strength of that household's kinship ties.

(B)   The ample availability of land makes security of land tenure unimportant, and the lack of a need for secure land tenure has made the concept of legal property rights unnecessary.

(C)   The strength of a household's kinship ties is a more reliable indicator of that household's receptivity to new agricultural technologies than is its quantity of nonland wealth, and the duration of a household's residence in its village is a more reliable indicator of that household's security of land tenure than is the strength of its kinship ties.

(D)   Security of land tenure based on kinship ties tends to make farmers more receptive to the use of improved plant varieties, and security of land tenure based on long duration of residence in a village tends to make farmers more receptive to the use of chemical herbicides.

(E)   A household is more likely to be receptive to the concept of land tenure based on legal property rights if it has easy access to uncultivated land, and a household is more likely to uphold the tradition of land tenure based on kinship ties if it possesses a significant degree of nonland wealth.

Evaluation

In discussing the study, the passage notes that the strength of kinship ties is a more important indicator of land-tenure security than are legal property rights. The researchers, knowing this, measured land-tenure security by indirectly measuring the strength of kinship ties. How long a household had resided in its village was taken as an indicator of the strength of kinship ties, and indirectly, of the household's degree of land-tenure security.

A   **Correct.** This summarizes two assumptions that the passage suggests were made by the researchers.

B   The passage notes that ample availability of land is characteristic of rain-forest communities, which presumably includes the Tawahka people on whom the study focused. However, based on the information in the passage, the study did not assume that land-tenure security was unimportant in that community.

C   The passage reports that the study took a household's duration of residence in its village as a reliable indicator of the strength of the household's kinship ties. Thus, the researchers did not assume that duration of residence was a more reliable measure of land-tenure security than kinship ties.

D   The passage does not indicate that the researchers assumed this. As already stated, the researchers in effect equated a household's strength of kinship ties with its length of residence in its village. Though only the latter was directly measured, both were regarded as guarantors and indicators of land-tenure security. According to the passage, the researchers found that "longer residence correlated with more adoption of improved plant varieties but with less adoption of chemical herbicides." This was a finding based on research data, not an assumption.

E   The passage does not attribute to the researchers an assumption that "a household is more likely to be receptive to the concept of land tenure based on legal property rights if it has easy access to uncultivated land."

The correct answer is A.

RC00455-05

510. According to the passage, the proposal mentioned in line 1 is aimed at preserving rain forests by encouraging farmers in rain-forest regions to do each of the following EXCEPT

(A)   adopt new agricultural technologies

(B)   grow improved plant varieties

(C)   decrease their use of chemical herbicides

(D)   increase their productivity

(E)   reduce their need to clear new land for cultivation

Supporting Idea

The goal of the proposal is to help preserve rain forests by encouraging the adoption of new agricultural technologies, including use of chemical herbicides. The latter would presumably help improve crop yields on existing land, reducing the need to clear portions of rain forest to expand agricultural production.

A   The proposal aims to encourage farmers to adopt new agricultural technologies.

B   The proposal aims to encourage farmers to grow improved plant varieties.

C   **Correct.** The proposal aims to encourage farmers to adopt new agricultural technologies, such as increased use of chemical herbicides. So persuading farmers to reduce their use of chemical herbicides is not part of the proposal.

D   The proposal aims to encourage farmers to increase their productivity.

E   The proposal aims to encourage farmers to reduce their need to clear rain-forest land for cultivation.

The correct answer is C.

Questions 511–514 refer to the passage on page 461.

Main Idea Summary

The passage as a whole functions as an introduction to the notion of monetizing (i.e., putting a monetary value on) ecosystem functions. The passage begins by considering the argument for monetizing such functions and then considers David Pearce's claim that all ecosystems have economic value and that, by showing this, we can help overcome the illusion that conservation is relatively unprofitable. The passage concludes with Gretchen Daily's view that monetization will help inform environmental decision making.

RC00344-02

511. Information in the passage suggests that David Pearce would most readily endorse which of the following statements concerning monetization?

(A)   Monetization represents a strategy that is attractive to both environmentalists and their critics.

(B)   Monetization is an untested strategy, but it is increasingly being embraced by environmentalists.

(C)   Monetization should at present be restricted to ecological services and should only gradually be extended to such commercial endeavors as tourism and recreation.

(D)   Monetization can serve as a means of representing persuasively the value of environmental conservation.

(E)   Monetization should inform environmental decision-making processes only if it is accepted by environmentalist groups.

Inference

This question requires an understanding of David Pearce's view of monetization. According to the passage, Pearce finds the idea that conservation is unprofitable to be an illusion. He argues for showing the economic value of ecosystems in order to make progress in conserving those ecosystems.

A   The passage attributes to Gretchen Daily the view that monetization is unpopular with environmentalists. The passage gives no reason to believe that Pearce would endorse the idea that environmentalists currently find monetization attractive.

B   The passage gives no indication that monetization is increasingly being embraced by environmentalists, even if Pearce thinks it should be.

C   The passage indicates Pearce's belief that some types of tourism are also types of ecological services that have economic value and that they should be monetized.

D   **Correct.** Pearce believes that monetization quantifies the value of the services provided by ecological systems—and if that value is quantified, people are more likely to be persuaded to conserve those systems.

E   Pearce is arguing, against some environmentalists, that monetization should inform the decision-making process with regard to preserving ecosystems.

The correct answer is D.

RC00344-04
512. Which of the following most clearly represents an example of an "ecological service" as that term is used in line 20 ?

(A)   A resort hotel located in an area noted for its natural beauty

(B)   A water-purifying plant that supplements natural processes with nontoxic chemicals

(C)   A wildlife preserve that draws many international travelers

(D)   A nonprofit firm that specializes in restoring previously damaged ecosystems

(E)   A newsletter that keeps readers informed of ecological victories and setbacks

Application

Based on the passage, *ecological services* are services provided by natural assets that have not been converted into commercial assets. Thus any example of such an ecological service requires that the area providing it is natural.

A   The passage mentions resort hotels as an example of explicitly commercial assets. Although some hotels might be situated in ecologically valuable natural environments, any ecological services in such cases would be contributed by the natural environments, not by the hotels themselves.

B   Water purifying is *an ecological* service if it is supplied by *undisturbed forests and wetlands.* The word *plant* here must mean a technological installation, not a botanical organism, because it is said to supplement—not to be part of—the natural processes. Thus it is not a natural asset and therefore does not provide an ecological service as described in the passage.

C   **Correct.** The passage states that a wildlife preserve that creates jobs and generates income would be providing an ecological service.

D   A nonprofit firm that restores damaged ecosystems would be performing a valuable ecology-related service, but it would not itself be an example of a natural asset providing an ecological service.

E   Environmentalists and others would most likely find such a newsletter informative, but it would not be an ecological service, because it is not a service provided by a natural asset.

The correct answer is C.

RC00344-05

513. According to the passage, Daily sees monetization as an indication of which of the following?

(A) The centrality of economic interests to people's actions

(B) The reluctance of the critics of environmentalism to acknowledge the importance of conservation

(C) The inability of financial interests and ecological interests to reach a common ideological ground

(D) The inevitability of environmental degradation

(E) The inevitability of the growth of ecological services in the future

Supporting Idea

This question asks about Daily's view of monetization, and according to the passage, she sees monetization as a practice that *reflects the dominant role that economic decisions play in human behavior.*

A **Correct.** According to the passage, Daily believes that economic interests are central to people's actions, and monetization of ecological services would take that central role realistically into account.

B The passage gives no evidence of this. It says nothing about how the concept of monetization relates to critics of environmentalism or about what Daily's opinion regarding such a relationship might be. It is reasonable to suppose that some critics of environmentalism would oppose the move to monetize the values of ecosystem functions because they believe that many ecosystem functions do not have true monetary value. However, the passage mentions Daily's views on the topic only as they relate to environmentalists, not to critics of environmentalism.

C This is the opposite of what, according to the passage, Daily says can be a benefit of monetization. For Daily, monetization represents a way for financial interests and ecological interests to reach a common ground; by using this common currency, both sides can make good decisions about the environment.

D Monetization, in Daily's view, would help to prevent environmental degradation; the passage does not suggest that she regards such degradation as at all inevitable.

E Daily does not see monetization as inevitably spurring the growth of ecological services but as more likely preventing their decline by leaving those services undisturbed.

The correct answer is A.

RC00344-06

514. Which of the following can be inferred from the passage concerning the environmentalists mentioned in line 8 ?

(A) They are organized in opposition to the generation of income produced by the sale of ecological services.

(B) They are fewer in number but better organized and better connected to the media than their opponents.

(C) They have sometimes been charged with failing to use a particular strategy in their pursuit of conservational goals.

(D) They have been in the forefront of publicizing the extent of worldwide environmental degradation.

(E) They define environmental progress differently and more conservatively than do other organized groups of environmentalists.

Inference

The sentence in question states that critics blame environmentalists for their failure *to address the economic issues of environmental degradation.*

A The passage states that, in the absence of monetization, conservation can appear unprofitable. But this does not mean that the environmentalists in question are opposed to conservation generating income.

B The passage does not address the issue of the number of environmentalists in question, the number of those opposed to them, or whether either group is better connected to the media.

C **Correct.** The passage indicates that critics of the environmentalists in question believe environmentalists are to blame for not using an effective economics-based strategy to promote conservation.

D   Although it may be the case that the environmentalists in question have been prominent in publicizing worldwide environmental degradation, the passage does not provide grounds for inferring that the possibility is necessarily true.

E   The passage suggests that certain critics consider environmentalists in general to be at fault for failing to address economic issues. In this respect, the passage makes no distinctions among different environmentalist groups, organized or otherwise, yet this answer choice is based on the assumption that the passage has made this distinction. Therefore, this answer choice cannot be inferred from the passage.

The correct answer is C.

Questions 515–518 refer to the passage on page 463.

Main Idea Summary

The passage consists of a brief overview of some research into a question related to marketing: how do various factors influence consumers' perceptions of performance risk (the possibility that a product will not function as consumers expect and/or will not provide the desired benefits)? The first paragraph reports some purported findings about the effects of price and advertising on such perceptions. The second paragraph reports some research into the ways in which perceptions of manufacturers' credibility may influence perceptions of performance risk. It then briefly discusses the possibility that some of the factors may interact with one another in more complex ways.

RC00359-01

515.   According to the passage, the studies referred to in line 12 reported which of the following about the effect of price on consumers' perception of the performance risk associated with a new product?

(A)   Although most consumers regard price as an important factor, their perception of the performance risk associated with a new product

is ultimately determined by the manufacturer's reputation.

(B)   Price interacts with the presentation of an advertised message to affect perceived performance risk.

(C)   Price does not significantly affect consumers' perception of the performance risk associated with a new product.

(D)   Consumers tend to regard price as more important than the manufacturer's credibility when they are buying from that manufacturer for the first time.

(E)   Consumers are generally less concerned about a new product's performance risk when that product is relatively expensive.

Supporting Idea

The question asks about information explicitly provided in the passage. The first paragraph explains that there are *conflicting findings* in the research about how the price of a product affects a consumer's perception of the performance risk of that product. Some studies have found that higher priced products reduce the perception of performance risk. The *other studies* referred to in line 12, however, have found little or no connection between price and perceived performance risk.

A   The passage does not mention that these studies consider the manufacturer's reputation.

B   The passage does not mention that these studies consider advertising messages.

C   **Correct.** The passage indicates that these studies have found little or no connection between relative price and consumers' perception of performance risk.

D   The passage does not mention that these studies consider the manufacturer's credibility.

E   Although some studies have found that a relatively high price reduces the perception of performance risk, the passage explains that the studies referred to in line 12 have not confirmed that finding.

The correct answer is C.

RC00359-03
516. The "past research" mentioned in line 25 suggests which of the following about perceived performance risk?

(A) The more expensive a new product is, the more likely consumers may be to credit advertised claims about that product.

(B) The more familiar consumers are with a particular manufacturer, the more willing they may be to assume some risk in the purchase of a new product being advertised by that manufacturer.

(C) Consumers' perception of the performance risk associated with a new product being advertised may be influenced by an interplay between the product's price and the manufacturer's credibility.

(D) Consumers may be more likely to believe that a product will function as it is advertised to do when they have bought products from a particular manufacturer before.

(E) The price of a particular advertised product may have less impact than the manufacturer's credibility on consumers' assessment of the performance risk associated with that product.

Supporting Idea

The question asks about information explicitly provided in the passage. The second paragraph explains that, according to some research, consumers perceive a product as having less performance risk when they trust the source of advertising about that product. *Past research*, however, suggests that performance risk is affected not merely by the credibility of the source, but by an interaction between source credibility and the price of the product.

A   The passage does not indicate that the past research addressed the question of how the price of a product affects consumers' perception of advertised claims. It only says that the research suggests that the two factors *interact*.

B   Although the passage discusses consumers' perception of how risky a purchase might be, it does not address the relationship between familiarity and willingness to assume risk.

C   **Correct.** The *past research* suggests that performance risk is affected by an

interaction between the price of the product and the credibility of the source of the advertising about the product—in other words, the manufacturer.

D   The *past research* suggests that consumers' beliefs about a product's performance are affected not merely by their perception of the manufacturer, but by an interplay between source credibility and product price. The passage does not mention any possible role of prior experience in this interplay.

E   The passage does not discuss whether price or the manufacturer's credibility has more of an effect on perceived performance risk.

The correct answer is C.

RC00359-05
517. The passage is primarily concerned with

(A) challenging the implications of previous research into why consumers try new products

(B) suggesting new marketing strategies for attracting consumers to new products

(C) reconciling two different views about the effect of price on consumers' willingness to try new products

(D) describing a new approach to researching why consumers try new products

(E) discussing certain findings regarding why consumers try new products

Main Idea

The question depends on understanding the passage as a whole. The passage begins with a statement explaining that much research has investigated *what motivates consumers to try new products*. It then defines one such motivating factor—perception of performance risk. The remainder of the passage summarizes research into how price and a manufacturer's advertising affect consumers' perception of performance risk.

A   The passage summarizes research findings that conflict with one another but does not support some findings over others.

B   The passage does not suggest any new marketing strategies.

C   The first paragraph mentions a study that could reconcile two conflicting findings, but this is only a supporting point in the passage's larger purpose of summarizing research.

D   The passage does not describe new research approaches.

E   **Correct.** The passage discusses studies about performance risk, which is a factor that motivates consumers to try new products.

The correct answer is E.

RC00359-06

518. Which of the following, if true, would most tend to weaken the conclusion drawn from "some of this research" (see line 8)?

(A)   In a subsequent study, consumers who were asked to evaluate new products with relatively low prices had the same perception of the products' performance risk as did consumers who were shown the same products priced more expensively.

(B)   In a subsequent study, the quality of the advertising for the products that consumers perceived as having a lower performance risk was relatively high, while the quality of the advertising for the products that consumers perceived as having a higher performance risk was relatively poor.

(C)   In a subsequent study, the products that consumers perceived as having a lower performance risk were priced higher than the highest priced products in the previous research.

(D)   None of the consumers involved in this research had ever before bought products from the manufacturers involved in the research.

(E)   Researchers found that the higher the source credibility for a product, the more consumers were willing to pay for it.

Evaluation

The question depends on evaluating the reasoning behind the conclusion of some research and deciding which evidence would weaken that conclusion. The research concludes that higher prices reduce consumers' perception of performance risk associated with a particular product. This conclusion involves a claim of cause and effect, so evidence showing that higher prices do not cause that effect would weaken the argument.

A   **Correct.** If lowering prices has no effect on consumers' perception of performance risk, the conclusion of the research is called into question.

B   Without further information, an observed correlation between quality of advertising and perceived performance risk would hardly be relevant to the research conclusion about the effects of price. We are given no information about whether there is any significant correlation between advertising quality and price and no evidence that the correlation between advertising quality and perceptions of performance risk indicates a causal connection. Even if advertising quality caused perceptions of lower performance risk, this would be theoretically compatible with the conclusion about the effect of price; the studies concluded that higher prices cause perceptions of lower performance risk, not that they are the only thing that causes such perceptions.

C   This answer choice provides no basis for comparison among prices within the subsequent study. For all we can tell, the prices that correlated with higher perceived performance risk in the subsequent study may have been lower than those that correlated with lower perceived risk. In that case, the subsequent study would tend to strengthen, not weaken, the conclusion drawn from the earlier research.

D   This indirectly suggests one type of reasoning to consider in checking whether the conclusion is well-founded, but its relevance is only remote. If the research involved only people who had never before bought products from the manufacturers involved in the research, this would raise the question of whether the sample might have been unrepresentative of consumers in general. However, we are given no reason to suppose that consumers who had previously bought from the manufacturers might be affected differently from the other group by differences in price.

E   Credibility of the source of advertisements is discussed as a separate issue in the second paragraph. We are given no information about how source credibility might relate to price or about how the prices that consumers are willing to pay might relate to the advertised prices of the products. Therefore, the relevance of this answer choice to the conclusion is only conjectural at best.

The correct answer is A.

Questions 519–523 refer to the passage on page 465.

RC00419-01

519. The primary purpose of the passage is to

(A) compare the economic role played by southern banks with the economic role played by banks in the rest of the United States during the late eighteenth and early nineteenth centuries

(B) reevaluate a conventional interpretation of the role played by banks in the American economy during the late eighteenth and early nineteenth centuries

(C) present different interpretations of the role played by banks in the American economy during the late eighteenth and early nineteenth centuries

(D) analyze how the increasing number of banks in the late eighteenth and early nineteenth centuries affected the American economy

(E) examine how scholarly opinion regarding the role played by banks in the American economy during the late eighteenth and early nineteenth centuries has changed over time

Main Idea

Answering this question correctly depends on understanding the passage as a whole. The passage describes two contrasting views about the role banks played in the economic growth of the United States around the turn of the nineteenth century. The first paragraph describes the view that banks played only a small role. The second paragraph describes the contrasting view that banks played a critical role.

A The mention of banks in the South is a small part of a larger discussion about the role of banks in the country as a whole.

B The passage describes two major views held by historians; it does not reevaluate either of those views.

C **Correct.** The passage describes two different views about the role that banks played in America's growing economy.

D The passage does not analyze any aspect of the relationship between the increasing number of banks and the economy. It alludes to the increase in numbers only within a broader description of two contrasting views about how banks affected the economy.

E Although the passage does indicate that a growing number of historians hold one of the two views it describes, the primary purpose of the passage is not to examine how scholarly opinion has changed, but rather to describe in some detail those two views.

The correct answer is C.

RC00419-02

520. The passage suggests that the scholars mentioned in line 4 would argue that the reason banks tended not to fund manufacturing and transportation projects in the late eighteenth and early nineteenth centuries was that

(A) these projects, being well established and well capitalized, did not need substantial long-term financing from banks

(B) these projects entailed a level of risk that was too great for banks' conservative lending practices

(C) banks preferred to invest in other, more speculative projects that offered the potential for higher returns

(D) bank managers believed that these projects would be unlikely to contribute significantly to economic growth in the new country

(E) bank managers believed funding these projects would result in credit being extended to too many borrowers

Inference

The question asks about information implied by the passage. According to the scholars' view described in the first paragraph, banks *followed conservative lending practices*: they shunned projects that were uncertain and that required substantial investments in capital. It follows that, according to those scholars, the reason banks chose not to fund certain projects was that the projects entailed too great a risk.

A   The passage indicates that manufacturing and transportation projects were less well established than those the banks preferred to fund, not more so.

B   **Correct.** Because the projects were uncertain and required a great deal of capital, banks considered them too risky.

C   The passage does not indicate that the scholars argue that banks preferred to invest in more speculative projects. In fact, it suggests that they argue the opposite: the banks avoided investing not only in manufacturing and transportation projects but also in any projects that were at least as risky as those.

D   The passage does not mention bank managers' beliefs about economic growth, and it does not provide any basis for inferring that the scholars in question held any particular views regarding such beliefs.

E   The passage does not mention, or provide a basis for inferences about, bank managers' concerns about numbers of borrowers.

The correct answer is B.

RC00419-04

521. The passage suggests that Paul Gilje would be most likely to agree with which of the following claims about the lending practices of the "earliest banks" (see line 21)?

(A)   These lending practices were unlikely to generate substantial profits for banks.

(B)   These lending practices only benefited a narrow sector of the economy.

(C)   The restrictive nature of these lending practices generated significant opposition outside of the South.

(D)   The restrictive nature of these lending practices forced state legislatures to begin granting more bank charters by the early nineteenth century.

(E)   These lending practices were likely to be criticized by economic elites as being overly restrictive.

Inference

This question asks about conclusions that can be logically inferred from information provided in the passage. According to the second paragraph, Paul Gilje believes that a driving force in American economic growth in the early nineteenth century was banks' lending to a larger and more diverse group of borrowers. The question asks what this would imply about Gilje's view toward earlier banks—which, the passage explains, offered credit only to *well-connected merchants*.

A   The profitability of banks' lending practices is not at issue in the discussion.

B   **Correct.** The passage says that the earliest banks had primarily made loans only to a narrow sector—well-connected merchants—and that they began lending more broadly in the early nineteenth century. It then cites Gilje's view to corroborate and explicate this claim. This strongly suggests that Gilje agrees with the claim.

C   Opposition to the earliest banks is not mentioned or alluded to in the discussion.

D   The passage provides no basis for inferring that Gilje held any particular view as to why legislatures began granting more bank charters.

E   The passage does not mention or provide a basis for inference about the views of economic elites regarding the lending practices of the earliest banks in the United States. It thus provides no basis for inferring that Gilje would have any particular opinion on this topic.

The correct answer is B.

RC00419-05

522. The passage suggests that the opposition to banks in the South in the early nineteenth century stemmed in part from the perception that banks

(A)   did not benefit more than a small minority of the people

(B)   did not support the interests of elite planters

(C) were too closely tied to transportation and industrial interests

(D) were unwilling to issue the long-term loans required by agrarian interests

(E) were too willing to lend credit widely

Inference

The question asks about statements that can be inferred from information provided in the passage. The second paragraph explains that people who opposed banks in the South saw them as monopolies controlled by elite planters. This would imply that those who opposed banks believed that most people in the South did not benefit from them.

A **Correct.** Since people opposed the banks on the grounds that they were monopolies controlled by an elite group of planters, they likely thought banks did not benefit most of the population.

B The passage states *the overwhelmingly agrarian nature of the economy generated outright opposition to banks, which were seen as monopolistic institutions controlled by an elite group of planters.* That statement implies that people believed the banks did serve the interests of elite planters, the opposite of what this answer choice states.

C The passage indicates that people believed banks in the South were tied to planters, not to transportation and industrial interests.

D Southern banks' willingness to provide long-term loans is not discussed or alluded to in the passage.

E The passage does not imply that anyone believed banks in the South were willing to lend credit widely. Since people believed the banks were controlled by the elite, they more likely thought banks were unwilling to lend credit widely.

The correct answer is A.

523. Which of the following statements best describes the function of the last sentence of the passage?

(A) It provides evidence tending to undermine the viewpoint of the scholars mentioned in line 5.

(B) It resolves a conflict over the role of banks summarized in the first paragraph.

(C) It clarifies some of the reasons state legislatures began granting more bank charters.

(D) It qualifies a claim made earlier in the passage about the impact of banks on the American economy in the early nineteenth century.

(E) It supports a claim made earlier in the passage about how the expansion of credit affected the economy.

Evaluation

This question asks about the function of the last sentence in relation to the rest of the passage. The first paragraph describes the view of one set of historians. The second paragraph describes the contrasting view of a second set of historians. The last sentence of the passage points out an exception mentioned by the second set of historians.

A The last sentence pertains to the view of historians described in the second paragraph, not those described in the first paragraph.

B The conflict between the two differing views is not resolved by the passage.

C The passage does not explain why legislatures began granting more bank charters.

D **Correct.** The second set of historians claim banks spurred American economic growth at the turn of the nineteenth century, but the last sentence adds an exception to that claim.

E The last sentence does not support the claim made by the second set of historians, but rather serves as an exception to that claim.

The correct answer is D.

Questions 524–527 refer to the passage on page 467.

RC00458-01

524. The passage is primarily concerned with

(A) examining economic factors that may have contributed to the success of certain Japanese companies

(B) discussing the relative merits of strategic partnerships as compared with those of market-exchange relationships

(C) challenging the validity of a widely held assumption about how Japanese firms operate

(D) explaining why Western companies have been slow to adopt a particular practice favored by Japanese companies

(E) pointing out certain differences between Japanese and Western supplier relationships

Main Idea

This question asks for an assessment of what the passage as a whole is doing. The passage discusses how Western business managers have been following the advice of academics and journalists to pursue strategic partnerships with their suppliers. The advice is based on studies comparing Japanese production and supply practices with those of the rest of the world. Newer research, however, indicates that Japanese practices actually differ from those indicated in the earlier studies and are not significantly different from practices associated with Western manufacturers.

A The passage is not primarily concerned with economic factors contributing to the success of Japanese companies, but rather with whether Japanese relationships with suppliers conform to the practices recently adopted by Western business manufacturers.

B Although the passage discusses strategic partnerships and market-exchange relationships, it does not discuss their relative merits.

C **Correct.** The passage does question the view promoted by several studies regarding the relationship Japanese firms have with their suppliers.

D The passage does not indicate that Western companies have been slow to adopt any particular practice favored by Japanese companies.

E Rather than pointing out differences between Japanese and Western supplier relationships, it actually suggests that they are more similar than generally realized.

The correct answer is C.

RC00458-02

525. According to the passage, the advice referred to in line 6 was a response to which of the following?

(A) A recent decrease in the number of available suppliers within the United States automobile industry

(B) A debate within Western management circles during the past decade regarding the value of strategic partnerships

(C) The success of certain European automobile manufacturers that have adopted strategic partnerships

(D) An increase in demand over the past decade for automobiles made by Western manufacturers

(E) Research comparing Japanese business practices with those of other nations

Supporting Idea

This question is concerned with identifying what the passage says about certain experts' advice. The passage indicates that the experts' advice is based on numerous studies carried out over the previous decade that compared Japanese manufacturing and supply practices with those of the rest of the world.

A The passage indicates that the major automobile manufacturers in the United States have decreased the number of suppliers they deal with, but the experts' advice was not in response to such a decrease; rather, the decrease was in response to the manufacturers' adoption of the experts' advice.

B The passage does not say anything about a debate within Western management circles regarding management partnerships.

C   The passage mentions that European
     manufacturers have adopted strategic
     partnerships, but it does not indicate how
     successful those manufacturers have been.

D   The passage does not indicate whether
     demand for automobiles has increased over
     the past decade.

E   Correct. The passage indicates that the
     experts' advice was made in reaction to
     studies that compared Japanese business
     practices regarding production and suppliers
     with those of other companies.

The correct answer is E.

RC00458-03

526. The author mentions "the success of a certain
     well-known Japanese automaker" in lines 10–11,
     most probably in order to

(A)   demonstrate some of the possible reasons for
       the success of a certain business practice

(B)   cite a specific case that has convinced Western
       business experts of the value of a certain
       business practice

(C)   describe specific steps taken by Western
       automakers that have enabled them to compete
       more successfully in a global market

(D)   introduce a paradox about the effect of a certain
       business practice in Japan

(E)   indicate the need for Western managers to
       change their relationships with their external
       business partners

Evaluation

The question requires the test-taker to determine
the author's reason for mentioning *the success
of a certain well-known Japanese automaker.*
Most likely, the author wishes to present
a specific case that was crucial in leading
Western management circles to value strategic
partnerships.

A   The passage does not discuss reasons for the
     success of the business practice.

B   Correct. The well-known success of a
     certain Japanese automaker is offered as a
     reason for Western management circles to
     believe in the value of the business practice
     of forming strategic partnerships.

C   Although the passage does indicate that
     Western automakers have adopted strategic
     partnerships with suppliers, it does not
     indicate whether this has enabled them to
     become more successful globally.

D   The passage does not specifically discuss any
     paradox related to the effects of Japanese
     business practices.

E   Although the passage does give reason
     to think that the changes adopted by
     Western managers may have made their
     relationships with external business
     partners less, rather than more, like the
     relationships Japanese managers have,
     the passage does not indicate whether
     the Western managers need to make any
     further changes.

The correct answer is B.

RC00458-05

527. Which of the following is cited in the passage as
     evidence supporting the author's claim about what the
     new research referred to in line 20 demonstrates?

(A)   The belief within Western management circles
       regarding the extent to which Japanese firms rely
       on strategic partnerships

(B)   The surprising number of European and
       United States businesses that have strategic
       partnerships with their suppliers

(C)   The response of Western automobile
       manufacturers to the advice that they adopt
       strategic partnerships with their suppliers

(D)   The prevalence of "market-exchange" relationships
       between Japanese firms and their suppliers

(E)   The success of a particular Japanese automobile
       manufacturer that favors strategic partnerships
       with its suppliers

Supporting Idea

To answer this question, you must identify what
evidence is cited in the passage regarding the
author's claim that new research casts doubt on
the widespread view that Japanese firms primarily
manage their supplier relationships through strategic
partnerships. To support this claim regarding the
new research, the author points out that Japanese
firms make extensive use of "market-exchange
relationships," which are alternatives to the strategic
relationships discussed in the preceding paragraph.

A This is the belief that the author claims that the new research casts doubt on, so it would not make sense for the author to cite this as evidence for the author's claim.

B This is cited as a result of the belief that the author claims the new research casts doubt on, not as evidence for the author's claim.

C The new research undermines the basis of the advice referred to here—advice that the Western automobile manufacturers heed—so it would make little sense for the author to cite this as evidence in support of the author's claim about the new research.

D **Correct.** The passage does cite this prevalence as evidence for the author's claim that the new research casts doubt on the widely held view about Japanese firms.

E Citing this firm's success would tend to support the widespread view about Japanese firms, not undermine that view.

The correct answer is D.

Questions 528–531 refer to the passage on page 469.

Main Idea Summary

The passage primarily addresses a question about what a company should do when it has acquired another company and needs to lay off some of the upper management team of the acquired company. *Is the acquisition more likely to be successful if top executives with longer experience in the acquired company are retained or if those with less experience in the company are retained?* The passage introduces the topic by way of a related discussion about which top executive positions should be retained. It then discusses some theoretical considerations in favor of two opposing views about whether longer-tenured executives or shorter-tenured executives should be retained. The final paragraph describes a study designed to help decide the issue. The main idea of the passage is that this study supports the view that acquisitions are more likely to succeed if longer-tenured top executives in the acquired company are retained than if shorter-tenured top executives are retained.

RC00497-02

528. According to the passage, the research mentioned in line 6 suggests which of the following about lower-ranked top executives and postacquisition success?

(A) Given that these executives are unlikely to contribute to postacquisition success, little effort should be spent trying to retain them.

(B) The shorter their length of service, the less likely it is that these executives will play a significant role in postacquisition success.

(C) These executives are less important to postacquisition success than are more highly ranked top executives.

(D) If they have long tenures, these executives may prove to be as important to postacquisition success as are more highly ranked top executives.

(E) Postacquisition success is unlikely if these executives are retained.

Supporting Idea

The question asks about information provided by the passage. According to the third sentence, research suggests that retaining the highest-level top executives in an acquisition is more strongly associated with success than retaining lower-ranked top executives—which suggests, in turn, that lower-ranked top executives are less important than top-level executives to postacquisition success, though it does not suggest that they are unimportant to such success.

A The research indicates that lower-ranked top executives are less strongly associated with success than are higher-ranked executives but does not provide advice about retention efforts.

B The research mentioned in the third sentence does not consider length of service.

C **Correct.** The research indicates that lower-ranked top executives are less strongly associated with postacquisition success than are the highest-ranked executives.

D The research mentioned in the third sentence does not consider length of service.

E   The research suggests that lower-ranked top executives are less strongly associated with postacquisition success but does not suggest that they decrease the likelihood of success.

The correct answer is C.

RC00497-03

529. The resource-based view, as described in the passage, is based on which of the following ideas?

(A)   The managerial skills of top executives become strongest after the first five years of their tenure.

(B)   Company-specific knowledge is an important factor in the success of an acquisition process.

(C)   The amount of nontransferable knowledge possessed by long-tenured top executives tends to be underestimated.

(D)   Effective implementation of an acquisition depends primarily on the ability of executives to adapt to change.

(E)   Short-tenured executives are likely to impede the implementation of a successful acquisition strategy.

Evaluation

This question requires analysis of the reasoning underlying one of the two explanations described in the passage. The resource-based view (RBV) holds that retaining high-level executives with long tenure will contribute to success because those people have important company-specific knowledge. This view rests on the assumption that company-specific knowledge is valuable to postacquisition success.

A   In RBV, executives with long tenure are valuable not specifically for their managerial skills but for their knowledge about the acquired company. The passage does not restrict to five years the period in which this knowledge is gained.

B   **Correct.** RBV values executives' knowledge of the acquired company and is based on the belief that company-specific knowledge is valuable for postacquisition success.

C   The passage does not indicate that RBV claims that executives' company-specific knowledge is generally undervalued. But the passage does indicate that RBV regards such knowledge as valuable to postacquisition success.

D   In RBV, executives with long tenure are valuable not for their ability to adapt to change, but for their knowledge about the acquired company.

E   RBV does not suggest that short-tenured executives impede postacquisition success, only that they are less important to success than the highest-ranked executives.

The correct answer is B.

RC00497-04

530. The passage suggests that Bergh and a proponent of the upper echelons perspective would be most likely to disagree over which of the following?

(A)   Whether there is a positive correlation between short organizational tenure and managerial adaptability

(B)   Whether there is a positive correlation between long organizational tenure and the acquisition of idiosyncratic and nontransferable knowledge

(C)   Whether adaptability is a useful trait for an executive who is managing an acquisition process

(D)   Whether retaining less-tenured top executives of an acquired company is an optimal strategy for achieving postacquisition success

(E)   Whether retaining highest-level top executives of acquired companies is more important than retaining lower-ranked top executives

Inference

The question asks about conclusions that can reasonably be drawn from the information provided in the passage. Bergh's study supports the resource-based view (RBV), which suggests that top executives with long tenure are more valuable to postacquisition success than other executives. The upper echelons perspective (UEP), in contrast, suggests that top executives with shorter tenure are more valuable to postacquisition success. Thus, Bergh and a proponent of UEP would likely disagree about whether long or short tenure top executives are more valuable to a positive outcome in a postacquisition situation.

A   The passage does not provide sufficiently specific information about statistical relationships to determine whether Bergh and proponents of UEP would agree or disagree about whether there is such a positive correlation.

B   There is a weak suggestion in the passage that Bergh believes such a positive correlation exists, but there is no indication that a proponent of UEP would question such a correlation.

C   The passage does not indicate that Bergh would disagree with proponents of UEP that adaptability is a valuable trait in an executive who is managing an acquisition.

D   **Correct.** The passage suggests that proponents of UEP believe that retaining less-tenured top executives during and after an acquisition is a better strategy, while Bergh believes that retaining longer-tenured top executives is better.

E   The passage suggests that Bergh and proponents of UEP agree that retaining the highest-level top executives is more important to postacquisition success than is retaining lower-ranked top executives.

The correct answer is D.

RC00497-05

531. According to the passage, prior to Bergh's study, research on the role of top executives of acquired companies in business acquisition success was limited in which of the following ways?

(A)   It did not address how the organizational tenure of top executives affects postacquisition success.

(B)   It did not address why some companies have longer-tenured CEOs than others.

(C)   It did not consider strategies for retaining long-tenured top executives of acquired companies.

(D)   It failed to differentiate between the contribution of highest-level top executives to postacquisition success and that of lower-ranked top executives.

(E)   It underestimated the potential contribution that lower-level top executives can make to postacquisition success.

Supporting Idea

This question asks about information explicitly provided in the passage. The first paragraph summarizes research indicating that retaining

highest-level top executives during and after an acquisition is more strongly associated with successful outcomes than retaining lower-ranking top executives. The paragraph then states that this research has limitations, including failing to take into account how long the highest-ranking executives have worked for the company. The second paragraph explains that Bergh's study responds to those limitations by analyzing the role of tenure (length of service in the organization).

A   **Correct.** The passage indicates that the research about the role of highest-level executives in acquisitions is limited by its failure to consider tenure.

B   The passage does not portray the failure of the research to address this as a limitation of the research in question.

C   The passage does not portray the failure of the research to consider this as a limitation of the research in question.

D   The passage indicates that the research does, in fact, differentiate between the respective contributions of these two groups of top executives.

E   Undervaluing the contributions of lower-level top executives is not one of the limitations mentioned in the passage.

The correct answer is A.

Questions 532–535 refer to the passage on page 471.

Main Idea Summary

The passage is primarily concerned with Marcus Garvey's role in the African American revitalization movement of the early twentieth century. The passage's first paragraph states that the return of African American soldiers from the First World War created an ideal constituency for Garvey's message of pride and unity among African Americans. The second paragraph describes the disillusionment of these soldiers upon their return and discusses Anthony F. C. Wallace's idea that the tension between a culture's expectations and reality can inspire a revitalization movement. The final paragraph argues that Garvey did not create the consciousness on which he built his movement, but merely gave it its political expression.

RC00017-02

532. According to the passage, which of the following contributed to Marcus Garvey's success?

(A) He introduced cultural and historical consciousness to the African American community.

(B) He believed enthusiastically in the traditional American success ethos.

(C) His audience had already formed a consciousness that made it receptive to his message.

(D) His message appealed to critics of African American support for United States military involvement in the First World War.

(E) He supported the movement to protest segregation that had emerged prior to his arrival in the United States.

Supporting Idea

To answer this question, find what the passage states explicitly about how Marcus Garvey achieved his success. The passage begins by stating that Garvey arrived at the right time: that returning African American soldiers were primed to receive what he had to say about the African American community. These soldiers already held strong beliefs about their rights to opportunities for success; the passage concludes that the divide between the soldiers' expectations and their experiences led to Garvey's success.

A   The passage states that African American people were in possession of a strong cultural and historical consciousness prior to Garvey's arrival in the United States.

B   The passage attributes belief in the traditional American success ethos to African American people who joined the armed forces; it does not mention Garvey's beliefs on this subject.

C   **Correct.** African American soldiers who had experienced segregation during the First World War were ready to hear what Garvey had to say.

D   Critics of African American support for United States involvement in the First World War are not mentioned in the passage.

E   While Garvey most likely would have supported a movement to protest

segregation, such a movement is not discussed in the passage.

The correct answer is C.

RC00017-03

533. The passage suggests that many African American people responded to their experiences in the armed forces in which of the following ways?

(A) They maintained as civilians their enthusiastic allegiance to the armed forces.

(B) They questioned United States involvement in the First World War.

(C) They joined political organizations to protest the segregation of African American troops and the indignities they suffered in the military.

(D) They became aware of the gap between their expectations and the realities of American culture.

(E) They repudiated Garvey's message of pride and unity.

Inference

According to the passage, African Americans enthusiastically joined the armed services but were confronted with continued segregation, both in the military and when they returned home. The passage does not explicitly state their response to these experiences, but a response can be inferred. The second paragraph refers to anthropologist Anthony F. C. Wallace, who argued that a revitalization movement may be brought about by the perception of a gap between expectations and reality, and such a revitalization did occur in African American communities following the First World War; thus, many African American people may have become aware of a gap such as Wallace described.

A   The passage states that African American troops experienced segregation and other indignities while in the military; these experiences could reasonably be inferred to have dampened their enthusiasm for the armed forces. Regardless, the passage does not suggest an enthusiastic allegiance.

B   The passage describes African American people's enthusiasm about joining the military. Although they experienced segregation and other indignities while in the military, the passage does not suggest that their opinion about involvement in the war changed.

C   While African American troops may have joined political organizations, the passage does not provide any actual evidence of this having occurred.

D   **Correct.** The fact that, as the passage states, a revitalization movement occurred in the African American community following the First World War suggests that the returning soldiers did become aware of the gap between their expectations of an improved situation with regard to segregation and the reality of continued segregation in the United States.

E   The passage does not suggest that African American troops repudiated Garvey's message. On the contrary, it states that Garvey built *the largest revitalization movement in African American history*. This suggests that the members of the African American community, including the returning soldiers, were extremely receptive to Garvey's message.

The correct answer is D.

RC00017-04

534. It can be inferred from the passage that the "scholars" mentioned in line 24 believe which of the following to be true?

(A)   Revitalization resulted from the political activism of returning African American soldiers following the First World War.

(B)   Marcus Garvey had to change a number of prevailing attitudes in order for his mass movement to find a foothold in the United States.

(C)   The prevailing sensibility of the African American community provided the foundation of Marcus Garvey's political appeal.

(D)   Marcus Garvey hoped to revitalize consciousness of cultural and historical identity in the African American community.

(E)   The goal of the mass movement that Marcus Garvey helped bring into being was to build on the pride and unity among African Americans.

Inference

To determine what it is logical to infer regarding the scholars discussed in the third paragraph,

look at the context in which they are mentioned. According to the passage, these scholars argue that Garvey was responsible for creating a particular consciousness within the African American community, a consciousness that the passage identifies as *identity, strength, and* [a] *sense of history*. Unlike the passage author, these scholars believe strongly in Garvey's responsibility for this consciousness, so they would most likely reject any suggestion that it existed prior to his arrival and activism.

A   According to the passage, the scholars believe that Garvey was responsible for the creation of the consciousness that led to revitalization, which suggests that revitalization resulted from Garvey's activism, not soldiers' activism.

B   **Correct.** According to the passage, the scholars believe that Garvey created the consciousness that led to his revitalization movement. This suggests that he had to change prevailing attitudes in order to foster this new consciousness.

C   According to the passage, the scholars believe that Garvey created a new consciousness in the African American community; thus, the prevailing sensibility could not have provided a foundation for his appeal.

D   According to the passage, the scholars believe that Garvey built his revitalization movement on a new consciousness of cultural and historical identity, not a previously existing one.

E   According to the passage, the scholars' position is that Garvey's movement was built on a new sense of pride and unity that he provided, and that that sense did not precede Garvey's work.

The correct answer is B.

RC00017-05

535. According to the passage, many African American people joined the armed forces during the First World War for which of the following reasons?

(A)   They wished to escape worsening economic conditions in African American communities.

(B)   They expected to fulfill ideals of personal attainment.

(C)   They sought to express their loyalty to the United States.

(D)   They hoped that joining the military would help advance the cause of desegregation.

(E)   They saw military service as an opportunity to fulfill Marcus Garvey's political vision.

Supporting Idea

This question depends on identifying what the passage states directly about African American people's reasons for joining the armed forces. The reason offered by the passage is that the African American people who entered the armed forces did so because they were *hoping to participate in the traditional American ethos of individual success.*

A   Although this is a plausible reason for entering the armed forces, the passage does not discuss economic conditions.

B   **Correct.** The passage states that African American people who joined the armed forces during the First World War wanted to achieve individual success.

C   The passage does not discuss African American people's loyalty to the United States.

D   The passage states that African American troops experienced segregation, but it does not suggest that they had hoped their joining the military would promote desegregation.

E   The passage suggests that African American troops did not become aware of Marcus Garvey's political vision until after they returned from the First World War.

The correct answer is B.

Questions 536–543 refer to the passage on page 473.

RC38200-01.01

536.   Which of the following best states the difference between free trade and fair trade, as explained in the passage?

(A)   Free trade requires no trade tariffs whatsoever, whereas fair trade assumes multilateral agreement on tariffs for goods of equal worth.

(B)   Free trade is based on the unrestricted movement of goods across all national boundaries, whereas fair trade is based on a nation's restriction of commerce with each nation that erects trade barriers to the first nation's exports.

(C)   The trade policies of countries like Arboria are based on the principles of free trade, whereas the trade policies of other types of world economies are based on fair trade.

(D)   Free-trade nations negotiate individual trade agreements with each of their trading partners, whereas fair-trade nations conduct multilateral trade negotiations.

(E)   Free trade assumes a constant level of global commerce, whereas fair trade promotes a steady expansion of international trade.

Evaluation

This question requires you to understand how the passage explains the difference between free trade and fair trade. The passage discusses international trade as viewed from the perspective of the nation of Arboria. The distinction between free trade and fair trade is discussed in the third paragraph. Free trade between two countries is understood as free movement of goods in each direction across countries' borders. From the Arborian perspective, fair trade is understood as mutually beneficial trading arrangements, where access to the Arborian market is granted only to nations that allow Arborian exports equal access to their own markets.

A   The distinction between free trade and fair trade in the passage does not hinge on the absence or presence of tariffs in a trading regime, even though the passage implies that asymmetric application of tariffs would render a trading regime unfair.

B   **Correct.** As explained above, free trade implies open access to markets; fair trade implies that each of any two trading partner nations should allow the same level of access for imports from the other nation.

C   Whether true or false, this is a claim of a factual kind, and does not provide anything resembling a definition of the two terms, *free trade* and *fair trade*. The passage suggests that Arboria has a free-trade economy and many other nations do not.

D   The passage tells us that both the free-trade advocates and the fair-trade advocates base their positions, in part, on the idea that multilateral negotiations are the most effective way of resolving pressing trade issues.

E   The passage suggests that free trade without fair trade would hinder the expansion of trade (especially Arborian trade) and that fair trade would eventually lead to free trade. But the passage also suggests that international trade between two countries can be simultaneously free and fair. As presented in the passage, the distinction between the two aspects of trade does not hinge on whether the regime promotes a steady expansion of international trade.

The correct answer is B.

RC38200-02.01

537. It can be inferred that the author of the passage would most likely agree with which of the following statements about multilateral trade negotiations?

(A)   They are the most effective way to resolve trade problems.

(B)   They are most effective in dealing with fair-trade issues between nations.

(C)   They have only recently begun to make an impact on world trade.

(D)   Arborian reliance on multilateral trade negotiations, while appropriate in the past, is inadequate for today's global marketplace.

(E)   The principles of multilateral trade negotiations are incompatible with current Arborian foreign trade policy.

Inference

Answering this question requires you to infer from the given information what claim about multilateral trade negotiations the author would most likely agree with. According to the passage, the advocates of free trade and the advocates of fair trade both assume that multilateral negotiations are the most effective way to resolve trading issues. But the passage claims that this assumption is wrong and outdated for current trading conditions. The passage argues that nearly 75 percent of trade is conducted by widely divergent economic systems in countries not subscribing to the same trading principles as Arboria and that this makes negotiation of multilateral trade agreements virtually impossible.

A   As explained above, the author of the passage takes a position opposed to this.

B   According to the passage, it is virtually impossible to negotiate multilateral agreements with countries that do not accept the same trading principles as Arboria and that therefore may have differing notions of what makes trade fair.

C   The passage suggests that the assumption concerning multilateral trade negotiations had for 40 years been accepted by the free-trade countries that dominated world trade—as well as possibly by other trading countries.

D   Correct. As explained above, this is a part of the argument in the passage.

E   The passage does not argue that a principle concerning multilateral approaches in negotiating trade policy, long accepted by Arborian trading authorities, was incompatible with "current" foreign-trade policy. Rather, the passage suggests that that principle and the associated policy should be questioned and rejected, with a view to formulating a policy more relevant to current conditions.

The correct answer is D.

RC38200-03.01

538. Which of the following statements best summarizes the author's opinion of "free traders" and "fair traders"?

(A)   The free and the fair traders' continuing debate provides a healthy and effective forum for examining Arborian trade policy.

(B)   The proponents of fair trade are essentially correct, while those who advocate free trade are not.

(C)   The proponents of free trade are better able to deal with current economic problems than are the fair traders.

(D)   Neither the free nor the fair traders can come up with a workable trade policy because neither takes multilateral negotiations into account.

(E)   The proponents of both free and fair trade have based their positions on out-of-date premises that do not reflect current economic conditions.

Supporting Idea

This question requires an understanding of what the author has to say about "free traders" and "fair traders." The final paragraph of the passage states that "both sides," i.e. the proponents of free trade and the proponents of fair trade, base their positions on two assumptions that, according to the passage, are outdated. The passage attributes this outdatedness to changes that have occurred in the composition of international trade.

A The passage implies that the debate between the free traders and the fair traders is unlikely to make progress because of two outdated assumptions that both sides make.

B The passage implies that fair trade ultimately leads to free trade. The passage implies that trade can be both free and fair.

C The passage indicates that assumptions on which the free traders and the fair traders rely are incompatible with the current realities of international trade.

D The passage argues that both free traders and fair traders wrongly assume that the best way to resolve trade issues is through the use of multilateral negotiations.

E **Correct.** This is a claim that is central to the argument in the passage, as explained above.

The correct answer is E.

RC38200-04.01

539. The author mentions all of the following as characteristic of world trade in the mid-1940s EXCEPT:

(A) Arboria played a major role in the global marketplace.

(B) Whorfland played a major role in the global marketplace.

(C) Tariffs were the main obstacle to trade.

(D) Fair-trade economies dominated international trade.

(E) Arborian manufacturers were unsurpassed in most industries.

Supporting Idea

The word "mentions" in the question is to be taken as meaning "explicitly states" (as opposed to implies or suggests), so this question requires that you recognize what is and is NOT explicitly

stated in the passage regarding world trade in the mid-1940s. The passage states that Arboria and Whorfland dominated the global economy for a long period, but no longer do so. It also states that tariffs were the main obstacle to trade during the time of Arboria's trade supremacy and that in most industries, Arboria had no close competitors. The passage neither states nor implies that at that time fair-trade economies dominated world trade.

A The passage states that this was so in the mid-1940s.

B This is stated in the passage.

C The passage states: "tariffs were the principal obstacle to trade."

D **Correct.** The passage does NOT mention this; it neither states nor implies that in the mid-1940s, fair-trade economies dominated world trade.

E The passage states: "Arborian supremacy was uncontested in virtually all industries."

The correct answer is D.

RC38200-05.01

540. In presenting the argument in the passage, the author uses all of the following EXCEPT:

(A) statistical information about global commerce

(B) definitions of terms concerning world trade

(C) generalizations about Arboria's economic system

(D) historical background of Arborian trade policy

(E) an example of an economic system whose principles differ from those of Arboria

Evaluation

This question concerns rhetorical techniques used in the passage, and we are asked to identify a technique that is NOT used.

A The passage gives some statistical information about global commerce: e.g., 75% of world trade involves countries with divergent economic systems that differ from those of Arboria.

B The passage defines free trade and fair trade.

C The passage states that the supremacy of Arboria in most industries was for a long time uncontested.

D   The passage indicates how the trade regime in which Arboria participates was established 40 years previously.

E   **Correct.** No individual economic system besides that of Whorfland—which has adopted the same trading principles as Arboria—is cited in the passage.

The correct answer is E.

RC38200-06.01

541. The author asserts which of the following about Arboria's trade policy?

(A)   A dramatic revision of Arboria's trade policy will be necessary unless Arborian manufacturers improve the quality of their goods.

(B)   The most crucial issue facing Arborian trade policymakers is that of free trade versus protectionism.

(C)   Arboria's current trade policy was essentially developed during the 1940s and has changed little since that time.

(D)   Arboria's trade policy is widely emulated throughout the world, to the extent that most international commerce is modeled on Arboria's principles.

(E)   Arboria's trade policy has evolved gradually over the last eighty years, constantly readjusting itself in response to shifts in global commerce.

Supporting Idea

This question asks us to identify something stated in the passage—though not necessarily in the exact words given. We should look for the statement that is the most precise paraphrase of a statement made in the passage.

A   Although the passage indicates that some revision of Arborian trade policy is needed, the passage does not indicate that such a revision would be unnecessary if the quality of Arborian manufactures improved.

B   The passage states: "Today the key trade issue is not free trade versus protectionism."

C   **Correct.** The passage states that the current trade policy is obsolete and "an artifact of the mid-1940s," and adds that although ecoomic circumstances have changed, Arborian trade policy has not.

D   The passage states: "nearly 75 percent [of world trade] is conducted by economic systems operating with principles at odds with those of Arboria."

E   The passage does not state that this is so; in fact, it emphasizes the lack of change over the previous 40 years in Arborian trade policy and the absence of readjustment in response to significant changes in conditions affecting global trade.

The correct answer is C.

RC38200-07.01

542. The passage is primarily concerned with

(A)   illustrating the erosion of Arboria's position in the world marketplace

(B)   examining the differences between "free" and "fair" traders

(C)   advocating a reassessment of Arboria's trade policy

(D)   criticizing the terms of the General Agreement on Tariffs and Trade (GATT)

(E)   comparing the different economic circumstances of Arboria's trade partners

Main Point

We are asked here to select the phrase that most accurately identifies the topic that is the central theme of the passage. The discussion revolves around trade policy—specifically the way in which it has affected the interests of the nation of Arboria. In the course of exploring this central topic, several issues are touched on: the loss of Arborian dominance in global trade; the distinction between free trade and fair trade; the impact of GATT on the governance of global trade; and the percentage of total trade conducted by countries other than Arboria and Whorfland.

A   Illustrating something generally involves providing a specific example. But the passage gives no example to show how the Arborian trade position has declined relative to that of other countries.

B   The distinction between free trade and fair trade, as understood by the advocates of each of these, is explained in the broader context of considering Arborian trade policy. But the passage emphasizes the common assumptions relied on by both free traders and fair traders.

C **Correct.** This is the theme of the passage, which advocates a reconsideration of Arborian trade policy and the longstanding assumptions on which it has been based. This central concern prompts the discussion of other relevant, but subsidiary, topics.

D The individual terms of GATT are not examined or criticized in any detail, but the relevance of GATT to current global trade is minimized.

E No such comparison is made, even though the divergence of economic systems involved in world trade is emphasized with a view to demonstrating the difficulty in negotiating multilateral trade deals and the obsolescence of the multilateral approach.

The correct answer is C.

RC38200-08.01

543. The author implies that the main obstacle to a truly effective Arborian trade policy is the

(A) weak position that Arboria currently holds in the global marketplace

(B) inability of Arborian leaders to recognize that foreign economic systems are based on principles fundamentally different from their own

(C) dominance of the supporters of free trade in the conflict between free-trade and fair-trade advocates

(D) apparent inability of Arborian industries to produce goods that are competitive in the world market

(E) protectionism that characterizes the foreign trade policies of so many of Arboria's trade partners

Inference

Correctly answering this question requires you to infer from the given information what the main obstacle to an effective Arborian trade policy is. The correct response is to be found in the first paragraph of the passage, which contains the following sentence: "Arboria faces the prospect of continuing economic loss until Arborian business and political leaders recognize the fundamental differences between Arborian and foreign economic systems." The phrase *continuing economic loss* indicates, from the author's perspective, an ineffective trade policy. The *until*-clause signifies that a necessary condition of improving the situation is a recognition by leaders that Arborian and foreign economic systems are fundamentally different. The final paragraph emphasizes that such differences exist: "75 percent [of world trade] is conducted by economic systems operating with principles at odds with those of Arboria."

A The passage does not state or imply that Arboria has a "weak position" in global trade; rather, it emphasizes that Arboria can gain a much stronger position and "misses opportunities for trade expansion."

B **Correct.** See the detailed analysis given above.

C The passage nowhere states or implies that the free-trade advocates are dominant in the dispute with fair-trade advocates, even though the passage suggests that developed economies such as Arboria and Whorfland have long practiced free trade and been dominant in global trade.

D The passage neither states nor implies that the goods produced by Arborian industries are deficient in quality or are overpriced, but it does suggest that some countries that export to Arboria have trade barriers, such as tariffs, that impede importation of Arborian products.

E The passage suggests that some trading partners of Arboria have trade barriers impeding imports from Arboria, but the passage asserts the following: "Today the key trade issue is not free trade versus protectionism but diminishing trade versus expanding trade."

The correct answer is B.

Questions 544 to 591 - Difficulty: **Medium**

Questions 544–551 refer to the passage on page 475.

RC74000-01.01

544. According to the passage, which of the following was true of the treaty establishing the Fort Berthold Indian Reservation?

(A) It was challenged in the Supreme Court a number of times.

(B) It was rescinded by the federal government, an action that gave rise to the Winters case.

(C) It cited American Indians' traditional use of the land's resources.

(D) It failed to mention water rights to be enjoyed by the reservation's inhabitants.

(E) It was modified by the Supreme Court in *Arizona v. California*.

Supporting Idea

This question depends on recognizing what the passage says about the treaty that established the Fort Berthold Indian Reservation. The passage indicates that the treaty does not mention water rights, but the federal government had intended, according to the Supreme Court, to reserve for the inhabitants of the reservation the waters that were essential to the usefulness of the land.

A The passage does discuss Supreme Court cases, but it does not explicitly mention any challenges in the Supreme Court to the treaty.

B The passage does not state that the federal government rescinded the treaty.

C The passage does not indicate that the treaty made any reference to the traditional use of the land's resources.

D Correct. The passage indicates that the treaty does not mention water rights.

E The passage's reference to *Arizona v. California* relates to the treaty that established the Fort Berthold Indian Reservation only in that *Arizona v. California* refers to the Winters doctrine,

which was established in a case regarding that treaty; *Arizona v. California* does not modify that treaty in any way.

The correct answer is D.

RC74000-02.01

545. The passage suggests that, if the criteria discussed in lines 10–20 of the text were the only criteria for establishing a reservation's water rights, which of the following would be true?

(A) The water rights of the inhabitants of the Fort Berthold Indian Reservation would not take precedence over those of other citizens.

(B) Reservations established before 1848 would be judged to have no water rights.

(C) There would be no legal basis for the water rights of the Rio Grande pueblos.

(D) Reservations other than American Indian reservations could not be created with reserved water rights.

(E) Treaties establishing reservations would have to mention water rights explicitly in order to reserve water for a particular purpose.

Inference

The question requires you to make an inference based on a hypothetical situation in which the criteria discussed in lines 10–20 are the only criteria relevant to establishing a reservation's water rights. These criteria relate to any reservation that has been formally withdrawn from federal public lands, in which the circumstances of that withdrawal make clear that the government had intended to reserve both water and land when the reservation was established. Because the Rio Grande pueblos never formally constituted a part of federal public lands, they were never formally withdrawn from these lands, and so this set of criteria does not apply to these pueblos. Thus, if these were the only legal criteria for establishing water rights, then there would be no legal basis for water rights for the Rio Grande pueblos.

A The criteria, which were established on the precedent set in the *Winters v. United States* ruling, all apply to the Fort Berthold Indian Reservation.

B   Although in actual fact there were no Indian reservations formally established before 1848, nothing in the passage suggests that there were not any, or that none would have met the criteria.

C   **Correct.** If the criteria were the only criteria relevant for establishing water rights, then the passage suggests that, because the Rio Grande pueblos were never formally withdrawn from federal public lands, there would be no legal basis for water rights for these pueblos.

D   The criteria as expressed in the passage do not restrict the type of reservation covered to American Indian reservations.

E   The criteria are meant to cover any circumstances in which the government intended to reserve water rights, whether water rights are explicitly mentioned or not.

The correct answer is C.

RC74000-03.01

546. Which of the following most accurately summarizes the relationship between *Arizona v. California*, as that decision is described in the passage, and the criteria discussed in lines 10–20?

(A)   *Arizona v. California* abolishes these criteria and establishes a competing set of criteria for applying the Winters doctrine.

(B)   *Arizona v. California* establishes that the Winters doctrine applies to a broader range of situations than those defined by these criteria.

(C)   *Arizona v. California* represents the sole example of an exception to the criteria as they were set forth in the Winters doctrine.

(D)   *Arizona v. California* does not refer to the Winters doctrine to justify water rights, whereas these criteria do rely on the Winters doctrine.

(E)   *Arizona v. California* applies the criteria derived from the Winters doctrine only to federal lands other than American Indian reservations.

Evaluation

This question requires you to determine how *Arizona v. California*, as it is described in the passage, relates to the criteria discussed in lines 10–20. Those criteria, which were established in various decisions based on the precedent of *Winters v. United States*, lay down conditions under which courts can uphold federal rights to

reserve water. One of the criteria is related to land formally withdrawn from federal public lands. *Arizona v. California* establishes that the Winters doctrine—which stipulates that water rights need not have been granted explicitly—applies to a broader range of situations than those defined by the criteria. For instance, the doctrine can apply in cases in which the land in question was never formally withdrawn from public lands.

A   The passage does not indicate that *Arizona v. California* abolishes these criteria. It merely indicates that *Arizona v. California* recognizes further situations to which the Winters doctrine can apply.

B   **Correct.** The passage indicates that *Arizona v. California* applies the Winters doctrine to a situation that falls outside these criteria.

C   The passage does not indicate that there are no other exceptions besides *Arizona v. California* to these criteria.

D   The passage indicates that *Arizona v. California* does refer to the Winters doctrine to justify water rights.

E   The passage does not indicate that *Arizona v. California* applies these criteria at all; instead, *Arizona v. California* broadens the range of situations to which the Winters doctrine applies.

The correct answer is B.

RC74000-04.01

547. The "pragmatic approach" mentioned in lines 37–38 of the passage is best defined as one that

(A)   grants recognition to reservations that were never formally established but that have traditionally been treated as such

(B)   determines the water rights of all citizens in a particular region by examining the actual history of water usage in that region

(C)   gives federal courts the right to reserve water along with land even when it is clear that the government originally intended to reserve only the land

(D)   bases the decision to recognize the legal rights of a group on the practical effect such a recognition is likely to have on other citizens

(E)   dictates that courts ignore precedents set by such cases as *Winters v. United States* in deciding what water rights belong to reserved land

Evaluation

This question depends on determining how the term *pragmatic approach* is used in lines 37–38. The passage states that what constitutes an American Indian reservation is a matter not of legal definition, but of practice. The Rio Grande pueblos, though they were never formally established by a withdrawal from federal public lands, have always been treated in practice as reservations. This is what is described in the passage as a *pragmatic approach*.

A   **Correct.** The passage refers to the idea that *[w]hat constitutes an American Indian reservation is a question of practice, not of legal definition* as a *pragmatic approach*. Thus, the pragmatic approach does not require that a reservation has been formally established, but only that it has been traditionally treated as such.

B   The passage does not concern itself with the water rights of all citizens.

C   The passage clearly indicates that determining whether the government intended to reserve water along with the land is crucial for courts.

D   The passage does not specifically consider the likely practical effect of recognizing a particular group's legal rights on other citizens.

E   The passage indicates that the pragmatic approach is supported by *Arizona v. California*, which used, and expanded on, the precedent set by *Winters v. United States*.

The correct answer is A.

RC74000-05.01

548. It can be inferred from the passage that the Winters doctrine has been used to establish which of the following?

(A)   A rule that the government may reserve water only by explicit treaty or agreement

(B)   A legal distinction between federal lands reserved for American Indians and federal lands reserved for other purposes

(C)   Criteria governing when the federal government may set land aside for a particular purpose

(D)   The special status of American Indian tribes' rights to reserved land

(E)   The federal right to reserve water implicitly as well as explicitly under certain conditions

Inference

This question requires you to make an inference based on facts the passage cites regarding the Winters doctrine. The passage indicates that the Supreme Court ruled in *Winters v. United States* that, despite the fact that the treaty establishing the Berthold Indian Reservation made no explicit mention of water rights, the federal government had intended to reserve such rights to the American Indians living on that reservation. Later court rulings that cited the Winters ruling as precedent further refined this doctrine such that water rights can be reserved implicitly if *circumstances reveal [that] the government intended to reserve water as well as land when establishing the reservation.*

A   The passage states that the Winters doctrine ruled that even if a treaty has not explicitly reserved water, water may be reserved if conditions reveal that the reservation of water had been intended.

B   The passage indicates that the Winters doctrine presupposes such a legal distinction; it does not establish it.

C   The passage does not give any information that suggests that the Winters doctrine has been used to establish any criteria governing when the federal government may set land aside for a particular purpose.

D   The passage indicates that the Winters doctrine gives special status to the water flowing through reserved lands, but it does not suggest that the doctrine has been used to establish any special status of American Indian tribes' rights to those lands.

E   **Correct.** The passage provides information suggesting that the Winters doctrine has been used to establish a federal right to implicitly reserve water under certain conditions.

The correct answer is E.

RC74000-06.01

549. The author cites the fact that the Rio Grande pueblos were never formally withdrawn from public lands primarily in order to do which of the following?

(A)   Suggest why it might have been argued that the Winters doctrine ought not to apply to pueblo lands

(B)   Imply that the United States never really acquired sovereignty over pueblo lands

(C)   Argue that the pueblo lands ought still to be considered part of federal public lands

(D)   Support the argument that the water rights of citizens other than American Indians are limited by the Winters doctrine

(E)   Suggest that federal courts cannot claim jurisdiction over cases disputing the traditional diversion and use of water by Pueblo Indians

Evaluation

The passage in the first paragraph outlines a set of criteria that, through various court decisions using the Winters decision as precedent, refined what came to be known as the Winters doctrine. These decisions established that courts can uphold federal rights to reserve water (specifically, for use by American Indians) if, among other conditions, *the land has been formally withdrawn from federal public lands*. Because the Rio Grande pueblos never formally constituted a part of federal public lands, it might appear that the Winters doctrine would not apply to them. The passage indicates, however, that *Arizona v. California* established that this doctrine did apply to them.

A   Correct. Because the Rio Grande pueblo lands were never formally withdrawn from federal public lands—because they never were a part of federal public lands—it might have appeared that the Winters doctrine did not apply to them, because that doctrine had traditionally been taken to apply only to land that had been formally withdrawn from federal public lands.

B   The passage does suggest that the federal government never acquired sovereignty over the Rio Grande pueblos. But the passage indicates this not by citing the fact that the pueblos were never formally withdrawn from public lands, but by pointing out that these pueblos were never part of federal public lands in the first place.

C   The passage states that the pueblo lands were never considered to be part of federal public lands.

D   It is not the fact that these lands were never withdrawn from federal public lands that

is cited in support of this argument; it is, rather, the fact that these lands were never part of federal public lands that is cited for this purpose.

E   The passage actually suggests the opposite of what this says, namely, that federal courts can claim jurisdiction over such cases.

The correct answer is A.

RC74000-07.01

550.   The primary purpose of the passage is to

(A)   trace the development of laws establishing American Indian reservations

(B)   explain the legal bases for the water rights of American Indian tribes

(C)   question the legal criteria often used to determine the water rights of American Indian tribes

(D)   discuss evidence establishing the earliest date at which the federal government recognized the water rights of American Indians

(F)   point out a legal distinction between different types of American Indian reservations

Main Idea

Answering this question requires identifying the primary purpose of the passage. The passage is mainly concerned with describing the legal bases of American Indian tribal water rights.

A   The passage does not discuss the development of laws establishing reservations. It is concerned with American Indian water rights.

B   Correct. The passage's primary concern is to discuss certain principles relating to American Indian water rights established in various court cases.

C   The passage does not question the legal criteria it discusses.

D   The passage indicates that a groundbreaking Supreme Court ruling regarding the water rights of American Indians was handed down in 1908, but that ruling suggested that the federal government had intended at an earlier stage, in the treaty establishing the Fort Berthold Indian Reservation, to recognize water rights; the passage gives no indication, though, of the date of that treaty, nor whether that treaty would have been the first recognition in law of such rights. The passage is concerned with the legal bases of American Indian water rights, not with when the federal government first recognized them.

E   The passage does discuss both lands that have been explicitly created as reservations by treaty and lands that have been treated as reservations although they had never been legally constituted as such; however, (1) the passage indicates that in crucial ways there are no legal distinctions between these two different types of American reservation, and (2) this is not the primary focus of the passage, which, instead, concerns the legal bases of American Indian water rights.

The correct answer is B.

RC74000-08.01
551. The passage suggests that the legal rights of citizens other than American Indians to the use of water flowing into the Rio Grande pueblos are

(A)   guaranteed by the precedent set in *Arizona v. California*

(B)   abolished by the Winters doctrine

(C)   deferred to the Pueblo Indians whenever treaties explicitly require this

(D)   guaranteed by federal land-use laws

(E)   limited by the prior claims of the Pueblo Indians

Inference

The question requires you to make an inference regarding the legal rights of citizens other than American Indians to the use of water flowing into the Rio Grande pueblos. The second paragraph of the passage discusses the Rio Grande pueblos, the rights to the water flowing into them, and the legal bases regarding those rights. Most relevantly to this question, the final sentence of the passage indicates that *the reserved water rights of Pueblo Indians have priority over other citizens' water rights.*

A   The passage indicates that the precedent set in *Arizona v. California* declares that the Winters doctrine applies to the pueblos, despite their never having been explicitly set aside as a reservation. This gave the inhabitants of the pueblos priority rights to

water. Thus, the legal rights of citizens other than American Indians are not guaranteed by the precedent set in that ruling.

B   The passage does not rule out the possibility that citizens other than American Indians may have some rights to the water; their rights are merely limited by the prior claims of the Pueblo Indians.

C   The passage does not explicitly discuss treaties to which Pueblo Indians are a party.

D   The passage gives no indication that federal land-use laws guarantee the legal rights of citizens other than American Indians to water flowing into the Rio Grande pueblos.

E   **Correct.** The passage explicitly states that the reserved water rights of Pueblo Indians have priority over other citizens' water rights.

The correct answer is E.

Questions 552–556 refer to the passage on page 477.

Main Idea Summary

The passage seeks to provide guidance about when companies should subject their suppliers to "competitive scrutiny" (readily comparing suppliers to provide the purchaser with economic leverage) and when they should accept "supplier partnerships" (arrangements in which the purchaser forgoes the right to pursue alternative suppliers). It does this primarily by distinguishing among four types of situations, each with its own set of implications for which approach is likely to be more advantageous.

RC00394-02
552. Which of the following can be inferred about supplier partnerships, as they are described in the passage?

(A)   They cannot be sustained unless the goods or services provided are available from a large number of suppliers.

(B)   They can result in purchasers paying more for goods and services than they would in a competitive-bidding situation.

(C)   They typically are instituted at the urging of the supplier rather than the purchaser.

(D) They are not feasible when the goods or services provided are directly related to the purchasers' end products.

(E) They are least appropriate when the purchasers' ability to change suppliers is limited.

Inference

According to the passage, in supplier partnerships a corporate purchaser forgoes the right to pursue alternative suppliers for certain goods or services. This tends to reduce or eliminate the threat of competition for the supplier in the partnership. It can be inferred that the corporate purchaser in a supplier partnership risks paying more for goods or services than it would if the supplier had to compete for the business.

A   The passage suggests something incompatible with this, i.e., that availability of the relevant goods or services from many suppliers would undermine rather than strengthen a supplier partnership.

B   **Correct.** The passage indicates that supplier partnerships, by definition, reduce the supplier's exposure to competition, and it can be inferred from this that a purchaser in such a partnership could sometimes pay more for the supplied goods or services than if not in the partnership.

C   The passage is silent on how supplier partnerships are initiated, and the passage gives no reason to believe that these would usually be initiated by suppliers.

D   The passage indicates that supplier partnerships are usually instituted for the supply of goods or services that do not contribute directly to the company's end products, though the passage gives no reason to believe that such partnerships would never make sense for supply of items directly related to end products.

E   The passage states that where alternative suppliers for certain goods or services are few and change from an existing supplier is difficult, partnerships may be "unavoidable." This seems to imply that in such cases, supplier partnerships are the most appropriate.

The correct answer is B.

RC00394-03

553. Which of the following best describes the relation of the second paragraph to the first?

(A) The second paragraph offers proof of an assertion made in the first paragraph.

(B) The second paragraph provides an explanation for the occurrence of a situation described in the first paragraph.

(C) The second paragraph discusses the application of a strategy proposed in the first paragraph.

(D) The second paragraph examines the scope of a problem presented in the first paragraph.

(E) The second paragraph discusses the contradictions inherent in a relationship described in the first paragraph.

Evaluation

The first paragraph recommends that a corporate purchaser of certain categories of goods and services should consider two variables to evaluate how, if at all, it might exert pressure on a supplier to gain economic advantage. Applying the two variables, the second paragraph identifies four different scenarios and, for each scenario, explains how the purchaser can gain some economic advantage.

A   The second paragraph is not focused on proving anything; rather it conducts an analysis of the ways in which, under various conditions, a corporate purchaser can gain economic advantage from a supplier.

B   The second paragraph conducts an analysis of various situations affecting the feasibility of a purchaser's exerting pressure to gain economic advantage from a supplier; it is not focused on explaining what causes the occurrence of any situation mentioned in the first paragraph.

C   **Correct.** The first paragraph recommends that corporate purchasers consider two variables in analyzing the feasibility of exerting pressure on suppliers with a view to economic advantage; the second paragraph shows how purchasers can apply those variables to identify four different types of situations affecting the degree to which economic advantage can be gained by exerting competitive pressure.

D   The first paragraph is not focused on presenting a problem, but rather on indicating an approach that purchasers might use in evaluating the feasibility of exerting economic pressure on suppliers with a view to economic advantage. The second paragraph elaborates on the suggested approach.

E   The second paragraph does not characterize as contradictory any relationship involved in the four types of situations it discusses. The first paragraph discusses supplier partnerships and identifies a disadvantage that they sometimes involve for purchasers; but the discussion in the second paragraph does not focus exclusively on situations that involve a supplier partnership.

The correct answer is C.

RC00394-04
554. It can be inferred that the author of the passage would be most likely to make which of the following recommendations to a company purchasing health care benefits for its employees?

(A)   Devise strategies for circumventing the obstacles to replacing the current provider of health care benefits.

(B)   Obtain health care benefits from a provider that also provides other indirect products and services.

(C)   Obtain bids from other providers of health care benefits in order to be in a position to negotiate a better deal with the current provider.

(D)   Switch providers of health care benefits whenever a different provider offers a more competitive price.

(E)   Acknowledge the difficulties involved in replacing the current provider of health care benefits and offer to form a partnership with the provider.

Inference

In the passage, health care benefits are used as an example of a Type 2 situation, where there are many competing providers, but where changing from one provider to another is difficult. In Type 2 situations, the author of the passage

recommends that the corporate purchaser examine the alternative providers to provide leverage in bargaining with the existing provider.

A   Presumably handling any obstacles to replacement would be necessary if a corporate purchaser had decided to change providers. The author of the passage does not preclude the possibility that this may sometimes be a reasonable decision but does not recommend it.

B   The author of the passage does not consider such a possibility, and does not even recommend switching from the existing provider in a Type 2 situation.

C   **Correct.** The recommendation offered in the passage is to review competitive alternatives to the existing provider, with a view to bargaining effectively for better terms with the existing provider.

D   As already noted, the author of the passage does not recommend switching from the existing provider, but recommends reviewing competitive alternatives to exert pressure on the existing provider to grant more favorable terms.

E   The author of the passage does not recommend this course of action in a Type 2 situation, which the corporate purchase of health care benefits exemplifies. The only situation in which the author views a supplier partnership as possibly the best of a set of bad options is a Type 4 situation, where there are few competitive alternatives available and change is difficult.

The correct answer is C.

RC00394-05
555. Which of the following is one difference between Type 2 situations and Type 4 situations, as they are described in the passage?

(A)   The number of alternative suppliers available to the purchaser

(B)   The most effective approach for the purchaser to use in obtaining competitive bids from potential suppliers

(C)   The degree of difficulty the purchaser encounters when changing suppliers

(D) The frequency with which each type of situation occurs in a typical business environment

(E) The likelihood that any given purchase will be an indirect purchase

Evaluation

According to the passage, Type 2 situations are those where there are several competitive alternative suppliers available but where changing from the existing supplier would be difficult. Type 4 situations are those where there are few competitive alternative suppliers and changing from the existing supplier would be difficult.

A **Correct.** The two types of situations differ in the number of competitive alternatives to the existing supplier that are available: in Type 2 situations there are several; in Type 4 situations there are few.

B How should the prospective purchaser ensure that potential suppliers submit truly competitive bids, or can a prospective purchaser even ensure it? The passage gives no answer to such questions that helps to identify a difference between the two types of situations.

C In both types of situations as described in the passage, changing to a new supplier is difficult, and no difference in the degree of difficulty is mentioned.

D How frequently each of the two types of situations typically occur is not addressed in the passage.

E Indirect purchases, as described in the passage, are goods or services that are not embodied in the corporation's end products. Many corporate producers currently make indirect purchases such as computers or business consultancy services. The passage does not compare the proportion of a corporation's total purchases that are indirect (the proportion would presumably vary widely depending on the nature of a corporation's production); so the passage provides no rational basis for estimating a universally applicable likelihood that a given purchase would be indirect.

The correct answer is A.

RC00394-06

556. According to the passage, which of the following factors distinguishes an indirect purchase from other purchases?

(A) The ability of the purchasing company to subject potential suppliers of the purchased item to competitive scrutiny

(B) The number of suppliers of the purchased item available to the purchasing company

(C) The methods of negotiation that are available to the purchasing company

(D) The relationship of the purchased item to the purchasing company's end product

(E) The degree of importance of the purchased item in the purchasing company's business operations

Supporting Idea

The passage characterizes a purchase of goods or services as indirect when the goods or services are not directly related to the end products of the purchasing corporation. Examples given are computers, advertising, and legal services. By implication, direct purchases by an automobile manufacturer could include steel, batteries, and tires: these would obviously be inputs embodied in the final products.

A The passage suggests that "competitive scrutiny" is typically applied only to suppliers of direct purchases, but makes the case that it could be applied also to suppliers of indirect purchases. The exposure to competitive scrutiny is not the characteristic that the passage uses to distinguish direct from indirect purchases.

B The number of available suppliers clearly can vary for both direct purchases and indirect purchases, and the passage provides no reason to think otherwise.

C The passage provides no information about the methods of negotiation that are available for direct purchases. The passage does not base the distinction between direct and indirect purchases on differences in methods of negotiation.

D **Correct.** The passage defines direct purchases as those directly related to the purchasing firm's end products; indirect purchases are purchases that are not related to the end products.

E The type of purchase—direct or indirect—is not, according to the passage, determined by the degree of importance of the purchase in facilitating the purchasing firm's business operations. For example, purchase of advertising by an accounting firm could be critically important for success of the firm's business operations, but such a purchase would likely count as indirect, given the way the passage defines indirect purchases.

The correct answer is D.

Questions 557–561 refer to the passage on page 479.

Main Idea Summary

The passage serves primarily to support the notion that carotenoids are meaningful in the context of mate selection not only because they are rare but because they are required. The passage begins with a discussion of carotenoids and the role they play in mate selection among animals. The passage then considers the question of why they play this role. The traditional view is that they do so because they are rare, but the passage asserts that there is growing evidence that they also do so because they are required for health. Males that are genetically resistant to disease and parasites can use carotenoids for flashy display instead of using them entirely for fighting disease.

RC00423-01

557. According to the "conventional view" referred to in line 13 of the passage, brighter carotenoid-based coloration in certain species suggests that an individual

(A) lives in a habitat rich in carotenoid-bearing plants and insects

(B) has efficient detoxification processes

(C) has a superior immune system

(D) possesses superior foraging capacity

(E) is currently capable of reproducing

Supporting Idea

According to the passage, the conventional view is that carotenoids in a male animal—recognizable by brighter coloration—are meaningful in the context of mate selection

because they are rare and not easily acquired. A male that displays brighter coloration than other males would appear to a female of the species to have foraged more effectively and would therefore seem healthier, and more eligible as a mate, than some less brightly colored males.

A Male animals in a carotenoid-rich environment might, on average, have brighter coloration, but the passage does not imply that this is part of the conventional view. The passage represents the conventional view as emphasizing the rarity of carotenoids, and the consequent difficulty of finding them.

B The conventional view holds that a brightly colored male might appear healthier than less brightly colored males to a female of the species. If the male were healthier, this would presumably require having efficient detoxification processes. But the passage does not treat this as part of the conventional view.

C If a male animal is healthier than other males of the species, presumably that male has a superior immune system, but the passage does not represent this as part of the conventional view.

D Correct. The passage represents the conventional view as holding that more brightly colored males seem to females to be more effective foragers, and therefore healthier.

E The passage does not represent the conventional view as holding that brighter coloration in a male animal would be taken by a female of the species as indicating a current ability to reproduce.

The correct answer is D.

RC00423-02

558. The idea that carotenoid-based coloration is significant partly because carotenoids are required for health suggests that a lack of bright coloration in a male is most likely to indicate which of the following?

(A) Inefficient detoxification processes

(B) Immunity to parasite infestation

(C) Low genetic resistance to disease

(D) Lack of interest in mating

(E) Lack of carotenoid-storing tissues

Inference

The passage states that carotenoids are used by the immune system and for detoxification processes that help maintain health. Males that are more susceptible to disease and parasites, i.e., males that lack high genetic resistance to such things, must use up the carotenoids they accumulate to boost their immune systems. The passage suggests that consequently male animals perceived by females of the species as having used up their carotenoids would be perceived as having relatively low genetic resistance to disease and parasites.

A   Even if an animal has efficient detoxification processes, the passage suggests that carotenoids would be used up in such processes. Thus, having relatively less bright coloration (and therefore less carotenoids) would not necessarily indicate inefficient detoxification processes.

B   The information in the passage suggests that having low genetic resistance to parasite infections is consistent with having immunity to at least some parasite infections, because carotenoids can be used to boost immunity. But this comes at the cost of lacking bright coloration.

C   **Correct.** The passage indicates that a male's having relatively bright coloration could indicate relatively high genetic resistance to disease, and having relatively less bright coloration could indicate relatively low genetic resistance, because the carotenoids that create bright coloration would have been used to boost immunity or aid detoxification processes.

D   The passage does not suggest that male animals lacking bright coloration would be perceived by a female of the species as lacking interest in mating.

E   The passage does not address the issue of whether carotenoid-storing tissues may be lacking in a male of a species that would normally have such tissues. The passage only states that "many" animal species use colorful signals made possible by carotenoids.

The correct answer is C.

RC00423-03
559. The passage suggests that relatively bright carotenoid-based coloration is a signal of which of the following characteristics in males of certain animal species?

(A)   Readiness for mating behavior

(B)   Ability to fight

(C)   Particular feeding preferences

(D)   Recovery from parasite infestation

(E)   Fitness as a mate

Application

According to the passage, "studies of several animal species have shown that when choosing mates, females prefer males with brighter, carotenoid-based coloration." The passage examines two mechanisms by which carotenoid-based coloration might affect mate selection: either signaling good health or signaling high genetic resistance to infection. It is implicit in the discussion that whichever mechanism is in question, bright coloration would function to signal fitness as a mate.

A   The passage discusses how bright carotenoid-based coloration may affect mate selection but does not cite perceived bright coloration as signaling readiness for mating behavior.

B   The passage suggests that bright carotenoid-based coloration tends to signal good health or genetic resistance to factors that cause illness. The passage does not refer to ability to fight.

C   The passage does not refer to feeding preferences, but only indicates that animals with bright carotenoid-based coloration would have consumed organisms that are rich in carotenoids.

D   The passage explores the possibility that bright carotenoid-based coloration could signal high genetic resistance to infection, but implies that recovery from infection could arise from strong immune resistance rather than from high genetic resistance, and could be signaled by lack of carotenoid-based brightness.

E   **Correct.** The passage discussion indicates that, whatever the precise mechanism, bright carotenoid-based coloration in males of certain species functions to signal fitness as a mate.

The correct answer is E.

RC00423-04

560. The passage implies which of the following about the insects from which animals acquire carotenoids?

(A) They do not produce carotenoids themselves.

(B) They use carotenoids primarily for coloration.

(C) They maintain constant levels of carotenoids in their tissues.

(D) They are unable to use carotenoids to boost their immune system.

(E) They are available in greater abundance than are carotenoid-bearing plants.

Inference

The passage says that animals "acquire carotenoids either directly (from the plants and algae that produce them) or indirectly (by eating insects)."

A **Correct.** The passage indicates that the phrase *acquire . . . . directly* signifies in this context acquisition from the ultimate source of carotenoids, so the phrase *acquire . . . indirectly* signifies an acquisition that is not from the ultimate source. This implies that insects do not produce their own carotenoids, but derive them by consuming plants, algae, or other insects.

B This may well be true of some insects, but no information in the passage implies it.

C No information in the passage implies that carotenoid levels in insect tissue remain constant over time.

D The passage contains no information that relates to the immune system of any insect species.

E Even if this is true, the passage contains no information that implies it.

The correct answer is A.

RC00423-05

561. Information in the passage suggests that which of the following is true of carotenoids that a male animal uses for detoxification processes?

(A) They were not acquired directly from plants and algae.

(B) They cannot be replenished through foraging.

(C) They cannot be used simultaneously to brighten coloration.

(D) They do not affect the animal's susceptibility to parasites.

(E) They increase the chances that the animal will be selected as a mate.

Inference

The passage states that carotenoids are used by the immune system and for detoxification processes. To the extent that any carotenoids are used for these purposes, the passage suggests, they would not also be available for bright-colored display to potential mates.

A The passage states that animals can acquire carotenoids from insects, as well as from plants and algae. Nothing indicates that a male animal's use of the carotenoids would determine which of these sources they are acquired from.

B No information in the passage suggests this. The passage tells us that males acquire carotenoids by foraging.

C **Correct.** The passage implies that the quantity of carotenoids used for detoxification is no longer available for any other purpose, such as display of bright coloration.

D The passage suggests that carotenoids could benefit immune response; this implies the possibility of better resistance to parasitic infections.

E The passage conjectures that a male animal's use of carotenoids for detoxification processes could reduce the chances of being selected as a mate.

The correct answer is C.

Questions 562–566 refer to the passage on page 481.

Main Idea Summary

The passage is a discussion of historian Linda Kerber's "republican motherhood" thesis, according to which the American Revolution led to an increase in educational opportunities for women and girls in the United States in the late eighteenth century. Kerber's work was influential at least partly because she explored a topic (female education) that historians had largely ignored. However, the passage cites an earlier historian who had provided evidence that the trend toward greater educational opportunities for women and girls had begun decades before the American Revolution. The main idea of the passage is that the influence of the "republican motherhood" thesis may have led historians to overlook evidence that the trend Kerber describes was already underway before the American Revolution.

RC00349-02

562. According to the passage, Kerber maintained that which of the following led to an increase in educational opportunities for women in the United States after the American Revolution?

(A) An unprecedented demand by women for greater educational opportunities in the decades following the Revolution

(B) A new political ideology calling for equality of opportunity between women and men in all aspects of life

(C) A belief that the American educational system could be reformed only if women participated more fully in that system

(D) A belief that women needed to be educated if they were to contribute to the success of the nation's new form of government

(E) A recognition that women needed to be educated if they were to take an active role in the nation's schools and churches

Supporting Idea

The passage ascribes to Linda Kerber the claim that there was "a surge of educational opportunities for women in the United States" after the American Revolution, and that this surge resulted from a new ideology of "republic motherhood." According to the passage, Kerber argued that the nation's leaders advocated education for women to equip them, in their family role, to raise politically virtuous sons.

A The passage attributes no claim to Kerber concerning a demand by women for education.

B The passage attributes no claim to Kerber concerning a new ideology calling for equality between women and men.

C Kerber's argument as represented in the passage did not claim that an increase in education opportunities for women resulted from a belief that such an increase was required for successful reform of the American educational system.

D **Correct.** According to the passage, Kerber argued that educational opportunities for women increased because the nation's leaders believed that successful democratic government would require that women raise politically virtuous sons within their families, and that women could do so only if they had access to education themselves.

E According to the passage, Kerber's thesis primarily concerns the roles that it was believed educated women could play in raising politically virtuous sons in the context of the family, not in the nation's schools or churches.

The correct answer is D.

RC00349-03

563. According to the passage, within the field of educational history, Thomas Woody's 1929 work was

(A) innovative because it relied on newspaper advertisements as evidence

(B) exceptional in that it concentrated on the period before the American Revolution

(C) unusual in that it focused on educational attitudes rather than on educational practices

(D) controversial in its claims regarding educational opportunities for boys

(E) atypical in that it examined the education of girls

Supporting Idea

According to the passage, Woody's work was a "notable exception" as contrast to the work of other educational historians, who "barely mentioned women and girls."

A Other historians prior to Woody's 1929 work may have used newspaper advertisements as evidence, but the passage provides no information as to whether this was so.

B The passage is silent as to whether educational historians besides Woody concentrated on the period before the American Revolution.

C   The passage does not provide information as to the extent to which either Woody or other historians focused on educational attitudes as opposed to educational practices.

D   According to the passage, Woody noted that educational opportunities increased for both girls and boys around 1750. But the passage does not indicate that this claim, or any other claim Woody may have made about educational opportunities for boys, was controversial.

E   **Correct.** As stated above, the passage describes Woody's work as a "notable exception," i.e., atypical, with respect to his discussion of education for girls.

The correct answer is E.

RC00349-04

564. The passage suggests that Woody would have agreed with which of the following claims regarding "An Essay on Woman"?

(A)   It expressed attitudes concerning women's education that were reflected in new educational opportunities for women after 1750.

(B)   It persuaded educators to offer greater educational opportunities to women in the 1750s.

(C)   It articulated ideas about women's education that would not be realized until after the American Revolution.

(D)   It offered one of the most original arguments in favor of women's education in the United States in the eighteenth century.

(E)   It presented views about women's education that were still controversial in Woody's own time.

Application

According to the passage, Woody characterized "An Essay on Woman" (1753) as reflecting a shift in view, and the context indicates that this shift concerned new attitudes that accompanied increased opportunities after 1750 for girls to become educated women.

A   **Correct.** Based on the passage, this is a claim with which Woody would likely have agreed.

B   The passage represents Woody as claiming that "An Essay on Woman" reflected changes that had already occurred around 1750. The passage does not indicate whether Woody would have agreed with this claim about a persuasive effect on educators.

C   Nothing in the passage represents Woody as thinking that "An Essay on Woman" had ideas about women's education that did not come to fruition until after the American Revolution. The tenor of Woody's thinking, as the passage represents it, is that the essay reflected changes already occurring.

D   The passage indicates that Woody characterizes "An Essay on Woman" as "reflecting" a view that had already gained some currency; so it is unlikely that Woody saw the essay as offering any highly original arguments in favor of women's education.

E   It may be true that "An Essay on Woman" presented some views that were at least somewhat controversial even around 1929, but the passage provides no information that addresses this point.

The correct answer is A.

RC00349-05

565. The passage suggests that, with regard to the history of women's education in the United States, Kerber's work differs from Woody's primarily concerning which of the following?

(A)   The extent to which women were interested in pursuing educational opportunities in the eighteenth century

(B)   The extent of the support for educational opportunities for girls prior to the American Revolution

(C)   The extent of public resistance to educational opportunities for women after the American Revolution

(D)   Whether attitudes toward women's educational opportunities changed during the eighteenth century

(E)   Whether women needed to be educated in order to contribute to the success of a republican form of government

Evaluation

The passage represents Kerber as claiming that the American Revolution led to a surge in educational opportunities for women because the nation's leaders believed women needed to be educated if they were to raise politically virtuous sons. Woody, however, is represented as claiming that there was a significant increase in such opportunities and significant advocacy for women's education well before the Revolution.

A   The passage does not represent either Kerber or Woody as addressing the extent to which women were interested in pursuing educational opportunities in the eighteenth century.

B   **Correct.** The passage attributes to Woody the view that "practical education for females had many advocates before the Revolution," notably in the 1750s, and that the Revolution at most accelerated an earlier trend of changing attitudes. This is contrary to the views attributed to Kerber.

C   The passage gives no information as to whether Kerber or Woody addresses this issue, nor does it discuss to what extent, if any, such resistance may have occurred.

D   The passage indicates that Kerber and Woody hold that there was a change in attitudes toward women's educational opportunities during the eighteenth century, disagreeing, however, as to whether the most significant change occurred before or after the Revolution.

E   Neither Kerber nor Woody is represented by the passage as holding divergent views on this point, and it would be reasonable to think that they may have agreed.

The correct answer is B.

RC00349-06

566. According to the passage, Kerber argued that political leaders thought that the form of government adopted by the United States after the American Revolution depended on which of the following for its success?

(A)   Women assuming the sole responsibility for instilling political virtue in children

(B)   Girls becoming the primary focus of a reformed educational system that emphasized political virtue

(C)   The family serving as one of the primary means by which children were imbued with political virtue

(D)   The family assuming many of the functions previously performed by schools and churches

(E)   Men and women assuming equal responsibility for the management of schools, churches, and the family

Supporting Idea

The passage attributes to Kerber the claim that the nation's leaders believed a virtuous citizenry was essential to the success of the nation's republican form of government, and that women would play a primary role in raising future citizens who would be politically virtuous.

A   According to the passage, Kerber indicates that the nation's leaders believed churches and schools, as well as families, would work to imbue political virtue, though they emphasized the crucial role of families.

B   Kerber argues that the educational system underwent reform in the sense that educational opportunities for women increased; but does not claim that schools or families would change focus to imbue girls with political virtue.

C   **Correct.** Kerber argues that political leaders emphasized the family as the primary means by which future citizens would be imbued with political virtue.

D   Kerber does not claim the nation's leaders proposed that the family would take over functions previously fulfilled by schools and churches.

E   Kerber does not attribute to the nation's leaders the view that men and women would exercise equal roles in managing schools, churches, and the family.

The correct answer is C.

Questions 567–569 refer to the passage on page 483.

RC00633-01

567. The primary purpose of the passage is to

(A) compare the adaptive responses of several species of columnar cacti in the Sonoran Desert with those in the arid tropical regions of southern Mexico

(B) discuss some of the possible causes of the relatively low abundance of migratory nectar-feeding bats in the Sonoran Desert

(C) provide a possible explanation for a particular evolutionary change in certain species of columnar cacti in the Sonoran Desert

(D) present recent findings that challenge a particular theory as to why several species of columnar cacti in the Sonoran Desert have expanded their range of pollinators

(E) compare the effectiveness of nocturnal and diurnal pollination for several different species of columnar cacti in the Sonoran Desert

Main Idea

This question depends on understanding the passage as a whole. The first paragraph discusses an evolutionary change undergone by columnar cacti in the Sonoran Desert with regard to pollination. The second paragraph offers a possible reason for this change—migratory nectar-feeding bats are unreliable pollinators—and the third paragraph goes on to provide evidence that supports the reason given in the second paragraph.

A The passage does compare the adaptations of cacti in the Sonoran Desert with those of cacti in southern Mexico, but it does so in support of a larger point about the Sonoran Desert cacti.

B The relatively low abundance of migratory nectar-feeding bats in the Sonoran Desert is important to the passage in that it provides a reason why the columnar cacti in that region have made certain adaptations. But the passage does not explain why the bats are not particularly abundant.

C **Correct.** The flowers of the columnar cacti in the Sonoran Desert have evolved to remain open after sunrise, and the passage is primarily concerned with explaining why this change may have taken place.

D The passage presents recent findings that support, rather than challenge, a theory as to why the columnar cacti of the Sonoran Desert have expanded their range of pollinators. The passage does not allude to any competing theory that may be challenged by the findings.

E Any comparison of the effectiveness of nocturnal and diurnal pollination for columnar cacti in the Sonoran Desert is made in support of the passage's primary concern: explaining why these cacti have come to remain open and receptive to pollination in daylight.

The correct answer is C.

RC00633 02

568. According to the passage, which of the following types of nectar-feeding pollinators is likely to be an unreliable pollinator of a particular cactus flower?

(A) A dietary specialist whose abundance is typically high in relation to that of the flower

(B) A dietary specialist whose abundance is at times significantly lower than that of the flower

(C) A dietary generalist for whom that flower's nectar is not a preferred food but is the most consistently available food

(D) A dietary generalist for whom that flower's nectar is slightly preferred to other available foods

(E) A dietary generalist that evolved from a species of dietary specialists

Supporting Idea

This question depends on recognizing the qualities of an unreliable pollinator, as described in the passage. The second paragraph addresses this issue: it explains that the unreliability of pollinators can arise in any of three ways: they may be dietary generalists with alternative sources of food; they may be dietary specialists whose own abundance varies; or they may be dietary specialists whose abundance is chronically low in relation to the flowers.

A A dietary specialist whose abundance is high in relation to the flowers on which it feeds would likely be a reliable pollinator.

B **Correct.** A dietary specialist whose abundance is at times significantly lower than that of the flower it pollinates would be, according to the passage, unreliable.

C   A dietary generalist who finds the flower of a particular species more consistently available than other suitable food sources would most likely be a reliable pollinator of that flower.

D   A dietary generalist who prefers the flower's nectar would likely be a reliable pollinator of that flower compared to other flowers.

E   The passage provides no reason to believe that the evolution of a pollinator's dietary preference has any bearing on its reliability as a pollinator.

The correct answer is B.

RC00633-06

569. According to the passage, present-day columnar cacti in the Sonoran Desert differ from their close relatives in southern Mexico in that the Sonoran cacti

(A)   have flowers that remain open after sunset

(B)   are pollinated primarily by dietary specialists

(C)   can be pollinated by nectar-feeding bats

(D)   have stigmas that are unreceptive to pollination at night

(E)   are sometimes pollinated by diurnal pollinators

Supporting Idea

This question depends on identifying a difference noted in the passage between columnar cacti in the Sonoran Desert and their relatives in southern Mexico. The first paragraph states that in southern Mexico, columnar cactus flowers are not receptive to pollination by diurnal pollinators, whereas in the Sonoran Desert, the flowers have evolved to allow diurnal pollination.

A   The cacti in both the Sonoran Desert and southern Mexico have flowers that remain open after sunset, because cacti in both locations can be pollinated nocturnally.

B   Sonoran Desert cacti are pollinated, at least partially, by nectar-feeding bats, which are dietary specialists. But the cacti in southern Mexico are pollinated by these specialists, too.

C   Sonoran Desert cacti can be pollinated by nectar-feeding bats—but so can cacti in southern Mexico.

D   Cacti in the Sonoran Desert have stigmas that have evolved to be receptive to pollination both at night and during the day.

E   **Correct.** The distinction between cacti in the Sonoran Desert and those in southern Mexico is that Sonoran Desert cacti have evolved to allow pollination during the day— that is, pollination by diurnal pollinators.

The correct answer is E.

Questions 570–574 refer to the passage on page 485.

RC00121-01

570. The passage suggests that in order for a manufacturer in a capital-intensive industry to have a decisive advantage over competitors making similar products, the manufacturer must

(A)   be the first in the industry to build production facilities of theoretically optimal size

(B)   make every effort to keep fixed and sunk costs as low as possible

(C)   be one of the first to operate its manufacturing plants at minimum efficient scale

(D)   produce goods of higher quality than those produced by direct competitors

(E)   stockpile raw materials at production sites in order to ensure a steady flow of such materials

Inference

This question asks for an inference about what a manufacturer in a capital-intensive industry must do to have an advantage over competitors making similar products. The passage addresses this question by stating that advantage accrues to those firms that are the first to exploit the full potential of optimally sized, technologically sophisticated plants. In this context, exploiting the full potential of such plants means operating them at *minimum efficient scale*. Based on the definition in the first paragraph, this means that the plant must have an output of such a size that the cost per unit of output is at a minimum.

A   The passage says that for new capital-intensive firms to dominate the market, it is not enough for them to have optimally sized plants; the plants must also be operated in a way that fully exploits their potential.

B   While keeping fixed and sunk costs low would obviously help keep overall costs low, the passage does not suggest that this is decisive in enabling a firm to have an advantage over competitors.

C   **Correct.** Being among the first manufacturers to operate plants at minimum efficient scale means that those plants are being exploited to their full potential. This strategy would most likely give such manufacturers a decisive advantage over new firms hoping to compete effectively.

D   The passage does not discuss the quality of goods made by manufacturers.

E   The passage does not suggest that stockpiling raw materials is the most efficient way to ensure a steady flow of raw materials into the manufacturing process, though the passage states that such a steady flow is a factor in achieving minimum efficient scale.

The correct answer is C.

RC00121-02

571. The passage suggests that which of the following is true of a manufacturer's fixed and sunk costs?

(A)   The extent to which they are determined by market conditions for the goods being manufactured is frequently underestimated.

(B)   If they are kept as low as possible, the manufacturer is very likely to realize significant profits.

(C)   They are the primary factor that determines whether a manufacturer will realize economies of scale.

(D)   They should be on a par with the fixed and sunk costs of the manufacturer's competitors.

(E)   They are not affected by fluctuations in a manufacturing plant's throughput.

Inference

This question asks about what the passage implies about fixed and sunk costs. The passage states that when production declines due to certain factors, such costs remain at the same level (which may be high), and the cost per unit produced (*unit costs*) rises sharply.

A   The passage discusses the impact of market conditions on determining what the optimal size of a manufacturing plant is (which affects fixed and sunk costs). But it makes no claim about the frequency with which such an impact is "underestimated."

B   The passage emphasizes that failing to keep throughput at an efficiently high level reduces profitability because that failure

results in increased cost per unit (to which, of course, the plant's fixed and sunk costs contribute). But the passage does not claim that keeping aggregate fixed and sunk costs very low is necessary in order to have the most competitive production operation.

C   The passage emphasizes that the crucial factor in achieving economies of scale is efficient operation of the production facilities, not the size of the firm's fixed and sunk costs (even though such costs are clearly in part determined by the size and design of the production facilities).

D   While a manufacturer's fixed and sunk costs may be on a par with those of the manufacturer's competitors, the passage provides no grounds for inferring that there is any need for them to be (for example, physical plants that employ different technologies may have different price tags).

E   **Correct.** According to the passage, "throughput" refers to the flow of materials through a plant. This flow can vary as a result of various factors, but fixed and sunk costs—financial resources already committed—remain the same regardless of such variation.

The correct answer is E.

RC00121-03

572. In the context of the passage as a whole, the second paragraph serves primarily to

(A)   provide an example to support the argument presented in the first paragraph

(B)   evaluate various strategies discussed in the first paragraph

(C)   introduce evidence that undermines the argument presented in the first paragraph

(D)   anticipate possible objections to the argument presented in the first paragraph

(E)   demonstrate the potential dangers of a commonly used strategy

Evaluation

This question asks about the rhetorical function of the second paragraph. While the first paragraph argues that a crucial factor in achieving economies of scale is intangible capital, or organized human capabilities, the second paragraph uses the example of new capital-intensive manufacturing industries to help show that this is indeed the case.

A **Correct.** The second paragraph provides an example that illustrates the claims made in the first paragraph. It discusses the way in which intangible capital—e.g., distribution networks, marketing systems, smooth production processes, and qualified management teams—enables manufacturers in new capital-intensive manufacturing industries to realize economies of scale and achieve market dominance.

B The second paragraph does, in a sense, "evaluate" investment in intangible capital: it suggests that such investment is necessary. However, investment in intangible capital is the only strategy it discusses.

C The second paragraph supports rather than undermines the first paragraph's argument.

D Nothing in the second paragraph suggests that there are, or could be, any objections to the first paragraph's argument.

E The second paragraph discusses the potential positive outcomes of investing in intangible capital. It suggests that there might be negative consequences to not making such investments, but it does not indicate that avoiding such investments is a commonly used strategy.

The correct answer is A.

RC00121-05

573. The passage LEAST supports the inference that a manufacturer's throughput could be adversely affected by

(A) a mistake in judgment regarding the selection of a wholesaler

(B) a breakdown in the factory's machinery

(C) a labor dispute on the factory floor

(D) an increase in the cost per unit of output

(E) a drop in the efficiency of the sales network

Application

This question may be best approached by using an elimination strategy—first finding the four choices that can reasonably be inferred from the passage, and then checking to make sure that the remaining choice cannot reasonably be inferred. This requires

understanding the information the passage gives about throughput, then making inferences about what can cause throughput to drop. The passage defines throughput generally as *the flow of materials through a plant* and goes on to explain that it involves coordination of the production process itself, as well as obtaining materials from suppliers and marketing and distributing the manufactured products. Anything that damages this flow of materials and products would be said to have an adverse effect on throughput.

A Making a poor judgment about a wholesaler would most likely have an adverse effect on throughput, in that it could affect *the flow of output to wholesalers and final consumers.*

B A breakdown in machinery would likely fall into the category of *problems on the factory floor* mentioned in the passage and would likely prove damaging to throughput because of its effect on the production process itself.

C A labor dispute would also likely fall into the category of *problems on the factory floor* mentioned in the passage and would probably cause a decline in production and thus adversely affect throughput.

D **Correct.** The passage emphasizes that changes in throughput can cause increases or decreases in costs per unit. But the passage is not committed to any claims about how changes in costs per unit might affect throughput.

E The passage suggests that inefficient sales networks could cause a decline in production. Thus a decrease in sales efficiency would most likely adversely affect a manufacturer's ability to provide goods to consumers, and thus would create problems with throughput.

The correct answer is D.

RC00121-07

574. The primary purpose of the passage is to

(A) point out the importance of intangible capital for realizing economies of scale in manufacturing

(B) show that manufacturers frequently gain a competitive advantage from investment in large manufacturing facilities

(C) argue that large manufacturing facilities often fail because of inadequate investment in both tangible and intangible capital

(D)   suggest that most new industries are likely to be dominated by firms that build large manufacturing plants early

(E)   explain why large manufacturing plants usually do not help manufacturers achieve economies of scale

Main Idea

This question depends on understanding the passage as a whole. In general, it makes an argument for investing in intangible capital as a way for manufacturers to realize economies of scale, and it supports its argument with an example.

A   **Correct.** The passage focuses on intangible capital as a crucial factor in realizing economies of scale.

B   According to the passage, manufacturers gain competitive advantage by building plants of optimal size that they then fully exploit; nothing in the passage suggests that large plants are frequently optimal.

C   The passage assumes that manufacturers invest appropriately in tangible capital and argues that it is important for them to invest in intangible capital as well.

D   The passage states that new capital-intensive manufacturing industries are dominated not by firms that are the first to build large plants, but by firms that exploit the full potential of their plants.

E   The passage indicates that economies of scale can be achieved in plants of optimal size. The passage does not suggest that large plants cannot be optimal.

The correct answer is A.

Questions 575–580 refer to the passage on page 487.

RC00120-05

575. The primary purpose of the passage is to

(A)   describe the development of new techniques that may help to determine the driving force behind population cycles in lepidoptera

(B)   present evidence that refutes a particular theory about the driving force behind population cycles in lepidoptera

(C)   present a hypothesis about the driving force behind population cycles in lepidoptera

(D)   describe the fluctuating patterns of population cycles in lepidoptera

(E)   question the idea that a single driving force is behind population cycles in lepidoptera

Main Idea

This question depends on understanding the passage as a whole in order to identify its purpose. The first paragraph defines population cycles of lepidoptera and discusses some ways those cycles have been studied. It suggests that a particular agent may regulate these cycles. The second paragraph describes a candidate for this agent: nuclear polyhedrosis viruses. The third paragraph explains why this hypothesis is compelling.

A   The passage mentions new techniques in molecular biology, but it does so in order to explain why a particular candidate for the agent behind population cycles has come to light.

B   The theory the passage presents is that there is a driving force behind lepidoptera population cycles. It does not refute this theory; rather, it offers a convincing case for nuclear polyhedrosis viruses as that force. It also discusses some previous approaches to seeking plausible hypotheses but does not focus on refuting any particular hypothesis.

C   **Correct.** The passage is primarily concerned with presenting the hypothesis that nuclear polyhedrosis viruses are the driving force behind lepidoptera population cycles.

D   The first paragraph describes the fluctuating patterns of lepidoptera population cycles, but it does so to explain what population cycles are, so that it can then go on to attempt to account for those cycles.

E   The passage is concerned with making a case for nuclear polyhedrosis viruses as the driving force behind at least some lepidoptera population cycles, not with questioning the idea that there is a driving force.

The correct answer is C.

RC00120-06

576. It can be inferred from the passage that the mortality caused by agents such as predatory birds or parasites was measured in an attempt to

(A) develop an explanation for the existence of lepidoptera population cycles

(B) identify behavioral factors in lepidoptera that affect survival rates

(C) identify possible methods for controlling lepidoptera population growth

(D) provide evidence that lepidoptera populations are self-regulating

(E) determine the life stages of lepidoptera at which mortality rates are highest

Inference

The passage states that mortality caused by various agents, birds and parasites among them, was measured because this was the common approach to studying causes of population cycles. This in turn suggests that those scientists engaged in such measuring in the case of lepidoptera were attempting to come up with a definitive explanation for why those lepidoptera population cycles occurred.

A **Correct.** Measuring mortality caused by various agents was part of the attempt to determine the driving force behind lepidoptera population cycles.

B The passage does not indicate that behavioral factors in lepidoptera are related to their mortality as caused by agents such as predatory birds or parasites.

C The passage is concerned not with controlling lepidoptera population growth, but rather with determining why population cycles occur.

D According to the information in the passage, scientists sought to measure mortality caused by particular agents in order to determine the driving force behind lepidoptera population cycles. In suggesting that mortality caused by these agents is not that force, the measurements may have indicated that the cycles could be self-regulating, but they were not undertaken in order to provide such evidence.

E The passage discusses mortality primarily in the caterpillar stage and does not suggest that any research was directed toward

comparing caterpillar mortality rates with mortality rates in other life stages of the insects.

The correct answer is A.

RC00120-01

577. Which of the following, if true, would most weaken the author's conclusion in lines 18–22 ?

(A) New research reveals that the number of species of birds and parasites that prey on lepidoptera has dropped significantly in recent years.

(B) New experiments in which the habitats of lepidoptera are altered in previously untried ways result in the shortening of lepidoptera population cycles.

(C) Recent experiments have revealed that the nuclear polyhedrosis virus is present in a number of predators and parasites of lepidoptera.

(D) Differences among the habitats of lepidoptera species make it difficult to assess the effects of weather on lepidoptera population cycles.

(E) Viral disease is typically observed in a large proportion of the lepidoptera population.

Evaluation

The sentence in question presents the author's conclusion that lepidoptera populations may be self-regulating or regulated by something more closely connected to the insects than predatory birds or parasites are. To weaken that conclusion requires weakening its support, namely, that mortality caused by predators and parasites seems not to affect population cycles, and that changing habitats and reducing populations has not altered population cycles either.

A A drop in birds and parasites preying on lepidoptera would not weaken the author's conclusion; mortality caused by these predators has not affected population cycles.

B **Correct.** New experiments involving changes in habitat that did succeed in altering population cycles would suggest that the populations are not in fact self-regulating, and that the search for another cycle-altering agent may be unnecessary.

C This finding would support the idea that the nuclear polyhedrosis virus is responsible for population cycles—that is, that the virus is the closely connected agent the author concludes is responsible.

D   The suggestion that the effects of weather may not have been adequately assessed is remotely relevant to the author's conclusion, but the mere difficulty of assessing the effects provides no positive reason to suppose that weather may be the cause of the cycles. On the other hand, answer choice B does offer evidence for an alternative explanation.

E   Viral disease is what the author ultimately suggests is the agent that drives the lepidoptera population cycles in question. The wide presence of viruses in lepidoptera could help support the author's conclusion.

The correct answer is B.

RC00120-02

578. According to the passage, before the discovery of new techniques for detecting viral DNA, population ecologists believed that viral diseases

(A)   were not widely prevalent among insect populations generally

(B)   affected only the caterpillar life stage of lepidoptera

(C)   were the driving force behind lepidoptera population cycles

(D)   attacked already declining caterpillar populations

(E)   infected birds and parasites that prey on various species of lepidoptera

Supporting Idea

This question addresses what the passage states directly about population ecologists' beliefs regarding viral diseases prior to the discovery of new viral DNA–detection techniques. The second paragraph of the passage states that these ecologists believed viral disease contributed to population decline that was already underway rather than initiating it.

A   The second paragraph states that viral disease had been reported; thus, population ecologists were aware of its existence in insect populations. The passage is consistent with ecologists having believed that it was prevalent.

B   The passage focuses mainly on the caterpillar life stage of lepidoptera, but there is nothing to suggest that scientists held

particular beliefs regarding viral diseases' restriction to that life stage.

C   It is after, not before, the discovery of new techniques for detecting viral DNA when populations ecologists came to believe that such diseases were the driving force behind the population cycles.

D   **Correct.** As stated in the passage, population ecologists believed that viral diseases contributed to already occurring population decline.

E   The passage does not discuss whether viral diseases may infect any lepidoptera predators.

The correct answer is D.

RC00120-03

579. According to the passage, nuclear polyhedrosis viruses can remain virulent in the environment only when

(A)   the polyhedrin protein crystals dissolve

(B)   caterpillar populations are in decline

(C)   they are present in large numbers

(D)   their concentration in a particular area remains low

(E)   they are sheltered from direct sunlight

Supporting Idea

The passage states in the second paragraph that these viruses remain virulent for many years if they are protected from direct sunlight. They are embedded in crystals of polyhedrin protein.

A   The viruses remain virulent partially because of their being contained in polyhedrin protein crystals. They would most likely not remain virulent if those crystals dissolved.

B   The viruses remain virulent even when caterpillar populations are not in decline; that is how the viruses initiate new population declines.

C   According to the passage, viral DNA has been detected in the environment at low concentrations, yet the viruses are still virulent. Thus, they need not be present in large numbers.

D   Nothing in the passage indicates that the concentration of these viruses must be low for them to be virulent.

E   **Correct.** The passage says that if the viruses are protected from direct sunlight, they remain virulent for many years. The context strongly suggests that if they are not so protected, they do not remain virulent.

The correct answer is E.

RC00120-04

580. It can be inferred from the passage that while inside its polyhedrin protein crystals, the nuclear polyhedrosis virus

(A) is exposed to direct sunlight

(B) is attractive to predators

(C) cannot infect caterpillars' cells

(D) cannot be ingested by caterpillars

(E) cannot be detected by new techniques of molecular biology

Inference

The passage indicates that the polyhedrin protein crystals protect the nuclear polyhedrosis virus when it is in the environment. When a caterpillar ingests those crystals, they dissolve. That releases the virus, whereupon it infects the caterpillar's cells. Thus it is reasonable to infer that the virus must be released from the crystals before it can infect the caterpillar.

A   The passage states that nuclear polyhedrosis viruses remain embedded in polyhedrin protein crystals if protected from direct sunlight, not that the virus is exposed to light when it is in the protein crystals.

B   Nothing in the passage indicates that any organism preys on the virus itself or that it attracts predators to caterpillars that it infects.

C   **Correct.** The virus must be released from the crystals before it can infect caterpillars' cells.

D   The passage states that caterpillars ingest the polyhedrin protein crystals.

E   According to the passage, new techniques of molecular biology enable the detection of viral DNA in the environment. The nuclear polyhedrosis virus persists in the environment inside protein crystals. The passage suggests that the new techniques are able to detect the virus inside its crystals but does not provide any evidence about whether they detect it directly or infer its presence indirectly.

The correct answer is C.

Questions 581–584 refer to the passage on page 489.

Main Idea Summary

The primary purpose of the passage is to describe resin and discuss a theory on its biological function. The first paragraph identifies some of the characteristics of resin and distinguishes it from gum and sap; one way in which resin differs from these two substances is that its physiological function is not clearly understood. The second paragraph considers whether resin may function to repel or attract insects, and indicates that the consideration of such issues led to the development of the discipline of chemical ecology.

RC00223-03

581. According to the passage, which of the following is true of plant antiherbivore chemistry?

(A) Changes in a plant's antiherbivore chemistry may affect insect feeding behavior.

(B) A plant's repellent effects often involve interactions between gum and resin.

(C) A plant's antiherbivore responses assist in combating bacterial infections.

(D) Plant antiherbivore chemistry plays only a minor role in the coevolution of plants and insects.

(E) Researchers first studied repellent effects in plants beginning in the 1950s.

Supporting Idea

This question addresses what the information in the passage indicates about plant antiherbivore chemistry—that is, plants' chemical defenses against herbivore attacks. The second paragraph of the passage cites the views of various scientists regarding the possible role of resin in antiherbivore chemistry; plants could have evolved resin specifically to repel insects.

A   **Correct.** According to the second paragraph, various scientists have suggested that a change in antiherbivore chemistry, here specifically involving resin, could repel insects; alternatively, some insects could have been attracted to resin, feeding more heavily on plants that produced it. Other researchers have suggested that even if resin does not directly repel or attract insects, it may indirectly affect insect-feeding behavior by mediating changes in plants' antiherbivore chemistry.

B   The first paragraph states that plants produce gum in response to bacterial infections. Although this does not rule out the hypothesis that gum also contributes to plants' antiherbivore chemistry, the passage provides no evidence that it does so.

C   According to the passage, a plant's antiherbivore responses have developed to combat predators, such as insects, that eat plants. The passage provides no evidence that such responses also combat bacterial infections.

D   The second paragraph indicates that plant antiherbivore chemistry plays a major role in the discipline of chemical ecology, and chemical ecology concerns itself with coevolution of plants and insects.

E   According to the passage, it was in the 1950s that entomologists began discussing resin's possible role in repelling and attracting insects. The passage does not suggest that this marked the beginning of their study of repellent effects more generally.

The correct answer is A.

RC00223-04

582. Of the following topics, which would be most likely to be studied within the discipline of chemical ecology as it is described in the passage?

(A)   Seeds that become attached to certain insects, which in turn carry away the seeds and aid in the reproductive cycle of the plant species in question

(B)   An insect species that feeds on weeds detrimental to crop health and yield, and how these insects might aid in agricultural production

(C)   The effects of deforestation on the life cycles of subtropical carnivorous plants and the insect species on which the plants feed

(D)   The growth patterns of a particular species of plant that has proved remarkably resistant to herbicides

(E)   Insects that develop a tolerance for feeding on a plant that had previously been toxic to them, and the resultant changes within that plant species

Application

The discipline of chemical ecology, as it is described in the passage, deals with how plants use chemicals to interact with other organisms—in particular, how they defend against attack—and how those interactions have evolved. To be studied within that discipline, a specific topic would need to address some aspect of that chemical interaction.

A   The passage provides no reason to suppose that the topic of seeds and how they travel would be studied within chemical ecology, given that it does not discuss how chemicals might be involved in the reproductive cycle.

B   The passage provides no indication that chemical ecology would be concerned with how weed-destroying insects would aid agricultural production.

C   The passage provides no indication that deforestation would involve plant chemicals or that its effects would be studied in chemical ecology.

D   The passage provides no indication that a plant's resistance to herbicides would be studied in chemical ecology, but the passage does suggest that the focus of chemical ecology is on how plants chemically interact with other organisms.

E   **Correct.** Chemical ecology developed to deal with the interdependence between plants and insects. Insects' developing a tolerance for feeding on a once-toxic plant, and the plants' resultant changes, is a situation of just such interdependence: plants and insects coevolving.

The correct answer is E.

RC00223-05

583. The author refers to "bacterial infections" (see line 11) most likely in order to

(A)   describe the physiological function that gum performs in plants

(B)   demonstrate that sap is not the only substance that is transported through a plant's tissues

(C)   explain how modern chemical analysis has been used to clarify the function of resin

(D)   show that gum cannot serve as an effective defense against herbivores

(E)   give an example of how confusion has arisen with regard to the nature of resin

Evaluation

The author mentions *bacterial infections* in the first paragraph as the reason why plants produce the substance known as gum.

A   **Correct.** The author states directly that plants produce gum in response to bacterial infections.

B   The author states directly that sap is transported through plant tissues. The passage does not address the question of whether bacterial infections or anything related to them are similarly transported.

C   The passage indicates that rigorous chemical analysis is now available, but scientists still do not know resin's function. The reference to bacterial infections is related to gum, not resin.

D   The reference to bacterial infections indicates the actual purpose served by gum; it does not function to show ways in which gum is inadequate.

E   Gum itself serves as an example of the confusion surrounding the nature of resin; bacterial infections, to which gum production is a response, do not serve as that example.

The correct answer is A.

RC00223-07

584. The author of the passage refers to Pliny most probably in order to

(A)   give an example of how the nature of amber has been misunderstood in the past

(B)   show that confusion about amber has long been more pervasive than confusion about resin

(C)   make note of the first known reference to amber as a semiprecious gem

(D)   point out an exception to a generalization about the history of people's understanding of amber

(E)   demonstrate that Pliny believed amber to be a mineral

Evaluation

The passage states generally that *amber has been widely misunderstood* but cites Pliny as noting correctly, in the first century, that amber resulted from a substance discharged by trees.

A   Pliny's observation was, according to the author, accurate and not a misunderstanding.

B   The author equates confusion about amber with confusion about resin; the reference to Pliny does not indicate which of the two, amber or resin, has been more widely misunderstood.

C   The author indicates that others, not Pliny, mischaracterized amber as a semiprecious gem—and when that mischaracterization first occurred is not identified.

D   **Correct.** Pliny's recognition that amber came from a substance discharged by trees stands, in the author's account, as an exception to the widespread incorrect identifications of the substance.

E   Others held the belief that amber was a mineral. The passage indicates that Pliny recognized that amber came from trees but provides no evidence that he also considered it a mineral.

The correct answer is D.

Questions 585–587 refer to the passage on page 491.

RC00333-01

585. The primary purpose of the passage is to

(A)   compare the impact of the Great Depression on Latin America with its impact on the United States

(B)   criticize a school of economic historians for failing to analyze the Great Depression in Latin America within a global context

(C)   illustrate the risks inherent in comparing different types of economic enterprises to explain economic phenomena

(D)   call into question certain scholars' views concerning the severity of the Great Depression in Latin America

(E)   demonstrate that the Great Depression had a more severe impact on industry in Latin American than in certain other regions

Main Idea

This question depends on understanding the passage as a whole. The passage first describes the view of many economic historians of the 1980s. It next describes the evidence on which that view is based. The remainder of the passage raises issues about the rationale for that view.

A   The comparison between Latin America and the United States is only a small part of a larger argument analyzing studies of the Great Depression in Latin America.

B   The passage does not discuss a global context for the Great Depression.

C   The passage does not primarily aim to illustrate risks that may be generally inherent in explaining economic phenomena.

D   Correct. The passage claims that certain scholars underestimate the severity of the Great Depression in Latin America.

E   The passage does not claim that the impact of the Great Depression on Latin American industry was generally more severe than its impact on industry elsewhere.

The correct answer is D.

RC00333-02

586. Which of the following conclusions about the Great Depression is best supported by the passage?

(A)   It did not impede Latin American industrial growth as much as historians had previously thought.

(B)   It had a more severe impact on the Brazilian and the Mexican textile industries than it had on Latin America as a region.

(C)   It affected the Latin American textile industry more severely than it did any other industry in Latin America.

(D)   The overall impact on Latin American industrial growth should be reevaluated by economic historians.

(E)   Its impact on Latin America should not be compared with its impact on the United States.

Inference

This question asks which conclusion is most strongly supported by the passage. The passage presents the rationale of some historians for their

conclusion that the Great Depression did not significantly interfere with economic growth in Latin America. It then critiques that rationale and conclusion. By questioning the historians' claims, the passage suggests that a reevaluation of the Great Depression's effect on Latin America is needed.

A   The passage does not significantly support this. The passage indicates that, in fact, the Great Depression impeded Latin American economic development more than some historians had thought.

B   The passage does not significantly support this. The passage does not compare the impact on the Brazilian and Mexican textile industries to the impact on the Latin American region.

C   The passage does not significantly support this. The passage does not compare the effect of the Great Depression on the textile industry to its effect on other industries.

D   Correct. As presented in the passage, the passage author's critique of the historians' rationale for their claims provides significant support for the conclusion that their claims should be reevaluated.

E   The passage does not significantly support the claim that the comparison in question should not be made.

The correct answer is D.

RC00333-04

587. Which of the following, if true, would most strengthen the author's assertion regarding economic indicators in lines 25–27 ?

(A)   During an economic depression, European textile manufacturers' profits rise while their industrial output remains steady.

(B)   During a national economic recession, United States microchips manufacturers' profits rise sharply while United States steel manufacturers' profits plunge.

(C)   During the years following a severe economic depression, textile manufacturers' output levels and profit levels increase in Brazil and Mexico but not in the rest of Latin America.

(D)   Although Japanese industry as a whole recovers after an economic recession, it does not regain its previously high levels of production.

(E)   While European industrial output increases in the years following an economic depression, total output remains below that of Japan or the United States.

Application

The question involves applying information from outside the passage to a claim made by the author. The text in lines 25–27 asserts that broad economic indicators pertaining to a nation or region can obscure differences between individual firms or industries within that nation or region. The question asks which evidence would most strengthen the support for that conclusion.

A   This refers only to the relationship between a single industry's profits and its output, not to general economic indicators.

B   **Correct.** The phrase *a national recession* refers to a general economic indicator. Suppose that in a situation described as a national recession, one industry (microchip manufacturing) prospers while another industry (steel manufacturing) does not. This would provide some additional support, over and above that given in the passage, for the assertion that broad economic indicators may mask differences between industries.

C   Economic differences between countries do not strengthen the support for the author's assertion regarding variations among different firms and industries in one country or region.

D   This has no obvious bearing on how sweeping economic indicators can mask differences between industries or enterprises in a single country or region.

E   A comparison of different countries does not pertain to the assertion regarding variation among firms and industries in the same country.

The correct answer is B.

Questions 588–591 refer to the passage on page 493.

RC00272-02

588. It can be inferred from the passage that a large plant might have to spend more than a similar but smaller plant on environmental compliance because the larger plant is

(A)   more likely to attract attention from local regulators

(B)   less likely to be exempt from permit and reporting requirements

(C)   less likely to have regulatory costs passed on to it by companies that supply its raw materials

(D)   more likely to employ older production technologies

(E)   more likely to generate wastes that are more environmentally damaging than those generated by smaller plants

Inference

This item depends on understanding the implications of the passage's discussion of differences between large and small plants. It asks what might be true of a larger plant that would compel it to spend more than a smaller plant on environmental compliance. The passage addresses this issue by stating that smaller plants are often not subject to the same permit or reporting requirements that larger plants are.

A   The likelihood of attracting regulatory attention is discussed only in the context of comparing plants that are *isolated* with small plants that are near large noncompliant ones. The passage does not suggest that size is generally the crucial determining factor in attracting regulatory attention.

B   **Correct.** According to the passage, certain permit or reporting requirements may not apply to smaller plants; this suggests that larger plants are less likely than smaller plants to be exempt from these requirements, and thus that the larger plants would have to spend more to comply.

C   The passage does not discuss the passing on of regulatory costs from suppliers to plants.

D   The passage does not suggest that larger plants are any more likely than smaller plants to employ older production technologies.

E   The passage does not distinguish between the types of wastes emitted by larger plants and those emitted by smaller plants.

The correct answer is B.

RC00272-04

589. According to the passage, which of the following statements about sulfur dioxide and nitrogen oxide outputs is true?

(A)   Older production technologies cannot be adapted so as to reduce production of these outputs as waste products.

(B)   Under the most recent environmental regulations, industrial plants are no longer permitted to produce these outputs.

(C)   Although these outputs are environmentally hazardous, some plants still generate them as waste products despite the high compliance costs they impose.

(D)   Many older plants have developed innovative technological processes that reduce the amounts of these outputs generated as waste products.

(E)   Since the production processes that generate these outputs are less costly than alternative processes, these less expensive processes are sometimes adopted despite their acknowledged environmental hazards.

Supporting Idea

This item depends on identifying what the passage states explicitly about outputs of sulfur dioxide and nitrogen oxide. The passage says that plants that produce these outputs are those that use older industrial coal-fired burners, and that such plants are subject to extensive compliance costs imposed by new regulations.

A   The passage does not address the question of whether older production technologies might be adapted to reduce outputs of sulfur dioxide and nitrogen oxide.

B   The passage states that new regulations have imposed high compliance costs on companies

that produce sulfur dioxide and nitrogen oxide outputs, not that these outputs are prohibited.

C   **Correct.** The passage states that some companies are still using the older kinds of burners that generate sulfur dioxide and nitrogen oxide outputs, and that new regulations have imposed high compliance costs on these companies.

D   The passage does not address the question of whether older plants have developed new processes to reduce the amounts of sulfur dioxide and nitrogen oxide they produce.

E   Sulfur dioxide and nitrogen oxide outputs, the passage suggests, are produced only by older industrial coal-fired burners; newer facilities (using alternative processes) do not employ this technology, the expense of which is not mentioned in the passage.

The correct answer is C.

RC00272-06

590. Which of the following best describes the relationship of the statement about large plants (lines 12–17) to the passage as a whole?

(A)   It presents a hypothesis that is disproved later in the passage.

(B)   It highlights an opposition between two ideas mentioned in the passage.

(C)   It provides examples to support a claim made earlier in the passage.

(D)   It exemplifies a misconception mentioned earlier in the passage.

(E)   It draws an analogy between two situations described in the passage.

Evaluation

This question asks about the role played in the passage by the following statement: *Additionally, large plants can spread compliance costs such as waste treatment across a larger revenue base; on the other hand, some smaller plants may not even be subject to certain provisions such as permit or reporting requirements by virtue of their size.* This statement describes situations in which compliance costs for plants of different sizes may differ, which serve as evidence in support of the passage's main claim: that environmental regulations do *not* affect all competitors in a given industry uniformly.

A   The statement in question is not a
        hypothesis; rather, it reports factors that
        are known to affect the varying impact of
        environmental regulations.
B   This is too vague to be a good description
        of the kind of relationship the question
        asks about. The statement in question does
        present a contrast—it suggests that larger
        plants' compliance costs are lower under
        some circumstances, while smaller plants'
        compliance costs are lower under other
        circumstances. But this purports to state
        two facts rather than mere *ideas*; they are
        contrasting facts but not in any meaningful
        sense *opposed*, since they can easily coexist.
C   **Correct.** The statement provides examples
        to support the initial claim made in the
        passage that regulatory costs fall unevenly on
        competitors in an industry: large plants can
        spread compliance costs around, and smaller
        plants may not even have to pay certain costs.
D   This statement helps to dispel, not
        exemplify, a misconception mentioned
        earlier in the passage—i.e., the myth
        that environmental regulations affect all
        companies in an industry the same way.
E   The statement does not suggest that the
        situation of larger and smaller plants is
        similar (or analogous) to any other situation
        mentioned in the passage.

The correct answer is C.

RC00272-07

591.   The primary purpose of the passage is to

(A)   address a widespread environmental
       management problem and suggest possible
       solutions

(B)   illustrate varying levels of compliance with
       environmental regulation among different
       corporations

(C)   describe the various alternatives to traditional
       methods of environmental management

(D)   advocate increased corporate compliance with
       environmental regulation

(E)   correct a common misconception about the
       impact of environmental regulations

Main Idea

This question depends on understanding the
passage as a whole. Its first sentence indicates
its main purpose: to dispel a myth about
environmental regulations that is often taken as fact.

A   The passage is not about the management
        of any environmental problem, which would
        be a problem about how to prevent or undo
        damage to the environment. The passage
        primarily aims to dispel a belief that the
        passage says is widely held by environmental
        managers.
B   The passage refers to variations in firms' levels
        of compliance with environmental regulations,
        but its primary purpose is not to illustrate
        those varying levels, nor does it do so.
C   The passage suggests that most
        environmental managers are mistaken
        about a key concept; its primary purpose
        is not to describe traditional methods of
        environmental management or alternatives to
        those traditional methods, nor does it do so.
D   The passage takes no position on whether
        companies should increase their compliance
        with environmental regulation.
E   **Correct.** The passage primarily aims to dispel
        the belief that environmental regulations
        affect all companies in an industry uniformly.

The correct answer is E.

Questions 592 to 651 - Difficulty: **Hard**

Questions 592–597 refer to the passage on page 495.

RC00109-01

592.   The primary purpose of the passage is to

(A)   examine two sides of a historiographical debate

(B)   call into question an author's approach to a
       historiographical debate

(C)   examine one author's approach to a
       historiographical debate

(D)   discuss two authors' works in relationship to a
       historiographical debate

(E)   explain the prevalent perspective on a
       historiographical debate

Main Idea

This question requires understanding what the passage as a whole is attempting to do. The passage opens by introducing two books published in 1984 that both concern the history of women in the United States. The passage then makes it clear that one book deals *directly* (line 15) with the issue of women's status, while the other does not. The passage then goes on to discuss the perspective that each book takes and what each book has to offer for an assessment of women's status in the eighteenth and nineteenth centuries.

A   The two books discussed in the passage do not take different sides on a particular debate but rather are described as being more or less useful to the debate itself.

B   The passage focuses on how two different books contain information useful to a particular historiographical debate but does not call into question the approach of either book.

C   The passage focuses on two authors' works, not one.

D   Correct. The passage discusses what two different books have to offer in relation to a particular historiographical debate.

E   The passage does not describe any perspective on a particular historiographical debate as being more prevalent than any other.

The correct answer is D.

RC00109-02

593. The author of the passage mentions the supervision of schools primarily in order to

(A)   remind readers of the role education played in the cultural changes of the nineteenth century in the United States

(B)   suggest an area in which nineteenth-century American women were relatively free to exercise power

(C)   provide an example of an occupation for which accurate data about women's participation are difficult to obtain

(D)   speculate about which occupations were considered suitable for United States women of the nineteenth century

(E)   illustrate how the answers to questions about women's status depend on particular contexts

Evaluation

Answering this question depends on understanding what role a particular piece of information plays in the passage as a whole. The author implicitly supports Lebsock's contention (beginning at line 20) that different frames of reference can produce different perspectives on the debate about women's status in the eighteenth and nineteenth centuries. The author then summarizes different contexts cited by Lebsock to support the contention about frames of reference. As part of this summary, the author refers to *supervising schools* (lines 24–25) as an example of a job that apparently showed women losing power.

A   The passage does not discuss the role of education in the nineteenth century.

B   The passage does mention some ways in which, according to Lebsock, *women . . . gained power* (lines 25–26) in the nineteenth century, but *supervising schools* is not among them.

C   The passage does not discuss the difficulty of obtaining data about particular occupations.

D   The passage makes no judgments about the suitability for women of any jobs in the nineteenth century.

E   Correct. The passage mentions supervising schools as part of an illustration of Lebsock's claim that the debate about women's status depends on the context being examined.

The correct answer is E.

RC00109-03

594. With which of the following characterizations of Lebsock's contribution to the controversy concerning women's status in the nineteenth-century United States would the author of the passage be most likely to agree?

(A)   Lebsock has studied women from a formerly neglected region and time period.

(B)   Lebsock has demonstrated the importance of frame of reference in answering questions about women's status.

(C)   Lebsock has addressed the controversy by using women's current status as a frame of reference.

(D)   Lebsock has analyzed statistics about occupations and property that were previously ignored.

(E)   Lebsock has applied recent historiographical methods to the biography of a nineteenth-century woman.

Supporting Idea

Answering this question requires recognizing information explicitly given in the passage. The passage introduces the work of Lebsock in line 6 and then goes on to describe several characteristics of Lebsock's book. In lines 20–22, the author introduces Lebsock's claim that the historiographical debate about women's status is dependent on frame of reference and calls that claim important; the passage then gives an example showing how frame of reference affects views of women's status. In so doing, the author displays an implicit agreement with Lebsock's discussion on this point.

A   The author of the passage portrays neither the place nor time period that Lebsock focuses on as having been neglected by historians.

B   Correct. The author describes as important Lebsock's idea that frame of reference informs the debate about women's status.

C   According to the passage, Lebsock's book deals with women's status in the eighteenth and nineteenth centuries, not the present status of women.

D   The passage does not mention or imply that Lebsock analyzed statistics in writing her book.

E   Although the passage does describe Lebsock's book as pertaining to an ongoing historiographical debate, it identifies the book's topic as *women in one southern community* (lines 7–8), not the life of a single woman.

The correct answer is B.

RC00109-04

595. According to the passage, Lebsock's work differs from Buel and Buel's work in that Lebsock's work

(A)   uses a large number of primary sources

(B)   ignores issues of women's legal status

(C)   refuses to take a position on women's status in the eighteenth century

(D)   addresses larger historiographical issues

(E)   fails to provide sufficient material to support its claims

Supporting Idea

This question asks for recognition of information contained in the passage. In the first sentence, the passage states that Buel and Buel's work and Lebsock's work have *contrasting approaches.* The passage then proceeds, using descriptions of each work's approach, to illustrate how the works differ. The passage notes that Buel and Buel's work *makes little effort* to place its biographical subject *in the context of recent historiography on women* (lines 5–6), whereas Lebsock's work attempts *to redirect two decades of historiographical debate* about women's status.

A   Primary sources are not mentioned in the passage in relation to either work discussed.

B   The legal status of women is not mentioned in the passage.

C   Lebsock's work is described in the passage as attempting to redirect the debate about women's status in the eighteenth and nineteenth centuries.

D   Correct. The passage suggests that by not placing its subject's story in the context of historiography, Buel and Buel's work does not therefore address larger historiographical issues, as Lebsock's does.

E   The passage tends to support Lebsock's views and does not refer to any lack of support for the claims made in Lebsock's work.

The correct answer is D.

RC00109-05

596. The passage suggests that Lebsock believes that compared to nineteenth-century American women, eighteenth-century American women were

(A)   in many respects less powerful in relation to men

(B)   more likely to own real estate

(C)   generally more economically independent

(D)   more independent in conducting their private lives

(E)   less likely to work as school superintendents

Inference

This question requires making an inference based on information given in the passage. As part of the passage's description of Lebsock's contribution to the historiographical debate about women's status in the eighteenth and nineteenth centuries, Lebsock's conclusions about women's autonomy are described. As part of this description, the passage cites Lebsock's conclusion that nineteenth-century women lost economic autonomy when compared to eighteenth-century women (lines 17–20).

A The passage states that in many ways women in the nineteenth century *lost power in relation to men* (line 23), which would imply that in those respects eighteenth-century women had more power in relation to men, not less. The only increase mentioned in nineteenth-century women's power is associated with owning more real estate.

B The passage states that more nineteenth-century women owned real estate.

C **Correct.** As the passage states, Lebsock concluded that nineteenth-century women lost economic autonomy compared to eighteenth-century women.

D The passage states that nineteenth-century women gained more independence in their private lives.

E The passage cites school superintendents as an example of an occupation more likely to be held by eighteenth-century women.

The correct answer is C.

RC00109-06

597. The passage suggests that Buel and Buel's biography of Mary Fish provides evidence for which of the following views of women's history?

(A) Women have lost power in relation to men since the colonial era.

(B) Women of the colonial era were not as likely to be concerned with their status as were women in the nineteenth century.

(C) The colonial era was not as favorable for women as some historians have believed.

(D) Women had more economic autonomy in the colonial era than in the nineteenth century.

(E) Women's occupations were generally more respected in the colonial era than in the nineteenth century.

Inference

This question requires understanding what the passage implies. The approach that Buel and Buel's work takes is specifically described in lines 3–6 and again in lines 28–34. In lines 29–32, the passage states that Buel and Buel's work *provides ample raw material for questioning the myth . . . of a colonial golden age in the eighteenth century*, referring to a myth about women's status. In describing this golden age as a myth fostered by some historians,

the passage suggests that this era was not as favorable to women as these historians suggest.

A The passage describes Lebsock's work as providing such evidence, not Buel and Buel's work.

B The passage does not pertain to the level of concern women had for their status.

C **Correct.** The final paragraph of the passage describes Buel and Buel's work as providing material that calls into question claims that the eighteenth century was especially favorable to women.

D The passage refers to the economic autonomy of women in relation to Lebsock's work, not Buel and Buel's work.

E The passage does not refer to whether any particular occupations held by women were more respected at one time or another.

The correct answer is C.

Questions 598–600 refer to the passage on page 497.

RC00558-01

598. The passage suggests that WIDC differed from WTUL in which of the following ways?

(A) WIDC believed that the existing safety regulations were adequate to protect women's health, whereas WTUL believed that such regulations needed to be strengthened.

(B) WIDC believed that unions could not succeed in pressuring employers to comply with such regulations, whereas WTUL believed that unions could succeed in doing so.

(C) WIDC believed that lead poisoning in white lead factories could be avoided by controlling conditions there, whereas WTUL believed that lead poisoning in such factories could not be avoided no matter how stringently safety regulations were enforced.

(D) At the time that the legislation concerning white lead factories was proposed, WIDC was primarily concerned with addressing health conditions in white lead factories, whereas WTUL was concerned with improving working conditions in all types of factories.

(E) At the time that WIDC was opposing legislative attempts to restrict women's labor, WTUL had already ceased to do so.

Inference

To answer this question you need to understand the differences between WIDC and WTUL as they are described in the passage. The only information about WTUL in the passage is that it had stopped opposing restrictions on women's labor in the late 1880s, and that, because existing safety regulations were not being enforced, it supported the proposal to prohibit women from working in white lead factories. WIDC, on the other hand, was formed in 1892 specifically to oppose restrictions on women's labor, and it opposed the proposal.

A According to the passage, WIDC did believe that existing safety regulations, if enforced, could prevent lead poisoning. WTUL may or may not have believed that the safety regulations needed to be strengthened; all the passage states is that WTUL did not believe that the safety regulations were likely to be enforced.

B The passage states that WTUL believed that because there were no unions to pressure employers, the employers would not comply with safety regulations. The passage does not present any information on which to base a conclusion about WIDC's beliefs regarding union pressure on employers.

C Based on information in the passage, both WIDC and SPEW believed that enforcing safety regulations could protect women against lead poisoning. WIDC supported SPEW's position on the matter. WTUL believed that safety regulations were unlikely to be enforced because of the lack of unions.

D The passage states that WIDC viewed the proposal to restrict women's employment in white lead factories as an instance of legislation designed to limit women's work opportunities—precisely the legislation that WIDC was formed to oppose. Thus, WIDC was not primarily concerned with the factories' health conditions.

E **Correct.** WIDC began opposing legislative attempts to restrict women's labor in 1892 and continued to do so through at least 1895, when the Home Secretary proposed prohibiting women from working in white lead factories. WTUL stopped opposing restrictions on women's labor in the late 1880s, before WIDC was even founded. Thus, the passage suggests that WTUL had stopped opposing restrictions on women's labor well before WIDC worked to oppose such legislation.

The correct answer is E.

RC00558-02

599. Which of the following, if true, would most clearly support the contention attributed to SPEW in lines 17–20 ?

(A) Those white lead factories that most strongly enforced regulations concerning worker safety and hygiene had the lowest incidences of lead poisoning among employees.

(B) The incidence of lead poisoning was much higher among women who worked in white lead factories than among women who worked in other types of factories.

(C) There were many household sources of lead that could have contributed to the incidence of lead poisoning among women who also worked outside the home in the late nineteenth century.

(D) White lead factories were more stringent than were certain other types of factories in their enforcement of workplace safety regulations.

(E) Even brief exposure to the conditions typically found in white lead factories could cause lead poisoning among factory workers.

Evaluation

This question requires the reader to find a statement that would provide additional support for the contention made in the following statement: *SPEW contended, and WIDC concurred, that controllable conditions in such factories were responsible for the development of lead poisoning.* Information suggesting that when conditions were controlled, lead poisoning was less likely to develop would provide support for SPEW's contention.

A **Correct.** If incidences of lead poisoning were low in those factories that enforced hygiene and safety regulations, that would suggest that lead poisoning was not an inevitable result of working in a white lead factory—but rather that lead poisoning was the result of poor hygiene and safety practices.

B It would not be particularly surprising for the incidence of lead poisoning to be higher among women working in white lead factories than among women working in other kinds of factories—but such a finding would say nothing about whether controllable conditions had any effect on the development of lead poisoning.

C The existence of household sources of lead that might contribute to lead poisoning would weaken, not support, SPEW's contention that controllable factory conditions were responsible for the development of lead poisoning.

D If white lead factories enforced workplace safety regulations more stringently than did some other types of factories, it might be the case that SPEW's contention was incorrect: that even controlled conditions could not prevent a high incidence of lead poisoning.

E If the conditions typically found in white lead factories were particularly bad with regard to safety and hygiene, it could conceivably be the case that SPEW's contention was true—that is, that the conditions that caused lead poisoning were controllable. But it might also be the case that an uncontrollable aspect of those conditions caused lead poisoning. Thus, this neither supports nor undermines SPEW's contention clearly.

The correct answer is A.

RC00558-06

600. The passage is primarily concerned with

(A) presenting various groups' views of the motives of those proposing certain legislation

(B) contrasting the reasoning of various groups concerning their positions on certain proposed legislation

(C) tracing the process whereby certain proposed legislation was eventually enacted

(D) assessing the success of tactics adopted by various groups with respect to certain proposed legislation

(E) evaluating the arguments of various groups concerning certain proposed legislation

Main Idea

Answering this question depends on identifying the overall point of the passage. The passage is mainly concerned with explaining the reasons behind the positions taken by WIDC and SPEW, which opposed the proposal to enact legislation prohibiting women from holding most white lead factory jobs, and the reasoning of WTUL, which supported the proposal.

A The passage explains how WIDC viewed the proposal, but it does not indicate what any of the groups believed about the motivations of the Home Secretary, who made the proposal.

B **Correct.** The passage contrasts the reasoning of the WIDC and SPEW, both of which believed that enforcing safety regulations would make the proposed legislation unnecessary, with the reasoning of WTUL, which thought that safety regulations were unlikely to be enforced and thus supported the proposal.

C The passage simply states that the proposal was eventually enacted; it does not trace the process by which this occurred.

D The passage implies that WIDC and SPEW were unsuccessful in their opposition to the proposed legislation, but it identifies only one tactic used in opposition to it: SPEW's attempt to challenge it by investigating the causes of lead poisoning.

E The passage does not evaluate the groups' arguments concerning the proposed legislation; rather, it presents those arguments without comment on their quality or value.

The correct answer is B.

Questions 601–606 refer to the passage on page 499.

RC00433-02

601. The author of the passage refers to Robert Filmer (see line 9) primarily in order to

(A)   show that Royalist ideology was somewhat more radical than most historians appear to realize

(B)   qualify the claim that patriarchalism formed the basis of Royalist ideology

(C)   question the view that most early feminists were associated with the Royalist faction

(D)   highlight an apparent tension between Royalist ideology and the ideas of early feminists

(E)   argue that Royalists held conflicting opinions on issues of family organization and women's political rights

Evaluation

This question asks about the role of Filmer in the passage. The author states that Filmer's radical patriarchalism is associated with Royalist ideology and then goes on to define radical patriarchalism as an ideology that asserts the power of the king and the male head of the household. Early feminists, however, questioned the subordination of women in marriage. Thus, there seems to be a conflict between these two sets of ideas.

A   Although the passage refers to Filmer's view as *radical patriarchalism*, it provides no evidence regarding any differences in the degrees to which historians consider that view, or Royalism in general, to be radical.

B   Filmer's work supports the claim that patriarchalism was the basis of Royalist ideology; it does not qualify such a claim.

C   That Filmer's approach was one of radical patriarchalism makes it surprising that early feminists were associated with the Royalist faction, but it does not provide any grounds for questioning whether they were so associated.

D   Correct. There is apparent tension between Filmer's radical patriarchalism, if that is indeed essential to Royalist ideology, and the ideas of early feminists, who questioned such patriarchalism.

E   The author refers to Filmer in order to suggest, initially, a uniformity among

Royalists regarding family and women; it is only later in the passage that this view becomes more complicated.

The correct answer is D.

RC00433-11

602. The passage suggests which of the following about the seventeenth-century English women mentioned in line 2?

(A)   Their status as forerunners of modern feminism is not entirely justified.

(B)   They did not openly challenge the radical patriarchalism of Royalist Filmerian ideology.

(C)   Cavendish was the first among these women to criticize women's subordination in marriage and assert women's equality with men.

(D)   Their views on family organization and women's political rights were diametrically opposed to those of both Royalist and Parliamentarian ideology.

(E)   Historians would be less puzzled if more of them were identified with the Parliamentarian side in the English Civil Wars.

Inference

The first sentence of the passage refers to women who are both regarded as forerunners of modern feminism and identified as Royalists. The passage goes on to suggest that, given Royalist ideology's association with Filmer's radical patriarchalism (equating absolute power of the king with absolute power of the male head of household), it is surprising that feminism would find any footing within such an ideology.

A   Nothing in the passage disputes the idea that the seventeenth-century English women in question should be considered the forerunners of modern feminism.

B   Gallagher provides the example of Margaret Cavendish as a writer who did openly challenge radical patriarchalism—albeit only in her writings.

C   The passage states that Cavendish had successors among early feminists, but it does not indicate whether she herself was the first seventeenth-century English woman to assert women's equality.

D   The passage does not indicate what the Parliamentarian view of family organization and women's political rights was, so there is no way to determine whether the Royalist forerunners of modern feminism were opposed to that view.

E   **Correct.** The basic puzzle the passage sets out to solve is why the forerunners of modern feminism would have been associated with the Royalist side, which seems to have been based on radical patriarchalism. Historians would most likely have been less surprised if these women had been identified with the Parliamentarian side, which presumably did not embrace radical patriarchalism.

The correct answer is E.

RC00433-04
603. The passage suggests that Margaret Cavendish's decision to become an author was motivated, at least in part, by a desire to

(A)   justify her support for the Royalist cause

(B)   encourage her readers to work toward eradicating Filmerian patriarchalism

(C)   persuade other women to break free from their political and social isolation

(D)   analyze the causes for women's exclusion from the pursuit of power

(E)   create a world over which she could exercise total control

Inference

This question asks about Margaret Cavendish's reasons for becoming an author. The second paragraph describes her as someone who *insisted that she was a self-sufficient being*; she understood that, given the real-world strictures in place, she could achieve this self-sufficiency in her own mind and on paper as a writer. So her decision to become a writer can be inferred to be motivated by her desire to exercise power and control.

A   The passage states that Cavendish justified her being the center of her own universe by invoking the Royalist figure of the absolute monarch; there is no suggestion in the passage that Cavendish felt the need to justify any support for the actual Royalist cause.

B   The passage gives no direct indication that Cavendish was even aware of Filmerian patriarchalism.

C   The second paragraph states that Cavendish's idea of absolute singularity carried with it the idea of social and political isolation; Cavendish was most likely not motivated by a desire to persuade other women to break free from such isolation.

D   Cavendish took the exclusion of women from the pursuit of power for granted; the passage does not suggest that she was concerned with its causes.

E   **Correct.** According to the passage, Cavendish considered herself a self-sufficient being who was at the center of her own universe; in her writing, she wanted to create a world in which this was also true.

The correct answer is E.

RC00433-08
604. The phrase "a satellite orbiting a dominant male planet" (lines 41–42) refers most directly to

(A)   Cavendish's concept that each woman is a sovereign self

(B)   the complete political and social isolation of absolute singularity

(C)   the immaterial world that a writer can create on paper

(D)   the absolute subordination of women in a patriarchal society

(E)   the metaphorical figure of the absolute monarch

Evaluation

The phrase in question is *a satellite orbiting a dominant male planet*. The passage states that this was the idea that Cavendish was reacting against; she preferred instead the idea that she was the center of her own universe, her own sovereign, subject to no one.

A   The idea of a satellite orbiting a dominant male planet refers not to Cavendish's idea that each woman is a sovereign self, but rather to the idea directly opposed to that: each woman must submit to a dominant male.

B A *satellite orbiting a dominant male planet* is by definition not isolated, nor is it singular.

C According to the passage, Cavendish wished to create her own world as a writer so that she did not have to be a *satellite*.

D **Correct.** The phrase refers to the idea that in a patriarchal society, women are as satellites to men, who are the dominant planets.

E While radical patriarchy does equate the monarch with the male head of the household, the in question phrase is most directly about the relationship, under patriarchy, between women and men.

The correct answer is D.

RC00433-06
605. The primary purpose of the passage is to

(A) trace the historical roots of a modern sociopolitical movement

(B) present one scholar's explanation for a puzzling historical phenomenon

(C) contrast two interpretations of the ideological origins of a political conflict

(D) establish a link between the ideology of an influential political theorist and that of a notoriously eccentric writer

(E) call attention to some points of agreement between opposing sides in an ideological debate

Main Idea

This question asks about the passage as a whole. The passage is mainly concerned with outlining Catherine Gallagher's attempt to explain why, given Royalist ideology's apparent association with radical patriarchalism, Royalist women offered feminist critiques of women's subordination in marriage and asserted their equality with men.

A The passage makes no connection between early feminism and its modern form.

B **Correct.** The passage presents a puzzling historical phenomenon, that Royalist women critiqued patriarchalism, in the first paragraph, and then presents Catherine Gallagher's explanation for that phenomenon in the second paragraph.

C While the passage discusses the political conflict between the Royalists and Parliamentarians in the English Civil Wars in the first paragraph, neither this conflict, nor its ideological origins are the focus of the passage. Furthermore, the passage does not offer any interpretations of the origins of the conflict.

D The passage attempts to unlink the ideology of political theorist Robert Filmer and the eccentric author Margaret Cavendish by suggesting that Filmer's radical patriarchalism was not the only way of understanding Royalist ideology. Cavendish provided a different understanding entirely.

E While both sides of the ideological debate did agree on the absolute monarchy, the passage as a whole does not focus on this agreement, but rather on the disagreement about where, theoretically, the idea of absolute monarchy leads.

The correct answer is B.

RC00433-09
606. Which of the following, if true, would most clearly undermine Gallagher's explanation of the link between Royalism and feminism?

(A) Because of their privileged backgrounds, Royalist women were generally better educated than were their Parliamentarian counterparts.

(B) Filmer himself had read some of Cavendish's early writings and was highly critical of her ideas.

(C) Cavendish's views were highly individual and were not shared by the other Royalist women who wrote early feminist works.

(D) The Royalist and Parliamentarian ideologies were largely in agreement on issues of family organization and women's political rights.

(E) The Royalist side included a sizable minority faction that was opposed to the more radical tendencies of Filmerian patriarchalism.

Inference

This question asks about how to undermine the way in which Gallagher connects Royalism and feminism. According to Gallagher, Cavendish's work exemplifies the connection between these ideas, because Cavendish took the idea of absolute monarchy and extended that to the idea of absolute self, an idea that should, Cavendish believed, apply to women as well as men.

580

A   Gallagher's explanation of the link between Royalism and feminism does not depend on the education level of Royalist women relative to Parliamentarian women.

B   Filmer most likely would have been critical of Cavendish's ideas, had he encountered them, but the passage does not indicate that Gallagher's argument had anything to do with whether Filmer read Cavendish's writings.

C   **Correct.** Gallagher uses Cavendish's work to explain how Royalism gave rise to feminism, but if Cavendish's views were completely atypical of other Royalist women, then those views cannot explain the link as Gallagher suggests they do.

D   The passage states in the first paragraph that if the Royalists and Parliamentarians were in agreement *on issues of family organization and women's political rights*, then feminists should have been divided between the two sides—but they were not. So this idea, if true, would undermine that statement, but not Gallagher's argument about the link between Royalists and feminists.

E   If more Royalists were opposed to Filmer's radical patriarchalism, then Cavendish's writings would seem to be more representative of tendencies in Royalist ideology, thus making Gallagher's case stronger, not weaker.

The correct answer is C.

Questions 607–611 refer to the passage on page 501.

RC00312-01

607.   The passage is primarily concerned with

(A)   identifying two practices in medical research that may affect the accuracy of clinical trials

(B)   describing aspects of medical research that tend to drive up costs

(C)   evaluating an analysis of certain shortcomings of current medical research practices

(D)   describing proposed changes to the ways in which clinical trials are conducted

(E)   explaining how medical researchers have traditionally conducted clinical trials and how such trials are likely to change

Main Idea

This question requires an understanding of what the passage as a whole is doing. The passage introduces Frazier and Mosteller as proposing changes to the ways clinical trials in medical research are currently conducted. The rest of the passage then describes these proposed changes together with the support Frazier and Mosteller provide for adopting these changes.

A   The passage identifies practices in medical research to help illustrate the basis for Frazier and Mosteller's proposed changes.

B   The passage mentions medical research costs as one example within the larger description of Frazier and Mosteller's proposed changes.

C   The passage is not concerned with evaluating Frazier and Mosteller's proposed changes.

D   **Correct.** The passage describes the changes proposed by Frazier and Mosteller to the way clinical trials are conducted.

E   The passage is not concerned with establishing the likelihood of any changes to the way medical research is conducted.

The correct answer is D.

RC00312-03

608.   Which of the following can be inferred from the passage about a study of the category of patients referred to in lines 20–22 ?

(A)   Its findings might have limited applicability.

(B)   It would be prohibitively expensive in its attempt to create ideal conditions.

(C)   It would be the best way to sample the total population of potential patients.

(D)   It would allow researchers to limit information collection without increasing the risk that important variables could be overlooked.

(E)   Its findings would be more accurate if it concerned treatments for a progressive disease than if it concerned treatments for a nonprogressive disease.

Inference

This question requires drawing an inference from information given in the passage. In describing the proposals put forth by Frazier and Mosteller, the passage states in lines 15–20 that they propose using more patients in clinical trials than are currently being used, and that the trials would thereby obtain *a more representative sample of the total population with the disease under study*. The passage then states that researchers often *restrict* (lines 20–22) their trials to certain types of patients, therefore limiting the applicability of their findings.

A   **Correct.** The passage states that the researchers preferred to restrict the types of patients used in their studies, thereby using a less representative sample than if they used a more inclusive group of patients.

B   The passage mentions the added expense of clinical trials only in relation to data storage, collection, and analysis.

C   The passage describes the category of patients referred to as restricted and therefore unrepresentative of the total population.

D   While the passage does mention the amount of data collected about an individual patient, that topic is not connected to the category of patients referred to in lines 20–22.

E   The passage does not suggest that a study using the category of patients referred to would be more effective in investigating progressive diseases.

The correct answer is A.

RC00312-04

609. It can be inferred from the passage that a study limited to patients like those mentioned in lines 20–22 would have which of the following advantages over the kind of study proposed by Frazier and Mosteller?

(A)   It would yield more data and its findings would be more accurate.

(B)   It would cost less in the long term, though it would be more expensive in its initial stages.

(C)   It would limit the number of variables researchers would need to consider when evaluating the treatment under study.

(D)   It would help researchers to identify subgroups of patients with secondary conditions that might also be treatable.

(E)   It would enable researchers to assess the value of an experimental treatment for the average patient.

Inference

This question requires understanding what the information in the passage implies. The passage explains that Frazier and Mosteller's proposal involves enrolling more patients in clinical trials (lines 18–19) than is the case with the category of patients referred to. The passage then explains that broadening the range of trial participants would allow an evaluation of particular treatments *under various conditions* and *for different patient subgroups* (line 29). This strongly suggests that limiting the patients used to those described in the referred text would limit the number of variables researchers would need to consider.

A   The passage suggests that not limiting the patients used in clinical trials will yield more data than restricting them will.

B   The passage refers to the costs of clinical trials only as they concern the collection, storage, and analysis of data collected from participants.

C   **Correct.** By limiting the patients used to those having the ailment under study, the passage suggests that researchers need to consider fewer variables in their assessment of a treatment.

D   The passage suggests that *not* limiting the types of patients used in clinical trials will better allow researchers to evaluate subgroups.

E   The passage suggests that limiting the types of patients available for clinical trials results in data for specific, rather than average, populations.

The correct answer is C.

RC00312-05

610. The author mentions patients' ages (line 32) primarily in order to

(A)   identify the most critical variable differentiating subgroups of patients

(B)   cast doubt on the advisability of implementing Frazier and Mosteller's proposals about medical research

(C)   indicate why progressive diseases may require different treatments at different stages

(D)   illustrate a point about the value of enrolling a wide range of patients in clinical trials

(E)   substantiate an argument about the problems inherent in enrolling large numbers of patients in clinical trials

Evaluation

Answering this question requires understanding how a particular piece of information functions in the passage as a whole. The passage is concerned with describing the proposals of Frazier and Mosteller. One of these proposals, described in the second paragraph, involves broadening the range of participants used in clinical trials. The passage states that in following this proposal, Frazier and Mosteller suggest that the effectiveness of treatments can be assessed for different patient subgroups. To affirm the value of broadening the range of participants, the passage then cites two examples of criteria by which relevant subgroups might be identified: disease stages and patients' ages.

A   The passage makes no judgment as to the value of the subgroups it refers to in relation to broadened participation in clinical trials.

B   The passage does not call into question the potential effectiveness of Frazier and Mosteller's proposals.

C   The passage's example of patients' ages is not intended to be causally connected to its previous example regarding progressive diseases.

D   Correct. Patients' ages are referred to in the passage to identify subgroups that could be evaluated if the range of participants in clinical trials were broadened.

E   The passage refers to patients' ages in support of Frazier and Mosteller's proposal that more patients be used in clinical trials.

The correct answer is D.

RC00312-06

611. According to the passage, which of the following describes a result of the way in which researchers generally conduct clinical trials?

(A)   They expend resources on the storage of information likely to be irrelevant to the study they are conducting.

(B)   They sometimes compromise the accuracy of their findings by collecting and analyzing more information than is strictly required for their trials.

(C)   They avoid the risk of overlooking variables that might affect their findings, even though doing so raises their research costs.

(D)   Because they attempt to analyze too much information, they overlook facts that could emerge as relevant to their studies.

(E)   In order to approximate the conditions typical of medical treatment, they base their methods of information collection on those used by hospitals.

Supporting Idea

This question asks for an identification of specific information given in the passage. The passage describes the proposals of Frazier and Mosteller as attempting to improve the way clinical trials have generally been conducted. In describing how current trials are generally conducted, the passage states that researchers *collect far more background information on patients than is strictly required for their trials* (lines 4–6) and that they therefore escalate the costs of the trials.

A   Correct. The passage states that researchers generally collect more information than they need to perform their clinical trials, which drives up the costs of the trials.

B   The passage makes no judgment about the accuracy of the information collected by researchers who currently hold clinical trials.

C   The passage states that the risk of overlooking relevant information in clinical trials is *never entirely eliminable* (line 11).

D   The passage states that researchers generally collect more information than is relevant, not that they overlook relevant information.

E   The passage states that, in general, researchers currently collect more information than hospitals do (line 6).

The correct answer is A.

Questions 612–617 refer to the passage on page 503.

RC00229-01

612. The primary purpose of the passage is to

(A)   assess the validity of a certain view

(B)   distinguish between two phenomena

(C)   identify the causes of a problem

(D)   describe a disturbing trend

(E)   allay concern about a particular phenomenon

Main Idea

This question requires understanding, in general terms, the purpose of the passage as a whole. The first paragraph identifies an area of concern: declines in amphibian populations may constitute a crisis, one that indicates humans' catastrophic effects on the environment. The rest of the passage then goes on to evaluate, as the second paragraph states, whether claims of crisis-level extinctions as a result of human activity are valid. In making this evaluation, the passage discusses the possible causes of extinctions, biologists' prioritization of population declines over extinctions, and the fact that we lack extensive long-term data on amphibian populations.

A **Correct.** The passage's main purpose is to assess whether the view that humans are causing crisis-level declines in amphibian populations is valid.

B The passage takes care, particularly in the third paragraph, to distinguish between population declines and extinctions, but this is not its primary purpose.

C The passage makes clear that it is difficult to identify the real extent of the problem facing amphibian populations, much less identify its causes.

D The first paragraph notes what may seem to be a disturbing trend—the decline in amphibian populations—but the rest of the passage is concerned not with describing that trend in greater detail, but rather with determining whether it is in fact occurring.

E While the passage provides possible grounds for concluding that concern about declining amphibian populations is overblown, it concludes by suggesting that we might, because we lack data, doom species and ecosystems to extinction. Thus, the overall purpose is not to allay concern.

The correct answer is A.

RC00229-02

613. It can be inferred from the passage that the author believes which of the following to be true of the environmentalists mentioned in lines 5–6 ?

(A) They have wrongly chosen to focus on anecdotal reports rather than on the long-term data that are currently available concerning amphibians.

(B) Their recommendations are flawed because their research focuses too narrowly on a single category of animal species.

(C) Their certainty that population declines in general are caused by environmental degradation is not warranted.

(D) They have drawn premature conclusions concerning a crisis in amphibian populations from recent reports of declines.

(E) They have overestimated the effects of chance events on trends in amphibian populations.

Inference

This question asks about the author's view of the environmentalists mentioned in the first paragraph. These environmentalists have claimed, based on amphibian population declines, that the situation is a crisis and that immediate action must be taken. The author, however, states that the declines are only *apparently* drastic and questions whether they are real, thus suggesting that the environmentalists are drawing conclusions in the absence of a complete consideration of the situation.

A The passage indicates that anecdotal reports are insufficient, but so too are other resources. The fourth paragraph of the passage makes clear that there is not enough long-term data available on which to base conclusions about amphibian populations.

B The passage does not indicate that the environmentalists under discussion have conducted research on any animal species.

C The passage does not indicate that the environmentalists in question hold, with certainty, any particular view regarding population declines in general.

D **Correct.** The author argues that the recent declines may have several different causes, and that environmentalists have jumped to a conclusion about the cause of the declines as well as their significance.

E The environmentalists, in attributing population declines to intentional human activity, have more likely underestimated than overestimated the effects of chance events on amphibian populations.

The correct answer is D.

RC00229-03

614. It can be inferred from the passage that the author believes which of the following to be true of the amphibian extinctions that have recently been reported?

(A) They have resulted primarily from human activities causing environmental degradation.

(B) They could probably have been prevented if timely action had been taken to protect the habitats of amphibian species.

(C) They should not come as a surprise, because amphibian populations generally have been declining for a number of years.

(D) They have probably been caused by a combination of chance events.

(E) They do not clearly constitute evidence of general environmental degradation.

Inference

The author suggests throughout the passage that recently reported amphibian extinctions may have several different causes: they may be due to any number of chance events, for example, or may simply be the result of a small population that finds itself unable to continue under difficult conditions, whatever causes those conditions.

A   The author states in the second paragraph that extinctions may occur without a proximate cause in human activities and does not make a commitment to any particular explanation of the amphibian extinctions.

B   That chance events can cause extinctions suggests that even if habitats had been protected, extinctions still might have occurred.

C   In the second paragraph, the author says that extinctions *should come as no great surprise*, but this option is imprecise. The amphibian populations have not generally *been declining for a number of years*. The author says in the third paragraph that amphibian populations show strong fluctuations; further, in the fourth paragraph, the author says that there is insufficient long-term data to conclude that amphibian populations have been, or are, in decline.

D   The author suggests that the extinctions may have been caused by chance events, but

there is not enough data to know whether or not this is probable.

E   **Correct.** The reported extinctions could have resulted from several different causes; thus, they are not clear evidence of general environmental degradation.

The correct answer is E.

RC00229-04

615. According to the passage, each of the following is true of endangered amphibian species EXCEPT:

(A) They are among the rarest kinds of amphibians.

(B) They generally have populations that are small in size.

(C) They are in constant danger of extinction.

(D) Those with decreasing populations are the most likely candidates for immediate extinction.

(E) They are in danger of extinction due to events that sometimes have nothing to do with human activities.

Application

This question asks what the passage does not say is true of endangered amphibian species. The second paragraph discusses endangered species, stating that they are *always rare, almost always small, and, by definition, under constant threat of extinction*, which may be caused by chance events. The possibility of their extinction, the passage states, depends only on the population size, and not whether that population is increasing or decreasing.

A   The second paragraph mentions rarity as a characteristic of endangered amphibian species.

B   According to the second paragraph, endangered amphibian species are generally those of small populations.

C   The second paragraph states that an endangered population is under constant threat of extinction.

D   **Correct.** The last sentence of the second paragraph states that the probability of extinction due to chance events is independent of how a population changes in size. Immediate extinction would more likely come from such events, whereas population decline is gradual, even if fairly rapid.

E Endangered species, according to the second paragraph, may become extinct due to chance events—that is, events that have nothing to do with human activities.

The correct answer is D.

RC00229-05

616. Which of the following most accurately describes the organization of the passage?

(A) A question is raised, a distinction regarding it is made, and the question is answered.

(B) An interpretation is presented, its soundness is examined, and a warning is given.

(C) A situation is described, its consequences are analyzed, and a prediction is made.

(D) Two interpretations of a phenomenon are described, and one of them is rejected as invalid.

(E) Two methods for analyzing a phenomenon are compared, and further study of the phenomenon is recommended.

Evaluation

This question asks about the organization of the passage as a whole. In the first paragraph, the author tells about a situation that has been interpreted in a particular way by environmentalists. The passage then proceeds to consider whether that interpretation is valid, and while it does not come to a definitive conclusion on that point, the final paragraph warns about the possible consequences of not taking the action recommended by the environmentalists.

A The passage does initially raise a question regarding whether the environmentalists' interpretation of events is valid, but it does not answer that question, for the appropriate long-term data are not available.

B **Correct.** The passage presents environmentalists' interpretation of recent news regarding amphibians, then examines the soundness of that interpretation. Finally, the author warns that postponing environmental action may have disastrous consequences.

C The first paragraph describes a situation of possibly drastic declines in amphibian populations but does not follow this description with an analysis of its consequences.

D The passage suggests that apparent declines in amphibian populations may or may not constitute a crisis, but it does not reject either idea.

E While the passage does imply, in its final paragraph, that long-term data on amphibian populations should be collected, the passage does not compare two methods for analyzing amphibian populations or population declines in those populations.

The correct answer is B.

RC00229-06

617. Which of the following best describes the function of the sentence in lines 35–38 ?

(A) To give an example of a particular kind of study

(B) To cast doubt on an assertion made in the previous sentence

(C) To raise an objection to a view presented in the first paragraph

(D) To provide support for a view presented in the first paragraph

(E) To introduce an idea that will be countered in the following paragraph

Evaluation

The sentence in question discusses the way in which anecdotal reports of population decreases cannot help biologists determine whether those decreases are normal fluctuations, take populations to lower levels that are not actually worrisome, or actually threaten extinctions. This indicates that the view mentioned in the first paragraph—reports of declines indicate a catastrophic crisis—may be mistaken.

A The sentence does not address a particular kind of study; it objects to the use of anecdotal reports in place of actual study.

B The previous sentence describes the possibilities referred to in the sentence in question. The sentence does not cast doubt on any of those possibilities.

C **Correct.** The view that reports of amphibian population declines indicate a crisis, as presented in the first paragraph, is countered by the objection here that there are several possible causes for population declines, and anecdotal reports cannot distinguish among those possibilities.

D   The first paragraph is concerned with articulating the view that amphibian population declines constitute a crisis. This sentence does not support that view; instead, it offers reason to question it.

E   The sentence introduces the idea that amphibian populations have fluctuated in the past, and the following paragraph supports this idea by stating that several amphibian species that appeared almost extinct in the 1950s and 1960s have recovered. Thus, the paragraph does not counter the sentence.

The correct answer is C.

Questions 618–621 refer to the passage on page 505.

Main Idea Summary

The main idea of the passage is that attempts to identify keystone species are complicated by multiple factors, including the difficulty of directly testing for keystone status with controlled experiments and the fact that keystone status appears to depend in complex ways on the contexts in which the species are found. The passage defines a keystone species as one whose effects on its ecosystem *are much larger than would be predicted from its abundance*. It notes that testing for keystone status by removing species from their environment and observing the effects of their absence is problematic. It then discusses one species of starfish to exemplify the difficulties inherent in determining whether a species is a keystone one. Drawing on those examples, the passage describes some ways in which keystone status depends on species' contexts.

RC00556-03

618. The passage mentions which of the following as a factor that affects the role of *P. ochraceus* as a keystone species within different habitats?

(A)   The degree to which the habitat is sheltered from waves

(B)   The degree to which other animals within a habitat prey on mussels

(C)   The fact that mussel populations are often not dominant within some habitats occupied by *P. ochraceus*

(D)   The size of the *P. ochraceus* population within the habitat

(E)   The fact that there is great species diversity within some habitats occupied by *P. ochraceus*

Supporting Idea

This question depends on recognizing what the passage states about the factors affecting *P. ochraceus*'s role as a keystone species, which is different in different habitats. According to the passage, *P. ochraceus* consumes and suppresses mussel populations in some habitats—specifically, those that are wave-exposed—making it a keystone predator in those habitats. But in wave-sheltered habitats, *P. ochraceus* does not play the same role in suppressing mussel populations.

A   **Correct.** The passage clearly states that *P. ochraceus*'s role in wave-exposed habitats differs from its role in wave-sheltered habitats.

B   The passage says that the impact of *P. ochraceus* predation on mussels is not strong in wave-sheltered habitats, but this is not—at least not at all sites—because other animals are preying on the mussels; rather, at least at some sites, it is because mussels are controlled by sand burial.

C   The passage does not suggest that mussel populations are dominant in any habitats occupied by *P. ochraceus*.

D   The size of the *P. ochraceus* population affects the size of the mussel population within wave-exposed habitats, but the passage does not suggest that *P. ochraceus*'s role as a keystone species depends on the size of its population within those habitats.

E   The only other species the passage mentions in conjunction with *P. ochraceus* habitats is the mussel; the passage does not address species diversity in these habitats.

The correct answer is A.

RC00556-04

619. Which of the following hypothetical experiments most clearly exemplifies the method of identifying species' roles that the author considers problematic?

(A) A population of seals in an Arctic habitat is counted in order to determine whether it is the dominant species in that ecosystem.

(B) A species of fish that is a keystone species in one marine ecosystem is introduced into another marine ecosystem to see whether the species will come to occupy a keystone role.

(C) In order to determine whether a species of monkey is a keystone species within a particular ecosystem, the monkeys are removed from that ecosystem and the ecosystem is then studied.

(D) Different mountain ecosystems are compared to determine how geography affects a particular species' ability to dominate its ecosystem.

(E) In a grassland experiencing a changing climate, patterns of species extinction are traced in order to evaluate the effect of climate changes on keystone species in that grassland.

Application

Answering this question depends on recognizing what the author says about identifying species' roles in habitats and then extending that to another situation. The author considers a particular method of studying keystone species problematic: removing a suspected keystone species from its habitat and observing what happens to the ecosystem. The author finds this problematic because interactions among species are complex.

A The author does not discuss counting the members of a population as a problematic way of determining whether that population is a dominant species.

B The method that the author finds problematic has to do with observing what happens to an ecosystem when a keystone species is removed from it, not with observing what happens to a different ecosystem when the species is introduced into it.

C **Correct.** The author states explicitly that removing a species from a habitat in order to determine its keystone status is problematic. Removing the monkeys from their habitat is a clear example of this problematic practice.

D Comparison of habitats in order to determine geography's effect on a particular species' dominance would most likely find favor with the author, for this is the approach the author seems to advocate in investigating *P. ochraceus*'s keystone status.

E The author does not discuss tracing patterns of extinction or changing climates in the passage.

The correct answer is C.

RC00556-05

620. Which of the following, if true, would most clearly support the argument about keystone status advanced in the last sentence of the passage (lines 24–31)?

(A) A species of bat is primarily responsible for keeping insect populations within an ecosystem low, and the size of the insect population in turn affects bird species within that ecosystem.

(B) A species of iguana occupies a keystone role on certain tropical islands, but does not play that role on adjacent tropical islands that are inhabited by a greater number of animal species.

(C) Close observation of a savannah ecosystem reveals that more species occupy keystone roles within that ecosystem than biologists had previously believed.

(D) As a keystone species of bee becomes more abundant, it has a larger effect on the ecosystem it inhabits.

(E) A species of moth that occupies a keystone role in a prairie habitat develops coloration patterns that camouflage it from potential predators.

Evaluation

To answer this question, focus on the argument advanced in the last sentence of the passage and identify what information would support that argument. In the last sentence of the passage, the author claims that keystone status depends on context. The author then offers three contextual factors that may affect a species' keystone status: geography, community diversity (i.e., the number of species in a given habitat), and length of species interaction. Evidence supporting this argument would show that context is important to a species' keystone status.

A   This scenario does not indicate anything about keystone status; this is simply a description of how species populations in a single ecosystem affect one another.

B   **Correct.** That the iguana is a keystone species in a location that has limited species diversity but not a keystone species in a location that has greater species diversity suggests that keystone status does indeed depend on context. Thus, this example supports the author's argument in the last sentence of the passage.

C   That biologists were mistaken about keystone species in a particular ecosystem does not have a bearing on whether keystone status is context dependent.

D   It is not surprising that an increase in a species' population would lead to that species having a larger effect on its ecosystem—but this does not speak directly to the question of whether keystone status itself depends on context.

E   A keystone species enhancing its ability to survive in a single ecosystem does not lend any support to the idea that keystone status depends on context. The moth's keystone status would have to undergo some change for this to have a bearing on the question of context.

The correct answer is B.

RC00556-06

621. The passage suggests which of the following about the identification of a species as a keystone species?

(A) Such an identification depends primarily on the species' relationship to the dominant species.

(B) Such an identification can best be made by removing the species from a particular ecosystem and observing changes that occur in the ecosystem.

(C) Such an identification is likely to be less reliable as an ecosystem becomes less diverse.

(D) Such an identification seems to depend on various factors within the ecosystem.

(E) Such an identification can best be made by observing predation behavior.

Inference

Answering this question requires identifying how the passage suggests that keystone species should be identified. The passage identifies a particular way in which keystone status should *not* be determined: removing a species and observing what happens to the ecosystem. The passage also argues that keystone status depends strongly on context: that is, an ecosystem's characteristics, including its geography and inhabitants, determine its keystone species.

A   While the passage uses an example of a keystone species, *P. ochraceus*, which preys on a species that would, in the keystone species' absence, be dominant, there is nothing to suggest that a keystone species *must* have a particular relationship with the dominant, or potentially dominant, species in an ecosystem.

B   The passage explicitly states that this method of identification would be problematic.

C   A reduction in an ecosystem's diversity might alter which species occupy keystone roles in that ecosystem, the passage suggests, but there is no indication that identifying such species would become more difficult.

D   **Correct.** If, as the passage suggests, keystone status for any given species depends on the context of the ecosystem in which it lives, then it is likely that identifying keystone species depends strongly on understanding what factors of the ecosystem contribute to creating keystone status. The passage lists such factors as geography, community diversity, and species interaction.

E   While the passage uses a predator, *P. ochraceus*, as its example of a keystone species, there is no indication that predation is an essential component of the actual definition of keystone species (*one whose effects are much larger than would be predicted from its abundance*).

The correct answer is D.

Questions 622–624 refer to the passage on page 507.

Main Idea Summary

The first paragraph of the passage indicates that the 1981 discovery of fossil remains of the tiny soft-bodied animals known as conodonts shed light on hypotheses regarding the development of vertebrate skeletons. The second paragraph states that the traditional view was that the vertebrate skeleton had developed as a defensive mechanism and that teeth were secondary features. The paragraph mentions, however, that other paleontologists argued that certain characteristics of vertebrates would not have evolved had the vertebrates not been predators and that teeth were more primitive than external armor. The final paragraph argues that certain features of conodonts suggest that hard parts first evolved in the mouth to improve predation, and aggression rather than protection drove the origin of the vertebrate skeleton. Supporting these latter claims is the primary purpose of the passage.

RC00073-01

622. According to the passage, the anatomical evidence provided by the preserved soft bodies of conodonts led scientists to conclude that

(A) conodonts had actually been invertebrate carnivores

(B) conodonts' teeth were adapted from protective bony scales

(C) conodonts were primitive vertebrate suspension feeders

(D) primitive vertebrates with teeth appeared earlier than armored vertebrates

(E) scientists' original observations concerning the phosphatic remains of conodonts were essentially correct

Supporting Idea

This question depends on understanding how a particular type of evidence—the preserved soft bodies of conodonts—supports a particular conclusion stated in the passage. The third paragraph makes this relationship explicit, explaining that certain features of conodonts show them to be more primitive than other vertebrates. Further, those features indicate that they came before ostracoderms and other armored jawless fishes. These remains support the conclusion stated in the second paragraph regarding teeth being more primitive than external armor.

A The passage states explicitly that conodonts were not invertebrates but rather vertebrates.

B This view is attributed to certain traditionalists but is contradicted by other paleontological evidence presented in the second and third paragraphs. According to the third paragraph, the evidence provided by the preserved soft bodies of conodonts undermines this traditional view.

C The final sentence of the passage indicates that the evidence in question supports the conclusion that conodonts were predators rather than suspension feeders.

D **Correct.** The third paragraph explains how conodonts' remains support the conclusion that teeth were more primitive than external armor.

E The second paragraph explains that originally, scientists thought that early vertebrates were not predators—but the remainder of the passage indicates that this idea is inconsistent with more recent evidence described in the passage.

The correct answer is D.

RC00073-03

623. The second paragraph in the passage serves primarily to

(A) outline the significance of the 1981 discovery of conodont remains to the debate concerning the development of the vertebrate skeleton

(B) contrast the traditional view of the development of the vertebrate skeleton with a view derived from the 1981 discovery of conodont remains

(C) contrast the characteristics of the ostracoderms with the characteristics of earlier soft-bodied vertebrates

(D) explain the importance of the development of teeth among the earliest vertebrate predators

(E) present the two sides of the debate concerning the development of the vertebrate skeleton

Evaluation

This question depends on understanding the second paragraph in the context of the passage as a whole. The second paragraph begins by noting the traditional view of the vertebrate skeleton—that it was a defense against predators—and then goes on to explain that other paleontologists argued against this idea, claiming instead that vertebrates began as predators and that teeth were a more primary feature than external armor.

A   The second paragraph focuses on describing the debate rather than on the distinctive contribution of the 1981 discovery to that debate.

B   The second paragraph does not explicitly indicate whether the opposition to the traditional view originally rested on the 1981 discovery of conodont remains. In fact, the surrounding discussion, in the first and third paragraphs, suggests that the discovery in 1981 turned out to support the opposing view, which some paleontologists already held at that time.

C   The mention of ostracoderms in the second paragraph merely serves to indicate how the traditionalists' arguments might have seemed plausible. The paragraph as a whole is not devoted to contrasting the ostracoderms with earlier soft-bodied vertebrates.

D   The development of teeth figures in the second paragraph, but this development is mentioned first as a feature that some believed to have been adapted from protective scales; only the final sentence of the paragraph connects teeth to early vertebrate predators.

E   **Correct.** According to the passage, the debate concerning the development of the vertebrate skeleton hinges on whether vertebrates began as predators, with teeth, or whether skeletal defenses such as external armor evolved first. The primary purpose of the second paragraph is to distinguish these two sides.

The correct answer is E.

RC00073-08

624. It can be inferred that on the basis of the 1981 discovery of conodont remains, paleontologists could draw which of the following conclusions?

(A)   The earliest vertebrates were sedentary suspension feeders.

(B)   Ostracoderms were not the earliest vertebrates.

(C)   Defensive armor preceded jaws among vertebrates.

(D)   Paired eyes and adaptations for activity are definitive characteristics of vertebrates.

(E)   Conodonts were unlikely to have been predators.

Inference

What could paleontologists conclude, based on the 1981 discovery of conodont remains? That discovery, according to the passage, supported the view of certain paleontologists that the earliest vertebrates were predators with teeth—unlike the ostracoderms, which had no jaws.

A   According to the second paragraph, traditionalists believed that early vertebrates were sedentary suspension feeders. But the 1981 discovery supported instead the hypothesis that early vertebrates were predators instead.

B   **Correct.** According to the third paragraph, the conodonts' body structures indicated that they were more primitive than the ostracoderms, so the ostracoderms must not have been the earliest vertebrates.

C   Traditionalists argued that teeth were adapted from bony scales that provided defensive armor, but the 1981 discovery suggested that teeth preceded such scales.

D   Paleontologists knew prior to the 1981 discovery that paired eyes and other adaptations are characteristics of vertebrates. They used this knowledge to help them interpret the 1981 discovery.

E   The third paragraph indicates that conodonts, given their teeth, were most likely predators.

The correct answer is B.

Questions 625–632 refer to the passage on page 509.

RC00013-01

625. The primary purpose of the passage is to

(A) advocate a more positive attitude toward technological change

(B) discuss the implications for employees of the modernization of a telephone exchange

(C) consider a successful challenge to the constructivist view of technological change

(D) challenge the position of advocates of technological determinism

(E) suggest that the social causes of technological change should be studied in real situations

Main Idea

This question asks for an assessment of what the passage as a whole is doing. The passage introduces Clark's study as a *solid contribution* (line 3) to the debate between technological determinists and social constructivists. In the second paragraph, Braverman is introduced as holding a position of social constructivism, a position that Clark takes issue with. In the final paragraph, the passage holds that *Clark refutes the extremes of the constructivists* (line 31), and Clark's arguments challenging social constructivism are then described.

A The passage takes no position on the merits of technological change but is concerned only with the role of such change in society.

B The passage mentions telephone exchange workers as an example that helps illustrate the more central debate between determinists and constructivists.

C **Correct.** The passage is mainly concerned with portraying Clark's view as a successful challenge to constructivism.

D The passage describes Clark's view as a successful challenge to social constructivism, not technological determinism.

E The passage is concerned with describing a challenge to social constructivism and not with suggesting the context in which technological change ought to be studied.

The correct answer is C.

RC00013-02

626. Which of the following statements about the modernization of the telephone exchange is supported by information in the passage?

(A) The new technology reduced the role of managers in labor negotiations.

(B) The modernization was implemented without the consent of the employees directly affected by it.

(C) The modernization had an impact that went significantly beyond maintenance routines.

(D) Some of the maintenance workers felt victimized by the new technology.

(E) The modernization gave credence to the view of advocates of social constructivism.

Supporting Idea

This question requires recognizing information contained in the passage. The passage states in the first paragraph that Clark's study focused on the modernization of a telephone exchange and the effect this had on maintenance work and workers. After describing Braverman's analysis in the second paragraph as being at odds with Clark's views, the passage discusses Clark's views in more detail in the final paragraph. As part of this discussion, the passage notes that Clark shows how a change from *maintenance-intensive electromechanical switches to semielectronic switching systems* at the telephone exchange *altered work tasks, skills, training opportunities, administration, and organization of workers* (lines 42–44). Thus, the passage shows that the modernization of the telephone exchange affected much more than maintenance routines.

A The passage does not discuss whether new technology reduces the role of managers in labor negotiations.

B The passage does not discuss the role of employee consent in the modernization of the telephone exchange.

C **Correct.** The passage states that the modernization of the telephone exchange affected tasks, skills, training, administration, and the organization of workers.

D   The passage does not suggest that maintenance workers felt victimized by the modernization of the telephone exchange.

E   The passage describes modernization as a fact viewable from a perspective of social constructivism or technological determinism, but that does not in itself support either view.

The correct answer is C.

RC00013-03

627. Which of the following most accurately describes Clark's opinion of Braverman's position?

(A)   He respects its wide-ranging popularity.

(B)   He disapproves of its misplaced emphasis on the influence of managers.

(C)   He admires the consideration it gives to the attitudes of the workers affected.

(D)   He is concerned about its potential to impede the implementation of new technologies.

(E)   He is sympathetic to its concern about the impact of modern technology on workers.

Inference

Answering this question requires inferring what the passage's author likely believes. The passage describes Braverman's position as one of mainstream social constructivism (lines 23–24), a position that Clark takes issue with. Although it describes Braverman's position, the rest of the passage is devoted to showing how Clark's position takes issue with Braverman's. In the second paragraph, the passage describes Clark as holding that *technology can be a primary determinant of social and managerial organization* (lines 9–11), which suggests that managers are sometimes subordinate to technological change. In lines 15–17, however, Braverman is described as holding that *the shape of a technological system is subordinate to the manager's desire to wrest control of the labor process from the workers*, which shows that Clark and Braverman are at odds on this point.

A   Since the passage says that Clark believes an important insight *has been obscured by the recent sociological fashion* that Braverman's

views exemplify (lines 11–14), one cannot infer that Clark respects the popularity of Braverman's views.

B   Correct. The passage shows that Clark believes managers to have less influence over how technology affects an organization than Braverman claims that they have.

C   The passage does not indicate that Clark admires any aspect of Braverman's position.

D   The passage does not indicate that Clark considers impediments to modernization.

E   The passage does not indicate that Clark is sympathetic to any concerns attributed to Braverman.

The correct answer is B.

RC00013-04

628. The information in the passage suggests that which of the following statements from hypothetical sociological studies of change in industry most clearly exemplifies the social constructivists' version of technological determinism?

(A)   It is the available technology that determines workers' skills, rather than workers' skills influencing the application of technology.

(B)   All progress in industrial technology grows out of a continuing negotiation between technological possibility and human need.

(C)   Some organizational change is caused by people; some is caused by computer chips.

(D)   Most major technological advances in industry have been generated through research and development.

(E)   Some industrial technology eliminates jobs, but educated workers can create whole new skills areas by the adaptation of the technology.

Application

This question requires understanding different points of view discussed in the passage. In the first paragraph, the passage mentions the debate involving technological determinism and social constructivism. In the second and third paragraphs, the passage uses Braverman's analysis to illustrate the social constructivists' position and in the third paragraph suggests that the constructivists are *misrepresenting technological determinism* (line 24). In lines 29–30, the constructivists are reported to hold that technological determinism views technology as *existing outside society, capable of directly influencing skills and work organization.*

A **Correct.** This statement is consistent with the constructivists' view that technological determinism sees technology as outside of society, influencing workers' skills.

B The passage states that the constructivists hold that *technological determinists are supposed to believe . . . that machinery imposes appropriate forms of order on society* (lines 25–27), suggesting that no negotiation is present.

C According to the description of them in the passage, constructivists portray technological determinists as believing that technology, not people, drives organizational change.

D The passage does not portray either constructivists or determinists as being concerned with technological research and development.

E The passage does not portray either constructivists or determinists as being concerned with technology-driven job elimination or creation.

The correct answer is A.

RC00013-05

629. The information in the passage suggests that Clark believes that which of the following would be true if social constructivism had not gained widespread acceptance?

(A) Businesses would be more likely to modernize without considering the social consequences of their actions.

(B) There would be greater understanding of the role played by technology in producing social change.

(C) Businesses would be less likely to understand the attitudes of employees affected by modernization.

(D) Modernization would have occurred at a slower rate.

(E) Technology would have played a greater part in determining the role of business in society.

Inference

Answering this question involves understanding a point of view as it is described in the passage. The passage aligns Clark's study closely with the technological determinists, summarizing his view in lines 9–11: *technology can be a primary determinant of social and managerial organization.* In the following sentence, the passage states that Clark believes that *this possibility is obscured by the recent sociological fashion, exemplified by Braverman's analysis* (lines 11–13). After illustrating Braverman's analysis, the passage then states that it represents *social constructivism.*

A According to the passage, Clark holds that constructivists obscure how modernization might have social consequences.

B **Correct.** According to the passage, Clark sees constructivism as obscuring the possibility that technology plays a primary role in social change.

C The passage does not discuss how the attitudes of employees are perceived by their employers.

D The passage describes a debate about the history and sociology of technology; it does not suggest that sociological analyses affect the pace of modernization.

E The passage describes a debate about the history and sociology of technology; it does not suggest that sociological analyses affect the role that technology plays in business.

The correct answer is B.

RC00013-07

630. According to the passage, constructivists employed which of the following to promote their argument?

(A) Empirical studies of business situations involving technological change

(B) Citation of managers supportive of their position

(C) Construction of hypothetical situations that support their view

(D) Contrasts of their view with a misstatement of an opposing view

(E) Descriptions of the breadth of impact of technological change

Supporting Idea

Answering this question involves recognizing information given in the passage. The passage indicates that a debate exists between technological determinists and social constructivists, suggesting that these views are in opposition. The passage goes on to state that *constructivists gain acceptance by misrepresenting technological determinism* (lines 23–24). This misrepresentation is presented as the *alternative to constructivism* (lines 27–28), suggesting that constructivists promoted their own view by contrasting it with a misrepresentation of determinists' views.

A   The passage mentions empirical studies in relation to Clark's study but not Braverman's analysis.

B   The passage does not mention that managers were supportive of any particular point of view within the sociology of technology.

C   The passage does not mention any hypothetical situations as being used by the constructivists in support of their view.

D   **Correct.** The passage indicates that the constructivists have come into fashion by contrasting their own views with a misrepresentation of the views of technological determinists.

E   The passage does not describe the constructivists as making determinations regarding the degree of impact that technological change has on social or managerial organization.

The correct answer is D.

RC00013-08

631. The author of the passage uses the expression "are supposed to" in line 25 primarily in order to

(A)   suggest that a contention made by constructivists regarding determinists is inaccurate

(B)   define the generally accepted position of determinists regarding the implementation of technology

(C)   engage in speculation about the motivation of determinists

(D)   lend support to a comment critical of the position of determinists

(E)   contrast the historical position of determinists with their position regarding the exchange modernization

Evaluation

This question requires understanding how a particular phrase functions in the passage as a whole. In the third paragraph the passage states that *constructivists gain acceptance by misrepresenting technological determinism* (lines 23–24) and follows this claim with an example of this misrepresentation, stating that *technological determinists are supposed to believe, for example* (lines 25–26). This line implies that the constructivist view of the determinists is inaccurate.

A   **Correct.** The passage uses the expression in part to provide an example of the constructivists' misrepresentation of the determinists.

B   The passage indicates that the view attributed to the determinists is a misrepresentation, not one that is generally accepted by determinists.

C   The expression in the passage is part of a discussion about the motivation of constructivists, not determinists.

D   The expression in the passage is part of a discussion that is critical of the constructivists, not the determinists.

E   The passage does not describe either the historical position of determinists or their position on the exchange modernization.

The correct answer is A.

RC00013-09

632. Which of the following statements about Clark's study of the telephone exchange can be inferred from information in the passage?

(A)   Clark's reason for undertaking the study was to undermine Braverman's analysis of the function of technology.

(B)   Clark's study suggests that the implementation of technology should be discussed in the context of conflict between labor and management.

(C)   Clark examined the impact of changes in the technology of switching at the exchange in terms of overall operations and organization.

(D) Clark concluded that the implementation of new switching technology was equally beneficial to management and labor.

(E) Clark's analysis of the change in switching systems applies only narrowly to the situation at the particular exchange that he studied.

Inference

This question requires understanding what the passage implies in its discussion of a point of view. The details of Clark's views are discussed primarily in the final paragraph. The passage states that on an empirical level, Clark demonstrates that technological change regarding switches at the telephone exchange *altered work tasks, skills, training opportunities, administration, and organization of workers* (lines 42–44). The passage goes on to state Clark's contention that these changes even influenced negotiations between management and labor unions.

A The passage indicates that Clark's study addressed the extremes of both technological determinism and social constructivism. It cites Braverman as a proponent of social constructivism but provides no evidence that Clark's motivation in beginning his study was specifically to target an analysis offered by Braverman.

B The passage indicates that Clark attributed some organizational change to the way labor and management negotiated the introduction of technology but does not mention conflict between them.

C **Correct.** According to the passage, Clark concludes that changes to the technology of switches had an influence on several aspects of the overall operations and organization of the telephone exchange.

D The passage does not indicate that Clark assesses the benefits of technological change to either labor or management.

E The passage indicates that Clark believes the change in switching technology influenced many aspects of the overall operations of the telephone exchange.

The correct answer is C.

Questions 633–637 refer to the passage on page 511.

Main Idea Summary

The central question addressed by the passage is whether, during the period 1794 to 1830, judges in the United States were prejudiced against patent holders. After a brief introduction to the history of patents, the author presents some purported evidence that the courts during this period had an antipatent bias. The passage then presents some considerations that weigh against such a conclusion. The main idea of the passage, implied in the chain of reasoning in the second paragraph but not explicitly stated, is that the pattern of judgments against patentees during the period in question was probably due to the fact that many patents had been awarded without merit rather than to an antipatent bias of the judges.

RC00650-02

633. The passage implies that which of the following was a reason that the proportion of verdicts in favor of patentees began to increase in the 1830s?

(A) Patent applications approved after 1836 were more likely to adhere closely to patent law.

(B) Patent laws enacted during the 1830s better defined patent rights.

(C) Judges became less prejudiced against patentees during the 1830s.

(D) After 1836, litigated cases became less representative of the population of patent disputes.

(E) The proportion of patent disputes brought to trial began to increase after 1836.

Inference

The question asks which statement can be reasonably inferred, from information provided in the passage, to be a reason for the increase in proportion of verdicts favoring patentees, starting in the 1830s. The second paragraph argues that what changed in that decade was not judges' attitudes toward patent law, but the types of patent cases that were litigated. It explains that a law passed in 1836 required that, for the first time in U.S. history, applications for patents had to be examined for their adherence to patent law before a patent would be issued. This information implies that patents granted after 1836 were more likely to adhere to patent law and were thus more likely to be upheld in court.

A **Correct.** The passage implies that patents granted after the 1836 law went into effect were more likely to adhere to patent law.

B The passage does not indicate that any law mentioned made changes to the definition of patent rights; rather, the passage indicates that the patent system was revised to require that patent applications be reviewed for adherence to existing law.

C The passage rejects the explanation that judges' attitudes toward patent rights became more favorable.

D The passage indicates that the population of disputes that were litigated changed after 1836, but it does not suggest that the population of litigated disputes differed from that of patent disputes as a whole.

E The passage does not indicate any change in the proportion of patent disputes brought to trial.

The correct answer is A.

RC00650-03

634. The passage implies that the scholars mentioned in line 8 would agree with which of the following criticisms of the American patent system before 1830?

(A) Its definition of property rights relating to inventions was too vague to be useful.

(B) Its criteria for the granting of patents were not clear.

(C) It made it excessively difficult for inventors to receive patents.

(D) It led to excessive numbers of patent-infringement suits.

(E) It failed to encourage national economic growth.

Inference

This question asks about a statement implied by the passage. The scholars mentioned in line 8 question whether U.S. patent law achieved its goal. That goal is described in the first sentence

of the passage: to encourage America's economic growth. Thus, it is reasonable to conclude that the scholars would criticize the pre-1830 patent system for failing to encourage economic growth.

A The scholars contend that judges rejected patents for arbitrary reasons, not because the definition of property rights was vague.

B The passage does not indicate that the scholars were critical of the criteria for granting patents.

C The scholars are concerned with inventors' attempts to protect their patents, not the difficulty of acquiring a patent in the first place.

D The passage does not imply that the scholars in question believed that too many patent-infringement suits were brought to court, but rather that too few succeeded.

E **Correct.** The scholars doubt that patent law helped to achieve its goal, which was to encourage economic growth.

The correct answer is E.

RC00650-06

635. It can be inferred from the passage that the frequency with which pre-1830 cases have been cited in court decisions is an indication that

(A) judicial support for patent rights was strongest in the period before 1830

(B) judicial support for patent rights did not increase after 1830

(C) courts have returned to judicial standards that prevailed before 1830

(D) verdicts favoring patentees in patent-infringement suits did not increase after 1830

(E) judicial bias against patentees persisted after 1830

Inference

The question asks what is indicated by the frequency with which pre-1830 cases have been cited in court decisions. The second paragraph rejects some scholars' claims that judges prior to the 1830s were *antipatent*, while judges after that time were more accepting of patent rights. The passage supports its critique by pointing out that decisions made by judges before the 1830s have been cited as precedents by later judges just as frequently as post-1830s decisions have been. This implies that later judges' attitudes toward patent rights were similar to those of pre-1830s judges. Thus, there is no reason to believe judges' attitudes toward patent rights changed at that time.

A   The passage argues that judicial support for patents did not change in the 1830s.

B   Correct. Pre-1830s court decisions have been cited as frequently as later decisions, suggesting no change in judges' attitudes.

C   The passage does not indicate that judicial standards changed from, and then returned to, those that prevailed before 1830.

D   Although actual numbers of favorable verdicts are not mentioned, the passage indicates that the proportion of verdicts decided in favor of patentees did, in fact, increase beginning in the 1830s.

E   The passage rejects the notion that judges were biased against patentees either before or after 1830.

The correct answer is B.

RC00650-07

636. It can be inferred from the passage that the author and the scholars referred to in line 21 disagree about which of the following aspects of the patents defended in patent-infringement suits before 1830?

(A)   Whether the patents were granted for inventions that were genuinely useful

(B)   Whether the patents were actually relevant to the growth of the United States economy

(C)   Whether the patents were particularly likely to be annulled by judges

(D)   Whether the patents were routinely invalidated for reasons that were arbitrary

(E)   Whether the patents were vindicated at a significantly lower rate than patents in later suits

Inference

The question depends on recognizing differences between two explanations—one favored by the scholars mentioned in line 21, the other favored by the author—for the frequency with which patents were invalidated in U.S. courts prior to 1830. The first paragraph describes the scholars' view that judges before 1830 were *antipatent* and rejected

patentees' claims for *arbitrary reasons*. The author of the passage rejects that view. As an alternate explanation, the author in the second paragraph implies that earlier patents often violated copyright law; this view is supported with reference to an 1836 revision to the patent system which instituted a procedure by which patent applications were inspected to ensure adherence to patent law.

A   The author and the scholars are both focused on protecting inventors' property rights, not with their inventions' utility.

B   Although the passage suggests that the scholars thought America's patent system did not help encourage economic growth, there is no suggestion that either the scholars or the author believes actual patents defended in court were irrelevant to economic growth.

C   Both the scholars and the author believe that patents defended in court prior to 1830 were more likely to be invalidated than were patents in later legal disputes.

D   Correct. The scholars claim that judges before 1830 decided against patentees for arbitrary reasons, but the passage suggests that the patents may have been invalidated because they failed to adhere to patent law.

E   Both the scholars and the author accept that patents were upheld in court less often before 1830 than after.

The correct answer is D.

RC00650-08

637. The author of the passage cites which of the following as evidence challenging the argument referred to in lines 14–15 ?

(A)   The proportion of cases that were decided against patentees in the 1820s

(B)   The total number of patent disputes that were litigated from 1794 to 1830

(C)   The fact that later courts drew upon the legal precedents set in pre-1830 patent cases

(D)   The fact that the proportion of judicial decisions in favor of patentees began to increase during the 1830s

(E)   The constitutional rationale for the 1836 revision of the patent system

Supporting Idea

The question asks what evidence the author brings to bear against the argument referred to in lines 14–15. In the first paragraph, the author summarizes scholars' arguments to the conclusion that judges' attitudes toward patent rights shifted in the 1830s, based on the fact that judges earlier had routinely ruled against patentees in lawsuits whereas judges after that time provided more protection for patent rights. In the second paragraph the author challenges the claim that judges' attitudes shifted. The author provides evidence that judges after the 1830s cited legal precedents set in pre-1830s cases, suggesting that their views had not changed.

A   The proportion of cases decided against patentees in the 1920s is cited as evidence that supports the scholars' argument in the first paragraph, not as evidence challenging their views.

B   The total number of disputes litigated is not mentioned in the passage.

C   **Correct.** The fact that judges after 1830 cited earlier cases as precedents is used as evidence to challenge scholars' claims that judges' attitudes shifted around 1830.

D   The change in the proportion of decisions in favor of patentees is a fact that both the scholars and the author of the passage attempt to explain.

E   No constitutional rationale for the 1836 law is mentioned in the passage.

The correct answer is C.

Questions 638–644 refer to the passage on page 513.

Main Idea Summary

The passage is primarily concerned with surveying various views of the social standing of European women during the Renaissance. The first paragraph discusses Jacob Burckhardt's view that the Renaissance was a period in which women had equality with men; Joan Kelly's contrary view that the Renaissance was a period in which women's status relative both to men and to medieval women was in decline; and a more complex view, held by various feminist scholars, who suggest that Burckhardt and Kelly each drew

too heavily on observations of upper-class Italian women. The second paragraph warns of the risks of conflating "women" and "women writers" in studying the status of Renaissance women, but, despite such a caveat regarding Tina Krontiris's research, praises her contributions to the field. The author sees her as representative of a cautiously optimistic assessment of Renaissance women's achievements while stressing the social obstacles Renaissance women faced and the caution they exercised when opposing cultural stereotypes.

RC00313-01

638. The author of the passage discusses Krontiris primarily to provide an example of a writer who

(A)   is highly critical of the writings of certain Renaissance women

(B)   supports Kelly's view of women's status during the Renaissance

(C)   has misinterpreted the works of certain Renaissance women

(D)   has rejected the views of both Burckhardt and Kelly

(E)   has studied Renaissance women in a wide variety of social and religious contexts

Evaluation

This question focuses on the author's reason for mentioning Krontiris's work. The passage states that Krontiris, in her discussion of six Renaissance women writers, is an example of scholars who are optimistic about women's achievements but also suggest that these women faced significant obstacles. She is a writer who, in other words, agrees with neither Kelly's negative views nor Burckhardt's positive approach.

A   The passage indicates that Krontiris uses the Renaissance women writers' works as historical evidence, not that she offered any criticism of the works themselves.

B   Krontiris's work, according to the author, is cautiously optimistic about women's achievements during the Renaissance. This contradicts Kelly's view that the status of women declined during this time.

C   The author suggests that Krontiris may have erred in taking her six subjects as representative of all women during the

Renaissance, not that she made any misinterpretations of their actual writing.

D   **Correct.** The author uses Krontiris as an example of those feminist scholars who have rejected the overgeneralized approaches of both Kelly and Burckhardt.

E   The author makes clear that Krontiris's study focuses on literate Renaissance women, who constituted a small minority.

The correct answer is D.

RC00313-02

639. According to the passage, Krontiris's work differs from that of the scholars mentioned in line 12 in which of the following ways?

(A)   Krontiris's work stresses the achievements of Renaissance women rather than the obstacles to their success.

(B)   Krontiris's work is based on a reinterpretation of the work of earlier scholars.

(C)   Krontiris's views are at odds with those of both Kelly and Burkhardt.

(D)   Krontiris's work focuses on the place of women in Renaissance society.

(E)   Krontiris's views are based exclusively on the study of a privileged group of women.

Supporting Idea

This question asks what the passage directly states about the difference between Krontiris's work and the feminist scholars mentioned in the first paragraph. The feminist scholars mentioned in the first paragraph explore differences among Renaissance women, particularly their social status and religion, and thus complicate Burckhardt's and Kelly's generalizations. Krontiris's work, on the other hand, focuses on Renaissance women writers, who are a distinctly privileged and small social group.

A   The second paragraph makes clear that Krontiris addresses the obstacles faced by Renaissance women.

B   The passage does not suggest that Krontiris is reinterpreting or drawing on reinterpretations of the work of earlier scholars.

C   The second paragraph shows that Krontiris's work does complicate both Burckhardt's and Kelly's views, but in this, she is in agreement with the feminist scholars mentioned in the first paragraph.

D   Both Krontiris and the feminist scholars mentioned in the first paragraph are concerned with the place of women in Renaissance society.

E   **Correct.** The feminist scholars mentioned in the first paragraph are concerned with women of different social classes and religions, whereas Krontiris's work focuses on a limited social group.

The correct answer is E.

RC00313-03

640. According to the passage, feminist scholars cite Burckhardt's view of Renaissance women primarily for which of the following reasons?

(A)   Burckhardt's view forms the basis for most arguments refuting Kelly's point of view.

(B)   Burckhardt's view has been discredited by Kelly.

(C)   Burckhardt's view is one that many feminist scholars wish to refute.

(D)   Burckhardt's work provides rich historical evidence of inequality between Renaissance women and men.

(E)   Burckhardt's work includes historical research supporting the arguments of the feminist scholars.

Supporting Idea

This question asks what the passage says explicitly about why feminist scholars reference Burckhardt's view of Renaissance women. The first paragraph states that Burckhardt's view is that Renaissance women enjoyed *perfect equality* with men, and then follows that by noting how feminist scholars have *repeatedly cited* this view to contrast it with extensive evidence of women's inequality during the Renaissance.

A   The passage does not indicate that any feminist scholars cite Burckhardt to refute Kelly's view. It uses Krontiris as an example of scholars who refute Kelly's point of view to a certain degree, but Krontiris does not use Burckhardt's view as her basis for doing so; Krontiris argues against Burckhardt as well.

B   According to the first paragraph, Kelly's work was in certain ways inconsistent with Burckhardt's view, but that is not a reason why Burckhardt's view is cited by feminist scholars. Rather, according to the passage, they cite it in order to argue against it.

C **Correct.** Many feminist scholars wish to refute Burckhardt's view that Renaissance women and men were equal.

D As the first paragraph makes clear, Burckhardt's work emphasizes equality, not inequality, between Renaissance women and men.

E The passage does not discuss the historical research on which Burckhardt based his work.

The correct answer is C.

RC00313-04

641. It can be inferred that both Burckhardt and Kelly have been criticized by the scholars mentioned in line 12 for which of the following?

(A) Assuming that women writers of the Renaissance are representative of Renaissance women in general

(B) Drawing conclusions that are based on the study of an atypical group of women

(C) Failing to describe clearly the relationship between social status and literacy among Renaissance women

(D) Failing to acknowledge the role played by Renaissance women in opposing cultural stereotypes

(E) Failing to acknowledge the ways in which social status affected the creative activities of Renaissance women

Inference

Line 12 refers to feminist scholars who have rejected both Kelly's and Burckhardt's views of the status of Renaissance women. The next sentence states that the feminist scholars use class and religious differences among Renaissance women to argue against Kelly's and Burckhardt's generalizations, which were based on upper-class Italian women.

A The second paragraph suggests that Krontiris at times conflates Renaissance women writers and women in general, but the passage does not indicate that the

feminist scholars believe this of Kelly or Burckhardt.

B **Correct.** The feminist scholars mentioned study different types of Renaissance women and so reject Kelly's and Burckhardt's conclusions that were based on a group that was not in fact typical.

C Krontiris, not Kelly and Burckhardt, is the scholar who, according to the passage, fails to address the relationship between literacy and social status.

D The passage provides no grounds for determining whether Kelly, Burckhardt, or the feminist scholars mentioned in the first paragraph dealt with Renaissance women's opposition to cultural stereotypes; Krontiris's work is concerned with this question.

E The first paragraph suggests that feminist scholars criticized Kelly and Burckhardt for failing to acknowledge the ways in which social status complicates any generalizations that can be made about Renaissance women's lives, not their creative activities specifically.

The correct answer is B.

RC00313-05

642. The author of the passage suggests that Krontiris incorrectly assumes that

(A) social differences among Renaissance women are less important than the fact that they were women

(B) literacy among Renaissance women was more prevalent than most scholars today acknowledge

(C) during the Renaissance, women were able to successfully oppose cultural stereotypes relating to gender

(D) Renaissance women did not face many difficult social obstacles relating to their gender

(E) in order to attain power, Renaissance women attacked basic assumptions in the ideologies that oppressed them

Inference

The first statement the author makes about Krontiris, in the second paragraph, concerns what the author characterizes as a problem with Krontiris's work. Krontiris takes the Renaissance women writers she studies as representative of all Renaissance women; the author says that designating *women* as the most important grouping fails to consider whether other social differences might make for differences in experience.

A **Correct.** The author indicates that Krontiris's error lies in assuming that women's identity as women trumps social and other differences.

B The author does not suggest that Krontiris assumes inappropriate literacy levels among Renaissance women, but rather that Krontiris does not give sufficient consideration to the idea that women who could read and write most likely led lives very different from those of women who could not read and write.

C The author says that Krontiris suggests that there were many cultural stereotypes that women were not able to oppose effectively.

D Krontiris, according to the author, acknowledges the many social obstacles faced by women on the basis of their gender.

E According to the author, Krontiris's concluding remarks suggest that Renaissance women *seldom attacked the basic assumptions in the ideologies that oppressed them.*

The correct answer is A.

RC00313-06

643. The last sentence in the passage serves primarily to

(A) suggest that Krontiris's work is not representative of recent trends among feminist scholars

(B) undermine the argument that literate women of the Renaissance sought to oppose social constraints imposed on them

(C) show a way in which Krontiris's work illustrates a "cautiously optimistic" assessment of Renaissance women's achievements

(D) summarize Krontiris's view of the effect of literacy on the lives of upper- and middle-class Renaissance women

(E) illustrate the way in which Krontiris's study differs from the studies done by Burckhardt and Kelly

Evaluation

The function of the final sentence of the passage is to indicate how Krontiris's work takes neither a completely positive nor completely negative view of Renaissance women's experiences—i.e., how her work is representative of those authors who are cautiously optimistic about the achievements of Renaissance women.

A The passage discusses Krontiris's work as an example of the trend described in the latter part of the first paragraph and mentioned in the first line of the second paragraph. The last sentence in the passage shows that Krontiris's work is in fact representative of recent trends among feminist scholars.

B The last sentence in the passage states that Renaissance women's opposition to cultural stereotypes was circumscribed, but it also suggests that these women did gain some power for themselves. Thus, the sentence does not serve primarily to undermine the argument that the women sought to oppose social constraints.

C **Correct.** Krontiris's work illustrates the "cautiously optimistic" view by embracing both the idea that Renaissance women could gain a certain amount of power and the idea that the extent of their opposition was limited.

D The last sentence in the passage summarizes Krontiris's view, but that view does not, according to the passage, take into account the effect of literacy on the members of a particular social class.

E The main function of the final sentence of the passage is to take up the idea of the *cautiously optimistic* assessment offered in the penultimate sentence. This does mark a significant departure from both Burckhardt and Kelly, but the distinction between their work and that of other feminist scholars is marked more clearly earlier in the passage.

The correct answer is C.

RC00313-08

644. The author of the passage implies that the women studied by Krontiris are unusual in which of the following ways?

(A) They faced obstacles less formidable than those faced by other Renaissance women.

(B) They have been seen by historians as more interesting than other Renaissance women.

(C) They were more concerned about recording history accurately than were other Renaissance women.

(D) Their perceptions are more likely to be accessible to historians than are those of most other Renaissance women.

(E) Their concerns are likely to be of greater interest to feminist scholars than are the ideas of most other Renaissance women.

Inference

The women Krontiris studied are unusual, the author suggests, because they were literate, thus putting them among the minority of Renaissance women. That they could write, however, means that their written reflections are part of the historical record, whereas the direct impressions of experiences had by Renaissance women who could not write about their lives are lost to history.

A   The author implies that the obstacles faced by Krontiris's subjects may have been different from those faced by other women, not that they were less formidable.

B   The author does not imply that the women studied by Krontiris are seen as more interesting; rather, the author indicates that their work is that which is available for study.

C   The women Krontiris studies were able to record their own history because they, unlike most other Renaissance women, were literate. This does not imply that they were more concerned with recording history accurately.

D   Correct. Because Krontiris's subjects were literate, they were able to write down, and thus preserve for historians, their perceptions in a way that most other Renaissance women were not.

E   The author does not suggest that feminist scholars in general are more interested in the concerns of middle- and upper-class literate women than they are with women of other classes.

The correct answer is D.

Questions 645–648 refer to the passage on page 515.

Main Idea Summary

The main idea of the passage is that observations of asteroid collisions and computer simulations of such collisions indicate that most observed asteroids are loose collections of rocks and only small asteroids are individual, solid rocks. The passage begins by describing how, in theory, one could determine the structure of asteroids by observing the rates at which they spin after collisions. The passage then reports that, using this method, scientists have found that most observed asteroids spin in ways that are inconsistent with their being solid rocks. The second paragraph indicates that the conclusions are supported by computer modeling and then presents a causal explanation for the observed phenomena.

RC00524-02

645. The passage implies which of the following about the five asteroids mentioned in line 12?

(A) Their rotation rates are approximately the same.

(B) They have undergone approximately the same number of collisions.

(C) They are monoliths.

(D) They are composed of fragments that have escaped the gravity of larger asteroids.

(E) They were detected only recently.

Inference

In line 12, *five observed asteroids*, refers to the five asteroids whose rotation rates are exceptions to the strict limit on the rate of rotation found in all other observed asteroids. These five asteroids all have diameters smaller than 200 meters. The passage indicates that if asteroids were all monoliths—that is, single rocks—then their rotation rates would form a bell curve when graphed, but if asteroids were piles of rubble, the tail of the bell curve indicating very fast rotation rates would be missing. Among asteroids larger than 200 meters, this tail is missing, and only the five asteroids described as exceptions have rotation rates falling at the very high end of the bell curve.

A   All that the passage states about the rotation rates of these five asteroids is that they do not obey a strict limit. The passage does not rule out that their rates of rotation are significantly different from one another.

B   According to the passage, frequent collisions occur among asteroids. But the passage does not suggest that asteroids that are of similar sizes, or that have particularly high rotation rates, will be similar in terms of the number of collisions that they have undergone to reach those distinctive states.

C   **Correct.** The second paragraph states that *most small asteroids* should be monolithic, and the five observed asteroids are all smaller than 200 meters in diameter.

D   The five asteroids are most likely not composed of fragments because, as the passage states, small asteroids should be monoliths.

E   The passage notes that researchers have observed these five asteroids, along with others, but it does not indicate when these asteroids were originally detected.

The correct answer is C.

RC00524-04

646. The discovery of which of the following would call into question the conclusion mentioned in line 16 ?

(A)   An asteroid 100 meters in diameter rotating at a rate of once per week

(B)   An asteroid 150 meters in diameter rotating at a rate of 20 times per hour

(C)   An asteroid 250 meters in diameter rotating at a rate of once per week

(D)   An asteroid 500 meters in diameter rotating at a rate of once per hour

(E)   An asteroid 1,000 meters in diameter rotating at a rate of once every 24 hours

Application

The conclusion that the text in line 16 points to is that asteroids with diameters greater than 200 meters are *multicomponent structures or rubble piles*. To call that conclusion into question, an observation would have to suggest that asteroids larger than 200 meters across are not such multicomponent structures. According to the first paragraph, rubble piles cannot be fast rotators: spinning faster than once every few hours would make them fly apart.

A   Nothing in the passage suggests that the behavior of an asteroid 100 meters in diameter is relevant to a conclusion about the behavior of asteroids greater than 200 meters in diameter.

B   Nothing in the passage suggests that the behavior of an asteroid 150 meters in diameter would have any effect on a conclusion about the constitution of asteroids with diameters greater than 200 meters.

C   An asteroid 250 meters in diameter rotating at a rate of once per week would be rotating at a slow enough rate to hold together a pile of rubble. Thus, this observation would be entirely consistent with the conclusion about asteroids larger than 200 meters in diameter.

D   **Correct.** Assuming that an asteroid composed of a pile of rubble is of a great enough density, a rotation rate greater than one revolution every few hours would make it fly apart. So a 500-meter asteroid rotating at a rate of once per hour—that is, faster than the crucial speed—would fly apart if it were not a monolith. The conclusion states that all asteroids larger than 200 meters are multicomponent structures (that is, are not monoliths), so the discovery of a 500-meter asteroid rotating at a rate of once an hour would call into question that conclusion.

E   An asteroid rotating at a rate of once every 24 hours would, regardless of size, be rotating much more slowly than the *once every few hours* that the passage claims would make a pile of rubble of a sufficient density fly apart. So an asteroid with a diameter of 1,000 meters that rotated once per day could be a pile of rubble and not conflict with the conclusion.

The correct answer is D.

RC00524-06
647. According to the passage, which of the following is a prediction that is based on the strength of the gravitational attraction of small asteroids?

(A) Small asteroids will be few in number.

(B) Small asteroids will be monoliths.

(C) Small asteroids will collide with other asteroids very rarely.

(D) Most small asteroids will have very fast rotation rates.

(E) Almost no small asteroids will have very slow rotation rates.

Supporting Idea

Regarding small asteroids, the second paragraph states that they have feeble gravity. Any fragments from impacts would escape that gravity, and thus, the passage states, the small asteroids *should be monolithic*.

A Small asteroids could be few in number, but the passage does not offer such a prediction.

B Correct. This prediction is offered in the second paragraph, based on the fact that small asteroids do not have strong gravitational attraction. Any impact fragments will easily escape the weak gravitational attraction of the small asteroids.

C The passage discusses large asteroids collisions in more detail than small-asteroid collisions, but it provides no basis for predicting how often large and small asteroids will, comparatively, be involved in such collisions.

D The first paragraph indicates that the rotation rates of small asteroids can exceed the upper limit on the rotation rates of large asteroids, but it does not indicate that most small asteroids have rotation rates that exceed this upper limit.

E The passage only indicates that there are few observed exceptions to the upper limit on rotation rates of large asteroids, and these exceptions are all smaller than 200 meters in diameter; the passage does not indicate that there are few small asteroids that have very slow rotation rates.

The correct answer is B.

RC00524-07
648. The author of the passage mentions "escape velocity" (see line 22) in order to help explain which of the following?

(A) The tendency for asteroids to become smaller rather than larger over time

(B) The speed with which impact fragments reassemble when they do not escape an asteroid's gravitational attraction after a collision

(C) The frequency with which collisions among asteroids occur

(D) The rotation rates of asteroids smaller than 200 meters in diameter

(E) The tendency for large asteroids to persist after collisions

Evaluation

This question asks about the purpose of the author's use of the phrase *escape velocity* in the second paragraph. The author is discussing what occurs after an asteroid collision, in which a large asteroid might be blasted to bits. The bits, according to the author, will move slower than their *mutual escape velocity*—that is, the speed at which they would have to move to get away from each other and not reassemble, under the influence of gravity, into a rubble pile.

A The author is emphasizing the asteroid bits that do not escape rather than those that do. Asteroids may become smaller over time, but the fact that most bits move slower than their escape velocity would not help to explain this shrinkage.

B That the bits of asteroid move slower than their escape velocity helps explain why the fragments reassemble, but it does not help explain the speed with which they reassemble.

C   According to the author, asteroid collisions occur frequently, but the escape velocity of the resulting fragments does not help to explain that frequency.

D   The concept of escape velocity may help explain why small asteroids are monoliths, but it has no relevance, at least as far as the passage indicates, to those asteroids' rotation rates.

E   **Correct.** After a collision, it is the asteroid fragments' failure to reach escape velocity that allows the fragments' gravitational pull to reassemble them into a rubble pile.

The correct answer is E.

Questions 649–651 refer to the passage on page 517.

Main Idea Summary

The primary purpose of the passage is to discuss the theory underlying attempts to get particles to travel faster than the speed of light by means of quantum tunneling. The passage states that quantum theory implies that there is a small probability that a particle can tunnel through a solid barrier. The time it takes a particle to tunnel through a barrier increases as the thickness of the barrier increases, but only up to a maximum amount of time; beyond that maximum, the amount of time does not vary no matter the thickness of the barrier. This implies that, given a certain thickness, the particle will exceed the speed of light, and this has received some empirical support.

RC00301-04

649. The author of the passage mentions calculations about tunneling time and barrier thickness in order to

(A)   suggest that tunneling time is unrelated to barrier thickness

(B)   explain the evidence by which Wigner and Eisenbud discovered the phenomenon of tunneling

(C)   describe data recently challenged by Raymond Chiao and colleagues

(D)   question why particles engaged in quantum tunneling rarely achieve extremely high speeds

(E)   explain the basis for Wigner and Eisenbud's hypothesis

Evaluation

This question asks why the author discusses calculations about tunneling time and barrier thickness. According to the passage, these calculations provided the grounds for Wigner and Eisenbud's hypothesis that tunneling particles may travel faster than light.

A   The passage states that tunneling time is related to barrier thickness, up to the point at which tunneling time reaches a maximum.

B   The passage indicates that the phenomenon of tunneling was noted at least as early as 1932. It provides no evidence that Wigner and Eisenbud discovered it.

C   The passage uses Chiao's work to support the idea that tunneling particles may move faster than light, not challenge it.

D   The author describes calculations about tunneling time and barrier thickness in order to explain that particles engaged in quantum tunneling may in fact achieve extremely high speeds, not to explain the rarity of the phenomenon.

E   **Correct.** The calculations about tunneling time and barrier thickness supported Wigner and Eisenbud's hypothesis that quantum tunneling could occur at speeds faster than that of light.

The correct answer is E.

RC00301-03

650. The passage implies that if tunneling time reached no maximum in increasing with barrier thickness, then

(A)   tunneling speed would increase with barrier thickness

(B)   tunneling speed would decline with barrier thickness

(C)   tunneling speed would vary with barrier thickness

(D)   tunneling speed would not be expected to increase without limit

(E)   successful tunneling would occur even less frequently than it does

Inference

The passage states that because tunneling time reaches a maximum, then tunneling speed must increase as barrier thickness increases. But if tunneling time did not reach such a maximum, then speed need not increase without limit; the particle could have as low a speed in thicker barriers as in thinner ones and take longer to tunnel through a barrier.

A   If tunneling time could not reach a maximum, then speed might increase, decrease, or remain the same as barrier thickness increases.

B   If tunneling time could not reach a maximum, then speed might increase, decrease, or remain the same as barrier thickness increases.

C   Tunneling speed could vary with barrier thickness if tunneling time could not reach a maximum, but there is no basis in the passage on which to conclude that this is definitely so.

D   **Correct.** The tunneling particle could have as low a speed in thicker barriers as in thinner ones and simply take longer to make its way through a thicker barrier.

E   The passage states that the probability of successful tunneling declines as the thickness of the barrier increases. However, it does not address the issue of whether the differences in probability of successful tunneling are due to the greater time required to go through thicker barriers.

The correct answer is D.

RC00301-02

651. Which of the following statements about the earliest scientific investigators of quantum tunneling can be inferred from the passage?

(A)   They found it difficult to increase barrier thickness continually.

(B)   They anticipated the later results of Chiao and his colleagues.

(C)   They did not suppose that tunneling particles could travel faster than light.

(D)   They were unable to observe instances of successful tunneling.

(E)   They made use of photons to study the phenomenon of tunneling.

Inference

This question asks about the earliest investigators of quantum tunneling. The passage notes that quantum tunneling's *extreme rapidity* was observed in 1932; thus, the earliest investigators of this phenomenon knew of its existence at that time. Not until 1955 did Wigner and Eisenbud hypothesize that the particles traveled faster than light. Thus, it is logical to infer that the earliest investigators did not imagine such a speed.

A   There is nothing in the passage to suggest that the earliest investigators of quantum tunneling had difficulty manipulating barrier thickness.

B   The passage states that Chiao and his colleagues measured photons moving at 1.7 times the speed of light—but the passage does not provide evidence that the earliest investigators anticipated such speeds.

C   **Correct.** The passage suggests that prior to 1955, investigators of quantum tunneling had not hypothesized that the particles could travel faster than the speed of light.

D   The passage indicates that by 1932, investigators had noted the rapidity of quantum tunneling; although this does not entail that they observed the phenomenon, it is consistent with their having been able to do so.

E   The passage indicates that Chiao's work involves photons, but it does not indicate the type of particles used or observed by the earliest investigators of the phenomenon.

The correct answer is C.

To register for the GMAT™ exam go to www.mba.com/gmat

8.0 Critical Reasoning

8.0 Critical Reasoning

GMAT™ Critical Reasoning questions test the reasoning skills involved in:

- constructing an argument
- evaluating an argument, and
- formulating or evaluating a plan of action.

The questions are based on materials drawn from a variety of sources. Answering the questions does not require any familiarity with these materials' subject matter beyond what is generally known.

Critical Reasoning questions are based on passages typically less than 100 words in length. Unlike Reading Comprehension passages, each Critical Reasoning passage is associated with just one question. On the actual exam, you will see only one passage and question at a time.

While answering Critical Reasoning questions requires no specialized knowledge, you do need to be familiar with such basic logical terms as "premise," "conclusion," and "assumption." The practice Critical Reasoning questions in this chapter illustrate the variety of topics the test may cover, the kinds of questions it may ask, and the level of analysis it requires.

8.1 What Is Measured

Critical Reasoning questions provide one measure of your ability to deal with reasoning.

For purposes of the GMAT exam, any series of statements of which at least one is given as logical support for another can be considered an example of reasoning. Some examples include reasoning for the purpose of justifying belief in a statement, justifying some plan of action, or explaining why a certain phenomenon occurs.

Many Critical Reasoning passages contain or report reasoning. Others display no reasoning and simply present information. Every Critical Reasoning question, however, will require you to engage in reasoning based on its passage. You may, for example, be asked to draw a conclusion from the given information; i.e., to identify, among the answer choices, the one statement the information logically supports. Or you may be asked to identify the one statement that most plausibly explains why a phenomenon described in the passage occurred, or to evaluate whether a particular plan of action is likely to achieve its intended goal.

Many different skills are involved in analyzing and evaluating reasoning. In the GMAT™ Enhanced Score Report, these skills are divided into four fundamental categories: *Analysis, Construction, Critique,* and *Plan*.

- *Analysis* questions primarily test your skill in understanding a piece of logical reasoning as a whole and identifying the relationships among its constituent parts.
- *Construction* questions mainly test your skill in forming cogent arguments—for example, in determining what additional information can be inferred from given information, or what additional information would be needed for an argument to work.
- *Critique* questions test your skill in challenging the cogency of arguments, identifying their strengths and weaknesses, and determining how they could be improved.
- *Plan* questions overlap with both *Construction* and *Critique*. Unlike other Critical Reasoning questions, *Plan* questions are designed to test your skill in constructing and critiquing arguments about proposed courses of action.

The following table lists in greater detail the major skills that Critical Reasoning questions measure:

Question Type	Skill	Examples
Analyzing reasoning structure	Identifying premises, conclusion, explanations, plan rationales, or background information in a passage containing reasoning	• [in a dialogue] *Ming uses which of the following techniques in responding to Wei?* • *Which of the following most accurately describes the functions of each boldfaced part of the passage?*
Drawing conclusions (inference)	Drawing a conclusion from given information	• *Which of the following is most strongly supported by the information provided?* • *Which of the following follows logically from the information provided?*
Identifying sufficient or required assumptions	Recognizing an assumption that can help fill a logical gap in a piece of reasoning	• *Which of the following is an assumption that Fang's reasoning requires?* • *The conclusion follows logically if which of the following is assumed?* • *The plan will fail unless which of the following occurs?*

Question Type	Skill	Examples
Evaluating hypotheses	Identifying a hypothesis that most plausibly explains a phenomenon or event	• *Which of the following, if true, most helps explain the failure to achieve the plan's objective?* • *Which of the following is most likely to contribute to the occurrence of the phenomenon observed?* • *In order to evaluate the force of the archaeologists' evidence, it would be most useful to determine which of the following?*
Resolving apparent inconsistency	Reconciling two apparently conflicting assertions or states of affairs	• *Which of the following most helps to resolve the discrepancy between the reported level of rainfall and the occurrence of flooding in City X?*
Identifying information that strengthens or weakens reasoning	Identifying information that either provides additional support or undermines reasoning	• *Which of the following, if discovered, would cast the most doubt on the engineer's reasoning?* • *Which of the following, if true, would most strengthen the support for the physician's diagnosis?*
Recognizing and describing logical flaws	Identifying reasoning errors such as confusing correlation with causation or confusing a sufficient condition with a necessary one	• *Which of the following, if true, most strongly indicates a flaw in the reasoning?* • *The reasoning attributed to the executive is most vulnerable to which of the following criticisms?*
Identifying a point of disagreement	Precisely identifying the key issue on which two parties disagree, based on the statements they have made	• *Which of the following is the main point of disagreement between Mandeep and Saumya?*
Finding a solution to a practical problem	Recognizing an effective strategy for solving a practical problem	• *Which of the following would most help the polling specialists overcome the difficulty they encountered in surveying a sample of likely voters?*

8.2 Test-Taking Strategies

To answer Critical Reasoning questions, you must analyze and logically evaluate the passage on which each question is based, then select the answer choice that most appropriately answers the question. Carefully read the passage and the question asked about the passage, then read the five answer choices. If the correct answer is not immediately obvious to you, see whether you can eliminate some of the wrong answers. Reading the passage a second time may illuminate subtleties not evident on first reading.

1. **Decide whether you benefit most from reading the passage or the question first.**

   Some test-takers may want to read the passage very carefully first and then read the question. But it can be advantageous to read the question first. Doing so can orient you toward noticing the content or structural features of the passage that are relevant to answering the question. Working through the practice questions in this guide should help you get a good feel for the approach that suits you best.

   Be careful to respond to the precise question asked. For example, here are two questions that, in a hurried reading, could easily be confused:

   i) Which of the following is valued by the most citizens of Nation X?

   ii) Which of the following is most valued by the citizens of Nation X?

   Something valued by the most citizens of Nation X may not be the same as what is generally most valued by the citizens of Nation X. The most justified answer to i) could be *wealth* even if the most justified answer to ii) is *good community relations*.

2. **Determine whether the passage contains reasoning or merely provides information.**

   To determine whether the passage contains reasoning, consider whether one or more of the statements are intended to support the truth of any other statement provided, or to justify a plan of action, or to explain some phenomenon. To help determine this, look for certain sorts of words or phrases, sometimes called "inference indicators," that authors may provide when they are presenting a piece of reasoning. For instance, the word *therefore* is frequently used to indicate a conclusion, and the word *because* is frequently used to indicate a premise or reason. Here are other examples (the list is not exhaustive):

   - Conclusion indicators: *consequently, it follows that, so, hence*
   - Premise indicators: *since, as, for, as is shown by, follows from*

   Some of these words have other uses; for example, *since* can signify time or can signify causation. Also, keep in mind that a passage may contain reasoning even if no such indicators are present. Ask yourself whether any of the statements support the truth of another statement, help explain a phenomenon described in the passage, or help support a plan proposed in the passage. Section 6.2 in the Verbal Review Chapter provides more information on how to identify reasoning in a passage.

3. **Identify the purpose and structure of any reasoning in a passage.**

   A good first step in analyzing passages that contain reasoning is to determine the purpose of the reasoning. Does the reasoning aim to provide logical support for a conclusion? If so, then identifying that conclusion will help. Or perhaps the reasoning aims to explain a phenomenon; i.e., to indicate what has caused the phenomenon to occur. If so, identifying the statement that predicts or hypothesizes the occurrence of the phenomenon will help. A third possibility is that the reasoning provides a rationale for a plan or policy. If so, identifying a statement that indicates the goal of the plan or policy will help.

   Once you have identified the reasoning's purpose, then you can identify the reasoning's structure (i.e., *how* the author makes the argument). Section 6.2.1 in the Verbal Review Chapter provides more information on how to analyze a passage's reasoning structure.

4. **To evaluate reasoning, try to imagine scenarios where the premises are true and the conclusion false.**

Many Critical Reasoning questions will require you to evaluate the soundness of a passage's reasoning. To evaluate reasoning, you do not need to decide whether premises or conclusions are actually true. Determining actual truth is beyond the scope of the test: no test-taker could determine the truth or falsity of every assertion present in Critical Reasoning passages. Moreover, many Critical Reasoning passages refer to fictional scenarios. One technique often helpful in evaluating a piece of reasoning is to try to *imagine* a situation in which the premises would all be true but the conclusion false. If the conclusion would almost certainly be true provided the premises were all true, then the reasoning is typically strong. On the other hand, if the conclusion could likely be false even provided that the premises were all true, then the reasoning is typically weak.

This does not mean that considerations about the real world will not, at times, be helpful in evaluating reasoning. Consider the following:

> Medical procedure A is as effective and cost-efficient as medical procedure B, but has fewer unwanted side-effects than B. Therefore, medical procedure A should be preferred over medical procedure B.

In evaluating this reasoning, you can rely on the obvious consideration that, all else being equal, a procedure with fewer unwanted side-effects is preferable.

Please refer to Sections 6.3 and 6.4 of Chapter 6 for more detailed information on how to evaluate the reasoning in various types of arguments.

8.3 Section Instructions

Go to www.mba.com/tutorial to view instructions for the section and get a feel for what the test center screens will look like on the actual GMAT exam.

8.4 Practice Questions

Each of the Critical Reasoning questions is based on a short argument, a set of statements, or a plan of action. For each question, select the best answer of the choices given.

Questions 652 to 706 - Difficulty: Easy

*CR70041.01

652. Arts advocate: Few universities require that students who are specializing in science and technology take many art courses. However, real progress in science and technology requires an element of creativity, which the arts foster. Thus, to help science and technology students succeed in their careers, universities should increase the number of art courses required for them.

Which of the following would, if true, most strengthen the argument above?

(A) Universities required more art courses for science and technology students in the past.

(B) Participation in art courses increases students' creative thinking in their science and technology courses.

(C) More students who are interested in art would specialize in science and technology if the number of art courses required for those programs were increased.

(D) Some of the most prominent scientists began their careers as artists.

(E) Discussion of science and technology topics in art courses increases creative thinking among students in those courses.

CR53631.01

653. Ramirez: The film industry claims that pirated DVDs, which are usually cheaper than legitimate DVDs and become available well before a film's official DVD release date, adversely affect its bottom line. But the industry should note what the spread of piracy indicates: consumers want lower prices and faster DVD releases. Lowering prices of DVDs and releasing them sooner would mitigate piracy's negative effect on film industry profits.

The argument above relies on which of the following assumptions?

(A) Releasing legitimate DVDs earlier would not cause any reduction in the revenue the film industry receives from the films' theatrical release.

(B) Some people who would otherwise purchase pirated DVDs would be willing to purchase legitimate DVDs if they were less expensive and released earlier than they are now.

(C) The film industry will in the future be able to produce DVDs more cheaply than is currently the case.

(D) Some current sellers of pirated DVDs would likely discontinue their businesses if legitimate DVDs were released faster and priced lower.

(E) Current purchasers of pirated DVDs are aware that those DVDs are not authorized by the film industry.

CR79041.01

654. Harunia Province has a relatively dry climate and is attracting a fast-growing population that has put increasing demands on its water supply. The two companies that supply water to the region have struggled to keep up with demand and still remain profitable. Yet now they are asking Harunian authorities to write residential water-use regulations that could reduce their revenues and restrict their future flexibility in supplying water profitably.

Which of the following would, if true, most logically help explain why the water-supply companies are asking the authorities to regulate residential water use?

(A) The companies are planning large water-transportation and irrigation systems that require the approval of neighboring provinces.

(B) The companies believe regulation is inevitable and that having it in place now will allow better planning and thus future profitability.

(C) Few, if any, Harunian government officials have investments in the companies or serve on their boards of directors.

(D) The companies believe that the population is not likely to continue to grow.

(E) Long-term climate projections suggest that greater rainfall will eventually increase the amount of water available.

---

*These numbers correlate with the online test bank question number. See the GMAT™ Official Guide Question Index in the back of this book.

CR31551.01

655. Loss of the Gocha mangrove forests has caused coastal erosion, reducing fish populations and requiring the Gocha Fishing Cooperative (GFC) to partially fund dredging and new shore facilities. However, as part of its subsidiary businesses, the GFC has now invested in a program to replant significant parts of the coast with mangrove trees. Given income from a controlled harvest of wood with continuing replanting, the mangrove regeneration effort makes it more likely that the cooperative will increase its net income.

Which of the following, if true, would most strengthen the argument that mangrove replanting will increase the Gocha cooperative's net income?

(A) The cost of dredging and shore facilities was shared with the local government.

(B) The GFC will be able to hire local workers to assist with the mangrove replanting.

(C) The GFC derives 10 percent of its revenue from salt-production facilities in an area previously cleared of mangroves.

(D) Mangrove forests tend to increase the commercial fish populations in coastal fishing grounds.

(E) A controlled harvesting of mangrove wood by the GFC would have little effect on coastal erosion.

CR07651.01

656. Executives at the Fizzles Beverage Company plan to boost profits in Country X on their range of fruit-flavored drinks by introducing new flavors based on tropical fruits that are little known there. The executives reason that since the fruit drinks of other companies have none of these flavors, Fizzles will not have to compete for customers and thus will be able to sell the drinks at a higher price.

Which of the following, if true, presents the most serious potential weakness of the plan?

(A) The new fruit drinks would be priced significantly higher than other Fizzles fruit drinks with more conventional flavors.

(B) In a telephone survey, at least one of the consumers contacted said that they preferred many of the new flavors to all of the more familiar flavors.

(C) To build widespread demand for the new flavors, Fizzles would have to launch an advertising campaign to familiarize consumers with them.

(D) Consumers choosing among fruit-flavored drinks of different brands generally buy on the basis of name recognition and price rather than the specific fruit flavor.

(E) Few consumers who are loyal to a specific brand of fruit-flavored drinks would willingly switch to another brand that costs more.

CR33061.01

657. Economist: In 2015, the average per-person amount paid for goods and services purchased by consumers in Country X was the equivalent of $17,570 in United States dollars, just 30 percent of the corresponding figure of $58,566 for Country Y. Yet in 2015, there was already a substantial middle class in Country X that had discretionary income for middle-class consumer goods such as new vehicles, computers, or major household appliances, while a significant portion of the middle class in Country Y did not have sufficient income to purchase such items.

Which of the following, if true, most helps explain the discrepancy in the relationships described by the economist?

(A) There are many consumer goods, such as household appliances, that are produced in Country X to be sold in the Country Y market.

(B) The volume of trade between Country X and Country Y is increasing rapidly in both directions.

(C) The economy of Country Y is recovering from a downturn that affected both Country Y and Country X.

(D) Country X residents pay much less than their Country Y counterparts for housing, transportation, and child care.

(E) In Country Y as well as in Country X, there are few assembly-line jobs in factories that pay a middle-class wage.

CR09616

658. Neuroscientist: Memory evolved to help animals react appropriately to situations they encounter by drawing on the past experience of similar situations. But this does not require that animals perfectly recall every detail of all their experiences. Instead, to function well, memory should generalize from past experiences that are similar to the current one.

The neuroscientist's statements, if true, most strongly support which of the following conclusions?

(A) At least some animals perfectly recall every detail of at least some past experiences.

(B) Perfectly recalling every detail of all their past experiences could help at least some animals react more appropriately than they otherwise would to new situations they encounter.

(C) Generalizing from past experiences requires clear memories of most if not all the details of those experiences.

(D) Recalling every detail of all past experiences would be incompatible with any ability to generalize from those experiences.

(E) Animals can often react more appropriately than they otherwise would to situations they encounter if they draw on generalizations from past experiences of similar situations.

CR52061.01

659. In Country X's last election, the Reform Party beat its main opponent, the Conservative Party, although pollsters, employing in-person interviews shortly before the vote, had projected a Conservative Party victory. Afterwards, the pollsters determined that, unlike Conservative Party supporters, Reform Party supporters were less likely to express their party preference during in-person interviews than they were during telephone interviews. Therefore, using only telephone interviews instead would likely result in more accurate projections for the next election.

Which of the following statements, if true, would most support the argument in the passage?

(A) The number of voters in Country X's next election will be significantly larger than the number of voters in the last election.

(B) The Conservative Party will win the next election.

(C) For each person interviewed in telephone polls before the next election, pollsters will be able to reasonably determine the likelihood of that person voting.

(D) People who expressed no party preference during the in-person interviews shortly before Country X's last election did not outnumber the people who expressed a preference for the Conservative Party.

(E) In the next election, pollsters will be able to conduct more in-person interviews than telephone interviews.

CR40751.01

660. A company that manufactures plastic products from recyclable plastic is, surprisingly, unconcerned that economic conditions may worsen, despite analysts' belief that consumers would then consider ecofriendly plastic products an expensive luxury. But the company reasons that it will be able to lower its prices because, in a weakened economy, other ecofriendly plastic manufacturers are likely to fail. Demand among manufacturers for recyclable plastics as raw materials would then plummet, creating an oversupply of such materials, making them less expensive for the manufacturer to purchase and thus lowering the company's costs.

Which of the following, if true, most weakens the company's reasoning?

(A) Smaller ecofriendly plastic manufacturers are more likely to fail in a weakened economy than larger ecofriendly manufacturers are.

(B) Some retailers whose sales include various companies' ecofriendly plastic products have struggled in recent years despite the overall good economy.

(C) Consumers would likely soon learn of the oversupply of recyclable plastics and cease recycling them, significantly raising manufacturers' raw-material costs.

(D) Retailers, including retailers that cater to consumers seeking certain types of ecofriendly products, may lose some business if economic conditions worsen.

(E) The plastics used by the company in its products were, after a recent investigation by a regulatory body, declared to be safe for consumers.

CR73241.01

661. Researchers asked volunteers to imagine they were running a five-kilometer race against 50 people and then against 500 people, races in each of which the top 10 percent would receive a $1,000 prize. Asked about the effort they would apply in the respective cases, the volunteers indicated, on average, that they would run slower in the race against the greater number of people. A likely explanation of this result is that those of the volunteers who were most *comparatively inclined*—those who most tended to compare themselves with others in the social environment—determined (perhaps unconsciously) that extreme effort would not be worthwhile in the 500-competitor race.

Which of the following would, if known to be true, most help justify the explanation offered above?

(A)   The volunteers who were most comparatively inclined were also those that had the greatest desire to win a $1,000 prize.

(B)   The volunteers who were the least comparatively inclined had no greater desire to win the $1,000 than those who were the most comparatively inclined.

(C)   The volunteers who were most comparatively inclined were likely to indicate that they would run the two races at the same speed.

(D)   The most comparatively inclined volunteers believed that they were significantly less likely to finish in the top 10 percent in the race against 500 than in the race against 50.

(E)   Volunteers were chosen for participation in the study on the basis of answers to various questions designed to measure the degree to which the volunteers were comparatively inclined.

CR41141.01
662. According to a study, after a week of high-altitude living, twenty men had slimmed down. The men, middle-aged residents of low-altitude areas, had been taken to a research station at 2,650 meters (8,694 feet) above sea level. They had unrestricted access to food and were forbidden vigorous exercise, yet they lost an average of 1.5 kilograms (3.3 pounds) during their one-week stay. Clearly, the lower availability of oxygen at higher altitudes, or hypobaric hypoxia, can be said to have caused the weight loss, since

_____.

Which of the following would, if true, most logically complete the argument?

(A)   a decrease in oxygen intake has been shown to depress appetite

(B)   the men all participated in the same kinds of exercise during their stay

(C)   the foods available to the men had fewer calories than the foods they usually ate

(D)   exercise at higher altitudes is more difficult than exercise at lower altitudes is

(E)   several weeks after returning home, the men still weighed less than they had before the study

CR11741.01
663. Editorial: Our city's public transportation agency is facing a budget shortfall. The fastest growing part of the budget has been employee retirement benefits, which are exceptionally generous. Unless the budget shortfall is resolved, transportation service will be cut, and many transportation employees will lose their jobs. Thus, it would be in the employees' best interest for their union to accept cuts in retirement benefits.

Which of the following is an assumption the editorial's argument requires?

(A)   The transportation employees' union should not accept cuts in retirement benefits if doing so would not be in the employees' best interest.

(B)   The only feasible way for the agency to resolve the budget shortfall would involve cutting transportation service and eliminating jobs.

(C)   Other things being equal, it is in the transportation employees' interest to have exceptionally generous retirement benefits.

(D)   Cutting the retirement benefits would help resolve the agency's budget shortfall.

(E)   The transportation employees' union will not accept cuts in retirement benefits if doing so will not allow more transportation employees to keep their jobs.

CR94231.01
664. Researchers hope to find clues about the A'mk peoples who lived in the Kaumpta region about one thousand years ago but who left few obvious traces. The researchers plan to hire the few remaining shamans of the modern-day indigenous people in Kaumpta, who are believed to be descended from the A'mk, to lead them to ancestral sites that may be the remains of A'mk buildings or ceremonial spaces. The shamans were taught the location of such sites as part of their traditional training as youths, and their knowledge of traditional Kaumpta customs may help determine the nature of any sites the researchers find.

Which of the following is an assumption on which the success of the plan depends?

(A)   The researchers have reliable evidence that the A'mk of one thousand years ago built important ceremonial spaces.

(B) The shamans have a reasonably accurate memory of A'mk sites they learned about as youths.

(C) Kaumpta shamans are generally held in high esteem for their traditional knowledge.

(D) Modern technologies available to the researchers are likely to be able to find some A'mk sites easily.

(E) Most or all A'mk sites are likely to be found within the Kaumpta region.

CR09994

665. Astronomer: Most stars are born in groups of thousands, each star in a group forming from the same parent cloud of gas. Each cloud has a unique, homogeneous chemical composition. Therefore, whenever two stars have the same chemical composition as each other, they must have originated from the same cloud of gas.

Which of the following, if true, would most strengthen the astronomer's argument?

(A) In some groups of stars, not every star originated from the same parent cloud of gas.

(B) Clouds of gas of similar or identical chemical composition may be remote from each other.

(C) Whenever a star forms, it inherits the chemical composition of its parent cloud of gas.

(D) Many stars in vastly different parts of the universe are quite similar in their chemical compositions.

(E) Astronomers can at least sometimes precisely determine whether a star has the same chemical composition as its parent cloud of gas.

CR08017

666. With employer-paid training, workers have the potential to become more productive not only in their present employment but also in any number of jobs with different employers. To increase the productivity of their workforce, many firms are planning to maintain or even increase their investments in worker training. But some training experts object that if a trained worker is hired away by another firm, the employer that paid for the training has merely subsidized a competitor. They note that such hiring has been on the rise in recent years.

Which of the following would, if true, contribute most to defeating the training experts' objection to the firms' strategy?

(A) Firms that promise opportunities for advancement to their employees get, on average, somewhat larger numbers of job applications from untrained workers than do firms that make no such promise.

(B) In many industries, employees who take continuing-education courses are more competitive in the job market.

(C) More and more educational and training institutions are offering reduced tuition fees to firms that subsidize worker training.

(D) Research shows that workers whose training is wholly or partially subsidized by their employer tend to get at least as much training as do workers who pay for all their own training.

(E) For most firms that invest in training their employees, the value added by that investment in employees who stay exceeds the value lost through other employees' leaving to work for other companies.

CR93241.01

667. In emerging economies in Africa and other regions, large foreign banks that were set up during the colonial era have long played a major economic role. These institutions have tended to confine their business to the wealthier of banks' potential customers. But development of these countries' economies requires financing of the small businesses that dominate their manufacturing, farming, and services sectors. So economic growth will be likely to occur if local banks take on this portion of the financial services markets, since _____.

Which of the following completions would produce the strongest argument?

(A) local banks tend not to strive as much as large foreign banks to diversify their investments

(B) small farming and manufacturing businesses contribute to economic growth if they obtain adequate investment capital

(C) large foreign banks in emerging economies could, with local employees and appropriate local consultation, profitably expand their business to less wealthy clients

(D) some small businesses are among the wealthier customers of foreign banks in emerging economies

(E) local banks in emerging economies tend to be less risk-averse than foreign banks

CR49551.01

668. Exporters in Country X are facing lower revenues due to a shortage of the large metal shipping containers in which they send their goods by sea to other countries. Fewer containers arrive in Country X due to reductions in imports. This has meant lost orders, costly delays, and a scramble for alternatives, such as air freight, all of which are costlier. Moreover, the revenues of exporters in Country X will probably continue to decline in the near future. This is because other countries are likely to find it increasingly unprofitable to export their goods to Country X, and because _____.

Which of the following would most logically complete the passage?

(A) production of shipping containers in Country X is growing rapidly as a response to the shortage

(B) shipping companies are willing to move containers from country to country only when the containers are full

(C) the cost of shipping alternatives such as air freight is likely to stabilize in the near future

(D) consumers in Country X are purchasing more products than ever before

(E) the worldwide demand for goods made in Country X has only recently begun to rise after a long decline

CR01107

669. Candle Corporation's television stations are likely to have more income from advertisers than previously. This is because advertisers prefer to reach people in the 18- to 49-year-old age group and the number of people in that group watching Candle television is increasing. Furthermore, among Candle viewers, the percentage of viewers 18 to 49 years old is increasing.

Which of the following, if true, would most strengthen the argument that Candle Corporation will receive more income from advertisers?

(A) Advertisers carefully monitor the demographic characteristics of television audiences and purchase advertising time to reach the audiences they prefer to reach.

(B) Among people over 49 years old, fewer viewers of Candle stations buy products advertised on television than do viewers of other stations.

(C) There will be increasingly more advertisements on television that are directed at viewers who are over 49 years old.

(D) Candle stations plan to show reruns of television shows during hours when other stations run shows for the first time.

(E) People 18 to 49 years old generally have less disposable income to spend than do people over 49 years old.

CR12584

670. A provincial government plans to raise the gasoline tax to give people an incentive to drive less, reducing traffic congestion in the long term. However, skeptics point out that most people in the province live in areas where cars are the only viable transportation to jobs and stores and therefore cannot greatly change their driving habits in response to higher gasoline prices.

In light of the skeptics' objection, which of the following, if true, would most logically support the prediction that the government's plan will achieve its goal of reducing traffic congestion?

(A) The revenue from the tax will be used to make public transportation a viable means of transportation to jobs and stores for far more people.

(B) The tax will encourage many residents to switch to more fuel-efficient cars, reducing air pollution and other problems.

(C) Because gasoline has been underpriced for decades, the province has many neighborhoods where cars are the only viable means of transportation.

(D) Most residents who cannot greatly change their driving habits could compensate for high gasoline prices by reducing other expenses.

(E) Traffic congestion is an especially serious problem for people for whom cars are the only viable means of transportation.

CR03940

671. Editorial: The roof of Northtown's municipal equipment-storage building collapsed under the weight of last week's heavy snowfall. The building was constructed recently and met local building-safety codes in every particular, except that the nails used for attaching roof supports to the building's columns were of a smaller size than the codes specify for this purpose. Clearly, this collapse exemplifies how even a single, apparently insignificant departure from safety standards can have severe consequences.

Which of the following, if true, most seriously weakens the editorial's argument?

(A) The only other buildings to suffer roof collapses from the weight of the snowfall were older buildings constructed according to less exacting standards than those in the codes.

(B) The amount of snow that accumulated on the roof of the equipment-storage building was greater than the predicted maximum that was used in drawing up the safety codes.

(C) Because the equipment-storage building was not intended for human occupation, some safety-code provisions that would have applied to an office building did not apply to it.

(D) The municipality of Northtown itself has the responsibility for ensuring that buildings constructed within its boundaries meet the provisions of the building-safety codes.

(E) Because the equipment-storage building was used for storing snow-removal equipment, the building was almost completely empty when the roof collapsed.

CR12078

672. Political theorist: Even with the best spies, area experts, and satellite surveillance, foreign policy assessments can still lack important information. In such circumstances intuitive judgment is vital. A national leader with such judgment can make good decisions about foreign policy even when current information is incomplete, since _____.

Which of the following, if true, most logically completes the argument?

(A) the central reason for failure in foreign policy decision making is the absence of critical information

(B) those leaders whose foreign policy decisions have been highly ranked have also been found to have good intuitive judgment

(C) both intuitive judgment and good information are required for sound decision making

(D) good foreign policy decisions often lead to improved methods of gathering information

(E) intuitive judgment can produce good decisions based on past experience, even when there are important gaps in current information

CR51141.01

673. Supply shortages and signs of growing demand are driving cocoa prices upward. Unusually severe weather in cocoa-producing regions—too much rain in Brazil and too little in West Africa—has limited production. Further, Europe and North America recently reported stronger demand for cocoa. In the first quarter, grinding of cocoa beans—the first stage in processing cocoa for chocolate—rose 8.1 percent in Europe and 16 percent

in North America. Analysts have concluded that cocoa's price will continue to rise at least into the near future.

Which of the following would, if true, most strengthen the reasoning above?

(A) Ground cocoa beans can be stored for long periods before they spoil.

(B) Several European and North American manufacturers that use cocoa have recently improved their processing capacity.

(C) It takes new cocoa trees five or six years before they start bearing fruit.

(D) Governments in Europe and North America are likely to change current restrictions on cocoa imports.

(E) Historically, cocoa production has varied widely from year to year.

CR01295

674. During the earliest period of industrialization in Britain, steam engines were more expensive to build and operate than either windmills or water mills, the other practicable sources of power for factories. Yet despite their significant cost disadvantage, steam-powered factories were built in large numbers well before technical improvements brought their cost down. Furthermore, they were built even in regions where geographical conditions permitted the construction of wind- and water-powered factories close to major markets.

Which of the following, if true, most helps to explain the proliferation of steam-powered factories during the earliest period of industrialization in Britain?

(A) In many areas of Britain, there were fewer steam-powered factories than wind- or water-powered factories in the earliest period of industrialization.

(B) Unlike wind- or water-powered factories, steam-powered factories were fueled with coal, which sometimes had to be transported significant distances from the mine to the site of the factory.

(C) It was both difficult and expensive to convert a factory from wind power or water power to steam power.

(D) In the early period of industrialization, many goods sold in towns and cities could not be mass-produced in factories.

(E) In Britain, the number of sites where a wind- or water-powered factory could be built was insufficient to provide for all of the demand for factory-produced goods at the time.

CR03938

675. Snowmaking machines work by spraying a mist that freezes immediately on contact with cold air. Because the sudden freezing kills bacteria, QuickFreeze is planning to market a wastewater purification system that works on the same principle. The process works only when temperatures are cold, however, so municipalities using it will still need to maintain a conventional system. Which of the following, if true, provides the strongest grounds for a prediction that municipalities will buy QuickFreeze's purification system despite the need to maintain a conventional purification system as well?

(A) Bacteria are not the only impurities that must be removed from wastewater.

(B) Many municipalities have old wastewater purification systems that need to be replaced.

(C) Conventional wastewater purification systems have not been fully successful in killing bacteria at cold temperatures.

(D) During times of warm weather, when it is not in use, QuickFreeze's purification system requires relatively little maintenance.

(E) Places where the winters are cold rarely have a problem of water shortage.

CR05080

676. **Plant scientists have used genetic engineering on seeds to produce crop plants that are highly resistant to insect damage**. Unfortunately, the seeds themselves are quite expensive, and the plants require more fertilizer and water to grow well than normal ones. Accordingly, **for most farmers the savings on pesticides would not compensate for the higher seed costs and the cost of additional fertilizer**. However, since consumer demand for grains, fruits, and vegetables grown without the use of pesticides continues to rise, the use of genetically engineered seeds of this kind is likely to become widespread.

In the argument given, the two portions in **boldface** play which of the following roles?

(A) The first supplies a context for the argument; the second is the argument's main conclusion.

(B) The first introduces a development that the argument predicts will have a certain outcome; the second is a state of affairs that, according to the argument, contributes to bringing about that outcome.

(C) The first presents a development that the argument predicts will have a certain outcome; the second acknowledges a consideration that tends to weigh against that prediction.

(D) The first provides evidence to support a prediction that the argument seeks to defend; the second is that prediction.

(E) The first and the second each provide evidence to support the argument's main conclusion.

CR04159

677. Which of the following most logically completes the passage?

Leptin, a protein occurring naturally in the blood, appears to regulate how much fat the body carries by speeding up the metabolism and decreasing the appetite when the body has too much fat. Mice that do not naturally produce leptin have more fat than other mice, but lose fat rapidly when they are given leptin injections. Unfortunately, however, leptin cannot be used as a dietary supplement to control fat, since _____.

(A) the digestive system breaks down proteins before they can enter the bloodstream

(B) there are pharmaceuticals already available that can contribute to weight loss by speeding up the metabolism

(C) people with unusually low levels of leptin in their blood tend to have a high percentage of body fat

(D) the mice that do not naturally produce leptin were from a specially bred strain of mice

(E) mice whose bodies did produce leptin also lost some of their body fat when given leptin injections

CR05452

678. Suncorp, a new corporation with limited funds, has been clearing large sections of the tropical Amazon forest for cattle ranching. This practice continues even though greater profits can be made from rubber tapping, which does not destroy the forest, than from cattle ranching, which does destroy the forest.

Which of the following, if true, most helps to explain why Suncorp has been pursuing the less profitable of the two economic activities mentioned above?

(A) The soil of the Amazon forest is very rich in nutrients that are important in the development of grazing lands.

(B) Cattle-ranching operations that are located in tropical climates are more profitable than cattle-ranching operations that are located in cold-weather climates.

(C) In certain districts, profits made from cattle ranching are more heavily taxed than profits made from any other industry.

(D) Some of the cattle that are raised on land cleared in the Amazon are killed by wildcats.

(E) The amount of money required to begin a rubber-tapping operation is twice as high as the amount needed to begin a cattle ranch.

CR09963

679. Archaeologists use technology to analyze ancient sites. It is likely that this technology will advance considerably in the near future, allowing archaeologists to gather more information than is currently possible. If they study certain sites now, they risk contaminating or compromising them for future studies. Therefore, in order to maximize the potential for gathering knowledge in the long run, a team of archaeologists plans to delay the examination of a newly excavated site.

Which of the following would be most useful to investigate for the purpose of evaluating the plan's prospects for achieving its goal?

(A) Whether any of the contents of the site will significantly deteriorate before the anticipated technology is available

(B) Whether there will continue to be improvements on the relevant technology

(C) Whether the team can study a site other than the newly excavated site for the time being

(D) Whether the site was inhabited by a very ancient culture

(E) Whether the anticipated technology will damage objects under study

CR01102

680. More and more law firms specializing in corporate taxes are paid on a contingency-fee basis. Under this arrangement, if a case is won, the firm usually receives more than it would have received if it had been paid on the alternate hourly rate basis. If the case is lost, the firm receives nothing. Most firms are likely to make more under the contingency-fee arrangement.

Which of the following, if true, would most strengthen the prediction above?

(A) Firms that work exclusively under the hourly rate arrangement spend, on average, fewer hours on cases that are won than on cases that are lost.

(B) Some litigation can last for years before any decision is reached, and, even then, the decision may be appealed.

(C) Firms under the contingency-fee arrangement still pay their employees on an hourly basis.

(D) Since the majority of firms specialize in certain kinds of cases, they are able to assess accurately their chances of winning each potential case.

(E) Firms working under the contingency-fee arrangement take in fewer cases per year than do firms working under the hourly rate arrangement.

CR67830.02

681. Pretzel Vendor: The new license fee for operating a pretzel stand outside the art museum is prohibitively expensive. Charging typical prices, I would need to sell an average of 25 pretzels per hour to break even. At my stand outside City Hall, with about as many passers-by as at the art museum, I average only 15 per hour. So I could not break even running a stand outside the art museum, much less turn a profit.

Which of the following, if true, most seriously weakens the pretzel vendor's argument?

(A) The pretzel vendor does not sell anything other than pretzels.

(B) People who visit the art museum are more likely to buy pretzels than are people who go to City Hall.

(C) The license fee for operating a pretzel stand outside City Hall will not increase.

(D) People who buy pretzels at pretzel stands are more likely to do so during the lunch hour than at other times.

(E) The city will grant more licenses for pretzel stands outside the art museum than the number it grants for stands outside City Hall.

CR00766

682. Beginning in 1966 all new cars sold in Morodia were required to have safety belts and power steering. Previously, most cars in Morodia were without these features. Safety belts help to prevent injuries in collisions, and power steering helps to avoid collisions in the first place. But even though in 1966 one-seventh of the cars in Morodia were replaced with new cars, the number of car collisions and collision-related injuries did not decline.

Which of the following, if true about Morodia, most helps to explain why the number of collisions and collision-related injuries in Morodia failed to decline in 1966?

(A)   Because of a driver-education campaign, most drivers and passengers in cars that did have safety belts used them in 1966.

(B)   Most of the new cars bought in 1966 were bought in the months of January and February.

(C)   In 1965, substantially more than one-seventh of the cars in Morodia were replaced with new cars.

(D)   An excessive reliance on the new safety features led many owners of new cars to drive less cautiously in 1966 than before.

(E)   The seat belts and power steering put into new cars sold in 1966 had to undergo strict quality-control inspections by manufacturers, whether the cars were manufactured in Morodia or not.

CR14430.02

683. Manufacturers of mechanical pencils make most of their profit on pencil leads rather than on the pencils themselves. The Write Company, which cannot sell its leads as cheaply as other manufacturers can, plans to alter the design of its mechanical pencil so that it will accept only a newly designed Write Company lead, which will be sold at the same price as the Write Company's current lead.

Which of the following, if true, most strongly supports the Write Company's projection that its plan will lead to an increase in its sales of pencil leads?

(A)   The new Write Company pencil will be introduced at a price higher than the price the Write Company charges for its current model.

(B)   In the foreseeable future, manufacturers of mechanical pencils will probably have to raise the prices they charge for mechanical pencils.

(C)   The newly designed Write Company lead will cost somewhat more to manufacture than the Write Company's current lead does.

((D)   A rival manufacturer recently announced similar plans to introduce a mechanical pencil that would accept only the leads produced by that manufacturer.

(E)   In extensive test marketing, mechanical-pencil users found the new Write Company pencil markedly superior to other mechanical pencils they had used.

CR04882

684. Enterprise Bank currently requires customers with checking accounts to maintain a minimum balance or pay a monthly fee. Enterprise plans to offer accounts with no monthly fee and no minimum-balance requirement; to cover their projected administrative costs of $3 per account per month they plan to charge $30 for overdrawing an account. Since each month on average slightly more than 10 percent of Enterprise's customers overdraw their accounts, bank officials predict the new accounts will generate a profit.

Which of the following, if true, most strongly supports the bank officials' prediction?

(A)   Some of Enterprise Bank's current checking account customers are expected to switch to the new accounts once they are offered.

(B)   One third of Enterprise Bank's revenues are currently derived from monthly fees tied to checking accounts.

(C)   Many checking account customers who occasionally pay a fee for not maintaining a minimum balance in their account generally maintain a balance well above the minimum.

(D)   Customers whose checking accounts do not have a minimum-balance requirement are more likely than others to overdraw their checking accounts.

(E)   Customers whose checking accounts do not have a minimum-balance requirement are more likely than others to write checks for small amounts.

CR08330.02

685. Highway Official: When resurfacing our concrete bridges, we should use electrically conductive concrete (ECC) rather than standard concrete. In the winter, ECC can be heated by passing an electric current through it, thereby preventing ice buildup. The cost of the electricity needed is substantially lower than the cost of the deicing salt we currently use.

Taxpayer: But ECC is vastly more expensive than standard concrete, so your proposal is probably not justifiable on economic grounds.

Which of the following, if true, could best be used by the highway official to support the official's proposal in the face of the taxpayer's objection?

(A)   The use of deicing salt causes corrosion of reinforcing steel in concrete bridge decks and damage to the concrete itself, thereby considerably shortening the useful life of concrete bridges.

(B)   Severe icing conditions can cause power outages and slow down the work of emergency crews trying to get power restored.

(C)   In weather conditions conducive to icing, ice

generally forms on the concrete surfaces of bridges well before it forms on parts of the roadway that go over solid ground.

(D) Aside from its potential use for deicing bridges, ECC might also be an effective means of keeping other concrete structures such as parking garages and airport runways ice free.

(E) If ECC were to be used for a bridge surface, the electric current would be turned on only at times at which ice was likely to form.

CR05667

686. In virtually any industry, technological improvements increase labor productivity, which is the output of goods and services per person-hour worked. In Parland's industries, labor productivity is significantly higher than it is in Vergia's industries. Clearly, therefore, Parland's industries must, on the whole, be further advanced technologically than Vergia's are.

The argument is most vulnerable to which of the following criticisms?

(A) It offers a conclusion that is no more than a paraphrase of one of the pieces of information provided in its support.

(B) It presents as evidence in support of a claim information that is inconsistent with other evidence presented in support of the same claim.

(C) It takes one possible cause of a condition to be the actual cause of that condition without considering any other possible causes.

(D) It takes a condition to be the effect of something that happened only after the condition already existed.

(E) It makes a distinction that presupposes the truth of the conclusion that is to be established.

CR08471

687. Chaco Canyon, a settlement of the ancient Anasazi culture in North America, had massive buildings. **It must have been a major Anasazi center**. Analysis of wood samples shows that some of the timber for the buildings came from the Chuska and San Mateo mountains, 50 miles from Chaco Canyon. **Only a major cultural center would have the organizational power to import timber from 50 miles away**.

In the argument given, the two portions in **boldface** play which of the following roles?

(A) The first is a premise used to support the argument's main conclusion; the second is the argument's main conclusion.

(B) The first is the argument's main conclusion; the second is a premise used to support that conclusion.

(C) The first is one of two premises used to support the argument's main conclusion; the second is the other of those two premises.

(D) The first is a premise used to support the argument's main conclusion; the second is a premise used to support another conclusion drawn in the argument.

(E) The first is inferred from another statement in the argument; the second is inferred from the first.

CR04364

688. The Maxilux car company's design for its new luxury model, the Max 100, included a special design for the tires that was intended to complement the model's image. The winning bid for supplying these tires was submitted by Rubco. Analysts concluded that the bid would only just cover Rubco's costs on the tires, but Rubco executives claim that winning the bid will actually make a profit for the company.

Which of the following, if true, most strongly justifies the claim made by Rubco's executives?

(A) In any Maxilux model, the spare tire is exactly the same make and model as the tires that are mounted on the wheels.

(B) Rubco holds exclusive contracts to supply Maxilux with the tires for a number of other models made by Maxilux.

(C) The production facilities for the Max 100 and those for the tires to be supplied by Rubco are located very near each other.

(D) When people who have purchased a carefully designed luxury automobile need to replace a worn part of it, they almost invariably replace it with a part of exactly the same make and type.

(E) When Maxilux awarded the tire contract to Rubco, the only criterion on which Rubco's bid was clearly ahead of its competitors' bids was price.

CR05186

689. Which of the following most logically completes the passage?

Most bicycle helmets provide good protection for the top and back of the head, but little or no protection for the temple regions on the sides of the head. A study of head injuries resulting from bicycle accidents showed that a large proportion were caused by blows to the temple area. Therefore, if bicycle helmets protected this area, the risk of serious head injury in bicycle accidents would be greatly reduced, especially since _____.

(A) among the bicyclists included in the study's sample of head injuries, only a very small proportion had been wearing a helmet at the time of their accident

(B) even those bicyclists who regularly wear helmets have a poor understanding of the degree and kind of protection that helmets afford

(C) a helmet that included protection for the temples would have to be somewhat larger and heavier than current helmets

(D) the bone in the temple area is relatively thin and impacts in that area are thus very likely to cause brain injury

(E) bicyclists generally land on their arm or shoulder when they fall to the side, which reduces the likelihood of severe impacts on the side of the head

CR01867
690. Which of the following most logically completes the argument?

In a typical year, Innovair's airplanes are involved in 35 collisions while parked or being towed in airports, with a resulting yearly cost of $1,000,000 for repairs.

To reduce the frequency of ground collisions, Innovair will begin giving its ground crews additional training, at an annual cost of $500,000. Although this will cut the number of ground collisions by about half at best, the drop in repair costs can be expected to be much greater, since _____.

(A) most ground collisions happen when ground crews are rushing to minimize the time a delayed airplane spends on the ground

(B) a ground collision typically occurs when there are no passengers on the airplane

(C) the additional training will focus on helping ground crews avoid those kinds of ground collisions that cause the most costly damage

(D) the $500,000 cost figure for the additional training of ground crews includes the wages that those crews will earn during the time spent in actual training

(E) most ground collisions have been caused by the least experienced ground-crew members

CR12558
691. Many agriculturally intensive areas of the world are beginning to encounter water scarcity problems. As a result, many farmers in these areas are likely to reduce their output as the water supply they need in order to maintain production shrinks. However, one group of farmers in such a region plans to increase their production by implementing techniques for water conservation.

Which of the following, if true, would most strongly support the prediction that the group's plan will succeed?

(A) Farmers that can gain a larger share of the food market in their regions will be better positioned to control more water resources.

(B) Most agricultural practices in areas with water shortages are water-intensive.

(C) Other regions of the world not facing water shortages are likely to make up for the reduction in agricultural output.

(D) Demand for agricultural products in the group's region is not expected to decline.

(E) More than half the water used for agriculture in the farmers' region is lost to evaporation or leakage from irrigation channels.

CR03367
692. Hollywood restaurant is replacing some of its standard tables with tall tables and stools. The restaurant already fills every available seat during its operating hours, and the change in seating arrangements will not result in an increase in the restaurant's seating capacity. Nonetheless, the restaurant's management expects revenue to increase as a result of the seating change without any concurrent change in menu, prices, or operating hours.

Which of the following, if true, provides the best reason for the expectation?

(A) One of the taller tables takes up less floor space than one of the standard tables.

(B) Diners seated on stools typically do not linger over dinner as long as diners seated at standard tables.

(C) Since the restaurant will replace only some of its standard tables, it can continue to accommodate customers who do not care for the taller tables.

(D) Few diners are likely to avoid the restaurant because of the new seating arrangement.

(E)   The standard tables being replaced by tall tables would otherwise have to be replaced with new standard tables at a greater expense.

CR07660

693. A major network news organization experienced a drop in viewership in the week following the airing of a controversial report on the economy. The network also received a very large number of complaints regarding the report. The network, however, maintains that negative reactions to the report had nothing to do with its loss of viewers.

Which of the following, if true, most strongly supports the network's position?

(A)   The other major network news organizations reported similar reductions in viewership during the same week.

(B)   The viewers who registered complaints with the network were regular viewers of the news organization's programs.

(C)   Major network news organizations publicly attribute drops in viewership to their own reports only when they receive complaints about those reports.

(D)   This was not the first time that this network news organization has aired a controversial report on the economy that has inspired viewers to complain to the network.

(E)   Most network news viewers rely on network news broadcasts as their primary source of information regarding the economy.

CR04366

694. Only a reduction of 10 percent in the number of scheduled flights using Greentown's airport will allow the delays that are so common there to be avoided. Hevelia airstrip, 40 miles away, would, if upgraded and expanded, be an attractive alternative for fully 20 percent of the passengers using Greentown airport. Nevertheless, experts reject the claim that turning Hevelia into a full-service airport would end the chronic delays at Greentown.

Which of the following, if true, most helps to justify the experts' position?

(A)   Turning Hevelia into a full-service airport would require not only substantial construction at the airport itself, but also the construction of new access highways.

(B)   A second largely undeveloped airstrip close to Greentown airport would be a more attractive alternative than Hevelia for many passengers who now use Greentown.

(C)   Hevelia airstrip lies in a relatively undeveloped area but would, if it became a full-service airport, be a magnet for commercial and residential development.

(D)   If an airplane has to wait to land, the extra jet fuel required adds significantly to the airline's costs.

(E)   Several airlines use Greentown as a regional hub, so that most flights landing at Greentown have many passengers who then take different flights to reach their final destinations.

CR07712

695. Farmer: Worldwide, just three grain crops—rice, wheat, and corn—account for most human caloric intake. To maintain this level of caloric intake and also keep pace with global population growth, yields per acre from each of these crops will have to increase at least 1.5 percent every year, given that the supply of cultivated land is diminishing. Therefore, the government should increase funding for research into new ways to improve yields.

Which of the following is an assumption on which the farmer's argument depends?

(A)   It is solely the government's responsibility to ensure that the amount of rice, wheat, and corn produced worldwide keeps pace with global population growth.

(B)   Increasing government funding for research into new ways to improve the yields per acre of rice, wheat, and corn crops would help to increase total worldwide annual production of food from these crops.

(C)   Increasing the yields per acre of rice, wheat, and corn is more important than increasing the yields per acre of other crops.

(D)   Current levels of funding for research into ways of improving grain crop yields per acre have enabled grain crop yields per acre to increase by more than 1.5 percent per year worldwide.

(E)   In coming decades, rice, wheat, and corn will become a minor part of human caloric intake, unless there is government-funded research to increase their yields per acre.

CR08770

696. The air quality board recently informed Coffee Roast, a small coffee roasting firm, of a complaint regarding the smoke from its roaster. Recently enacted air quality regulations require machines roasting more than 10 pounds of coffee to be equipped with expensive smoke-dissipating afterburners. The firm, however, roasts only 8 pounds of coffee at a time. Nevertheless, the company has decided to purchase and install an afterburner.

Which of the following, if true, most strongly supports the firm's decision?

(A) Until settling on the new air quality regulations, the board had debated whether to require afterburners for machines roasting more than 5 pounds of coffee at a time.

(B) Coffee roasted in a machine equipped with an afterburner has its flavor subtly altered.

(C) The cost to the firm of an afterburner is less than the cost of replacing its roaster with a smaller one.

(D) Fewer complaints are reported in areas that maintain strict rules regarding afterburners.

(E) The firm has reason to fear that negative publicity regarding the complaints could result in lost sales.

CR03695

697. People who do regular volunteer work tend to live longer, on average, than people who do not. It has been found that "doing good," a category that certainly includes volunteer work, releases endorphins, the brain's natural opiates, which induce in people a feeling of well-being. Clearly, there is a connection: Regular releases of endorphins must in some way help to extend people's lives.

Which of the following, if true, most seriously undermines the force of the evidence given as support for the hypothesis that endorphins promote longevity?

(A) People who do regular volunteer work are only somewhat more likely than others to characterize the work they do for a living as "doing good."

(B) Although extremely high levels of endorphins could be harmful to health, such levels are never reached as a result of the natural release of endorphins.

(C) There are many people who have done some volunteer work but who do not do such work regularly.

(D) People tend not to become involved in regular volunteer work unless they are healthy and energetic to begin with.

(E) Releases of endorphins are responsible for the sense of well-being experienced by many long-distance runners while running.

CR04140

698. A study compared a sample of Swedish people older than 75 who needed in-home assistance with a similar sample of Israeli people. The people in the two samples received both informal assistance, provided by family and friends, and formal assistance, professionally provided. Although Sweden and Israel have equally well-funded and comprehensive systems for providing formal assistance, the study found that the people in the Swedish sample received more formal assistance, on average, than those in the Israeli sample.

Which of the following, if true, does most to explain the difference that the study found?

(A) A companion study found that among children needing special in-home care, the amount of formal assistance they received was roughly the same in Sweden as in Israel.

(B) More Swedish than Israeli people older than 75 live in rural areas where formal assistance services are sparse or nonexistent.

(C) Although in both Sweden and Israel much of the funding for formal assistance ultimately comes from the central government, the local structures through which assistance is delivered are different in the two countries.

(D) In recent decades, the increase in life expectancy of someone who is 75 years old has been greater in Israel than in Sweden.

(E) In Israel, people older than 75 tend to live with their children, whereas in Sweden people of that age tend to live alone.

CR05077

699. Film Director: It is true that certain characters and plot twists in my newly released film *The Big Heist* are similar to characters and plot twists in *Thieves*, a movie that came out last year. Pointing to these similarities, the film studio that produced *Thieves* is now accusing me of taking ideas from that film. The accusation is clearly without merit. All production work on *The Big Heist* was actually completed months before *Thieves* was released.

Which of the following, if true, provides the strongest support for the director's position?

(A) Before *Thieves* began production, its script had been circulating for several years among various film studios, including the studio that produced *The Big Heist*.

(B) The characters and plot twists that are most similar in the two films have close parallels in many earlier films of the same genre.

(C) The film studio that produced *Thieves* seldom produces films in this genre.

(D)   The director of *Thieves* worked with the director of *The Big Heist* on several earlier projects.

(E)   Production work on *Thieves* began before production work on *The Big Heist* was started.

CR05412

700. In Mernia commercial fossil hunters often sell important fossils they have found, not to universities or museums, but to individual collectors, who pay much better but generally do not allow researchers access to their collections. To increase the number of fossils available for research, some legislators propose requiring all fossils that are found in Mernia to be sold only to universities or museums.

Which of the following, if true, most strongly indicates that the legislators' proposal will fail to achieve its goal?

(A)   Some fossil hunters in Mernia are not commercial fossil hunters, but rather are amateurs who keep the fossils that they find.

(B)   Most fossils found in Mernia are common types that have little scientific interest.

(C)   Commercial fossil hunters in Mernia currently sell some of the fossils they find to universities and museums.

(D)   Many universities in Mernia do not engage in fossil research.

(E)   Most fossils are found by commercial fossil hunters, and they would give up looking for fossils if they were no longer allowed to sell to individual collectors.

CR02702

701. Economist: Tropicorp, which constantly seeks profitable investment opportunities, has been buying and clearing sections of tropical forest for cattle ranching, although pastures newly created there become useless for grazing after just a few years. The company has not gone into rubber tapping, even though greater profits can be made from rubber tapping, which leaves the forest intact. Thus, some environmentalists argue that **Tropicorp's actions do not serve even its own economic interest**. However, the initial investment required for a successful rubber-tapping operation is larger than that needed for a cattle ranch; there is a shortage of workers employable in rubber-tapping operations; and taxes are higher on profits from rubber tapping than on profits from cattle ranching. Consequently, **the environmentalists' conclusion is probably wrong**.

In the economist's argument, the two **boldface** portions play which of the following roles?

(A)   The first supports the conclusion of the economist's argument; the second calls that conclusion into question.

(B)   The first states the conclusion of the economist's argument; the second supports that conclusion.

(C)   The first supports the conclusion of the environmentalists' argument; the second states that conclusion.

(D)   The first states the conclusion of the environmentalists' argument; the second states the conclusion of the economist's argument.

(E)   Each supports the conclusion of the economist's argument.

CR41700.02

702. Brown tides are growths of algae on the sea's surface that prevent sunlight from reaching marine plants below, thereby destroying not only the plants but also the shellfish that live off these plants. Biologists recently isolated a virus that, when added to seawater, kills the algae that cause brown tides. Adding large quantities of this virus to waters affected by brown tides will therefore make it possible to save the populations of shellfish that inhabit those waters.

Which of the following, if true, provides the most support for the conclusion of the argument?

(A)   When applied in large quantities, the virus not only kills the algae that cause brown tides but also many harmless kinds of algae.

(B)   Marine animals that prey on shellfish avoid areas of the sea in which brown tides are occurring.

(C)   The number of different kinds of virus present in seawater is far greater than many marine biologists had, until recently, believed.

(D)   The presence of large quantities of the virus in seawater does not adversely affect the growth of marine plants.

(E)   The amount of the virus naturally present in seawater in which brown tides occur is neither significantly greater nor significantly less than the amount present in seawater in which brown tides do not occur.

CR18310.02

703. In persons with astigmatism, the clear outer layer of the eye is deformed in a way that impairs and sometimes distorts vision. The elongated figures in the paintings of El Greco (1541–1614) were so unusual that some critics sought to explain them by hypothesizing that, without knowing it, El Greco had an astigmatism that caused everything to appear to him in the distorted way that was characteristic of his painted figures.

The proposed explanation is most vulnerable to the criticism that it fails to

(A) establish that during the period in which El Greco lived, there was any correction available to those who did realize their vision was distorted

(B) provide evidence that astigmatism was common in the 1500s and 1600s

(C) consider that the critics who proposed the explanation might have suffered from astigmatism

(D) consider the effect of the hypothesized astigmatism on El Greco's perception of his own paintings

(E) allow for the possibility that artists see the world differently than do nonartists

CR74231.01

704. Marketing executive for Magu Corporation: Whenever Magu opens a manufacturing facility in a new city, the company should sponsor, or make donations to, a number of nonprofit organizations in that city. Doing so would improve Magu's image in the community, and thus the money spent on such charitable ventures would lead to increased sales.

Which statement would, if true, point to the most serious weakness in the marketing executive's advice?

(A) Magu sells its products internationally, so sales in any one city represent only a small portion of total revenue.

(B) Spending on charitable ventures would require Magu to decrease direct advertisements, which are the most effective means of reaching its target customers.

(C) If market conditions change, Magu may have to close any such facility or relocate it.

(D) Some nonprofit organizations are poorly organized, so money donated to them would be of little benefit to the community.

(E) If workers at the manufacturing facility believed their wages or working conditions were poor, their complaints would outweigh any good impressions generated by Magu's donations or sponsorships.

CR30650.02

705. In the last few years, plant scientists have been able to genetically engineer seeds to produce crops highly resistant to insect damage. Farmers growing crops with these seeds will be able to spend significantly less on pesticides. This cost reduction would more than make up for the higher cost of the genetically engineered seeds. Clearly, therefore, farmers who grow crops from genetically engineered seeds will be able to reduce their costs by using them.

Which of the following, if true, most weakens the argument?

(A) Plant scientists have not yet developed insect-resistant strains of every crop that is currently grown commercially.

(B) The cost of several commonly used pesticides is expected to rise in the next few years.

(C) Crops grown from the genetically engineered seeds require significantly more fertilizer and water to grow well than do crops grown from nonengineered seeds.

(D) In the future, the cost of genetically engineered seeds is likely to fall to the level of nonengineered seeds.

(E) The crops that now require the greatest expenditure on pesticides are not the ones for which genetically engineered seeds will become available.

CR44040.02

706. Educational Theorist: Recent editorials have called for limits on the amount of homework assigned to schoolchildren younger than 12. They point out that free-time activities play an important role in childhood development and that homework in large quantities can severely restrict children's free time, hindering their development. But the actual average homework time for children under 12—little more than 30 minutes per night—leaves plenty of free time. In reality, therefore, the editorials' rationale cannot justify the restriction they advocate.

Which of the following, if true, would most seriously call into question the educational theorist's conclusion?

(A) Some teachers give as homework assignments work of a kind that research suggests is most effective educationally when done in class.

(B) For children younger than 12, regularly doing homework in the first years of school has no proven academic value, but many educators believe that it fosters self-discipline and time management.

(C) Some homework assignments are related to free-time activities that children engage in, such as reading or hobbies.

(D) A substantial proportion of schoolchildren under 12, particularly those in their first few years of school, have less than 10 minutes of homework assigned per night.

(E) Some free-time activities teach children skills or information that they later find useful in their schoolwork.

Questions 707 to 760 - Difficulty: Medium

CR78590.02

707. Airline Representative: The percentage of flight delays caused by airline error decreased significantly this year. This indicates that airlines listened to complaints about preventable errors and addressed the problems. Although delays caused by weather and other uncontrollable factors will always be part of travel, preventable delays are clearly decreasing.

Which of the following most clearly points to a logical flaw in the representative's reasoning?

(A) Airlines may be motivated by financial concerns to underreport the percentage of flight delays caused by airline error.

(B) The delays caused by uncontrollable factors could have led to an increase in complaints to airlines.

(C) Complaints may not be the most reliable measure of how many errors occurred in a given year.

(D) Delays caused by weather and other uncontrollable factors could have increased dramatically during the year under discussion.

(E) Airline customers might not believe that particular delays were caused by uncontrollable factors rather than airline error.

CR08831

708. Although the school would receive financial benefits if it had soft drink vending machines in the cafeteria, we

should not allow them. Allowing soft drink machines there would not be in our students' interest. If our students start drinking more soft drinks, they will be less healthy.

The argument depends on which of the following?

(A) If the soft drink vending machines were placed in the cafeteria, students would consume more soft drinks as a result.

(B) The amount of soft drinks that most students at the school currently drink is not detrimental to their health.

(C) Students are apt to be healthier if they do not drink soft drinks at all than if they just drink small amounts occasionally.

(D) Students will not simply bring soft drinks from home if the soft drink vending machines are not placed in the cafeteria.

(E) The school's primary concern should be to promote good health among its students.

CR01112

709. Many athletes inhale pure oxygen after exercise in an attempt to increase muscular reabsorption of oxygen. Measured continuously after exercise, however, the blood lactate levels of athletes who inhale pure oxygen are practically identical, on average, to those of athletes who breathe normal air. The lower the blood lactate level is, the higher the muscular reabsorption of oxygen is.

If the statements above are all true, they most strongly support which of the following conclusions?

(A) Athletes' muscular reabsorption of oxygen is not increased when they inhale pure oxygen instead of normal air.

(B) High blood lactate levels cannot be reduced.

(C) Blood lactate levels are a poor measure of oxygen reabsorption by muscles.

(D) The amount of oxygen reabsorbed by an athlete's muscles always remains constant.

(E) The inhaling of pure oxygen has no legitimate role in athletics.

CR79751.01

710. Historian: Fifteenth-century advances in mapmaking contributed to the rise of modern nation-states. In medieval Europe (from the fifth to the fifteenth century), sovereignty centered in cities and towns and radiated outward, with boundaries often ambiguously defined.

The conceptual shift toward the modern state began in the late fifteenth century, when mapmakers learned to reflect geography accurately by basing maps on latitude-longitude grids. By the mid-seventeenth century, nearly all maps showed boundary lines.

Which of the following would, if true, most strengthen the historian's reasoning?

(A) Borders did not become codified in Europe until certain treaties were signed in the early nineteenth century.

(B) During the medieval period, various authorities in Europe claimed power over collections of cities and towns, not contiguous territories.

(C) Many members of the political elite collected maps as a hobby during the late sixteenth and early seventeenth centuries.

(D) Seventeenth-century treatises and other sources of political authority describe areas of sovereignty rather than illustrate them using maps.

(E) During the fifteenth century in Europe, mapmakers simplified the borders of sovereignty by drawing clear lines of demarcation between political powers.

CR11751.01

711. Sascha: The attempt to ban parliament's right to pass directed-spending bills—bills that contain provisions specifically funding the favorite projects of some powerful politicians—is antidemocratic. Our nation's constitution requires that money be drawn from our treasury only when so stipulated by laws passed by parliament, the branch of government most directly representative of the citizens. This requirement is based on the belief that exercising the power to spend public resources involves the ultimate exercise of state authority and that therefore _____.

Which of the following most logically completes Sascha's argument?

(A) designating funding specifically for the favorite projects of some powerful politicians should be considered antidemocratic

(B) the right to exercise such a power should belong exclusively to the branch of government most directly representative of the citizens

(C) exercising the power to spend public resources is in most cases—but not all—protected by the constitution

(D) modifications to any spending bills should be considered expenditures authorized by law

(E) only officials who are motivated by concerns for reelection should retain that power

CR02143

712. Boreal owls range over a much larger area than do other owls of similar size. Scientists have hypothesized that **it is scarcity of prey that leads the owls to range so widely.** This hypothesis would be hard to confirm directly, since it is not possible to produce a sufficiently accurate count of the populations of small mammals inhabiting the forests where boreal owls live. Careful study of owl behavior has, however, shown that **boreal owls do range over larger areas when they live in regions where food of the sort eaten by small mammals is comparatively sparse.** This indicates that the scientists' hypothesis is not sheer speculation.

In the argument given, the two **boldfaced** portions play which of the following roles?

(A) The first presents an explanatory hypothesis; the second states the main conclusion of the argument.

(B) The first presents an explanatory hypothesis; the second presents evidence tending to support this hypothesis.

(C) The first presents an explanatory hypothesis; the second presents evidence to support an alternative explanation.

(D) The first describes a position that the argument opposes; the second presents evidence to undermine the support for the position being opposed.

(E) The first describes a position that the argument opposes; the second states the main conclusion of the argument.

CR18731.01

713. Cognitive scientist: Using the pioneering work of comparative psychologist Gordon Gallup as a model, several studies have investigated animals' capacity for mirror self-recognition (MSR). Most animals exposed to a mirror respond only with social behavior, such as aggression. However, in the case of the great apes, repeated exposure to mirrors leads to self-directed behaviors, such as exploring the inside of the mouth, suggesting that these animals recognize the reflection as an image of self. The implication of these studies is that the great apes have a capacity for self-awareness unique among nonhuman species.

The cognitive scientist makes which of the following assumptions in the argument above?

(A) Gallup's work has established that the great apes have a capacity for MSR unique among nonhuman species.

(B) If an animal does not have the capacity for MSR, it does not have the capacity for self-awareness.

(C) If a researcher exposes an animal to a mirror and that animal exhibits social behavior, that animal is incapable of being self-aware.

(D) When exposed to a mirror, all animals display either social behavior or self-directed behavior.

(E) Animals that do not exhibit MSR may demonstrate a capacity for self-awareness in other ways.

CR02888
714. Last year a record number of new manufacturing jobs were created. Will this year bring another record? Well, any new manufacturing job is created either within an existing company or by the start-up of a new company. **Within existing firms, new jobs have been created this year at well below last year's record pace**. At the same time, there is considerable evidence that the number of new companies starting up will be no higher this year than it was last year and **there is no reason to think that the new companies starting up this year will create more jobs per company than did last year's start-ups**. So clearly, the number of new jobs created this year will fall short of last year's record.

In the argument given, the two portions in **boldface** play which of the following roles?

(A) The first is a claim that the argument challenges; the second is an explicit assumption on which that challenge is based.

(B) The first is a claim that the argument challenges; the second is a judgment advanced in support of the main conclusion of the argument.

(C) The first provides evidence in support of the main conclusion of the argument; the second is an objection that has been raised against that main conclusion.

(D) The first provides evidence in support of the main conclusion of the argument; the second is a judgment advanced in support of that main conclusion.

(E) The first and the second are each claims that have been advanced in support of a position that the argument opposes.

CR07809
715. A study of ticket sales at a summer theater festival found that people who bought tickets to individual plays had a no-show rate of less than 1 percent, while those who paid in advance for all ten plays being performed that summer had a no-show rate of nearly 30 percent. This may be at least in part because the greater the awareness customers retain about the cost of an item, the more likely they are to use it.

Which of the following would, if true, best serve as an alternative explanation of the results of the study?

(A) The price per ticket was slightly cheaper for those who bought all ten tickets in advance.

(B) Many people who attended the theater festival believed strongly that they should support it financially.

(C) Those who attended all ten plays became eligible for a partial refund.

(D) Usually, people who bought tickets to individual plays did so immediately prior to each performance that they attended.

(E) People who arrived just before the performance began could not be assured of obtaining seats in a preferred location.

CR12019
716. Although there is no record of poet Edmund Spenser's parentage, we do know that as a youth Spenser attended the Merchant Tailors' School in London for a period between 1560 and 1570. Records from this time indicate that the Merchant Tailors' Guild then had only three members named Spenser: Robert Spenser, listed as a gentleman; Nicholas Spenser, elected the Guild's Warden in 1568; and John Spenser, listed as a "journeyman cloth-maker." Of these, the last was likely the least affluent of the three—and most likely Edmund's father, since school accounting records list Edmund as a scholar who attended the school at a reduced fee.

Which of the following is an assumption on which the argument depends?

(A) Anybody in sixteenth-century London who made clothing professionally would have had to be a member of the Merchant Tailors' Guild.

(B)   The fact that Edmund Spenser attended the Merchant Tailors' School did not necessarily mean that he planned to become a tailor.

(C)   No member of the Guild could become Guild warden in sixteenth-century London unless he was a gentleman.

(D)   Most of those whose fathers were members of the Merchant Tailors' Guild were students at the Merchant Tailors' School.

(E)   The Merchant Tailors' School did not reduce its fees for the children of the more affluent Guild members.

CR20831.01

717. Hea Sook: One should not readily believe urban legends. Most legends are propagated because the moral lesson underlying them supports a political agenda. People will repeat a tale if it fits their purpose. They may not deliberately spread untruths, but neither are they particularly motivated to investigate deeply to determine if the tale they are telling is true.

Kayla: But people would not repeat stories that they did not believe were true. Therefore, one can safely assume that if a story has been repeated by enough people then it is more likely to be true.

Kayla's reply is most vulnerable to the criticism that it

(A)   does not specify how many people need to repeat a story before someone is justified believing it

(B)   overstates the significance of political agendas in the retelling of stories

(C)   fails to address the claim that people will not verify the truth of a story that fits their purpose

(D)   implicitly supports the claim that the people repeating legends are not deliberately spreading untruths

(E)   cannot distinguish people's motivations for repeating urban legends from their motivations for repeating other types of story

CR03749

718. Rainwater contains hydrogen of a heavy form called deuterium. The deuterium content of wood reflects the deuterium content of rainwater available to trees during their growth. Wood from trees that grew between 16,000 and 24,000 years ago in North America contains significantly more deuterium than wood from trees growing today. But water trapped in several North American caves that formed during that same early period contains significantly less

deuterium than rainwater in North America contains today.

Which of the following, if true, most helps to reconcile the two findings?

(A)   There is little deuterium in the North American caves other than the deuterium in the water trapped there.

(B)   Exposure to water after a tree has died does not change the deuterium content of the wood.

(C)   Industrialization in North America over the past 100 years has altered the deuterium content of rain.

(D)   Trees draw on shallow groundwater from rain that falls during their growth, whereas water trapped in caves may have fallen as rainwater thousands of years before the caves formed.

(E)   Wood with a high deuterium content is no more likely to remain preserved for long periods than is wood with a low deuterium content.

CR04925

719. Enforcement of local speed limits through police monitoring has proven unsuccessful in the town of Ardane. In many nearby towns, speed humps (raised areas of pavement placed across residential streets, about 300 feet apart) have reduced traffic speeds on residential streets by 20 to 25 percent. In order to reduce traffic speed and thereby enhance safety in residential neighborhoods, Ardane's transportation commission plans to install multiple speed humps in those neighborhoods.

Which of the following, if true, identifies a potentially serious drawback to the plan for installing speed humps in Ardane?

(A)   On residential streets without speed humps, many vehicles travel at speeds more than 25 percent above the posted speed limit.

(B)   Because of their high weight, emergency vehicles such as fire trucks and ambulances must slow almost to a stop at speed humps.

(C)   The residential speed limit in Ardane is higher than that of the nearby towns where speed humps were installed.

(D)   Motorists who are not familiar with the streets in Ardane's residential districts would be likely to encounter the speed humps unawares unless warned by signs and painted indicators.

(E)   Bicyclists generally prefer that speed humps be constructed so as to leave a space on the side of the road where bicycles can travel without going over the humps.

CR00748

720. Which of the choices most logically completes the following argument?

NowNews, although still the most popular magazine covering cultural events in Kalopolis, has recently suffered a significant drop in advertising revenue because of falling circulation. Many readers have begun buying a competing magazine that, at 50 cents per copy, costs less than *NowNews* at $1.50 per copy. In order to boost circulation and thus increase advertising revenue, *NowNews's* publisher has proposed making it available at no charge. However, this proposal has a serious drawback, since _____.

(A)   those Kalopolis residents with the greatest interest in cultural events are regular readers of both magazines.

(B)   one reason *NowNews's* circulation fell was that its competitor's reporting on cultural events was superior.

(C)   the newsstands and stores that currently sell *NowNews* will no longer carry it if it is being given away for free.

(D)   at present, 10 percent of the total number of copies of each issue of *NowNews* are distributed free to students on college campuses in the Kalopolis area.

(E)   *NowNews's* competitor would begin to lose large amounts of money if it were forced to lower its cover price.

CR07304

721. Archaeologist: Researchers excavating a burial site in Cyprus found a feline skeleton lying near a human skeleton. Both skeletons were in the same sediment at the same depth and equally well-preserved, suggesting that the feline and human were buried together about 9,500 years ago. This shows that felines were domesticated around the time farming began, when they would have been useful in protecting stores of grain from mice.

Which of the following, if true, would most seriously weaken the archaeologist's argument?

(A)   Archaeologists have not found any remains of stores of grain in the immediate vicinity of the burial site.

(B)   The burial site in Cyprus is substantially older than any other known burial site in which a feline skeleton and a human skeleton appear to have been buried together.

(C)   Paintings found near the burial site seem to show people keeping felines as domestic companions, but do not show felines hunting mice.

(D)   In Cyprus, there are many burial sites dating from around 9,500 years ago in which the remains of wild animals appear to have been buried alongside human remains.

(E)   Before felines were domesticated, early farmers had no effective way to protect stores of grain from mice.

CR90061.01

722. Farmer: Several people in the past few years have claimed to have seen a mountain lion in the suburban outskirts—the latest just last month—and, while mountain lions were thought to have been driven from this entire region about twenty years ago, there is no reason for the people who reported seeing a mountain lion to have deliberately concocted a false report. Therefore, local wildlife managers should begin to urgently address the mountain lion's presence.

Which of the following would, if true, most seriously weaken the farmer's argument?

(A)   Farmers in the suburban outskirts mostly raise cattle and hogs, which when fully grown are generally not attacked by mountain lions.

(B)   Mountain lions are dissimilar in size and color to other wild animals found near the suburban outskirts.

(C)   No person who claimed to have seen a mountain lion had anyone else with them at the purported sighting.

(D)   There have been no regional reports in the past year of mountain lions migrating to the area.

(E)   Recent surveys show that more than half of the people in the region report that they have never seen a mountain lion before.

CR09117

723. The heavy traffic in Masana is a growing drain on the city's economy—the clogging of the streets of the central business district alone cost the economy more than $1.2 billion over the past year. In order to address this problem, officials plan to introduce congestion pricing, by which drivers would pay to enter the city's most heavily trafficked areas during the busiest times of the day.

Which of the following, if true, would most strongly indicate that the plan will be a success?

(A) Approximately one-fifth of the vehicles in the central business district are in transit from one side of the city to the other.

(B) Planners expect that, without congestion pricing, traffic in Masana is likely to grow by 6 percent in the next five years.

(C) In other urban areas, congestion pricing has strongly encouraged carpooling (sharing of rides by private commuters).

(D) Several studies have shown that a reduction in traffic of 15 percent in Masana could result in 5,500 or more new jobs.

(E) Over 30 percent of the vehicles in the city's center are occupied by more than one person.

CR09151

724. Economist: The most economically efficient way to reduce emissions of air pollutants is to tax them in proportion to the damage they are likely to cause. But in Country Y, many serious pollutants are untaxed and unregulated, and policy makers strongly oppose new taxes. Therefore, the best way to achieve a reduction in air pollutant emissions in Country Y would be to institute fixed upper limits on them.

Which of the following is an assumption of the economist's argument?

(A) Policy makers in Country Y oppose all new taxes equally strongly, regardless of any benefits they may provide.

(B) Country Y's air pollutant emissions would not fall significantly if they were taxed in proportion to the damage they are likely to cause.

(C) Policy makers in Country Y strongly favor reductions in air pollutant emissions.

(D) Country Y's policy makers believe that air pollutant emissions should be reduced with maximum economic efficiency.

(E) Policy makers in Country Y do not oppose setting fixed upper limits on air pollutant emissions as strongly as they oppose new taxes.

CR04986

725. Humans get Lyme disease from infected ticks. Ticks get infected by feeding on animals with Lyme disease, but the ease of transmission from host animal to tick varies. With most species of host animal, transmission of Lyme disease to ticks is extremely rare, but white-footed mice are an exception, readily passing Lyme disease to ticks. And white-footed mouse populations greatly expand, becoming the main food source for ticks, in areas where biodiversity is in decline.

The information in the passage most strongly supports which of the following?

(A) In areas where many humans are infected with Lyme disease, the proportion of ticks infected with Lyme disease is especially high.

(B) Very few animals that live in areas where there are no white-footed mice are infected with Lyme disease.

(C) Humans are less at risk of contracting Lyme disease in areas where biodiversity is high.

(D) Ticks feed on white-footed mice only when other host species are not available to them.

(E) The greater the biodiversity of an area, the more likely any given host animal in that area is to pass Lyme disease to ticks.

CR04935

726. Many industrialized nations are trying to reduce atmospheric concentrations of carbon dioxide, a gas released by the burning of fossil fuels. One proposal is to replace conventional cement, which is made with calcium carbonate, by a new "eco-cement." This new cement, made with magnesium carbonate, absorbs large amounts of carbon dioxide when exposed to the atmosphere. Therefore, using eco-cement for new concrete building projects will significantly help reduce atmospheric concentrations of carbon dioxide.

Which of the following, if true, most strengthens the argument?

(A) The cost of magnesium carbonate, currently greater than the cost of calcium carbonate, probably will fall as more magnesium carbonate is used in cement manufacture.

(B) Eco-cement is strengthened when absorbed carbon dioxide reacts with the cement.

(C) Before the development of eco-cement, magnesium-based cement was considered too susceptible to water erosion to be of practical use.

(D) The manufacture of eco-cement uses considerably less fossil fuel per unit of cement than the manufacture of conventional cement does.

(E) Most building-industry groups are unaware of the development or availability of eco-cement.

CR81021.02

727. Professor: A marine biologist argues that transmission of sea lice from farm salmon to wild salmon is unlikely in the Broughton Archipelago, British Columbia, citing numerous studies suggesting that salinities less than 30 parts per thousand are unfavorable to sea-lice survival. The biologist concludes that the archipelago's 25–30 parts per thousand salinity range between March and June, the critical period for wild salmon migration, tends to suppress sea-lice proliferation. But a review of the literature shows that salinities of 25–30 parts per thousand in combination with British Columbia's cool spring temperatures favor the flourishing of sea lice.

In this passage, the professor attempts to undermine the biologist's argument by

(A) pointing out that a condition claimed to be necessary for sea-lice survival is not sufficient for it

(B) citing studies that suggest that salinity levels were not measured reliably

(C) claiming that there is evidence showing that one of its premises is false

(D) questioning the reliability of the biologist's scientific sources

(E) showing that its conclusion is inconsistent with its premises

CR00895

728. Advertisement: When your car's engine is running at its normal operating temperature, any major brand of motor oil will protect it about as well as Tuff does. When the engine is cold, it is a different story: Tuff motor oil flows better at lower temperatures than its major competitors do. So, if you want your car's engine to have maximum protection, you should use Tuff.

Which of the following, if true, most strengthens the argument in the advertisement?

(A) Tuff motor oil provides above-average protection for engines that happen to overheat.

(B) Tuff motor oil is periodically supplied free of charge to automobile manufacturers to use in factory-new cars.

(C) Tuff motor oil's share of the engine oil market peaked three years ago.

(D) Tuff motor oil, like any motor oil, is thicker and flows less freely at cold temperatures than at hot temperatures.

(E) Tuff motor oil is manufactured at only one refinery and shipped from there to all markets.

CR55541.01

729. Linguist: In English, the past is described as "behind" and the future "ahead," whereas in Aymara the past is "ahead" and the future "behind." Research indicates that English speakers sway backward when discussing the past and forward when discussing the future. Conversely, Aymara speakers gesture forward with their hands when discussing the past and backward when discussing the future. These bodily movements, therefore, suggest that the language one speaks affects how one mentally visualizes time.

The linguist's reasoning depends on assuming which of the following?

(A) At least some Aymara speakers sway forward when discussing the past and backward when discussing the future.

(B) Most people mentally visualize time as running either forward or backward.

(C) Not all English and Aymara speakers tend to sway or gesture forward or backward when discussing the present.

(D) How people move when discussing the future correlates to some extent with how they mentally visualize time.

(E) The researchers also examined the movements of at least some speakers of languages other than English and Aymara discussing the past and the future.

CR13108

730. *The Testament of William Thorpe* was published around 1530 as an appendix to Thorpe's longer *Examination*. Many scholars, however, doubt the attribution of the *Testament* to Thorpe because, whereas the *Examination* is dated 1406, the *Testament* is dated 1460. One scholar has recently argued that the 1460 date be amended to 1409, based on the observation that when these numbers are expressed as Roman numerals, MCCCCLX and MCCCCIX, it becomes easy to see how the dates might have become confused through scribal error.

Which of the following, if true, would most support the scholar's hypothesis concerning the date of the *Testament*?

(A) The sole evidence that historians have had that William Thorpe died no earlier than 1460 was the presumed date of publication of the *Testament*.

(B) In the preface to the 1530 publication, the editor attributes both works to William Thorpe.

(C) Few writers in fifteenth-century England marked dates in their works using only Roman numerals.

(D) The *Testament* alludes to a date, "Friday, September 20," as apparently contemporaneous with the writing of the *Testament*, and September 20 fell on a Friday in 1409 but not in 1460.

(E) The *Testament* contains few references to historical events that occurred later than 1406.

CR00777

731. A prominent investor who holds a large stake in the Burton Tool Company has recently claimed that the company is mismanaged, citing as evidence the company's failure to slow down production in response to a recent rise in its inventory of finished products. It is doubtful whether an investor's sniping at management can ever be anything other than counterproductive, but in this case, it is clearly not justified. It is true that **an increased inventory of finished products often indicates that production is outstripping demand**, but in Burton's case it indicates no such thing. Rather, **the increase in inventory is entirely attributable to products that have already been assigned to orders received from customers**.

In the argument given, the two **boldfaced** portions play which of the following roles?

(A) The first states a generalization that underlies the position that the argument as a whole opposes; the second provides evidence to show that the generalization does not apply in the case at issue.

(B) The first states a generalization that underlies the position that the argument as a whole opposes; the second clarifies the meaning of a specific phrase as it is used in that generalization.

(C) The first provides evidence to support the conclusion of the argument as a whole; the second is evidence that has been used to support the position that the argument as a whole opposes.

(D) The first provides evidence to support the conclusion of the argument as a whole; the second states that conclusion.

(E) The first and the second each provide evidence against the position that the argument as a whole opposes.

CR10028

732. To reduce productivity losses from employees calling in sick, Corporation X implemented a new policy requiring employees to come into work unless they were so sick that they had to go to a doctor. But a year after the policy was implemented, a study found that Corporation X's overall productivity losses due to reported employee illnesses had increased.

Which of the following, if true, would best explain why the policy produced the reverse of its intended effect?

(A) After the policy was implemented, employees more frequently went to the doctor when they felt sick.

(B) Before the policy was implemented, employees who were not sick at all often called in sick.

(C) Employees coming into work when sick often infect many of their coworkers.

(D) Unusually few employees became genuinely sick during the year after the policy was implemented.

(E) There are many other factors besides employee illness that can adversely affect productivity.

CR08443

733. Advertising by mail has become much less effective, with fewer consumers responding. Because consumers are increasingly overwhelmed by the sheer amount of junk mail they receive, most discard almost all offers without considering them. Thus, an effective way for corporations to improve response rates would be to more carefully target the individuals to whom they mail advertising, thereby cutting down on the amount of junk mail each consumer receives.

Which of the following, if true, would most support the recommendation above?

(A) There are cost-effective means by which corporations that currently advertise by mail could improve response rates.

(B) Many successful corporations are already carefully targeting the individuals to whom they mail advertising.

(C)   Any consumer who, immediately after receiving an advertisement by mail, merely glances at it, is very likely to discard it.

(D)   Improvements in the quality of the advertising materials used in mail that is carefully targeted to individuals can improve the response rate for such mail.

(E)   Response rates to carefully targeted advertisements by mail are considerably higher, on average, than response rates to most other forms of advertising.

CR01905

734.   Petrochemical industry officials have said that the extreme pressure exerted on plant managers during the last five years to improve profits by cutting costs has done nothing to impair the industry's ability to operate safely. However, environmentalists contend that the recent rash of serious oil spills and accidents at petrochemical plants is traceable to cost-cutting measures.

Which of the following, if true, would provide the strongest support for the position held by industry officials?

(A)   The petrochemical industry benefits if accidents do not occur, since accidents involve risk of employee injury as well as loss of equipment and product.

(B)   Petrochemical industry unions recently demanded that additional money be spent on safety and environmental protection measures, but the unions readily abandoned those demands in exchange for job security.

(C)   Despite major cutbacks in most other areas of operation, the petrochemical industry has devoted more of its resources to environmental and safety measures in the last five years than in the preceding five years.

(D)   There is evidence that the most damaging of the recent oil spills would have been prevented had cost-cutting measures not been instituted.

(E)   Both the large fines and the adverse publicity generated by the most recent oil spill have prompted the petrochemical industry to increase the resources devoted to oil-spill prevention.

CR01368

735.   A company has developed a new sensing device that, according to the company's claims, detects weak, ultralow-frequency electromagnetic signals associated with a beating heart. These signals, which pass through almost any physical obstruction, are purportedly detected by the device even at significant distances. Therefore, if the company's claims are true, their device will radically improve emergency teams' ability to locate quickly people who are trapped within the wreckage of collapsed buildings.

Which of the following, if true, most strengthens the argument?

(A)   People trapped within the wreckage of collapsed buildings usually have serious injuries that require prompt medical treatment.

(B)   The device gives a distinctive reading when the signals it detects come from human beings rather than from any other living beings.

(C)   Most people who have survived after being trapped in collapsed buildings were rescued within two hours of the building's collapse.

(D)   Ultralow-frequency signals are not the only electromagnetic signals that can pass through almost any physical obstruction.

(E)   Extensive training is required in order to operate the device effectively.

CR11639

736.   Economist: The price of tap water in our region should be raised drastically. **Supplies in local freshwater reservoirs have been declining for years** because water is being used faster than it can be replenished. Since the price of tap water has been low, **few users have bothered to adopt even easy conservation measures**.

The two sections in **boldface** play which of the following roles in the economist's argument?

(A)   The first is a conclusion for which support is provided, and which in turn supports the main conclusion; the second is the main conclusion.

(B)   The first is an observation for which the second provides an explanation; the second is the main conclusion but not the only conclusion.

(C)   The first is a premise supporting the argument's main conclusion; so is the second.

(D)   The first is the only conclusion; the second provides an explanation for the first.

(E)   The first is the main conclusion; the second is a conclusion for which support is provided, and which in turn supports the first.

CR13127

737. Politician: Hybrid cars use significantly less fuel per kilometer than nonhybrids. And fuel produces air pollution, which contributes to a number of environmental problems. Motorists can save money by driving cars that are more fuel efficient, and they will be encouraged to drive hybrid cars if we make them aware of that fact. Therefore, we can help reduce the total amount of pollution emitted by cars in this country by highlighting this advantage of hybrid cars.

Which of the following, if true, would most indicate a vulnerability of the politician's argument?

(A) People with more fuel-efficient cars typically drive more than do those with less fuel-efficient cars.

(B) Not all air pollution originates from automobiles.

(C) Hybrid cars have already begun to gain popularity.

(D) Fuel-efficient alternatives to hybrid cars will likely become available in the future.

(E) The future cost of gasoline and other fuel cannot be predicted with absolute precision or certainty.

CR99530.01

738. Mayor: False alarms from home security systems waste so much valuable police time that in many communities police have stopped responding to alarms from homes whose systems frequently produce false alarms. This policy reduces wastage of police time but results in a loss of protection for some residents. To achieve a comparable reduction in wastage without reducing protection for residents, the council has enacted a measure to fine residents for repeated false alarms.

Which of the following, if true, casts the most doubt on whether the measure enacted by the council will achieve its goal?

(A) A fine in the amount planned by the council will not cover the expenses police typically incur when they respond to a false alarm.

(B) Homes equipped with security systems are far less likely to be broken into than are homes without security systems.

(C) The threat of fines is likely to cause many residents to deactivate their security systems.

(D) The number of home security systems is likely to increase dramatically over the next five years.

(E) Many home security systems have never produced false alarms.

CR53341.01

739. Excavation of the house of a third-century Camarnian official revealed that he had served four magistrates— public officials who administer the law—over his thirty-year public career, in four provincial capital cities. However, given the Camarnian administrative system of that era, it is unclear whether he served them simultaneously, as a traveling administrator living for part of the year in each provincial capital, or else did so sequentially, leaving one magistrate after several years to join another.

Which of the following would, if found in the excavation, most likely help reveal the pattern of the official's administrative service?

(A) Maps and documents describing each of the four provincial capitals

(B) A cache of the official's documents related to work from early in his career

(C) A set of cups of a type made only in the city of the first magistrate whom the official is known to have served

(D) Several pieces of furniture in the styles of two of the provincial capital cities

(E) Heavy clothing appropriate only for the coldest of the four cities

CR80531.01

740. In 1563, in Florence's Palazzo Vecchio, Giorgio Vasari built in front of an existing wall a new wall on which he painted a mural. Investigators recently discovered a gap between Vasari's wall and the original, large enough to have preserved anything painted on the original. Historians believe that Leonardo da Vinci had painted, but left unfinished, a mural on the original wall; some historians had also believed that by 1563 the mural had been destroyed. However, it is known that in the late 1560s, when renovating another building, Santa Maria Novella, Vasari built a façade over its frescoes, and the frescoes were thereby preserved. Thus, Leonardo's Palazzo Vecchio mural probably still exists behind Vasari's wall.

Which of the following is an assumption on which the argument depends?

(A) Leonardo rarely if ever destroyed artworks that he left unfinished.

(B) Vasari was likely unaware that the mural in the Palazzo Vecchio had willingly been abandoned by Leonardo.

(C) Vasari probably would not have built the Palazzo Vecchio wall with a gap behind it except to preserve something behind the new wall.

(D) Leonardo would probably have completed the Palazzo Vecchio mural if he had had the opportunity to do so.

(E) When Vasari preserved the frescoes of Santa Maria Novella he did so secretly.

CR09534

741. Coffee shop owner: A large number of customers will pay at least the fair market value for a cup of coffee, even if there is no formal charge. Some will pay more than this out of appreciation of the trust that is placed in them. And our total number of customers is likely to increase. We could therefore improve our net cash flow by implementing an honor system in which customers pay what they wish for coffee by depositing money in a can.

Manager: We're likely to lose money on this plan. Many customers would cheat the system, paying a very small sum or nothing at all.

Which of the following, if true, would best support the owner's plan, in light of the manager's concern?

(A) The new system, if implemented, would increase the number of customers.

(B) By roasting its own coffee, the shop has managed to reduce the difficulties (and cost) of maintaining an inventory of freshly roasted coffee.

(C) Many customers stay in the cafe for long stretches of time.

(D) The shop makes a substantial profit from pastries and other food bought by the coffee drinkers.

(E) No other coffee shop in the area has such a system.

CR03272

742. Birds have been said to be descended from certain birdlike dinosaur species with which they share distinctive structural features. The fossil record, however, shows that this cannot be so, since there are bird fossils that are much older than the earliest birdlike dinosaur fossils that have been found.

Which of the following is an assumption on which the argument relies?

(A) The birdlike dinosaurs have no living descendants.

(B) There are no flightless dinosaur species that have the distinctive structural features shared by birds and birdlike dinosaurs.

(C) There are no birdlike dinosaur fossils that are older than the bird fossils but have not yet been unearthed.

(D) It could not have been the case that some birds were descended from one of the birdlike dinosaur species and other birds from another.

(E) Birds cannot have been descended from dinosaur species with which the birds do not share the distinctive structural features.

CR08239

743. City council member: Demand for electricity has been increasing by 1.5 percent a year, and there simply is no more space to build additional power plants to meet future demand increases. We must therefore begin to curtail usage, which is why I propose passing ordinances requiring energy-conservation measures in all city departments.

The city council member's proposal assumes which of the following?

(A) Existing power plants do not have the capacity to handle all of the projected increase in demand for electricity.

(B) No city departments have implemented energy-conservation measures voluntarily.

(C) Passing ordinances designed to curtail electricity usage will not have negative economic consequences for the city.

(D) Residential consumers are not responsible for the recent increases in demand for electricity.

(E) City departments that successfully conserve energy will set a good example for residential and industrial consumers of electricity.

CR32441.01

744. Certain groups of Asian snails include both "left-handed" and "right-handed" species, with shells coiling to the left and right, respectively. Some left-handed species have evolved from right-handed ones. Also, researchers found that snail-eating snakes in the same habitat have asymmetrical jaws, allowing them to grasp right-handed snail shells more easily. If these snakes ate more right-handed snails over time, this would have given left-handed snails an evolutionary advantage over right-handed snails, with the left-handed snails eventually becoming a new species. Thus, the snakes' asymmetrical jaws probably helped drive the emergence of the left-handed snail species.

Which of the following would, if true, most strengthen the argument that asymmetrical snake jaws helped drive left-handed snail evolution?

(A) In one snake species, the snakes with asymmetrical jaws eat snails, while the snakes with symmetrical jaws do not eat snails.

(B) Some species of Asian snails contain either all right-handed snails, or all left-handed snails.

(C) Anatomical differences prevent left-handed snails from mating easily with right-handed snails.

(D) Some right-handed snails in this habitat have shells with a very narrow opening that helps prevent snakes from extracting the snails from inside their shells.

(E) Experiments show that the snail-eating snakes in this habitat fail more often in trying to eat left-handed snails than in trying to eat right-handed snails.

CR95631.01

745. A moderately large city is redesigning its central downtown area and is considering a plan that would reduce the number of lanes for automobiles and trucks and increase those for bicycles and pedestrians. The intent is to attract more workers and shoppers to downtown businesses by making downtown easier to reach and more pleasant to move around in.

Which of the following would, if true, most strongly support the prediction that the plan would achieve its goal?

(A) People who make a habit of walking or bicycling whenever feasible derive significant health benefits from doing so.

(B) Most people who prefer to shop at suburban malls instead of downtown urban areas do so because parking is easier and cheaper at the former.

(C) In other moderately sized cities where measures were taken to make downtowns more accessible for walkers and cyclists, downtown businesses began to thrive.

(D) If the proposed lane restrictions on drivers are rigorously enforced, more people will likely be attracted to downtown businesses than would otherwise be.

(E) Most people who own and frequently ride bicycles for recreational purposes live at a significant distance from downtown urban areas.

CR00713

746. Previously, Autoco designed all of its cars itself and then contracted with specialized parts suppliers to build parts according to its specifications. Now it plans to include its suppliers in designing the parts they are to build. Since many parts suppliers have more designers with specialized experience than Autoco has, Autoco expects this shift to reduce the overall time and cost of the design of its next new car.

Which of the following, if true, most strongly supports Autoco's expectation?

(A) When suppliers provide their own designs, Autoco often needs to modify its overall design.

(B) In order to provide designs for Autoco, several of the parts suppliers will have to add to their existing staffs of designers.

(C) Parts and services provided by outside suppliers account for more than 50 percent of Autoco's total costs.

(D) When suppliers built parts according to specifications provided by Autoco, the suppliers competed to win contracts.

(E) Most of Autoco's suppliers have on hand a wide range of previously prepared parts designs that can readily be modified for a new car.

CR02830

747. In response to viral infection, the immune systems of mice typically produce antibodies that destroy the virus by binding to proteins on its surface. Mice infected with the herpesvirus generally develop keratitis, a degenerative disease affecting part of the eye. Since proteins on the surface of cells in this part of the eye closely resemble those on the herpesvirus surface, scientists hypothesize that these cases of keratitis are caused by antibodies to the herpesvirus.

Which of the following, if true, most helps to support the scientists' reasoning?

(A) Other types of virus have surface proteins that closely resemble proteins found in various organs of mice.

(B) Mice that are infected with the herpesvirus but do not develop keratitis produce as many antibodies as infected mice that do develop keratitis.

(C)   Mice infected with a new strain of the herpesvirus that has different surface proteins did not develop keratitis.

(D)   Mice that have never been infected with the herpesvirus can sometimes develop keratitis.

(E)   There are mice that are unable to form antibodies in response to herpes infections, and these mice contract herpes at roughly the same rate as other mice.

CR38931.01

748. One might expect that within a particular species, any individuals that managed to slow down the aging process would leave more offspring. Natural selection should therefore favor extreme longevity—but this does not seem to be the case. A possible explanation is that aging is a product of the inevitable wear and tear of living, similar to how household appliances generally accumulate faults that lead to their eventual demise. However, most researchers do not find this analogy satisfactory as an explanation.

Which of the following would, if true, provide the strongest explanation for the researchers' reaction?

(A)   Some organisms are capable of living much longer than other organisms.

(B)   Some organisms reproduce very quickly despite having short lifespans.

(C)   There are several ways of defining "extreme longevity," and according to some definitions it occurs frequently.

(D)   Organisms are capable of maintenance and self-repair and can remedy much of the damage that they accumulate.

(E)   Some organisms generate much more wear and tear on their bodies than others.

CR02885

749. Last year a record number of new manufacturing jobs were created. Will this year bring another record? Well, **any new manufacturing job is created either within an existing company or by the start-up of a new company**. Within existing firms, new jobs have been created this year at well below last year's record pace. At the same time, there is considerable evidence that the number of new companies starting up this year will be no higher than it was last year and **there is no reason to**

think that the new companies starting up this year will create more jobs per company than did last year's start-ups. So clearly, the number of new jobs created this year will fall short of last year's record.

In the argument given, the two portions in **boldface** play which of the following roles?

(A)   The first provides evidence in support of the main conclusion of the argument; the second is a claim that the argument challenges.

(B)   The first is a generalization that the argument seeks to establish; the second is a conclusion that the argument draws in order to support that generalization.

(C)   The first is a generalization that the argument seeks to establish; the second is a judgment that has been advanced in order to challenge that generalization.

(D)   The first is presented as an obvious truth on which the argument is based; the second is a claim that has been advanced in support of a position that the argument opposes.

(E)   The first is presented as an obvious truth on which the argument is based; the second is a judgment advanced in support of the main conclusion of the argument.

CR02886

750. Last year a record number of new manufacturing jobs were created. Will this year bring another record? Well, **any new manufacturing job is created either within an existing company or by the start-up of a new company**. Within existing firms, new jobs have been created this year at well below last year's record pace. At the same time, there is considerable evidence that the number of new companies starting up will be no higher this year than it was last year and there is no reason to think that the new companies starting up this year will create more jobs per company than did last year's start-ups. So clearly, **the number of new jobs created this year will fall short of last year's record**.

In the argument given, the two portions in **boldface** play which of the following roles?

(A)   The first is presented as an obvious truth on which the argument is based; the second is the main conclusion of the argument.

(B)   The first is presented as an obvious truth on which the argument is based; the second is a conclusion drawn in order to support the main conclusion of the argument.

(C) The first and the second each provide evidence in support of the main conclusion of the argument.

(D) The first is a generalization that the argument seeks to establish; the second is the main conclusion of the argument.

(E) The first is a generalization that the argument seeks to establish; the second is a conclusion that has been drawn in order to challenge that generalization.

CR00827
751. In Stenland, many workers have been complaining that they cannot survive on minimum wage, the lowest wage an employer is permitted to pay. The government is proposing to raise the minimum wage. Many employers who pay their workers the current minimum wage argue that if it is raised, unemployment will increase because they will no longer be able to afford to employ as many workers.

Which of the following, if true in Stenland, most strongly supports the claim that raising the minimum wage there will not have the effects that the employers predict?

(A) For any position with wages below a living wage, the difficulty of finding and retaining employees adds as much to employment costs as would raising wages.

(B) Raising the minimum wage does not also increase the amount employers have to contribute in employee benefits.

(C) When inflation is taken into account, the proposed new minimum wage is not as high as the current one was when it was introduced.

(D) Many employees currently being paid wages at the level of the proposed new minimum wage will demand significant wage increases.

(E) Many employers who pay some workers only the minimum wage also pay other workers wages that are much higher than the minimum.

CR07810
752. Biologists with a predilection for theory have tried—and largely failed—to define what it is that makes something a living thing. Organisms take in energy-providing materials and excrete waste products, but so do automobiles. Living things replicate and take part in evolution, but so do some computer programs. We must be open to the possibility that there are living

things on other planets. Therefore, we will not be successful in defining what it is that makes something a living thing merely by examining living things on Earth—the only ones we know. Trying to do so is analogous to trying to specify _____.

Which of the following most logically completes the passage?

(A) the laws of physics by using pure mathematics

(B) what a fish is by listing its chemical components

(C) what an animal is by examining a plant

(D) what a machine is by examining a sketch of it

(E) what a mammal is by examining a zebra

CR74541.01
753. For the period from the eighth century through the eleventh century, the shifting boundaries between Kingdom F and Kingdom G have not been well charted. Although a certain village in a border region between the two kingdoms usually belonged to Kingdom G, ninth-century artifacts found in the village were in the typical Kingdom F style of that time. It is unclear whether the village was actually a part of Kingdom F in the ninth century or whether it was a part of Kingdom G but had merely adopted Kingdom F's artistic styles under Kingdom F's cultural influence.

Which of the following would, if found in ninth-century sites in the village, best help in determining whether the village was a part of Kingdom F or Kingdom G in the ninth century?

(A) A trading contract written in the Kingdom G dialect

(B) A drawing of a dwelling complex known to have existed on the border of Kingdom F and Kingdom G in the ninth century

(C) Knives and other utensils made from metal typical of ninth-century mining sites in Kingdom F

(D) Some fragments of pottery made in the Kingdom G style from the seventh century out of materials only found in Kingdom F

(E) Numerous teeth from the ninth century with a chemical signature typical only of teeth from people who had grown up in the heart of Kingdom F

CR02829
754. Sammy: For my arthritis, I am going to try my aunt's diet: large amounts of wheat germ and garlic. She was able to move more easily right after she started that diet.

Pat: When my brother began that diet, his arthritis got worse. But he has been doing much better since he stopped eating vegetables in the nightshade family, such as tomatoes and peppers.

Which of the following, if true, would provide a basis for explaining the fact that Sammy's aunt and Pat's brother had contrasting experiences with the same diet?

(A) A change in diet, regardless of the nature of the change, frequently brings temporary relief from arthritis symptoms.

(B) The compounds in garlic that can lessen the symptoms of arthritis are also present in tomatoes and peppers.

(C) Arthritis is a chronic condition whose symptoms improve and worsen from time to time without regard to diet.

(D) In general, men are more likely to have their arthritis symptoms alleviated by avoiding vegetables in the nightshade family than are women.

(E) People who are closely related are more likely to experience the same result from adopting a particular diet than are people who are unrelated.

CR91630.02

755. In the 1960s, surveys of Florida's alligator population indicated that the population was dwindling rapidly. Hunting alligators was banned. By the early 1990s, the alligator population had recovered, and restricted hunting was allowed. Over the course of the 1990s, reports of alligators appearing on golf courses and lawns increased dramatically. Therefore, in spite of whatever alligator hunting went on, the alligator population must have increased significantly over the decade of the 1990s.

Which of the following, if true, most seriously weakens the argument?

(A) The human population of Florida increased significantly during the 1990s.

(B) The hunting restrictions applied to commercial as well as private hunters.

(C) The number of sightings of alligators in lakes and swamps increased greatly in Florida during the 1990s.

(D) Throughout the 1990s, selling alligator products was more strictly regulated than hunting was.

(E) Most of the sightings of alligators on golf courses and lawns in the 1990s occurred at times at which few people were present on those golf courses and lawns.

CR05756

756. Infotek, a computer manufacturer in Katrovia, has just introduced a new personal computer model that sells for significantly less than any other model. Market research shows, however, that very few Katrovian households without personal computers would buy a computer, regardless of its price. Therefore, introducing the new model is unlikely to increase the number of computers in Katrovian homes.

Which of the following is an assumption on which the argument depends?

(A) Infotek achieved the lower price of the new model by using components of lower quality than those used by other manufacturers.

(B) The main reason cited by consumers in Katrovia for replacing a personal computer is the desire to have an improved model.

(C) Katrovians in households that already have computers are unlikely to purchase the new Infotek model as an additional computer for home use.

(D) The price of other personal computers in Katrovia is unlikely to drop below the price of Infotek's new model in the near future.

(E) Most personal computers purchased in Katrovia are intended for home use.

CR05501

757. Fast-food restaurants make up 45 percent of all restaurants in Canatria. Customers at these restaurants tend to be young; in fact, studies have shown that the older people get, the less likely they are to eat in fast-food restaurants. Since the average age of the Canatrian population is gradually rising and will continue to do so, the number of fast-food restaurants is likely to decrease.

Which of the following, if true, most seriously weakens the argument?

(A) Fast-food restaurants in Canatria are getting bigger, so each one can serve more customers.

(B) Some older people eat at fast-food restaurants more frequently than the average young person.

(C) Many people who rarely eat in fast-food restaurants nevertheless eat regularly in restaurants.

(D) The overall population of Canatria is growing steadily.

(E) As the population of Canatria gets older, more people are eating at home.

CR04805

758. Last year a chain of fast-food restaurants, whose menu had always centered on hamburgers, added its first vegetarian sandwich, much lower in fat than the chain's other offerings. Despite heavy marketing, the new sandwich accounts for a very small proportion of the chain's sales. The sandwich's sales would have to quadruple to cover the costs associated with including it on the menu. Since such an increase is unlikely, the chain would be more profitable if it dropped the sandwich.

Which of the following, if true, most seriously weakens the argument?

(A) Although many of the chain's customers have never tried the vegetarian sandwich, in a market research survey most of those who had tried it reported that they were very satisfied with it.

(B) Many of the people who eat at the chain's restaurants also eat at the restaurants of competing chains and report no strong preference among the competitors.

(C) Among fast-food chains in general, there has been little or no growth in hamburger sales over the past several years as the range of competing offerings at other restaurants has grown.

(D) When even one member of a group of diners is a vegetarian or has a preference for low-fat food, the group tends to avoid restaurants that lack vegetarian or low-fat menu options.

(E) An attempt by the chain to introduce a lower-fat hamburger failed several years ago, since it attracted few new customers and most of the chain's regular customers greatly preferred the taste of the regular hamburgers.

CR03727

759. Transportation expenses accounted for a large portion of the total dollar amount spent on trips for pleasure by residents of the United States in 1997, and about half of the total dollar amount spent on transportation was for airfare. However, the large majority of United States residents who took trips for pleasure in 1997 did not travel by airplane but used other means of transportation.

If the statements above are true, which of the following must also be true about United States residents who took trips for pleasure in 1997?

(A) Most of those who traveled by airplane did so because the airfare to their destination was lower than the cost of other available means of transportation.

(B) Most of those who traveled by airplane did so because other means of transportation to their destination were unavailable.

(C) Per mile traveled, those who traveled by airplane tended to spend more on transportation to their destination than did those who used other means of transportation.

(D) Overall, people who did not travel by airplane had lower average transportation expenses than people who did.

(E) Those who traveled by airplane spent about as much, on average, on other means of transportation as they did on airfare.

CR12051

760. Voters commonly condemn politicians for being insincere, but politicians often must disguise their true feelings when they make public statements. If they expressed their honest views—about, say, their party's policies—then achieving politically necessary compromises would be much more difficult. Clearly, the very insincerity that people decry shows that our government is functioning well.

Which of the following, if true, most seriously undermines this reasoning?

(A) Achieving political compromises is not all that is necessary for the proper functioning of a government.

(B) Some political compromises are not in the best long-term interest of the government.

(C) Voters often judge politicians by criteria other than the sincerity with which they express their views.

(D) A political party's policies could turn out to be detrimental to the functioning of a government.

(E) Some of the public statements made by politicians about their party's policies could in fact be sincere.

Questions 761 to 817 - Difficulty: **Hard**

CR09760.02

761. Duckbill dinosaurs, like today's monitor lizards, had particularly long tails, which they could whip at considerable speed. Monitor lizards use their tails to strike predators. However, although duckbill tails were otherwise very similar to those of monitor lizards, the duckbill's tailbones were proportionately much thinner and thus more delicate. Moreover, to ward off their proportionately much larger predators, duckbills would have had to whip their tails considerably faster than monitor lizards do.

The information given, if accurate, provides the strongest support for which of the following hypotheses?

(A) If duckbills whipped their tails faster than monitor lizards do, the duckbill's tail would have been effective at warding off the duckbills' fiercest predators.

(B) Duckbills used their tails to strike predators, and their tailbones were frequently damaged from the impact.

(C) Using their tails was not the only means duckbills had for warding off predators.

(D) Duckbills were at much greater risk of being killed by a predator than monitor lizards are.

(E) The tails of duckbills, if used to ward off predators, would have been more likely than the tails of monitor lizards to sustain damage from the impact.

CR00860.02

762. In an attempt to produce a coffee plant that would yield beans containing no caffeine, the synthesis of a substance known to be integral to the initial stages of caffeine production was blocked either in the beans, in the leaves, or both. For those plants in which synthesis of the substance was blocked only in the leaves, the resulting beans contained no caffeine.

Any of the following, if true, would provide the basis for an explanation of the observed results EXCEPT:

(A) In coffee plants, the substance is synthesized only in the leaves and then moves to the beans, where the initial stages of caffeine production take place.

(B) In coffee plants, the last stage of caffeine production takes place in the beans using a compound that is produced only in the leaves by the substance.

(C) In coffee plants, the initial stages of caffeine production take place only in the beans, but later stages depend on another substance that is synthesized only in the leaves and does not depend on the blocked substance.

(D) In coffee plants, caffeine production takes place only in the leaves, but the caffeine then moves to the beans.

(E) Caffeine was produced in the beans of the modified coffee plants, but all of it moved to the leaves, which normally produce their own caffeine.

CR20170.02

763. Which of the following most logically completes the passage?

Laminated glass is much harder to break than the glass typically used in the windows of cars driven in Relnia. It is more difficult for thieves to break into cars with laminated glass windows than into cars with ordinary glass windows, and laminated glass windows are less likely to break in a collision. Nevertheless, considerations of security and safety do not unambiguously support a proposal to require that in Relnia all glass installed in cars be laminated glass, since _____.

(A) most people cannot visually distinguish laminated glass from the glass typically used for car windows

(B) a significant proportion of cars driven in Relnia are manufactured elsewhere

(C) some cars in Relnia already have laminated glass in their windows

(D) the rates of car theft and of collisions have both fallen slightly in Relnia in recent years

(E) there are times when breaking a car's window is the best way to provide timely help for people trapped inside

CR65030.02

764. Consultant: **Ace Repairs ends up having to redo a significant number of the complex repair jobs it undertakes, but when those repairs are redone, they are invariably done right.** Since we have established that there is no systematic difference between the mechanics who are assigned to do the initial repairs and those who are assigned to redo unsatisfactory jobs, we must reject the hypothesis that mistakes made in the initial repairs are due to the mechanics' lack of competence. Rather, it is likely that **complex repairs require a level of focused attention that the company's mechanics apply consistently only to repair jobs that have not been done right on the first try.**

In the consultant's reasoning, the two portions in **boldface** play which of the following roles?

(A) The first is the consultant's main conclusion; the second provides evidence in support of that main conclusion.

(B) The first is evidence that serves as the basis for rejecting one explanation of a certain finding; the second is the consultant's own explanation of that finding.

(C) The first is a claim whose truth is at issue in the reasoning; the second provides evidence to show that the claim is true.

(D) The first presents a contrast whose explanation is at issue in the reasoning; the second is the consultant's explanation of that contrast.

(E) The first presents a contrast whose explanation is at issue in the reasoning; the second is evidence that has been used to challenge the consultant's explanation of that contrast.

CR06728

765. To reduce waste of raw materials, the government of Sperland is considering requiring household appliances to be broken down for salvage when discarded. To cover the cost of salvage, the government is planning to charge a fee, which would be imposed when the appliance is first sold. Imposing the fee at the time of salvage would reduce waste more effectively, however, because consumers tend to keep old appliances longer if they are faced with a fee for discarding them.

Which of the following, if true, most seriously weakens the argument?

(A) Increasing the cost of disposing of an appliance properly increases the incentive to dispose of it improperly.

(B) The fee provides manufacturers with no incentive to produce appliances that are more durable.

(C) For people who have bought new appliances recently, the salvage fee would not need to be paid for a number of years.

(D) People who sell their used, working appliances to others would not need to pay the salvage fee.

(E) Many nonfunctioning appliances that are currently discarded could be repaired at relatively little expense.

CR02866

766. When there is less rainfall than normal, the water level of Australian rivers falls and the rivers flow more slowly. Because algae whose habitat is river water grow best in slow-moving water, the amount of algae per unit of water generally increases when there has been little rain. By contrast, however, following a period of extreme drought, algae levels are low even in very slow-moving river water.

Which of the following, if true, does most to explain the contrast described above?

(A) During periods of extreme drought, the populations of some of the species that feed on algae tend to fall.

(B) The more slowly water moves, the more conducive its temperature is to the growth of algae.

(C) When algae populations reach very high levels, conditions within the river can become toxic for some of the other species that normally live there.

(D) Australian rivers dry up completely for short intervals in periods of extreme drought.

(E) Except during periods of extreme drought, algae levels tend to be higher in rivers in which the flow has been controlled by damming than in rivers that flow freely.

CR04924

767. Increased use of incineration is sometimes advocated as a safe way to dispose of chemical waste. But opponents of incineration point to the 40 incidents involving unexpected releases of dangerous chemical agents that were reported just last year at two existing incinerators commissioned to destroy a quantity of chemical waste material. Since designs for proposed new incinerators include no additional means of preventing such releases, leaks will only become more prevalent if use of incineration increases.

Which of the following, if true, most seriously weakens the argument?

(A) At the two incinerators at which leaks were reported, staff had had only cursory training on the proper procedures for incinerating chemical waste.

(B) Other means of disposing of chemical waste, such as chemical neutralization processes, have not been proven safer than incineration.

(C) The capacity of existing incinerators is sufficient to allow for increased incineration of chemical waste without any need for new incinerators.

(D) The frequency of reports of unexpected releases of chemical agents at newly built incinerators is about the same as the frequency at older incinerators.

(E) In only three of the reported incidents of unexpected chemical leaks did the releases extend outside the property on which the incinerators were located.

CR10049

768. Public health expert: **Increasing the urgency of a public health message may be counterproductive.** In addition to irritating the majority who already behave responsibly, **it may undermine all government pronouncements on health by convincing people that such messages are overly cautious.** And there is no reason to believe that those who ignore measured voices will listen to shouting.

The two sections in **boldface** play which of the following roles in the public health expert's argument?

(A)   The first is a conclusion for which support is provided, but is not the argument's main conclusion; the second is an unsupported premise supporting the argument's main conclusion.

(B)   The first is a premise supporting the only explicit conclusion; so is the second.

(C)   The first is the argument's main conclusion; the second supports that conclusion and is itself a conclusion for which support is provided.

(D)   The first is a premise supporting the argument's only conclusion; the second is that conclusion.

(E)   The first is the argument's only explicit conclusion; the second is a premise supporting that conclusion.

CR01163

769. Several industries have recently switched at least partly from older technologies powered by fossil fuels to new technologies powered by electricity. It is thus evident that less fossil fuel is being used as a result of the operations of these industries than would have been used if these industries had retained their older technologies.

Which of the following, if true, most strengthens the argument above?

(A)   Many of the industries that have switched at least partly to the new technologies have increased their output.

(B)   Less fossil fuel was used to manufacture the machinery employed in the new technologies than was originally used to manufacture the machinery employed in the older technologies.

(C)   More electricity is used by those industries that have switched at least partly to the new technologies than by those industries that have not switched.

(D)   Some of the industries that have switched at least partly to the new technologies still use primarily technologies that are powered by fossil fuels.

(E)   The amount of fossil fuel used to generate the electricity needed to power the new technologies is less than the amount that would have been used to power the older technologies.

CR00792

770. The difference in average annual income in favor of employees who have college degrees, compared with those who do not have such degrees, doubled between 1980 and 1990. Some analysts have hypothesized that increased competition between employers for employees with college degrees drove up income for such employees.

Which of the following, if true, most seriously undermines the explanation described above?

(A)   During the 1980s a growing percentage of college graduates, unable to find jobs requiring a college degree, took unskilled jobs.

(B)   The average age of all employees increased slightly during the 1980s.

(C)   The unemployment rate changed very little throughout most of the 1980s.

(D)   From 1980 to 1990 the difference in average income between employees with advanced degrees and those with bachelor's degrees also increased.

(E)   During the 1980s there were some employees with no college degree who earned incomes comparable to the top incomes earned by employees with a college degree.

CR01239

771. Which of the following most logically completes the passage?

According to the last pre-election poll in Whippleton, most voters believe that the three problems government needs to address, in order of importance, are pollution, crime, and unemployment. Yet in the election, candidates from parties perceived as strongly against pollution were defeated, while those elected were all from parties with a history of opposing legislation designed to reduce pollution. These results should not be taken to indicate that the poll was inaccurate, however, since _____.

(A) some voters in Whippleton do not believe that pollution needs to be reduced

(B) every candidate who was defeated had a strong antipollution record

(C) there were no issues other than crime, unemployment, and pollution on which the candidates had significant differences of opinion

(D) all the candidates who were elected were perceived as being stronger against both crime and unemployment than the candidates who were defeated

(E) many of the people who voted in the election refused to participate in the poll

CR01153

772. Manufacturing plants in Arundia have recently been acquired in substantial numbers by investors from abroad. Arundian politicians are proposing legislative action to stop such investment, justifying the proposal by arguing that foreign investors, opportunistically exploiting a recent fall in the value of the Arundian currency, were able to buy Arundian assets at less than their true value.

Which of the following, if true, casts the most serious doubt on the adequacy of the Arundian politicians' justification for the proposed legislation?

(A) The Arundian government originally welcomed the fall in the value of the Arundian currency because the fall made Arundian exports more competitive on international markets.

(B) Foreign investors who acquired Arundian manufacturing plants generally did so with no intention of keeping and running those plants over the long term.

(C) Without the recent fall in the value of the Arundian currency, many of the Arundian assets bought by foreign investors would have been beyond the financial reach of those investors.

(D) In Concordia, a country broadly similar to Arundia, the share of manufacturing assets that is foreign-controlled is 60 percent higher than it is in Arundia.

(E) The true value of an investment is determined by the value of the profits from it, and the low value of the Arundian currency has depressed the value of any profits earned by foreign investors from Arundian assets.

CR27430.02

773. Proposal: Carbon dioxide and methane in the atmosphere block the escape of heat into space. So emission of these "greenhouse" gases contributes to global warming. In order to reduce global warming, emission of greenhouse gases needs to be reduced. Therefore, the methane now emitted from open landfills should instead be burned to produce electricity.

Objection: The burning of methane generates carbon dioxide that is released into the atmosphere.

Which of the following, if true, most adequately counters the objection made to the proposal?

(A) Every time a human being or other mammal exhales, there is some carbon dioxide released into the air.

(B) The conversion of methane to electricity would occur at a considerable distance from the landfills.

(C) The methane that is used to generate electricity would generally be used as a substitute for a fuel that does not produce any greenhouse gases when burned.

(D) Methane in the atmosphere is more effective in blocking the escape of heat from the Earth than is carbon dioxide.

(E) The amount of methane emitted from the landfills could be reduced if the materials whose decomposition produces methane were not discarded, but recycled.

CR04964

774. Proposed new safety rules for Beach City airport would lengthen considerably the minimum time between takeoffs from the airport. In consequence, the airport would be able to accommodate 10 percent fewer flights than currently use the airport daily. The city's operating budget depends heavily on taxes generated by tourist spending, and most of the tourists come by plane. Therefore, the proposed new safety rules, if adopted, will reduce the revenue available for the operating budget.

The argument depends on assuming which of the following?

(A) There are no periods of the day during which the interval between flights taking off from the airport is significantly greater than the currently allowed minimum.

(B) Few, if any, of the tourists who use Beach City airport do so when their main destination is a neighboring community and not Beach City itself.

(C) If the proposed safety rules are adopted, the reduction in tourist numbers will not result mainly from a reduction in the number of tourists who spend relatively little in Beach City.

(D) Increasing the minimum time between takeoffs is the only way to achieve necessary safety improvements without a large expenditure by the city government on airport enhancements.

(E) The response to the adoption of the new safety rules would not include a large increase in the number of passengers per flight.

CR01096
775. The introduction of new drugs into the market is frequently prevented by a shortage of human subjects for the clinical trials needed to show that the drugs are safe and effective. Since the lives and health of people in future generations may depend on treatments that are currently experimental, practicing physicians are morally in the wrong when, in the absence of any treatment proven to be effective, they fail to encourage suitable patients to volunteer for clinical trials.

Which of the following, if true, casts most doubt on the conclusion of the argument?

(A) Many drugs undergoing clinical trials are intended for the treatment of conditions for which there is currently no effective treatment.

(B) Patients do not share the physician's professional concern for public health, but everyone has a moral obligation to alleviate suffering when able to do so.

(C) Usually, half the patients in a clinical trial serve as a control group and receive a nonactive drug in place of the drug being tested.

(D) An experimental drug cannot legally be made available to patients unless those patients are subjects in clinical trials of the drug.

(E) Physicians have an overriding moral and legal duty to care for the health and safety of their current patients.

CR01285
776. As a construction material, bamboo is as strong as steel and sturdier than concrete. Moreover, in tropical areas bamboo is a much less expensive construction material than either steel or concrete and is always readily available. In tropical areas, therefore, building with bamboo makes better economic sense than building with steel or concrete, except where land values are high.

Which of the following, if true, most helps to explain the exception noted above?

(A) Buildings constructed of bamboo are less likely to suffer earthquake damage than are steel and concrete buildings.

(B) Bamboo is unsuitable as a building material for multistory buildings.

(C) In order to protect it from being damaged by termites and beetles, bamboo must be soaked, at some expense, in a preservative.

(D) In some tropical areas, bamboo is used to make the scaffolding that is used during large construction projects.

(E) Bamboo growing in an area where land values are increasing is often cleared to make way for construction.

CR25550.02
777. The country of Virodia has, until now, been barely self-sufficient in both meat and grain. Greater prosperity there has gone hand in hand with steadily increasing per capita consumption of meat, and it takes several pounds of grain used as feed to produce one pound of meat. Per capita income is almost certain to rise further, yet increases in domestic grain production are unlikely.

Which of the following is most strongly supported by the information given?

(A) Some land in Virodia that is currently used for grain production will soon be turned into pastureland for grazing cattle for meat.

(B) In the future, per capita income in Virodia is unlikely to increase as rapidly as it has in the past.

(C) In Virodia, the amount of grain it takes to produce one pound of meat is likely to increase in coming years.

(D) Grain is soon likely to make up a larger proportion of the average Virodian's diet than ever before.

(E)   Virodia is likely to become an importer of grain or meat or both.

CR00788

778. Newspaper editors should not allow reporters to write the headlines for their own stories. The reason for this is that, while the headlines that reporters themselves write are often clever, what typically makes them clever is that they allude to little-known information that is familiar to the reporter but that never appears explicitly in the story itself.

Which of the following, if true, most strengthens the argument?

(A)   The reporter who writes a story is usually better placed than the reporter's editor is to judge what the story's most newsworthy features are.

(B)   To write a headline that is clever, a person must have sufficient understanding of the story that the headline accompanies.

(C)   Most reporters rarely bother to find out how other reporters have written stories and headlines about the same events that they themselves have covered.

(D)   For virtually any story that a reporter writes, there are at least a few people who know more about the story's subject matter than does the reporter.

(E)   The kind of headlines that newspaper editors want are those that anyone who has read a reporter's story in its entirety will recognize as clever.

CR03251

779. Scientists have modified feed corn genetically, increasing its resistance to insect pests. Farmers who tried out the genetically modified corn last season applied less insecticide to their corn fields and still got yields comparable to those they would have gotten with ordinary corn. Ordinary corn seed, however, costs less, and what these farmers saved on insecticide rarely exceeded their extra costs for seed. Therefore, for most feed-corn farmers, switching to genetically modified seed would be unlikely to increase profits.

Which of the following would it be most useful to know in order to evaluate the argument?

(A)   Whether there are insect pests that sometimes reduce feed-corn yields, but against which

commonly used insecticides and the genetic modification are equally ineffective

(B)   Whether the price that farmers receive for feed corn has remained steady over the past few years

(C)   Whether the insecticides typically used on feed corn tend to be more expensive than insecticides typically used on other crops

(D)   Whether most of the farmers who tried the genetically modified corn last season applied more insecticide than was actually necessary

(E)   Whether, for most farmers who plant feed corn, it is their most profitable crop

CR07318

780. Debater: The average amount of overtime per month worked by an employee in the manufacturing division of the Haglut Corporation is 14 hours. Most employees of the Haglut Corporation work in the manufacturing division. Furthermore, the average amount of overtime per month worked by any employee in the company generally does not fluctuate much from month to month. Therefore, each month, most employees of the Haglut Corporation almost certainly work at least some overtime.

The debater's argument is most vulnerable to criticism on which of these grounds?

(A)   It takes for granted that the manufacturing division is a typical division of the corporation with regard to the average amount of overtime its employees work each month.

(B)   It takes for granted that if a certain average amount of overtime is worked each month by each employee of the Haglut Corporation, then approximately the same amount of overtime must be worked each month by each employee of the manufacturing division.

(C)   It confuses a claim from which the argument's conclusion about the Haglut Corporation would necessarily follow with a claim that would follow from the argument's conclusion only with a high degree of probability.

(D)   It overlooks the possibility that even if, on average, a certain amount of overtime is worked by the members of some group, many members of that group may work no overtime at all.

(E)   It overlooks the possibility that even if most employees of the corporation work some overtime each month, any one corporate employee may, in some months, work no overtime.

CR05446

781. Proponents of the recently introduced tax on sales of new luxury boats had argued that a tax of this sort would be an equitable way to increase government revenue because the admittedly heavy tax burden would fall only on wealthy people and neither they nor anyone else would suffer any economic hardship. In fact, however, 20 percent of the workers employed by manufacturers of luxury boats have lost their jobs as a direct result of this tax.

The information given, if true, most strongly supports which of the following?

(A) The market for luxury boats would have collapsed even if the new tax on luxury boats had been lower.

(D) The new tax would produce a net gain in tax revenue for the government only if the yearly total revenue that it generates exceeds the total of any yearly tax-revenue decrease resulting from the workers' loss of jobs.

(C) Because many people never buy luxury items, imposing a sales tax on luxury items is the kind of legislative action that does not cost incumbent legislators much popular support.

(D) Before the tax was instituted, luxury boats were largely bought by people who were not wealthy.

(E) Taxes can be equitable only if their burden is evenly distributed over the entire population.

CR05191

782. In Wareland last year, 16 percent of licensed drivers under 21 and 11 percent of drivers ages 21–24 were in serious accidents. By contrast, only 3 percent of licensed drivers 65 and older were involved in serious accidents. These figures clearly show that the greater experience and developed habits of caution possessed by drivers in the 65-and-older group make them far safer behind the wheel than the younger drivers are.

Which of the following is an assumption on which the argument depends?

(A) Drivers 65 and older do not, on average, drive very many fewer miles per year than drivers 24 and younger.

(B) Drivers 65 and older do not constitute a significantly larger percentage of licensed drivers in Wareland than drivers ages 18–24 do.

(C) Drivers 65 and older are less likely than are drivers 24 and younger to drive during weather conditions that greatly increase the risk of accidents.

(D) The difference between the accident rate of drivers under 21 and of those ages 21–24 is attributable to the greater driving experience of those in the older group.

(E) There is no age bracket for which the accident rate is lower than it is for licensed drivers 65 and older.

CR05614

783. In the past the country of Malvernia has relied heavily on imported oil. Malvernia recently implemented a program to convert heating systems from oil to natural gas. Malvernia currently produces more natural gas each year than it uses, and oil production in Malvernian oil fields is increasing at a steady pace. If these trends in fuel production and usage continue, therefore, Malvernian reliance on foreign sources for fuel is likely to decline soon.

Which of the following would it be most useful to establish in evaluating the argument?

(A) When, if ever, will production of oil in Malvernia outstrip production of natural gas?

(B) Is Malvernia among the countries that rely most on imported oil?

(C) What proportion of Malvernia's total energy needs is met by hydroelectric, solar, and nuclear power?

(D) Is the amount of oil used each year in Malvernia for generating electricity and fuel for transportation increasing?

(E) Have any existing oil-burning heating systems in Malvernia already been converted to natural-gas-burning heating systems?

CR03618

784. Exposure to certain chemicals commonly used in elementary schools as cleaners or pesticides causes allergic reactions in some children. Elementary school nurses in Renston report that the proportion of schoolchildren sent to them for treatment of allergic reactions to those chemicals has increased significantly over the past ten years. Therefore, either Renston's schoolchildren have been exposed to greater quantities of the chemicals, or they are more sensitive to them than schoolchildren were ten years ago.

Which of the following is an assumption on which the argument depends?

(A) The number of school nurses employed by Renston's elementary schools has not decreased over the past ten years.

(B) Children who are allergic to the chemicals are no more likely than other children to have allergies to other substances.

(C) Children who have allergic reactions to the chemicals are not more likely to be sent to a school nurse now than they were ten years ago.

(D) The chemicals are not commonly used as cleaners or pesticides in houses and apartment buildings in Renston.

(F) Children attending elementary school do not make up a larger proportion of Renston's population now than they did ten years ago.

CR51520.02
785. Lockeport's commercial fishing boats use gill nets, which kill many of the netted fish, including some fish of endangered species. The fishing commission has proposed requiring the use of tent nets, which do not kill fish; boat crews would then throw back fish of endangered species. Profitable commercial fishing boats in similar areas have already switched over to tent nets. The proposal can therefore be implemented without economic harm to Lockeport's commercial fishing boat operators.

Which of the following, if true, casts the most serious doubt on the argument made for the proposal?

(A) In places where the use of tent nets has been mandated, there are typically fewer commercial fishing boats in operation than there were before tent nets came into use.

(B) Even when used properly, gill nets require many more repairs than do tent nets.

(C) Recreational anglers in Lockeport catch more fish of endangered species than do commercial fishing boats.

(D) The endangered species of fish in Lockeport's commercial fishing area did not become endangered as a result of the use of gill nets by fishing fleets.

(E) The endangered species of fish caught by Lockeport's commercial fishing fleet are of no commercial value.

CR01854
786. Normally, the pineal gland governs a person's sleep-wake cycle by secreting melatonin in response to the daily cycle of light and darkness as detected by the eye. Nonetheless, many people who are totally blind due to lesions in the visual cortex of the brain easily maintain a 24-hour sleep-wake cycle. So the neural pathway by which the pineal gland receives information from the eye probably does not pass through the visual cortex.

For purposes of evaluating the argument it would be most useful to establish which of the following?

(A) Whether melatonin supplements help people who have difficulty maintaining a 24-hour sleep cycle to establish such a pattern

(B) Whether the melatonin levels of most totally blind people who successfully maintain a 24-hour sleep-wake cycle change in response to changes in exposure to light and darkness

(C) Whether melatonin is the only substance secreted by the pineal gland

(D) Whether most people who do not have a 24-hour sleep-wake cycle nevertheless have a cycle of consistent duration

(E) Whether there are any people with normal vision whose melatonin levels respond abnormally to periods of light and darkness

CR00942
787. **In countries where automobile insurance includes compensation for whiplash injuries sustained in automobile accidents, reports of having suffered such injuries are twice as frequent as they are in countries where whiplash is not covered.** Presently, no objective test for whiplash exists, so it is true that spurious reports of whiplash injuries cannot be readily identified. Nevertheless, these facts do not warrant the conclusion drawn by some commentators that in the countries with the higher rates of reported whiplash injuries, half of the reported cases are spurious. Clearly, **in countries where automobile insurance does not include compensation for whiplash, people often have little incentive to report whiplash injuries that they actually have suffered.**

In the argument given, the two **boldfaced** portions play which of the following roles?

(A) The first is a claim that the argument disputes; the second is a conclusion that has been based on that claim.

(B)   The first is a claim that has been used to support a conclusion that the argument accepts; the second is that conclusion.

(C)   The first is evidence that has been used to support a conclusion for which the argument provides further evidence; the second is the main conclusion of the argument.

(D)   The first is a finding whose implications are at issue in the argument; the second is a claim presented in order to argue against deriving certain implications from that finding.

(E)   The first is a finding whose accuracy is evaluated in the argument; the second is evidence presented to establish that the finding is accurate.

CR03859

788.   Last year Comfort Airlines had twice as many delayed flights as the year before, but the number of complaints from passengers about delayed flights went up three times. It is unlikely that this disproportionate increase in complaints was rooted in an increase in overall dissatisfaction with the service Comfort Airlines provides, since the airline made a special effort to improve other aspects of its service last year.

Which of the following, if true, most helps to explain the disproportionate increase in customer complaints?

(A)   Comfort Airlines had more flights last year than the year before.

(B)   Last year a single period of unusually bad weather caused a large number of flights to be delayed.

(C)   Some of the improvements that Comfort Airlines made in its service were required by new government regulations.

(D)   The average length of a flight delay was greater last year than it was the year before.

(E)   The average number of passengers per flight was no higher last year than the year before.

CR01337

789.   Last year a global disturbance of weather patterns disrupted harvests in many of the world's important agricultural areas. Worldwide production of soybeans, an important source of protein for people and livestock alike, was not adversely affected, however. Indeed, last year's soybean crop was actually slightly larger than average. Nevertheless, the weather phenomenon is probably responsible for a recent increase in the world price of soybeans.

Which of the following, if true, provides the strongest justification for the attribution of the increase in soybean prices to the weather phenomenon?

(A)   Last year's harvest of anchovies, which provide an important protein source for livestock, was disrupted by the effects of the weather phenomenon.

(B)   Most countries that produce soybeans for export had above-average harvests of a number of food crops other than soybeans last year.

(C)   The world price of soybeans also rose several years ago, immediately after an earlier occurrence of a similar global weather disturbance.

(D)   Heavy rains attributable to the weather phenomenon improved grazing pastures last year, allowing farmers in many parts of the world to reduce their dependence on supplemental feed.

(E)   Prior to last year, soybean prices had been falling for several years.

CR03541

790.   Most of the year, the hermit thrush, a North American songbird, eats a diet consisting mainly of insects, but in autumn, as the thrushes migrate to their Central and South American wintering grounds, they feed almost exclusively on wild berries. Wild berries, however, are not as rich in calories as insects, yet thrushes need to consume plenty of calories in order to complete their migration. One possible explanation is that berries contain other nutrients that thrushes need for migration and that insects lack.

Which of the following, if true, most seriously calls into question the explanation given for the thrush's diet during migration?

(A)   Hermit thrushes, if undernourished, are unable to complete their autumn migration before the onset of winter.

(B)   Insect species contain certain nutrients that are not found in wild berries.

(C)   For songbirds, catching insects requires the expenditure of significantly more calories than eating wild berries does.

(D)   Along the hermit thrushes' migration routes, insects are abundant throughout the migration season.

(E)   There are some species of wild berries that hermit thrushes generally do not eat, even though these berry species are exceptionally rich in calories.

CR01879

791. The kinds of hand and wrist injuries that result from extended use of a computer while maintaining an incorrect posture are common among schoolchildren in Harnville. Computers are important to the school curriculum there, so instead of reducing the amount their students use computers, teachers plan to bring about a sharp reduction in the number of these injuries by carefully monitoring their students' posture when using computers in the classroom.

Which of the following would it be most useful to know in order to assess the likelihood that the teachers' plan will be successful?

(A) Whether extended use of a computer while maintaining incorrect posture can cause injuries other than hand and wrist injuries

(B) Whether hand and wrist injuries not caused by computer use are common among schoolchildren in Harnville

(C) What proportion of schoolchildren in Harnville with hand and wrist injuries use computers extensively outside the classroom

(D) Whether changes in the curriculum could reduce the schools' dependence on computers

(E) What proportion of schoolchildren in Harnville already use correct posture while using a computer

CR04718

792. A certain cultivated herb is one of a group of closely related plants that thrive in soil with high concentrations of metals that are toxic to most other plants. Agronomists studying the growth of this herb have discovered that it produces large amounts of histidine, an amino acid that, in test-tube solutions, renders these metals chemically inert. Hence, the herb's high histidine production must be the key feature that allows it to grow in metal-rich soils.

In evaluating the argument, it would be most important to determine which of the following?

(A) Whether the herb can thrive in soil that does not have high concentrations of the toxic metals

(B) Whether others of the closely related group of plants also produce histidine in large quantities

(C) Whether the herb's high level of histidine production is associated with an unusually low level of production of some other amino acid

(D) Whether growing the herb in soil with high concentrations of the metals will, over time, reduce their concentrations in the soil

(E) Whether the concentration of histidine in the growing herb declines as the plant approaches maturity

CR01293

793. Many people suffer an allergic reaction to certain sulfites, including those that are commonly added to wine as preservatives. However, since there are several winemakers who add sulfites to none of the wines they produce, people who would like to drink wine but are allergic to sulfites can drink wines produced by these winemakers without risking an allergic reaction to sulfites.

Which of the following is an assumption on which the argument depends?

(A) These winemakers have been able to duplicate the preservative effect produced by adding sulfites by means that do not involve adding any potentially allergenic substances to their wine.

(B) Not all forms of sulfite are equally likely to produce the allergic reaction.

(C) Wine is the only beverage to which sulfites are commonly added.

(D) Apart from sulfites, there are no substances commonly present in wine that give rise to an allergic reaction.

(E) Sulfites are not naturally present in the wines produced by these winemakers in amounts large enough to produce an allergic reaction in someone who drinks these wines.

CR11447

794. A new law gives ownership of patents—documents providing exclusive right to make and sell an invention—to universities, not the government, when those patents result from government-sponsored university research. Administrators at Logos University plan to sell any patents they acquire to corporations in order to fund programs to improve undergraduate teaching.

Which of the following, if true, would cast the most doubt on the viability of the college administrators' plan described above?

(A) Profit-making corporations interested in developing products based on patents held by universities are likely to try to serve as exclusive sponsors of ongoing university research projects.

(B)   Corporate sponsors of research in university facilities are entitled to tax credits under new federal tax-code guidelines.

(C)   Research scientists at Logos University have few or no teaching responsibilities and participate little if at all in the undergraduate programs in their field.

(D)   Government-sponsored research conducted at Logos University for the most part duplicates research already completed by several profitmaking corporations.

(E)   Logos University is unlikely to attract corporate sponsorship of its scientific research.

CRO1848

795. Since it has become known that **several of a bank's top executives have been buying shares in their own bank**, the bank's depositors, who had been worried by rumors that the bank faced impending financial collapse, have been greatly relieved. They reason that, since top executives evidently have faith in the bank's financial soundness, those worrisome rumors must be false. Such reasoning might well be overoptimistic, however, since **corporate executives have been known to buy shares in their own company in a calculated attempt to dispel negative rumors about the company's health.**

In the argument given, the two **boldfaced** portions play which of the following roles?

(A)   The first describes evidence that has been taken as supporting a conclusion; the second gives a reason for questioning that support.

(B)   The first describes evidence that has been taken as supporting a conclusion; the second states a contrary conclusion that is the main conclusion of the argument.

(C)   The first provides evidence in support of the main conclusion of the argument; the second states that conclusion.

(D)   The first describes the circumstance that the argument as a whole seeks to explain; the second gives the explanation that the argument seeks to establish.

(E)   The first describes the circumstance that the argument as a whole seeks to explain; the second provides evidence in support of the explanation that the argument seeks to establish.

CRO3814

796. Between 1980 and 2000 the sea otter population of the Aleutian Islands declined precipitously. There were no signs of disease or malnutrition, so there was probably an increase in the number of otters being eaten by predators. Orcas will eat otters when seals, their normal prey, are unavailable, and the Aleutian Islands seal population declined dramatically in the 1980s. Therefore, orcas were most likely the immediate cause of the otter population decline.

Which of the following, if true, most strengthens the argument?

(A)   The population of sea urchins, the main food of sea otters, has increased since the sea otter population declined.

(B)   Seals do not eat sea otters, nor do they compete with sea otters for food.

(C)   Most of the surviving sea otters live in a bay that is inaccessible to orcas.

(D)   The population of orcas in the Aleutian Islands has declined since the 1980s.

(E)   An increase in commercial fishing near the Aleutian Islands in the 1980s caused a slight decline in the population of the fish that seals use for food.

CR76951.02

797. Political Strategist: The domestic policies of our opponents in Party X are contrary to the priorities of many middle-class voters. Yet some of these same voters are supporters of Party X and its candidates due to the party's appeals about foreign policy. In order to win these voters back, we in Party Y must prove to middle-class voters that Party X does not represent their priorities with respect to domestic policy.

Which of the following would, if true, most strongly suggest that the political strategist's plan is unlikely to succeed?

(A)   Many in the middle class who support Party X for its foreign policies also support its domestic policies and are fully aware of the implications of those policies.

(B)   Most middle-class supporters of Party X care about foreign policy and know very little about its domestic policies.

(C)   Long-term domestic policy sometimes conflicts with short-term domestic policy.

(D)   There are topics on which Party X and Party Y have significant agreement.

(E)   Some middle-class voters are concerned about both domestic and foreign policy.

CR05960

798.   Studies in restaurants show that the tips left by customers who pay their bill in cash tend to be larger when the bill is presented on a tray that bears a credit-card logo. Consumer psychologists hypothesize that simply seeing a credit-card logo makes many credit-card holders willing to spend more because it reminds them that their spending power exceeds the cash they have immediately available.

Which of the following, if true, most strongly supports the psychologists' interpretation of the studies?

(A)   The effect noted in the studies is not limited to patrons who have credit cards.

(B)   Patrons who are under financial pressure from their credit-card obligations tend to tip less when presented with a restaurant bill on a tray with a credit-card logo than when the tray has no logo.

(C)   In virtually all of the cases in the studies, the patrons who paid bills in cash did not possess credit cards.

(D)   In general, restaurant patrons who pay their bills in cash leave larger tips than do those who pay by credit card.

(E)   The percentage of restaurant bills paid with a given brand of credit card increases when that credit card's logo is displayed on the tray with which the bill is presented.

CR11633

799.   In an experiment, each volunteer was allowed to choose between an easy task and a hard task and was told that another volunteer would do the other task. Each volunteer could also choose to have a computer assign the two tasks randomly. Most volunteers chose the easy task for themselves and under questioning later said they had acted fairly. But when the scenario was described to another group of volunteers, almost all said choosing the easy task would be unfair. This shows that most people apply weaker moral standards to themselves than to others.

Which of the following is an assumption required by this argument?

(A)   At least some volunteers who said they had acted fairly in choosing the easy task would have said that it was unfair for someone else to do so.

(B)   The most moral choice for the volunteers would have been to have the computer assign the two tasks randomly.

(C)   There were at least some volunteers who were assigned to do the hard task and felt that the assignment was unfair.

(D)   On average, the volunteers to whom the scenario was described were more accurate in their moral judgments than the other volunteers were.

(E)   At least some volunteers given the choice between assigning the tasks themselves and having the computer assign them felt that they had made the only fair choice available to them.

CR08527

800.   Country X's recent stock-trading scandal should not diminish investors' confidence in the country's stock market. For one thing, **the discovery of the scandal confirms that Country X has a strong regulatory system**, as the following considerations show. In any stock market, some fraudulent activity is inevitable. If a stock market is well regulated, any significant stock-trading fraud in it will very likely be discovered. This deters potential perpetrators and facilitates improvement in regulatory processes.

In the argument, the portion in **boldface** plays which of the following roles?

(A)   It is the argument's only conclusion.

(B)   It is a conclusion for which the argument provides support and which itself is used to support the argument's main conclusion.

(C)   It is the argument's main conclusion and is supported by another explicitly stated conclusion for which further support is provided.

(D)   It is an assumption for which no explicit support is provided and is used to support the argument's only conclusion.

(E)   It is a compound statement containing both the argument's main conclusion and an assumption used to support that conclusion.

CR05644

801. **Delta Products Inc. has recently switched at least partly from older technologies using fossil fuels to new technologies powered by electricity.** The question has been raised whether it can be concluded that **for a given level of output Delta's operation now causes less fossil fuel to be consumed than it did formerly.** The answer, clearly, is yes, since the amount of fossil fuel used to generate the electricity needed to power the new technologies is less than the amount needed to power the older technologies, provided level of output is held constant.

In the argument given, the two **boldfaced** portions play which of the following roles?

(A) The first identifies the content of the conclusion of the argument; the second provides support for that conclusion.

(B) The first provides support for the conclusion of the argument; the second identifies the content of that conclusion.

(C) The first states the conclusion of the argument; the second calls that conclusion into question.

(D) The first provides support for the conclusion of the argument; the second calls that conclusion into question.

(E) Each provides support for the conclusion of the argument.

CR44930.02

802. A product that represents a clear technological advance over competing products can generally command a high price. Because **technological advances tend to be quickly surpassed** and companies want to make large profits while they still can, many companies charge the greatest price the market will bear when they have such a product. But **large profits on the new product will give competitors a strong incentive to quickly match the new product's capabilities.** Consequently, the strategy to maximize overall profit from a new product is to charge less than the greatest possible price.

In the argument above, the two portions in **boldface** play which of the following roles?

(A) The first is an assumption that forms the basis for a course of action that the argument criticizes; the second presents the course of action endorsed by the argument.

(B) The first is a consideration raised to explain the appeal of a certain strategy; the second is a consideration raised to call into question the wisdom of adopting that strategy.

(C) The first is an assumption that has been used to justify a certain strategy; the second is a consideration that is used to cast doubt on that assumption.

(D) The first is a consideration raised in support of a strategy the argument endorses; the second presents grounds in support of that consideration.

(E) The first is a consideration raised to show that adopting a certain strategy is unlikely to achieve the intended effect; the second is presented to explain the appeal of that strategy.

CR00907

803. Theater Critic: The play *La Finestrina,* now at Central Theater, was written in Italy in the eighteenth century. The director claims that this production is as similar to the original production as is possible in a modern theater. Although the actor who plays Harlequin the clown gives a performance very reminiscent of the twentieth-century American comedian Groucho Marx, Marx's comic style was very much within the comic acting tradition that had begun in sixteenth-century Italy.

The considerations given best serve as part of an argument that

(A) modern audiences would find it hard to tolerate certain characteristics of a historically accurate performance of an eighteenth-century play

(B) Groucho Marx once performed the part of the character Harlequin in *La Finestrina*

(C) in the United States the training of actors in the twentieth century is based on principles that do not differ radically from those that underlay the training of actors in eighteenth-century Italy

(D) the performance of the actor who plays Harlequin in *La Finestrina* does not serve as evidence against the director's claim

(E) the director of *La Finestrina* must have advised the actor who plays Harlequin to model his performance on comic performances of Groucho Marx

CR07257

804. Although the discount stores in Goreville's central shopping district are expected to close within five years as a result of competition from a SpendLess discount department store that just opened, those

locations will not stay vacant for long. In the five years since the opening of Colson's, a nondiscount department store, a new store has opened at the location of every store in the shopping district that closed because it could not compete with Colson's.

Which of the following, if true, most seriously weakens the argument?

(A) Many customers of Colson's are expected to do less shopping there than they did before the SpendLess store opened.

(B) Increasingly, the stores that have opened in the central shopping district since Colson's opened have been discount stores.

(C) At present, the central shopping district has as many stores operating in it as it ever had.

(D) Over the course of the next five years, it is expected that Goreville's population will grow at a faster rate than it has for the past several decades.

(E) Many stores in the central shopping district sell types of merchandise that are not available at either SpendLess or Colson's.

CR05685

805. Last year all refuse collected by Shelbyville city services was incinerated. This incineration generated a large quantity of residual ash. In order to reduce the amount of residual ash Shelbyville generates this year to half of last year's total, the city has revamped its collection program. This year city services will separate for recycling enough refuse to reduce the number of truckloads of refuse to be incinerated to half of last year's number.

Which of the following is required for the revamped collection program to achieve its aim?

(A) This year, no materials that city services could separate for recycling will be incinerated.

(B) Separating recyclable materials from materials to be incinerated will cost Shelbyville less than half what it cost last year to dispose of the residual ash.

(C) Refuse collected by city services will contain a larger proportion of recyclable materials this year than it did last year.

(D) The refuse incinerated this year will generate no more residual ash per truckload incinerated than did the refuse incinerated last year.

(E) The total quantity of refuse collected by Shelbyville city services this year will be no greater than that collected last year.

CR01801

806. Veterinarians generally derive some of their income from selling several manufacturers' lines of pet-care products. Knowing that pet owners rarely throw away mail from their pet's veterinarian unread, one manufacturer of pet-care products offered free promotional materials on its products to veterinarians for mailing to their clients. Very few veterinarians accepted the offer, however, even though the manufacturer's products are of high quality.

Which of the following, if true, most helps to explain the veterinarians' reaction to the manufacturer's promotional scheme?

(A) Most of the veterinarians to whom the free promotional materials were offered were already selling the manufacturer's pet-care products to their clients.

(B) The special promotional materials were intended as a supplement to the manufacturer's usual promotional activities rather than as a replacement for them.

(C) The manufacturer's products, unlike most equally good competing products sold by veterinarians, are also available in pet stores and in supermarkets.

(D) Many pet owners have begun demanding quality in products they buy for their pets that is as high as that in products they buy for themselves.

(E) Veterinarians sometimes recommend that pet owners use products formulated for people when no suitable product specially formulated for animals is available.

CR00778

807. The average hourly wage of television assemblers in Vernland has long been significantly lower than that in neighboring Borodia. Since Borodia dropped all tariffs on Vernlandian televisions three years ago, the number of televisions sold annually in Borodia has not changed. However, recent statistics show a drop in the number of television assemblers in Borodia. Therefore, updated trade statistics will probably indicate that the number of televisions Borodia imports annually from Vernland has increased.

Which of the following is an assumption on which the argument depends?

(A) The number of television assemblers in Vernland has increased by at least as much as the number of television assemblers in Borodia has decreased.

(B) Televisions assembled in Vernland have features that televisions assembled in Borodia do not have.

(C) The average number of hours it takes a Borodian television assembler to assemble a television has not decreased significantly during the past three years.

(D) The number of televisions assembled annually in Vernland has increased significantly during the past three years.

(E) The difference between the hourly wage of television assemblers in Vernland and the hourly wage of television assemblers in Borodia is likely to decrease in the next few years.

CR05725

808. Guidebook writer: I have visited hotels throughout the country and have noticed that in those built before 1930 the quality of the original carpentry work is generally superior to that in hotels built afterward. Clearly carpenters working on hotels before 1930 typically worked with more skill, care, and effort than carpenters who have worked on hotels built subsequently.

Which of the following, if true, most seriously weakens the guidebook writer's argument?

(A) The quality of original carpentry in hotels is generally far superior to the quality of original carpentry in other structures, such as houses and stores.

(B) Hotels built since 1930 can generally accommodate more guests than those built before 1930.

(C) The materials available to carpenters working before 1930 were not significantly different in quality from the materials available to carpenters working after 1930.

(D) The better the quality of original carpentry in a building, the less likely that building is to fall into disuse and be demolished.

(E) The average length of apprenticeship for carpenters has declined significantly since 1930.

CR02997

809. Scientists typically do their most creative work before the age of forty. It is commonly thought that this happens because aging by itself brings about a loss of creative capacity. However, studies show that **of scientists who produce highly creative work beyond the age of forty, a disproportionately large number entered their field at an older age than is usual**. Since by the age of forty the large majority of scientists have been working in their field for at least fifteen years, the studies' finding strongly suggests that the real reason why scientists over forty rarely produce highly creative work is not that they have aged but rather that **scientists over forty have generally spent too long in their field**.

In the argument given, the two portions in **boldface** play which of the following roles?

(A) The first is a claim, the accuracy of which is at issue in the argument; the second is a conclusion drawn on the basis of that claim.

(B) The first is an objection that has been raised against a position defended in the argument; the second is that position.

(C) The first is evidence that has been used to support an explanation that the argument challenges; the second is that explanation.

(D) The first is evidence that has been used to support an explanation that the argument challenges; the second is a competing explanation that the argument favors.

(E) The first provides evidence to support an explanation that the argument favors; the second is that explanation.

CR03818

810. NorthAir charges low fares for its economy-class seats, but it provides very cramped seating and few amenities. Market research shows that economy passengers would willingly pay more for wider seating and better service, and additional revenue provided by these higher ticket prices would more than cover the additional cost of providing these amenities. Even though NorthAir is searching for ways to improve its profitability, it has decided not to make these improvements.

Which of the following, if true, would most help to explain NorthAir's decision in light of its objectives?

(A) None of NorthAir's competitors offers significantly better seating and service to economy-class passengers than NorthAir does.

(B) On many of the routes that NorthAir flies, it is the only airline to offer direct flights.

(C) A few of NorthAir's economy-class passengers are satisfied with the service they receive, given the low price they pay.

(D)   Very few people avoid flying on NorthAir because of the cramped seating and poor service offered in economy class.

(E)   The number of people who would be willing to pay the high fares NorthAir charges for its business-class seats would decrease if its economy-class seating were more acceptable.

CR00774
811. Which of the following most logically completes the argument given?

Asthma, a chronic breathing disorder, is significantly more common today among adult competitive swimmers than it is among competitive athletes who specialize in other sports. Although chlorine is now known to be a lung irritant and swimming pool water is generally chlorinated, it would be rash to assume that frequent exposure to chlorine is the explanation of the high incidence of asthma among these swimmers, since _____.

(A)   young people who have asthma are no more likely to become competitive athletes than are young people who do not have asthma

(B)   competitive athletes who specialize in sports other than swimming are rarely exposed to chlorine

(C)   competitive athletes as a group have a significantly lower incidence of asthma than do people who do not participate in competitive athletics

(D)   until a few years ago, physicians routinely recommended competitive swimming to children with asthma, in the belief that this form of exercise could alleviate asthma symptoms

(E)   many people have asthma without knowing they have it and thus are not diagnosed with the condition until they begin engaging in very strenuous activities, such as competitive athletics

CR01289
812. In the country of Marut, the Foreign Trade Agency's records were reviewed in 1994 in light of information then newly available about neighboring Goro. The review revealed that in every year since 1963, the agency's projection of what Goro's gross national product (GNP) would be five years later was a serious underestimate. The review also revealed that in every year since 1963, the agency estimated Goro's GNP for the previous year—a Goro state secret—very accurately.

Of the following claims, which is most strongly supported by the statements given?

(A)   Goro's GNP fluctuated greatly between 1963 and 1994.

(B)   Prior to 1995, Goro had not released data intended to mislead the agency in making its five-year projections.

(C)   The amount by which the agency underestimated the GNP it projected for Goro tended to increase over time.

(D)   Even before the new information came to light, the agency had reason to think that at least some of the five-year projections it had made were inaccurate.

(E)   The agency's five-year projections of Goro's GNP had no impact on economic planning in Marut.

CR05082
813. Vargonia has just introduced a legal requirement that student-teacher ratios in government-funded schools not exceed a certain limit. All Vargonian children are entitled to education, free of charge, in these schools. When a recession occurs and average incomes fall, the number of children enrolled in government-funded schools tends to increase. Therefore, though most employment opportunities contract in economic recessions, getting a teaching job in Vargonia's government-funded schools will not be made more difficult by a recession.

Which of the following would be most important to determine in order to evaluate the argument?

(A)   Whether in Vargonia there are any schools not funded by the government that offer children an education free of charge

(B)   Whether the number of qualified applicants for teaching positions in government-funded schools increases significantly during economic recessions

(C)   What the current student-teacher ratio in Vargonia's government-funded schools is

(D)   What proportion of Vargonia's workers currently hold jobs as teachers in government-funded schools

(E)   Whether in the past a number of government-funded schools in Vargonia have had student-teacher ratios well in excess of the new limit

814. In Colorado subalpine meadows, nonnative dandelions co-occur with a native flower, the larkspur. Bumblebees visit both species, creating the potential for interactions between the two species with respect to pollination. In a recent study, researchers selected 16 plots containing both species; all dandelions were removed from eight plots; the remaining eight control plots were left undisturbed. The control plots yielded significantly more larkspur seeds than the dandelion-free plots, leading the researchers to conclude that the presence of dandelions facilitates pollination (and hence seed production) in the native species by attracting more pollinators to the mixed plots.

Which of the following, if true, most seriously undermines the researchers' reasoning?

(A) Bumblebees preferentially visit dandelions over larkspurs in mixed plots.

(B) In mixed plots, pollinators can transfer pollen from one species to another to augment seed production.

(C) If left unchecked, nonnative species like dandelions quickly crowd out native species.

(D) Seed germination is a more reliable measure of a species' fitness than seed production.

(E) Soil disturbances can result in fewer blooms, and hence lower seed production.

815. An experiment was done in which human subjects recognize a pattern within a matrix of abstract designs and then select another design that completes that pattern. The results of the experiment were surprising. The lowest expenditure of energy in neurons in the brain was found in those subjects who performed most successfully in the experiments.

Which of the following hypotheses best accounts for the findings of the experiment?

(A) The neurons of the brain react less when a subject is trying to recognize patterns than when the subject is doing other kinds of reasoning.

(B) Those who performed best in the experiment experienced more satisfaction when working with abstract patterns than did those who performed less well.

(C) People who are better at abstract pattern recognition have more energy-efficient neural connections.

(D) The energy expenditure of the subjects' brains increases when a design that completes the initially recognized pattern is determined.

(E) The task of completing a given design is more capably performed by athletes, whose energy expenditure is lower when they are at rest.

816. With seventeen casinos, Moneyland operates the most casinos in a certain state. Although intent on expanding, it was outmaneuvered by Apex Casinos in negotiations to acquire the Eldorado chain. To complete its acquisition of Eldorado, Apex must sell five casinos to comply with a state law forbidding any owner to operate more than one casino per county. Since Apex will still be left operating twenty casinos in the state, it will then have the most casinos in the state.

Which of the following, if true, most seriously undermines the prediction?

(A) Apex, Eldorado, and Moneyland are the only organizations licensed to operate casinos in the state.

(B) The majority of Eldorado's casinos in the state will need extensive renovations if they are to continue to operate profitably.

(C) Some of the state's counties do not permit casinos.

(D) Moneyland already operates casinos in the majority of the state's counties.

(E) Apex will use funds it obtains from the sale of the five casinos to help fund its acquisition of the Eldorado chain.

817. It is widely assumed that people need to engage in intellectual activities such as solving crossword puzzles or mathematics problems in order to maintain mental sharpness as they age. In fact, however, simply talking to other people—that is, participating in social interaction, which engages many mental and perceptual skills—suffices. Evidence to this effect comes from a study showing that the more social contact people report, the better their mental skills.

Which of the following, if true, most seriously weakens the force of the evidence cited?

(A)   As people grow older, they are often advised to keep exercising their physical and mental capacities in order to maintain or improve them.

(B)   Many medical conditions and treatments that adversely affect a person's mental sharpness also tend to increase that person's social isolation.

(C)   Many people are proficient both in social interactions and in solving mathematical problems.

(D)   The study did not itself collect data but analyzed data bearing on the issue from prior studies.

(E)   The tasks evaluating mental sharpness for which data were compiled by the study were more akin to mathematics problems than to conversation.

8.5 Answer Key

652. B	686. C	720. C	754. C	788. D
653. B	687. B	721. D	755. A	789. A
654. B	688. D	722. C	756. C	790. C
655. D	689. D	723. C	757. D	791. C
656. D	690. C	724. E	758. D	792. B
657. D	691. E	725. C	759. D	793. E
658. E	692. B	726. D	760. A	794. D
659. C	693. A	727. C	761. E	795. A
660. C	694. E	728. A	762. C	796. C
661. D	695. B	729. D	763. E	797. A
662. A	696. E	730. D	764. D	798. B
663. D	697. D	731. A	765. A	799. A
664. B	698. E	732. C	766. D	800. B
665. C	699. B	733. E	767. A	801. B
666. E	700. E	734. C	768. E	802. B
667. B	701. D	735. B	769. E	803. D
668. B	702. D	736. C	770. A	804. B
669. A	703. D	737. A	771. D	805. D
670. A	704. B	738. C	772. E	806. C
671. B	705. C	739. B	773. D	807. C
672. E	706. D	740. C	774. E	808. D
673. C	707. D	741. D	775. E	809. E
674. E	708. A	742. C	776. B	810. E
675. C	709. A	743. A	777. E	811. D
676. C	710. E	744. E	778. E	812. D
677. A	711. B	745. C	779. D	813. B
678. E	712. B	746. E	780. D	814. E
679. A	713. B	747. C	781. B	815. C
680. D	714. D	748. D	782. A	816. A
681. B	715. D	749. E	783. D	817. B
682. D	716. E	750. A	784. C	
683. E	717. C	751. A	785. A	
684. D	718. D	752. E	786. B	
685. A	719. B	753. E	787. D	

8.6 Answer Explanations

The following discussion is intended to familiarize you with the most efficient and effective approaches to Critical Reasoning questions. The particular questions in this chapter are generally representative of the kinds of Critical Reasoning questions you will encounter on the GMAT exam. Remember that it is the problem solving strategy that is important, not the specific details of a particular question.

Questions 652 to 706 - Difficulty: Easy

*CR70041.01

652. Arts advocate: Few universities require that students who are specializing in science and technology take many art courses. However, real progress in science and technology requires an element of creativity, which the arts foster. Thus, to help science and technology students succeed in their careers, universities should increase the number of art courses required for them.

Which of the following would, if true, most strengthen the argument above?

(A)   Universities required more art courses for science and technology students in the past.

(B)   Participation in art courses increases students' creative thinking in their science and technology courses.

(C)   More students who are interested in art would specialize in science and technology if the number of art courses required for those programs were increased.

(D)   Some of the most prominent scientists began their careers as artists.

(E)   Discussion of science and technology topics in art courses increases creative thinking among students in those courses.

Argument Evaluation

Situation   The arts advocate argues that universities should increase the number of art courses required for students specializing in science and technology, with the goal of helping these students succeed in their careers. Few universities require students in these fields to take many art courses.

Reasoning   *What piece of information, if true and added to the argument, would most strengthen it?* One of the arts advocate's premises is that progress in science and technology requires creativity. Another premise is that courses in the arts foster creativity. The conclusion is that universities should, for the sake of promoting career success, require students specializing in science and technology to take more courses in art. Suppose that participation in art courses enriches students' participation in the science and technology courses: that would be a further reason for universities to require that the students take more art courses.

A   This does not indicate that increasing art offerings now for science and technology students is the most prudent course of action. Universities' past decision to offer fewer art courses for science and technology students may have resulted from review of data, careful analysis, and prudent policy assumptions. For example, the decision may have been required in order to finance provision of more science and technology courses.

B   **Correct.** This suggests that participation in art courses increases the value of science and technology courses, an additional piece of information that strengthens the argument.

C   The argument does not suggest that the goal of requiring science and technology students to take more art courses is to persuade more students interested in art to specialize in science and technology. This information is therefore largely irrelevant to the arts advocate's Reasoning.

D   This information does not address the role art may have played in the scientists' achievements in science and technology. Several of these scientists may well have been aspiring artists who failed or became disenchanted and discovered that they could better exploit their talents in science and technology.

E   The arts advocate does not advocate that science and technology topics be addressed in art courses. The arts advocate's Reasoning focuses on the value of art courses in fostering creativity.

The correct answer is B.

_____
*These numbers correlate with the online test bank question number. See the GMAT™ Official Guide Question Index in the back of this book.

665

CR53631.01

653. Ramirez: The film industry claims that pirated DVDs, which are usually cheaper than legitimate DVDs and become available well before a film's official DVD release date, adversely affect its bottom line. But the industry should note what the spread of piracy indicates: consumers want lower prices and faster DVD releases. Lowering prices of DVDs and releasing them sooner would mitigate piracy's negative effect on film industry profits.

The argument above relies on which of the following assumptions?

(A) Releasing legitimate DVDs earlier would not cause any reduction in the revenue the film industry receives from the films' theatrical release.

(B) Some people who would otherwise purchase pirated DVDs would be willing to purchase legitimate DVDs if they were less expensive and released earlier than they are now.

(C) The film industry will in the future be able to produce DVDs more cheaply than is currently the case.

(D) Some current sellers of pirated DVDs would likely discontinue their businesses if legitimate DVDs were released faster and priced lower.

(E) Current purchasers of pirated DVDs are aware that those DVDs are not authorized by the film industry.

Argument Construction

Situation   Pirated DVDs of films are released earlier than the film's official DVD release day. They are also sold more cheaply. These practices cut into the revenue expected from a film's official DVD sales. According to Ramirez, the prevalence of piracy indicates that consumers want lower prices and earlier releases. Ramirez concludes that if the official DVDs were sold more cheaply and released earlier, the impact of piracy on film industry profits might be reduced.

Reasoning   *What must Ramirez assume for the argument to be logically correct?* To evaluate which answer choice the argument relies on assuming, ask yourself about each answer choice, "If this statement were false, then would the argument's conclusion also have to false?" If the answer is yes, then the argument must be making that assumption. For example, suppose the statement made in answer choice B were false. That would mean that none of the people who would otherwise purchase pirated DVDs would be willing to purchase legitimate DVDs even if these were released earlier and at a significantly lower price. If that were so, then the measures Ramirez suggests would not mitigate piracy.

A   This does not have to be assumed for Ramirez's reasoning to be logically good. Earlier release of the official DVDs at a lower price could somewhat reduce revenue from movie theater showings of the films. But if the revenue from official DVDs released earlier and priced lower were greatly boosted through greatly increased official DVD sales, overall revenue for each film could be higher than would be the case with widespread piracy.

B   **Correct.** If all existing purchasers of pirated film DVDs continued to purchase such DVDs even after implementation of the changes Ramirez advocates, then the changes would not mitigate the destructive consequences of piracy. Thus, Ramirez's reasoning must assume that the recommended changes would cause at least some former purchasers of pirated DVDs to begin purchasing the official DVDs.

C   This might improve profits provided revenue did not also decline. Ramirez's argument does not depend on the assumption that the cost of producing DVDs will decline. Ramirez's reasoning assumes that total sales volume for official DVDs would increase if piracy were reduced.

D   Ideally this would occur with the change Ramirez recommends, but it does not have to be assumed for Ramirez's reasoning to be logically sound. For example, the result Ramirez predicts could occur if all existing sellers of pirated DVDs continued to sell them but sold fewer.

E   This is likely true but is not an assumption that Ramirez needs to make for the reasoning to be logically sound. Even if some DVDs sold by DVD sellers were pirated without the sellers being aware of it, e.g., if they purchased them from a fraudulent wholesaler, the fact that the pirated DVDs are sold more cheaply and before the release of the official DVD would reduce the filmmakers' total revenue.

The correct answer is B.

CR79041.01

654. Harunia Province has a relatively dry climate and is attracting a fast-growing population that has put increasing demands on its water supply. The two companies that supply water to the region have struggled to keep up with demand and still remain profitable. Yet now they are asking Harunian authorities to write residential water-use regulations that could reduce their revenues and restrict their future flexibility in supplying water profitably.

Which of the following would, if true, most logically help explain why the water-supply companies are asking the authorities to regulate residential water use?

(A)   The companies are planning large water-transportation and irrigation systems that require the approval of neighboring provinces.

(B)   The companies believe regulation is inevitable and that having it in place now will allow better planning and thus future profitability.

(C)   Few, if any, Harunian government officials have investments in the companies or serve on their boards of directors.

(D)   The companies believe that the population is not likely to continue to grow.

(E)   Long-term climate projections suggest that greater rainfall will eventually increase the amount of water available.

Argument Construction

Situation   Two water-supply companies are asking the authorities in Harunia Province to regulate residential water use, even though regulation could reduce their revenues and restrict their flexibility in supplying water profitably in the future.

Reasoning   *Which piece of information would most help explain why the companies are advocating water-use regulations that would restrict their operations?* The companies are already struggling to keep up with demand from a fast-growing population in the region. So why would they advocate regulations that could, at least in the immediate term, reduce their profits and restrict them? Is there any advantage that the companies perceive—an advantage that would outweigh any disadvantages—in getting regulations instituted soon?

A   It is unclear how this information bears on the companies' request for regulations in Harunia Province, since neighboring provinces seem primarily involved.

B   **Correct.** The companies presumably must strategically plan their capital investments to cope with increasing water demand in Harunia Province and to receive adequate return on that investment. In that context it seems critically important for the companies to have certainty at the planning stage about future regulatory requirements. Moreover, given possible shortfalls in water supply, the companies would reasonably expect government regulation even if they did not request it.

C   This suggests that, in framing water regulations, Harunian government officials will not be influenced by financial interests, so the companies cannot expect to obtain special favors from the regulatory authorities in the framing of water regulations.

D   If anything, this suggests that the companies could continue to operate without any regulatory regime that might restrict their operations.

E   This would presumably result in a weakening of the case for residential water-use regulation and would also make it easier for the water-supply companies to meet demand.

The correct answer is B.

CR31551.01
655. Loss of the Gocha mangrove forests has caused coastal erosion, reducing fish populations and requiring the Gocha Fishing Cooperative (GFC) to partially fund dredging and new shore facilities. However, as part of its subsidiary businesses, the GFC has now invested in a program to replant significant parts of the coast with mangrove trees. Given income from a controlled harvest of wood with continuing replanting, the mangrove regeneration effort makes it more likely that the cooperative will increase its net income.

Which of the following, if true, would most strengthen the argument that mangrove replanting will increase the Gocha cooperative's net income?

(A)	The cost of dredging and shore facilities was shared with the local government.
(B)	The GFC will be able to hire local workers to assist with the mangrove replanting.
(C)	The GFC derives 10 percent of its revenue from salt-production facilities in an area previously cleared of mangroves.
(D)	Mangrove forests tend to increase the commercial fish populations in coastal fishing grounds.
(E)	A controlled harvesting of mangrove wood by the GFC would have little effect on coastal erosion.

Argument Evaluation

Situation	A subsidiary business of the Gocha Fishing Cooperative (GFC) has invested in a program to replant significant parts of the coast with mangrove trees.

Reasoning	*What additional information, if true, would most strengthen the argument's support for the conclusion that the mangrove regeneration effort will increase the GFC's net income?* If the regeneration effort helped the GFC's fishing operations, this could lead to an increase in GFC's income.

A	If the local government helped with the cost of dredging and shore facilities, that would help reduce the GFC's costs, but that is not directly related to the impact of the GFC's mangrove regeneration effort on GFC's net income.

B	It is unclear whether hiring local workers to assist with mangrove replanting would be less costly than hiring workers from elsewhere, so it is unclear whether this would help the GFC increase its net income.

C	The information provided does not indicate whether the mangrove regeneration effort will have any effect on its salt-production facilities, or any revenue or profit that it derives from these facilities, so this does not strengthen the argument.

D	**Correct.** If the mangrove restoration effort helps increase the commercial fish population in coastal fishing grounds, then there is a good chance that the GFC's income from its fishing operations will increase as a result.

E	The information provided does not indicate what, if any, effect coastal erosion has on GFC's net income, so the fact that controlled harvesting of mangrove wood would have little effect on coastal erosion does not strengthen the argument.

The correct answer is D.

CR07651.01

656. Executives at the Fizzles Beverage Company plan to boost profits in Country X on their range of fruit-flavored drinks by introducing new flavors based on tropical fruits that are little known there. The executives reason that since the fruit drinks of other companies have none of these flavors, Fizzles will not have to compete for customers and thus will be able to sell the drinks at a higher price.

Which of the following, if true, presents the most serious potential weakness of the plan?

(A) The new fruit drinks would be priced significantly higher than other Fizzles fruit drinks with more conventional flavors.

(B) In a telephone survey, at least one of the consumers contacted said that they preferred many of the new flavors to all of the more familiar flavors.

(C) To build widespread demand for the new flavors, Fizzles would have to launch an advertising campaign to familiarize consumers with them.

(D) Consumers choosing among fruit-flavored drinks of different brands generally buy on the basis of name recognition and price rather than the specific fruit flavor.

(E) Few consumers who are loyal to a specific brand of fruit-flavored drinks would willingly switch to another brand that costs more.

Evaluation of a Plan

Situation   Fizzle Beverage Company's executives plan to offer drinks with tropical fruit flavors that are little known in Country X in the hope that doing so will boost profits in that country. They reason that because their competitors in that country do not offer drinks with these flavors, Fizzle will be able to sell the drinks at a premium price.

Reasoning   *What casts the most doubt on the claim that the executive's plan will effectively allow them to sell fruit-flavored drinks at a higher price?* The executives believe that the lack of a direct competitor to these drinks will allow the company to sell the drinks for a higher price. But any information indicating that something other than the specific fruit flavor of the drink drives sales of fruit-flavored drinks would cast doubt on the plan.

A   We have already been told that the prices will be higher. The question is whether they will be able to sell the drink successfully at these higher prices as a result of the plan.

B   This provides at least some very slight support for the belief that the plan would succeed (if no one at all preferred the new drinks, then the plan would almost certainly fail); however, the question asks for something that would cast doubt on the effectiveness of the plan.

C   When introducing a new product, companies usually have to launch advertising campaigns, and quite frequently such campaigns effectively create demand for the product, so the fact that Fizzles will have to launch an advertising campaign does not cast doubt on the plan.

D   **Correct.** The plan depends on consumers wanting the drinks because of their unique, unfamiliar flavors, and being willing to pay a higher price for them because of their uniqueness in the market. If price (presumably a lower one) and name recognition, rather than the specific fruit flavor, are what generally drive sales, then it seems unlikely that the executives' plan will succeed.

E   Nothing in the information provided indicates how many consumers are loyal to any specific brand of fruit-flavored drinks. Perhaps the vast majority of consumers are willing to switch brands. If that is so, then the fact that the very few who are loyal to a specific brand would not be willing to switch would not cast much doubt on the effectiveness of the plan.

The correct answer is D.

CR33061.01

657. Economist: In 2015, the average per-person amount paid for goods and services purchased by consumers in Country X was the equivalent of $17,570 in United States dollars, just 30 percent of the corresponding figure of $58,566 for Country Y. Yet in 2015, there was already a substantial middle class in Country X that had discretionary income for middle-class consumer goods such as new vehicles, computers, or major household appliances, while a significant portion of the middle class in Country Y did not have sufficient income to purchase such items.

Which of the following, if true, most helps explain the discrepancy in the relationships described by the economist?

(A) There are many consumer goods, such as household appliances, that are produced in Country X to be sold in the Country Y market.

(B) The volume of trade between Country X and Country Y is increasing rapidly in both directions.

(C) The economy of Country Y is recovering from a downturn that affected both Country Y and Country X.

(D) Country X residents pay much less than their Country Y counterparts for housing, transportation, and child care.

(E) In Country Y as well as in Country X, there are few assembly-line jobs in factories that pay a middle-class wage.

Argument Construction

Situation An economist points out that even though in 2015 the average per-person amount paid for goods and services in Country X was only 30 percent of the corresponding figure in Country Y, a substantial middle class in Country X had discretionary income for consumer goods whereas a substantial portion of the middle class in Country Y did not.

Reasoning *What, if true, would most help explain the discrepancies described by the economist?* Information indicating that residents in Country X pay much less for nondiscretionary items than do residents of Country Y would help explain why, even though people in Country Y pay on average three times more for goods and services than people in Country X, Country X has a more substantial middle class capable of buying discretionary goods than does Country Y.

A   That many consumer goods produced in Country X are intended to be sold in Country Y does not help explain why many people in Country Y are not able to afford such goods.

B   An increasing volume of trade between Country X and Country Y—which, for all we know, is perfectly balanced—would not help explain any discrepancies between the two countries.

C   That the economies of both Country X and Country Y both suffered a downturn, and Country Y is recovering, could not plausibly explain why many people in Country Y have trouble paying for discretionary goods unless we had the information that Country Y's recovery was significantly slower than Country X's; but we do not have that information.

D   Correct. That people in one nation pay far less for nondiscretionary goods than people in another nation would potentially be helpful in explaining how the people in the former nation would more easily be able to afford discretionary goods.

E   If a claim is true of both Country X and Country Y, it would not help explain a discrepancy between the two countries.

The correct answer is D.

CR09616
658. Neuroscientist: Memory evolved to help animals react appropriately to situations they encounter by drawing on the past experience of similar situations. But this does not require that animals perfectly recall every detail of all their experiences. Instead, to function well, memory should generalize from past experiences that are similar to the current one.

The neuroscientist's statements, if true, most strongly support which of the following conclusions?

(A)   At least some animals perfectly recall every detail of at least some past experiences.

(B)   Perfectly recalling every detail of all their past experiences could help at least some animals react more appropriately than they otherwise would to new situations they encounter.

(C)   Generalizing from past experiences requires clear memories of most if not all the details of those experiences.

(D)   Recalling every detail of all past experiences would be incompatible with any ability to generalize from those experiences.

(E)   Animals can often react more appropriately than they otherwise would to situations they encounter if they draw on generalizations from past experiences of similar situations.

Argument Construction

Situation   A neuroscientist claims that memory evolved to help animals learn how to react appropriately by generalizing from past experiences but that this does not require animals to remember all details of those experiences.

Reasoning   *What conclusion would the neuroscientist's theory about memory most strongly support?* The neuroscientist asserts that the evolutionary function of memory is to help animals learn to react appropriately by drawing on generalizations from similar experiences they have had. If memory is to serve this function, drawing on generalizations must actually help animals learn to react more appropriately than they otherwise would, even when they do not remember all the details of past experiences.

A   Even if no animal ever recalls all the details of any past experience, animals could still learn through generalizations, as the neuroscientist claims.

B   This statement could be false even if all of what the neuroscientist says is true. Even if it were never helpful for any animal to recall every detail of all its past experiences, animals could still benefit by learning through generalizations.

C   Generalizations from experiences might be made while the experiences are occurring, so that only the generalizations and not the details need to be remembered.

D   The neuroscientist only claims that remembering perfect details is not required for memory to serve its function, not that such perfect recall is incompatible with memory serving its function.

E   **Correct.** If the evolutionary function of memory is to help animals react more appropriately by drawing on generalizations from past experiences, it follows that animal memories can often successfully serve this function in this manner.

The correct answer is E.

CR52061.01

659. In Country X's last election, the Reform Party beat its main opponent, the Conservative Party, although pollsters, employing in-person interviews shortly before the vote, had projected a Conservative Party victory. Afterwards, the pollsters determined that, unlike Conservative Party supporters, Reform Party supporters were less likely to express their party preference during in-person interviews than they were during telephone interviews. Therefore, using only telephone interviews instead would likely result in more accurate projections for the next election.

Which of the following statements, if true, would most support the argument in the passage?

(A) The number of voters in Country X's next election will be significantly larger than the number of voters in the last election.

(B) The Conservative Party will win the next election.

(C) For each person interviewed in telephone polls before the next election, pollsters will be able to reasonably determine the likelihood of that person voting.

(D) People who expressed no party preference during the in-person interviews shortly before Country X's last election did not outnumber the people who expressed a preference for the Conservative Party.

(E) In the next election, pollsters will be able to conduct more in-person interviews than telephone interviews.

Argument Evaluation

Situation Pollsters, using in-person interviews shortly before the last election in Country X, incorrectly predicted that the Conservative Party would win that election, whereas the Reform Party won instead. The pollsters determined that Reform Party supporters, unlike Conservative Party supporters, are less likely to give their party preference in person than in telephone interviews.

Reasoning *What additional information, if true, would most strengthen the support, in light of the given information, for the prediction that using only telephone interviews would result in more accurate projections in the next election in Country X?* Even if in telephone interviews pollsters are more likely to get accurate information about which party a person interviewed supports, the pollsters' projections may not be accurate if the pollsters are unable to determine whether that person is actually likely to vote. So, information indicating that pollsters will be able to determine the likelihood that a person will vote would strengthen support for the conclusion.

A If this larger number of voters in the next election is not anticipated by pollsters, then it may affect the accuracy of their predictions. However, the effect would likely be a decrease, rather than an increase, in accuracy. If the pollsters are able to accurately predict voter turnout, then their predictions for the next election could be more accurate. But we have no indication as to whether their turnout predictions will be accurate.

B If the Conservative Party will win the next election, an underestimate of Reform Party support will be less important for the accuracy of the projection of which party will win.

C **Correct.** It would certainly be helpful if the pollsters were able to determine how likely the person they were interviewing would be to vote.

D This is irrelevant to the argument. The conclusion concerns the relative accuracy of telephone interviews in predicting voting numbers in the next election.

E If pollsters are able to do more in-person interviews than telephone interviews for the next election, that at least weakly suggests that they might not be able to conduct a sufficient number of telephone interviews to get a representative sample—which would weaken support for the conclusion, not strengthen it.

The correct answer is C.

CR40751.01

660. A company that manufactures plastic products from recyclable plastic is, surprisingly, unconcerned that economic conditions may worsen, despite analysts' belief that consumers would then consider ecofriendly plastic products an expensive luxury. But the company reasons that it will be able to lower its prices because, in a weakened economy, other ecofriendly plastic manufacturers are likely to fail. Demand among manufacturers for recyclable plastics as raw materials would then plummet, creating an oversupply of such materials, making them less expensive for the manufacturer to purchase and thus lowering the company's costs.

Which of the following, if true, most weakens the company's reasoning?

(A) Smaller ecofriendly plastic manufacturers are more likely to fail in a weakened economy than larger ecofriendly manufacturers are.

(B) Some retailers whose sales include various companies' ecofriendly plastic products have struggled in recent years despite the overall good economy.

(C) Consumers would likely soon learn of the oversupply of recyclable plastics and cease recycling them, significantly raising manufacturers' raw-material costs.

(D) Retailers, including retailers that cater to consumers seeking certain types of ecofriendly products, may lose some business if economic conditions worsen.

(E) The plastics used by the company in its products were, after a recent investigation by a regulatory body, declared to be safe for consumers.

Argument Evaluation

Situation   A company that manufactures products from recyclable plastics believes that if economic conditions worsen it will be able to lower its prices. It believes its costs will decline because other ecofriendly plastic manufacturers will fail, thereby reducing the demand for recyclable plastics as raw materials.

Reasoning   *What would most weaken the reasoning?* Suppose the company's costs did not decline and the company consequently could not reduce its prices. Even if demand for recyclable plastics as raw materials weakens in an economic downturn, the company's costs may nonetheless not decline if for some reason the supply of recyclable plastics also declines. If so, then the company may well not be able to lower its prices and stay profitable.

A   We are not told whether the company in question is a smaller ecofriendly plastic manufacturer or a larger one. Given that, the fact that smaller such companies are more likely to fail than larger ones may strengthen the argument rather than weaken it (assuming the company in question is a larger such company).

B   If some retailers whose sales include various companies' ecofriendly plastic products have struggled in a healthy economy, they may well struggle even more in a weak economy. This could help drive the company's competitors out of business, which is what the company argues is likely to happen in an economic downturn; so rather than weakening the argument, this arguably strengthens it.

C   **Correct.** Suppose consumers learn of the oversupply of recyclable plastics and stop recycling them as a result; the oversupply may therefore not last long, and indeed a shortage might arise. This would lead not to lower raw-material costs, as the company argues, but to higher raw-material costs.

D   The information that retailers' lost business might result in a decrease in sales of the competing products does not weaken the argument. A loss of business due to worsening economic conditions is a presupposition of the argument.

E   The fact that the plastics used by the company have been declared safe has probably helped boost demand for the company's products, and perhaps for the competing products as well, yet an economic downturn could still hurt the company's competitors. So, this does little to weaken the company's argument.

The correct answer is C.

CR73241.01

661. Researchers asked volunteers to imagine they were running a five-kilometer race against 50 people and then against 500 people, races in each of which the top 10 percent would receive a $1,000 prize. Asked about the effort they would apply in the respective cases, the volunteers indicated, on average, that they would run slower in the race against the greater number of people. A likely explanation of this result is that those of the volunteers who were most *comparatively inclined*—those who most tended to compare themselves with others in the social environment—determined (perhaps unconsciously) that extreme effort would not be worthwhile in the 500-competitor race.

Which of the following would, if known to be true, most help justify the explanation offered above?

(A)   The volunteers who were most comparatively inclined were also those that had the greatest desire to win a $1,000 prize.

(B)   The volunteers who were the least comparatively inclined had no greater desire to win the $1,000 than those who were the most comparatively inclined.

(C)   The volunteers who were most comparatively inclined were likely to indicate that they would run the two races at the same speed.

(D)   The most comparatively inclined volunteers believed that they were significantly less likely to finish in the top 10 percent in the race against 500 than in the race against 50.

(E)   Volunteers were chosen for participation in the study on the basis of answers to various questions designed to measure the degree to which the volunteers were comparatively inclined.

Argument Construction

Situation   Volunteers were asked how much effort they would expend when running a five-kilometer race against 50 people and how much they would expend in such a race against 500 people, when the prize for each race is $1,000 for finishing in the top 10 percent. The volunteers indicated, on average, that they would run more slowly in the race against 500 people than in the race against 50 people. This result is likely because comparatively inclined volunteers believed that extreme effort would not have been worthwhile in the race against 500 competitors.

Reasoning   *What would most help to justify the explanation proposed above?* If comparatively inclined volunteers thought it was at least as likely that they would finish in the top 10 percent in the race against 500 as in the race against 50, the proposed explanation would fail. Thus, it would help justify the explanation if we knew that the comparatively inclined volunteers believed they were less likely to win in the race against 500 than in the race against 50.

A   If one knew that the volunteers who were most comparatively inclined had the greatest desire to win the $1,000, one might actually be more puzzled about why these volunteers said they would expend less effort against the 500 competitors. If they expended less effort, they would probably be less likely to finish in the top 10 percent.

B   If one knew that the volunteers who were more comparatively inclined had no less desire to win a $1,000 prize than those who were least comparatively inclined, one would have at least some reason to think the comparatively inclined volunteers wanted to win the $1,000; this clearly cannot explain why they would not expend as much effort in the 500-competitor race as in the 50-competitor race.

C   The claim that one would run the two races at the same speed contradicts the position expressed on average by the group as a whole (that they would run more slowly against the larger group of contestants). Therefore, if the most comparatively inclined volunteers said that they would run the two races at the same speed, their position would be inconsistent with that of the group as a whole. So if this answer choice were true, it would weaken, rather than strengthen, the explanation that the views of the most comparatively inclined volunteers account for the fact that the volunteers said, on average, that they would run more slowly against the greater number of contestants.

D   **Correct.** If the most comparatively inclined volunteers believed they would be far less likely to finish in the top 10 percent in the race against 500 than in the race against 50, then they would likely believe that extreme effort would not be worthwhile in the race with more people. This therefore is likely to be at least part of the explanation.

E   Even if volunteers were chosen on the basis of answers to questions designed to measure how comparatively inclined they were, we are not told whether the volunteers were chosen because of the degree to which they were comparatively inclined.

The correct answer is D.

CR41141.01

662. According to a study, after a week of high-altitude living, twenty men had slimmed down. The men, middle-aged residents of low-altitude areas, had been taken to a research station at 2,650 meters (8,694 feet) above sea level. They had unrestricted access to food and were forbidden vigorous exercise, yet they lost an average of 1.5 kilograms (3.3 pounds) during their one-week stay. Clearly, the lower availability of oxygen at higher altitudes, or hypobaric hypoxia, can be said to have caused the weight loss, since _____.

Which of the following would, if true, most logically complete the argument?

(A) a decrease in oxygen intake has been shown to depress appetite

(B) the men all participated in the same kinds of exercise during their stay

(C) the foods available to the men had fewer calories than the foods they usually ate

(D) exercise at higher altitudes is more difficult than exercise at lower altitudes is

(E) several weeks after returning home, the men still weighed less than they had before the study

Argument Construction

Situation   Twenty middle-aged men lived at a high-altitude research station for one week. They had unrestricted access to food but did no vigorous exercise. By the end of their stay they had lost an average 1.5 kilograms (3.3 pounds) of weight.

Reasoning   *Which additional information, if true, would most help support the claim that lower availability of oxygen at higher altitudes caused the weight loss?* The puzzlement arises from the fact that the twenty men had free access to food and did no vigorous exercise. And consuming less of the types of food they would normally eat would have caused weight loss. But suppose one or both of these behaviors had not occurred?

A   **Correct.** This information helps support the explanatory hypothesis that lower oxygen levels accounted for the weight loss. The men's intake of oxygen certainly decreased at an altitude of 2,650 meters (8694 feet), since they normally lived in low-altitude areas. Moreover, reduced appetite would provide a mechanism by which weight loss could have occurred.

B   The men were forbidden vigorous exercise and we can assume that, in a research context, they followed this restriction. Mild exercise would be unlikely to explain the weight loss.

C   This does not support the explanatory hypothesis concerning the role of oxygen reduction in the weight loss.

D   Even if this is generally true, it does not support the hypothesis that lower oxygen levels accounted for the weight loss.

E   This provides no support for the explanatory hypothesis that lower oxygen levels accounted for the weight loss. It might even cast some doubt on the hypothesis, since over a period of several weeks following the study, the men's weight did not increase with their return to their normal oxygen levels.

The correct answer is A.

CR11741.01

663. Editorial: Our city's public transportation agency is facing a budget shortfall. The fastest growing part of the budget has been employee retirement benefits, which are exceptionally generous. Unless the budget shortfall is resolved, transportation service will be cut, and many transportation employees will lose their jobs. Thus, it would be in the employees' best interest for their union to accept cuts in retirement benefits.

Which of the following is an assumption the editorial's argument requires?

(A) The transportation employees' union should not accept cuts in retirement benefits if doing so would not be in the employees' best interest.

(B) The only feasible way for the agency to resolve the budget shortfall would involve cutting transportation service and eliminating jobs.

(C) Other things being equal, it is in the transportation employees' interest to have exceptionally generous retirement benefits.

(D) Cutting the retirement benefits would help resolve the agency's budget shortfall.

(E) The transportation employees' union will not accept cuts in retirement benefits if doing so will not allow more transportation employees to keep their jobs.

Argument Construction

Situation   An editorial indicates that the fastest growing part of a particular city's public transportation agency's budget is employee retirement benefits. The agency's budget has a shortfall. If the shortfall is not resolved, transportation service will be cut and many of the employees will lose their jobs

Reasoning   *What must be true if we are to accept the editorial's conclusion, that it is in the employee's best interest to accept cuts in retirement benefits?* If cutting the employees' retirement benefits would not be sufficient to resolve the budget shortfall, then it may well not be in employees' best interest to accept such cuts. The reasons given for accepting the cuts are related to the undesirable consequences of a continued shortfall.

A   The argument is about whether the union's accepting the cuts is in fact in the employees' best interest, and does not require any assumption about whether employees should accept what is in their best interest.

B   This is incompatible with an assumption made by the argument. The argument assumes that cutting the retirement benefits of the employees would help resolve the budget shortfall.

C   The argument would actually be stronger if it were NOT the case that it is in the employees' interest to have exceptionally generous retirement benefits.

D   Correct. If cutting retirement benefits would not help resolve the agency's budget shortfall, then cutting those benefits would not help the employees avoid job cuts.

E   The argument does not depend on assuming anything regarding what factors would motivate the union's acceptance.

The correct answer is D.

CR94231.01

664. Researchers hope to find clues about the A'mk peoples who lived in the Kaumpta region about one thousand years ago but who left few obvious traces. The researchers plan to hire the few remaining shamans of the modern-day indigenous people in Kaumpta, who are believed to be descended from the A'mk, to lead them to ancestral sites that may be the remains of A'mk buildings or ceremonial spaces. The shamans were taught the location of such sites as part of their traditional training as youths, and their knowledge of traditional Kaumpta customs may help determine the nature of any sites the researchers find.

Which of the following is an assumption on which the success of the plan depends?

(A) The researchers have reliable evidence that the A'mk of one thousand years ago built important ceremonial spaces.

(B) The shamans have a reasonably accurate memory of A'mk sites they learned about as youths.

(C) Kaumpta shamans are generally held in high esteem for their traditional knowledge.

(D) Modern technologies available to the researchers are likely to be able to find some A'mk sites easily.

(E) Most or all A'mk sites are likely to be found within the Kaumpta region.

Evaluation of a Plan

Situation   Researchers wish to find sites of an ancient people, the A'mk, who lived in the Kaumpta region one thousand years ago. Indigenous people believed to be descended from the A'mk live in that region today. Their shamans, as youths, were taught about such sites. To discover some of these sites, the researchers plan to hire the shamans.

Reasoning   *What must be true for the success of the researchers' plan to find the sites by relying on the shamans' assistance?* The plan would fail, for example, if there were no such sites in the Kaumpta region. Therefore, the researchers' plan depends on assuming that Kaumpta have some such sites—but not that most of the sites are there. The plan also requires that the shamans collectively have reasonably accurate recall of what they learned about the sites as youths.

A   The researchers hope to find buildings or ceremonial spaces or both. However, the plan does not require ceremonial spaces to be found or that the researchers have evidence of them.

B   Correct. If the shamans collectively have no "reasonably accurate memory" of what they learned of the location of such sites, then the researchers' plan is not a useful one and can have no reasonable expectation of success.

C   This is likely to be so if the indigenous group from which they come is still committed to maintaining their traditional knowledge. But the plan does not rely on the shamans being honored among their own people. It must be assumed, of course, that the shamans currently possess "traditional knowledge" and are willing to share it.

D   The researchers' reliance on the shamans' assistance suggests that it is not so easy for the researchers to rely entirely on "modern technologies" in this case.

E   The plan can succeed even if this is not correct. What must be assumed is that at least some of the A'mk sites are within the Kaumpta region; it need not be assumed that most or all are.

The correct answer is B.

CR09994

665. Astronomer: Most stars are born in groups of thousands, each star in a group forming from the same parent cloud of gas. Each cloud has a unique, homogeneous chemical composition. Therefore, whenever two stars have the same chemical composition as each other, they must have originated from the same cloud of gas.

Which of the following, if true, would most strengthen the astronomer's argument?

(A) In some groups of stars, not every star originated from the same parent cloud of gas.

(B) Clouds of gas of similar or identical chemical composition may be remote from each other.

(C) Whenever a star forms, it inherits the chemical composition of its parent cloud of gas.

(D) Many stars in vastly different parts of the universe are quite similar in their chemical compositions.

(E) Astronomers can at least sometimes precisely determine whether a star has the same chemical composition as its parent cloud of gas.

Argument Evaluation

Situation   Most stars are born in groups, any one of which forms from a parent gas cloud with a unique, homogenous chemical composition.

Reasoning   *What would be additional evidence that any two stars with the same chemical composition originated from the same gas cloud?* The implicit reasoning is that since the chemical composition of each gas cloud is unique and homogenous, any two stars that formed from gas with the same chemical composition must have originated from the same cloud. The astronomer then infers that if two stars have the same composition now, they must have originated from the same cloud. This inference requires the assumption that the composition each star has now depends only on the composition of the cloud in which it originated. Any evidence that supports this assumption will strengthen the argument.

A   Whether or not stars born in different clouds of gas are ever in the same "group" is not clearly relevant to whether or not they ever have the same chemical composition.

B   How remote clouds of similar compositions are from each other is not clearly relevant to whether stars that have the same chemical composition may have formed from different clouds of gas. Also, the suggestion that different gas clouds may have identical compositions conflicts with the astronomer's premise that the composition of each cloud from which stars form is unique.

C   **Correct.** If each star's composition is identical to that of its parent cloud, and each cloud's composition is unique, then any two stars identical in composition must have formed from the same parent cloud.

D   If anything, this would suggest that stars with the same composition might have formed from different clouds, so it would weaken rather than strengthen the argument.

E   If astronomers could do this, they might be able to obtain additional evidence for or against the position taken in the argument, but the mere fact that they can do this does not, in itself, provide any support for the astronomer's argument because it tells us nothing about whether two stars with the same chemical composition as one another actually did originate from the same parent cloud of gas.

The correct answer is C.

CR08017

666. With employer-paid training, workers have the potential to become more productive not only in their present employment but also in any number of jobs with different employers. To increase the productivity of their workforce, many firms are planning to maintain or even increase their investments in worker training. But some training experts object that if a trained worker is hired away by another firm, the employer that paid for the training has merely subsidized a competitor. They note that such hiring has been on the rise in recent years.

Which of the following would, if true, contribute most to defeating the training experts' objection to the firms' strategy?

(A) Firms that promise opportunities for advancement to their employees get, on average, somewhat larger numbers of job applications from untrained workers than do firms that make no such promise.

(B) In many industries, employees that take continuing-education courses are more competitive in the job market.

(C) More and more educational and training institutions are offering reduced tuition fees to firms that subsidize worker training.

(D) Research shows that workers whose training is wholly or partially subsidized by their employer tend to get at least as much training as do workers who pay for all their own training.

(E) For most firms that invest in training their employees, the value added by that investment in employees who stay exceeds the value lost through other employees' leaving to work for other companies.

Evaluation of a Plan

Situation Many firms pay to train their workers in order to increase their workforces' productivity. But in recent years firms have been increasingly hiring away from each other workers who have had such training.

Reasoning *What would most help address the concern that firms that pay to train workers are thereby subsidizing competitors that hire away those workers?* In order for the employer-paid training to be worthwhile for a given firm despite the risk of subsidizing competitors that may hire away the trained workers, that firm has to gain more benefits from the training than it loses by subsidizing such competitors. Any evidence that this is true for most firms would help to address the experts' concern.

A A typical firm does not necessarily want larger numbers of applications from unqualified workers. And if hired, those workers can still be hired away by competitors after the firm has paid to train them, just as the experts warned.

B This suggests that in many industries, companies, rather than investing in employee training, prefer to hire employees who already have specifically relevant training (perhaps funded by other companies). If anything, this slightly supports, rather than defeats, the training experts' view. No firm has an interest in making its own employees more competitive in the job market unless the firm is likely to benefit from their being so.

C Even firms that pay reduced tuition fees for worker training may lose the money they pay for those fees and effectively subsidize competitors that hire the trained employees away. So this does not defeat the training experts' objection.

D The more highly trained workers—regardless of whether their training was company subsidized or not—would presumably be prime targets for recruitment by competing firms, just as the experts warned. The research finding in question does not help defeat the experts' objection.

E **Correct.** This explicitly indicates that most firms gain more than they lose from the general practice of firms paying to train their workers.

The correct answer is E.

CR93241.01

667. In emerging economies in Africa and other regions, large foreign banks that were set up during the colonial era have long played a major economic role. These institutions have tended to confine their business to the wealthier of banks' potential customers. But development of these countries' economies requires financing of the small businesses that dominate their manufacturing, farming, and services sectors. So economic growth will be likely to occur if local banks take on this portion of the financial services markets, since _____.

Which of the following completions would produce the strongest argument?

(A) local banks tend not to strive as much as large foreign banks to diversify their investments

(B) small farming and manufacturing businesses contribute to economic growth if they obtain adequate investment capital

(C) large foreign banks in emerging economies could, with local employees and appropriate local consultation, profitably expand their business to less wealthy clients

(D) some small businesses are among the wealthier customers of foreign banks in emerging economies

(E) local banks in emerging economies tend to be less risk-averse than foreign banks

Argument Construction

Situation   Large foreign banks have long played an economic role in emerging economies, but they have typically confined their business to wealthier customers. Economic development in these countries requires the financing of small businesses that dominate their manufacturing, farming, and services sectors.

Reasoning   *What would most help support the claim that growth in emerging economies will likely occur if local banks help finance small businesses in the relevant sectors of these emerging markets?* If it were the case that these small businesses would actually be likely to contribute to economic growth, given adequate investment capital, then economic growth would indeed be likely to occur if local banks provided the investment capital.

A   It could be the case that whatever sorts of investments local banks make—diversified or not—economic growth will not tend to occur; for instance, it could be that the businesses they invest in do not use the capital wisely. So, this claim does not help support the conclusion.

B   **Correct.** If small farming and manufacturing businesses will contribute to economic growth if they obtain adequate investment capital, then we have fairly good reason to think that economic growth is likely to occur if local banks take on the financing of such small businesses (we merely need to also assume that they will provide adequate investment capital when they take on this financing).

C   Even if large foreign banks could profitably expand their businesses to less-wealthy clients, we have been given no reason to think they will. Furthermore, the claim in need of support is that economic growth will occur if local, rather than foreign, banks financially support these small businesses.

D   The claim that economic growth will occur if local banks finance small business in certain sectors is not supported by the claim that there are some small businesses supported by foreign banks. If these businesses are already financially supported and yet there is not the sort of economic growth discussed, then that might even suggest that economic growth is unlikely to occur.

E   It could be that, if local banks are less risk-averse than foreign banks, they will invest in risky businesses that fail, which would not tend to support the claim that economic growth will likely result if local banks in emerging counties provide financial support for the relevant sectors.

The correct answer is B.

CR49551.01

668. Exporters in Country X are facing lower revenues due to a shortage of the large metal shipping containers in which they send their goods by sea to other countries. Fewer containers arrive in Country X due to reductions in imports. This has meant lost orders, costly delays, and a scramble for alternatives, such as air freight, all of which are costlier. Moreover, the revenues of exporters in Country X will probably continue to decline in the near future. This is because other countries are likely to find it increasingly unprofitable to export their goods to Country X, and because _____.

Which of the following would most logically complete the passage?

(A)   production of shipping containers in Country X is growing rapidly as a response to the shortage

(B)   shipping companies are willing to move containers from country to country only when the containers are full

(C)   the cost of shipping alternatives such as air freight is likely to stabilize in the near future

(D)   consumers in Country X are purchasing more products than ever before

(E)   the worldwide demand for goods made in Country X has only recently begun to rise after a long decline

Argument Construction

Situation   Exporters in Country X are finding that there is an insufficient number of shipping containers for them to use for their exports, because the number of such containers arriving in Country X has declined because of reduced imports. Also, alternative methods of shipping are relatively costly. Furthermore, other countries will likely find shipping goods to Country X to be less and less profitable.

Reasoning   *What would most support the prediction that Country X's exporters' revenues will likely see further declines in revenue in the near future?* If the number of shipping containers available to exporters is likely to decrease, then the prediction would have further support. We know that other countries exporting to Country X will find it increasingly unprofitable, so there is reason to believe their exports will decline further—meaning there will be fewer imports into Country X, which means fewer shipping containers arriving in Country X carrying imported goods, unless the shipping containers shipped in the future are less full than when they are shipped now. If shipping companies are willing to move such containers to another country only when the containers are full, then that will not occur.

A   If production of shipping containers in Country X were rapidly increasing, then the reason given for the decline in revenue for exporters in Country X—that there is an insufficient number of shipping containers—would be undermined, and so therefore would be the conclusion.

B   **Correct.** If shipping companies are unwilling to move containers from country to country unless the containers are full, then, given Country X's decline in imports, there will likely be fewer shipping containers available to Country X's exporters, which provides support for the claim that their revenues will likely decline.

C   If the cost of shipping alternatives such as air freight is likely to stabilize, then those alternative methods of shipping might become economically viable, which would undermine rather than support the conclusion.

D   The fact that consumers in Country X are purchasing more goods than ever before does not affect how much revenue is generated by exporting goods from Country X.

E   If there is increased demand for goods from Country X, then the price of such goods might increase sufficiently to make alternative methods of shipping economically viable, which would undermine rather than support the conclusion.

The correct answer is B.

CR01107

669. Candle Corporation's television stations are likely to have more income from advertisers than previously. This is because advertisers prefer to reach people in the 18- to 49-year-old age group and the number of people in that group watching Candle television is increasing. Furthermore, among Candle viewers, the percentage of viewers 18 to 49 years old is increasing.

Which of the following, if true, would most strengthen the argument that Candle Corporation will receive more income from advertisers?

(A) Advertisers carefully monitor the demographic characteristics of television audiences and purchase advertising time to reach the audiences they prefer to reach.

(B) Among people over 49 years old, fewer viewers of Candle stations buy products advertised on television than do viewers of other stations.

(C) There will be increasingly more advertisements on television that are directed at viewers who are over 49 years old.

(D) Candle stations plan to show reruns of television shows during hours when other stations run shows for the first time.

(E) People 18 to 49 years old generally have less disposable income to spend than do people over 49 years old.

Argument Evaluation

Situation Both the number and the percentage of Candle television viewers who are 18 to 49 years old are increasing. Advertisers prefer to reach people in this age group.

Reasoning *What evidence, when combined with the cited facts, would most support the prediction that Candle will receive more income from advertisers?* The argument assumes that the increasing number and percentage of Candle viewers in the age group that advertisers prefer to reach will probably encourage advertisers to spend more on advertising with Candle. This assumption could be supported by evidence that the advertisers realize that Candle is getting more viewers in that preferred age range or by evidence that this awareness will influence the advertisers' purchase of advertising time.

A **Correct.** Advertisers monitoring demographics will probably realize that Candle has increasing numbers of viewers in their preferred age range. If they purchase advertising to reach viewers in that age range, then they will probably purchase more advertising time with Candle.

B This gives advertisers less reason to advertise on Candle to reach viewers over 49 years old. Other things being equal, that makes Candle likely to receive less income from advertisers, not more income.

C Since the percentage of Candle viewers 18 to 49 years old is growing, the percentage over 49 years old is probably shrinking. This could make advertisers seeking to reach older viewers less inclined to advertise on Candle even as they increase their overall television advertising.

D Advertisers are not necessarily inclined to purchase more advertising during showings of reruns than during original airings of television shows and may even be inclined to purchase less advertising during such showings.

E This gives advertisers less incentive to try to reach audiences between 18 and 49 years old and hence less reason to purchase advertising on Candle.

The correct answer is A.

CR12584

670. A provincial government plans to raise the gasoline tax to give people an incentive to drive less, reducing traffic congestion in the long term. However, skeptics point out that most people in the province live in areas where cars are the only viable transportation to jobs and stores and therefore cannot greatly change their driving habits in response to higher gasoline prices.

In light of the skeptics' objection, which of the following, if true, would most logically support the prediction that the government's plan will achieve its goal of reducing traffic congestion?

(A) The revenue from the tax will be used to make public transportation a viable means of transportation to jobs and stores for far more people.

(B) The tax will encourage many residents to switch to more fuel-efficient cars, reducing air pollution and other problems.

(C) Because gasoline has been underpriced for decades, the province has many neighborhoods where cars are the only viable means of transportation.

(D) Most residents who cannot greatly change their driving habits could compensate for high gasoline prices by reducing other expenses.

(E) Traffic congestion is an especially serious problem for people for whom cars are the only viable means of transportation.

Evaluation of a Plan

Situation   A provincial government plans to raise the gasoline tax in order to reduce traffic congestion by discouraging people from driving. But skeptics point out that most people in the province have no viable form of transportation other than driving.

Reasoning   *What would suggest that raising the gasoline tax will reduce traffic congestion even though most people in the province have no viable form of transportation other than driving?* The skeptics point out that since most people in the province have no way to reach jobs or stores except by car, they will not be able to reduce their driving much even if the gasoline tax increases. Any evidence that raising the gasoline tax would reduce traffic congestion despite this obstacle would help to support the plan in light of the skeptics' objection.

A   **Correct.** If the tax will fund these public transit improvements, then far more people will have a viable means of transportation other than driving, undermining the basis of the skeptics' objection.

B   People switching to fuel-efficient cars would not reduce traffic congestion.

C   This essentially only tends to support the skeptics' objection. Unless the plan somehow helps to alleviate the necessity of driving (by, for example, making alternative transportation available), the information provided gives no reason to suppose that the higher costs would significantly reduce traffic congestion.

D   If residents cannot greatly change their driving habits, then the tax will not reduce traffic congestion.

E   This suggests that many residents in the province could benefit if the plan did reduce traffic congestion, but it does not provide a reason to believe the plan will have that effect.

The correct answer is A.

CR03940

671. Editorial: The roof of Northtown's municipal equipment-storage building collapsed under the weight of last week's heavy snowfall. The building was constructed recently and met local building-safety codes in every particular, except that the nails used for attaching roof supports to the building's columns were of a smaller size than the codes specify for this purpose. Clearly, this collapse exemplifies how even a single, apparently insignificant departure from safety standards can have severe consequences.

Which of the following, if true, most seriously weakens the editorial's argument?

(A) The only other buildings to suffer roof collapses from the weight of the snowfall were older buildings constructed according to less exacting standards than those in the codes.

(B) The amount of snow that accumulated on the roof of the equipment-storage building was greater than the predicted maximum that was used in drawing up the safety codes.

(C) Because the equipment-storage building was not intended for human occupation, some safety-code provisions that would have applied to an office building did not apply to it.

(D) The municipality of Northtown itself has the responsibility for ensuring that buildings constructed within its boundaries meet the provisions of the building-safety codes.

(E) Because the equipment-storage building was used for storing snow-removal equipment, the building was almost completely empty when the roof collapsed.

Argument Evaluation

Situation   The roof of a recently constructed building collapsed under heavy snowfall. The only way the building did not meet safety standards was that some nails for the roof supports were smaller than prescribed by the building codes.

Reasoning   *What would make it less likely that the building's collapse resulted from a single, apparently minor departure from safety standards?* The building met safety standards except for the size of the nails. So if the collapse exemplifies how a departure from safety standards can have severe consequences, as the conclusion claims, then the size of the nails had to be responsible for the collapse. Thus, evidence that a factor other than the size of the nails could fully account for the collapse would weaken the argument.

A   This suggests that the snow would not have been heavy enough to collapse the roof if the construction had completely met the safety standards, so it strengthens, rather than weakens, the argument.

B   Correct. This suggests that the snow could have collapsed the roof even if the nails had met the safety standards, thus casting doubt on the assumption that the nails' inadequacy was responsible for the collapse.

C   The claim that the safety requirements for this building were weaker than some others tends slightly to strengthen, rather than weaken, the hypothesis that the bad consequences resulted partly from a failure to comply. Even if safety-code provisions for an equipment-storage building differ from those for an office building, they may still be adequate to ensure the roof's stability.

D   The question of who was responsible for ensuring compliance with the safety codes is irrelevant to whether a failure to comply was responsible for the roof's collapse.

E   This suggests that the alleged consequences of failing to meet safety standards were less severe than they could have been, but it is irrelevant to determining the cause of the collapse.

The correct answer is B.

CR12078

672. Political theorist: Even with the best spies, area experts, and satellite surveillance, foreign policy assessments can still lack important information. In such circumstances intuitive judgment is vital. A national leader with such judgment can make good decisions about foreign policy even when current information is incomplete, since _____.

Which of the following, if true, most logically completes the argument?

(A) the central reason for failure in foreign policy decision making is the absence of critical information

(B) those leaders whose foreign policy decisions have been highly ranked have also been found to have good intuitive judgment

(C) both intuitive judgment and good information are required for sound decision making

(D) good foreign policy decisions often lead to improved methods of gathering information

(E) intuitive judgment can produce good decisions based on past experience, even when there are important gaps in current information

Argument Construction

Situation   National leaders sometimes must make foreign policy decisions while lacking important information.

Reasoning   *What would most help support the claim that a national leader with intuitive judgment can make good foreign policy decisions without complete information?* The word *since* preceding the blank indicates that the blank should be filled with a premise supporting the statement immediately before the blank. So an observation that supports the claim that a national leader with intuitive judgment can make good foreign policy decisions without complete information would logically complete the argument.

A   This gives us no reason to suppose that intuitive judgment helps national leaders avoid such failures.

B   This does not specify who ranked the foreign policy decisions, nor how they determined the rankings, so it gives us no reason to accept those rankings. For all we know, the anonymous rankers may have used the dubious rankings they created as the sole evidence for their so-called findings about which leaders have good intuitive judgment.

C   This implies that intuitive judgment alone is inadequate without good information, so it undermines rather than supports the claim that national leaders can make good foreign policy decisions with intuitive judgment while lacking complete information.

D   This gives us no reason to suppose that good foreign policy decisions can be made in the first place by leaders lacking important information.

E   **Correct.** This suggests that national leaders can make good foreign policy decisions using intuitive judgment based on their past foreign policy experience, even without complete information about the current situations they're facing.

The correct answer is E.

CR51141.01

673. Supply shortages and signs of growing demand are driving cocoa prices upward. Unusually severe weather in cocoa-producing regions—too much rain in Brazil and too little in West Africa—has limited production. Further, Europe and North America recently reported stronger demand for cocoa. In the first quarter, grinding of cocoa beans—the first stage in processing cocoa for chocolate—rose 8.1 percent in Europe and 16 percent in North America. Analysts have concluded that cocoa's price will continue to rise at least into the near future.

Which of the following would, if true, most strengthen the reasoning above?

(A) Ground cocoa beans can be stored for long periods before they spoil.

(B) Several European and North American manufacturers that use cocoa have recently improved their processing capacity.

(C) It takes new cocoa trees five or six years before they start bearing fruit.

(D) Governments in Europe and North America are likely to change current restrictions on cocoa imports.

(E) Historically, cocoa production has varied widely from year to year.

Argument Evaluation

Situation   There has been limited production of cocoa beans due to severe weather and also increased demand for cocoa; as a result, cocoa prices have risen.

Reasoning   *What would help support the analysts' inference that cocoa prices will continue to rise at least into the near future?* If the price of cocoa is to continue to rise, then the conditions that have led to the recent increase in price must not be ameliorated. They would be ameliorated if demand for cocoa beans declined, e.g., because price increases made people less likely to want ground cocoa; they would also be ameliorated if supply increased, e.g., because many new cocoa trees were planted and very quickly started bearing fruit. If we had reason to believe that one or more of these ameliorating factors is unlikely to happen, then we have more reason to think that prices might stay high, and possibly even rise further.

A   That ground cocoa beans can be stored for long periods without spoiling does not tell us whether supply and demand conditions will stay stable, improve, or get worse.

B   The fact that these manufacturers have recently improved their processing capacity might help explain why the grinding of cocoa beans has increased recently; but it does not indicate that this increased capacity will be fully utilized. Often, if end-product demand decreases, industrial capacity will become underutilized.

C   **Correct.** If it takes new cocoa trees several years to start bearing fruit, then it is less likely that supply can quickly be increased, which in turn makes it less likely that supply can quickly meet any increased demand and thereby relieve pricing pressures.

D   These governments may change current restrictions on cocoa imports, but for all we know they may make them more restrictive rather than less restrictive. If they made them more restrictive, demand might decrease, in which case prices might actually fall.

E   If cocoa production varies from year to year, it could be that next year cocoa production increases, in which case, as long as demand does not increase as well, prices might fall.

The correct answer is C.

CR01295

674. During the earliest period of industrialization in Britain, steam engines were more expensive to build and operate than either windmills or water mills, the other practicable sources of power for factories. Yet despite their significant cost disadvantage, steam-powered factories were built in large numbers well before technical improvements brought their cost down. Furthermore, they were built even in regions where geographical conditions permitted the construction of wind- and water-powered factories close to major markets.

Which of the following, if true, most helps to explain the proliferation of steam-powered factories during the earliest period of industrialization in Britain?

(A) In many areas of Britain, there were fewer steam-powered factories than wind- or water-powered factories in the earliest period of industrialization.

(B) Unlike wind- or water-powered factories, steam-powered factories were fueled with coal, which sometimes had to be transported significant distances from the mine to the site of the factory.

(C) It was both difficult and expensive to convert a factory from wind power or water power to steam power.

(D) In the early period of industrialization, many goods sold in towns and cities could not be mass-produced in factories.

(E) In Britain, the number of sites where a wind- or water-powered factory could be built was insufficient to provide for all of the demand for factory-produced goods at the time.

Argument Construction

Situation   Although steam engines were more expensive than windmills and water mills in early industrial Britain, many steam-powered factories were built even in regions where the construction of wind- and water-powered factories was geographically feasible.

Reasoning   *Why might steam-powered factories have proliferated despite their cost disadvantage?* Early industrialists would have needed some positive reason to choose steam over less expensive power sources for their factories. For example, steam engines might have operated faster or more effectively than windmills or water mills. Or steam engines might have received government subsidies. Or conditions restricting the number or locations of windmills and water mills might have forced industrialists to use steam power instead.

A   This suggests that the steam-powered factories did not initially proliferate as widely as they might have, but it does not explain why they proliferated to the extent that they did.

B   The inconvenience of transporting coal for steam-powered factories would have made those factories less likely to proliferate, not more likely.

C   The difficulty of converting factories to steam power would have made steam-powered factories less likely to proliferate, not more likely.

D   The technological inability to mass-produce popular products in factories would have made factories in general less likely to proliferate, including steam-powered factories.

E   **Correct.** The inadequate number of sites for wind- and water-powered factories might have encouraged early industrialists to build steam-powered factories instead, since the high demand for factory-produced goods could have made these factories profitable despite their cost disadvantage.

The correct answer is E.

CR03938

675. Snowmaking machines work by spraying a mist that freezes immediately on contact with cold air. Because the sudden freezing kills bacteria, QuickFreeze is planning to market a wastewater purification system that works on the same principle. The process works only when temperatures are cold, however, so municipalities using it will still need to maintain a conventional system.

Which of the following, if true, provides the strongest grounds for a prediction that municipalities will buy QuickFreeze's purification system despite the need to maintain a conventional purification system as well?

(A) Bacteria are not the only impurities that must be removed from wastewater.

(B) Many municipalities have old wastewater purification systems that need to be replaced.

(C) Conventional wastewater purification systems have not been fully successful in killing bacteria at cold temperatures.

(D) During times of warm weather, when it is not in use, QuickFreeze's purification system requires relatively little maintenance.

(E) Places where the winters are cold rarely have a problem of water shortage.

Evaluation of a Plan

Situation   QuickFreeze is planning to market wastewater purification systems that work by spraying a mist that freezes on contact with cold air. The sudden freezing kills bacteria. Because the system works only at cold temperatures, municipalities using it will still need to maintain a conventional system.

Reasoning   *Which statement provides the strongest grounds for thinking that at least some municipalities will buy the purification system despite the need to maintain a conventional purification system as well?* The passage tells us why a municipality using a QuickFreeze wastewater purification system would still need a conventional system. But why would a municipality want the QuickFreeze system in addition to a conventional system? If conventional systems are not fully effective at cold temperatures, the QuickFreeze system would allow municipalities that sometimes experience cold temperatures to purify their wastewater more effectively.

A   This neither weakens nor strengthens the prediction. There is no basis in the passage for determining whether the QuickFreeze system could help remove impurities other than bacteria from wastewater. If it did, the effect of this information would be neutral, because we are already told that the municipalities would be unable to use the QuickFreeze system as a stand-alone purification system. Without further information, the need to remove other impurities would have no effect on the strength of the prediction.

B   The passage states that municipalities using the QuickFreeze system would still need a conventional system. Thus, the old conventional wastewater systems would still need to be replaced with new conventional systems. This answer choice provides no reason to think municipalities would buy the QuickFreeze system.

C   **Correct.** This statement, if true, would strengthen the prediction, because it provides a valid reason why the QuickFreeze system could be needed alongside conventional ones: it is more effective than the conventional systems in cold weather.

D   Although this claim does undercut one reason for thinking municipalities might not be likely to purchase the QuickFreeze system, it provides little reason to think that they will purchase such a system. Perhaps in times of cold weather, the QuickFreeze system is very expensive to maintain.

E   The issue of whether or not there are water shortages in places where winters are cold is not directly relevant. If conventional wastewater systems are sufficient to purify water in such places, municipalities would not need the QuickFreeze system (as they would still need to maintain a conventional purification system).

The correct answer is C.

CR05080

676. **Plant scientists have used genetic engineering on seeds to produce crop plants that are highly resistant to insect damage**. Unfortunately, the seeds themselves are quite expensive, and the plants require more fertilizer and water to grow well than normal ones. Accordingly, **for most farmers the savings on pesticides would not compensate for the higher seed costs and the cost of additional fertilizer**. However, since consumer demand for grains, fruits, and vegetables grown without the use of pesticides continues to rise, the use of genetically engineered seeds of this kind is likely to become widespread.

In the argument given, the two portions in **boldface** play which of the following roles?

(A) The first supplies a context for the argument; the second is the argument's main conclusion.

(B) The first introduces a development that the argument predicts will have a certain outcome; the second is a state of affairs that, according to the argument, contributes to bringing about that outcome.

(C) The first presents a development that the argument predicts will have a certain outcome; the second acknowledges a consideration that tends to weigh against that prediction.

(D) The first provides evidence to support a prediction that the argument seeks to defend; the second is that prediction.

(E) The first and the second each provide evidence to support the argument's main conclusion.

Argument Construction

Situation   Seeds genetically engineered by plant scientists produce crops that are highly resistant to insect damage, and such crops can be grown with less use of pesticides. The seeds would be costly to use, and the savings on pesticides would not be sufficient, in themselves, to increase most farmers' profitability. Nonetheless, consumer demand for pesticide-free food materials is increasing, so genetically engineered seeds are likely to become widely used.

Reasoning   *What function is served by the statement that plant scientists have used genetic engineering on seeds to produce insect-resistant crop plants? What function is served by the statement that for most farmers the savings on pesticides would not outweigh other associated costs?* The first statement describes an innovation—genetically engineered seeds—that allows crops to be grown with little or no use of pesticides. The second statement notes that savings on pesticide use would not outweigh the higher costs of the genetically engineered seeds. The argument's main conclusion, however, is the prediction, expressed in the second clause of the final sentence of the passage, that use of such genetically engineered seeds will become widespread.

A   The second statement is a not the main conclusion. Instead it is an intermediate conclusion, which is based on the preceding statements. The main conclusion is presented in the final clause of the passage.

B   This correctly characterizes the first statement but not the second. The second statement is not meant to indicate a factor that contributes to the predicted outcome; instead, it indicates a factor that could hypothetically count against the argument's prediction.

C   **Correct.** The first boldface portion reports a development in agricultural technology. In the final sentence, the argument goes on to predict that an outcome of this development will be the widespread adoption of insect-resistant genetically engineered seeds. The second boldface portion acknowledges a financial consideration that would tend to count against that prediction.

D   The first statement does provide partial support for the prediction stated in the argument's main conclusion. The second statement does not provide any support for the prediction that the argument seeks to defend. That prediction is expressed in the final clause of the passage and is the main conclusion of the argument.

E   The second statement cannot accurately be described as giving evidence to support the prediction stated in the argument's main conclusion. Instead, it tangentially acknowledges a consideration that could plausibly be thought to count against the conclusion.

The correct answer is C.

CR04159

677. Which of the following most logically completes the passage?

Leptin, a protein occurring naturally in the blood, appears to regulate how much fat the body carries by speeding up the metabolism and decreasing the appetite when the body has too much fat. Mice that do not naturally produce leptin have more fat than other mice, but lose fat rapidly when they are given leptin injections. Unfortunately, however, leptin cannot be used as a dietary supplement to control fat, since _____.

(A) the digestive system breaks down proteins before they can enter the bloodstream

(B) there are pharmaceuticals already available that can contribute to weight loss by speeding up the metabolism

(C) people with unusually low levels of leptin in their blood tend to have a high percentage of body fat

(D) the mice that do not naturally produce leptin were from a specially bred strain of mice

(E) mice whose bodies did produce leptin also lost some of their body fat when given leptin injections

Argument Construction

Situation   Leptin, a protein naturally occurring in the bloodstream, speeds up metabolism to induce loss of excessive fat. Mice that lack leptin have more fat than other mice, but lose fat when given leptin injections. However, leptin cannot be used as a dietary supplement to control fat.

Reasoning   *What would explain the fact that a dietary supplement of leptin will not help to control fat?* Leptin injected into the bloodstream—but not leptin taken as a dietary supplement—helps control fat. So leptin taken as a dietary supplement is either inactivated in the gastrointestinal system or for some other reason fails to enter the bloodstream.

A   **Correct.** The digestive system breaks down proteins and would therefore break down leptin, which is a protein. This means that leptin given as a dietary supplement would never reach the bloodstream.

B   The question concerns leptin alone, and this new information fails to explain why leptin cannot help control fat if administered as a dietary supplement.

C   It is unsurprising that this would be so, but this information does nothing to explain why leptin consumed as a supplement would fail to control fat.

D   Presumably leptin administered as a dietary supplement was first tested on mice bred to lack leptin. However, the question about leptin does not concern only mice, but presumably humans and other mammals.

E   This suggests that boosting existing normal leptin levels with injections can induce further fat loss. However, this has no obvious relevance to the question raised about why dietary supplements of leptin fail to produce fat loss.

The correct answer is A.

CR05452

678. Suncorp, a new corporation with limited funds, has been clearing large sections of the tropical Amazon forest for cattle ranching. This practice continues even though greater profits can be made from rubber tapping, which does not destroy the forest, than from cattle ranching, which does destroy the forest.

Which of the following, if true, most helps to explain why Suncorp has been pursuing the less profitable of the two economic activities mentioned above?

(A) The soil of the Amazon forest is very rich in nutrients that are important in the development of grazing lands.

(B) Cattle-ranching operations that are located in tropical climates are more profitable than cattle-ranching operations that are located in cold-weather climates.

(C) In certain districts, profits made from cattle ranching are more heavily taxed than profits made from any other industry.

(D) Some of the cattle that are raised on land cleared in the Amazon are killed by wildcats.

(E) The amount of money required to begin a rubber-tapping operation is twice as high as the amount needed to begin a cattle ranch.

Argument Construction

Situation   Suncorp is a new corporation with limited funds. It has been clearing large sections of the tropical Amazon forest for ranching, even though rubber-tapping would be more profitable.

Reasoning   *What would explain why Suncorp is clearing sections of the rain forest for ranching, even though rubber tapping would be more profitable?* Because Suncorp has limited funds, if rubber tapping has much higher start-up costs, Suncorp might not have enough money to start rubber-tapping operations. If cattle ranching has much lower start-up costs than rubber tapping, Suncorp might be able to afford such an operation.

A   This statement gives a reason why cattle ranching in the Amazon might be more profitable than one might otherwise think it would be. However, we already know from the passage that rubber tapping would be more profitable than cattle ranching. So, this answer choice does not help explain why cattle ranching might be preferable to rubber tapping.

B   The comparison between the profitableness of cattle ranching in tropical climates and in cold-weather climates is irrelevant. The passage only covers cattle ranching in the tropical Amazon forest. This answer choice would at most explain why Suncorp is undertaking cattle ranching in the Amazon rather than in some cold-weather location.

C   This statement makes what needs to be explained harder to understand, for it indicates that cattle ranching in the Amazon might be less profitable than one would otherwise think.

D   Like answer choice C, this statement indicates a disadvantage of cattle ranching in the Amazon. So, it does not explain why cattle ranching would be preferred to some other economic activity.

E   **Correct.** Because it costs less to begin cattle ranching than it does to begin rubber tapping, Suncorp—which has limited funds—would have a reason to pursue cattle ranching over a potentially more profitable activity.

The correct answer is E.

CR09963

679. Archaeologists use technology to analyze ancient sites. It is likely that this technology will advance considerably in the near future, allowing archaeologists to gather more information than is currently possible. If they study certain sites now, they risk contaminating or compromising them for future studies. Therefore, in order to maximize the potential for gathering knowledge in the long run, a team of archaeologists plans to delay the examination of a newly excavated site.

Which of the following would be most useful to investigate for the purpose of evaluating the plan's prospects for achieving its goal?

(A) Whether any of the contents of the site will significantly deteriorate before the anticipated technology is available

(B) Whether there will continue to be improvements on the relevant technology

(C) Whether the team can study a site other than the newly excavated site for the time being

(D) Whether the site was inhabited by a very ancient culture

(E) Whether the anticipated technology will damage objects under study

Evaluation of a Plan

Situation   To avoid prematurely compromising a newly excavated site, an archaeological team plans to postpone examining it until more advanced technology is developed that will let them gather more information from it. Their goal is to maximize the potential for gathering knowledge.

Reasoning   *What would be most helpful to investigate in order to assess how likely it is that delaying examination of the site will maximize the potential for gathering knowledge from it?* In order to maximize (or even increase) the potential for gathering knowledge from the site by delaying its examination, the risk of compromising the site by examining it now has to be greater than the risk that the site will be compromised as much or more by delaying the examination. The delay might also increase the risk that the site will never be examined at all—for example, the team might lose its funding while it delays, or changes in local political conditions might prevent the site's future examination. Investigating any of these risks could be helpful in assessing the likelihood that the team's plan will achieve its goal.

A   **Correct.** If any of the site's contents will significantly deteriorate before the technology becomes available, that could reduce the ability to gather future information from the site even more than examining and compromising the site now would.

B   The passage already tells us that it is likely the technology *will advance considerably in the near future*. Given this information, further inquiry into whether there will be any ongoing (perhaps minor) improvements is somewhat redundant and probably of minimal value with respect to evaluating the plan's likelihood of success.

C   Even if the team can study a second site in the meanwhile, they might maximize the overall potential for gathering knowledge by delaying the examination of either site, both sites, or neither site until more advanced technology is available.

D   The age of the culture that inhabited the site is irrelevant to assessing the risks of delaying the site's examination until more advanced technology is available.

E   Even if the anticipated technology will damage or destroy the objects under study, it might still maximize the amount of knowledge that can be gathered from those objects. Without any comparison between the damage risk that would be incurred by proceeding with the current technology and the damage risk that would be incurred by waiting, the mere fact that some damage would occur is irrelevant.

The correct answer is A.

CR01102

680. More and more law firms specializing in corporate taxes are paid on a contingency-fee basis. Under this arrangement, if a case is won, the firm usually receives more than it would have received if it had been paid on the alternate hourly rate basis. If the case is lost, the firm receives nothing. Most firms are likely to make more under the contingency-fee arrangement.

Which of the following, if true, would most strengthen the prediction above?

(A) Firms that work exclusively under the hourly rate arrangement spend, on average, fewer hours on cases that are won than on cases that are lost.

(B) Some litigation can last for years before any decision is reached, and, even then, the decision may be appealed.

(C) Firms under the contingency-fee arrangement still pay their employees on an hourly basis.

(D) Since the majority of firms specialize in certain kinds of cases, they are able to assess accurately their chances of winning each potential case.

(E) Firms working under the contingency-fee arrangement take in fewer cases per year than do firms working under the hourly rate arrangement.

Argument Evaluation

Situation   Law firms of a certain type are increasingly working on a contingency-fee basis, whereby the firm is only paid if the case won. For the individual cases that are thus taken and won, the payments are generally greater than the total payments would have been if the firms had been paid on an hourly basis. Furthermore, although cases taken on a contingency-fee basis present a significant risk of working for many hours on a case and not being paid, the passage claims that most firms are likely to make more money, on average, than they would if they took their cases on an hourly basis.

Reasoning   *What would most strongly indicate that, despite the risks, the law firms working on a contingency fee basis are likely to make more money, on average, than they would have otherwise?* Our task is to find the statement that would most strongly support this prediction. A primary risk of using contingency fees is that a firm might have so many unsuccessful cases that the average revenue (and profit) is less than it would have been with hourly fees. Anything indicating that the firms might be able to reduce that risk would provide some support for the prediction that they would make more money with contingency fees than with hourly fees.

A   Supposing that the firms mentioned in this option changed from working on an hourly-rate basis to working on a contingency-fee basis, we would not have enough information to predict what the results would be. For example, we may have no reason to expect that the firm would accept the same cases that they would have accepted if they were working on an hourly-rate basis. As such, patterns of work on cases taken on an hourly basis may be irrelevant for determining how much the firms would make if they were to take their cases on a contingency-fee basis.

B   This answer choice indicates that firms taking cases on a contingency-fee basis can work on the cases for years without payment. Rather than supporting the point that firms would make more money if they worked on a contingency-fee basis, the option illustrates an aspect of the risks associated with this payment arrangement.

C   This answer choice does not support the prediction that *most firms are likely to make more,* it could mean either that they are likely to have greater total revenue or that they are likely to have a greater amount of profit. With regard to gross revenue, the cost of staff time tells us nothing about how much money the firms are likely to take in. With regard to profits, the need to pay employees even for work on unsuccessful cases slightly weakens the prediction: all else being equal, profits would be higher if employees were not paid for work on such cases. However, we are given no information about whether firms might be able to have some alternative arrangement whereby they pay employees only for successful cases, or about whether they would have to pay considerably more with such arrangements.

D **Correct.** This answer choice suggests that firms working on a contingency-fee basis would be able to select cases that they would be likely to win and therefore be paid for. Thus, they could mitigate the risk of having too few successful cases to offset the lack of income from the unsuccessful ones. This increases the probability that the firms would be able to bring in more total revenue in the long run with a contingency-fee system than they would if they charged hourly fees. And since we are given no evidence that the ability to select high-win-probability cases would lead to greater costs, this also tends slightly to strengthen the prediction that the firms' profits would be greater in the long run.

E Although the difference in numbers of cases described in this option could, given certain possible facts, be relevant to the prediction made by the argument, we have not been given any such facts.

The correct answer is D.

CR67830.02

681. Pretzel Vendor: The new license fee for operating a pretzel stand outside the art museum is prohibitively expensive. Charging typical prices, I would need to sell an average of 25 pretzels per hour to break even. At my stand outside City Hall, with about as many passers-by as at the art museum, I average only 15 per hour. So I could not break even running a stand outside the art museum, much less turn a profit.

Which of the following, if true, most seriously weakens the pretzel vendor's argument?

(A) The pretzel vendor does not sell anything other than pretzels.

(B) People who visit the art museum are more likely to buy pretzels than are people who go to City Hall.

(C) The license fee for operating a pretzel stand outside City Hall will not increase.

(D) People who buy pretzels at pretzel stands are more likely to do so during the lunch hour than at other times.

(E) The city will grant more licenses for pretzel stands outside the art museum than the number it grants for stands outside City Hall.

Argument Evaluation

Situation   Because of a new license fee for operating a pretzel stand outside the art museum, a pretzel vendor would have to sell on average 25 pretzels per hour to break even, which is 10 more on average than the vendor sells outside City Hall. But the museum would have no more passers-by than City Hall has. The vendor concludes that a pretzel stand outside the museum would not break even.

Reasoning   *What additional information, if true, would most weaken the support, in light of the given information, for the prediction that the vendor would not break even running a stand outside the art museum?* The vendor's prediction that a pretzel stand outside the art museum would not break even is based on the following considerations: (1) the vendor would have to sell 10 more pretzels on average per hour than the vendor sells outside City Hall, and (2) there are no more passers-by outside the museum than outside City Hall. But what matters is not how many *potential* customers pass by the art museum. What matters is how many *actual* customers there will be. If the people who pass by the stand outside the museum are more likely to buy pretzels than the people who pass by the stand at City Hall are, the prediction might fail.

A   This would be more likely to strengthen the argument than weaken it. If the vendor did sell something other than pretzels outside the museum but not outside City Hall, then it is possible that this product would help the vendor at least break even. But this answer choice tells us that the vendor sells only pretzels.

B   **Correct.** If the people who visit the museum are more likely to buy pretzels than the people who go to City Hall are, then it could be that the vendor will be able to sell 25 pretzels per hour on average. This could be true even if there are not more people outside the art museum than outside City Hall.

C   The vendor's prediction is only about whether a stand outside the art museum could break even, not about whether the business in the current location would continue to break even. For that prediction, it does not matter whether there will be a fee for a stand outside City Hall.

D   The vendor's argument does not include or depend on anything about when the pretzels are sold at the stand. So a claim that more pretzels are sold during the lunch hour than at any other time does not weaken the argument.

E   This claim strengthens the argument instead of weakening it. If there are more pretzel stands outside the art museum than there are outside City Hall, then there would be more competition. That might make it harder to sell even 15 pretzels per hour, let alone 25.

The correct answer is B.

CR00766
682. Beginning in 1966 all new cars sold in Morodia were required to have safety belts and power steering. Previously, most cars in Morodia were without these features. Safety belts help to prevent injuries in collisions, and power steering helps to avoid collisions in the first place. But even though in 1966 one-seventh of the cars in Morodia were replaced with new cars, the number of car collisions and collision-related injuries did not decline.

Which of the following, if true about Morodia, most helps to explain why the number of collisions and collision-related injuries in Morodia failed to decline in 1966?

(A) Because of a driver-education campaign, most drivers and passengers in cars that did have safety belts used them in 1966.

(B) Most of the new cars bought in 1966 were bought in the months of January and February.

(C) In 1965, substantially more than one-seventh of the cars in Morodia were replaced with new cars.

(D) An excessive reliance on the new safety features led many owners of new cars to drive less cautiously in 1966 than before.

(E) The seat belts and power steering put into new cars sold in 1966 had to undergo strict quality-control inspections by manufacturers, whether the cars were manufactured in Morodia or not.

Argument Construction

Situation   Starting in 1966, new cars sold in Morodia were required to have safety belts and power steering. But the numbers of car collisions and collision-related injuries did not decline that year.

Reasoning   *What could explain why the newly required safety features did not reduce the numbers of collisions and collision-related injuries in 1966?* The passage says that power steering helps to prevent collisions and that safety belts help to prevent collision-related injuries. Since most Morodian cars previously lacked these features, and one-seventh of them were replaced with new cars in 1966, the proportion of cars with these features must have increased that year. This should have reduced the numbers of collisions and collision-related injuries unless some other factor counteracted the reductions. Evidence of any such countervailing factor would help to explain why the numbers did not decrease.

A   Increased usage of safety belts should have reduced the number of collision-related injuries, so it would not help explain why this number did not decrease.

B   If the new cars bought in 1966 were mostly purchased early in the year, the increased proportion of cars with the newly required safety features should have started more significantly reducing the numbers of collisions and collision-related injuries early in the year, producing greater reductions for the year as a whole.

C   However, many cars were replaced in the year before the safety features were required, in 1966 the replacement of one-seventh of all Morodian cars should still have increased the overall proportion of Morodian cars with the safety features and thus reduced the numbers of collisions and collision-related injuries.

D   **Correct.** If many owners of the cars with the new safety features drove less cautiously, their recklessness could have increased the overall numbers of collisions and collision-related injuries despite any benefits from the safety features.

E   Strict quality-control inspections should have made the safety features more reliable, further reducing the numbers of collisions and collision-related injuries.

The correct answer is D.

CR14430.02

683. Manufacturers of mechanical pencils make most of their profit on pencil leads rather than on the pencils themselves. The Write Company, which cannot sell its leads as cheaply as other manufacturers can, plans to alter the design of its mechanical pencil so that it will accept only a newly designed Write Company lead, which will be sold at the same price as the Write Company's current lead.

Which of the following, if true, most strongly supports the Write Company's projection that its plan will lead to an increase in its sales of pencil leads?

(A) The new Write Company pencil will be introduced at a price higher than the price the Write Company charges for its current model.

(B) In the foreseeable future, manufacturers of mechanical pencils will probably have to raise the prices they charge for mechanical pencils.

(C) The newly designed Write Company lead will cost somewhat more to manufacture than the Write Company's current lead does.

(D) A rival manufacturer recently announced similar plans to introduce a mechanical pencil that would accept only the leads produced by that manufacturer.

(E) In extensive test marketing, mechanical-pencil users found the new Write Company pencil markedly superior to other mechanical pencils they had used.

Argument Evaluation

Situation   The Write Company makes mechanical pencils and pencil-lead refills. Companies in this type of business make most of their profits from selling the leads, but the Write Company's leads cost more than leads made by other firms, so the refills are not selling well. The company plans to alter the design of its pencil and leads so that only the company's leads will fit. The new leads will be sold at the same price as the existing ones. The company projects that its plan will lead to an increase in the sale of its leads.

Reasoning   *Which of the stated pieces of additional information most strongly supports the company's projection of an increase in sales of leads?* Presumably, because of the price difference, users of Write Company pencils are often refilling them with competitors' cheaper leads instead of Write Company leads. If the number of sales of the company's redesigned pencil did not drop significantly below the number of sales for its original pencil, a likely consequence would be a significant increase in refill sales for the redesigned pencil, because users would no longer have the option of using competitors' leads. The pencil would have to be priced competitively and function well.

A   This slightly weakens support for the company's projection because it suggests that the redesigned pencil might not sell sufficiently well to boost lead sales unless the redesigned pencil is perceived by potential buyers as being worth the higher price.

B   It is not clear whether, if this predicted outcome were to occur, it would help or hinder the Write Company in selling more of its pencil leads. For all we know, the Write Company's pencil and leads could become less price-competitive compared with those of other firms.

C   Since the new lead will cost the same as the current one, the increased unit cost would, all else being equal, tend to reduce profits unless this reduction were compensated for by increased sales volume. Given that the price to consumers would stay the same, the lower profit per lead does not suggest that consumers would buy more of the leads.

D   This provides too little information to tell what the effect of the competitor's action might be. For one thing, we have no information about whether the competitor would continue to sell its leads at a lower price than that of Write Company leads. The competitor's action might create additional competition for the Write Company's new products, increasing the risk that the Write Company's plan will fail. On the other hand, the competitor's pencils would have a similar potential drawback to that of the new Write Company pencils (restriction on the choice of refill leads), so it might tend to reduce the number of consumers who would avoid the new Write Company pencils in favor of the competitor's product.

E   **Correct.** This information suggests that sales of the Write Company's redesigned pencil may increase (or at least will probably not significantly decrease), that many consumers will find the company's pencils worth the additional expense of refilling them with Write Company leads, and that consequently the company's plan to increase lead sales will succeed.

The correct answer is E.

CR04882

684. Enterprise Bank currently requires customers with checking accounts to maintain a minimum balance or pay a monthly fee. Enterprise plans to offer accounts with no monthly fee and no minimum-balance requirement; to cover their projected administrative costs of $3 per account per month they plan to charge $30 for overdrawing an account. Since each month on average slightly more than 10 percent of Enterprise's customers overdraw their accounts, bank officials predict the new accounts will generate a profit.

Which of the following, if true, most strongly supports the bank officials' prediction?

(A) Some of Enterprise Bank's current checking account customers are expected to switch to the new accounts once they are offered.

(B) One third of Enterprise Bank's revenues are currently derived from monthly fees tied to checking accounts.

(C) Many checking account customers who occasionally pay a fee for not maintaining a minimum balance in their account generally maintain a balance well above the minimum.

(D) Customers whose checking accounts do not have a minimum-balance requirement are more likely than others to overdraw their checking accounts.

(E) Customers whose checking accounts do not have a minimum-balance requirement are more likely than others to write checks for small amounts.

Evaluation of a Plan

Situation   Enterprise Bank gives customers checking accounts with no monthly fee provided they maintain a certain minimum balance. However, the bank plans to offer accounts with no minimum-balance requirement and no monthly fee. It plans to cover the bank's $3 per account per month administrative cost by charging a $30 penalty for overdrafts. Only slightly more than 10 percent of customers, on average, overdraw their accounts in a month. The bank officials predict the new accounts will generate a profit.

Reasoning   *What new information, if accurate, would most strongly support the prediction?* If about only one customer in ten, on average, currently has an overdraft in a month, and if this trend continues among customers who sign up for the new account, then the proposed $30 penalty per overdraft will cover the $30 cost of maintaining checking accounts for 10 customers per month. Would removing the minimum-balance requirement significantly increase the 10 percent overdraft rate? If so, then significantly more than one in ten customers, on average, would pay a $30 penalty. If this were so, then the new plan would yield a profit, as predicted.

A   "Some" might mean only a few, and this would probably not be sufficient to make the new plan significantly profitable.

B   This suggests that many customers with the current minimum-balance no-monthly-fee account do not maintain the minimum-balance requirement and pay fees instead. However, this information by itself seems to have little bearing on the new plan.

C   Such customers would be likely to overdraw their accounts less frequently. This suggests that if a preponderance of the customers for the proposed new account were such customers, the overdraft rate would decrease, and the proposed new account would be less profitable, or even unprofitable.

D   **Correct.** This information provides strong support for the bank officials' prediction. It indicates that the currently roughly 10 percent overdraft rate might increase drastically with the no-minimum-balance account and, on average, cause the imposition of a $30 penalty on significantly more than 10 percent of customers per month. This would make the new account significantly profitable.

E   This suggests that a check written by one of these customers is more likely to be for a small amount and is therefore somewhat less likely to cause an overdraft (unless such customers typically have small checking balances, which we are not told). If there were many such customers for the proposed new account, the overdraft rate might be less than 10 percent; this would indicate that the new account might not turn out to be profitable.

The correct answer is D.

CR08330.02

685. Highway Official: When resurfacing our concrete bridges, we should use electrically conductive concrete (ECC) rather than standard concrete. In the winter, ECC can be heated by passing an electric current through it, thereby preventing ice buildup. The cost of the electricity needed is substantially lower than the cost of the deicing salt we currently use.

Taxpayer: But ECC is vastly more expensive than standard concrete, so your proposal is probably not justifiable on economic grounds.

Which of the following, if true, could best be used by the highway official to support the official's proposal in the face of the taxpayer's objection?

(A) The use of deicing salt causes corrosion of reinforcing steel in concrete bridge decks and damage to the concrete itself, thereby considerably shortening the useful life of concrete bridges.

(B) Severe icing conditions can cause power outages and slow down the work of emergency crews trying to get power restored.

(C) In weather conditions conducive to icing, ice generally forms on the concrete surfaces of bridges well before it forms on parts of the roadway that go over solid ground.

(D) Aside from its potential use for deicing bridges, ECC might also be an effective means of keeping other concrete structures such as parking garages and airport runways ice free.

(E) If ECC were to be used for a bridge surface, the electric current would be turned on only at times at which ice was likely to form.

Evaluation of a Plan

Situation   A highway official recommends using electrically conductive concrete (ECC) for resurfacing concrete bridges. This would allow the transmission of an electric current to prevent ice buildup in winter. The highway official supports the proposal by stating that the cost of the electricity used would be substantially lower than the cost of the deicing salt used at present. A taxpayer objects that ECC is much more expensive than standard concrete.

Reasoning   *Which piece of additional information would most logically address the objection of the taxpayer?* Consider whether there could be other, indirect or long-term, costs associated with either of the two deicing methods (salt, electricity). For example, would use of ECC involve installation of additional infrastructure to provide electric power to the bridges—and, if so, how would the total costs compare with total existing costs? What are the cost implications of the current use of deicing salt? Any additional information that addresses these questions will be relevant. Note that the taxpayer's objection primarily concerns the capital cost of ECC bridge surfacing.

A   **Correct.** The use of deicing salt causes corrosion that considerably shortens the useful life of the bridge. Clearly, replacement of a bridge would involve a large capital expenditure. This is a major reason for reconsidering the use of deicing salt. Of course, absent additional information about total costs of installation and use of each deicing method, it is not a conclusive reason to discontinue using deicing salt.

B   Power outages in severe icing conditions would cause dangerous road-surface conditions on bridges surfaced with ECC, thus requiring a backup method of deicing in such circumstances. This would probably require road maintenance systems to use an auxiliary power backup or deicing salt in rare cases. However, this provides no evidence that the cost of emergency backup measures would exceed the overall savings available with the use of ECC.

C   This is a reason for ensuring that deicing of bridges is given priority over deicing other places, but this prioritization can be done whatever method of deicing is used.

D   The issues raised by the statements of the highway official and the taxpayer concern only the use of ECC for deicing bridges, so the information in this answer choice has no clear or direct relevance to that issue.

E   This most likely offers no relevant additional information, since it is presumably already taken into account in the claim that the cost of electricity for deicing is lower than the cost of deicing salt. So this merely acknowledges one way to help optimize the costs associated with ECC deicing, but it is not, by itself, a substantial refutation of the taxpayer's objection.

The correct answer is A.

CR05667
686. In virtually any industry, technological improvements increase labor productivity, which is the output of goods and services per person-hour worked. In Parland's industries, labor productivity is significantly higher than it is in Vergia's industries. Clearly, therefore, Parland's industries must, on the whole, be further advanced technologically than Vergia's are.

The argument is most vulnerable to which of the following criticisms?

(A) It offers a conclusion that is no more than a paraphrase of one of the pieces of information provided in its support.

(B) It presents as evidence in support of a claim information that is inconsistent with other evidence presented in support of the same claim.

(C) It takes one possible cause of a condition to be the actual cause of that condition without considering any other possible causes.

(D) It takes a condition to be the effect of something that happened only after the condition already existed.

(E) It makes a distinction that presupposes the truth of the conclusion that is to be established.

Argument Evaluation

Situation   Technological improvements in nearly every industry increase labor productivity, which is the output of goods and services per person-hour worked. Because labor productivity is significantly higher in Parland than Vergia, Parland's industries are, in general, more technologically advanced than Vergia's.

Reasoning   *To which criticism is the argument most vulnerable?* Though one factor, such as technological advancements, may lead to greater labor productivity, it may not be the only such factor, or even a necessary factor, leading to great labor productivity. Therefore, the mere fact that one region's labor is more productive than another's is not sufficient to establish that the former region is more technologically advanced than the latter region is.

A   The conclusion is not merely a paraphrase of the pieces of information provided in its support. Indeed, the problem with the argument is that the conclusion goes too far beyond what the premises merit.

B   The premises of the argument are not inconsistent with one another.

C   Correct. This accurately describes the flaw in the argument because the reasons given in the argument for its conclusion would be good reasons only if there were no other plausible explanations for Parland's greater labor productivity.

D   The argument does not mention how long Parland has had more productive labor, or when technological improvements would have occurred.

E   Neither of the premises contains anything that presupposes the conclusion to be true. The argument's two premises are *Technological improvements in nearly every industry increase labor productivity* and *Labor productivity is significantly higher in Parland than Vergia.* The argument's conclusion states *Parland's industries must on the whole be further advanced than Vergia's are.* If anything in the premises presupposed that conclusion, the conclusion could not be false if the premises were true. But the conclusion can be false even if both premises are true. Suppose, for instance, that Parland and Vergia engage in different industries and Parland's industries inherently have greater labor productivity. That might not be because Parland's industries are more technologically advanced than Vergia's are, but only because of the nature of the different industries. Yet it can nonetheless be true that technological improvements increase labor productivity.

The correct answer is C.

CR08471

687. Chaco Canyon, a settlement of the ancient Anasazi culture in North America, had massive buildings. **It must have been a major Anasazi center**. Analysis of wood samples shows that some of the timber for the buildings came from the Chuska and San Mateo mountains, 50 miles from Chaco Canyon. **Only a major cultural center would have the organizational power to import timber from 50 miles away**.

In the argument given, the two portions in **boldface** play which of the following roles?

(A) The first is a premise used to support the argument's main conclusion; the second is the argument's main conclusion.

(B) The first is the argument's main conclusion; the second is a premise used to support that conclusion.

(C) The first is one of two premises used to support the argument's main conclusion; the second is the other of those two premises.

(D) The first is a premise used to support the argument's main conclusion; the second is a premise used to support another conclusion drawn in the argument.

(E) The first is inferred from another statement in the argument; the second is inferred from the first.

Argument Construction

Situation   The ancient Anasazi settlement at Chaco Canyon had massive buildings, for which some of the timber came from mountains 50 miles away.

Reasoning   *What roles do the statement that Chaco Canyon must have been a major Anasazi center and the statement that only a major center would have the organizational power to import timber from 50 miles away play in the argument?* The first and third sentences in the passage are both factual observations. Since no further support is provided for either of them, neither can be a conclusion in the argument. The final sentence (i.e., the second boldface portion of the argument) is a speculative generalization about major cultural centers. None of the other statements gives us any reason to think this generalization is true, so it cannot be a conclusion in the argument, either. However, the third and fourth sentences together imply that Chaco Canyon was a major cultural center, and the first sentence indicates that it was Anasazi. So together, the first, third, and fourth sentences all support the claim that Chaco Canyon was a major Anasazi cultural center and thus more generally a major Anasazi center, as the second sentence asserts. Therefore, the first, third, and fourth sentences are all premises that jointly support the second sentence (i.e., the first **boldface** portion of the argument) as a conclusion.

A   As explained above in the Reasoning section, the first boldface sentence is a conclusion supported by the second boldface sentence, not the other way around.

B   **Correct.** As explained above in the Reasoning section, the first boldface sentence is the argument's only stated conclusion, and thus is its main conclusion, while all the other sentences are premises used to support it; therefore, the second boldface sentence (*Only a major cultural center . . . 50 miles away*) is a premise used to support the conclusion.

C   As explained above in the Reasoning section, the first boldface sentence is the argument's conclusion, not a premise used to support the conclusion.

D   As explained above in the Reasoning section, the first boldface sentence is the argument's only stated conclusion, and there is no reason to suppose that the argument is intended to lead to any other tacit conclusion that the second boldface sentence is intended to support.

E   As explained above in the Reasoning section, the first boldface sentence is inferred from the three other statements in the argument together, not from any one of them alone. The second boldface sentence is a speculative generalization that cannot be, and is not meant to be, inferred from the first boldface sentence or from any other statement in the argument.

The correct answer is B.

CR04364

688. The Maxilux car company's design for its new luxury model, the Max 100, included a special design for the tires that was intended to complement the model's image. The winning bid for supplying these tires was submitted by Rubco. Analysts concluded that the bid would only just cover Rubco's costs on the tires, but Rubco executives claim that winning the bid will actually make a profit for the company.

Which of the following, if true, most strongly justifies the claim made by Rubco's executives?

(A) In any Maxilux model, the spare tire is exactly the same make and model as the tires that are mounted on the wheels.

(B) Rubco holds exclusive contracts to supply Maxilux with the tires for a number of other models made by Maxilux.

(C) The production facilities for the Max 100 and those for the tires to be supplied by Rubco are located very near each other.

(D) When people who have purchased a carefully designed luxury automobile need to replace a worn part of it, they almost invariably replace it with a part of exactly the same make and type.

(E) When Maxilux awarded the tire contract to Rubco, the only criterion on which Rubco's bid was clearly ahead of its competitors' bids was price.

Argument Construction

Situation   Rubco won a bid for supplying tires for the Max 100, a new luxury model by Maxilux. The bid would barely cover the cost of the tires, but Rubco executives claim that winning the bid will be profitable.

Reasoning   *What would support the executives' claim?* Rubco is not expected to make a profit from supplying the tires for the new cars, so we must look for some other way that Rubco could derive a profit as a result of winning the bid. If by winning the bid Rubco created an inevitable market for itself in replacement tires—on which Rubco could earn a profit—then the executives' claim may be justified.

A   We have already been told that the bid is expected to barely cover the costs of supplying the tires on the new cars, so the analysts mentioned in the passage have presumably already taken into account that there is a spare tire supplied for the Max 100.

B   If winning the bid led Rubco to win more exclusive contracts with the Maxilux, that might help support the executives' claim. But this statement indicates only that Rubco already has several exclusive contracts to supply Maxilux with tires, not that winning the bid has led to, or will lead to, more such contracts, which is what would be needed.

C   As in answer choice (A), this is relevant to the costs of supplying the tires for the Max 100, but presumably this was taken into account by the analysts when they concluded that the bid would barely cover Rubco's costs on the tires.

D   **Correct.** This indicates that by winning the bid Rubco has created a way to profit from the contract with Maxilux, specifically, by creating a market for replacement tires.

E   This is likely one of the reasons that Rubco's bid only just covers Rubco's costs on the tires; it does nothing to justify the executives' claims that the bid will lead to a profit for Rubco.

The correct answer is D.

CR05186

689. Which of the following most logically completes the passage?

Most bicycle helmets provide good protection for the top and back of the head, but little or no protection for the temple regions on the sides of the head. A study of head injuries resulting from bicycle accidents showed that a large proportion were caused by blows to the temple area. Therefore, if bicycle helmets protected this area, the risk of serious head injury in bicycle accidents would be greatly reduced, especially since _____.

(A) among the bicyclists included in the study's sample of head injuries, only a very small proportion had been wearing a helmet at the time of their accident

(B) even those bicyclists who regularly wear helmets have a poor understanding of the degree and kind of protection that helmets afford

(C) a helmet that included protection for the temples would have to be somewhat larger and heavier than current helmets

(D) the bone in the temple area is relatively thin and impacts in that area are thus very likely to cause brain injury

(E) bicyclists generally land on their arm or shoulder when they fall to the side, which reduces the likelihood of severe impacts on the side of the head

Argument Construction

Situation   Bicycle helmets protect the top and back of the head, but not the sides or temples. A study found that a large proportion of head injuries caused by biking accidents were caused by blows to the temple area.

Reasoning   *Why would the risk of serious head injury in bicycle accidents be greatly reduced if bicycle helmets protected the temple regions?* If for some reason a serious head injury is particularly likely when there is impact to the temple area, then bicycle helmets that protect that area would be apt to reduce the number of serious head injuries from bicycle accidents. One such reason is that the bone in the temple area is relatively thin.

A   This point is irrelevant because it gives us no information about the seriousness or the likelihood of injuries due to impact to the temple area.

B   Whether bicyclists who regularly wear helmets have a good understanding of what protection their helmets afford is not relevant as to whether serious head injuries are particularly likely to occur from impact to the temple area.

C   This point is relevant only to what a helmet that protected the temple area would be like, not to the seriousness of injuries resulting from impact to that area. If anything, this point counts as a reason *against* the conclusion, not *for* it. If such helmets are heavier and larger, they may be used less than they otherwise would be. If fewer helmets are used, then improvements to helmet design will have less of an effect in reducing serious head injuries.

D   **Correct.** This statement provides a reason why the temple area of the rider's head needs protection: impacts to this area are very likely to cause brain injuries.

E   This is largely irrelevant. Even if it suggests that head injuries do not generally result from bicyclists falling to the side, it does not indicate that such injuries are rare or that there is not great risk of serious injury in those cases in which there is impact to the temple area.

The correct answer is D.

CR01867

690. Which of the following most logically completes the argument?

In a typical year, Innovair's airplanes are involved in 35 collisions while parked or being towed in airports, with a resulting yearly cost of $1,000,000 for repairs.

To reduce the frequency of ground collisions, Innovair will begin giving its ground crews additional training, at an annual cost of $500,000. Although this will cut the number of ground collisions by about half at best, the drop in repair costs can be expected to be much greater, since _____.

(A) most ground collisions happen when ground crews are rushing to minimize the time a delayed airplane spends on the ground

(B) a ground collision typically occurs when there are no passengers on the airplane

(C) the additional training will focus on helping ground crews avoid those kinds of ground collisions that cause the most costly damage

(D) the $500,000 cost figure for the additional training of ground crews includes the wages that those crews will earn during the time spent in actual training

(E) most ground collisions have been caused by the least experienced ground-crew members

Evaluation of a Plan

Situation   An airline will give its ground crews additional training to reduce the frequency of the collisions its airplanes are involved in while parked or being towed in airports.

Reasoning   *What premise would most logically support the conclusion that the additional training will reduce repair costs from ground collisions much more than it reduces the number of such collisions?* The key word *since* before the blank shows that the argument should be completed with a premise that supports the preceding claim that the *drop in repair costs can be expected to be much greater.* What statement would support that claim? Note that the annual cost of training, $500,000, is half as much as the yearly cost of the repairs needed as a result of ground collisions, $1,000,000. We are told that the training will cut the number of ground collisions by at most about half, so if the drop in repair costs will be much greater than half, which would need to be the case to make the training worthwhile, what would have to be true of the ground collisions that the training will help the ground crews avoid? Presumably, they would have to be among the higher repair cost collisions, as opposed to the less serious collisions that result in lower repair costs. That is, the collisions that are avoided would have to make up more than half of the repair costs, so, they would have to be costlier than average, given that the number of collisions avoided is no more than half. Thus, it would be quite useful to include in the argument a premise providing evidence that the training will help avoid the sorts of ground collisions that lead to above average repair costs.

A   We are given no reason to believe that the additional training would affect how much ground crews rush to minimize delays.

B   The number of passengers is not clearly relevant to the repair costs resulting from a ground collision and in any case would not be affected by additional ground crew training.

C   **Correct.** If the training especially helps the ground crews avoid those kinds of collisions that cause the most costly damage (that is, damage from ground collisions that has higher repair costs than the average repair costs for damage from ground collisions), then it will probably reduce repair costs by more than half.

D   Whether the cited expense for training includes wages is irrelevant to whether the training will reduce repair costs more than it reduces the number of collisions.

E   This suggests that the additional training may help reduce the number of collisions, not that it will reduce repair costs more than it reduces the number of collisions.

The correct answer is C.

CR12558
691. Many agriculturally intensive areas of the world are beginning to encounter water scarcity problems. As a result, many farmers in these areas are likely to reduce their output as the water supply they need in order to maintain production shrinks. However, one group of farmers in such a region plans to increase their production by implementing techniques for water conservation.

Which of the following, if true, would most strongly support the prediction that the group's plan will succeed?

(A) Farmers who can gain a larger share of the food market in their regions will be better positioned to control more water resources.

(B) Most agricultural practices in areas with water shortages are water-intensive.

(C) Other regions of the world not facing water shortages are likely to make up for the reduction in agricultural output.

(D) Demand for agricultural products in the group's region is not expected to decline.

(E) More than half the water used for agriculture in the farmers' region is lost to evaporation or leakage from irrigation channels.

Evaluation of a Plan

Situation   Farmers in many agriculturally intensive regions will probably reduce their output because the regions' water supplies are dwindling, but one group of farmers in such a region plans to use water conservation techniques to increase their output.

Reasoning   *What would provide evidence that water conservation techniques will help the farmers increase production despite their region's dwindling water supplies?* In order for the water conservation techniques to be effective, they must result in significantly more water becoming available for the farmers to use. Because overall supplies are shrinking, rather than growing, that can only happen if the farmers are currently losing or wasting a great deal of water in ways that could be prevented with water conservation techniques.

A   This suggests an advantage the farmers will gain if their water conservation plan enables them to increase production, but it provides no evidence that the plan actually will enable them to increase production.

B   This suggests that the plan would have to yield quite a lot of conserved water in order for the farmers to increase production, but it offers no evidence that the plan will do so. Thus, it provides some reason to question whether the plan will succeed.

C   Whether regions without water shortages will increase production is not directly relevant to the question of whether a particular measure would lead to increased production in one region that does have a water shortage.

D   This has some slight, indirect relevance to the question of whether the farmers' plan will succeed: it suggests that if the farmers do manage to increase production, they will continue to have a market for what they produce. However, it does not address the issue of whether they will be able to increase production. Furthermore, even if demand for agricultural products in the group's region were expected to decline, it could still remain high enough to support the farmers' increased output from their water conservation plan.

E   **Correct.** This suggests that the farmers are losing a lot of water in ways that the water conservation techniques might prevent, so it provides evidence that employing some such techniques could enable the farmers to save enough water to increase their output.

The correct answer is E.

CRO3367

692. Hollywood restaurant is replacing some of its standard tables with tall tables and stools. The restaurant already fills every available seat during its operating hours, and the change in seating arrangements will not result in an increase in the restaurant's seating capacity. Nonetheless, the restaurant's management expects revenue to increase as a result of the seating change without any concurrent change in menu, prices, or operating hours.

Which of the following, if true, provides the best reason for the expectation?

(A) One of the taller tables takes up less floor space than one of the standard tables.

(B) Diners seated on stools typically do not linger over dinner as long as diners seated at standard tables.

(C) Since the restaurant will replace only some of its standard tables, it can continue to accommodate customers who do not care for the taller tables.

(D) Few diners are likely to avoid the restaurant because of the new seating arrangement.

(E) The standard tables being replaced by tall tables would otherwise have to be replaced with new standard tables at a greater expense.

Argument Construction

Situation Hollywood restaurant is replacing some of its tables with taller tables and stools, and the management expects this will increase revenue, despite the fact that the restaurant already fills all of its available seats and that this change will not increase seating capacity. Furthermore, there will not be any change in menu, prices, or operating hours.

Reasoning *What would strongly support the management's expectation?* Since the new seating will not increase the restaurant's seating capacity, the management's expectations must be based on a belief that the change to taller tables and stools will somehow change diners' behavior, perhaps by leading them to order more food, or to stay at their tables for a shorter time, thereby allowing the restaurant to serve more diners during its operating hours without increasing seating capacity. If diners seated at tall tables and on tall stools spend less time lingering over their dinners, then they will leave sooner, opening up the tables for more diners. Because the restaurant, before the change, already fills every available seat during its operating hours, it is reasonable to think that it will be able to serve more diners than it currently does, thereby selling more food and thus increasing revenue.

A This would be relevant if we could infer from it that seating capacity will increase. However, the passage indicates that the new seating arrangement will not result in greater capacity.

B **Correct.** Because the restaurant will be able to serve more meals during its operating hours, the restaurant's revenue can be expected to increase.

C This may indicate that the restaurant is less likely to alienate customers who do not care for tall tables and stools, but that only supports the claim that the restaurant will not lose customers and therefore lose revenue; it does not indicate that the restaurant will see revenue increase.

D Again, this merely indicates that there will not be a loss—or much loss—of revenue, not that there will be an increase in revenue.

E Less expensive tables will decrease the restaurant's costs, but it will not increase the restaurant's revenue.

The correct answer is B.

CR07660

693. A major network news organization experienced a drop in viewership in the week following the airing of a controversial report on the economy. The network also received a very large number of complaints regarding the report. The network, however, maintains that negative reactions to the report had nothing to do with its loss of viewers.

Which of the following, if true, most strongly supports the network's position?

(A) The other major network news organizations reported similar reductions in viewership during the same week.

(B) The viewers who registered complaints with the network were regular viewers of the news organization's programs.

(C) Major network news organizations publicly attribute drops in viewership to their own reports only when they receive complaints about those reports.

(D) This was not the first time that this network news organization has aired a controversial report on the economy that has inspired viewers to complain to the network.

(E) Most network news viewers rely on network news broadcasts as their primary source of information regarding the economy.

Argument Construction

Situation   A major network news organization aired a controversial report on the economy, and the following week the network's viewership declined. The network claims that the loss of viewers was not connected with negative reactions to the report.

Reasoning   *Which statement most strongly supports the network's position?* If other major news networks had similar drops in viewership, it is implausible to think that the controversial report accounted for the other networks' drops in viewership. On the other hand, it is plausible to suppose that whatever did cause the drop in the viewership experienced by other network news organizations— e.g., holidays, weather, popular non-news programming—also had that effect on the organization that ran the controversial report. This would give some reason to believe that the airing of the report does not account for the organization's drop in viewership.

A   **Correct.** The network's position is that the drop in viewership was not caused by its airing of the controversial report and thus that the drop was caused by something else. This answer choice provides some evidence that there might have been a different cause. If none of the other networks had aired the controversial report, their reductions in viewership were likely due to some other factor; it is implausible to suppose that disapproval of the one network would have caused viewers to avoid all networks. A simultaneous drop in viewership among all the networks would support the hypothesis that a single factor or set of factors caused the drop for all the networks, including the one that aired the report.

B   If anything, this statement tends to undermine the network's claim, because it suggests that the report offended people who otherwise might have continued to watch the organization's programming.

C   Since the network did in fact receive complaints about the report, this statement is irrelevant.

D   The fact that the network has received complaints before about controversial reports on the economy that the network's news organization has aired tells us nothing about whether this recent report caused a subsequent drop in viewership.

E   The fact that viewers turn to network news broadcasts as their primary source of information about the economy tells us nothing about whether viewers might stop watching a particular network news organization's programs as a result of its airing a controversial report on the economy.

The correct answer is A.

CR04366

694. Only a reduction of 10 percent in the number of scheduled flights using Greentown's airport will allow the delays that are so common there to be avoided. Hevelia airstrip, 40 miles away, would, if upgraded and expanded, be an attractive alternative for fully 20 percent of the passengers using Greentown airport. Nevertheless, experts reject the claim that turning Hevelia into a full-service airport would end the chronic delays at Greentown.

Which of the following, if true, most helps to justify the experts' position?

(A) Turning Hevelia into a full-service airport would require not only substantial construction at the airport itself, but also the construction of new access highways.

(B) A second largely undeveloped airstrip close to Greentown airport would be a more attractive alternative than Hevelia for many passengers who now use Greentown.

(C) Hevelia airstrip lies in a relatively undeveloped area but would, if it became a full-service airport, be a magnet for commercial and residential development.

(D) If an airplane has to wait to land, the extra jet fuel required adds significantly to the airline's costs.

(E) Several airlines use Greentown as a regional hub, so that most flights landing at Greentown have many passengers who then take different flights to reach their final destinations.

Evaluation of a Plan

Situation   To avoid the delays now common at Greentown's airport, the number of scheduled flights there would need to be reduced by 10 percent. If the nearby Hevelia airstrip were expanded and upgraded, it would be an attractive alternative for 20 percent of Greentown airport's passengers. Still, experts do not believe that the delays at Greentown would end even if Hevelia were turned into a full-service airport.

Reasoning   *Which statement most supports the experts' position?* If the number of flights at Greentown's airport did not drop by at least 10 percent, despite the fact that 20 percent of the passengers who currently use Greentown's airport would find nearby Hevelia airstrip an attractive alternative, then the delays would not be avoided. Airlines generally use certain airports as regional hubs—an airport through which an airline routes most of its traffic—so, even if many passengers would be willing to use Hevelia airstrip, the number of flights at Greentown may not decline significantly, or at all.

A   The experts' position concerns what would happen to the flight delays at Greentown airport if the Hevelia airstrip were converted into a full-service airport. So the fact that there are great costs involved in making such a conversion—possibly making such a conversion unlikely—has no bearing on the effects such a conversion would have on flight delays at Greentown if the conversion were to be carried out.

B   This statement indicates that the undeveloped airstrip near Greentown might be a better way to alleviate flight delays at Greentown, but it tells us nothing about the effects that converting the Hevelia airstrip to a full-service airport would have were it to be carried out.

C   This in no way explains why converting the Hevelia airstrip into a full-service airport would not alleviate the problem with flight delays at Greentown.

D   This provides a reason to think that reducing the number of flights at Greentown might make the airport more efficient. But that has no bearing on the effect that converting the Hevelia airstrip to a full-service airport might have on flight delays at Greentown.

E   **Correct.** This statement provides support for the experts' position because it gives a reason for thinking that the number of scheduled flights at Greentown would not be reduced, even if Hevelia airstrip became an attractive alternative for some 20 percent of Greentown's passengers.

The correct answer is E.

CR07712
695. Farmer: Worldwide, just three grain crops—rice, wheat, and corn—account for most human caloric intake. To maintain this level of caloric intake and also keep pace with global population growth, yields per acre from each of these crops will have to increase at least 1.5 percent every year, given that the supply of cultivated land is diminishing. Therefore, the government should increase funding for research into new ways to improve yields.

Which of the following is an assumption on which the farmer's argument depends?

(A) It is solely the government's responsibility to ensure that the amount of rice, wheat, and corn produced worldwide keeps pace with global population growth.

(B) Increasing government funding for research into new ways to improve the yields per acre of rice, wheat, and corn crops would help to increase total worldwide annual production of food from these crops.

(C) Increasing the yields per acre of rice, wheat, and corn is more important than increasing the yields per acre of other crops.

(D) Current levels of funding for research into ways of improving grain crop yields per acre have enabled grain crop yields per acre to increase by more than 1.5 percent per year worldwide.

(E) In coming decades, rice, wheat, and corn will become a minor part of human caloric intake, unless there is government-funded research to increase their yields per acre.

Argument Construction

Situation The farmer states that although the worldwide human population is increasing, the supply of cultivated land is decreasing. We thus need to increase yields for the food crops that account for most of human caloric intake—rice, wheat, and corn—if we are to maintain our existing caloric intake. The increase in yields, according to the farmer, would need to be at least 1.5 percent every year.

Reasoning *What must be true if we are to accept the farmer's conclusion, that the government should increase funding for research into new ways to improve crop yields, on the basis of the above statements?* The farmer uses the above statements as premises of an argument for an increase in government funding for research on crop yields. Supposing that the farmer's statements are true, we need to find in the available options the statement that, if added to the argument, may allow us to accept the farmer's conclusion, based on the argument.

A Whether or not nongovernmental entities such as NGOs (nongovernmental organizations) are responsible for helping to ensure that humans have an adequate amount of food, governments may or may not also have this responsibility.

B **Correct.** If government funding of this research does not increase crop yields, then the premises of the argument provide no support for the conclusion that the government should provide such funding. The cogency of the argument thus depends on this statement.

C Crops in addition to rice, wheat, and corn could also be very important, and perhaps essential for human existence. However, this would not diminish the importance of food crops such as rice, wheat, and corn.

D This option may suggest that current levels of funding of research into crop yields are sufficient for purposes of our obtaining the necessary crop yields.

E This option suggests that rice, wheat, and corn may be replaced by other crops, because the other crops have better yields. Because we might thus have a means for increasing crop yields that does not involve an increase in government research funding, this option may actually decrease the support for the conclusion.

The correct answer is B.

CR08770

696. The air quality board recently informed Coffee Roast, a small coffee roasting firm, of a complaint regarding the smoke from its roaster. Recently enacted air quality regulations require machines roasting more than 10 pounds of coffee to be equipped with expensive smoke-dissipating afterburners. The firm, however, roasts only 8 pounds of coffee at a time. Nevertheless, the company has decided to purchase and install an afterburner.

Which of the following, if true, most strongly supports the firm's decision?

(A) Until settling on the new air quality regulations, the board had debated whether to require afterburners for machines roasting more than 5 pounds of coffee at a time.

(B) Coffee roasted in a machine equipped with an afterburner has its flavor subtly altered.

(C) The cost to the firm of an afterburner is less than the cost of replacing its roaster with a smaller one.

(D) Fewer complaints are reported in areas that maintain strict rules regarding afterburners.

(E) The firm has reason to fear that negative publicity regarding the complaints could result in lost sales.

Evaluation of a Plan

Situation   After being informed of a complaint about smoke from its coffee roaster, a firm decided to purchase and install an afterburner to reduce or eliminate emissions of smoke, even though the roaster roasts too little coffee at a time for an afterburner to be legally required.

Reasoning   *What would have been a good reason for the firm to buy and install the afterburner?* The only factors mentioned that might give the firm reason to buy an afterburner are the complaint about smoke and the regulations requiring an afterburner. Since the regulations do not apply in this case, the complaint is more likely to have motivated the firm's decision. Any serious potential consequences the firm might have faced from failure to address the complaint could have provided a good reason to buy and install the afterburner.

A   If this debate had still been ongoing when the firm made its decision, uncertainty about the pending regulations might have justified the decision. But the debate had already been settled before the firm decided to purchase the afterburner, and the regulations clearly did not require one.

B   An unspecified alteration in flavor is not clearly a good reason to use an afterburner—the afterburner might worsen the flavor.

C   The firm's roaster was already small enough that the regulations did not require it to be replaced, even without an afterburner.

D   This reason relates only to rules regarding afterburners, not to Coffee Roast's purchase of an afterburner, which was not mandated by regulations. Furthermore, it could be that the air quality regulations recently enacted are among the strictest in any region, which could result in fewer complaints regardless of whether Coffee Roast installs an afterburner.

E   **Correct.** Since installing an afterburner is a plausible way to address the complaint and prevent future complaints, the firm has plausible reasons to believe this strategy will help it avoid the negative publicity and lost sales it fears. These considerations could have reasonably justified its decision.

The correct answer is E.

CR03695

697. People who do regular volunteer work tend to live longer, on average, than people who do not. It has been found that "doing good," a category that certainly includes volunteer work, releases endorphins, the brain's natural opiates, which induce in people a feeling of well-being. Clearly, there is a connection: Regular releases of endorphins must in some way help to extend people's lives.

Which of the following, if true, most seriously undermines the force of the evidence given as support for the hypothesis that endorphins promote longevity?

(A) People who do regular volunteer work are only somewhat more likely than others to characterize the work they do for a living as "doing good."

(B) Although extremely high levels of endorphins could be harmful to health, such levels are never reached as a result of the natural release of endorphins.

(C) There are many people who have done some volunteer work but who do not do such work regularly.

(D) People tend not to become involved in regular volunteer work unless they are healthy and energetic to begin with.

(E) Releases of endorphins are responsible for the sense of well-being experienced by many long-distance runners while running.

Argument Evaluation

Situation   People who volunteer regularly live longer on average than people who do not. Doing good work, including volunteer work, releases endorphins, which induce a feeling of well-being.

Reasoning   *What additional findings would suggest that the cited evidence does not indicate that endorphins increase longevity?* The argument implicitly assumes that the reason regular volunteers tend to live longer is that volunteering lengthens their lives. It further assumes that no factor that is correlated with volunteering, other than the endorphin release, would plausibly explain how volunteering could have this effect. Findings that cast doubt on either of these assumptions would undermine the connection between the cited evidence and the conclusion that endorphins promote longevity.

A   Volunteering might greatly boost volunteers' endorphin levels even if the work the volunteers do for a living is no different from other people's work.

B   Even if unnaturally high endorphin levels could harm health, the levels attainable through volunteer work may promote health.

C   The argument is about an observed correlation in a certain group of people (those who regularly do volunteer work). How many people are outside that group (i.e., do not regularly do volunteer work) is independent of the question of what causes the observed correlation. Even if some people volunteer only occasionally, volunteering regularly may promote longevity by causing regular releases of endorphins.

D   **Correct.** This suggests that the initially better health of people who choose to volunteer could fully explain the cited correlation between volunteering and longevity.

E   Unless we are also given evidence that long-distance runners tend not to live longer than other people, this does not undermine the purported evidence in the argument. Endorphins might promote longevity in both regular volunteers and long-distance runners.

The correct answer is D.

CR04140

698. A study compared a sample of Swedish people older than 75 who needed in-home assistance with a similar sample of Israeli people. The people in the two samples received both informal assistance, provided by family and friends, and formal assistance, professionally provided. Although Sweden and Israel have equally well-funded and comprehensive systems for providing formal assistance, the study found that the people in the Swedish sample received more formal assistance, on average, than those in the Israeli sample.

Which of the following, if true, does most to explain the difference that the study found?

(A) A companion study found that among children needing special in-home care, the amount of formal assistance they received was roughly the same in Sweden as in Israel.

(B) More Swedish than Israeli people older than 75 live in rural areas where formal assistance services are sparse or nonexistent.

(C) Although in both Sweden and Israel much of the funding for formal assistance ultimately comes from the central government, the local structures through which assistance is delivered are different in the two countries.

(D) In recent decades, the increase in life expectancy of someone who is 75 years old has been greater in Israel than in Sweden.

(E) In Israel, people older than 75 tend to live with their children, whereas in Sweden people of that age tend to live alone.

Argument Construction

Situation A study of elder care in Israel and Sweden found that in Sweden, of the total amount of care that people older than 75 and needing in home assistance received, the proportion of care that was formal, i.e., provided by professional care personnel, was greater than in Israel. Both Sweden and Israel had equally good systems for providing formal care, and in both countries, the elderly also received informal care, i.e., care provided by friends and family.

Reasoning *Among the factors given, which would most contribute to explaining the difference the study found between Sweden and Israel with respect to elder care?* A good guess would be that there is a difference in some societal factor that affects the difference the study found. For example, perhaps elders in one of the countries regard maintaining independence as a higher priority than elders in the other and consequently try to rely less on friends and family? Perhaps patterns of decline in ability to remain independent are different in the two countries? Or perhaps a greater proportion of elders live alone in one of the countries than in the other?

A The difference to be explained concerns only elder care, not care of children.

B The fact that formal elder care is less available in Swedish rural areas than in Israeli rural areas might suggest that there would be a greater reliance on informal care in such areas in Sweden. But this new information throws little light on how the overall proportions of formal and informal care in each country would be affected.

C This information is not specific enough to help explain the precise difference found in the study. It is reasonable to assume that the study was conducted with sufficient rigor to take account of any relevant structural differences in the delivery of formal elder care.

D This could suggest either that the greater proportion of informal elder care in Israel contributes to greater life expectancy or that greater life expectancy signals greater fitness during old age that would make it more practical for friends and family to provide informal elder care.

E **Correct.** The prevalence in Israel of elders living in family settings—in contrast to Sweden, where elders tend to live alone—offers a plausible explanation of the difference that the study found in the patterns of elder care in Israel and Sweden. It seems reasonable to think that, all things being equal, elders living alone would use formal elder care services more often than elders living with friends or family.

The correct answer is E.

CR05077

699. Film Director: It is true that certain characters and plot twists in my newly released film *The Big Heist* are similar to characters and plot twists in *Thieves*, a movie that came out last year. Pointing to these similarities, the film studio that produced *Thieves* is now accusing me of taking ideas from that film. The accusation is clearly without merit. All production work on *The Big Heist* was actually completed months before *Thieves* was released.

Which of the following, if true, provides the strongest support for the director's position?

(A) Before *Thieves* began production, its script had been circulating for several years among various film studios, including the studio that produced *The Big Heist*.

(B) The characters and plot twists that are most similar in the two films have close parallels in many earlier films of the same genre.

(C) The film studio that produced *Thieves* seldom produces films in this genre.

(D) The director of *Thieves* worked with the director of *The Big Heist* on several earlier projects.

(E) Production work on *Thieves* began before production work on *The Big Heist* was started.

Argument Evaluation

Situation   The director of the film *The Big Heist* has been accused, by the studio that produced the film *Thieves*, of taking ideas from the film. The director responds that the accusation lacks merit, since all production work on *The Big Heist* was completed before *Thieves* appeared last year in theaters.

Reasoning   *Which of the five statements most strongly supports the director's position?* Crime thrillers, as a film genre, are likely to have stock characters and plot lines that reflect a long tradition. So it would be no surprise if some of the characters or plot twists in one such film would resemble, to a greater or lesser extent, the characters and plot twists in another. The studio might be correct in identifying such resemblances between *The Big Heist* and *Thieves*. But it would not necessarily be correct that characters or plot lines in *The Big Heist* were derived from *Thieves*.

A   This undercuts the director's position, since it provides information that indicates an opportunity for the director to copy ideas from the script for *Thieves*.

B   **Correct.** This information strengthens the support for the director's claim that the studio's accusation lacks merit. Since both *Thieves* and *The Big Heist* fall within a long tradition of crime thriller films, the characters and plot lines in both films reflect that tradition, and so any resemblances do not imply deliberate copying of the ideas in *Thieves* by the director of *The Big Heist*.

C   This information seems largely irrelevant to the issue raised and does not strengthen support for the director's conclusion.

D   This does little to indicate that the director's conclusion is correct. For example, the then-future director of *Thieves* might have discussed with the future director of *The Big Heist* specific ideas about character and plot for a planned crime thriller film.

E   This does not support the director's claim. For example, it raises the possibility that information about *Thieves* leaked during the early stages of production—information that could have been exploited in the production of *The Big Heist*.

The correct answer is B.

CR05412

700. In Mernia commercial fossil hunters often sell important fossils they have found, not to universities or museums, but to individual collectors, who pay much better but generally do not allow researchers access to their collections. To increase the number of fossils available for research, some legislators propose requiring all fossils that are found in Mernia to be sold only to universities or museums.

Which of the following, if true, most strongly indicates that the legislators' proposal will fail to achieve its goal?

(A) Some fossil hunters in Mernia are not commercial fossil hunters, but rather are amateurs who keep the fossils that they find.

(B) Most fossils found in Mernia are common types that have little scientific interest.

(C) Commercial fossil hunters in Mernia currently sell some of the fossils they find to universities and museums.

(D) Many universities in Mernia do not engage in fossil research.

(E) Most fossils are found by commercial fossil hunters, and they would give up looking for fossils if they were no longer allowed to sell to individual collectors.

Evaluation of a Plan

Situation   Fossil hunters in Mernia often sell important fossils to collectors who do not make them accessible to researchers. To increase the number of fossils available for research, some legislators propose requiring all fossils found in Mernia to be sold only to universities or museums.

Reasoning   *What would most strongly suggest that requiring all fossils found in Mernia to be sold only to universities or museums would not increase the number of fossils available for research?* To increase the number of fossils available for research, the proposed requirement will have to be implemented and effectively enforced. It will presumably have to increase the total number of fossils sold to universities and museums. And those institutions will have to make more of the fossils in their collections available to researchers than the private collectors do. Evidence that any of those conditions will not be fulfilled would suggest that the legislators' proposal will fail to achieve its goal.

A   Even if the legislation does not affect fossils kept by amateurs, it might still result in many more fossils being sold to universities or museums rather than to private collectors, and thus might still increase the number of fossils available for research.

B   Even if few Mernian fossils are interesting to researchers, the legislation could still achieve its goal of making more fossils available for research.

C   Even if commercial fossil hunters already sell a few fossils to universities and museums, the legislation could encourage them to sell many more fossils.

D   The universities that do not engage in fossil research presumably will not be interested in buying fossils even if the legislation passes. But the fossil hunters can just sell their fossils to other universities and museums that do engage in fossil research.

E   **Correct.** This suggests that if the legislation passes, fossils will simply be left in the ground rather than sold to private collectors. That would not increase the total number of fossils available for research.

The correct answer is E.

CR02702

701. Economist: Tropicorp, which constantly seeks profitable investment opportunities, has been buying and clearing sections of tropical forest for cattle ranching, although pastures newly created there become useless for grazing after just a few years. The company has not gone into rubber tapping, even though greater profits can be made from rubber tapping, which leaves the forest intact. Thus, some environmentalists argue that **Tropicorp's actions do not serve even its own economic interest**. However, the initial investment required for a successful rubber-tapping operation is larger than that needed for a cattle ranch; there is a shortage of workers employable in rubber-tapping operations; and taxes are higher on profits from rubber tapping than on profits from cattle ranching. Consequently, **the environmentalists' conclusion is probably wrong**.

In the economist's argument, the two **boldface** portions play which of the following roles?

(A) The first supports the conclusion of the economist's argument; the second calls that conclusion into question.

(B) The first states the conclusion of the economist's argument; the second supports that conclusion.

(C) The first supports the conclusion of the environmentalists' argument; the second states that conclusion.

(D) The first states the conclusion of the environmentalists' argument; the second states the conclusion of the economist's argument.

(E) Each supports the conclusion of the economist's argument.

Argument Construction

Situation   According to an economist, the firm Tropicorp has been investing in tropical forest that it has cleared for cattle ranching. But its new pastures are useless for grazing after a few years. In contrast, rubber tapping—which would avoid cutting trees—could be more profitable. According to the economist, environmentalists consequently argue that Tropicorp's investment does not serve the firm's economic interest. However, the economist argues, investing in rubber tapping involves some potential costs and risks greater than those that investing in cattle ranching involves. Consequently, the economist argues, the environmentalists' conclusion is probably wrong.

Reasoning   *What function is served by the statement that Tropicorp's actions do not serve even its own economic interest? What function is served by the statement that the environmentalists' conclusion is probably wrong?* The first statement is a conclusion that the economist attributes to environmentalists. The second statement is the conclusion of an argument presented by the economist.

A   The first states the conclusion of the argument that is attributed to environmentalists; it does not support—nor is it meant to—the conclusion of the economist.

B   The second statement, not the first, is the conclusion of the economist's argument.

C   The first is the conclusion attributed to environmentalists and is not meant merely as support for that conclusion.

D   **Correct.** The first states the conclusion of the environmentalists' argument as the economist presents it; the second is the conclusion of the economist's argument.

E   Neither statement is meant as support for the economist's conclusion, nor does it offer such support.

The correct answer is D.

CR41700.02

702. Brown tides are growths of algae on the sea's surface that prevent sunlight from reaching marine plants below, thereby destroying not only the plants but also the shellfish that live off these plants. Biologists recently isolated a virus that, when added to seawater, kills the algae that cause brown tides. Adding large quantities of this virus to waters affected by brown tides will therefore make it possible to save the populations of shellfish that inhabit those waters.

Which of the following, if true, provides the most support for the conclusion of the argument?

(A) When applied in large quantities, the virus not only kills the algae that cause brown tides but also many harmless kinds of algae.

(B) Marine animals that prey on shellfish avoid areas of the sea in which brown tides are occurring.

(C) The number of different kinds of virus present in seawater is far greater than many marine biologists had, until recently, believed.

(D) The presence of large quantities of the virus in seawater does not adversely affect the growth of marine plants.

(E) The amount of the virus naturally present in seawater in which brown tides occur is neither significantly greater nor significantly less than the amount present in seawater in which brown tides do not occur.

Argument Evaluation

Situation   Brown tides—growths of algae on the sea's surface—kill the marine plants on which certain shellfish depend, by depriving them of sunlight. Biologists have discovered a virus that, if added to seawater in large quantities, can kill the algae. An author argues that this can be a means of saving the shellfish populations.

Reasoning   *Which of the answer choices most strongly supports the conclusion of the argument?* The argument concludes that adding large quantities of the virus to seawater infected by brown tides will help the shellfish survive. Any new information suggesting that the virus would, directly or indirectly, help the shellfish survive supports the conclusion. But the conclusion would be questionable if the virus could directly or indirectly harm the shellfish in a way that would outweigh any benefits the virus provides. New information indicating that this would not occur could provide support for the argument.

A   This information suggests that deployment of the virus could have undesirable side effects, but it neither supports nor casts doubt on the conclusion. We have no information suggesting that killing algae other than those that produce brown tides would, directly or indirectly, help the shellfish survive.

B   This information neither supports nor casts doubt on the conclusion. It indicates a way in which brown tides indirectly provide a benefit to shellfish, even if the indirect harm they cause to shellfish outweighs that benefit.

C   This information indicates that certain viruses can survive in seawater environments, but this information, by itself, neither supports nor casts doubt on the conclusion.

D   **Correct.** This information indicates that the virus the biologists isolated does not directly harm the marine plants on which shellfish depend. Therefore it provides significant support for the conclusion by indicating that the virus will not harm the shellfish indirectly by harming their food source.

E   This information suggests that only large quantities of the virus the biologists isolated will be effective in eliminating brown tides. But the conclusion of the argument specifies that the virus would need to be added in *large quantities*, so the information given in this answer choice provides no additional support for the conclusion.

The correct answer is D.

CR18310.02

703. In persons with astigmatism, the clear outer layer of the eye is deformed in a way that impairs and sometimes distorts vision. The elongated figures in the paintings of El Greco (1541–1614) were so unusual that some critics sought to explain them by hypothesizing that, without knowing it, El Greco had an astigmatism that caused everything to appear to him in the distorted way that was characteristic of his painted figures.

The proposed explanation is most vulnerable to the criticism that it fails to

(A) establish that during the period in which El Greco lived, there was any correction available to those who did realize their vision was distorted

(B) provide evidence that astigmatism was common in the 1500s and 1600s

(C) consider that the critics who proposed the explanation might have suffered from astigmatism

(D) consider the effect of the hypothesized astigmatism on El Greco's perception of his own paintings

(E) allow for the possibility that artists see the world differently than do nonartists

Argument Evaluation

Situation   Figures in the paintings of El Greco are strikingly elongated. Some art critics have hypothesized that this was an unintentional result of his having a type of astigmatism that made things look elongated to him.

Reasoning   *What is a significant weakness in the critics' explanation?* Reasons to doubt the explanation could include any evidence that another explanation is more likely to be true or that the situation envisioned in the explanation may be impossible or inconsistent with the phenomena to be explained. For example, if only human figures in El Greco's paintings were elongated while other similarly shaped objects were not, that observation would be inconsistent with the claim that the elongations were due to a general distortion in his vision. Answer choice D presents a similar reason to think that the proposed explanation is inconsistent with the facts. If El Greco perceived human models as more elongated than they appear to non-astigmatic perceivers, he would also have perceived his depictions of such models as more elongated than those depictions appear to non-astigmatic perceivers. So if he had intended to depict the figures accurately, he would have adjusted his painting accordingly, and his depictions should appear accurately shaped to typical viewers. But they do not. Therefore, the distortions were more likely intentional.

A   The hypothesis of some critics is that El Greco may have had astigmatism without being aware of it. So the explanation does not depend on whether astigmatism could have been corrected during the period in which El Greco lived.

B   The reasoning concerning the hypothesis of some critics does not depend on whether astigmatism was common in the 1500s or 1600s. It is entirely consistent with the hypothesis that astigmatism was rare and that El Greco was one of the few people who had it.

C   Even if the critics who proposed the explanation had astigmatism, the explanation and the reasoning concerning the explanation would not be rendered faulty. The information provided is that the figures in El Greco's paintings were unusually elongated, not merely that they appear elongated to the critics mentioned.

D   **Correct.** According to the art critics' hypothesis, El Greco did not intend the figures in his paintings to be unnaturally elongated and did not know that they were. But this is the opposite of what one should expect if he had a type of astigmatism that made things look elongated to him. His astigmatism should have made the elongated figures in his paintings appear to him even more elongated than they appear to typical observers. So, regardless of whether he had astigmatism or not, the elongations were most likely intentional. If they were intentional, this feature of his paintings provides no more evidence that he had astigmatism than that he did not.

E   The explanation offered by the critics is entirely compatible with the possibility that artists see the world differently than do nonartists. One might wonder whether this possibility provides an alternative explanation for why El Greco painted elongated figures: he did so because he, like all artists, saw the world differently than nonartists do. But that hypothesis does not offer a coherent alternative to the critics' explanation. If all artists see the world as El Greco did, we should expect them all to depict the world as he did. However, most do not. If, on the other hand, El Greco's way of perceiving the world was only one of many ways in which artists' perceptions differ from those of nonartists, this provides no reason to think that the difference between El Greco's work and others' was not caused by astigmatism.

The correct answer is D.

CR74231.01

704. Marketing executive for Magu Corporation: Whenever Magu opens a manufacturing facility in a new city, the company should sponsor, or make donations to, a number of nonprofit organizations in that city. Doing so would improve Magu's image in the community, and thus the money spent on such charitable ventures would lead to increased sales.

Which statement would, if true, point to the most serious weakness in the marketing executive's advice?

(A) Magu sells its products internationally, so sales in any one city represent only a small portion of total revenue.

(B) Spending on charitable ventures would require Magu to decrease direct advertisements, which are the most effective means of reaching its target customers.

(C) If market conditions change, Magu may have to close any such facility or relocate it.

(D) Some nonprofit organizations are poorly organized, so money donated to them would be of little benefit to the community.

(E) If workers at the manufacturing facility believed their wages or working conditions were poor, their complaints would outweigh any good impressions generated by Magu's donations or sponsorships.

Evaluation of a Plan

Situation A marketing executive for Magu Corporation argues that Magu can increase its sales if it sponsors or donates to nonprofit organizations in any city in which it opens a new manufacturing facility, because doing so would improve its image in that city and increase sales.

Reasoning *What would most strongly suggest that Magu would not increase sales even if it followed the plan proposed by the marketing executive?* Sponsoring or donating to nonprofit organizations would require the use of financial assets that therefore cannot be spent elsewhere. If as a result Magu had to cut other expenditures that drive sales more effectively than funding nonprofit organizations drives sales, the plan may not succeed.

A Because Magu sells its products internationally and no one city represents more than a small portion of revenue, any increase in sales in any given city will have only a slight effect on total sales; nonetheless, sales could still rise.

B **Correct.** If sponsoring or donating to a nonprofit would require Magu to reduce advertising, and advertising is the most effective means of reaching its target customers, then any positive influence on sales resulting from the charitable venture might be overwhelmed by a decrease in sales because of the advertising cuts.

C The fact that Magu might have to close or relocate one of these new facilities does not suggest that the marketing executive's plan would not work; Magu's image could, nonetheless, improve and sales could increase as a result.

D Even if some nonprofit organizations are poorly organized, others may not be, and Magu could limit its support to those.

E Even if such complaints from workers would outweigh any benefit arising from Magu's support of nonprofit organizations, this does not indicate that the marketing executive's plan will not work, because we have no reason to think that the workers will in fact be dissatisfied with their wages or working conditions.

The correct answer is B.

CR30650.02

705. In the last few years, plant scientists have been able to genetically engineer seeds to produce crops highly resistant to insect damage. Farmers growing crops with these seeds will be able to spend significantly less on pesticides. This cost reduction would more than make up for the higher cost of the genetically engineered seeds. Clearly, therefore, farmers who grow crops from genetically engineered seeds will be able to reduce their costs by using them.

Which of the following, if true, most weakens the argument?

(A) Plant scientists have not yet developed insect-resistant strains of every crop that is currently grown commercially.

(B) The cost of several commonly used pesticides is expected to rise in the next few years.

(C) Crops grown from the genetically engineered seeds require significantly more fertilizer and water to grow well than do crops grown from nonengineered seeds.

(D) In the future, the cost of genetically engineered seeds is likely to fall to the level of nonengineered seeds.

(E) The crops that now require the greatest expenditure on pesticides are not the ones for which genetically engineered seeds will become available.

Argument Evaluation

Situation   Farmers who grow crops with seeds that have been genetically engineered to produce crops resistant to insect damage will be able to spend less on pesticides. Though these seeds are more expensive than regular seeds, this greater cost will be more than compensated for by lower expenditures on pesticides.

Reasoning   *What claim most weakens the argument's support for the claim that farmers who grow crops from these genetically engineered seeds will be able to reduce their costs by using them?* The argument gives us good reason to think that even though these seeds are more expensive, the added expense is less than the amount that farmers will save by reducing their pesticide usage. But the argument does not tell us how the use of these seeds affects other costs the farmer might have. If, for instance, crops grown from these seeds require greater use of fertilizer or water, costs may stay stable or even increase.

A   The argument's conclusion is only that farmers who grow crops using these seeds will be able to reduce their costs. The argument does not claim that every farmer will be able to reduce costs for every crop the farmer produces.

B   If the cost of pesticides will increase in the next few years, this gives us some reason to believe that farmers who use these genetically engineered seeds to grow crops will have lower costs than they would have if they used other seeds to grow the same crops. That strengthens rather than weakens the argument's support for its conclusion.

C   **Correct.** As discussed above, if crops grown with the genetically engineered seeds require the use of more fertilizer or water, the farmer who uses such seeds may not see a reduction in costs.

D   If the genetically engineered seeds eventually become no more expensive than regular seeds, then it is more likely that farmers growing crops with these genetically engineered seeds will see their costs reduced.

E   This answer choice indicates that farmers will not be able to reduce costs as much as they might if all crops could be grown using seeds that are genetically engineered to produce crops resistant to insect damage. That, however, is fully consistent with the possibility that if farmers grow crops using the genetically engineered seeds that are available, they will thereby be able to reduce their costs.

The correct answer is C.

CR44040.02

706. Educational Theorist: Recent editorials have called for limits on the amount of homework assigned to schoolchildren younger than 12. They point out that free-time activities play an important role in childhood development and that homework in large quantities can severely restrict children's free time, hindering their development. But the actual average homework time for children under 12—little more than 30 minutes per night—leaves plenty of free time. In reality, therefore, the editorials' rationale cannot justify the restriction they advocate.

Which of the following, if true, would most seriously call into question the educational theorist's conclusion?

(A) Some teachers give as homework assignments work of a kind that research suggests is most effective educationally when done in class.

(B) For children younger than 12, regularly doing homework in the first years of school has no proven academic value, but many educators believe that it fosters self-discipline and time management.

(C) Some homework assignments are related to free-time activities that children engage in, such as reading or hobbies.

(D) A substantial proportion of schoolchildren under 12, particularly those in their first few years of school, have less than 10 minutes of homework assigned per night.

(E) Some free-time activities teach children skills or information that they later find useful in their schoolwork.

Argument Evaluation

Situation   An educational theorist points out that recent editorials have called for limits on the amount of homework assigned to children under the age of 12, since large amounts of homework can restrict the sort of free-time activities that are crucial to their development. The theorist argues that such restrictions are not justified, because children under 12 spend on average only 30 minutes on homework. That leaves plenty of time for other activities.

Reasoning   *What would most seriously call the theorist's conclusion into question?* The theorist gives only the average amount of time children under the age of 12 spend on homework. However, the editorials advocated a limit on the maximum amount of homework assigned, not on the average amount across all schoolchildren. There could be a wide variation among the amounts of time different children spend on homework. While a large number of children may spend only a short amount of time on homework, some children may spend much longer. For those who have the greater amounts of homework, this might leave little time for important free-time activities.

A   This claim, if true, may suggest that certain types of homework that teachers assign would be better done in class. It might be best not to give such assignments for homework, but that does not give us much reason to think that the *amount* of homework should be restricted.

B   This choice indicates that, despite a possible objection to assigning homework, homework does have value. That does not tell us, though, whether the maximum amount of homework that is assigned is too much, too little, or just right.

C   This claim could be true and yet children could still be left with too little time for important free-time activities.

D   **Correct.** As explained in the reasoning section above, the educational theorist draws a conclusion regarding whether there should be a limit on the **maximum** amount of homework assigned to children under 12 and bases this conclusion solely on the **average** amount of time children under the age of 12 spend on homework. This conclusion would not be well supported if there is a wide variation in the amount of time children under the age of 12 spend on homework and if some—perhaps in the lower grades—spend only a very short amount of time on it. Suppose, for instance, as this answer choice has, that less than 10 minutes of homework is assigned to some of these children each night. If that were the case, then because the average amount of time schoolchildren under the age of 12 spend on homework each night is 30 minutes, that would mean that many schoolchildren may be spending far more than 30 minutes a night on homework. If so, then those children may not have enough free time for other important activities. That might mean that it would be appropriate to put limits on the amount of homework assigned to children under the age of 12.

E   This claim shows that some free-time activities are important for schoolwork later in life. But that does not tell us whether the maximum amount of homework that is assigned is too much, too little, or just right.

The correct answer is D.

Questions 707 to 760 - Difficulty: **Medium**

CR78590.02

707. Airline Representative: The percentage of flight delays caused by airline error decreased significantly this year. This indicates that airlines listened to complaints about preventable errors and addressed the problems. Although delays caused by weather and other uncontrollable factors will always be part of travel, preventable delays are clearly decreasing.

Which of the following most clearly points to a logical flaw in the representative's reasoning?

(A) Airlines may be motivated by financial concerns to underreport the percentage of flight delays caused by airline error.

(B) The delays caused by uncontrollable factors could have led to an increase in complaints to airlines.

(C) Complaints may not be the most reliable measure of how many errors occurred in a given year.

(D) Delays caused by weather and other uncontrollable factors could have increased dramatically during the year under discussion.

(E) Airline customers might not believe that particular delays were caused by uncontrollable factors rather than airline error.

Argument Evaluation

Situation According to an airline representative, the percentage of flight delays caused by airline error decreased significantly this year. The representative concludes that airlines have addressed preventable errors reported by travelers.

Reasoning *Which of the answer choices most clearly suggests a logical flaw in the reasoning of the airline representative?* Flight delays can be caused in many ways: for example, by unpredictable bad weather, mechanical or computer failures, bad management, or some combination of these. Some but not all errors of these kinds—and the flight delays they might cause—are preventable. Note that the argument is focused on *the percentage* of all flight delays that are airline-error (AE) delays. This percentage can decrease by (1) a reduction in the number of AE delays or (2) an increase in the number of non-AE delays, i.e., those delays that the airline could not have prevented. Even if a significant increase occurred in the number of AE delays, such delays could have decreased as a percentage of all flight delays if there had been a large enough increase in non-AE flight delays.

A The hypothesis stated in this answer choice offers a slight, indirect basis for wondering whether the information on which the representative bases the reasoning is accurate. However, it provides no direct grounds for supposing that the reasoning itself is logically flawed. Even to the extent that this gives any reason to doubt the truth of the purported information, the relevance is very indirect. Even if airlines *may* have a motivation to underreport the percentage of flight delays caused by airline error, there is little reason to suppose that the representative's information may be a result of any airline's acting on such a motivation. And the representative argues on the basis of a decrease in the percentage, not on the basis of any particular percentage. If airlines systematically underreported the percentages, a decrease would still likely be significant.

B This is only remotely relevant because the representative's quantitative comparison is about a difference in percentage of actual delays due to certain factors, not about a difference in numbers of complaints about such delays. In principle, if the total number of complaints increased and the increase was at least partially attributable to delays caused by uncontrollable factors, this information could suggest that the number of delays caused by uncontrollable factors might have increased. This, in turn, could indirectly suggest the hypothesis stated in answer choice D. But at best the relevance of answer choice B to such a hypothesis is very oblique and conjectural.

C The issue being discussed primarily concerns flight delays. Airlines could make many kinds of errors that do not lead to flight delays and that generally do not elicit complaints from air travelers.

D **Correct.** As explained above, if there is a large enough increase in non-AE flight delays—delays entirely due to factors outside an airline's control—then the overall number of flight delays also increases, provided the number of AE flight delays remains constant or also increases. So even if the number of AE flight delays did not decrease, the percentage of all flight delays that were AE flight delays could decrease.

E Air travelers who experience flight delays and disbelieve the explanations given by airlines for those delays may be justified in doing so—but in many, or even most, cases also may be mistaken. We have no information as to how this would affect the number of complaints from travelers. Certainly, the general level of trust between airlines and their customers does not affect the facts regarding the rate of AE flight delays or the rate of non-AE flight delays.

The correct answer is D.

CR08831

708. Although the school would receive financial benefits if it had soft drink vending machines in the cafeteria, we should not allow them. Allowing soft drink machines there would not be in our students' interest. If our students start drinking more soft drinks, they will be less healthy.

The argument depends on which of the following?

(A)   If the soft drink vending machines were placed in the cafeteria, students would consume more soft drinks as a result.

(B)   The amount of soft drinks that most students at the school currently drink is not detrimental to their health.

(C)   Students are apt to be healthier if they do not drink soft drinks at all than if they just drink small amounts occasionally.

(D)   Students will not simply bring soft drinks from home if the soft drink vending machines are not placed in the cafeteria.

(E)   The school's primary concern should be to promote good health among its students.

Argument Construction

Situation   Allowing soft drink vending machines in a school cafeteria would financially benefit the school, but students who drink more soft drinks would become less healthy.

Reasoning   *What must be true in order for the claim that students drinking more soft drinks would cause them to become less healthy to justify the conclusion that soft drink vending machines should not be allowed in the cafeteria?* The argument is that because drinking more soft drinks would be unhealthy for the students, allowing the vending machines would not be in the students' interest, so the vending machines should not be allowed. This reasoning depends on the implicit factual assumption that allowing the vending machines would result in the students drinking more soft drinks. It also depends on the implicit value judgment that receiving financial benefits should be less important to the school than preventing a situation that would make the students less healthy.

A   **Correct.** If the cafeteria vending machines would not result in students consuming more soft drinks, then allowing the machines would not harm the students' health in the way the argument assumes.

B   Even if the amount of soft drinks the students currently drink were unhealthy, enabling the students to drink more could make them even less healthy.

C   Even if drinking small amounts of soft drinks occasionally would not harm the students, vending machines in the cafeteria could lead the students to drink excessive amounts.

D   Even if students who cannot buy soft drinks in the cafeteria sometimes bring them from home instead, adding vending machines in the cafeteria could increase the students' overall soft drink consumption.

E   A concern does not have to be the primary one in order to be valid and important. It could be held that promoting students' good health should not be the schools' primary concern but should still be a more important concern than the financial benefits from the vending machines.

The correct answer is A.

CRO1112

709. Many athletes inhale pure oxygen after exercise in an attempt to increase muscular reabsorption of oxygen. Measured continuously after exercise, however, the blood lactate levels of athletes who inhale pure oxygen are practically identical, on average, to those of athletes who breathe normal air. The lower the blood lactate level is, the higher the muscular reabsorption of oxygen is.

If the statements above are all true, they most strongly support which of the following conclusions?

(A)   Athletes' muscular reabsorption of oxygen is not increased when they inhale pure oxygen instead of normal air.

(B)   High blood lactate levels cannot be reduced.

(C)   Blood lactate levels are a poor measure of oxygen reabsorption by muscles.

(D)   The amount of oxygen reabsorbed by an athlete's muscles always remains constant.

(E)   The inhaling of pure oxygen has no legitimate role in athletics.

Argument Construction

Situation   Blood lactate levels after exercise are practically identical in athletes who breathe normal air and in those who inhale pure oxygen after exercise. The lower the blood lactate level, the higher the muscular reabsorption of oxygen.

Reasoning   *What conclusion do the stated facts most strongly support?* We are told that lower blood lactate levels correspond consistently to higher muscular reabsorption of oxygen. Since athletes who breathe pure oxygen after exercise have blood lactate levels practically identical to those in athletes who breathe normal air, probably muscular reabsorption of oxygen does not differ significantly between athletes who breathe pure oxygen and those who breathe pure air.

A   **Correct.** As explained above, the stated facts suggest that muscular reabsorption of oxygen does not differ significantly between athletes who breathe pure oxygen and those who breathe pure air. So breathing pure oxygen instead of normal air after exercise probably does not increase athletes' muscular reabsorption of oxygen.

B   None of the statements indicates that blood lactate levels cannot be reduced by means other than inhaling pure oxygen.

C   We are told that blood lactate levels are negatively correlated with muscular reabsorption of oxygen. This negative correlation might allow muscular reabsorption of oxygen to be precisely determined by measuring blood lactate levels.

D   Muscular reabsorption of oxygen might vary for reasons unrelated to whether an athlete has been inhaling pure oxygen.

E   Inhaling pure oxygen might have some legitimate role unrelated to muscular reabsorption of oxygen.

The correct answer is A.

CR79751.01

710. Historian: Fifteenth-century advances in mapmaking contributed to the rise of modern nation-states. In medieval Europe (from the fifth to the fifteenth century), sovereignty centered in cities and towns and radiated outward, with boundaries often ambiguously defined. The conceptual shift toward the modern state began in the late fifteenth century, when mapmakers learned to reflect geography accurately by basing maps on latitude-longitude grids. By the mid-seventeenth century, nearly all maps showed boundary lines.

Which of the following would, if true, most strengthen the historian's reasoning?

(A) Borders did not become codified in Europe until certain treaties were signed in the early nineteenth century.

(B) During the medieval period, various authorities in Europe claimed power over collections of cities and towns, not contiguous territories.

(C) Many members of the political elite collected maps as a hobby during the late sixteenth and early seventeenth centuries.

(D) Seventeenth-century treatises and other sources of political authority describe areas of sovereignty rather than illustrate them using maps.

(E) During the fifteenth century in Europe, mapmakers simplified the borders of sovereignty by drawing clear lines of demarcation between political powers.

Argument Evaluation

Situation   A historian claims that fifteenth-century advances in mapmaking contributed to the rise of modern nation states. In earlier centuries boundaries of sovereignty in Europe were poorly defined but in the fifteenth century maps were made based on grids showing latitude and longitude.

Reasoning   *What additional piece of information, if true and added to the argument, would most improve the support offered for the conclusion that improved mapping contributed to the rise of nation states?* The historian claims that there was a cause–effect relationship between progress in mapmaking and the rise of the nation state. This claim is supported by information that territories of sovereignty were vague and ill-defined before the fifteenth century, when latitude-longitude grids began to allow progressively greater accuracy in the delineation of territories on maps. The argument assumes that the rise of nation states would have required a high degree of clarity about each state's non-overlapping area of sovereignty.

A   This indicates the role of treaties in the evolution of nation states but provides no additional support for the historian's causal claim.

B   This information is consistent with the historian's belief that nothing resembling the modern state existed before the fifteenth century, but it provides no additional support for the historian's causal claim.

C   The relevance of this information to the argument is tenuous at best. There could be many non-political explanations for the interest of political elites in collecting maps. Many people other than political elites may also have collected maps during the period mentioned.

D   This information tends to minimize the role of maps in defining areas of sovereignty and to cast some doubt on the historian's causal claim.

E   **Correct.** This information makes explicit the role of mapmakers in providing clarity about the geographical boundaries of each political entity's sovereignty. It thus provides additional evidence for the historian's causal claim and strengthens the historian's reasoning.

The correct answer is E.

CR11751.01

711. Sascha: The attempt to ban parliament's right to pass directed-spending bills—bills that contain provisions specifically funding the favorite projects of some powerful politicians—is antidemocratic. Our nation's constitution requires that money be drawn from our treasury only when so stipulated by laws passed by parliament, the branch of government most directly representative of the citizens. This requirement is based on the belief that exercising the power to spend public resources involves the ultimate exercise of state authority and that therefore _____.

Which of the following most logically completes Sascha's argument?

(A) designating funding specifically for the favorite projects of some powerful politicians should be considered antidemocratic

(B) the right to exercise such a power should belong exclusively to the branch of government most directly representative of the citizens

(C) exercising the power to spend public resources is in most cases—but not all—protected by the constitution

(D) modifications to any spending bills should be considered expenditures authorized by law

(E) only officials who are motivated by concerns for reelection should retain that power

Argument Construction

Situation   According to Sascha, restricting parliament's ability to direct public money to the projects favored by powerful politicians would be undemocratic. Sascha argues that such a restriction on directed spending would be inconsistent with constitutional requirements.

Reasoning   *What piece of information would most logically complete Sascha's argument?* What piece of information would most strongly associate parliament's spending authority with the concept of democracy? A good guess would be: some information that connects parliament's public representation role with its spending authority.

A   Sascha believes that democratic constitutional principles require that parliament remain free to do what is described in this sentence.

B   **Correct.** This statement makes explicit the connection, implicitly relied on by Sascha's argument, between parliament's spending authority and its role in representing the public.

C   This statement may be true but fails to associate parliament's spending authority under the constitution with the notion of democracy.

D   Bills are merely works-in-progress, texts of proposed laws. Modifications of bills do not in themselves provide legal authority for any public spending item.

E   Sascha opposes restrictions on parliament's spending power, and this would seem to imply that Sascha believes every parliamentary representative should be free to vote on such measures regardless of their levels of concern for reelection.

The correct answer is B.

CR02143

712. Boreal owls range over a much larger area than do other owls of similar size. Scientists have hypothesized that **it is scarcity of prey that leads the owls to range so widely**. This hypothesis would be hard to confirm directly, since it is not possible to produce a sufficiently accurate count of the populations of small mammals inhabiting the forests where boreal owls live. Careful study of owl behavior has, however, shown that **boreal owls do range over larger areas when they live in regions where food of the sort eaten by small mammals is comparatively sparse**. This indicates that the scientists' hypothesis is not sheer speculation.

In the argument given, the two **boldfaced** portions play which of the following roles?

(A) The first presents an explanatory hypothesis; the second states the main conclusion of the argument.

(B) The first presents an explanatory hypothesis; the second presents evidence tending to support this hypothesis.

(C) The first presents an explanatory hypothesis; the second presents evidence to support an alternative explanation.

(D) The first describes a position that the argument opposes; the second presents evidence to undermine the support for the position being opposed.

(E) The first describes a position that the argument opposes; the second states the main conclusion of the argument.

Argument Construction

Situation   Boreal owls range over a much larger area than other owls of similar size. Scientists hypothesize that they do so because of prey scarcity. Counting the owls' prey—small mammals—in the boreal owls' habitat is inherently difficult. This makes the scientists' hypothesis hard to confirm directly. However, it has been found that boreal owls range widely when they inhabit regions that have relatively little food for the small mammals they prey on.

Reasoning   *What function is served by the statement that it is scarcity of prey that leads the owls to range so widely? What function is served by the statement that boreal owls range widely if food for their small-mammal prey is relatively sparse in the region they inhabit?* The first boldface statement expresses an explanatory hypothesis. The passage explicitly says that this is a hypothesis and indicates that scientists have proposed this hypothesis as a tentative explanation for the comparatively wide range of boreal owls. The second boldface statement provides some indirect evidence for the scientists' hypothesis. The final sentence of the passage says that the immediately preceding idea (expressed in the second boldface portion) indicates that the scientists' hypothesis (the first boldface portion) is not mere speculation. The evidence expressed in this second boldface portion is indirect in that it depends heavily on further assumptions and is not sufficient to prove the hypothesis.

A   The main conclusion of the argument is that the scientists' hypothesis is not sheer speculation, i.e., that the scientists have based their hypothesis on some evidence that they have discovered. The first statement presents the scientists' hypothesis. The second statement cites some evidence for the hypothesis and is not the main conclusion of the argument.

B   **Correct.** As explained above, the first statement presents an explanatory hypothesis, while the second cites some indirect evidence for the hypothesis.

C   The second statement cites some indirect evidence for the scientists' hypothesis, not for some other hypothesis.

D   The argument does not oppose the scientists' hypothesis, presented in the first statement; the second statement cites evidence for the hypothesis and does not cite evidence for any position the argument opposes.

E   The second statement does not present the argument's main conclusion. The main conclusion is that the scientists' hypothesis is not mere speculation.

The correct answer is B.

CR18731.01

713. Cognitive scientist: Using the pioneering work of comparative psychologist Gordon Gallup as a model, several studies have investigated animals' capacity for mirror self-recognition (MSR). Most animals exposed to a mirror respond only with social behavior, such as aggression. However, in the case of the great apes, repeated exposure to mirrors leads to self-directed behaviors, such as exploring the inside of the mouth, suggesting that these animals recognize the reflection as an image of of self. The implication of these studies is that the great apes have a capacity for self-awareness unique among nonhuman species.

The cognitive scientist makes which of the following assumptions in the argument above?

(A)   Gallup's work has established that the great apes have a capacity for MSR unique among nonhuman species.

(B)   If an animal does not have the capacity for MSR, it does not have the capacity for self-awareness.

(C)   If a researcher exposes an animal to a mirror and that animal exhibits social behavior, that animal is incapable of being self-aware.

(D)   When exposed to a mirror, all animals display either social behavior or self-directed behavior.

(E)   Animals that do not exhibit MSR may demonstrate a capacity for self-awareness in other ways.

Argument Construction

Situation   A cognitive scientist claims that several studies, modeled on Gordon Gallup's work, have investigated animals' capacity for mirror self-recognition (MSR), and found that, whereas most animals exposed to a mirror exhibit only social behavior in response, great apes can come to respond with self-directed behavior. The cognitive scientist infers from this that the great apes, unique among nonhumans, have a capacity for self-awareness.

Reasoning   *What must be true for the studies to support the cognitive scientist's conclusion?* The implicit reasoning is that an animal has self-awareness only if the animal has the capacity for MSR; if the latter is lacking, so is the capacity for self-awareness.

A   The studies the cognitive scientist's inference is based on were not necessarily conducted by Gallup himself. We are told only that they are modeled on his work.

B   **Correct.** If it were possible for an animal to have the capacity for self-awareness even if the animal lacks the capacity for MSR, then the studies would not imply that the great apes have a capacity for self-awareness that other nonhuman animal species lack.

C   The cognitive scientist's reasoning does not require that an animal with the capacity for self-awareness never exhibits social behavior when exposed to a mirror; it merely requires that it does not exhibit only such behavior.

D   The cognitive scientist's reasoning is compatible with an animal's displaying no behavior in response to exposure to a mirror.

E   The cognitive scientist's reasoning is compatible with the claim that an animal that does not exhibit MSR has no capacity at all for self-awareness.

The correct answer is B.

CR02888

714. Last year a record number of new manufacturing jobs were created. Will this year bring another record? Well, any new manufacturing job is created either within an existing company or by the start-up of a new company. **Within existing firms, new jobs have been created this year at well below last year's record pace**. At the same time, there is considerable evidence that the number of new companies starting up will be no higher this year than it was last year and **there is no reason to think that the new companies starting up this year will create more jobs per company than did last year's start-ups**. So clearly, the number of new jobs created this year will fall short of last year's record.

In the argument given, the two portions in **boldface** play which of the following roles?

(A) The first is a claim that the argument challenges; the second is an explicit assumption on which that challenge is based.

(B) The first is a claim that the argument challenges; the second is a judgment advanced in support of the main conclusion of the argument.

(C) The first provides evidence in support of the main conclusion of the argument; the second is an objection that has been raised against that main conclusion.

(D) The first provides evidence in support of the main conclusion of the argument; the second is a judgment advanced in support of that main conclusion.

(E) The first and the second are each claims that have been advanced in support of a position that the argument opposes.

Argument Construction

Situation Manufacturing jobs are created either within existing companies or in start-ups. Manufacturing jobs are being created at a much slower rate this year than last year. It seems likely that the number of new start-ups will not exceed last year's number and that the average number of manufacturing jobs per start-up will not exceed last year's number. So fewer manufacturing jobs are likely to be created this year than last year.

Reasoning *What function is served by the statement that within existing firms, new jobs have been created this year at well below last year's record pace? What function is served by the statement that there is no reason to think that the new companies starting up this year will create more jobs per company than did last year's start-ups?* The first statement is one of the statements used as support for the argument's main conclusion (the prediction about this year's job creation). The second statement gives another premise used as support for that prediction.

A The argument does not challenge the claim made by the first statement; it uses the first and the second statement as support for the argument's main conclusion, the prediction about this year's job creation.

B The argument does not challenge the claim made by the first statement, but uses the first and second statements as support for the argument's main conclusion.

C The first provides evidence in support of the main conclusion of the argument; the second is not an objection that has been raised against the main conclusion.

D Correct. The first provides evidence in support of the main conclusion of the argument; the second also provides support for the main conclusion.

E Neither the first nor the second is meant to support a position that the argument opposes; rather, they are both meant to support the argument's main conclusion.

The correct answer is D.

CR07809
715. A study of ticket sales at a summer theater festival found that people who bought tickets to individual plays had a no-show rate of less than 1 percent, while those who paid in advance for all ten plays being performed that summer had a no-show rate of nearly 30 percent. This may be at least in part because the greater the awareness customers retain about the cost of an item, the more likely they are to use it.

Which of the following would, if true, best serve as an alternative explanation of the results of the study?

(A) The price per ticket was slightly cheaper for those who bought all ten tickets in advance.

(B) Many people who attended the theater festival believed strongly that they should support it financially.

(C) Those who attended all ten plays became eligible for a partial refund.

(D) Usually, people who bought tickets to individual plays did so immediately prior to each performance that they attended.

(E) People who arrived just before the performance began could not be assured of obtaining seats in a preferred location.

Argument Construction

Situation   People who bought tickets to individual plays at a theater festival had a much lower no-show rate than did people who paid in advance for all ten plays.

Reasoning   *What factor other than greater awareness of the ticket costs could explain why people who bought tickets individually were more likely to attend the plays?* The passage suggests that people who bought tickets individually were more likely to attend the plays because they were more vividly aware of what they had paid for each ticket. But there are other possible explanations—perhaps the people who bought the tickets individually were more eager to attend each play for its own sake, or had other characteristics or incentives that made them more likely to attend the plays.

A   A slight price difference would not plausibly explain why the no-show rate was thirty times greater among those who bought all the tickets in advance than among those who bought them individually.

B   This could be true of many people who bought their tickets individually as well as many who bought them in advance.

C   This would provide an added incentive for those who bought tickets in advance to attend all the plays.

D   Correct. If people who bought individual tickets usually did so right before each performance, they would have much less time after buying the tickets to change their minds about whether to attend than would people who bought all the tickets in advance.

E   If anything, this might present an additional difficulty for those who bought individual tickets without advance planning, so it would not help to explain the lower no-show rate among buyers of individual tickets.

The correct answer is D.

CR12019

716. Although there is no record of poet Edmund Spenser's parentage, we do know that as a youth Spenser attended the Merchant Tailors' School in London for a period between 1560 and 1570. Records from this time indicate that the Merchant Tailors' Guild then had only three members named Spenser: Robert Spenser, listed as a gentleman; Nicholas Spenser, elected the Guild's Warden in 1568; and John Spenser, listed as a "journeyman cloth-maker." Of these, the last was likely the least affluent of the three—and most likely Edmund's father, since school accounting records list Edmund as a scholar who attended the school at a reduced fee.

Which of the following is an assumption on which the argument depends?

(A) Anybody in sixteenth century London who made clothing professionally would have had to be a member of the Merchant Tailors' Guild.

(B) The fact that Edmund Spenser attended the Merchant Tailors' School did not necessarily mean that he planned to become a tailor.

(C) No member of the Guild could become Guild warden in sixteenth century London unless he was a gentleman.

(D) Most of those whose fathers were members of the Merchant Tailors' Guild were students at the Merchant Tailors' School.

(E) The Merchant Tailors' School did not reduce its fees for the children of the more affluent Guild members.

Argument Construction

Situation   Records indicate that the poet Edmund Spenser attended the Merchant Tailors' School for a reduced fee as a youth. There is no record of his parentage, but at the time the Merchant Tailors' Guild had only three members named Spenser, of whom the least affluent was probably John Spenser.

Reasoning   *What must be true in order for the cited facts to support the conclusion that John Spenser was probably Edmund Spenser's father?* The implicit reasoning is that since Edmund Spenser attended the Merchant Tailors' School at a reduced fee, his father must have been poor. And since John Spenser was probably the poorest of the three men named Spenser in the Merchant Tailors' Guild, he was probably Edmund Spenser's father. This reasoning assumes that only the children of poor parents had reduced fees at the Merchant Tailors' School, that the children at the school generally had fathers in the Merchant Tailors' Guild, that children in that time and place generally shared their fathers' surnames, and that the two other Spensers in the Merchant Tailors' Guild were not poor enough for their children to qualify for reduced fees.

A   John Spenser, as a tailor and member of the guild, could have been Edmund Spenser's father even if some other professional tailors did not belong to the guild and did not have children at the school.

B   Although Edmund Spenser became a poet as an adult, he and all his classmates might have attended the school as children because they planned to become tailors.

C   The argument assumes that a Guild's Warden probably would have been wealthier than a journeyman cloth-maker, but that might have been probable even if the Guild's Warden were not a "gentleman."

D   Even if most children of fathers in the guild did not attend the school, all the children who did attend the school might have had fathers in the guild.

E   **Correct.** If the school reduced its fees for children of wealthier guild members, then the fact that Edmund Spenser's fees were reduced would not provide evidence that his father was the poorest of the three Spensers in the guild, as the argument requires.

The correct answer is E.

CR20831.01

717. Hea Sook: One should not readily believe urban legends. Most legends are propagated because the moral lesson underlying them supports a political agenda. People will repeat a tale if it fits their purpose. They may not deliberately spread untruths, but neither are they particularly motivated to investigate deeply to determine if the tale they are telling is true.

Kayla: But people would not repeat stories that they did not believe were true. Therefore, one can safely assume that if a story has been repeated by enough people then it is more likely to be true.

Kayla's reply is most vulnerable to the criticism that it

(A) does not specify how many people need to repeat a story before someone is justified believing it

(B) overstates the significance of political agendas in the retelling of stories

(C) fails to address the claim that people will not verify the truth of a story that fits their purpose

(D) implicitly supports the claim that the people repeating legends are not deliberately spreading untruths

(E) cannot distinguish people's motivations for repeating urban legends from their motivations for repeating other types of story

Argument Evaluation

Situation Hea Sook and Kayla have a difference of opinion on how likely urban legends are to be true.

Reasoning *What criticism is Kayla's reply most vulnerable to?* Hea Sook argues that because urban legends generally are propagated for political purposes, people are not particularly motivated to carefully investigate whether the story they are telling is true. These people may not be deliberately telling an untruth, but they have not taken care to establish whether the story is true. Kayla responds that people would not repeat a story that they did not believe to be true, but Hea Sook not only does not attempt to deny that, but she suggests that it may be true. Kayla ignores the fact that sometimes people believe that something is true without carefully determining whether it actually is true, and that they are less likely to verify whether it is true when the story fits their purposes.

A   Kayla does not specify how many people need to repeat a story before one is justified in believing it, but she does not need to. Her claim—that there is some number sufficient for such belief to be justified—could be true even if she does not specify what that number is.

B   It is Hea Sook, not Kayla, who asserts that political agendas are a significant factor in whether one retells a story.

C   Correct. Kayla does not address whether people are unlikely to verify whether a story is true if the story fits their purpose.

D   Kayla does not merely implicitly claim that people who repeat legends are not deliberately spreading untruths; she explicitly states this, but in this she and Hea Sook agree.

E   We have no reason to think that Kayla cannot distinguish people's motivations for repeating urban legends from their motivations for repeating other types of stories. She may well be able to do this.

The correct answer is C.

CR03749
718. Rainwater contains hydrogen of a heavy form called deuterium. The deuterium content of wood reflects the deuterium content of rainwater available to trees during their growth. Wood from trees that grew between 16,000 and 24,000 years ago in North America contains significantly more deuterium than wood from trees growing today. But water trapped in several North American caves that formed during that same early period contains significantly less deuterium than rainwater in North America contains today.

Which of the following, if true, most helps to reconcile the two findings?

(A)   There is little deuterium in the North American caves other than the deuterium in the water trapped there.

(B)   Exposure to water after a tree has died does not change the deuterium content of the wood.

(C)   Industrialization in North America over the past 100 years has altered the deuterium content of rain.

(D)   Trees draw on shallow groundwater from rain that falls during their growth, whereas water trapped in caves may have fallen as rainwater thousands of years before the caves formed.

(E)   Wood with a high deuterium content is no more likely to remain preserved for long periods than is wood with a low deuterium content.

Argument Construction

Situation   In North America, wood from trees that grew 16,000 to 24,000 years ago contains more deuterium than wood from trees growing today. But water in caves that formed during that same period contains less deuterium than rainwater contains today.

Reasoning   *What could explain the puzzling discrepancy between the observed deuterium levels in wood and in caves?* Since the deuterium content of wood from trees reflects the deuterium content of rainwater available to the trees while they grew, the deuterium levels observed in wood suggests that North American rainwater contained more deuterium 16,000 to 24,000 years ago than it contains today. But this conclusion seems at odds with the low deuterium levels in water in caves that formed 16,000 to 24,000 years ago. Several factors might explain the discrepancy: the water in those caves might not be rainwater from the period when the caves formed; or some natural process might have altered the deuterium levels in the cave water or the wood; or the wood or caves in which deuterium levels were measured might be statistically abnormal somehow.

A   If the caves had absorbed deuterium out of the rainwater trapped in them, there would probably be deuterium in the cave walls. So the observation that there is little deuterium in the caves apart from that in the water eliminates one possible explanation for the oddly low deuterium levels in the cave water.

B   This suggests that the deuterium levels in the wood accurately reflect higher deuterium levels in rainwater that fell 16,000 to 24,000 years ago, but it does not explain why the deuterium levels are so low in water in the caves that formed then.

C   This could explain why deuterium levels in rainwater have changed, but it does not help explain the discrepancy between the high deuterium levels in the wood and the low deuterium levels in the cave water.

D   Correct. If the water in the caves fell as rainwater thousands of years before the caves formed, it may date from a period when rainwater contained much less deuterium than during the period 16,000 to 24,000 years ago, and much less than today.

E   If wood with high deuterium content were more likely to be preserved, then wood from 16,000 to 24,000 years ago might have a high deuterium content even if the rainwater then had a low deuterium content. So the observation that wood with more deuterium is not more likely to be preserved eliminates one possible explanation for the discrepancy.

The correct answer is D.

CR04925

719. Enforcement of local speed limits through police monitoring has proven unsuccessful in the town of Ardane. In many nearby towns, speed humps (raised areas of pavement placed across residential streets, about 300 feet apart) have reduced traffic speeds on residential streets by 20 to 25 percent. In order to reduce traffic speed and thereby enhance safety in residential neighborhoods, Ardane's transportation commission plans to install multiple speed humps in those neighborhoods.

Which of the following, if true, identifies a potentially serious drawback to the plan for installing speed humps in Ardane?

(A) On residential streets without speed humps, many vehicles travel at speeds more than 25 percent above the posted speed limit.

(B) Because of their high weight, emergency vehicles such as fire trucks and ambulances must slow almost to a stop at speed humps.

(C) The residential speed limit in Ardane is higher than that of the nearby towns where speed humps were installed.

(D) Motorists who are not familiar with the streets in Ardane's residential districts would be likely to encounter the speed humps unawares unless warned by signs and painted indicators.

(E) Bicyclists generally prefer that speed humps be constructed so as to leave a space on the side of the road where bicycles can travel without going over the humps.

Evaluation of a Plan

Situation   Ardane's difficulty in getting compliance with speed limits has led it to propose the installation of speed humps to slow traffic. In nearby towns, speed humps have reduced speeds in residential areas by up to 25 percent.

Reasoning   *Which one of the statements presented identifies a major disadvantage of the proposed installation of speed humps? Is it possible that they might slow traffic too much? Clearly, there is a general need for traffic to flow smoothly. Would speed humps affect all types of traffic equally? Perhaps not. For example, certain emergency vehicles must sometimes need to travel quickly through residential neighborhoods. A problem with speed humps is that some heavier vehicles must go very slowly over speed humps.*

A   This indicates a drawback of not installing speed humps.

B   **Correct.** This information indicates a significant drawback—possibly leading to loss of life and property—of the plan to install the speed humps.

C   This suggests that installing speed humps might lower speeds significantly below the current speed limits. If speeds became very low, the result could be traffic gridlock that would have unforeseen consequences. However, we have insufficient information to evaluate such possibilities.

D   This is unlikely to be a drawback, since such warning signs are typically put in place whenever speed humps are installed.

E   This information provides no evidence of a drawback in Ardane's plan for speed humps, since the design of Ardane's planned speed humps is not indicated.

The correct answer is B.

CR00748

720. Which of the following most logically completes the argument below?

NowNews, although still the most popular magazine covering cultural events in Kalopolis, has recently suffered a significant drop in advertising revenue because of falling circulation. Many readers have begun buying a competing magazine that, at 50 cents per copy, costs less than *NowNews* at $1.50 per copy. In order to boost circulation and thus increase advertising revenue, *NowNews's* publisher has proposed making it available at no charge, but this proposal has a serious drawback, since _____.

(A) Those Kalopolis residents with the greatest interest in cultural events are regular readers of both magazines.

(B) One reason *NowNews's* circulation fell was that its competitor's reporting on cultural events was superior.

(C) The newsstands and stores that currently sell *NowNews* will no longer carry it if it is being given away for free.

(D) At present, 10 percent of the total number of copies of each issue of *NowNews* are distributed free to students on college campuses in the Kalopolis area.

(E) *NowNews's* competitor would begin to lose large amounts of money if it were forced to lower its cover price.

Argument Construction

Situation   *NowNews* is suffering declines in circulation and advertising revenue due to competition from a lower-priced magazine. The publisher proposes offering *NowNews* for free to reverse these declines.

Reasoning   *What would suggest that the publisher's proposal will fail to increase circulation and advertising revenue?* The proposal's intended effect is simply to increase advertising revenue by increasing circulation. Any evidence that offering the magazine for free will not result in more copies being circulated or will not attract advertisers would therefore be evidence of a drawback in the proposal. So a statement offering such evidence would logically complete the argument.

A   The fact that certain highly motivated Kalopolis residents still read *NowNews* even at a cost of $1.50 per issue leaves open the possibility that providing the magazine free might still boost readership.

B   This suggests that improving its cultural reporting might help *NowNews* increase its circulation, not that the publisher's proposal will fail to do so.

C   **Correct.** If the proposal leads newsstands and stores to stop carrying *NowNews*, circulation and advertising revenue would probably decline as a result.

D   Even if 10 percent of the copies of *NowNews* are already distributed for free, distributing the remaining 90 percent for free could still increase circulation and advertising revenue as the publisher intends.

E   Forcing a competing magazine to lower its cover price and lose lots of money would be an advantage rather than a drawback of the proposal, as far as the publisher of *NowNews* was concerned.

The correct answer is C.

CR07304

721. Archaeologist: Researchers excavating a burial site in Cyprus found a feline skeleton lying near a human skeleton. Both skeletons were in the same sediment at the same depth and equally well-preserved, suggesting that the feline and human were buried together about 9,500 years ago. This shows that felines were domesticated around the time farming began, when they would have been useful in protecting stores of grain from mice.

Which of the following, if true, would most seriously weaken the archaeologist's argument?

(A) Archaeologists have not found any remains of stores of grain in the immediate vicinity of the burial site.

(B) The burial site in Cyprus is substantially older than any other known burial site in which a feline skeleton and a human skeleton appear to have been buried together.

(C) Paintings found near the burial site seem to show people keeping felines as domestic companions, but do not show felines hunting mice.

(D) In Cyprus, there are many burial sites dating from around 9,500 years ago in which the remains of wild animals appear to have been buried alongside human remains.

(E) Before felines were domesticated, early farmers had no effective way to protect stores of grain from mice.

Argument Evaluation

Situation   A human skeleton and a feline skeleton were apparently buried together in Cyprus about 9,500 years ago.

Reasoning   *What would most strongly suggest that the skeletons do not show that felines were domesticated around the time farming began?* The argument implicitly assumes that farming in Cyprus began around 9,500 years ago, so evidence against that assumption would weaken the argument. The argument could also be weakened by evidence that felines were domesticated much earlier, that the feline skeleton was not from a domesticated cat, or that the two skeletons were not actually buried together around 9,500 years ago.

A   Even if archaeologists searched for evidence of a grain store, the fact that no such evidence was found near the burial site is at best only weak evidence that no grain store existed there or slightly farther away.

B   The lack of corroborating evidence from other burial sites would weaken the argument slightly but would still be compatible with the hypothesis that this site revealed one of the very first burials of a domesticated cat.

C   This would cast doubt on the hypothesis that cats were domesticated mainly to protect stores of grain, but not on the argument's conclusion that cats were domesticated around the time farming began.

D   Correct. If many wild animals were buried alongside humans in Cyprus around 9,500 years ago, then the feline skeleton is just as likely to be that of a wild animal than that of a domesticated cat.

E   Since this would provide an additional reason why early farmers might have domesticated the local cats, it would strengthen rather than weaken the argument.

The correct answer is D.

CR90061.01

722. Farmer: Several people in the past few years have claimed to have seen a mountain lion in the suburban outskirts—the latest just last month—and, while mountain lions were thought to have been driven from this entire region about twenty years ago, there is no reason for the people who reported seeing a mountain lion to have deliberately concocted a false report. Therefore, local wildlife managers should begin to urgently address the mountain lion's presence.

Which of the following would, if true, most seriously weaken the farmer's argument?

(A) Farmers in the suburban outskirts mostly raise cattle and hogs, which when fully grown are generally not attacked by mountain lions.

(B) Mountain lions are dissimilar in size and color to other wild animals found near the suburban outskirts.

(C) No person who claimed to have seen a mountain lion had anyone else with them at the purported sighting.

(D) There have been no regional reports in the past year of mountain lions migrating to the area.

(E) Recent surveys show that more than half of the people in the region report that they have never seen a mountain lion before.

Argument Evaluation

Situation   A farmer argues that, because several people in recent years, including someone just last month, have claimed to have seen a mountain lion in the suburban outskirts, local wildlife managers need to address the mountain lion's presence. The farmer claims that people would not intentionally create a false story about seeing a mountain lion.

Reasoning   *What would most seriously call into question the farmer's argument that because there have been reports of mountain lion sightings, wildlife managers should address the issue?* Even if it is true that people would not intentionally create a false report of having seen a mountain lion, it is possible that people have mistakenly believed they have seen a mountain lion when in fact what they saw was something else. If some fact called into question the accuracy of the reports of mountain lion sightings, then the farmer's conclusion would have weaker support.

A   Even if most fully grown animals raised by farmers would not be attacked by mountain lions, there could still be good reason to be concerned about the presence of mountain lions in the suburban outskirts. The mountain lion might attack animals before they are fully grown.

B   A dissimilarity in size and color between mountain lions and other wild animals in the area where the mountain lions were purportedly sighted would make it less likely that people mistakenly believed that an animal they spotted was a mountain lion. So, this would strengthen the farmer's argument, not weaken it.

C   **Correct.** If there actually were at least one mountain lion in the area, and several people over a period of a few years accurately claim to have seen one, then it seems likely that on at least some occasions a person would have been in the presence of someone else at the time, given the frequency with which people are in the company of others. So, if there have been no instances of a person reporting seeing a mountain lion when in the company of another, perhaps that is because when someone has mistakenly believed that an animal is a mountain lion, the other person helps correct the mistaken belief. With no one else present, an illusory sighting would be less likely to be corrected.

D   There have been purported sightings of a mountain lion in the area for several years, so presumably, if the sightings are accurate, there has been at least one mountain lion for several years, so the sightings could be accurate even if no mountain lion has migrated to the area in the past year.

E   It might be likely that most people living in the area would not have seen a mountain lion even if one lived in the area. For instance, the mountain lion might intentionally try to avoid people.

The correct answer is C.

CR09117

723. The heavy traffic in Masana is a growing drain on the city's economy—the clogging of the streets of the central business district alone cost the economy more than $1.2 billion over the past year. In order to address this problem, officials plan to introduce congestion pricing, by which drivers would pay to enter the city's most heavily trafficked areas during the busiest times of the day.

Which of the following, if true, would most strongly indicate that the plan will be a success?

(A) Approximately one-fifth of the vehicles in the central business district are in transit from one side of the city to the other.

(B) Planners expect that, without congestion pricing, traffic in Masana is likely to grow by 6 percent in the next five years.

(C) In other urban areas, congestion pricing has strongly encouraged carpooling (sharing of rides by private commuters).

(D) Several studies have shown that a reduction in traffic of 15 percent in Masana could result in 5,500 or more new jobs.

(E) Over 30 percent of the vehicles in the city's center are occupied by more than one person.

Evaluation of a Plan

Situation   Traffic congestion in Masana has been harming the city's economy. To address the problem, officials plan to make drivers pay to enter the city's most heavily trafficked areas during the busiest times of day.

Reasoning   *What would most strongly suggest that the plan will reduce the harm to Masana's economy from traffic congestion?* In order to succeed, the plan will have to be implemented and effectively enforced. Furthermore, the prices drivers pay will have to be high enough to significantly change their behavior in ways that reduce the amount of traffic congestion in the city. Finally, the economic benefits from the reduced traffic congestion will have to substantially outweigh any economically damaging side effects of the congestion pricing. Any evidence that any of these conditions will hold would provide at least some support for the prediction that the plan will succeed.

A   This provides no evidence that the congestion pricing would affect the behavior of either the one-fifth of drivers whose vehicles traverse the city or of the other four-fifths of drivers, nor does it give any evidence that the plan would produce overriding economic benefits.

B   This indicates that the traffic problem will grow worse if the plan is not implemented, but it does not provide any evidence that the plan will help address the problem.

C   **Correct.** This indicates that similar plans have successfully changed drivers' behavior in other cities in a way likely to reduce the number of cars on the road in heavily trafficked areas at busy times of day without producing harmful economic side effects. Thus, it provides evidence that the strategy could also be successful in Masana.

D   Although this suggests that reducing traffic congestion would be economically beneficial, it doesn't provide any evidence that the plan will succeed in reducing traffic congestion.

E   This suggests that many drivers in the city center are already carpooling, which, if anything, indicates that the plan will be less able to further affect those drivers' behavior and thus could be less effective than it might otherwise be.

The correct answer is C.

CR09151

724. Economist: The most economically efficient way to reduce emissions of air pollutants is to tax them in proportion to the damage they are likely to cause. But in Country Y, many serious pollutants are untaxed and unregulated, and policy makers strongly oppose new taxes. Therefore, the best way to achieve a reduction in air pollutant emissions in Country Y would be to institute fixed upper limits on them.

Which of the following is an assumption of the economist's argument?

(A) Policy makers in Country Y oppose all new taxes equally strongly, regardless of any benefits they may provide.

(B) Country Y's air pollutant emissions would not fall significantly if they were taxed in proportion to the damage they are likely to cause.

(C) Policy makers in Country Y strongly favor reductions in air pollutant emissions.

(D) Country Y's policy makers believe that air pollutant emissions should be reduced with maximum economic efficiency.

(E) Policy makers in Country Y do not oppose setting fixed upper limits on air pollutant emissions as strongly as they oppose new taxes.

Argument Construction

Situation Although taxing air pollution emissions in proportion to the damage they cause is the most economically efficient way to reduce those emissions, many serious pollutants in Nation Y are untaxed and unregulated, and the nation's policy makers strongly oppose new taxes. Therefore, fixed upper limits on such emissions would more effectively reach this goal.

Reasoning *What must be true in order for the factors the economist cites to support the claim that fixing upper limits on air pollutant emissions in Nation Y would be the best way to reduce those emissions?* Political opposition to taxation in Nation Y is the only factor the economist cites to support the argument's conclusion that it would be best to institute fixed upper limits on air pollutants. In order for the premise to support the conclusion, there must be less political opposition in Nation Y to instituting such limits than there would be to the proportional taxation approach the economist prefers.

A Even if the policy makers oppose some new taxes less than others, they could still oppose the proportional taxation approach strongly enough for it to be utterly infeasible.

B Even if the proportional taxation scheme would significantly reduce emissions, it still might not be the best approach for Nation Y if it would generate too much political opposition to be viable there.

C Even if policy makers in Nation Y do not strongly favor reducing emissions, fixing upper limits on emissions might still be a better and more politically feasible way to reduce emissions than any alternative is.

D Since fixing upper emissions limits would be no more economically efficient than the proportional taxation scheme, the policy makers' support for economic efficiency would not make the former approach any more politically feasible than the latter.

E **Correct.** If the policy makers opposed fixing upper emissions limits as strongly as they oppose new taxes, then their opposition to new taxes would no longer support the conclusion that fixing the emissions limits is a better way to reduce emissions.

The correct answer is E.

CR04986

725. Humans get Lyme disease from infected ticks. Ticks get infected by feeding on animals with Lyme disease, but the ease of transmission from host animal to tick varies. With most species of host animal, transmission of Lyme disease to ticks is extremely rare, but white-footed mice are an exception, readily passing Lyme disease to ticks. And white-footed mouse populations greatly expand, becoming the main food source for ticks, in areas where biodiversity is in decline.

The information in the passage most strongly supports which of the following?

(A) In areas where many humans are infected with Lyme disease, the proportion of ticks infected with Lyme disease is especially high.

(B) Very few animals that live in areas where there are no white-footed mice are infected with Lyme disease.

(C) Humans are less at risk of contracting Lyme disease in areas where biodiversity is high.

(D) Ticks feed on white-footed mice only when other host species are not available to them.

(E) The greater the biodiversity of an area, the more likely any given host animal in that area is to pass Lyme disease to ticks.

Argument Construction

Situation   White-footed mice readily pass Lyme disease to ticks, which pass it to humans. White-footed mouse populations expand where biodiversity is declining.

Reasoning   *What conclusion do the stated facts support?* Since declining biodiversity causes white-footed mouse populations to increase, and white-footed mice are especially likely to pass Lyme disease to ticks, and ticks pass it to humans, declining biodiversity could reasonably be expected to increase the incidence of Lyme disease in both ticks and humans.

A   In areas where many humans are infected with Lyme disease, the total number of ticks may be unusually high, so even if the number of infected ticks is unusually high, the proportion of infected ticks may not be unusually high

B   Most animals with Lyme disease may get it from sources other than ticks that have fed on infected mice.

C   **Correct.** If biodiversity is high, then any biodiversity decline that has already begun has likely not yet reached a point where white-footed mouse populations have greatly expanded, so the risk of people contracting Lyme disease is still relatively less than in areas where biodiversity is low and where significant decline in biodiversity has likely already occurred.

D   Even if ticks feed on white-footed mice when few other species are available for them to feed on, they may also sometimes feed on white-footed mice when there are many other species for them to feed on.

E   The passage suggests that the overall incidence of Lyme disease is probably lower in more biodiverse areas, so any given host animal in those areas would probably be less likely to pass Lyme disease to a tick.

The correct answer is C.

CR04935
726. Many industrialized nations are trying to reduce atmospheric concentrations of carbon dioxide, a gas released by the burning of fossil fuels. One proposal is to replace conventional cement, which is made with calcium carbonate, by a new "eco-cement." This new cement, made with magnesium carbonate, absorbs large amounts of carbon dioxide when exposed to the atmosphere. Therefore, using eco-cement for new concrete building projects will significantly help reduce atmospheric concentrations of carbon dioxide.

Which of the following, if true, most strengthens the argument?

(A) The cost of magnesium carbonate, currently greater than the cost of calcium carbonate, probably will fall as more magnesium carbonate is used in cement manufacture.

(B) Eco-cement is strengthened when absorbed carbon dioxide reacts with the cement.

(C) Before the development of eco-cement, magnesium-based cement was considered too susceptible to water erosion to be of practical use.

(D) The manufacture of eco-cement uses considerably less fossil fuel per unit of cement than the manufacture of conventional cement does.

(E) Most building-industry groups are unaware of the development or availability of eco-cement.

Argument Evaluation

Situation   Many nations are trying to reduce atmospheric concentrations of carbon dioxide. One proposed method is to use a new type of "eco-cement" that absorbs carbon dioxide from air.

Reasoning   *What evidence, combined with the cited facts, would most support the prediction that using eco-cement will significantly help reduce atmospheric concentrations of carbon dioxide?* The prediction assumes that the use of eco-cement would be an effective way to reduce carbon dioxide levels. Any evidence supporting this assumption will support the prediction.

A   Since eco-cement uses magnesium carbonate, the prediction that magnesium carbonate prices will fall suggests that a potential financial barrier to widespread eco-cement use will diminish. However, those prices may not fall enough to make eco-cement cost-competitive with regular cement.

B   Even if absorbed carbon dioxide strengthens eco-cement, the strengthened eco-cement might still be much weaker than regular cement and thus might never become widely used, in which case it will not significantly help reduce atmospheric concentrations of carbon dioxide.

C   Even if eco-cement is less susceptible to water erosion than earlier forms of magnesium-based cement were, it might still be much more susceptible to water erosion than regular cement is, and thus might never become widely used.

D   **Correct.** This suggests that manufacturing eco-cement produces much less carbon dioxide than manufacturing regular cement does, so it supports the claim that widespread use of eco-cement would be an effective way to reduce carbon dioxide levels.

E   If anything, this lack of awareness makes it less likely that eco-cement will become widely used, which in turn makes it less likely that eco-cement will significantly help reduce atmospheric concentrations of carbon dioxide.

The correct answer is D.

CR81021.02
727. Professor: A marine biologist argues that transmission of sea lice from farm salmon to wild salmon is unlikely in the Broughton Archipelago, British Columbia, citing numerous studies suggesting that salinities less than 30 parts per thousand are unfavorable to sea-lice survival. The biologist concludes that the archipelago's 25–30 parts per thousand salinity range between March and June, the critical period for wild salmon migration, tends to suppress sea-lice proliferation. But a review of the literature shows that salinities of 25–30 parts per thousand in combination with British Columbia's cool spring temperatures favor the flourishing of sea lice.

In this passage, the professor attempts to undermine the biologist's argument by

(A) pointing out that a condition claimed to be necessary for sea-lice survival is not sufficient for it
(B) citing studies that suggest that salinity levels were not measured reliably
(C) claiming that there is evidence showing that one of its premises is false
(D) questioning the reliability of the biologist's scientific sources
(E) showing that its conclusion is inconsistent with its premises

Argument Evaluation

Situation   A professor gives us information about one biologist's opinion, based on numerous studies, about the low probability of sea-lice transmission from farm salmon to wild salmon in the Broughton Archipelago. The biologist thinks salinities less than 30 parts per thousand (ppt) would make such transmission unlikely; in the archipelago, the salinity is 25–30 ppt between March and June, the period when wild salmon migration occurs. However, the professor challenges the biologist's view, maintaining, based on a literature review, that cool spring temperatures in the archipelago, combined with the lower salinity, do favor flourishing of sea lice.

Reasoning   *In what way does the professor attempt to undermine the biologist's argument?* The professor points out that a premise used by the biologist—that the low spring salinities in the archipelago when the wild salmon migrate suppress sea-lice proliferation—is not correct. The professor claims the academic literature reveals that two conditions—the 25–30 ppt salinities combined with the cool spring temperatures—would be jointly sufficient for the flourishing of sea lice.

A   This does not accurately describe the professor's technique. In effect, the professor points out that salinities of 30 ppt or more are NOT necessary for sea-lice survival; lower salinities combined with lower temperatures are sufficient to enable sea-lice survival.
B   The professor cites no studies that suggest unreliable measurement of salinity levels.
C   Correct. As explained in the Reasoning section above, the professor appeals to evidence from the literature to show that one of the biologist's premises is false.
D   The professor primarily questions the conclusion that the biologist draws from the sources; the professor does not question the reliability of the sources.
E   The professor undermines the biologist's argument by claiming that one of its premises is false and thus that the conclusion might not follow. The professor does not claim that if the premises were true the conclusion would have to be false.

The correct answer is C.

CR00895

728. Advertisement: When your car's engine is running at its normal operating temperature, any major brand of motor oil will protect it about as well as Tuff does. When the engine is cold, it is a different story: Tuff motor oil flows better at lower temperatures than its major competitors do. So, if you want your car's engine to have maximum protection, you should use Tuff.

Which of the following, if true, most strengthens the argument in the advertisement?

(A) Tuff motor oil provides above-average protection for engines that happen to overheat.

(B) Tuff motor oil is periodically supplied free of charge to automobile manufacturers to use in factory-new cars.

(C) Tuff motor oil's share of the engine oil market peaked three years ago.

(D) Tuff motor oil, like any motor oil, is thicker and flows less freely at cold temperatures than at hot temperatures.

(E) Tuff motor oil is manufactured at only one refinery and shipped from there to all markets.

Argument Evaluation

Situation   An advertisement argues that since Tuff motor oil flows better than its major competitors at low temperatures and works about as well as they do at normal temperatures, it provides *maximum protection* for car engines.

Reasoning   *What additional evidence would suggest that Tuff motor oil provides the best available protection for car engines?* The argument requires the assumptions that no type of motor oil other than the "major brands" provides superior protection, that flowing better at lower temperatures ensures superior protection at those temperatures, and that Tuff protects car engines at least as well as its competitors do at above-normal temperatures. Any evidence supporting any of these assumptions would strengthen the argument.

A   **Correct.** If Tuff provides above-average protection when engines overheat, in addition to the solid protection it provides at normal and low temperatures, it may well provide the best available protection overall.

B   The company that makes Tuff might give automobile manufacturers free motor oil as a promotional gimmick even if Tuff is an inferior product.

C   Tuff's sales might have declined over the past three years because consumers have realized that Tuff is an inferior product.

D   The similar responses of Tuff and other motor oils to temperature changes do not suggest that Tuff provides better protection overall than those other motor oils do.

E   Even if Tuff is manufactured at only one refinery, it may still be an inferior product.

The correct answer is A.

CR55541.01

729. Linguist: In English, the past is described as "behind" and the future "ahead," whereas in Aymara the past is "ahead" and the future "behind." Research indicates that English speakers sway backward when discussing the past and forward when discussing the future. Conversely, Aymara speakers gesture forward with their hands when discussing the past and backward when discussing the future. These bodily movements, therefore, suggest that the language one speaks affects how one mentally visualizes time.

The linguist's reasoning depends on assuming which of the following?

(A) At least some Aymara speakers sway forward when discussing the past and backward when discussing the future.

(B) Most people mentally visualize time as running either forward or backward.

(C) Not all English and Aymara speakers tend to sway or gesture forward or backward when discussing the present.

(D) How people move when discussing the future correlates to some extent with how they mentally visualize time.

(E) The researchers also examined the movements of at least some speakers of languages other than English and Aymara discussing the past and the future.

Argument Construction

Situation   A linguist argues that the language one speaks affects how one mentally visualizes time. The linguist's argument is based on the fact that English speakers, who refer to the past as "behind" and the future as "ahead," display backward and forward bodily movements when speaking of the past and the future, while speakers of Aymara, who refer to the past as "ahead" and the future as "behind" display correspondingly different body movements.

Reasoning   *What must be true if we are to accept the linguist's conclusion from the given information that the language one speaks affects how one mentally visualizes time?* The linguist's evidence will support the conclusion only if there is some correlation between people's bodily movements and how they mentally visualize time. So, the linguist's reasoning requires an assumption to that effect.

A   The linguist's reasoning is based on the differences in bodily movements discussed in the argument—that is, that Aymara speakers gesture in certain ways and that English speakers sway in certain ways; thus, the linguist's reasoning does not require that Aymara speakers sway in any way whatsoever when they discuss the past or future.

B   The linguist's reasoning is based only on speakers of English and Aymara, so no claim related to speakers of other languages—who make up a majority of people—is required.

C   The linguist's argument would actually be stronger if all English and Aymara speakers sway or gesture in the ways discussed, so the argument certainly does not depend on assuming that not all such speakers sway or gesture in these ways.

D   Correct. The fact that English and Aymara speakers sway or gesture in the ways described would be irrelevant to the linguist's conclusion if how people move when discussing the future does not correlate at least to some extent with how they visualize time.

E   It might be helpful to the linguist's argument to examine the movements of speakers of other languages when they discuss the past and the future, but the linguist's argument does not require this.

The correct answer is D.

CR13108

730. *The Testament of William Thorpe* was published around 1530 as an appendix to Thorpe's longer *Examination*. Many scholars, however, doubt the attribution of the *Testament* to Thorpe because, whereas the *Examination* is dated 1406, the *Testament* is dated 1460. One scholar has recently argued that the 1460 date be amended to 1409, based on the observation that when these numbers are expressed as Roman numerals, MCCCCLX and MCCCCIX, it becomes easy to see how the dates might have become confused through scribal error.

Which of the following, if true, would most support the scholar's hypothesis concerning the date of the *Testament*?

(A) The sole evidence that historians have had that William Thorpe died no earlier than 1460 was the presumed date of publication of the *Testament*.

(B) In the preface to the 1530 publication, the editor attributes both works to William Thorpe.

(C) Few writers in fifteenth-century England marked dates in their works using only Roman numerals.

(D) The *Testament* alludes to a date, "Friday, September 20," as apparently contemporaneous with the writing of the *Testament*, and September 20 fell on a Friday in 1409 but not in 1460.

(E) The *Testament* contains few references to historical events that occurred later than 1406.

Argument Construction

Situation   *The Testament of William Thorpe*, dated 1460, was published around 1530 as an appendix to Thorpe's *Examination*, dated 1406. But when expressed in Roman numerals, 1460 could easily be confused with 1409.

Reasoning   *Given the facts cited, what would provide additional evidence that Thorpe's Testament dates from 1409 rather than 1460?* The scholar's hypothesis that the work dates from 1409 is based on the observation that in Roman numerals, 1409 might easily have been improperly transcribed as 1460. What evidence would support this hypothesis? Any independent evidence that 1409 is a more likely date for the *Testament* than 1460 would certainly help. For instance, if some event or date that occurred in 1409 but not in 1460 is referred to in the *Testament* as being recent or contemporaneous, this would lend significant support to the hypothesis. For instance, if the *Testament* indicated that some day of the month had just fallen on a given day of the week, and that date fell on that day in 1409 but not in 1460, this would support the hypothesis significantly.

A   Suppose there is no reason to think that Thorpe was still alive in 1460 other than the presumption that the *Testament* was published in that year. That gives us no more reason to accept the scholar's hypothesis about a scribal error in reporting the date than to accept the other scholars' hypothesis that the *Testament* is improperly ascribed to Thorpe. Furthermore, it provides very little reason to support either of these hypotheses, because the mere lack of evidence, other than the purported 1460 date of creation, that Thorpe died no earlier than 1460 does not provide us with any evidence that he **did** die earlier than 1460.

B   The editor of the 1530 publication could easily have been mistaken about the authorship of one or both works. And even if the editor were correct, Thorpe might have lived long enough to write one work in 1406 and the other in 1460.

C   This would cast doubt on the scholar's argument by providing evidence that the original manuscripts were not dated only in Roman numerals.

D   Correct. As explained in the Reasoning section above, this provides strong evidence directly supporting the hypothesis that the *Testament* dates from 1409 specifically.

E   Even if the *Testament* contained only one reference to a historical event that occurred later than 1406 (for example, one event in 1459), that reference alone could provide strong evidence that the work dates from 1460 rather than 1409.

The correct answer is D.

CR00777

731. A prominent investor who holds a large stake in the Burton Tool Company has recently claimed that the company is mismanaged, citing as evidence the company's failure to slow down production in response to a recent rise in its inventory of finished products. It is doubtful whether an investor's sniping at management can ever be anything other than counterproductive, but in this case, it is clearly not justified. It is true that **an increased inventory of finished products often indicates that production is outstripping demand**, but in Burton's case it indicates no such thing. Rather, **the increase in inventory is entirely attributable to products that have already been assigned to orders received from customers**.

In the argument given, the two **boldfaced** portions play which of the following roles?

(A) The first states a generalization that underlies the position that the argument as a whole opposes; the second provides evidence to show that the generalization does not apply in the case at issue.

(B) The first states a generalization that underlies the position that the argument as a whole opposes; the second clarifies the meaning of a specific phrase as it is used in that generalization.

(C) The first provides evidence to support the conclusion of the argument as a whole; the second is evidence that has been used to support the position that the argument as a whole opposes.

(D) The first provides evidence to support the conclusion of the argument as a whole; the second states that conclusion.

(E) The first and the second each provide evidence against the position that the argument as a whole opposes.

Argument Construction

Situation   An investor has criticized a company, based on the company's recent increase in inventory and on its not decreasing production as a result of this increase.

Reasoning   *What roles do the two boldfaced statements play in the argument?* The argument suggests that the investor's criticism is based on a principle that increased inventory of finished products often indicates that production is faster than it should be, given the existing demand for a company's products. However, the argument then states that the increase in inventory at the company in question is "entirely attributable" to existing orders of products. The argument thus suggests that the investor's criticism is misplaced, based on a suggestion as to (1) a principle that the investor could be using to support her argument and (2) an explanation as to why the principle does not apply to the company. The two boldfaced portions state these respective elements.

A   **Correct.** The first boldfaced portion states the principle that may provide the basis of the investor's criticism, which the argument as a whole opposes. The second boldfaced portion is a statement that, if true, the generalization would not apply to the company in question.

B   This option correctly describes the first of the boldfaced portions. However, rather than clarifying an aspect of the meaning of the first generalization, the second boldfaced portion indicates why the first generalization may not apply to the company.

C   This option incorrectly describes both of the boldfaced portions. The first boldfaced portion states a general principle that could support the position that the argument *opposes*. The second boldfaced portion then criticizes the application of the principle.

D   Because the second boldfaced portion describes a fundamental premise rather than the conclusion, the description in this option of the second boldfaced portion is incorrect.

E   If we think of an argument as a set of statements that are meant to support, or provide evidence for, a conclusion, then, because the boldfaced statements are indeed part of the argument, they may be seen as providing evidence for the position the argument opposes. However, a description of the roles of the boldfaced statements in this argument would need to provide more detail, such as what option A provides.

The correct answer is A.

CR10028

732. To reduce productivity losses from employees calling in sick, Corporation X implemented a new policy requiring employees to come into work unless they were so sick that they had to go to a doctor. But a year after the policy was implemented, a study found that Corporation X's overall productivity losses due to reported employee illnesses had increased.

Which of the following, if true, would best explain why the policy produced the reverse of its intended effect?

(A) After the policy was implemented, employees more frequently went to the doctor when they felt sick.

(B) Before the policy was implemented, employees who were not sick at all often called in sick.

(C) Employees coming into work when sick often infect many of their coworkers.

(D) Unusually few employees became genuinely sick during the year after the policy was implemented.

(E) There are many other factors besides employee illness that can adversely affect productivity.

Evaluation of a Plan

Situation   After a company started requiring employees to come to work unless they were sick enough to have to go to a doctor, the company's productivity losses from reported employee illness increased.

Reasoning   *What would explain why the policy increased productivity losses from reported employee illness?* Any factors that could have plausibly caused the policy to increase employee absenteeism from reported illness or to reduce the employees' productivity at work as a result of reported illness could explain why the policy increased productivity losses from reported illness.

A   Even though the policy required sick employees to consult a doctor, there is no reason to think that employees' doing so would have made them less productive than they would otherwise have been when absent from work.

B   This suggests that the policy made it more difficult for employees to falsely claim illness as an excuse for a work absence. Reduction in absences should result in productivity gains rather than losses.

C   **Correct.** This could have been a result of the policy and would have led to productivity losses possibly greater than those seen before the policy was introduced.

D   This would help to explain lower productivity losses from reported illness after the policy was implemented, not higher productivity losses.

E   The question is what could explain how the policy increased productivity losses from reported employee illness specifically, not productivity losses from any other factors.

The correct answer is C.

CR08443

733. Advertising by mail has become much less effective, with fewer consumers responding. Because consumers are increasingly overwhelmed by the sheer amount of junk mail they receive, most discard almost all offers without considering them. Thus, an effective way for corporations to improve response rates would be to more carefully target the individuals to whom they mail advertising, thereby cutting down on the amount of junk mail each consumer receives.

Which of the following, if true, would most support the recommendation above?

(A) There are cost-effective means by which corporations that currently advertise by mail could improve response rates.

(B) Many successful corporations are already carefully targeting the individuals to whom they mail advertising.

(C) Any consumer who, immediately after receiving an advertisement by mail, merely glances at it is very likely to discard it.

(D) Improvements in the quality of the advertising materials used in mail that is carefully targeted to individuals can improve the response rate for such mail.

(E) Response rates to carefully targeted advertisements by mail are considerably higher, on average, than response rates to most other forms of advertising.

Evaluation of a Plan

Situation   Advertising by mail has become less effective because consumers overwhelmed with the amount of junk mail they receive discard almost all of it without considering it.

Reasoning   *What would most help to support the claim that making mail advertising more carefully targeted would improve response rates?* The passage recommends targeted advertising, reasoning that since targeted advertising would reduce the total amount of junk mail consumers receive, it would generate higher response rates. Any additional evidence for the claim that carefully targeted advertising would improve response rates would support this recommendation.

A   Even if targeted advertising and every other means of improving response rates were too expensive to be cost-effective, targeted advertising could still be effective for any corporation willing to pay the expense.

B   If many corporations already mail targeted advertising, and mail advertising is nonetheless yielding declining response rates, that suggests that targeted mail is an ineffective way to increase response rates.

C   This could be equally true for targeted and untargeted mail advertising, so it does not suggest that the former is more effective.

D   The question under consideration is whether more carefully targeted mail advertising would in itself increase response rates, not whether higher quality advertising would do so.

E   **Correct.** This provides some evidence that carefully targeted mail advertising is associated with higher response rates than untargeted mail advertising is, and therefore that targeting mail advertising more carefully would improve response rates.

The correct answer is E.

CR01905

734. Petrochemical industry officials have said that the extreme pressure exerted on plant managers during the last five years to improve profits by cutting costs has done nothing to impair the industry's ability to operate safely. However, environmentalists contend that the recent rash of serious oil spills and accidents at petrochemical plants is traceable to cost-cutting measures.

Which of the following, if true, would provide the strongest support for the position held by industry officials?

(A) The petrochemical industry benefits if accidents do not occur, since accidents involve risk of employee injury as well as loss of equipment and product.

(B) Petrochemical industry unions recently demanded that additional money be spent on safety and environmental protection measures, but the unions readily abandoned those demands in exchange for job security.

(C) Despite major cutbacks in most other areas of operation, the petrochemical industry has devoted more of its resources to environmental and safety measures in the last five years than in the preceding five years.

(D) There is evidence that the most damaging of the recent oil spills would have been prevented had cost-cutting measures not been instituted.

(E) Both the large fines and the adverse publicity generated by the most recent oil spill have prompted the petrochemical industry to increase the resources devoted to oil-spill prevention.

Argument Evaluation

Situation   Petrochemical industry officials claim that pressure on plant managers to cut costs over the past five years has not made the industry's operations any less safe. Environmentalists claim that recent oil spills and accidents show otherwise.

Reasoning   *What evidence would most strongly suggest that the cost-cutting pressure was not responsible for the recent rash of oil spills and accidents?* Evidence that the plant managers did not cut costs in any specific ways likely to have increased the likelihood of oil spills and accidents would support the industry officials' position that the cost-cutting pressure has not made petrochemical operations any less safe.

A   Even if the petrochemical industry has good reasons to try to prevent accidents, the recent rash of serious accidents suggests that it is failing to do so and that the cost-cutting pressure might be responsible.

B   This suggests that the unions, whose members could directly observe the cost-cutting pressure's effects, share the environmentalists' belief that this pressure contributed to the oil spills and accidents. Because the unions abandoned their demands, their concerns probably have not been addressed.

C   **Correct.** This suggests that, as the industry officials claim, the cost-cutting pressure has not in itself reduced the industry's effectiveness at preventing oil spills and accidents. Thus, it suggests that other factors are probably responsible for the recent problems.

D   This clearly suggests that the cost-cutting measures have indeed caused the industry to operate less safely, as the environmentalists claim.

E   Although this suggests that the industry is now trying to address the recent problems, the cost-cutting measures might nonetheless have caused all those problems.

The correct answer is C.

CR01368
735. A company has developed a new sensing device that, according to the company's claims, detects weak, ultralow-frequency electromagnetic signals associated with a beating heart. These signals, which pass through almost any physical obstruction, are purportedly detected by the device even at significant distances. Therefore, if the company's claims are true, their device will radically improve emergency teams' ability to locate quickly people who are trapped within the wreckage of collapsed buildings.

Which of the following, if true, most strengthens the argument?

(A) People trapped within the wreckage of collapsed buildings usually have serious injuries that require prompt medical treatment.

(B) The device gives a distinctive reading when the signals it detects come from human beings rather than from any other living beings.

(C) Most people who have survived after being trapped in collapsed buildings were rescued within two hours of the building's collapse.

(D) Ultralow-frequency signals are not the only electromagnetic signals that can pass through almost any physical obstruction.

(E) Extensive training is required in order to operate the device effectively.

Argument Evaluation

Situation   A new sensing device can detect—at significant distances and even behind obstructions such as walls—weak, ultralow-frequency electromagnetic signals that are characteristic of heartbeats. It is predicted, based on this information, that the new device will shorten the time it currently takes to locate people buried under collapsed buildings but still alive.

Reasoning   *What new information, if accurate, would provide further evidence that would support the prediction?* The existing evidence fails to tell us whether the new device can distinguish between human heartbeats and heartbeats from other species. If the device does not allow the user to distinguish between the heartbeats of humans and those of animals of other species, then the prediction might not be correct, because if there are any nonhuman animals in the building, emergency teams may believe they have located a trapped human and begin a rescue effort, when in fact they have merely located an animal of some other species. Any new information that implies the device can help the user to discern between signals associated with a human heartbeat and signals associated with the heartbeats of animals of other species will strengthen support for the prediction.

A   This implies that prompt rescue of people trapped under collapsed buildings is vitally important. The prediction is that the new device will speed rescue of such people, but the new information here does nothing to indicate that the prediction is accurate.

B   **Correct.** As explained in the Reasoning section above, there is a crucial gap in the argument: The argument does not indicate whether the device allows the user to distinguish between signals associated with human heartbeats and signals associated with the heartbeats of other species. This information fills that gap.

C   Even if this is true, shortening the time for locating and rescuing people from collapsed buildings would clearly be beneficial. However, the new information given here does not make it more likely that the prediction is correct.

D   If this is correct, then, if anything, it somewhat undermines the evidence given for the prediction, since it raises the possibility that the detection ability of the device might be impeded by "noise" from irrelevant electromagnetic signals near the collapsed building.

E   This could lead to practical obstacles when using the device even in emergency situations, with the result that the device might never actually be used by competent personnel to "improve emergency teams' ability" because the "extensive training" would cost too much.

The correct answer is B.

CR11639

736. Economist: The price of tap water in our region should be raised drastically. **Supplies in local freshwater reservoirs have been declining for years** because water is being used faster than it can be replenished. Since the price of tap water has been low, **few users have bothered to adopt even easy conservation measures**.

The two sections in **boldface** play which of the following roles in the economist's argument?

(A) The first is a conclusion for which support is provided, and which in turn supports the main conclusion; the second is the main conclusion.

(B) The first is an observation for which the second provides an explanation; the second is the main conclusion but not the only conclusion.

(C) The first is a premise supporting the argument's main conclusion; so is the second.

(D) The first is the only conclusion; the second provides an explanation for the first.

(E) The first is the main conclusion; the second is a conclusion for which support is provided, and which in turn supports the first.

Argument Construction

Situation   Local water supplies have been declining for years because of excessive water use and low prices. Few users have adopted even easy conservation measures.

Reasoning   *What roles do the two boldface statements play in the argument?* Both are factual observations. Since no further evidence or support is provided for either, neither can be a conclusion in the argument. However, interconnected causal explanations, signaled by *because* and *since*, are provided for both. The observation in the first boldface statement is causally explained by the further observation that water is being used faster than it can be replenished, which in turn is causally explained by the entire final sentence. The observation in the second boldface statement is causally explained by the observation that the price of tap water has been low. The only remaining portion of the argument is the initial sentence, a recommendation supported by these four observations together, and by the causal claims in which they are embedded. Thus, the four observations (including the two boldface statements) and the causal claims containing them are all premises, and the initial statement is the argument's only conclusion.

A   As explained in the Reasoning section above, the two boldface statements are premises of the argument. Although causal explanations are provided for both, no support or evidence is provided for either. Neither statement is inferred from anything else in the argument, so neither can be a conclusion in the argument.

B   As explained in the Reasoning section above, the second boldface statement does provide part of the causal explanation for the observation in the first boldface statement. But the second is not a conclusion. It is not inferred from anything else in the argument, so it cannot be a conclusion in the argument.

C   **Correct.** As explained in the Reasoning section above, each of the statements is a premise that serves along with other claims to support the recommendation in the initial sentence, which is the argument's only conclusion, and in that sense its main conclusion.

D   As explained in the Reasoning section above, the second boldface statement does provide part of the causal explanation for the observation in the first boldface statement. But the first is not a conclusion. It is not inferred from anything else in the argument, so it cannot be a conclusion in the argument.

E   As explained in the Reasoning section above, the two boldface statements are premises of the argument. Although causal explanations are provided for both, no support or evidence is provided for either. Neither statement is inferred from anything else in the argument, so neither can be a conclusion in the argument.

The correct answer is C.

CR13127
737. Politician: Hybrid cars use significantly less fuel per kilometer than nonhybrids. And fuel produces air pollution, which contributes to a number of environmental problems. Motorists can save money by driving cars that are more fuel efficient, and they will be encouraged to drive hybrid cars if we make them aware of that fact. Therefore, we can help reduce the total amount of pollution emitted by cars in this country by highlighting this advantage of hybrid cars.

Which of the following, if true, would most indicate a vulnerability of the politician's argument?

(A)   People with more fuel-efficient cars typically drive more than do those with less fuel-efficient cars.

(B)   Not all air pollution originates from automobiles.

(C)   Hybrid cars have already begun to gain popularity.

(D)   Fuel-efficient alternatives to hybrid cars will likely become available in the future.

(E)   The future cost of gasoline and other fuel cannot be predicted with absolute precision or certainty.

Argument Evaluation

Situation   According to a politician, hybrid cars use less fuel per kilometer than nonhybrids, and fuel produces air pollution. Motorists can save money by driving fuel-efficient cars, and will be encouraged to do so if made aware of the fact. The politician concludes that highlighting this fact will result in a reduction in air pollution.

Reasoning   *What would suggest that telling motorists they can save money by driving fuel-efficient cars would not reduce automotive air pollution, despite the facts cited by the politician?* The politician's implicit reasoning is that since hybrid cars use less fuel per kilometer, and fuel produces air pollution, motorists who drive hybrid cars must produce less air pollution than those who drive nonhybrids. The politician concludes that encouraging motorists to drive hybrid cars by telling them they would save money on fuel will therefore reduce automotive air pollution. Evidence that motorists who drive hybrid cars produce just as much automotive air pollution as those who drive nonhybrids would undermine this argument.

A   **Correct.** If drivers of hybrid cars tend to drive more kilometers than drivers of nonhybrids, then they may consume just as much fuel and produce just as much air pollution as the nonhybrid car drivers do, despite their lower fuel use per kilometer.

B   The politician's argument is only about air pollution from cars specifically, not air pollution from all sources.

C   Even if hybrid cars are beginning to gain popularity, informing motorists of the cost savings from fuel efficiency could help these cars become more popular than they would otherwise be.

D   Encouraging motorists to switch to hybrid cars now could reduce fuel use and automotive air pollution in the near future even if other, more fuel-efficient vehicles will become available further in the future.

E   Even if the future cost of fuel cannot be predicted accurately, encouraging motorists to switch to hybrid cars could reduce air pollution as the politician argues.

The correct answer is A.

CR99530.01

738. Mayor: False alarms from home security systems waste so much valuable police time that in many communities police have stopped responding to alarms from homes whose systems frequently produce false alarms. This policy reduces wastage of police time but results in a loss of protection for some residents. To achieve a comparable reduction in wastage without reducing protection for residents, the council has enacted a measure to fine residents for repeated false alarms.

Which of the following, if true, casts the most doubt on whether the measure enacted by the council will achieve its goal?

(A) A fine in the amount planned by the council will not cover the expenses police typically incur when they respond to a false alarm.

(B) Homes equipped with security systems are far less likely to be broken into than are homes without security systems.

(C) The threat of fines is likely to cause many residents to deactivate their security systems.

(D) The number of home security systems is likely to increase dramatically over the next five years.

(E) Many home security systems have never produced false alarms.

Evaluation of a Plan

Situation In many communities, police have been responding to false home-security alarms but have ceased to respond to alarms from homes that often have such false alarms. To reduce wastage of police time without compromising residents' home protection, one town council has enacted a new measure that will fine home residents for repeated false alarms.

Reasoning *What fact or occurrence would most reduce the likelihood that the town council's newly enacted measure would achieve its goal, which is to reduce wastage of police time without compromising home protection?* Note that the goal is not to eliminate all wastage of police time or to pay all the costs of it; some random wastage is to be expected. But if many residents deactivated their security alarms (even well-functioning systems) because they wish to avoid being fined, this could reduce the level of home protection for those residents.

A   The goal is to reduce wastage of police time resulting from false security-system alarms, not necessarily to cover all the costs in police time for such alarms.

B   This seems obviously true, but it is also irrelevant to the frequency of false home-security alarms. It is therefore irrelevant, also, to whether the council's measure will effectively address wastage of police time stemming from such alarms.

C   **Correct.** If this occurred, it would result in a lower level of home protection for some residents and would mean that the town council's measure would have failed to achieve its goal.

D   This scenario does not make the council's measure more likely to fail to achieve its goal. If the increase in alarm systems occurs, it will likely result in more protection for the homes of more residents. Assuming vigorous enforcement of the new measure, we have no reason to believe that the number of false alarms would increase.

E   This has little bearing on the likelihood of the council's measure succeeding. Any home-security system that has never produced a false alarm could do so tomorrow, for all kinds of reasons.

The correct answer is C.

CR53341.01

739. Excavation of the house of a third-century Camarnian official revealed that he had served four magistrates—public officials who administer the law—over his thirty-year public career, in four provincial capital cities. However, given the Camarnian administrative system of that era, it is unclear whether he served them simultaneously, as a traveling administrator living for part of the year in each provincial capital, or else did so sequentially, leaving one magistrate after several years to join another.

Which of the following would, if found in the excavation, most likely help reveal the pattern of the official's administrative service?

(A) Maps and documents describing each of the four provincial capitals

(B) A cache of the official's documents related to work from early in his career

(C) A set of cups of a type made only in the city of the first magistrate whom the official is known to have served

(D) Several pieces of furniture in the styles of two of the provincial capital cities

(E) Heavy clothing appropriate only for the coldest of the four cities

Argument Construction

Situation   Evidence from an excavation makes clear that a particular third-century Camarnian official served four magistrates in four provincial capitals over his thirty-year career, but it is unclear whether he served the magistrates simultaneously or sequentially.

Reasoning   *What evidence, if it were also found in the excavation, would be most helpful in determining whether the official served the magistrates simultaneously or sequentially?* It would be helpful to find documents from throughout the magistrate's career indicating at what times he worked for each magistrate, or even documents from just one period, as long as there were a large number, because this would likely show whether he was working for just one magistrate or for all four.

A   We already know that the official worked in each of the four capitals. The fact that maps and documents describing the capitals were at his house tells us nothing about whether he worked for magistrates in these capitals simultaneously or not.

B   **Correct.** Presumably the work-related documents would show whom he was working for at the time, and for how long—and would provide evidence as to whether he was working for multiple magistrates or for just one.

C   Merely finding a set of cups made only in one of the cities tells us little. Even if we knew when he acquired the set, he need not have been working for the magistrate of that city at the time he acquired it; perhaps he had simply traveled to that city.

D   One frequently moves furniture when moving from one city to another, so the fact that the official had pieces of furniture that may have come from different cities does not give us any indication of whether the official worked for all four magistrates simultaneously or not.

E   The fact that heavy clothing appropriate only for the coldest of the four cities was found in the excavation of the official's house does not imply that other clothing, appropriate for one or more of the other cities, was not found. Consistent with the finding of the heavy clothing, the official may have worked exclusively in the city for which that clothing was appropriate, or worked intermittently in this city.

The correct answer is B.

CR80531.01

740. In 1563, in Florence's Palazzo Vecchio, Giorgio Vasari built in front of an existing wall a new wall on which he painted a mural. Investigators recently discovered a gap between Vasari's wall and the original, large enough to have preserved anything painted on the original. Historians believe that Leonardo da Vinci had painted, but left unfinished, a mural on the original wall; some historians had also believed that by 1563 the mural had been destroyed. However, it is known that in the late 1560s, when renovating another building, Santa Maria Novella, Vasari built a façade over its frescoes, and the frescoes were thereby preserved. Thus, Leonardo's Palazzo Vecchio mural probably still exists behind Vasari's wall.

Which of the following is an assumption on which the argument depends?

(A) Leonardo rarely if ever destroyed artworks that he left unfinished.

(B) Vasari was likely unaware that the mural in the Palazzo Vecchio had willingly been abandoned by Leonardo.

(C) Vasari probably would not have built the Palazzo Vecchio wall with a gap behind it except to preserve something behind the new wall.

(D) Leonardo would probably have completed the Palazzo Vecchio mural if he had had the opportunity to do so.

(E) When Vasari preserved the frescoes of Santa Maria Novella he did so secretly.

Argument Construction

Situation   Georgio Vasari built a new wall in front of an existing wall in the Palazzo Vecchio that historians believe had had an unfinished mural by Leonardo da Vinci painted on it. Some historians, however, believe the mural had been destroyed by the time Vasari built the new wall. There is a gap between the old and new wall, large enough to have preserved anything painted on it, as there is in Santa Maria Novella, where Vasari also constructed a new wall in front of an old wall; on that wall, the building's frescoes were preserved.

Reasoning   *What claim needs to be true for the cited facts to support the conclusion that Leonardo's Palazzo Vecchio mural likely still exists behind Vasari's wall?* If there are other equally likely reasons that Vasari would have left a gap between the old wall and a new wall, besides preserving any painting on the old wall, the stated facts would not support the conclusion. After all, it may be only fortuitous that the frescoes in the Santa Maria Novella were preserved when Vasari built the new wall with a gap between it and the old wall. Therefore, the argument depends on assuming that it is unlikely that Vasari would have created a gap between the old and new walls unless he had been trying to preserve something painted on the old wall.

A   The argument does not depend on the claim that Leonardo rarely if ever destroyed his unfinished artworks. Obviously, it does depend on the claim that he did not always do so, but even if he fairly regularly destroyed unfinished artworks, this mural could be one of the ones he did not—perhaps the reason the mural was left unfinished was that he died before completing it.

B   The argument does not depend on Vasari knowing that Leonardo had willingly abandoned the mural. Even if Leonardo did willingly leave it unfinished, Vasari could nonetheless have thought the mural was of value and wanted to preserve it.

C   **Correct.** If there had been other likely reasons for Vasari to have built a gap behind the new wall other than to preserve something painted on the old wall, the cited facts would not be a good reason to believe that Vasari built the gap for the purpose of preserving anything painted on it.

D   Leonardo may have had no interest in finishing the mural. Vasari could nevertheless have thought that there was value in preserving it.

E   There is no need to assume that Vasari preserved the frescoes at Santa Maria Novella secretly. Even if he did not do so in this instance, he could have preserved other paintings secretly by the same means, or he may have let others know that he was preserving Leonardo's mural, although there is no historical record that he did let them know.

The correct answer is C.

8.6 Critical Reasoning **Answer Explanations**

CR09534

741. Coffee shop owner: A large number of customers will pay at least the fair market value for a cup of coffee, even if there is no formal charge. Some will pay more than this out of appreciation of the trust that is placed in them. And our total number of customers is likely to increase. We could therefore improve our net cash flow by implementing an honor system in which customers pay what they wish for coffee by depositing money in a can.

Manager: We're likely to lose money on this plan. Many customers would cheat the system, paying a very small sum or nothing at all.

Which of the following, if true, would best support the owner's plan, in light of the manager's concern?

(A) The new system, if implemented, would increase the number of customers.

(B) By roasting its own coffee, the shop has managed to reduce the difficulties (and cost) of maintaining an inventory of freshly roasted coffee.

(C) Many customers stay in the cafe for long stretches of time.

(D) The shop makes a substantial profit from pastries and other food bought by the coffee drinkers.

(E) No other coffee shop in the area has such a system.

Evaluation of a Plan

Situation   The owner and the manager of a coffee shop disagree about whether allowing customers to pay for coffee on an honor system would increase or decrease profits.

Reasoning   *What would be the best evidence that the honor-system plan would increase profits even if many customers cheated the system?* The owner argues that profits would increase because many customers will choose to pay as much or more than before and the total number of customers will likely increase. But the manager points out that many customers would also choose to pay little or nothing. Assuming that the manager is correct about that, what further support could the owner present for the claim that the plan would still be profitable?

A   Since the owner has already basically asserted this, asserting it again would not provide any significant additional support for the plan.

B   This suggests that the shop is already profitable, not that the honor-system plan would make it more profitable.

C   Customers who stay in the cafe for long stretches would not necessarily pay any more per cup on the honor-system plan than other customers would.

D   Correct. If the customer base increases (as both the owner and the manager seem to agree), more customers will likely purchase highly profitable pastries and other foods, thus boosting profits.

E   The reason no other coffee shop in the area has an honor system may be that their owners and managers have determined that it would not be profitable.

The correct answer is D.

CR03272

742. Birds have been said to be descended from certain birdlike dinosaur species with which they share distinctive structural features. The fossil record, however, shows that this cannot be so, since there are bird fossils that are much older than the earliest birdlike dinosaur fossils that have been found.

Which of the following is an assumption on which the argument relies?

(A) The birdlike dinosaurs have no living descendants.

(B) There are no flightless dinosaur species that have the distinctive structural features shared by birds and birdlike dinosaurs.

(C) There are no birdlike dinosaur fossils that are older than the bird fossils but have not yet been unearthed.

(D) It could not have been the case that some birds were descended from one of the birdlike dinosaur species and other birds from another.

(E) Birds cannot have been descended from dinosaur species with which the birds do not share the distinctive structural features.

Argument Construction

Situation   Although birds have been said to be descended from birdlike dinosaurs, some bird fossils predate the earliest known birdlike dinosaur fossils.

Reasoning   *What must be true in order for the premise that some bird fossils predate the earliest known birdlike dinosaur fossils to support the conclusion that birds are not descended from birdlike dinosaurs?* The argument implicitly reasons that since the cited bird fossils predate the earliest known birdlike dinosaur fossils, they must be from birds that lived before the earliest birdlike dinosaurs, and which therefore could not have been descended from birdlike dinosaurs. This reasoning assumes that any birdlike dinosaurs that lived before the first birds would have left fossils that still exist. It also assumes that no undiscovered birdlike dinosaur fossils predate the cited bird fossils.

A   The argument is only about whether birds are descended from birdlike dinosaurs. Whether birdlike dinosaurs have any living descendants other than birds is irrelevant.

B   The argument is only about birds and birdlike dinosaurs. It is not about other types of dinosaurs that were not birdlike.

C   **Correct.** If any undiscovered birdlike dinosaur fossils predate the cited bird fossils, then the latter fossils' age does not support the conclusion that birds are not descended from birdlike dinosaurs.

D   The argument purports to establish that the relative ages of bird fossils and birdlike dinosaur fossils show that birds cannot be descended from any of the known birdlike dinosaur species. In doing this, it acknowledges multiple birdlike dinosaur species and leaves open the question of whether some birds may be descended from one such species and other birds from another such species.

E   The argument does not claim that the known fossil record shows that birds cannot be descended from dinosaurs. It only claims that the record shows that they cannot be descended from the birdlike dinosaurs that shared their distinctive structural features.

The correct answer is C.

CR08239
743. City council member: Demand for electricity has been increasing by 1.5 percent a year, and there simply is no more space to build additional power plants to meet future demand increases. We must therefore begin to curtail usage, which is why I propose passing ordinances requiring energy-conservation measures in all city departments.

The city council member's proposal assumes which of the following?

(A) Existing power plants do not have the capacity to handle all of the projected increase in demand for electricity.

(B) No city departments have implemented energy-conservation measures voluntarily.

(C) Passing ordinances designed to curtail electricity usage will not have negative economic consequences for the city.

(D) Residential consumers are not responsible for the recent increases in demand for electricity.

(E) City departments that successfully conserve energy will set a good example for residential and industrial consumers of electricity.

Argument Construction

Situation   A city council member proposes energy-conservation measures for all city government departments because there is no room to build new power plants to meet future increases in the demand for electricity.

Reasoning   *What must be true in order for the factors the city council member cites to help justify the proposal?* The city council member says electricity usage must be curtailed on account of an increasing demand for electricity and a lack of space for new power plants that could meet future demand increases. In order for this reasoning to help justify the proposal, the cited factors must actually establish a need to curtail electricity usage.

A   **Correct.** If current power plants could satisfy the projected increased demand for electricity, then the increasing demand and the lack of room to build new plants would not establish a need to curtail electricity usage.

B   The proposed ordinances could still be necessary even if one city department had voluntarily implemented energy-conservation measures.

C   Passing the ordinances could still be necessary even if they would have some negative economic effects.

D   No matter who is responsible for the recent increases in demand, curtailing the city government's electricity usage could still help to reduce demand.

E   Ordinances to curtail the city government's energy usage could be economically necessary regardless of whether or not departments that obey the ordinances set a good example.

The correct answer is A.

CR32441.01

744. Certain groups of Asian snails include both "left-handed" and "right-handed" species, with shells coiling to the left and right, respectively. Some left-handed species have evolved from right-handed ones. Also, researchers found that snail-eating snakes in the same habitat have asymmetrical jaws, allowing them to grasp right-handed snail shells more easily. If these snakes ate more right-handed snails over time, this would have given left-handed snails an evolutionary advantage over right-handed snails, with the left-handed snails eventually becoming a new species. Thus, the snakes' asymmetrical jaws probably helped drive the emergence of the left-handed snail species.

Which of the following would, if true, most strengthen the argument that asymmetrical snake jaws helped drive left-handed snail evolution?

(A) In one snake species, the snakes with asymmetrical jaws eat snails, while the snakes with symmetrical jaws do not eat snails.

(B) Some species of Asian snails contain either all right-handed snails, or all left-handed snails.

(C) Anatomical differences prevent left-handed snails from mating easily with right-handed snails.

(D) Some right-handed snails in this habitat have shells with a very narrow opening that helps prevent snakes from extracting the snails from inside their shells.

(E) Experiments show that the snail-eating snakes in this habitat fail more often in trying to eat left-handed snails than in trying to eat right-handed snails.

Argument Evaluation

Situation   There are both Asian snails with shells that coil to the right and Asian snails with shells that coil to the left, and the latter have evolved from the former; furthermore, there are snakes that have asymmetrical jaws that allow the snakes to grasp the snails with right-coiled shells more easily.

Reasoning   *What fact would help support the claim that the snakes' asymmetrical jaws helped drive the emergence of species of snails with left-coiled shells?* We are told that if over time the snakes with asymmetrical jaws ate more snails with right-coiled shells than snails with left-coiled shells, then this would give snails with left-coiled shells an evolutionary survival advantage. So, if some evidence showed that the snakes with such jaws in fact were more likely to have successfully eaten the snails with the right-coiled shells, then we would have good reason to think the snakes' asymmetrical jaws helped drive the emergence of snails with left-coiled shells.

A   The fact that snakes with asymmetrical jaws eat snails and other snakes do not does not give any indication as to whether snails with left-coiled shells have any evolutionary advantages over snails with right-coiled shells. At best it only tells us that if snakes drove the evolution of snails with left-coiled shells, it would likely have been the snakes with asymmetrical jaws.

B   The fact that some species of Asian snails have no variation in the direction in which their shells coil tells us nothing about what, if any, evolutionary advantages they have relative to other snails, or whether the snakes' asymmetrical jaws had any effect on any such evolutionary advantages.

C   The inability of snails with left-coiled shells to mate easily with snails with right-coiled shells in and of itself tells us nothing about whether the snakes' asymmetrical jaws had any effect on the emergence of snails with left-coiled shells. Although it does suggest a different factor that could have contributed to the emergence of the snail species with left-coiled shells, it does not exclude the possibility that the snakes were also a factor.

D   The fact that snakes cannot extract some snails with right-coiled shells from their shells would suggest that these snails might have an evolutionary advantage; but the argument's conclusion is about an evolutionary advantage that snails with left-coiled shells presumably have, not an advantage that snails with right-coiled shells would have.

E   **Correct.** The fact that experiments show that the snakes are more successful at eating snails with right-coiled shells than they are at eating snails with left-coiled shells would support the claim that these snakes did in fact eat more snails with right-coiled shells, and hence the snails with left-coiled shells would as a result have an evolutionary advantage.

The correct answer is E.

CR95631.01

745. A moderately large city is redesigning its central downtown area and is considering a plan that would reduce the number of lanes for automobiles and trucks and increase those for bicycles and pedestrians. The intent is to attract more workers and shoppers to downtown businesses by making downtown easier to reach and more pleasant to move around in.

Which of the following would, if true, most strongly support the prediction that the plan would achieve its goal?

(A) People who make a habit of walking or bicycling whenever feasible derive significant health benefits from doing so.

(B) Most people who prefer to shop at suburban malls instead of downtown urban areas do so because parking is easier and cheaper at the former.

(C) In other moderately sized cities where measures were taken to make downtowns more accessible for walkers and cyclists, downtown businesses began to thrive.

(D) If the proposed lane restrictions on drivers are rigorously enforced, more people will likely be attracted to downtown businesses than would otherwise be.

(E) Most people who own and frequently ride bicycles for recreational purposes live at a significant distance from downtown urban areas.

Evaluation of a Plan

Situation   A moderately large city desires to attract more workers and shoppers to downtown businesses by making the downtown area more pleasant and easier to travel to. In light of this goal, the city is considering a plan that would reduce the number of lanes for automobiles and trucks and increase those for bicycles and pedestrians.

Reasoning   *What would most strongly support the prediction that reducing the number of lanes for automobiles and trucks and increasing those for bicycles and pedestrians would achieve the goal of attracting more people to downtown businesses?* If other moderately sized cities that have improved the accessibility of their downtown areas to pedestrians and cyclists have seen increased downtown business, then it is reasonable to think that the city in question will have improved downtown business as well.

A   If people who make a habit of walking or bicycling derive significant health benefits, that would provide further motivation for trying to encourage people to walk or ride a bicycle, but it does not provide much support for the claim that adding lanes for pedestrians and cyclists will successfully bring people to shop or work more in the city's downtown. Perhaps people will merely use the new lanes for exercise, but not to get to the downtown area to do business.

B   Because the plan as described does not provide for additional parking, the fact that parking is a major concern motivating people to shop at suburban malls does not give us good reason to think that the city's plan will help achieve the city's goal.

C   **Correct.** If other moderately sized cities that have made their downtown areas more accessible to pedestrians and cyclists have seen their downtown businesses begin to thrive soon afterwards, this is evidence—even if not conclusive—that the changes produced the thriving. Consequently, it is reasonable to think that the same will result for the city in question.

D   It might be the case that rigorously enforcing lane restrictions will attract more people to downtown businesses than would otherwise be the case, but the information provided does not indicate how strictly lane restrictions will be enforced.

E   The city's plan is aimed at increasing the use of bicycles for the purposes of shopping or getting to work, not only for recreational purposes. And even if people who use their bicycles for recreational purposes would also be likely to use them for shopping or getting to work, the fact that most recreational cyclists live at a significant distance from the city's downtown area may suggest that the city's plan will not be successful, because the cyclists may live too far away to use their bicycles for these purposes, even if it would be somewhat easier for them to do so once the plan has been implemented.

The correct answer is C.

CR00713

746. Previously, Autoco designed all of its cars itself and then contracted with specialized parts suppliers to build parts according to its specifications. Now it plans to include its suppliers in designing the parts they are to build. Since many parts suppliers have more designers with specialized experience than Autoco has, Autoco expects this shift to reduce the overall time and cost of the design of its next new car.

Which of the following, if true, most strongly supports Autoco's expectation?

(A) When suppliers provide their own designs, Autoco often needs to modify its overall design.

(B) In order to provide designs for Autoco, several of the parts suppliers will have to add to their existing staffs of designers.

(C) Parts and services provided by outside suppliers account for more than 50 percent of Autoco's total costs.

(D) When suppliers built parts according to specifications provided by Autoco, the suppliers competed to win contracts.

(E) Most of Autoco's suppliers have on hand a wide range of previously prepared parts designs that can readily be modified for a new car.

Evaluation of a Plan

Situation   A car manufacturer plans to have its parts suppliers start helping to design the parts they build for the manufacturer. Many parts suppliers have more designers with specialized experience than the manufacturer has.

Reasoning   *What would make it more likely that having the parts suppliers help design the parts will reduce the time and cost of designing the manufacturer's next new car?* In order for the change to reduce the time and cost, the parts suppliers involved in designing the next car will probably have to do their portion of the design process faster and cheaper than the manufacturer would have, and the design collaboration process will have to avoid producing substantial new inefficiencies.

A   The additional need to modify the overall design would probably make the design process slower and more expensive, not faster and cheaper.

B   The additional need to hire more designers would probably increase design costs, not reduce them.

C   Although this suggests that the change is likely to substantially affect the design's expense, it does not indicate whether the expense will increase or decrease.

D   If anything, this competition probably made Autoco's previous design process cheaper. It does not suggest that the new design process, which may involve less competition, will be faster or cheaper than the previous one.

E   **Correct.** Modifying the previously prepared parts designs will probably be faster and cheaper than creating new designs from scratch.

The correct answer is E.

CR02830

747. In response to viral infection, the immune systems of mice typically produce antibodies that destroy the virus by binding to proteins on its surface. Mice infected with the herpesvirus generally develop keratitis, a degenerative disease affecting part of the eye. Since proteins on the surface of cells in this part of the eye closely resemble those on the herpesvirus surface, scientists hypothesize that these cases of keratitis are caused by antibodies to the herpesvirus.

Which of the following, if true, most helps to support the scientists' reasoning?

(A) Other types of virus have surface proteins that closely resemble proteins found in various organs of mice.

(B) Mice that are infected with the herpesvirus but do not develop keratitis produce as many antibodies as infected mice that do develop keratitis.

(C) Mice infected with a new strain of the herpesvirus that has different surface proteins did not develop keratitis.

(D) Mice that have never been infected with the herpesvirus can sometimes develop keratitis.

(E) There are mice that are unable to form antibodies in response to herpes infections, and these mice contract herpes at roughly the same rate as other mice.

Argument Evaluation

Situation Mice infected with the herpesvirus tend to develop keratitis, an eye disease. The surface of the eye cells have proteins that resemble those on the herpesvirus surface. Based on this finding, scientists have hypothesized that keratitis develops in mice because antibodies that attack herpesvirus surface proteins can also attack eyes.

Reasoning *What other information, if correct, would provide the strongest support for the scientists' hypothesis?* The clue that led the scientists to form their hypothesis was the close resemblance of the proteins on the mouse eye surface to those on the herpesvirus surface. The resemblance could cause antibodies to bind to both types of proteins, in one case eliminating the herpesvirus and in the other case causing keratitis.

A   Even if this is correct, we lack information as to whether the antibodies to those other types of virus can damage the organs that display the closely resembling proteins. If such a damage process were confirmed, it could count as evidence—even if not sufficient—to confirm the scientists' hypothesis.

B   If anything, this would, absent further information, raise doubts about the correctness of the scientists' proposed explanation.

C   **Correct.** This provides strong confirmation of the scientists' hypothesis. The proteins on the new strain of the herpesvirus no longer sufficiently resemble the proteins on the eye surface to cause the antibodies to attack those proteins and cause keratitis.

D   For all we know, keratitis may have multiple independent causes and may sometimes be caused by processes other than the protein misidentification hypothesized by the scientists. This information neither confirms nor refutes the scientists' hypothesis.

E   The rates at which mice contract herpes is not discussed. We lack any information as to whether mice that lack antibodies to the herpesvirus sometimes contract keratitis along with herpes infection.

The correct answer is C.

CR38931.01

748. One might expect that within a particular species, any individuals that managed to slow down the aging process would leave more offspring. Natural selection should therefore favor extreme longevity—but this does not seem to be the case. A possible explanation is that aging is a product of the inevitable wear and tear of living, similar to how household appliances generally accumulate faults that lead to their eventual demise. However, most researchers do not find this analogy satisfactory as an explanation.

Which of the following would, if true, provide the strongest explanation for the researchers' reaction?

(A) Some organisms are capable of living much longer than other organisms.

(B) Some organisms reproduce very quickly despite having short lifespans.

(C) There are several ways of defining "extreme longevity," and according to some definitions it occurs frequently.

(D) Organisms are capable of maintenance and self-repair and can remedy much of the damage that they accumulate.

(E) Some organisms generate much more wear and tear on their bodies than others.

Argument Construction

Situation   One possible explanation for the fact that natural selection does not favor extreme longevity, despite the fact that a slowed-down aging process would leave more offspring, is that aging is the product of wear and tear, much like household appliances eventually no longer function because of wear and tear; most researchers, however, reject this analogy as an explanation.

Reasoning   *What would explain the researchers' rejection of the explanation?* The explanation is based on analogy between organisms and household appliances. If there were a crucial difference between appliances and organisms, such as the fact that organisms are capable of self-repair in a way that household appliances are not, then it would be reasonable for the researchers to reject the explanation.

A   The fact that some organisms can live much longer than other organisms is not a good reason to reject the analogy; after all, some household appliances may last much longer than others, perhaps because they receive a different amount of wear and tear.

B   Even if some organisms reproduce very quickly despite having short lifespans, that does not mean that they would not have even more offspring if they lived longer; also, this is irrelevant as to whether the analogy between the aging process and the wear and tear on household appliances is any good.

C   It is unclear what these different ways of defining "extreme longevity" are—perhaps the definition is merely a relative one; some organisms live much longer than others, and those that do have "extreme longevity." But presumably some household appliances last much longer than others, so this would not indicate a difference, and thus would not explain why most researchers reject the analogy.

D   **Correct.** Household appliances cannot repair themselves as organisms can, so the wear and tear of living is quite different from the wear and tear in household appliances.

E   Presumably some household appliances receive much more wear and tear than other household appliances, so the fact that some organisms generate more wear and tear on their bodies than others does not indicate a difference between appliances and organisms, and thus does not explain why the researchers reject the analogy.

The correct answer is D.

CR02885

749. Last year a record number of new manufacturing jobs were created. Will this year bring another record? Well, **any new manufacturing job is created either within an existing company or by the start-up of a new company**. Within existing firms, new jobs have been created this year at well below last year's record pace. At the same time, there is considerable evidence that the number of new companies starting up this year will be no higher than it was last year and **there is no reason to think that the new companies starting up this year will create more jobs per company than did last year's start-ups**. So clearly, the number of new jobs created this year will fall short of last year's record.

In the argument given, the two portions in **boldface** play which of the following roles?

(A) The first provides evidence in support of the main conclusion of the argument; the second is a claim that the argument challenges.

(B) The first is a generalization that the argument seeks to establish; the second is a conclusion that the argument draws in order to support that generalization.

(C) The first is a generalization that the argument seeks to establish; the second is a judgment that has been advanced in order to challenge that generalization.

(D) The first is presented as an obvious truth on which the argument is based; the second is a claim that has been advanced in support of a position that the argument opposes.

(E) The first is presented as an obvious truth on which the argument is based; the second is a judgment advanced in support of the main conclusion of the argument.

Argument Construction

Situation   Manufacturing jobs are created either within existing companies or in start-ups. Manufacturing jobs are being created at a much slower rate this year than last year. It seems likely that the number of new start-ups will not exceed last year's number and that the average number of manufacturing jobs per start-up will not exceed last year's number. So fewer manufacturing jobs are likely to be created this year than last year.

Reasoning   *What function is served by the statement that any new manufacturing job is created either within an existing company or by the start-up of a new company? What function is served by the statement that there is no reason to think that the new companies starting up this year will create more jobs per company than did last year's start-ups?* The first statement makes explicit a general background assumption that there are just two ways in which manufacturing jobs are created. This assumption is used, along with other information, to support the argument's main conclusion, i.e., the prediction about job creation this year. The second statement gives a premise meant to help support the prediction about this year's manufacturing-job creation.

A   The first is a general statement making explicit an assumption on which the argument's reasoning depends, but the second is a statement affirmed as part of the argument and does not express a claim that the argument challenges.

B   The first is a generalization that is simply stated, without any support being offered. The second is not a conclusion and is not offered in support of the first.

C   The second is not presented as a challenge to the generalization that is given in the first statement. The argument does not seek to establish the first statement, but merely asserts it.

D   The second is information offered in support of the argument's main conclusion rather than a statement offered in support of a position opposed by the argument.

E   **Correct.** The first, stating a truism, is merely asserted and requires no support in the argument, for which it provides a foundation; the second is a piece of information meant to support the prediction that is the argument's main conclusion.

The correct answer is E.

CR02886

750. Last year a record number of new manufacturing jobs were created. Will this year bring another record? Well, **any new manufacturing job is created either within an existing company or by the start-up of a new company**. Within existing firms, new jobs have been created this year at well below last year's record pace. At the same time, there is considerable evidence that the number of new companies starting up will be no higher this year than it was last year and there is no reason to think that the new companies starting up this year will create more jobs per company than did last year's start-ups. So clearly, **the number of new jobs created this year will fall short of last year's record**.

In the argument given, the two portions in **boldface** play which of the following roles?

(A) The first is presented as an obvious truth on which the argument is based; the second is the main conclusion of the argument.

(B) The first is presented as an obvious truth on which the argument is based; the second is a conclusion drawn in order to support the main conclusion of the argument.

(C) The first and the second each provide evidence in support of the main conclusion of the argument.

(D) The first is a generalization that the argument seeks to establish; the second is the main conclusion of the argument.

(E) The first is a generalization that the argument seeks to establish; the second is a conclusion that has been drawn in order to challenge that generalization.

Argument Construction

Situation   Manufacturing jobs are created either within existing companies or in start-ups. Manufacturing jobs at existing firms are being created at a much slower rate this year than last year. It seems likely that the number of new start-ups will not exceed last year's number and that the average number of new manufacturing jobs per start-up will not exceed last year's number. So fewer manufacturing jobs are likely to be created this year than last year.

Reasoning   *What function is served by the statement that any new manufacturing job is created either within an existing company or by the start-up of a new company? What function is served by the statement that the number of new jobs created this year will fall short of last year's record number?* The first statement makes explicit a general background assumption that manufacturing jobs are created in just two ways. This assumption is used, along with other information, to support the argument's main conclusion. The second statement gives the argument's main conclusion, a prediction about how this year's manufacturing-job creation will compare with last year's.

A   **Correct.** The first statement expresses a truism: assuming that all manufacturing jobs are created by companies, it is obviously true that all such jobs are created either by companies that already existed or by new companies that did not exist before. The argument then goes on to claim that new-job creation in each of these categories in the current year will be less than in the previous year. Since these two categories are exhaustive (as indicated in the first boldface portion), the argument concludes that new-job creation in the current year will be less than in the previous year. This is the argument's main conclusion (expressed in the second boldface portion).

B   The second statement is the argument's main conclusion, not an intermediate conclusion used to support the argument's main conclusion.

C   The second statement is the main conclusion of the argument, not a statement used as support for the main conclusion.

D   The argument merely asserts, and does not "seek to establish," the first statement. The first statement is a truism that does not need to be supported with evidence.

E   The second statement is the argument's main conclusion and is not meant to present a challenge to the first statement. The first statement serves to provide partial support for the argument's main conclusion.

The correct answer is A.

CR00827

751. In Stenland, many workers have been complaining that they cannot survive on minimum wage, the lowest wage an employer is permitted to pay. The government is proposing to raise the minimum wage. Many employers who pay their workers the current minimum wage argue that if it is raised, unemployment will increase because they will no longer be able to afford to employ as many workers.

Which of the following, if true in Stenland, most strongly supports the claim that raising the minimum wage there will not have the effects that the employers predict?

(A) For any position with wages below a living wage, the difficulty of finding and retaining employees adds as much to employment costs as would raising wages.

(B) Raising the minimum wage does not also increase the amount employers have to contribute in employee benefits.

(C) When inflation is taken into account, the proposed new minimum wage is not as high as the current one was when it was introduced.

(D) Many employees currently being paid wages at the level of the proposed new minimum wage will demand significant wage increases.

(E) Many employers who pay some workers only the minimum wage also pay other workers wages that are much higher than the minimum.

Argument Evaluation

Situation   Stenland's government proposes to raise the minimum wage because many workers have complained they cannot survive on it. But many employers claim that raising the minimum wage will increase unemployment.

Reasoning   *What evidence would most strongly suggest that raising the minimum wage will not increase unemployment?* The employers with minimum-wage workers implicitly reason that because raising the minimum wage will increase the wages they have to pay each worker, it will reduce the number of workers they can afford to employ, and thus will increase unemployment. Evidence that the increased wage would not actually increase the employers' expenses per employee would cast doubt on their prediction, as would evidence that reducing the number of minimum-wage workers would not increase the nation's overall unemployment rate.

A   **Correct.** This suggests that raising the minimum wage would make it easier for employers to find and retain minimum-wage employees, and that the savings would fully offset the cost of paying the higher wages. If there were such offsetting savings, the employers should still be able to afford to employ as many workers as they currently do.

B   Even if raising the minimum wage does not increase employers' costs for employee benefits, paying the higher wage might still in itself substantially increase employers' overall costs per employee.

C   For all we know, the current minimum wage might have substantially increased unemployment when it was introduced.

D   These additional demands would probably raise employers' overall costs per employee, making it more likely that increasing the minimum wage would increase overall unemployment.

E   Even if some workers receive more than the minimum wage, raising that wage could still raise employers' expenses for employing low-wage workers, making it too expensive for the employers to employ as many workers overall.

The correct answer is A.

CRO7810

752. Biologists with a predilection for theory have tried—and largely failed—to define what it is that makes something a living thing. Organisms take in energy-providing materials and excrete waste products, but so do automobiles. Living things replicate and take part in evolution, but so do some computer programs. We must be open to the possibility that there are living things on other planets. Therefore, we will not be successful in defining what it is that makes something a living thing merely by examining living things on Earth—the only ones we know. Trying to do so is analogous to trying to specify _____.

Which of the following most logically completes the passage?

(A) the laws of physics by using pure mathematics
(B) what a fish is by listing its chemical components
(C) what an animal is by examining a plant
(D) what a machine is by examining a sketch of it
(E) what a mammal is by examining a zebra

Argument Construction

Situation Some biologists have tried, unsuccessfully, to find a theoretically defensible account of what it means for something to be a living thing. Some of the suggested definitions are too broad because they include things that we would not regard as living. To find life on other planets, we must not narrow our conception of life by basing it simply on the kinds of life encountered on Earth.

Reasoning *Which of the answer choices would be the logically most appropriate completion of the argument?* The argument points out that life-forms elsewhere in the universe may be very different from any of the life-forms on Earth. Both life-forms on Earth and life-forms discovered elsewhere would all qualify as members of a very large class, the class of all life-forms. Taking life-forms on Earth, a mere subset of the class of all life-forms, as representative of all life-forms would be a logical mistake and might not lead to success in defining what it means for something to be a living thing. The correct answer choice, therefore, would involve a case of specifying what some general class of things is by examining the members of only a small, and not necessarily representative, subset of that class of things. In other words, the correct answer choice will involve the logical mistake of taking a subset as representative of a larger class.

A Pure mathematics is not a subset of the law of physics, so this does not involve the logical mistake of taking a subset as representative of a larger class.

B The chemical components of a fish are what make up the fish; they are not a small subset of the fish, so this does not involve the logical mistake of taking a subset as representative of a larger class.

C Plants are not a subset of the class of animals, so this does not involve the logical mistake of taking a subset as representative of a larger class.

D A sketch of a machine is not a subclass of the machine itself, so this does not involve the logical mistake of taking a subset as representative of a larger class.

E **Correct.** This involves the logical mistake of taking the class of zebras, a subclass of the class of mammals, as representative of the class of all mammals. Logically, it resembles taking the class of life-forms on Earth as representative of the class of all life-forms.

The correct answer is E.

CR74541.01

753. For the period from the eighth century through the eleventh century, the shifting boundaries between Kingdom F and Kingdom G have not been well charted. Although a certain village in a border region between the two kingdoms usually belonged to Kingdom G, ninth-century artifacts found in the village were in the typical Kingdom F style of that time. It is unclear whether the village was actually a part of Kingdom F in the ninth century or whether it was a part of Kingdom G but had merely adopted Kingdom F's artistic styles under Kingdom F's cultural influence.

Which of the following would, if found in ninth-century sites in the village, best help in determining whether the village was a part of Kingdom F or Kingdom G in the ninth century?

(A) A trading contract written in the Kingdom G dialect

(B) A drawing of a dwelling complex known to have existed on the border of Kingdom F and Kingdom G in the ninth century

(C) Knives and other utensils made from metal typical of ninth-century mining sites in Kingdom F

(D) Some fragments of pottery made in the Kingdom G style from the seventh century out of materials only found in Kingdom F

(E) Numerous teeth from the ninth century with a chemical signature typical only of teeth from people who had grown up in the heart of Kingdom F

Argument Construction

Situation   From the eighth century to the eleventh century, the boundaries between two kingdoms, F and G, shifted, but these shifts are not well documented. A certain village in a border region was usually part of Kingdom G, but ninth-century artifacts in the village are typical of the style of ninth-century artifacts from Kingdom F.

Reasoning   *What evidence, if it were found in the ninth-century sites in the village, would be most helpful in determining which of the two kingdoms the village was a part of during that century?* Information strongly indicating that during the ninth century the village was primarily settled by people clearly from Kingdom F would lend support to the claim that the village was part of Kingdom F in the ninth century.

A   A trading contract found at a ninth-century site in the village written in Kingdom G dialect would not settle whether the village was part of Kingdom G, because it could be the case that such a document would be written in that dialect even if the village were part of Kingdom F but regularly traded with Kingdom G.

B   Finding at a ninth-century site in the village a drawing of a dwelling complex known to have been on the border of Kingdom F and Kingdom G would not be useful in determining to which kingdom the village belonged at the time. We are not told in which kingdom that dwelling complex existed, and even if we were told, it could be that a villager in the other kingdom had a drawing of that complex for some reason (e.g., the villager could have had it because that complex was going to be attacked in a skirmish between the kingdoms).

C   Because there could have been trade between Kingdom F and Kingdom G, the fact that utensils made from metal typical of ninth-century mining sites in Kingdom F would not be very helpful in determining to which of the two kingdoms the village belonged in that century.

D   If fragments of pottery from the seventh century made in the Kingdom G style but from materials found only in Kingdom F were discovered, it would be unclear in which kingdom the pottery had been made. Given that the fragments may be from two centuries earlier than the period in question, and that we do not even know what kingdom the pottery was created in, these fragments would be of no use in determining to which kingdom the village belonged in the ninth century.

E   **Correct.** Although the mere presence of people from Kingdom F in the village would not provide strong support for the claim that the village was part of Kingdom F during the ninth century—the village could have shifted from Kingdom F to Kingdom G while maintaining much of its Kingdom F population—the presence of significant numbers of people from the heart of Kingdom F would support the claim that there was widespread migration of people from Kingdom F to the village. This is what one might reasonably expect if the village was part of Kingdom F during the ninth century. The discovery of numerous teeth that clearly belonged to people who grew up in the heart of Kingdom F in the ninth century would support the claim that many such people lived in the village during that century.

The correct answer is E.

CR02829

754. Sammy: For my arthritis, I am going to try my aunt's diet: large amounts of wheat germ and garlic. She was able to move more easily right after she started that diet.

Pat: When my brother began that diet, his arthritis got worse. But he has been doing much better since he stopped eating vegetables in the nightshade family, such as tomatoes and peppers.

Which of the following, if true, would provide a basis for explaining the fact that Sammy's aunt and Pat's brother had contrasting experiences with the same diet?

(A) A change in diet, regardless of the nature of the change, frequently brings temporary relief from arthritis symptoms.

(B) The compounds in garlic that can lessen the symptoms of arthritis are also present in tomatoes and peppers.

(C) Arthritis is a chronic condition whose symptoms improve and worsen from time to time without regard to diet.

(D) In general, men are more likely to have their arthritis symptoms alleviated by avoiding vegetables in the nightshade family than are women.

(E) People who are closely related are more likely to experience the same result from adopting a particular diet than are people who are unrelated.

Argument Construction

Situation   Sammy's aunt's arthritis apparently improved after she consumed large amounts of wheat germ and garlic. Pat's brother's arthritis deteriorated after he followed the same diet. Since he stopped eating vegetables in the nightshade family, such as tomatoes and peppers, his arthritis has improved.

Reasoning   *What could account for the fact that Sammy's aunt's arthritis improved and Pat's brother's arthritis got worse after they both followed the wheat germ and garlic diet?* The fact that a person has a health improvement following a diet is, by itself, very weak evidence for the claim that the diet caused the improvement. More generally, the fact that one event follows another is seldom, by itself, evidence that the earlier event caused the later. This applies to both the experience of Sammy's aunt and that of Pat's brother with the wheat germ and garlic diet.

A   In theory, this could be somewhat relevant to Sammy's aunt's experience but not to Pat's brother's experience. It is, however, insufficient to explain either.

B   Even if this is true, it might be the case that a large quantity of the compounds in question must be consumed in concentrated form to benefit arthritis. No evidence is given to indicate whether this is so. Regardless, the puzzle as to why the wheat germ and garlic diet was followed by arthritis improvement in one case and not in the other remains.

C   **Correct.** If we know there are typically fluctuations in the severity of arthritis symptoms and these can occur independent of diet, then the divergent experiences of the two people can be attributed to such fluctuations—even if it is conceded that some diets can affect arthritis symptoms in some manner. The wheat germ and garlic diet may, or may not, be such a diet.

D   This could throw light on Pat's brother's experience but not on Sammy's aunt's experience.

E   If this is correct, it is still far too general to provide a basis for explaining why the experiences of the two people were different. Does it apply to arthritis? We're not told. Nor are we told that it applies to the wheat germ and garlic diet. Is Pat's brother closely related to Sammy's aunt? We don't know.

The correct answer is C.

CR91630.02

755. In the 1960s, surveys of Florida's alligator population indicated that the population was dwindling rapidly. Hunting alligators was banned. By the early 1990s, the alligator population had recovered, and restricted hunting was allowed. Over the course of the 1990s, reports of alligators appearing on golf courses and lawns increased dramatically. Therefore, in spite of whatever alligator hunting went on, the alligator population must have increased significantly over the decade of the 1990s.

Which of the following, if true, most seriously weakens the argument?

(A) The human population of Florida increased significantly during the 1990s.

(B) The hunting restrictions applied to commercial as well as private hunters.

(C) The number of sightings of alligators in lakes and swamps increased greatly in Florida during the 1990s.

(D) Throughout the 1990s, selling alligator products was more strictly regulated than hunting was.

(E) Most of the sightings of alligators on golf courses and lawns in the 1990s occurred at times at which few people were present on those golf courses and lawns.

Argument Evaluation

Situation   In the 1960s, hunting alligators was banned in Florida to allow the alligator population to recover—as it did by the early 1990s. Then restricted hunting was allowed. But over the decade, reports of alligators appearing on golf courses and lawns increased greatly. The author of the argument concludes from this information that the alligator population must have increased significantly during the 1990s.

Reasoning   *What new piece of information would seriously weaken the argument?* Increased sightings of alligators could occur either because there are more alligators or because more people are seeing the ones that are there. Any information indicating an increase in the ratio of people to alligators in locations where the two species coexist could offer an alternative to the hypothesis that the alligator population increased.

A   **Correct.** The argument suggests that Florida is an area in which golf courses and lawns are common. A large rapid increase in the human population of such an area would probably lead to a significant increase in the number of golf courses and lawns, some of which would encroach on the alligators' habitats. Even without any increase in the overall number of alligators, this could lead to an increase in both the percentage of alligators that venture onto golf courses and lawns and the number of people who happen to be in such locations when alligators are present.

B   This information is peripheral to the issue we are being asked to address; it neither weakens nor strengthens the argument.

C   This information tends to strengthen, not weaken, the argument; it suggests that the frequency of reported sightings in other places was reliable and that the sightings indicated a surge in the alligator population.

D   To the extent that this is relevant, it could provide some weak support for the argument. Strictly regulating the sale of alligator products could deter alligator hunting by making it less profitable and could thus allow further increases in the alligator population.

E   Without further evidence, the net effect of this information cannot be reliably determined. On the one hand, if *sightings* is understood as elliptical for *reports of seeing alligators*, this could suggest that some of the reports may be dubious because they are not corroborated by additional observers. On the other hand, it suggests that the alligator population may in fact have increased. Times when few people are present are also times when wildlife such as alligators would be more likely to venture onto lawns and golf courses. Without any evidence that sightings before the 1990s did not typically occur in such conditions, this suggests that the number of alligators observable at those times increased in the 1990s.

The correct answer is A.

CR05756

756. Infotek, a computer manufacturer in Katrovia, has just introduced a new personal computer model that sells for significantly less than any other model. Market research shows, however, that very few Katrovian households without personal computers would buy a computer, regardless of its price. Therefore, introducing the new model is unlikely to increase the number of computers in Katrovian homes.

Which of the following is an assumption on which the argument depends?

(A) Infotek achieved the lower price of the new model by using components of lower quality than those used by other manufacturers.

(B) The main reason cited by consumers in Katrovia for replacing a personal computer is the desire to have an improved model.

(C) Katrovians in households that already have computers are unlikely to purchase the new Infotek model as an additional computer for home use.

(D) The price of other personal computers in Katrovia is unlikely to drop below the price of Infotek's new model in the near future.

(E) Most personal computers purchased in Katrovia are intended for home use.

Argument Construction

Situation   In Katrovia, a new personal computer model costs less than any other model. But market research shows that very few Katrovian households without personal computers would buy even cheap ones.

Reasoning   *What must be true in order for the stated facts to support the conclusion that introducing the new computer model is unlikely to increase the overall number of computers in Katrovian homes?* The market research supports the conclusion that no new computer model is likely to significantly increase the number of computers in Katrovian homes that currently lack computers. But the overall number of computers in Katrovian homes will still increase if Katrovian homes that already have computers buy additional computers while keeping their existing ones. So the argument has to assume that the new computer model will not increase the number of additional computers purchased for Katrovian homes that already have computers.

A   Even if Infotek used high-quality components in the new computer model, Katrovians might still refuse to buy it.

B   Replacing a personal computer does not change the overall number of personal computers in homes, so Katrovians' motives for replacing their computers are irrelevant to the argument.

C   **Correct.** As explained above, unless computers of the new model are purchased as additional computers for Katrovian homes that already have computers, the new model's introduction is unlikely to increase the overall number of computers in Katrovian homes.

D   The assumption that other personal computer prices would stay relatively high does not help establish the link between its premises and its conclusion. If answer choice D were false, the argument would be no weaker than it is without any consideration of other computers' potential prices.

E   If most personal computers purchased in Katrovia were not intended for home use, then the new model's introduction would be even less likely to increase the number of personal computers in Katrovian homes. So the argument does not depend on assuming that most of the computers purchased are for home use.

The correct answer is C.

CR05501

757. Fast-food restaurants make up 45 percent of all restaurants in Canatria. Customers at these restaurants tend to be young; in fact, studies have shown that the older people get, the less likely they are to eat in fast-food restaurants. Since the average age of the Canatrian population is gradually rising and will continue to do so, the number of fast-food restaurants is likely to decrease.

Which of the following, if true, most seriously weakens the argument?

(A) Fast-food restaurants in Canatria are getting bigger, so each one can serve more customers.

(B) Some older people eat at fast-food restaurants more frequently than the average young person.

(C) Many people who rarely eat in fast-food restaurants nevertheless eat regularly in restaurants.

(D) The overall population of Canatria is growing steadily.

(E) As the population of Canatria gets older, more people are eating at home.

Argument Evaluation

Situation In Canatria, the older people get, the less likely they are to eat in fast-food restaurants. The average age of Canatrians is increasing.

Reasoning *What evidence would most weaken the support provided by the cited facts for the prediction that the number of fast-food restaurants in Canatria is likely to decrease?* The argument implicitly reasons that since studies have shown that Canatrians tend to eat in fast-food restaurants less as they get older, and since Canatrians are getting older on average, the proportion of Canatrians eating in fast-food restaurants will decline. The argument assumes that this means the overall number of fast-food restaurant customers will decline and that demand will decrease enough to reduce the number of fast-food restaurants that can sustain profitability. Consequently, fewer new fast-food restaurants will open or more old ones will close, or both. Thus, the number of fast-food restaurants in Canatria will fall. Any evidence casting doubt on any inference in this chain of implicit reasoning will weaken the argument.

A   This strengthens the argument by providing additional evidence that the total number of fast-food restaurants will decrease. If the average number of customers per fast-food restaurant is increasing, then fewer fast-food restaurants will be needed to serve the same—or a lesser—number of customers.

B   Even if a few individuals do not follow the general trends described, those trends could still reduce the overall demand for and number of fast-food restaurants.

C   The argument is only about fast-food restaurants, not restaurants of other types.

D   Correct. This suggests that even if the proportion of Canatrians eating at fast-food restaurants declines, the total number doing so may not decline. Thus, the total demand for and profitability of fast-food restaurants may not decline either, so the total number of fast-food restaurants in Canatria may not decrease.

E   If anything, this strengthens the argument by pointing out an additional trend likely to reduce the demand for, and thus the number of, fast-food restaurants in Canatria.

The correct answer is D.

CR04805

758. Last year a chain of fast-food restaurants, whose menu had always centered on hamburgers, added its first vegetarian sandwich, much lower in fat than the chain's other offerings. Despite heavy marketing, the new sandwich accounts for a very small proportion of the chain's sales. The sandwich's sales would have to quadruple to cover the costs associated with including it on the menu. Since such an increase is unlikely, the chain would be more profitable if it dropped the sandwich.

Which of the following, if true, most seriously weakens the argument?

(A) Although many of the chain's customers have never tried the vegetarian sandwich, in a market research survey most of those who had tried it reported that they were very satisfied with it.

(B) Many of the people who eat at the chain's restaurants also eat at the restaurants of competing chains and report no strong preference among the competitors.

(C) Among fast-food chains in general, there has been little or no growth in hamburger sales over the past several years as the range of competing offerings at other restaurants has grown.

(D) When even one member of a group of diners is a vegetarian or has a preference for low-fat food, the group tends to avoid restaurants that lack vegetarian or low-fat menu options.

(E) An attempt by the chain to introduce a lower-fat hamburger failed several years ago, since it attracted few new customers and most of the chain's regular customers greatly preferred the taste of the regular hamburgers.

Argument Evaluation

Situation   Last year a fast-food restaurant chain specializing in hamburgers started offering a low-fat vegetarian sandwich and marketed it heavily. The new sandwich's sales are far too low to cover the costs associated with including it on the menu.

Reasoning   *What evidence would most weaken the support provided by the cited facts for the prediction that it would be more profitable for the chain to drop the sandwich?* The implicit argument is that since the new sandwich's sales are too low to cover the costs associated with including it on the menu, offering the sandwich diminishes the chain's profitability and will continue to do so if the sandwich continues to be offered. This reasoning assumes that the sandwich provides the chain no substantial indirect financial benefits except through its direct sales. It also assumes that the sandwich's sales will not increase sufficiently to make the sandwich a viable product. Any evidence casting doubt on either of these assumptions will weaken the argument.

A   This gives information only about the respondents to the survey who had tried the sandwich (possibly very few), who were probably already more open to liking a vegetarian sandwich than any of the chain's other customers. So their responses are probably unrepresentative of the chain's customers in general and do not suggest that the sandwich has enough market potential.

B   Although the issue of competition with other restaurants is not raised in the information provided, this new information, if anything, strengthens the argument, by suggesting that the introduction of the new sandwich has not significantly enhanced customer preference for eating at the restaurants that offer the new sandwich.

C   This suggests that the cause of stagnation in fast-food restaurants' hamburger sales has been competition from non-fast-food restaurants, but not that the non-fast-food restaurants competed by offering vegetarian options.

D   **Correct.** This suggests that even if the sandwich's sales are low, it may indirectly increase the chain's overall profits by encouraging large groups to eat at the chain.

E   This strengthens the argument by suggesting that the chain's customers are generally not interested in low-fat menu options such as the new sandwich.

The correct answer is D.

CR03727

759. Transportation expenses accounted for a large portion of the total dollar amount spent on trips for pleasure by residents of the United States in 1997, and about half of the total dollar amount spent on transportation was for airfare. However, the large majority of United States residents who took trips for pleasure in 1997 did not travel by airplane but used other means of transportation.

If the statements above are true, which of the following must also be true about United States residents who took trips for pleasure in 1997?

(A) Most of those who traveled by airplane did so because the airfare to their destination was lower than the cost of other available means of transportation.

(B) Most of those who traveled by airplane did so because other means of transportation to their destination were unavailable.

(C) Per mile traveled, those who traveled by airplane tended to spend more on transportation to their destination than did those who used other means of transportation.

(D) Overall, people who did not travel by airplane had lower average transportation expenses than people who did.

(E) Those who traveled by airplane spent about as much, on average, on other means of transportation as they did on airfare.

Argument Construction

Situation In 1997, about half of total transportation spending by U.S. residents taking trips for pleasure was for airfare. But the large majority of U.S. residents who took trips for pleasure in 1997 did not travel by airplane.

Reasoning *What can be deduced from the stated facts?* The information provided indicates that among U.S. residents who took trips for pleasure in 1997, those who traveled by airplane were a small minority. Yet this small minority's spending for airfare accounted for half of all transportation spending among residents taking trips for pleasure. It follows that on average, those who traveled by airplane must have spent far more per person on transportation than those who did not travel by airplane.

A This does not follow logically from the information given. Most of those who traveled by airplane may have done so even if flying was more expensive than other modes of transportation—for example, because flying was faster or more comfortable.

B This does not follow from the information given. Most of those who traveled by airplane may have done so even if many other modes of transportation were available—the other modes may all have been less desirable.

C This does not follow from the information given. Those who traveled by airplane may have traveled much farther on average than those who used other means of transportation, so their transportation spending per mile traveled need not have been greater.

D **Correct.** As explained above, those who traveled by airplane must have spent more per person on transportation than those who did not travel by airplane, on average. In other words, those who did not travel by airplane must have had lower average transportation expenses than those who did.

E This does not follow from the information given. Although half the total dollar spending on transportation was for airfare, much of the transportation spending that was not for airfare was by the large majority of U.S. residents who did not travel by airplane.

The correct answer is D.

CR12051

760. Voters commonly condemn politicians for being insincere, but politicians often must disguise their true feelings when they make public statements. If they expressed their honest views—about, say, their party's policies—then achieving politically necessary compromises would be much more difficult. Clearly, the very insincerity that people decry shows that our government is functioning well.

Which of the following, if true, most seriously undermines this reasoning?

(A) Achieving political compromises is not all that is necessary for the proper functioning of a government.

(B) Some political compromises are not in the best long-term interest of the government.

(C) Voters often judge politicians by criteria other than the sincerity with which they express their views.

(D) A political party's policies could turn out to be detrimental to the functioning of a government.

(E) Some of the public statements made by politicians about their party's policies could in fact be sincere.

Argument Evaluation

Situation   Politicians must often make insincere public statements because expressing their true feelings would make it harder for them to achieve politically necessary compromises.

Reasoning   *What would suggest that the argument's premises do not establish that politicians' insincerity shows our government is functioning well?* The implicit reasoning is that insincerity helps politicians achieve politically necessary compromises, and these compromises help our government to function well, so insincerity must show that our government is functioning well. Evidence that these necessary compromises do not ensure that our government functions well would undermine the argument's reasoning, as would evidence that politicians' insincerity has other substantial effects that hinder the government's functioning.

A   **Correct.** If governments may function poorly even when insincerity allows necessary political compromises to be made, then the argument's premises do not establish that politicians' insincerity shows our government is functioning well.

B   The argument does not require that all political compromises help government to function well, only that politically necessary compromises do.

C   Even if voters often judge politicians by criteria other than their sincerity, they may also often decry politicians' insincerity, not realizing or caring that such insincerity helps the government function well.

D   Even if a political party's policies impair the government's functioning, politically necessary compromises by politicians in that party could improve the government's functioning.

E   Even if politicians sometimes speak sincerely about their party's policies, their general willingness to be insincere as needed to achieve politically necessary compromises could be a sign that the government is functioning well.

The correct answer is A.

Questions 761 to 817 - Difficulty: **Hard**

CR09760.02

761. Duckbill dinosaurs, like today's monitor lizards, had particularly long tails, which they could whip at considerable speed. Monitor lizards use their tails to strike predators. However, although duckbill tails were otherwise very similar to those of monitor lizards, the duckbill's tailbones were proportionately much thinner and thus more delicate. Moreover, to ward off their proportionately much larger predators, duckbills would have had to whip their tails considerably faster than monitor lizards do.

The information given, if accurate, provides the strongest support for which of the following hypotheses?

(A) If duckbills whipped their tails faster than monitor lizards do, the duckbill's tail would have been effective at warding off the duckbills' fiercest predators.

(B) Duckbills used their tails to strike predators, and their tailbones were frequently damaged from the impact.

(C) Using their tails was not the only means duckbills had for warding off predators.

(D) Duckbills were at much greater risk of being killed by a predator than monitor lizards are.

(E) The tails of duckbills, if used to ward off predators, would have been more likely than the tails of monitor lizards to sustain damage from the impact.

Argument Construction

Situation   Duckbill dinosaur tails were like the tails of contemporary monitor lizards in that they were very long. They differed, though, in that their tailbones were much thinner and more delicate than monitor lizards' tailbones. Monitor lizards use their tails to strike predators. If duckbills did so, they would have had to whip their tails much faster, as their predators were proportionately much larger.

Reasoning   *Which hypothesis is most strongly supported by the given information?* The information states that duckbills would have had to whip their tails much faster than monitor lizards do to ward off their proportionately larger predators, but their tailbones were more delicate. It would be reasonable to conclude, then, that duckbills' tails would have been more likely to sustain damage if used to ward off predators than monitor lizards' tails are.

A   The information gives us little reason to be confident that duckbills would have been effective at warding off their fiercest predators even if they whipped their tails faster than monitor lizards do. Note that we are not even told how effective monitor lizards are at warding off particularly fierce predators.

B   The information gives us both a reason to think that duckbills might have used their tails to strike predators—their tails are similar in length to the tails of monitor lizards, which are used to strike predators—and reasons to think they might not have done so—their tailbones were much thinner and more delicate than monitor lizards' tailbones, and they would have had to whip their tails much faster than monitor lizards whip theirs. Therefore, the support for this answer choice is not very strong.

C   The information does give some modest support for the claim that duckbills' tails would not provide a particularly good defense against their predators. This suggests weakly that they had other defenses against their predators. Note, though, that this answer choice, as worded, entails that duckbills *did* use their tails as a defense; it was simply not the only defense. But the information on which we are to base the hypothesis is compatible with duckbills not having used their tails to ward off predators.

D   The information does not give much support for this answer choice. It could be that duckbills had other effective defenses against their predators. Perhaps they were fast, or had sharp claws.

E   **Correct.** As noted above, duckbills would have had to whip their tails much faster than monitor lizards do to ward off their proportionately larger predators, but their tailbones were more delicate, so duckbills' tails would have been more likely to sustain damage if used to ward off predators than monitor lizards' tails are.

The correct answer is E.

CR00860.02

762. In an attempt to produce a coffee plant that would yield beans containing no caffeine, the synthesis of a substance known to be integral to the initial stages of caffeine production was blocked either in the beans, in the leaves, or both. For those plants in which synthesis of the substance was blocked only in the leaves, the resulting beans contained no caffeine.

Any of the following, if true, would provide the basis for an explanation of the observed results EXCEPT:

(A) In coffee plants, the substance is synthesized only in the leaves and then moves to the beans, where the initial stages of caffeine production take place.

(B) In coffee plants, the last stage of caffeine production takes place in the beans using a compound that is produced only in the leaves by the substance.

(C) In coffee plants, the initial stages of caffeine production take place only in the beans, but later stages depend on another substance that is synthesized only in the leaves and does not depend on the blocked substance.

(D) In coffee plants, caffeine production takes place only in the leaves, but the caffeine then moves to the beans.

(E) Caffeine was produced in the beans of the modified coffee plants, but all of it moved to the leaves, which normally produce their own caffeine.

Argument Evaluation

Situation   The synthesis of a substance integral to the initial production of caffeine was blocked only in the beans of some coffee plants, only in the leaves of others, and in both the beans and leaves of yet other coffee plants. No caffeine was found in beans from the plants in which the synthesis of the substance was blocked only in the leaves.

Reasoning   *Which claim would NOT form the basis for an explanation of the observed results?* There are many possible explanations. For instance, the results could be explained by any claim that indicates (1) that the substance integral to the initial production of caffeine is synthesized only in the leaves, or (2) that the substance is also produced in the beans but, when it is blocked from being produced in the leaves, that substance or the caffeine that is produced in the beans is entirely depleted from the beans. However, the observed results would *not* be explained by any claim that (1) indicates that the early stages of caffeine synthesis can occur in the beans, entailing that the crucial substance is present in the beans even when it is blocked in the leaves, and (2) provides no explanation for why blocking the crucial substance in the leaves would prevent the completion of the caffeine synthesis in the beans.

A   If a substance that is integral to the initial production of caffeine is produced only in the leaves, and that production has been blocked, then the observed results are to be expected.

B   If the last stage of caffeine production requires a compound that is produced in the leaves by a substance the synthesis of which is blocked in the leaves, then the observed results are to be expected.

C   **Correct.** Suppose the initial stages of caffeine production take place in the beans. The substance integral to those initial stages must therefore be present in the beans. But this does not tell us whether that substance is synthesized in the beans or elsewhere. It does tell us that some other substance that plays a part in the production of caffeine is synthesized in the leaves, but we are not told that the synthesis of that substance is blocked. Therefore, this answer choice does not give us reason to expect the observed results, and so does not serve as the basis for an explanation of those results.

D   Suppose we know that caffeine production in coffee plants takes place entirely in the leaves but at least some of the caffeine migrates from there to the beans. Then, if the synthesis of a substance that is integral to the initial production of caffeine is blocked in the leaves, it seems reasonable to expect the observed results.

E   If caffeine is normally produced in both the leaves and the beans of a coffee plant, but all the caffeine produced in the beans will migrate from the beans to the leaves if for any reason caffeine is not produced in the leaves, then it is reasonable to expect the observed results.

The correct answer is C.

CR20170.02

763. Which of the following most logically completes the passage?

Laminated glass is much harder to break than the glass typically used in the windows of cars driven in Relnia. It is more difficult for thieves to break into cars with laminated glass windows than into cars with ordinary glass windows, and laminated glass windows are less likely to break in a collision. Nevertheless, considerations of security and safety do not unambiguously support a proposal to require that in Relnia all glass installed in cars be laminated glass, since _____ .

(A) most people cannot visually distinguish laminated glass from the glass typically used for car windows

(B) a significant proportion of cars driven in Relnia are manufactured elsewhere

(C) some cars in Relnia already have laminated glass in their windows

(D) the rates of car theft and of collisions have both fallen slightly in Relnia in recent years

(E) there are times when breaking a car's window is the best way to provide timely help for people trapped inside

Argument Construction

Situation   Laminated glass is much more difficult to break than the glass that is typically used in car windows in Relnia and, when used in a car window, makes it harder for thieves to break into the car and is less likely to shatter in collisions.

Reasoning   *What claim, despite the given information, most helps support the conclusion that considerations of security and safety do not unambiguously support a proposal to require that in Relnia all glass installed in cars be laminated glass? If there are any significant safety or security problems that would arise from having laminated glass, this would count against the proposal. For instance, sometimes it is essential to break a car's window to help people trapped in the car.*

A   None of the security-or safety-related characteristics of laminated glass discussed in the argument depend on laminated glass being visually distinguishable from the glass typically used for car windows. Therefore, this answer choice does not help justify the conclusion and so would not logically complete the passage.

B   Even if most cars in Relnia are manufactured elsewhere, there may be no reason not to require that all glass installed in cars in Relnia be laminated glass.

C   Whether some cars, no cars, or all cars currently in Relnia have laminated glass in their windows is irrelevant to whether it is a good idea to require that all glass installed in cars in Relnia be laminated glass.

D   Even if rates of car theft and of collision have fallen, that does not mean they could not fall further if laminated glass were required. In fact, we are not told why they fell. Could it be that more cars in Relnia had windows made of laminated glass, and that this led to these reduced rates?

E   **Correct.** This answer choice provides a reason to think that sometimes, for the security or safety of passengers in cars, it might be better not to have all the windows of every car made of laminated glass. Therefore, it logically completes the passage.

The correct answer is E.

CR65030.02

764. Consultant: **Ace Repairs ends up having to redo a significant number of the complex repair jobs it undertakes, but when those repairs are redone, they are invariably done right**. Since we have established that there is no systematic difference between the mechanics who are assigned to do the initial repairs and those who are assigned to redo unsatisfactory jobs, we must reject the hypothesis that mistakes made in the initial repairs are due to the mechanics' lack of competence. Rather, it is likely that **complex repairs require a level of focused attention that the company's mechanics apply consistently only to repair jobs that have not been done right on the first try.**

In the consultant's reasoning, the two portions in **boldface** play which of the following roles?

(A) The first is the consultant's main conclusion; the second provides evidence in support of that main conclusion.

(B) The first is evidence that serves as the basis for rejecting one explanation of a certain finding; the second is the consultant's own explanation of that finding.

(C) The first is a claim whose truth is at issue in the reasoning; the second provides evidence to show that the claim is true.

(D) The first presents a contrast whose explanation is at issue in the reasoning; the second is the consultant's explanation of that contrast.

(E) The first presents a contrast whose explanation is at issue in the reasoning; the second is evidence that has been used to challenge the consultant's explanation of that contrast.

Argument Construction

Situation   The following information is attributed to a consultant: Some complex repair jobs done by Ace Repairs have to be redone. The repairs, when redone, are usually successful. But the mechanics who do the initial repairs and any others who redo those repairs are, overall, competent to do the repairs successfully.

Reasoning   *What role in the consultant's reasoning do the boldfaced statements play?* The consultant's first sentence describes a phenomenon that could be puzzling and needs explanation. One might be inclined to argue that the mechanics who redo the repairs are more competent than those who did the initial repairs. But the second boldfaced statement rebuts this explanation by telling us that it has been *established* that there are no systematic differences in competence. The final sentence of the consultant's reasoning puts forward another explanation: that the redoing of a repair elicits from mechanics a higher level of focused attention than did the performance of the initial repair.

A   The first describes a puzzling phenomenon for which the consultant seeks an explanation. It is not presented as a conclusion, i.e., a statement that is asserted on the basis of other statements. The second is not a statement presented *in support of* the first; it gives an explanation offered by the consultant for the puzzling phenomenon described in the first boldfaced portion.

B   The first describes a puzzling phenomenon for which the consultant seeks an explanation, and it is not offered to show that a certain explanation does not fit. The second gives the consultant's own explanation of that finding.

C   The reasoning does not question the accuracy of the first boldfaced portion; that portion is a description of a phenomenon that the consultant believes needs explanation. The second is not meant as evidence to indicate that the first is true; rather, it is offered as an explanation for the puzzling phenomenon described in the first.

D   Correct. The first boldfaced portion contrasts the success of repairs that are redone with the failure of those repairs when they were first done. The second gives an explanation proposed by the consultant for the difference.

E   The first contrasts the success of repairs that are redone with the failure of those repairs when they were first done. Rather than giving evidence to challenge the consultant's explanation, the second provides that explanation itself.

The correct answer is D.

CR06728
765. To reduce waste of raw materials, the government of Sperland is considering requiring household appliances to be broken down for salvage when discarded. To cover the cost of salvage, the government is planning to charge a fee, which would be imposed when the appliance is first sold. Imposing the fee at the time of salvage would reduce waste more effectively, however, because consumers tend to keep old appliances longer if they are faced with a fee for discarding them.

Which of the following, if true, most seriously weakens the argument?

(A) Increasing the cost of disposing of an appliance properly increases the incentive to dispose of it improperly.

(B) The fee provides manufacturers with no incentive to produce appliances that are more durable.

(C) For people who have bought new appliances recently, the salvage fee would not need to be paid for a number of years.

(D) People who sell their used, working appliances to others would not need to pay the salvage fee.

(E) Many nonfunctioning appliances that are currently discarded could be repaired at relatively little expense.

Evaluation of a Plan

Situation   A government is considering requiring household appliances to be broken down for salvage when discarded. To cover the salvage costs, the government plans to charge a fee on appliance sales.

Reasoning   *What would suggest that charging the fee at the time of salvage would less effectively reduce waste than charging the fee at the time of sale would?* The argument is that charging the fee at the time of salvage would reduce waste of raw materials because it would encourage consumers to keep their appliances longer before salvaging them. This argument could be weakened by pointing out other factors that might increase waste if the fee is charged at the time of salvage or reduce waste if the fee is charged at the time of sale.

A   **Correct.** This suggests that charging the fee at the time of salvage rather than the time of sale would encourage consumers to discard their appliances illegally, thereby increasing waste of raw materials by reducing the proportion of discarded appliances that are salvaged.

B   This factor would remain the same regardless of whether the fee was charged at the time of sale or the time of salvage.

C   This might be a reason for consumers to prefer the fee be charged at the time of salvage rather than the time of sale, but it does not suggest that charging the fee at the time of salvage would reduce waste less effectively.

D   This provides an additional reason to expect that charging the fee at the time of salvage would help reduce waste, so it strengthens rather than weakens the argument.

E   This would give consumers an additional reason to keep using their old appliances and postpone paying a fee at the time of salvage, so it strengthens rather than weakens the argument.

The correct answer is A.

CR02866

766. When there is less rainfall than normal, the water level of Australian rivers falls and the rivers flow more slowly. Because algae whose habitat is river water grow best in slow-moving water, the amount of algae per unit of water generally increases when there has been little rain. By contrast, however, following a period of extreme drought, algae levels are low even in very slow-moving river water.

Which of the following, if true, does most to explain the contrast described above?

(A) During periods of extreme drought, the populations of some of the species that feed on algae tend to fall.

(B) The more slowly water moves, the more conducive its temperature is to the growth of algae.

(C) When algae populations reach very high levels, conditions within the river can become toxic for some of the other species that normally live there.

(D) Australian rivers dry up completely for short intervals in periods of extreme drought.

(E) Except during periods of extreme drought, algae levels tend to be higher in rivers in which the flow has been controlled by damming than in rivers that flow freely.

Argument Construction

Situation   When Australian rivers flow slowly due to little rain, algae populations in those rivers increase. But after periods of extreme drought, algae levels are low even in water moving at speeds that would normally show population increases.

Reasoning   *What would explain the contrast between algae levels in slow-moving water resulting from little rain and slow-moving water after a drought?* There must be some difference between what happens during periods in which there is simply less rainfall than normal and periods in which there is extreme drought, a difference that affects the algae population.

A   This indicates one of the consequences of drought, and slightly suggests that this might be due to a lower algae level. But it does nothing to explain why algae levels might be lower after a drought.

B   This could explain why some rivers that are slow-moving and have little water might have a high algae level—but not why the algae level is low in such rivers after a period of drought.

C   This explains why levels of other species might be low when algae populations are high, not why algae populations are high when there is little rain, but low following a period of extreme drought.

D   Correct. This statement properly identifies something that helps explain the contrast. According to the information given, the habitat of the algae under discussion is river water. If the river dries up, the algae will probably not survive. Then after the drought, algae population levels would likely take a while to rise again.

E   This emphasizes that there is a contrast between what happens to algae during periods of extreme drought and what happens to them at other times, but it does not help explain that contrast.

The correct answer is D.

CR04924
767. Increased use of incineration is sometimes advocated as a safe way to dispose of chemical waste. But opponents of incineration point to the 40 incidents involving unexpected releases of dangerous chemical agents that were reported just last year at two existing incinerators commissioned to destroy a quantity of chemical waste material. Since designs for proposed new incinerators include no additional means of preventing such releases, leaks will only become more prevalent if use of incineration increases.

Which of the following, if true, most seriously weakens the argument?

(A) At the two incinerators at which leaks were reported, staff had had only cursory training on the proper procedures for incinerating chemical waste.

(B) Other means of disposing of chemical waste, such as chemical neutralization processes, have not been proven safer than incineration.

(C) The capacity of existing incinerators is sufficient to allow for increased incineration of chemical waste without any need for new incinerators.

(D) The frequency of reports of unexpected releases of chemical agents at newly built incinerators is about the same as the frequency at older incinerators.

(E) In only three of the reported incidents of unexpected chemical leaks did the releases extend outside the property on which the incinerators were located.

Argument Evaluation

Situation   Last year, at two chemical waste incinerators, there were forty reported incidents involving unexpected releases of dangerous chemicals. Designs for proposed new incinerators include no additional safeguards against such releases. Therefore, increased use of incineration will likely make such releases more prevalent.

Reasoning   *What would undermine the support provided for the conclusion that leaks will become more prevalent if more chemical waste is disposed of through incineration?* The argument draws a general conclusion about chemical waste incineration from evidence about only two particular incinerators. This reasoning would be undermined by any evidence that the leaks at those two incinerators were the result of something other than insufficient safeguards against such releases.

A   **Correct.** If the staff training at the two incinerators was cursory, then the leaks may have been the results of staff not knowing how to use safeguards with which the incinerators are equipped that, if properly used, would have prevented the release of dangerous chemicals. Therefore, if staff at newer incinerators will be better trained, leaks might not become more prevalent even if chemical waste incineration becomes more common.

B   Other chemical waste disposal methods may be safer than incineration even if no one has proven so; and even if they're not safer overall, they may involve fewer leaks.

C   Continuing to use existing incinerators might well produce just as many leaks as switching to new incinerators would.

D   This suggests that new incinerators produce as many leaks as older incinerators do, a finding that provides additional evidence that increased incineration even with proposed new incinerators would lead to more leaks.

E   The argument is not about how far the releases from leaks extend, only about how many of them are likely to occur.

The correct answer is A.

CR10049

768. Public health expert: **Increasing the urgency of a public health message may be counterproductive**. In addition to irritating the majority who already behave responsibly, **it may undermine all government pronouncements on health by convincing people that such messages are overly cautious**. And there is no reason to believe that those who ignore measured voices will listen to shouting.

The two sections in **boldface** play which of the following roles in the public health expert's argument?

(A) The first is a conclusion for which support is provided, but is not the argument's main conclusion; the second is an unsupported premise supporting the argument's main conclusion.

(B) The first is a premise supporting the only explicit conclusion; so is the second.

(C) The first is the argument's main conclusion; the second supports that conclusion and is itself a conclusion for which support is provided.

(D) The first is a premise supporting the argument's only conclusion; the second is that conclusion.

(E) The first is the argument's only explicit conclusion; the second is a premise supporting that conclusion.

Argument Construction

Situation   A public health expert argues against increasing the urgency of public health messages by pointing out negative effects that may arise from such an increase, as well as by questioning its efficacy.

Reasoning   *What roles are played in the argument by the two claims in boldface?* The first claim in boldface states that increasing the urgency of public health messages may be counterproductive. After making this claim, the public health expert mentions two specific reasons this could be so: it could irritate people who already behave responsibly, and it could convince people that all public health messages are too cautious. (The latter reason in the second claim in boldface). The phrase [i]n *addition to* indicates that neither claim in the second sentence is intended to support or explain the other. However, since each claim in the second sentence gives a reason to believe the claim in the first sentence, each independently supports the first sentence as a conclusion. The word [a]nd beginning the third sentence reveals that its intended role in the argument is the same as that of the two claims in the second sentence.

A   Everything stated after the first sentence is intended to help support it, so the first sentence is the argument's main conclusion.

B   Everything stated after the first sentence is intended to help support it, so the first sentence is a conclusion, not a premise.

C   Each of the three claims in the second and third sentences is presented as an independent reason to accept the general claim in the first sentence. Therefore, nothing in the passage is intended to support the second statement in boldface as a conclusion.

D   Everything stated after the first sentence is intended to help support it, so the first sentence is a conclusion, not a premise.

E   **Correct.** Each of the three claims in the second and third sentences is presented as an independent reason to accept the general claim in the first sentence. Thus, each of those claims is a premise supporting the claim in the first sentence as the argument's only conclusion.

The correct answer is E.

CR01163

769. Several industries have recently switched at least partly from older technologies powered by fossil fuels to new technologies powered by electricity. It is thus evident that less fossil fuel is being used as a result of the operations of these industries than would have been used if these industries had retained their older technologies.

Which of the following, if true, most strengthens the argument above?

(A) Many of the industries that have switched at least partly to the new technologies have increased their output.

(B) Less fossil fuel was used to manufacture the machinery employed in the new technologies than was originally used to manufacture the machinery employed in the older technologies.

(C) More electricity is used by those industries that have switched at least partly to the new technologies than by those industries that have not switched.

(D) Some of the industries that have switched at least partly to the new technologies still use primarily technologies that are powered by fossil fuels.

(E) The amount of fossil fuel used to generate the electricity needed to power the new technologies is less than the amount that would have been used to power the older technologies.

Argument Evaluation

Situation   Several industries have now switched, at least partly, to technologies using electricity rather than fossil fuels. Thus, less fossil fuel will be consumed as a result of the operation of these industries than otherwise would have been.

Reasoning   *Which option most strengthens the argument?* One way to strengthen an argument is to eliminate or minimize one of its flaws or weaknesses. Because the conclusion is stated in terms of "fossil fuel consumed as a result of the operation of these industries," the claim would encompass even any fossil fuel that might be used to generate the electricity that the newer technologies use. Yet the premise of the argument does not address this issue. So the argument is strengthened if it turns out that less fossil fuel was used to produce the electricity than would have been used to power the older technologies.

A   In an indirect way, this answer choice slightly weakens rather than strengthens the argument. For if fossil fuels are used to produce the electricity now used by the industries and if it is because of these newer technologies that output has increased, the argument's conclusion is less likely.

B   It does not matter how much fossil fuel was used to manufacture the older technologies originally. That has no bearing on whether more fossil fuel would have been expended as a result of the continued operation of the industries if the partial switch to newer technologies had not occurred.

C   This is what we would expect, but it in no way strengthens the argument.

D   This may seem to weaken the argument by indicating that the switch from older technologies will have less of an impact on fossil fuel consumption by these industries than we might have assumed. But since the conclusion makes no claim about how much consumption has been reduced, it is not clear that this option has any bearing on the strength of the argument one way or the other.

E   **Correct.** As explained in the Reasoning section above, the conclusion is stated in terms of "fossil fuel consumed as a result of the operation of these industries," so the claim would encompass even any fossil fuel that might be used to generate the electricity that the newer technologies use. If at least as much fossil fuel must be used to generate the needed electricity, the conclusion that less fossil fuel is used does not follow. Yet the premise of the argument does not address this issue. So the argument is strengthened if it turns out that less fossil fuel is used to produce the electricity than would have been used to power the older technologies.

The correct answer is E.

CR00792

770. The difference in average annual income in favor of employees who have college degrees, compared with those who do not have such degrees, doubled between 1980 and 1990. Some analysts have hypothesized that increased competition between employers for employees with college degrees drove up income for such employees.

Which of the following, if true, most seriously undermines the explanation described above?

(A) During the 1980s a growing percentage of college graduates, unable to find jobs requiring a college degree, took unskilled jobs.

(B) The average age of all employees increased slightly during the 1980s.

(C) The unemployment rate changed very little throughout most of the 1980s.

(D) From 1980 to 1990 the difference in average income between employees with advanced degrees and those with bachelor's degrees also increased.

(E) During the 1980s there were some employees with no college degree who earned incomes comparable to the top incomes earned by employees with a college degree.

Argument Evaluation

Situation   The amount by which average annual income for employees with college degrees exceeds that for employees without such degrees doubled between 1980 and 1990.

Reasoning   *What evidence would most strongly suggest that increased competition among employers for employees with college degrees does not explain the relative increase in those employees' incomes?* Such increased competition could not explain the relative increase in income for employees with college degrees if the competition did not actually increase, or if such competition occurred but did not result in employers paying higher wages or salaries, or if the increase in competition to hire employees without college degrees was even greater. So evidence that any of those conditions existed would undermine the analysts' explanation.

A   **Correct.** This suggests that the supply of college graduates grew relative to employers' demand for them, and hence that employers' competition for college-educated employees did not actually increase.

B   The average age might have increased equally for employees with college degrees and for those without them, so the increase is not clearly relevant to explaining why the difference between these two groups' average incomes grew.

C   Even if the overall unemployment rate did not change, competition for college-educated employees could have increased while competition for other employees decreased.

D   This statement gives information comparing income trends among two groups of those with college degrees, and is irrelevant to the comparison of income trends for those with college degrees and those without college degrees.

E   Even if there was strong competition and high pay for certain unusual types of employees without college degrees, increasing competition for employees with college degrees might have explained the overall growing difference in average pay between employees with college degrees and those without.

The correct answer is A.

CR01239

771. Which of the following most logically completes the passage?

According to the last pre-election poll in Whippleton, most voters believe that the three problems government needs to address, in order of importance, are pollution, crime, and unemployment. Yet in the election, candidates from parties perceived as strongly against pollution were defeated, while those elected were all from parties with a history of opposing legislation designed to reduce pollution. These results should not be taken to indicate that the poll was inaccurate, however, since _____.

(A) some voters in Whippleton do not believe that pollution needs to be reduced

(B) every candidate who was defeated had a strong antipollution record

(C) there were no issues other than crime, unemployment, and pollution on which the candidates had significant differences of opinion

(D) all the candidates who were elected were perceived as being stronger against both crime and unemployment than the candidates who were defeated

(E) many of the people who voted in the election refused to participate in the poll

Argument Construction

Situation   A pre-election poll indicated that most voters believed the three problems government needs to address, in order of importance, are pollution, crime, and unemployment. But in the election, candidates from parties with a history of opposing anti-pollution legislation beat candidates from parties perceived as more strongly against pollution.

Reasoning   *What would most help explain how the poll might have been accurate despite the election results?* Since the poll indicated that voters were most concerned about pollution, it suggested that candidates from anti-pollution parties would be more likely to be elected, other things being equal—and yet those candidates were not elected. There are many possible explanations for this outcome that are compatible with the poll having been accurate. For example, voters might have been swayed by the candidates' personalities, qualifications, or advertising more than by their positions on the issues. Or some candidates might have convinced voters that their personal positions on the issues were different from those of their parties. Or voters might have chosen candidates based on their positions on crime and unemployment, considering those issues together more important than pollution alone. Any statement suggesting that any such factors explained the election results would logically complete the passage by providing a reason to believe that the poll could have been accurate despite those results.

A   If the number of voters who did not believe that pollution needed to be reduced was large enough to explain the election results, then the poll was probably inaccurate. So this does not explain how the poll might have been accurate despite those results.

B   This eliminates the possibility that candidates were defeated for having weak antipollution records conflicting with their parties' antipollution stances, so it eliminates one explanation of how the poll might have been accurate despite the election results. Thus, it slightly weakens the conclusion of the argument instead of providing a premise to support it.

C   This eliminates the possibility that differences of opinion among the candidates on these other issues might explain the election results, but it does not explain how the poll could have been accurate despite the election results.

D   **Correct.** The poll indicated that voters believed that the government needs to address crime and unemployment as well as pollution. So if the poll was accurate, the election outcome might have resulted from voters considering candidates' positions on crime and unemployment to be jointly more important than their positions on pollution.

E   If anything, this provides a reason to doubt that the poll accurately reflected voters' opinions. It does not explain how the poll might have accurately reflected those opinions despite the election results.

The correct answer is D.

CR01153

772. Manufacturing plants in Arundia have recently been acquired in substantial numbers by investors from abroad. Arundian politicians are proposing legislative action to stop such investment, justifying the proposal by arguing that foreign investors, opportunistically exploiting a recent fall in the value of the Arundian currency, were able to buy Arundian assets at less than their true value.

Which of the following, if true, casts the most serious doubt on the adequacy of the Arundian politicians' justification for the proposed legislation?

(A) The Arundian government originally welcomed the fall in the value of the Arundian currency because the fall made Arundian exports more competitive on international markets.

(B) Foreign investors who acquired Arundian manufacturing plants generally did so with no intention of keeping and running those plants over the long term.

(C) Without the recent fall in the value of the Arundian currency, many of the Arundian assets bought by foreign investors would have been beyond the financial reach of those investors.

(D) In Concordia, a country broadly similar to Arundia, the share of manufacturing assets that is foreign-controlled is 60 percent higher than it is in Arundia.

(E) The true value of an investment is determined by the value of the profits from it, and the low value of the Arundian currency has depressed the value of any profits earned by foreign investors from Arundian assets.

Argument Evaluation

Situation   After a recent fall in the value of Arundian currency, foreign investors have been acquiring many Arundian manufacturing plants. Arundian politicians are proposing legislation to stop such investment.

Reasoning   *What would most undermine the Arundian politicians' justification for the proposed legislation?* The politicians are justifying their proposal by claiming that foreign investors have been exploiting the fall in the currency's value by buying Arundian assets at less than their *true value* (whatever that means). Any evidence that their claim is false or meaningless would undermine their justification for the proposal, as would any evidence that the claim, even if true, does not provide a good reason to stop the foreign investments.

A   This suggests that the foreign investors got a good deal on the manufacturing plants, since it provides evidence that those plants will now be more competitive and profitable. So, if anything, it supports the politicians' justification for their proposal rather than undermining it.

B   This suggests that the foreign investors generally believe the manufacturing plants are undervalued, and intend to sell them at a profit as soon as the currency rises enough. So it supports the politicians' justification for their proposal rather than undermining it.

C   This suggests that the recent fall in the currency's value made Arundian assets cost less than usual for foreign investors, thus arguably allowing the investors to buy the assets at less than their *true value*. So, if anything, it supports the politicians' justification for their proposal rather than undermining it.

D   The Arundian politicians might consider the example of Concordia to be a warning of the disaster that could befall Arundia unless the legislation is enacted. So the situation in Concordia might be cited as support for the politicians' justification of their proposal.

E   **Correct.** This implies that the fall in the Arundian currency's value has reduced the *true value* of Arundian manufacturing plants and any profits they may make, so it undermines the politicians' claim that the foreign investors exploited the fall in the currency's value to acquire the plants for less than their *true value*.

The correct answer is E.

CR27430.02

773. Proposal: Carbon dioxide and methane in the atmosphere block the escape of heat into space. So emission of these "greenhouse" gases contributes to global warming. In order to reduce global warming, emission of greenhouse gases needs to be reduced. Therefore, the methane now emitted from open landfills should instead be burned to produce electricity.

Objection: The burning of methane generates carbon dioxide that is released into the atmosphere.

Which of the following, if true, most adequately counters the objection made to the proposal?

(A) Every time a human being or other mammal exhales, there is some carbon dioxide released into the air.

(B) The conversion of methane to electricity would occur at a considerable distance from the landfills.

(C) The methane that is used to generate electricity would generally be used as a substitute for a fuel that does not produce any greenhouse gases when burned.

(D) Methane in the atmosphere is more effective in blocking the escape of heat from the Earth than is carbon dioxide.

(E) The amount of methane emitted from the landfills could be reduced if the materials whose decomposition produces methane were not discarded, but recycled.

Evaluation of a Plan

Situation   The greenhouse gases methane and carbon dioxide trap heat in Earth's atmosphere and warm the planet. To reduce that global warming, emission of these gases needs to be reduced. For these reasons, someone has proposed that the methane emitted from landfills should be captured and burned to produce electricity. However, an objection to the proposal is that burning methane causes the release of carbon dioxide (another greenhouse gas) into the atmosphere.

Reasoning   *What would be a logically effective response to counter the objection to the proposal?* It is true that burning methane causes the release of carbon dioxide. However, if burning methane from landfills to generate electricity helps reduce net global warming, then the objection would not provide a good reason for rejecting the proposal. It turns out that, as a greenhouse gas, methane has a much more powerful impact on global warming than does carbon dioxide. This fact provides strong support for rejecting the objection to the proposal.

A   Clearly the effects referred to here are unavoidable in the lives of humans and other mammals on Earth. The emissions that must be curtailed to avoid global warming are those that are avoidable as a result of voluntary human activity.

B   This suggests that there could be costs in implementing the proposal, but the possibility of such costs does not, by itself, counter the proposal. Such costs could presumably be reduced by better siting of landfills and electricity-generation plants.

C   This information, if true, would not counter the objection and would provide some support for it. We would still need some reason to believe that allowing carbon dioxide emissions from burning methane would be better than continuing to release methane itself. In the absence of such a reason, we should expect no net greenhouse-gas-related benefit in substituting the landfill-emitted methane for a fuel that produces no greenhouse gases.

D   **Correct.** This information provides a strong rebuttal of the objection. Since methane has more powerful global-warming effects than does carbon dioxide, there is a net greenhouse-gas-reduction benefit in generating electricity by burning methane from landfills even though that burning itself emits the greenhouse gas carbon dioxide.

E   Undoubtedly it would be better to reduce the amount of methane that landfills will generate in the future. However, the possibility of doing so tells us nothing about whether the potential emission of carbon dioxide provides a reason not to burn the methane that is currently emitted from landfills.

The correct answer is D.

CR04964

774. Proposed new safety rules for the Beach City airport would lengthen considerably the minimum time between takeoffs from the airport. In consequence, the airport would be able to accommodate 10 percent fewer flights than currently use the airport daily. The city's operating budget depends heavily on taxes generated by tourist spending, and most of the tourists come by plane. Therefore, the proposed new safety rules, if adopted, will reduce the revenue available for the operating budget.

The argument depends on assuming which of the following?

(A) There are no periods of the day during which the interval between flights taking off from the airport is significantly greater than the currently allowed minimum.

(B) Few, if any, of the tourists who use the Beach City airport do so when their main destination is a neighboring community and not Beach City itself.

(C) If the proposed safety rules are adopted, the reduction in tourist numbers will not result mainly from a reduction in the number of tourists who spend relatively little in Beach City.

(D) Increasing the minimum time between takeoffs is the only way to achieve necessary safety improvements without a large expenditure by the city government on airport enhancements.

(E) The response to the adoption of the new safety rules would not include an increase in the number of passengers per flight.

Argument Construction

Situation   Proposed safety rules for a city airport would reduce the number of daily flights the airport can accommodate. The city's operating budget depends heavily on taxes generated by tourists, who mostly come by plane. Therefore, adopting the safety rules will result in lower revenue available for the operating budget.

Reasoning   *What must be true in order for the cited facts to support the conclusion that the proposed rules would reduce the revenue for the operating budget?* The implicit reasoning is that since the rules would reduce the number of flights that can be accommodated, they would thereby reduce the number of tourists arriving by plane, which in turn would reduce the tax revenue that tourist spending generates for the operating budget. This assumes that the actual number of daily flights would fall along with the number that the airport can accommodate; that fewer daily flights would mean fewer people flying into the airport; that fewer people flying into the airport would mean fewer tourists flying into the airport; that fewer tourists flying into the airport would mean fewer tourists visiting the city; that fewer tourists visiting the city would mean less taxable spending by tourists; and that less taxable spending by tourists would mean less revenue overall for the operating budget.

A   Even if flights depart the airport less frequently during some periods of the day, increasing the minimum time between flights at busy times of day could reduce the total number of daily flights from the airport.

B   Even if half the tourists flying into the airport were bound for other nearby towns, the other half could still spend enough in town to generate lots of revenue for the operating budget.

C   It is possible that most tourists spend relatively little in the city, but a few spend a lot. In that case, even if a reduction in tourist numbers resulted mainly from a declining number of tourists who spend relatively little, it could also greatly reduce the already small number of tourists who spend a lot.

D   This suggests that the proposed rules might be financially better for the city than any alternative way to improve safety, whereas the argument's conclusion is that the proposed rules are financially disadvantageous.

E   **Correct.** If adopting the proposed rules would result in a large increase in the number of passengers per flight, fewer daily flights would not necessarily mean fewer passengers or fewer tourists overall.

The correct answer is E.

CR01096

775. The introduction of new drugs into the market is frequently prevented by a shortage of human subjects for the clinical trials needed to show that the drugs are safe and effective. Since the lives and health of people in future generations may depend on treatments that are currently experimental, practicing physicians are morally in the wrong when, in the absence of any treatment proven to be effective, they fail to encourage suitable patients to volunteer for clinical trials.

Which of the following, if true, casts most doubt on the conclusion of the argument?

(A) Many drugs undergoing clinical trials are intended for the treatment of conditions for which there is currently no effective treatment.

(B) Patients do not share the physician's professional concern for public health, but everyone has a moral obligation to alleviate suffering when able to do so.

(C) Usually, half the patients in a clinical trial serve as a control group and receive a nonactive drug in place of the drug being tested.

(D) An experimental drug cannot legally be made available to patients unless those patients are subjects in clinical trials of the drug.

(E) Physicians have an overriding moral and legal duty to care for the health and safety of their current patients.

Argument Evaluation

Situation	A shortage of human subjects for clinical trials needed to show that new drugs are safe and effective often prevents those drugs from being introduced into the market. The lives and health of future generations may depend on treatments that are now experimental.
Reasoning	*What would cast doubt on the judgment that doctors are morally obligated to encourage their patients to volunteer for clinical trials?* Note that the argument's conclusion, unlike its premises, is a moral judgment. This judgment could be cast into doubt by a moral principle that would be likely to conflict with it under the conditions described. For example, a principle suggesting that it is sometimes morally unacceptable for doctors to encourage their patients to volunteer for clinical trials would also suggest that they are not morally obligated to encourage their patients to volunteer for clinical trials, since anything morally obligatory must also be morally acceptable.

A   If anything, this highlights how important it is to ensure that these drugs undergo clinical trials to benefit future generations, so it supports rather than casts doubt on the argument's conclusion.

B   This suggests that patients are morally obligated to volunteer for clinical trials to help prevent suffering in future generations. If anything, this supports the claim that doctors are morally obligated to encourage their patients to volunteer.

C   The clinical trial will probably not harm any patients in the control group, yet their participation will benefit future generations. So, if anything, this supports the claim that doctors should encourage their patients to volunteer.

D   This legal barrier makes it even more essential for the drugs to undergo clinical trials in order to benefit patients, so it supports rather than casts doubt on the argument's conclusion.

E   **Correct.** Since the experimental drugs' safety is being tested during the trials, the drugs may prove unsafe for subjects in the trials. If doctors have an overriding moral duty to keep their current patients safe, then it may be morally unacceptable for them to encourage those patients to volunteer for the trials.

The correct answer is E.

CR01285

776. As a construction material, bamboo is as strong as steel and sturdier than concrete. Moreover, in tropical areas bamboo is a much less expensive construction material than either steel or concrete and is always readily available. In tropical areas, therefore, building with bamboo makes better economic sense than building with steel or concrete, except where land values are high.

Which of the following, if true, most helps to explain the exception noted above?

(A) Buildings constructed of bamboo are less likely to suffer earthquake damage than are steel and concrete buildings.

(B) Bamboo is unsuitable as a building material for multistory buildings.

(C) In order to protect it from being damaged by termites and beetles, bamboo must be soaked, at some expense, in a preservative.

(D) In some tropical areas, bamboo is used to make the scaffolding that is used during large construction projects.

(E) Bamboo growing in an area where land values are increasing is often cleared to make way for construction.

Argument Construction

Situation | Bamboo is as strong as steel and sturdier than concrete when used as a construction material. In tropical areas, bamboo is much less expensive and is always readily available.

Reasoning | *What explains the exception specified in the conclusion?* The argument's conclusion is that in tropical areas bamboo is a more economical building material than steel or concrete, *except where land values are high*. The information in the passage makes clear why bamboo is a more economical building material in tropical areas than are concrete or steel. So the question is: Why must an exception be made for areas where land values are high? Multistory buildings are particularly desirable in areas where land values are high, but bamboo may not be suitable for such buildings.

A   This explains why bamboo would be preferable to steel or concrete in tropical areas especially prone to earthquakes. However, there is no clear connection to be made between areas where land values are high and areas especially prone to earthquakes.

B   **Correct.** Multistory buildings provide a greater area of floor space for a given site area, and in that sense are more economical. A single-story building with the same floor space will occupy a much bigger site, so the higher the land values, the more likely it is that a multistory building will be built on that land. Thus, given this information, bamboo is less suitable for areas where land values are high.

C   This undermines, to some extent, the claim that bamboo is an economical building material. But it does nothing to explain why it would be less economical specifically in areas where land values are high.

D   This is irrelevant. Bamboo is used to build scaffolding for construction projects and as a building material for permanent structures. There is no way to infer from this that bamboo is less economical specifically in areas where land values are high.

E   The fact that bamboo is cleared from an area to make room for construction in no way implies that bamboo would not be a suitable and economical building material for the area once it has been cleared.

The correct answer is B.

CR25550.02

777. The country of Virodia has, until now, been barely self-sufficient in both meat and grain. Greater prosperity there has gone hand in hand with steadily increasing per capita consumption of meat, and it takes several pounds of grain used as feed to produce one pound of meat. Per capita income is almost certain to rise further, yet increases in domestic grain production are unlikely.

Which of the following is most strongly supported by the information given?

(A) Some land in Virodia that is currently used for grain production will soon be turned into pastureland for grazing cattle for meat.

(B) In the future, per capita income in Virodia is unlikely to increase as rapidly as it has in the past.

(C) In Virodia, the amount of grain it takes to produce one pound of meat is likely to increase in coming years.

(D) Grain is soon likely to make up a larger proportion of the average Virodian's diet than ever before.

(E) Virodia is likely to become an importer of grain or meat or both.

Argument Construction

Situation Virodia has been barely self-sufficient in both meat and grain. Recently per capita meat consumption in Virodia has been increasing. Recent increases in per capita income will probably continue, but production of grain will probably not increase. It takes several pounds of grain to produce each pound of meat.

Reasoning *What claim is most strongly supported by the given information?* We are told that producing a pound of meat requires several pounds of grain. If (1) more meat is going to be consumed in Virodia, (2) more grain will not be produced, and (3) there is no excess grain, then Virodia will have to import meat, or import grain so it can produce more meat, or both.

A The information given says nothing about pastureland for grazing cattle, and it provides no evidence that meat producers would be able to produce more meat per area of land by using the land for pasture than by using it for grain production. Furthermore, there is no evidence that the meat in Virodia is produced from cattle rather than from some other types of animals that are fed on grain. Given that the information suggests that there may be an increase in demand for grain, it seems unlikely that there will be a reduction in the amount of land used to produce grain.

B The information says that per capita income is likely to increase and that greater prosperity correlates positively with greater meat consumption. It provides no reason to think that the correlation between rising income and increasing meat consumption occurs only with more rapid rises in income.

C Nothing in the information given provides any evidence as to whether the amount of grain needed to produce a pound of meat will change.

D The information indicates that per capita meat consumption is likely to continue to increase, which actually supports the opposite of what this answer choice states.

E **Correct.** The information indicates that grain production will probably not increase. We are told however that meat consumption will increase. Meat production in Virodia requires a substantial amount of grain, and we know that Virodia produces no excess grain or meat. This indicates that Virodia will likely have to become an importer of meat, or, if not, it will have to become an importer of grain so that it will be able to produce more meat.

The correct answer is E.

CR00788

778. Newspaper editors should not allow reporters to write the headlines for their own stories. The reason for this is that, while the headlines that reporters themselves write are often clever, what typically makes them clever is that they allude to little-known information that is familiar to the reporter but that never appears explicitly in the story itself.

Which of the following, if true, most strengthens the argument?

(A) The reporter who writes a story is usually better placed than the reporter's editor is to judge what the story's most newsworthy features are.

(B) To write a headline that is clever, a person must have sufficient understanding of the story that the headline accompanies.

(C) Most reporters rarely bother to find out how other reporters have written stories and headlines about the same events that they themselves have covered.

(D) For virtually any story that a reporter writes, there are at least a few people who know more about the story's subject matter than does the reporter.

(E) The kind of headlines that newspaper editors want are those that anyone who has read a reporter's story in its entirety will recognize as clever.

Argument Evaluation

Situation   The headlines newspaper reporters write for their own stories are often clever only because they allude to little-known information that never appears explicitly in the stories themselves.

Reasoning   *What would most help the argument support the conclusion that newspaper editors should not allow reporters to write headlines for their own stories?* The argument's only explicit premise is that the headlines newspaper reporters write for their own stories are often clever only because they allude to little-known information that never appears explicitly in the stories themselves. In order for this premise to support the conclusion that newspaper editors should not allow reporters to write their own headlines, it would be helpful to be given a reason why editors should avoid headlines alluding to such little-known information.

A   This suggests that reporters are likely to write better headlines for their stories than editors are, so it weakens the argument that editors should not allow reporters to write their own headlines.

B   Since a reporter who wrote a story is likely to understand that story well, this does not provide a reason why editors should not allow reporters to write their own headlines.

C   If most reporters did what is suggested, they could perhaps hone their headline-writing skills—unless almost all reporters are weak in such skills, as suggested in the given information. The fact that they do not bother to do so may help explain why reporters' headline-writing skills are weak. An explanation of why this is so does not provide additional support for the argument's conclusion.

D   The people who know more about a story's subject matter than the reporter writing the story might be just as likely to see the cleverness of allusions to little-known information as the reporters are. So, to the extent that this is relevant at all, it slightly weakens the argument by suggesting that obscurely clever headlines sometimes function as intended.

E   **Correct.** The argument's explicit premise suggests that typically a reporter's headline for his or her own story cannot be recognized as clever by a reader who has read the whole story. So if editors want headlines that anyone who has read the accompanying stories would recognize as clever, they have a reason not to let reporters write the headlines.

The correct answer is E.

CR03251

779. Scientists have modified feed corn genetically, increasing its resistance to insect pests. Farmers who tried out the genetically modified corn last season applied less insecticide to their corn fields and still got yields comparable to those they would have gotten with ordinary corn. Ordinary corn seed, however, costs less, and what these farmers saved on insecticide rarely exceeded their extra costs for seed. Therefore, for most feed-corn farmers, switching to genetically modified seed would be unlikely to increase profits.

Which of the following would it be most useful to know in order to evaluate the argument?

(A) Whether there are insect pests that sometimes reduce feed-corn yields, but against which commonly used insecticides and the genetic modification are equally ineffective

(B) Whether the price that farmers receive for feed corn has remained steady over the past few years

(C) Whether the insecticides typically used on feed corn tend to be more expensive than insecticides typically used on other crops

(D) Whether most of the farmers who tried the genetically modified corn last season applied more insecticide than was actually necessary

(E) Whether, for most farmers who plant feed corn, it is their most profitable crop

Argument Evaluation

Situation   Farmers who grew feed corn genetically engineered to be pest resistant got yields comparable to those of farmers growing ordinary feed corn, but did so while using less pesticide. Since the amount saved on pesticide was rarely in excess of the extra costs for the genetically modified corn, most farmers will probably not increase profits by choosing the genetically engineered variety.

Reasoning   *Which would be most useful to know in evaluating the argument?* To answer a question such as this, one should look for information that would strengthen or weaken the argument. If one had information that the farmers growing the genetically modified corn could have increased their yields last year at lower cost, this would be helpful in evaluating the argument, because this would show that the argument is weak.

A   It does not matter to the argument whether there are pests against which pesticides and genetic resistance are equally ineffective, because that is compatible with there being pests against which they are not equally effective.

B   Whether prices of feed corn go up or down affects the comparison groups equally.

C   The relative cost of insecticides for other crops has no bearing on the argument because the argument is concerned with only feed corn.

D   Correct. This option provides the information that it would be most useful to know in evaluating the argument. It shows that farmers growing genetically modified corn last year could have attained higher profits than they in fact did.

E   The argument concerns only the relative profitability of growing one variety of feed corn versus another.

The correct answer is D.

CR07318

780. Debater: The average amount of overtime per month worked by an employee in the manufacturing division of the Haglut Corporation is 14 hours. Most employees of the Haglut Corporation work in the manufacturing division. Furthermore, the average amount of overtime per month worked by any employee in the company generally does not fluctuate much from month to month. Therefore, each month, most employees of the Haglut Corporation almost certainly work at least some overtime.

The debater's argument is most vulnerable to criticism on which of these grounds?

(A) It takes for granted that the manufacturing division is a typical division of the corporation with regard to the average amount of overtime its employees work each month.

(B) It takes for granted that if a certain average amount of overtime is worked each month by each employee of the Haglut Corporation, then approximately the same amount of overtime must be worked each month by each employee of the manufacturing division.

(C) It confuses a claim from which the argument's conclusion about the Haglut Corporation would necessarily follow with a claim that would follow from the argument's conclusion only with a high degree of probability.

(D) It overlooks the possibility that even if, on average, a certain amount of overtime is worked by the members of some group, many members of that group may work no overtime at all.

(E) It overlooks the possibility that even if most employees of the corporation work some overtime each month, any one corporate employee may, in some months, work no overtime.

Argument Evaluation

Situation   Most of the employees of the Haglut Corporation work in the manufacturing division, where employees average 14 hours per month in overtime. The average amount of overtime per month for employees at Haglut does not fluctuate much from month to month.

Reasoning   *What is the argument's greatest weakness?* The argument's conclusion is that almost certainly each month most of the employees of Haglut work at least some overtime. Answer choice (D) identifies the argument's greatest weakness because it points out how the conclusion of the argument could be false even if all of the supporting information were true. For example, it could be that less than half of the employees work any overtime at all, but those that do work overtime work much more than 14 hours per month.

A   The argument leaves open the possibility that in some divisions of the corporation, the average monthly overtime of its employees is quite different from 14 hours, even if (as the argument states) that average does not change much from month to month.

B   The argument does not assume that there is a monthly amount of overtime worked by each employee of the manufacturing division equivalent to the company-wide average monthly overtime per employee.

C   This does not identify a weakness that can be detected in the argument. Since the claims mentioned here are not specified, the passage provides no evidence that clearly indicates that this type of confusion is playing a role in the argument.

D   **Correct.** The argument ignores the possibility that most of the employees of Haglut work no overtime at all in a particular month—which is quite consistent with the argument's assertion that the average number of monthly overtime hours per employee within the manufacturing division is 14.

E   The possibility described by this is not overlooked by the argument, because this possibility is consistent with the conclusion. It could easily be that most employees of the corporation work some overtime each month—as the conclusion envisions—but that there are always some employees who do not work any overtime.

The correct answer is D.

CR05446

781. Proponents of the recently introduced tax on sales of new luxury boats had argued that a tax of this sort would be an equitable way to increase government revenue because the admittedly heavy tax burden would fall only on wealthy people and neither they nor anyone else would suffer any economic hardship. In fact, however, 20 percent of the workers employed by manufacturers of luxury boats have lost their jobs as a direct result of this tax.

The information given, if true, most strongly supports which of the following?

(A) The market for luxury boats would have collapsed even if the new tax on luxury boats had been lower.

(B) The new tax would produce a net gain in tax revenue for the government only if the yearly total revenue that it generates exceeds the total of any yearly tax-revenue decrease resulting from the workers' loss of jobs.

(C) Because many people never buy luxury items, imposing a sales tax on luxury items is the kind of legislative action that does not cost incumbent legislators much popular support.

(D) Before the tax was instituted, luxury boats were largely bought by people who were not wealthy.

(E) Taxes can be equitable only if their burden is evenly distributed over the entire population.

Argument Construction

Situation   Proponents of a recently introduced tax on sales of new luxury boats argued that it would be an equitable way to increase government revenue because the tax would fall only on the wealthy and cause no economic hardship. But because of the tax, 20 percent of luxury-boat manufacturing workers have lost their jobs.

Reasoning   *What conclusion do the statements about the proponents' argument and the tax's effects support?* Since the tax caused many workers to lose their jobs, apparently the proponents were incorrect in asserting that it would cause no one to suffer any economic hardship. Thus, their justification for concluding that the tax is an equitable way to increase government revenue is factually inaccurate, casting doubt on that conclusion.

A   The passage indicates that the tax directly caused a significant decrease (though not necessarily a collapse) in the market for luxury boats. But the passage contains no evidence about whether such a decrease might not have occurred if the new tax had been somewhat lower.

B   **Correct.** Since the tax caused the workers to lose their jobs, it might have made the government lose revenue from payroll taxes that the laid-off workers would have paid if they had kept their jobs. So if the yearly total revenue generated directly and indirectly by the tax were less than those total yearly payroll taxes and any other tax revenue that was lost as a result of the tax, the tax would have caused a net loss in tax revenue.

C   The passage contains no information about what types of legislative actions cost, or do not cost, incumbent legislators popular support.

D   Although the passage suggests that some of the tax proponents' assumptions were wrong, it contains no information suggesting that those proponents were wrong in thinking that luxury boats are purchased mainly by wealthy people.

E   The passage does not provide any basis for determining what makes a tax equitable or about whether the luxury boat tax is equitable. The tax's proponents evidently felt that a tax whose burden falls only on the wealthy rather than evenly on the entire population can be equitable.

The correct answer is B.

CR05191
782. In Wareland last year, 16 percent of licensed drivers under 21 and 11 percent of drivers ages 21–24 were in serious accidents. By contrast, only 3 percent of licensed drivers 65 and older were involved in serious accidents. These figures clearly show that the greater experience and developed habits of caution possessed by drivers in the 65-and-older group make them far safer behind the wheel than the younger drivers are.

Which of the following is an assumption on which the argument depends?

(A) Drivers 65 and older do not, on average, drive very many fewer miles per year than drivers 24 and younger.

(B) Drivers 65 and older do not constitute a significantly larger percentage of licensed drivers in Wareland than drivers ages 18–24 do.

(C) Drivers 65 and older are less likely than are drivers 24 and younger to drive during weather conditions that greatly increase the risk of accidents.

(D) The difference between the accident rate of drivers under 21 and of those ages 21–24 is attributable to the greater driving experience of those in the older group.

(E) There is no age bracket for which the accident rate is lower than it is for licensed drivers 65 and older.

Argument Evaluation

Situation   Last year in Wareland, a much higher percentage of drivers 24 and under than of drivers 65 and older were in serious accidents.

Reasoning   *What must be true for the observation about the accident rates to support the conclusion that the greater experience and caution of drivers 65 and older make them safer behind the wheel than the younger drivers?* Several factors other than greater experience and caution could explain the lower accident rate among the older drivers. For example, the older drivers might simply drive much less than the younger ones, but still get in just as many accidents per mile driven. Or perhaps because the older drivers are more often retired, their schedules less often lead them to drive at times of day when accident rates are greater for everyone. Or they might be more likely to live in rural areas with less traffic and lower accident rates. The argument depends on assuming that none of these factors fully explains the difference in accident rates.

A   **Correct.** Although we are given no information about the possible extent of any difference in average miles driven, the (somewhat vague) information that drivers 65 and older drive *very many fewer miles per year*, on average, than drivers 24 and younger would cast serious doubt on the statistical argument given. The argument assumes that the difference in miles driven is not sufficiently substantial to undermine the argument.

B   The argument is only about the discrepancy between the percentages of the drivers in two specific age groups who were in serious accidents last year. The percentages of licensed drivers who fall in these age groups are irrelevant.

C   Even if drivers 65 and older are just as likely as younger drivers to drive in inclement weather, they may do so far more carefully than the younger drivers, so the older drivers' greater experience and caution could still explain their lower accident rates.

D   Even if greater experience does not explain the difference between the accident rates of the two younger groups of drivers, it might still explain the differences between the accident rate of those two younger groups taken together and that of drivers aged 65 and older.

E   The accident rate could be lower for drivers in late middle age than for those 65 and older because drivers in late middle age are also cautious and experienced, but their reflexes and vision tend to be less impaired. Even if that were true, the experience and caution of the drivers 65 and older might still make them safer than drivers 24 and under.

The correct answer is A.

CR05614

783. In the past the country of Malvernia has relied heavily on imported oil. Malvernia recently implemented a program to convert heating systems from oil to natural gas. Malvernia currently produces more natural gas each year than it uses, and oil production in Malvernian oil fields is increasing at a steady pace. If these trends in fuel production and usage continue, therefore, Malvernian reliance on foreign sources for fuel is likely to decline soon.

Which of the following would it be most useful to establish in evaluating the argument?

(A)   When, if ever, will production of oil in Malvernia outstrip production of natural gas?

(B)   Is Malvernia among the countries that rely most on imported oil?

(C)   What proportion of Malvernia's total energy needs is met by hydroelectric, solar, and nuclear power?

(D)   Is the amount of oil used each year in Malvernia for generating electricity and fuel for transportation increasing?

(E)   Have any existing oil-burning heating systems in Malvernia already been converted to natural-gas-burning heating systems?

Argument Evaluation

Situation   Malvernia has relied heavily on imported oil, but recently began a program to convert heating systems from oil to natural gas. Malvernia produces more natural gas than it uses. Furthermore, Malvernia's oil production is expanding, Therefore, Malvernia will probably reduce its reliance on imported oils If these trends continue.

Reasoning   *Which option provides the information that it would be most useful to know in evaluating the argument?* In other words, we are looking for the option which—depending on whether it was answered yes or no—would either most weaken or most strengthen the argument. The argument indicates that Malvernia will be using less oil for heating and will be producing more oil domestically. But the conclusion that Malvernia's reliance on foreign oil will decline, assuming the current trends mentioned continue, would be undermined if there was something in the works that could offset these trends, for instance, if it turned out that the country's need for oil was going to rise in the coming years.

A   Since both domestic oil production and domestic natural gas production counteract the need for imported oil, it makes little difference to the argument whether domestic oil production exceeds domestic natural gas.

B   Whether there are many countries that rely more on foreign oil than Malvernia would have little impact on whether Malvernia's need for foreign oil can be expected to decline.

C   Since there is no information in the argument about whether Malvernia can expect an increase or decrease from these other energy sources, it does not matter how much they now provide.

D   Correct. This option provides the information that it would be most useful to know in evaluating the argument. As explained in the Reasoning section above, if Malvernia's need for oil rises in the coming years, the conclusion that Malvernia's reliance on foreign oil will decline is undermined.

E   The argument tells us that a program has begun *recently* to convert heating systems from oil to gas. So, even if no such conversions have been completed, the argument still indicates that they can be expected to occur.

The correct answer is D.

CR03618

784. Exposure to certain chemicals commonly used in elementary schools as cleaners or pesticides causes allergic reactions in some children. Elementary school nurses in Renston report that the proportion of schoolchildren sent to them for treatment of allergic reactions to those chemicals has increased significantly over the past ten years. Therefore, either Renston's schoolchildren have been exposed to greater quantities of the chemicals, or they are more sensitive to them than schoolchildren were ten years ago.

Which of the following is an assumption on which the argument depends?

(A) The number of school nurses employed by Renston's elementary schools has not decreased over the past ten years.

(B) Children who are allergic to the chemicals are no more likely than other children to have allergies to other substances.

(C) Children who have allergic reactions to the chemicals are not more likely to be sent to a school nurse now than they were ten years ago.

(D) The chemicals are not commonly used as cleaners or pesticides in houses and apartment buildings in Renston.

(E) Children attending elementary school do not make up a larger proportion of Renston's population now than they did ten years ago.

Argument Construction

Situation Some children have allergic reactions to some of the chemicals commonly used in elementary schools as cleaners and pesticides. The number of children sent to elementary school nurses in Renston for allergic reactions to such chemicals has risen significantly over the past ten years.

Reasoning *What must the argument assume?* The argument's conclusion presents just two alternatives: either the children are exposed to more of the chemicals than children in earlier years *or* they are more sensitive. But there is a third possible explanation for the significant increase in school-nurse visits that the school nurses have reported: that children are just more inclined to go to the school nurse when they experience an allergic reaction than were children several years ago. For the conclusion to follow from its premises, the argument must assume that this is not the correct explanation.

A If the number of elementary school nurses in Renston elementary schools had decreased over the past ten years, that would in no way explain the rise in the proportion of children reporting to school nurses for allergic reactions.

B Only school-nurse visits for allergic reactions to the cleaners and pesticides used in elementary schools are in question in the argument. Of course there could be school-nurse visits for allergic reactions to other things, but that issue does not arise in the argument.

C **Correct.** This can be seen by considering whether the argument would work if we assume that this were false, i.e., that a school-nurse visit *is* more likely in such cases. As noted above, this provides an alternative to the two explanations that the conclusion claims are the sole possibilities.

D This does not need to be assumed by the argument. The argument's conclusion suggests that children may in recent years have had greater exposure to the chemicals, not that this exposure has occurred exclusively in the schools. The argument does not rely on this latter assumption.

E The argument does not need to make this assumption. The argument is framed in terms of proportions of children having school-nurse visits for certain allergic reactions. *How many* children there are or what proportion such children are of Renston's total population is not directly relevant to the argument.

The correct answer is C.

CR51520.02

785. Lockeport's commercial fishing boats use gill nets, which kill many of the netted fish, including some fish of endangered species. The fishing commission has proposed requiring the use of tent nets, which do not kill fish; boat crews would then throw back fish of endangered species. Profitable commercial fishing boats in similar areas have already switched over to tent nets. The proposal can therefore be implemented without economic harm to Lockeport's commercial fishing boat operators.

Which of the following, if true, casts the most serious doubt on the argument made for the proposal?

(A) In places where the use of tent nets has been mandated, there are typically fewer commercial fishing boats in operation than there were before tent nets came into use.

(B) Even when used properly, gill nets require many more repairs than do tent nets.

(C) Recreational anglers in Lockeport catch more fish of endangered species than do commercial fishing boats.

(D) The endangered species of fish in Lockeport's commercial fishing area did not become endangered as a result of the use of gill nets by fishing fleets.

(E) The endangered species of fish caught by Lockeport's commercial fishing fleet are of no commercial value.

Evaluation of a Plan

Situation   Gill nets, used by Lockeport's commercial fishing boats, kill some fish of endangered species. The fishing commission has proposed requiring the use of tent nets, which do not kill fish. This would allow the fish of endangered species to be thrown back. It is argued that the proposed requirement will not harm commercial fishing boat operators, since commercial fishing boats in other similar places are using tent nets and are profitable.

Reasoning   *What new piece of information would weaken the argument for the proposed requirement?* The crucial support given for the argument is that in other similar places, commercial fishing boats that use tent nets and not gill nets are profitable. But if, in places where only tent nets are now used, the numbers of commercial fishing boats diminished, it would be reasonable to suspect that switching entirely to tent nets may have driven some of the fishing operations out of business or caused them to move to other areas in which there was no expectation that they would use only tent nets.

A   **Correct.** This is new information. As explained above, it would justify doubt about the argument made in favor of the proposal.

B   This suggests that implementation of the proposed requirement could, over time, lower a certain type of operational costs for commercial fishing boats using tent nets. This would provide a new reason in support of the proposed requirement, not a reason to doubt the argument for it.

C   This suggests that perhaps recreational fishing in Lockeport needs to be regulated more strictly, but that is a separate issue from the one addressed in the argument for the proposed tent-net requirement.

D   This information casts no doubt on the relevance of the stated information that using gill nets contributes to undermining populations of at least some of the endangered fish species in Lockeport. If the species are currently endangered, they may need protection regardless of how they became endangered.

E   This information suggests that fish of the endangered species in Lockeport cannot profitably be sold. It does not cast doubt on the argument made in favor of the proposed requirement. Neither does it cast doubt on the practicality or the desirability of the proposed requirement.

The correct answer is A.

CR01854
786. Normally, the pineal gland governs a person's sleep-wake cycle by secreting melatonin in response to the daily cycle of light and darkness as detected by the eye. Nonetheless, many people who are totally blind due to lesions in the visual cortex of the brain easily maintain a 24-hour sleep-wake cycle. So the neural pathway by which the pineal gland receives information from the eye probably does not pass through the visual cortex.

For purposes of evaluating the argument it would be most useful to establish which of the following?

(A) Whether melatonin supplements help people who have difficulty maintaining a 24-hour sleep cycle to establish such a pattern

(B) Whether the melatonin levels of most totally blind people who successfully maintain a 24-hour sleep-wake cycle change in response to changes in exposure to light and darkness

(C) Whether melatonin is the only substance secreted by the pineal gland

(D) Whether most people who do not have a 24-hour sleep-wake cycle nevertheless have a cycle of consistent duration

(E) Whether there are any people with normal vision whose melatonin levels respond abnormally to periods of light and darkness

Argument Evaluation

Situation   Normally, a person's sleep-wake cycle is governed by the pineal gland secreting melatonin in response to the daily cycle of light and darkness as detected by the eye. Yet many people who are totally blind due to lesions of the visual cortex easily maintain a 24-hour sleep-wake cycle.

Reasoning   *What additional information would be most helpful in evaluating the argument?* The argument's conclusion is that the neural pathway by which the pineal gland receives information probably does not pass through the visual cortex. This is suggested by the fact that people without a well-functioning visual cortex (e.g., people with a certain type of blindness) can nonetheless maintain a 24-hour sleep-wake cycle. Is it by the pineal gland's secretion of melatonin that they do so? The argument tells us that *normally* (i.e., in sighted people), this is the mechanism for sleep regulation. But the argument depends on assuming that a similar mechanism is operating in people who are blind but have well-regulated sleep cycles. The best choice will be the one that helps us decide whether that assumption is correct.

A   This question would not give us an answer that would help in evaluating the argument. A "no" answer would not clarify whether the pineal gland-melatonin mechanism operates in people who are blind. A "yes" answer would do no better. The question refers only to people who have sleep dysfunctions (which the argument does not address).

B   **Correct.** Answering this question would provide the most useful information for evaluating the argument. A "yes" answer would help confirm a key assumption of the argument: that blind people rely on the pineal gland-melatonin mechanism for sleep regulation. A "no" answer would help disconfirm that assumption.

C   Whether or not there are other substances secreted by the pineal gland makes no difference to the reasoning. The argument relies on the premise that the pineal gland governs the sleep cycle *by secreting melatonin*. For example, if the pineal gland sometimes secreted adrenaline, that would still have no bearing on the argument.

D   The consistency or inconsistency of the duration of some people's sleep patterns has no relevance to the reasoning. Their sleep patterns could be due to any of a number of factors.

E   This does not help, for there could be sighted people whose melatonin levels respond abnormally simply because of a pineal-gland abnormality.

The correct answer is B.

CR00942

787. **In countries where automobile insurance includes compensation for whiplash injuries sustained in automobile accidents, reports of having suffered such injuries are twice as frequent as they are in countries where whiplash is not covered**. Presently, no objective test for whiplash exists, so it is true that spurious reports of whiplash injuries cannot be readily identified. Nevertheless, these facts do not warrant the conclusion drawn by some commentators that in the countries with the higher rates of reported whiplash injuries, half of the reported cases are spurious. Clearly, **in countries where automobile insurance does not include compensation for whiplash, people often have little incentive to report whiplash injuries that they actually have suffered.**

In the argument given, the two **boldfaced** portions play which of the following roles?

(A) The first is a claim that the argument disputes; the second is a conclusion that has been based on that claim.

(B) The first is a claim that has been used to support a conclusion that the argument accepts; the second is that conclusion.

(C) The first is evidence that has been used to support a conclusion for which the argument provides further evidence; the second is the main conclusion of the argument.

(D) The first is a finding whose implications are at issue in the argument; the second is a claim presented in order to argue against deriving certain implications from that finding.

(E) The first is a finding whose accuracy is evaluated in the argument; the second is evidence presented to establish that the finding is accurate.

Argument Evaluation

Situation   Reported whiplash injuries are twice as common in countries where car insurance companies pay compensation for such injuries as they are in countries where insurance companies do not. Although there is no objective test for whiplash, this does not mean, as some suggest, that half of the reports of such injuries are fake. It could simply be that where insurance will not pay for such injuries, people are less inclined to report them.

Reasoning   *What roles do the two boldfaced portions play in the argument?* The first portion tells us about the correlation between reported cases of whiplash in countries and the willingness of insurance companies in those countries to compensate for whiplash injuries. The argument next states that whiplash is difficult to verify objectively. The argument then asserts that although this last fact, taken together with the first boldfaced portion, has led some to infer that over half of the reported cases in countries with the highest whiplash rates are spurious, such an inference is unwarranted. The second boldfaced portion then helps to explain, by offering an alternative explanation, why such an inference is not necessarily warranted.

A   The claim made in the first boldfaced portion is never disputed in the argument. The second is not the argument's conclusion.

B   Perhaps the argument uses the first portion to support its conclusion; but there is no indication that it has been used elsewhere to do so. Regardless, the second boldfaced portion is not the argument's conclusion.

C   The first portion has been used to support a conclusion that the argument rejects; the second portion is not the argument's conclusion.

D   **Correct.** This answer choice correctly identifies the roles played in the argument by the boldfaced portions. As explained in the reasoning section above, the first boldface portion tells us about the correlation between reported cases of whiplash in countries and the willingness of insurance companies in those countries to compensate for whiplash injuries. This is presented as a fact whose implications are at issue in the ensuing portions of the passage. The argument then reports that this fact, considered together with the difficulty of proving whiplash injuries, has led some to infer that over half of the reported cases in countries with the highest whiplash rates are spurious. The conclusion of the argument is that this inference is unwarranted. The second boldface portion expresses the basis for the argument's conclusion: there is a reasonable alternative explanation for the differences in frequency of whiplash injury reports between the two types of countries.

E   The accuracy of the first boldfaced portion is never questioned in the argument; nor is the second intended to somehow help show that the first is accurate. Rather, the argument assumes that the first portion is accurate.

The correct answer is D.

CR03859

788. Last year Comfort Airlines had twice as many delayed flights as the year before, but the number of complaints from passengers about delayed flights went up three times. It is unlikely that this disproportionate increase in complaints was rooted in an increase in overall dissatisfaction with the service Comfort Airlines provides, since the airline made a special effort to improve other aspects of its service last year.

Which of the following, if true, most helps to explain the disproportionate increase in customer complaints?

(A) Comfort Airlines had more flights last year than the year before.

(B) Last year a single period of unusually bad weather caused a large number of flights to be delayed.

(C) Some of the improvements that Comfort Airlines made in its service were required by new government regulations.

(D) The average length of a flight delay was greater last year than it was the year before.

(E) The average number of passengers per flight was no higher last year than the year before.

Argument Construction

Situation Last year Comfort Airlines had twice as many delayed flights as it did the year before, but three times as many passenger complaints about delayed flights. The airline made a special effort to improve other aspects of its service last year.

Reasoning *What could explain why the number of complaints about delayed flights increased disproportionately to the number of delayed flights last year?* In other words, why did the average number of passenger complaints per delayed flight go up last year? One obvious possibility is that the average number of passengers per delayed flight was greater last year than it had been the year before. Another is that the flight delays tended to cause worse problems for passengers last year than they had the year before, so that on average each delay was more upsetting for the passengers.

A This helps explain why the airline had more delayed flights last year, but not why the increase in complaints about delayed flights was disproportionate to the increase in delayed flights.

B This helps explain why the airline had more delayed flights last year. But, if anything, the situation should have reduced the number of passenger complaints per delayed flight, since many passengers should have realized that the unusually bad weather was not the airline's fault.

C If any of the improvements concerned handling of flight delays, for example, and passengers were aware that government regulations addressed this, then passengers might have complained more than previously. But the information we are given here is too general and too vague to explain the disproportionate increase in complaints.

D Correct. Longer flight delays would have more severely inconvenienced passengers and thus would probably have generated more passenger complaints per delay.

E This rules out the possibility that an increased number of passengers per delayed flight could have caused the disproportionate increase in the number of complaints about delayed flights. But no alternative explanation is offered.

The correct answer is D

CR01337

789. Last year a global disturbance of weather patterns disrupted harvests in many of the world's important agricultural areas. Worldwide production of soybeans, an important source of protein for people and livestock alike, was not adversely affected, however. Indeed, last year's soybean crop was actually slightly larger than average. Nevertheless, the weather phenomenon is probably responsible for a recent increase in the world price of soybeans.

Which of the following, if true, provides the strongest justification for the attribution of the increase in soybean prices to the weather phenomenon?

(A)   Last year's harvest of anchovies, which provide an important protein source for livestock, was disrupted by the effects of the weather phenomenon.

(B)   Most countries that produce soybeans for export had above-average harvests of a number of food crops other than soybeans last year.

(C)   The world price of soybeans also rose several years ago, immediately after an earlier occurrence of a similar global weather disturbance.

(D)   Heavy rains attributable to the weather phenomenon improved grazing pastures last year, allowing farmers in many parts of the world to reduce their dependence on supplemental feed.

(E)   Prior to last year, soybean prices had been falling for several years.

Argument Construction

Situation   A weather disturbance last year disrupted harvests worldwide but did not reduce production of soybeans, a protein source for both people and livestock. Soybean prices increased nonetheless, likely a result of the weather.

Reasoning   *What evidence would suggest that the weather disturbance caused the increase in soybean prices even though it did not reduce soybean production?* Prices tend to increase when the supply of a product falls relative to the demand for the product. But the production of soybeans did not fall. Evidence that the weather disturbance either hindered the global distribution of soybeans or increased global demand for soybeans could support the claim that the weather disturbance caused the increase in soybean prices.

A   **Correct.** If the weather disturbance reduced the anchovy harvest, and anchovies provide protein for livestock just as soybeans do, then more soybeans for livestock feed would be needed to compensate for the lack of anchovies. The resulting increase in demand for soybeans could thus have increased global soybean prices.

B   This is not surprising, given that the weather disturbance did not severely affect the soybean-producing countries, but it does not explain how the weather disturbance could have caused soybean prices to increase.

C   The rise in soybean prices after the earlier weather disturbance could easily have been a coincidence. Or, unlike last year's disturbance, the earlier disturbance could have reduced soybean production.

D   This suggests that demand for soybeans should have fallen as a result of the weather disturbance, so it does not explain why soybean prices rose.

E   If soybean prices were unusually low for some temporary reason when the weather disturbance occurred, they might have been likely to rise back to normal levels even without the weather disturbance.

The correct answer is A.

CR03541

790. Most of the year, the hermit thrush, a North American songbird, eats a diet consisting mainly of insects, but in autumn, as the thrushes migrate to their Central and South American wintering grounds, they feed almost exclusively on wild berries. Wild berries, however, are not as rich in calories as insects, yet thrushes need to consume plenty of calories in order to complete their migration. One possible explanation is that berries contain other nutrients that thrushes need for migration and that insects lack.

Which of the following, if true, most seriously calls into question the explanation given for the thrush's diet during migration?

(A) Hermit thrushes, if undernourished, are unable to complete their autumn migration before the onset of winter.

(B) Insect species contain certain nutrients that are not found in wild berries.

(C) For songbirds, catching insects requires the expenditure of significantly more calories than eating wild berries does.

(D) Along the hermit thrushes' migration routes, insects are abundant throughout the migration season.

(E) There are some species of wild berries that hermit thrushes generally do not eat, even though these berry species are exceptionally rich in calories.

Argument Evaluation

Situation   Hermit thrushes are songbirds that usually eat insects but switch to eating berries when migrating. The thrushes need lots of calories to migrate, but berries contain fewer calories than insects do. Perhaps the berries contain nutrients that insects do not provide.

Reasoning   *What would cast doubt on the claim that the thrushes switch to berries because berries contain nutrients that insects lack and that the thrushes need for their migration?* Evidence that berries do not contain such nutrients or that thrushes do not decrease their net calorie consumption by eating berries would cast doubt on the proposed explanation. So would any evidence that supported an alternative explanation for the diet change during migration—for example, seasonal or regional differences in the amount or quality of berries or insects available for the thrushes to consume.

A   Even if thrushes need to be well-nourished to finish migrating before winter, extra nutrients found in berries but not insects might help provide the nourishment they need.

B   Even if insects contain *certain nutrients* not found in wild berries, those specific nutrients may not be the ones the thrushes need for their migration.

C   **Correct.** This suggests that the thrushes might gain more net calories from eating berries than from eating insects, which could explain why they switch to eating berries even if the berries contain no extra nutrients.

D   By ruling out a lack of insects to eat while migrating as an alternative explanation for why the thrushes switch to eating berries, this would support the proposed explanation.

E   The calorie-rich species of berries the thrushes do not eat might be poisonous or indigestible for them, even if the species of berries the thrushes do eat contain nutrients they need to migrate.

The correct answer is C.

CR01879

791. The kinds of hand and wrist injuries that result from extended use of a computer while maintaining an incorrect posture are common among schoolchildren in Harnville. Computers are important to the school curriculum there, so instead of reducing the amount their students use computers, teachers plan to bring about a sharp reduction in the number of these injuries by carefully monitoring their students' posture when using computers in the classroom.

Which of the following would it be most useful to know in order to assess the likelihood that the teachers' plan will be successful?

(A)   Whether extended use of a computer while maintaining incorrect posture can cause injuries other than hand and wrist injuries

(B)   Whether hand and wrist injuries not caused by computer use are common among schoolchildren in Harnville

(C)   What proportion of schoolchildren in Harnville with hand and wrist injuries use computers extensively outside the classroom

(D)   Whether changes in the curriculum could reduce the schools' dependence on computers

(E)   What proportion of schoolchildren in Harnville already use correct posture while using a computer

Evaluation of a Plan

Situation   Hand and wrist injuries from using computers while maintaining poor posture are common among schoolchildren in Harnville. Teachers plan to greatly reduce the number of such injuries by monitoring their students' posture while the students use computers in the classroom.

Reasoning   *What would be most helpful to know to determine the likelihood that the teachers' plan will succeed?* The primary concern is the *posture* students adopt while using computers. To succeed, the teachers' plan must reduce the time students spend with poor posture while using computers and reduce it enough to greatly reduce the number of injuries. To know how likely this is, it would help to know how effectively the teachers will be able to monitor and improve their students' posture inside the classroom. But how many of the students use computers *outside of school* while maintaining poor posture and how often do they do so? If many students do so quite often, they may develop hand and wrist injuries regardless of what happens in school.

A   The teachers do not plan to reduce any injuries other than hand and wrist injuries, so whether computer use with poor posture causes any such other injuries is irrelevant to the likelihood that their plan will produce its intended effect.

B   The plan being discussed concerns only the reduction of hand and wrist injuries caused specifically by computer use with poor posture, so the frequency of hand and wrist injuries from other causes is irrelevant to the likelihood that the plan will produce its intended effect.

C   **Correct.** If the students' school use of computers is a large part of their overall computer use, any retraining that accompanies the monitoring might have some effect on their posture and related injury rates overall. However, the greater the proportion of children with hand and wrist injuries who use computers extensively outside the classroom, the more children are likely to keep developing the injuries regardless of any monitoring at school, so the less effective the teachers' plan involving only computer use at school is likely to be.

D   Knowing whether this is the case might help in developing a potential alternative to the teachers' plan, but if it did, this would not help significantly toward assessing the likelihood that the actual plan will succeed. The teachers' actual plan involves monitoring computer use in school without reducing such use. Other possible means of achieving the plan's goal are not part of the plan and are therefore irrelevant to the likelihood that the teachers' actual plan will succeed.

E   The passage indicates that the proportion of the schoolchildren maintaining poor posture while using computers is high enough for many to develop hand and wrist injuries as a result. Whatever the exact proportion is, the teachers' plan may or may not succeed in reducing it.

The correct answer is C.

CR04718
792. A certain cultivated herb is one of a group of closely related plants that thrive in soil with high concentrations of metals that are toxic to most other plants. Agronomists studying the growth of this herb have discovered that it produces large amounts of histidine, an amino acid that, in test-tube solutions, renders these metals chemically inert. Hence, the herb's high histidine production must be the key feature that allows it to grow in metal-rich soils.

In evaluating the argument, it would be most important to determine which of the following?

(A) Whether the herb can thrive in soil that does not have high concentrations of the toxic metals

(B) Whether others of the closely related group of plants also produce histidine in large quantities

(C) Whether the herb's high level of histidine production is associated with an unusually low level of production of some other amino acid

(D) Whether growing the herb in soil with high concentrations of the metals will, over time, reduce their concentrations in the soil

(E) Whether the concentration of histidine in the growing herb declines as the plant approaches maturity

Argument Evaluation

Situation   A certain herb and closely related species thrive in soil full of metals toxic to most plants. The herb produces much histidine, which makes those metals chemically inert. Histidine production, therefore, is largely what accounts for the herb's thriving in metal-rich soils.

Reasoning   *What evidence would help determine whether the herb's histidine production is what enables it to thrive in metal-rich soils?* The argument is that since the herb's histidine chemically neutralizes the metals that are toxic to most plants, it must explain why the herb can thrive in metal-rich soils. To evaluate this argument, it would be helpful to know about the relationship between other closely related plant species' histidine production and the ability to thrive in metal-rich soils. It would also be helpful to know about any other factors that might plausibly explain why the herb can thrive in those soils.

A   Whether or not the herb thrives in metal-free soils, histidine production could enable it to thrive in soils that contain toxic metals.

B   **Correct.** If the closely related plants do not produce much histidine, whatever other factor allows them to thrive in metal-rich soils would likely account for why the herb thrives in those soils as well.

C   The given information suggests no particular reason to suppose that a low level of some unspecified amino acid would enable a plant to thrive in metal-rich soils.

D   The herb might absorb metals from any metal-rich soil it grows in, regardless of why it thrives in that soil.

E   Whether or not histidine concentrations in the herb decline as it approaches maturity, there could still be enough histidine in the growing herb to neutralize the metals and explain why it can grow in metal-rich soil.

The correct answer is B.

CR01293
793. Many people suffer an allergic reaction to certain sulfites, including those that are commonly added to wine as preservatives. However, since there are several winemakers who add sulfites to none of the wines they produce, people who would like to drink wine but are allergic to sulfites can drink wines produced by these winemakers without risking an allergic reaction to sulfites.

Which of the following is an assumption on which the argument depends?

(A) These winemakers have been able to duplicate the preservative effect produced by adding sulfites by means that do not involve adding any potentially allergenic substances to their wine.

(B) Not all forms of sulfite are equally likely to produce the allergic reaction.

(C) Wine is the only beverage to which sulfites are commonly added.

(D) Apart from sulfites, there are no substances commonly present in wine that give rise to an allergic reaction.

(E) Sulfites are not naturally present in the wines produced by these winemakers in amounts large enough to produce an allergic reaction in someone who drinks these wines.

Argument Construction

Situation   People who are allergic to certain sulfites can avoid risking an allergic reaction by drinking wine from one of the several producers that does not add sulfites.

Reasoning   *On what assumption does the argument depend?* Drinking wine to which no sulfites have been *added* will not prevent exposure to sulfites if, for instance, sulfites occur naturally in wines. In particular, if the wines that do not have sulfites added have sulfites present naturally in quantities sufficient to produce an allergic reaction, drinking these wines will not result in an allergic reaction. The argument therefore depends on assuming that this is not the case.

A   The argument does not require this because the conclusion does not address allergic reactions to substances other than sulfites.

B   The argument specifically refers to "certain sulfites" producing allergic reactions. It is entirely compatible with certain other forms of sulfites not producing allergic reactions in anyone.

C   This is irrelevant. The argument does not claim that one can avoid having an allergic reaction to sulfites *from any source* just by restricting one's wine consumption to those varieties to which no sulfites have been added.

D   Once again, the argument's conclusion does not address allergic reactions to substances other than sulfites in wine.

E   **Correct.** As explained in the Reasoning section above, the argument relies on the assumption that sulfites are not naturally present, in quantities sufficient to cause allergic reactions, in the wines to which no sulfites are added. If this assumption is not made, then the fact that no sulfites are added to certain wines is not a good reason to believe that people with sulfite allergies who consume the wines will not have an allergic reaction; if there are enough sulfites that naturally occur in the wine, people who consume the wine may well have an allergic reaction despite the fact that no sulfites have been added.

The correct answer is E.

CR11447

794. A new law gives ownership of patents—documents providing exclusive right to make and sell an invention—to universities, not the government, when those patents result from government-sponsored university research. Administrators at Logos University plan to sell any patents they acquire to corporations in order to fund programs to improve undergraduate teaching.

Which of the following, if true, would cast the most doubt on the viability of the college administrators' plan described above?

(A) Profit-making corporations interested in developing products based on patents held by universities are likely to try to serve as exclusive sponsors of ongoing university research projects.

(B) Corporate sponsors of research in university facilities are entitled to tax credits under new federal tax-code guidelines.

(C) Research scientists at Logos University have few or no teaching responsibilities and participate little if at all in the undergraduate programs in their field.

(D) Government-sponsored research conducted at Logos University for the most part duplicates research already completed by several profit-making corporations.

(E) Logos University is unlikely to attract corporate sponsorship of its scientific research.

Evaluation of a Plan

Situation	Universities own the patents resulting from government-sponsored research at their institutions. One university plans to sell its patents to corporations and use the proceeds to fund a program to improve teaching.
Reasoning	*What would cast doubt on the university's plan?* The plan assumes that the university has been granted, and/or will be granted, patents for its inventions; that there will be a market for its patents; and that corporations will want to buy them. What might make this untrue? For example, the university's inventions might have no practical value or might be useful only for government agencies, and if some of the corporations have already done the same or similar research, they will likely not be prospective buyers of the university's patents.

A   This point is irrelevant to the plan to sell patents in order to fund a program.

B   The university plans to sell the patents to the corporations, not to invite the corporations to sponsor research.

C   This point is irrelevant to the university's plan to sell off patents since the plan does not specify that the research scientists will be involved in the programs to improve undergraduate teaching.

D   Correct. This statement properly identifies a factor that casts doubt on the university's plan. The plan presupposes that corporations will want to buy the rights to the inventions. If some of the corporations have already done the same or similar research, they would likely have developed ways of achieving what the university's inventions promise to achieve. In the case of potential future patents, they might even have already patented the inventions that the university would develop, in which case, the university would be unable to patent them. Or the corporations might have developed similar, but not identical, inventions that serve the same purpose. In such cases, they probably would not need the university's inventions.

E   The plan concerns selling patents resulting from government-sponsored research, not attracting corporate sponsorship for research.

The correct answer is D.

CR01848

795. Since it has become known that **several of a bank's top executives have been buying shares in their own bank**, the bank's depositors, who had been worried by rumors that the bank faced impending financial collapse, have been greatly relieved. They reason that, since top executives evidently have faith in the bank's financial soundness, those worrisome rumors must be false. Such reasoning might well be overoptimistic, however, since **corporate executives have been known to buy shares in their own company in a calculated attempt to dispel negative rumors about the company's health.**

In the argument given, the two **boldfaced** portions play which of the following roles?

(A) The first describes evidence that has been taken as supporting a conclusion; the second gives a reason for questioning that support.

(B) The first describes evidence that has been taken as supporting a conclusion; the second states a contrary conclusion that is the main conclusion of the argument.

(C) The first provides evidence in support of the main conclusion of the argument; the second states that conclusion.

(D) The first describes the circumstance that the argument as a whole seeks to explain; the second gives the explanation that the argument seeks to establish.

(E) The first describes the circumstance that the argument as a whole seeks to explain; the second provides evidence in support of the explanation that the argument seeks to establish.

Argument Evaluation

Situation   Top executives at a bank that has been rumored to be in financial trouble have been buying shares in the bank. Bank depositors see this as a good sign, because they believe that it indicates that the executives have faith in the bank. However, corporate executives sometimes do this just to dispel rumors about a company's health.

Reasoning   *What is the role that the two boldfaced portions play in the argument?* The first boldfaced portion states that bank executives are buying bank shares, which the passage indicates is taken by bank depositors to be evidence of the executives' faith in the bank; in other words, the bank depositors take the fact that the executives are buying shares in the bank as supporting the conclusion that the executives have faith in the bank and thus that the rumors that the bank is facing financial collapse are wrong. The passage then tells us what some have inferred from this (namely, that worrisome rumors about the bank's impending financial collapse are false). Finally, the passage offers in the second boldfaced portion evidence that undermines this inference: Corporate executives have sometimes bought shares in their own companies just to dispel negative rumors, presumably whether the rumors are true or not.

A   **Correct.** This option correctly identifies the roles played by the boldfaced portions. As discussed in the Reasoning section above, the bank depositors have drawn the conclusion from the first boldfaced portion that the bank's finances are sound, but the second boldfaced portion is presented to call their conclusion into question.

B   This correctly describes the first portion's role, but the second portion is not offered as a conclusion— no evidence is given for it; rather it is evidence for something else.

C   The second portion is not offered as a conclusion; no evidence is given for it.

D   The second portion is not itself offered as an explanation of why these bank executives are investing in the bank; if it were, that would mean that the bank executives are doing so *because* corporate executives are known to do such things in a calculated effort to dispel worries. Furthermore the argument does not conclude that this other explanation (which the boldfaced portion points to) is correct, only that the one inferred by depositors may not be.

E   The argument is not so much seeking to establish an explanation of its own as it is trying to undermine that inferred by the depositors.

The correct answer is A.

CR03814

796. Between 1980 and 2000 the sea otter population of the Aleutian Islands declined precipitously. There were no signs of disease or malnutrition, so there was probably an increase in the number of otters being eaten by predators. Orcas will eat otters when seals, their normal prey, are unavailable, and the Aleutian Islands seal population declined dramatically in the 1980s. Therefore, orcas were most likely the immediate cause of the otter population decline.

Which of the following, if true, most strengthens the argument?

(A) The population of sea urchins, the main food of sea otters, has increased since the sea otter population declined.

(B) Seals do not eat sea otters, nor do they compete with sea otters for food.

(C) Most of the surviving sea otters live in a bay that is inaccessible to orcas.

(D) The population of orcas in the Aleutian Islands has declined since the 1980s.

(E) An increase in commercial fishing near the Aleutian Islands in the 1980s caused a slight decline in the population of the fish that seals use for food.

Argument Evaluation

Situation   A sea otter population declined even though there were no signs of disease or malnutrition. The local seal population also declined. Orcas eat otters when seals are unavailable, and thus are probably the cause of the decline in the otter population.

Reasoning   *What would be evidence that predation by orcas reduced the sea otter population?* Disease and malnutrition are ruled out as alternative explanations of the decline in the sea otter population. The argument could be further strengthened by casting doubt on other possible explanations, such as predation by other animals, or by presenting observations that predation of otters by orcas would help to explain.

A   Regardless of whether or not orcas ate the sea otters, the sea urchin population would most likely have increased when the population of sea otters preying on them decreased.

B   Because the seal population declined during the initial years of the otter population decline, predation by and competition with seals were already implausible explanations of the otter population decline.

C   **Correct.** Orcas eating most of the accessible otters could plausibly explain this observation, which therefore provides additional evidence that orca predation reduced the sea otter population.

D   If the orca population declined at the same time as the sea otter population, it would be less likely that increasing predation by orcas reduced the otter population.

E   Since the sea otters showed no signs of malnutrition, they were probably getting enough fish. But if they were not, commercial fishing rather than orcas might have caused the otter population decline.

The correct answer is C.

CR76951.02

797. Political Strategist: The domestic policies of our opponents in Party X are contrary to the priorities of many middle-class voters. Yet some of these same voters are supporters of Party X and its candidates due to the party's appeals about foreign policy. In order to win these voters back, we in Party Y must prove to middle-class voters that Party X does not represent their priorities with respect to domestic policy.

Which of the following would, if true, most strongly suggest that the political strategist's plan is unlikely to succeed?

(A) Many in the middle class who support Party X for its foreign policies also support its domestic policies and are fully aware of the implications of those policies.

(B) Most middle-class supporters of Party X care about foreign policy and know very little about its domestic policies.

(C) Long-term domestic policy sometimes conflicts with short-term domestic policy.

(D) There are topics on which Party X and Party Y have significant agreement.

(E) Some middle-class voters are concerned about both domestic and foreign policy.

Evaluation of a Plan

Situation   A political strategist for Party Y notes that the domestic policies of Party X are contrary to the priorities of middle-class voters. Many middle-class voters nonetheless support Party X because of its foreign policy. The strategist argues that to win these voters back, Party Y should prove to middle-class voters that Party X's domestic policies do not represent their priorities.

Reasoning   *What claim would most strongly suggest that the strategist's plan will not succeed?* Suppose that a large number of the middle-class voters who support Party X's foreign policies also support its domestic policies, despite the fact that the domestic policies are contrary to their priorities. If that were true, then Party Y might well be unable to win back these voters by following the strategist's plan.

A   **Correct.** As noted above, if many middle-class voters who support Party X's foreign policies also support its domestic policies, the strategy of attempting to show these voters that there is a conflict between their priorities and Party X's domestic policies may well fail to get them to vote for Party Y. Presumably these voters are aware of the conflict and support Party X nonetheless—perhaps because Party Y's domestic policies conflict with their priorities even more.

B   If most middle-class supporters of Party X know little about its domestic policies, Party Y may well be able to win them back simply by showing them the inconsistencies between those policies and their own priorities.

C   A conflict between long-term domestic policy and short-term domestic policy tells us nothing about whether educating middle-class voters about conflicts between their priorities and Party X's domestic policies would help win them back to Party Y.

D   The fact that the two parties have significant agreement on certain topics does not suggest the strategist's plan will not succeed. In fact, if the parties agreed on very little, the strategy of pointing only to issues related to domestic policy might be less likely to work. Therefore, this answer choice helps rule out a reason for thinking that the plan might not work.

E   If anything, this would help support the claim that the strategist's plan will succeed.

The correct answer is A.

CR05960

798. Studies in restaurants show that the tips left by customers who pay their bill in cash tend to be larger when the bill is presented on a tray that bears a credit-card logo. Consumer psychologists hypothesize that simply seeing a credit-card logo makes many credit-card holders willing to spend more because it reminds them that their spending power exceeds the cash they have immediately available.

Which of the following, if true, most strongly supports the psychologists' interpretation of the studies?

(A) The effect noted in the studies is not limited to patrons who have credit cards.

(B) Patrons who are under financial pressure from their credit-card obligations tend to tip less when presented with a restaurant bill on a tray with a credit-card logo than when the tray has no logo.

(C) In virtually all of the cases in the studies, the patrons who paid bills in cash did not possess credit cards.

(D) In general, restaurant patrons who pay their bills in cash leave larger tips than do those who pay by credit card.

(E) The percentage of restaurant bills paid with a given brand of credit card increases when that credit card's logo is displayed on the tray with which the bill is presented.

Argument Evaluation

Situation   Studies have found that restaurant customers give more generous tips when their bills are brought on trays bearing a credit-card logo. Psychologists speculate that this is because the logo reminds customers of their ability to spend more money than they have.

Reasoning   *Which of the options most helps to support the psychologists' explanation of the studies?* The psychologists' hypothesis is that the credit-card logos on the trays bring to the minds of those who tip more the fact that they have more purchasing power than merely the cash that they have at hand. This explanation would not be valid even if those people who are not reminded of their own excess purchasing power—if in fact they have any such power—when they see such a logo nonetheless tip more in such trays. Thus, if restaurant patrons who are under financial pressure from their credit-card obligations do not tip more when their bills are presented on trays bearing credit-card logos, then the psychologists' interpretation of the studies is supported.

A   This undermines the psychologists' interpretation, for it shows that the same phenomenon occurs even when the alleged cause has been removed.

B   **Correct.** If the consumer psychologists' hypothesis is true, it implies that only those who do, in fact, have additional spending power in the form of credit will be influenced by the logos to leave larger tips. If those who do not have such additional spending power are influenced in the same way, the hypothesis is flawed. Answer choice B indicates that the hypothesis is not flawed in this way, so it thereby tends to strengthen the hypothesis. It also strengthens the hypothesis by weakening some alternative hypotheses such as the following: Most of the customers who pay with cash do so because they have excessive credit-card debt and cannot use a credit card. However, seeing a credit-card logo makes them wonder whether credit-card customers may leave larger tips, and to avoid displeasing the server by leaving a small tip, they decide to leave a larger tip than they might otherwise have done.

C   This undermines the psychologists' interpretation by showing that the same phenomenon occurs even when the alleged cause has been removed; patrons cannot be reminded of something that is not there.

D   To the extent that this bears on the interpretation of the study, it weakens it. Patrons using credit cards are surely aware that they have credit, and yet they spend less generously.

E   This does not support the idea that being reminded that one has a credit card induces one to be more generous, only that it induces one to use that credit card.

The correct answer is B.

CR11633

799. In an experiment, each volunteer was allowed to choose between an easy task and a hard task and was told that another volunteer would do the other task. Each volunteer could also choose to have a computer assign the two tasks randomly. Most volunteers chose the easy task for themselves and under questioning later said they had acted fairly. But when the scenario was described to another group of volunteers, almost all said choosing the easy task would be unfair. This shows that most people apply weaker moral standards to themselves than to others.

Which of the following is an assumption required by this argument?

(A) At least some volunteers who said they had acted fairly in choosing the easy task would have said that it was unfair for someone else to do so.

(B) The most moral choice for the volunteers would have been to have the computer assign the two tasks randomly.

(C) There were at least some volunteers who were assigned to do the hard task and felt that the assignment was unfair.

(D) On average, the volunteers to whom the scenario was described were more accurate in their moral judgments than the other volunteers were.

(E) At least some volunteers given the choice between assigning the tasks themselves and having the computer assign them felt that they had made the only fair choice available to them.

Argument Construction

Situation In an experiment, most volunteers chose to do an easy task themselves and leave a hard task for someone else. They later said they had acted fairly, but almost all volunteers in another group to which the scenario was described said choosing the easy task would be unfair, indicating that most people apply weaker moral standards to themselves.

Reasoning *What must be true in order for the facts presented to support the conclusion that most people apply weaker moral standards to themselves than to others?* One set of volunteers said they had acted fairly in taking the easy task, whereas different volunteers said that doing so would be unfair. In neither case did any of the volunteers actually judge their own behavior differently from how they judged anyone else's. So the argument implicitly infers from the experimental results that most of the volunteers would judge their own behavior differently from someone else's if given the chance. This inference assumes that the volunteers in the second group would have applied the same moral standards that those in the first group did if they had been in the first group's position, and vice versa.

A   Correct. If none of the volunteers who said their own behavior was fair would have judged someone else's similar behavior as unfair, then their relaxed moral judgment of themselves would not suggest that they applied weaker moral standards to themselves than to others.

B   Even if this is so, the experimental results could still suggest that the volunteers would apply weaker moral standards to themselves than to others.

C   The argument would be equally strong even if volunteers who were assigned the hard task did not know that someone else had gotten an easier task—or even if no volunteers were actually assigned the hard task at all.

D   Even if the moral standards applied by the volunteers who judged themselves were as accurate as those applied by the volunteers to whom the scenario was described, the former standards were still weaker.

E   Even if all the volunteers in the first group had felt that all the choices available to them would have been fair for them to make personally, they might have applied stricter moral standards to someone else in the same position.

The correct answer is A.

CR08527

800. Country X's recent stock-trading scandal should not diminish investors' confidence in the country's stock market. For one thing, **the discovery of the scandal confirms that Country X has a strong regulatory system**, as the following considerations show. In any stock market, some fraudulent activity is inevitable. If a stock market is well regulated, any significant stock-trading fraud in it will very likely be discovered. This deters potential perpetrators and facilitates improvement in regulatory processes.

In the argument, the portion in **boldface** plays which of the following roles?

(A) It is the argument's only conclusion.

(B) It is a conclusion for which the argument provides support and which itself is used to support the argument's main conclusion.

(C) It is the argument's main conclusion and is supported by another explicitly stated conclusion for which further support is provided.

(D) It is an assumption for which no explicit support is provided and is used to support the argument's only conclusion.

(E) It is a compound statement containing both the argument's main conclusion and an assumption used to support that conclusion.

Argument Construction

Situation	Country X recently had a stock-trading scandal.
Reasoning	*What role does the statement that the scandal's discovery confirms that Country X has a strong regulatory system play in the argument?* In the sentence containing the boldface statement, the phrase *For one thing* indicates that the statement is being used to justify the claim in the preceding sentence. Thus, the boldface statement must support that preceding sentence as a conclusion. Directly after the boldface statement, the phrase as *the following considerations show* indicates that the subsequent sentences are being used to support the boldface statement. Thus, the boldface statement is a conclusion supported by the sentences following it, and this statement itself supports the sentence preceding it, which must be the argument's main conclusion.

A   As explained above, the boldface statement supports the claim in the preceding sentence, so it cannot be the argument's only conclusion.

B   **Correct.** As explained above, the boldface statement is supported by the statements following it and in turn is used to support the argument's main conclusion in the statement preceding it.

C   As explained above, the boldface statement cannot be the argument's main conclusion, because it supports a further conclusion presented in the sentence preceding it.

D   As explained above, the sentences following the boldface statement are the explicit support provided for it.

E   As explained above, the argument's main conclusion is stated only in the first sentence, which precedes the boldface statement. It is not repeated anywhere in the boldface statement.

The correct answer is B.

CR05644

801. **Delta Products Inc. has recently switched at least partly from older technologies using fossil fuels to new technologies powered by electricity.** The question has been raised whether it can be concluded that, **for a given level of output, Delta's operation now causes less fossil fuel to be consumed than it did formerly.** The answer, clearly, is yes, since the amount of fossil fuel used to generate the electricity needed to power the new technologies is less than the amount needed to power the older technologies, provided level of output is held constant.

In the argument given, the two **boldfaced** portions play which of the following roles?

(A) The first identifies the content of the conclusion of the argument; the second provides support for that conclusion.

(B) The first provides support for the conclusion of the argument; the second identifies the content of that conclusion.

(C) The first states the conclusion of the argument; the second calls that conclusion into question.

(D) The first provides support for the conclusion of the argument; the second calls that conclusion into question.

(E) Each provides support for the conclusion of the argument.

Argument Evaluation

Situation   Delta switched from technologies using fossil fuels to ones using electricity. It has been asked whether this results in less fossil fuel used per level of output. The answer is that it does.

Reasoning   *What roles do the two boldfaced portions play in the argument?* The first boldfaced statement is simply asserted by the passage; no premise, or reason, is given to support it. But the second boldfaced statement, when it is first introduced, is not asserted to be true, but rather is identified as something that might be inferred from the first statement. By the end of the passage the argument concludes that the second statement is true.

A   This option simply reverses the roles that the statements play in the argument.

B   **Correct.** This option identifies the roles the boldfaced portions play: The second statement is not, on its own, the conclusion, because the argument initially merely *asks* whether it can be concluded on the basis of the first statement (that is, it asks whether the first boldface statement provides support for it). The conclusion of the argument is actually the statement *The answer, clearly, is yes.* The word *yes* is elliptical for *Yes, it can be concluded that for a given level of output, Delta's operation now causes less fossil fuel to be consumed than it did formerly.* The boldface portion tells us what can be concluded, and thus it can accurately be described as the content of the conclusion.

C   Nothing in the passage is intended to support the first statement; and the second statement is not supposed to call the first into question.

D   This correctly identifies the role of the first statement, but the second boldfaced portion does not call the argument's conclusion into question—it is part of a sentence that refers to the question whether that conclusion can be drawn from the first statement.

E   Again, this is only half right. The second boldfaced portion is not offered as support for the conclusion; if it were offered as such support, the argument would be guilty of circular reasoning, since the second boldfaced portion states exactly what the argument concludes.

The correct answer is B.

CR44930.02

802. A product that represents a clear technological advance over competing products can generally command a high price. Because **technological advances tend to be quickly surpassed** and companies want to make large profits while they still can, many companies charge the greatest price the market will bear when they have such a product. But **large profits on the new product will give competitors a strong incentive to quickly match the new product's capabilities**. Consequently, the strategy to maximize overall profit from a new product is to charge less than the greatest possible price.

In the argument above, the two portions in **boldface** play which of the following roles?

(A) The first is an assumption that forms the basis for a course of action that the argument criticizes; the second presents the course of action endorsed by the argument.

(B) The first is a consideration raised to explain the appeal of a certain strategy; the second is a consideration raised to call into question the wisdom of adopting that strategy.

(C) The first is an assumption that has been used to justify a certain strategy; the second is a consideration that is used to cast doubt on that assumption.

(D) The first is a consideration raised in support of a strategy the argument endorses; the second presents grounds in support of that consideration.

(E) The first is a consideration raised to show that adopting a certain strategy is unlikely to achieve the intended effect; the second is presented to explain the appeal of that strategy.

Argument Evaluation

Situation   Companies generally charge the greatest price the market will bear when they have a product that represents a technological advance. This is because they want to make large profits while they can. But making large profits inspires competition. As a result, profits can be maximized by charging less than the greatest price possible.

Reasoning   *What logical roles do the two portions in boldface play in the argument?* The first sentence of the passage introduces a connection between technological advances and price. The second sentence discusses a pricing strategy related to such advances and offers certain considerations that help explain that strategy. The first boldfaced portion of the passage, which is contained in the second sentence, presents one of these considerations. The third sentence begins with the word "But," which suggests that what follows—the second boldfaced section—presents a consideration that may be at least superficially at odds with the strategy just described. The final sentence of the argument presents an alternative strategy that is supported by the preceding discussion.

A   The course of action endorsed by the argument is described in the passage's fourth and final sentence, not in the second boldfaced portion, which is found in the passage's third sentence.

B   **Correct.** The first boldfaced portion is part of an explanation of why many companies follow the strategy of charging as much as the market will bear when they have a product representing a technological advance. The second boldfaced portion gives a reason not to follow that strategy.

C   The second boldfaced portion does not cast doubt on an assumption used to justify a strategy, but rather casts doubt on the strategy itself.

D   The first boldfaced portion is raised in support of a strategy that the argument calls into question, not a strategy that the argument endorses.

E   The first boldfaced portion helps explain the appeal of adopting a certain strategy; it does not show that the strategy is likely to fail. The second boldfaced portion does not explain the appeal of the strategy, but rather calls the strategy into question.

The correct answer is B.

CR00907

803. Theater Critic: The play *La Finestrina*, now at Central Theater, was written in Italy in the eighteenth century. The director claims that this production is as similar to the original production as is possible in a modern theater. Although the actor who plays Harlequin the clown gives a performance very reminiscent of the twentieth-century American comedian Groucho Marx, Marx's comic style was very much within the comic acting tradition that had begun in sixteenth-century Italy.

The considerations given best serve as part of an argument that

(A) modern audiences would find it hard to tolerate certain characteristics of a historically accurate performance of an eighteenth-century play

(B) Groucho Marx once performed the part of the character Harlequin in *La Finestrina*

(C) in the United States the training of actors in the twentieth century is based on principles that do not differ radically from those that underlay the training of actors in eighteenth-century Italy

(D) the performance of the actor who plays Harlequin in *La Finestrina* does not serve as evidence against the director's claim

(E) the director of *La Finestrina* must have advised the actor who plays Harlequin to model his performance on comic performances of Groucho Marx

Argument Construction

Situation   The director of the local production of *La Finestrina* says it is as similar to the original production as is possible in a modern theater. The actor playing Harlequin gives a performance reminiscent of Groucho Marx, whose comic style falls within an acting tradition which began in sixteenth-century Italy.

Reasoning   *For which of the options would the consideration given best serve as an argument?* The actor's performance was reminiscent of someone who fell within a tradition going back to sixteenth-century Italy. The play was written, and therefore was likely first performed, in eighteenth-century Italy. All of this suggests that there could be a similarity between the performances of Harlequin in the local production and in the original production. While the two performances *might* have been quite dissimilar, there is nothing *here* that supports that.

A   Regardless of how plausible this option might be on its own merits, the passage provides no support for it because the passage provides no information about the characteristics of a historically accurate performance of an eighteenth-century play.

B   The passage neither says this nor implies it.

C   The passage says nothing about the training of actors, so this option would be supported by the passage only in a very roundabout, indirect way.

D   Correct. This is the option that the considerations most support.

E   That the performance reminded the theater critic of Groucho Marx hardly shows that the similarity was intentional, let alone that it was at the director's instruction.

The correct answer is D.

CR07257

804. Although the discount stores in Goreville's central shopping district are expected to close within five years as a result of competition from a SpendLess discount department store that just opened, those locations will not stay vacant for long. In the five years since the opening of Colson's, a nondiscount department store, a new store has opened at the location of every store in the shopping district that closed because it could not compete with Colson's.

Which of the following, if true, most seriously weakens the argument?

(A) Many customers of Colson's are expected to do less shopping there than they did before the SpendLess store opened.

(B) Increasingly, the stores that have opened in the central shopping district since Colson's opened have been discount stores.

(C) At present, the central shopping district has as many stores operating in it as it ever had.

(D) Over the course of the next five years, it is expected that Goreville's population will grow at a faster rate than it has for the past several decades.

(E) Many stores in the central shopping district sell types of merchandise that are not available at either SpendLess or Colson's.

Argument Evaluation

Situation   Due to competition from a recently opened SpendLess discount department store, discount stores in Goreville's central shopping district are expected to close within five years. But those locations will not be vacant long, for new stores have replaced all those that closed because of the opening five years ago of a Colson's nondiscount department store.

Reasoning   *Which option would most weaken the argument?* The arguer infers that stores that leave because of the SpendLess will be replaced in their locations by other stores because that is what happened after the Colson's department store came in. Since the reasoning relies on a presumed similarity between the two cases, any information that brings to light a relevant dissimilarity would weaken the argument. If the stores that were driven out by Colson's were replaced mostly by discount stores, that suggests that the stores were replaced because of a need that no longer exists after the opening of SpendLess.

A   The fact that Colson's may be seeing fewer customers does not mean that the discount stores that close will not be replaced; they might be replaced by stores that in no way compete with Colson's or SpendLess.

B   **Correct.** As explained in the Reasoning section above, the reasoning in the argument relies on a presumed similarity between the two cases, so any information that brings to light a relevant dissimilarity would weaken the argument. In the previous five years, the stores that went out of business were apparently direct competitors of Colson's, whereas their replacements were of a different type. In contrast, in the predicted scenario, the stores that are expected to go out of business are apparently direct competitors of the new SpendLess discount store. Furthermore, if there has been a significant increase in the number of discount stores in the shopping district, the market for discount stores may well be nearly saturated, so that few, if any, new ones can survive.

C   If anything, this strengthens the argument by indicating that Goreville's central shopping district is thriving.

D   This strengthens the argument because one is more likely to open a new store in an area with a growing population.

E   Because this statement does not indicate whether any of these stores that offer goods not sold at SpendLess or Colson's will be among those that are closing, it is not possible to determine what effect it has on the strength of the argument.

The correct answer is B.

CR05685

805. Last year all refuse collected by Shelbyville city services was incinerated. This incineration generated a large quantity of residual ash. In order to reduce the amount of residual ash Shelbyville generates this year to half of last year's total, the city has revamped its collection program. This year city services will separate for recycling enough refuse to reduce the number of truckloads of refuse to be incinerated to half of last year's number.

Which of the following is required for the revamped collection program to achieve its aim?

(A) This year, no materials that city services could separate for recycling will be incinerated.

(B) Separating recyclable materials from materials to be incinerated will cost Shelbyville less than half what it cost last year to dispose of the residual ash.

(C) Refuse collected by city services will contain a larger proportion of recyclable materials this year than it did last year.

(D) The refuse incinerated this year will generate no more residual ash per truckload incinerated than did the refuse incinerated last year.

(E) The total quantity of refuse collected by Shelbyville city services this year will be no greater than that collected last year.

Argument Construction

Situation   To cut in half the residual ash produced at its incinerator, the city will separate, for recycling, enough refuse to cut in half the number of truckloads of refuse going to the incinerator.

Reasoning   *Which option is required if the city's revamped collection program is to achieve its aim?* Cutting the number of truckloads of refuse in half must reduce the amount of residual ash to half last year's level. But if removal of the recycled refuse does not proportionately reduce the amount of ash, this will not happen. So, if the amount of residual ash produced per truckload increases after recycling, then the amount of ash produced will not be cut in half by cutting in half the number of truckloads.

A   This merely indicates that no further reduction of ash through recycling could be achieved this year; it indicates nothing about how much the ash will be reduced.

B   This suggests a further benefit from recycling, but does not bear on the amount of ash that will be produced.

C   Since no information is provided about how much, if any, recyclable materials were removed from the refuse last year, this does not affect the reasoning.

D   **Correct.** This states a requirement for the collection program to achieve its aim. To see why this is required, assume this were not true. Suppose, instead, that the refuse incinerated this year would generate more residual ash per truckload incinerated than the refuse incinerated last year did. If that were the case, then cutting in half the truckloads to be incinerated would not cut in half the amount of residual ash generated by incineration.

E   This is not a requirement because even if the city collects more refuse this year, it could still cut in half the amount of residual ash by cutting in half the number of truckloads going to the incinerator.

The correct answer is D.

CR01801

806. Veterinarians generally derive some of their income from selling several manufacturers' lines of pet-care products. Knowing that pet owners rarely throw away mail from their pet's veterinarian unread, one manufacturer of pet-care products offered free promotional materials on its products to veterinarians for mailing to their clients. Very few veterinarians accepted the offer, however, even though the manufacturer's products are of high quality.

Which of the following, if true, most helps to explain the veterinarians' reaction to the manufacturer's promotional scheme?

(A) Most of the veterinarians to whom the free promotional materials were offered were already selling the manufacturer's pet-care products to their clients.

(B) The special promotional materials were intended as a supplement to the manufacturer's usual promotional activities rather than as a replacement for them.

(C) The manufacturer's products, unlike most equally good competing products sold by veterinarians, are also available in pet stores and in supermarkets.

(D) Many pet owners have begun demanding quality in products they buy for their pets that is as high as that in products they buy for themselves.

(E) Veterinarians sometimes recommend that pet owners use products formulated for people when no suitable product specially formulated for animals is available.

Evaluation of a Plan

Situation	Veterinarians generally derive some income from selling various manufacturers' pet-care products, but very few veterinarians accepted free promotional materials from one such manufacturer to mail to their clients.
Reasoning	*What would most help explain why so few veterinarians accepted the free promotional materials to mail to their clients?* The passage says that veterinarians generally derive income from selling pet-care products, which suggests that it should have been in many veterinarians' financial interest to accept and mail out the free promotional materials to increase sales. Any evidence that mailing out these specific promotional materials from this manufacturer would not actually have been in many veterinarians' financial interest could help explain why so few veterinarians accepted the materials.

A   This suggests that most of the veterinarians should have had a financial interest in accepting and mailing out the promotional materials in order to increase their sales of the manufacturer's products.

B   Even if the promotional materials supplemented the manufacturer's usual promotional activities, they could still have increased the veterinarians' sales of the manufacturer's products and thus generated more income for the veterinarians.

C   **Correct.** If this manufacturer's products are available in pet stores and supermarkets but most other products sold by veterinarians are not, then distributing the manufacturer's promotional materials could have encouraged customers to buy this manufacturer's products from pet stores and supermarkets rather than to buy competing products from the veterinarians. Thus, the veterinarians may have been concerned that the promotions would reduce their profits.

D   The passage says the manufacturer's products are of high quality, so we have no reason to suppose that clients' demand for quality products would discourage veterinarians from accepting the manufacturer's promotional materials.

E   Presumably the manufacturer's products are specially formulated for pets, so any products veterinarians recommend only when no specially formulated pet-care products are available would not reduce the veterinarians' interest in promoting the manufacturer's products.

The correct answer is C.

CR00778

807. The average hourly wage of television assemblers in Vernland has long been significantly lower than that in neighboring Borodia. Since Borodia dropped all tariffs on Vernlandian televisions three years ago, the number of televisions sold annually in Borodia has not changed. However, recent statistics show a drop in the number of television assemblers in Borodia. Therefore, updated trade statistics will probably indicate that the number of televisions Borodia imports annually from Vernland has increased.

Which of the following is an assumption on which the argument depends?

(A) The number of television assemblers in Vernland has increased by at least as much as the number of television assemblers in Borodia has decreased.

(B) Televisions assembled in Vernland have features that televisions assembled in Borodia do not have.

(C) The average number of hours it takes a Borodian television assembler to assemble a television has not decreased significantly during the past three years.

(D) The number of televisions assembled annually in Vernland has increased significantly during the past three years.

(E) The difference between the hourly wage of television assemblers in Vernland and the hourly wage of television assemblers in Borodia is likely to decrease in the next few years.

Argument Construction

Situation   Television assemblers in Vernland are paid less than those in neighboring Borodia. The number of televisions sold in Borodia has not dropped since its tariffs on Vernlandian TVs were lowered three years ago, but the number of TV assemblers in Borodia has. So TV imports from Vernland have likely increased.

Reasoning   *What assumption does the argument depend on?* The fact that fewer individuals in Borodia are working as TV assemblers is offered as evidence that TV imports from Vernland into Borodia have likely increased. That piece of evidence is relevant only as an indication that the number of TVs being produced within Borodia has decreased. But a drop in the number of TV assemblers does not indicate a drop in the number of TVs being assembled if the number of TVs an average assembler puts together has increased. Thus, the argument must be assuming that the average time it takes an assembler to put together a TV has not significantly decreased.

A   The argument does not rely on any information about the number of television assemblers in Vernland nor for that matter on the number of TVs assembled in Vernland.

B   The argument need not assume there is any difference in the features of the TVs produced in the two countries. Increased sales of Vernlandian TVs in Borodia could be due to any number of other reasons, such as price or quality.

C   **Correct.** If the average productivity of TV assemblers had increased significantly, the fact that there are fewer Borodian TV assemblers would not strongly support the conclusion that there has been a decrease in the number of TVs assembled in Borodia and an increase in imports; fewer assemblers may be producing just as many TVs as before. Therefore, for the argument to work, it needs to assume that productivity per assembler in Borodia has not decreased significantly.

D   The argument does not depend upon this being so: Vernland's domestic TV sales (or perhaps its exports to countries other than Borodia) may have decreased by more than its exports to Borodia have increased.

E   The argument's conclusion addresses what has happened; the argument in no way relies on any assumptions about what may or may not happen in the coming years.

The correct answer is C.

CR05725

808. Guidebook writer: I have visited hotels throughout the country and have noticed that in those built before 1930 the quality of the original carpentry work is generally superior to that in hotels built afterward. Clearly carpenters working on hotels before 1930 typically worked with more skill, care, and effort than carpenters who have worked on hotels built subsequently.

Which of the following, if true, most seriously weakens the guidebook writer's argument?

(A) The quality of original carpentry in hotels is generally far superior to the quality of original carpentry in other structures, such as houses and stores.

(B) Hotels built since 1930 can generally accommodate more guests than those built before 1930.

(C) The materials available to carpenters working before 1930 were not significantly different in quality from the materials available to carpenters working after 1930.

(D) The better the quality of original carpentry in a building, the less likely that building is to fall into disuse and be demolished.

(E) The average length of apprenticeship for carpenters has declined significantly since 1930.

Argument Evaluation

Situation   The original carpentry in hotels built before 1930 shows superior care, skill, and effort to that in hotels built after 1930. This leads to the conclusion that carpenters working on hotels before 1930 were superior in skill, care, and effort to those that came after.

Reasoning   *Which option most seriously weakens the argument?* The argument draws an inference from a comparison between carpentry in hotels of different eras to a judgment about the carpenters working on hotels in those eras. One way to weaken this inference is by finding some way in which the carpentry in the hotels may be unrepresentative of the skill, care, and effort of the carpenters working in the eras. The comparison is between the carpentry evident in hotels of the two eras *that still exist.* Thus, if there is some reason to think that hotels with good carpentry survive longer than those with bad carpentry, then still-existing hotels from the older era will have disproportionately more good carpentry, even assuming no difference between the skill, care, and effort of the carpenters from the two eras.

A   This option applies equally to both eras, so it has no bearing on the argument.

B   It is not clear whether carpenters working on larger hotels would exercise more, less, or the same skill and care as those working on smaller hotels; thus this option does not weaken the argument.

C   The argument does not rely, even implicitly, on there being any difference in the quality of materials used in the two eras, so it does not weaken the argument to point out that no such difference exists.

D   Correct. This weakens the reasoning in the argument by showing a respect in which the comparison between *existing* hotels may be unrepresentative. Specifically, the comparison may be unrepresentative in that still-existing hotels that were built prior to 1930 may well have been better built than most hotels built prior to 1930 were; the hotels that did not have unusually high-quality carpentry work may have all fallen into disuse and been demolished.

E   The longer a carpenter works as an apprentice, the more skill he or she is apt to have upon becoming a full-fledged carpenter. So this option would tend to slightly strengthen rather than weaken the argument.

The correct answer is D.

CR02997

809. Scientists typically do their most creative work before the age of forty. It is commonly thought that this happens because aging by itself brings about a loss of creative capacity. However, studies show that **of scientists who produce highly creative work beyond the age of forty, a disproportionately large number entered their field at an older age than is usual.** Since by the age of forty the large majority of scientists have been working in their field for at least fifteen years, the studies' finding strongly suggests that the real reason why scientists over forty rarely produce highly creative work is not that they have aged but rather that **scientists over forty have generally spent too long in their field.**

In the argument given, the two portions in **boldface** play which of the following roles?

(A) The first is a claim, the accuracy of which is at issue in the argument; the second is a conclusion drawn on the basis of that claim.

(B) The first is an objection that has been raised against a position defended in the argument; the second is that position.

(C) The first is evidence that has been used to support an explanation that the argument challenges; the second is that explanation.

(D) The first is evidence that has been used to support an explanation that the argument challenges; the second is a competing explanation that the argument favors.

(E) The first provides evidence to support an explanation that the argument favors; the second is that explanation.

Argument Evaluation

Situation   It is generally thought that the reason scientists tend to do their most creative work before age forty is that creative capacity declines with age. Yet those scientists who do creative work after forty tend, disproportionately, to have started their careers in science later in life. So a better explanation is that many scientists over forty have just been at it too long.

Reasoning   *What roles do the two portions of the argument that are in boldface play?* The argument describes a phenomenon and what is commonly thought to explain it. Then, the first boldfaced statement introduces evidence that suggests that there may be another explanation. After this evidence is further developed, the argument then concludes that there is indeed a better explanation for the phenomenon; that explanation is stated in the second boldfaced portion.

A   The accuracy of the first statement is never called into question by the argument; rather, it is relied upon as the basis for the argument's conclusion.

B   The first statement is not an objection against the position the argument defends; instead, it is a basis for that position.

C   The first statement is not used to support a position the argument challenges, and the second statement is the explanation the argument supports, not the one it challenges.

D   The second statement is indeed an explanation that the argument favors; but the first statement is not used to support a competing explanation that the argument challenges.

E   **Correct.** This option correctly identifies the roles played by the boldfaced portions of the argument.

The correct answer is E.

CR03818

810. NorthAir charges low fares for its economy-class seats, but it provides very cramped seating and few amenities. Market research shows that economy passengers would willingly pay more for wider seating and better service, and additional revenue provided by these higher ticket prices would more than cover the additional cost of providing these amenities. Even though NorthAir is searching for ways to improve its profitability, it has decided not to make these improvements.

Which of the following, if true, would most help to explain NorthAir's decision in light of its objectives?

(A) None of NorthAir's competitors offers significantly better seating and service to economy-class passengers than NorthAir does.

(B) On many of the routes that NorthAir flies, it is the only airline to offer direct flights.

(C) A few of NorthAir's economy-class passengers are satisfied with the service they receive, given the low price they pay.

(D) Very few people avoid flying on NorthAir because of the cramped seating and poor service offered in economy class.

(E) The number of people who would be willing to pay the high fares NorthAir charges for its business-class seats would decrease if its economy-class seating were more acceptable.

Evaluation of a Plan

Situation   Market research shows that improving some amenities for economy-class passengers would allow NorthAir to raise its economy ticket prices more than enough to cover the additional cost of providing those amenities. But NorthAir has decided not to improve those amenities, even though it is looking for ways to improve its profitability.

Reasoning   *What would most help explain why NorthAir decided not to improve the seating and other amenities, even though the resulting increase in economy-class ticket prices would more than cover the expense?* NorthAir is looking for ways to improve its profitability. Making improvements that would increase ticket prices enough to generate more revenue than they cost should improve profitability, other things being equal. But if improving the amenities would generate side effects that reduced profitability, those side effects would provide a good reason for NorthAir's decision not to improve the amenities and hence would help explain why NorthAir made that decision.

A   The passage says that for NorthAir, the cost of providing better economy seating and other amenities would be more than met by the increased revenue from the higher ticket prices that passengers would be willing to pay. This could give NorthAir a competitive edge, with improved profitability.

B   Even if NorthAir faces little or no competition on certain routes, offering extra amenities might increase passengers' interest in flying those routes. It might also lead passengers to choose NorthAir on other routes that competing airlines also serve. Both of these effects could improve NorthAir's profitability.

C   Even if a few NorthAir economy passengers would not pay more for extra amenities, the market research indicates that most of them would, so offering the amenities could still improve NorthAir's profits attributable to economy-class seating.

D   This suggests that improving the amenities would not increase the total number of NorthAir passengers. But improving the amenities might still enable the airline to increase its ticket prices per passenger enough to improve its profitability.

E   **Correct.** This suggests that improving the economy-class amenities would reduce NorthAir's revenue from sales of business-class tickets, which are likely much more expensive than economy-class tickets. This reduction in revenue could be enough to reduce NorthAir's total profitability despite the increased revenue from economy-class ticket sales.

The correct answer is E.

CR00774

811. Which of the following most logically completes the argument given?

Asthma, a chronic breathing disorder, is significantly more common today among adult competitive swimmers than it is among competitive athletes who specialize in other sports. Although chlorine is now known to be a lung irritant and swimming pool water is generally chlorinated, it would be rash to assume that frequent exposure to chlorine is the explanation of the high incidence of asthma among these swimmers, since _____.

(A) young people who have asthma are no more likely to become competitive athletes than are young people who do not have asthma

(B) competitive athletes who specialize in sports other than swimming are rarely exposed to chlorine

(C) competitive athletes as a group have a significantly lower incidence of asthma than do people who do not participate in competitive athletics

(D) until a few years ago, physicians routinely recommended competitive swimming to children with asthma, in the belief that this form of exercise could alleviate asthma symptoms

(E) many people have asthma without knowing they have it and thus are not diagnosed with the condition until they begin engaging in very strenuous activities, such as competitive athletics

Argument Construction

Situation   Asthma is more common among competitive swimmers than among other competitive athletes. Chlorine is a lung irritant generally present in swimming pool water.

Reasoning   *What would cast doubt on the hypothesis that exposure to chlorine in swimming pools accounts for the high incidence of asthma among adult competitive swimmers?* Evidence of any other factor that would provide an alternative explanation of why asthma is more common among adult competitive swimmers than among other competitive athletes would make it rash to assume that frequent exposure to chlorine explains the high incidence of asthma among these swimmers, so a statement providing such evidence would logically fill in the blank at the end of the passage to complete the argument.

A   This might help explain why competitive athletes in general are not especially likely to have asthma, but it does not explain why adult competitive swimmers are more likely to have asthma than other competitive athletes are.

B   This provides additional evidence that exposure to chlorine explains why adult competitive swimmers are more likely to have asthma than other competitive athletes are, so it does not cast doubt on that hypothesis.

C   A lower incidence of asthma among competitive athletes than among nonathletes does not help explain the higher incidence of asthma among adult competitive swimmers than among other competitive athletes.

D   Correct. Routinely encouraging children with asthma to take up competitive swimming would likely have made the proportion of adult competitive swimmers with asthma exceed the proportion of other competitive athletes with asthma, even if chlorine in swimming pool water never causes asthma in swimmers.

E   This might help explain why people with asthma are just as likely as other people to become competitive athletes, but it does not help explain why adult competitive swimmers are more likely to have asthma than other competitive athletes are.

The correct answer is D.

CR01289

812. In the country of Marut, the Foreign Trade Agency's records were reviewed in 1994 in light of information then newly available about neighboring Goro. The review revealed that in every year since 1963, the agency's projection of what Goro's gross national product (GNP) would be five years later was a serious underestimate. The review also revealed that in every year since 1963, the agency estimated Goro's GNP for the previous year—a Goro state secret—very accurately.

Of the following claims, which is most strongly supported by the statements given?

(A) Goro's GNP fluctuated greatly between 1963 and 1994.

(B) Prior to 1995, Goro had not released data intended to mislead the agency in making its five-year projections.

(C) The amount by which the agency underestimated the GNP it projected for Goro tended to increase over time.

(D) Even before the new information came to light, the agency had reason to think that at least some of the five-year projections it had made were inaccurate.

(E) The agency's five-year projections of Goro's GNP had no impact on economic planning in Marut.

Argument Construction

Situation   A review in 1994 revealed that every year since 1963, Marut's Foreign Trade Agency had seriously underestimated what Goro's GNP would be five years later, but accurately estimated what Goro's GNP had been the previous year.

Reasoning   *What conclusion do the stated facts most strongly support?* Goro's GNP in each year at least from 1969 through 1993 had been seriously underestimated by the agency five years in advance, yet was then accurately estimated by the agency one year after the fact. It follows that for each of these years, the agency's earlier projection of Goro's GNP must have been much lower than its later estimate.

A   This is not supported by the information given. The fact that the agency consistently underestimated each year's GNP in its five-year projections and then correctly estimated it after the fact does not indicate that Goro's GNP fluctuated greatly.

B   This is not supported by the information given. The reason the agency's five-year projections were inaccurate might well have been that Goro deliberately released data intended to mislead the agency in making those projections.

C   This is not supported by the information given. The fact that the underestimates remained large throughout the years in question does not indicate that the underestimates increased over time.

D   Correct. As explained above, for many years there were serious discrepancies between the agency's five-year projections of Goro's GNP and its retrospective estimates of each previous year's trade. In any year at least from 1970 through 1993, these discrepancies, if noticed, would have given the agency reason to doubt some of the five-year projections.

E   This is not supported by the information given. Even though at least some of the five-year projections were eventually known to be serious underestimates, they could still have affected Marut's economic planning. The economic planners might have retained an unreasonable faith in the accuracy of the most recent projections.

The correct answer is D.

CR05082

813. Vargonia has just introduced a legal requirement that student-teacher ratios in government-funded schools not exceed a certain limit. All Vargonian children are entitled to education, free of charge, in these schools. When a recession occurs and average incomes fall, the number of children enrolled in government-funded schools tends to increase. Therefore, though most employment opportunities contract in economic recessions, getting a teaching job in Vargonia's government-funded schools will not be made more difficult by a recession.

Which of the following would be most important to determine in order to evaluate the argument?

(A) Whether in Vargonia there are any schools not funded by the government that offer children an education free of charge

(B) Whether the number of qualified applicants for teaching positions in government-funded schools increases significantly during economic recessions

(C) What the current student-teacher ratio in Vargonia's government-funded schools is

(D) What proportion of Vargonia's workers currently hold jobs as teachers in government-funded schools

(E) Whether in the past a number of government-funded schools in Vargonia have had student-teacher ratios well in excess of the new limit

Argument Evaluation

Situation   During a recession, the number of children in government-funded schools in Vargonia tends to increase. Vargonian children are entitled to a free education in these schools. A new law requires student-teacher ratios in these schools to remain below a certain limit.

Reasoning   *Which of the five questions would provide us with the best information for evaluating the argument?* The argument's conclusion is that recessions do not make teaching jobs in Vargonia's government-funded schools harder to get. During recessions, the reasoning goes, more students will enroll in Vargonia's government-funded schools than in nonrecession times. Implicit in the argument is the thought that, because the new law sets an upper limit on the average number of students per teacher, schools that get an influx of new students would have to hire more teachers. During a recession, however, there might be much more competition in the labor market for teachers because many more qualified people are applying for teaching jobs.

A   This information is not significant in the context of the argument, which does not need to assume that only government-funded schools provide free education.

B   **Correct.** Getting an answer to this question would provide us with specific information useful in evaluating the argument. A "yes" answer to this question would suggest that competition for teaching jobs in Vargonian government-funded schools would be keener during recessions. A "no" answer would suggest that the level of competition would decrease during recessions.

C   Discovering the current student-teacher ratio in Vargonia's schools would be of no value, by itself, in evaluating the argument. We do not know what the new upper limit on the student-teacher ratio is, and we do not know whether Vargonia is currently in a recession.

D   Finding out whether the proportion this refers to is 1 percent, for example, or 4 percent, would tell us nothing about whether getting teaching jobs at government-funded schools in Vargonia becomes more difficult during a recession. Among other things, we do not know whether Vargonia is currently in a recession, and we do not know what proportion of Vargonia's workers would be qualified candidates for teaching jobs.

E   This is of no relevance in evaluating the argument because, presumably, the new limit on student-teacher ratios will be complied with. Thus, even if student-teacher ratios in the past would have exceeded the new limit, the argument concerns whether, *in the future*, getting a teaching job in Vargonia's government-funded schools will be made more difficult by a recession.

The correct answer is B.

CR09951

814. In Colorado subalpine meadows, nonnative dandelions co-occur with a native flower, the larkspur. Bumblebees visit both species, creating the potential for interactions between the two species with respect to pollination. In a recent study, researchers selected 16 plots containing both species; all dandelions were removed from eight plots; the remaining eight control plots were left undisturbed. The control plots yielded significantly more larkspur seeds than the dandelion-free plots, leading the researchers to conclude that the presence of dandelions facilitates pollination (and hence seed production) in the native species by attracting more pollinators to the mixed plots.

Which of the following, if true, most seriously undermines the researchers' reasoning?

(A)   Bumblebees preferentially visit dandelions over larkspurs in mixed plots.

(B)   In mixed plots, pollinators can transfer pollen from one species to another to augment seed production.

(C)   If left unchecked, nonnative species like dandelions quickly crowd out native species.

(D)   Seed germination is a more reliable measure of a species' fitness than seed production.

(E)   Soil disturbances can result in fewer blooms, and hence lower seed production.

Argument Evaluation

Situation   Bumblebees visit both larkspur and dandelions in certain meadows. A study found that more larkspur seeds were produced in meadow plots in which both larkspur and dandelions grew than in similar plots from which all dandelions had been removed. The researchers inferred that dandelions facilitate larkspur pollination.

Reasoning   *What evidence would cast the most doubt on the inference from the study's findings to the conclusion that dandelions facilitate larkspur pollination by attracting more pollinators?* The argument assumes that the only relevant difference between the two types of plots was whether dandelions were present. Evidence that the plots differed in some other way that could provide a plausible alternative explanation of why more larkspur seeds were produced in the plots with dandelions would weaken the argument.

A   This would suggest that the larkspur pollination should have been lower in the plots with dandelions, so it does not provide a plausible alternative explanation for the study's findings.

B   This is fully compatible with the claim that the dandelions attracted more pollinators to the mixed plots, and it would also help to support the argument's conclusion that dandelions facilitated larkspur pollination in those plots.

C   Although this suggests that the mixed plots won't remain mixed for long, it does not provide a plausible alternative explanation for the study's finding that larkspur seed production was higher in the mixed plots.

D   The argument is not about how fit larkspurs are as a species, but about why they produced different numbers of seeds in the different plots.

E   **Correct.** This provides a plausible alternative explanation for why larkspur seed production was lower in the plots from which dandelions had been removed, since digging them out would have disturbed the soil.

The correct answer is E.

CR11453

815. An experiment was done in which human subjects recognize a pattern within a matrix of abstract designs and then select another design that completes that pattern. The results of the experiment were surprising. The lowest expenditure of energy in neurons in the brain was found in those subjects who performed most successfully in the experiments.

Which of the following hypotheses best accounts for the findings of the experiment?

(A) The neurons of the brain react less when a subject is trying to recognize patterns than when the subject is doing other kinds of reasoning.

(B) Those who performed best in the experiment experienced more satisfaction when working with abstract patterns than did those who performed less well.

(C) People who are better at abstract pattern recognition have more energy-efficient neural connections.

(D) The energy expenditure of the subjects' brains increases when a design that completes the initially recognized pattern is determined.

(E) The task of completing a given design is more capably performed by athletes, whose energy expenditure is lower when they are at rest.

Argument Construction

Situation   Experimental subjects worked with pattern recognition and completion. The subjects who performed best showed the lowest expenditure of energy in neurons in the brain.

Reasoning   *Which hypothesis best accounts for the findings?* In order to account for the findings, the hypothesis must suggest a plausible link between successful performance and the energy expenditure of neurons in the brain. Consider each answer choice, and evaluate its plausibility and logic. Where is there a reasonably direct relationship between the given factors and the conclusion that is drawn? Understand that hypotheses based on factors not included in the experiment cannot be used to account for the findings.

A   The experiment did not compare types of reasoning so this hypothesis does not account for the results.

B   No information is provided about subjects' satisfaction, so this hypothesis is not warranted.

C   **Correct.** This statement properly identifies a hypothesis that connects subjects' performance with their energy expenditure and so could account for the experiment's results.

D   The most successful subjects would presumably not have completed fewer patterns than average, so the posited increase in energy would likely lead to higher energy expenditures for them, not lower.

E   No information is offered on the subjects, so no hypothesis about athletes is warranted.

The correct answer is C.

CR01202

816. With seventeen casinos, Moneyland operates the most casinos in a certain state. Although intent on expanding, it was outmaneuvered by Apex Casinos in negotiations to acquire the Eldorado chain. To complete its acquisition of Eldorado, Apex must sell five casinos to comply with a state law forbidding any owner to operate more than one casino per county. Since Apex will still be left operating twenty casinos in the state, it will then have the most casinos in the state.

Which of the following, if true, most seriously undermines the prediction?

(A) Apex, Eldorado, and Moneyland are the only organizations licensed to operate casinos in the state.

(B) The majority of Eldorado's casinos in the state will need extensive renovations if they are to continue to operate profitably.

(C) Some of the state's counties do not permit casinos.

(D) Moneyland already operates casinos in the majority of the state's counties.

(E) Apex will use funds it obtains from the sale of the five casinos to help fund its acquisition of the Eldorado chain.

Argument Evaluation

Situation   Moneyland operates seventeen casinos, the most in a certain state, and is intent on expanding. Another operator, Apex Casinos, is acquiring the Eldorado casino chain, but must sell five casinos to comply with a state law forbidding any owner to operate more than one casino per county. After these transactions, Apex will operate twenty casinos in the state.

Reasoning   *What observation would cast the most doubt on the prediction that Apex will have the most casinos in the state after the transactions?* Apex will operate twenty casinos, whereas Moneyland now operates just seventeen, and no one else operates even that many. It follows that Apex will operate more casinos after its transactions than Moneyland or any other one owner now operates. However, if Moneyland also acquires three or more casinos during the transactions, then Apex will not have the most casinos in the state afterward. Thus, any observation suggesting that Moneyland is about to acquire several casinos would undermine the prediction.

A   **Correct.** Since Apex is acquiring Eldorado, Moneyland and Apex will be the only remaining licensed casino operators in the state. Therefore, Moneyland is the only likely buyer for the five casinos Apex needs to sell. So Moneyland is likely to acquire the five casinos during the sale and end up with twenty-two casinos—more than Apex.

B   This does not undermine the prediction. Even if the Eldorado casinos cannot operate profitably for long without extensive renovations, Apex will still have twenty casinos immediately after its transactions.

C   This supports rather than undermines the prediction. If fewer counties permit casinos, there will be fewer opportunities for Moneyland or any other operator to acquire more casinos to surpass the twenty Apex will own.

D   This supports rather than undermines the prediction. If Moneyland's seventeen casinos are in most of the state's counties already, then there are fewer counties in which Moneyland could acquire additional casinos to surpass the twenty Apex will own.

E   This supports rather than undermines the prediction. Apex's use of the funds from selling the five casinos to acquire the Eldorado chain will not help anyone else to acquire more casinos to surpass the twenty Apex will own.

The correct answer is A.

CR05093

817. It is widely assumed that people need to engage in intellectual activities such as solving crossword puzzles or mathematics problems in order to maintain mental sharpness as they age. In fact, however, simply talking to other people—that is, participating in social interaction, which engages many mental and perceptual skills—suffices. Evidence to this effect comes from a study showing that the more social contact people report, the better their mental skills.

Which of the following, if true, most seriously weakens the force of the evidence cited?

(A) As people grow older, they are often advised to keep exercising their physical and mental capacities in order to maintain or improve them.

(B) Many medical conditions and treatments that adversely affect a person's mental sharpness also tend to increase that person's social isolation.

(C) Many people are proficient both in social interactions and in solving mathematical problems.

(D) The study did not itself collect data but analyzed data bearing on the issue from prior studies.

(E) The tasks evaluating mental sharpness for which data were compiled by the study were more akin to mathematics problems than to conversation.

Argument Evaluation

Situation   A study shows that the more social contact people report, the better their mental skills are, so engaging in social interaction is sufficient for maintaining mental sharpness.

Reasoning   *What would suggest that the study does not establish the truth of the conclusion?* The study shows a correlation between mental sharpness and social interaction but does not indicate why this correlation exists. Evidence that mental sharpness contributes to social interaction or that some third factor affects both mental sharpness and social interaction, could provide an alternative explanation for the correlation and thus cast doubt on the explanation that social interaction contributes to mental sharpness.

A   People are often wrongly advised to do things that are not actually beneficial. And even if exercising mental capacities does help to maintain them, the passage says that social interaction provides such exercise.

B   **Correct.** This provides evidence that the correlation observed in the study results from mental sharpness facilitating social interaction, in which case the study results do not indicate that social interaction facilitates mental sharpness.

C   This would be expected, given the argument's conclusion that social interaction helps to maintain better mental skills overall.

D   A study that analyzes data from prior studies can provide evidence just as well as a study that collects its own data can.

E   The argument's conclusion would be compatible with this observation, and would then suggest that social interaction contributes to the mental sharpness needed for tasks similar to math problems.

The correct answer is B.

9.0   Sentence Correction

9.0 Sentence Correction

Each GMAT™ Sentence Correction question presents a statement in which words are underlined. The question asks you to select the best expression of the idea or relationship described in the underlined section from the answer options. The first answer choice always repeats the original phrasing, whereas the other four provide alternatives. In some cases, the original phrasing is the best choice. In other cases, the underlined section has obvious or subtle errors that require correction. These questions require you to be familiar with the stylistic conventions and grammatical rules of standard written English and to demonstrate your ability to improve incorrect or ineffective expressions. Sentence Correction questions may include English-language idioms, which are standard constructions not derived from the most basic rules of grammar and vocabulary, but questions about idioms are not intended to measure any specialized knowledge of colloquialisms or regionalisms.

You should begin each question by reading the sentence carefully. Note whether there are any obvious grammatical errors as you read the underlined portion. Then read the five answer choices carefully. If there is a subtle error you did not recognize the first time you read the sentence, it may become apparent after you have read the answer choices. If the error is still unclear, see whether you can eliminate some of the answers as being incorrect. Remember that in some cases, the original selection may be the best answer.

9.1 Some Comments About How It Works

Sentence Correction questions require a good understanding of how the conventions of standard written English can be used for effective communication. However, that understanding does not have to come from extensive explicit training in grammar and usage or from knowledge of specialized linguistic terminology. Many people may have the needed insights without being able to explain them in technical terms. Analogously, without knowing the scientific name of baker's yeast or the chemistry of the Maillard reaction, a talented baker or food critic may be able to tell whether a loaf of bread was properly prepared. This is not to say that explicit training in grammar and usage is unhelpful. As an adjunct to experience in critical reading and writing, it can be a useful way to develop insights into good written communication. It is good to be cautious, though; books and websites offering advice about how to write may occasionally stipulate outmoded or idiosyncratic rules not generally followed in effective professional writing.

The problems posed in Sentence Correction take a different approach from those in the other Verbal Reasoning sections, and fall within a different domain. But like the questions in those sections, they test skills of critical reasoning, problem solving, and reading comprehension. Sentence Correction tasks can be aptly thought of as requiring detective work. A key part of this work consists in understanding the differences among formulations the answer choices offer and in seeing that some do not make sense when they are plugged into the larger sentence. In this way, the Sentence Correction questions pose some of the most refined and closely targeted reading comprehension tasks in the GMAT exam. To see why certain wordings do not work, you will need to use critical analysis, forming hypotheses about what the writer is trying to express and being ready to revise the hypotheses as you read through the answer choices.

The more difficult questions are not essentially designed to test for knowledge of rules or facts that are harder to learn or that require more technical training. Difficulty often stems from complexity and subtlety among the interconnected parts of the sentence and involves critical application of principles that all astute users of English should understand. Sentence Correction tasks are puzzles of a sort, but they are not arbitrarily contrived. Typically, the incorrect answer choices represent flaws that even an experienced writer might introduce by temporarily losing track of a sentence's structure or by accidentally moving a piece of text to an unsuitable position.

Sometimes you may be able to think of a wording that works better than any of the options presented, but the task is to find the most effective of the wording choices offered. In writing, there are almost always tradeoffs. For example, conciseness is sometimes the enemy of adequate precision and specificity. Certain types of redundancy can be annoying and can make the writer seem inept, but other types of repetition and paraphrasing can improve readability and comprehension. Language serves many purposes, not all of which are cooperative or directly informative. In sincere, straightforwardly informative writing—although not in all advertising, entertainment, and poetry—one should minimize ambiguity, yet in the end every sentence is at least somewhat open to multiple interpretations. Because one can never absolutely eliminate the risk of unintended interpretations, Sentence Correction answers should minimize that risk relative to the context, setting, and ordinary assumptions about the intent of the writer. It is safe to assume that any GMAT Sentence Correction sentence you encounter will be intended to sincerely inform, instruct, or inquire, rather than to parody bad writing, confuse the reader, or provoke laughter, outrage, or derision.

You will not be expected to take sides in contentious controversies about grammar, usage, or style or to apply rules widely regarded as highly pedantic or outdated. A few of these are mentioned in the discussions of the specific categories that follow.

9.2 The Eight Sentence Correction Categories

Sentence Correction questions are classified into eight grammar and usage categories. Each incorrect answer choice contains a flaw in at least one of these categories, and some span two or more categories. Each test contains questions representing a wide range of different types of problem. In the answer explanations in section 9.9, the categories shown in each question's heading are the most salient, but many questions contain problems in other categories as well. Although these eight categories represent the full range of Sentence Correction questions, the discussions about each category below are not exhaustive and are not intended as a comprehensive guide to English grammar and usage. For each category, the discussion aims to provide a general understanding of the kinds of reasoning that may be involved in solving Sentence Correction problems of that type. For more information about English grammar and style, please refer to section 6.5 of Chapter 6.

1. Agreement

Effective verbal communication requires clarity about how a sentence's elements relate to one another. The conventions of agreement help maintain such clarity; constructions that violate these conventions can be confusing or even nonsensical. There are two types of agreement: subject-verb agreement and agreement of terms that have the same referent.

A. ***Subject-verb agreement:*** Singular subjects take singular verbs, whereas plural subjects take plural verbs.

B. ***Agreement between terms that have the same referent:*** A pronoun that stands for another element in the discourse—a noun, a noun phrase, or another pronoun—must agree with its antecedent in person, number, and gender.

For details about and examples of these two types of agreement, see section 6.5.2 of Chapter 6.

Almost all educated users of English have internalized the conventions of agreement, yet we all occasionally make grammatical mistakes involving agreement because we lose track of the structure of our wording. Keep in mind that as you evaluate different wording choices, context is vitally important.

Examples:

i) We can see immediately that an entire clause consisting of the words *you is working* would be incorrect. On the other hand, that same sequence of words is correct in the following sentence:

> The team member, who used to assist **you, is working** on a different project now.

Seeing this depends on recognizing that the subject of *is* is not *you* but rather the entire noun phrase preceding the verb. This recognition may be either intuitive or based on explicit analysis.

ii) Similarly, no one would seriously claim that the plural *they* should stand for the singular noun *proposal*, but one might more easily overlook the failure of agreement in the following sentence:

> From among the six submitted proposals, they chose number four, believing that they could be more easily implemented than the other five.

Many readers may see the problem quickly, but in doing so they are noting some complex features of the sentence structure. Grammatically, *they* could refer to the six proposals or to those who chose from among them, but neither of those tentative interpretations makes sense. The choosers are not the sorts of things that could be implemented, and the comparative phrase *than the other five* rules out the hypothesis that the antecedent of *they* is the plural *six submitted proposals*. Changing *they* to *it* resolves the discrepancy by providing a pronoun that clearly has the singular noun phrase *number four* as its antecedent. Here the reasoning overlaps with that involved in the category of logical predication discussed in section 9.2.5 below.

Some complicating factors to consider:

When analyzing potential agreement issues in Sentence Correction, keep in mind that not all cases conform obviously and straightforwardly to the basic rules of agreement reviewed in section 6.5 of Chapter 6. Here are a few special considerations not reviewed in that section.

A. *Plurals that appear singular:* Fluent English speakers are aware that for some words the plural is the same as the singular (*sheep* and *deer*, for example). But there are subtle cases, as when a formally singular noun referring to a group or culture is construed as plural. No simple rule governs the use of such terms; one can say, for example, *the British are* or *the Inuit are* but not *the German are* or *the Cuban are*. *Police* is plural, but many similar group words, such as *navy*, are typically construed as singular.

B. *Plurals construed as singular:* Some formally plural nouns, such as *news*, are construed as singular in normal usage. A title with a plural form (such as *The Grapes of Wrath*) takes a singular verb if it refers to a single work, and some names of organizations or political entities may be construed as singular even though they have a plural form. For example, the phrase *the Cayman Islands* may be singular when referring to the country as a political entity but plural when referring to the islands as multiple pieces of land.

C. *Singular verbs that could appear plural:* For most English verbs (with the notable exception of *to be*), the infinitive is the same as the present plural, and the present subjunctive for all persons is the same as the infinitive. Furthermore, the singular past subjunctive is the same as the plural. Thus, there is a risk that at first glance a correct verb form used with a singular subject may appear plural.

Examples:

i) "The researcher suspend further testing" and "I were you" would be incorrect as complete sentences, but in the following sentences they are in the subjunctive mood and are correct:

We considered it imperative that **the researcher suspend further testing**.
I wouldn't do that if **I were you**.

ii) As a complete sentence, "The mayor attend the hearings" would be incorrect, but in the following sentence it is correct because the verb form ***attend*** is an infinitive preceded by the auxiliary verb ***will***:

In none of these cases will either the councilor or **the mayor attend the hearings**."

Some issues that are not tested:

The following are a few examples of issues outside the scope of the agreement-related Sentence Correction questions:

A. Especially in informal discourse, the plural pronoun ***they*** and related forms ***them***, ***their***, and ***theirs*** are sometimes used as nonspecific, genderless ways of referring to a singular person. Consider, for example, "Somebody left **their** notebook on the conference room table."

The reasoning surrounding such usage and the alternatives (***he, she, she or he, she/he***) is complex and evolving. You should not expect to see questions that require you to judge which usage is preferable.

B. Although you should be able to recognize commonly used irregular plurals or special classes of plurals (such as ***phenomena, cacti, genera***), you will not be asked to correct an improper plural spelling. For example, you will not be asked to correct ***the genuses are*** to ***the genera are***.

C. You will also not be expected to know whether certain highly technical terms or local organization names take singular or plural verbs and pronouns unless the context makes it clear whether they are singular or plural. For example, those who are very familiar with the Centers for Disease Control (a U.S. government organization) will know that it is normally referred to in the singular, but others would not be able to determine this merely from seeing the name.

2. Diction

Sentences that are structurally well formed can still be confusing, or can make the writer seem inept, if the words are not chosen appropriately and effectively. Effective diction involves using the right part of speech and observing other conventions regarding which words to use in which contexts. Word choices involving agreement and verb form may also be thought of partly as matters of diction, but they are treated separately under the Agreement and Verb Form headings. The diction issues you may encounter in Sentence Correction questions are too many and varied to list here. Many such issues are discussed and examples provided in Chapter 6. Here are a few salient categories often encountered in diction-related Sentence Correction questions:

A. *Parts of speech:* Even accomplished writers sometimes accidentally use an inappropriate part of speech, such as an adjective where an adverb is needed or a preposition where a conjunction is needed.

> *Example:*
> **Correct:** I could **easily** tell that the cat was friendly.
> **Incorrect:** I could **easy** tell that the cat was friendly.

B. *Pronoun cases:* Pronouns should be in the right case. A writer might compromise clarity by using a subject form of a pronoun as an object or vice versa or a reflexive pronoun in a nonreflexive context.

C. *Counting and quantifying:* Although the conventions for quantification of mass nouns and count nouns have some subtle complexities, keep in mind the general rule that mass nouns are quantified by an amount, whereas count nouns are quantified by numbers or by words (such as ***many***) that indicate multiple units.

> *Example:*
> **Correct:** **Fewer** deliveries arrived today than yesterday.
> **Incorrect:** **Less** deliveries arrived today than yesterday.

D. *Prepositions:* Subtle differences of relationship are often expressed by different prepositions that function similarly to one another. Consider, for example, ***in/into/within, to/toward, on/onto/above, through/throughout, beside/besides, beside/along/against,*** and ***on/over/above***.

> *Examples:*
> i) **Correct:** We were standing **beside** the river.
> **Incorrect:** We were standing **besides** the river.
>
> The incorrect version above can also be thought of as displaying a problem of logical predication in that it appears to say illogically that the river was also standing.
>
> ii) **Correct:** The editor was sitting **in** his office all afternoon.
> **Incorrect:** The editor was sitting **into** his office all afternoon.
>
> The preposition ***into*** indicates motion from outside a location to within that location. Since it is unlikely that sitting would be a motion from outside an office to within an office over the course of an entire afternoon, ***into*** is the wrong preposition to use in this context.

Word choices that are inherently very simple and obvious can become a little more difficult in complex settings, and a Sentence Correction answer choice that appears appropriate on its own may not work when plugged into the larger sentence.

Examples:

i) In isolation, **distributed throughout** is recognizable as a standard phrase, but in the following sentence it does not make sense:

The computers were **distributed throughout** the generosity of a group of donors.

Replacing **throughout** with **through** solves the problem. The issue here is a matter not only of diction but also of logical predication: the wording causes the sentence to make an illogical claim about the computers.

ii) Similarly, the phrase **we were confident** is fine as a freestanding clause, but it is nonsense in the following context:

The lawyer who consulted with **we were confident** that we could negotiate a settlement.

This displays combined problems of diction (**with we**), agreement (the plural **were** with the singular subject **lawyer**), and grammatical construction.

iii) The phrase **us was confident** sounds strange out of context, but substituting **us was** for the offending part of the sentence solves the problem:

The lawyer who consulted with **us was confident** that we could negotiate a settlement.

Some complicating factors to consider:

The following are only a few examples of the types of subtleties and complexities that may be involved in deciding what words are appropriate:

A. *Potentially misleading grammatical constructions:* In some contexts, a verb might superficially appear to require an adverb when in fact an adjective is appropriate. For example, it is correct to say "The surface feels rough" rather than "The surface feels roughly." And "The animal does not smell well" means something very different from "The animal does not smell good." Both can be correct depending on what the writer wants to convey.

B. Words ending in *-ing* that are derived from verbs (such as **going**, **assessing**, and **hurting**) can be either gerunds or participles. Generally, in carefully crafted formal writing, a pronoun or noun that modifies a gerund will be possessive. However, in some similar constructions the *-ing* word is intended as a participle with the noun or pronoun as its subject.

Examples:

i) **Correct:** The schedule depends on **our** receiving the materials on time.
Incorrect in formal writing: The schedule depends on **us** receiving the materials on time.

ii) **Correctly expresses one meaning:** I was concerned about **my friend's lying on the ground**.
iii) **Correctly expresses a different meaning:** I was concerned about **my friend lying on the ground**.

In ii) the object noun phrase is headed by the gerund **lying**, indicating that the concern is about the situation the friend was in. But in iii), **lying** is a participle modifying the noun **friend**, indicating that the concern is explicitly about the friend rather than the situation.

C. *Words with multiple functions:* In English, almost any noun can function as an adjective. Nouns that also function as verbs are well known (as in *chaired the meeting* or *tabled the motion*), but words that are not normally used as verbs can also be pressed into special service as verbs on an ad hoc basis. One could say, for example, "She plans to greenhouse her tender plants when the weather turns cold." Some words regularly function as both adjectives and adverbs. One can say, for example, both "This is a hard job" and "We are working hard." Likewise, *fast* is used correctly as both adjective and adverb in the following sentence: "This is not usually a fast train, but it is moving fast at this moment."

D. *Considerations in applying between and among: Among* is generally not appropriate for relationships that involve only two entities. It is standard to say *the distance between my house and yours*, not *the distance among my house and yours*. For relationships involving more than two entities, *among* is usually needed instead of *between*, but there are exceptions. *Between* is sometimes the more accurate preposition to use where the relationship holds, independently, between each member of the group and another individual member. Thus, for example, it would be appropriate to say, "In planning your trip among the five destinations, consider the distances between cities."

Some issues that are not tested:

The following are a few examples of issues outside the scope of the diction-related Sentence Correction questions:

A. *Which/that:* Some American publishers have adopted the convention that *which*, used as a relative pronoun, should always be nonrestrictive and should be replaced with *that* in restrictive contexts (as in "Laws which have been repealed are no longer enforced" versus "Laws that have been repealed are no longer enforced"). You should not expect to see questions for which the deciding factor is merely whether the writer adheres to this convention.

B. *Object words with* to be: Some usage advisors prescribe the use of nominative (subject) pronouns in both the subject position and the object position with the verb *to be.* According to this convention, "If I were her, I would be happy to accept the job" is incorrect; it should be "If I were she, I would be happy to accept the job." In some contexts, this latter form of expression could seem annoyingly stilted and pedantic, and thus could violate other standards of effective expression. You should not expect to see questions for which the deciding factor is merely whether the writer adheres to this convention.

C. *Slang, archaic diction, and words that are distinctively regional or limited to certain subsets of English:* You will not be expected, for example, to correct *thou* or *you-all* to *you*, to understand that *skint* could be paraphrased as *lacking resources*, to judge whether *mickle* is a synonym of *muckle* or whether either of these should be paraphrased with *large*, or to understand that *give* (a test) in some usages is synonymous with *take* (a test) in others.

D. *Variant forms and spellings:* You will not be asked to choose between variant forms that have the same function and meaning. Some examples of such variant pairs are: *whilst/while, toward/towards, until/till, and outward/outwards.*

3. Grammatical Construction

Many issues of agreement, verb form, parallelism, diction, and idiom can be described as matters of grammar, but those categories by no means cover the full range of grammar-related tasks in Sentence Correction. The Grammatical Construction category concerns issues of grammar not treated elsewhere in this classification scheme. For the most part, these are matters of syntax—the ways a sentence's elements are arranged. Effective communication depends on shared understandings between the writer and reader about how the relative positions of words and phrases help convey meaning. A series of words and punctuation marks that does not follow predictable conventions of syntax can be puzzling, annoying, or even incomprehensible. In section 6.5 of Chapter 6, grammatical issues are reviewed extensively and many examples provided. Here are a few major issues often encountered in Sentence Correction questions related to grammatical construction:

A. ***Complete structure:*** In English, a well-formed sentence or independent clause generally needs both a subject and a predicate that contains a main verb.

B. ***Clear and correct linkages and punctuation:*** A sentence's elements need to be linked to and separated from one another with standard punctuation and, when appropriate, with links such as conjunctions and relative pronouns.

C. ***Proper ordering of words and phrases:*** A sentence whose components are ordered in ways incompatible with the conventions of standard English can be confusing and can make the writer appear unfamiliar with the language.

To see how a Sentence Correction answer choice affects a sentence's grammatical construction, you may need to analyze the relationship between widely separated parts.

Examples:

i) **Incorrect:** If you clean the filter before it becomes so clogged that it impedes the flow can prevent costly repairs in the long run.

Correct: Cleaning the filter before it becomes so clogged that it impedes the flow can prevent costly repairs in the long run.

It is important to see that the main verb phrase in these sentences is ***can prevent***; the intervening verbs are embedded in the clause modifying ***clean the filter***. In the incorrect version, the opening phrase ***if you clean*** is not grammatically structured to function as a subject. But in the correct version that phrase is replaced with ***cleaning***, which allows the noun phrase ***cleaning the filter*** to serve correctly as the sentence's subject. This sentence correction task involves both grammatical construction and verb form (discussed later under that heading).

ii) **Incorrect:** The headphones that were provided with the audio player that although she bought them last year, they never worked.

Correct: The headphones that were provided with the audio player she bought last year never worked.

The phrase ***she bought last year never worked*** would be ungrammatical in isolation, but if substituted for the underlined phrase in the incorrect version, it makes the sentence grammatically correct. The crucial relationship here is between the opening words (***the headphones***) and the final phrase of the sentence.

Some complicating factors to consider:

In informal contexts and in many formal contexts where economy of words and smoothness of flow are key considerations, certain sentence elements may be omitted when the writer's intent is entirely clear without them. For example, ***that*** is often omitted at the start of a relative clause, as in "The film I saw last night was boring" or "I was afraid they might be angry." It is also often acceptable to omit infinitive verbs to avoid awkward repetition, leaving the preposition ***to*** dangling, as in "I reviewed the report even though I didn't want to."

Some issues that are not tested:

The following two issues are outside the scope of Sentence Correction questions related to grammatical construction:

A. *Fragments that function as complete sentences in special contexts:* A group of words with no subject or verb can sometimes stand as a well-formed sentence. For example, "No" can be a complete sentence in answer to a stated or hypothetical question, as can "The one on the left." Similarly, a clause beginning with a conjunction and not followed by any other clause can sometimes be an acceptable sentence, as, for example, "Because the delivery was late." Exclamations such as "Not again!" are also complete and well formed in special contexts. You should not expect to see a Sentence Correction question that appears likely to be drawn from a context in which it is intended to function in any of these ways or as a headline, title, or line of poetry.

B. *Punctuation as editorial style:* You will need to judge issues of punctuation only insofar as they involve standard conventions that make a difference for the sentence's meaning and coherence. Beyond the basic grammatical principles, some punctuation conventions vary by region or academic discipline, are matters of pure style, or are determined by publishers or editors for their own purposes. You will not need to judge, for example, whether a comma should be inside or outside a closing quotation mark, whether emphasis should be indicated by italics, or whether an apostrophe should be inserted before the *s* in a plural non-word such as *IOUs/IOU's* or *1980s/1980's*.

4. Idiom

Idioms are standard forms of expression that consist of ordinary words but whose uses cannot be inferred from the meanings of their component parts or the basic conventions of grammar and usage. There is ultimately no logical reason why English speakers say *on average* rather than *at average* or *depending on* rather than *depending from*. This is simply how we do things. Thus, knowing idiomatic constructions is rather like knowing vocabulary words. Accidentally using the wrong combination of words in an idiomatic construction or structuring a phrase in an unidiomatic way can make it difficult for readers to discern the writer's intended meaning. Here are a few major categories of idiomatic wording issues that you may encounter in Sentence Correction questions:

A. *Prepositions with abstract concepts:* For abstract concepts, there is no top, bottom, inside, or outside, yet with terms denoting such concepts we often use the same prepositions that denote spatial relationships between concrete objects. There are some patterns, but for the most part knowing which preposition to use with which abstract noun or verb depends on familiarity. The idiomatic pairings of prepositions with abstract concepts are far too many and varied to list here. A few illustrations are: *in* love, different *from*, *in* a while, *on* guard, *at* work.

Examples:
i) **Correct:** With regard to your party invitation, I may not be able to go, because I will be on call at the clinic that evening.
Incorrect: On regard with your party invitation, I may not be able to go, because I will be in call at the clinic that evening.

ii) **Correct:** The cost of the repairs will depend on what clever solutions the contractors come up with.
Incorrect: The cost of the repairs will depend from what clever solutions the contractors come out through.

B. *Correlatives:* Certain standard correlative structures provide economical ways of expressing relationships between concepts. For example, it can be more efficient to say "Neither she nor he is going" than to say "He is not going, and she is also not going." However, if such structures are not skillfully handled in accordance with standard conventions, they can be puzzling and misleading.

> *Examples:*
> i) **Correct:** Neither the pomegranates **nor** the melons have arrived yet from the vendor.
> **Incorrect:** Neither the pomegranates have arrived yet **neither** the melons from the vendor.
>
> ii) **Correct:** She was almost **as** sure that if we installed this system it would fail **as** that we would need some such system.
> **Incorrect:** She was almost **as** sure that if we installed this system it would fail **than** that we would need some such system.

C. *Verb phrases:* Many combinations of verbs with adverbs and/or prepositions have conventional meanings that do not follow directly from the meanings of their component parts. These include such phrases as *give up, give up on, come through with, come up, come up with, come down with, do without, have at, get over, get on with, go through, go through with,* and *get through with*. Similarly, there are many idiomatic combinations of verbs and objects, such as *have had it, make waves, make one's mark*, and *put one's finger on*.

> *Example:*
> **Correct:** When they checked the patient's temperature, it **turned out** that he was **running a fever**.
> **Incorrect:** When they checked the patient's temperature, it **veered off** that he was **doing a fever**.

D. *Pronouns with no reference:* As discussed in section 6.5, English requires stated subjects in most sentences with active verb forms. Where there is no real subject, one uses specific referentless placeholder pronouns: *it* and **there**.

E. *Compound modifiers:* Some adverbs and adjectives are idiomatically built out of multiple words. A few examples are: *all in all, by and by, by and large, on the whole, through and through, on the up and up*, and *on the other hand* (which is sometimes, but not always, correlated with *on the one hand*).

> *Examples:*
> i) **Correct:** She listened to the radio **off and on** throughout the day.
> **Incorrect:** She listened to the radio **off but again on** throughout the day.
>
> ii) **Correct:** You wondered whether anyone would mention you at the meeting; in fact, two people **did so**.
> **Incorrect:** You wondered whether anyone would mention you at the meeting; in fact, two people **did thus and so**.

Idiom-related questions do not always involve identifying malformed idioms. Sometimes the crucial insight may involve determining which of multiple idiomatic meanings is intended, or whether a phrase should be treated as an idiom or not.

Example:
Incorrect: She asked for information **on purpose** of the order I had submitted.

The meaning of the sentence above is unclear. However, a plausible hypothesis is that the writer meant to say *information on the purpose*, with *on* serving as an informal equivalent of *regarding*. On that reading, the apparent use of the idiom *on purpose* results from an accidental juxtaposition of the two words. Substituting a phrase such as *regarding the* for *on* can turn this into a meaningful, well-formed sentence:

Correct: She asked for information **regarding the purpose** of the order I had submitted.

Some complicating factors to consider:

Here are just a few of the many subtleties that one may encounter in judging whether idiomatic usages are correct and effective:

A. Similar phrases often have very different idiomatic uses and meanings; consider, for example, *come through with*, *come down with*, and *come up with*.

B. Some idiomatic preposition-plus-noun phrases have alternate forms. For example, it is correct to say either *with regard to* or *in regard to*.

C. Many idiomatic phrases have multiple meanings, which are not always similar. For example, *come out with* in some contexts means *express* and in others means *publish* or *begin marketing*.

D. For many idiomatic expressions, there are special exceptions to the standard forms.

Example:
Phrases of the form *not only . . . but* are standardly completed with *also*, but there are special cases in which *also* is unnecessary or misleading.

Correct: Surprisingly, the endangered species was found **not only** at the valley's lowest elevations **but** throughout the entire valley.
Incorrect: Surprisingly, the endangered species was found **not only** at the valley's lowest elevations **but also** throughout the entire valley.

If the lowest elevations referred to are in the valley, *but also* would misleadingly seem to indicate that the entire valley was a separate category rather than a more general category encompassing the lower elevations.

E. Words that form standard pairs, such as *neither* and *nor*, often have other meanings and uses as well. In some contexts, *neither* or *nor* might appear at first glance to need the other term. However, *neither* often occurs as an adjective (as in "**Neither book** has been opened"), a pronoun (as in "**Neither of them** has been opened"), or a freestanding clause negator (as in "My supervisor is not fond of filing reports, but **neither am I**"). Similarly, *nor* can occur without *neither* (as in "None of the strata in the escarpment were fractured in the earthquake, **nor** were any of the exposed formations displaced").

Some issues that are not tested:

GMAT Sentence Correction questions neither assess nor presuppose knowledge of obsolete forms of idiomatic expression, highly specialized technical jargon, distinctive dialect constructions, or slang idioms that have not become standard forms of expression.

5. Logical Predication

Logical predication is the modification of one sentence element by another. Accidentally modifying the wrong sentence element may create unintended meanings even in a grammatically correct sentence. Issues of logical predication intersect with all the other categories discussed here and are involved in many of the Sentence Correction questions. Here are a few ways they may occur. See Chapter 6 for more details and examples.

A. *Position and scope of modifiers:* Modifiers should be positioned so that it is clear what word or words they are meant to modify. If modifiers are not positioned clearly, they can cause illogical references or comparisons, or otherwise distort the meaning of the sentence.

> *Example:*
> **Correct:** I put the cake **that I baked** by the door.
> **Incorrect:** I put the cake by the door **that I baked**.

B. *Pronoun-antecedent relationships:* A misplaced pronoun can bind to the wrong noun, pronoun, or noun phrase and thus create an unintended meaning.

> *Example:*
> **Correct:** After **it** has reviewed the report from the consultants, **the company** may consider changing the logo.
> **Incorrect:** After **it** has reviewed the report from the consultants, **changing the logo** may be considered by the company.

C. *Compatibility of concepts:* Careless wording can cause a predicate to say something inconsistent with the nature of the subject and vice versa.

> *Examples:*
> i) **Correct:** **The three types of wildlife** most often seen in the park **are sparrows, mallards, and squirrels**, in that order.
> **Incorrect:** **The type of wildlife** most often seen in the park **is the sparrow, the mallard, and the squirrel**, in that order.
>
> ii) **Correct:** Stock prices **rose** abruptly today **to an all-time high**.
> **Incorrect:** Stock prices **dropped** abruptly today **to an all-time high**.

D. *Ellipses and extraneous elements:* Omission of a crucial word or phrase or inclusion of an extraneous element can shift the subject to an unintended element while leaving the sentence grammatically well formed. Accidents of this sort can also make an unintended noun or pronoun the subject or object of a verb.

Examples:
i) **Correct:** Work on the stadium renovations is temporarily **at a standstill**.
Incorrect: Work on the stadium renovations is temporarily **a standstill**.

In the incorrect version of i), the omission of **at** causes the sentence to claim illogically that the work itself is a standstill.

ii) **Correct:** The **car was traveling** slowly along the highway.
Incorrect: The **car's speed was traveling** slowly along the highway.

In the incorrect version of ii), the redundant reference to speed makes the sentence say, absurdly, that the speed rather than the car was traveling along the highway.

E. *Reversed relationships:* An unintended meaning can result from accidentally or misguidedly reversing a relationship between sentence elements.

Examples:
i) **Correct:** Last week's unusually high sales of electric fans can almost certainly be **blamed on** the unseasonably hot weather.
Incorrect: Last week's unusually high sales of electric fans can almost certainly be **blamed for** the unseasonably hot weather.

Example i) also involves idiomatic usage of prepositions (discussed under the Idiom category above).

ii) **Correct:** **Forecasters said the cold front** will move through the region tomorrow.
Incorrect: **Forecasters, said the cold front,** will move through the region tomorrow.

F. *Ambiguous words and phrases:* Writers should be cautious in using words or phrases that have multiple standard meanings. Often the context makes it clear which meaning is intended, but sometimes it does not. Paraphrasing to rule out unwanted meanings can sometimes require adding words or increasing a sentence's structural complexity.

Examples:
i) **Incorrect:** She has studied Greek and speaks it as well as Gujarati.
Correct: She has studied Greek and speaks it in addition to Gujarati.
Correct: She has studied Greek and speaks it as well as she speaks Gujarati.

As well as is an entirely acceptable equivalent of *and also* or *in addition to,* but it can be an unfortunate choice of words for a context in which *well* makes perfect sense as an evaluative judgment. The second correct version of i) captures this alternate, evaluative meaning.

ii) **Incorrect:** Although visitors may not enter the loading docks, they occasionally may wander past the area.
Correct: Although visitors might not enter the loading docks, they occasionally might wander past the area.
Correct: Although visitors are not allowed to enter the loading docks, they occasionally are allowed to wander past the area.

Here again, there is no firm basis for deciding which way the incorrect version is intended. Both occurrences of *may* could mean either *are permitted to* or *might*.

Few incorrect answers in actual Sentence Correction questions will be as easy to dismiss as the most obvious of these illustrative examples. Most Logical Predication questions will require careful analysis of the relationships between the answer choice and the nonunderlined portions of the sentence. Be alert for all types of problematic relationships among sentence parts, not just for stereotypical dangling modifiers.

Some complicating factors to consider:

Given that all Sentence Correction questions are presented out of context, there may be no basis for certainty about which of several possible interpretations the writer intended to convey. You will not be given multiple equally good versions of a sentence and asked to guess which one accurately represents the writer's true intention. In principle, almost any illogically constructed sentence could be intended to convey a bizarre meaning. One could hypothesize that the writer of the first incorrect example under *Reversed Relationships* really did intend to say that the fan sales somehow caused the hot weather. Even on that hypothesis, the most reasonable judgment for Sentence Correction purposes would be that the sentence is poorly constructed. A careful writer who wants to convey a straightforward message should make it clear that the unusual meaning is the intended one instead of leading the reader to believe that she or he is ineptly trying to convey the more plausible meaning.

Some issues that are not tested:

Occasionally, you may find a poorly worded version of a sentence amusing. However, you should not expect to see Sentence Correction sentences that can be interpreted as jokes. Among the answer choices, there will always be a serious way of resolving ambiguities and illogical meanings.

6. Parallelism

Words or phrases that have similar roles in a sentence should be treated in ways that make the similarity clear. This often requires ensuring that parallel clauses have parallel structure, that verbs having the same function are in the same form, and that elements within the scope of a modifier all relate to the modifier in the same way. Here are some major categories in which parallelism can be an issue:

A. *Elements of a series:* Where the elements of a series all have the same role or function, they often should be in parallel form.

> *Example:*
> **Correct:** She tackled the problem calmly, **efficiently**, and **analytically**.
> **Incorrect:** She tackled the problem calmly, **by being efficient in tackling it**, and **was analytic**.
>
> In this example, the nonparallel version of the sentence is also awkward and wordy. Problems of these types are further discussed under the category of rhetorical construction.

B. *Correlations and comparisons:* As explained in section 6.5.5.D of Chapter 6, the sides of a correlative structure often need parallel treatment to make the relationship clear and accurate.

C. *Issues of scope and repetition of elements:* To determine what elements of a sentence should be made parallel to each other, it is sometimes necessary to determine how much of the wording should fall within the scope of a verb, preposition, or modifier. The scope may determine which elements need to be in parallel form and whether certain elements need to be repeated. Issues of this type overlap with those discussed previously.

> *Examples:*
> i) **Correct:** He mended the torn fabric **with a needle and thread**.
> **Incorrect:** He mended the torn fabric **with a needle and with thread**.
>
> Assuming that the needle and thread were used together as a unit, the incorrect version's repetition of *with* misrepresents the relationship, suggesting that the needle was used separately from the thread.
>
> Contrast this with example ii) below, in which the incorrect version inappropriately combines one action that used the needle with a separate action that used the thread:
>
> ii) **Correct:** He **punched holes** in the decoration **with a needle** and **tied it** to the lamp **with thread**.
> **Incorrect:** He **punched holes in and tied** the decoration to the lamp **with a needle and thread**.
>
> In example iii) below, the preposition *on* functions so differently in the two phrases that it makes no sense to subsume both the fire and the list under a single occurrence of the preposition. Therefore, we need the repetition of *was on*.
>
> iii) **Correct:** The house **that was on fire was on the list** of historically significant buildings.
> **Incorrect:** The house **was on fire and the list** of historically significant buildings.

D. *Corresponding series:* Where the elements of one series are supposed to correspond to those of another series, the order of elements in each series should parallel the order of elements in the other. This parallelism can help prevent confusion about how the two series relate to each other without using cumbersome repetition.

Example:

Correct: Our **first, second, and third meetings** last week were on **Tuesday, Wednesday, and Thursday respectively**.
Incorrect: Of our **first, second, and third meetings** last week, **one was on Thursday and on Tuesday and Wednesday the others occurred**.

E. *Grammatical considerations:* Some requirements of parallelism, including some of those illustrated above, are also requirements of grammatical construction.

Example:

Correct: **The shipping delays** and **the two-day closure** have caused a backlog of orders.
Incorrect: **The shipping was delayed** and **the two-day closure** have caused a backlog of orders.

To function properly as subjects of **have caused**, both of the stated causes need to be in the form of noun phrases.

Some complicating factors to consider:

Problems of idiomatic structure and of logical predication sometimes involve parallelism as well. The following sentence displays all three:

Not only the CEO, and also the executive vice president's proposed policies, have been distributed to the relevant people in middle management.

In presenting a faulty parallelism between the **not only** term and the **and also** term, the sentence appears illogically to claim that the CEO has been distributed. It also falls short of the clarity that could be achieved with a more standard **not only . . . but also** structure.

Agreement, as discussed previously, represents a special kind of parallelism. For example, where a singular noun and a pronoun refer to the same thing, the two terms should be parallel in both being singular, and when a verb has a plural subject, the two should be parallel in both being plural. However, in the Sentence Correction classification scheme, agreement is treated as a distinct category. Thus, agreement-related answer explanations in section 9.9 will not automatically carry the parallelism label as well.

Some issues that are not tested:

Sentence Correction questions do not require decisions about purely aesthetic or decorative types of parallelism. For example, you will not be asked to decide whether a rhymed pair such as **highways and byways** would be preferable to another phrase that is equivalent in meaning and function.

7. Rhetorical Construction

A sentence that is grammatically and idiomatically correct and conforms to good standards of parallelism and logical predication may still be unclear or annoying or may appear ineptly written. Rhetorical construction problems arise in many ways, including the following:

A. *Economy of wording:* Superfluous words, unneeded punctuation, pointless redundancies, or convoluted structures that do not enhance precision and adequacy of detail can make a sentence confusing or simply annoying.

> *Example:*
> **Correct:** We will carefully review your memo and let you know whether we are interested in the solutions you propose.
> **Incorrect:** We will "review"—i.e., carefully scrutinize—your memo submitted, letting you know, vis-à-vis the memo's contained proposal details, whether there is interest, on our part, or not, in those.

B. *Precision and adequacy of detail:* Wording that is too vague, sparse, indeterminate, or incomplete can fail to effectively communicate the intended message. Precision often requires including details and qualifying phrases. How much specificity and qualification are required depends on the communication's purpose. Scientific and legal contexts, for example, often require far more precision than do casual communications between friends.

> *Example:*
> **Correct:** The contractor shall deliver the completed materials, as defined in Section 5 of this agreement, no later than the thirtieth calendar day after the date on which the signed and ratified contract is distributed to the contracting parties.
> **Incorrect:** The contractor shall finish taking the actions for relevant agreement sections within a month of contract distribution and related events.
>
> The latter version of this sentence is poorly constructed and very vague. The acceptability of the former version depends on the wording's adequacy for the intended purpose.

C. *Active and passive voice:* Passive voice is a means of bringing a verb's object into the subject position. It can sometimes be more straightforward and economical than active voice where the verb's subject in the active voice is unknown or irrelevant. However, passive-voice constructions are often objectionably vague, awkward, or indirect.

Examples:
i) **Correct:** **We had** lunch in the hotel and then **spent** the afternoon **looking at** paintings and sculptures in the museum.
Incorrect: Lunch **was had** in the hotel **by us** before the afternoon **was spent** in the museum where paintings and sculptures **were looked at.**

In the correct version of i), the sentence's subject *we* is known and relevant, and only needs to be stated once to serve as the subject of both verbs and of the gerund. Thus, the use of passive voice in the incorrect version is needlessly vague and convoluted.

ii) **Correct:** The fruits **are left** to dry for two weeks and then collected, sorted, and packaged for shipment.
Incorrect: **Relevant people leave** the fruits to dry for two weeks, and then **people, devices, and systems collect, sort, and package** them for **someone or something to ship.**

In the incorrect version of ii), the active voice requires specifying vague or unimportant grammatical subjects, making the sentence much wordier than the correct version, which appropriately uses the passive voice.

D. *Other types of awkwardness and inelegance:* Problems of rhetorical construction take many different forms, some of which do not fall neatly into standard categories.

Examples:
i) **Correct:** As expected, she did the job very well.
Incorrect: Expectedly, the goodness of her doing the job was considerable.

ii) **Correct:** She hoped that humans would be able to explore some of the planets in other solar systems.
Incorrect: Her hope was for other solar systems' planets' possible human exploration.

Some complicating factors to consider:

Because rhetorical construction is one of the points tested in Sentence Correction, some people might be tempted to guess that shorter answer choices are a safer bet than longer ones. Wordiness is a stereotypical feature of some inelegant writing, and teachers and writing coaches often emphasize conciseness as a goal. On the other hand, some might guess that a longer version or one with more qualifiers and caveats is more likely correct. No such guessing strategy is justified. Sentence Correction questions are designed to represent a wide range of issues. Highly professional expert question writers and test assemblers would be unlikely to create predictable patterns that could be exploited in guessing. There is simply no substitute for careful analysis and understanding of the content of each question and answer choice.

Some issues that are not tested:

Sentence Correction questions do not require judgments about rhetorical appropriateness that depend on knowledge of highly technical or specialized vocabulary or syntax. Similarly, you should not expect to see questions for which the deciding factor is merely whether the writer uses jargon or buzzwords. For example, you would not be asked to determine whether *contact* might be preferable to *reach out to*—or whether *sunsetting* might be an effective substitute for *phasing out*—in a sentence such as: "I will reach out to various stakeholders to leverage decisions about the timeframe for phasing out the product."

8. Verb Form

Verbs should be in the right tenses and moods and should have the right relationships to other verbs. Uses of infinitives and participles should follow standard conventions so that the intended meanings are clear. For an extended discussion and examples of appropriate uses of verb tenses and moods, see section 6.5.3 of Chapter 6. Some of the problems posed in Sentence Correction questions involve choices among verb tenses, but many are concerned with other verb-form issues. Here are some categories in which verb-form problems may occur:

A. *Temporal relationships:* Because Sentence Correction questions are presented without any context, it is sometimes impossible to tell when they were written or whether the events they refer to were in the past, present, or future from the writer's point of view. Therefore, to the extent that verb tenses are at issue, they are often a matter of internal coherence of the parts of the sentence.

Example:
Correct: Chili peppers belong to the Solanaceae family of flowering plants.
Incorrect: Chili peppers are belonging to the Solanaceae family of flowering plants.

The present-progressive form *are belonging* is used unidiomatically in the incorrect version. That form indicates that the event or condition referred to is ongoing at the time of writing and may not continue. The simple present form *belong* is coherent with the permanence and timelessness of the stated fact.

B. *Conditionals and subjunctives:* As explained in section 6.5.3.D of Chapter 6, conditional verb forms referring to conjectural or counterfactual events are typically created with the auxiliary *would*. *Would* constructions often require the antecedent (the *if* clause) to be in subjunctive form. Subjunctives have other purposes as well, such as expressing wishes and requests.

C. *Auxiliary verbs:* English uses auxiliary verbs for many purposes, some of which are mentioned in the discussions of temporal relationships and conditionals in section 6.5.3 of Chapter 6. For effective communication, the use of auxiliary verbs should conform to standard conventions.

Examples:
i) **Correct:** Does the professor teach that course often?
Incorrect: Teaches the professor that course often?

In contemporary English, interrogative forms of most verbs are created using appropriate forms of the auxiliary verb *to do*. The simple inversion of subject and verb seen in the incorrect version of i) is an obsolete form.

ii) **Correct:** The new book might turn out to be a best seller.
Incorrect: The new book might turn out will be a best seller.

The auxiliary verbal phrase *might turn out* is correctly used with infinitive verb forms such as *to be*, not with simple future forms such as *will be*.

D. *Treatment of participles, gerunds, and infinitives:* Present participles (such as *finding* and *taking*) are used with the verb *to be* to express progressive verb forms (*is finding, had been taking*). They also function as modifiers in phrases such as *he bought the book, hoping he would like it* and as nouns in phrases such as *his buying the book was unexpected.* When used as nouns, present participles are known as gerunds.

Past participles (such as *found* and *taken*) are used with the verb *to have* to express perfect verb forms (*has found, will have taken*). They also function as adjectives in phrases such as *the book published last year* and *the withered plant.*

The infinitive form is used for verbs that are modified by other verbs. With some modifying verbs, the infinitive must be preceded by *to.* With other verbs (certain modal and auxiliary verbs) it must not. With yet others (such as *help, go,* and *need*) it can be used either with or without *to.* Infinitives can be treated as nouns, serving as subjects or objects of verbs, as in *to laugh at one's own mistakes can be therapeutic.*

Examples:
i) **Correct:** Being widely disliked, the software went unused.
Incorrect: Been widely disliked, the software went unused.

In i), the present participle *being* can correctly head a modifying phrase, but the past participle *been* cannot.

ii) **Correct:** My colleague went to find another microphone.
Incorrect: My colleague went find another microphone.

Although such expressions as *go find* and *go get* are standard, they are unidiomatic in affirmative past tenses, which require the preposition *to* with the infinitive (*went to find*).

Some complicating factors to consider:

English verb forms and surrounding idiomatic wording conventions have many peculiarities and nuances. The following are reminders of just a few such complications:

A. Keep in mind that the subtleties of how English tenses are used cannot always be inferred from the names of the tenses. For example, in some other European languages, actions that are currently occurring are indicated by the simple present tense. But English typically uses the present-progressive form for that purpose, as in "The dog is barking" or "The car is running." The simple present tense in English is typically reserved instead for events and conditions that occur at indefinite or unspecified times or that recur, as in "Dogs bark for various reasons" or "The car runs on unleaded fuel."

B. *Going to (do or happen)* is a standard way of expressing the future tense, but unlike in French for example, there is no parallel form *coming from (doing or happening).* To indicate that an action was recently completed, English uses the idiom *has/have/had just,* as in "I had just finished composing the email."

C. The preposition *to* has many different uses in combination with verbs. These differences can sometimes lead to ambiguous constructions and potential confusion. Stereotypically, *to* before a verb is thought of as an infinitive marker, but it can also indicate purpose or intention. Thus, for example, "I need your truck to haul the boxes" is indeterminate between two meanings. More precise expressions of these could be "I need your truck so that I can haul the boxes" and "It is essential for me that your truck haul the boxes." The latter may seem very formal but could be appropriate where precision is needed. *To* with a verb can also be prescriptive, as in "The borrower is to pay a fine if the materials are not returned by the due date," or simply predictive, as in "The visitors are to arrive soon." It can even be used in expressing a past tense in a construction such as *was never to see him again* or *was the last one to leave the building*.

D. *Shall* also has multiple meanings. As a simple future-tense indicator, it is an alternative to *will* for first-person verbs ("I shall tell you about it tomorrow"). However, it can also be used prescriptively, similarly to *must*, as in "The borrower shall pay a fine if the materials are not returned by the due date."

Some issues that are not tested:

You may hear that some usage advisors object to placing anything between *to* and an infinitive verb, as in *to finally reach the destination*. You should not expect to see Sentence Correction questions for which the deciding factor is merely whether the writer follows this advice. However, you might encounter a sentence that is awkward and unclear because too many words—or words that would go better elsewhere—are crammed in between the preposition and the verb. This occurs in the following sentence:

I try to remember **to scrupulously every day before I leave work log off** my computer.

This sentence has an issue of general unclarity and inelegance falling under the heading of rhetorical construction, and not a mere case of a split infinitive.

9.3 Study Suggestions

There are two basic ways you can study for Sentence Correction questions:

1. **Read material that reflects standard usage.**
   One way to gain familiarity with the basic conventions of standard written English is simply to read. Suitable material will usually be found in good magazines and nonfiction books, editorials in outstanding newspapers, and the collections of essays used by many college and university writing courses.

2. **Review basic rules of grammar and practice with writing exercises.**
   Begin by reviewing the grammar rules laid out in this chapter. Then, if you have school assignments (such as essays and research papers) that have been carefully evaluated for grammatical errors, it may be helpful to review the comments and corrections.

9.4 What Is Measured

Sentence Correction questions test three broad aspects of language proficiency:

- **Correct expression**
  A correct sentence is grammatically and structurally sound. It conforms to all the rules of standard written English, including noun-verb agreement, noun-pronoun agreement, pronoun consistency, pronoun case, and verb tense sequence. A correct sentence will not have dangling, misplaced, or improperly formed modifiers; unidiomatic or inconsistent expressions; or faults in parallel construction.

- **Effective expression**
  An effective sentence expresses an idea or relationship clearly and concisely as well as grammatically.

This does not mean the choice with the fewest and simplest words is necessarily the best answer. It means there are no superfluous words or needlessly complicated expressions in the best choice.

- **Proper diction**

  An effective sentence also uses proper diction. In evaluating the diction of a sentence, you must be able to recognize whether the words are well chosen, accurate, and suitable for the context.

In the GMAT™ Enhanced Score Report, the Sentence Correction skills are divided into two fundamental categories, *Grammar* and *Communication*.

The skills classified as *Grammar* are represented primarily by the Agreement, Diction, Grammatical Construction, and Verb Form question types and by some aspects of the Idiom and Parallelism questions. *Grammar* tasks primarily give you an opportunity to show your skill in judging whether a sentence structure conforms to the basic conventions of standard English syntax and word use.

The skills classified as *Communication* are represented primarily by the Logical Predication and Rhetorical Construction question types and by some aspects of the Idiom and Parallelism questions. *Communication* tasks give you an opportunity to show your skill in judging whether a sentence effectively and reasonably communicates a coherent message.

9.5 Test-Taking Strategies

1. **Read the entire sentence carefully.**

   Try to understand the specific idea or relationship that the sentence should express.

2. **Evaluate the underlined passage for errors and possible corrections before reading the answer choices.**

   This strategy will help you discriminate among the answer choices. Remember, in some cases the underlined section of the sentence is correct.

3. **Read each answer choice carefully.**

   The first answer choice always repeats the underlined portion of the original sentence. Choose this answer if you think that the sentence is best as originally written, but do so **only after** examining all the other choices.

4. **Try to determine how to correct what you consider to be wrong with the original sentence.**

   Some of the answer choices may change things that are not wrong, whereas others may not change everything that is wrong.

5. **Make sure that you evaluate the sentence and the choices thoroughly.**

   Pay attention to general clarity, grammatical and idiomatic usage, economy and precision of language, and appropriateness of diction.

6. **Read the whole sentence, substituting the choice that you prefer for the underlined passage.**

   An answer choice may be wrong because it does not fit grammatically or structurally with the rest of the sentence. Remember that some sentences will require no correction. When the given sentence requires no correction, choose the first answer choice.

9.6 Section Instructions

Go to www.mba.com/tutorial to view instructions for the section and get a feel for what the test center screens will look like on the actual GMAT exam.

9.7 Practice Questions

Each of the Sentence Correction questions presents a sentence, part or all of which is underlined. Beneath the sentence you will find five ways of phrasing the underlined part. The first of these repeats the original; the other four are different. Follow the requirements of standard written English to choose your answer, paying attention to grammar, word choice, and sentence construction. Select the answer that produces the most effective sentence; your answer should make the sentence clear, exact, and free of grammatical error. It should also minimize awkwardness, ambiguity, and redundancy.

Questions 818 to 869 - Difficulty: Easy

*SC39850.02

818. The market for so-called functional beverages, drinks that promise health benefits beyond their inherent nutritional value, nearly doubled over the course of four years, in rising from $2.68 billion in 1997 to be $4.7 billion in 2000.

    (A) in rising from $2.68 billion in 1997 to be

    (B) in having risen from $2.68 billion in 1997 to

    (C) as it rose from $2.68 billion in 1997 to be

    (D) with its rise from $2.68 billion in 1997 to

    (E) rising from $2.68 billion in 1997 to

SC01527

819. According to some critics, watching television not only undermines one's ability to think critically but also impairs one's overall ability to perceive.

    (A) not only undermines one's ability to think critically but also impairs one's

    (B) not only undermines one's ability of critical thinking but also impairs the

    (C) undermines not only one's ability to think critically but also impairs one's

    (D) undermines not only one's ability of critical thinking but also impairs the

    (E) undermines one's ability not only to think critically but also impairs one's

SC20160.02

820. To show that it is serious about addressing the state's power crisis, the administration has plans for ordering all federal facilities in California to keep thermostats at 78 degrees Fahrenheit and shutting down escalators during electricity shortages this summer.

    (A) has plans for ordering all federal facilities in California to keep thermostats at 78 degrees Fahrenheit and shutting

    (B) has plans to order that all federal facilities in California are keeping thermostats at 78 degrees Fahrenheit and shutting

    (C) is planning on ordering all federal facilities in California to keep thermostats at 78 degrees Fahrenheit, and they will shut

    (D) is planning to order that all federal facilities in California are keeping thermostats at 78 degrees to order all federal facilities in California to keep thermostats at 78 degrees Fahrenheit and shut

SC33440.02

821. Once made exclusively from the wool of sheep that roam the Isle of Lewis and Harris off the coast of Scotland, Harris tweed is now made only with wools that are imported, sometimes from the mainland and sometimes they come—as a result of a 1996 amendment to the Harris Tweed Act—from outside Scotland.

    (A) sometimes from the mainland and sometimes they come

    (B) sometimes from the mainland and sometimes

    (C) and come sometimes from the mainland or sometimes

    (D) from the mainland sometimes, or sometimes it comes

    (E) from the mainland sometimes, or sometimes coming

*These numbers correlate with the online test bank question number. See the GMAT™ Official Guide Question Index in the back of this book.

859

SC12999

822. In her presentation, the head of the Better Business Bureau emphasized that companies should think of the cost of conventions and other similar gatherings <u>as not an expense, but as</u> an investment in networking that will pay dividends.

(A) as not an expense, but as

(B) as not expense but

(C) not an expense, rather

(D) not as an expense, but as

(E) not in terms of expense, but

SC15382

823. Recent interdisciplinary studies advance the argument that emotions, including those deemed personal or <u>private is a social phenomenon, though one inseparable</u> from bodily response.

(A) private is a social phenomenon, though one inseparable

(B) private, are social phenomena that are inseparable

(C) private are a social phenomenon but are not those separable

(D) private—are social phenomena but not separable

(E) also as private emotions, are social phenomena not inseparable

SC01455

824. In a speech before the Senate Banking Committee, the chairman of the Federal Reserve painted an optimistic picture of the economy, <u>suggesting to investors the central bank in the near future is not lowering interest rates.</u>

(A) suggesting to investors the central bank in the near future is not lowering interest rates

(B) suggesting to investors that the central bank would not lower interest rates in the near future

(C) which suggests that to investors in the near future interest rates will not be lowered by the central bank

(D) with the suggestion to investors in the near future that interest rates would not be lowered by the central bank

(E) with the suggestion to investors of interest rates not being lowered in the near future by the central bank

SC00740.02

825. The company's CEO backed away from her <u>plan for dividing the firm into five parts, saying that she still had meant</u> to spin off or sell two units but that the company would retain ownership of two others as well as the core company.

(A) plan for dividing the firm into five parts, saying that she still had meant

(B) plan that was to divide the firm into five parts, and she said that she still would mean

(C) plan to divide the firm into five parts, saying that she still meant

(D) planning on dividing the firm into five parts, and saying that she meant still

(E) planning to divide the firm into five parts, and she said that she meant still

SC52050.02

826. <u>The cactus is now heavily plundered in deserts in the southwestern United States, so much that enforcement agencies in five states have created special squads for its protection.</u>

(A) The cactus is now heavily plundered in deserts in the southwestern United States, so much that enforcement agencies in five states have created special squads for its protection.

(B) The cactus is now heavily plundered in deserts in the southwestern United States, so much so that special squads have been created by law enforcement agencies in five states for protecting them.

(C) The cactus is now so heavily plundered in deserts in the southwestern United States that enforcement agencies in five states have created special squads to protect it.

(D) Because they are now so heavily plundered in deserts in the southwestern United States, enforcement agencies in five states have created special squads to protect cacti.

(E) Because they are now so heavily plundered in the southwestern United States, special squads have been created by enforcement agencies in five states for the protection of cacti.

SC08150.02

827. Satellite radio transmissions, a popular feature in car stereos, differ from those of AM and FM radio, <u>which is sent directly from earthbound towers and then to a car</u> stereo.

- (A) which is sent directly from earthbound towers and then to a car
- (B) which are sent directly from earthbound towers to a car's
- (C) sent from earthbound towers and then directly to a car
- (D) sending them directly from earthbound towers to a car's
- (E) being sent directly from earthbound towers to a car

SC21130.02

828. Although <u>the company's executives have admitted that there had been accounting irregularities involving improper reporting of revenue, as well as of failure to record</u> expenses, they could not yet say precisely how much money was involved.

- (A) the company's executives have admitted that there had been accounting irregularities involving improper reporting of revenue, as well as of failure to record
- (B) the company's executives admitted that there had been accounting irregularities involving improper reporting of revenue and failure to record
- (C) the company's executives, admitting accounting irregularities involving improper reporting of revenue and failure in recording
- (D) admission by the company's executives was made of accounting irregularities involving improper reporting of revenue and failure in recording
- (E) admission by the company's executives that there had been accounting irregularities involving improper reporting of revenue and failure in recording

SC03014

829. <u>As with ants, the elaborate social structure of termites includes a few individuals reproducing</u> and the rest serve the colony by tending juveniles, gathering food, building the nest, or battling intruders.

- (A) As with ants, the elaborate social structure of termites includes a few individuals reproducing
- (B) As do ants, termites have an elaborate social structure, which includes a few individuals to reproduce

- (C) Just as with ants, termite social structure is elaborate, including a few individuals for reproducing
- (D) Like ants, termites have an elaborate social structure in which a few individuals reproduce
- (E) Like that of ants, the termite social structure is elaborate, including a few individuals that reproduce

SC02078

830. While Noble Sissle may be best known for his collaboration with Eubie Blake, as both a vaudeville performer <u>and as a lyricist for songs and Broadway musicals, also enjoying</u> an independent career as a singer with such groups as Hahn's Jubilee Singers.

- (A) and as a lyricist for songs and Broadway musicals, also enjoying
- (B) and writing lyrics for songs and Broadway musicals, also enjoying
- (C) and a lyricist for songs and Broadway musicals, he also enjoyed
- (D) as well as writing lyrics for songs and Broadway musicals, he also enjoyed
- (E) as well as a lyricist for songs and Broadway musicals, he had also enjoyed

SC03881

831. <u>Air traffic routes over the North Pole are currently used by only two or three planes a day, but it was found by a joint Canadian–Russian study to be both feasible as well as desirable if those routes are opened to thousands more commercial planes a year.</u>

- (A) Air traffic routes over the North Pole are currently used by only two or three planes a day, but it was found by a joint Canadian–Russian study to be both feasible as well as desirable if those routes are opened to thousands more commercial planes a year.
- (B) Currently used by only two or three planes a day, a joint Canadian–Russian study has found that if air traffic routes over the North Pole are opened to thousands more commercial planes a year, it would be both feasible and desirable.
- (C) A joint Canadian–Russian study, finding it to be both feasible as well as desirable to open air traffic routes over the North Pole, which are currently used by only two or three planes a day, to thousands more commercial planes a year.

(D) Although air traffic routes over the North Pole are currently used by only two or three planes a day, a joint Canadian–Russian study has found that opening those routes to thousands more commercial planes a year is both feasible and desirable.

(E) With air traffic routes over the North Pole currently used by only two or three planes a day, opening those routes to thousands more commercial planes a year has been found by a joint Canadian—Russian study as both feasible and desirable.

SC01680

832. From an experiment using special extrasensory perception cards, each bearing one of a set of symbols, parapsychologist Joseph Banks Rhine claimed statistical proof <u>for subjects who could use thought transference to identify a card in the dealer's hand</u>.

(A) for subjects who could use thought transference to identify a card in the dealer's hand

(B) for a card in the dealer's hand to be identified by subjects with thought transference

(C) of subjects able to identify with thought transference a card in the dealer's hand

(D) that subjects could identify a card in the dealer's hand by using thought transference

(E) that subjects are capable to use thought transference for identifying a card in the dealer's hand

SC02272

833. A long-term study of some 1,000 physicians indicates that the more coffee these doctors drank, the <u>more they had a likelihood of coronary disease</u>.

(A) more they had a likelihood of coronary disease

(B) more was their likelihood of having coronary disease

(C) more they would have a likelihood to have coronary disease

(D) greater was their likelihood of having coronary disease

(E) greater was coronary disease likely

SC02096

834. <u>Hurricanes at first begin traveling from east to west, because that direction is the way the prevailing winds in the tropics blow, but</u> they then veer off toward higher latitudes, in many cases changing direction toward the east before dissipating over the colder, more northerly waters or over land.

(A) Hurricanes at first begin traveling from east to west, because that direction is the way the prevailing winds in the tropics blow, but

(B) At first, hurricanes travel from east to west, because that is the direction of the prevailing winds in the tropics, but

(C) While hurricanes travel from east to west at first, the direction of the prevailing winds blowing in the tropics, and

(D) Because hurricanes at first travel from east to west, since it is the direction of the prevailing winds in the tropics,

(E) Hurricanes, beginning by traveling from east to west, because this is the direction of the prevailing winds in the tropics,

SC03083

835. Travelers from Earth to <u>Mars would have to endure low levels of gravity for long periods of time, avoiding large doses of radiation, plus contending</u> with the chemically reactive Martian soil, and perhaps even ward off contamination by Martian life-forms.

(A) Mars would have to endure low levels of gravity for long periods of time, avoiding large doses of radiation, plus contending

(B) Mars would have to endure low levels of gravity for long periods of time, avoid large doses of radiation, contend

(C) Mars, having to endure low levels of gravity for long periods of time, would also have to avoid large doses of radiation, plus contending

(D) Mars, having to endure low levels of gravity for long periods of time, avoid large doses of radiation, plus contend

(E) Mars, who would have to endure low levels of gravity for long periods of time, avoid large doses of radiation, contend with

SC01739
836. Unlike the virginal, <u>whose single set of strings runs parallel to the front edge of the instrument, the harpsichord's several sets of strings are</u> placed at right angles to its front edge.

(A) whose single set of strings runs parallel to the front edge of the instrument, the harpsichord's several sets of strings are

(B) with a single set of strings running parallel to the front edge of the instrument, the several sets of strings of the harpsichord are

(C) which has a single set of strings that runs parallel to the front edge of the instrument, in the case of the harpsichord, several sets of strings are

(D) which has a single set of strings that run parallel to the front edge of the instrument, the harpsichord has several sets of strings

(E) in which a single set of strings run parallel to the front edge of the instrument, the harpsichord's several sets of strings are

SC91050.02
837. Many population studies have linked a high-salt diet to high rates of hypertension and <u>shown that in societies where they consume little salt, their</u> blood pressure typically does not rise with age.

(A) shown that in societies where they consume little salt, their

(B) shown that in societies that have consumed little salt, their

(C) shown that in societies where little salt is consumed,

(D) showing that in societies where little salt is consumed,

(E) showing that in societies where they consume little salt, their

SC61940.02
838. According to scientists, human <u>expansion and the human appropriation of Earth's finite resources is</u> the cause of what may be the most sweeping wave of species extinctions since the demise of the dinosaurs 65 million years ago.

(A) expansion and the human appropriation of Earth's finite resources is

(B) expansion and human appropriation of Earth's finite resources are

(C) expansion and its appropriation of Earth's finite resources is

(D) expansion, along with their appropriation of Earth's finite resources, is

(E) expansion, along with its appropriation of Earth's finite resources, are

SC02000
839. Although Alice Walker published a number of essays, poetry collections, and stories during the 1970s, her third novel, *The Color Purple*, <u>which was published in 1982, brought her the widest acclaim in that it won both the National Book Award as well as the Pulitzer Prize.</u>

(A) which was published in 1982, brought her the widest acclaim in that it won both the National Book Award as well as the Pulitzer Prize

(B) published in 1982, bringing her the widest acclaim by winning both the National Book Award and the Pulitzer Prize

(C) published in 1982, brought her the widest acclaim, winning both the National Book Award and the Pulitzer Prize

(D) was published in 1982 and which, winning both the National Book Award and the Pulitzer Prize, brought her the widest acclaim

(E) was published in 1982, winning both the National Book Award as well as the Pulitzer Prize, and bringing her the widest acclaim

SC01436
840. Heating oil and natural gas futures rose sharply yesterday, as long-term forecasts for much colder temperatures in key heating regions raised fears <u>of insufficient supplies capable of meeting</u> the demand this winter.

  (A) of insufficient supplies capable of meeting

  (B) of supplies that would be insufficient for meeting

  (C) of insufficient supplies that are unable to meet

  (D) that there would be supplies insufficient for meeting

  (E) that supplies would be insufficient to meet

SC00970
841. Because it regarded the environmentalists as members of an out-of-state organization, the city council voted <u>that they are denied permission for participating</u> in the parade.

  (A) that they are denied permission for participating

  (B) that they be denied permission for participating

  (C) denying them permission for participation

  (D) the denial of permission that they participate

  (E) to deny them permission to participate

SC07348
842. In 1913, the largely self-taught Indian mathematician Srinivasa Ramanujan mailed 120 of his theorems to three different British mathematicians; <u>only one, G. H. Hardy, recognized the brilliance of these theorems, but</u> thanks to Hardy's recognition, Ramanujan was eventually elected to the Royal Society of London.

  (A) only one, G. H. Hardy, recognized the brilliance of these theorems, but

  (B) they were brilliant, G. H. Hardy alone recognized, but

  (C) these theorems were brilliant, but only one, G. H. Hardy recognized;

  (D) but, only one, G. H. Hardy, recognizing their brilliance,

  (E) only one G. H. Hardy recognized, but these theorems were brilliant

SC05201
843. Cost cutting and restructuring <u>has allowed the manufacturing company to lower its projected losses for the second quarter, and they are forecasting</u> a profit before the end of the year.

  (A) has allowed the manufacturing company to lower its projected losses for the second quarter, and they are forecasting

  (B) has allowed for the manufacturing company to lower its projected losses in the second quarter and to forecast

  (C) have allowed that the manufacturing company can lower the projected losses for the second quarter, and to forecast

  (D) have allowed the manufacturing company to lower its projected second-quarter losses and to forecast

  (E) have allowed for the manufacturing company to lower the projected losses in the second quarter, as well as forecasting

SC13010
844. The Life and Casualty Company hopes that by increasing its environmental fund reserves to $1.2 billion, <u>that it has set aside enough to pay for environmental claims and no longer has</u> to use its profits and capital to pay those claims bit by bit, year by year.

  (A) that it has set aside enough to pay for environmental claims and no longer has

  (B) enough has been set aside with which environmental claims can be paid and it will have no longer

  (C) it has set aside enough for payment of environmental claims and thus no longer having

  (D) enough has been set aside to pay for environmental claims, thus no longer having

  (E) it has set aside enough to pay for environmental claims and will no longer have

SC03079
845. <u>Like ancient Egyptian architectural materials that were recycled in the construction of</u> ancient Greek Alexandria, so ancient Greek materials from the construction of that city were reused in subsequent centuries by Roman, Muslim, and modern builders.

  (A) Like ancient Egyptian architectural materials that were recycled in the construction of

  (B) Like recycling ancient Egyptian architectural materials to construct

(C)   Just as ancient Egyptian architectural materials were recycled in the construction of

(D)   Just as they recycled ancient Egyptian architectural materials in constructing

(E)   Just like ancient Egyptian architectural materials that were recycled in constructing

SC09877

846.   Especially in the early years, new entrepreneurs may need to find resourceful ways, like renting temporary office space or using answering services, <u>that make their company seem large</u> and more firmly established than they may actually be.

(A)   that make their company seem large

(B)   to make their companies seem larger

(C)   thus making their companies seem larger

(D)   so that the companies seem larger

(E)   of making their company seem large

SC01975

847.   Unlike <u>the nests of leaf cutters and most other ants,</u> situated underground or in pieces of wood, raider ants make a portable nest by entwining their long legs to form "curtains" of ants that hang from logs or boulders, providing protection for the queen and the colony larvae and pupae.

(A)   the nests of leaf cutters and most other ants,

(B)   the nests of leaf cutters and most other ants, which are

(C)   leaf cutters and most other ants, whose nests are

(D)   leaf cutters and most other ants in having nests

(E)   those of leaf cutters and most other ants with nests

SC04452

848.   Turtles, like other reptiles, can endure long <u>fasts, in their ability to survive</u> on weekly or even monthly feedings; however, when food is readily available, they may eat frequently and grow very fat.

(A)   fasts, in their ability to survive

(B)   fasts, having their ability to survive

(C)   fasts, due to having the ability of surviving

(D)   fasts because they are able to survive

(E)   fasts because of having the ability of surviving

SC02025

849.   Thai village crafts, <u>as with</u> other cultures, have developed through the principle that form follows function and incorporate readily available materials fashioned using traditional skills.

(A)   as with

(B)   as did those of

(C)   as they have in

(D)   like in

(E)   like those of

SC27250.02

850.   <u>With near to all tortilla chips made from corn kernels that have been heated in a solution of calcium hydroxide (lime), this</u> removes the skin of the kernel so water can penetrate.

(A)   With near to all tortilla chips made from corn kernels that have been heated in a solution of calcium hydroxide (lime), this

(B)   Having nearly all tortilla chips made from corn kernels that are heated in a solution of calcium hydroxide (lime), this

(C)   Nearly all tortilla chips being made from corn kernels that are heated in a solution of calcium hydroxide (lime)

(D)   Nearly all tortilla chips are made from corn kernels that have been heated in a solution of calcium hydroxide (lime), a process that

(E)   Nearly all tortilla chips are made from corn kernels having been heated in a solution of calcium hydroxide (lime), a process that

SC01554

851.   <u>To estimate the expansion rate of the universe is a notoriously difficult problem because there is a lack of a single yardstick that all distances can be measured by</u>.

(A)   To estimate the expansion rate of the universe is a notoriously difficult problem because there is a lack of a single yardstick that all distances can be measured by.

(B)   Estimating the expansion rate of the universe is a notoriously difficult problem because there is no single yardstick by which all distances can be measured.

(C)   Because there is a lack of a single yardstick to measure all distances by, estimating the expansion rate of the universe is a notoriously difficult problem.

(D) A notoriously difficult problem is to estimate the expansion rate of the universe because a single yardstick is lacking by which all distances can be measured.

(E) It is a notoriously difficult problem to estimate the expansion rate of the universe because by no single yardstick can all distances be measured.

SC94340.02

852. Although the earliest inhabitants of Mapungubwe, building their dwellings of either wattle and daub or unfired mud brick, by the thirteenth century buildings of coral blocks in lime mortar began to appear.

(A) earliest inhabitants of Mapungubwe, building their dwellings

(B) earliest inhabitants of Mapungubwe, who built their dwellings

(C) earliest inhabitants of Mapungubwe built their dwellings

(D) dwellings of the earliest inhabitants of Mapungubwe, built

(E) dwellings of the earliest inhabitants of Mapungubwe, which were built

SC01059

853. The Commerce Department reported that the nation's economy grew at a brisk annual pace of 3.7 percent in the second quarter, but that while businesses were expanding their production, unsold goods piled up on store shelves as consumer spending is slowed sharply.

(A) unsold goods piled up on store shelves as consumer spending is slowed sharply

(B) unsold goods were piling up on store shelves as consumer spending slowed sharply

(C) unsold goods had piled up on store shelves with a sharp slowing of consumer spending

(D) consumer spending was slowing sharply, with the piling up of unsold goods on store shelves

(E) consumer spending has slowed sharply, with unsold goods piling up on store shelves

SC01470

854. Thomas Mann's novel *Doctor Faustus* offers an examination not only of how difficult it is to reconcile reason, will, and passion together in any art form, but also a skillfully navigated exploration of the major concerns of modernism.

(A) an examination not only of how difficult it is to reconcile reason, will, and passion together in any art form, but

(B) an examination not only about the difficulty of reconciling reason, will, and passion in any art form, and

(C) not only an examination of how difficult it is to reconcile reason, will, and passion in any art form, and

(D) not only an examination about the difficulty with reconciling reason, will, and passion together in any art form, but

(E) not only an examination of the difficulty of reconciling reason, will, and passion in any art form, but

SC03260.02

855. Upon their first encountering leaf-cutting ants in South America, the insects seemed to some Europeans to be carrying bits of greenery to shade themselves from the tropical sun—hence the sobriquet "parasol ants."

(A) Upon their first encountering leaf-cutting ants in South America, the insects seemed to some Europeans to be

(B) Upon their first encountering leaf-cutting ants in South America, some Europeans thought they were

(C) On first encountering leaf-cutting ants in South America, it seemed to some Europeans that the insects were

(D) On first encountering leaf-cutting ants in South America, some Europeans thought the insects were

(E) On their first encounter with leaf-cutting ants in South America, some Europeans thought it was because the insects were

SC91660.02

856. By skimming along the top of the atmosphere, a proposed new style of aircraft could fly between most points on Earth in under two hours, according to its proponents.

(A) By skimming along the top of the atmosphere, a proposed new style of aircraft could fly between most points on Earth in under two hours, according to its proponents.

(B) By skimming along the top of the atmosphere, proponents of a proposed new style of aircraft say it could fly between most points on Earth in under two hours.

(C) A proposed new style of aircraft could fly between most points on Earth in under two hours, according to its proponents, with it skimming along the top of the atmosphere.

(D) A proposed new style of aircraft, say its proponents, could fly between most points on Earth in under two hours because of its skimming along the top of the atmosphere.

(E) According to its proponents, skimming along the top of the atmosphere makes it possible that a proposed new style of aircraft could fly between most points on Earth in under two hours.

SC00981

857. According to a recent study, retirees in the United States are four times more likely to give regular financial aid to their children as to receive it from them.

(A) retirees in the United States are four times more likely to give regular financial aid to their children as

(B) retirees in the United States are four times as likely to give regular financial aid to their children as it is for them

(C) retirees in the United States are four times more likely to give regular financial aid to their children than

(D) it is four times more likely for retirees in the United States to give regular financial aid to their children than they are

(E) it is four times as likely that retirees in the United States will give their children regular financial aid as they are

SC04093

858. Discussion of greenhouse effects have usually had as a focus the possibility of Earth growing warmer and to what extent it might, but climatologists have indicated all along that precipitation, storminess, and temperature extremes are likely to have the greatest impact on people.

(A) Discussion of greenhouse effects have usually had as a focus the possibility of Earth growing warmer and to what extent it might,

(B) Discussion of greenhouse effects has usually had as its focus whether Earth would get warmer and what the extent would be,

(C) Discussion of greenhouse effects has usually focused on whether Earth would grow warmer and to what extent,

(D) The discussion of greenhouse effects have usually focused on the possibility of Earth getting warmer and to what extent it might,

(E) The discussion of greenhouse effects has usually focused on whether Earth would grow warmer and the extent that is,

SC02102

859. In the seventh century B.C., the Roman alphabet was adapted from the Etruscan alphabet, which in turn had been adapted in the previous century from a western Greek alphabet, which itself had been adapted earlier in the same century from the Phoenician alphabet.

(A) which itself had been adapted earlier

(B) adapting itself earlier

(C) itself being adapted earlier

(D) having been earlier adapted itself

(E) earlier itself having been adapted

SC09185

860. The foundation works to strengthen local and regional agricultural markets and cooperating with governments, improving access for farmers for productive resources such as land and credit.

(A) cooperating with governments, improving access for farmers for

(B) cooperates with governments to improve access for farmers to

(C) cooperate with governments for improvements of access for farmers to

(D) cooperate with governments and improve accessibility for farmers for their

(E) in cooperation with governments to improve access for farmers for

SC07338

861. A professor at the university has taken a sabbatical to research on James Baldwin's books that Baldwin wrote in France while he was living there.

(A) on James Baldwin's books that Baldwin wrote in France while he was living there

(B) about the books James Baldwin wrote in France

(C) into James Baldwin's books written while in France

(D) on the books of James Baldwin, written while he lived in France

(E) the books James Baldwin wrote while he lived in France

SC12710.01

862. When working with overseas clients, an understanding of cultural norms is at least as important as grasping the pivotal business issues for the global manager.

(A) When working with overseas clients, an understanding of cultural norms is at least as important as grasping the pivotal business issues for the global manager.

misplaced modifier

(B) When they work with overseas clients, understanding cultural norms is at least of equivalent importance to grasping the pivotal business issues for the global manager.

who is they → points to underst. cult. norms

(C) For global managers working with overseas clients, understanding cultural norms is at least as important as grasping the pivotal business issues.

(D) For global managers working with overseas clients, an understanding of cultural norms is at least as important to them as grasping the pivotal business issues. *+ redundant*

(F) Global managers working with overseas clients find an understanding of cultural norms to be equally important to grasping the pivotal business issues.

SC87460.01

863. Often major economic shifts are so gradual as to be indistinguishable at first from ordinary fluctuations in the financial markets.

(A) so gradual as to be indistinguishable

(B) so gradual they can be indistinguishable

(C) so gradual that they are unable to be distinguished

(D) gradual enough not to be distinguishable

(E) gradual enough so that one cannot distinguish them

SC19060.02

864. Dinosaur tracks show them walking with their feet directly under their bodies, like mammals and birds, not extended out to the side in the manner of modern reptiles.

(A) Dinosaur tracks show them walking with their feet directly under their bodies, like

(B) Dinosaur tracks show that they walked with their feet directly under their bodies, as do

(C) Dinosaurs left tracks that showed them walking with their feet directly under their bodies, like

(D) The tracks that dinosaurs left show that they walked with their feet directly under their bodies, as do

(E) In the tracks they left, dinosaurs are shown walking with their feet under their bodies, like

SC22260.02

865. Although when a hagfish is threatened, it will secrete slime that is small in quantity, it expands several hundred times as it absorbs seawater, forming a slime ball that can coat the gills of predatory fish and either suffocate them or distress them enough to make them flee.

(A) Although when a hagfish is threatened, it will secrete slime that is small in quantity,

(B) Although a small quantity of slime is secreted by the hagfish, when threatened

(C) Although, when threatened, a hagfish will secrete slime that is small in quantity,

(D) Although the slime secreted by a threatened hagfish is small in quantity,

(E) Although the hagfish secretes a small quantity of slime when threatened,

SC69440.02

866. Officials at the United States Mint believe that the Sacagawea dollar coin will be used more as a substitute for four quarters rather than for the dollar bill because of its weight, only 8.1 grams, which is far less than four quarters, which weigh 5.67 grams each.

(A) more as a substitute for four quarters rather than for the dollar bill because of its weight, only 8.1 grams, which is far less than

(B) more as a substitute for four quarters than the dollar bill because it weighs only 8.1 grams, far lighter than

(C) as a substitute for four quarters more than for the dollar bill because it weighs only 8.1 grams, far less than

(D) as a substitute for four quarters more than the dollar bill because its weight of only 8.1 grams is far lighter than it is for

(E) as a substitute more for four quarters rather than for the dollar bill because its weight, only 8.1 grams, is far less than it is for

SC14740.02

867. In the United States, less than half as many multifamily housing units were produced in the 1990s than in each of the previous two decades.

(A) less than half as many multifamily housing units were produced in the 1990s than

(B) less than half as many multifamily housing units had been produced in the 1990s as

(C) there were less than half as many multifamily housing units produced in the 1990s than

(D) fewer than half as many multifamily housing units were produced in the 1990s as

(E) fewer than half as many multifamily housing units had been produced in the 1990s than

SC40050.02

868. Educator Maria Montessori believed <u>that students be allowed to choose from among a number of different lessons designed for the encouragement of</u> their development as thinkers and creators with individual learning and thinking styles.

(A) that students be allowed to choose from among a number of different lessons designed for the encouragement of

(B) that students be allowed to choose between a number of different lessons designed to encourage

(C) that students should be allowed to choose among a number of different lessons designed to encourage

(D) in allowing students to choose from among a number of different lessons were designed for encouraging

(E) in allowing students to choose between a number of different lessons designed for the encouragement of

SC03050.02

869. Analysts and media executives predict <u>the coming year to be no less challenging than the previous one had been</u> for the company's C.E.O.

(A) the coming year to be no less challenging than the previous one had been

(B) the coming year to be no less challenging compared to the previous one

(C) that the coming year would be no less challenging compared to the previous one

(D) that the coming year will be no less challenging than the previous one had been

(E) that the coming year will be no less challenging than the previous one

Questions 870 to 928 - Difficulty: Medium

SC80540.02

870. Scientists say that, by bathing the skin cells in extracts of immune cells, <u>that human skin cells in a test tube are made to behave as if they were</u> immune system cells.

(A) that human skin cells in a test tube are made to behave as if they were

(B) that human skin cells were to behave in a test tube as if they were

(C) human skin cells in a test tube were made to behave as if

(D) they have made human skin cells in a test tube that were behaving as

(E) they have made human skin cells in a test tube behave as if they were

SC01506

871. Researchers now regard interferon <u>as not a single substance, but it is rather a biological family of complex molecules that play</u> an important, though not entirely defined, role in the immune system.

(A) as not a single substance, but it is rather a biological family of complex molecules that play

(B) as not a single substance but as a biological family of complex molecules playing

(C) not as a single substance but as a biological family of complex molecules that play

(D) not to be a single substance but rather a biological family of complex molecules playing

(E) not as a single substance but instead as being a biological family of complex molecules that play

SC01018

872. <u>The remarkable similarity of Thule artifacts throughout a vast region can, in part, be explained as</u> a very rapid movement of people from one end of North America to the other.

(A) The remarkable similarity of Thule artifacts throughout a vast region can, in part, be explained as

(B) Thule artifacts being remarkably similar throughout a vast region, one explanation is

(C) That Thule artifacts are remarkably similar throughout a vast region is, in part, explainable as

(D) One explanation for the remarkable similarity of Thule artifacts throughout a vast region is that there was

(E) Throughout a vast region Thule artifacts are remarkably similar, with one explanation for this being

SC12841.01

873. Regulators are likely to end what are, in effect, long-standing exemptions permitting pilots of small turboprop aircraft at small carriers to fly <u>as much as 20 percent more hours per month than pilots at larger airlines fly, with the consequence that</u> some carriers could be forced to hire additional pilots.

(A) as much as 20 percent more hours per month than pilots at larger airlines fly, with the consequence that

(B) as many as 20 percent more hours per month as pilots at larger airlines, and

(C) more hours per month, as much as 20 percent, than pilots at larger airlines; consequently

(D) as much as 20 percent more hours per month as larger airlines' pilots, so

(E) as many as 20 percent more hours per month than pilots at larger airlines do, and consequently

SC24751.01

874. Self-compassion is made up of mindfulness, the ability to manage thoughts and emotions without being carried <u>away or repressing them, common humanity, or empathy with the suffering of others,</u> and self-kindness, a recognition of your own suffering and a commitment to solving the problem.

(A) away or repressing them, common humanity, or empathy with the suffering of others,

(B) away, or repression of them, and common humanity, or empathy with the suffering of others,

(C) away, or repressing them, common humanity, empathy with the suffering of others;

(D) away or repressing them; common humanity, an empathy with the suffering of others;

(E) away or repress them; common humanity, to empathize with the suffering of others

SC83751.01

875. According to the laws of this nation, individuals are minors until they reach the age of eighteen, <u>although this is less in some countries and more in others</u>.

(A) although this is less in some countries and more in others

(B) but this age is lower in some countries; higher in others

(C) although in some countries, it is lower and in others it is higher

(D) although it is less than that in some countries and more than that in others

(E) but the relevant age is lower in some countries and higher in others

SC32261.01

876. <u>Rather than ignore a company that seems about to fail,</u> investment analysts should recognize that its reorganization and recent uptick in revenue, combined with its dynamic new leadership, indicate that the firm's prospects must be taken seriously.

(A) Rather than ignore a company that seems about to fail,

(B) Rather than ignoring a company that is about to seemingly fail,

(C) Instead of a company that is seemingly about to fail being ignored,

(D) Instead of ignore a company that seems about to fail,

(E) In place of ignoring a company's imminent failure seemingly about to occur,

SC01490

877. Between 14,000 and 8,000 B.C. the ice cap that covered northern Asia, Europe, and America <u>began to melt, uncovering vast new areas that were to be occupied</u> by migrating peoples moving northward.

(A) began to melt, uncovering vast new areas that were to be occupied

(B) began melting, to uncover vast new areas to be occupied

(C) began, by melting, to uncover vast new areas for occupation

(D) began, after melting, uncovering vast new areas which are to be occupied

(E) would begin to uncover, through melting, vast new areas for occupation

SC71360.02

878. Because property values sometimes fluctuate in response to economic conditions beyond the purchaser's control, <u>an investment in a home may underperform when compared to that of other widely available classes of investments</u>.

(A) an investment in a home may underperform when compared to that of other widely available classes of investments

(B) an investment in a home may underperform compared with other widely available classes of investments

(C) an investment in a home may underperform when comparing it with other widely available classes of investments

(D) compared to that of other widely available classes of investments, an investment in a home may underperform

(E) in comparison with that of other widely available classes of investments, an investment in a home may underperform

SC01472

879. Bengal-born writer, philosopher, and educator Rabindranath Tagore had the greatest admiration <u>for Mohandas K. Gandhi the person and also as a politician, but Tagore had been</u> skeptical of Gandhi's form of nationalism and his conservative opinions about India's cultural traditions.

(A) for Mohandas K. Gandhi the person and also as a politician, but Tagore had been

(B) for Mohandas K. Gandhi as a person and as a politician, but Tagore was also

(C) for Mohandas K. Gandhi not only as a person and as a politician, but Tagore was also

(D) of Mohandas K. Gandhi as a person and as also a politician, but Tagore was

(E) of Mohandas K. Gandhi not only as a person and as a politician, but Tagore had also been

SC04704

880. Traffic safety officials predict that drivers will be <u>equally likely to exceed the proposed speed limit as</u> the current one.

(A) equally likely to exceed the proposed speed limit as

(B) equally likely to exceed the proposed speed limit as they are

(C) equally likely that they will exceed the proposed speed limit as

(D) as likely that they will exceed the proposed speed limit as

(E) as likely to exceed the proposed speed limit as they are

SC04562

881. Written early in the French Revolution, <u>Mary Wollstonecraft's *A Vindication of the Rights of Man* (1790) and *A Vindication of the Rights of Woman* (1792) attributed Europe's social and political ills to be the result of</u> the dominance of aristocratic values and patriarchal hereditary privilege.

(A) Mary Wollstonecraft's *A Vindication of the Rights of Man* (1790) and *A Vindication of the Rights of Woman* (1792) attributed Europe's social and political ills to be the result of

(B) Mary Wollstonecraft's *A Vindication of the Rights of Man* (1790) and *A Vindication of the Rights of Woman* (1792) attributed Europe's social and political ills to result from

(C) Mary Wollstonecraft's *A Vindication of the Rights of Man* (1790) and *A Vindication of the Rights of Woman* (1792) attributed Europe's social and political ills to

(D) in *A Vindication of the Rights of Man* (1790) and *A Vindication of the Rights of Woman* (1792), Mary Wollstonecraft attributed Europe's social and political ills to have been the result of

(E) Mary Wollstonecraft, in *A Vindication of the Rights of Man* (1790) and *A Vindication of the Rights of Woman* (1792), attributed Europe's social and political ills to

SC01498

882. Using study groups managed by the principal popular organizations and political parties, <u>the Swedish public was informed by the government about energy and nuclear power</u>.

(A) the Swedish public was informed by the government about energy and nuclear power

(B) the government informed the Swedish public about energy and nuclear power

(C) energy and nuclear power information was given to the Swedish public by the government

(D) information about energy and nuclear power was given to the Swedish public by the government

(E) the public of Sweden was given energy and nuclear power information by the government

SC07446

883. The use of the bar code, or Universal Product Code, which was created in part to enable supermarkets to process customers at a faster rate, has expanded beyond supermarkets to other retail outlets and <u>have become readily accepted despite some initial opposition when it was first introduced in 1974</u>.

(A) have become readily accepted despite some initial opposition when it was first introduced in 1974

(B) has become readily accepted despite some initial opposition when they were first introduced in 1974

(C) have become readily accepted despite some initial opposition when first introduced in 1974

(D) has become readily accepted despite some initial opposition when the bar code was first introduced in 1974

(E) bar codes have become readily accepted despite some initial opposition when it was first introduced in 1974

SC01595

884. Normally a bone becomes fossilized through the action of groundwater, <u>which permeates the bone, washes away its organic components, and replaces them</u> with minerals.

(A) which permeates the bone, washes away its organic components, and replaces them

(B) which permeates the bone, washes away its organic components, and those are replaced

(C) which permeates the bone, washing away its organic components, to be replaced

(D) permeating the bone, washing away its organic components, to be replaced

(E) permeating the bone, washing away its organic components and replacing them

SC04416

885. The Organization of Petroleum Exporting Countries (OPEC) had long been expected to announce a reduction in output to bolster sagging oil prices, but officials of the organization just recently announced that the group will pare daily production by 1.5 million barrels by the beginning of next <u>year, but only if non-OPEC nations, including Norway, Mexico, and Russia, were to trim output</u> by a total of 500,000 barrels a day.

(A) year, but only if non-OPEC nations, including Norway, Mexico, and Russia, were to trim output

(B) year, but only if the output of non-OPEC nations, which includes Norway, Mexico, and Russia, is trimmed

(C) year only if the output of non-OPEC nations, including Norway, Mexico, and Russia, would be trimmed

(D) year only if non-OPEC nations, which includes Norway, Mexico, and Russia, were trimming output

(E) year only if non-OPEC nations, including Norway, Mexico, and Russia, trim output

SC25540.02

886. Even with the proposed budget cuts and new taxes and fees, the city's projected deficit for the next budget year is getting worse: administration officials announced that they believe the gap will be $3.7 billion, a billion dollars <u>over what it was predicted</u> just two months ago.

(A) over what it was predicted

(B) over the prediction from

(C) more than it was predicted

(D) more than they had predicted

(E) more than they predicted it

SC01507

887. Over the past ten years cultivated sunflowers have become a major commercial crop, <u>second only to soybeans as a source of vegetable oil</u>.

(A) second only to soybeans as a source of vegetable oil

(B) second in importance to soybeans only as a source of vegetable oil

(C) being second in importance only to soybeans as a source of vegetable oil

(D) which, as a source of vegetable oil, is only second to soybeans

(E) as a source of vegetable oil only second to soybeans

SC00985

888. Not trusting themselves to choose wisely among the wide array of investment opportunities on the market, <u>stockbrokers are helping many people who turn to them to buy stocks that could be easily</u> bought directly.

(A) stockbrokers are helping many people who turn to them to buy stocks that could be easily

(B) stockbrokers are helping many people who are turning to them for help in buying stocks that they could easily have

(C) many people are turning to stockbrokers for help from them to buy stocks that could be easily

(D) many people are turning to stockbrokers for help to buy stocks that easily could have been

(E) many people are turning to stockbrokers for help in buying stocks that could easily be

SC61120.02

889. Scientists claim that the discovery of the first authenticated mammal bones in amber could provide important clues of determining, in addition to how, when mammals colonized the islands of the West Indies.

(A) of determining, in addition to how, when mammals colonized the islands of the West Indies

(B) in the determination of how and when the islands of the West Indies were colonized by mammals

(C) to determine how mammals colonized the islands of the West Indies and when they did

(D) for determining when the islands of the West Indies were colonized by mammals and how they were

(E) for determining how and when mammals colonized the islands of the West Indies

SC01007

890. In the 1940s popular magazines in the United States began to report on the private lives of persons from the entertainment industry, in despite of the fact that they previously had featured individuals in business and politics.

(A) in despite of the fact that they previously had featured individuals

(B) in spite of the fact previously that these publications featured articles on those

(C) whereas previously there were those individuals featured in articles

(D) whereas previously those individuals they featured were

(E) whereas previously these publications had featured articles on individuals

SC04770

891. In the early part of the twentieth century, many vacationers found that driving automobiles and sleeping in tents allowed them to enjoy nature close at hand and tour at their own pace, with none of the restrictions of passenger trains and railroad timetables or with the formalities, expenses, and impersonality of hotels.

(A) with none of the restrictions of passenger trains and railroad timetables or with the

(B) with none of the restrictions of passenger trains, railroad timetables, nor

(C) without the restrictions of passenger trains and railroad timetables nor

(D) without the restrictions of passenger trains and railroad timetables or with the

(E) without the restrictions of passenger trains and railroad timetables or the

SC04760

892. Over the next few years, increasing demands on the Chattahoochee River, which flows into the Apalachicola River, could alter the saline content of Apalachicola Bay, which would rob the oysters there of their flavor, and to make them decrease in size, less distinctive, and less in demand.

(A) which would rob the oysters there of their flavor, and to make them decrease in size,

(B) and it would rob the oysters there of their flavor, make them smaller,

(C) and rob the oysters there of their flavor, making them decrease in size,

(D) robbing the oysters there of their flavor and making them smaller,

(E) robbing the oysters there of their flavor, and making them decrease in size,

SC01469

893. Elizabeth Barber, the author of both *Prehistoric Textiles*, a comprehensive work on cloth in the early cultures of the Mediterranean, and also of *Women's Work*, a more general account of early cloth manufacture, is an expert authority on textiles in ancient societies.

(A) also of *Women's Work*, a more general account of early cloth manufacture, is an expert authority on

(B) also *Women's Work*, a more general account of cloth manufacture, is an expert authority about

(C)   of *Women's Work*, a more general account about early cloth manufacture, is an authority on

(D)   of *Women's Work*, a more general account about early cloth manufacture, is an expert authority about

(E)   *Women's Work*, a more general account of early cloth manufacture, is an authority on

SC00994

894. Digging in sediments in northern China, <u>evidence has been gathered by scientists suggesting that complex life-forms emerged much earlier than they had</u> previously thought.

(A)   evidence has been gathered by scientists suggesting that complex life-forms emerged much earlier than they had

(B)   evidence gathered by scientists suggests a much earlier emergence of complex life-forms than had been

(C)   scientists have gathered evidence suggesting that complex life-forms emerged much earlier than

(D)   scientists have gathered evidence that suggests a much earlier emergence of complex life-forms than that which was

(E)   scientists have gathered evidence which suggests a much earlier emergence of complex life-forms than that

SC01521

895. Employing many different techniques throughout his career, Michelangelo produced a great variety of art works, <u>including paintings, for example, in the Sistine Chapel, to sculpture, for example,</u> the statue of David.

(A)   including paintings, for example, in the Sistine Chapel, to sculpture, for example,

(B)   including paintings, for example, in the Sistine Chapel, to sculpture, like

(C)   including paintings, such as those in the Sistine Chapel, and sculpture, as

(D)   ranging from paintings, such as those in the Sistine Chapel, to sculpture, such as

(E)   ranging from paintings, such as in the Sistine Chapel, and sculpture, such as

SC04422

896. According to a recent study of consumer spending on prescription medications, increases in the sales of the 50 drugs that were advertised most <u>heavily accounts for almost half of the $20.8 billion increase in drug spending last year, the remainder of which came</u> from sales of the 9,850 prescription medicines that companies did not advertise or advertised very little.

(A)   heavily accounts for almost half of the $20.8 billion increase in drug spending last year, the remainder of which came

(B)   heavily were what accounted for almost half of the $20.8 billion increase in drug spending last year; the remainder of the increase coming

(C)   heavily accounted for almost half of the $20.8 billion increase in drug spending last year, the remainder of the increase coming

(D)   heavily, accounting for almost half of the $20.8 billion increase in drug spending last year, while the remainder of the increase came

(E)   heavily, which accounted for almost half of the $20.8 billion increase in drug spending last year, with the remainder of it coming

SC00971

897. Technically, "quicksand" is the term for sand <u>that is so saturated with water as to acquire a liquid's character.</u>

(A)   that is so saturated with water as to acquire a liquid's character

(B)   that is so saturated with water that it acquires the character of a liquid

(C)   that is saturated with water enough to acquire liquid characteristics

(D)   saturated enough with water so as to acquire the character of a liquid

(E)   saturated with water so much as to acquire a liquid character

SC07232

898. At the end of 2001, motion picture industry representatives said that there were about a million copies of Hollywood movies available <u>online and expected piracy to increase with high-speed Internet connections that become more widely available.</u>

(A)   online and expected piracy to increase with high-speed Internet connections that become more widely available

(B)   online and expect the increase of piracy with the wider availability of high-speed Internet connections

(C) online, and they expect more piracy to increase with the wider availability of high-speed Internet connections

(D) online, and that they expected the increase of piracy as high-speed Internet connections would become more widely available

(E) online, and that they expected piracy to increase as high-speed Internet connections became more widely available

SC14066

899. Making things even more difficult has been general market inactivity lately, if not paralysis, which has provided little in the way of pricing guidance.

(A) has been general market inactivity lately, if not paralysis, which has provided

(B) there is general market inactivity, if not paralysis, lately it has provided

(C) general market inactivity, if not paralysis, has lately provided

(D) lately, general market inactivity, if not paralysis, has provided

(E) is that lately general market inactivity, if not paralysis, which provides

SC01946

900. Ryūnosuke Akutagawa's knowledge of the literatures of Europe, China, and that of Japan were instrumental in his development as a writer, informing his literary style as much as the content of his fiction.

(A) that of Japan were instrumental in his development as a writer, informing his literary style as much as

(B) that of Japan was instrumental in his development as a writer, and it informed both his literary style as well as

(C) Japan was instrumental in his development as a writer, informing both his literary style and

(D) Japan was instrumental in his development as a writer, as it informed his literary style as much as

(E) Japan were instrumental in his development as a writer, informing both his literary style in addition to

SC24321.01

901. Many stock traders in the United States have set out to become global investors, convinced that limiting their investments to the U.S. stock market, even though it is certainly home to the stocks of some of the world's great corporations, restricted their gains.

(A) even though it is certainly

(B) which, while it is certainly

(C) despite that that market is certainly

(D) which, though certainly

(E) although, certainly as

SC01973

902. According to scientists who monitored its path, an expanding cloud of energized particles ejected from the Sun recently triggered a large storm in the magnetic field that surrounds Earth, which brightened the Northern Lights and also possibly knocking out a communications satellite.

(A) an expanding cloud of energized particles ejected from the Sun recently triggered a large storm in the magnetic field that surrounds Earth, which brightened the Northern Lights and also possibly knocking

(B) an expanding cloud of energized particles ejected from the Sun was what recently triggered a large storm in the magnetic field that surrounds Earth, and it brightened the Northern Lights and also possibly knocked

(C) an expanding cloud of energized particles ejected from the Sun recently triggered a large storm in the magnetic field that surrounds Earth, brightening the Northern Lights and possibly knocking

(D) a large storm in the magnetic field that surrounds Earth, recently triggered by an expanding cloud of energized particles, brightened the Northern Lights and it possibly knocked

(E) a large storm in the magnetic field surrounding Earth was recently triggered by an expanding cloud of energized particles, brightening the Northern Lights and it possibly knocked

SC01033

903. Because many of Australia's marsupials, such as the koala, are cute and cuddly, as well as <u>being biologically different than North American marsupials, they have attracted a lot of attention after</u> their discovery in the 1700s.

   (A)   being biologically different than North American marsupials, they have attracted a lot of attention after

   (B)   being biologically different from North American marsupials, they attracted a lot of attention since

   (C)   biologically different than North American marsupials, they attracted a lot of attention since

   (D)   biologically different than North American marsupials, they have attracted a lot of attention after

   (E)   biologically different from North American marsupials, they have attracted a lot of attention since

SC02448

904. <u>Having been named for a mythological nymph who cared for the infant Jupiter, the asteroid named Ida, in the middle of the belt of asteroids that orbit the Sun between Mars and Jupiter, was discovered in 1884.</u>

   (A)   Having been named for a mythological nymph who cared for the infant Jupiter, the asteroid named Ida, in the middle of the belt of asteroids that orbit the Sun between Mars and Jupiter, was discovered in 1884.

   (B)   Discovered in 1884, the asteroid Ida, named for a mythological nymph who cared for the infant Jupiter, is in the middle of the belt of asteroids that orbit the Sun between Mars and Jupiter.

   (C)   In the middle of the belt of asteroids that orbit the Sun between Mars and Jupiter, the asteroid Ida, discovered in 1884 and named for a mythological nymph who cared for the infant Jupiter.

   (D)   The asteroid Ida, named for a mythological nymph who cared for the infant Jupiter and discovered in 1884, is in the middle of the belt of asteroids to orbit the Sun between Mars and Jupiter.

   (E)   Ida, an asteroid discovered in 1884 and which was named for a mythological nymph who cared for the infant Jupiter, is in the middle of the belt of asteroids to orbit the Sun between Mars and Jupiter.

SC20121.01

905. Custodian fees and expenses, as described in the statement of operations, <u>include interest expense incurred by the fund on any cash overdrafts of its custodian account during the period</u>.

   (A)   include interest expense incurred by the fund on any cash overdrafts of its custodian account during the period

   (B)   are to include interest expenses on any cash overdrafts of its custodian account the fund incurred during the period

   (C)   includes interest expense the fund incurred during the period on any cash overdrafts of its custodian account

   (D)   may include interest expense during the period that the fund was to incur on any cash overdrafts of its custodian account

   (E)   including interest expense on any cash overdrafts of its custodian account incurred by the fund during the period

SC36241.01

906. Although some had accused Smith, the firm's network manager, of negligence when the crucial data went missing, the CEO defused <u>a situation that was quite tense with her public statement that the debacle was not Smith's fault.</u>

   (A)   a situation that was quite tense with her public statement that the debacle was not Smith's fault

   (B)   a situation that was quite tense, by publicly stating that the debacle was not Smith's fault

   (C)   a situation, which was quite tense, by stating publicly that Smith was not responsible for the debacle

   (D)   a quite tense situation with a public statement about the debacle not being Smith's fault

   (E)   a quite tense situation by publicly stating the debacle not to have been Smith's fault

SC01077

907. Many utilities obtain most of their electric power from large coal and nuclear operations at costs that are sometimes <u>two to three times higher as that of power from smaller, more efficient plants that can both</u> make use of waste heat and take advantage of the current abundance of natural gas.

   (A)   two to three times higher as that of power from smaller, more efficient plants that can both

   (B)   higher by two to three times as that from smaller, more efficient plants that both can

(C) two to three times higher than those for power from smaller, more efficient plants that can both

(D) between two to three times higher as those for power from smaller, more efficient plants that both can

(E) between two to three times higher than from smaller, more efficient plants that they can both

SC16020.02

908. Five hundred million different species of living creatures have appeared on Earth, nearly 99 percent of them vanishing.

(A) Five hundred million different species of living creatures have appeared on Earth, nearly 99 percent of them vanishing.

(B) Nearly 99 percent of five hundred million different species of living creatures that appeared on Earth have vanished.

(C) Vanished are nearly 99 percent of the five hundred million different species of living creatures that appeared on Earth.

(D) Of five hundred million different species of living creatures that have appeared on Earth, nearly 99 percent of them have vanished.

(E) Of the five hundred million different species of living creatures that have appeared on Earth, nearly 99 percent have vanished.

SC01523

909. When viewed from the window of a speeding train, the speed with which nearby objects move seems faster than that of more distant objects.

(A) the speed with which nearby objects move seems faster than that of

(B) the speed that nearby objects move seems faster than for

(C) the speed of nearby objects seems faster than

(D) nearby objects' speeds seem to be faster than those of

(E) nearby objects seem to move at a faster speed than do

SC41451.01

910. Ramón pointed out that food high in whole-grain fiber creates the energy we need to fight illnesses—as do vegetables and lean proteins.

(A) fiber creates the energy we need to fight illnesses—as do vegetables and lean proteins

(B) fiber in addition to vegetables and lean proteins, create the energy we need to fight illnesses

(C) fiber creates the energy we need to fight illnesses, along with vegetables and lean proteins

(D) fiber, vegetables, and lean proteins creates the energy we need to fight illnesses

(E) fiber, as vegetables and lean proteins, create the energy we need to fight illnesses

SC01487

911. The English physician Edward Jenner found that if experimental subjects were deliberately infected with cowpox, which caused only a mild illness, they are immune from smallpox.

(A) which caused only a mild illness, they are immune from

(B) causing only a mild illness, they become immune from

(C) which causes only a mild illness, they are immune to

(D) causing only a mild illness, they became immune from

(E) which caused only a mild illness, they would become immune to

SC34740.02

912. As opposed to adults, pound for pound, children breathe twice as much air, drink two and a half times as much water, eat three to four times as much food, and have more skin surface area.

(A) As opposed to adults, pound for pound, children

(B) Compared pound for pound with adults, children

(C) Unlike an adult, pound for pound, children

(D) Pound for pound, a child, unlike an adult, will

(E) Pound for pound, children compared to adults will

SC00989

913. The final decades of the twentieth century not only saw an explosion of the literary production among women, but there was also an intense interest in the lives and works of women writers.

(A) not only saw an explosion of the literary production among women, but there was also

(B) not only saw an explosion of literary production in women, but there was also

(C) saw not only an explosion of literary production among women, but also

(D) saw not only an explosion of the literary production by women, but it also saw

(E) saw not only an explosion of literary production by women, but also saw

SC07530.02

914. In the six-month period that ended on September 30, the average number of Sunday papers sold by the company was 81,000 less than the comparable period a year ago.

(A) the average number of Sunday papers sold by the company was 81,000 less than

(B) on average, the number of Sunday papers sold by the company was 81,000 less than it was

(C) the company sold an average of 81,000 fewer Sunday papers than in

(D) the company averaged sales of 81,000 fewer Sunday papers than what it did in

(F) the average sale of Sunday papers for the company was 81,000 less than what they were in

SC07920.02

915. Michelangelo, it is believed, had made his sculpture of David using an eight-inch plaster model that was recently discovered after being lost for nearly 300 years.

(A) Michelangelo, it is believed, had made his sculpture of David using an eight-inch plaster model that was recently discovered after being

(B) An eight-inch plaster model is believed to have been used by Michelangelo for his sculpture of David and recently discovered after it was

(C) An eight-inch plaster model believed to have been used by Michelangelo for his sculpture of David has been discovered after having been

(D) It is believed that an eight-inch plaster model that Michelangelo used for his sculpture of David and has recently been discovered after it was

(E) It is believed that Michelangelo used an eight-inch plaster model for his sculpture of David, and it was recently discovered after having been

SC11850.01

916. Although the rise in the Producer Price Index was greater than expected, most analysts agreed that the index was unlikely to continue going up and that inflation remained essentially under control.

(A) that the index was unlikely to continue going up and that inflation remained

(B) that it was unlikely for the index continuing to go up and for inflation to remain

(C) that the index was unlikely to continue to go up, with inflation to remain

(D) on the unlikelihood that the index would continue going up and that inflation remained

(E) on the unlikelihood that the index would continue to go up and for inflation to remain

SC71030.02

917. Just like the Internet today, often being called an "information superhighway," the telegraph was described in its day as an "instantaneous highway of thought."

(A) Just like the Internet today, often being

(B) Just as the Internet is today often

(C) As with the Internet being today often

(D) As is often the case today with the Internet,

(E) Similar to the Internet today, often

SC17041.01

918. Severely hindered by problems with local suppliers, the fact that the AQ division also had a new management team to adapt to was not seen by the board of directors as a legitimate excuse for such low productivity.

(A) Severely hindered by problems with local suppliers, the fact that the AQ division also had a new management team to adapt to

(B) Though severely hindered by local supply problems, the fact that the AQ division also had a new management team to which to adapt

(C) Severely hindered by problems with local suppliers, the AQ division also had to adapt to a new management team, but this

(D) Severely hindered by local supply problems, that the AQ division also had to adapt to a new management team

(E) Though severely hindered by problems with local suppliers, the AQ division's also having a new management team to which it had to adapt

SC01037

919. The Eastern State Penitentiary was established in 1822 by reformers <u>advocating that prisoners be held in solitary confinement and hard labor so as to reform them</u>.

   (A) advocating that prisoners be held in solitary confinement and hard labor so as to reform them

   (B) who were advocating prisoners to be held in solitary confinement and hard labor for their reform

   (C) advocating solitary confinement and hard labor as the means to reform prisoners

   (D) who advocated solitary confinement and hard labor for the means of prisoner reform

   (E) advocating as the means for prisoner reform solitary confinement and hard labor

SC03288

920. Some anthropologists believe that the genetic homogeneity evident in the world's people is the result of a "population bottleneck"—<u>at some time in the past our ancestors suffered an event, greatly reducing their numbers</u> and thus our genetic variation.

   (A) at some time in the past our ancestors suffered an event, greatly reducing their numbers

   (B) that at some time in the past our ancestors suffered an event that greatly reduced their numbers

   (C) that some time in the past our ancestors suffered an event so that their numbers were greatly reduced,

   (D) some time in the past our ancestors suffered an event from which their numbers were greatly reduced

   (E) some time in the past, that our ancestors suffered an event so as to reduce their numbers greatly,

SC01493

921. <u>Through experimenting designed to provide information that will ultimately prove</u> useful in the treatment of hereditary diseases, mice have received bone marrow transplants that give them a new gene.

   (A) Through experimenting designed to provide information that will ultimately prove

   (B) Through experiments designed to provide information ultimately proving

   (C) In experimentation designed to provide information that ultimately proves

   (D) In experimenting designed to provide information ultimately proving

   (E) In experiments designed to provide information that will ultimately prove

SC48420.01

922. Linking arrangements <u>among secondary schools and the workplace never evolved in the United States as they have</u> in most other developed countries.

   (A) among secondary schools and the workplace never evolved in the United States as they have

   (B) in the United States among secondary schools and the workplace never evolved as they did

   (C) between secondary schools and the workplace never evolved in the United States as

   (D) in the United States between secondary schools and the workplace never evolved as they have

   (E) between secondary schools and the workplace never evolved in the United States as they did

SC38250.02

923. The ages of tropical rain forest trees provide critical information for understanding the dynamics of tree populations, <u>to determine historical patterns of disturbance, developing sustainable forestry practices, and calculating</u> carbon recycling rates.

   (A) to determine historical patterns of disturbance, developing sustainable forestry practices, and calculating

   (B) to determine historical patterns of disturbance, develop sustainable forestry practices, and to calculate

   (C) determining historical patterns of disturbance, developing sustainable forestry practices, and calculating

   (D) determining historical patterns of disturbance, developing sustainable forestry practices, and to calculate

   (E) determining historical patterns of disturbance, for developing sustainable forestry practices, and for calculating

SC01603

924. The United Parcel Service plans <u>to convert its more than 2,000 gasoline-powered trucks in the Los Angeles area to</u> run on cleaner-burning natural gas.

   (A) to convert its more than 2,000 gasoline-powered trucks in the Los Angeles area to

(B) to convert its more than 2,000 trucks in the Los Angeles area that are powered by gasoline to

(C) on converting its more than 2,000 gasoline-powered trucks in the Los Angeles area that will

(D) for its more than 2,000 gasoline-powered trucks in the Los Angeles area to convert to

(E) that its more than 2,000 trucks in the Los Angeles area that are powered by gasoline will convert to

SC02443

925. Foraging at all times of the day and night, but interspersing their feeding with periods of rest that last <u>between one and eight hours, a sperm whale could eat so</u> much as a ton of squid a day.

(A) between one and eight hours, a sperm whale could eat so

(B) between one and eight hours, sperm whales can eat as

(C) between one to eight hours, sperm whales could eat as

(D) from one to eight hours, sperm whales could eat so

(E) from one to eight hours, a sperm whale can eat so

SC14796

926. In some types of pine tree, <u>a thick layer of needles protects the buds from which new growth proceeds; consequently they are able to withstand forest fires relatively well.</u>

(A) a thick layer of needles protects the buds from which new growth proceeds; consequently they are able to withstand forest fires relatively well

(B) a thick needle layer protects buds from where new growth proceeds, so that they can withstand forest fires relatively well

(C) a thick layer of needles protect the buds from which new growth proceeds; thus, they are able to withstand relatively well any forest fires

(D) since the buds from which new growth proceeds are protected by a thick needle layer, consequently they can therefore withstand forest fires relatively well

(E) because the buds where new growth happens are protected by a thick layer of needles, they are able to withstand forest fires relatively easily as a result

SC08577

927. The tourism commission has conducted surveys of hotels in the most popular resorts, <u>with the ultimate goal of reducing the guests who end up expressing overall dissatisfaction with the service in the hotels.</u>

(A) with the ultimate goal of reducing the guests who end up expressing overall dissatisfaction with the service in the hotels

(B) with the goal to ultimately reduce the number of guests who end up expressing overall dissatisfaction with the hotels' service

(C) ultimately with the goal to reduce expressions of overall dissatisfaction by the guests with the hotel service

(D) in an ultimate attempt to reduce the number of guests that ends up expressing overall dissatisfaction with the hotels' service

(E) with the ultimate goal of reducing the number of guests who express overall dissatisfaction with the hotels' service

SC61740.02

928. Unlike historical evidence of weather patterns in other regions of the world, which scientists find abundantly represented in tree rings, ancient glacial ice, or layers of sediment from seasonal plankton, <u>the North Pole's clues about its past climates are almost nonexistent.</u>

(A) the North Pole's clues about its past climates are almost nonexistent

(B) the North Pole does not offer many clues as to its past climates

(C) clues to the past climates of the North Pole are almost nonexistent

(D) there are few clues about past climates for the North Pole

(E) the past climates of the North Pole do not offer many clues

Questions 929 to 995 - Difficulty: Hard

SC01607

929. A new study suggests that the conversational pace of everyday life may be so brisk <u>it hampers the ability of some children for distinguishing discrete sounds and words and, the result is, to make</u> sense of speech.

(A) it hampers the ability of some children for distinguishing discrete sounds and words and, the result is, to make

(B)   that it hampers the ability of some children to distinguish discrete sounds and words and, as a result, to make

(C)   that it hampers the ability of some children to distinguish discrete sounds and words and, the result of this, they are unable to make

(D)   that it hampers the ability of some children to distinguish discrete sounds and words, and results in not making

(E)   as to hamper the ability of some children for distinguishing discrete sounds and words, resulting in being unable to make

SC07035

930. The nineteenth-century chemist Humphry Davy presented the results of his early experiments in his "Essay on Heat and Light," a critique of all chemistry since Robert Boyle as well as a vision of a new chemistry that Davy hoped to found.

(A)   a critique of all chemistry since Robert Boyle as well as a vision of a

(B)   a critique of all chemistry following Robert Boyle and also his envisioning of a

(C)   a critique of all chemistry after Robert Boyle and envisioning as well

(D)   critiquing all chemistry from Robert Boyle forward and also a vision of

(E)   critiquing all the chemistry done since Robert Boyle as well as his own envisioning of

SC02280

931. To attract the most talented workers, some companies are offering a wider range of benefits, letting employees pick those most important to them.

(A)   benefits, letting employees pick those most important to them

(B)   benefits, letting employees pick the most important of them to themselves

(C)   benefits and letting employees pick the most important to themselves

(D)   benefits and let employees pick the most important to them

(E)   benefits and let employees pick those that are most important to themselves

SC01583

932. Many of the earliest known images of Hindu deities in India date from the time of the Kushan Empire,

fashioned either from the spotted sandstone of Mathura or Gandharan grey schist.

(A)   Empire, fashioned either from the spotted sandstone of Mathura or

(B)   Empire, fashioned from either the spotted sandstone of Mathura or from

(C)   Empire, either fashioned from the spotted sandstone of Mathura or

(D)   Empire and either fashioned from the spotted sandstone of Mathura or from

(E)   Empire and were fashioned either from the spotted sandstone of Mathura or from

SC01051

933. Tides typically range from three to six feet, but while some places show no tides at all, some others, such as the Bay of Fundy, have tides of at least thirty feet and more.

(A)   some others, such as the Bay of Fundy, have tides of at least thirty feet and more

(B)   the others, such as the Bay of Fundy, that have tides of more than thirty feet

(C)   others, such as the Bay of Fundy, have tides of more than thirty feet

(D)   those at the Bay of Fundy, which has tides of more than thirty feet

(E)   the ones at the Bay of Fundy have tides of at least thirty feet and more

SC01028

934. A leading figure in the Scottish Enlightenment, Adam Smith's two major books are to democratic capitalism what Marx's *Das Kapital* is to socialism.

(A)   Adam Smith's two major books are to democratic capitalism what

(B)   Adam Smith's two major books are to democratic capitalism like

(C)   Adam Smith's two major books are to democratic capitalism just as

(D)   Adam Smith wrote two major books that are to democratic capitalism similar to

(E)   Adam Smith wrote two major books that are to democratic capitalism what

SC04331

935. Researchers studying the brain scans of volunteers who pondered ethical dilemmas have found that the

basis for making tough moral judgments is emotion, not logic or analytical reasoning.

(A) the brain scans of volunteers who pondered ethical dilemmas have found that the basis for making tough moral judgments is

(B) the brain scans of volunteers who pondered ethical dilemmas and found the basis to make tough moral decisions to be

(C) the brain scans of volunteers pondering ethical dilemmas and found that the basis for making tough moral decisions is

(D) volunteers' brain scans while pondering ethical dilemmas have found the basis to make tough moral judgments to be

(E) volunteers' brain scans while they pondered ethical dilemmas have found that the basis for making tough moral judgments is

SC02060

936. Rivaling the pyramids of Egypt or even the ancient cities of the Maya as an achievement, <u>the army of terra-cotta warriors created to protect Qin Shi Huang, China's first emperor, in his afterlife is more than 2,000 years old and took 700,000 artisans more than 36 years to complete.</u>

(A) the army of terra-cotta warriors created to protect Qin Shi Huang, China's first emperor, in his afterlife is more than 2,000 years old and took 700,000 artisans more than 36 years to complete

(B) Qin Shi Huang, China's first emperor, was protected in his afterlife by an army of terra-cotta warriors that was created more than 2,000 years ago by 700,000 artisans who took more than 36 years to complete it

(C) it took 700,000 artisans more than 36 years to create an army of terra-cotta warriors more than 2,000 years ago that would protect Qin Shi Huang, China's first emperor, in his afterlife

(D) more than 2,000 years ago, 700,000 artisans worked more than 36 years to create an army of terra-cotta warriors to protect Qin Shi Huang, China's first emperor, in his afterlife

(E) more than 36 years were needed to complete the army of terra-cotta warriors that 700,000 artisans created 2,000 years ago to protect Qin Shi Huang, China's first emperor, in his afterlife

SC03675

937. In California, a lack of genetic variation in the Argentine ant has allowed the species to spread widely; <u>due to their being so genetically similar to one another, the ants consider all their fellows to be a close relative and thus do not engage in the kind of fierce intercolony struggles that limits</u> the spread of this species in its native Argentina.

(A) due to their being so genetically similar to one another, the ants consider all their fellows to be a close relative and thus do not engage in the kind of fierce intercolony struggles that limits

(B) due to its being so genetically similar, the ant considers all its fellows to be a close relative and thus does not engage in the kind of fierce intercolony struggles that limit

(C) because it is so genetically similar, the ant considers all its fellows to be close relatives and thus does not engage in the kind of fierce intercolony struggles that limits

(D) because they are so genetically similar to one another, the ants consider all their fellows to be close relatives and thus do not engage in the kind of fierce intercolony struggles that limit

(E) because of being so genetically similar to one another, the ants consider all their fellows to be a close relative and thus do not engage in the kind of fierce intercolony struggles that limits

SC07758

938. Next month, state wildlife officials are scheduled to take over the job of increasing the wolf population in the federally designated recovery <u>area, the number of which will however</u> ultimately be dictated by the number of prey in the area.

(A) area, the number of which will however

(B) area; the size of the population, however, will

(C) area, however the number of wolves will

(D) area; the number of which will, however,

(E) area, when the size of the population will, however,

SC02710

939. About 5 million acres in the United <u>States have been invaded by leafy spurge, a herbaceous plant from Eurasia with milky sap that gives mouth sores to cattle, displacing grasses and other cattle food and rendering</u> rangeland worthless.

(A)   States have been invaded by leafy spurge, a herbaceous plant from Eurasia with milky sap that gives mouth sores to cattle, displacing grasses and other cattle food and rendering

(B)   States have been invaded by leafy spurge, a herbaceous plant from Eurasia, with milky sap, that gives mouth sores to cattle and displaces grasses and other cattle food, rendering

(C)   States have been invaded by leafy spurge, a herbaceous plant from Eurasia having milky sap that gives mouth sores to cattle and displacing grasses and other cattle food, rendering

(D)   States, having been invaded by leafy spurge, a herbaceous plant from Eurasia with milky sap that gives mouth sores to cattle, displaces grasses and other cattle food, and renders

(E)   States, having been invaded by leafy spurge, a herbaceous plant from Eurasia that has milky sap giving mouth sores to cattle and displacing grasses and other cattle food, rendering

SC01445
940.   While it costs about the same to run nuclear plants as other types of power plants, it is the fixed costs that stem from building nuclear plants that makes it more expensive for them to generate electricity.

(A)   While it costs about the same to run nuclear plants as other types of power plants, it is the fixed costs that stem from building nuclear plants that makes it more expensive for them to generate electricity.

(B)   While the cost of running nuclear plants is about the same as for other types of power plants, the fixed costs that stem from building nuclear plants make the electricity they generate more expensive.

(C)   Even though it costs about the same to run nuclear plants as for other types of power plants, it is the fixed costs that stem from building nuclear plants that makes the electricity they generate more expensive.

(D)   It costs about the same to run nuclear plants as for other types of power plants, whereas the electricity they generate is more expensive, stemming from the fixed costs of building nuclear plants.

(E)   The cost of running nuclear plants is about the same as other types of power plants, but the electricity they generate is made more expensive because of the fixed costs stemming from building nuclear plants.

SC03207
941.   The 32 species that make up the dolphin family are closely related to whales and in fact include the animal known as the killer whale, which can grow to be 30 feet long and is famous for its aggressive hunting pods.

(A)   include the animal known as the killer whale, which can grow to be 30 feet long and is

(B)   include the animal known as the killer whale, growing as big as 30 feet long and

(C)   include the animal known as the killer whale, growing up to 30 feet long and being

(D)   includes the animal known as the killer whale, which can grow as big as 30 feet long and is

(E)   includes the animal known as the killer whale, which can grow to be 30 feet long and it is

SC06611
942.   The first trenches that were cut into a 500-acre site at Tell Hamoukar, Syria, have yielded strong evidence for centrally administered complex societies in northern regions of the Middle East that were arising simultaneously with but independently of the more celebrated city-states of southern Mesopotamia, in what is now southern Iraq.

(A)   that were cut into a 500-acre site at Tell Hamoukar, Syria, have yielded strong evidence for centrally administered complex societies in northern regions of the Middle East that were arising simultaneously with but

(B)   that were cut into a 500-acre site at Tell Hamoukar, Syria, yields strong evidence that centrally administered complex societies in northern regions of the Middle East were arising simultaneously with but also

(C)   having been cut into a 500-acre site at Tell Hamoukar, Syria, have yielded strong evidence that centrally administered complex societies in northern regions of the Middle East were arising simultaneously but

(D)   cut into a 500-acre site at Tell Hamoukar, Syria, yields strong evidence of centrally administered complex societies in northern regions of the Middle East arising simultaneously but also

(E)   cut into a 500-acre site at Tell Hamoukar, Syria, have yielded strong evidence that centrally administered complex societies in northern regions of the Middle East arose simultaneously with but

SC02317

943. Companies are relying more and more on networked computers for such critical tasks as inventory management, electronic funds transfer, and electronic data interchange, <u>in which standard business transactions are handled via computer rather than on paper.</u>

(A) in which standard business transactions are handled via computer rather than on paper

(B) where computers handle standard business transactions rather than on paper

(C) in which computers handle standard business transactions instead of on paper

(D) where standard business transactions are handled, not with paper, but instead via computer

(E) in which standard business transactions are being handled via computer, in place of on paper

SC07231

944. Combining enormous physical strength with higher intelligence, the Neanderthals <u>appear as equipped for facing any obstacle the environment could put in their path,</u> but their relatively sudden disappearance during the Paleolithic era indicates that an inability to adapt to some environmental change led to their extinction.

(A) appear as equipped for facing any obstacle the environment could put in their path,

(B) appear to have been equipped to face any obstacle the environment could put in their path,

(C) appear as equipped to face any obstacle the environment could put in their paths,

(D) appeared as equipped to face any obstacle the environment could put in their paths,

(E) appeared to have been equipped for facing any obstacle the environment could put in their path,

SC02135

945. To map Earth's interior, geologists use a network of seismometers to chart seismic waves that originate in the earth's crust and ricochet around its <u>interior, most rapidly traveling through cold, dense regions and slower</u> through hotter rocks.

(A) interior, most rapidly traveling through cold, dense regions and slower

(B) interior, which travel most rapidly through cold, dense regions, and more slowly

(C) interior, traveling most rapidly through cold, dense regions and more slowly

(D) interior and most rapidly travel through cold, dense regions, and slower

(E) interior and that travel most rapidly through cold, dense regions and slower

SC02470

946. Prices at the producer level are only 1.3 percent higher now <u>than a year ago and are going down, even though floods in the Midwest and drought in the South are hurting crops and therefore raised</u> corn and soybean prices.

(A) than a year ago and are going down, even though floods in the Midwest and drought in the South are hurting crops and therefore raised

(B) than those of a year ago and are going down, even though floods in the Midwest and drought in the South are hurting crops and therefore raising

(C) than a year ago and are going down, despite floods in the Midwest and drought in the South, and are hurting crops and therefore raising

(D) as those of a year ago and are going down, even though floods in the Midwest and drought in the South hurt crops and therefore raise

(E) as they were a year ago and are going down, despite floods in the Midwest and drought in the South, and are hurting crops and therefore raising

SC07117

947. Fossils of the arm of a <u>sloth found in Puerto Rico in 1991, and dated at 34 million years old, made it the earliest known mammal of</u> the Greater Antilles Islands.

(A) sloth found in Puerto Rico in 1991, and dated at 34 million years old, made it the earliest known mammal of

(B) sloth, that they found in Puerto Rico in 1991, has been dated at 34 million years old, thus making it the earliest mammal known on

(C) sloth that was found in Puerto Rico in 1991, was dated at 34 million years old, making this the earliest known mammal of

(D) sloth, found in Puerto Rico in 1991, have been dated at 34 million years old, making the sloth the earliest known mammal on

(E) sloth which, found in Puerto Rico in 1991, was dated at 34 million years old, made the sloth the earliest known mammal of

SC01550

948. Recently physicians have determined that stomach ulcers are <u>not caused by stress, alcohol, or rich foods, but</u> a bacterium that dwells in the mucous lining of the stomach.

(A) not caused by stress, alcohol, or rich foods, but

(B) not caused by stress, alcohol, or rich foods, but are by

(C) caused not by stress, alcohol, or rich foods, but by

(D) caused not by stress, alcohol, and rich foods, but

(E) caused not by stress, alcohol, and rich foods, but are by

SC05848

949. <u>The eyes of the elephant seal adapt to darkness more quickly than any other animal yet tested, thus allowing it</u> to hunt efficiently under the gloomy conditions at its feeding depth of between 300 and 700 meters.

(A) The eyes of the elephant seal adapt to darkness more quickly than any other animal yet tested, thus allowing it

(B) The eyes of the elephant seal adapt to darkness more quickly than does any other animal yet tested, allowing them

(C) The eyes of the elephant seal adapt to darkness more quickly than do those of any other animal yet tested, allowing it

(D) Because they adapt to darkness more quickly than any other animal yet tested, the eyes of the elephant seal allow it

(E) Because the eyes of the elephant seal adapt to darkness more quickly than do those of any other animal yet tested, it allows them

SC01068

950. A mutual fund having billions of dollars in assets will typically invest that money in hundreds of <u>companies, rarely holding more than one percent</u> of the shares of any particular corporation.

(A) companies, rarely holding more than one percent

(B) companies, and it is rare to hold at least one percent or more

(C) companies and rarely do they hold more than one percent

(D) companies, so that they rarely hold more than one percent

(E) companies; rarely do they hold one percent or more

SC08083

951. Positing an enormous volcanic explosion at the end of the Permian period would explain the presence of a buried crater, <u>account for the presence of the element iridium (originating deep within the earth), and the presence of quartz having been</u> shattered by high-impact shock waves.

(A) account for the presence of the element iridium (originating deep within the earth), and the presence of quartz having been

(B) of the element iridium (originating deep within the earth), and of quartz

(C) the element iridium (originating deep within the earth), and explain the presence of quartz having been

(D) the presence of the element iridium (originating deep within the earth), and explain the presence of quartz

(E) explain the element iridium (originating deep within the earth), and the presence of quartz

SC01561

952. The 19-year-old pianist and composer performed his most recent work all over Europe, Asia, and North America last year, <u>winning prestigious awards in both London as well as Tokyo for his achievement at so young an age, and he is hoping</u> to continue composing now that he has returned to Chicago.

(A) winning prestigious awards in both London as well as Tokyo for his achievement at so young an age, and he is hoping

(B) winning prestigious awards both in London and Tokyo for his achievement at such a young age, and hoping

(C) having won prestigious awards both in London and Tokyo for his achievement at so young an age, hoping

(D) winning prestigious awards in both London and Tokyo for his achievement at such a young age, and he hopes

(E) having won prestigious awards both in London as well as Tokyo for his achievement at so young an age, and he hopes

SC01474

953. Starfish, with anywhere from five to eight arms, have a strong regenerative ability, and if <u>one arm is lost it quickly replaces it, sometimes by the animal overcompensating and</u> growing an extra one or two.

(A) one arm is lost it quickly replaces it, sometimes by the animal overcompensating and

(B) one arm is lost it is quickly replaced, with the animal sometimes overcompensating and

(C) they lose one arm they quickly replace it, sometimes by the animal overcompensating,

(D) they lose one arm they are quickly replaced, with the animal sometimes overcompensating,

(E) they lose one arm it is quickly replaced, sometimes with the animal overcompensating,

SC04249

954. In 2000, a mere two dozen products accounted for half the increase in spending on prescription drugs, a phenomenon that is explained not just because of more expensive drugs but by the fact that doctors are writing many more prescriptions for higher-cost drugs.

(A) a phenomenon that is explained not just because of more expensive drugs but by the fact that doctors are writing

(B) a phenomenon that is explained not just by the fact that drugs are becoming more expensive but also by the fact that doctors are writing

(C) a phenomenon occurring not just because of drugs that are becoming more expensive but because of doctors having also written

(D) which occurred not just because drugs are becoming more expensive but doctors are also writing

(E) which occurred not just because of more expensive drugs but because doctors have also written

SC05393

955. Similar to other early Mississippi Delta blues singers, the music of Robert Johnson arose from an oral tradition beginning with a mixture of chants, fiddle tunes, and religious music and only gradually evolved into the blues.

(A) Similar to other early Mississippi Delta blues singers, the music of Robert Johnson arose from an oral tradition beginning with

(B) Similar to that of other early Mississippi Delta blues singers, Robert Johnson made music that arose from an oral tradition that began with

(C) As with other early Mississippi Delta blues singers, Robert Johnson made music that arose from an oral tradition beginning as

(D) Like other early Mississippi Delta blues singers,

Robert Johnson's music arose from an oral tradition beginning with

(E) Like the music of other early Mississippi Delta blues singers, the music of Robert Johnson arose from an oral tradition that began as

SC03805

956. Thelonious Monk, who was a jazz pianist and composer, produced a body of work both rooted in the stride-piano tradition of Willie (The Lion) Smith and Duke Ellington, yet in many ways he stood apart from the mainstream jazz repertory.

(A) Thelonious Monk, who was a jazz pianist and composer, produced a body of work both rooted

(B) Thelonious Monk, the jazz pianist and composer, produced a body of work that was rooted both

(C) Jazz pianist and composer Thelonious Monk, who produced a body of work rooted

(D) Jazz pianist and composer Thelonious Monk produced a body of work that was rooted

(E) Jazz pianist and composer Thelonious Monk produced a body of work rooted both

SC06898

957. Nobody knows exactly how many languages there are in the world, partly because of the difficulty of distinguishing between a language and the sublanguages or dialects within it, but those who have tried to count typically have found about five thousand.

(A) and the sublanguages or dialects within it, but those who have tried to count typically have found

(B) and the sublanguages or dialects within them, with those who have tried counting typically finding

(C) and the sublanguages or dialects within it, but those who have tried counting it typically find

(D) or the sublanguages or dialects within them, but those who tried to count them typically found

(E) or the sublanguages or dialects within them, with those who have tried to count typically finding

SC08719

958. Although a number of excellent studies narrate the development of domestic technology and its impact on housewifery, these works do not discuss the contributions of the women employed by manufacturers and utility companies as product demonstrators and publicists, who initially promoted new and unfamiliar technology to female consumers.

(A) by manufacturers and utility companies as product demonstrators and publicists,

(B) to be product demonstrators and publicists by manufacturers and utility companies,

(C) to demonstrate and publicize their products by manufacturers and utility companies

(D) by manufacturers and utility companies to be demonstrators and publicists of their products

(E) by manufacturers and utility companies to demonstrate and publicize their products

SC01577
959. The absence from business and financial records of the nineteenth century of statistics about women leave us with no record of the jobs that were performed by women and how they survived economically.

(A) from business and financial records of the nineteenth century of statistics about women leave us with no record of the jobs that were performed by women and

(B) from business and financial records of statistics about women from the nineteenth century leave us with no record of what jobs women performed or

(C) of statistics for women from business and financial records in the nineteenth century leaves us with no record of either the jobs that women were performing and of

(D) of statistics on women from business and financial records in the nineteenth century leave us with no record of the jobs that women performed or of

(E) of statistics about women from business and financial records of the nineteenth century leaves us with no record of either what jobs women performed or

SC02138
960. Heating-oil prices are expected to be higher this year than last because refiners are paying about $5 a barrel more for crude oil than they were last year.

(A) Heating-oil prices are expected to be higher this year than last because refiners are paying about $5 a barrel more for crude oil than they were

(B) Heating-oil prices are expected to rise higher this year over last because refiners pay about $5 a barrel for crude oil more than they did

(C) Expectations are for heating-oil prices to be higher this year than last year's because refiners are paying about $5 a barrel for crude oil more than they did

(D) It is the expectation that heating-oil prices will be higher for this year over last because refiners are paying about $5 a barrel more for crude oil now than what they were

(E) It is expected that heating-oil prices will rise higher this year than last year's because refiners pay about $5 a barrel for crude oil more than they did

SC01443
961. Even though Clovis points, spear points with longitudinal grooves chipped onto their faces, have been found all over North America, they are named for the New Mexico site where they were first discovered in 1932.

(A) Even though Clovis points, spear points with longitudinal grooves chipped onto their faces, have been found all over North America, they are named for the New Mexico site where they were first discovered in 1932.

(B) Although named for the New Mexico site where first discovered in 1932, Clovis points are spear points of longitudinal grooves chipped onto their faces and have been found all over North America.

(C) Named for the New Mexico site where they have been first discovered in 1932, Clovis points, spear points of longitudinal grooves chipped onto the faces, have been found all over North America.

(D) Spear points with longitudinal grooves that are chipped onto the faces, Clovis points, even though named for the New Mexico site where first discovered in 1932, but were found all over North America.

(E) While Clovis points are spear points whose faces have longitudinal grooves chipped into them, they have been found all over North America, and named for the New Mexico site where they have been first discovered in 1932.

SC04408
962. Heavy commitment by an executive to a course of action, especially if it has worked well in the past, makes it likely to miss signs of incipient trouble or misinterpret them when they do appear.

(A) Heavy commitment by an executive to a course of action, especially if it has worked well in the past, makes it likely to miss signs of incipient trouble or misinterpret them when they do appear.

(B)   An executive who is heavily committed to a course of action, especially one that worked well in the past, makes missing signs of incipient trouble or misinterpreting ones likely when they do appear.

(C)   An executive who is heavily committed to a course of action is likely to miss or misinterpret signs of incipient trouble when they do appear, especially if it has worked well in the past.

(D)   Executives' being heavily committed to a course of action, especially if it has worked well in the past, makes them likely to miss signs of incipient trouble or misinterpreting them when they do appear.

(E)   Being heavily committed to a course of action, especially one that has worked well in the past, is likely to make an executive miss signs of incipient trouble or misinterpret them when they do appear.

SC06740

963. According to recent studies comparing the nutritional value of meat from wild animals and meat from domesticated animals, wild animals have less total fat than do livestock fed on grain and more of a kind of fat they think is good for cardiac health.

(A)   wild animals have less total fat than do livestock fed on grain and more of a kind of fat they think is

(B)   wild animals have less total fat than livestock fed on grain and more of a kind of fat thought to be

(C)   wild animals have less total fat than that of livestock fed on grain and have more fat of a kind thought to be

(D)   total fat of wild animals is less than livestock fed on grain and they have more fat of a kind thought to be

(E)   total fat is less in wild animals than that of livestock fed on grain and more of their fat is of a kind they think is

SC03292

964. Yellow jackets number among the 900 or so species of the world's social wasps, wasps living in a highly cooperative and organized society where they consist almost entirely of females—the queen and her sterile female workers.

(A)   wasps living in a highly cooperative and organized society where they consist almost entirely of

(B)   wasps that live in a highly cooperative and organized society consisting almost entirely of

(C)   which means they live in a highly cooperative and organized society, almost all

(D)   which means that their society is highly cooperative, organized, and it is almost entirely

(E)   living in a society that is highly cooperative, organized, and it consists of almost all

SC02539

965. Before 1988, insurance companies in California were free to charge whatever rates the market would bear, needing no approval from regulators before raising rates.

(A)   needing no approval from regulators before raising

(B)   and it needed no approval by regulators before raising

(C)   and needing no approval from regulators before they raised

(D)   with approval not needed by regulators before they raised

(E)   with no approval needed from regulators before the raising of

SC01022

966. Marconi's conception of the radio was as a substitute for the telephone, a tool for private conversation; instead, it is precisely the opposite, a tool for communicating with a large, public audience.

(A)   Marconi's conception of the radio was as a substitute for the telephone, a tool for private conversation; instead, it is

(B)   Marconi conceived of the radio as a substitute for the telephone, a tool for private conversation, but which is

(C)   Marconi conceived of the radio as a tool for private conversation that could substitute for the telephone; instead, it has become

(D)   Marconi conceived of the radio to be a tool for private conversation, a substitute for the telephone, which has become

(E)   Marconi conceived of the radio to be a substitute for the telephone, a tool for private conversation, other than what it is,

SC02611

967. Because there are provisions of the new maritime code that provide that even tiny islets can be the basis for claims to the fisheries and oil fields of large sea areas,

they have already stimulated international disputes over uninhabited islands.

(A) Because there are provisions of the new maritime code that provide that even tiny islets can be the basis for claims to the fisheries and oil fields of large sea areas, they have already stimulated

(B) Because the new maritime code provides that even tiny islets can be the basis for claims to the fisheries and oil fields of large sea areas, it has already stimulated

(C) Even tiny islets can be the basis for claims to the fisheries and oil fields of large sea areas under provisions of the new maritime code, already stimulating

(D) Because even tiny islets can be the basis for claims to the fisheries and oil fields of large sea areas under provisions of the new maritime code, this has already stimulated

(E) Because even tiny islets can be the basis for claims to the fisheries and oil fields of large sea areas under provisions of the new maritime code, which is already stimulating

SC02576

968. Unlike the automobile company, whose research was based on crashes involving sport utility vehicles, the research conducted by the insurance company took into account such factors as a driver's age, sex, and previous driving record.

(A) company, whose research was based on

(B) company, which researched

(C) company, in its research of

(D) company's research, having been based on

(E) company's research on

SC12131

969. Gusty westerly winds will continue to usher in a seasonably cool air mass into the region, as a broad area of high pressure will build and bring fair and dry weather for several days.

(A) to usher in a seasonably cool air mass into the region, as a broad area of high pressure will build and

(B) ushering in a seasonably cool air mass into the region and a broad area of high pressure will build that

(C) to usher in a seasonably cool air mass to the region, a broad area of high pressure building, and

(D) ushering a seasonably cool air mass in the region, with a broad area of high pressure building and

(E) to usher a seasonably cool air mass into the region while a broad area of high pressure builds, which will

SC02008

970. With the patience of its customers and with its network strained to the breaking point, the on-line service company announced a series of new initiatives trying to relieve the congestion that has led to at least four class-action lawsuits and thousands of complaints from frustrated customers.

(A) the patience of its customers and with its network strained to the breaking point, the on-line service company announced a series of new initiatives trying to relieve

(B) the patience of its customers and its network strained to the breaking point, the on-line service company announced a series of new initiatives that try to relieve

(C) its network and the patience of its customers strained to the breaking point, the on-line service company announced a series of new initiatives to try to relieve

(D) its network and with the patience of its customers strained to the breaking point, the on-line service company announced a series of initiatives to try relieving

(E) its network and its customers' patience strained to the breaking point, the on-line service company announced a series of new initiatives to try relieving

SC02094

971. November is traditionally the strongest month for sales of light trucks, but sales this past November, even when compared with sales in previous Novembers, accounted for a remarkably large share of total vehicle sales.

(A) but sales this past November, even when compared with sales in previous Novembers,

(B) but even when it is compared with previous Novembers, this past November's sales

(C) but even when they are compared with previous Novembers, sales of light trucks this past November

(D) so that compared with previous Novembers, sales of light trucks this past November

(E) so that this past November's sales, even compared with previous Novembers' sales,

SC05760

972. Most of the country's biggest daily newspapers had lower circulation in the six months from October 1995 through March 1996 than <u>a similar period</u> a year earlier.

  (A) a similar period
  (B) a similar period's
  (C) in a similar period
  (D) that in a similar period
  (E) that of a similar period

SC01714

973. Mauritius was a British colony for almost 200 years, <u>excepting for</u> the domains of administration and teaching, the English language was never really spoken on the island.

  (A) excepting for
  (B) except in
  (C) but except in
  (D) but excepting for
  (E) with the exception of

SC04853

974. <u>Although appearing less appetizing than most of their round and red supermarket cousins, heirloom tomatoes, grown from seeds saved during the previous year</u>—they are often green and striped, or have plenty of bumps and bruises—heirlooms are more flavorful and thus in increasing demand.

  (A) Although appearing less appetizing than most of their round and red supermarket cousins, heirloom tomatoes, grown from seeds saved during the previous year
  (B) Although heirloom tomatoes, grown from seeds saved during the previous year, appear less appetizing than most of their round and red supermarket cousins
  (C) Although they appear less appetizing than most of their round and red supermarket cousins, heirloom tomatoes, grown from seeds saved during the previous year
  (D) Grown from seeds saved during the previous year, heirloom tomatoes appear less appetizing than most of their round and red supermarket cousins
  (E) Heirloom tomatoes, grown from seeds saved during the previous year, although they appear less appetizing than most of their round and red supermarket cousins

SC01987

975. The World Wildlife Fund has declared that global warming, <u>a phenomenon most scientists agree to be caused by human beings in burning fossil fuels,</u> will create havoc among migratory birds by altering the environment in ways harmful to their habitats.

  (A) a phenomenon most scientists agree to be caused by human beings in burning fossil fuels,
  (B) a phenomenon most scientists agree that is caused by fossil fuels burned by human beings,
  (C) a phenomenon that most scientists agree is caused by human beings' burning of fossil fuels,
  (D) which most scientists agree on as a phenomenon caused by human beings who burn fossil fuels,
  (E) which most scientists agree to be a phenomenon caused by fossil fuels burned by human beings,

SC02216

976. The largest of all the planets, <u>not only is Jupiter three times so massive as Saturn, the next larger</u> planet, but also possesses four of the largest satellites, or moons, in our solar system.

  (A) not only is Jupiter three times so massive as Saturn, the next larger
  (B) not only is Jupiter three times as massive as Saturn, the next largest
  (C) Jupiter, not only three times as massive as Saturn, the next largest
  (D) Jupiter not only is three times as massive as Saturn, the next largest
  (E) Jupiter is not only three times so massive as Saturn, the next larger

SC01587

977. While many of the dinosaur fossils found recently in northeast China seem to provide evidence of the kinship between dinosaurs and birds, the wealth of enigmatic fossils <u>seem more likely at this stage that they will inflame debates over the origin of birds rather</u> than settle them.

  (A) seem more likely at this stage that they will inflame debates over the origin of birds rather than
  (B) seem more likely that it will inflame debates over the origin of birds at this stage than
  (C) seems more likely to inflame debates on the origin of birds at this stage rather than
  (D) seems more likely at this stage to inflame debates over the origin of birds than to
  (E) seems more likely that it will inflame debates on the origin of birds at this stage than to

SC01622

978. Found only in the Western Hemisphere and surviving through extremes of climate, hummingbirds' range extends from Alaska to Tierra del Fuego, from sea-level rain forests to the edges of Andean snowfields and ice fields at altitudes of 15,000 feet.

   (A)   Found only in the Western Hemisphere and surviving through extremes of climate, hummingbirds' range extends

   (B)   Found only in the Western Hemisphere, hummingbirds survive through extremes of climate, their range extending

   (C)   Hummingbirds, found only in the Western Hemisphere and surviving through extremes of climate, with their range extending

   (D)   Hummingbirds, found only in the Western Hemisphere and surviving through extremes of climate, their range extends

   (E)   Hummingbirds are found only in the Western Hemisphere, survive through extremes of climate, and their range extends

SC01761

979. She was less successful after she had emigrated to New York compared to her native Germany, photographer Lotte Jacobi nevertheless earned a small group of discerning admirers, and her photographs were eventually exhibited in prestigious galleries across the United States.

   (A)   She was less successful after she had emigrated to New York compared to

   (B)   Being less successful after she had emigrated to New York as compared to

   (C)   Less successful after she emigrated to New York than she had been in

   (D)   Although she was less successful after emigrating to New York when compared to

   (E)   She had been less successful after emigrating to New York than in

SC02259

980. Scientists have recently found evidence that black holes—regions of space in which matter is so concentrated and the pull of gravity so powerful that nothing, not even light, can emerge from them—probably exist at the core of nearly all galaxies and the mass of each black hole is proportional to its host galaxy.

   (A)   exist at the core of nearly all galaxies and the mass of each black hole is proportional to

   (B)   exist at the core of nearly all galaxies and that the mass of each black hole is proportional to that of

   (C)   exist at the core of nearly all galaxies, and that the mass of each black hole is proportional to

   (D)   exists at the core of nearly all galaxies, and that the mass of each black hole is proportional to that of

   (E)   exists at the core of nearly all galaxies and the mass of each black hole is proportional to that of

SC02346

981. The use of lie detectors is based on the assumption that lying produces emotional reactions in an individual that, in turn, create unconscious physiological responses.

   (A)   that, in turn, create unconscious physiological responses

   (B)   that creates unconscious physiological responses in turn

   (C)   creating, in turn, unconscious physiological responses

   (D)   to create, in turn, physiological responses that are unconscious

   (E)   who creates unconscious physiological responses in turn

SC04213

982. Australian embryologists have found evidence that suggests that the elephant is descended from an aquatic animal, and its trunk originally evolving as a kind of snorkel.

   (A)   that suggests that the elephant is descended from an aquatic animal, and its trunk originally evolving

   (B)   that has suggested the elephant descended from an aquatic animal, its trunk originally evolving

   (C)   suggesting that the elephant had descended from an aquatic animal with its trunk originally evolved

   (D)   to suggest that the elephant had descended from an aquatic animal and its trunk originally evolved

   (E)   to suggest that the elephant is descended from an aquatic animal and that its trunk originally evolved

SC01957

983. Most efforts to combat such mosquito-borne diseases like malaria and dengue have focused either on the vaccination of humans or on exterminating mosquitoes with pesticides.

   (A)   like malaria and dengue have focused either on the vaccination of humans or on exterminating

   (B)   like malaria and dengue have focused either on vaccinating of humans or on the extermination of

(C) as malaria and dengue have focused on either vaccinating humans or on exterminating

(D) as malaria and dengue have focused on either vaccinating of humans or on extermination of

(E) as malaria and dengue have focused on either vaccinating humans or exterminating

SC02344
984. Among the Tsonga, a Bantu-speaking group of tribes in southeastern Africa, dance teams represent their own chief at <u>the court of each other, providing entertainment in return for</u> food, drink, and lodging.

(A) the court of each other, providing entertainment in return for

(B) the court of another and provide entertainment in return for

(C) the court of the other, so as to provide entertainment as a return on

(D) each other's court, entertainment being provided in return for

(E) another's court and provide entertainment as a return on

SC06633
985. Almost like clones in their similarity to one another, <u>the cheetah species' homogeneity makes them especially vulnerable to disease</u>.

(A) the cheetah species' homogeneity makes them especially vulnerable to disease

(B) the cheetah species is especially vulnerable to disease because of its homogeneity

(C) the homogeneity of the cheetah species makes it especially vulnerable to disease

(D) homogeneity makes members of the cheetah species especially vulnerable to disease

(E) members of the cheetah species are especially vulnerable to disease because of their homogeneity

SC04330
986. As sources of electrical power, windmills now account for only about 2,500 megawatts nationwide, but production is <u>almost expected to double by the end of the year, which would provide</u> enough electricity for 1.3 million households.

(A) almost expected to double by the end of the year, which would provide

(B) almost expected that it will double by the end of the year, thus providing

(C) expected that it will almost double by the end of the year to provide

(D) expected almost to double by the end of the year and thus to provide

(E) expected almost to double by the end of the year, which would thus be providing

SC03154
987. While most of the earliest known ball courts in Mesoamerica date to 900–400 B.C., <u>waterlogged latex balls found at El Manati and representations of ballplayers painted on ceramics found at San Lorenzo attest</u> to the fact that the Mesoamerican ballgame was well established by the mid-thirteenth century B.C.

(A) waterlogged latex balls found at El Manati and representations of ballplayers painted on ceramics found at San Lorenzo attest

(B) waterlogged latex balls found at El Manati and the painting of representations of ballplayers on ceramics found at San Lorenzo attests

(C) waterlogged latex balls found at El Manati and ceramics painted with representations of ballplayers found at San Lorenzo attests

(D) the finding of waterlogged latex balls at El Manati and the painting of representations of ballplayers on ceramics found at San Lorenzo attests

(E) the finding of waterlogged latex balls at El Manati and of representations of ballplayers painted on ceramics at San Lorenzo attest

SC04899
988. As criminal activity on the Internet becomes more and more sophisticated, not only are thieves able to divert cash from company bank accounts, <u>they can also pilfer valuable information such as business development strategies, new product specifications, and contract bidding plans, and sell</u> the data to competitors.

(A) they can also pilfer valuable information such as business development strategies, new product specifications, and contract bidding plans, and sell

(B) they can also pilfer valuable information that includes business development strategies, new product specifications, and contract bidding plans, and selling

(C) also pilfering valuable information including business development strategies, new product specifications, and contract bidding plans, selling

(D) but also pilfer valuable information such as business development strategies, new product specifications, and contract bidding plans to sell

(E) but also pilfering valuable information such as business development strategies, new product specifications, and contract bidding plans and selling

SC05785

989. Last week local shrimpers held a news conference to take some credit for the resurgence of the rare Kemp's ridley turtle, saying that their compliance with laws <u>requiring that turtle-excluder devices be on shrimp nets protect</u> adult sea turtles.

(A) requiring that turtle-excluder devices be on shrimp nets protect

(B) requiring turtle-excluder devices on shrimp nets is protecting

(C) that require turtle-excluder devices on shrimp nets protect

(D) to require turtle-excluder devices on shrimp nets are protecting

(E) to require turtle-excluder devices on shrimp nets is protecting

SC03752

990. <u>A ruined structure found at Aqaba, Jordan, was probably a church, as indicated in its eastward orientation and by its overall plan, as well as</u> artifacts, such as glass oil-lamp fragments, found at the site.

(A) A ruined structure found at Aqaba, Jordan, was probably a church, as indicated in its eastward orientation and by its overall plan, as well as

(B) A ruined structure found at Aqaba, Jordan, once probably being a church, was indicated by its eastward orientation, overall plan, and

(C) Indicating that a ruined structure found at Aqaba, Jordan, was probably a church were its eastward orientation and overall plan, but also the

(D) A ruined structure found at Aqaba, Jordan, was probably a church, as indicates its eastward orientation and overall plan, as well as the

(E) That a ruined structure found at Aqaba, Jordan, was probably a church is indicated by its eastward orientation and overall plan, as well as by the

SC04343

991. In the major cities of industrialized countries at the end of the nineteenth century, important public places such as theaters, restaurants, shops, and banks had installed electric lighting, but <u>electricity was in less than 1 percent of homes, where lighting was still</u> provided mainly by candles or gas.

(A) electricity was in less than 1 percent of homes, where lighting was still

(B) electricity was in less than 1 percent of homes and lighting still

(C) there had been less than 1 percent of homes with electricity, where lighting was still being

(D) there was less than 1 percent of homes that had electricity, having lighting that was still

(E) less than 1 percent of homes had electricity, where lighting had still been

SC02965

992. By 1999, astronomers <u>had discovered 17 nearby stars that are orbited by planets</u> about the size of Jupiter.

(A) had discovered 17 nearby stars that are orbited by planets

(B) had discovered 17 nearby stars with planets orbiting them that were

(C) had discovered that there were 17 nearby stars that were orbited by planets

(D) have discovered 17 nearby stars with planets orbiting them that are

(E) have discovered that 17 nearby stars are orbited by planets

SC01647

993. <u>Although she was considered among her contemporaries to be the better poet than her husband, later Elizabeth Barrett Browning was overshadowed by his success.</u>

(A) Although she was considered among her contemporaries to be the better poet than her husband, later Elizabeth Barrett Browning was overshadowed by his success.

(B) Although Elizabeth Barrett Browning was considered among her contemporaries as a better poet than her husband, she was later overshadowed by his success.

(C) Later overshadowed by the success of her husband, Elizabeth Barrett Browning's poetry had been considered among her contemporaries to be better than that of her husband.

(D)   Although Elizabeth Barrett Browning's success was later overshadowed by that of her husband, among her contemporaries she was considered the better poet.

(E)   Elizabeth Barrett Browning's poetry was considered among her contemporaries as better than her husband, but her success was later overshadowed by his.

SC01618

994.   In no other historical sighting did Halley's Comet cause such a worldwide sensation as <u>did its return in 1910–1911</u>.

(A)   did its return in 1910–1911

(B)   had its 1910–1911 return

(C)   in its return of 1910–1911

(D)   its return of 1910–1911 did

(E)   its return in 1910–1911

SC04836

995.   Rock samples taken from the remains of an asteroid about twice the size of the 6-mile-wide asteroid that eradicated the dinosaurs <u>has been dated to be 3.47 billion years old and thus is</u> evidence of the earliest known asteroid impact on Earth.

(A)   has been dated to be 3.47 billion years old and thus is

(B)   has been dated at 3.47 billion years old and thus

(C)   have been dated to be 3.47 billion years old and thus are

(D)   have been dated as being 3.47 billion years old and thus

(E)   have been dated at 3.47 billion years old and thus are

9.8 Answer Key

818.	E	854.	E	890.	E	926.	A	962.	E
819.	A	855.	D	891.	E	927.	E	963.	B
820.	E	856.	A	892.	D	928.	C	964.	B
821.	B	857.	C	893.	E	929.	B	965.	A
822.	D	858.	C	894.	C	930.	A	966.	C
823.	B	859.	A	895.	D	931.	A	967.	B
824.	B	860.	B	896.	C	932.	E	968.	E
825.	C	861.	E	897.	B	933.	C	969.	E
826.	C	862.	C	898.	E	934.	E	970.	C
827.	B	863.	A	899.	D	935.	A	971.	A
828.	B	864.	D	900.	C	936.	A	972.	C
829.	D	865.	D	901.	A	937.	D	973.	C
830.	C	866.	C	902.	C	938.	B	974.	B
831.	D	867.	D	903.	E	939.	B	975.	C
832.	D	868.	C	904.	B	940.	B	976.	D
833.	D	869.	E	905.	A	941.	A	977.	D
834.	B	870.	E	906.	B	942.	E	978.	B
835.	B	871.	C	907.	C	943.	A	979.	C
836.	D	872.	D	908.	E	944.	B	980.	B
837.	C	873.	E	909.	E	945.	C	981.	A
838.	B	874.	D	910.	A	946.	B	982.	E
839.	C	875.	E	911.	E	947.	D	983.	E
840.	E	876.	A	912.	B	948.	C	984.	B
841.	E	877.	A	913.	C	949.	C	985.	E
842.	A	878.	B	914.	C	950.	A	986.	D
843.	D	879.	B	915.	C	951.	B	987.	A
844.	E	880.	E	916.	A	952.	D	988.	A
845.	C	881.	C	917.	B	953.	B	989.	B
846.	B	882.	B	918.	C	954.	B	990.	E
847.	C	883.	D	919.	C	955.	E	991.	A
848.	D	884.	A	920.	B	956.	D	992.	A
849.	E	885.	E	921.	E	957.	A	993.	D
850.	D	886.	D	922.	E	958.	A	994.	C
851.	B	887.	A	923.	C	959.	E	995.	E
852.	C	888.	E	924.	A	960.	A		
853.	B	889.	E	925.	B	961.	A		

9.9 Answer Explanations

The following discussion of Sentence Correction is intended to familiarize you with the most efficient and effective approaches to these kinds of questions. The particular questions in this chapter are generally representative of the kinds of Sentence Correction questions you will encounter on the GMAT exam.

Questions 818 to 869 - Difficulty: Easy

*SC39850.02

818. The market for so-called functional beverages, drinks that promise health benefits beyond their inherent nutritional value, nearly doubled over the course of four years, <u>in rising from $2.68 billion in 1997 to be</u> $4.7 billion in 2000.

(A) in rising from $2.68 billion in 1997 to be

(B) in having risen from $2.68 billion in 1997 to

(C) as it rose from $2.68 billion in 1997 to be

(D) with its rise from $2.68 billion in 1997 to

(E) rising from $2.68 billion in 1997 to

Idiom: Diction

The words *in* and *be* in the underlined portion have no meaningful function in relation to the surrounding words. Hypothetically, *in rising* could be intended to mean that the market nearly doubled while it was in the process of rising from one level to the other, but in that case, there should not be a comma before *in*. *Rising to be* seems to say, illogically, that the market became the higher level—perhaps even that it rose for the purpose of being the higher level. It would make better sense to say that the market rose *from* the lower level *to* the higher level. If both *in* and *be* are omitted, *rising from . . . to* functions as a straightforward explication of the preceding claim that the market nearly doubled.

A   As explained above, *in* and *be* have no meaningful function in relation to the surrounding words and are misleading.

B   As explained above, *in* has no meaningful function in relation to the surrounding words, especially considering the preceding comma.

C   As explained above, *be* has no meaningful function in relation to the surrounding words and is illogical. Also, *as* is ambiguous; it could be a logical indicator equivalent

to *because* or *given that*, but it could also readily appear to be a temporal indicator functioning similarly to *while*. On this latter interpretation, *nearly doubled . . . as it rose* is misleading; the market did not nearly double throughout the time that it was rising from $2.68 billion to $4.7 billion.

D   Because *with its rise* is set off by a comma from the part that it is presumably supposed to modify, it does not make good sense.

E   **Correct.** This version is succinct, with no superfluous words. In this version, *rising from $2.68 billion in 1997 to $4.7 billion in 2000* functions straightforwardly as an explication of the preceding claim that the market nearly doubled.

The correct answer is E.

SC01527

819. According to some critics, watching television <u>not only undermines one's ability to think critically but also impairs one's</u> overall ability to perceive.

(A) not only undermines one's ability to think critically but also impairs one's

(B) not only undermines one's ability of critical thinking but also impairs the

(C) undermines not only one's ability to think critically but also impairs one's

(D) undermines not only one's ability of critical thinking but also impairs the

(E) undermines one's ability not only to think critically but also impairs one's

Grammatical Construction; Parallelism

The sentence correctly uses the structure *not only . . . but also . . .* to convey two points about the effects that critics believe result from watching television. When a sentence makes use of the *not only X but also Y* structure, the

*These numbers correlate with the online test bank question number. See the GMAT™ Official Guide Question Index in the back of this book.

896

words or phrases that replace *X* and *Y* must be grammatically parallel; that is, they should belong to the same parts of speech. This is because whatever precedes *not only* "attaches" to whatever fills in the blanks after *not only* and *but also*. One straightforward way to test whether the *not only X but also Y* structure is being used correctly is to create two sentences, both of which begin with the portion of the sentence in question that precedes *not only*, but one sentence is completed with the *X* portion of the *not only X but also Y* structure, and the other sentence is completed with the *Y* portion. (For instance, given the sentence *Mary is good at playing not only tennis but also soccer*, the *X* portion is *tennis* and the *Y* portion is *soccer;* the two sentences that would be created are *Mary is good at playing tennis* and *Mary is good at playing soccer*.) The original sentence is correct only if both of the two sentences are also grammatically correct. Some of the incorrect answer choices fail to use the *not only . . . but also . . .* structure correctly. In addition to that problem, some of the answer choices use the unidiomatic phrase *ability of critical thinking; ability to think critically*, which is used in the correct answer choice, is more idiomatic.

A **Correct.** Two verb phrases *undermines . . .* and *impairs . . .* are coordinated and placed in the correct positions, in parallel form. Also, *ability to think* (where *to think* is the infinitive form of the verb) is an idiomatically correct usage.

B As discussed in the above answer choice, some idiomatically correct expressions are *ability to think critically* and *critical thinking ability; ability of critical thinking*, however, is not a correct idiom.

C The part of speech that follows *not only* (in this case, a noun phrase, *one's ability to think critically*) is different from the part of speech that follows *but also* (a verb phrase, *impairs one's overall ability to perceive*).

D The part of speech that follows *not only* (in this case, a noun phrase, *one's ability of critical thinking*) is different from the part of speech that follows *but also* (a verb phrase, *impairs the overall ability to perceive*). Additional problems with the sentence are

its use of *ability of critical thinking* (*ability to think critically* would be correct) and its use of *the* instead of *one's* following *impairs*.

E The parts of speech that follow *not only* and *but also* are both verb phrases, but the forms of the verbs contained in those phrases are different and thus are not grammatically parallel, as they should be. The verb that follows *not only* is an infinitive (*to think*), while the verb that follows *but also* is in a conjugated form (*impairs*), not the infinitive.

The correct answer is A.

SC20160.02

820. To show that it is serious about addressing the state's power crisis, the administration has plans for ordering all federal facilities in California to keep thermostats at 78 degrees Fahrenheit and shutting down escalators during electricity shortages this summer.

(A) has plans for ordering all federal facilities in California to keep thermostats at 78 degrees Fahrenheit and shutting

(B) has plans to order that all federal facilities in California are keeping thermostats at 78 degrees Fahrenheit and shutting

(C) is planning on ordering all federal facilities in California to keep thermostats at 78 degrees Fahrenheit, and they will shut

(D) is planning to order that all federal facilities in California are keeping thermostats at 78 degrees Fahrenheit and shut

(E) is planning to order all federal facilities in California to keep thermostats at 78 degrees Fahrenheit and shut

Idiom; Logical Predication

The sentence appears most likely intended to say that the administration is planning to order all federal facilities in California to do two things— to keep thermostats at 78 degrees Fahrenheit and to shut down escalators. To convey this clearly and grammatically, the verb forms should be the same: *to keep* and *to shut down* or *to keep . . . and shut down . . .* where *to* applies to both verbs. Because instead the participial form *shutting down* is used, that form is parallel with *ordering*. This relationship among verb forms makes the sentence appear to say that the administration has *plans for ordering all federal facilities in California to keep thermostats at 78 degrees Fahrenheit* and that the administration also *has plans for shutting down escalators during electricity shortages.*

A   As explained above, the infinitive *to shut down* would be preferable to the participial form *shutting down.*

B   The present continuous tense *are keeping* is not the appropriate tense to use with *to order that.* The correct wording would be *the administration has plans to order that* [*they*] *keep thermostats at 78 degrees.* Similarly, the correct verb to use would be *shut down*, not *shutting down.*

C   The antecedent of *they* in the phrase *they will shut* is somewhat unclear even though the nearest preceding plural noun phrase is *all federal facilities in California.* The structure of the sentence strongly suggests that everything after the opening phrase *to show that it is serious . . .* is supposed to be part of what the administration is doing to show that it is serious. However, *they will shut down* is an independent clause referring to an action outside the scope of that opening phrase. The grammatical break after *Fahrenheit* makes the phrase *during electricity shortages* modify only *they will shut down*, with the implausible implication that the facilities will be ordered to keep their thermostats at 78 degrees continuously, even in winter. If the author intended to communicate a separate claim that the federal facilities will shut down their escalators during electricity shortages, independently of the order regarding thermostats, it would have been preferable to end the sentence with *Fahrenheit* and to add a new sentence such as: *The federal facilities will also shut down escalators during energy shortages this summer.*

D   The present continuous tense *are keeping* is not the appropriate tense to use with *to order that.* The correct wording would be *the administration is planning to order that* [*they*] *keep thermostats at 78 degrees.*

E   **Correct.** This version uses the correct verb forms with *to order* and clearly conveys a coherent idea.

The correct answer is E.

SC33440.02

821. Once made exclusively from the wool of sheep that roam the Isle of Lewis and Harris off the coast of Scotland, Harris tweed is now made only with wools that are imported, <u>sometimes from the mainland and sometimes they come</u>—as a result of a 1996 amendment to the Harris Tweed Act—from outside Scotland.

(A) sometimes from the mainland and sometimes they come

(B) sometimes from the mainland and sometimes

(C) and come sometimes from the mainland or sometimes

(D) from the mainland sometimes, or sometimes it comes

(E) from the mainland sometimes, or sometimes coming

Agreement; Grammatical Construction

The sentence suggests that Harris tweed made in the Isle of Lewis and Harris, an island that is part of Scotland, is now made only from wool that is imported, sometimes from the Scottish mainland and sometimes from outside Scotland. The word sequence *sometimes from the mainland* modifies the verb *are imported.* However, the form *sometimes X and sometimes Y* is not used correctly in the sentence. The two elements conjoined by *and* should be grammatically parallel, but they are not: one is an adverbial phrase (*sometimes from the mainland*) and the other is an independent clause (*sometimes they come from outside Scotland*). The sentence can be improved by deleting *they come.* In that version (see answer choice B), *are imported* is modified by a complex phrase consisting of two parallel elements, *sometimes from the mainland* and *sometimes from outside. . . .*

A   As explained above, this version is incorrect because the two elements conjoined by *and* are not parallel. The first element is an adverbial phrase and the second is an independent clause.

B Correct. This version is correct because the two elements conjoined by *and* are parallel.

C   The fact that *and come* is set off by a comma suggests that *come* is not intended to be directly parallel with *are imported* and that its subject may be *Harris tweed*. On that interpretation, the singular subject would not agree with the plural verb. Further, in the construction *sometimes X and/or sometimes Y*, the conjunction *and* is preferable to *or* in this context because *and*, unlike *or*, indicates that the wool that comes from the mainland and the wool that comes from outside Scotland comprise all the wool that is imported for the making of Harris tweed.

D   For the reason given in the discussion of answer choice C above, *and* is preferable to *or*. Further, the grammatical parallelism required by *or* is lacking because the elements linked by *or* are different parts of speech and the placement of *sometimes* is different in the two elements. Another problem with this version of the sentence is that *it* does not agree in number with its antecedent *wools*.

E   For the reason given in the discussion of answer choice C above, *and* is preferable to *or*. Further, the grammatical parallelism required by *or* is lacking because the elements linked by *or* are different parts of speech. Also contributing to the failure of parallelism is the dissimilar placement of *sometimes* in the two elements.

The correct answer is B.

SC12999

822. In her presentation, the head of the Better Business Bureau emphasized that companies should think of the cost of conventions and other similar gatherings <u>as not an expense, but as</u> an investment in networking that will pay dividends.

(A)   as not an expense, but as

(B)   as not expense but

(C)   not an expense, rather

(D)   not as an expense, but as

(E)   not in terms of expense, but

Parallelism; Idiom

This sentence is constructed around *not as X, but as Y*, which must start with the word *not* in accordance with this idiomatic pattern, and express both parts in a parallel way.

A   This sentence improperly places *as* before *not*.

B   This sentence improperly places *as* before *not*.

C   This version lacks the required words *as* and *but*.

D Correct. The idiom has all of its parts and expresses the two opposed concepts in parallel terms.

E   Although *in terms of* is an acceptable substitute for *as*, the construction is no longer parallel due to the lack of a second *in terms of* (or *as*) after *but*.

The correct answer is D.

SC15382

823. Recent interdisciplinary studies advance the argument that emotions, including those deemed personal or <u>private is a social phenomenon, though one inseparable</u> from bodily response.

(A)   private is a social phenomenon, though one inseparable

(B)   private, are social phenomena that are inseparable

(C)   private are a social phenomenon but are not those separable

(D)   private—are social phenomena but not separable

(E)   also as private emotions, are social phenomena not inseparable

Agreement; Rhetorical Construction

The main problem is one of agreement: in the clause starting with *that*, the subject is the plural *emotions*, which demands the verb *are*, not *is*. Also, the phrase starting with *including* is a parenthetical expression that needs to be set off from the rest of the clause, with some punctuation to indicate a pause at its end (after *private*).

A	The verb form *is* is incorrect, and should instead be *are*; the parenthetical expression is not separated at its end from the rest of the clause.

B	**Correct.** *Are* is the correct agreeing verb form, and the comma after *private* correctly sets off the parenthetical expression.

C	*Are* is correct, but nothing after *private* sets off the parenthetical expression from the subsequent material. In addition, describing *emotions* (plural) as *a social phenomenon* (singular) may create some confusion, in part because the phrase *are not those separable* then switches back to the plural, and the reader is left unsure what the referent of *those* is. It seems most natural to take *social phenomenon* to be the referent, but *those* (plural) and *social phenomenon* (singular) do not agree in number. Furthermore, the sentence would be improved by simply removing *those*, or by replacing *those not separable* with *inseparable*.

D	This version of the sentence is incorrect because the same sort of punctuation must be used to set off the parenthetical expression. The dash that follows *private* would be correct only if *including* had been immediately preceded by a dash; otherwise a comma rather than a dash is needed after *private*. The phrase *not separable* should either be preceded by *are* or be replaced by *are inseparable*.

E	The phrase *deemed personal or also as private emotions* has several flaws: First, the use of *as* before *private* is incorrect because it should be parallel with *personal*. Second, the use of *also* seems to indicate that personal emotions and private emotions are different things, but they are not. Another problem with this version of the sentence is that the phrase *social phenomena not inseparable* not only does not express the intended meaning, but should also include a pronoun such as *that* and a verb; the sentence would be improved if this phrase were replaced with *social phenomena that are not separable*.

The correct answer is B.

SC01455

824.	In a speech before the Senate Banking Committee, the chairman of the Federal Reserve painted an optimistic picture of the economy, <u>suggesting to investors the central bank in the near future is not lowering interest rates</u>.

(A)	suggesting to investors the central bank in the near future is not lowering interest rates

(B)	suggesting to investors that the central bank would not lower interest rates in the near future

(C)	which suggests that to investors in the near future interest rates will not be lowered by the central bank

(D)	with the suggestion to investors in the near future that interest rates would not be lowered by the central bank

(E)	with the suggestion to investors of interest rates not being lowered in the near future by the central bank

Grammatical Construction; Verb Form

The sentence seeks to report an idea that the chairman of the Federal Reserve (the central bank) expressed concerning the central bank's intentions. Instead of quoting directly from the speech, the writer expresses the chairman's words indirectly: the chairman suggested that such and such would occur. In the speech, the chairman presumably used the future tense, for example: "The central bank will probably not lower interest rates in the near future." But, the sentence is a report of a past speech, not of something that is currently occurring, so to accurately represent the past communication, *will not lower* should morph into the past tense *would not lower* or *was not going to lower*. *In the near future* refers to a time that had not yet come when the chairman made the speech; that time period might or might not have extended to or beyond the time when the sentence was written.

A	The placement of *in the near future* makes the sentence ambiguous. The phrase appears to modify *the central bank*, but it is more likely intended to modify *is not lowering interest rates*. The present-continuous form *is not lowering* is a poor choice in this context. The present-continuous form most standardly means that an action is ongoing at the present time, but the sentence reports a past speech of the chairman that referred to what the central bank intended to do at some future time after the speech was made. The present-continuous form is sometimes used in informal speech to refer to a future event or intention, as in the sentence, "My sister told me that she's not going to the office tomorrow." However, that usage is nonstandard in more formal contexts. Also, if the author had intended it in that way, unless the sentence was written almost immediately after the chairman's speech, she or he should have used the past-continuous form *was not lowering* instead of *is not lowering*.

B **Correct.** This clearly and effectively reports the chairman's past speech about what the central bank intended at that time.

C The antecedent of the relative pronoun *which* is unclear: is it *the economy*, *an optimistic picture of the economy*, or *the chairman . . . the economy*? The placement of *in the near future* makes that phrase appear to modify *investors*, but it is far more plausibly intended to modify *will not be lowered by the central bank*. The sequence *suggests that to investors* implausibly puts *to investors* within the scope of the indirectly reported speech, i.e., within the *that*-clause. With this arrangement of words, the sentence says literally that the chairman's speech suggests that the following is true: "To investors in the near future, interest rates will not be lowered by the central bank." But that does not make good sense.

D The placement of the adverbial phrase *in the near future* incorrectly removes it outside the scope of the reported speech and leaves it unclear what verb or adjective it is meant to modify.

E Indirect speech (as distinguished from direct quotation) is normally best expressed in a *that*-clause; the attempt to express it by the prepositional phrase *of interest rates not being lowered . . .* makes the structure of the sentence ambiguous and difficult to interpret. The placement of the phrase *of interest rates* makes it appear to modify *investors*, but on that interpretation, the sentence does not make sense.

The correct answer is B.

SC00740.02

825. The company's CEO backed away from her <u>plan for dividing the firm into five parts, saying that she still had meant</u> to spin off or sell two units but that the company would retain ownership of two others as well as the core company.

(A) plan for dividing the firm into five parts, saying that she still had meant

(B) plan that was to divide the firm into five parts, and she said that she still would mean

(C) plan to divide the firm into five parts, saying that she still meant

(D) planning on dividing the firm into five parts, and saying that she meant still

(E) planning to divide the firm into five parts, and she said that she meant still

Idiom; Verb Form

The sentence describes an action taken by a CEO and a statement she made when she took the action; in particular, the CEO decided not to follow through on a plan, and she sketched out a less ambitious plan. Two issues arise with the sentence: (1) Does the phrase *plan for dividing* correctly convey the intended meaning? (2) Is the past-perfect verb form *had meant* correct in this context? Regarding (1), we can distinguish between an action that is planned (a *plan to divide* the firm into five parts) and a plan or series of steps for implementing that action (a *plan for dividing* the firm into five parts). Either sense of plan could correctly apply. Regarding (2), the past-perfect form is used to refer to an action or event preceding another action or event described using the simple past (here the verb form *backed away*). In this context, there is some rhetorical tension between *still*, which indicates the continuation of an action, and *had meant*, which indicates a completed action. In direct speech, the CEO presumably said something like "I still mean to spin off . . . units" and not "I still have meant to spin off . . . units." Therefore, the verb form *had meant* is inappropriate here.

A This version is incorrect because the simple-past form *meant* should be used instead of the past-perfect form *had meant*, to signify a time contemporaneous with the time of the *saying*—the time designated by the sentence's main verb *backed away*.

B   This version uses more words than is necessary to clearly convey its meaning. For example, the word sequence *that was* adds nothing useful to the intended meaning. The verb form *would mean* occurs in an indirect-speech context governed by the verb *said*. The corresponding direct speech form has the CEO saying: "I still will mean to spin off . . .". However, the phrase *will mean to spin off* is odd because *I mean to spin off . . .* already has a future-like connotation. Given that, using the future tense *will mean* is unnecessary.

C   **Correct.** As explained above, the verb form *to divide* is correctly used for one of the two senses of the word *plan*, a sense applicable in this context. The verb form *meant* is correct in this indirect-speech context, which is set in a time governed by the verb *saying*, which is contemporaneous with the time indicated by the simple past of the main verb *backed away*.

D   The phrase *her planning on dividing* is less idiomatic than *plan to divide* or *plan for dividing*. The long phrase that begins with *saying* is not an independent clause and so cannot correctly be conjoined with the first part of the sentence. In principle, *saying . . .* could be intended to refer to part of what the CEO backed away from, but the comma after *parts* undermines that interpretation.

E   The phrase *backed away from her planning* means something different from *backed away from her plan*. The latter implies dropping part or all of her plan, whereas the former means something like *disengaging herself from the activity of planning*, which does not necessarily mean that she is backing away from her plan; she could be disengaging from planning because she has completed making the plan and now is going to execute it. The rest of the sentence suggests, however, that the intended meaning is that she has backed away from the plan itself.

The correct answer is C.

SC52050.02

826.   The cactus is now heavily plundered in deserts in the southwestern United States, so much that enforcement agencies in five states have created special squads for its protection.

(A)   The cactus is now heavily plundered in deserts in the southwestern United States, so much that enforcement agencies in five states have created special squads for its protection.

(B)   The cactus is now heavily plundered in deserts in the southwestern United States, so much so that special squads have been created by law enforcement agencies in five states for protecting them.

(C)   The cactus is now so heavily plundered in deserts in the southwestern United States that enforcement agencies in five states have created special squads to protect it.

(D)   Because they are now so heavily plundered in deserts in the southwestern United States, enforcement agencies in five states have created special squads to protect cacti.

(E)   Because they are now so heavily plundered in the southwestern United States, special squads have been created by enforcement agencies in five states for the protection of cacti.

Idiom; Logical Predication; Agreement

The sentence is about a type of cactus that people have been harvesting illegitimately from the desert areas where it grows. In this context, *heavily* describes the amount of plundering, not the way in which the plundering is done. The function of the phrase *so much that* is unclear in relation to the rest of the sentence. Given that it is set off by a comma, it could plausibly be construed as a reiteration and intensification of the idea that the cactus has been heavily plundered. But for that purpose, the proper phrase would be *so much so that . . .* or *so heavily that . . .* rather than *so much that . . .*, so it is more likely intended to indicate the degree to which the plundering was heavy. In that case, a much clearer, more standard, and more efficient wording would be *so heavily plundered that. . . .* That wording is used in answer choice C. Answer choices B, D, and E fail because a phrase fails to modify what it is intended to modify or because a pronoun does not agree in number with its antecedent.

A   As explained above, the intended function of *so much that* is unclear in relation to the rest of the sentence. The more standard wording *so heavily plundered that* would be preferable.

B   The sentence says *special squads have been created . . . for protecting them.* The only plausible object of the verb *protecting* is the cactus. Because *the cactus* is grammatically singular but the pronoun *them* is plural, the pronoun fails to agree in number with its antecedent. The correct pronoun is *it*.

C   Correct. This version correctly uses the idiom *so . . . that* and the pronoun *it* agrees in number with its antecedent *the cactus.*

D   The phrase *they are now so heavily plundered in the southwestern United States* is almost certainly intended to refer to *cacti*, but grammatically it refers to *enforcement agencies in five states* instead.

E   The phrase *they are now so heavily plundered in the southwestern United States* is almost certainly intended to refer to *cacti*, but grammatically it refers to *enforcement agencies in five states* instead.

The correct answer is C.

SC08150.02

827. Satellite radio transmissions, a popular feature in car stereos, differ from those of AM and FM radio, <u>which is sent directly from earthbound towers and then to a car</u> stereo.

(A)   which is sent directly from earthbound towers and then to a car

(B)   which are sent directly from earthbound towers to a car's

(C)   sent from earthbound towers and then directly to a car

(D)   sending them directly from earthbound towers to a car's

(E)   being sent directly from earthbound towers to a car

Grammatical Construction; Logical Predication

A   The sentence compares two kinds of radio transmissions—satellite radio and AM and FM radio—with respect to how each is sent to car stereos. Issues to note include: (1) what the antecedent of the relative pronoun *which* is

and whether the verb with *which* as its subject should be singular or plural and (2) whether the phrasing *directly from . . . and then . . .* is coherent in context. Given the singular verb *is* with *which* as its subject, the noun phrase *AM and FM radio* is the only plausible antecedent of *which*. Thus, the sentence seems to say illogically that AM and FM radio is sent from towers to car stereos. The more coherent meaning—and presumably the intended one—is that the transmissions of AM and FM radio are sent directly from towers. A significant issue in this answer choice is the incoherence of the phrasing *directly from . . . and then to . . .* At least without further clarifying language, this is incoherent because the word sequence *and then to . . .* indicates indirectness.

B   Correct. In this answer choice, the plural verb *are*, with *which* as its subject, indicates that the antecedent of *which* must be a plural noun, noun phrase, or pronoun. The nearest plausible candidate is the pronoun *those*, which refers back to *transmissions*. This logically contrasts one kind of transmission with another kind: *those of AM and FM radio.* The *which* clause coherently indicates that AM and FM radio transmissions to a car stereo *are sent directly.*

C   It is unclear what the past participle *sent* modifies; it could be either *AM and FM radio* or the pronoun *those*, which refers back to *transmissions.* Also, the phrasing *from . . . and then directly to . . .* is at least superficially incoherent because the word sequence *from . . . and then to . . .* indicates indirectness.

D   The phrase *sending them . . . stereo* is significantly flawed. It incoherently modifies the sentence's subject, *Satellite radio transmissions.* The pronoun *them* logically refers to the pronoun *those*, which in turn refers to *transmissions*, i.e., those of AM and FM radio.

E   Structurally, the role of the phrase *being sent . . . car stereo* seems to modify the subject of the sentence, *Satellite radio transmissions.* However, this produces a sentence without a coherent meaning, given the common understanding that satellite transmissions are not sent directly from earthbound towers to car stereos.

The correct answer is B.

SC21130.02

828. Although <u>the company's executives have admitted that there had been accounting irregularities involving improper reporting of revenue, as well as of failure to record</u> expenses, they could not yet say precisely how much money was involved.

(A) the company's executives have admitted that there had been accounting irregularities involving improper reporting of revenue, as well as of failure to record

(B) the company's executives admitted that there had been accounting irregularities involving improper reporting of revenue and failure to record

(C) the company's executives, admitting accounting irregularities involving improper reporting of revenue and failure in recording

(D) admission by the company's executives was made of accounting irregularities involving improper reporting of revenue and failure in recording

(E) admission by the company's executives that there had been accounting irregularities involving improper reporting of revenue and failure in recording

Verb Form; Logical Predication

The sentence seems meant to tell us that company executives admitted two kinds of accounting irregularities—improper reporting of revenue and failure to record expenses—but were unable to say immediately how much money was involved. Issues arising with the sentence include the following: (1) the relationship between the verb forms *have admitted* and *had been*, (2) the appropriate way to conjoin two noun phrases designating the mentioned irregularities, and (3) the nouns or noun phrases that are the appropriate objects of the verbs *involving* and *reporting*.

A   Without any clarification of the temporal relationships among the events, the relationship between the present perfect form *have admitted* and the past perfect *had been* is puzzling and potentially confusing. The wording *as well as of* does not function correctly to conjoin the noun phrases that refer to aspects of the *irregularities* mentioned. The preposition *of* suggests that *failure to record expenses* is an object of *reporting* (and not of the verb *involving*). However, this reading yields a very implausible implication that there were accounting irregularities involving improper

reporting of failure to record expenses. If that was the author's intended message, it should have been stated more clearly.

B   **Correct.** The past perfect verb form *had been* is the appropriate way of designating an event preceding the event designated by the simple-past form *admitted*. The conjunction *and* is appropriately used to conjoin the two parallel noun phrases that are the objects of *involving*. This version is idiomatically correct in using the infinitive verb form *to record* following *failure*.

C   This is not a grammatically valid sentence; the long opening clause beginning with *although* establishes *the company's executives* as its subject, but it has no main verb. The phrase *failure in recording expenses* is unclear and vague; it does not imply that a failure to record expenses occurred, merely that in the course of recording expenses, there was some failure or other.

D   The passive-voice phrasing *admission by . . . was made* is unnecessarily awkward and indirect. The phrasing *was made of* is usually followed by some reference to materials or ingredients of which something is composed; that meaning is inapplicable here. A further defect is that the phrase *failure in recording expenses* is unclear and vague; it does not imply that a failure to record expenses occurred, merely that in the course of recording expenses, there was some failure or other.

E   This is not a grammatically valid sentence; it has no main verb that has *admission by . . . expenses* as its subject. Also, the passive-voice phrasing *admission by . . . was made* is unnecessarily awkward and indirect.

The correct answer is B.

SC03014

829. <u>As with ants, the elaborate social structure of termites includes a few individuals reproducing</u> and the rest serve the colony by tending juveniles, gathering food, building the nest, or battling intruders.

(A) As with ants, the elaborate social structure of termites includes a few individuals reproducing

(B) As do ants, termites have an elaborate social structure, which includes a few individuals to reproduce

(C)   Just as with ants, termite social structure is elaborate, including a few individuals for reproducing

(D)   Like ants, termites have an elaborate social structure in which a few individuals reproduce

(E)   Like that of ants, the termite social structure is elaborate, including a few individuals that reproduce

Grammatical Construction; Parallelism

The sentence describes the organization of reproduction and labor among termites. As written, the sentence seems, illogically, to compare a social structure with ants, not with another social structure. Overall, the sentence structure is unnecessarily awkward.

A   The phrases *a few individuals reproducing* and *the rest serve . . .* are nonparallel, contrary to what would be expected given the coordinating conjunction *and*.

B   The *and* seems as if it should coordinate two parallel elements in a complex relative clause; yet *a few individuals to reproduce* is not parallel with *the rest serve . . . intruders*.

C   This illogically compares a social structure with ants. The structure *including . . . and . . .* raises an expectation that there would be a phrase following *and* that would be parallel with the phrase *a few individuals for reproducing*. However, *the rest serve . . . intruders* is not parallel. The participle *including* is often used to introduce instances of a class; its use here is confusing since a social structure is not a class that has termites as its members.

D   **Correct.** The sentence concisely notes that termites resemble ants in having an elaborate social structure. The complex relative clause *in which . . . and . . .* has two coordinated elements correctly parallel in structure: *a few individuals reproduce* and *the rest serve . . . intruders*.

E   The phrase *that of ants* is not parallel with *the termite social structure*; also, the forward reference of *that* is unnecessarily awkward and impairs readability. As already noted, the use of the participle *including* is confusing. The conjunction *and* indicates coordination of two parallel elements, but *a few*

individuals that reproduce cannot be correctly coordinated with anything that follows it.

The correct answer is D.

SC02078

830.   While Noble Sissle may be best known for his collaboration with Eubie Blake, as both a vaudeville performer <u>and as a lyricist for songs and Broadway musicals, also enjoying</u> an independent career as a singer with such groups as Hahn's Jubilee Singers.

(A)   and as a lyricist for songs and Broadway musicals, also enjoying

(B)   and writing lyrics for songs and Broadway musicals, also enjoying

(C)   and a lyricist for songs and Broadway musicals, he also enjoyed

(D)   as well as writing lyrics for songs and Broadway musicals, he also enjoyed

(E)   as well as a lyricist for songs and Broadway musicals, he had also enjoyed

Grammatical Construction; Idiom; Parallelism

As worded, this sentence opens with a dependent clause (a clause that cannot stand on its own), which requires a main clause (also known as an independent clause) to complete the sentence; however, there is no main clause. Also, given the placement of *as* before *both*, the *as* before *a lyricist* is incorrect. It would be acceptable to write *as both a vaudeville performer and a lyricist* or to write *both as a vaudeville performer and as a lyricist*; it is not acceptable to mix the two forms, as is done here.

A   The dependent clause, *While . . . Broadway musicals*, is followed by a participial phrase rather than a main clause and is therefore ungrammatical. Furthermore, the word *as* before *a lyricist* violates the parallel structure required by the phrase *both . . . and*.

B   The construction *as both a performer and writing lyrics* is incorrect. Also, like answer choice A, this version of the sentence does not supply a main clause.

C   **Correct.** Unlike answer choices A and B, this version has a main clause and correctly uses the *both x and y* form.

D   Although this version does supply the main clause anticipated by *While . . .*, its use *as both a vaudeville performer as well as writing lyrics* is incorrect.

E   This version's use of *both x as well as y* instead of *both x and y* is incorrect. It also introduces an inexplicable past perfect verb, *had . . . enjoyed*, in the main clause.

The correct answer is C.

SC03881

831. Air traffic routes over the North Pole are currently used by only two or three planes a day, but it was found by a joint Canadian–Russian study to be both feasible as well as desirable if those routes are opened to thousands more commercial planes a year.

   (A)   Air traffic routes over the North Pole are currently used by only two or three planes a day, but it was found by a joint Canadian–Russian study to be both feasible as well as desirable if those routes are opened to thousands more commercial planes a year.

   (B)   Currently used by only two or three planes a day, a joint Canadian–Russian study has found that if air traffic routes over the North Pole are opened to thousands more commercial planes a year, it would be both feasible and desirable.

   (C)   A joint Canadian–Russian study, finding it to be both feasible as well as desirable to open air traffic routes over the North Pole, which are currently used by only two or three planes a day, to thousands more commercial planes a year.

   (D)   Although air traffic routes over the North Pole are currently used by only two or three planes a day, a joint Canadian–Russian study has found that opening those routes to thousands more commercial planes a year is both feasible and desirable.

   (E)   With air traffic routes over the North Pole currently used by only two or three planes a day, opening those routes to thousands more commercial planes a year has been found by a joint Canadian—Russian study as both feasible and desirable.

Rhetorical Construction; Verb Form; Logical Predication

The point of the sentence is to share the results of a study about air routes over the North Pole, but the sentence, which uses the passive construction *it was found by a joint Canadian–Russian study to be*, could be expressed more directly and clearly in the active voice: *a joint Canadian–Russian study has found*. It is acceptable and even desirable to use the passive voice in certain circumstances. For instance, if you want to emphasize that a certain thing or person was acted upon, rather than some other thing or person, then you may want to use the passive voice, e.g., *The window was what John broke, not the door*. However, the passive voice serves no such purpose here, and its use here requires the use of the impersonal pronoun *it*, which has no clear antecedent. Therefore, the active voice is preferable. An additional problem is the strange use of the conditional *if*. Logically, the point that the sentence is trying to convey is that opening the routes is feasible. This would be better conveyed by *feasible . . . to open those routes* or, as in the correct answer choice D, *opening those routes . . . is . . . feasible*.

A   For the reasons discussed above, the sentence would be better if the passive construction *it was found by a joint Canadian–Russian study to be* were replaced with the active voice construction *a joint Canadian–Russian study has found*. Additionally, as pointed out above, the use of the conditional *if* is strange in this particular context.

B   *Used by only two or three planes* illogically modifies *a joint Canadian–Russian study*; the pronoun *it* has no clear antecedent.

C   The subject *A joint Canadian–Russian study* has no verb; *to thousands more commercial planes* is located too far away from *to open*, which it is intended to modify.

D   Correct. The sentence uses correctly placed modifiers and the active voice to explain clearly what a *joint Canadian–Russian study has found*.

E   For reasons similar to those discussed above, the sentence would be better if the passive construction *opening those routes . . . has been found by a joint Canadian–Russian study as both* were replaced with an active voice construction.

The correct answer is D.

SC01680

832. From an experiment using special extrasensory perception cards, each bearing one of a set of symbols, parapsychologist Joseph Banks Rhine claimed statistical proof for subjects who could use thought transference to identify a card in the dealer's hand.

(A) for subjects who could use thought transference to identify a card in the dealer's hand

(B) for a card in the dealer's hand to be identified by subjects with thought transference

(C) of subjects able to identify with thought transference a card in the dealer's hand

(D) that subjects could identify a card in the dealer's hand by using thought transference

(E) that subjects are capable to use thought transference for identifying a card in the dealer's hand

Idiom; Rhetorical Construction

This sentence is meant to indicate that Joseph Banks Rhine claimed that a certain experiment statistically proved that subjects could identify what symbol was on a card in a dealer's hand by using thought transference. The present version of the sentence does not convey the intended meaning well, however. What should follow *proof* is a statement of the assertion that Rhine claims the experiment has statistically proved, linked to the word *proof* by the word *that*. Instead *proof* is followed by a prepositional phrase *for subjects who. . . .*

A This version of the sentence inappropriately attempts to describe the claim by using a prepositional phrase, *for subjects who. . . .*

B Like answer choice A, this version of the sentence inappropriately attempts to describe the claim by using a prepositional phrase, *for a card in. . . .*

C Like answer choices A and B, this version of the sentence inappropriately attempts to describe the claim by using a prepositional phrase. While *proof* might reasonably be followed by *of*, the phrase that follows the preposition is ungrammatical, requiring a participle to modify *subjects*, such as *being able to. . . .*

D **Correct.** This version correctly uses the idiom *proof that* followed by an assertion.

E While this version of the sentence correctly follows *proof* with *that* followed by an assertion, it fails to use the appropriate idiom with *capable*; instead of *capable to use*, it should have *capable of using*.

The correct answer is D.

SCO2272

833. A long-term study of some 1,000 physicians indicates that the more coffee these doctors drank, the <u>more they had a likelihood of coronary disease</u>.

(A) more they had a likelihood of coronary disease

(B) more was their likelihood of having coronary disease

(C) more they would have a likelihood to have coronary disease

(D) greater was their likelihood of having coronary disease

(E) greater was coronary disease likely

Idiom; Rhetorical Construction

This sentence describes the results of a study in which researchers found a correlation between the amounts of coffee that people drank and their likelihood of coronary disease. It most eloquently expresses this correlation as a comparison of parallel forms, using the idiom *the + comparative adjective phrase . . . the + comparative adjective phrase*. The two adjective phrases should have the same grammatical form.

A This version obscures the intended correlation between *coffee* and *likelihood*. The phrase *the more they had a likelihood* somewhat illogically indicates that the research subjects had likelihood to a greater degree rather than that their likelihood was greater.

B Although the adverb *more* is used to indicate a greater degree or extent in phrases such as *more likely*, the adjective *more* normally indicates greater quantity. Thus, the use of *more* as an adjective modifying *their likelihood* is nonstandard. Differences in a particular type of likelihood are normally thought of as matters of degree, not of quantity. *Greater* is the preferred adjective for indicating such differences.

C The conditional verb phrase *would have a likelihood to have* is redundant, wordy, and not comparable to the simple past tense *drank*.

D **Correct.** This version uses proper wording and is clear and concise.

E This completion of the comparison is not idiomatic; moreover, it is ungrammatical, attempting to use an adjective *greater* to describe an adverb, *likely*.

The correct answer is D.

SC02096

834. Hurricanes at first begin traveling from east to west, because that direction is the way the prevailing winds in the tropics blow, but they then veer off toward higher latitudes, in many cases changing direction toward the east before dissipating over the colder, more northerly waters or over land.

(A) Hurricanes at first begin traveling from east to west, because that direction is the way the prevailing winds in the tropics blow, but

(B) At first, hurricanes travel from east to west, because that is the direction of the prevailing winds in the tropics, but

(C) While hurricanes travel from east to west at first, the direction of the prevailing winds blowing in the tropics, and

(D) Because hurricanes at first travel from east to west, since it is the direction of the prevailing winds in the tropics,

(E) Hurricanes, beginning by traveling from east to west, because this is the direction of the prevailing winds in the tropics,

Rhetorical Construction; Grammatical Construction

Hurricanes at first begin traveling is redundant, with *at first* illogically modifying *begin*. It would be better to start the sentence with *At first, hurricanes travel* or *Hurricanes begin traveling*. The phrase *the way the prevailing winds . . . blow* is ambiguous between *how the prevailing winds blow* and *the direction in which the prevailing winds blow*. That ambiguity, together with the unnecessary convolution, could puzzle or annoy many readers; readers should expect additional complexity to convey additional information or rhetorical force, but the complex phrase *that direction is the way* turns out to be merely equivalent to the simpler *that is the direction* or *that is the way*.

A As explained above, the wording is ambiguous and contains complexities that convey no additional information or rhetorical force.

B Correct. This version of the sentence is grammatically correct, straightforward, and free of complexities that add nothing to the meaning, such as *at first begin* and *that direction is the way*.

C This sentence begins with a dependent clause (that is, a clause that cannot stand on its own), anticipating a main clause (also known as an independent clause) to complete the sentence; a main clause does follow, but it is connected to the initial dependent clause by the coordinating conjunction and, which would be appropriate here only if the initial clause were of the same grammatical type (that is, also a main clause).

D *Because* suggests that the direction in which hurricanes initially travel causes them later to veer off to the north, but this makes little logical sense.

E This sentence opens with a main subject, *Hurricanes*, but this subject has no verb. The subject of the sentence's main verb, *veer*, is *they*.

The correct answer is B.

SC03083

835. Travelers from Earth to Mars would have to endure low levels of gravity for long periods of time, avoiding large doses of radiation, plus contending with the chemically reactive Martian soil, and perhaps even ward off contamination by Martian life-forms.

(A) Mars would have to endure low levels of gravity for long periods of time, avoiding large doses of radiation, plus contending

(B) Mars would have to endure low levels of gravity for long periods of time, avoid large doses of radiation, contend

(C) Mars, having to endure low levels of gravity for long periods of time, would also have to avoid large doses of radiation, plus contending

(D) Mars, having to endure low levels of gravity for long periods of time, avoid large doses of radiation, plus contend

(E) Mars, who would have to endure low levels of gravity for long periods of time, avoid large doses of radiation, contend with

Grammatical Construction; Parallelism

The sentence lists a series of things that travelers from Earth to Mars would have to do in order to successfully handle challenging conditions. Listing elements in a series requires parallelism in wording for each element, together with the use of a conjunction immediately preceding the final element.

A   The parallelism requirement is not fulfilled; for example, *endure . . . time* is not parallel with *avoiding . . . radiation* or *contending . . . soil*. The word *plus* is not a coordinating conjunction and its inclusion impairs the structure of the series.

B   Correct. The parallelism requirement is fulfilled, with the following elements: *endure . . ., avoid . . ., contend . . ., and perhaps even ward off.*

C   The parallelism requirement is not fulfilled; for example, *would have to avoid* is not parallel with *contending*. The word *plus* is not a coordinating conjunction.

D   This is not a valid sentence since it lacks an independent clause.

E   This is not a valid sentence since it lacks an independent clause.

The correct answer is B.

SC01739

836. Unlike the virginal, <u>whose single set of strings runs parallel to the front edge of the instrument, the harpsichord's several sets of strings are</u> placed at right angles to its front edge.

(A)   whose single set of strings runs parallel to the front edge of the instrument, the harpsichord's several sets of strings are

(B)   with a single set of strings running parallel to the front edge of the instrument, the several sets of strings of the harpsichord are

(C)   which has a single set of strings that runs parallel to the front edge of the instrument, in the case of the harpsichord, several sets of strings are

(D)   which has a single set of strings that run parallel to the front edge of the instrument, the harpsichord has several sets of strings

(E)   in which a single set of strings run parallel to the front edge of the instrument, the harpsichord's several sets of strings are

Parallelism; Agreement

The point of the sentence is to contrast two instruments, but the sentence has been written to contrast the *virginal* with the *sets of strings* on the harpsichord. The proper contrast is between the *virginal* and the *harpsichord*.

A   The *virginal* is illogically contrasted with the *sets of strings* on the harpsichord. Note the possessive form *harpsichord's* in contrast to virginal.

B   The *virginal* is illogically contrasted with the *sets of strings* on the harpsichord.

C   *In the case of the harpsichord* is not parallel to the *virginal*.

D   Correct. The contrast is properly drawn between *the virginal* and *the harpsichord*.

E   The *virginal* is illogically contrasted with the *sets of strings* on the harpsichord; the verb *run* does not agree with the singular subject *set*.

The correct answer is D.

SC91050.02

837. Many population studies have linked a high-salt diet to high rates of hypertension and <u>shown that in societies where they consume little salt, their</u> blood pressure typically does not rise with age.

(A)   shown that in societies where they consume little salt, their

(B)   shown that in societies that have consumed little salt, their

(C)   shown that in societies where little salt is consumed,

(D)   showing that in societies where little salt is consumed,

(E)   showing that in societies where they consume little salt, their

Idiom; Verb Form

The pronouns *they* and *their* do not have logical antecedents. *High rates of hypertension* (or possibly *societies*) is grammatically the apparent antecedent, but neither rates nor societies have blood pressure, and it is odd to say that societies (rather than the people living in the societies) consume salt. Three of the answer choices can be ruled out for this reason. Two answer choices have another problem: they use the incorrect verb form *showing*. The correct verb form is *shown*, to match the verb form *linked* earlier in the sentence.

A   As explained above, *they* and *their* have no logical antecedents.

B   In this version also, *they* does not have a logical antecedent. The verb form *have consumed* is inappropriate—or puzzling at best—in relation to the rest of the sentence.

C   **Correct.** This version does not make use of pronouns, so clearly it does not make use of pronouns that lack a logical antecedent. Also, the sentence uses the appropriate verb form, *shown*.

D   This version uses the incorrect verb form, *showing*.

E   This version has both problems explained above: it uses the incorrect verb form, *showing*, and there is no logical antecedent for the pronoun *their*.

The correct answer is C.

SC61940.02

838. According to scientists, human <u>expansion and the human appropriation of Earth's finite resources is</u> the cause of what may be the most sweeping wave of species extinctions since the demise of the dinosaurs 65 million years ago.

(A)   expansion and the human appropriation of Earth's finite resources is

(B)   expansion and human appropriation of Earth's finite resources are

(C)   expansion and its appropriation of Earth's finite resources is

(D)   expansion, along with their appropriation of Earth's finite resources, is

(E)   expansion, along with its appropriation of Earth's finite resources, are

Grammatical Construction; Agreement

The sentence ascribes to scientists the belief that human expansion and human appropriation of Earth's resources may cause the worst wave of species extinctions in 65 million years.

A   The singular verb *is* does not agree with the conjoined noun phrases that are its subject. In some cases, conjoined nouns or noun phrases could function as a singular compound subject, but here they are far more plausibly construed as two separate factors.

B   **Correct.** The plural verb *are* is correctly in agreement with its subject, two conjoined noun phrases.

C   The singular verb *is* does not agree with its subject, two conjoined noun phrases. The

antecedent of *its* is *human expansion*, so this version refers implausibly to human expansion's appropriation of finite resources.

D   *Their* has no clear referent. Being plural, it cannot coherently have the singular *human expansion* as its antecedent. Given the sentence structure, *their* appears to refer to the plural *scientists*, but it is implausible to suppose that the scientists would claim that their own appropriation of Earth's finite resources is a cause of a massive wave of extinctions. The singular *is*, with *human expansion* as its subject, is correct.

E   Because *along with . . .* is parenthetical, the subject is the singular *human expansion*. The plural *are* does not agree with the singular subject.

The correct answer is B.

SC02000

839. Although Alice Walker published a number of essays, poetry collections, and stories during the 1970s, her third novel, *The Color Purple*, <u>which was published in 1982, brought her the widest acclaim in that it won both the National Book Award as well as the Pulitzer Prize.</u>

(A)   which was published in 1982, brought her the widest acclaim in that it won both the National Book Award as well as the Pulitzer Prize

(B)   published in 1982, bringing her the widest acclaim by winning both the National Book Award and the Pulitzer Prize

(C)   published in 1982, brought her the widest acclaim, winning both the National Book Award and the Pulitzer Prize

(D)   was published in 1982 and which, winning both the National Book Award and the Pulitzer Prize, brought her the widest acclaim

(E)   was published in 1982, winning both the National Book Award as well as the Pulitzer Prize, and bringing her the widest acclaim

Idiom; Grammatical Construction

This sentence claims that the 1982 novel *The Color Purple* brought Alice Walker more acclaim than her many publications in the 1970s.

A   The construction *both the American Book Award as well as the Pulitzer Prize* is unidiomatic; the correct idiomatic form is *both x and y*.

B   Because this sentence uses only participial phrases in the clause following the initial, dependent clause, the sentence lacks a main verb and is therefore ungrammatical.

C   **Correct.** This version correctly uses the form *both x and y* and is grammatically correct.

D   The use of *which* is inappropriate here; although it would still be rhetorically inferior to the correct answer choice C, this version would be acceptable if the word *which* were deleted.

E   Like answer choice A, this version of the sentence uses the unidiomatic form *both x as well as y.*

The correct answer is C.

SC01436

840. Heating oil and natural gas futures rose sharply yesterday, as long-term forecasts for much colder temperatures in key heating regions raised fears of insufficient supplies capable of meeting the demand this winter.

(A)   of insufficient supplies capable of meeting

(B)   of supplies that would be insufficient for meeting

(C)   of insufficient supplies that are unable to meet

(D)   that there would be supplies insufficient for meeting

(E)   that supplies would be insufficient to meet

Rhetorical Construction; Verb Form

The wording of the underlined portion of this sentence is incoherent because it suggests that supplies that are "insufficient" are "capable of meeting the demand." The phrase *fears of insufficient supplies* is awkward and unclear: it suggests that the object of the fears already exists, i.e., that supplies are already insufficient. How can the intended meaning—regarding a fear that something might occur—be best expressed in the context of the sentence as a whole?

A   This produces an incoherent sentence that forces us to guess at what might have been intended.

B   This is wordy and unnecessarily awkward. The phrase *insufficient to meet* would be more idiomatic than *insufficient for meeting*.

C   The present tense *are* fails to express the future-oriented nature of the fears:

that future supplies might turn out to be insufficient relative to demand.

D   The awkward expression here is misleading. What the fears were about was not that there would be supplies but that the supplies would be insufficient.

E   **Correct.** What was feared was the following: future supplies will be insufficient to meet the demand. Because we are told that the fears were raised in the past, the futurity of the feared occurrence must be expressed by *would be* (rather than by *will be*) in the context of the *that*-clause, which clearly conveys what was feared (the object of the "fears").

The correct answer is E.

SC00970

841. Because it regarded the environmentalists as members of an out-of-state organization, the city council voted that they are denied permission for participating in the parade.

(A)   that they are denied permission for participating

(B)   that they be denied permission for participating

(C)   denying them permission for participation

(D)   the denial of permission that they participate

(E)   to deny them permission to participate

Verb Form; Logical Predication

The sentence describes a vote that has been taken by a city council and suggests an explanation as to why the city council voted the particular way it did. The underlined portion, together with the three words that follow it, serves to describe the particular way the council voted and begins immediately after the verb *voted*. The word *that* at the beginning of the underlined portion introduces a subordinate clause that introduces the particular way the city council voted.

A   When we vote for something, what we vote for is something that perhaps should happen, rather than a fact or a description of an actual state of affairs. The statement *they are denied permission* would, if used properly, simply describe an actual state of affairs. It is therefore something that would not be voted for. The wording of the sentence thus needs to be changed, so that what is described as being voted for is not described as if it were an existing state of affairs. Furthermore, as discussed in connection with answer choice B, the use of "for participating" may also be incorrect.

B   The use of "for participating" in this version may be incorrect. The noun *permission* as used in this statement describes an official act of allowing someone or something *to do something*. In this statement, it would be better if *permission* were followed by an infinitive form of a verb (beginning with the word "to"). For example, *permission to participate* would be correct.

C   In addition to the flaw described in connection with answer choice B, this version has a flaw associated with the use of the word *denying*. Between *voted* and whatever form of the verb "deny" we may choose, we need a term, such as an infinitive (e.g., *to*) or a preposition (e.g., *for* or *on*) to introduce the statement describing the vote. In this way, *to deny*, *for denying*, and *on denying* could be correct, but lacks such an introducing term.

D   This version is a noun phrase, which, when preceded by the verb "voted," needs a preposition such as *for* or *on* to precede it. For example, *voted for the denial of permission* might be correct. The use of *that they participate* is also incorrect. This flaw could be fixed if, as discussed in connection with answer choice B, we used *to participate* instead.

E   **Correct.** This version is without the flaws explained above.

The correct answer is E.

SC07348

842. In 1913, the largely self-taught Indian mathematician Srinivasa Ramanujan mailed 120 of his theorems to three different British mathematicians; <u>only one, G. H. Hardy, recognized the brilliance of these theorems, but</u> thanks to Hardy's recognition, Ramanujan was eventually elected to the Royal Society of London.

(A)   only one, G. H. Hardy, recognized the brilliance of these theorems, but

(B)   they were brilliant, G. H. Hardy alone recognized, but

(C)   these theorems were brilliant, but only one, G. H. Hardy recognized;

(D)   but, only one, G. H. Hardy, recognizing their brilliance,

(E)   only one G. H. Hardy recognized, but these theorems were brilliant

Logical Predication; Grammatical Construction

The point of the sentence is that only one of the British mathematicians with whom Srinivasa Ramanujan initially shared his theorems recognized their brilliance, but that recognition was sufficient to earn Ramanujan acclaim. The sentence has been correctly constructed, with the phrase *only one* referring clearly to *British mathematicians* and the noun *theorems* repeated to avoid confusion.

A   **Correct.** The phrase *only one* refers clearly to *British mathematicians*, and the noun *theorems* is repeated to avoid confusion.

B   *They* is intended to refer to *theorems* but instead refers to *mathematicians*, causing confusion.

C   Structured in this way, the sentence does not make sense. *Only one* is intended to refer to *G. H. Hardy* but instead seems to refer to *theorems*, causing confusion. If *only one* is taken to refer to *G. H. Hardy*, the absence of a comma after the name and the absence of an object for *recognized* make the sentence ungrammatical.

D   The sentence is ungrammatical because *G. H. Hardy* serves as the subject of a clause but is not paired with a verb.

E   *Only one G. H. Hardy recognized* incorrectly implies (in an awkwardly inverted wording structure) that Hardy recognized only one theorem; *these theorems were brilliant thanks to Hardy's recognition* illogically suggests that Hardy's recognition is what made the theorems brilliant.

The correct answer is A.

SC05201

843. Cost cutting and restructuring <u>has allowed the manufacturing company to lower its projected losses for the second quarter, and they are forecasting</u> a profit before the end of the year.

(A)   has allowed the manufacturing company to lower its projected losses for the second quarter, and they are forecasting

(B) has allowed for the manufacturing company to lower its projected losses in the second quarter and to forecast

(C) have allowed that the manufacturing company can lower the projected losses for the second quarter, and to forecast

(D) have allowed the manufacturing company to lower its projected second-quarter losses and to forecast

(E) have allowed for the manufacturing company to lower the projected losses in the second quarter, as well as forecasting

Agreement; Idiom; Verb Form

The point of the sentence is to explain the two main effects of the changes made by the company. However, the singular verb *has allowed* does not agree with the compound subject *cost cutting and restructuring*, which are far more plausibly understood as two actions rather than as two facets of a single action. In principle, *the manufacturing company* could be construed as plural (referring collectively to the decision makers and spokespeople who are projecting losses and forecasting a profit), but the plural pronoun *they* does not agree with the earlier *its*, which treats the antecedent as singular.

A   The singular verb *has allowed* does not agree with the compound subject *cost cutting and restructuring*; the plural pronoun *they* does not agree with the intended singular antecedent *company*.

B   The singular verb *has allowed* does not agree with the compound subject *cost cutting and restructuring*; *allowed for* is not the correct idiom.

C   *Allowed that* is not the correct idiom; *can lower* and *to forecast* are not grammatically parallel.

D   Correct. The sentence uses the correct subject–verb combination *cost cutting and restructuring have allowed*; the two occurrences of the pronoun *its* agree with each other in treating their antecedent *company* as singular; and the two effects *to lower* and *to forecast* are parallel and idiomatic.

E   *Allowed for* is not the correct idiom; *to lower* and *as well as forecasting* are not parallel.

The correct answer is D.

SC13010
844. The Life and Casualty Company hopes that by increasing its environmental fund reserves to $1.2 billion, <u>that it has set aside enough to pay for environmental claims and no longer has</u> to use its profits and capital to pay those claims bit by bit, year by year.

(A) that it has set aside enough to pay for environmental claims and no longer has

(B) enough has been set aside with which environmental claims can be paid and it will have no longer

(C) it has set aside enough for payment of environmental claims and thus no longer having

(D) enough has been set aside to pay for environmental claims, thus no longer having

(E) it has set aside enough to pay for environmental claims and will no longer have

Grammatical Construction; Logical Predication

All predicates need a proper logical subject. Here, the relevant predicates are the verbs *increase*, *set aside*, and *have*. With *it* as the subject for *set aside*—referring back to the Life and Casualty Company—all three verbs should have this as their understood subject. With a different subject for *set aside*, at least one of the other verbs lacks a proper logical subject. Also, this sentence uses the word *that* after *hope* to start the subordinate clause, but then incorrectly repeats the *that* after the initial adverbial phrase (*by increasing . . . billion*). Only the first *that* is grammatically correct.

A   The additional *that* makes the sentence ungrammatical. Also, because in this context the hope is forward-looking (*bit by bit, year by year*), it would be preferable to use the future tense, *will no longer have to*, instead of the present *no longer has to*.

B   With *enough* as the subject of *set aside*, the next subject (*it*) is naturally interpreted as *enough*, but this is not a logical choice for the subject of *use*.

C   The phrase *no longer having* is ungrammatical when connected to the rest of the sentence by *and*, which should connect two regular clauses; *no longer having* ... is a mere phrase, not a clause, and *no longer has* would be correct.

D For *no longer having*, illogically, the implied subject is *enough*; the implied subject, instead, should be the company referred to at the beginning of the sentence.

E **Correct.** There is only one *that*, and *will no longer have to use* has its proper logical subject (*it*) from the clause preceding it.

The correct answer is E.

SC03079

845. Like ancient Egyptian architectural materials that were recycled in the construction of ancient Greek Alexandria, so ancient Greek materials from the construction of that city were reused in subsequent centuries by Roman, Muslim, and modern builders.

(A) Like ancient Egyptian architectural materials that were recycled in the construction of

(B) Like recycling ancient Egyptian architectural materials to construct

(C) Just as ancient Egyptian architectural materials were recycled in the construction of

(D) Just as they recycled ancient Egyptian architectural materials in constructing

(E) Just like ancient Egyptian architectural materials that were recycled in constructing

Diction; Parallelism

When two situations are asserted to be similar, the proper way to express this is with the paired expressions *just as ... so ...*, not *like ... so.* Moreover, the two compared situations should be expressed as clauses, not as noun phrases. Thus the clause *ancient Egyptian architectural materials were recycled* ... is correct, as opposed to a noun phrase like *ancient Egyptian architectural materials that were recycled* ...

A *Just as* and a following clause with a passive verb are preferred, but instead this option has *like* and a following noun phrase (*ancient Egyptian materials* ...). It appears, somewhat implausibly, to say that the ancient Greek materials were similar to the earlier ancient Egyptian ones in that both were used by Roman, Muslim, and modern builders.

B *Just as* and a following clause with a passive verb are preferred, but instead this option has *like* and a following noun phrase

(*recycling ancient Egyptian materials* ...). It appears illogically to say that the action of recycling was similar to the ancient Greek materials in that both were reused in subsequent centuries.

C **Correct.** The expressions *just as* and *so* are paired to link the two clauses in parallel, and both clauses use the passive construction.

D *Just as* is used to connect two clauses, which is good, but the first clause employs the active construction rather than the preferred passive, so there is a failure of parallelism. Also, it is unclear what *they* refers to. The sentence appears to say illogically that some unidentified group's action of recycling was similar to the ancient Greek materials' being reused.

E *Just as* introducing a clause with a passive verb is preferable, but this sentence uses *like* and a following noun phrase (*ancient Egyptian materials* ...). It appears, somewhat implausibly, to say that the ancient Greek materials were similar to the earlier ancient Egyptian ones in that both were used by Roman, Muslim, and modern builders.

The correct answer is C.

SC09877

846. Especially in the early years, new entrepreneurs may need to find resourceful ways, like renting temporary office space or using answering services, that make their company seem large and more firmly established than they may actually be.

(A) that make their company seem large

(B) to make their companies seem larger

(C) thus making their companies seem larger

(D) so that the companies seem larger

(E) of making their company seem large

Grammatical Construction; Diction

The clause beginning with *that* suggests that a company can be made to seem better than it actually is. The comparison signaled by *than* appears to be intended to apply to both the size of the company and the degree to which the company is firmly established. In that case, it is a mistake to use *large* instead of *larger*. If, on the other hand, *large* is not intended to be part of the comparison, it would be better to clarify this by separating the two topics in a construction such as *make their company seem large and also make it seem more firmly established. . . .* The phrase *resourceful ways* suggests purpose, so *ways* should connect with *to* or *of*, rather than a *that* clause to capture the intended meaning.

A   *Large* is the incorrect form to express comparison; it should be *larger*; the *that* clause does not adequately capture the idea of purpose implicit in *ways*. The singular *company* does not agree with the plural pronoun *they*. Thus, the sentence either commits an agreement mistake or illogically says that entrepreneurs need to find ways to make themselves seem large and more firmly established.

B   **Correct.** *Larger* is the correct form to express the comparative meaning, and *to* correctly follows *way*. *Companies* agrees with the plural *they*.

C   The phrase beginning *thus making* does not capture the idea of purpose implicit in *ways*.

D   Clauses beginning *so that* can express purpose, but do not fit with *ways* in the manner required here: *to* or *of* is needed after *ways*.

E   *Large* is the incorrect form to express comparison; it should be *larger*. The singular *company* does not agree with the plural pronoun *they*. Thus, the sentence either commits an agreement mistake or illogically says that entrepreneurs need to find ways to make themselves seem large and more firmly established.

The correct answer is B.

SC01975

847. Unlike <u>the nests of leaf cutters and most other ants,</u> situated underground or in pieces of wood, raider ants make a portable nest by entwining their long legs to form "curtains" of ants that hang from logs or boulders, providing protection for the queen and the colony larvae and pupae.

(A)   the nests of leaf cutters and most other ants,

(B)   the nests of leaf cutters and most other ants, which are

(C)   leaf cutters and most other ants, whose nests are

(D)   leaf cutters and most other ants in having nests

(E)   those of leaf cutters and most other ants with nests

Logical Predication

As worded, this sentence draws a contrast between raider ants and the nests of leaf cutters and most other ants. The appropriate contrast would be with leaf cutters and most other ants themselves, not their nests.

A   As indicated above, the appropriate contrast is between raider ants and other kinds of ants (namely leaf cutters and most ants). As worded, this version of the sentence says something obviously true: of course the nests of leaf cutters and most other ants do not make portable nests.

B   Like answer choice A, this sentence compares nests with raider ants. Additionally, the referent of the relative pronoun *which* is ambiguous, possibly modifying *ants*, and possibly modifying *nests*.

C   **Correct.** This version correctly draws the contrast between raider ants and other kinds of ants. Furthermore, unlike answer choices B and D, it is clear here that *situated underground or in pieces of wood* applies to the nests of leaf cutters and most other ants.

D   This sentence correctly compares leaf cutters and other ants with raider ants, but the prepositional phrase *in having nests* suggests that it is raider ants, not leaf cutters and most other ants, that have nests situated underground or in pieces of wood; however, the rest of the sentence indicates that in fact raider ants' nests are not situated in such locations.

E   The referent of *those* is unclear; presumably it refers to *nests*, but grammatically it has no clear antecedent. If it is taken to refer to nests, *those* creates an illogical comparison with *raider ants*.

The correct answer is C.

SC04452

848. Turtles, like other reptiles, can endure long <u>fasts, in their ability to survive</u> on weekly or even monthly feedings; however, when food is readily available, they may eat frequently and grow very fat.

(A)   fasts, in their ability to survive

(B)   fasts, having their ability to survive

(C)   fasts, due to having the ability of surviving

(D)   fasts because they are able to survive

(E)   fasts because of having the ability of surviving

Idiom; Diction

In the sentence as originally presented, the construction *can endure . . . in* does not correspond to any standard usage, and the intended meaning is unclear. Typically, one would expect *in* to introduce a situation in which the endurance is possible—for example, *in captivity* or *in the winter*. However, *their ability* is not such a situation, and the comma before *in* counts against such an interpretation. Given the comma after *fasts*, one might wonder whether *in their ability . . .* is intended as an explication or elaboration of the preceding clause. But in that case, *in their ability* is not a correct way to express it. A standard way to express that meaning would be *in that they are able . . .* or *being able. . . .* Alternatively, *in their ability . . .* might be intended to express why turtles can endure long fasts, but it is not recognizable as a standard way to say that. To make that meaning clear, it should say *because of their ability to survive . . .* or *because they are able to survive. . . .* Answer choice D uses the latter form in a way that makes it clear that it is offering a causal explanation. All the other answer choices contain phrases that have no standard recognizable meaning and may even seem ungrammatical to many readers.

A   As explained above, the construction *can endure . . . in* does not correspond to any standard usage, and the intended meaning is unclear. Depending on what meaning the sentence is supposed to convey, it could be made clearer by saying, for example, *can endure long fasts, in that they are able . . .* or *can endure long fasts because they are able. . . .*

B   If *their ability* were changed to *the ability* or *an ability*, this could serve as an elaboration of the claim that turtles can endure long fasts. However, *having their ability* is nonstandard for this meaning and appears to indicate illogically that turtles' having *their* ability, rather than something else's ability is an important factor. The point is that they are able to survive with infrequent feedings.

C   *Ability of* is incorrect; *ability* must be followed by *to* in order to express the intended meaning. *Due to* is sometimes used to introduce adverbial modifying phrases,

but it is more standardly used adjectively as in "the power failure was due to a severe storm." In light of that consideration and the comma before *due*, the phrase *due to having the ability* could appear illogically to modify *fasts*, making it equivalent to *fasts, which are due to. . . .* The word *having* is superfluous and potentially confusing.

D   **Correct.** This option uses *because* in a standard way to express a causal relation and uses *to* correctly after *ability*.

E   *Ability of* is incorrect; *ability* must be followed by *to* in order to express the intended meaning. The superfluous words in the phrase *because of having the ability* contribute nothing to the meaning and could be puzzling or jarring to readers.

The correct answer is D.

SC02025

849. Thai village crafts, as with other cultures, have developed through the principle that form follows function and incorporate readily available materials fashioned using traditional skills.

(A)   as with

(B)   as did those of

(C)   as they have in

(D)   like in

(E)   like those of

Logical Predication; Diction; Verb Form

The phrase *as with other cultures* is initially confusing given that no culture has been specifically mentioned; Thai village culture is indirectly referenced by the mention of *Thai village crafts*, so perhaps that is what is meant. But then, looking at the phrase in context, it becomes clear that the sentence is intended to indicate that the *crafts* of other cultures are similar in certain ways to Thai village crafts. Thus, the sentence should say *those of other cultures*. Furthermore, the use here of *as with* is questionable. To do the job it is supposed to do here (to indicate that the crafts of Thai villages are like the crafts of other cultures in a particular way), *as with* should be at the beginning of the sentence: *As with the crafts of other cultures, Thai village crafts have developed. . . .* Alternatively, *like* could be used here instead of *as with*.

A   The appropriate comparison is between Thai village crafts and those (i.e., crafts) of other cultures, not the other cultures themselves. Additionally, *like* would be more appropriate here than *as with*.

B   The verb form here is incorrect. [*D*]*id* is not parallel to *have* later in the sentence. The phrase *as have those of other cultures* would be parallel, but it is in the wrong position. To be correct, it would need to occur after the main verb is introduced: *Thai village crafts have developed, as have those of other cultures,* . . .

C   The use of the pronoun *they* is inaccurate; the reader is likely to take its antecedent to be *Thai village crafts*, not *crafts*. Furthermore, even if the pronoun here were not problematic, if the construction *as they have in other cultures* is used, it should occur after the main verb (*have developed*) is introduced.

D   The comparative term *like* compares two nouns or noun phrases, but in this version of the sentence, *like* compares a noun (*crafts*) with a prepositional phrase (*in other cultures*).

E   **Correct.** [*T*]*hose of other cultures* clearly refers to the crafts of other cultures; *like* is appropriate for making a comparison between two sorts of things (*crafts*).

The correct answer is E.

SC27250.02

850. With near to all tortilla chips made from corn kernels that have been heated in a solution of calcium hydroxide (lime), this removes the skin of the kernel so water can penetrate.

(A)   With near to all tortilla chips made from corn kernels that have been heated in a solution of calcium hydroxide (lime), this

(B)   Having nearly all tortilla chips made from corn kernels that are heated in a solution of calcium hydroxide (lime), this

(C)   Nearly all tortilla chips being made from corn kernels that are heated in a solution of calcium hydroxide (lime)

(D)   Nearly all tortilla chips are made from corn kernels that have been heated in a solution of calcium hydroxide (lime), a process that

(E)   Nearly all tortilla chips are made from corn kernels having been heated in a solution of calcium hydroxide (lime), a process that

Logical Predication; Diction

The phrase *near to all* is not proper usage; *nearly all*, *almost all*, or *most* would be correct. Furthermore, nothing in the sentence can clearly serve as the referent of the pronoun *this*.

A   As explained above, *near to all* is not proper usage and the referent of *this* is unclear.

B   The entire opening clause—*Having . . . (lime)*—illogically modifies *this*. The sentence literally indicates that two things are true of *this*: (1) it has nearly all tortilla chips made from corn kernels that have been heated in a solution of calcium hydroxide and (2) it removes the skin of the kernel. *This* has no plausible referent within the sentence, and no plausible referent of *this* in any hypothetical context could plausibly do both of the things that are predicated of it in this construction.

C   In this version, the subject of the verb *removes* is the entire phrase *Nearly all tortilla chips being made . . . (lime)*. This involves an illogical predication. The fact that tortilla chips are made from corn kernels heated in this way does not remove the skin; the process of their being heated in this way removes the skin.

D   **Correct.** This version straightforwardly expresses the idea, with no predication errors or linguistic usage problems.

E   This version can be interpreted as being equivalent to the version in answer choice D, but in this context, *that have been* is clearer and less vulnerable to misreading than *having been*. *Corn kernels having been heated . . .* could readily appear to be a noun phrase in which *having* is a gerund, so that answer choice E appears to say illogically that tortilla chips are simply the result of heating corn kernels in lime. Tortilla chips are made from corn kernels that have had their skins removed by heating them with lime, but they are not simply the direct result of that process.

The correct answer is D.

SC01554

851. To estimate the expansion rate of the universe is a notoriously difficult problem because there is a lack of a single yardstick that all distances can be measured by.

(A) To estimate the expansion rate of the universe is a notoriously difficult problem because there is a lack of a single yardstick that all distances can be measured by.

(B) Estimating the expansion rate of the universe is a notoriously difficult problem because there is no single yardstick by which all distances can be measured.

(C) Because there is a lack of a single yardstick to measure all distances by, estimating the expansion rate of the universe is a notoriously difficult problem.

(D) A notoriously difficult problem is to estimate the expansion rate of the universe because a single yardstick is lacking by which all distances can be measured.

(E) It is a notoriously difficult problem to estimate the expansion rate of the universe because by no single yardstick can all distances be measured.

Rhetorical Construction; Logical Predication

The sentence seeks to explain the difficulty of estimating the expansion rate of the universe and uses a *because*-clause to present the explanation. Issues in the given sentence include the following: is the infinitive verb form *to estimate* best here? And is there a more straightforward and more readable way to express the explanation?

A This version of the sentence begins with the infinitive verb *to estimate*, which sets up the expectation that the sentence will explain how to estimate something (consider a sentence like *To estimate the total cost of your grocery items, round each item to the nearest dollar amount and add*), yet the sentence then goes off in another direction; a preferable way to begin the sentence would be with the word *estimating* or the phrase *how to estimate*. The phrase *there is a lack of a single yardstick* could be more succinctly worded *there is no single yardstick*.

B **Correct.** Use of the verbal noun *estimating* is acceptable here. The phrase *there is no*

single yardstick is more concise than *there is a lack of a single yardstick*.

C The phrase *there is a lack of a single yardstick* could be more succinctly worded *there is no single yardstick*.

D Beginning the sentence with *A notoriously difficult problem is to . . .* suggests that the sentence is defining the term *a notoriously difficult problem* rather than stating that estimating the expansion rate of the universe is a notoriously difficult problem, which is what is intended. Additionally, the placement of the *because*-clause suggests that the clause modifies the verb *estimate*; in other words, it appears to give an explanation of why one is estimating the expansion rate, whereas the clause should be explaining why it is difficult to estimate the expansion rate.

E The phrase *to estimate* is less clear than *how to estimate* would be. The *because*-clause, which is meant to explain why estimating the expansion rate of the universe is difficult, is too widely separated from the reference to difficulty. In the *because*-clause, the inversion of the normal subject-verb order is nonstandard and serves no good rhetorical purpose.

The correct answer is B.

SC94340.02

852. Although the earliest inhabitants of Mapungubwe, building their dwellings of either wattle and daub or unfired mud brick, by the thirteenth century buildings of coral blocks in lime mortar began to appear.

(A) earliest inhabitants of Mapungubwe, building their dwellings

(B) earliest inhabitants of Mapungubwe, who built their dwellings

(C) earliest inhabitants of Mapungubwe built their dwellings

(D) dwellings of the earliest inhabitants of Mapungubwe, built

(E) dwellings of the earliest inhabitants of Mapungubwe, which were built

Diction; Grammatical Construction

The earliest inhabitants of Mapungubwe built their dwellings of either wattle and daub or unfired mud brick, but this began to change by the thirteenth century. One issue in the sentence concerns the verb form. Another issue concerns the overall structural integrity of the sentence.

A To make the sentence grammatically coherent, the word sequence *Although . . . brick* needs to be a complete clause, but it lacks a finite verb and thus does not make sense. The participle *building* is part of a parenthetical phrase that modifies *the earliest inhabitants of Mapungubwe*, which one would expect to be the subject of a clause.

B The word sequence *Although . . . brick* is not a complete clause; unlike the embedded relative clause *who built . . .* , it lacks a finite verb. The flaw in the *although* clause impairs the overall structural integrity of the sentence.

C **Correct.** The clause introduced by *Although* has *built* as its verb, with *the earliest . . . Mapungubwe* as its subject. The sentence as a whole has structural integrity.

D The word sequence *Although . . . brick* is not a complete clause; it lacks a finite verb that would have *the dwellings* as its subject. The past participle *built* is part of a parenthetical phrase that modifies *the dwellings*, which one would expect to be the subject of a clause. The flaw in the *although* clause impairs the overall structural integrity of the sentence.

E The word sequence *Although . . . brick* is not a complete clause; unlike the embedded relative clause *which were built . . .* , it lacks a finite verb. The flaw in the *although* clause impairs the overall structural integrity of the sentence.

The correct answer is C.

SC01059

853. The Commerce Department reported that the nation's economy grew at a brisk annual pace of 3.7 percent in the second quarter, but that while businesses were expanding their production, <u>unsold goods piled up on store shelves as consumer spending is slowed sharply.</u>

(A) unsold goods piled up on store shelves as consumer spending is slowed sharply

(B) unsold goods were piling up on store shelves as consumer spending slowed sharply

(C) unsold goods had piled up on store shelves with a sharp slowing of consumer spending

(D) consumer spending was slowing sharply, with the piling up of unsold goods on store shelves

(E) consumer spending has slowed sharply, with unsold goods piling up on store shelves

Verb Form; Rhetorical Construction

The sentence summarizes a government report about four business and economic processes occurring over a single quarter: economic growth, increasing production, unsold goods accumulating in retail stores, and a sharp slowing in consumer spending. A problem in the verb *is slowed* is use of the passive form, which in this context is awkward and unidiomatic. It is also present tense, whereas *piled up* is simple-past tense—a breach of proper tense sequence.

A This fails because of the inappropriate and in context unidiomatic use of the passive voice. Additionally, *piled up* does not clearly indicate a process.

B **Correct.** The verb *were piling up* correctly indicates a process as opposed to a single event; with the *as*-clause, the verb *slowed* indicates a process simultaneous with another process (and, implicitly, contributing to it).

C The verb *had piled up* suggests an event that occurred before businesses were expanding their production, even though the *while*-clause indicates that the piling-up occurred simultaneously with that expansion.

D The import of the *with*-phrase is insufficiently clear. It could be read as indicating that the piling-up was also slowing. But this reading fails to capture the idea of a causal relationship implicitly conveyed in the given sentence.

E The verb *has slowed* suggests a process that occurred in the recent past and impinges on the present (not necessarily in "the second quarter"). The verb tense does not match the verb tense *were expanding* in the *while*-clause, and does not convey simultaneity with the expansion referred to.

The correct answer is B.

SC01470

854. Thomas Mann's novel *Doctor Faustus* offers <u>an examination not only of how difficult it is to reconcile reason, will, and passion together in any art form, but</u> also a skillfully navigated exploration of the major concerns of modernism.

(A) an examination not only of how difficult it is to reconcile reason, will, and passion together in any art form, but

(B) an examination not only about the difficulty of reconciling reason, will, and passion in any art form, and

(C) not only an examination of how difficult it is to reconcile reason, will, and passion in any art form, and

(D) not only an examination about the difficulty with reconciling reason, will, and passion together in any art form, but

(E) not only an examination of the difficulty of reconciling reason, will, and passion in any art form, but

Grammatical Construction; Idiom

The sentence, in its most correct form, would use the structure *not only . . . but also . . .* to coordinate parallel references to an "examination" and to an "exploration." However, the given sentence errs in placing the phrase *not only* after the first of the items meant to be coordinated. This impairs the required parallelism and the grammatical structure of the sentence as a whole—as if the "examination" referred to was not only an examination of the difficulty of a certain reconciliation but was also an examination of a skillfully navigated exploration. This does not seem to be the intended meaning, and if it were, the latter *of*, not included, would be required.

A In addition to the structural problem explained above, the word *together* is superfluous because its meaning is already included in *reconcile*.

B The word *examination* should be followed in this context by the preposition *of* rather than by *about*. The coordinate conjunction *and* is unidiomatic, given the earlier occurrence of *not only*.

C The coordinate conjunction *and* is unidiomatic in this context, given the earlier occurrence of *not only*.

D The prepositions *about* and *with* are unidiomatic here (as opposed to *of* in both cases). As explained above, *together* is superfluous with *reconcile*.

E **Correct.** The coordination of the parallel reference to an examination and an exploration is successfully executed here using the structure *not only . . . but also*.

The correct answer is E.

SC03260.02

855. <u>Upon their first encountering leaf-cutting ants in South America, the insects seemed to some Europeans to be</u> carrying bits of greenery to shade themselves from the tropical sun—hence the sobriquet "parasol ants."

(A) Upon their first encountering leaf-cutting ants in South America, the insects seemed to some Europeans to be

(B) Upon their first encountering leaf-cutting ants in South America, some Europeans thought they were

(C) On first encountering leaf-cutting ants in South America, it seemed to some Europeans that the insects were

(D) On first encountering leaf-cutting ants in South America, some Europeans thought the insects were

(E) On their first encounter with leaf-cutting ants in South America, some Europeans thought it was because the insects were

Logical Predication; Rhetorical Construction

The referent of *their* in the opening clause is clearly intended to be *some Europeans*, but because *the insects* immediately follows the opening clause, *the insects* appears to be the referent of *their*. Additionally, *Upon their first encountering* is unnecessarily wordy.

A As explained above, *insects* rather than *some Europeans* appears to be the referent of *their*. Also, *Upon their first encountering* is unnecessarily wordy.

B *Upon their first encountering* is unnecessarily wordy. The referent of *they* should be *leaf-cutting ants*, but because of the prior use of *their* to refer to *some Europeans*, the expectation is created that the referent of *they* would also be *some Europeans*.

C   This version is wordy and awkward, and the opening clause appears illogically to modify *it*.

D   **Correct.** This version has no pronouns with unclear referents and is clearly and concisely expressed.

E   The referent of *it* is unclear. The only grammatically possible referent of *it* would be *their first encounter*, but this makes no logical sense.

The correct answer is D.

SC91660.02

856. By skimming along the top of the atmosphere, a proposed new style of aircraft could fly between most points on Earth in under two hours, according to its proponents.

(A) By skimming along the top of the atmosphere, a proposed new style of aircraft could fly between most points on Earth in under two hours, according to its proponents.

(B) By skimming along the top of the atmosphere, proponents of a proposed new style of aircraft say it could fly between most points on Earth in under two hours.

(C) A proposed new style of aircraft could fly between most points on Earth in under two hours, according to its proponents, with it skimming along the top of the atmosphere.

(D) A proposed new style of aircraft, say its proponents, could fly between most points on Earth in under two hours because of its skimming along the top of the atmosphere.

(E) According to its proponents, skimming along the top of the atmosphere makes it possible that a proposed new style of aircraft could fly between most points on Earth in under two hours.

Rhetorical Construction; Logical Predication

Because it is placed immediately before the subject *a proposed new style of aircraft*, the modifier *By skimming along the top of the atmosphere* can clearly be seen to be describing, as intended, the means by which *a proposed new style of aircraft* is able to *fly between most points on Earth in under two hours*.

A   **Correct.** As explained above, by placing the adverbial phrase *By skimming along the top of the atmosphere* immediately before *a proposed new style of aircraft*, this version of the sentence clearly conveys its intended meaning.

B   In this version, because of its placement immediately before the subject *proponents*, the adverbial phrase *By skimming along the top of the atmosphere* absurdly describes the means by which the proponents *say* what they do about the proposed aircraft. If a second comma were added after *say*, making *proponents . . . say* parenthetical, the opening phrase would modify *it could fly . . .* as it is presumably intended to do.

C   In this version, the relationship of the phrase *skimming along the top of the atmosphere* to the rest of the sentence is unclear, and the wording is potentially misleading. *With it skimming* seems to refer to an additional, possibly unconnected, thing the aircraft would do.

D   *Because of its skimming* is awkward and unidiomatic.

E   In this version, the antecedent of *its* appears to be *skimming along the top of the atmosphere*, not *a proposed new style of aircraft* as it should be.

The correct answer is A.

SC00981

857. According to a recent study, retirees in the United States are four times more likely to give regular financial aid to their children as to receive it from them.

(A) retirees in the United States are four times more likely to give regular financial aid to their children as

(B) retirees in the United States are four times as likely to give regular financial aid to their children as it is for them

(C) retirees in the United States are four times more likely to give regular financial aid to their children than

(D) it is four times more likely for retirees in the United States to give regular financial aid to their children than they are

(E) it is four times as likely that retirees in the United States will give their children regular financial aid as they are

Diction; Parallelism

The sentence notes a difference, for retirees in the United States, between the likelihood that they will give regular financial aid to their children and the likelihood that they will receive regular financial aid from their children. The elements of the comparison need to be expressed in parallel and in a proper construction.

A   This sentence improperly implements the construction *four times more likely to X than to Y*, with *X* corresponding to *give regular financial aid to their children* and *Y* corresponding to *receive it from them*. Instead of the word *than* that would be used in this construction, the sentence improperly uses *as*.

B   This sentence, like answer choice A, improperly uses *as*. It also lacks parallelism, because *to give regular financial aid to their children* is not parallel to *it is for them to receive it from them*.

C   **Correct.** This sentence resolves both of the issues discussed in connection with answer choices A and B. In addition to properly using *than* in the construction *four times more likely to X than to Y*, the sentence properly lists in parallel the two elements being compared—*to give regular financial aid to their children* and *to receive it from them*.

D   This sentence is wordy and lacks parallelism. The phrase *to give regular financial aid to their children* is not parallel to *they are to receive it from them*. The words *they are* in the second phrase are superfluous and make the sentence more difficult to read than necessary, and can simply be removed.

E   This sentence is hard to parse and lacks parallelism. It is difficult to see what two phrases represent the elements to be compared and thus what needs to be parallel with what.

The correct answer is C.

SC04093

858. <u>Discussion of greenhouse effects have usually had as a focus the possibility of Earth growing warmer and to what extent it might,</u> but climatologists have indicated all along that precipitation, storminess, and temperature extremes are likely to have the greatest impact on people.

(A)   Discussion of greenhouse effects have usually had as a focus the possibility of Earth growing warmer and to what extent it might,

(B)   Discussion of greenhouse effects has usually had as its focus whether Earth would get warmer and what the extent would be,

(C)   Discussion of greenhouse effects has usually focused on whether Earth would grow warmer and to what extent,

(D)   The discussion of greenhouse effects have usually focused on the possibility of Earth getting warmer and to what extent it might,

(E)   The discussion of greenhouse effects has usually focused on whether Earth would grow warmer and the extent that is,

Agreement; Parallelism

The sentence contrasts climatologists' views concerning greenhouse effects with other views that emphasize global warming. The main subject of the sentence is *discussion . . .*, which is singular, so the main verb should be singular. The two things that are said to be the focus of discussion should be in parallel form.

A   The plural verb *have . . . had* does not agree with the singular subject *discussion*. The phrases *the possibility . . . warmer* and *to what . . . might* are not parallel.

B   The verb form *has had as its focus* is unnecessarily wordy; the noun clauses are parallel in form, but it is not clear what *the extent* refers to.

C   **Correct.** This has correct subject-verb agreement, eliminates the wordiness of the original sentence, and the phrases *whether . . . warmer* and *to what extent* are parallel.

D   The singular subject *discussion* does not agree with the plural verb *have focused*. The possibility *of . . .* is not parallel with *to what extent. . . .*

E   The two phrases following *on* are not in parallel form. What *that* refers to in *the extent that is* is unclear.

The correct answer is C.

SC02102

859. In the seventh century B.C., the Roman alphabet was adapted from the Etruscan alphabet, which in turn had been adapted in the previous century from a western Greek alphabet, <u>which itself had been adapted earlier</u> in the same century from the Phoenician alphabet.

(A)   which itself had been adapted earlier

(B)   adapting itself earlier

(C)   itself being adapted earlier

(D)   having been earlier adapted itself

(E)   earlier itself having been adapted

Rhetorical Construction; Verb Form; Logical Predication

This sentence describes a string of adaptations of the alphabet, tracing back from the seventh century BC through two points in the eighth century BC. Because the latest of the three adaptations is temporally located in past tense, earlier adaptations should be located in the past perfect tense.

A **Correct.** This sentence is properly constructed and uses the appropriate verb forms for the relationships among the events that it describes.

B It is unclear what the participial phrase *adapting itself earlier . . .* refers to. The present participle could be used for an event that was simultaneous with, or part of, the event mentioned before the underlined portion. However, it is inappropriate for describing an event that took place even earlier than the seventh century BC, which has already been designated in the sentence as past tense. The reflexive form *adapting itself* is nonsensical in this sentence.

C The present tense of the reflexive participial phrase is inappropriate for describing an event prior to the seventh century BC, given that the seventh century BC has already been designated in the sentence as past tense.

D Without commas around *itself*, the pronoun appears to be reflexive. The combination of passive and reflexive then makes no sense. If *itself* is intended simply for emphasis, rather than as a reflexive pronoun, it would be preferable, in this context, to set it off with commas. But if it were intended in that way, it would seem to refer to the Roman alphabet, and the claim made in the sentence would be confusing and nearly nonsensical. This modifier is confusingly placed before the designation of time (*in the same century*) and source (*from the Phoenician alphabet*).

E The adverb *earlier* is misplaced before the pronoun *itself*; it should be immediately before the phrase *in the same century*.

The correct answer is A.

SC09185

860. The foundation works to strengthen local and regional agricultural markets and <u>cooperating with governments, improving access for farmers for</u> productive resources such as land and credit.

(A) cooperating with governments, improving access for farmers for

(B) cooperates with governments to improve access for farmers to

(C) cooperate with governments for improvements of access for farmers to

(D) cooperate with governments and improve accessibility for farmers for their

(E) in cooperation with governments to improve access for farmers for

Parallelism; Rhetorical Construction

As written, this sentence does not clearly indicate whether *and* is intended to conjoin two things that the foundation does (working to strengthen markets and cooperating with governments) or two things that the foundation works to accomplish (strengthening markets and cooperating with governments). The latter is less plausible because of the redundancy of *works to cooperate*. In the former, the proper verb form, parallel with the present-tense *works*, would be *cooperates*. In the latter, the proper verb form, parallel with the infinitive *to strengthen*, would be *to cooperate* or simply *cooperate*. Only one of the answer choices resolves the uncertainty of meaning in a coherent and well-formed way.

A *Cooperating* is incorrect, since it is not in the same form as either *works* or *to strengthen*.

B **Correct.** This version correctly represents the foundation's two actions by putting the verbs *works* and *cooperates* in parallel form. *Cooperates . . . to improve* is the most concise phrasing to express the purpose of improving access.

C *Cooperate . . . for improvements of access for farmers* is awkwardly phrased and unnecessarily wordy.

D *Cooperate . . . and improve accessibility for farmers* is awkwardly phrased and unnecessarily wordy.

E *In cooperation* destroys the parallelism required by *works to*: there should be a verb following *works to*, not this prepositional phrase.

The correct answer is B.

SC07338

861. A professor at the university has taken a sabbatical to research <u>on James Baldwin's books that Baldwin wrote in France while he was living there.</u>

(A) on James Baldwin's books that Baldwin wrote in France while he was living there

(B) about the books James Baldwin wrote in France

(C) into James Baldwin's books written while in France

(D) on the books of James Baldwin, written while he lived in France

(E) the books James Baldwin wrote while he lived in France

Diction; Rhetorical Construction

The phrasing of this sentence is wordy and redundant: *books that Baldwin wrote in France while he was living there* could more concisely be expressed with *books James Baldwin wrote while he lived in France.* The verb *research* requires a direct object, not a preposition followed by its object.

A *On* incorrectly follows *to research,* and *books that Baldwin wrote in France while he was living there* includes redundant information.

B *About* incorrectly follows *to research.*

C *Into* incorrectly follows *to research.* Given this sentence structure, *while in France* seems to say, illogically, that the books were written while they were in France.

D *On* incorrectly follows *to research*; also, there is no need to make *written while he lived in France* into an independent phrase instead of a relative clause.

E **Correct.** *Research* takes a direct object, which describes the books directly without redundancy.

The correct answer is E.

SC12710.01

862. <u>When working with overseas clients, an understanding of cultural norms is at least as important as grasping the pivotal business issues for the global manager.</u>

(A) When working with overseas clients, an understanding of cultural norms is at least as important as grasping the pivotal business issues for the global manager.

(B) When they work with overseas clients, understanding cultural norms is at least of equivalent importance to grasping the pivotal business issues for the global manager.

(C) For global managers working with overseas clients, understanding cultural norms is at least as important as grasping the pivotal business issues.

(D) For global managers working with overseas clients, an understanding of cultural norms is at least as important to them as grasping the pivotal business issues.

(E) Global managers working with overseas clients find an understanding of cultural norms to be equally important to grasping the pivotal business issues.

Idiom; Rhetorical Construction; Logical Predication

The sentence compares the relative importance of two kinds of understanding that are important for global managers working with overseas clients: understanding of cultural norms and grasping the pivotal business issues. The sentence and its variants seem intended to assert that the first is at least as important as the second. The idiomatic usage *as important as* is the most effective way to make the comparison, but some of the variants do not make it in this way. In the given sentence, the initial phrase *when . . . clients,* by virtue of its position, should modify the main subject of the sentence, *an understanding of cultural norms,* but that reading is untenable and results in a logical-predication error. The adverbial modifier *for the global manager* is not well placed to make clear that it modifies the adjective *important.*

A This version fails for the reasons explained above: misleading placement of the initial phrase, and misleading placement of an adverbial modifier.

B The pronoun *they* should refer forward to a plural noun or pronoun but does not do so here. To make a comparison, the awkward phrase *of equivalent importance to* is used instead of the more idiomatic *as important as.* The modifying phrase *for the global manager* fails to show clearly what it is intended to modify.

C **Correct.** The initial adverbial phrase *for global . . . clients* signals clearly that it modifies the adjective *important.* The comparison is made clearly and idiomatically.

D The phrase *to them* is redundant with *for global managers.* The phrase *an understanding of cultural norms* is not parallel with the verbal-noun construction *grasping the pivotal business issues.*

E   The wording used to express the comparison is awkward and unidiomatic. The phrase *an understanding of cultural norms* is not parallel with the verbal-noun construction *grasping the pivotal business issues.* Also, preferable to *equally important to* would be *as important as.*

The correct answer is C.

SC87460.01

863.   Often major economic shifts are <u>so gradual as to be indistinguishable</u> at first from ordinary fluctuations in the financial markets.

(A)   so gradual as to be indistinguishable

(B)   so gradual they can be indistinguishable

(C)   so gradual that they are unable to be distinguished

(D)   gradual enough not to be distinguishable

(E)   gradual enough so that one cannot distinguish them

Idiom; Rhetorical Construction

The idiom *so . . . as to . . .* is correctly used as a predicate of the subject in the given sentence. None of the variants offered uses the idiom correctly, and some of them have rhetorical issues such as redundancy or awkwardness.

A   Correct. The underlined portion is an example of correct use of the idiom mentioned above, and contains no other errors.

B   The word *can* is redundant here, given the ending *-able* of *indistinguishable.* The intended sense could be conveyed by *so gradual that they are indistinguishable*—even though this would not be a use of the idiom mentioned above.

C   This contains awkward verbiage in the phrase *are unable to.* The intended sense would be better conveyed by *cannot*—even though this would not be a use of the idiom mentioned above.

D   This is unnecessarily awkward, and the use of *enough* often carries the nuance that the sufficiency is of something desirable—which seems not to be so in this context. The idiomatic use above would be better.

E   This is wordy and unnecessarily awkward. As explained, the use of *enough* is inappropriate in the context, and use of the idiom explained above would be much better.

The correct answer is A.

SC19060.02

864.   <u>Dinosaur tracks show them walking with their feet directly under their bodies, like</u> mammals and birds, not extended out to the side in the manner of modern reptiles.

(A)   Dinosaur tracks show them walking with their feet directly under their bodies, like

(B)   Dinosaur tracks show that they walked with their feet directly under their bodies, as do

(C)   Dinosaurs left tracks that showed them walking with their feet directly under their bodies, like

(D)   The tracks that dinosaurs left show that they walked with their feet directly under their bodies, as do

(E)   In the tracks they left, dinosaurs are shown walking with their feet under their bodies, like

Logical Predication; Diction

The only grammatically possible antecedent of *them* and *their* in this sentence is *dinosaur tracks,* but that does not make sense in the context of the sentence; dinosaur tracks do not have feet or bodies. Clearly *them* and *their* should have the plural noun *dinosaurs* as their antecedent, but because that word does not occur in the context, it cannot properly serve as their antecedent. *Dinosaur* occurs only as an adjective in the noun phrase *dinosaur tracks.*

A   As explained above, the only grammatically possible antecedent for *them* and *their* in this version is *dinosaur tracks,* which renders the sentence nonsensical.

B   Clearly the intended referent of the pronouns *they* and *their* is *dinosaurs,* but that word does not occur in the context, as it should if it is to serve as the antecedent of these pronouns.

C   *Dinosaurs left tracks that showed them walking with their feet directly under their bodies* is poorly constructed. What is most likely intended is that the tracks showed *that* dinosaurs walked with their feet directly under their bodies—that is, the tracks provide evidence that dinosaurs walked in this manner. The tracks do not actually show the dinosaurs walking.

D **Correct.** The antecedent of the pronouns *them* and *their* in this version of the sentence is clearly *dinosaurs*; this version clearly and accurately conveys a coherent meaning.

E *In the tracks they left, dinosaurs are shown walking . . .* is poorly constructed. The tracks show *that* dinosaurs walked with their feet directly under their bodies—that is, the tracks provide evidence that dinosaurs walked in this manner. The tracks do not actually depict the dinosaurs walking.

The correct answer is D.

SC22260.02

865. Although when a hagfish is threatened, it will secrete slime that is small in quantity, it expands several hundred times as it absorbs seawater, forming a slime ball that can coat the gills of predatory fish and either suffocate them or distress them enough to make them flee.

(A) Although when a hagfish is threatened, it will secrete slime that is small in quantity,

(B) Although a small quantity of slime is secreted by the hagfish, when threatened

(C) Although, when threatened, a hagfish will secrete slime that is small in quantity,

(D) Although the slime secreted by a threatened hagfish is small in quantity,

(E) Although the hagfish secretes a small quantity of slime when threatened,

Logical Predication

To determine which version of this sentence is best, it is important to determine what is the antecedent of *it* in *it expands several hundred times*. That is, what expands several hundred times? Upon analysis, clearly what expands is the slime secreted by the hagfish. In this version of the sentence, the prior use of *it* in *it will secrete slime that is small in quantity* has as its antecedent *hagfish*. This initial use of *it* in the sentence creates a flawed expectation that the second *it* will have the same antecedent, leading to an inaccurate reading in which the hagfish and not the slime is said to expand several hundred times.

A As explained above, the fact that the two instances of *it* have different antecedents creates confusion.

B Because *when threatened* modifies *hagfish*, the *hagfish* appears to be the antecedent of *it*. But what expands several hundred times is not the hagfish, but the slime.

C In this version, too, the antecedent of *it* appears to be *hagfish*, not *slime*.

D **Correct.** In this version, *slime* is clearly and appropriately the antecedent of *it* and the tenses of the verbs do not conflict.

E The antecedent of *it* appears to be *hagfish*, not *slime*.

The correct answer is D.

SC69440.02

866. Officials at the United States Mint believe that the Sacagawea dollar coin will be used more as a substitute for four quarters rather than for the dollar bill because of its weight, only 8.1 grams, which is far less than four quarters, which weigh 5.67 grams each.

(A) more as a substitute for four quarters rather than for the dollar bill because of its weight, only 8.1 grams, which is far less than

(B) more as a substitute for four quarters than the dollar bill because it weighs only 8.1 grams, far lighter than

(C) as a substitute for four quarters more than for the dollar bill because it weighs only 8.1 grams, far less than

(D) as a substitute for four quarters more than the dollar bill because its weight of only 8.1 grams is far lighter than it is for

(E) as a substitute more for four quarters rather than for the dollar bill because its weight, only 8.1 grams, is far less than it is for

Logical Predication; Diction

The sentence ascribes to officials of the United States Mint a belief about the Sacagawea dollar coin: based on the relative weights of the dollar coin and the four twenty-five-cent coins (quarters), the officials believe, the dollar coin will be used as a substitute for four quarters more frequently than for the equivalently valued paper dollar. In other words, they believe that the frequency of one type of use will be greater than that of another type of use. In expressing this comparison, the sentence errs by failing to use two parallel expressions for the two things being compared. It also errs in using *more . . . rather than*, where the correct phrasing requires simply *more than*. The sentence contains a second comparison using *less than*. The only possible referent of *which* is the coin's weight, so the sentence also errs by comparing *its weight* with *four quarters*.

A   As explained above, this answer choice contains an error in each of two comparisons. In the first comparison, the form *X rather than Y* has an exclusionary effect; *X rather than Y* means *X but not Y*. But using this sense here is not acceptable when combined with the comparison using *more*; such a comparison must use *than* (not *rather than*) to introduce the second element of the comparison. There is also an error in the second comparison: whether we read *which* as referring to *its weight* as an abstract concept or to the specific quantity *8.1 grams*, it is erroneous to directly compare a weight with *four quarters*.

B   The structure of the phrasing *will be used more . . . dollar bill* makes this appear to mean that the Sacagawea dollar coin *will be used more as a substitute for four quarters than the dollar bill* [*will be so used*]. However, this meaning is not coherent with the rest of the sentence, which (however flawed) seems meant to convey the idea that the Sacagawea dollar coin is lighter than four quarters. Describing a quantity of weight as being *lighter* is erroneous; such a description illogically presupposes that a quantity of weight has itself a weight. An alternative parsing could take *far lighter* as a modifier of *weighs*, but to say that one thing weighs lighter than another is unidiomatic.

C   **Correct.** This version creates a sentence that correctly compares two items: frequency of use as a substitute for four quarters and frequency of use as a substitute for the dollar bill. It also correctly uses the wording *far less than* to compare how much one thing (the Sacagawea dollar coin) weighs with how much another thing (four quarters combined) weighs. The pronoun *it* refers to

the *Sacagawea dollar coin*, the subject of the *that* clause introduced by *believe*.

D   The wording *four quarters more than the dollar bill* is most easily read as a noun phrase referring to a sum of money worth two dollars, but this reading, implying that the Sacagawea dollar coin would be accepted in exchange for the sum of two dollars, is incoherent. Another error here is to predicate the adjective *lighter* of a weight; quantities of weight do not themselves have weight. The wording *lighter than it is for four quarters* has no clear meaning, in part because what *it* refers to and the meaning of the preposition *for* are unclear in this context.

E   As explained above, *rather than* is not the appropriate usage for a comparison of the kind in question here: a comparison of a (predicted) frequency of one kind of use with a frequency of another kind of use. The phrasing *far less than it is for four quarters* has no clear meaning, in part because what the pronoun *it* refers to and the meaning of the preposition *for* are unclear in this context.

The correct answer is C.

SC14740.02

867. In the United States, <u>less than half as many multifamily housing units were produced in the 1990s than</u> in each of the previous two decades.

(A)   less than half as many multifamily housing units were produced in the 1990s than

(B)   less than half as many multifamily housing units had been produced in the 1990s as

(C)   there were less than half as many multifamily housing units produced in the 1990s than

(D)   fewer than half as many multifamily housing units were produced in the 1990s as

(E)   fewer than half as many multifamily housing units had been produced in the 1990s than

Diction; Idiom

The sentence compares the number of multifamily units constructed in the 1990s with the numbers constructed in each of the previous two decades. Notice the uses of *less than*, *fewer than*, and *as many as*. In formal contexts, the adjective *less*—the comparative form of *little*—is normally used only with singular non-count nouns (for example, *less cheese*), while the adjective *fewer*—the comparative form of *few*—is normally used only with plural count nouns (for example, *fewer people*). *Many*, like *few*, as an adjective, applies to count nouns.

A   The noun *units* is a count noun, and the connotation of plurality carries over to *half as many*; so the use of *less* rather than *fewer* is incorrect. The form *as many . . . in . . . than in . . .* is incorrect (it should be *as many . . . in . . . as in. . .*).

B   The noun *units* is a count noun, and the connotation of plurality carries over to *half as many;* so the use of *less* rather than *fewer* is incorrect. The past-perfect verb form *had been produced* is unlikely to be what the author intended; it should be used only to refer to a past that is before another past referred to or implied in the context. The sentence does not establish any past time from which the 1990s were viewed as an even earlier past time; it appears to be intended to refer to the 1990s from the viewpoint of the present.

C   The noun *units* is a count noun, and the connotation of plurality carries over to *half as many;* so the use of *less* rather than *fewer* is incorrect. The form *as many . . . in . . . than in . . .* is incorrect with the use of *than* (it should be *as*).

D   **Correct.** As explained, the comparative form *fewer* of the adjective *few* is appropriate to use with the count noun *units*. The form *as many . . . in . . . than in . . .* is incorrect (it should be *as many . . . in . . . as i . . .*).

E   The form *as many . . . in . . . than in . . .* is incorrect (it should be *as many . . . in . . . as in . . .*). The past-perfect verb form *had been produced* is unlikely to be what the author intended; it should be used only to refer to a past that is before another past referred to in the context. The sentence does not establish any past time from which the 1990s were viewed as an even earlier past time; it appears to be intended to refer to the 1990s from the viewpoint of the present.

The correct answer is D.

SC40050.02

868. Educator Maria Montessori believed <u>that students be allowed to choose from among a number of different lessons designed for the encouragement of</u> their development as thinkers and creators with individual learning and thinking styles.

(A)   that students be allowed to choose from among a number of different lessons designed for the encouragement of

(B)   that students be allowed to choose between a number of different lessons designed to encourage

(C)   that students should be allowed to choose among a number of different lessons designed to encourage

(D)   in allowing students to choose from among a number of different lessons were designed for encouraging

(E)   in allowing students to choose between a number of different lessons designed for the encouragement of

Diction; Grammatical Construction

The sentence is most likely meant to report a belief of Maria Montessori: that students should be allowed to choose among lessons that are designed to encourage their development. The phrase *believed that students be allowed* is ungrammatical and incoherent. The subjunctive form *that students be allowed* does not make sense with *believed* as it would with a preceding verb such as *ordered* or *required*. The *that* clause is presumably meant to report a belief about what *should occur*; an auxiliary verb such as *should, ought,* or *must* is needed (for example, she believed that they *should be allowed*). The wording *designed for the encouragement of their development* is unnecessarily wordy and indirect; the verb form *to encourage* is preferable to the noun *encouragement*.

A   This answer choice has flaws mentioned above.

B   As explained above, the verb form *be allowed* is incorrect in a report of the content of a belief. The preposition *between* is incorrect in this context because the students would choose from a group of more than two alternatives; presumably they do not choose each lesson by comparing it to a single other lesson within the group of available lessons.

Either *from* or *among* would be idiomatically correct.

C **Correct.** This answer choice has the improvements explained above.

D The word sequence *to choose from among a number of different lessons were designed* is ungrammatical and makes no sense. It could be made coherent by, for example, deleting *were* or changing *were* to *that were*.

E The preposition *between* is incorrect in this context because the students would choose from a group of more than two alternatives; presumably they do not choose each lesson by comparing it to a single other lesson within the group of available lessons. Either *from* or *among* would be idiomatically correct. The wording *designed for the encouragement of their development* is unnecessarily wordy and indirect; the verb form *to encourage* is preferable to the use of the noun *encouragement*.

The correct answer is C.

SC03050.02

869. Analysts and media executives predict <u>the coming year to be no less challenging than the previous one had been</u> for the company's C.E.O.

(A) the coming year to be no less challenging than the previous one had been

(B) the coming year to be no less challenging compared to the previous one

(C) that the coming year would be no less challenging compared to the previous one

(D) that the coming year will be no less challenging than the previous one had been

(E) that the coming year will be no less challenging than the previous one

Verb Form; Idiom

Predict the coming year to be is not idiomatically standard; the more standard way to express the idea would be *predict that the coming year will be* or *predict the coming year will be*. The verb form *had been* makes the time sequence unclear and is at least superficially inconsistent with the present tense *predict*. *Had been* is in the past perfect tense, which is used to indicate that an occurrence that started at some point in the past continued up to another point in the past. The simple past tense

was would be more clearly coherent with the most plausible intended meaning of the sentence.

A As explained above, *predict the coming year to be* is not idiomatically standard. Also, the verb form *had been* is incorrect.

B *Predict the coming year to be* is not idiomatically standard. Also, *compared to* is unidiomatic in this context; *than* would be clearer and more standard.

C *Would be* indicates either that the prediction was made in the past or that it is dependent on some hypothetical condition. Since there is no *if* clause, this verb form does not make sense in relation to the present tense *predict*. The analysts and media executives are making a prediction about something that is yet to occur; the more appropriate tense to use here is the future tense *will be*.

D The past perfect tense *had been* is incorrect.

E **Correct.** This version is idiomatically correct and properly uses the future tense *will be*.

The correct answer is E.

Questions 870 to 928 - Difficulty: **Medium**

SC80540.02

870. Scientists say that, by bathing the skin cells in extracts of immune cells, <u>that human skin cells in a test tube are made to behave as if they were</u> immune system cells.

(A) that human skin cells in a test tube are made to behave as if they were

(B) that human skin cells were to behave in a test tube as if they were

(C) human skin cells in a test tube were made to behave as if

(D) they have made human skin cells in a test tube that were behaving as

(E) they have made human skin cells in a test tube behave as if they were

Verb Form; Rhetorical Construction

The sentence, though flawed, seems to attribute to scientists a report that they have made skin cells in a test tube behave as if they were immune cells. Note the confusing and unhelpful repetition of *that*. Also note that given the overall sentence structure, the agency implicit in the phrase *by bathing* appears to be attributed to the *human skin cells*, but that reading yields a nonsensical sentence. This flaw is in part facilitated by unnecessary use of the passive-voice form *are made to behave*. The idiomatic *as if* introduces a clause that can correctly convey the second element of a comparison to indicate a similarity between skin-cell behavior and immune-cell behavior.

A   This version produces a sentence with flaws explained above.

B   The confusing and pointless repetition of *that* occurs with this version as well as in the one above. No clear meaning can be attached to the verb form *were to behave* in this context. (For contexts in which such a verb form would be acceptable, consider the following examples: *The children's parents said that the children were to behave as if they were adults. The parents indicated that they were to be away for the weekend.*)

C   Using the passive-voice form *were made to behave* is unnecessary and awkward. One effect of its use is to make *human skin cells* into the implicit subject of *bathing*. The conjunction *as if* needs completion with *they were* in order to convey the second element of a comparison indicating a similarity between skin-cell behavior and immune-cell behavior.

D   This version makes the relationship between *the skin cells* and *human skin cells* unclear. The sentence appears literally to indicate that the scientists bathed some unspecified cells in extracts and that by doing so they created some new human skin cells, which they observed behaving in a certain way. This is a somewhat implausible claim. Furthermore, it is odd to say that the human skin cells in a test tube behaved *as immune system cells*; if the cells completely assumed the role of immune system cells, a clearer and more standard way to express this would be to say that they *functioned as immune system cells*. The more plausible intended meaning is that the skin cells behaved as if they were immune system cells.

E   **Correct.** This version creates a sentence where *they*, referring to *scientists,* is clearly the subject of both *bathing* and *have made*. The verb *made . . .* is used in an idiomatically

correct way indicating that the scientists caused the cells to do something, rather than that the scientists created cells that did something. The idiomatic *as if* introduces a clause conveying the second element of a comparison indicating similarity of skin-cell behavior to immune-cell behavior.

The correct answer is E.

SC01506

871.   Researchers now regard interferon <u>as not a single substance, but it is rather a biological family of complex molecules that play</u> an important, though not entirely defined, role in the immune system.

(A)   as not a single substance, but it is rather a biological family of complex molecules that play

(B)   as not a single substance but as a biological family of complex molecules playing

(C)   not as a single substance but as a biological family of complex molecules that play

(D)   not to be a single substance but rather a biological family of complex molecules playing

(E)   not as a single substance but instead as being a biological family of complex molecules that play

Parallelism; Rhetorical Construction

This sentence draws a contrast between how interferon is and is not regarded by researchers. However, the two parts of the contrast are not expressed in parallel form since the first is a prepositional phrase (*as not a single substance*), and the second is a clause (*it is rather a biological family*). Furthermore, the wording *regard interferon as not* is awkward and confusing. For clarity and proper parallelism, the contrast should be constructed using the expression *not as X but as Y,* where *X* and *Y* are both noun phrases.

A   The contrast is not expressed using parallel grammatical structure, and *regard interferon as not* is awkward and confusing.

B   The wording *regard interferon as not* is awkward and confusing and violates proper parallelism.

C   **Correct.** The contrast is expressed using the parallel structure *not as a single substance but as a biological family.*

D   The main defect here is that *regard interferon not to be a single substance* is unidiomatic; *regard . . . as . . .* is the correct form; and completing the parallelism correctly would require the repetition of *as*, in the phrase *but rather as . . .*

E   The contrast is not expressed using parallel grammatical structure since *a single substance* is a noun phrase, while *being a biological family* is a participial phrase; omitting the unnecessary words *being* and *instead* would improve the sentence.

The correct answer is C.

SC01018

872. The remarkable similarity of Thule artifacts throughout a vast region can, in part, be explained as a very rapid movement of people from one end of North America to the other.

(A)   The remarkable similarity of Thule artifacts throughout a vast region can, in part, be explained as

(B)   Thule artifacts being remarkably similar throughout a vast region, one explanation is

(C)   That Thule artifacts are remarkably similar throughout a vast region is, in part, explainable as

(D)   One explanation for the remarkable similarity of Thule artifacts throughout a vast region is that there was

(E)   Throughout a vast region Thule artifacts are remarkably similar, with one explanation for this being

Logical Predication; Grammatical Construction; Rhetorical Construction

The intended meaning of the sentence is that the rapid movement of people across North America is one explanation of the *similarity of Thule artifacts throughout a vast region*. As worded, however, the sentence is illogical: The sentence indicates that the similarity in artifacts was a rapid movement of people, which makes no sense. Instead of equating similarity with movement, the sentence needs to identify this movement of people as a cause of similarity among artifacts.

A   As worded, this version of the sentence makes the illogical statement that the similarity among artifacts is explainable *as a very rapid movement*. It should specify that the similarity of artifacts may be a consequence of the rapid population movement.

B   This version of the sentence is syntactically awkward, and leaves unclear what the main

subject, *one explanation*, is supposed to be an explanation of.

C   Like answer choice A, this version of the sentence equates the similarity of artifacts with the movement of people, when a causal connection is what is intended.

D   Correct. This version adequately expresses the intended causal connection.

E   This version is awkward, introducing the causal connection with the unnecessarily wordy and indirect string of prepositional phrases, *with one explanation for this. . . .*

The correct answer is D.

SC12841.01

873. Regulators are likely to end what are, in effect, long-standing exemptions permitting pilots of small turboprop aircraft at small carriers to fly as much as 20 percent more hours per month than pilots at larger airlines fly, with the consequence that some carriers could be forced to hire additional pilots.

(A)   as much as 20 percent more hours per month than pilots at larger airlines fly, with the consequence that

(B)   as many as 20 percent more hours per month as pilots at larger airlines, and

(C)   more hours per month, as much as 20 percent, than pilots at larger airlines; consequently

(D)   as much as 20 percent more hours per month as larger airlines' pilots, so

(E)   as many as 20 percent more hours per month than pilots at larger airlines do, and consequently

Grammatical Construction; Diction

The sentence is meant to convey that an exemption to maximum flying-time regulations for pilots at smaller airlines may soon be ended and that this will entail that such airlines will have to hire more pilots. The most significant error in the given sentence is in the final clause, which seems to indicate that pilots' flying as many as 20 percent more hours per month could result in carriers having to hire additional pilots. This "consequence" is wrongly assigned to the extra flying time rather than to the (probable) ending of the exemption—a logical predication error. A second significant error, a diction error, in some of the variants is the use of *as* in a context where *than* is required to express a comparison.

A usage that is preferable to *as much as*, given that the noun it modifies is plural, is *as many as*.

A   This version fails because of the errors identified above.

B   The comparison of flying times here is erroneously expressed by the third occurrence of *as* where *than* is required. The verb *do* should be inserted immediately following *airlines* to complete the clause. Also, the idea of consequence present in the given sentence is not conveyed by using *and* without some such word as *consequently*.

C   Inserting the percentage as a parenthesis fails to indicate clearly that what is intended is 20 percent more hours than the flying time of pilots at larger airlines.

D   The comparison of flying times here is erroneously expressed by the third occurrence of *as*, where *than* is required. The verb *do* should be inserted immediately following *airlines* to complete the clause.

E   **Correct.** None of the errors identified in the given sentence is present here. The consequence referred to is correctly assigned to the possible ending of the exemption. The comparison between the maximum flying times for the two classes of pilots is correctly expressed using *than*.

The correct answer is E.

SC24751.01

874. Self-compassion is made up of mindfulness, the ability to manage thoughts and emotions without being carried <u>away or repressing them, common humanity, or empathy with the suffering of others,</u> and self-kindness, a recognition of your own suffering and a commitment to solving the problem.

(A)   away or repressing them, common humanity, or empathy with the suffering of others,

(B)   away, or repression of them, and common humanity, or empathy with the suffering of others,

(C)   away, or repressing them, common humanity, empathy with the suffering of others;

(D)   away or repressing them; common humanity, an empathy with the suffering of others;

(E)   away or repress them; common humanity, to empathize with the suffering of others

Parallelism; Grammatical Construction

This sentence seems meant to present a list of three elements that make up self-compassion: mindfulness, common humanity, and self-kindness. However, the sentence is not well formed, especially with respect to punctuation. Also, the use of the conjunction *or* is haphazard and its function unclear. The description of each of the three elements is complex, comprising a noun that names the element, followed by a noun phrase that gives a definition of that noun. For clarity, the sentence should be structured in a way that highlights the parallelism among the three elements. Because of the complexity and length of the description of each element, the sentence would be made clearest by separating the descriptions of the elements with semicolons.

A   The second occurrence of *or* could function to introduce a definition of a term but its use here is confusing and nonparallel with its first occurrence. The lack of appropriate punctuation creates a reading difficulty.

B   The first occurrence of *or* is meant to coordinate two items, but the naming of the items impairs the formal parallelism that should be present; *being carried away*, a verbal noun, is nonparallel with *repression*, which is a noun but not a verbal noun. As indicated above, the function of the second occurrence of *or* is not clear: for example, does it introduce a definition of *common humanity*? If so, the description of the second element in the series is nonparallel with the descriptions of the other two elements.

C   The effect of the final semicolon here is to coalesce, in a very confusing way, the descriptions of the first two elements; to avoid this, a semicolon should also immediately precede *common humanity*.

D   **Correct.** This version produces a sentence in which each of the descriptions of the three elements of self-compassion is set off with a semicolon and clearly distinguished from the others in a way that makes salient the parallelism among the three descriptions and facilitates the reader in understanding the sentence.

E   The punctuation here is confusing: the first semicolon is not matched by a semicolon immediately after *others*. The verb *repress* is nonparallel with the verbal noun *being carried away*.

The correct answer is D.

SC83751.01

875. According to the laws of this nation, individuals are minors until they reach the age of eighteen, <u>although this is less in some countries and more in others</u>.

(A) although this is less in some countries and more in others

(B) but this age is lower in some countries; higher in others

(C) although in some countries, it is lower and in others it is higher

(D) although it is less than that in some countries and more than that in others

(E) but the relevant age is lower in some countries and higher in others

Logical Predication; Diction

What the pronoun *this* refers to in the underlined clause is unclear. Could it be the age of majority? No, because this is not mentioned in the preceding context. Could it be *the age of eighteen*? No, because it makes no sense to say the age of eighteen is *less in some countries* (this would be a logical predication error). If *lower* were substituted for *less*, but no other change was made, the sentence would not be any better—even if, in general, the adjective *lower* is a more appropriate modifier with *age* than is *less*.

A   As explained, this version fails because of a logical predication error and a diction error.

B   This version also contains a logical predication error. The semicolon, rather than a comma or a coordinating conjunction *and*, is inappropriate: it turns *higher in others* into a mere sentence fragment.

C   The context fails to provide an antecedent that makes sense for the pronoun *it*; if *the age of eighteen* were the antecedent, there would be a logical predication error. The comma after *countries* is unnecessary and confusing.

D   Again, as explained, the reference of the pronoun *it* is unclear. The predicates *less than that* and *more than that* create a logical

predication error if they are predicates of *the age of eighteen*.

E   **Correct.** The phrase *the relevant age* clearly refers to the age at which minors reach the age of majority. The sentence indicates that in some countries that age is lower than eighteen and in some others higher.

The correct answer is E.

SC32261.01

876. <u>Rather than ignore a company that seems about to fail,</u> investment analysts should recognize that its reorganization and recent uptick in revenue, combined with its dynamic new leadership, indicate that the firm's prospects must be taken seriously.

(A) Rather than ignore a company that seems about to fail,

(B) Rather than ignoring a company that is about to seemingly fail,

(C) Instead of a company that is seemingly about to fail being ignored,

(D) Instead of ignore a company that seems about to fail,

(E) In place of ignoring a company's imminent failure seemingly about to occur,

Diction; Verb Form; Parallelism

The underlined phrase raises two main issues: Is *rather than* the appropriate way of introducing the modifying underlined phrase? Is the verb form *ignore* correct? The phrases *instead of* and *in place of* both function as prepositions and must therefore be followed, even if not immediately, by a word or phrase that functions as a noun or pronoun (this could include verbal nouns, ending in *-ing*). The phrase *rather than* indicates a comparison or contrast. (However, *rather than* can function as a preposition in some contexts.)

A   **Correct.** *Rather than* does not function as a preposition here. Its function is to coordinate two verbs, in parallel form, that indicate actions compared in the sentence (some have called *rather than* in this function a "quasi-conjunction").

B   The phrase *rather than ignoring* is correct and accepted in some usages, where *rather than* functions prepositionally, as here. This version is incorrect because the phrase *about to seemingly fail* does not coherently capture the intended idea. Notice that the idea to be conveyed is that actual failure seems about to occur, not that the appearance of failure is about to occur.

C   The passive verb form is quite unnecessary and produces an unnecessarily awkward phrase that is also incorrect in another way: the complex noun phrase *instead of . . . being ignored* is mistakenly placed in parallel with *investment analysts*.

D   *Instead of* normally functions as a preposition and can govern only a word or phrase that functions as a noun or pronoun, not a finite verb form (a verb form that is neither a verbal noun nor an infinitive) such as *ignore*.

E   *In place of* is a preposition that can do the same work as *instead of* in some contexts but is somewhat awkward here. In the noun phrase *a company's imminent failure seemingly about to occur*, the adjectival phrase *seemingly about to occur* is redundant with the adjective *imminent*.

The correct answer is A.

SC01490

877. Between 14,000 and 8,000 B.C. the ice cap that covered northern Asia, Europe, and America <u>began to melt, uncovering vast new areas that were to be occupied</u> by migrating peoples moving northward.

(A)   began to melt, uncovering vast new areas that were to be occupied

(B)   began melting, to uncover vast new areas to be occupied

(C)   began, by melting, to uncover vast new areas for occupation

(D)   began, after melting, uncovering vast new areas which are to be occupied

(E)   would begin to uncover, through melting, vast new areas for occupation

Verb Form; Logical Predication

The sentence tells what happened when an ice cap *began to melt*. The participial phrase *uncovering vast new areas* suggests an ongoing process and makes no commitment to when the uncovering was completed. It is thus coherent with the idea that the process unfolded as the

melting progressed. The verb form *were to be occupied* is used to indicate that occupation would take place at a time in the future from the time of the melting. In principle, *were to be occupied* could mean, illogically, that someone had prescribed that the new areas should be occupied—analogously to "These boxes were to be removed yesterday, but they are still here." However, the former meaning is more standard in a context such as this. The decision between answer choices A and B is subtle. The main advantages of answer choice A are that (1) *uncovering* more accurately conveys the gradual process than *to uncover* does and (2) the placement of *were* before *to be occupied* less strongly suggests that melting of the ice caps was done intentionally for the purpose of occupying the new areas.

A   **Correct.** The sentence uses an appropriate modifying phrase and verb form to express immediate and future effects of the melting of an ice cap.

B   In the phrase *began melting, to uncover*, the word *to* could appear to be a purpose indicator equivalent to the longer form *in order to*, as in, "They have begun building a dam to control flooding on the river." On that interpretation, the sentence illogically implies that the ice cap melted for the purpose of uncovering new areas. The comma after *melting* helps prevent that interpretation. Presumably, *to uncover* is intended to indicate that the second event resulted from or accompanied the first, as in the following sentences: "The clouds parted to reveal a bright full moon." "I opened the package to discover that it was totally empty." However, that interpretation suggests that the uncovering was complete when the melting had just begun. The participle *uncovering* in answer choice A is a better way to express the ongoing nature of the process. The phrase *areas to be occupied* in answer choice B is also ambiguous. Phrases of this form typically indicate that the action is prescribed or required, as in "she brought me a batch of documents to be filed," or "the areas to be sprayed are marked on the map." On that interpretation, the sentence nonsensically implies that someone had designated the areas as needing to be occupied. The inclusion of the words *that were* in answer choice A mitigates this appearance.

C   Since *melting* is what caused new areas to be uncovered, that word should be part of the main verb, not placed in the nonrestrictive prepositional phrase *by melting*. *For occupation* appears to indicate that the melting was done for the purpose of occupying the new areas.

D   It does not make sense to say that the ice cap *began . . . uncovering* new areas *after* it had melted—since the ice cap no longer existed in the areas where it had melted. The present tense *are to be* is incoherent with the past events.

E   Since *melting* is what caused new areas to be uncovered, that word should be part of the main verb, not placed in the nonrestrictive prepositional phrase *through melting*. *For occupation* appears to indicate that the melting was done for the purpose of occupying the new areas.

The correct answer is A.

SC71360.02

878.   Because property values sometimes fluctuate in response to economic conditions beyond the purchaser's control, an investment in a home may underperform when compared to that of other widely available classes of investments.

(A)   an investment in a home may underperform when compared to that of other widely available classes of investments

(B)   an investment in a home may underperform compared with other widely available classes of investments

(C)   an investment in a home may underperform when comparing it with other widely available classes of investments

(D)   compared to that of other widely available classes of investments, an investment in a home may underperform

(E)   in comparison with that of other widely available classes of investments, an investment in a home may underperform

Diction; Verb Form

An investment in a home may underperform— be less profitable or grow more slowly—than other classes of investments. Something like this comparison seems what the given sentence is meant to convey. The sentence uses the form *X when compared to Y*. However, it is somewhat odd to say that an investment underperforms *when compared* (that is, at the time it is compared) to another investment. The point most likely intended would be better conveyed by the form *X compared with Y*. Another issue concerns the use of the locution *that of*. In such a phrase, the pronoun *that* logically should refer to a preceding noun or noun phrase, e.g., *an investment*. But this would render the sentence incoherent. No other preceding noun or noun phrase fits as an antecedent of *that*, and the words *that of* would be better dropped; they convey no useful information and only serve to structurally impair the sentence.

A   As explained above, the form *when compared to* does not function well to convey the comparison that is likely meant. The words *that of* convey no useful information and only serve to structurally impair the sentence.

B   Correct. This version creates a sentence that avoids the errors explained above.

C   The phrase *when comparing it* is erroneous in two ways: (1) it somewhat oddly suggests that an investment in a home underperforms *when* it is being compared and (2) because of the clause structure, the participle *comparing* has *an investment* as its implicit subject but also has *it* referring to the same noun. The idea of an investment comparing an investment is incoherent.

D   The position of *compared to* makes the sentence as a whole somewhat awkward and encourages a misreading in which the phrase *compared to . . . investments* modifies *the purchaser's control* rather than *an investment in a home*. As previously explained, it is unclear what *that* refers to; the words *that of* serve no useful purpose and would be better omitted.

E   The position of *in comparison with . . . investments* makes the sentence as a whole somewhat awkward and encourages a misreading in which the phrase *in comparison with . . . investments* modifies *the purchaser's control* rather than *an investment in a home*. As previously explained, it is unclear what *that* refers to; the words *that of* serve no useful purpose and would be better omitted.

The correct answer is B.

SC01472

879. Bengal-born writer, philosopher, and educator Rabindranath Tagore had the greatest admiration <u>for Mohandas K. Gandhi the person and also as a politician, but Tagore had been</u> skeptical of Gandhi's form of nationalism and his conservative opinions about India's cultural traditions.

(A) for Mohandas K. Gandhi the person and also as a politician, but Tagore had been

(B) for Mohandas K. Gandhi as a person and as a politician, but Tagore was also

(C) for Mohandas K. Gandhi not only as a person and as a politician, but Tagore was also

(D) of Mohandas K. Gandhi as a person and as also a politician, but Tagore was

(E) of Mohandas K. Gandhi not only as a person and as a politician, but Tagore had also been

Rhetorical Construction; Parallelism

This sentence describes the writer and philosopher Tagore's two types of feelings for Gandhi. The underlined part of the sentence has to express correctly the time line of these two feelings (they happened simultaneously). The underlined part also has to express the correct relationship between the complements of admiration and skepticism.

A To maintain parallelism, it is important for two conjoined phrases to be of the same grammatical type. Thus, it is appropriate to conjoin *Gandhi the person and the politician,* or *Gandhi as a person and as a politician,* but it is nonstandard in English to mix and match. In addition, the use of the past perfect tense *had been* places the skepticism earlier on the time line than the admiration, which is misleading.

B **Correct.** This version correctly conjoins two parallel phrases, *Gandhi as a person and as a politician*, and, in using two simple past tenses to introduce the two emotions, marks them as holding at the same time.

C The phrase *not only X but also Y* matches the meaning of this sentence: Tagore had not only admiration but also skepticism. However *not only* has to precede *admiration* for this rhetorical construction to be parallel.

D The noun *admiration* as it is positioned in this sentence should take the preposition *for*, not *of*, since it refers to a person. The adverb *also* is redundant because it expresses the same meaning as the conjunction *and*.

E As in answer choice D, the noun *admiration* should take the preposition *for*. As in answer choice C, the rhetorical structure of *not only X but also Y* is violated. Finally, the use of the past perfect tense *had been* is misleading with respect to the time line.

The correct answer is B.

SC04704

880. Traffic safety officials predict that drivers will be <u>equally likely to exceed the proposed speed limit as</u> the current one.

(A) equally likely to exceed the proposed speed limit as

(B) equally likely to exceed the proposed speed limit as they are

(C) equally likely that they will exceed the proposed speed limit as.

(D) as likely that they will exceed the proposed speed limit as

(E) as likely to exceed the proposed speed limit as they are

Idiom; Parallelism

This sentence reports on a prediction that compares the likelihood of drivers exceeding a proposed new speed limit with the likelihood of drivers exceeding the current speed limit. The idiom *as x as y*, rather than the incorrect form *equally . . . as*, should be used to express the comparison.

A *Equally likely . . . as* is not an idiomatic form of comparison.

B This also offers a nonidiomatic form of comparison.

C The comparison is expressed nonidiomatically. Also, *the drivers will be equally likely* should be followed by *to exceed* rather than by *that they will exceed*. The resulting sentence is wordy and structurally flawed.

D   The resulting sentence is wordy and structurally flawed. The idiomatic phrase *as x as y* is somewhat in use, but *as likely that they* is awkward, and the comparison is unclear and not parallel.

E   **Correct.** The idiomatic phrase *as x as y* is properly used, and the comparison is clear and parallel.

The correct answer is E.

SC04562

881. Written early in the French Revolution, <u>Mary Wollstonecraft's *A Vindication of the Rights of Man* (1790) and *A Vindication of the Rights of Woman* (1792) attributed Europe's social and political ills to be the result of</u> the dominance of aristocratic values and patriarchal hereditary privilege.

(A)   Mary Wollstonecraft's *A Vindication of the Rights of Man* (1790) and *A Vindication of the Rights of Woman* (1792) attributed Europe's social and political ills to be the result of

(B)   Mary Wollstonecraft's *A Vindication of the Rights of Man* (1790) and *A Vindication of the Rights of Woman* (1792) attributed Europe's social and political ills to result from

(C)   Mary Wollstonecraft's *A Vindication of the Rights of Man* (1790) and *A Vindication of the Rights of Woman* (1792) attributed Europe's social and political ills to

(D)   in *A Vindication of the Rights of Man* (1790) and *A Vindication of the Rights of Woman* (1792), Mary Wollstonecraft attributed Europe's social and political ills to have been the result of

(E)   Mary Wollstonecraft, in *A Vindication of the Rights of Man* (1790) and *A Vindication of the Rights of Woman* (1792), attributed Europe's social and political ills to

Logical Predication; Idiom

The phrase at the beginning needs a subject for *written*; most logically here it would be the books mentioned written by Mary Wollstonecraft; any other main-clause subject is therefore incorrect. The verb *attribute* idiomatically requires the preposition *to* followed by a noun phrase, not the infinitive marker *to* followed by a verb.

A   The main subject is correctly predicated of *written*, but *attribute* is incorrectly followed by the infinitive *to* plus a verb (*be*).

B   The main subject is correctly predicated of *written*, but *attribute* is incorrectly followed by the infinitive *to* plus a verb (*result*).

C   **Correct.** The main subject is correctly predicated of *written*, and *attribute* is correctly followed by the preposition *to*.

D   The subject of the main clause is *Mary Wollstonecraft*, and so this phrase is illogically forced to be taken as the subject of *written*. Also, *attribute* is incorrectly followed by *to* plus a verb (*have been*).

E   The subject of the main clause is *Mary Wollstonecraft*, and so this phrase is illogically forced to be taken as the subject of *written*.

The correct answer is C.

SC01498

882. Using study groups managed by the principal popular organizations and political parties, <u>the Swedish public was informed by the government about energy and nuclear power</u>.

(A)   the Swedish public was informed by the government about energy and nuclear power

(B)   the government informed the Swedish public about energy and nuclear power

(C)   energy and nuclear power information was given to the Swedish public by the government

(D)   information about energy and nuclear power was given to the Swedish public by the government

(E)   the public of Sweden was given energy and nuclear power information by the government

Logical Predication; Rhetorical Construction

This sentence tries to describe a situation in which the government used study groups to inform the Swedish public. Therefore, it is incorrect to use *the Swedish public* as the subject of *inform* in this sentence, because doing so in this case illogically makes *the Swedish public* the subject of *using* as well. Additionally, *inform* is a more concise and direct way to express the idea in *give information*.

A   Using *the Swedish public* as the subject of the main clause incorrectly makes it the subject of *using* as well.

B **Correct.** Using *the government* as the main subject correctly allows it to count as the subject of using; inform is a concise phrasing for the main action of the sentence.

C Energy and nuclear power information does not work as the subject of the main clause, since this also, illogically, makes it the subject of *using*. Also, this phrase delays the reader's understanding of the important noun *information* (a clearer phrasing is *information about energy and nuclear power*) and employs *give information* rather than the more concise *inform*.

D *Energy and nuclear power information* does not work as the main clause subject, since this also, illogically, makes it the subject of *using*. In addition, this version awkwardly uses *give information to* instead of the more concise *inform*.

E *The public of Sweden* is awkward compared to *the Swedish public*, and in any case is illogically taken as the subject of using; *given . . . information* could be phrased more concisely with *inform*.

The correct answer is B.

SC07446

883. The use of the bar code, or Universal Product Code, which was created in part to enable supermarkets to process customers at a faster rate, has expanded beyond supermarkets to other retail outlets and <u>have become readily accepted despite some initial opposition when it was first introduced in 1974</u>.

(A) have become readily accepted despite some initial opposition when it was first introduced in 1974

(B) has become readily accepted despite some initial opposition when they were first introduced in 1974

(C) have become readily accepted despite some initial opposition when first introduced in 1974

(D) has become readily accepted despite some initial opposition when the bar code was first introduced in 1974

(E) bar codes have become readily accepted despite some initial opposition when it was first introduced in 1974

Agreement; Rhetorical Construction

The subject of this sentence is *the use of the bar code*, the main noun of which is the singular *use*; thus, the corresponding main verb should be in the singular form *has*, not the plural *have*. The actual subject for this verb is merely understood, but when it is present, any pronoun that refers back to it must agree with it in number.

A The verb form *have* does not agree with the sentence's subject. The referent of *it* is potentially unclear.

B *Has* is correct; however, the rest of its clause is badly worded, because its subject *they* does not clearly refer back to the singular *Universal Product Code* (or *bar code*); a better choice is *it*.

C The plural *have* does not agree with the singular subject *use*.

D **Correct.** The verb is in the correct form *has*, and using *bar code* as the last clause's subject avoids an agreement problem.

E Restating the subject as the plural *bar codes* allows the following verb to be *have*, but it is then incorrect to use *it* later in the sentence, since *it* does not agree in number with *bar codes*.

The correct answer is D.

SC01595

884. Normally a bone becomes fossilized through the action of groundwater, <u>which permeates the bone, washes away its organic components, and replaces them</u> with minerals.

(A) which permeates the bone, washes away its organic components, and replaces them

(B) which permeates the bone, washes away its organic components, and those are replaced

(C) which permeates the bone, washing away its organic components, to be replaced

(D) permeating the bone, washing away its organic components, to be replaced

(E) permeating the bone, washing away its organic components and replacing them

Logical Predication; Grammatical Construction

The sentence explains the process by which groundwater produces fossilization of bones. The grammatically correct sentence describes a series of three stages in the process.

A **Correct.** Three parallel verbal phrases—*permeates . . ., washes . . ., and replaces . . .*—are correctly coordinated within a relative clause that has *which* as its subject referring to *groundwater*.

B The third component of the series, *and those are replaced,* is nonparallel, and therefore incorrect. This renders the sentence ungrammatical.

C This lacks the appropriate parallelism; based on structure, the phrase *to be replaced . . .* should modify *which,* a relative pronoun referring to *groundwater.* But this would not express the thought intended in the given sentence, which indicates that organic components are replaced.

D The participles *permeating* and *washing away* should, based on structure, have the subject of the sentence, *a bone,* as their implicit subject. But this produces nonsense. It is unclear what the phrase *to be replaced* modifies: based on the intended meaning, it should be *its organic components,* but the structure does not indicate this, given that the subject of the sentence is *a bone.*

E The three participles *permeating, washing away,* and *replacing* have the subject of the sentence (*a bone*) as their implicit subject. This produces nonsense. Also, any three-element series must have a comma immediately following each of its first two elements.

The correct answer is A.

SC04416

885. The Organization of Petroleum Exporting Countries (OPEC) had long been expected to announce a reduction in output to bolster sagging oil prices, but officials of the organization just recently announced that the group will pare daily production by 1.5 million barrels by the beginning of next <u>year, but only if non-OPEC nations, including Norway, Mexico, and Russia, were to trim output</u> by a total of 500,000 barrels a day.

(A) year, but only if non-OPEC nations, including Norway, Mexico, and Russia, were to trim output

(B) year, but only if the output of non-OPEC nations, which includes Norway, Mexico, and Russia, is trimmed

(C) year only if the output of non-OPEC nations, including Norway, Mexico, and Russia, would be trimmed

(D) year only if non-OPEC nations, which includes Norway, Mexico, and Russia, were trimming output

(E) year only if non-OPEC nations, including Norway, Mexico, and Russia, trim output

Rhetorical Construction; Logical Predication

The underlined part of this sentence deals with the conditions that must hold if OPEC members are to lower their own oil production by 1.5 million barrels by the beginning of next year. The sentence as it is currently worded is rhetorically odd in that it states that officials at OPEC have announced that OPEC *will pare daily production . . . next year,* but then it states that it will do so *only if* certain other things *were to* happen. The use of *were to* suggests a state of affairs that is uncertain; however, the verb *will* in *will pare daily production* seems to express certainty (with *were to,* the verb *would pare* would be more appropriate). The sentence would be improved and would convey its idea more appropriately if it said OPEC *will pare daily production . . . next year only if* certain things **do** happen. The important thing to notice in answering this question correctly is to focus on the following logical relation: *X will do something only if Y does something else.*

A This version is rhetorically illogical, as described in the paragraph above.

B This version uses the passive construction in the conditional clause *only if the output . . . is trimmed.* This use of the passive voice makes the sentence vague in that it is unclear who needs to trim the output of non-OPEC nations. Additionally, the intended subject of *includes* is either *nations,* in which case the verb should be *include,* so that it agrees in number with its subject, or *output,* in which case the verb is correct, but then the sentence nonsensically says that Norway, Mexico, and Russia are included in the output of non-OPEC nations.

C As in answer choice B, this version also introduces vagueness by using the passive construction. In addition, *would be trimmed* is rhetorically illogical given the preceding *will pare daily production.*

D This version uses an active verb, but in the past-progressive form, *were trimming*, which makes no sense in the context of the sentence, because the sentence presumes that the non-OPEC nations have not yet trimmed production by 500,000 barrels a day.

E **Correct.** This version is best because it avoids the problems contained in the other answer choices, and introduces no problems of its own.

The correct answer is E.

SC25540.02

886. Even with the proposed budget cuts and new taxes and fees, the city's projected deficit for the next budget year is getting worse: administration officials announced that they believe the gap will be $3.7 billion, a billion dollars <u>over what it was predicted</u> just two months ago.

(A) over what it was predicted

(B) over the prediction from

(C) more than it was predicted

(D) more than they had predicted

(E) more than they predicted it

Idiom; Rhetorical Construction; Logical Predication

The sentence refers to an announcement by a city's administration officials, conveying their belief that, for the next year, the city will have a greater budget deficit than predicted two months earlier. The budget deficit is a *gap* between what is budgeted for next year and the amount expected to be available from the city's revenue for next year. The sentence is flawed in how it expresses the comparison between the deficit amount predicted earlier and the deficit amount predicted later. The preposition *over* is not idiomatic for comparing one sum of money with a lesser sum. The role of *it* in the sentence is unclear; does it refer to *the gap* or is it the impersonal *it* that could be correctly used in a passive-voice phrase such as it *was predicted that* . . . ? In either case, the underlined phrase is incoherent.

A As explained above, this version creates an incoherent sentence and fails to render the required comparison idiomatically.

B The noun *the prediction* does not strictly refer to a sum of money and so cannot

correctly be compared with one. Even if *the prediction* could be read as meaning the same as *the predicted amount*, the preposition *over* is not idiomatic for comparing one sum of money with another.

C *More than* can be used to compare two sums of money. However, no sum of money is clearly designated here as the second element of the comparison. The phrasing *than it was predicted* is unclear, in part because, as explained above, the import of the pronoun *it* is unclear. If we take *it* as referring back to *the gap*, we still have an inadequate expression of the second element of the comparison. Either *the gap will be more than it was predicted to be* or *the gap will be more than was predicted* would make sense, but *the gap will be more than it was predicted* does not.

D **Correct.** The comparative phrase *more than* is used correctly to compare two sums of money—in this case the later predicted budget-deficit amount and the earlier one, 3.7 billion dollars and 2.7 billion dollars respectively. This version is idiomatically read as elliptical: *more than [the amount] they had predicted*. The pronoun *they* refers correctly to the administration officials mentioned.

E The phrase *more than* can be used to compare two sums of money. However, in this case, the second element of the comparison is not correctly expressed: *than they predicted it* is unidiomatic and does not make sense. The meaning conveyed by the simple-past verb form *predicted* is unlikely to be what is intended. The past perfect *had predicted* would be preferable because it is almost certainly meant to refer to a time previous to a past event, the officials' announcement.

The correct answer is D.

SC01507

887. Over the past ten years cultivated sunflowers have become a major commercial crop, <u>second only to soybeans as a source of vegetable oil</u>.

(A) second only to soybeans as a source of vegetable oil

(B) second in importance to soybeans only as a source of vegetable oil

(C) being second in importance only to soybeans as a source of vegetable oil

(D) which, as a source of vegetable oil, is only second to soybeans

(E) as a source of vegetable oil only second to soybeans

Rhetorical Construction; Idiom

The sentence makes the point that cultivated sunflowers are the second largest source of vegetable oil, soybeans alone being larger. Where *only* is placed in the sentence greatly affects the sense.

A **Correct.** The placement of *only* allows the sentence to correctly express the thought that cultivated sunflowers rank second as a source of vegetable oil, with soybeans alone ranking first.

B The placement of *only* creates an ambiguity: does it modify *soybeans* or the phrase *as a source of vegetable oil?* In the latter case, the sense would be that being a source of vegetable oil is the only respect in which soybeans are more important than sunflower seeds. However, this does not seem to be the intended sense of the given sentence. The phrase *in importance* is unnecessary and would make the sentence wordy.

C The word *being* and the phrase *in importance* are unnecessary and make the sentence wordy.

D The phrase *only second to soybeans* appears to minimize the importance, initially suggested, of sunflowers' being second to soybeans as a source of vegetable oil.

E The word *only* is misplaced, given the intended sense, and it is unclear whether it modifies the phrase *as a source of vegetable oil,* or the phrase *second to soybeans.* In either case it fails to capture the sense of the given sentence.

The correct answer is A.

SC00985

888. Not trusting themselves to choose wisely among the wide array of investment opportunities on the market, stockbrokers are helping many people who turn to them to buy stocks that could be easily bought directly.

(A) stockbrokers are helping many people who turn to them to buy stocks that could be easily

(B) stockbrokers are helping many people who are turning to them for help in buying stocks that they could easily have

(C) many people are turning to stockbrokers for help from them to buy stocks that could be easily

(D) many people are turning to stockbrokers for help to buy stocks that easily could have been

(E) many people are turning to stockbrokers for help in buying stocks that could easily be

Logical Predication; Grammatical Construction; Verb Form

This sentence is intended to be about people who, because they do not trust themselves to make wise investment decisions, turn to stockbrokers for advice. As the sentence is worded, however, it is stockbrokers who do not trust themselves to choose wisely. The sentence is made even more incomprehensible by the peculiar placement of the adverbs in the phrase, *could be easily bought directly.*

A This version of the sentence incorrectly identifies the subject described by the opening modifier as *stockbrokers*; the adverb *easily* is misplaced in the phrase *could be easily bought.*

B As in answer choice A, the opening clause illogically modifies *stockbrokers* rather than *many people.* The tense of the verb phrase *could easily have bought* does not match the tense of *are helping* earlier in the main clause.

C Although the opening modifier is correctly attached to *people* rather than *stockbrokers,* the sentence is unnecessarily wordy (*for help from them*).

D *To buy* is not idiomatic in this context—*in buying* would be correct—and the tense of the verb *could have been* does not match the tense of the verb earlier in the clause; the point is not that people are turning to stockbrokers for help in buying stocks that at some earlier time could have been bought directly, but rather that the stocks could be bought by the people directly at the very time they are seeking help from the stockbrokers.

E **Correct.** The opening clause correctly modifies *many people,* and the adverb is correctly placed.

The correct answer is E.

SC61120.02

889. Scientists claim that the discovery of the first authenticated mammal bones in amber could provide important clues <u>of determining, in addition to how, when mammals colonized the islands of the West Indies</u>.

(A) of determining, in addition to how, when mammals colonized the islands of the West Indies

(B) in the determination of how and when the islands of the West Indies were colonized by mammals

(C) to determine how mammals colonized the islands of the West Indies and when they did

(D) for determining when the islands of the West Indies were colonized by mammals and how they were

(E) for determining how and when mammals colonized the islands of the West Indies

Diction; Rhetorical Construction

How did mammals colonize the islands of the West Indies, and when did this occur? The sentence suggests that the discovery of mammal bones in amber could provide clues for determining the answers regarding *how* and *when*. However, the given version of the sentence is unnecessarily awkward, especially in the word sequence *determining, in addition to how, when . . .* The intended meaning would be better expressed using *and* to conjoin *how* and *when* in a parallel form. The use of the preposition *of* in *clues of determining* is unidiomatic.

A   As explained above, this has two flaws: *of* is not idiomatic with *clues* in this context, and the way in which the answers are conjoined is unnecessarily awkward and unclear.

B   The phrasing *in the determination of* is wordy and unnecessarily awkward.

C   *To determine* (instead of *for* determining, *toward determining*, or *to help determine*) suggests that the clues would be used as a sufficient basis for determining the information needed. That makes it rhetorically somewhat at odds with the standard meaning of *clues*; clues are normally thought of as incomplete bits of evidence. At the end of the sentence, *did so* would be more standard and rhetorically effective as an indication that the verb *did* refers back to *colonized the islands of the West Indies*.

D   The passive verb form *were colonized* is unnecessarily indirect. *How they were* is somewhat unclear. Overall this version is unnecessarily awkward and wordy.

E   **Correct.** The use of *clues for determining* is idiomatically correct. The two hypothetical answers to the *how* and *when* questions are economically conjoined by *and*.

The correct answer is E.

SC01007

890. In the 1940s popular magazines in the United States began to report on the private lives of persons from the entertainment industry, <u>in despite of the fact that they previously had featured individuals</u> in business and politics.

(A) in despite of the fact that they previously had featured individuals

(B) in spite of the fact previously that those publications featured articles on those

(C) whereas previously there were those individuals featured in articles

(D) whereas previously those individuals they featured were

(E) whereas previously these publications had featured articles on individuals

Idiom; Parallelism; Logical Predication

The sentence compares the reporting by popular magazines in the 1940s to the reporting by these magazines before the 1940s. Whereas previously the publications featured articles on people in business and politics, in the 1940s the magazines began to report on the private lives of persons in the entertainment industry. The two elements being compared should be described clearly and in a parallel fashion.

A   This sentence appears to misuse the *in spite of* idiom by using *despite* instead of *spite*. The use of *despite* is incorrect. Furthermore, although we can discern what the pronoun *they* is meant to refer to, the sentence would be easier to read if *these publications* were used in place of *they*.

B   The word *previously*, which is misplaced in this sentence, should be between *publications* and *featured*, and perhaps preceded with *had*. The wording of the relevant portion of the sentence would thus be *fact that these publications had previously featured.* Furthermore, although we can discern what (or who) *those in business and politics* is meant to refer to, more specific wording would have made this phrase in the sentence easier to read. For example, we could substitute *individuals* for *those.*

C   In this sentence, the phrase, *there were those individuals featured in articles in business and politics* is an assertion that individuals thus featured existed. Although we can guess that the writer would have meant to indicate that it was the magazines that were doing the featuring, the sentence fails to make this point clear. The sentence thus lacks clarity.

D   This sentence may present an improvement over answer choices A–C, and would be more readable if the phrase *those individuals they featured* was made parallel with the corresponding portion of the other element of the comparison. For example, *they featured those individuals* would be parallel with *popular magazines . . . began to report on the private lives of persons . . .* It would also help if *they* were replaced with a more specific term such as *the magazines.*

E   **Correct.** This sentence is clear and relatively easy to read.

The correct answer is E.

SC04770

891.   In the early part of the twentieth century, many vacationers found that driving automobiles and sleeping in tents allowed them to enjoy nature close at hand and tour at their own pace, <u>with none of the restrictions of passenger trains and railroad timetables or with the</u> formalities, expenses, and impersonality of hotels.

(A)   with none of the restrictions of passenger trains and railroad timetables or with the

(B)   with none of the restrictions of passenger trains, railroad timetables, nor

(C)   without the restrictions of passenger trains and railroad timetables nor

(D)   without the restrictions of passenger trains and railroad timetables or with the

(E)   without the restrictions of passenger trains and railroad timetables or the

Rhetorical Construction; Diction

The sentence lays out some advantages that car travel and tent camping were perceived to offer over rail travel. The sentence attempts to describe these advantages in terms of the absence of any of a series of annoyances accompanying rail travel. But the sentence fails because of the mismatch between *with none of . . .* and *or with. . . .* One way to successfully convey the intended meaning is to use the preposition *without* governing all the items in the series, expressed as nouns or noun phrases.

A   By using *none of . . .* to introduce the first drawback of rail travel, and *or* to introduce the rest of them, this sentence suggests that the presence of drawbacks on the final list is an alternative to the absence of *restrictions.*

B   *With none . . . nor . . .* is nonidiomatic (as opposed to *neither . . . nor . . .*).

C   The structure *without . . . nor . . .* in the way used here is nonidiomatic. The negative *without* governs the whole list of drawbacks at the end of the sentence.

D   The coupling of *without* and *or with* is confusing, suggesting, as in answer choice A, that the drawbacks on the final list are an alternative to the absence of *restrictions.*

E   **Correct.** The sentence is unambiguous and constructed in a way that *without* clearly distributes over all the items in the series.

The correct answer is E.

SC04760

892.   Over the next few years, increasing demands on the Chattahoochee River, which flows into the Apalachicola River, could alter the saline content of Apalachicola Bay, <u>which would rob the oysters there of their flavor, and to make them decrease in size,</u> less distinctive, and less in demand.

(A)   which would rob the oysters there of their flavor, and to make them decrease in size,

(B)   and it would rob the oysters there of their flavor, make them smaller,

(C)   and rob the oysters there of their flavor, making them decrease in size,

(D)   robbing the oysters there of their flavor and making them smaller,

(E) robbing the oysters there of their flavor, and making them decrease in size,

Parallelism; Grammatical Construction

The sentence claims that demands for river water may change the saline content of the bay, possibly altering the flavor and size of oysters there and diminishing the oysters' marketability. The sentence is not parallel. It should read *which would rob the oysters . . . and make them decrease* to be parallel and grammatical. The series of three phrases after *make them* that describes what will happen to the oysters also needs to be parallel.

A   The referent of the relative pronoun, *which*, is ambiguous; the two effects of altered saline content are not expressed in parallel form, with a relative clause expressing the first effect, and an infinitive phrase expressing the second.

B   The referent of the pronoun *it* is ambiguous. Also, the effects of the bay's altered saline content are not expressed in parallel form— the first being an independent clause and the second a verb phrase.

C   The comma before the conjunction *and* signals that an independent clause will follow *and*, but a verb phrase follows instead. The series of phrases following *making them* lacks appropriate parallelism.

D   Correct. The potential effects on the oysters are expressed by two parallel participial phrases, the second of which lists three adjectives correctly in a series.

E   The series of phrases following *making them* lacks appropriate parallelism.

The correct answer is D.

SC01469

893. Elizabeth Barber, the author of both *Prehistoric Textiles*, a comprehensive work on cloth in the early cultures of the Mediterranean, and <u>also of *Women's Work*, a more general account of early cloth manufacture, is an expert authority on</u> textiles in ancient societies.

(A)   also of *Women's Work*, a more general account of early cloth manufacture, is an expert authority on

(B)   also *Women's Work*, a more general account of cloth manufacture, is an expert authority about

(C)   of *Women's Work*, a more general account about early cloth manufacture, is an authority on

(D)   of *Women's Work*, a more general account about early cloth manufacture, is an expert authority about

(E)   *Women's Work*, a more general account of early cloth manufacture, is an authority on

Rhetorical Construction; Idiom; Parallelism

Using a lot of parenthetical elements, this sentence communicates the main idea that Elizabeth Barber is an authority on textiles in ancient societies. It is the main rhetorical goal of the sentence to position the parenthetical elements so that they do not obscure the main idea. The parenthetical descriptions need to be streamlined enough to be informative, but not too long. In addition, several versions repeat *of* before the title *Women's Work* and doing so makes the sentence unparallel; the first *of* comes before *both* and so should distribute over both clauses.

A   The use of *also of* before *Women's Work* is redundant and unparallel. It is sufficient to connect the two book titles like this: *both X and Y*. The meanings of the two nouns *expert* and *authority* largely overlap, so there is no need to modify one with the other.

B   The use of *also* before *Women's Work* is redundant. It is sufficient to connect the two book titles like this: *both X and Y*. The meanings of the two nouns *expert* and *authority* largely overlap, so there is no need to modify one with the other. Finally, the noun *authority* takes the preposition *on*, not *about*.

C   Repeating the preposition *of* before *Women's Work* makes the sentence unparallel. The noun *account* takes the preposition *of*, not *about*.

D   As in answer choices A and C, repeating the preposition *of* before *Women's Work* makes the sentence unparallel. The noun *account* takes the preposition *of*, not *about*. It is redundant to modify *authority* with *expert* because they express the same idea. Finally, the noun *authority* takes the preposition *on*, not *about*.

E   Correct. This version is parallel, uses the most concise structure of the parenthetical descriptions, eschews the redundant modification of *authority*, and employs the correct prepositions.

The correct answer is E.

SC00994

894. Digging in sediments in northern China, <u>evidence has been gathered by scientists suggesting that complex life-forms emerged much earlier than they had</u> previously thought.

(A) evidence has been gathered by scientists suggesting that complex life-forms emerged much earlier than they had

(B) evidence gathered by scientists suggests a much earlier emergence of complex life-forms than had been

(C) scientists have gathered evidence suggesting that complex life-forms emerged much earlier than

(D) scientists have gathered evidence that suggests a much earlier emergence of complex life-forms than that which was

(E) scientists have gathered evidence which suggests a much earlier emergence of complex life-forms than that

Logical Predication; Modification

In principle, the relationship described in the first part of the underlined portion could be expressed with *scientists* as the subject (*scientists gathered evidence*) or with *evidence* as the subject (*evidence was gathered by scientists*). The latter construction could be effective in some contexts, but here its relationship to the rest of the sentence appears to commit the writer to the claim that the evidence was digging in China.

A This version has a dangling participle, *digging. . . . Digging in sediments in northern China* must modify *scientists*, not *evidence*. The passive structure of the main clause also creates an inadvisable distance between the words *evidence* and *suggesting*. Furthermore, the dependent clause starting with *suggesting* may be construed with either the evidence or the scientists, which makes this version unnecessarily ambiguous.

B This version has a dangling participle, *digging. . . . Digging in sediments in northern China* must modify *scientists*, not *evidence*.

C Correct. Choosing *scientists* as the subject of *gathered*, this version corrects the dangling participle. It also uses a parallel active form of the verb *emerge*, and does not use redundant material.

D In this context it would be preferable to use a verb (*emerged*). The phrasing used here (*suggests a much earlier emergence of*) sounds more stilted and is less clear and direct. In addition, inserting *that which* before *previously thought* is not only redundant but incorrect English.

E The flaws explained above in answer choice D are also present here.

The correct answer is C.

SC01521

895. Employing many different techniques throughout his career, Michelangelo produced a great variety of art works, <u>including paintings, for example, in the Sistine Chapel, to sculpture, for example,</u> the statue of David.

(A) including paintings, for example, in the Sistine Chapel, to sculpture, for example,

(B) including paintings, for example, in the Sistine Chapel, to sculpture, like

(C) including paintings, such as those in the Sistine Chapel, and sculpture, as

(D) ranging from paintings, such as those in the Sistine Chapel, to sculpture, such as

(E) ranging from paintings, such as in the Sistine Chapel, and sculpture, such as

Parallelism; Rhetorical Construction

This sentence names painting and sculpture as two of the many kinds of art created by Michelangelo and provides examples of his work in those two art forms. Although the two sets of examples are expressed in parallel form, the position of the phrase *for example* that introduces them creates a choppy and awkward sentence since it must be surrounded by commas. A more concise way to construct parallel sets of examples is to express each using a phrase introduced by *such as*.

A The sentence is choppy and awkward due to the twofold use of the phrase *for example*, which must be surrounded by commas. The preposition *to*, in context, suggests a range, but it would then be needed to be preceded by *from*.

B The examples of art are not in parallel form since the first is introduced by *for example* followed by the prepositional phrase *in the Sistine Chapel*, and the second is introduced by the prepositional phrase *like*... The preposition *to* is unidiomatic and awkwardly used here.

C   The examples of art are not in parallel form since the first is introduced by *such as,* and the second is introduced by *as.*

D   Correct. The examples of art are in parallel form, each introduced with the words *such as.*

E   Although the examples of art are both introduced by *such as*, the form is not parallel since the first is a prepositional phrase (*in the Sistine Chapel*) and the second is a noun phrase (*the statue of David*).

The correct answer is D.

SC04422

896. According to a recent study of consumer spending on prescription medications, increases in the sales of the 50 drugs that were advertised most <u>heavily accounts for almost half of the $20.8 billion increase in drug spending last year, the remainder of which came from sales of the 9,850 prescription medicines that</u> companies did not advertise or advertised very little.

(A)   heavily accounts for almost half of the $20.8 billion increase in drug spending last year, the remainder of which came

(B)   heavily were what accounted for almost half of the $20.8 billion increase in drug spending last year; the remainder of the increase coming

(C)   heavily accounted for almost half of the $20.8 billion increase in drug spending last year, the remainder of the increase coming

(D)   heavily, accounting for almost half of the $20.8 billion increase in drug spending last year, while the remainder of the increase came

(E)   heavily, which accounted for almost half of the $20.8 billion increase in drug spending last year, with the remainder of it coming

Grammatical Construction; Verb Form

The sentence indicates that according to research, increases in sales of the relatively small number of the most heavily advertised drugs accounted for nearly half of last year's total increase in drug spending. The sentence is flawed because of subject-verb disagreement, and an ambiguity in the referent of *which*.

A   The singular verb form *accounts* fails to agree in number with the plural subject *increases.* What the relative pronoun *which* refers to is

unclear; to make clear sense, it should refer to *the... increase.*

B   The phrase *were what accounted* is unnecessarily wordy; the semicolon before *the remainder* signals that a complete clause will follow, but what follows is not a complete clause.

C   Correct. The sentence is clear and grammatically correct. The subject and verb agree.

D   In the resulting sentence, no main verb follows the main subject *increases.*

E   The resulting sentence lacks a main verb for the main subject *increases.*

The correct answer is C.

SC00971

897. Technically, "quicksand" is the term for sand <u>that is so saturated with water as to acquire a liquid's character.</u>

(A)   that is so saturated with water as to acquire a liquid's character

(B)   that is so saturated with water that it acquires the character of a liquid

(C)   that is saturated with water enough to acquire liquid characteristics

(D)   saturated enough with water so as to acquire the character of a liquid

(E)   saturated with water so much as to acquire a liquid character

Rhetorical Construction; Logical Predication

The statement provides a definition of the term *quicksand* as sand that has been saturated with water to a certain degree. Many of the flaws in the incorrect options have to do with how this degree of saturation is described.

A   The matter of degree is introduced with the word *so*, which is used to indicate that the relevant degree of saturation will be specified with a clause that states a condition—a statement that includes both a subject and a verb—that implies a certain degree of saturation. Lacking a subject, this sentence fails to state a clear condition.

B   Correct. The clause introduced with *that* contains a proper statement—with both a subject and verb—which implies a degree of saturation with water. This sentence has none of the flaws explained above in answer choice A.

C   The word (adjective) *enough*, which qualifies the word *water* is misplaced. In English (with exceptions), qualifiers of nouns are generally placed before the noun. In this case, it should be *enough water*.

D   The words *so as* make this option a poor choice. Like answer choice D, if we cut out "so as" and write, *"quicksand" is the term for sand saturated enough to acquire the character of a liquid*, then our statement would be much improved. However, as it stands, answer choice D is at best awkward.

E   This version is awkward—*so much* qualifies *saturated*, yet it is placed after the word *water*, well after *saturated*. This makes the statement unnecessarily difficult to read. A modification of this part of the sentence so as to read *saturated so much with water* would be an improvement. As explained above in answer choices A and B, this sentence would be better if *as to acquire a liquid character* were replaced with *that it acquires a liquid character* (or, as in answer choice B, *that it acquires the character of a liquid*).

The correct answer is B.

SC07232

898. At the end of 2001, motion picture industry representatives said that there were about a million copies of Hollywood movies available <u>online and expected piracy to increase with high-speed Internet connections that become more widely available.</u>

(A)   online and expected piracy to increase with high-speed Internet connections that become more widely available

(B)   online and expect the increase of piracy with the wider availability of high-speed Internet connections

(C)   online, and they expect more piracy to increase with the wider availability of high-speed Internet connections

(D)   online, and that they expected the increase of piracy as high-speed Internet connections would become more widely available

(E)   online, and that they expected piracy to increase as high-speed Internet connections became more widely available

Rhetorical Construction; Grammatical Construction

Every clause needs a subject, either an overt subject or an understood subject (whose interpretation can come from a coordinated clause or some other nearby clause). In this sentence, the clause containing *expected* lacks a clear subject. The intended subject is *motion picture industry representatives*, but to clearly indicate that, the subject should either be repeated or be replaced with the pronoun *they*. Furthermore, *piracy to increase with high-speed Internet connections that become more widely available* is awkward, and it fails to clearly communicate the idea that piracy will increase as a result of high-speed Internet connections becoming available.

A   The second clause is awkward and unclear; there is no clear subject for *expected*.

B   There is no clear subject for *expect*.

C   It is redundant to use both *more* and *increase*.

D   This wording makes the meaning very unclear. *They expected the increase in piracy* appears to refer to a particular (past) increase, but this does not clearly make sense with the ensuing use of the conditional verb form *would become*, which is inappropriate here.

E   **Correct.** In this version the verb *expect* has an overt subject, and the following phrasing clearly indicates that the expected increase in piracy is the result of high-speed Internet connections becoming more widely available.

The correct answer is E.

SC14066

899. Making things even more difficult <u>has been general market inactivity lately, if not paralysis, which has provided</u> little in the way of pricing guidance.

(A)   has been general market inactivity lately, if not paralysis, which has provided

(B)   there is general market inactivity, if not paralysis, lately it has provided

(C)   general market inactivity, if not paralysis, has lately provided

(D)   lately, general market inactivity, if not paralysis, has provided

(E)   is that lately general market inactivity, if not paralysis, which provides

Grammatical Construction; Rhetorical Construction

This sentence uses a special inverted structure, putting the predicate (*Making things even more difficult*) before the verb (*has been*) and the subject. In this construction, the subject (*general market inactivity*) can be directly compared with *paralysis*. Such contrasts are best made using phrases that are adjacent, not separated by other material (here, the adverb *lately*). If a more normal clause structure is used, *making things even more difficult* becomes a modifier, not the main predicate, so it should be clearly set off from the rest of the clause with a comma.

A This inverted structure makes *general market activity* the subject of *Making things even more difficult*. This would be legitimate by itself, but it requires *general market inactivity* to be next to both *if not paralysis* (for contrast) and *which* (marking a relative clause modifying *inactivity*). It cannot be next to both of these simultaneously.

B This is a run-on sentence, with two independent clauses (*Making things even more difficult there is general market inactivity, if not paralysis, and lately it has provided little in the way of pricing guidance*) conjoined merely by a comma, rather than by a coordinating conjunction, such as and. Also, the initial topic phrase (*Making things even more difficult*) is awkward without a following comma.

C The initial topic phrase (*Making things even more difficult*) should be followed by a comma.

D Correct. The topic phrase (*Making things even more difficult*) is properly separated from the subject by a comma, and *inactivity* and *if not paralysis* are adjacent for the clearest connection between them.

E This is a sentence fragment.

The correct answer is D.

SC01946

900. Ryūnosuke Akutagawa's knowledge of the literatures of Europe, China, and that of Japan were instrumental in his development as a writer, informing his literary style as much as the content of his fiction.

(A) that of Japan were instrumental in his development as a writer, informing his literary style as much as

(B) that of Japan was instrumental in his development as a writer, and it informed both his literary style as well as

(C) Japan was instrumental in his development as a writer, informing both his literary style and

(D) Japan was instrumental in his development as a writer, as it informed his literary style as much as

(E) Japan were instrumental in his development as a writer, informing both his literary style in addition to

Logical Predication; Agreement

When a verb follows a complex noun phrase made up of several parts, it agrees with the first noun in the phrase. In this case, *knowledge of the literatures of Europe, China, and Japan* is a singular noun and the correct verb form is *was*, not *were*. The various parts of an enumeration have to be alike: *the literatures of Europe, China, and Japan*. The logical relationship between the predicates is important.

A This version of the sentence violates the correct subject-verb agreement, and the correct structure of enumeration is disrupted by the addition of *that of* in front of *Japan*.

B The correct structure of enumeration is disrupted by the addition of *that of* in front of *Japan*. Both . . . as well as . . . is incorrect usage.

C Correct. The structure of the enumeration (*Europe, China, and Japan*) as well as the conjunction structure (*both X and Y*) are correct. The logical relationships among the parts of the sentence are clearly expressed.

D This phrasing makes it unclear what the writer is claiming. It appears to indicate that the effect of Akutagawa's knowledge on his development as a writer was due to the fact that both of the aspects of his writing were influenced to the same extent. However, it is implausible to suppose that this is what the writer intends. Furthermore, the comparison is ambiguous: did his knowledge inform his style as much as it informed the content, or did it inform his style as much as the content informed his style?

E The subject-verb agreement in this version is incorrect. *Both X in addition to Y* is incorrect usage.

The correct answer is C.

SC24321.01

901. Many stock traders in the United States have set out to become global investors, convinced that limiting their investments to the U.S. stock market, <u>even though it is certainly</u> home to the stocks of some of the world's great corporations, restricted their gains.

(A) even though it is certainly

(B) which, while it is certainly

(C) despite that that market is certainly

(D) which, though certainly

(E) although, certainly as

Grammatical Construction; Diction

This sentence contains no errors. A major error in three of the variants of the underlined portion is to create a mere sentence fragment through failure to complete, with a verb, the noun clause that would normally be introduced by the phrase *convinced that*.

A **Correct.** The phrase *convinced that* introduces a noun clause: *limiting their investments to the U.S. stock market restricted their gains.* The clause introduced by *even though* is a parenthesis inserted in the noun clause.

B This creates a sentence fragment by leaving the noun clause introduced by *convinced that* with no verb to complete it. The relative pronoun *which* introduces a relative clause; this clause takes *restricted* as its verb and *the U.S. stock market* as the antecedent of *which*.

C There is a diction error here. The phrase *despite that* is not a subordinating conjunction; the word *despite* is normally used as a preposition. A preposition must be followed by a noun, noun phrase, or pronoun that it governs (as in "despite that fact, . . .") but is not so followed in this case. The conjunction *although* would better serve the function intended for *despite that*.

D This creates a sentence fragment by leaving the noun clause introduced by *convinced that* without a verb to complete it.

E This creates a sentence fragment and deprives the verb *restricted* of a subject. The word *although* is a subordinating conjunction used only to introduce a subordinate clause, which is required to have its own verb. But these requirements are not fulfilled here, so we have a diction error.

The correct answer is A.

SC01973

902. According to scientists who monitored its path, <u>an expanding cloud of energized particles ejected from the Sun recently triggered a large storm in the magnetic field that surrounds Earth, which brightened the Northern Lights and also possibly knocking</u> out a communications satellite.

(A) an expanding cloud of energized particles ejected from the Sun recently triggered a large storm in the magnetic field that surrounds Earth, which brightened the Northern Lights and also possibly knocking

(B) an expanding cloud of energized particles ejected from the Sun was what recently triggered a large storm in the magnetic field that surrounds Earth, and it brightened the Northern Lights and also possibly knocked

(C) an expanding cloud of energized particles ejected from the Sun recently triggered a large storm in the magnetic field that surrounds Earth, brightening the Northern Lights and possibly knocking

(D) a large storm in the magnetic field that surrounds Earth, recently triggered by an expanding cloud of energized particles, brightened the Northern Lights and it possibly knocked

(E) a large storm in the magnetic field surrounding Earth was recently triggered by an expanding cloud of energized particles, brightening the Northern Lights and it possibly knocked

Logical Predication; Rhetorical Construction; Verb Form

The timing and logical relationships among the events described in this sentence are of utmost importance. The scientists monitored a cloud ejected from the Sun. The cloud triggered a large storm, whose consequences were the brightening of the Northern Lights and the possible knocking out of a satellite. The latter two events are in a conjunction, so they should be represented by similar verb forms.

A In this context, the shift in verb form from *which brightened* to *and also possibly knocking* is ungrammatical. The two verbs should be in the same verb form for parallel construction.

B *X was what triggered Y* is wordy and awkward, and its meaning is unclear in this context. Given the most plausible intended meaning of the sentence, the two conjunctions *and . . . and . . .* in the last clause are redundant. The comma after *Earth* turns the final part of the sentence into an independent clause, and it is unclear whether this is part of what the scientists claimed or a separate claim made by the writer.

C **Correct.** The conjoined elements are of parallel forms, and the logical relations between the events are clear and concisely communicated.

D The wording in this answer choice makes the intended meaning unclear. The information that the cloud particles were ejected from the Sun is lost. The sentence is ungrammatical; the second conjoined main verb, *knocked*, needs no pronoun subject *it* because its subject is *a large storm*.

E The wording in this answer choice makes the intended meaning unclear. The information that the cloud particles were ejected from the Sun is lost. The two conjoined verbs are of different form; the second conjoined verb includes an unnecessary pronoun subject.

The correct answer is C.

SC01033

903. Because many of Australia's marsupials, such as the koala, are cute and cuddly, as well as <u>being biologically different than North American marsupials, they have attracted a lot of attention after</u> their discovery in the 1700s.

(A) being biologically different than North American marsupials, they have attracted a lot of attention after

(B) being biologically different from North American marsupials, they attracted a lot of attention since

(C) biologically different than North American marsupials, they attracted a lot of attention since

(D) biologically different than North American marsupials, they have attracted a lot of attention after

(E) biologically different from North American marsupials, they have attracted a lot of attention since

Verb Form; Parallelism

In seeking to explain why Australian marsupials have attracted much attention in North America, the sentence ascribes two attributes to them: they differ biologically from North American marsupials and seem friendly and appealing. The structure *are . . . as well as . . .* is used to coordinate the description of the two properties—but incorrectly, because the insertion of *being* impairs the required parallelism: *are cute and cuddly* is not parallel to *[are] being biologically different*. Also, there is a lack of fit between the verb form *have attracted* and the preposition *after*.

A The phrase *cute and cuddly* is adjectival, as is *biologically different . . .;* adding the word *being* is not useful and impairs parallelism. The verb form *have attracted* suggests a process continuing from some point in the past, but the word *after* is most naturally read as indicating the time of a single event relative to an earlier point in time.

B The word *being* is superfluous here. The word *since* indicates continuation over a past period, whereas the verb *attracted* indicates a single event occurring within a period.

C The word *being* is superfluous here and impairs parallelism. The verb *attracted*, indicating a single event, does not match the use of the word *since*, which indicates a continuing duration relative to the time of an earlier event.

D The verb *have attracted*, indicating continuation, does not match the use of the word *after*, which is appropriate in order to give the time of a single event relative to an earlier point in time.

E **Correct.** The superfluous word *being* is omitted, preserving the parallelism between the two adjectival phrases in the description of the attribute following *as well as*. The preposition *since* is the appropriate usage with the verb form *have attracted*.

The correct answer is E.

SC02448

904. <u>Having been named for a mythological nymph who cared for the infant Jupiter, the asteroid named Ida, in the middle of the belt of asteroids that orbit the Sun between Mars and Jupiter, was discovered in 1884.</u>

(A) Having been named for a mythological nymph who cared for the infant Jupiter, the asteroid named Ida, in the middle of the belt of asteroids that orbit the Sun between Mars and Jupiter, was discovered in 1884.

(B) Discovered in 1884, the asteroid Ida, named for a mythological nymph who cared for the infant Jupiter, is in the middle of the belt of asteroids that orbit the Sun between Mars and Jupiter.

(C) In the middle of the belt of asteroids that orbit the Sun between Mars and Jupiter, the asteroid Ida, discovered in 1884 and named for a mythological nymph who cared for the infant Jupiter.

(D) The asteroid Ida, named for a mythological nymph who cared for the infant Jupiter and discovered in 1884, is in the middle of the belt of asteroids to orbit the Sun between Mars and Jupiter.

(E) Ida, an asteroid discovered in 1884 and which was named for a mythological nymph who cared for the infant Jupiter, is in the middle of the belt of asteroids to orbit the Sun between Mars and Jupiter

Rhetorical Construction; Logical Predication; Grammatical Construction

This sentence describes a discovery that occurred in 1884 and provides some additional information about the object that was discovered. The most effectively worded answer choice opens with a past-participial phrase (*discovered . . .*) describing the subject of the sentence, *the asteroid Ida*. Ida's discovery is logically prior to its naming, described in a second past, following the subject (*named . . .*). The sentence is then completed with a present tense linking verb *is* + prepositional phrase to explain Ida's location.

A   Opening with a past perfect passive verb, *Having been named*, this version of the sentence illogically suggests that being named for a mythological nymph preceded the discovery of Ida.

B   **Correct.** This version is clear, logically coherent, and grammatically correct.

C   This version is ungrammatical; it has no main verb for the subject *the asteroid Ida*.

D   The sequence of events is obscured by the placement of *named* before *discovered* in the compound participial phrases. The infinitive

form *to orbit* is ungrammatical in place of the relative clause.

E   This sentence awkwardly attempts to use a compound conjunction *and* to join the past participial phrase *discovered in 1884* with the relative clause *which was named. . . .* The infinitive form *to orbit* is ungrammatical in place of the relative clause.

The correct answer is B.

SC20121.01

905. Custodian fees and expenses, as described in the statement of operations, <u>include interest expense incurred by the fund on any cash overdrafts of its custodian account during the period</u>.

(A) include interest expense incurred by the fund on any cash overdrafts of its custodian account during the period

(B) are to include interest expenses on any cash overdrafts of its custodian account the fund incurred during the period

(C) includes interest expense the fund incurred during the period on any cash overdrafts of its custodian account

(D) may include interest expense during the period that the fund was to incur on any cash overdrafts of its custodian account

(E) including interest expense on any cash overdrafts of its custodian account incurred by the fund during the period

Logical Predication; Agreement; Grammatical Construction; Verb Form

The given sentence is correct. The subject of the main verb is plural; the word *custodian* functions as an adjective modifying *fees and expenses*. The complex adjectival phrase *incurred . . . period* (which includes embedded adverbial modifiers such as *by the fund*) modifies the noun phrase *interest expense*. The adverbial phrase *during the period* modifies the verb *incurred*. Errors occurring in the other versions include misplaced modifiers, errors in subject-verb agreement, and a grammatical construction error.

A   **Correct.** This has none of the errors listed above. The use of the singular *expense*, an abstract noun with no plural, is legitimate— as is also the use of the plural concrete noun *expenses* (a "count noun") elsewhere in the sentence.

B   The phrase *are to include* can convey either a future sense or an imperative sense, but nothing in the given sentence indicates that either of these senses is appropriate. The relative clause [*that*] *the fund incurred* . . . is misleadingly attached to *account* rather than to *expenses*—a logical predication error.

C   The verb *includes* is singular but its subject is plural.

D   The introduction of *may* and *was to* do not improve on the given sentence and introduce superfluous words. The force of *was to* is unclear. The relative clause *that* . . . *incur* is misleadingly attached to *period* rather than to *expense*.

E   This version is no longer a sentence—as opposed to an extended noun phrase—because the present participle *including* has replaced the finite verb *include*. The adjectival modifier *incurred by* . . . *period* is misleadingly attached to *account* rather than *expense*.

The correct answer is A.

SC36241.01

906.   Although some had accused Smith, the firm's network manager, of negligence when the crucial data went missing, the CEO defused <u>a situation that was quite tense with her public statement that the debacle was not Smith's fault.</u>

(A)   a situation that was quite tense with her public statement that the debacle was not Smith's fault

(B)   a situation that was quite tense, by publicly stating that the debacle was not Smith's fault

(C)   a situation, which was quite tense, by stating publicly that Smith was not responsible for the debacle

(D)   a quite tense situation with a public statement about the debacle not being Smith's fault

(E)   a quite tense situation by publicly stating the debacle not to have been Smith's fault

Logical Predication; Rhetorical Construction

The sentence is awkwardly and ambiguously worded. The phrase *with her public statement that the debacle was not Smith's fault* could be read as modifying *tense* or as expressing the means by which the CEO defused the situation, which is surely what is intended.

A   The sentence is flawed for the reasons discussed above.

B   **Correct.** This clearly conveys the intended meaning that the CEO defused the situation *by publicly stating that the debacle was not Smith's fault.*

C   By setting *which was quite tense* apart with commas, the tenseness of the situation appears to be inessential, but surely the fact that the situation was quite tense is an important part of the intended meaning. Thus, this version fails rhetorically.

D   *With a public statement about the debacle not being Smith's fault* could be taken to be modifying *situation* or to be indicating the means by which the CEO defused the situation. Therefore, this version is ambiguous.

E   *By publicly stating the debacle not to have been Smith's fault* is awkward and lacks rhetorical force.

The correct answer is B.

SC01077

907.   Many utilities obtain most of their electric power from large coal and nuclear operations at costs that are sometimes <u>two to three times higher as that of power from smaller, more efficient plants that can both</u> make use of waste heat and take advantage of the current abundance of natural gas.

(A)   two to three times higher as that of power from smaller, more efficient plants that can both

(B)   higher by two to three times as that from smaller, more efficient plants that both can

(C)   two to three times higher than those for power from smaller, more efficient plants that can both

(D)   between two to three times higher as those for power from smaller, more efficient plants that both can

(E)   between two to three times higher than from smaller, more efficient plants that they can both

Grammatical Construction; Diction

The sentence compares utilities' high costs of power obtained from large producers with the costs of power obtained from smaller, more economic producers. The comparative form *higher* must be followed by the preposition *than*, not by *as*. The sentence uses the plural *costs*; therefore, the singular pronoun *that* in the phrase *as that of power from . . .* incorrectly refers to a plural antecedent *costs*. An issue that arises in some of the five choices concerns the placing of *both* in a *both . . . and . . .* construction that is meant to indicate parallelism between the clauses *that make use of . . .* and *[that] take advantage of. . . .*

A   As indicated, the use of *as* with *higher* in the comparison between costs is incorrect. Use of the singular pronoun *that* to refer to the plural *costs* is incorrect.

B   The phrase *higher by two to three times* is unclear, and the use of *as* is unidiomatic here. Also, *higher as* is incorrect.

C   **Correct.** The comparative *higher* is correctly followed by *than*. The plural pronoun *those* is correctly used to refer back to *costs*. The placement of *both* indicates correctly the parallel clauses.

D   The phrase *higher as* is unidiomatic. The placement of *both* is ambiguous: either suggesting that the number of "more efficient plants" is just two, or that the verb *can* is not to be read as going along with *take* (this reading would create a grammatical-construction flaw, and render *take advantage . . . gas* into a sentence fragment).

E   This omits a pronoun that would refer back to costs and so fails to capture the comparison intended in the given sentence. It compares the costs of power from large plants with power from smaller plants, i.e., it nonsensically compares costs with power.

The correct answer is C.

SC16020.02

908. Five hundred million different species of living creatures have appeared on Earth, nearly 99 percent of them vanishing.

(A)   Five hundred million different species of living creatures have appeared on Earth, nearly 99 percent of them vanishing.

(B)   Nearly 99 percent of five hundred million different species of living creatures that appeared on Earth have vanished.

(C)   Vanished are nearly 99 percent of the five hundred million different species of living creatures that appeared on Earth.

(D)   Of five hundred million different species of living creatures that have appeared on Earth, nearly 99 percent of them have vanished.

(E)   Of the five hundred million different species of living creatures that have appeared on Earth, nearly 99 percent have vanished.

Verb Form; Logical Predication

The verb forms and overall structure of the sentence do not clearly express a coherent temporal relationship among the species' appearing on Earth, their vanishing, and the current situation. The structure of the sentence could appear strangely to indicate that at the various times when 99 percent of the five hundred million species appeared, each of them had the characteristic *vanishing*. Among the answer choices, the one that is most coherent relates the past events to our present time, conveying the idea that 99 percent of the many species that have ever appeared on Earth *have since* vanished.

A   As explained above, the given sentence is worded in an unclear and potentially misleading way.

B   This version leaves open whether the five hundred million species referred to are *all* of the species that have appeared and, if not, why these five hundred million are mentioned. Also notice that two different verb forms are used: the simple past *appeared* and the past perfect *have vanished*. This difference suggests that not all of the species up to the present are being referred to—contrary to what would be the case if *have appeared* were used.

C   The inverted order of predicate and subject is permissible and even useful in special contexts (e.g., some forms of poetry) but is awkward in this case and not useful in conveying a clear sense. The verb form *have appeared* would be preferable to *appeared*; the former would indicate that the author is referring to all the species up to the present.

D   The repetition of the preposition *of* is confusingly redundant; the words *of them* should have been omitted. Also, the phrasing *Of five hundred . . . Earth* leaves open whether all of such species are being referred to.

E   **Correct.** The inclusion of *the* in the phrasing *Of the . . . Earth* indicates reference to the totality of species that have appeared on Earth up to the present. The past-perfect verb forms *have appeared* and *have vanished* are correct in this context.

The correct answer is E.

SC01523

909. When viewed from the window of a speeding train, <u>the speed with which nearby objects move seems faster than that of</u> more distant objects.

(A) the speed with which nearby objects move seems faster than that of

(B) the speed that nearby objects move seems faster than for

(C) the speed of nearby objects seems faster than

(D) nearby objects' speeds seem to be faster than those of

(E) nearby objects seem to move at a faster speed than do

Logical Predication; Parallelism

The intended meaning of the sentence is easily discerned: objects viewed from a speeding train seem to move faster than more distant objects. However, the sentence is defective in structure. One problem is that the participle *viewed* seems to apply to the subject of the main clause, the noun phrase *the speed with which nearby objects move*. Since this produces nonsense, the sentence needs to be reshaped. Comparing the speed of nearby objects with the speed of more distant objects would ideally be done with parallelism in phrasing, but that is lacking in the given sentence.

A   The subject of the main clause should be *nearby objects* and not *the speed with which nearby objects move*, given the participle in the *when*-clause.

B   The phrase *the speed . . . move* is erroneously made the subject of the main clause, but the phrase contains an additional problem: structurally it makes the relative pronoun *that* the object of the verb *move*.

C   The phrase *the speed . . . objects* is erroneously made the subject of the main clause.

D   The phrase *nearby objects' speeds* is erroneously made the subject of the main clause.

E   **Correct.** The phrase *nearby objects* is correctly made the subject of the verb *seem*, and this fits with the participle in the *when*-clause. Additionally, there is a strict parallelism between *nearby objects* and *more distant objects*, which are being compared with respect to their apparent speed.

The correct answer is E.

SC41451.01

910. Ramón pointed out that food high in whole-grain <u>fiber creates the energy we need to fight illnesses—as do vegetables and lean proteins</u>.

(A) fiber creates the energy we need to fight illnesses—as do vegetables and lean proteins

(B) fiber in addition to vegetables and lean proteins, create the energy we need to fight illnesses

(C) fiber creates the energy we need to fight illnesses, along with vegetables and lean proteins

(D) fiber, vegetables, and lean proteins creates the energy we need to fight illnesses

(E) fiber, as vegetables and lean proteins, create the energy we need to fight illnesses

Logical Predication; Grammatical Construction; Agreement

The sentence is clear and correctly constructed. Its variants go wrong in three different ways. One error is to make the verb number plural where the subject of the verb is singular. Another error consists of the misapplication of a predicate. In the given sentence, the predicate *creates the energy we need to fight illnesses* is correctly applied, and the verb is singular because the subject of the verb is given by the noun phrase *food high in whole grain fiber*. A third error concerns the use of *as*. In the given sentence, it functions correctly as a conjunction introducing a clause that compares foods high in whole-grain fiber with vegetables and lean proteins.

A   **Correct.** As explained above, this avoids errors that appear in the variant versions of the sentence.

B   This fails in two ways. First, the comma immediately following *proteins* in effect creates two sentence fragments which do not comprise a sentence and neither of which can stand on its own as an independent clause. This is a grammatical construction error. Even if the comma were removed, a plural verb is paired with the singular subject designated by *food high in whole-grain fiber.* The phrase *in addition to . . . proteins* is an adjectival modifier of the subject and does not generate a plural subject.

C   The main error here arises from the placement of the final phrase *along with . . . proteins.* Inserting it instead immediately after *fiber* would make the meaning clearer for the reader. It would then be an adjectival modifier of the noun phrase *food high in whole-grain fiber.* But as it stands, it can be read as an adverbial modifier, though it is unclear which verb it would modify.

D   It would make sense to describe a meal plan as rich in vegetables. But vegetables are not parallel to fiber as components of a food, and this indicates that the series *fiber, vegetables, and lean proteins* has logical predication and parallelism issues.

E   The verb *create* is incorrect in being plural, given that its subject *food high in whole-grain fiber* is singular. The role of *as* here is ambiguous: is it meant to function as a preposition—which must govern a noun, noun phrase, or pronoun—or as a conjunction that would introduce a subordinate clause? In the given sentence, it functions, correctly, as a conjunction. Here, though, it is unclear, and looks more like a preposition, since the phrase *as vegetables and lean proteins* contains no verb. However, if taken as a propositional phrase, the phrase could imply that vegetables and lean proteins are high in whole-grain fiber (obviously false). This would be a logical predication error.

The correct answer is A.

SC01487

911.   The English physician Edward Jenner found that if experimental subjects were deliberately infected with cowpox, <u>which caused only a mild illness, they are immune from</u> smallpox.

(A)   which caused only a mild illness, they are immune from

(B)   causing only a mild illness, they become immune from

(C)   which causes only a mild illness, they are immune to

(D)   causing only a mild illness, they became immune from

(E)   which caused only a mild illness, they would become immune to

Verb Form

This sentence describes the result of infecting volunteers with cowpox. A conditional verb form is used to describe the cowpox infection: *if experimental subjects were deliberately infected.* The sentence then incorrectly uses simple present tense for the effects of that infection: *they are immune.* However, since the effects are dependent on an action that may or may not occur, the correct way to express those effects is by using another conditional verb form: *they would become immune.*

A   The effects of a conditional situation are incorrectly expressed using the simple present tense verb *are.*

B   The participle *causing* suggests that infecting the subjects with cowpox caused a mild illness only in some of the cases— but this does not seem to be the intended meaning. The effects of a conditional situation are incorrectly expressed using the simple present tense verb *become.* The preposition *from* is incorrect with *immune*; it should be *to.*

C   The effects of a conditional situation are incorrectly expressed using the simple present tense verb *are.*

D   As explained above in answer choice B, *causing* does not seem to convey the intended meaning. The effects of a conditional situation are incorrectly expressed using the simple past tense verb *became.* The preposition with *immune* should be *to.*

E   **Correct.** The effects of a conditional situation are correctly expressed using the conditional verb *would become.* The preposition *to* (rather than *from*) is correct with *immune.*

The correct answer is E.

SC34740.02

912. As opposed to adults, pound for pound, children breathe twice as much air, drink two and a half times as much water, eat three to four times as much food, and have more skin surface area.

(A) As opposed to adults, pound for pound, children

(B) Compared pound for pound with adults, children

(C) Unlike an adult, pound for pound, children

(D) Pound for pound, a child, unlike an adult, will

(E) Pound for pound, children compared to adults will

Idiom; Logical Predication

The sentence compares children and adults with respect to respiration rate, food and water consumption, and skin surface area. It indicates that, adjusted for body weight, all three quantities are greater in children than in adults.

A   The phrasing *As opposed to adults . . . children . . .* would normally indicate that what is said about children is simply not true of adults. However, the ensuing portion of the sentence names some characteristics that both adults and children have in different ratios to body weight. So the sentence appears to say that children have these characteristics in relatively greater degrees than adults, whereas adults do not have these characteristics in relatively greater degrees than adults.

B   **Correct.** The participial phrase introduced by *Compared,* modifying *children,* indicates clearly that children are to be compared with adults. So the clause *children breathe twice as much air* has the other term of the comparison understood: *twice as much air* [*as adults do*]. The adverbial phrase *pound for pound* modifying *compared* is an idiomatic usage indicating how the comparison is made, namely by adjusting the quantities mentioned in the comparison in order to compensate for the differences in body weight between children and adults.

C   This fails in part because of the lack of parallelism between the singular *an adult* and the plural *children.* But even if we had *unlike adults,* the resulting sentence would fail to make a meaningful comparison; for example, it would imply, incoherently, that children

breathe twice as much air and adults do not do so. The use of the preposition *unlike* in this way can only indicate that children have characteristics that adults lack.

D   The use of the future auxiliary verb form *will* is unnecessary and confusing in this context. As explained in answer choice C, the preposition *unlike* is not an idiomatic way of conveying a comparison of degree with respect to variable characteristics.

E   This version can be interpreted as suggesting, nonsensically, that only children who are compared to adults have the differences indicated with respect to the three variable characteristics.

The correct answer is B.

SC00989

913. The final decades of the twentieth century not only saw an explosion of the literary production among women, but there was also an intense interest in the lives and works of women writers.

(A) not only saw an explosion of the literary production among women, but there was also

(B) not only saw an explosion of literary production in women, but there was also

(C) saw not only an explosion of literary production among women, but also

(D) saw not only an explosion of the literary production by women, but it also saw

(E) saw not only an explosion of literary production by women, but also saw

Parallelism; Diction

The sentence, about twentieth century literary production by women and the interest in women writers, contains a common type of construction that requires parallelism.

A   The predicate of this sentence begins with what would be the first part of the construction *not only saw . . . but also saw.* In this construction, *not also saw* would be parallel with *but also saw,* thus allowing for a statement that is easy for a human to process. However, instead of *but also saw,* the sentence uses *but there was also.* The sentence thus lacks parallelism and is unnecessarily difficult to read.

B This sentence has the same flaw as does sentence A with respect to *but there was also*. Furthermore, the use of *in* in *production in women* is incorrect and should be replaced with *among*.

C **Correct.** This sentence correctly uses, after the main verb *saw*, the construction *not only . . . but also*. It also uses *among* as suggested for answer choice B.

D The portion of this sentence that follows the main verb *saw* starts with what would be the construction *not only . . . but also*. However, instead of *but also*, the sentence uses *but it also saw*. This is incorrect on various grounds. First, the portion is in the predicate and it is clear what the subject is. The pronoun *it*, which refers to the subject, is thus unnecessary. Second, because it fails to correctly follow the construction *not only . . . but also*, the sentence lacks parallelism.

E The main flaw in this sentence is the inclusion of *saw* after *also*. This use of *saw* is redundant and lacks parallelism.

The correct answer is C.

SC07530.02

914. In the six-month period that ended on September 30, the average number of Sunday papers sold by the company was 81,000 less than the comparable period a year ago.

(A) the average number of Sunday papers sold by the company was 81,000 less than

(B) on average, the number of Sunday papers sold by the company was 81,000 less than it was

(C) the company sold an average of 81,000 fewer Sunday papers than in

(D) the company averaged sales of 81,000 fewer Sunday papers than what it did in

(E) the average sale of Sunday papers for the company was 81,000 less than what they were in

Diction; Grammatical Construction; Logical Predication

The major flaw in the sentence is in the phrasing *81,000 less than the comparable period a year ago*. This phrasing compares two disparate things: 81,000 Sunday papers and a period of time. One of the ways in which the sentence could be improved is to have the preposition *in*

immediately following *than*. In that case, *in the comparable period* would be parallel to *In the six-month period* and thus would more accurately express the comparison. Given the structure of the rest of the sentence, an active-voice verb instead of the past-participle construction with *sold* would be more concise and would be rhetorically preferable.

A As explained above, because of the omission of *in* immediately following *than*, the sentence fails to provide the parallelism needed to express the intended comparison.

B The parenthetical *on average* should, for clarity, be placed immediately before the numeral 81,000. The preposition *in* should immediately follow *was* in order to complete the parallelism required to convey the comparison.

C **Correct.** This version has the merit of directly conveying the intended comparison by using the active-voice verb *sold*. With the preposition *in* following *than*, the phrasing is parallel as it should be in this kind of comparison. Additionally, this sentence is more concise with the phrasing *81,000 fewer Sunday papers*.

D The inclusion of the unnecessary clause *what it did* is unclear and awkward.

E The logic of comparison dictates that the average sale should be compared with another average sale. But the pronoun *they* in *what they were* must refer back to the only plural given, i.e., *Sunday papers*, so the sentence is incoherent in comparing Sunday papers with an average sale.

The correct answer is C.

SC07920.02

915. Michelangelo, it is believed, had made his sculpture of David using an eight-inch plaster model that was recently discovered after being lost for nearly 300 years.

(A) Michelangelo, it is believed, had made his sculpture of David using an eight-inch plaster model that was recently discovered after being

(B) An eight-inch plaster model is believed to have been used by Michelangelo for his sculpture of David and recently discovered after it was

(C)   An eight-inch plaster model believed to have been used by Michelangelo for his sculpture of David has been discovered after having been

(D)   It is believed that an eight-inch plaster model that Michelangelo used for his sculpture of David and has recently been discovered after it was

(E)   It is believed that Michelangelo used an eight-inch plaster model for his sculpture of David, and it was recently discovered after having been

Verb Form; Logical Predication

The structure of the sentence leaves the message somewhat unclear. Which of the following is it primarily meant to convey: (1) a belief about how Michelangelo made the sculpture of David or (2) a report about a recent discovery of a plaster model? The use and placement of the parenthetical *it is believed* is awkward and contributes toward making the meaning unclear. For example, is the discovery of the plaster model and its having been lost for almost 300 years part of what is *believed*? Or does the belief merely comprise the claim that Michelangelo used the model? A further issue arises with the phrasing *his sculpture of David using an eight-inch plaster model*. We can readily get an absurd reading from this if we take the participial phrase *using . . . model* as predicated of *David*; it suggests that the sculpture portrayed David in the action of *using an eight-inch plaster model*. Note that a verb-form issue arises with the past-perfect form *had made*, where the simple past *made* would be more appropriate.

A   This version has flaws explained above.

B   This version applies a complex predicate, consisting of two elements conjoined by *and*, to *an eight-inch plaster model*. It describes the model as believed to have been used by Michelangelo and to have been recently discovered. However, this is rhetorically odd with the order in which the two elements of the belief are reported. The sentence seems to convey that it is believed that a recently discovered plaster model lost for 300 years is a model used by Michelangelo. But the order of presentation of the two elements of the belief leaves the phrase *an eight-inch plaster model* somewhat ambiguous: does it refer to a particular plaster model or merely indefinitely, to some plaster model or other?

C   **Correct.** This version creates a clear and coherent sentence. The primary focus of the sentence is the news that a certain plaster model *has been discovered* (this is reported as fact and not characterized as a belief). The complex modifier *believed . . . David* is applied to the noun phrase that is the sentence's subject, *an eight-inch plaster model*. The adverbial phrase *after . . . years* modifies the verb *has been discovered*.

D   This version has a serious sentence-structure flaw: what we have is an attempted but incomplete sentence. What initially seems like a *that* clause reporting the content of a belief is not, in fact, a valid clause; its apparent subject, the complex noun phrase beginning with *an eight-inch plaster model*, lacks a main verb. In other words, the resulting "sentence" is structurally similar to the following sentence portion: *It is believed that the Taj Mahal, which is a tall building*. Note that the word sequence *that . . . years* is a relative clause modifying the noun phrase *an eight-inch plaster model*.

E   The second portion of the sentence, *it was recently discovered . . .* is set off by a comma as an independent clause, so it is not part of what the first part of the sentence says *is believed*. Thus, if the second occurrence of *it* is understood as referring to the model, the sentence is rhetorically somewhat odd. It appears to indicate that Michelangelo is merely believed to have used a plaster model, but it then asserts that the model that is (currently) only believed to exist was recently discovered. Another issue with this version concerns the second occurrence of the pronoun *it*: hypothetically, *it* could refer to *his sculpture of David*, or to *an eight-inch plaster model*. Instead of the pronoun *it*, something like *that model* or even *what is believed to be that model* would make the sentence clearer and more precise.

The correct answer is C.

SC11850.01

916.   Although the rise in the Producer Price Index was greater than expected, most analysts agreed <u>that the index was unlikely to continue going up and that inflation remained</u> essentially under control.

(A) that the index was unlikely to continue going up and that inflation remained

(B) that it was unlikely for the index continuing to go up and for inflation to remain

(C) that the index was unlikely to continue to go up, with inflation to remain

(D) on the unlikelihood that the index would continue going up and that inflation remained

(E) on the unlikelihood that the index would continue to go up and for inflation to remain

Rhetorical Construction; Verb Form

The sentence as given is a better version than any of the variants. The analysts agreed on two points, each expressed in a noun clause, with each clause introduced by *that*. The first point of agreement is on a prediction, the second on a determination of fact. Each of these noun clauses is an object of the verb *agreed*. There is a rhetorically appropriate parallelism between the two clauses, whereas three of the four variants lack this parallelism. Also note that when a past-tense verb takes a *that*-clause as its object, the tense of that clause should be past (e.g., *was, remained*).

A **Correct.** As explained above, this has a rhetorically appropriate parallelism and correctly uses a past-tense verb in each of the noun clauses.

B When using the construction *unlikely for*, it is incorrect to say *unlikely for the index continuing to go up*. The correct construction is *unlikely for the index to continue to go up*. The second parallel member in this choice is correctly constructed: *unlikely . . . for inflation to remain . . . under control*. Here is another correct example: It is unlikely for the company **to survive** this recession.

C The phrase *with inflation to remain* does not clearly convey any information and leaves us guessing what it is intended to mean: for example, is it meant to indicate in context that it was agreed that inflation's remaining under control would impede the continuation of the increase in the index? If this is the intended meaning it would be better expressed by, e.g., the clause *if inflation remained . . .*, plus dropping the comma immediately preceding it.

D Compare *agreed on the unlikelihood that the index would continue going up* in

this version with *agreed that the index was unlikely to continue going up* in the original, best version of the sentence. Note that with the former wording, unlike the latter wording, it is unclear whether it is meant to say that analysts agreed **that** the index was unlikely to continue to go up or that they agreed on whether the index was **likely** or whether it was **unlikely** to go up. The parallelism between the two *that*-clauses here is introduced not by *agreed* but by *unlikelihood*. Worded this way, the sentence appears to indicate that analysts agreed that inflation was unlikely to remain under control.

E As explained in answer choice D above, *agreed on the unlikelihood* is ambiguous. Also, the lack of parallelism between *unlikelihood that* and [*unlikelihood*] *for* is not ideal. Moreover, the former is idiomatic and the latter is not. Finally, the sentence worded in this way indicates that analysts agreed that inflation was unlikely to remain under control.

The correct answer is A.

SC71030.02

917. <u>Just like the Internet today, often being</u> called an "information superhighway," the telegraph was described in its day as an "instantaneous highway of thought."

(A) Just like the Internet today, often being

(B) Just as the Internet is today often

(C) As with the Internet being today often

(D) As is often the case today with the Internet,

(E) Similar to the Internet today, often

Verb Form; Diction

The sentence is somewhat illogical but is designed to indicate a similarity between how the telegraph was once described and how the Internet is described today. The comparison is made using the conjunction *just as*, which introduces a clause about the Internet parallel to a clause about the telegraph.

A This version is illogical in that the telegraph was not *just like the Internet today* with respect to its description; the descriptions are different, even if analogous. The participle *being* in the sequence *being called* is superfluous and awkward, and with this sentence structure it could appear that *the telegraph* is the subject of both *being called* and *was described*.

B   **Correct.** The conjunction *just as* is correctly used to introduce a clause about the Internet in parallel with a clause about the telegraph, functioning to draw an analogy between the cited descriptions of the Internet and the telegraph.

C   The wording *as with* functions as a correlative conjunction and does not introduce a clause that can be conjoined with the clause *the telegraph . . . thought."* This failure is sufficient to render the sentence as a whole ungrammatical. Moreover, the participle *being* serves no useful purpose here.

D   This version implies that the Internet is described today as *an "instantaneous highway of thought"* (in addition to being called *an "information superhighway."*)

E   This version awkwardly appears to make three claims: (1) the telegraph was similar to the Internet in some unspecified way, (2) the Internet is called an "information superhighway," and (3) the telegraph was described as an "instantaneous highway of thought." This literal meaning is unlikely to be what the sentence is intended to express, and if this were the intended meaning, it should be expressed more clearly and directly.

The correct answer is B.

SC17041.01

918. Severely hindered by problems with local suppliers, the fact that the AQ division also had a new management team to adapt to was not seen by the board of directors as a legitimate excuse for such low productivity.

(A)   Severely hindered by problems with local suppliers, the fact that the AQ division also had a new management team to adapt to

(B)   Though severely hindered by local supply problems, the fact that the AQ division also had a new management team to which to adapt

(C)   Severely hindered by problems with local suppliers, the AQ division also had to adapt to a new management team, but this

(D)   Severely hindered by local supply problems, that the AQ division also had to adapt to a new management team

(E)   Though severely hindered by problems with local suppliers, the AQ division's also having a new management team to which it had to adapt

Logical Predication; Rhetorical Construction

The adjectival phrase *Severely . . . suppliers* appears, because of its position, to modify the subject of the main clause, the noun phrase *the fact . . . to.* On this interpretation, the sentence lacks a coherent meaning and has a logical predication error. The opening phrase was most likely intended to modify *the AQ division* instead of *the fact . . . to.*

A   As explained above, this sentence fails because of an illogical relationship between the initial modifier and the phrase that it modifies.

B   A logical predication flaw similar to the one noted above is present in this variant.

C   **Correct.** This makes clear that the adjectival phrase *Severely . . . suppliers* modifies the noun phrase *the AQ division.*

D   This has a logical predication problem like that noted in the sentence as originally presented: the initial adjectival phrase, rather than modifying *the AQ division*, appears to modify a noun clause *that . . . team,* but this would yield an incoherent interpretation of the sentence.

E   This also has a logical predication flaw; because of its position, the phrase *Though severely . . . suppliers* seems to modify the complex noun phrase, *the AQ division's also having a new management team to which it had to adapt.*

The correct answer is C.

SC01037

919. The Eastern State Penitentiary was established in 1822 by reformers advocating that prisoners be held in solitary confinement and hard labor so as to reform them.

(A) advocating that prisoners be held in solitary confinement and hard labor so as to reform them

(B) who were advocating prisoners to be held in solitary confinement and hard labor for their reform

(C) advocating solitary confinement and hard labor as the means to reform prisoners

(D) who advocated solitary confinement and hard labor for the means of prisoner reform

(E) advocating as the means for prisoner reform solitary confinement and hard labor

Idiom; Rhetorical Construction

The sentence describes an effect—reform of prisoners—that those who founded a prison in 1822 hoped would result from two types of punishment they advocated. The sentence as worded, however, does not clearly and idiomatically convey this information. For instance, the antecedent of the pronoun *them* is unclear; it could be taken to be *reformers* or *solitary confinement and hard labor* as well as *prisoners*; *prisoners* is surely what is intended. Additionally, *held in solitary confinement and hard labor* is less than ideal, because *held in hard labor* is not the proper idiom; *sentenced to hard labor* would be better, as would rewording the sentence in the way that the correct answer choice C does. Finally, the phrase *so as to reform them* is grammatically problematic because the subject of the passive-voice verb *be held* is *prisoners*, whereas the implicit subject of the verb *to reform* is presumably the punishments or the prison staff.

A As explained above, the antecedent of the pronoun *them* is unclear; *held in . . . hard labor* is not the proper idiom; and the subject of *reform* is unclear.

B In the phrase *advocating prisoners . . .*, *prisoners* appears to be the object of *advocating*, whereas *solitary confinement and hard labor* should be the object of that verb. Also, as indicated in the paragraph above, the phrase *held in . . . hard labor* is not a proper idiom. Finally, as with *them* in the sentence as given, the antecedent of *their* is unclear.

C **Correct.** The wording here conveys the intended meaning correctly and idiomatically, as well as with clarity and brevity. It indicates that reform of prisoners is the hoped-for result of the advocated punishments.

D The phrase *for the means of prisoner reform* is unclear. For example, it could be intended to suggest that prisoner reform is a means to some unstipulated end or it could be intended to suggest that the two punishment types are means to reforming prisoners. Presumably the latter is what is intended, but, if so, *as* would work much better than *for*.

E The object of the verb *advocating*—*solitary confinement and hard labor*—is unnecessarily far removed from the verb.

The correct answer is C.

SC03288

920. Some anthropologists believe that the genetic homogeneity evident in the world's people is the result of a "population bottleneck"—at some time in the past our ancestors suffered an event, greatly reducing their numbers and thus our genetic variation.

(A) at some time in the past our ancestors suffered an event, greatly reducing their numbers

(B) that at some time in the past our ancestors suffered an event that greatly reduced their numbers

(C) that some time in the past our ancestors suffered an event so that their numbers were greatly reduced,

(D) some time in the past our ancestors suffered an event from which their numbers were greatly reduced

(E) some time in the past, that our ancestors suffered an event so as to reduce their numbers greatly,

Grammatical Construction; Parallelism

The underlined part of this sentence is an explanatory rewording of the clause that follows *believe*. *Scientists believe that X*—[in other words,] *that Y*. In this construction, X and Y are parallel clauses.

A   The omission of *that* after the dash makes the function of the final clause unclear. The structure makes that clause appear to be an awkward and rhetorically puzzling separate assertion that the writer has appended to the prior claim about what the anthropologists believe. The agent or cause of *reducing* is unclear.

B   **Correct.** Repetition of *that* effectively signals the paraphrasing of the belief.

C   The preposition *at* before *some time* is missing; without *at* the adverb *sometime* would be needed instead of this two-word noun phrase. The modifier of *event* is expressed with a wordy passive construction, which destroys the parallelism between it and what follows.

D   Repetition of *that* signals the paraphrasing of the belief and is therefore needed. The preposition *at* before *some time* is missing. The modifier of *event* is expressed with a wordy passive construction, which destroys the parallelism between it and what follows.

E   *That* is repeated in the paraphrase, but in the wrong place. A possible, and absurd, reading of this version is that our ancestors suffered an event in order to willfully reduce their own numbers and thus our genetic variation.

The correct answer is B.

SC01493

921. Through experimenting designed to provide information that will ultimately prove useful in the treatment of hereditary diseases, mice have received bone marrow transplants that give them a new gene.

(A)   Through experimenting designed to provide information that will ultimately prove

(B)   Through experiments designed to provide information ultimately proving

(C)   In experimentation designed to provide information that ultimately proves

(D)   In experimenting designed to provide information ultimately proving

(E)   In experiments designed to provide information that will ultimately prove

Rhetorical Construction; Diction

The sentence reports that mice received a new gene by means of a bone marrow transplant, in the context of experiments aimed at improving treatment of hereditary disease. Issues arise concerning use of the preposition *through*, use of the verb form *experimenting*, and use of certain forms of the verb *prove*. The hoped-for result is more clearly expressed by the future tense *will . . . prove* than by other forms of the verb.

A   The verb form *experimenting* is inappropriate here because it seems to have *mice* as its implicit subject, which would be nonsensical, presuming scientists ran the experiment. The preposition *through* awkwardly signals that the experiments were the means by which—rather than the context in which—the bone marrow transplants were administered.

B   The use of *through* is awkward for the reason already indicated. Compared with *will . . . prove*, the present participle *proving* less clearly signals the prospective nature of the experimenters' goal.

C   The word *experimentation*, because it can simply mean "trying out new things or ideas," is unnecessarily imprecise compared with *experiments*. The present tense *prove* does not clearly signal the prospective nature of the experimenters' goal.

D   The use of the verbal noun *experimenting* is less idiomatic than *experiments*. Compared with *will . . . prove*, the present participle *proving* less clearly signals the prospective nature of the experimenters' goal.

E   **Correct.** The use of the preposition *in*, the word *experiments*, and the future *will . . . prove* create a sentence that avoids some of the potential problems identified.

The correct answer is E.

SC48420.01

922. Linking arrangements <u>among secondary schools and the workplace never evolved in the United States as they have</u> in most other developed countries.

(A) among secondary schools and the workplace never evolved in the United States as they have

(B) in the United States among secondary schools and the workplace never evolved as they did

(C) between secondary schools and the workplace never evolved in the United States as

(D) in the United States between secondary schools and the workplace never evolved as they have

(E) between secondary schools and the workplace never evolved in the United States as they did

Diction; Verb Form

The sentence presents a contrast between the United States and other countries with respect to the relationship (or lack thereof) between school and workplace. The sentence has two flaws. The first flaw is the use of *among*, which should be used to indicate only a relationship of more than two entities. Here, the use of *among* suggests a relationship among secondary schools. But the intended relationship is between two entities: secondary schools on the one hand and the workplace on the other. The preposition *between* is a better usage. The second flaw relates to the use of *have*. It would be appropriate as a proxy for a preceding occurrence of the past-perfect verb *have evolved*, rather than the simple-past verb from, *evolved*, used in the first part of the sentence. The simple-past verb form *did* is a better proxy for *evolved*.

A The sentence is flawed as explained above.

B The default reading of the phrase *in the United States* would treat it as a modifier of *arrangements*, but this reading is nonsensical in the context of the sentence as a whole; it makes no sense to say that linking arrangements in the United States have evolved in other countries. The parallelism that would help to highlight the intended comparison is lost. Also, the preposition *among* is not correct, for the reason explained above.

C This can convey what is likely an unintended meaning: that the linking arrangements never evolved in the United States and never evolved in most other developed countries.

D The default reading of the phrase *in the United States* would treat it as a modifier of *arrangements*, but this reading is nonsensical in the context of the sentence as a whole; it makes no sense to say that linking arrangements in the United States have evolved in other countries. The phrase would be better treated as an adverbial modifier of the verb *evolved*. The parallelism that would help to highlight the comparison is lost.

E **Correct.** None of the flaws identified above, nor any other flaw, is present here.

The correct answer is E.

SC38250.02

923. The ages of tropical rain forest trees provide critical information for understanding the dynamics of tree populations, <u>to determine historical patterns of disturbance, developing sustainable forestry practices, and calculating</u> carbon recycling rates.

(A) to determine historical patterns of disturbance, developing sustainable forestry practices, and calculating

(B) to determine historical patterns of disturbance, develop sustainable forestry practices, and to calculate

(C) determining historical patterns of disturbance, developing sustainable forestry practices, and calculating

(D) determining historical patterns of disturbance, developing sustainable forestry practices, and to calculate

(E) determining historical patterns of disturbance, for developing sustainable forestry practices, and for calculating

Parallelism; Idiom

The sentence tells us that the ages of tropical rain forest trees provide critical information for determining the dynamics of tree populations—and for three other purposes. These three purposes are not coherently expressed; for example, the infinitive form *to determine* is not parallel with the three participle phrases. All three purposes can be expressed—in parallel with *understanding . . . populations*—in a series of participle phrases, with the preposition *for* understood as preceding each one.

A   As explained above, the infinitive phrase *to determine* is not parallel with *understanding* and therefore undermines the completion of a four-member series with *understanding, developing, and calculating.* Such a four-member series has the preposition *for* governing all four members, and *for to determine* does not make sense.

B   The infinitives *to determine* and *to calculate* are not parallel with the participle *understanding;* the parallelism is needed to complete a four-member series in which the preposition *for* governs all four members.

C   **Correct.** The three participles *determining, developing,* and *calculating* function as nouns here, and form a four-member series with *understanding.* The preposition *for* governs the participle *understanding* and carries over to each of the other three participles in the series.

D   The infinitive *to calculate* is not parallel with the participle *understanding* and therefore cannot complete a four-member series of participles functioning as nouns and governed by the preposition *for.*

E   The preposition *for* is missing before the participle *determining.* In a four-member series of participles, all functioning as nouns, the preposition *for* governing *understanding* can be understood as carrying over to the other three participles in the series; for parallelism, the preposition *for* can remain implicit before each of the three. The preposition can also be explicit, but if it is explicitly stated in any of the final three, it must be explicitly stated in each of them.

The correct answer is C.

SC01603

924. The United Parcel Service plans <u>to convert its more than 2,000 gasoline-powered trucks in the Los Angeles area to</u> run on cleaner-burning natural gas.

(A)   to convert its more than 2,000 gasoline-powered trucks in the Los Angeles area to

(B)   to convert its more than 2,000 trucks in the Los Angeles area that are powered by gasoline to

(C)   on converting its more than 2,000 gasoline-powered trucks in the Los Angeles area that will

(D)   for its more than 2,000 gasoline-powered trucks in the Los Angeles area to convert to

(E)   that its more than 2,000 trucks in the Los Angeles area that are powered by gasoline will convert to

Verb Form; Logical Predication

The sentence reports a company's plan to convert certain of its trucks to run on natural gas. Issues to note include: what construction should follow the verb *plan* and how the class of trucks that are to be converted is described.

A   **Correct.** The planned action is described by the infinitive form *to convert.* Of the company's trucks, those in question are specified by the adjective *gasoline-powered* and by the adjectival phrase *in the Los Angeles area.* The goal of the conversion is given by the infinitive verbal phrase *to run . . . gas.*

B   The introduction of the relative clause *that are powered by gasoline* is unnecessarily awkward, especially because the relative pronoun *that* is not adjacent to its antecedent *trucks.*

C   The construction *plans on converting . . .* is not a standard form, even if sometimes used informally. The future tense in the relative clause *that will run . . .* does not clearly specify that the trucks' running on natural gas is the goal of the planned conversion.

D   This fails to capture the thought in the given sentence, which indicates that the company plans to convert the trucks, rather than (as here) the trucks converting. In this version, *to convert* is being used intransitively (without an object), with its implicit subject being the noun phrase *its more than . . . area,* which refers to the trucks.

E   This refers to a plan that the trucks will convert (where *convert* is used intransitively), rather than to a plan to convert the trucks. This intransitive use makes no sense in the context. The introduction of the relative clause *that are powered by gasoline* is unnecessarily awkward.

The correct answer is A.

SC02443
925. Foraging at all times of the day and night, but interspersing their feeding with periods of rest that last <u>between one and eight hours, a sperm whale could eat so</u> much as a ton of squid a day.

(A) between one and eight hours, a sperm whale could eat so

(B) between one and eight hours, sperm whales can eat as

(C) between one to eight hours, sperm whales could eat as

(D) from one to eight hours, sperm whales could eat so

(E) from one to eight hours, a sperm whale can eat so

Agreement; Diction

Although this sentence, as presented, uses the conditional or past verb form *could*, it is more plausibly intended to make a general statement about the actual behavior of a species, a statement that holds in the present day. For that purpose, the present indicative *can* is preferable. *So much as* is not the correct wording to express the upper level of a variable amount; *as much as* should be used instead. Also, although the singular *a sperm whale* can be used to refer to sperm whales generally, the plural *their* needs to refer to the plural *sperm whales*.

A   This sentence incorrectly uses *so*. Also, the plural *their* does not agree with the singular *sperm whale*.

B   **Correct.** Both *can* and *as* are used; also, *sperm whales* agrees with the plural *their*.

C   *To* is the wrong word to use with *between*. The proper construction would be *between . . . and* or *from . . . to*.

D   This sentence incorrectly uses *so*.

E   *So* is not the correct form; also the use of the singular *a sperm whale* does not agree with the plural *their*.

The correct answer is B.

SC14796
926. In some types of pine tree, <u>a thick layer of needles protects the buds from which new growth proceeds; consequently they are able to withstand forest fires relatively well</u>.

(A) a thick layer of needles protects the buds from which new growth proceeds; consequently they are able to withstand forest fires relatively well

(B) a thick needle layer protects buds from where new growth proceeds, so that they can withstand forest fires relatively well

(C) a thick layer of needles protect the buds from which new growth proceeds; thus, they are able to withstand relatively well any forest fires

(D) since the buds from which new growth proceeds are protected by a thick needle layer, consequently they can therefore withstand forest fires relatively well

(E) because the buds where new growth happens are protected by a thick layer of needles, they are able to withstand forest fires relatively easily as a result

Grammatical Construction; Rhetorical Construction

This sentence is fine as written. It uses the correct *from which* to introduce the relative clause modifying *buds* and avoids redundant expressions of causation, such as *consequently . . . therefore,* or *because . . . as a result.*

A   **Correct.** The relative clause starting with *from which* is in the correct form, and the causality is expressed efficiently and clearly with one word, *consequently.*

B   In this context, *needle layer* is less precise than the more standard *layer of needles,* which makes it clear that the layer is composed of needles rather than being, for example, a layer of a needle. *From where* is not the correct form, because it is redundant in using two words that express the idea of location (*from* and *where*) instead of one.

C   The short direct object *any forest fires* is separated from its verb *withstand* by an adverb phrase; this word order is awkward, and is acceptable only with very long direct objects and in some cases where there is no other reasonable way to eliminate ambiguity.

D   This version is unnecessarily redundant in expressing causation, using all of *since, consequently,* and *therefore.* As in answer choice B, *layer of needles* would be more precise than *needle layer.*

E   This version is unnecessarily redundant in expressing causation, using both *because* and *as a result.*

The correct answer is A.

SC08577

927. The tourism commission has conducted surveys of hotels in the most popular resorts, <u>with the ultimate goal of reducing the guests who end up expressing overall dissatisfaction with the service in the hotels</u>.

(A) with the ultimate goal of reducing the guests who end up expressing overall dissatisfaction with the service in the hotels

(B) with the goal to ultimately reduce the number of guests who end up expressing overall dissatisfaction with the hotels' service

(C) ultimately with the goal to reduce expressions of overall dissatisfaction by the guests with the hotel service

(D) in an ultimate attempt to reduce the number of guests that ends up expressing overall dissatisfaction with the hotels' service

(E) with the ultimate goal of reducing the number of guests who express overall dissatisfaction with the hotels' service

Verb Form; Rhetorical Construction

This sentence seems to be saying illogically that the goal is to reduce the guests themselves, instead of to reduce the number of guests who express dissatisfaction or to reduce the expressions of dissatisfaction. *End up* has no meaningful role in the sentence and is somewhat misleading. *End up expressing* suggests that the expression comes as the culmination of a process whose outcome has been uncertain, perhaps as the result of the guests deliberating and changing their minds. Most likely, the goal is to reduce the number of guests who express dissatisfaction, not merely the number of those who end up doing so.

A   *Reducing the guests* should be changed to *reducing the number of guests* or *reducing the expressions of dissatisfaction*. As explained above, e*nd up* is superfluous and misleading.

B   As explained above, e*nd up* is superfluous and misleading. Also, a minor consideration is that *the goal to (infinitive)* is less standard than *the goal of (participle)* and might be jarring to some readers.

C   *With the hotel service* appears illogically to modify *the guests*. This modifier should be placed next to *dissatisfaction*. Also, *ultimately*

with the goal seems to indicate that the commission does not yet have the goal but that it ultimately will have. The more likely intended meaning would be better expressed as *with the ultimate goal*. In general, direct modifiers should not be separated from the word they modify, if possible.

D   The relative clause *that ends up . . .* modifies the plural *guests* (not, in this context, *number*), so the correct verb form is *end up*. Furthermore, e*nd up* is superfluous and misleading.

E   **Correct.** The *with* phrase is concise, and it is the number of guests, not the guests themselves, that is to be reduced. *With the hotel's service* is adjacent to *dissatisfaction*. Also, in the relative clause starting with *who*, the implicit subject of *express* is *guests*, so this verb correctly agrees with its subject.

The correct answer is E.

SC61740.02

928. Unlike historical evidence of weather patterns in other regions of the world, which scientists find abundantly represented in tree rings, ancient glacial ice, or layers of sediment from seasonal plankton, <u>the North Pole's clues about its past climates are almost nonexistent</u>.

(A) the North Pole's clues about its past climates are almost nonexistent

(B) the North Pole does not offer many clues as to its past climates

(C) clues to the past climates of the North Pole are almost nonexistent

(D) there are few clues about past climates for the North Pole

(E) the past climates of the North Pole do not offer many clues

Logical Predication; Rhetorical Construction

The sentence compares and contrasts the evidence of past climates in many regions of the world with the evidence of the North Pole's past climates. An abundance of evidence in one case is contrasted with scarcity of evidence in the other. To convey the contrast, the preposition *unlike* is used. Issues with the given sentence concern (1) the appropriate preposition to use following *clues* and (2) the correct use of parallelism in expressing the things compared.

A The expression *the North Pole's clues* is somewhat odd—as if the clues to North Pole climates were owned by the North Pole or would be found only there. The wording *clues to* is a more standard usage than *clues about*. The sense of the preposition *about* is somewhat vaguer; *clues to* suggests evidence that will provide answers to specific questions, e.g., what patterns of precipitation were there at the North Pole 1 million years ago?

B The placement of *the North Pole* in the subject position of the clause results in an illogical contrast between historical evidence of weather patterns and the North Pole. The locution *clues as to* is nonstandard, as opposed to *clues to*.

C **Correct.** The locution *clues to* is correct. The placement of *clues*—referring to one kind of evidence—in the subject position clearly expresses the idea that *clues to the past climates of the North Pole* are being compared and contrasted with *historical evidence of weather patterns in other regions of the world.* Saying that such clues *are almost nonexistent* is an acceptable way of indicating that few such clues have been found (this may have been true when the sentence was composed).

D One of the standard ways in which the existence of something is expressed, as here, is by using *there is* or *there are*. In some contexts, however, this usage can blunt the rhetorical impact of a sentence or clause. In this case, the subject of the sentence, *clues*, does not begin the clause, and this makes the sentence literally seem to contrast *historical evidence . . .* with *there*. Thus, this structure is rhetorically less effective in expressing the contrast between the *clues* and the *historical evidence* earlier mentioned. The preposition *for* (as opposed to *at* or *of*) fails to capture the meaning most relevant to the overall context.

E The placement of *the North Pole* in the subject position of the clause means that

evidence is illogically contrasted with *climates* (rather than *clues* about those climates).

The correct answer is C.

Questions 929 to 995 - Difficulty: **Hard**

SC01607

929. A new study suggests that the conversational pace of everyday life may be so brisk <u>it hampers the ability of some children for distinguishing discrete sounds and words and, the result is, to make</u> sense of speech.

(A) it hampers the ability of some children for distinguishing discrete sounds and words and, the result is, to make

(B) that it hampers the ability of some children to distinguish discrete sounds and words and, as a result, to make

(C) that it hampers the ability of some children to distinguish discrete sounds and words and, the result of this, they are unable to make

(D) that it hampers the ability of some children to distinguish discrete sounds and words, and results in not making

(E) as to hamper the ability of some children for distinguishing discrete sounds and words, resulting in being unable to make

Rhetorical Construction; Parallelism; Diction

The sentence describes a hypothesized causal series: The fast conversational pace impairs children's ability to distinguish individual sounds and words, and this, in turn, impairs their ability to make sense of speech. These two consequences, both impaired abilities, are most clearly and efficiently expressed in parallel infinitive phrases (*to distinguish* and *to make*). The explanatory phrase *as a result* before the second infinitive clarifies the sequence. The term *ability* should be followed by the preposition *to*, not *for*.

A *For* is the wrong preposition to follow *ability*; the phrase *and, the result is*, introduces a new clause which indicates that children's inability to distinguish sounds enables them to make sense of speech.

B **Correct.** The two abilities hampered by the fast pace of conversation are described with the parallel infinitive phrases *to distinguish* and *to make*.

C   *The result of this* is a new subject that grammatically requires a new verb; the phrase is wordy and unclear.

D   This version nonsensically suggests that the pace of speech results in not making sense of speech, removing the children from the picture as the ones who are affected.

E   The phrase is awkward, wordy, and unclear; *for* is the incorrect preposition to follow ability.

The correct answer is B.

SC07035

930. The nineteenth-century chemist Humphry Davy presented the results of his early experiments in his "Essay on Heat and Light," <u>a critique of all chemistry since Robert Boyle as well as a vision of a</u> new chemistry that Davy hoped to found.

(A)   a critique of all chemistry since Robert Boyle as well as a vision of a

(B)   a critique of all chemistry following Robert Boyle and also his envisioning of a

(C)   a critique of all chemistry after Robert Boyle and envisioning as well

(D)   critiquing all chemistry from Robert Boyle forward and also a vision of

(E)   critiquing all the chemistry done since Robert Boyle as well as his own envisioning of

Parallelism; Rhetorical Construction

The main objective of the sentence is to describe "Essay on Heat and Light" as Davy's presentation of his own experiments and to further explain that the essay served as both a critique of previous chemistry and a vision of a new kind of chemistry. The clearest, most effective form for providing this explanation of the essay's function is to make *critique* and *vision* both appositives of "Essay on Heat and Light," and to present them in a parallel structure.

A   **Correct.** The phrases describing the essay's function are presented in parallel form.

B   *Critique* and *his envisioning* are not parallel; the phrase *and also his envisioning* is unnecessarily wordy; it is also unclear to whom *his* refers.

C   The two descriptors are not parallel.

D   The two descriptors are not parallel.

E   The meaning is confused in the assertion that Davy critiqued his own vision of chemistry.

The correct answer is A.

SC02280

931. To attract the most talented workers, some companies are offering a wider range of <u>benefits, letting employees pick those most important to them</u>.

(A)   benefits, letting employees pick those most important to them

(B)   benefits, letting employees pick the most important of them to themselves

(C)   benefits and letting employees pick the most important to themselves

(D)   benefits and let employees pick the most important to them

(E)   benefits and let employees pick those that are most important to themselves

Diction; Parallelism; Verb Form

The sentence describes the benefit options offered by some companies, which allow employees to *pick those most important to them. Letting* maintains the progressive sense of *are offering; those* refers clearly and concisely to *benefits*; and *them* is the correct pronoun to serve as the object of the preposition *to*.

A   **Correct.** The sentence clearly and concisely explains benefit options that allow employees to *pick those most important to them*.

B   *The most important of them to themselves* is wordy, and the function of *themselves* is unclear. Normally, *themselves* would be either reflexive or emphatic, but in this case it cannot reasonably be taken in either of those ways. This nonstandard use of the pronoun makes it unclear whether *to themselves* is supposed to modify *pick* or *most important of them*.

C   The pronoun *themselves* is used incorrectly, and its intended function is unclear. Normally, *themselves* would be either reflexive or emphatic, but in this case it cannot reasonably be taken in either of those ways. This nonstandard use of the pronoun makes it unclear whether *to themselves* is supposed to modify *pick* or *most important of them*.

D   The present tense verb *let* incorrectly shifts tense from the present progressive *are offering*.

E   The present tense verb *let* incorrectly shifts tense from the present progressive *are offering*; the function of *themselves* is unclear. Normally, *themselves* would be either reflexive or emphatic, but in this case it cannot reasonably be taken in either of those ways. This nonstandard use of the pronoun makes it unclear whether *to themselves* is supposed to modify *pick* or *most important of them*.

The correct answer is A.

SC01583

932. Many of the earliest known images of Hindu deities in India date from the time of the Kushan Empire, fashioned either from the spotted sandstone of Mathura or Gandharan grey schist.

(A) Empire, fashioned either from the spotted sandstone of Mathura or

(B) Empire, fashioned from either the spotted sandstone of Mathura or from

(C) Empire, either fashioned from the spotted sandstone of Mathura or

(D) Empire and either fashioned from the spotted sandstone of Mathura or from

(E) Empire and were fashioned either from the spotted sandstone of Mathura or from

Logical Predication; Parallelism

The sentence makes two claims about the earliest known images of Hindu deities in India: They date from the Kushan Empire, and they are made from sandstone or schist. The clearest, most effective way to incorporate these two claims into a single sentence is to provide two parallel predicates for the single subject, *the earliest known images of Hindu deities in India*. The two options of media, presented as either/or choices, must also be given in parallel structure: *either from . . . or from . . . or from either . . . or. . . .*

A   Placement of the modifier *fashioned . . .* suggests that the *Empire* (the closest noun), not the images of the deities, was fashioned out of these materials; to parallel *either from*, the preposition *from* should also follow *or*.

B   Parallelism requires that *either* precede the first appearance of *from* or that the second appearance of *from* be eliminated.

C   As in answer choices A and B, the placement of the modifier after *Empire* is misleading; parallelism requires that the phrase *fashioned from*, or another comparable verb and preposition, follow *or*.

D   Parallelism requires that a verb follow *or*, since a verb follows *either*.

E   **Correct.** Two verbs, *date* and *were fashioned*, introduce parallel predicates for the subject, *earliest known images*; the choices of media are correctly presented with the structure *either from . . . or from*.

The correct answer is E.

SC01051

933. Tides typically range from three to six feet, but while some places show no tides at all, some others, such as the Bay of Fundy, have tides of at least thirty feet and more.

(A) some others, such as the Bay of Fundy, have tides of at least thirty feet and more

(B) the others, such as the Bay of Fundy, that have tides of more than thirty feet

(C) others, such as the Bay of Fundy, have tides of more than thirty feet

(D) those at the Bay of Fundy, which has tides of more than thirty feet

(E) the ones at the Bay of Fundy have tides of at least thirty feet and more

Idiom; Grammatical Construction

This sentence defines typical tides and then draws a contrast between locations with tides lower than that norm and locations with tides higher than the norm. The proper idiom for drawing this contrast is *some places* and *others*—not *some places* and *some others* as written. The height of tides in places such as the Bay of Fundy is expressed in a confusing manner since *at least thirty feet* sets a lower limit on the height. This wording is pointlessly redundant with the phrase *and more*, which follows it. *At least* would normally be used to indicate that the writer does not know, or prefers not to say, whether the tides are sometimes higher. *And more* rhetorically conflicts with this by signaling a definite commitment to the claim that they are (at least sometimes) higher. A charitable reading suggests that *tides of more than thirty feet* is the intended meaning.

A   The sentence contains repetitive and redundant wording—*some places* and *some others*, and *at least thirty feet and more*.

B   The final clause is incomplete because *that* introduces a subordinate clause, leaving the subject *others* with no main verb.

C   Correct. A contrast is drawn between places with low tides and places with high tides using the expression *some places* and *others*, and the height of the high tides is expressed clearly and without redundancy.

D   The pronoun *those*, which refers to *places*, does not make sense along with *at the Bay of Fundy*, which names a single place; the final clause is incomplete because *which* introduces a subordinate clause, leaving the subject *those* with no verb.

E   The word *ones*, which refers to *places*, does not make sense along with *at the Bay of Fundy*, which names a single place; *at least thirty feet and more* is redundant and confusing.

The correct answer is C.

SC01028

934. A leading figure in the Scottish Enlightenment, <u>Adam Smith's two major books are to democratic capitalism what</u> Marx's *Das Kapital* is to socialism.

(A)   Adam Smith's two major books are to democratic capitalism what

(B)   Adam Smith's two major books are to democratic capitalism like

(C)   Adam Smith's two major books are to democratic capitalism just as

(D)   Adam Smith wrote two major books that are to democratic capitalism similar to

(E)   Adam Smith wrote two major books that are to democratic capitalism what

Idiom; Logical Predication

A leading figure in the Scottish Enlightenment describes Adam Smith, not his two books, so the name of Adam Smith must immediately follow the opening phrase. The comparison between Smith's books and Marx's book is expressed as a ratio, so the correct idiomatic expression is *x is to y what a is to b.*

A   The opening phrase is a dangling modifier because it describes Smith, not his books.

B   The opening phrase is a dangling modifier;

like is an incorrect word for making the comparison.

C   The opening phrase is a dangling modifier; *just as* is an incorrect term for the comparison.

D   *Similar to* is an incorrect conclusion to the comparison introduced by *are to.*

E   Correct. The opening phrase is followed by the subject that it modifies, Adam Smith, and the comparison of the two men's work is presented idiomatically.

The correct answer is E.

SC04331

935. Researchers studying <u>the brain scans of volunteers who pondered ethical dilemmas have found that the basis for making tough moral judgments is</u> emotion, not logic or analytical reasoning.

(A)   the brain scans of volunteers who pondered ethical dilemmas have found that the basis for making tough moral judgments is

(B)   the brain scans of volunteers who pondered ethical dilemmas and found the basis to make tough moral decisions to be

(C)   the brain scans of volunteers pondering ethical dilemmas and found that the basis for making tough moral decisions is

(D)   volunteers' brain scans while pondering ethical dilemmas have found the basis to make tough moral judgments to be

(E)   volunteers' brain scans while they pondered ethical dilemmas have found that the basis for making tough moral judgments is

Logical Predication; Grammatical Construction

The sentence reports that researchers got volunteers to ponder ethical dilemmas and make moral judgments. Brain scans revealed that the volunteers' judgments were based on emotion rather than logical analysis. The main clause of this sentence is *Researchers . . . have found that . . .;* embedded within this sentence, the present participial phrase *studying . . .* describes the researchers, the relative clause *who pondered . . .* describes the volunteers, and the object of the main verb appears as a noun clause *that the basis . . . is. . . .*

A   Correct. The sentence is coherent and grammatically correct.

B   The use of the conjunction *and* immediately

before *found* indicates that the past tense verbs *pondered* and *found* both have *volunteers* as subject, but this changes the original sentence, making it a long noun phrase rather than a complete sentence.

C The conjunction *and* leaves the verb *found* without a subject, and this changes the original sentence into a sequence of incoherently connected phrases rather than a complete sentence.

D The phrase *the basis to make* is unidiomatic, a sufficient reason for rejecting this option. The placement of the modifier *while pondering* appears in a form parallel to *studying* and means that the researchers, not the volunteers, were pondering ethical dilemmas. This does not make the sentence incoherent, but creates a sentence that fails to capture the meaning clearly intended in the original sentence.

E Because the word *volunteers'* is a possessive form, and functions adjectivally as a modifier of *brain scans*, *they* must refer back to *researchers* rather than to *volunteers'*. This is not incorrect in itself, but, as with answer choice D, the resulting sentence fails to capture the intended meaning of the original sentence.

The correct answer is A.

SC02060

936. Rivaling the pyramids of Egypt or even the ancient cities of the Maya as an achievement, the army of terra-cotta warriors created to protect Qin Shi Huang, China's first emperor, in his afterlife is more than 2,000 years old and took 700,000 artisans more than 36 years to complete.

(A) the army of terra-cotta warriors created to protect Qin Shi Huang, China's first emperor, in his afterlife is more than 2,000 years old and took 700,000 artisans more than 36 years to complete

(B) Qin Shi Huang, China's first emperor, was protected in his afterlife by an army of terra-cotta warriors that was created more than 2,000 years ago by 700,000 artisans who took more than 36 years to complete it

(C) it took 700,000 artisans more than 36 years to create an army of terra-cotta warriors more than

2,000 years ago that would protect Qin Shi Huang, China's first emperor, in his afterlife

(D) more than 2,000 years ago, 700,000 artisans worked more than 36 years to create an army of terra-cotta warriors to protect Qin Shi Huang, China's first emperor, in his afterlife

(E) more than 36 years were needed to complete the army of terra-cotta warriors that 700,000 artisans created 2,000 years ago to protect Qin Shi Huang, China's first emperor, in his afterlife

Logical Predication; Rhetorical Construction

The opening modifier, *Rivaling the pyramids . . .* describes *the army of terra-cotta warriors*, which must immediately follow the modifier. The placement of the predicates that follow is important; they must clarify two things about the army of terra-cotta warriors: how old it is and how long it took to complete. The clearest and most effective way to express these two assertions is as parallel verb phrases, *is more than 2,000 years old* and *took . . . more than 36 years to complete*.

A **Correct.** The opening phrase correctly modifies the subject, *the army of terra-cotta warriors*; the placement of modifiers and predicates in the main clause makes the meaning of the sentence clear.

B Opening phrase is a dangling modifier because it does not describe the subject *Qin Shi Huang*; in addition, the sentence is awkward and unclear.

C Opening phrase is a dangling modifier because it does not describe the subject *it*; the sequence of information presented is confusing and unclear.

D Opening phrase is a dangling modifier because it does not describe the subject *700,000 artisans*.

E Opening phrase is a dangling modifier because it does not describe the subject *more than 36 years*.

The correct answer is A.

SC03675

937. In California, a lack of genetic variation in the Argentine ant has allowed the species to spread widely; due to their being so genetically similar to one another, the

ants consider all their fellows to be a close relative and thus do not engage in the kind of fierce intercolony struggles that limits the spread of this species in its native Argentina.

(A) due to their being so genetically similar to one another, the ants consider all their fellows to be a close relative and thus do not engage in the kind of fierce intercolony struggles that limits

(B) due to its being so genetically similar, the ant considers all its fellows to be a close relative and thus does not engage in the kind of fierce intercolony struggles that limit

(C) because it is so genetically similar, the ant considers all its fellows to be close relatives and thus does not engage in the kind of fierce intercolony struggles that limits

(D) because they are so genetically similar to one another, the ants consider all their fellows to be close relatives and thus do not engage in the kind of fierce intercolony struggles that limit

(E) because of being so genetically similar to one another, the ants consider all their fellows to be a close relative and thus do not engage in the kind of fierce intercolony struggles that limits

Diction; Agreement

Words that express comparisons, such as *similar*, require either a plural object, with an optional expression of the entities being compared, or a singular object, in which case this explicit comparison is required. Thus *its being so genetically similar*, without this explicit comparison, is incorrect. Also, the two sides of the construction *consider . . . to be* must agree in number (*fellows . . . close relatives*, not *fellows . . . a close relative*).

A *Consider all their fellows to be a close relative* shows incorrect agreement, with plural *fellows* and singular *a close relative*.

B *Its being so genetically similar* is incorrect because there is no explicit statement of what the ant is similar to; also, the plural *fellows* and *singular a close relative* do not agree.

C *It is so genetically similar* is incorrect because there is no explicit statement of what the ant is similar to.

D **Correct.** The clause with *similar* uses the plural *they* and an explicit *to one another*, and agreement is respected between *ants* and *fellows*.

E The plural *fellows* and singular *a close relative* do not agree.

The correct answer is D.

SC07758

938. Next month, state wildlife officials are scheduled to take over the job of increasing the wolf population in the federally designated recovery area, the number of which will however ultimately be dictated by the number of prey in the area.

(A) area, the number of which will however

(B) area; the size of the population, however, will

(C) area, however the number of wolves will

(D) area; the number of which will, however,

(E) area, when the size of the population will, however,

Grammatical Construction; Diction

The point of the sentence is that the ultimate size of the wolf population will be determined according to the number of prey in the area. However, the phrase *the number of which* has no referent since it cannot logically refer to the noncount noun *population* or to the singular *wolf*, which is used adjectivally here to modify *population*. The idea can be expressed clearly by making *the size of the population* the subject of a new independent clause: *the size of the population* will *be dictated by the number of prey*.

A *The number of which* cannot logically refer to the noncount noun *population* or to the singular *wolf*, which is used adjectivally here to modify *population*.

B **Correct.** The idea is expressed clearly with an independent clause: *the size of the population* will *be dictated by the number of prey*.

C *However* is intended to serve as a conjunctive adverb between the two independent clauses, but the punctuation of the sentence creates confusion by suggesting that *however* is modifying *are scheduled*. A semicolon after *area* and a comma after *however* would make the intended function of *however* clear.

D *The number of which* cannot logically refer to the noncount noun *population*; the semicolon creates confusion since it is not followed by an independent clause.

E *When* illogically suggests that the size of the population will be determined at the moment wildlife officials take over the task. This conflicts with the ensuing claim that the determination will *ultimately* depend on a long-term condition (*the number of prey in the area*).

The correct answer is B.

SC02710

939. About 5 million acres in the United States have been invaded by leafy spurge, a herbaceous plant from Eurasia with milky sap that gives mouth sores to cattle, displacing grasses and other cattle food and rendering rangeland worthless.

(A) States have been invaded by leafy spurge, a herbaceous plant from Eurasia with milky sap that gives mouth sores to cattle, displacing grasses and other cattle food and rendering

(B) States have been invaded by leafy spurge, *a herbaceous plant from Eurasia*, with milky sap, that gives mouth sores to cattle and displaces grasses and other cattle food, rendering

(C) States have been invaded by leafy spurge, a herbaceous plant from Eurasia having milky sap that gives mouth sores to cattle and displacing grasses and other cattle food, rendering

(D) States, having been invaded by leafy spurge, a herbaceous plant from Eurasia with milky sap that gives mouth sores to cattle, displaces grasses and other cattle food, and renders

(E) States, having been invaded by leafy spurge, a herbaceous plant from Eurasia that has milky sap giving mouth sores to cattle and displacing grasses and other cattle food, rendering

Logical Predication; Grammatical Construction

The sentence explains that leafy spurge causes mouth sores in cattle and also displaces other plants eaten by cattle. However, the structure of the sentence seems, illogically, to indicate that *displacing grasses* modifies either the immediately preceding phrase (*that gives mouth sores to cattle*) or the main subject of the sentence (*about 5 million acres in the United States*). A clearer way to express the effects of the leafy spurge invasion is with a compound predicate in the subordinate clause: *that gives mouth sores . . . and displaces grasses.*

A Displacing grasses appears illogically to modify either about 5 million acres in the United States or that gives mouth sores to cattle.

B **Correct.** The effects of the leafy spurge invasion are expressed clearly with a compound predicate in the subordinate clause: that gives mouth sores . . . and displaces grasses. The parenthetical commas around with milky sap make it clear that the entire phrase that gives . . . and displaces . . . rendering . . . is intended to modify a herbaceous plant from Eurasia. Although the sap may well be the means by which the plant gives mouth sores to cattle, the sentence can be well formed and meaningful without making a definite commitment to whether that is the case.

C *Having* and *displacing* should not be expressed in parallel form since the first is a permanent characteristic of leafy spurge and the second refers to an effect of the plant's invasion.

D The subject of the sentence, *5 million acres* is not clearly paired with a verb. The structure of the sentence suggests that *5 million acres* may be the intended subject of both *displaces* and *renders* but it is illogical to say that 5 million acres displaces grasses and renders rangeland worthless.

E The subject of the sentence, *5 million acres* is not clearly paired with a verb. The structure of the sentence suggests that *5 million acres* may be the intended subject of both *displaces* and *renders* but it is illogical to say that 5 million acres displaces grasses and renders rangeland worthless.

The correct answer is B.

SC01445

940. While it costs about the same to run nuclear plants as other types of power plants, it is the fixed costs that stem from building nuclear plants that makes it more expensive for them to generate electricity.

(A) While it costs about the same to run nuclear plants as other types of power plants, it is the fixed costs that stem from building nuclear plants that makes it more expensive for them to generate electricity.

(B) While the cost of running nuclear plants is about the same as for other types of power plants, the fixed costs that stem from building nuclear plants make the electricity they generate more expensive.

(C) Even though it costs about the same to run nuclear plants as for other types of power plants, it is the fixed costs that stem from building nuclear plants that makes the electricity they generate more expensive.

(D) It costs about the same to run nuclear plants as for other types of power plants, whereas the electricity they generate is more expensive, stemming from the fixed costs of building nuclear plants.

(E) The cost of running nuclear plants is about the same as other types of power plants, but the electricity they generate is made more expensive because of the fixed costs stemming from building nuclear plants.

Agreement; Logical Predication

The singular verb *makes* does not agree in number with its subject, *fixed costs*. Other versions of the sentence have problems arising from ambiguous antecedents or other predication issues.

A   The verb *makes* does not agree in number with its subject, *the fixed costs*.

B   **Correct.** The verb *make* agrees in number with its subject, *the fixed costs*. Furthermore, this version has none of the predication problems found in the other answer choices.

C   This version has an agreement issue: The verb *makes* does not agree in number with its subject *the fixed costs*. Also, the antecedent of *they* would grammatically appear to be *fixed costs*, but surely the intended antecedent is *nuclear power plants*.

D   The phrase beginning with *stemming from* is a dangling modifier, as it is unclear what the phrase is supposed to be describing. Additionally, the antecedent of *they* is unclear: is the antecedent *nuclear power plants* or *other types of power plants*?

E   This version illogically compares *The cost of running nuclear power plants* to *other types of power plants*. The sentence would be improved if it began *The cost of running nuclear power plants is about the same as the cost of running other types of power plants*.

The correct answer is B.

SC03207

941. The 32 species that make up the dolphin family are closely related to whales and in fact <u>include the animal known as the killer whale, which can grow to be 30 feet long and is</u> famous for its aggressive hunting pods.

(A) include the animal known as the killer whale, which can grow to be 30 feet long and is

(B) include the animal known as the killer whale, growing as big as 30 feet long and

(C) include the animal known as the killer whale, growing up to 30 feet long and being

(D) includes the animal known as the killer whale, which can grow as big as 30 feet long and is

(E) includes the animal known as the killer whale, which can grow to be 30 feet long and it is

Rhetorical Construction; Agreement

The subject of the sentence is *the 32 species that make up the dolphin family*, and the sentence makes two claims about them: They are closely related, and they include the killer whale. The relative pronoun *which* restates the object of the second verb, reintroducing *the animal known as the killer whale* as the subject of a relative clause followed by two parallel verbs: *can grow* and *is famous*.

A   **Correct.** The sentence is concise, verbs agree in number with their subjects, and the relative pronoun *which* indicates clearly that *the animal known as the killer whale* is the subject of the verbs in the dependent clause.

B   Changing the verb to the participial *growing* introduces ambiguity, because it could refer back to the subject of the sentence (*32 species*).

C   The participial *growing* might refer to *the 32 species*; the introduction of *being* is unnecessarily wordy and adds nothing in terms of meaning.

D   *as big as* is an idiomatically incorrect expression of the comparison; the plural verb form *include* is needed to match the plural subject *the 32 species*.

E   *It* simply restates the subject of the previous phrase, introducing more words but no additional meaning; the singular verb form *includes* should be the plural form *include*.

The correct answer is A.

SC06611

942. The first trenches <u>that were cut into a 500-acre site at Tell Hamoukar, Syria, have yielded strong evidence for centrally administered complex societies in northern regions of the Middle East that were arising simultaneously with but</u> independently of the more celebrated city-states of southern Mesopotamia, in what is now southern Iraq.

(A) that were cut into a 500-acre site at Tell Hamoukar, Syria, have yielded strong evidence for centrally administered complex societies in northern regions of the Middle East that were arising simultaneously with but

(B) that were cut into a 500-acre site at Tell Hamoukar, Syria, yields strong evidence that centrally administered complex societies in northern regions of the Middle East were arising simultaneously with but also

(C) having been cut into a 500-acre site at Tell Hamoukar, Syria, have yielded strong evidence that centrally administered complex societies in northern regions of the Middle East were arising simultaneously but

(D) cut into a 500-acre site at Tell Hamoukar, Syria, yields strong evidence of centrally administered complex societies in northern regions of the Middle East arising simultaneously but also

(E) cut into a 500-acre site at Tell Hamoukar, Syria, have yielded strong evidence that centrally administered complex societies in northern regions of the Middle East arose simultaneously with but

Rhetorical Construction; Agreement; Grammatical Construction

This sentence, explaining interconnections among a number of events, needs to be streamlined as much as possible in order to become understandable. To this end, unnecessary words and structures should be eliminated. Prominent among these are the relative clauses beginning with *that*. Additionally, the subject of this sentence is the plural *trenches*, which requires a plural verb.

A *That were cut . . .* and *that were arising . . .* are unnecessarily wordy and create an unnecessarily complicated and confusing sentence structure.

B In addition to the unnecessarily wordy relative clauses, the singular verb *yields* does not agree with the plural subject *trenches*.

C *Having been cut . . .* is unnecessarily wordy; *arising simultaneously* must be followed by the preposition *with* in order to make sense.

D The singular verb *yields* does not agree with the plural subject *trenches*; *also* adds no meaning to the sentence.

E **Correct.** Unnecessary clauses and phrases are avoided, and the subject and verb of the main clause agree in number.

The correct answer is E.

SC02317

943. Companies are relying more and more on networked computers for such critical tasks as inventory management, electronic funds transfer, and electronic data interchange, <u>in which standard business transactions are handled via computer rather than on paper</u>.

(A) in which standard business transactions are handled via computer rather than on paper

(B) where computers handle standard business transactions rather than on paper

(C) in which computers handle standard business transactions instead of on paper

(D) where standard business transactions are handled, not with paper, but instead via computer

(E) in which standard business transactions are being handled via computer, in place of on paper

Idiom; Logical Predication; Rhetorical Construction

The concluding comparison in this sentence uses the idiom *rather than*, which requires parallel structures. In this sentence the prepositional phrase *via computer* parallels *on paper*. Substituting *where* for *in which* creates a nonstandard idiom.

A **Correct.** This sentence uses standard idiomatic constructions and avoids the problems that are found in the other versions.

B *Where* is a nonstandard way to refer to a noun that does not name a location. If electronic data interchange were a location, this version would entail the odd claim that *on paper* is an alternative location at which computers would be expected to process information.

C The comparison of the clause *computers handle . . .* with the prepositional phrase *on paper* illogically treats a location (*on paper*) as an alternative to an activity (*computers handle*).

D   As in answer choice B, *where* is a nonstandard idiom. The commas around *not with paper* appear to make this phrase parenthetical; thus, it is somewhat unclear what *instead via computer* is contrasted with.

E   The pile of prepositions in the phrase *in place of on paper* is unnecessarily confusing and wordy.

The correct answer is A.

SC07231

944. Combining enormous physical strength with higher intelligence, the Neanderthals <u>appear as equipped for facing any obstacle the environment could put in their path,</u> but their relatively sudden disappearance during the Paleolithic era indicates that an inability to adapt to some environmental change led to their extinction.

(A)   appear as equipped for facing any obstacle the environment could put in their path,

(B)   appear to have been equipped to face any obstacle the environment could put in their path,

(C)   appear as equipped to face any obstacle the environment could put in their paths,

(D)   appeared as equipped to face any obstacle the environment could put in their paths,

(E)   appeared to have been equipped for facing any obstacle the environment could put in their path,

Verb Form; Diction

Because Neanderthals "disappeared," the verb describing their apparent abilities cannot be present tense, so *as equipped* must be changed to *to have been equipped*. The expression *equipped to face* is clearer and more direct than *equipped for facing*.

A   *As equipped* indicates that Neanderthals still appear this way; *equipped* should be followed by an infinitive form instead of a prepositional phrase.

B   **Correct.** The verb tense clearly indicates that the current evidence is about Neanderthals in the past.

C   *As equipped* does not indicate that Neanderthals appeared this way in the past; while individual Neanderthals may well have followed different paths, this sentence is about the single evolutionary path taken by Neanderthals as a species.

D   Present-tense *appear* is needed to parallel present-tense *indicates* and to reinforce that this is current evidence about Neanderthals in the past; as in answer choice C, *paths* should be singular.

E   *For facing* is an incorrect substitution of a prepositional phrase for an infinitive.

The correct answer is B.

SC02135

945. To map Earth's interior, geologists use a network of seismometers to chart seismic waves that originate in the earth's crust and ricochet around its <u>interior, most rapidly traveling through cold, dense regions and slower</u> through hotter rocks.

(A)   interior, most rapidly traveling through cold, dense regions and slower

(B)   interior, which travel most rapidly through cold, dense regions, and more slowly

(C)   interior, traveling most rapidly through cold, dense regions and more slowly

(D)   interior and most rapidly travel through cold, dense regions, and slower

(E)   interior and that travel most rapidly through cold, dense regions and slower

Grammatical Construction; Parallelism

This sentence explains in detail an activity of geologists (using seismometers to chart waves), focusing primarily on the object, seismic waves. A description of these waves is developed in a relative clause (*that originate . . . hotter rocks*) that contains a compound verb phrase (*originate . . . ricochet . . .*). The action, *ricochet*, is further described in a participial phrase in which *traveling . . .* is then further described in a comparison of travel speeds in cold and hot regions of Earth's crust.

A   The two expressions of comparison should be parallel. Because *most rapidly* is placed before the verb, it appears to modify the entire ensuing phrase, including *slower*. This and the contrast between the forms of *rapidly* and *slower* make the comparisons nonparallel. Some usage advisers consider *slower* to be only an adjective. Although *slower* is sometimes used as an adverb, that usage would be more appropriate with the parallel *faster*. The stark contrast between this typically adjectival form and the clearly adverbial *ly* form is somewhat jarring.

B   The referent of the relative pronoun *which* is unclear.

C   Correct. The modifiers are parallel and correctly positioned in relation to the verb.

D   This version of the sentence offers *travel* as a compound verb parallel with *originate* and *ricochet* rather than as a description of how the waves ricochet. It has the same problems with parallelism as answer choice A.

E   Adding a relative clause *and that . . .* makes this sentence wordy and awkward.

The correct answer is C.

SC02470

946. Prices at the producer level are only 1.3 percent higher now <u>than a year ago and are going down, even though floods in the Midwest and drought in the South are hurting crops and therefore raised</u> corn and soybean prices.

(A)   than a year ago and are going down, even though floods in the Midwest and drought in the South are hurting crops and therefore raised

(B)   than those of a year ago and are going down, even though floods in the Midwest and drought in the South are hurting crops and therefore raising

(C)   than a year ago and are going down, despite floods in the Midwest and drought in the South, and are hurting crops and therefore raising

(D)   as those of a year ago and are going down, even though floods in the Midwest and drought in the South hurt crops and therefore raise

(E)   as they were a year ago and are going down, despite floods in the Midwest and drought in the South, and are hurting crops and therefore raising

Logical Predication; Verb Form

The sentence as written makes an illogical comparison between *prices at the producer level* and a time period (*a year ago*); surely the intended comparison is between such prices now and those of a year ago. The clause at the end of the sentence states that flooding and a drought *are hurting* crops, and as a result of this, they have

raised prices of certain crops. *Are hurting* is in the present progressive tense, indicating an ongoing process; *raised* is in the simple past tense, indicating a completed action. It would be more appropriate to use the present progressive tense here as well, *[are] raising*.

A   The first part of this version illogically compares prices to a time; the second part of the sentence indicates that a completed action (*raised . . . prices*) results from an ongoing present condition (*floods . . . and drought . . . are hurting crop*s).

B   Correct. This version makes an appropriate comparison (between prices now and those of a year ago), and uses tenses in an appropriate way.

C   Like answer choice A, this version illogically compares prices to time past. Furthermore, in this version, *Prices* is the subject not only for the verb *are* but also for the verbs *are hurting* and *[are] raising*, which makes no sense.

D   The comparative adjective *higher* requires the comparative term *than* instead of *as*; the tenses of the verbs in the latter half of the sentence, *hurt* (simple past) and *raise* (simple present), do not work together logically.

E   Like answer choice D, this version inappropriately uses *as* instead of *than* with *higher*. Furthermore, like answer choice C, in this version *[p]rices* is the subject not only for the verb *are* but also for the verbs *are hurting* and *[are] raising*.

The correct answer is B.

SC07117

947. Fossils of the arm of a <u>sloth found in Puerto Rico in 1991, and dated at 34 million years old, made it the earliest known mammal of</u> the Greater Antilles Islands.

(A)   sloth found in Puerto Rico in 1991, and dated at 34 million years old, made it the earliest known mammal of

(B)   sloth, that they found in Puerto Rico in 1991, has been dated at 34 million years old, thus making it the earliest mammal known on

(C)   sloth that was found in Puerto Rico in 1991, was dated at 34 million years old, making this the earliest known mammal of

(D)   sloth, found in Puerto Rico in 1991, have been dated at 34 million years old, making the sloth the earliest known mammal on

(E)   sloth which, found in Puerto Rico in 1991, was dated at 34 million years old, made the sloth the earliest known mammal of

Agreement; Logical Predication

The subject of the sentence is the plural *fossils*, not *sloth*, and therefore requires a plural verb. *It* therefore does not have a singular antecedent. To clarify the identification of the oldest known mammal, the noun *the sloth* must be explicitly identified.

A   Because *sloth* is the object of a preposition and not the subject of the sentence, there is no reasonable antecedent for the pronoun *it*; in this construction, the subject of *made* is *fossils*, but it makes no sense to say that the *fossils* made it the earliest known mammal.

B   The introduction of the mysterious *they*, a pronoun without a reference, adds confusion to this sentence; the singular verb does not agree with the plural subject.

C   The relative clause *that was . . .* is wordy and awkward; the singular verb does not agree with the plural subject.

D   **Correct.** The plural verb agrees with its plural subject, and *the sloth* is explicitly identified as *the earliest known mammal.*

E   The singular verb does not agree with the plural subject.

The correct answer is D.

SC01550

948. Recently physicians have determined that stomach ulcers are not caused by stress, alcohol, or rich foods, but a bacterium that dwells in the mucous lining of the stomach.

(A)   not caused by stress, alcohol, or rich foods, but

(B)   not caused by stress, alcohol, or rich foods, but are by

(C)   caused not by stress, alcohol, or rich foods, but by

(D)   caused not by stress, alcohol, and rich foods, but

(E)   caused not by stress, alcohol, and rich foods, but are by

Parallelism; Diction

The formula used in this sentence *not this but that* requires parallel elements following *not* and *but*. This means that *not by stress, alcohol, or rich foods* must be balanced by *but by a bacterium. . . .* There is no need to repeat the verb *are caused*, or even the auxiliary verb *are*, because the verb precedes the *not by . . . but by . . .* formula. The substitution of the conjunction *and* for the conjunction *or* changes the meaning of the sentence: *Stress, alcohol and rich foods* identifies the combination of these three factors as a suggested cause of stomach ulcers, whereas *stress, alcohol, or rich foods* offers three individual possibilities. There is no way to tell which one of these is the intended meaning of the sentence.

A   To preserve parallelism, *but* should be followed by *by*.

B   There is no reason to repeat the auxiliary verb *are*.

C   **Correct.** This sentence correctly uses the *not by . . . but by . . .* formula.

D   To preserve parallelism, *but* should be followed by *by*.

E   To preserve parallelism, *but* should be followed by *by*.

The correct answer is C.

SC05848

949. The eyes of the elephant seal adapt to darkness more quickly than any other animal yet tested, thus allowing it to hunt efficiently under the gloomy conditions at its feeding depth of between 300 and 700 meters.

(A)   The eyes of the elephant seal adapt to darkness more quickly than any other animal yet tested, thus allowing it

(B)   The eyes of the elephant seal adapt to darkness more quickly than does any other animal yet tested, allowing them

(C)   The eyes of the elephant seal adapt to darkness more quickly than do those of any other animal yet tested, allowing it

(D)   Because they adapt to darkness more quickly than any other animal yet tested, the eyes of the elephant seal allow it

(E)   Because the eyes of the elephant seal adapt to darkness more quickly than do those of any other animal yet tested, it allows them

Logical Predication; Agreement

Logically, the eyes of the elephant seal should be contrasted with the eyes of other animals, not with the animals themselves. The sentence must make this comparison directly and precisely, with each subject interpretable as the subject of *adapt*. Given the correct subject (*those of any other animal yet tested*), which is plural, any reference to it must also be plural.

A   *Any other animal yet tested* is incorrectly set up as the subject of *adapt*.

B   *Any other animal yet tested* is incorrectly set up as the subject of *adapt*. The plural pronoun *them* seems to refer to eyes. Although there is a sense in which eyes can hunt, it is more reasonable to suppose that, in this context, the writer's intention is to mention how the eyes' quick adaptation allows the seal to hunt efficiently.

C   **Correct.** The subject of the comparative phrase is correctly *those of any other animal yet tested*, the plural verb *do* correctly agrees with this subject (*those*), and the singular pronoun *it* correctly agrees with its antecedent (*elephant seal*).

D   *Any other animal yet tested* is incorrectly set up as the subject of *adapt*.

E   The subject is correct, but in the following clause *it* has no clear referent.

The correct answer is C.

SC01068

950.   A mutual fund having billions of dollars in assets will typically invest that money in hundreds of <u>companies, rarely holding more than one percent</u> of the shares of any particular corporation.

(A)   companies, rarely holding more than one percent

(B)   companies, and it is rare to hold at least one percent or more

(C)   companies and rarely do they hold more than one percent

(D)   companies, so that they rarely hold more than one percent

(E)   companies; rarely do they hold one percent or more

Agreement; Logical Predication

The participial phrase starting with *rarely holding* is predicated of the main subject *a mutual fund*. It elaborates on the effect of the main clause verb: since a mutual fund invests in hundreds of companies, it rarely holds more than one percent in any particular corporation.

A   **Correct.** The participle *holding* in the embedded clause correctly refers to *a mutual fund*. It also correctly expresses the cause-and-effect relationship between investing in many companies and holding little in each company.

B   The antecedent of *it is rare to hold* is not clear. The use of *it is rare* instead of *rarely* could be misleading.

C   The use of *and* between the clauses makes them both main clauses. Thus, the cause-and-effect relationship between investing and holding is lost. The referent of *they* is unclear. It makes no sense to suppose that it refers to the hundreds of companies. Since it presumably refers to *a mutual fund*, it should be singular.

D   The pronoun *they* refers to *a mutual fund* and thus should be singular.

E   The pronoun *they* refers to *a mutual fund* and thus should be singular.

The correct answer is A.

SC08083

951.   Positing an enormous volcanic explosion at the end of the Permian period would explain the presence of a buried crater, <u>account for the presence of the element iridium (originating deep within the earth), and the presence of quartz having been</u> shattered by high-impact shock waves.

(A)   account for the presence of the element iridium (originating deep within the earth), and the presence of quartz having been

(B)   of the element iridium (originating deep within the earth), and of quartz

(C)   the element iridium (originating deep within the earth), and explain the presence of quartz having been

(D)   the presence of the element iridium (originating deep within the earth), and explain the presence of quartz

(E)   explain the element iridium (originating deep within the earth), and the presence of quartz

Parallelism; Rhetorical Construction

The sentence indicates that a volcanic explosion would explain the presence of three features, but those features are not expressed using parallel grammatical structures. The first two items in the list are verb phrases that involve needless repetition—*explain the presence of* and *account for the presence of*—while the third is an awkwardly worded noun phrase—*the presence of quartz having been shattered*. The three features can be identified more concisely with a list of prepositional phrases following *explain the presence*: *of a buried crater*, *of the element iridium*, and *of quartz*.

A   The three features are not listed in parallel form; the sentence is wordy and awkward.

B   Correct. The three features are identified with parallel prepositional phrases.

C   The three features are not listed in parallel form since the first and third are verb phrases, while the second is a noun phrase; the wording is awkward and needlessly repetitive.

D   The three features are not listed in parallel form since the first and third are verb phrases, while the second is a noun phrase; the wording is needlessly repetitive.

E   The three features are not listed in parallel form since the first and second are verb phrases, while the third is a noun phrase; the sentence illogically states that an explosion would *explain the element iridium*, rather than explain the *presence* of the element.

The correct answer is B.

SC01561

952. The 19-year-old pianist and composer performed his most recent work all over Europe, Asia, and North America last year, <u>winning prestigious awards in both London as well as Tokyo for his achievement at so young an age, and he is hoping</u> to continue composing now that he has returned to Chicago.

(A)   winning prestigious awards in both London as well as Tokyo for his achievement at so young an age, and he is hoping

(B)   winning prestigious awards both in London and Tokyo for his achievement at such a young age, and hoping

(C)   having won prestigious awards both in London and Tokyo for his achievement at so young an age, hoping

(D)   winning prestigious awards in both London and Tokyo for his achievement at such a young age, and he hopes

(E)   having won prestigious awards both in London as well as Tokyo for his achievement at so young an age, and he hopes

Idiom; Grammatical Construction

This sentence is about the past accomplishments and the future ambitions of a musician who recently won awards on a world tour. In some of the versions of the sentence, the phrase *as well as* is redundant with the word *both* before *London* and *Tokyo*. Idiomatically, the simple conjunction *and* completes the phrase beginning with *both*.

A   The phrase *as well as* between *London* and *Tokyo* is not idiomatic (the idiomatic formula is *both X and Y*). The present progressive verb *is hoping* is unnecessarily wordy.

B   Because *hoping* is parallel with *winning*, it suggests that the *hoping* and *winning* are contemporaneous, whereas in fact the musician won his awards last year but is now, in the present, upon his return, hoping to continue composing.

C   The present-perfect participial phrase *having won* suggests that his winning took place before his performance tour. Furthermore, the use of *hoping* in this version of the sentence suggests that hoping is something the pianist did while on his performance tour *last year*, but the final phrase, *now that he has returned to Chicago*, indicates this is not so.

D   Correct. This version of the sentence uses the correct idiomatic formula (*both X and Y*).

E   The participial phrase *having won ...* inaccurately states that the musician won his awards prior to his performance tour. Furthermore, *both in London as well as Tokyo* is unidiomatic, as explained above in answer choice A, and unparallel (*in* should either precede *both*, or else *in* should be added before *Tokyo*).

The correct answer is D.

SC01474

953. Starfish, with anywhere from five to eight arms, have a strong regenerative ability, and if <u>one arm is</u> <u>lost it quickly replaces it, sometimes by the</u> <u>animal</u> <u>overcompensating and</u> growing an extra one or two.

(A) one arm is lost it quickly replaces it, sometimes by the animal overcompensating and

(B) one arm is lost it is quickly replaced, with the animal sometimes overcompensating and

(C) they lose one arm they quickly replace it, sometimes by the animal overcompensating,

(D) they lose one arm they are quickly replaced, with the animal sometimes overcompensating,

(E) they lose one arm it is quickly replaced, sometimes with the animal overcompensating,

Agreement; Idiom

In a conditional sentence *if X, (then) Y*, rhetorical flow is enhanced by the two clauses sharing the same structure. If one clause is passive, the other should be passive; if one clause is active, the other should be active, too.

A   The conditional clause has a passive verb, while the result clause has an active verb. The pronoun *it* should be plural since it refers to *starfish*. We know that *starfish* is plural in this sentence because it agrees with *have* in the main clause.

B   **Correct.** The conditional structure is clear and correct.

C   This answer choice allows the unintended reading that the animal replaces the missing arm by overcompensating. The logical connection between *overcompensating* and *growing* is unclear.

D   The conditional clause has an active verb, while the result clause has a passive verb. The second *they* should refer to *arm*, so the agreement is not correct. The logical connection between *overcompensating* and *growing* is unclear.

E   The conditional clause has an active verb, while the result clause has a passive verb. The logical connection between *overcompensating* and *growing* is unclear.

The correct answer is B.

SC04249

954. In 2000, a mere two dozen products accounted for half the increase in spending on prescription drugs, a phenomenon that is explained not just because of more expensive drugs but by the fact that doctors are writing many more prescriptions for higher-cost drugs.

(A) a phenomenon that is explained not just because of more expensive drugs but by the fact that doctors are writing

(B) a phenomenon that is explained not just by the fact that drugs are becoming more expensive but also by the fact that doctors are writing

(C) a phenomenon occurring not just because of drugs that are becoming more expensive but because of doctors having also written

(D) which occurred not just because drugs are becoming more expensive but doctors are also writing

(E) which occurred not just because of more expensive drugs but because doctors have also written

Rhetorical Construction; Idiom

This sentence explains that a few high-cost products account for increased spending for two reasons—rising drug prices and more prescriptions for high-priced drugs. To present these two causes, the sentence employs a formula that requires parallel elements: *not just because of x*, *but because of y*, with *x* and *y* assuming the same grammatical form. One way to create this parallelism is to phrase both contributing causes as noun clauses beginning with *the fact that*. To streamline the sentence, unnecessary words and redundancies should be eliminated. One such redundancy is the repetition of meaning in *explained* and *because of*.

A   It is redundant and confusing to say that the phenomenon in question is *explained . . . because of*; the sentence structure is not parallel.

B   **Correct.** This sentence correctly uses parallel structure.

C   The phrasing *drugs that are becoming* and *doctors having also written* are awkward and confusing; the placement of *also* is incorrect.

D   The structure of this sentence is not parallel.

E   The placement of *also* is incorrect; the structure of the sentence is not parallel.

The correct answer is B.

SC05393

955. Similar to other early Mississippi Delta blues singers, the music of Robert Johnson arose from an oral tradition beginning with a mixture of chants, fiddle tunes, and religious music and only gradually evolved into the blues.

(A)   Similar to other early Mississippi Delta blues singers, the music of Robert Johnson arose from an oral tradition beginning with

(B)   Similar to that of other early Mississippi Delta blues singers, Robert Johnson made music that arose from an oral tradition that began with

(C)   As with other early Mississippi Delta blues singers, Robert Johnson made music that arose from an oral tradition beginning as

(D)   Like other early Mississippi Delta blues singers, Robert Johnson's music arose from an oral tradition beginning with

(E)   Like the music of other early Mississippi Delta blues singers, the music of Robert Johnson arose from an oral tradition that began as

Logical Predication; Verb Form

The sentence aims to compare the *music* of *early Mississippi Delta blues singers* with the *music of Robert Johnson*. But what it does is illogically compare *singers* themselves with the *music* of Johnson. The second part of the sentence describes two stages of the *oral tradition* from which blues developed.

A   The sentence illogically compares *other early Mississippi Delta blues singers* to *the music of Robert Johnson*. The proper comparison would be between the music of the other blues singers and Johnson's music. The second half of the sentence attempts to describe the stages of the oral tradition, but does so in a nonparallel form, describing the first stage by using a participial phrase (*beginning with . . .*) and the second by using a verb phrase (*evolved into . . .*).

B   Presumably the pronoun *that* is meant to refer to *music*. If so, however, the sentence illogically compares the music of other early Mississippi Delta blues singers to Robert Johnson himself, whereas the proper comparison is between the music of the other blues singers and Johnson's music.

C   Because the intended comparison is between what Robert Johnson did (*made music that arose from an oral tradition . . .*) and what other early Mississippi Delta blues singers did, the sentence should begin *As did* rather than *As with*. The second half of the sentence violates parallelism, describing the first stage

of the oral tradition by using a present-participle phrase and the second by using a past-tense verb phrase.

D   This version of the sentence illogically compares *singers* with *music*. It also violates parallelism by coupling a participial phrase (*beginning with . . .*) with a verb phrase (*evolved into . . .*).

E   **Correct.** The resulting sentence compares like with like, in this case the *music* of other early Mississippi Delta blues singers with the *music* of Robert Johnson. It uses a relative clause to describe the oral tradition from which blues developed, indicating the two stages of development with two verbs in parallel.

The correct answer is E.

SC03805

956.   Thelonious Monk, who was a jazz pianist and composer, produced a body of work both rooted in the stride-piano tradition of Willie (The Lion) Smith and Duke Ellington, yet in many ways he stood apart from the mainstream jazz repertory.

(A)   Thelonious Monk, who was a jazz pianist and composer, produced a body of work both rooted

(B)   Thelonious Monk, the jazz pianist and composer, produced a body of work that was rooted both

(C)   Jazz pianist and composer Thelonious Monk, who produced a body of work rooted

(D)   Jazz pianist and composer Thelonious Monk produced a body of work that was rooted

(E)   Jazz pianist and composer Thelonious Monk produced a body of work rooted both

Grammatical Construction; Rhetorical Construction

The subject of the sentence is *Thelonious Monk*, and the sentence tells about two things that he did: *produced* and *stood apart*. The work he produced was rooted in the mainstream (*stride piano*) jazz tradition, yet at the same time, he deviated from this tradition. The use of a relative clause (*who was a jazz pianist . . .*) or an appositive (*the jazz pianist . . .*) introduces unnecessary wordiness and grammatical complexity. Since only one point is being made about Monk's body of work, the appearance of the word *both* in the clause presenting the claim about Monk's work is deceptive as well as grammatically incorrect.

A   The relative clause introduces wordiness and confusion.

B   The appositive introduces wordiness and unnecessary grammatical complexity.

C   The sentence is a fragment because the main subject, *Thelonious Monk*, has no verb.

D   Correct. The sentence concisely identifies Thelonious Monk and expresses the single point about his work without unnecessary or misleading words.

E   The appearance of *both* is misleading, since only one point is being made about where Monk's musical roots are located.

The correct answer is D.

SC06898

957. Nobody knows exactly how many languages there are in the world, partly because of the difficulty of distinguishing between a language <u>and the sublanguages or dialects within it, but those who have tried to count typically have found</u> about five thousand.

(A) and the sublanguages or dialects within it, but those who have tried to count typically have found

(B) and the sublanguages or dialects within them, with those who have tried counting typically finding

(C) and the sublanguages or dialects within it, but those who have tried counting it typically find

(D) or the sublanguages or dialects within them, but those who tried to count them typically found

(E) or the sublanguages or dialects within them, with those who have tried to count typically finding

Agreement; Idiom

This sentence first introduces a condition that makes it difficult to count languages and then, with the conjunction *but*, introduces the topic of those who defy these difficulties and try to count the world's languages anyway. Connecting these two parts of the sentence with *but* indicates that the second clause of the sentence is counter to expectation. The challenges of the task are explained using the example of a single language and its many sublanguages or dialects. When this example is referred to with a pronoun, the pronoun should be singular; when the languages being counted are referred to with a pronoun, this pronoun must be plural.

A   **Correct.** The pronoun *it* agrees in number to its singular antecedent, and *but* indicates that the idea expressed in the final clause defies expectations.

B   The plural pronoun *them* incorrectly refers to the singular antecedent *language*; connecting the two clauses with the preposition *with* loses the sense that counting languages despite the difficulties defies expectations.

C   The second appearance of *it*, referring to world languages, is incorrect because it does not agree in number with *languages*.

D   The conjunction *or* is incorrect—the idiomatic expression is *distinguishing between x and y*; the plural pronoun *them* does not agree with the singular antecedent *language*.

E   The plural pronoun *them* incorrectly refers to the singular antecedent, *language*; *with* is an imprecise connector for the two clauses, losing the *counter-to-expectation* relationship between them.

The correct answer is A.

SC08719

958. Although a number of excellent studies narrate the development of domestic technology and its impact on housewifery, these works do not discuss the contributions of the women employed <u>by manufacturers and utility companies as product demonstrators and publicists</u>, who initially promoted new and unfamiliar technology to female consumers.

(A) by manufacturers and utility companies as product demonstrators and publicists,

(B) to be product demonstrators and publicists by manufacturers and utility companies,

(C) to demonstrate and publicize their products by manufacturers and utility companies

(D) by manufacturers and utility companies to be demonstrators and publicists of their products

(E) by manufacturers and utility companies to demonstrate and publicize their products

Logical Predication; Rhetorical Construction

The point of the sentence is that studies do not include the contributions of women who promoted new domestic technology. The sentence indicates clearly that the women were *employed by manufacturers and utility companies*, worked as *product demonstrators and publicists*, and promoted new technology *to female consumers.*

A   **Correct.** The sentence clearly describes the women's employment and contributions.

B   This sentence structure appears to make *who initially promoted* refer to *manufacturers and utility companies* rather than to *the women.* This conflicts with the use of the word *who,* which would normally be expected to refer to persons rather than to abstract entities such as companies.

C   *Their* refers to *the women,* incorrectly suggesting that the *products* belong to them. This sentence structure appears to make *who initially promoted* refer to *manufacturers and utility companies* rather than to *the women.* This conflicts with the word *who,* which would normally be expected to refer to persons rather than to abstract entities such as companies.

D   *Who initially promoted* follows, and appears to refer to, *products,* which cannot logically be the referent.

E   *Who initially promoted* follows, and appears to refer to, *products,* which cannot logically be the referent.

The correct answer is A.

SC01577

959. The absence <u>from business and financial records of the nineteenth century of statistics about women leave us with no record of the jobs that were performed by women and</u> how they survived economically.

(A)   from business and financial records of the nineteenth century of statistics about women leave us with no record of the jobs that were performed by women and

(B)   from business and financial records of statistics about women from the nineteenth century leave us with no record of what jobs women performed or

(C)   of statistics for women from business and financial records in the nineteenth century leaves us with no record of either the jobs that women were performing and of

(D)   of statistics on women from business and financial records in the nineteenth century leave us with no record of the jobs that women performed or of

(E)   of statistics about women from business and financial records of the nineteenth century leaves us with no record of either what jobs women performed or

Rhetorical Construction; Agreement

This sentence is phrased awkwardly in two ways. The first relates to *absence of statistics:* it is best to place a noun modifier right next to the noun that it modifies, with no intervening material. Second, *jobs that were performed by women* is more complicated than necessary—*jobs women performed* is better, for example. Also, the singular noun *absence* requires the correct agreeing verb form *leaves.*

A   *Absence* and *of statistics* are widely separated, and *leave* does not properly agree with its subject, *absence.*

B   *Absence* and *of statistics* are widely separated, and *leave* does not properly agree with its subject, *absence.*

C   *Jobs that women were performing* is unnecessarily long and complex. The *either* construction should be completed with *or,* not *and.*

D   *Leave* does not properly agree with its subject, *absence.*

E   **Correct.** *Leaves* agrees with *absence.* The phrase *of statistics* is next to the noun it modifies (*absence*), and *jobs women performed* is a nicely simple phrasing.

The correct answer is E.

SC02138

960. <u>Heating-oil prices are expected to be higher this year than last because refiners are paying about $5 a barrel more for crude oil than they were</u> last year.

(A)   Heating-oil prices are expected to be higher this year than last because refiners are paying about $5 a barrel more for crude oil than they were

(B)   Heating-oil prices are expected to rise higher this year over last because refiners pay about $5 a barrel for crude oil more than they did

(C)   Expectations are for heating-oil prices to be higher this year than last year's because refiners are paying about $5 a barrel for crude oil more than they did

(D)   It is the expectation that heating-oil prices will be higher for this year over last because refiners are paying about $5 a barrel more for crude oil now than what they were

(E)   It is expected that heating-oil prices will rise higher this year than last year's because refiners pay about $5 a barrel for crude oil more than they did

Rhetorical Construction; Idiom

The sentence connects a comparison between this year's and last year's heating-oil prices with a comparison between this year's and last year's crude-oil prices. It draws this comparison efficiently, using two parallel comparative expressions, *higher than* and *more than*.

A **Correct.** This sentence efficiently uses parallel comparative phrases in an overall structure that makes it clear what is being compared to what and how one of the comparisons (the difference in crude-oil prices) provides a reason for the other (the expected difference in heating-oil prices).

B The comparative form *higher* needs the comparative term *than* rather than *over*. In the second clause, the comparative term *more* should immediately follow *$5 a barrel*. An alternative effective way to reposition *more* would be to say *$5 more per barrel*.

C *Expectations are for* . . . is an unnecessarily wordy and indirect expression. In the second clause, the comparative term *more* should immediately follow *$5 a barrel*. An alternative effective way to reposition *more* would be to say *$5 more per barrel*.

D *It is the expectation that* . . . is nonstandard. Because of this atypical wording, the pronoun *it* could readily appear to need an antecedent, which it does not have. In a more standard phrase such as *it is expected that*, the status of *it* as a referentless placeholder would be clear. The comparative form *higher* needs the comparative term *than* rather than *over*.

E The possessive *year's* is not parallel with the adverbial phrase *this year*. This makes it unclear whether the sentence might be illogically drawing a comparison between (1) the price level that heating oil in general will reach this year and (2) the price level that last year's heating oil will reach this year. In the second clause, the comparative term *more* should immediately follow *$5 a barrel*. An alternative effective way to reposition *more* would be to say *$5 more per barrel*. A minor consideration is that some readers would find *It is expected that heating-oil prices will* . . . unnecessarily wordy and indirect and would expect a simpler

construction such as *heating-oil prices are expected to. . . .*

The correct answer is A.

SC01443

961. Even though Clovis points, spear points with longitudinal grooves chipped onto their faces, have been found all over North America, they are named for the New Mexico site where they were first discovered in 1932.

(A) Even though Clovis points, spear points with longitudinal grooves chipped onto their faces, have been found all over North America, they are named for the New Mexico site where they were first discovered in 1932.

(B) Although named for the New Mexico site where first discovered in 1932, Clovis points are spear points of longitudinal grooves chipped onto their faces and have been found all over North America.

(C) Named for the New Mexico site where they have been first discovered in 1932, Clovis points, spear points of longitudinal grooves chipped onto the faces, have been found all over North America.

(D) Spear points with longitudinal grooves that are chipped onto the faces, Clovis points, even though named for the New Mexico site where first discovered in 1932, but were found all over North America.

(E) While Clovis points are spear points whose faces have longitudinal grooves chipped into them, they have been found all over North America, and named for the New Mexico site where they have been first discovered in 1932.

Verb Form; Rhetorical Construction; Logical Predication

Even though, although, and *while* introduce clauses that appear to be logically incompatible but in fact are not. In this sentence, the apparent incompatibility that must be clearly expressed is that although the spear points are named for a particular place in New Mexico, they are in fact found throughout North America. Because their discovery took place in 1932 and is not ongoing, the correct verb tense is simple past, not present perfect.

A **Correct.** The *even though* clause expresses clearly that the seeming incompatibility is between where the spear points have been found (*all over North America*) and the naming of the spear points for a single site in New Mexico.

B   The sentence structure indicates that the expected incompatibility is between the geographically based name of the points and their physical properties, which makes no sense; *where discovered* is missing a subject— the correct form is *where they were first discovered*.

C   *Have been first discovered* is the wrong tense, since the discovery is a discrete event completed in the past.

D   The sequence of information in this sentence is confusing; *even though* and *but* both introduce information that is contrary to expectation, so to use them both to describe a single apparent contradiction is redundant and nonsensical.

E   *While* introduces a description of Clovis points and suggests that this appears incompatible with their appearance all over North America, which makes no sense; *have been first discovered* is the wrong tense.

The correct answer is A.

SC04408

962. Heavy commitment by an executive to a course of action, especially if it has worked well in the past, makes it likely to miss signs of incipient trouble or misinterpret them when they do appear.

(A) Heavy commitment by an executive to a course of action, especially if it has worked well in the past, makes it likely to miss signs of incipient trouble or misinterpret them when they do appear.

(B) An executive who is heavily committed to a course of action, especially one that worked well in the past, makes missing signs of incipient trouble or misinterpreting ones likely when they do appear.

(C) An executive who is heavily committed to a course of action is likely to miss or misinterpret signs of incipient trouble when they do appear, especially if it has worked well in the past.

(D) Executives' being heavily committed to a course of action, especially if it has worked well in the past, makes them likely to miss signs of incipient trouble or misinterpreting them when they do appear.

(E) Being heavily committed to a course of action, especially one that has worked well in the past, is likely to make an executive miss signs of incipient trouble or misinterpret them when they do appear.

Rhetorical Construction; Logical Predication

This sentence explains that an executive who is blindly committed to a proven course of action is likely to overlook or misinterpret indicators that the plan may no longer be working. The sentence needs to make clear *who* may misinterpret these indicators.

A   The passive construction causes the sentence to be wordy and confusing; the reference for *it* is ambiguous, leaving the reader with questions about who or what is likely to miss these signs.

B   The sentence structure indicates that the *executive*, not his or her strategy, causes signs to be overlooked; the modifier *when they do appear* is misplaced.

C   The reference for the pronoun *it* is unclear because many nouns have intervened between the appearance of the logical referent (*course of action*) and *it*.

D   *Misinterpreting* should be an infinitive verb form to parallel *miss*; the phrasing throughout the sentence is wordy and awkward.

E   **Correct.** The grammatical structure of this sentence and the appropriate placement of modifiers expresses the meaning clearly and concisely.

The correct answer is E.

SC06740

963. According to recent studies comparing the nutritional value of meat from wild animals and meat from domesticated animals, wild animals have less total fat than do livestock fed on grain and more of a kind of fat they think is good for cardiac health.

(A) wild animals have less total fat than do livestock fed on grain and more of a kind of fat they think is

(B) wild animals have less total fat than livestock fed on grain and more of a kind of fat thought to be

(C) wild animals have less total fat than that of livestock fed on grain and have more fat of a kind thought to be

(D) total fat of wild animals is less than livestock fed on grain and they have more fat of a kind thought to be

(E) total fat is less in wild animals than that of livestock fed on grain and more of their fat is of a kind they think is

Logical Predication; Rhetorical Construction

The sentence reports research findings on the comparison between the fat content of wild animals and that of domestic livestock. The most significant error in the sentence is in the phrase *they think*: the pronoun *they* either lacks a referent or is meant to refer back to *wild animals*, which would be nonsensical.

A   The pronoun *they* fails to refer correctly.

B   **Correct.** The phrase *thought to be* eliminates the most significant error in the original sentence. Note that while the phrase *less total fat than livestock* differs from the phrase *less total fat than do livestock* in the original, either would be correct here.

C   The resulting sentence is unnecessarily wordy and confusing. The pronoun *that* is not only superfluous, but it fails to refer back to anything.

D   The resulting sentence makes a nonsensical comparison between *total fat* and *livestock*.

E   The resulting sentence is wordy and confusing. It lacks the required parallelism *in wild animals . . . in livestock*. The referent of the possessive pronoun *their* is ambiguous, as is the referent of the pronoun *they*.

The correct answer is B.

SC03292

964. Yellow jackets number among the 900 or so species of the world's social wasps, <u>wasps living in a highly cooperative and organized society where they consist almost entirely of</u> females—the queen and her sterile female workers.

(A)   wasps living in a highly cooperative and organized society where they consist almost entirely of

(B)   wasps that live in a highly cooperative and organized society consisting almost entirely of

(C)   which means they live in a highly cooperative and organized society, almost all

(D)   which means that their society is highly cooperative, organized, and it is almost entirely

(E)   living in a society that is highly cooperative, organized, and it consists of almost all

Idiom; Logical Predication; Rhetorical Construction

This sentence identifies yellow jackets as one of 900 types of social wasps and provides an explanation

of the term *social wasps*. In this explanation, the society or population—not the individual wasps themselves—consists almost entirely of females. The three descriptors of social wasps (*cooperative, organized,* and *consisting almost entirely of females*) are most effectively expressed in parallel structures.

A   *They*, referring to wasps, is an incorrect subject for *consist*.

B   **Correct.** The three descriptors of the wasp society are in parallel form, and *consisting* properly modifies *society*.

C   The sentence structure makes it unclear what *almost all females* describes.

D   *And it is . . .* violates the parallelism of the three descriptors of social wasps.

E   *And it consists . . .* violates the parallelism of the three descriptors.

The correct answer is B.

SC02539

965. Before 1988, insurance companies in California were free to charge whatever rates the market would bear, <u>needing no approval from regulators before raising</u> rates.

(A)   needing no approval from regulators before raising

(B)   and it needed no approval by regulators before raising

(C)   and needing no approval from regulators before they raised

(D)   with approval not needed by regulators before they raised

(E)   with no approval needed from regulators before the raising of

Logical Predication; Rhetorical Construction

The sentence explains that, prior to 1988, insurance companies in California could raise rates without regulators' approval. This idea is expressed concisely using a participial phrase and two prepositional phrases: *needing no approval from regulators before raising rates.* Unlike some of the answer choices that contain errors involving antecedents, this construction uses no pronouns and contains no such errors.

A   **Correct.** The combination of a participial phrase and two prepositional phrases expresses the idea clearly with no errors involving pronouns or antecedents.

B The singular pronoun *it* has no clear antecedent. If *it* is taken to refer to the market (the only grammatically plausible antecedent), the sentence is illogical. *Whatever rates the market would bear* clearly indicates that *market* is being used in the sense of an abstract set of forces affecting prices. To say that the market, in that sense, raised taxes and that it needed no approval to do so is nonsensical.

C The construction *were . . . and needing* is ungrammatical. The pronoun *they* is intended to refer to *companies* but could also seem, illogically, to refer to *regulators*.

D *By regulators* illogically indicates that regulators are the ones who did not need approval; the pronoun *they* is intended to refer to *companies* but could also seem, illogically, to refer to *regulators*.

E *Before the raising of* is wordy and awkward. Both that phrase and *with no approval needed* are strangely uninformative and rhetorically ineffective in that they appear to pointedly avoid telling who did not need the approval or who might have raised the rates.

The correct answer is A.

SC01022

966. Marconi's conception of the radio was as a substitute for the telephone, a tool for private conversation; instead, it is precisely the opposite, a tool for communicating with a large, public audience.

(A) Marconi's conception of the radio was as a substitute for the telephone, a tool for private conversation; instead, it is

(B) Marconi conceived of the radio as a substitute for the telephone, a tool for private conversation, but which is

(C) Marconi conceived of the radio as a tool for private conversation that could substitute for the telephone; instead, it has become

(D) Marconi conceived of the radio to be a tool for private conversation, a substitute for the telephone, which has become

(E) Marconi conceived of the radio to be a substitute for the telephone, a tool for private conversation, other than what it is,

Rhetorical Construction; Logical Predication

The main point of this sentence is to explain that while Marconi felt the radio would substitute for the phone as an instrument of private communication, in fact it has become an instrument of mass communication. It is less wordy to use *Marconi* as the subject of the active verb *conceived* than to use the subject *conception* with the static verb *was*. The pronoun *it* positioned as the subject of the final verb *has become* refers back to *radio*. Versions of the sentence that use the relative pronoun *which* indicate that the telephone has become a mass medium.

A The nominalized subject, *conception*, leads to a wordy and awkward sentence.

B The reference for the relative pronoun *which* is ambiguous; the sentence as a whole is awkward.

C **Correct.** An active verb makes the first clause more concise; *it* in the second clause clearly refers to *the radio*.

D *Conceived of . . .* should be followed by *as* rather than *to be*.

E *Conceived of . . .* should be followed by *as* rather than *to be*; *other than what it is* is awkward, wordy, and redundant, overlapping the meaning of *precisely the opposite . . . .*

The correct answer is C.

SC02611

967. Because there are provisions of the new maritime code that provide that even tiny islets can be the basis for claims to the fisheries and oil fields of large sea areas, they have already stimulated international disputes over uninhabited islands.

(A) Because there are provisions of the new maritime code that provide that even tiny islets can be the basis for claims to the fisheries and oil fields of large sea areas, they have already stimulated

(B) Because the new maritime code provides that even tiny islets can be the basis for claims to the fisheries and oil fields of large sea areas, it has already stimulated

(C) Even tiny islets can be the basis for claims to the fisheries and oil fields of large sea areas under provisions of the new maritime code, already stimulating

(D) Because even tiny islets can be the basis for claims to the fisheries and oil fields of large sea areas under provisions of the new maritime code, this has already stimulated

(E) Because even tiny islets can be the basis for claims to the fisheries and oil fields of large sea areas under provisions of the new maritime code, which is already stimulating

Logical Predication; Grammatical Construction

In this sentence, the *there are . . . that . . .* construction contributes nothing more than unnecessary words. The sentence needs to make clear whether *provisions* or *code* is the subject of the main verb *stimulated*.

A The *there are . . . that . . .* construction is unnecessarily wordy; in the predicate nominative instead of the subject position, *provisions* is not an obvious referent for the pronoun *they*.

B **Correct.** *The new maritime code* is clearly the antecedent of *it* in the main clause and thus the subject of *has already stimulated*.

C *Under provisions of the new maritime code* is a misplaced modifier, seeming to describe *sea areas*; the sentence does not make clear what is *stimulating . . . disputes*.

D The referent of *this* is unclear.

E The sentence is a fragment, opening with a dependent clause (*Because . . . code*) and concluding with a relative clause, but lacking a main, independent clause.

The correct answer is B.

SC02576

968. Unlike the automobile <u>company, whose research was based on</u> crashes involving sport utility vehicles, the research conducted by the insurance company took into account such factors as a driver's age, sex, and previous driving record.

(A) company, whose research was based on

(B) company, which researched

(C) company, in its research of

(D) company's research, having been based on

(E) company's research on

Logical Predication; Rhetorical Construction

The point of the sentence is to contrast the research conducted by the automobile company and that conducted by the insurance company,

but the sentence has been written in a way that contrasts *the automobile company* with *research*. The correct contrast is between *automobile company's research* and *research conducted by the insurance company*.

A *Automobile company* is incorrectly contrasted with *research*.

B *Automobile company* is incorrectly contrasted with *research*.

C *Automobile company* is incorrectly contrasted with *research*.

D *Having been based on* is wordy. This construction makes it unclear whether *having been based on crashes involving sport utility vehicles* is intended to modify *the automobile company's research* or *the research conducted by the insurance company*. The sentence structure slightly favors the latter interpretation, but it is somewhat implausible to suppose that this is the intended meaning.

E **Correct.** The sentence concisely contrasts the *automobile company's research* and *research conducted by the insurance company*.

The correct answer is E.

SC12131

969. Gusty westerly winds will continue <u>to usher in a seasonably cool air mass into the region, as a broad area of high pressure will build and</u> bring fair and dry weather for several days.

(A) to usher in a seasonably cool air mass into the region, as a broad area of high pressure will build and

(B) ushering in a seasonably cool air mass into the region and a broad area of high pressure will build that

(C) to usher in a seasonably cool air mass to the region, a broad area of high pressure building, and

(D) ushering a seasonably cool air mass in the region, with a broad area of high pressure building and

(E) to usher a seasonably cool air mass into the region while a broad area of high pressure builds, which will

Verb Form; Grammatical Construction; Diction

The sentence offers a prediction that two concurrent weather events will bring a certain type of weather, but its use of the phrase *as . . . will build* causes confusion. The wording makes the sequence of events and the causal relationships among them unclear. Future tense is used to indicate that winds *will continue.* The relation of *as* to the rest of the sentence makes it unclear whether *as* is intended as a logical indicator (similar to *because*) or as a temporal indicator (equivalent to *while*). If *as* is intended in the former way, it would be preferable to resolve the ambiguity by using a word or phrase such as *because* or *given that.* If it is intended in the latter way, a present tense verb would be needed following *as* or *while* to show that the second event is concurrent with, or part of, the future situation: *while high pressure builds.* In addition, *usher in . . . into* is redundant and unidiomatic. A clear, concise way to express this idea is *will continue to usher a seasonably cool air mass into the region while a broad area of high pressure builds.*

A   *Usher in . . . into* is redundant and unidiomatic. *As . . . will build* causes confusion.

B   The absence of a comma after *region* makes this ungrammatical. *Ushering in . . . into* is redundant; *will build* is the wrong verb tense; the plural verb *bring* does not agree with *area*, the singular antecedent of *that.*

C   The grammatical function of *a broad area of high pressure building* is unclear.

D   *Ushering . . . in the region* is incorrect since *into* is needed to indicate movement from outside in; the subject of the verb *bring* is unclear.

E   **Correct.** The idea is expressed with clear, correct combinations of verbs and subjects.

The correct answer is E.

SC02008

970. With the patience of its customers and with its network strained to the breaking point, the on-line service company announced a series of new initiatives trying to relieve the congestion that has led to at least four class-action lawsuits and thousands of complaints from frustrated customers.

(A)   the patience of its customers and with its network strained to the breaking point, the on-line service company announced a series of new initiatives trying to relieve

(B)   the patience of its customers and its network strained to the breaking point, the on-line service company announced a series of new initiatives that try to relieve

(C)   its network and the patience of its customers strained to the breaking point, the on-line service company announced a series of new initiatives to try to relieve

(D)   its network and with the patience of its customers strained to the breaking point, the on-line service company announced a series of initiatives to try relieving

(E)   its network and its customers' patience strained to the breaking point, the on-line service company announced a series of new initiatives to try relieving

Logical Predication; Rhetorical Construction

The sentence explains the online service provider's efforts to relieve congestion, but it has been written with confusing ambiguities. Because *the patience of its customers* is in a separate prepositional phrase from *its network*, it is not clear whether both or only the latter is *strained to the breaking point.* The phrase *trying to relieve* is probably meant to explain the purpose of the initiatives, but does not do so unambiguously (for example, *trying* could modify either *the company* or *initiatives*, and it is not clear which is intended). An unambiguous wording of the sentence would clarify that both *the patience of its customers* and *its network* are *strained to the breaking point* and that the purpose of the initiatives is *to try to relieve* the congestion.

A   *The patience of its customers* is not clearly linked to *strained to the breaking point*; *trying to relieve* is an ambiguous and unidiomatic way of expressing the purpose of the initiatives.

B   *That try to relieve* fails to express the purpose of the initiatives in a rhetorically acceptable way; moreover the present tense *try* is illogical here. The phrase *the patience of its customers and its network* is rhetorically flawed in that its structure makes it seem to be attributing *patience* to the *network.*

C   **Correct.** The sentence indicates clearly that both *the patience of its customers* and *its network* are *strained to the breaking point* and that the company introduced initiatives aimed at relieving the congestion.

D   *Its network* is not clearly linked to *strained to the breaking point*; with *to try*, the infinitive form *to relieve* is more rhetorically appropriate here than the verbal noun form *relieving*, in order to indicate the goal of the intervention.

E   With *to try*, the infinitive form *to relieve* is more rhetorically appropriate here than the verbal noun form *relieving*, in order to indicate the goal of the intervention.

The correct answer is C.

SC02094

971. November is traditionally the strongest month for sales of light trucks, <u>but sales this past November, even when compared with sales in previous Novembers,</u> accounted for a remarkably large share of total vehicle sales.

(A)   but sales this past November, even when compared with sales in previous Novembers,

(B)   but even when it is compared with previous Novembers, this past November's sales

(C)   but even when they are compared with previous Novembers, sales of light trucks this past November

(D)   so that compared with previous Novembers, sales of light trucks this past November

(E)   so that this past November's sales, even compared with previous Novembers' sales,

Logical Predication; Agreement

This sentence identifies November as traditionally being the month with the strongest sales of light trucks, and then goes on to indicate that even when compared to previous Novembers, this past November's sales accounted for a notably large portion of overall sales. It makes sense to make a comparison between sales in one November with sales in other Novembers. It does not make sense to compare sales to months, as in answer choices C and D.

A   **Correct.** This version makes the correct comparison between sales in one particular November and sales in previous Novembers.

B   The antecedent of the word *it* is unclear. The sentence begins with the word *November*, which is used to refer not to a specific November, but to the month generally. If the antecedent of *it* is taken to be *November*, then the sentence compares November, taken generally, to previous Novembers. But previous to what? Since taking *November* to be the antecedent renders the sentence nonsensical, we may be inclined to look for the antecedent elsewhere; the only other possible candidate, however, is *this past*

November's sales, which is ruled out because *it* is singular and *sales* is plural.

C   The antecedent of the pronoun *they* is *sales*, making the comparison between *they* and *previous Novembers* illogical.

D   The sentence illogically compares sales of light trucks with previous Novembers. The conjunction *so that* nonsensically introduces a causal relationship between November's typically strong sales and the aforementioned comparison.

E   Like answer choice D, this sentence introduces a nonsensical causal relationship, in this case between the fact that November typically has the strongest sales and the fact that this past November's sales accounted for a remarkably large share of total vehicle sales.

The correct answer is A.

SC05760

972. Most of the country's biggest daily newspapers had lower circulation in the six months from October 1995 through March 1996 than <u>a similar period</u> a year earlier.

(A)   a similar period

(B)   a similar period's

(C)   in a similar period

(D)   that in a similar period

(E)   that of a similar period

Logical Predication; Parallelism

The sentence compares newspaper circulation during two separate periods, but the comparison is not parallel because it has been drawn using a prepositional phrase, *in the six months*, and a noun phrase, *a similar period*. Both phrases compared by *than* should be prepositional phrases: *lower in the six months . . . than in a similar period.*

A   *In the six months* and *a similar period* are not grammatically parallel. The sentence appears illogically to compare a period of time with an amount of circulation.

B   *In the six months* and *a similar period's* are not grammatically parallel.

C   **Correct.** *In the six months* and *in a similar period* are both prepositional phrases, making the comparison clear and properly idiomatic.

D   *In the six months* and *that in a similar period* are not grammatically parallel; it is unclear what the antecedent of *that* is supposed to be.

E *In the six months* and *that of a similar period* are not grammatically parallel; it is unclear what the antecedent of *that* is supposed to be.

The correct answer is C.

SC01714

973. Mauritius was a British colony for almost 200 years, <u>excepting for</u> the domains of administration and teaching, the English language was never really spoken on the island.

(A) excepting for

(B) except in

(C) but except in

(D) but excepting for

(E) with the exception of

Idiom; Grammatical Construction

This two-clause sentence describes an apparent incompatibility: as a British colony, Mauritius might be expected to be English-speaking, but in fact it was not. To describe this apparent contradiction and to avoid a comma splice, the clauses should be joined by the conjunction *but*. *Domains* describes places *in* which English is spoken; *for* is the incorrect preposition. *Excepting* is not idiomatic English in this case.

A The lack of a conjunction causes a comma splice; *excepting for* is non-idiomatic.

B The lack of a conjunction causes a comma splice.

C **Correct.** The two independent clauses are separated by *but*, and *except in* is an appropriate idiom.

D *Excepting for* is non-idiomatic.

E The lack of a conjunction causes a comma splice.

The correct answer is C.

SC04853

974. <u>Although appearing less appetizing than most of their round and red supermarket cousins, heirloom tomatoes, grown from seeds saved during the previous year</u>—they are often green and striped, or have plenty of bumps and bruises—heirlooms are more flavorful and thus in increasing demand.

(A) Although appearing less appetizing than most of their round and red supermarket cousins, heirloom tomatoes, grown from seeds saved during the previous year

(B) Although heirloom tomatoes, grown from seeds saved during the previous year, appear less appetizing than most of their round and red supermarket cousins

(C) Although they appear less appetizing than most of their round and red supermarket cousins, heirloom tomatoes, grown from seeds saved during the previous year

(D) Grown from seeds saved during the previous year, heirloom tomatoes appear less appetizing than most of their round and red supermarket cousins

(E) Heirloom tomatoes, grown from seeds saved during the previous year, although they appear less appetizing than most of their round and red supermarket cousins

Rhetorical Construction; Grammatical Construction

The intended meaning could be communicated more effectively by mentioning heirloom tomatoes as early as possible in the sentence, so that we know that the writer is comparing heirloom tomatoes with supermarket tomatoes. The placement of *heirloom tomatoes* and *heirlooms* makes the sentence ungrammatical.

A This is ungrammatical. If *heirloom tomatoes* is the subject of *are more flavorful . . .* then *heirlooms* has no predicate and is nonsensically superfluous. If *heirlooms* is the subject, *heirloom tomatoes* has no predicate.

B **Correct.** The noun *heirloom tomatoes* is mentioned early in the sentence, followed by a parenthetical definition, and is the subject of the verb *appear*, and *heirlooms* is the subject of *are*.

C The noun *heirloom tomatoes* appears too late in the sentence. Parsing is made harder by introducing the pronoun *they* and revealing its antecedent later in the sentence. The sentence is also ungrammatical. If *heirloom tomatoes* is the subject of *are more flavorful . . .* then *heirlooms* has no predicate and is nonsensically superfluous. If *heirlooms* is the subject, *heirloom tomatoes* has no predicate.

D Beginning the sentence with the explanatory clause *grown from seeds . . .* gives it too much importance. It could be construed as the reason why heirloom tomatoes appear less appetizing, which is contrary to the truth. The sentence is also ungrammatical.

E   Rhetorical structure requires that *although* appear in the beginning of the clause to which it pertains. Placing it later necessitates the pronoun *they* with antecedent *heirloom tomatoes*, which is redundant. The sentence is also ungrammatical.

The correct answer is B.

SC01987

975. The World Wildlife Fund has declared that global warming, <u>a phenomenon most scientists agree to be caused by human beings in burning fossil fuels,</u> will create havoc among migratory birds by altering the environment in ways harmful to their habitats.

(A)   a phenomenon most scientists agree to be caused by human beings in burning fossil fuels,

(B)   a phenomenon most scientists agree that is caused by fossil fuels burned by human beings,

(C)   a phenomenon that most scientists agree is caused by human beings' burning of fossil fuels,

(D)   which most scientists agree on as a phenomenon caused by human beings who burn fossil fuels,

(E)   which most scientists agree to be a phenomenon caused by fossil fuels burned by human beings,

Logical Predication; Rhetorical Construction

The underlined portion of the sentence is an appositive defining *global warming* as a phenomenon caused by the burning of fossil fuels by humans. Because this appositive intervenes between the subject (*global warming*) and verb (*will create*) of a clause, it should be expressed as clearly and economically as possible so as not to confuse the meaning of the sentence as a whole.

A   *To be caused* and *in burning* are wordy, awkward, and indirect.

B   *That is* should immediately follow *phenomenon*, not *agree*.

C   **Correct.** The phrase *human beings' burning* is more economical than constructions with prepositional phrases or relative clauses.

D   The phrasing is wordy and indirect.

E   The phrasing is wordy and the meaning is imprecise; it is not fossil fuels that cause global warming—it is the burning of fossil fuels by humans.

The correct answer is C.

SC02216

976. The largest of all the planets, <u>not only is Jupiter three times so massive as Saturn, the next larger</u> planet, but also possesses four of the largest satellites, or moons, in our solar system.

(A)   not only is Jupiter three times so massive as Saturn, the next larger

(B)   not only is Jupiter three times as massive as Saturn, the next largest

(C)   Jupiter, not only three times as massive as Saturn, the next largest

(D)   Jupiter not only is three times as massive as Saturn, the next largest

(E)   Jupiter is not only three times so massive as Saturn, the next larger

Diction; Idiom

This sentence begins with a phrase, [*t*]*he largest . . .*, describing the main subject *Jupiter*. The remainder of the sentence describes Jupiter's size and possession of moons, using the idiom *not only x but y* to introduce parallel adjective phrases.

A   In this version, *so massive as Saturn* violates the parallelism established by the idiom *as + adjective + as + noun*. For the sake of clarity, the noun described by the opening adjectival phrase should immediately follow that phrase. The phrase *next larger* is unidiomatic and unclear. The superlative (*largest*) is appropriate in this consideration of all the planets.

B   As in answer choice A, *Jupiter* should immediately follow the opening phrase.

C   This version violates the parallelism of the idiom *not only x but y*, following the first half of the template with an adjective phrase and the second half with a verb phrase.

D   **Correct.** The placement of the subject in relation to the opening modifier, the properly constructed phrasing, and the proper use of comparison words make the meaning of the sentence clear.

E   The phrase *so massive as* violates the idiom *as x as y*. Consideration of Jupiter's size among all the planets, including Saturn, requires the superlative form, *largest*.

The correct answer is D.

SC01587

977. While many of the dinosaur fossils found recently in northeast China seem to provide evidence of the kinship between dinosaurs and birds, the wealth of enigmatic fossils <u>seem more likely at this stage that they will inflame debates over the origin of birds rather</u> than settle them.

(A) seem more likely at this stage that they will inflame debates over the origin of birds rather than

(B) seem more likely that it will inflame debates over the origin of birds at this stage than

(C) seems more likely to inflame debates on the origin of birds at this stage rather than

(D) seems more likely at this stage to inflame debates over the origin of birds than to

(E) seems more likely that it will inflame debates on the origin of birds at this stage than to

Agreement; Parallelism

This sentence states that whereas many dinosaur fossils from China suggest that there is a kinship between dinosaurs and birds, the *wealth* of fossils are more ambiguous about what they suggest about the ancestry of birds. The word *wealth* is a mass noun followed by a prepositional phrase; because *wealth* follows the article *the*, the emphasis is on it rather than on the noun in the prepositional phrase, *fossils*. The singular *wealth* requires a singular main verb (*seems*). The comparative expression *more likely . . .* must be followed by an infinitive verb (*to inflame*) so it will be parallel to the verb with which it is compared (*to settle*).

A The singular subject *wealth* does not agree with the plural verb *seem*; both items being compared should be in parallel form (*inflame* and *settle*); the relative clause *that they will inflame* violates the parallelism.

B Again, the relative clause violates the desired parallelism; the singular subject, *wealth*, requires a singular verb, *seems*.

C The subject and the verb agree with one another, but the placement of the modifier *at this stage* makes the modifier appear to describe *origin of the birds* rather than the verb *seems*.

D **Correct.** The verb *seems* agrees in number with the noun *wealth*; the infinitive *to inflame* is parallel with the verb to which it is compared, *to settle*.

E The clause *wealth . . . seems more likely that it will inflame* is not idiomatic, and *that it will inflame* is not parallel with the infinitive verb *to settle*.

The correct answer is D.

SC01622

978. <u>Found only in the Western Hemisphere and surviving through extremes of climate, hummingbirds' range extends</u> from Alaska to Tierra del Fuego, from sea-level rain forests to the edges of Andean snowfields and ice fields at altitudes of 15,000 feet.

(A) Found only in the Western Hemisphere and surviving through extremes of climate, hummingbirds' range extends

(B) Found only in the Western Hemisphere, hummingbirds survive through extremes of climate, their range extending

(C) Hummingbirds, found only in the Western Hemisphere and surviving through extremes of climate, with their range extending

(D) Hummingbirds, found only in the Western Hemisphere and surviving through extremes of climate, their range extends

(E) Hummingbirds are found only in the Western Hemisphere, survive through extremes of climate, and their range extends

Logical Predication; Grammatical Construction

This sentence makes three points about hummingbirds: they live in the Western Hemisphere, they survive extreme climates, and their range is wide and varied. *Hummingbirds*, not *hummingbirds' range*, should be the subject of the sentence.

A The opening modifier, *found . . . and surviving . . .* should modify *hummingbirds*, not, as it does, *hummingbirds' range*.

B **Correct.** *Hummingbirds* is the subject of the sentence, and the use of the absolute phrase *their range extending* appropriately connects the final clause to the rest of the sentence.

C This version has no main verb for the subject *Hummingbirds* and as a result is ungrammatical.

D Like answer choice C, this version has no main verb for the subject *Hummingbirds*.

E This version begins with the subject *Hummingbirds* attached to a pair of verb phrases (*are found . . .* and *survive . . .*) followed by the conjunction *and*, which suggests that what follows should also be a verb phrase; instead, a new subject is introduced, *their range*. Replacing the comma before *survive* with *and* would render the sentence acceptable.

The correct answer is B.

SC01761

979. She was less successful after she had emigrated to New York compared to her native Germany, photographer Lotte Jacobi nevertheless earned a small group of discerning admirers, and her photographs were eventually exhibited in prestigious galleries across the United States.

(A) She was less successful after she had emigrated to New York compared to

(B) Being less successful after she had emigrated to New York as compared to

(C) Less successful after she emigrated to New York than she had been in

(D) Although she was less successful after emigrating to New York when compared to

(E) She had been less successful after emigrating to New York than in

Idiom; Grammatical Construction; Logical Predication

This sentence compares the success Jacobi experienced after moving to New York to the success she had previously experienced in Germany. The phrase *less successful* anticipates the conclusion of the comparison with the phrase *than. . . .* The main subject of the sentence is *photographer Lotte Jacobi*, and the main verb is *earned*. The opening clause *She was less successful . . .* therefore creates a comma splice if the comma is not followed by a conjunction. The most efficient way to incorporate the information about Jacobi's comparative successes in Germany and in New York is to turn this clause into an adjectival phrase describing Jacobi.

A *Less successful . . .* anticipates *than* rather than *compared to . . .* ; a comma is insufficient to join two independent clauses into a single sentence.

B *As compared to* is an incorrect way to complete the comparison introduced by *less; Being . . .* is unnecessarily wordy and awkward.

C **Correct.** The idiomatic construction *less successful . . . than* is incorporated into an introductory adjectival phrase modifying *Lotte Jacobi*.

D *When compared to* is an incorrect phrase to complete the comparison introduced by *less*.

E A comma is insufficient to join two independent clauses into a single sentence; past-perfect tense is misleading, since it refers to Jacobi's experience in New York, which in fact followed her experience in Germany.

The correct answer is C.

SC02259

980. Scientists have recently found evidence that black holes—regions of space in which matter is so concentrated and the pull of gravity so powerful that nothing, not even light, can emerge from them—probably exist at the core of nearly all galaxies and the mass of each black hole is proportional to its host galaxy.

(A) exist at the core of nearly all galaxies and the mass of each black hole is proportional to

(B) exist at the core of nearly all galaxies and that the mass of each black hole is proportional to that of

(C) exist at the core of nearly all galaxies, and that the mass of each black hole is proportional to

(D) exists at the core of nearly all galaxies, and that the mass of each black hole is proportional to that of

(E) exists at the core of nearly all galaxies and the mass of each black hole is proportional to that of

Logical Predication; Agreement

This sentence focuses attention on two hypotheses about black holes—one about their location and the other about their mass. These hypotheses appear as parallel relative clauses *that black holes . . . exist at . . .* and *that the mass . . . is proportional*. The subject of the first relative clause (*black holes*) is plural, so the clause must be completed with the plural form of *exist*.

A This version does not provide the relative pronoun *that* to provide parallel structure for presenting the two things scientific evidence reveals about black holes. This leaves it somewhat unclear whether the final clause is intended to convey part of what the scientists discovered or to express a claim that the writer is making independently of the scientists' discovery. The sentence illogically compares *mass* to *galaxy*.

B   Correct. The structure of the sentence makes the meaning clear, and the plural verb form agrees with the plural subject.

C   The comma appears to signal that the final part of the sentence is intended as an independent clause expressing a separate claim rather than describing part of the scientists' discovery. But if it were intended in that way, it should be set off as a separate sentence, not conjoined with the preceding clause. Like answer choice A, this version makes an illogical comparison between *mass* and *galaxy*.

D   The singular verb *exists* does not agree with the plural subject *black holes.* As in answer choice C, the comma is inappropriate because it does not introduce a new independent clause.

E   The singular verb *exists* does not agree with the plural subject *black holes.* Like answer choice A, this version lacks the relative pronoun *that*, which would clarify the relationship between the two clauses.

The correct answer is B.

SC02346

981. The use of lie detectors is based on the assumption that lying produces emotional reactions in an individual <u>that, in turn, create unconscious physiological responses</u>.

(A)   that, in turn, create unconscious physiological responses

(B)   that creates unconscious physiological responses in turn

(C)   creating, in turn, unconscious physiological responses

(D)   to create, in turn, physiological responses that are unconscious

(E)   who creates unconscious physiological responses in turn

Agreement; Rhetorical Construction; Logical Predication

This sentence describes a cause-and-effect sequence; in the underlined portion of the

sentence, the relative pronoun *that* refers to the plural noun *reactions.* The verb in the relative clause must therefore be a plural verb. The causal sequence is most clearly expressed by a relative clause that turns the object *emotional reactions* (from the clause *lying causes emotional reactions in an individual*) into the subject (*that*) of a new clause (*that in turn create unconscious physiological responses*). *In turn* is best placed before the verb of the second relative clause, *create*, to clarify that a chain of events is being described.

A   Correct. This construction clearly indicates the causal sequence.

B   The singular verb *creates* does not agree with the subject referenced by the relative pronoun *that* (*reactions*).

C   This construction is less successful at clarifying the chain of events because *creating* seems to refer back to *lying*; if used as a participial, *creating* would have to be preceded by a comma.

D   This construction does not make clear the causal chain of events, because it is unclear which noun *to create* should attach to; the infinitive construction implies intent, which does not really make sense.

E   Because *reactions* is not a person, *who* is the wrong relative pronoun to use.

The correct answer is A.

SC04213

982. Australian embryologists have found evidence <u>that suggests that the elephant is descended from an aquatic animal, and its trunk originally evolving</u> as a kind of snorkel.

(A)   that suggests that the elephant is descended from an aquatic animal, and its trunk originally evolving

(B)   that has suggested the elephant descended from an aquatic animal, its trunk originally evolving

(C)   suggesting that the elephant had descended from an aquatic animal with its trunk originally evolved

(D)   to suggest that the elephant had descended from an aquatic animal and its trunk originally evolved

(E)   to suggest that the elephant is descended from an aquatic animal and that its trunk originally evolved

Parallelism; Verb Form

The sentence, as originally presented, is ungrammatical. Because the evidence suggests two things, not a series of three or more, *and* should not be preceded by a comma. Alternatively, one might wonder whether the comma before *and* is supposed to set off the final phrase as an independent clause, but the phrase contains no grammatical subject, so it cannot function as an independent clause. Furthermore, it would be rhetorically inappropriate to conjoin an assertion about what the embryologists' evidence suggests with a separate assertion, outside the scope of the evidence, about the elephant's trunk. Therefore, the sentence must be intended to claim that the evidence suggests both of these things. If the two things that the evidence suggests are to be conjoined with *and*, they should be parallel. The first and second parallel elements are both underlined—in other words, it is not possible to tell, upon reading only the original sentence, what form of parallelism the correct answer will take, as both elements are underlined and therefore could be changed.

A   As explained above, the sentence is ungrammatical. The phrase following the conjunction *and* is not parallel with the relative clause *that the elephant is descended. . . .*

B   The evidence presumably still suggests these things about the evolution of the elephant and its trunk, so the present-perfect verb tense *has suggested* is inaccurate.

C   *Had descended* is the wrong verb tense. The word *evolved* is most readily understood here as a simple past-tense verb; an adjectival use of *evolved* would hardly make sense in this context. With *evolved* understood as a verb, the sentence is ungrammatical; *with* cannot be followed by an independent clause.

D   *Had descended* is the wrong tense; the phrase following the conjunction *and* does not parallel the relative clause that precedes the conjunction.

E   **Correct.** The two dependent clauses beginning with *that* are in parallel form and contain verbs in the correct tenses.

The correct answer is E.

SC01957

983. Most efforts to combat such mosquito-borne diseases <u>like malaria and dengue have focused either on the vaccination of humans or on exterminating</u> mosquitoes with pesticides.

(A)   like malaria and dengue have focused either on the vaccination of humans or on exterminating

(B)   like malaria and dengue have focused either on vaccinating of humans or on the extermination of

(C)   as malaria and dengue have focused on either vaccinating humans or on exterminating

(D)   as malaria and dengue have focused on either vaccinating of humans or on extermination of

(E)   as malaria and dengue have focused on either vaccinating humans or exterminating

Diction; Parallelism

The phrase *such . . . diseases like malaria and dengue* is not a correct way in English to indicate that the two diseases mentioned are examples of a larger category; the correct expression is *such . . . as. . . .*

A   This use of *such . . . like . . .* is incorrect English; the correct expression is *such . . . as. . . .* It is better to keep the preposition *on* close to the verb it goes with, *focus*, so as not to repeat it.

B   The correct expression is *such . . . as. . . .* It is better to keep the preposition *on* close to the verb it goes with, *focus*, so as not to repeat it. This use of the gerund *vaccinating* (followed by *of*) would normally be preceded by *the*, but this would make the phrase awkward. It would be preferable to use *vaccination*, which is parallel to *extermination*.

C   This answer choice incorrectly repeats the preposition *on* before *exterminating*.

D   This answer choice incorrectly repeats the preposition *on* before *extermination*. This use of the gerund *vaccinating* (followed by *of*) would normally be preceded by *the*, but this would make the phrase awkward. It would be preferable to use *vaccination*, which is parallel to *extermination*.

E   **Correct.** This version uses *either . . . or . . .* correctly and appropriately uses the parallel forms *vaccinating* and *extermination.*

The correct answer is E.

SC02344

984. Among the Tsonga, a Bantu-speaking group of tribes in southeastern Africa, dance teams represent their own chief at <u>the court of each other, providing entertainment in return for</u> food, drink, and lodging.

(A)   the court of each other, providing entertainment in return for

(B)   the court of another and provide entertainment in return for

(C)   the court of the other, so as to provide entertainment as a return on

(D)   each other's court, entertainment being provided in return for

(E)   another's court and provide entertainment as a return on

Diction; Idiom

The point of the sentence is that dancers representing one chief perform at the court of another chief *in return for* gifts. *The court of each other* is unidiomatic and unclear. It could be intended to indicate, somewhat implausibly, that each team has a court that the other teams visit, but *represent their own chief* strongly suggests that the court referred to is the court of another chief. The correct pronoun to refer to a different chief is *another*.

A   *The court of each other* is unidiomatic and unclear. *Each other* seems to refer, somewhat illogically, to the dancers.

B   Correct. The sentence clearly explains the idea, using the correct pronoun *another* and the correct idiom *in return for*.

C   This could be confusing in that *the other* indicates that there is only one other chief, whereas *group of tribes* suggests that there may be a number of chiefs. *As a return on* is the incorrect idiom; *a return on* normally refers to a gain from an investment, not a direct exchange of one good for another.

D   *Each other's court* somewhat illogically indicates that the dancers each have a court. *Entertainment being provided in return for* is awkward and indirect.

E   *As a return on* is the incorrect idiom; *a return on* normally refers to a gain from an investment, not a direct exchange of one good for another.

The correct answer is B.

SC06633

985. Almost like clones in their similarity to one another, <u>the cheetah species' homogeneity makes them especially vulnerable to disease</u>.

(A)   the cheetah species' homogeneity makes them especially vulnerable to disease

(B)   the cheetah species is especially vulnerable to disease because of its homogeneity

(C)   the homogeneity of the cheetah species makes it especially vulnerable to disease

(D)   homogeneity makes members of the cheetah species especially vulnerable to disease

(E)   members of the cheetah species are especially vulnerable to disease because of their homogeneity

Agreement; Logical Predication

Genetic homogeneity is presented as a cause of cheetahs' vulnerability to disease. The opening adjectival phrase refers to the fact that individual cheetahs are almost like clones of one another because of how genetically similar they are. This adjectival phrase should be followed by what it describes, individual cheetahs. But the structure of the sentence makes it seem that this adjectival phrase is meant—illogically—to describe *the cheetah species' homogeneity*. The sentence structure also fails to make clear that the intended reference is to just one (the only) cheetah species.

A   The sentence nonsensically presents the opening phrase as describing *homogeneity*.

B   The resulting sentence opens with a reference to a plurality of individuals (*to one another*), but confusingly identifies this with a single (collective) entity, a species.

C   The resulting sentence nonsensically presents the opening phrase as describing *homogeneity*.

D   The resulting sentence nonsensically presents the opening phrase as describing *homogeneity*.

E   Correct. The sentence is clear and the opening phrase correctly modifies *members of the cheetah species*.

The correct answer is E.

SC04330

986. As sources of electrical power, windmills now account for only about 2,500 megawatts nationwide, but production is <u>almost expected to double by the end of the year, which would provide</u> enough electricity for 1.3 million households.

(A)   almost expected to double by the end of the year, which would provide

(B)   almost expected that it will double by the end of the year, thus providing

(C) expected that it will almost double by the end of the year to provide

(D) expected almost to double by the end of the year and thus to provide

(E) expected almost to double by the end of the year, which would thus be providing

Rhetorical Construction; Idiom

The intended meaning of the sentence seems to be that the electricity production of windmills is expected to approximately double by year's end. But instead of saying *almost double*, we have *almost expected*, which is an unclear idea. Also unclear is what the relative pronoun *which* refers to.

A The placement of *almost* makes it nonsensically modify *is expected*. What the relative pronoun *which* refers to is ambiguous: for example, does it refer to the expectation, the possible doubling, or the year?

B The resulting sentence misplaces the adverb *almost*.

C The phrase *production is expected that it will*... makes no sense—as opposed to, for example, *it is expected that production will*. . . .

D Correct. This sentence clearly conveys the expectations of production: *almost to double* and *thus to provide*. There is no ambiguity as to what will be providing *enough electricity*.

E The referent of the relative pronoun *which* is ambiguous, and the conditional verb form *would thus be providing* is unnecessarily wordy.

The correct answer is D.

SC03154

987. While most of the earliest known ball courts in Mesoamerica date to 900–400 B.C., <u>waterlogged latex balls found at El Manati and representations of ballplayers painted on ceramics found at San Lorenzo attest</u> to the fact that the Mesoamerican ballgame was well established by the mid-thirteenth century B.C.

(A) waterlogged latex balls found at El Manati and representations of ballplayers painted on ceramics found at San Lorenzo attest

(B) waterlogged latex balls found at El Manati and the painting of representations of ballplayers on ceramics found at San Lorenzo attests

(C) waterlogged latex balls found at El Manati and ceramics painted with representations of

ballplayers found at San Lorenzo attests

(D) the finding of waterlogged latex balls at El Manati and the painting of representations of ballplayers on ceramics found at San Lorenzo attests

(E) the finding of waterlogged latex balls at El Manati and of representations of ballplayers painted on ceramics at San Lorenzo attest

Logical Predication; Agreement

The sentence points out two pieces of evidence that prove the early existence of ballgames in Mesoamerica: *waterlogged latex balls* and *representations of ballplayers*. The two noun phrases together serve as subjects for the verb *attest*, creating a sentence that logically and correctly expresses its main idea.

A Correct. *Waterlogged latex balls* and *representations of ballplayers* together serve as subjects for the verb *attest*.

B *Painting* could refer to something that has been painted, but on that interpretation the sentence does not make sense, because the painting is itself the representation and a single painting would not plausibly be on multiple ceramics. Alternatively, it could refer to an ongoing act of painting, which could not plausibly constitute the kind of evidence referred to. The singular verb *attests* does not agree with the compound subject *balls* and *painting*.

C The singular verb *attests* does not agree with the compound subject *balls* and *ceramics*.

D *Balls*, not *finding*, should be the subject of the verb since the balls are the evidence. *Painting* could refer to something that has been painted, but on that interpretation the sentence does not make sense, because the painting is itself the representation and a single painting would not plausibly be on multiple ceramics. Alternatively, it could refer to an ongoing act of painting, which could not plausibly constitute the kind of evidence referred to. The singular verb *attests* does not agree with the compound subject *finding* and *painting*.

E *Balls* and *representations* should be the subject of the verb *attest* since they are the evidence—not *finding*; the plural verb *attest* does not agree with the singular subject *finding*.

The correct answer is A.

SC04899

988. As criminal activity on the Internet becomes more and more sophisticated, not only are thieves able to divert cash from company bank accounts, <u>they can also pilfer valuable information such as business development strategies, new product specifications, and contract bidding plans, and sell</u> the data to competitors.

(A) they can also pilfer valuable information such as business development strategies, new product specifications, and contract bidding plans, and sell

(B) they can also pilfer valuable information that includes business development strategies, new product specifications, and contract bidding plans, and selling

(C) also pilfering valuable information including business development strategies, new product specifications, and contract bidding plans, selling

(D) but also pilfer valuable information such as business development strategies, new product specifications, and contract bidding plans to sell

(E) but also pilfering valuable information such as business development strategies, new product specifications, and contract bidding plans and selling

Grammatical Construction; Verb Form

The two clauses in this *not only* . . . construction normally require subjects, which this sentence has. The second clause (beginning with *they can*) further divides into two clauses about pilfering and selling; here, the two verbs must have the same form, since each one is the main verb of its clause.

A   **Correct.** *They* supplies the needed subject, and *pilfer* and *sell* are both in the bare verb form.

B   *Selling* is the wrong form for the main verb of a finite clause; it should be *sell*.

C   There is no subject for the *pilfer* clause, and *pilfering* would be the wrong form even if a subject were added.

D   There is no subject for the *pilfer* clause.

E   There is no subject for the *pilfer* clause, and both *selling* and *pilfering* have the wrong verb for the main verb of a finite clause; they should be *sell* and *pilfer*, respectively.

The correct answer is A.

SC05785

989. Last week local shrimpers held a news conference to take some credit for the resurgence of the rare Kemp's ridley turtle, saying that their compliance with laws <u>requiring that turtle-excluder devices be on shrimp nets protect</u> adult sea turtles.

(A) requiring that turtle-excluder devices be on shrimp nets protect

(B) requiring turtle-excluder devices on shrimp nets is protecting

(C) that require turtle-excluder devices on shrimp nets protect

(D) to require turtle-excluder devices on shrimp nets are protecting

(E) to require turtle-excluder devices on shrimp nets is protecting

Rhetorical Construction; Agreement

The subject of the clause introduced by *saying that* is the singular noun *compliance*. This subject requires the singular form of the verb *protect*. The clearest, most economical way to describe the laws in question is to follow the word *laws* with a present participle *requiring*. To use an infinitive, *to require*, seems to indicate that requiring these devices is the objective of the laws, when in fact the objective is to protect the sea turtles.

A   The plural verb *protect* does not agree with the singular subject *compliance*.

B   **Correct.** The singular verb *is protecting* agrees with the singular subject *compliance*, and the participial phrase beginning with *requiring* concisely and accurately describes the laws.

C   The relative clause *that require* introduces unnecessary wordiness; the plural verb *protect* does not agree with the singular subject *compliance*.

D   *To require* obscures the purpose of the laws; the plural verb phrase *are protecting* does not agree with the singular subject *compliance*.

E   *To require* obscures the purpose of the laws.

The correct answer is B.

SC03752

990. A ruined structure found at Aqaba, Jordan, was probably a church, as indicated in its eastward orientation and by its overall plan, as well as artifacts, such as glass oil-lamp fragments, found at the site.

(A) A ruined structure found at Aqaba, Jordan, was probably a church, as indicated in its eastward orientation and by its overall plan, as well as

(B) A ruined structure found at Aqaba, Jordan, once probably being a church, was indicated by its eastward orientation, overall plan, and

(C) Indicating that a ruined structure found at Aqaba, Jordan, was probably a church were its eastward orientation and overall plan, but also the

(D) A ruined structure found at Aqaba, Jordan, was probably a church, as indicates its eastward orientation and overall plan, as well as the

(E) That a ruined structure found at Aqaba, Jordan, was probably a church is indicated by its eastward orientation and overall plan, as well as by the

Logical Predication; Parallelism

This sentence explains why a currently ruined structure probably used to be a church. In the best-worded answer choice, the abstract subject (the probability that a certain hypothesis is true) is explained abstractly in a relative clause (*That a ruined structure was probably...*) followed by a passive verb (*is indicated*), followed by the prepositional phrase (*by...*), which is completed by a parallel listing of forms of evidence, all presented as noun phrases in the expression, (*by*) (*its*) A + B, as well as (*by*) C.

A This version makes the relationship between *as well as...* and the rest of the sentence unclear. The most plausible hypothesis is that the artifacts are another of the types of evidence, parallel with the structure's orientation and its plan. The sentence violates the parallelism required in the list by failing to supply the preposition in the final item following *as well as*.

B The subject of this version of the sentence, *structure*, is completed by the verb *was indicated*, creating the illogical assertion that the structure itself, rather than its probable identity, was indicated by its orientation, plan, and attendant artifacts.

C Opening the sentence with the predicate adjective *indicating* leads to a confusing and awkward withholding of the subjects *orientation...plan...artifacts*.

D The only plausible subject for the singular verb *indicates* is the plural *orientation...plan, as well as the artifacts*. Very little about this sentence makes sense.

E **Correct.** The relationships among the parts of the sentence are clear and logical.

The correct answer is E.

SC04343

991. In the major cities of industrialized countries at the end of the nineteenth century, important public places such as theaters, restaurants, shops, and banks had installed electric lighting, but electricity was in less than 1 percent of homes, where lighting was still provided mainly by candles or gas.

(A) electricity was in less than 1 percent of homes, where lighting was still

(B) electricity was in less than 1 percent of homes and lighting still

(C) there had been less than 1 percent of homes with electricity, where lighting was still being

(D) there was less than 1 percent of homes that had electricity, having lighting that was still

(E) less than 1 percent of homes had electricity, where lighting had still been

Rhetorical Construction; Verb Form

In this type of usage, a participle such as *provided* normally must be preceded by some form of the verb *be*. The best choice for this is the past tense *was*, since the main part of the clause describes the situation in the past tense (*electricity was...*). To link the ideas of lighting and electricity in homes, *where* is the most efficient and direct expression, superior to alternatives such as *and* or *having*.

A **Correct.** The participle is preceded by the appropriate form *was*, and the clauses are linked efficiently by *where*.

B There is no form of *be* in the second clause, and *and* does not clearly indicate the connection between the two clauses.

C   *Had been* and *was being* represent inappropriate tenses, and the *there had been* construction is longer than necessary.

D   Both *having lighting* and the *there was* construction are longer and more complicated than necessary. This sentence structure makes *there*, instead of *homes*, the subject of *having*.

E   *Had been* is not the appropriate tense for this situation.

The correct answer is A.

SC02965

992. By 1999, astronomers <u>had discovered 17 nearby stars that are orbited by planets</u> about the size of Jupiter.

   (A)   had discovered 17 nearby stars that are orbited by planets

   (B)   had discovered 17 nearby stars with planets orbiting them that were

   (C)   had discovered that there were 17 nearby stars that were orbited by planets

   (D)   have discovered 17 nearby stars with planets orbiting them that are

   (E)   have discovered that 17 nearby stars are orbited by planets

Verb Form; Rhetorical Construction

Opening with a past date (*1999*) describing the end point of a period of discovery, this sentence calls for a past perfect main verb to follow the subject *astronomers*. In order to economize on words and maximize clarity, the object of the main clause, *stars*, is modified by a passive relative clause *that are orbited by planets* followed by the adjective phrase *about the size of Jupiter*. This structure avoids an awkward and confusing string of relative clauses and prepositional phrases.

A   **Correct.** This version is clear and uses the correct verb form *had discovered*.

B   The use of a prepositional phrase *with planets* necessitates the introduction of a relative clause *that were . . .*, in which the referent of the relative pronoun *that* is somewhat uncertain (stars? or planets?). The past tense verb *were* suggests, improbably, that the size of the planets may have changed significantly since 1999.

C   The string of relative clauses is awkward and wordy.

D   If the sentence was written after 1999, the present perfect tense is illogical, because 1999 is in the past. If it was written in 1999, this way of referring to the then-present time is odd and misleading. The prepositional phrase is wordy and indirect.

E   As in answer choice D, the present perfect tense is illogical.

The correct answer is A.

SC01647

993. <u>Although she was considered among her contemporaries to be the better poet than her husband, later Elizabeth Barrett Browning was overshadowed by his success.</u>

   (A)   Although she was considered among her contemporaries to be the better poet than her husband, later Elizabeth Barrett Browning was overshadowed by his success.

   (B)   Although Elizabeth Barrett Browning was considered among her contemporaries as a better poet than her husband, she was later overshadowed by his success.

   (C)   Later overshadowed by the success of her husband, Elizabeth Barrett Browning's poetry had been considered among her contemporaries to be better than that of her husband.

   (D)   Although Elizabeth Barrett Browning's success was later overshadowed by that of her husband, among her contemporaries she was considered the better poet.

   (E)   Elizabeth Barrett Browning's poetry was considered among her contemporaries as better than her husband, but her success was later overshadowed by his.

Idiom; Verb Form; Logical Predication

The sentence misuses the idiom *the better*; it is acceptable to say *a better X than* but not *the better X than*. If two poets *X* and *Y* have already been mentioned, and someone wants to say that *X* is better than *Y*, you can say either *X is a better poet than Y*, or simply, *X is the better poet*, but not *X is the better poet than Y*. Additionally, *to be* in *considered . . . to be* is superfluous and should be deleted.

Other answer choices use *considered . . . as*, which is ambiguous (see the explanations for answer choices B and E below).

A   As explained in the paragraph above, this version misuses the idiom *the better poet*, most likely confusing it with the idiom *a better poet than*. Furthermore, *to be* is superfluous here.

B   As indicated in the paragraph above, *was considered among her contemporaries as a better poet than her husband* is ambiguous; it could mean either that her contemporaries considered her a better poet than her husband or that her contemporaries considered her as a candidate for being called a better poet than her husband.

C   As explained in the paragraph above, to be is generally considered superfluous and should be deleted. The opening modifier *Later overshadowed by the success of her husband* refers to the subject *poetry*; in other words, it compares her husband's general *success* to her *poetry*. It would be more logical to say either that her success was overshadowed by her husband's success (as the correct answer does) or that her poetry was overshadowed by her husband's poetry.

D   Correct. This version avoids the problems discussed in the paragraph above and in the explanations of the other answer choices.

E   As noted in the paragraph above, *was considered among her contemporaries as a better poet than her husband* is ambiguous; it could mean either that her contemporaries considered her a better poet than her husband or that her contemporaries considered her as a candidate for being called a better poet than her husband. Furthermore, this version comically compares Elizabeth Barrett Browning's poetry to her husband; the appropriate comparison, of course, is Elizabeth Barrett Browning's poetry to her husband's poetry.

The correct answer is D.

SC01618

994.   In no other historical sighting did Halley's Comet cause such a worldwide sensation as <u>did its return in 1910–1911</u>.

(A)   did its return in 1910–1911

(B)   had its 1910–1911 return

(C)   in its return of 1910–1911

(D)   its return of 1910–1911 did

(E)   its return in 1910–1911

Parallelism; Verb Form; Logical Predication

The single subject of this sentence is *Halley's Comet*, and its single verb phrase is *did cause*. The comparison presented by the sentence is between adverbial phrases describing times when the comet was seen. Grammatically, the items being compared are parallel prepositional phrases beginning with the preposition *in: in no other sighting* and *in its return in 1910–1911*. This is the clearest, most economical way of presenting the information. The options that introduce a second verb (*did* or *had*) violate the parallelism and introduce a comparison between the comet itself (subject of the verb *did cause*) and the comet's return (subject of the verb *did* or *had*).

A   This sentence implies a comparison between the comet and its return.

B   This sentence implies a comparison between the comet and its return; *had* is the wrong auxiliary verb form because it must be followed by *caused* instead of *cause*.

C   Correct. The parallel prepositional phrases in this sentence correctly compare times when the comet was sighted.

D   This sentence implies a comparison between the comet and its return.

E   This sentence violates parallelism, implying a comparison between a prepositional phrase and a noun phrase.

The correct answer is C.

SC04836

995.   Rock samples taken from the remains of an asteroid about twice the size of the 6-mile-wide asteroid that eradicated the dinosaurs <u>has been dated to be 3.47 billion years old and thus is</u> evidence of the earliest known asteroid impact on Earth.

(A)   has been dated to be 3.47 billion years old and thus is

(B)   has been dated at 3.47 billion years old and thus

(C)   have been dated to be 3.47 billion years old and thus are

(D)   have been dated as being 3.47 billion years old and thus

(E)   have been dated at 3.47 billion years old and thus are

Agreement; Idiom

The plural subject of this sentence, *Rock samples*, requires plural verb phrases—*have been dated* and *are* rather than *has been dated* and *is*. The idiomatic way of expressing estimation of age is with the phrase *dated at*.

A   The subject and verbs do not agree; *dated to be . . .* is not idiomatic.

B   The subject and verb do not agree; the conjunction *and thus* should be followed by a verb.

C   *Dated to be* is not idiomatic.

D   *As being* is not idiomatic; the conjunction *and thus* should be followed by a verb.

E   **Correct.** The plural verbs match the plural subject, and the wording of the sentence is idiomatic.

The correct answer is E.

10.0 Integrated Reasoning

Please visit gmat.wiley.com and use the unique access code found on the inside front cover of this book to access Integrated Reasoning questions and answer explanations.

10.0 Integrated Reasoning

This chapter contains an overview of integrated reasoning question types, explains what they measure, and offers some tips and strategies for answering them. Because of the way integrated reasoning questions are presented on a computer screen, this book does **not** contain any integrated reasoning practice questions.

> **For Integrated Reasoning practice questions, you can go to** gmat.wiley.com **and log into your account using the access code located on the inside front cover of this book.**

Overview of the Integrated Reasoning Section:

The Integrated Reasoning section of the GMAT™ exam measures your ability to understand and evaluate multiple sources and types of information—numeric, graphic, and verbal—as they relate to one another.

In this section, you will:

- Use quantitative and verbal reasoning skills to solve complex problems,

- Solve multiple problems in relation to one another, and

- Provide answers in different response formats, rather than only traditional multiple choice.

The Integrated Reasoning section consists of 12 questions to be completed over 30 minutes. Four types of questions are used throughout the section, and some require multiple responses. The questions involve both quantitative and verbal reasoning, either separately or in combination. Questions with a **quantitative component** require a basic knowledge of arithmetic, elementary algebra, and commonly known concepts of geometry and statistics. Questions with a **verbal component** require the ability to understand written material and to reason and evaluate arguments.

Special Features:

- The Integrated Reasoning section differs from the Quantitative Reasoning and Verbal Reasoning sections of the GMAT exam in that it is not computer-adaptive. This means that your performance on earlier questions does not determine the selection of later questions.

- Unlike the other sections of the GMAT exam, integrated reasoning questions may have multiple questions on a single screen. For these questions, you can change answers while on the current screen before clicking "Next" to advance to the next question. However, once you move to a new screen, you cannot return to the previous screen.

- The Integrated Reasoning section may contain quantitative elements but is not a test of quantitative skills. An on-screen calculator with basic functions will be available for this section only, whereas it is not available for the Quantitative Reasoning section.

10.1 What Is Measured

The Integrated Reasoning section of the GMAT exam measures how well you integrate data to solve complex problems. Specifically, the Integrated Reasoning section tests you in the following skill categories:

Skill Category	Details	Examples
Apply	Ability to understand principles, rules, or other concepts and apply them to a new context or predict consequences that would follow if new information were incorporated	• Decide whether new examples would comply with or violate established rules • Determine how a trend would be affected by new scenarios • Use established principles to draw conclusions about new data
Evaluate	Ability to make judgments about the quality of information	• Decide whether a claim made in one source is supported or weakened by information provided in another source • Determine whether information provided is sufficient to justify a course of action • Judge the strength of evidence in support of an argument or plan • Identify errors or gaps in the information provided
Infer	Ability to draw conclusions based on information or ideas that are not explicitly stated in the materials provided, but can be derived from them	• Calculate the probability of an outcome based on given data • Indicate whether statements follow logically from the information provided • Determine the meaning of a term within a given context • Identify the rate of change in data gathered over time
Recognize	Ability to identify information that is directly presented in the materials provided, including specific facts, details, or relationships between pieces of information	• Identify areas of agreement and disagreement between sources of information • Determine the strength of correlation between two variables • Indicate rank within a table within a combination of categories (e.g., which product maximizes revenue and minimizes costs) • Identify facts provided as evidence in an argument
Strategize	Ability to work toward a goal within the context of particular needs or constraints	• Choose a plan of action that minimizes risks and maximizes value • Identify trade-offs required to reach a goal • Specify the mathematical formula that will yield a desired result • Determine which means of completing a task are consistent within given constraints

10.2 Question Types and Test-Taking Strategies

There are four types of questions in the Integrated Reasoning section:

Multi-Source Reasoning	Table Analysis	Graphics Interpretation	Two-Part Analysis

Multi-Source Reasoning

What will be displayed:

- Two or three sources of information presented on multiple tabs on the left side of your screen

- A question prompt with answer choices on the right side of your screen

- Multiple tabs for you to click on to view information and determine what is needed to answer the question. At least one tab will contain a written passage (e.g., an email or report)

- Other sources may be tables, graphs, diagrams, or other visual information

Example of information sources presented on multiple tabs:

Techniques	Artifacts	Budget

For outside laboratory tests, the museum's first-year budget for the Kaxna collection allows unlimited IRMS testing, and a total of $7,000—equal to the cost of 4 TL tests plus 15 radiocarbon tests, or the cost of 40 ICP-MS tests—for all other tests. For each technique applied by an outside lab, the museum is charged a fixed price per artifact.

The response type:

- For some questions, you will receive a traditional multiple-choice question with five answer choices

- For some questions, you will receive a set of three conditional statements for you to indicate true/false or yes/no

  - Select one answer choice PER ROW (i.e., conditional statement)

  - All three conditional statements must be answered correctly to receive credit for the question

Example of a conditional statement question:

For each of the following artifacts in the museum's Kaxna collection, select *Yes* if, based on the museum's assumptions, a range of dates for the object's creation can be obtained using one of the techniques in the manner described. Otherwise, select *No*.

Yes	No	
○	○	Bronze statue of a deer
○	○	Fired-clay pot
○	○	Wooden statue of a warrior

Strategies for Answering Multi-Source Reasoning Questions

- **Do not expect to be completely familiar with the material presented in multi-source reasoning sets.**

  All the information you will need to answer the questions correctly will be provided. Even so, you may find some graphs, charts, tables, or verbal passages easier to understand than others; all the material is designed to be challenging.

- **Analyze each source of information carefully, as the questions require detailed understanding of the information presented.**

  Text passages often build ideas sequentially, so note as you read how each statement adds to the main idea of the passage as a whole. Some of the passages used with multi-source reasoning questions will be entirely descriptive; others may contain strong opinions.

  The graphic elements in the multi-source reasoning questions come in various forms, such as tables, graphs, diagrams, or charts. Briefly familiarize yourself with the information presented. If scales are provided, note the marked values and labels. Also note the major graphical elements of the information presented.

- **Read the questions carefully, making sure you understand what is being asked.**

  Some questions may require you to recognize discrepancies among different sources of information or to draw inferences using information from different sources. Other questions may require you to determine which one of the information sources is relevant.

  You can refer back to any of the information at any time while you are answering the multi-source reasoning questions by clicking on the tabs in the graphics.

- **Select the answer choices that have the most support based on the information provided.**

  If you happen to be familiar with the subject matter, do not let this knowledge influence your answer. Consider only the information provided in the question when selecting an answer.

Table Analysis

What will be displayed:

- A data table similar to a spreadsheet, which you will be able to sort by each data column

Example of data table with sorting drop-down menu:

The table displays data on *Brazilian agricultural* products in 2009.

Sort By: | Production, world share (%) ▼ |

Commodity	Production, world share (%)	Production, world rank	Exports, world share (%)	Exports, world rank
Pork	4	4	12	4
Cotton	5	5	10	4
Corn	8	4	10	2
Chickens	15	3	38	1
Beef	16	2	22	1
Sugar	21	1	44	1
Soybeans	27	2	40	2
Coffee	40	1	32	1
Orange juice	56	1	82	1

The response type:

- A set of three conditional statements for you to indicate true/false or yes/no

  - Select one answer choice PER ROW (i.e., conditional statement)

  - All three conditional statements must be answered correctly to receive credit for the question

Example of a conditional statement question:

For each of the following statements, select *Yes* if the statement can be shown to be true based on the information in the table. Otherwise select *No*.

Yes	No	
○	○	No individual country produces more than one-fourth of the world's sugar.
○	○	If Brazil produces less than 20% of the world's supply of any commodity listed in the table, Brazil is not the world's top exporter of that commodity.
○	○	Of the commodities in the table for which Brazil ranks first in world exports, Brazil produces more than 20% of the world's supply.

Strategies for Answering Table Analysis Questions

- **Examine the table and accompanying text to determine the type of information provided.**

  Orienting yourself to the data at the start will make it easier to locate the information you need.

- **Read the question carefully.**

  The question will contain the condition that each phrase, statement, numerical value, or algebraic expression does or does not meet. If you clearly understand the condition (e.g., "*is consistent with the information provided*" or "*can be inferred from the information provided*"), you will find it easier to understand what choice you need to make. Some questions involve quantitative skills, but others involve subsets, conditions, or consistency of data, which are not necessarily mathematical.

- **Read each phrase, statement, numerical value, or algebraic expression carefully to determine the data analysis required.**

  Often, the phrase, statement, numerical value, or algebraic expression indicates a relationship that you can clarify by sorting the table by one or more of its columns. Understanding how the data is organized and sorted can help you work more efficiently.

- **Judge each phrase, statement, numerical value, or algebraic expression carefully based on the condition specified.**

  For each, the two answer choices (such as *yes* or *no*, *true* or *false*, *consistent* or *inconsistent*) are mutually exclusive and only one answer selection for each phrase, statement, numerical value, or algebraic expression is correct. Focus your attention on whether the given condition has been met.

Graphics Interpretation

What will be displayed:

- A graph, diagram, or other visual representation

  - Graphics may include (but are not limited to) bar graphs, line graphs, scatterplots, bubble charts, pie charts, flow charts, or organizational charts

- One or more statements with blank/missing information

Example of graphics:

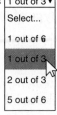

X = 10 students

30 years of age   no high school
or older   diploma

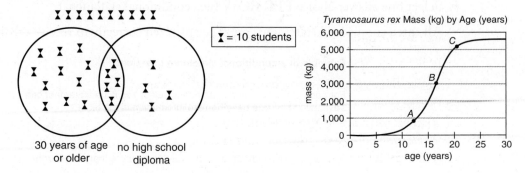

Example of statement with blank/missing information and drop-down menus:

Use the drop-down menus to complete each statement according to the information presented in the diagram.

If one student is selected at random from the 300 surveyed, the chance that the student will be under 30 or a high school graduate or both is [Select... ▾]

If one student is selected at random from the 300 surveyed, the chance that the student will be both under 30 and high school graduate is [1 out of 3 ▾]

> Select...
> 1 out of 6
> 1 out of 3
> 2 out of 3
> 5 out of 6

The response type:

- Drop-down menus containing a word, number, or phrase
  - If there is more than one blank, all drop-down menus must be answered correctly in order to receive credit for the question
- Interpret the graphic and complete each statement with the most accurate word, number, or phrase from an embedded drop-down menu

Strategies for Answering Graphics Interpretation Questions

- **Make sure you understand what the problem is asking you to do.**

  Graphics interpretation problems involve interpreting and integrating data, discerning relationships, and making inferences from a set of data. You may have to do some quantitative analysis, such as calculating change in a given value over time or comparing different rates of growth.

- **Read the graphic carefully.**

  Familiarize yourself with the information presented in the graphic. If there are scales on the axes, make note of the marked values. If there are labels, be sure to note any discrepancy between the units in the graph and the units discussed in the text.

- **Read any accompanying text carefully.**

  If there is accompanying text, it may clarify the meaning of the graphic. The text might also present information that is not contained in the graphic but is necessary to answer the question.

- **Read all the choices in the drop-down menu.**

  By checking the menu options, you may find additional information about the task involved.

- **Choose the option that best completes the statement.**

  More than one option in the drop-down menu may seem plausible; choose the one that makes the statement most accurate or logical. If the drop-down menu is preceded by a phrase, such as *nearest to* or *closest to*, choose the option that is closest to your calculated answer. You might find it helpful to read the statement again with your answer choice in place.

Two-Part Analysis

Two-part analysis questions, which measure your ability to solve complex problems, cover a wide range of content and could be quantitative, verbal, or some combination of both. The versatility of the format lends itself to a wide range of content and skills measured, including the ability to evaluate trade-offs, solve simultaneous equations, and discern relationships between two entities.

What is displayed:

- A brief written scenario or problem
- A table with two related choices relevant to the information provided
  - The two related choices are represented by the first two columns
  - Your answer options are listed in the third column of the table

Example of a written scenario:

A literature department at a small university in an English-speaking country is organizing a two-day festival in which it will highlight the works of ten writers who have been the subjects of recent scholarly work by the faculty. Five writers will be featured each day. To reflect the department's strengths, the majority of writers scheduled for one of the days will be writers whose primary writing language is not English. On the other day of the festival, at least four of the writers will be women. Neither day should have more than two writers from the same country. Departmental members have already agreed on a schedule for eight of the writers. That schedule showing names, along with each writer's primary writing language and country of origin, is shown.

- Day 1:

  Achebe (male, English, Nigeria)

  Weil (female, French, France)

  Gavalda (female, French, France)

  Barrett Browning (female, English, UK)

- Day 2:

  Rowling (female, English, UK)

  Austen (female, English, UK)

  Ocantos (male, Spanish, Argentina)

  Lu Xun (male, Chinese, China)

Example of a response based on passage information:

Select a writer who could be added to the schedule for either day. Then select a writer who could be added to the schedule for neither day. Make only two selections, one in each column.

Either day	Neither day	Writer
○	○	LeGuin (female, English, USA)
○	○	Longfellow (make, English, USA)
○	○	Murasaki (female, Japanese, Japan)
○	○	Colette (female, French, France)
○	○	Vargas Llosa (male, Spanish, Peru)
○	○	Zola (male, French, France)

The response type:

- Select one response PER COLUMN (not per row)
    - A single correct answer must be selected for each column to receive credit for the question
    - The same answer choice can be selected for both response columns (i.e., the two answer choices are not mutually exclusive)

Strategies for Answering Two-Part Analysis Questions

- **Read the information carefully.**

    All the material presented is designed to be challenging. If you happen to be familiar with the subject matter, do not let this knowledge influence your choice. Answer the question only on the basis of what is given.

- **Determine exactly what the question is asking.**

    Do not assume that the headings in the two response columns are complete descriptions of the tasks to be performed. Pay close attention to how the question describes the tasks. Often the headings in the two response columns are shorthand references to the tasks.

- **Remember that you are only supposed to make two choices.**

    Select one answer in each of the first two columns of the response table. You do not need to make a choice for each *row* of the table. The third column contains possible answers to the two questions.

- **Review all available answers before making a final choice.**

    Do not assume you have chosen the best answers in the two columns without reading all the options.

- **Determine whether tasks are dependent or independent.**

    Some two-part analysis questions pose two tasks that can be carried out individually. Others pose one task with two dependent parts, each of which you must carry out correctly to create a single correct response. With dependent questions, you cannot answer the question logically without making both choices. Be sure to examine your answers in relation to one another.

- **Keep in mind that the same answer choice might be the correct response for both columns.**

    If the tasks associated with the two response columns are *not* mutually exclusive, it is possible that one answer option satisfies the conditions of both response columns.

Additional Tips for the Integrated Reasoning Section

Examine and analyze all given data

- Do not expect to be completely familiar with all the material presented. You may find some graphs, charts, tables, or verbal passages to be easier to understand than others. All the material is designed to be challenging, but if you have familiarity with the subject matter, do not let this knowledge influence your answer choices. Answer all questions based on the information that is provided.

- For graphs and charts, make sure you take note of the scales on the axes and read all accompanying text carefully, as it may help clarify the meaning of the graphic or provide additional valuable information.

Read each question carefully

- Make sure you are clear about exactly what the question is asking. Fully read each question problem, including the accompanying text, which usually comes before the answer tables.

Scan the answer choices

- It may be helpful to scan the answer choices prior to doing any work; sometimes the answer choices will give you additional information about the task involved.

Manage your time wisely

- You have 30 minutes to complete 12 questions in the Integrated Reasoning section, which is $2\frac{1}{2}$ minutes per question.

- Remember that many questions have a considerable amount of information to comprehend and consist of multiple parts.

Additional Integrated Reasoning Samples

For additional sample questions in each question format, visit: mba.com/ir-questions

Additional Integrated Reasoning Practice

Use your unique access code found in the inside front cover of this book to access 74 Integrated Reasoning practice questions with answer explanations at gmat.wiley.com. Additional Integrated Reasoning practice questions are available for purchase on mba.com.

10.3 Section Instructions

Go to www.mba.com/tutorial to view instructions for the section and get a feel for what the test center screens will look like on the actual GMAT exam.

For additional Integrated Reasoning practice questions, the *GMAT™ Official IR Practice* product is available for purchase through mba.com.

11.0 Analytical Writing Assessment

11.0 Analytical Writing Assessment

The Analytical Writing Assessment (AWA) consists of one 30-minute writing task called the Analysis of an Argument. In this section, you must read a brief argument, analyze the reasoning behind it, and then write a critique of the argument. You are not asked to state your opinion but rather to analyze the one given. For example, you may consider what questionable assumptions underlie the author's thinking, what alternative explanations or counterexamples might weaken the conclusion, or what sort of evidence could help strengthen or refute the argument.

For this task, you will use the computer keyboard to type your response. You will be able to use typical word-processing functions—that is, you can cut, copy, paste, undo, and redo. These functions can be accessed either by using the keyboard or by using the mouse to click on icons on the screen. You will be able to take notes when planning your response.

It is important that you plan carefully before you begin writing. Read the specific analytical writing task several times to make sure you understand exactly what is expected. Think about how you might present your analysis. You may want to sketch an outline to help you plan and organize. Keep in mind the 30-minute time limit as you plan your response—keep your analysis brief enough to allow for plenty of time to write a first draft, read it over carefully, and make any necessary corrections or revisions before you run out of time. As you write, try to keep your language clear, your sentences concise, and the flow of your ideas logical. State your premise clearly at the beginning, and make sure you present a strong conclusion at the end.

To view a list of all possible AWA questions on the GMAT™ exam, go to www.mba.com/awa-questions.

11.1 What Is Measured

The Analytical Writing Assessment is designed as a direct measure of your ability to think critically and communicate your ideas. More specifically, the Analysis of an Argument task tests your ability to formulate an appropriate and constructive critique of a prescribed conclusion based upon a specific line of thinking.

The argument that you will analyze may concern a topic of general interest, possibly related to business, or to a variety of other subjects. It is important to note, however, that no Analysis of an Argument question presupposes any specific knowledge of business or other specific content areas. Only your capacity to write analytically is assessed.

Each essay is scored using a combination of a computer scoring program and professional essay raters. Your responses will be scored on the basis of:

- the overall quality of your ideas
- your ability to organize, develop, and express those ideas
- how well you provide relevant supporting reasons and examples
- your ability to control the elements of standard written English

11.2 Test-Taking Strategies

1. **Read the question carefully.**
   Make sure you have taken all parts of a question into account before you begin to respond to it.

2. **Do not start to write immediately.**
   Take a few minutes to think about the question and plan a response before you begin writing. You may find it helpful to write a brief outline or jot down some ideas on the erasable notepad provided. Take care to organize your ideas and develop them fully, but leave time to reread your response and make any revisions that you think would improve it.

3. **Focus on the task of analyzing and critiquing a line of thinking or reasoning.**
   Get used to asking yourself questions such as the following: *What questionable assumptions might underlie the thinking? What alternative explanations might be given? What counterexamples might be raised? What additional evidence might prove useful in fully and fairly evaluating the reasoning?*

4. **Develop fully any examples you use.**
   Do not simply list your examples—explain how they illustrate your point.

5. **Discuss alternative explanations or counterexamples.**
   These techniques allow you to introduce illustrations and examples drawn from your observations, experiences, and reading.

6. **Make sure your response reads like a narrative.**
   Your response should not read like an outline. It should use full sentences, a coherent organizational scheme, logical transitions between points, and appropriately introduced and developed examples.

11.3 The Directions

These are the directions that you will see for the Analysis of an Argument essay. If you read them carefully and understand them clearly before going to sit for the test, you will not need to spend too much time reviewing them when you take the GMAT exam. They read as follows:

ANALYSIS OF AN ARGUMENT

In this section, you will be asked to write a critique of the argument presented. *You are* not *asked to present your own views on the subject.*

Writing Your Response: Take a few minutes to evaluate the argument and plan a response before you begin writing. Be sure to leave enough time to reread your response and make any revisions that you think are necessary.

Evaluation of Your Response: Scores will reflect how well you:

- organize, develop, and express your ideas about the argument presented
- provide relevant supporting reasons and examples
- control the elements of standard written English

11.4 GMAT™ Scoring Guide: Analysis of an Argument

6 Outstanding

A 6 paper presents a cogent, well-articulated critique of the argument and demonstrates mastery of the elements of effective writing.

A typical paper in this category exhibits the following characteristics:

- clearly identifies important features of the argument and analyzes them insightfully
- develops ideas cogently, organizes them logically, and connects them with clear transitions
- effectively supports the main points of the critique
- demonstrates control of language, including diction and syntactic variety
- demonstrates facility with the conventions of standard written English but may have minor flaws

5 Strong

A 5 paper presents a well-developed critique of the argument and demonstrates good control of the elements of effective writing.

A typical paper in this category exhibits the following characteristics:

- clearly identifies important features of the argument and analyzes them in a generally thoughtful way
- develops ideas clearly, organizes them logically, and connects them with appropriate transitions
- sensibly supports the main points of the critique
- demonstrates control of language, including diction and syntactic variety
- demonstrates facility with the conventions of standard written English but may have occasional flaws

4 Adequate

A 4 paper presents a competent critique of the argument and demonstrates adequate control of the elements of writing.

A typical paper in this category exhibits the following characteristics:

- identifies and analyzes important features of the argument
- develops and organizes ideas satisfactorily but may not connect them with transitions
- supports the main points of the critique
- demonstrates sufficient control of language to convey ideas with reasonable clarity
- generally follows the conventions of standard written English but may have some flaws

3 Limited

A 3 paper demonstrates some competence in analytical writing skills and in its control of the elements of writing but is plainly flawed.

A typical paper in this category exhibits one or more of the following characteristics:

- does not identify or analyze most of the important features of the argument, although some analysis of the argument is present
- mainly analyzes tangential or irrelevant matters, or reasons poorly
- is limited in the logical development and organization of ideas
- offers support of little relevance and value for points of the critique
- does not convey meaning clearly
- contains occasional major errors or frequent minor errors in grammar, usage, and mechanics

2 Seriously Flawed

A 2 paper demonstrates serious weaknesses in analytical writing skills.

A typical paper in this category exhibits one or more of the following characteristics:

- does not present a critique based on logical analysis, but may instead present the writer's own views on the subject
- does not develop ideas, or is disorganized and illogical
- provides little, if any, relevant or reasonable support
- has serious and frequent problems in the use of language and in sentence structure
- contains numerous errors in grammar, usage, and mechanics that interfere with meaning

1 Fundamentally Deficient

A 1 paper demonstrates fundamental deficiencies in analytical writing skills.

A typical paper in this category exhibits more than one of the following characteristics:

- provides little evidence of the ability to understand and analyze the argument
- provides little evidence of the ability to develop an organized response
- has severe and persistent errors in language and sentence structure
- contains a pervasive pattern of errors in grammar, usage, and mechanics that results in incoherence

0 No Score

A paper in this category is off topic, not written in English, is merely attempting to copy the topic, or consists only of keystroke characters.

NR Blank

A paper is assigned NR when no response has been submitted.

11.5 Sample: Analysis of an Argument

Read the statement and the instructions that follow it, and then make any notes that will help you plan your response.

The following appeared as part of an article in a daily newspaper:

"The computerized on-board warning system that will be installed in commercial airliners will virtually solve the problem of midair plane collisions. One plane's warning system can receive signals from another's transponder—a radio set that signals a plane's course—in order to determine the likelihood of a collision and recommend evasive action."

Discuss how well reasoned you find this argument. In your discussion, be sure to analyze the line of reasoning and the use of evidence in the argument. For example, you may need to consider what questionable assumptions underlie the thinking and what alternative explanations or counterexamples might weaken the conclusion. You can also discuss what sort of evidence would strengthen or refute the argument, what changes in the argument would make it more logically sound, and what, if anything, would help you better evaluate its conclusion.

Sample Paper 6

The argument that this warning system will virtually solve the problem of midair plane collisions omits some important concerns that must be addressed to substantiate the argument. The statement that follows the description of what this warning system will do simply describes the system and how it operates. This alone does not constitute a logical argument in favor of the warning system, and it certainly does not provide support or proof of the main argument.

Most conspicuously, the argument does not address the cause of the problem of midair plane collisions, the use of the system by pilots and flight specialists, or who is involved in the midair plane collisions. First, the argument assumes that the cause of the problem is that the planes' courses, the likelihood of collisions, and actions to avoid collisions are unknown or inaccurate. In a weak attempt to support its claim, the argument describes a system that makes all of these things accurately known. But if the cause of the problem of midair plane collisions is that pilots are not paying attention to their computer systems or flight operations, the warning system will not solve the collision problem. Second, the argument never addresses the interface between individuals and the system and how this will affect the warning system's objective of obliterating the problem of collisions. If the pilot or flight specialist does not conform to what the warning system suggests, midair collisions will not be avoided. Finally, if planes other than commercial airliners are involved in the collisions, the problem of these collisions cannot be solved by a warning system that will not be installed on non-commercial airliners. The argument also does not address what would happen in the event that the warning system collapses, fails, or does not work properly.

Because the argument leaves out several key issues, it is not sound or persuasive. If it included the items discussed above instead of solely explaining what the system supposedly does, the argument would have been more thorough and convincing.

Explanation of Score 6

This response is, as the scoring guide requires of a 6, "cogent" and "well articulated": all the points made not only bear directly on the argument to be analyzed, but also contribute to a single, integrated development of the writer's critique. The writer begins by making the controlling point that a mere description of the warning system's mode of operation cannot serve as a true argument proving the system's effectiveness, since the description overlooks several major considerations. The writer then identifies these considerations—what causes midair collisions, how pilots will actually use the commercial airline warning system, what kinds of airplanes are typically involved in midair collisions—and, citing appropriate counterexamples (e.g., what if pilots do not pay attention to their instruments?), explains fully how each oversight undermines the conclusion that the warning system will virtually eliminate midair plane collisions.

Throughout, the writer complements the logically organized development of this critique with good, clear prose that demonstrates the ability not only to control language and vary sentence structure but also to express ideas forcibly (e.g., "the argument never addresses the interface between individuals and the system"). Of course, as in any response written under time constraints, occasional minor flaws can be found. For example, "the argument assumes that the cause of the problem is that the planes' courses, the likelihood of collisions, and actions to avoid collisions are unknown or inaccurate" is wordy and imprecise: how can a course, a likelihood, or actions be inaccurate? But flaws such as these, minor and infrequent, do not interfere with the overall clarity and forcefulness of this outstanding response.

Sample Paper 4

The argument is not logically convincing. It does not state whether all planes can receive signals from each other. It does not state whether planes constantly receive signals. If they only receive signals once every certain time interval, collisions will not definitely be prevented. Further if they receive a signal right before they are about to crash, they cannot avoid each other.

The main flaw in the argument is that it assumes that the two planes, upon receiving each other's signals, will know which evasive action to take. For example, the two planes could be going towards each other and then receive the signals. If one turns at an angle to the left and the other turns at an angle to the right, the two planes will still crash. Even if they receive an updated signal, they will not have time to avoid each other.

The following argument would be more sound and persuasive. The new warning system will solve the problem of midair plane collisions. Each plane will receive constant, continual signals from each other. If the two planes are headed in a direction where they will crash, the system will coordinate the signals, and tell one plane to go one way, and the other plane to go another way. The new system will ensure that the two planes will turn in different directions so they don't crash by trying to prevent the original crash. In addition, the two planes will be able to see themselves and the other on a computer screen, to aid in the evasive action.

Explanation of Score 4

This response competently cites a number of deficiencies in the argument presented: the information given about the nature of the signals sent and received and the evasive action recommended does not warrant the conclusion that the onboard warning system "will virtually solve the problem of midair plane collisions." However, in discussing these insufficiencies in the argument, the response reveals an unevenness in the quality of its reasoning. For example, while it is perfectly legitimate to point out that the argument assumes too much and says too little about the evasive action that will be recommended by the warning system, it is farfetched to suggest that the system might be so poorly designed as to route two approaching airplanes to the same spot. Likewise, while it is fair to question the effectiveness of a warning signal about which the argument says so little, it is not reasonable to assume that the system would be designed to space signals so far apart that they would prove useless. Rather than invent implausibly bad versions of the warning system to prove that it might be ineffective, a stronger response would analyze unexplored possibilities inherent in the information that is given—for example, the possibility that pilots might not be able to respond quickly and effectively to the radio signals the argument says they will receive when the new system is installed. The "more sound and persuasive argument" in the last paragraph, while an improvement on the original, continues to overlook this possibility and also assumes that other types of aircraft without transponders will pose no problems.

The organization of ideas, while generally sound, is sometimes weakened by needless repetition of the same points, as in sentences 4 and 5 of the last paragraph. The writing contains minor instances of awkwardness (e.g., "Each plane will receive constant, continual signals from each other" in paragraph 3), but is free of flaws that make understanding difficult. However, though the writing is generally clean and clear, the syntax does not show much variety. A few sentences begin with "if" clauses, but almost all the rest, even those that begin with a transitional phrase such as "for example" or "in addition," conform to a "subject, verb, complement" pattern. The first paragraph, in which the second and third sentences begin the same way ("It does not state"), is particularly repetitious.

Sample Paper 2

This argument has no information about air collisions. I think most cases happen in new airports because the air traffic I heavy. In this case sound airport control could solve the problem.

I think this argument is logically reasonable. Its assumption is that plane collisions are caused by planes that don't know each others positions. So pilots can do nothing, if they know each others position through the system it will solve the problem.

If it can provide evidence the problem is lack of knowledge of each others positions, it will be more sound and persuasive.

More information about air collisions is helpful, (the reason for air collisions).

Explanation of Score 2

This response is seriously flawed in several ways. First of all, it has very little substance. The writer appears to make only one point—that while it seems reasonable to assume that midair collisions would be less likely if pilots were sure of each other's positions, readers cannot adequately judge this assumption without more information about where, why, and how such collisions occur. This point, furthermore, is neither explained by a single reason beyond what is given in the topic nor supported by a single example. Legitimate though it is, it cannot, alone and undeveloped, serve as an adequate response to the argument.

Aside from being undeveloped, the response is confusing. At the outset, it seems to be critical of the argument. The writer begins by pointing to the inadequacy of the information given; then speculates, without evidence, that "most cases happen in new airports"; and then suggests that the problem should be addressed by improving "airport control," not (it is implied) by installing onboard warning systems. After criticizing the argument in the first paragraph, the writer confusingly seems to endorse it in the second. Then, in the remainder of the response, the writer returns to a critical stance.

The general lack of coherence is reflected in the serious and frequent writing problems that make meaning hard to determine—for example, the elliptical and ungrammatical "So pilots can do nothing, if they know each others position through the system it will solve the problem" (paragraph 2) or "If it can provide evidence the problem is lack of knowledge of each others positions, it will be more sound and persuasive" (paragraph 3). The prose suffers from a variety of basic errors in grammar, usage, and mechanics.

To further practice your analytical writing skills, the *GMAT™ Official AWA Practice* product is available for purchase through mba.com.

12.0   GMAT™ Official Guide Question Index

12.0 **GMAT™ Official Guide Question Index**

The Official Guide Index is organized by GMAT™ section, difficulty level, and then by mathematical or verbal concept. The question number, page number, and answer explanation page number are listed so that questions within the book can be quickly located.

To locate a question from the online question bank in the book—Every question in the online question bank has a unique ID, called the Practice Question Identifier, or PQID, which appears above the question number. Look up the PQID in the table to find its problem number and page number in the book.

Math Review

Difficulty	Concept	Question #	Page	Answer Explanation Page	PQID
Easy	Algebra Applied Problems	11	51	52	PS51061.03
Easy	Algebra Ratio and Proportion	7	37	39	DS71210.03
Easy	Algebra; Arithmetic Simplifying Algebraic Expressions; Percents	14	51	53	PS23461.03
Easy	Arithmetic Percents	12	51	52	DS15161.03
Easy	Arithmetic Rate Problem	13	51	53	DS07061.03
Easy	Arithmetic Statistics	16	67	69	PS07310.03
Easy	Arithmetic Statistics	17	67	69	PS57720.03
Easy	Arithmetic; Algebra Interpretation of Tables; Applied Problems	6	37	38	PS21840.03
Easy	Geometry Angle Measure in Degrees	21	88	90	PS22061.03
Easy	Geometry Volume	22	88	90	DS17061.03
Easy	Geometry; Arithmetic Percents; Interpretation of Graphs	23	88	91	PS29261.03
Medium	Algebra Exponents	8	38	39	DS84820.03
Medium	Algebra Inequalities	2	24	26	DS38350.03
Medium	Algebra Inequalities	10	38	40	DS53060.02
Medium	Algebra Order	3	25	26	DS75160.03
Medium	Algebra Simultaneous Equations	9	38	40	DS67730.03
Medium	Algebra; Geometry Quadrilaterals	24	89	91	DS48061.03

(*Continued*)

Difficulty	Concept	Question #	Page	Answer Explanation Page	PQID
Medium	Arithmetic Applied Problems; Operations with Decimals	4	25	27	PS10241.03
Medium	Arithmetic Measurement Conversion	1	24	25	PS87710.03
Medium	Arithmetic Statistics	18	68	70	PS97920.03
Medium	Geometry Circles; Area	25	89	92	DS39161.03
Hard	Algebra Applied Problems	15	52	54	PS61361.03
Hard	Arithmetic Probability	20	68	71	DS11040.03
Hard	Arithmetic Properties of Numbers	5	25	27	DS10680.03
Hard	Arithmetic Sets	19	68	71	DS22030.03

Verbal Review

Difficulty	Concept	Question #	Page	Answer Explanation Page	PQID
Easy	Argument Construction	1	386	387	CR63800.03
Easy	Evaluation of a Plan	4	391	391	CR96370.03
Easy	Evaluation of a Plan	5	393	393	CR03570.03
Easy	Idiom; Rhetorical Construction	24	442	443	SC92120.03
Easy	Inference	8	395	397	RC73100-05.03
Easy	Logical Predication; Parallelism	23	441	441	SC74010.03
Easy	Main Idea	9	395	397	RC73100-06.03
Easy	Passage				RC73100-00.03
Easy	Supporting Idea	6	395	395	RC73100-01.03
Easy	Supporting Idea	7	395	396	RC73100-03.03
Easy	Verb Form; Diction	18	425	426	SC93410.03
Medium	Argument Evaluation	2	386	387	CR32900.03
Medium	Evaluation	13	407	409	RC00034-04
Medium	Inference	12	407	408	RC00034-03
Medium	Inference	14	407	409	RC00034-07
Medium	Logical Predication; Grammatical Construction	22	438	439	RC02605

Difficulty	Concept	Question #	Page	Answer Explanation Page	PQID
Medium	Main Idea	11	406	407	RC00034-01
Medium	Passage				RC00034-00
Medium	Rhetorical Construction; Parallelism	25	442	443	CR09351.03
Medium	Verb Form; Rhetorical Construction	20	432	432	SC02457
Hard	Argument Evaluation	10	400	400	CR51800.03
Hard	Argument Evaluation	3	389	389	CR49110.03
Hard	Argument Evaluation	15	411	412	CR28310.03
Hard	Argument Evaluation	16	416	417	CR88310.03
Hard	Argument Evaluation	17	419	420	CR13750.03
Hard	Grammatical Construction; Logical Predication	21	436	436	SC95430.03
Hard	Rhetorical Construction; Parallelism	19	430	430	SC06684

Problem Solving

Difficulty	Concept	Question #	Page	Answer Explanation Page	PQID
Easy	Algebraic Expressions	60	120	173	PS08385
Easy	Algebraic Expressions	73	123	180	PS01315
Easy	Algebraic Expressions	93	126	187	PS99551.02
Easy	Angles	56	120	172	PS07408
Easy	Angles and Their Measure	32	116	165	PS00534
Easy	Applied Problems	4	112	156	PS07308
Easy	Applied Problems	5	112	156	PS07799
Easy	Applied Problems	9	113	158	PS05001
Easy	Applied Problems	23	115	162	PS09707
Easy	Applied Problems	31	116	164	PS13801
Easy	Applied Problems	33	116	165	PS17479

(*Continued*)

Difficulty	Concept	Question #	Page	Answer Explanation Page	PQID
Easy	Applied Problems	35	117	166	PS01233
Easy	Applied Problems	45	118	169	PS13159
Easy	Applied Problems	51	119	171	PS05308
Easy	Applied Problems	55	120	172	PS08173
Easy	Applied Problems	64	121	176	PS15523
Easy	Applied Problems	69	122	178	PS00526
Easy	Applied Problems	71	122	179	PS02209
Easy	Applied Problems	75	123	180	PS02102
Easy	Applied Problems	77	123	181	PS14236
Easy	Applied Problems	83	124	183	PS13101
Easy	Applied Problems; First-Degree Equations	97	127	189	PS93850.02
Easy	Applied Problems; Percents	34	117	165	PS13707
Easy	Applied Problems; Percents	54	120	172	PS12114
Easy	Applied Problems; Percents	78	124	181	PS02996
Easy	Applied Problems; Properties of Numbers	14	114	159	PS01248
Easy	Applied Problems; Sequences	79	124	182	PS00307
Easy	Area	52	119	171	PS05544
Easy	Area	70	122	178	PS06601
Easy	Circles; Circumference; Perimeter	25	115	162	PS12542
Easy	Coordinate Geometry	62	121	174	PS00096
Easy	Coordinate Geometry	68	122	178	PS02695
Easy	Coordinate Geometry	84	124	184	PS02947
Easy	Estimation	28	116	163	PS05239
Easy	Estimation	50	119	170	PS06243
Easy	Estimation	53	119	172	PS10470
Easy	Estimation	57	120	173	PS08768
Easy	Exponents	41	118	168	PS04797
Easy	First-Degree Equations	10	113	158	PS17812
Easy	First-Degree Equations	13	114	159	PS02382

Difficulty	Concept	Question #	Page	Answer Explanation Page	PQID
Easy	First-Degree Equations	20	115	161	PS15957
Easy	First-Degree Equations	22	115	161	PS15358
Easy	First-Degree Equations	74	123	180	PS00907
Easy	First-Degree Equations	92	126	187	PS04734
Easy	Fractions	89	125	186	PS14989
Easy	Functions	99	127	189	PS09899
Easy	Inequalities	26	115	163	PS03972
Easy	Inequalities	61	121	174	PS03371
Easy	Inequalities	85	125	184	PS11091
Easy	Inequalities	96	126	188	PS66740.02
Easy	Interpretation of Graphs and Tables	49	119	170	PS05100
Easy	Interpretation of Tables	2	112	155	PS09868
Easy	Interpretation of Tables	46	118	169	PS02534
Easy	Measurement Conversion	94	126	188	PS92820.02
Easy	Operations on Radical Expressions	76	123	181	PS00419
Easy	Operations on Rational Numbers	8	113	157	PS05410
Easy	Operations with Integers	27	116	163	PS00087
Easy	Operations with Integers	86	125	185	PS14467
Easy	Operations with Radical Expressions	82	124	183	PS12764
Easy	Operations with Rational Numbers	11	113	158	PS02295
Easy	Operations with Rational Numbers	18	114	160	PS02286
Easy	Operations with Rational Numbers	42	118	168	PS05747
Easy	Operations with Rational Numbers	43	118	168	PS14972
Easy	Operations with Rational Numbers	80	124	182	PS03635
Easy	Percents	7	113	157	PS08877
Easy	Percents	16	114	160	PS14861
Easy	Percents	19	114	160	PS11906

(*Continued*)

Difficulty	Concept	Question #	Page	Answer Explanation Page	PQID
Easy	Percents	67	122	177	PS12287
Easy	Percents	87	125	185	PS07465
Easy	Percents	95	126	188	PS11396
Easy	Percents	98	127	189	PS07672
Easy	Perimeter	1	112	155	PS02991
Easy	Probability	24	115	162	PS02127
Easy	Profit and Loss	36	117	166	PS02007
Easy	Properties of Numbers	58	120	173	PS08025
Easy	Properties of Numbers	66	121	177	PS05682
Easy	Properties of Numbers	81	124	182	PS03214
Easy	Properties of Numbers	88	125	186	PS06946
Easy	Pythagorean Theorem	40	118	167	PS05680
Easy	Pythagorean Theorem	72	123	179	PS05957
Easy	Rate	65	121	177	PS07197
Easy	Ratio and Proportion	12	114	158	PS08461
Easy	Ratio and Proportion	39	117	167	PS13831
Easy	Ratio and Proportion	48	119	170	PS14250
Easy	Sequences	59	120	173	PS00015
Easy	Simple Coordinate Geometry; Triangles	6	113	157	PS02599
Easy	Simplifying Algebraic Expressions	38	117	167	PS12786
Easy	Simplifying Algebraic Expressions	90	126	187	PS12949
Easy	Simultaneous Equations	47	119	170	PS02338
Easy	Simultaneous First-Degree Equations	29	116	164	PS15402
Easy	Statistics	3	112	156	PS10002
Easy	Statistics	15	114	159	PS07369
Easy	Statistics	17	114	160	PS02764
Easy	Statistics	21	115	161	PS00984
Easy	Statistics	30	116	164	PS04571
Easy	Statistics	63	121	176	PS10568

Difficulty	Concept	Question #	Page	Answer Explanation Page	PQID
Easy	Statistics	91	126	187	PS12760
Easy	Triangles	37	117	166	PS10628
Easy	Volume	44	118	168	PS06592
Medium	Absolute Value; Number Line	140	133	203	PS08399
Medium	Algebraic Expressions	107	128	192	PS30730.02
Medium	Applied Problems	117	129	196	PS01080.02
Medium	Applied Problems	125	131	198	PS09737
Medium	Applied Problems	136	132	202	PS08865
Medium	Applied Problems	154	135	208	PS04617
Medium	Applied Problems	155	136	208	PS12577
Medium	Applied Problems	157	136	209	PS00428
Medium	Area	122	130	197	PS02820
Medium	Area	153	135	208	PS50750.02
Medium	Circles; Rectangles	100	127	190	PS77502.01
Medium	Circles; Triangles	118	130	196	PS11308
Medium	Elementary Combinatorics	167	138	212	PS28101.02
Medium	Estimation	156	136	209	PS05973
Medium	Estimation; Exponents	159	137	210	PS94421.02
Medium	Exponents	135	132	201	PS81711.02
Medium	First-Degree Equations	121	130	197	PS69400.02
Medium	Formulas	106	128	192	PS45430.02
Medium	Formulas	110	129	193	PS37631.02
Medium	Functions	152	135	207	PS10546
Medium	Inequalities	142	133	204	PS05962
Medium	Measurement Conversion	108	128	193	PS49140.02
Medium	Measurement Conversion	124	131	198	PS30720.02
Medium	Measurement Conversion	149	135	207	PS39811.02
Medium	Measurement Conversion	150	135	207	PS41450.02
Medium	Operations on Radical Expressions	133	132	201	PS00633

(*Continued*)

Difficulty	Concept	Question #	Page	Answer Explanation Page	PQID
Medium	Operations with Decimals; Place Value	166	138	212	PS02017
Medium	Operations with Integers	111	129	193	PS01761
Medium	Operations with Integers	126	131	198	PS01622
Medium	Operations with Integers	139	133	203	PS02325
Medium	Operations with Integers	164	137	212	PS02749
Medium	Percents	116	129	195	PS05560
Medium	Percents	128	131	199	PS02555
Medium	Percents	146	134	205	PS08441
Medium	Percents	147	134	206	PS15111
Medium	Percents	161	137	211	PS03823
Medium	Percents; First-Degree Equations	127	131	199	PS04448
Medium	Percents; Ratio and Proportion	129	131	199	PS10307
Medium	Place Value	143	134	204	PS07601.02
Medium	Probability	158	136	210	PS63210.02
Medium	Properties of Numbers	113	129	194	PS10391
Medium	Properties of Numbers	148	135	206	PS02704
Medium	Quadrilaterals; Area	104	128	191	PS40602.01
Medium	Quadrilaterals; Pythagorean Theorem	101	127	190	PS58502.01
Medium	Ratio and Proportion	112	129	194	PS04482
Medium	Rectangles	102	127	191	PS98502.01
Medium	Remainders	120	130	197	PS11756
Medium	Second-Degree Equations	114	129	195	PS07325
Medium	Second-Degree Equations	132	132	200	PS11121
Medium	Second-Degree Equations	151	135	207	PS02600
Medium	Series and Sequences	123	130	198	PS44321.02
Medium	Sets	105	128	192	PS24210.02
Medium	Sets	134	132	201	PS21260.02
Medium	Sets	144	134	205	PS04089
Medium	Sets	145	134	205	PS06133

Difficulty	Concept	Question #	Page	Answer Explanation Page	PQID
Medium	Sets; Interpretation of Tables	137	133	202	PS51950.02
Medium	Simple Coordinate Geometry	115	129	195	PS68850.02
Medium	Simplifying Algebraic Expressions	109	128	193	PS14031.02
Medium	Simplifying Algebraic Expressions	163	137	211	PS70371.02
Medium	Simplifying Algebraic Expressions; Operations on Rational Numbers	131	132	200	PS09708
Medium	Simultaneous Equations	130	132	200	PS36090.02
Medium	Simultaneous Equations; Inequalities	165	138	212	PS02777
Medium	Statistics	119	130	196	PS15517
Medium	Statistics	160	137	210	PS08966
Medium	Statistics	162	137	211	PS11600
Medium	Triangles; Area	103	128	191	PS19502.01
Medium	Volume	138	133	203	PS07112
Medium	Volume	141	133	203	PS94530.02
Hard	Algebra; Statistics; Applied Problems; Simultaneous Equations	248	150	245	PS16890
Hard	Applied Problems	172	139	214	PS16410
Hard	Applied Problems	181	140	217	PS01987
Hard	Applied Problems	189	141	220	PS16810
Hard	Applied Problems	196	142	224	PS07459
Hard	Applied Problems	208	144	230	PS07081
Hard	Applied Problems	213	145	232	PS06562
Hard	Applied Problems	219	146	234	PS16830
Hard	Applied Problems	220	146	234	PS16831
Hard	Applied Problems	228	147	237	PS08570
Hard	Applied Problems	238	148	241	PS04677
Hard	Applied Problems	250	150	246	PS16894
Hard	Applied Problems	251	150	247	PS16896
Hard	Applied Problems	258	152	250	PS16904

(Continued)

Difficulty	Concept	Question #	Page	Answer Explanation Page	PQID
Hard	Applied Problems; Simultaneous Equations	215	145	232	PS16823
Hard	Area	175	139	215	PS13827
Hard	Area	259	152	251	PS49220.02
Hard	Arithmetic; Volume; Ratio and Proportion	188	141	219	PS08313
Hard	Circles	206	144	230	PS12078
Hard	Coordinate Geometry	212	145	231	PS06948
Hard	Elementary Combinatorics	169	138	213	PS13724
Hard	Elementary Combinatorics	177	139	216	PS08280
Hard	Elementary Combinatorics	211	145	231	PS07547
Hard	Elementary Combinatorics	230	147	238	PS13691
Hard	Elementary Combinatorics	245	149	244	PS05140
Hard	Equations	209	144	231	PS13996
Hard	Estimation	221	146	234	PS16832
Hard	Inequalities	214	145	232	PS16107
Hard	Inequalities	222	146	235	PS16833
Hard	Inequalities	260	152	251	PS14203
Hard	Interpretation of Graphs and Tables; Statistics	193	142	223	PS00422
Hard	Negative Exponents	240	149	242	PS03686
Hard	Negative Exponents	262	152	252	PS08886
Hard	Operations on Rational Numbers	190	141	222	PS16811
Hard	Operations on Rational Numbers	192	141	222	PS06570
Hard	Operations on Rational Numbers	216	145	232	PS16824
Hard	Operations on Rational Numbers	226	147	236	PS06558
Hard	Operations on Rational Numbers	232	148	238	PS09403
Hard	Operations on Rational Numbers	246	150	244	PS00574
Hard	Operations on Rational Numbers	254	151	248	PS16899
Hard	Operations on Rational Numbers	256	151	249	PS01648
Hard	Operations with Integers	202	143	228	PS06497

Difficulty	Concept	Question #	Page	Answer Explanation Page	PQID
Hard	Operations with Integers	234	148	240	PS91151.02
Hard	Percents	182	140	218	PS16088
Hard	Percents	198	142	224	PS07730
Hard	Percents	201	143	227	PS04688
Hard	Percents	237	148	240	PS08552
Hard	Percents	241	149	242	PS07555
Hard	Perimeter	185	140	218	PS08219
Hard	Polygons	255	151	248	PS00947
Hard	Probability	171	138	213	PS02111
Hard	Probability	191	141	222	PS16122
Hard	Probability	199	143	225	PS06215
Hard	Probability	252	151	247	PS16897
Hard	Profit and Loss	225	147	236	PS16116
Hard	Properties of Numbers	170	138	213	PS10982
Hard	Properties of Numbers	183	140	218	PS11065
Hard	Properties of Numbers	194	142	223	PS08209
Hard	Properties of Numbers	204	144	229	PS00041
Hard	Properties of Numbers	205	144	229	PS04651
Hard	Properties of Numbers	207	144	230	PS12177
Hard	Properties of Numbers	210	144	231	PS12536
Hard	Properties of Numbers	218	146	233	PS16828
Hard	Properties of Numbers	224	147	236	PS05882
Hard	Properties of Numbers	229	147	237	PS00564
Hard	Properties of Numbers	244	149	244	PS02405
Hard	Properties of Numbers; Decimals	176	139	215	PS00562
Hard	Pythagorean Theorem; Rectangles	168	138	213	PS60231.02
Hard	Quadrilaterals; Triangles	203	143	228	PS07536
Hard	Rate	235	148	240	PS06498
Hard	Rectangular Solids and Cylinders	239	149	241	PS56710.02

(Continued)

Difficulty	Concept	Question #	Page	Answer Explanation Page	PQID
Hard	Second-Degree Equations	197	142	224	PS05888
Hard	Second-Degree Equations	217	145	233	PS07491
Hard	Second-Degree Equations	231	147	238	PS08480
Hard	Second-Degree Equations	253	151	247	PS16898
Hard	Second-Degree Equations	257	152	250	PS16115
Hard	Second-Degree Equations; Simultaneous Equations	184	140	218	PS16802
Hard	Sequences	236	148	240	PS08732
Hard	Sets	261	152	252	PS07712
Hard	Simple Coordinate Geometry	249	150	246	PS16893
Hard	Simplifying Algebraic Expressions	227	147	236	PS16100
Hard	Simplifying Algebraic Expressions	243	149	243	PS16146
Hard	Simplifying Expressions; Computation with Integers	233	148	239	PS03513
Hard	Simultaneous Equations	178	140	216	PS02903
Hard	Simultaneous Equations	247	150	245	PS03144
Hard	Simultaneous Equations; Inequalities	186	141	219	PS04711
Hard	Statistics	173	139	214	PS07357
Hard	Statistics	180	140	217	PS03768
Hard	Statistics	187	141	219	PS16214
Hard	Statistics	195	142	223	PS06674
Hard	Statistics	200	143	226	PS13244
Hard	Statistics	242	149	243	PS04305
Hard	Statistics; Applied Problems	223	146	235	PS16835
Hard	Systems of Equations	179	140	216	PS16259
Hard	Triangles	174	139	214	PS02649

Data Sufficiency

Difficulty	Concept	Question #	Page	Answer Explanation Page	PQID
Easy	Coordinate Geometry	309	265	304	DS12533
Easy	Angles	271	261	289	DS17639
Easy	Angles	296	264	299	DS27860.02
Easy	Applied Problems	263	261	286	DS02562
Easy	Applied Problems	279	262	293	DS02541
Easy	Applied Problems	284	263	295	DS06802
Easy	Applied Problems	287	263	296	DS00858
Easy	Applied Problems	301	264	300	DS06905
Easy	Applied Problems	313	265	306	DS02441
Easy	Applied Problems	317	265	307	DS03628
Easy	Applied Problems	324	266	310	DS05312
Easy	Applied Problems; Percents	297	264	299	DS07839
Easy	Applied Problems; Percents	300	264	300	DS11109
Easy	Applied Problems; Percents	304	264	301	DS02450
Easy	Circles	298	264	299	DS06397
Easy	Circles; Area	308	265	303	DS08730
Easy	Circles; Pythagorean Theorem	310	265	304	DS19520
Easy	Equations	293	263	298	DS06633
Easy	Equations	299	264	300	DS07813
Easy	Exponents	288	263	296	DS06065
Easy	Exponents	295	263	299	DS06475
Easy	Exponents and Radicals	341	267	314	DS22602.01
Easy	Inequalities	292	263	298	DS11254
Easy	Inequalities	315	265	306	DS09315
Easy	Inequalities	318	265	307	DS02585
Easy	Inequalities	319	265	308	DS01619
Easy	Lines	325	266	310	DS48710.02
Easy	Lines and Segments	306	264	303	DS04366

(Continued)

Difficulty	Concept	Question #	Page	Answer Explanation Page	PQID
Easy	Lines and Segments	346	268	316	DS04602.0
Easy	Measurement Conversion	348	268	316	DS45602.01
Easy	Operations with Integers	303	264	301	DS15377
Easy	Operations with Integers	329	266	311	DS10602.01
Easy	Operations with Radicals	323	266	309	DS08308
Easy	Order	307	264	303	DS11805
Easy	Order; Ratio	275	262	291	DS05338
Easy	Percents	282	262	294	DS04630
Easy	Percents	316	265	307	DS01216
Easy	Probability	280	262	294	DS08054
Easy	Probability	314	265	306	DS03999
Easy	Properties of Integers	327	266	311	DS76502.01
Easy	Properties of Integers	330	266	312	DS01602.01
Easy	Properties of Integers	332	266	312	DS21602.01
Easy	Properties of Integers	338	267	314	DS32602.01
Easy	Properties of Integers	340	267	314	DS72602.01
Easy	Properties of Numbers	302	264	301	DS12031
Easy	Properties of Numbers	321	266	308	DS01425
Easy	Properties of Numbers	322	266	309	DS14502
Easy	Properties of Numbers	339	267	314	DS52602.01
Easy	Properties of Numbers	347	268	316	DS65602.01
Easy	Ratio and Proportion	268	261	288	DS03422
Easy	Ratio and Proportion	272	262	289	DS07822
Easy	Ratio and Proportion	278	262	293	DS10687
Easy	Ratios	273	262	290	DS15940
Easy	Ratios	336	267	313	DS81602.01
Easy	Rectangular Solids	286	263	295	DS15650.02
Easy	Sequences	285	263	295	DS06662
Easy	Series and Sequences	331	266	312	DS11602.01
Easy	Series and Sequences	337	267	313	DS12602.01

Difficulty	Concept	Question #	Page	Answer Explanation Page	PQID
Easy	Sets	294	263	298	DS07949
Easy	Sets	311	265	305	DS13122
Easy	Sets	312	265	305	DS01544
Easy	Sets	320	266	308	DS04536
Easy	Simple Coordinate Geometry	265	261	287	DS18950.02
Easy	Simple Coordinate Geometry	269	261	288	DS16840.02
Easy	Simplifying Algebraic Expressions	335	267	313	DS41602.01
Easy	Simplifying Algebraic Expressions	344	267	315	DS53602.01
Easy	Simultaneous Equations	264	261	286	DS10471
Easy	Simultaneous Equations	266	261	287	DS03802
Easy	Simultaneous Equations	270	261	289	DS12265
Easy	Simultaneous Equations	283	263	294	DS12062
Easy	Simultaneous Equations	290	263	297	DS08723
Easy	Simultaneous Equations	291	263	297	DS04605
Easy	Simultaneous Equations	333	267	312	DS70602.01
Easy	Simultaneous Equations	334	267	313	DS90602.01
Easy	Simultaneous Equations	342	267	315	DS42602.01
Easy	Statistics	267	261	288	DS05863
Easy	Statistics	274	262	290	DS50241.02
Easy	Statistics	276	262	291	DS03138
Easy	Statistics	277	262	292	DS00254
Easy	Statistics	289	263	297	DS00660
Easy	Statistics	343	267	315	DS43602.01
Easy	Triangles	328	266	311	DS27502.01
Easy	Triangles	345	268	316	DS63602.01
Easy	Triangles; Area	305	264	302	DS06901
Easy	Triangles; Pythagorean Theorem	281	262	294	DS04594
Easy	Volume	326	266	310	DS51531.02
Medium	Algebra; Applied Problems	406	274	339	DS05631

(Continued)

Difficulty	Concept	Question #	Page	Answer Explanation Page	PQID
Medium	Algebra; Applied Problems	421	275	347	DS71521.01
Medium	Angles	400	273	337	DS04852
Medium	Applied Problems	379	271	330	DS14569
Medium	Applied Problems	381	271	331	DS11287
Medium	Applied Problems	393	272	335	DS05330
Medium	Applied Problems	395	273	335	DS46420.02
Medium	Applied Problems	396	273	336	DS01257
Medium	Applied Problems	423	275	347	DS14527
Medium	Applied Problems; Circles	384	272	331	DS05049
Medium	Applied Problems; Percents	408	274	340	DS13541
Medium	Applied Problems; Percents	418	275	345	DS04540
Medium	Applied Problems; Percents	419	275	346	DS08365
Medium	Applied Problems; Proportions	375	271	328	DS08420
Medium	Arithmetic Operations	350	268	317	DS37502.01
Medium	Circles	360	269	321	DS30602.01
Medium	Circles; Area	361	269	322	DS59502.01
Medium	Computation with Integers	405	274	339	DS04157
Medium	Computation with Integers	420	275	346	DS01168
Medium	Exponents	355	268	319	DS38502.01
Medium	Exponents	387	272	333	DS09379
Medium	First-Degree Equations	385	272	332	DS24751.01
Medium	First-Degree Equations	403	273	338	DS72951.01
Medium	First-Degree Equations	413	274	343	DS45530.01
Medium	Functions	392	272	334	DS24571.01
Medium	Inequalities	359	269	320	DS69502.01
Medium	Inequalities	402	273	338	DS13588
Medium	Inequalities	407	274	340	DS15561
Medium	Inequalities	415	274	343	DS13130
Medium	Number Line	426	276	349	DS01324
Medium	Operations with Integers	410	274	342	DS13841.01

Difficulty	Concept	Question #	Page	Answer Explanation Page	PQID
Medium	Operations with Integers; Order	389	272	333	DS13949
Medium	Percents	383	271	331	DS13408
Medium	Polygons	409	274	341	DS75271.01
Medium	Probability	394	272	335	DS03045
Medium	Properties of Integers	349	268	317	DS07502.01
Medium	Properties of Integers	357	269	320	DS49502.01
Medium	Properties of Integers	380	271	330	DS05377
Medium	Properties of Integers	425	275	348	DS15045
Medium	Properties of Numbers	382	271	331	DS17615
Medium	Properties of Numbers	386	272	332	DS05772
Medium	Properties of Numbers	390	272	334	DS12943
Medium	Properties of Numbers	391	272	334	DS14788
Medium	Properties of Numbers	404	273	339	DS11257
Medium	Properties of Numbers	412	274	343	DS06027
Medium	Properties of Numbers	414	274	343	DS08197
Medium	Quadrilaterals	363	269	323	DS51602.01
Medium	Quadrilaterals	374	271	327	DS75602.01
Medium	Quadrilaterals; Area	356	268	319	DS28502.01
Medium	Quadrilaterals; Perimeter	370	270	325	DS64602.01
Medium	Ratios	362	269	322	DS61602.01
Medium	Ratios; Simultaneous Equations	358	269	320	DS00602.01
Medium	Rectangles; Perimeter	398	273	336	DS04428
Medium	Series and Sequences	351	268	317	DS57502.01
Medium	Series and Sequences	365	269	323	DS92602.01
Medium	Sets	401	273	338	DS06096
Medium	Simplifying Algebraic Expressions	376	271	329	DS04057
Medium	Simplifying Algebraic Expressions	399	273	337	DS06537
Medium	Simultaneous Equations	352	268	318	DS86502.01
Medium	Simultaneous Equations	353	268	318	DS47502.01
Medium	Simultaneous Equations	354	268	319	DS08502.01

(Continued)

Difficulty	Concept	Question #	Page	Answer Explanation Page	PQID
Medium	Simultaneous Equations	366	269	324	DS13602.01
Medium	Simultaneous Equations	388	272	333	DS19199
Medium	Statistics	377	271	329	DS02939
Medium	Statistics	378	271	329	DS01341
Medium	Statistics	417	275	344	DS08091.01
Medium	Statistics	422	275	347	DS05269
Medium	Statistics	424	275	348	DS89950.01
Medium	Statistics; Simplifying Algebraic Expressions	397	273	336	DS02706
Medium	Surface Area	416	275	344	DS47651.01
Medium	Triangles	367	270	324	DS83602.01
Medium	Triangles	369	270	325	DS34602.01
Medium	Triangles; Area	364	269	323	DS71602.01
Medium	Triangles; Area	368	270	324	DS24602.01
Medium	Triangles; Area	371	270	326	DS74602.01
Medium	Triangles; Area; Pythagorean Theorem	373	270	327	DS94602.01
Medium	Volume	372	270	327	DS84602.01
Medium	Volume; Surface Area	411	274	342	DS50351.01
Hard	Absolute Value	489	282	374	DS07441
Hard	Angles	498	283	379	DS06875
Hard	Applied Problems	433	276	351	DS05639
Hard	Applied Problems	435	276	352	DS05668
Hard	Applied Problems	436	276	352	DS07953
Hard	Applied Problems	448	278	358	DS03680
Hard	Applied Problems	457	278	361	DS00764
Hard	Applied Problems	471	280	366	DS16164
Hard	Applied Problems	488	282	374	DS19120.02
Hard	Applied Problems	491	282	375	DS04409
Hard	Applied Problems	495	283	377	DS16188
Hard	Applied Problems; Estimating	477	280	368	DS08995

Difficulty	Concept	Question #	Page	Answer Explanation Page	PQID
Hard	Area	496	283	378	DS16572
Hard	Circles	466	279	365	DS16542
Hard	Circles	476	280	368	DS12070
Hard	Computation with Integers	434	276	351	DS03057
Hard	Computation with Integers	456	278	361	DS07508
Hard	Coordinate Geometry	444	277	356	DS05265
Hard	Coordinate Geometry	479	281	370	DS12806
Hard	Coordinate Geometry	480	281	370	DS07713
Hard	Cylinders; Volume	440	277	354	DS13982
Hard	Elementary Combinatorics	428	276	350	DS06659
Hard	Exponents	447	278	358	DS06318
Hard	Functions	461	279	363	DS06657
Hard	Inequalities	458	278	361	DS06038
Hard	Inequalities	470	280	366	DS00328
Hard	Inequalities	473	280	367	DS13958
Hard	Inequalities	499	283	379	DS16370
Hard	Operations on Rational Numbers	484	281	372	DS01427
Hard	Operations with Radicals	439	277	353	DS12730
Hard	Order	432	276	351	DS07262
Hard	Order	441	277	355	DS16197
Hard	Percents	427	276	349	DS11210.02
Hard	Percents	429	276	350	DS16078
Hard	Percents	437	277	352	DS14406
Hard	Place Value	446	277	357	DS04631
Hard	Place Value	485	281	372	DS11723
Hard	Polygons	464	279	364	DS02888
Hard	Properties of Integers	453	278	360	DS06789
Hard	Properties of Integers	462	279	363	DS12718
Hard	Properties of Numbers	431	276	350	DS08231
Hard	Properties of Numbers	451	278	359	DS08105

(Continued)

Difficulty	Concept	Question #	Page	Answer Explanation Page	PQID
Hard	Properties of Numbers	454	278	360	DS13965
Hard	Properties of Numbers	460	279	363	DS16361
Hard	Properties of Numbers	467	279	365	DS13641
Hard	Properties of Numbers	469	280	366	DS08301
Hard	Properties of Numbers	474	280	367	DS08451
Hard	Properties of Numbers	487	282	373	DS00340
Hard	Properties of Numbers	493	282	377	DS16368
Hard	Properties of Numbers	497	283	378	DS16168
Hard	Properties of Numbers	501	283	380	DS16085
Hard	Proportions	500	283	379	DS16589
Hard	Rate Problems	438	277	353	DS06315
Hard	Ratio and Proportion	465	279	364	DS01049
Hard	Ratios	452	278	360	DS16384
Hard	Rectangular Solids and Cylinders	468	279	365	DS04897
Hard	Rounding; Estimating	430	276	350	DS16529
Hard	Second-Degree Equations	463	279	364	DS03046
Hard	Sets	459	279	362	DS12008
Hard	Sets	486	282	373	DS05162
Hard	Simplifying Algebraic Expressions	502	283	380	DS16204
Hard	Simultaneous Equations	442	277	355	DS18414
Hard	Simultaneous Equations	449	278	358	DS01383
Hard	Statistics	445	277	357	DS09603
Hard	Statistics	455	278	360	DS00172
Hard	Statistics	472	280	367	DS12047
Hard	Statistics	475	280	368	DS01473
Hard	Statistics	478	281	369	DS12239
Hard	Statistics	482	281	371	DS09973
Hard	Statistics	490	282	374	DS11538
Hard	Statistics	492	282	376	DS01641
Hard	Statistics	494	282	377	DS16565

Difficulty	Concept	Question #	Page	Answer Explanation Page	PQID
Hard	Triangles	483	281	371	DS13857
Hard	Triangles; Area	443	277	356	DS16536
Hard	Triangles; Area	450	278	358	DS06869
Hard	Triangles; Perimeter	481	281	371	DS06861

Reading Comprehension

Difficulty	Concept	Question #	Page	Answer Explanation Page	PQID
Easy	Application	512	461	525	RC00344-04
Easy	Evaluation	509	459	523	RC00455-03
Easy	Evaluation	518	464	529	RC00359-06
Easy	Evaluation	523	466	532	RC00419-06
Easy	Evaluation	526	468	534	RC00458-03
Easy	Evaluation	529	469	536	RC00497-03
Easy	Evaluation	536	473	540	RC38200-01.01
Easy	Evaluation	540	474	542	RC38200-05.01
Easy	Inference	507	457	521	RC00525-02
Easy	Inference	511	461	524	RC00344-02
Easy	Inference	514	462	526	RC00344-06
Easy	Inference	520	465	530	RC00419-02
Easy	Inference	521	466	531	RC00419-04
Easy	Inference	522	466	531	RC00419-05
Easy	Inference	530	470	536	RC00497-04
Easy	Inference	533	471	538	RC00017-03
Easy	Inference	534	472	539	RC00017-04
Easy	Inference	537	473	541	RC38200-02.01
Easy	Inference	543	474	544	RC38200-08.01
Easy	Main Idea	503	455	519	RC00504-01

(Continued)

Difficulty	Concept	Question #	Page	Answer Explanation Page	PQID
Easy	Main Idea	505	456	520	RC00504-04
Easy	Main Idea	506	457	521	RC00525-01
Easy	Main Idea	517	464	528	RC00359-05
Easy	Main Idea	519	465	530	RC00419-01
Easy	Main Idea	524	467	533	RC00458-01
Easy	Main Idea	542	474	543	RC38200-07.01
Easy	Supporting Idea	504	455	519	RC00504-05
Easy	Supporting Idea	508	458	522	RC00525-07
Easy	Supporting Idea	510	460	524	RC00455-05
Easy	Supporting Idea	513	462	526	RC00344-05
Easy	Supporting Idea	515	463	527	RC00359-01
Easy	Supporting Idea	516	463	528	RC00359-03
Easy	Supporting Idea	525	467	533	RC00458-02
Easy	Supporting Idea	527	468	534	RC00458-05
Easy	Supporting Idea	528	469	535	RC00497-02
Easy	Supporting Idea	531	470	537	RC00497-05
Easy	Supporting Idea	532	471	538	RC00017-02
Easy	Supporting Idea	535	472	539	RC00017-05
Easy	Supporting Idea	538	474	541	RC38200-03.01
Easy	Supporting Idea	539	474	542	RC38200-04.01
Easy	Supporting Idea	541	474	543	RC38200-06.01
Medium	Application	559	479	554	RC00423-03
Medium	Application	564	482	557	RC00349-04
Medium	Application	573	486	562	RC00121-05
Medium	Application	582	489	567	RC00223-04
Medium	Application	587	492	569	RC00333-04
Medium	Evaluation	546	475	546	RC74000-03.01
Medium	Evaluation	547	476	546	RC74000-04.01
Medium	Evaluation	549	476	547	RC74000-06.01
Medium	Evaluation	553	477	550	RC00394-03

Difficulty	Concept	Question #	Page	Answer Explanation Page	PQID
Medium	Evaluation	555	478	551	RC00394-05
Medium	Evaluation	565	482	557	RC00349-05
Medium	Evaluation	572	485	561	RC00121-03
Medium	Evaluation	577	488	564	RC00120-01
Medium	Evaluation	583	490	567	RC00223-05
Medium	Evaluation	584	490	568	RC00223-07
Medium	Evaluation	590	494	571	RC00272-06
Medium	Inference	545	475	545	RC74000-02.01
Medium	Inference	548	476	547	RC74000-05.01
Medium	Inference	551	476	549	RC74000-08.01
Medium	Inference	552	477	549	RC00394-02
Medium	Inference	554	478	551	RC00394-04
Medium	Inference	558	479	553	RC00423-02
Medium	Inference	560	479	555	RC00423-04
Medium	Inference	561	480	555	RC00423-05
Medium	Inference	570	485	560	RC00121-01
Medium	Inference	571	485	561	RC00121-02
Medium	Inference	576	487	564	RC00120-06
Medium	Inference	580	488	566	RC00120-04
Medium	Inference	586	491	569	RC00333-02
Medium	Inference	588	493	570	RC00272-02
Medium	Main Idea	550	476	548	RC74000-07.01
Medium	Main Idea	567	483	559	RC00633-01
Medium	Main Idea	574	486	562	RC00121-07
Medium	Main Idea	575	487	563	RC00120-05
Medium	Main Idea	585	491	568	RC00333-01
Medium	Main Idea	591	494	572	RC00272-07
Medium	Supporting Idea	544	475	545	RC74000-01.01
Medium	Supporting Idea	556	478	552	RC00394-06

(Continued)

Difficulty	Concept	Question #	Page	Answer Explanation Page	PQID
Medium	Supporting Idea	557	479	553	RC00423-01
Medium	Supporting Idea	562	481	556	RC00349-02
Medium	Supporting Idea	563	481	556	RC00349-03
Medium	Supporting Idea	566	482	558	RC00349-06
Medium	Supporting Idea	568	483	559	RC00633-02
Medium	Supporting Idea	569	484	560	RC00633-06
Medium	Supporting Idea	578	488	565	RC00120-02
Medium	Supporting Idea	579	488	565	RC00120-03
Medium	Supporting Idea	581	489	566	RC00223-03
Medium	Supporting Idea	589	493	571	RC00272-04
Hard	Application	615	504	585	RC00229-04
Hard	Application	619	505	588	RC00556-04
Hard	Application	628	510	593	RC00013-04
Hard	Application	646	515	604	RC00524-04
Hard	Evaluation	593	495	573	RC00109-02
Hard	Evaluation	599	498	576	RC00558-02
Hard	Evaluation	601	499	578	RC00433-02
Hard	Evaluation	604	500	579	RC00433-08
Hard	Evaluation	610	502	582	RC00312-05
Hard	Evaluation	616	504	586	RC00229-05
Hard	Evaluation	617	504	586	RC00229-06
Hard	Evaluation	620	506	588	RC00556-05
Hard	Evaluation	623	507	590	RC00073-03
Hard	Evaluation	631	510	595	RC00013-08
Hard	Evaluation	638	513	599	RC00313-01
Hard	Evaluation	643	514	602	RC00313-06
Hard	Evaluation	648	516	605	RC00524-07
Hard	Evaluation	649	517	606	RC00301-04
Hard	Inference	596	496	574	RC00109-05
Hard	Inference	597	496	575	RC00109-06

Difficulty	Concept	Question #	Page	Answer Explanation Page	PQID
Hard	Inference	598	497	575	RC00558-01
Hard	Inference	602	500	578	RC00433-11
Hard	Inference	603	500	579	RC00433-04
Hard	Inference	606	500	580	RC00433-09
Hard	Inference	608	501	581	RC00312-03
Hard	Inference	609	502	582	RC00312-04
Hard	Inference	613	503	584	RC00229-02
Hard	Inference	614	503	585	RC00229-03
Hard	Inference	621	506	589	RC00556-06
Hard	Inference	624	508	591	RC00073-08
Hard	Inference	627	509	593	RC00013-03
Hard	Inference	629	510	594	RC00013-05
Hard	Inference	632	510	595	RC00013-09
Hard	Inference	633	511	596	RC00650-02
Hard	Inference	634	511	597	RC00650-03
Hard	Inference	635	511	597	RC00650-06
Hard	Inference	636	512	598	RC00650-07
Hard	Inference	641	514	601	RC00313-04
Hard	Inference	642	514	601	RC00313-05
Hard	Inference	644	514	603	RC00313-08
Hard	Inference	645	515	603	RC00524-02
Hard	Inference	650	517	606	RC00301-03
Hard	Inference	651	517	607	RC00301-02
Hard	Main Idea	592	495	572	RC00109-01
Hard	Main Idea	600	498	577	RC00558-06
Hard	Main Idea	605	500	580	RC00433-06
Hard	Main Idea	607	501	581	RC00312-01
Hard	Main Idea	612	503	583	RC00229-01
Hard	Main Idea	625	509	592	RC00013-01

(Continued)

Difficulty	Concept	Question #	Page	Answer Explanation Page	PQID
Hard	Supporting Idea	594	496	573	RC00109-03
Hard	Supporting Idea	595	496	574	RC00109-04
Hard	Supporting Idea	611	502	583	RC00312-06
Hard	Supporting Idea	618	505	587	RC00556-03
Hard	Supporting Idea	622	507	590	RC00073-01
Hard	Supporting Idea	626	509	592	RC00013-02
Hard	Supporting Idea	630	510	594	RC00013-07
Hard	Supporting Idea	637	512	598	RC00650-08
Hard	Supporting Idea	639	513	600	RC00313-02
Hard	Supporting Idea	640	514	600	RC00313-03
Hard	Supporting Idea	647	516	605	RC00524-06

Critical Reasoning

Difficulty	Concept	Question #	Page	Answer Explanation Page	PQID
Easy	Argument Construction	653	614	666	CR53631.01
Easy	Argument Construction	654	614	667	CR79041.01
Easy	Argument Construction	657	615	670	CR33061.01
Easy	Argument Construction	658	615	671	CR09616
Easy	Argument Construction	661	616	674	CR73241.01
Easy	Argument Construction	662	617	675	CR41141.01
Easy	Argument Construction	663	617	676	CR11741.01
Easy	Argument Construction	667	618	680	CR93241.01
Easy	Argument Construction	668	619	681	CR49551.01
Easy	Argument Construction	672	620	685	CR12078
Easy	Argument Construction	674	620	687	CR01295
Easy	Argument Construction	676	621	689	CR05080
Easy	Argument Construction	677	621	690	CR04159
Easy	Argument Construction	678	621	691	CR05452

Difficulty	Concept	Question #	Page	Answer Explanation Page	PQID
Easy	Argument Construction	682	622	696	CR00766
Easy	Argument Construction	687	624	701	CR08471
Easy	Argument Construction	688	624	702	CR04364
Easy	Argument Construction	689	624	703	CR05186
Easy	Argument Construction	692	625	706	CR03367
Easy	Argument Construction	693	626	707	CR07660
Easy	Argument Construction	695	626	709	CR07712
Easy	Argument Construction	698	627	712	CR04140
Easy	Argument Construction	701	628	715	CR02702
Easy	Argument Evaluation	652	614	665	CR70041.01
Easy	Argument Evaluation	655	615	668	CR31551.01
Easy	Argument Evaluation	659	616	672	CR52061.01
Easy	Argument Evaluation	660	616	673	CR40751.01
Easy	Argument Evaluation	665	618	678	CR09994
Easy	Argument Evaluation	669	619	682	CR01107
Easy	Argument Evaluation	671	619	684	CR03940
Easy	Argument Evaluation	673	620	686	CR51141.01
Easy	Argument Evaluation	680	622	693	CR01102
Easy	Argument Evaluation	681	622	695	CR67830.02
Easy	Argument Evaluation	683	623	697	CR14430.02
Easy	Argument Evaluation	686	624	700	CR05667
Easy	Argument Evaluation	697	627	711	CR03695
Easy	Argument Evaluation	699	627	713	CR05077
Easy	Argument Evaluation	702	628	716	CR41700.02
Easy	Argument Evaluation	703	629	717	CR18310.02
Easy	Argument Evaluation	705	629	720	CR30650.02
Easy	Argument Evaluation	706	629	721	CR44040.02
Easy	Evaluation of a Plan	656	615	669	CR07651.01
Easy	Evaluation of a Plan	664	617	677	CR94231.01

(*Continued*)

Difficulty	Concept	Question #	Page	Answer Explanation Page	PQID
Easy	Evaluation of a Plan	666	618	679	CR08017
Easy	Evaluation of a Plan	670	619	683	CR12584
Easy	Evaluation of a Plan	675	621	688	CR03938
Easy	Evaluation of a Plan	679	622	692	CR09963
Easy	Evaluation of a Plan	684	623	698	CR04882
Easy	Evaluation of a Plan	685	623	699	CR08330.02
Easy	Evaluation of a Plan	690	625	704	CR01867
Easy	Evaluation of a Plan	691	625	705	CR12558
Easy	Evaluation of a Plan	694	626	708	CR04366
Easy	Evaluation of a Plan	696	626	710	CR08770
Easy	Evaluation of a Plan	700	628	714	CR05412
Easy	Evaluation of a Plan	704	629	719	CR74231.01
Medium	Argument Construction	708	630	724	CR08831
Medium	Argument Construction	709	630	725	CR01112
Medium	Argument Construction	711	631	727	CR11751.01
Medium	Argument Construction	712	631	728	CR02143
Medium	Argument Construction	713	631	729	CR18731.01
Medium	Argument Construction	714	632	730	CR02888
Medium	Argument Construction	715	632	731	CR07809
Medium	Argument Construction	716	632	732	CR12019
Medium	Argument Construction	718	633	734	CR03749
Medium	Argument Construction	720	634	736	CR00748
Medium	Argument Construction	724	635	740	CR09151
Medium	Argument Construction	725	635	741	CR04986
Medium	Argument Construction	729	636	745	CR55541.01
Medium	Argument Construction	730	636	746	CR13108
Medium	Argument Construction	731	637	747	CR00777
Medium	Argument Construction	736	638	752	CR11639
Medium	Argument Construction	739	639	755	CR53341.01
Medium	Argument Construction	740	639	756	CR80531.01

Difficulty	Concept	Question #	Page	Answer Explanation Page	PQID
Medium	Argument Construction	742	640	758	CR03272
Medium	Argument Construction	743	640	759	CR08239
Medium	Argument Construction	748	642	764	CR38931.01
Medium	Argument Construction	749	642	765	CR02885
Medium	Argument Construction	750	642	766	CR02886
Medium	Argument Construction	752	643	768	CR07810
Medium	Argument Construction	753	643	769	CR74541.01
Medium	Argument Construction	754	643	771	CR02829
Medium	Argument Construction	756	644	773	CR05756
Medium	Argument Construction	759	645	776	CR03727
Medium	Argument Evaluation	707	630	723	CR78590.02
Medium	Argument Evaluation	710	630	726	CR79751.01
Medium	Argument Evaluation	717	633	733	CR20831.01
Medium	Argument Evaluation	721	634	737	CR07304
Medium	Argument Evaluation	722	634	738	CR90061.01
Medium	Argument Evaluation	726	635	742	CR04935
Medium	Argument Evaluation	727	636	743	CR81021.02
Medium	Argument Evaluation	728	636	744	CR00895
Medium	Argument Evaluation	734	638	750	CR01905
Medium	Argument Evaluation	735	638	751	CR01368
Medium	Argument Evaluation	737	639	753	CR13127
Medium	Argument Evaluation	744	640	760	CR32441.01
Medium	Argument Evaluation	747	641	763	CR02830
Medium	Argument Evaluation	751	643	767	CR00827
Medium	Argument Evaluation	755	644	772	CR91630.02
Medium	Argument Evaluation	757	644	774	CR05501
Medium	Argument Evaluation	758	645	775	CR04805
Medium	Argument Evaluation	760	645	777	CR12051
Medium	Evaluation of a Plan	719	633	735	CR04925

(Continued)

Difficulty	Concept	Question #	Page	Answer Explanation Page	PQID
Medium	Evaluation of a Plan	723	635	739	CR09117
Medium	Evaluation of a Plan	732	637	748	CR10028
Medium	Evaluation of a Plan	733	637	749	CR08443
Medium	Evaluation of a Plan	738	639	754	CR99530.01
Medium	Evaluation of a Plan	741	640	757	CR09534
Medium	Evaluation of a Plan	745	641	761	CR95631.01
Medium	Evaluation of a Plan	746	641	762	CR00713
Hard	Argument Construction	761	645	778	CR09760.02
Hard	Argument Construction	763	646	780	CR20170.02
Hard	Argument Construction	764	646	781	CR65030.02
Hard	Argument Construction	766	647	783	CR02866
Hard	Argument Construction	768	648	785	CR10049
Hard	Argument Construction	771	648	788	CR01239
Hard	Argument Construction	774	649	791	CR04964
Hard	Argument Construction	776	650	793	CR01285
Hard	Argument Construction	777	650	794	CR25550.02
Hard	Argument Construction	781	652	798	CR05446
Hard	Argument Construction	784	652	801	CR03618
Hard	Argument Construction	788	654	806	CR03859
Hard	Argument Construction	789	654	807	CR01337
Hard	Argument Construction	793	655	811	CR01293
Hard	Argument Construction	799	657	817	CR11633
Hard	Argument Construction	800	657	818	CR08527
Hard	Argument Construction	803	658	821	CR00907
Hard	Argument Construction	805	659	823	CR05685
Hard	Argument Construction	807	659	825	CR00778
Hard	Argument Construction	811	661	829	CR00774
Hard	Argument Construction	812	661	830	CR01289
Hard	Argument Construction	815	662	833	CR11453
Hard	Argument Evaluation	762	646	779	CR00860.02

Difficulty	Concept	Question #	Page	Answer Explanation Page	PQID
Hard	Argument Evaluation	767	647	784	CR04924
Hard	Argument Evaluation	769	648	786	CR01163
Hard	Argument Evaluation	770	648	787	CR00792
Hard	Argument Evaluation	772	649	789	CR01153
Hard	Argument Evaluation	775	650	792	CR01096
Hard	Argument Evaluation	778	651	795	CR00788
Hard	Argument Evaluation	779	651	796	CR03251
Hard	Argument Evaluation	780	651	797	CR07318
Hard	Argument Evaluation	782	652	799	CR05191
Hard	Argument Evaluation	783	652	800	CR05614
Hard	Argument Evaluation	786	653	803	CR01854
Hard	Argument Evaluation	787	653	804	CR00942
Hard	Argument Evaluation	790	654	808	CR03541
Hard	Argument Evaluation	792	655	810	CR04718
Hard	Argument Evaluation	795	656	813	CR01848
Hard	Argument Evaluation	796	656	814	CR03814
Hard	Argument Evaluation	798	657	816	CR05960
Hard	Argument Evaluation	801	658	819	CR05644
Hard	Argument Evaluation	802	658	820	CR44930.02
Hard	Argument Evaluation	804	658	822	CR07257
Hard	Argument Evaluation	808	660	826	CR05725
Hard	Argument Evaluation	809	660	827	CR02997
Hard	Argument Evaluation	813	661	831	CR05082
Hard	Argument Evaluation	814	662	832	CR09951
Hard	Argument Evaluation	816	662	834	CR01202
Hard	Argument Evaluation	817	662	835	CR05093
Hard	Evaluation of a Plan	765	647	782	CR06728
Hard	Evaluation of a Plan	773	649	790	CR27430.02
Hard	Evaluation of a Plan	785	653	802	CR51520.02

(Continued)

Difficulty	Concept	Question #	Page	Answer Explanation Page	PQID
Hard	Evaluation of a Plan	791	655	809	CR01879
Hard	Evaluation of a Plan	794	655	812	CR11447
Hard	Evaluation of a Plan	797	656	815	CR76951.02
Hard	Evaluation of a Plan	806	659	824	CR01801
Hard	Evaluation of a Plan	810	660	828	CR03818

Sentence Correction

Difficulty	Concept	Question #	Page	Answer Explanation Page	PQID
Easy	Grammatical Construction; Idiom; Parallelism	830	861	905	SC02078
Easy	Rhetorical Construction; Verb Form	840	864	911	SC01436
Easy	Agreement; Grammatical Construction	821	859	898	SC33440.02
Easy	Agreement; Grammatical Construction	838	863	910	SC61940.02
Easy	Agreement; Idiom; Verb Form	843	864	912	SC05201
Easy	Agreement; Parallelism	858	867	922	SC04093
Easy	Agreement; Rhetorical Construction	823	860	899	SC15382
Easy	Diction; Parallelism	845	864	914	SC03079
Easy	Diction; Parallelism	857	867	921	SC00981
Easy	Diction; Rhetorical Construction	861	867	924	SC07338
Easy	Grammatical Construction; Diction	846	865	914	SC09877
Easy	Grammatical Construction; Diction	852	866	918	SC94340.02
Easy	Grammatical Construction; Diction	868	869	928	SC40050.02
Easy	Grammatical Construction; Idiom	854	866	920	SC01470
Easy	Grammatical Construction; Logical Predication	827	861	903	SC08150.02
Easy	Grammatical Construction; Logical Predication	844	864	913	SC13010
Easy	Grammatical Construction; Parallelism	819	859	896	SC01527

Difficulty	Concept	Question #	Page	Answer Explanation Page	PQID
Easy	Grammatical Construction; Parallelism	829	861	904	SC03014
Easy	Grammatical Construction; Parallelism	835	862	908	SC03083
Easy	Grammatical Construction; Verb Form	824	860	900	SC01455
Easy	Idiom, Logical Predication; Agreement	826	860	902	SC52050.02
Easy	Idiom; Diction	818	859	896	SC39850.02
Easy	Idiom; Diction	848	865	915	SC04452
Easy	Idiom; Diction	867	868	927	SC14740.02
Easy	Idiom; Grammatical Construction	839	863	910	SC02000
Easy	Idiom; Logical Predication	820	859	897	SC20160.02
Easy	Idiom; Rhetorical Construction	832	862	906	SC01680
Easy	Idiom; Rhetorical Construction	833	862	907	SC02272
Easy	Idiom; Rhetorical Construction	863	868	925	SC87460.01
Easy	Idiom; Rhetorical Construction; Logical Predication	862	868	924	SC12710.01
Easy	Idiom; Verb Form	825	860	901	SC00740.02
Easy	Idiom; Verb Form	837	863	909	SC91050.02
Easy	Idiom; Verb Form	869	869	929	SC03050.02
Easy	Logical Predication	847	865	915	SC01975
Easy	Logical Predication	865	868	926	SC22260.02
Easy	Logical Predication; Diction	850	865	917	SC27250.02
Easy	Logical Predicaion; Diction	864	868	925	SC19060.02
Easy	Logical Predication; Diction	866	868	926	SC69440.02
Easy	Logical Predication; Diction; Verb Form	849	865	916	SC02025
Easy	Logical Predication; Grammatical Construction	842	864	912	SC07348
Easy	Logical Prediction; Rhetorical Construction	855	866	920	SC03260.02
Easy	Parallelism; Agreement	836	863	909	SC01739
Easy	Parallelism; Idiom	822	860	899	SC12999
Easy	Parallelism; Rhetorical Construction	860	867	923	SC09185

(*Continued*)

Difficulty	Concept	Question #	Page	Answer Explanation Page	PQID
Easy	Rhetorical Construction; Grammatical Construction	834	862	908	SC02096
Easy	Rhetorical Construction; Logical Predication	851	865	918	SC01554
Easy	Rhetorical Construction; Logical Predication	856	866	921	SC91660.02
Easy	Rhetorical Construction; Verb Form; Logical Predication	831	861	906	SC03881
Easy	Rhetorical Construction; Verb Form; Logical Predication	859	867	922	SC02102
Easy	Verb Form; Logical Predication	828	861	904	SC21130.02
Easy	Verb Form; Logical Predication	841	864	911	SC00970
Easy	Verb Form; Rhetorical Construction	853	866	919	SC01059
Medium	Agreement; Diction	925	880	965	SC02443
Medium	Agreement; Rhetorical Construction	883	872	938	SC07446
Medium	Diction; Grammatical Construction; Logical Predication	914	878	957	SC07530.02
Medium	Diction; Verb Form	878	870	935	SC71360.02
Medium	Diction; Verb Form	917	878	959	SC71030.02
Medium	Diction; Verb Form	922	879	963	SC48420.01
Medium	Diction; Verb Form; Parallelism	876	870	933	SC32261.01
Medium	Grammatical Construction; Diction	873	870	931	SC12841.01
Medium	Grammatical Construction; Diction	901	875	949	SC24321.01
Medium	Grammatical Construction; Diction	907	876	952	SC01077
Medium	Grammatical Construction; Parallelism	920	879	961	SC03288
Medium	Grammatical Construction; Rhetorical Construction	899	875	947	SC14066
Medium	Grammatical Construction; Rhetorical Construction	926	880	965	SC14796
Medium	Grammatical Construction; Verb Form	896	874	946	SC04422
Medium	Idiom; Logical Predication	912	877	956	SC34740.02

Difficulty	Concept	Question #	Page	Answer Explanation Page	PQID
Medium	Idiom; Parallelism	880	871	936	SC04704
Medium	Idiom; Parallelism	923	879	963	SC38250.02
Medium	Idiom; Parallelism; Logical Predication	890	873	942	SC01007
Medium	Idiom; Rhetorical Construction	919	879	960	SC01037
Medium	Idiom; Rhetorical Construction; Logical Predication	886	872	940	SC25540.02
Medium	Logical Predication; Agreement	900	875	948	SC01946
Medium	Logical Predication; Agreement; Grammatical Construction; Verb Form	905	876	951	SC20121.01
Medium	Logical Predication; Diction	875	870	933	SC83751.01
Medium	Logical Predication; Grammatical Construction	884	872	938	SC01595
Medium	Logical Predication; Grammatical Construction; Agreement	910	877	954	SC41451.01
Medium	Logical Predication; Grammatical Construction; Rhetorical Construction	872	869	931	SC01018
Medium	Logical Predication; Grammatical Construction; Verb Form	888	872	941	SC00985
Medium	Logical Predication; Idiom	881	871	937	SC04562
Medium	Logical Predication; Modification	894	874	945	SC00994
Medium	Logical Predication; Parallelism	909	877	954	SC01523
Medium	Logical Predication; Rhetorical Construction	882	871	937	SC01498
Medium	Logical Predication; Rhetorical Construction	906	876	952	SC36241.01
Medium	Logical Predication; Rhetorical Construction	918	878	960	SC17041.01
Medium	Logical Predication; Rhetorical Construction	928	880	966	SC61740.02
Medium	Logical Predication; Rhetorical Construction; Verb Form	902	875	949	SC01973
Medium	Parallelism; Diction	913	877	956	SC00989
Medium	Parallelism; Grammatical Construction	874	870	932	SC24751.01

(Continued)

Difficulty	Concept	Question #	Page	Answer Explanation Page	PQID
Medium	Parallelism; Grammatical Construction	892	873	943	SC04760
Medium	Parallelism; Rhetorical Construction	871	869	930	SC01506
Medium	Parallelism; Rhetorical Construction	895	874	945	SC01521
Medium	Rhetorical Construction; Diction	889	873	942	SC61120.02
Medium	Rhetorical Construction; Diction	891	873	943	SC04770
Medium	Rhetorical Construction; Diction	921	879	962	SC01493
Medium	Rhetorical Construction; Grammatical Construction	898	874	947	SC07232
Medium	Rhetorical Construction; Idiom	887	872	940	SC01507
Medium	Rhetorical Construction; Idiom; Parallelism	893	873	944	SC01469
Medium	Rhetorical Construction; Logical Predication	885	872	939	SC04416
Medium	Rhetorical Construction; Logical Predication	897	874	946	SC00971
Medium	Rhetorical Construction; Logical Predication; Grammatical Construction	904	876	950	SC02448
Medium	Rhetorical Construction; Parallelism	879	871	936	SC01472
Medium	Rhetorical Construction; Verb Form	916	878	958	SC11850.01
Medium	Verb Form	911	877	955	SC01487
Medium	Verb Form; Logical Predication	877	870	934	SC01490
Medium	Verb Form; Logical Predication	908	877	953	SC16020.02
Medium	Verb Form; Logical Predication	915	878	957	SC07920.02
Medium	Verb Form; Logical Predication	924	879	964	SC01603
Medium	Verb Form; Parallelism	903	876	950	SC01033
Medium	Verb Form; Rhetorical Construction	870	869	929	SC80540.02
Medium	Verb Form; Rhetorical Construction	927	880	966	SC08577
Hard	Agreement; Idiom	953	885	980	SC01474
Hard	Agreement; Idiom	957	886	983	SC06898

Difficulty	Concept	Question #	Page	Answer Explanation Page	PQID
Hard	Agreement; Idiom	995	894	1003	SC04836
Hard	Agreement; Logical Predication	940	883	973	SC01445
Hard	Agreement; Logical Predication	947	884	977	SC07117
Hard	Agreement; Logical Predication	950	885	979	SC01068
Hard	Agreement; Logical Predication	985	892	998	SC06633
Hard	Agreement; Parallelism	977	890	994	SC01587
Hard	Agreement; Rhetorical Construction; Logical Predication	981	891	996	SC02346
Hard	Diction; Agreement	937	882	971	SC03675
Hard	Diction; Idiom	976	890	993	SC02216
Hard	Diction; Idiom	984	892	997	SC02344
Hard	Diction; Parallelism	983	891	997	SC01957
Hard	Diction; Parallelism; Verb Form	931	881	968	SC02280
Hard	Grammatical Construction; Diction	938	882	972	SC07758
Hard	Grammatical Construction; Parallelism	945	884	976	SC02135
Hard	Grammatical Construction; Rhetorical Construction	956	886	982	SC03805
Hard	Grammatical Construction; Verb Form	988	892	1000	SC04899
Hard	Idiom; Grammatical Construction	933	881	969	SC01051
Hard	Idiom; Grammatical Construction	952	885	980	SC01561
Hard	Idiom; Grammatical Construction	973	890	992	SC01714
Hard	Idiom; Grammatical Construction; Logical Predication	979	891	995	SC01761
Hard	Idiom; Logical Predication	934	881	970	SC01028
Hard	Idiom; Logical Predication; Rhetorical Construction	943	884	975	SC02317
Hard	Idiom; Logical Predication; Rhetorical Construction	964	888	987	SC03292
Hard	Idiom; Verb Form; Logical Predication	993	893	1002	SC01647
Hard	Logical Predication; Agreement	949	885	978	SC05848
Hard	Logical Predication; Agreement	971	889	991	SC02094

(*Continued*)

Difficulty	Concept	Question #	Page	Answer Explanation Page	PQID
Hard	Logical Predication; Agreement	980	891	995	SC02259
Hard	Logical Predication; Agreement	987	892	999	SC03154
Hard	Logical Predication; Grammatical Construction	935	881	970	SC04331
Hard	Logical Predication; Grammatical Construction	939	882	973	SC02710
Hard	Logical Predication; Grammatical Construction	967	888	988	SC02611
Hard	Logical Predication; Grammatical Construction	978	891	994	SC01622
Hard	Logical Predication; Parallelism	932	881	969	SC01583
Hard	Logical Predication; Parallelism	972	890	991	SC05760
Hard	Logical Predication; Parallelism	990	893	1001	SC03752
Hard	Logical Predication; Rhetorical Construction	936	882	971	SC02060
Hard	Logical Predication; Rhetorical Construction	958	886	983	SC08719
Hard	Logical Predication; Rhetorical Construction	963	888	986	SC06740
Hard	Logical Predication; Rhetorical Construction	965	888	987	SC02539
Hard	Logical Predication; Rhetorical Construction	968	889	989	SC02576
Hard	Logical Predication; Rhetorical Construction	970	889	990	SC02008
Hard	Logical Predication; Rhetorical Construction	975	890	993	SC01987
Hard	Logical Predication; Verb Form	946	884	977	SC02470
Hard	Logical Predication; Verb Form	955	886	981	SC05393
Hard	Parallelism; Diction	948	885	978	SC01550
Hard	Parallelism; Rhetorical Construction	930	881	968	SC07035
Hard	Parallelism; Rhetorical Construction	951	885	979	SC08083
Hard	Parallelism; Verb Form	982	891	996	SC04213
Hard	Parallelism; Verb Form; Logical Predication	994	894	1003	SC01618

Difficulty	Concept	Question #	Page	Answer Explanation Page	PQID
Hard	Rhetorical Construction; Agreement	941	883	974	SC03207
Hard	Rhetorical Construction; Agreement	959	887	984	SC01577
Hard	Rhetorical Construction; Agreement	989	893	1000	SC05785
Hard	Rhetorical Construction; Agreement; Grammatical Construction	942	883	975	SC06611
Hard	Rhetorical Construction; Grammatical Construction	974	890	992	SC04853
Hard	Rhetorical Construction; Idiom	954	886	981	SC04249
Hard	Rhetorical Construction; Idiom	960	887	984	SC02138
Hard	Rhetorical Construction; Idiom	986	892	998	SC04330
Hard	Rhetorical Construction; Logical Predication	962	887	986	SC04408
Hard	Rhetorical Construction; Logical Predication	966	888	988	SC01022
Hard	Rhetorical Construction; Parallelism; Diction	929	880	967	SC01607
Hard	Rhetorical Construction; Verb Form	991	893	1001	SC04343
Hard	Verb Form; Diction	944	884	976	SC07231
Hard	Verb Form; Grammatical Construction; Diction	969	889	989	SC12131
Hard	Verb Form; Rhetorical Construction	992	893	1002	SC02965
Hard	Verb Form; Rhetorical Construction; Logical Predication	961	887	985	SC01443

To register for the GMAT™ exam go to www.mba.com/gmat

Appendix A   Answer Sheets

Problem Solving Answer Sheet

1.	33.	65.	97.	129.
2.	34.	66.	98.	130.
3.	35.	67.	99.	131.
4.	36.	68.	100.	132.
5.	37.	69.	101.	133.
6.	38.	70.	102.	134.
7.	39.	71.	103.	135.
8.	40.	72.	104.	136.
9.	41.	73.	105.	137.
10.	42.	74.	106.	138.
11.	43.	75.	107.	139.
12.	44.	76.	108.	140.
13.	45.	77.	109.	141.
14.	46.	78.	110.	142.
15.	47.	79.	111.	143.
16.	48.	80.	112.	144.
17.	49.	81.	113.	145.
18.	50.	82.	114.	146.
19.	51.	83.	115.	147.
20.	52.	84.	116.	148.
21.	53.	85.	117.	149.
22.	54.	86.	118.	150.
23.	55.	87.	119.	151.
24.	56.	88.	120.	152.
25.	57.	89.	121.	153.
26.	58.	90.	122.	154.
27.	59.	91.	123.	155.
28.	60.	92.	124.	156.
29.	61.	93.	125.	157.
30.	62.	94.	126.	158.
31.	63.	95.	127.	159.
32.	64.	96.	128.	160.

161.	182.	203.	224.	245.
162.	183.	204.	225.	246.
163.	184.	205.	226.	247.
164.	185.	206.	227.	248.
165.	186.	207.	228.	249.
166.	187.	208.	229.	250.
167.	188.	209.	230.	251.
168.	189.	210.	231.	252.
169.	190.	211.	232.	253.
170.	191.	212.	233.	254.
171.	192.	213.	234.	255.
172.	193.	214.	235.	256.
173.	194.	215.	236.	257.
174.	195.	216.	237.	258.
175.	196.	217.	238.	259.
176.	197.	218.	239.	260.
177.	198.	219.	240.	261.
178.	199.	220.	241.	262.
179.	200.	221.	242.	
180.	201.	222.	243.	
181.	202.	223.	244.	

Data Sufficiency Answer Sheet

263.	299.	335.	371.	407.
264.	300.	336.	372.	408.
265.	301.	337.	373.	409.
266.	302.	338.	374.	410.
267.	303.	339.	375.	411.
268.	304.	340.	376.	412.
269.	305.	341.	377.	413.
270.	306.	342.	378.	414.
271.	307.	343.	379.	415.
272.	308.	344.	380.	416.
273.	309.	345.	381.	417.
274.	310.	346.	382.	418.
275.	311.	347.	383.	419.
276.	312.	348.	384.	420.
277.	313.	349.	385.	421.
278.	314.	350.	386.	422.
279.	315.	351.	387.	423.
280.	316.	352.	388.	424.
281.	317.	353.	389.	425.
282.	318.	354.	390.	426.
283.	319.	355.	391.	427.
284.	320.	356.	392.	428.
285.	321.	357.	393.	429.
286.	322.	358.	394.	430.
287.	323.	359.	395.	431.
288.	324.	360.	396.	432.
289.	325.	361.	397.	433.
290.	326.	362.	398.	434.
291.	327.	363.	399.	435.
292.	328.	364.	400.	436.
293.	329.	365.	401.	437.
294.	330.	366.	402.	438.
295.	331.	367.	403.	439.
296.	332.	368.	404.	440.
297.	333.	369.	405.	441.
298.	334.	370.	406.	442.

443.	455.	467.	479.	491.
444.	456.	468.	480.	492.
445.	457.	469.	481.	493.
446.	458.	470.	482.	494.
447.	459.	471.	483.	495.
448.	460.	472.	484.	496.
449.	461.	473.	485.	497.
450.	462.	474.	486.	498.
451.	463.	475.	487.	499.
452.	464.	476.	488.	500.
453.	465.	477.	489.	501.
454.	466.	478.	490.	502.

Reading Comprehension Answer Sheet

503.	533.	563.	593.	623.
504.	534.	564.	594.	624.
505.	535.	565.	595.	625.
506.	536.	566.	596.	626.
507.	537.	567.	597.	627.
508.	538.	568.	598.	628.
509.	539.	569.	599.	629.
510.	540.	570.	600.	630.
511.	541.	571.	601.	631.
512.	542.	572.	602.	632.
513.	543.	573.	603.	633.
514.	544.	574.	604.	634.
515.	545.	575.	605.	635.
516.	546.	576.	606.	636.
517.	547.	577.	607.	637.
518.	548.	578.	608.	638.
519.	549.	579.	609.	639.
520.	550.	580.	610.	640.
521.	551.	581.	611.	641.
522.	552.	582.	612.	642.
523.	553.	583.	613.	643.
524.	554.	584.	614.	644.
525.	555.	585.	615.	645.
526.	556.	586.	616.	646.
527.	557.	587.	617.	647.
528.	558.	588.	618.	648.
529.	559.	589.	619.	649.
530.	560.	590.	620.	650.
531.	561.	591.	621.	651.
532.	562.	592.	622.	

Critical Reasoning Answer Sheet

652.	686.	720.	754.	788.
653.	687.	721.	755.	789.
654.	688.	722.	756.	790.
655.	689.	723.	757.	791.
656.	690.	724.	758.	792.
657.	691.	725.	759.	793.
658.	692.	726.	760.	794.
659.	693.	727.	761.	795.
660.	694.	728.	762.	796.
661.	695.	729.	763.	797.
662.	696.	730.	764.	798.
663.	697.	731.	765.	799.
664.	698.	732.	766.	800.
665.	699.	733.	767.	801.
666.	700.	734.	768.	802.
667.	701.	735.	769.	803.
668.	702.	736.	770.	804.
669.	703.	737.	771.	805.
670.	704.	738.	772.	806.
671.	705.	739.	773.	807.
672.	706.	740.	774.	808.
673.	707.	741.	775.	809.
674.	708.	742.	776.	810.
675.	709.	743.	777.	811.
676.	710.	744.	778.	812.
677.	711.	745.	779.	813.
678.	712.	746.	780.	814.
679.	713.	747.	781.	815.
680.	714.	748.	782.	816.
681.	715.	749.	783.	817.
682.	716.	750.	784.	
683.	717.	751.	785.	
684.	718.	752.	786.	
685.	719.	753.	787.	

Sentence Correction Answer Sheet

818.	854.	890.	926.	962.
819.	855.	891.	927.	963.
820.	856.	892.	928.	964.
821.	857.	893.	929.	965.
822.	858.	894.	930.	966.
823.	859.	895.	931.	967.
824.	860.	896.	932.	968.
825.	861.	897.	933.	969.
826.	862.	898.	934.	970.
827.	863.	899.	935.	971.
828.	864.	900.	936.	972.
829.	865.	901.	937.	973.
830.	866.	902.	938.	974.
831.	867.	903.	939.	975.
832.	868.	904.	940.	976.
833.	869.	905.	941.	977.
834.	870.	906.	942.	978.
835.	871.	907.	943.	979.
836.	872.	908.	944.	980.
837.	873.	909.	945.	981.
838.	874.	910.	946.	982.
839.	875.	911.	947.	983.
840.	876.	912.	948.	984.
841.	877.	913.	949.	985.
842.	878.	914.	950.	986.
843.	879.	915.	951.	987.
844.	880.	916.	952.	988.
845.	881.	917.	953.	989.
846.	882.	918.	954.	990.
847.	883.	919.	955.	991.
848.	884.	920.	956.	992.
849.	885.	921.	957.	993.
850.	886.	922.	958.	994.
851.	887.	923.	959	995.
852.	888.	924.	960.	
853.	889.	925.	961.	

Notes

Notes

Notes

GMAT™

Where do you see yourself in 8 weeks?

How about celebrating your completion of the GMAT™ exam?

Get your FREE 8-week study planner: **mba.com/8-weeks**

© 2021 Graduate Management Admission Council (GMAC). All rights reserved. GMAT™ and Graduate Management Admission Council™ are trademarks of GMAC in the United States and other countries.